Economics
and changing
economies

8

THE OPEN UNIVERSITY COURSE TEAM

Internal

Betty Atkinson, Secretary

Andrew Bertie, Programmer

Vivienne Brown, Senior Lecturer in Economics

David Calderwood, Project Control

Giles Clark, Deputy Managing Editor, Book Trade

Stephen Clift, Editor

Robert Cookson, Senior Editor, Social Sciences

Neil Costello, Senior Lecturer and Staff Tutor in Economics

Jonathan Davies, Graphic Design Co-ordinator, Social Sciences

Graham Dawson, Lecturer in Economics

Nigel Draper, Editor

Alison George, Graphic Artist

Caroline Hailey, Designer

Eddie Head, Compositor

Susan Himmelweit, Senior Lecturer in Economics

David Lee, Research Assistant

Maureen Mackintosh, Professor of Economics and Course Team Chair

Ione Mako, BBC Production Assistant

Iris Manzi, Secretary

Anne-Marie McCallum, Course Manager

Ray Munns, Graphic Artist

Chris Nichols, Course Manager

Yvette Purdy, Course Manager

Moira Sambrooks, Secretary

Paul Smith, Media Librarian

Grahame F. Thompson, Senior Lecturer in Economics

Andrew B. Trigg, Lecturer in Economics

Alison Tucker, BBC Producer

External Assessor

Malcolm Sawyer, Professor of Economics, University of Leeds

External Authors

Giles Atkinson, Research Fellow, Centre for Social and Economic Research on the Global Environment (CSERGE), University College, London

Paul Auerbach, Reader in Economics, Kingston University

David Bailey, Lecturer in Economics, University of East Anglia

Nick Crafts, Professor of Economic History, University of Warwick

Francis Green, Professor of Economics, University of Leeds

Mary Gregory, Fellow and Tutor in Economics, St Hilda's College, Oxford

Shaun P. Hargreaves Heap, Senior Lecturer in Economics, University of East Anglia

Wendy K. Olsen, Lecturer in Social Research, University of Salford

Catherine Price, Senior Lecturer in Economics, University of Leicester

Andrew A. Stevenson, Senior Lecturer, Department of Political Economy, University of Glasgow

Anthony J. Venables, Professor of Economics, London School of Economics and Political Science

Jane Wheelock, Reader in Social Policy, University of Newcastle upon Tyne

L. Alan Winters, Chief, International Trade Division, World Bank, and Professor of Economics, University of Birmingham

George Yarrow, Director, Regulatory Policy Research Centre, Hertford College, Oxford

Tutor consultants

Brian Atkinson, Senior Lecturer in Economics, University of Central Lancashire, and OU Tutor

Isabel Denny, Head of Humanities, Tonbridge Grammar School for Girls, Tonbridge, Kent, and OU Tutor

Alan McDonald, Lecturer in Economics, Queen Margaret College, Edinburgh, and OU Tutor

Graham Smith, Lecturer in Economics, University of Manchester, and OU Tutor

Andrew Fitch, OU Tutor

Other External Contributors

Paul Helm, Teaching Technology Adviser, University of Bradford

Economics
and changing
economies

**M. Mackintosh, V. Brown, N. Costello,
G. Dawson, G. Thompson and A. Trigg**

The Open
University

INTERNATIONAL THOMSON BUSINESS PRESS

an International Thomson Publishing company I(T)P

London • Bonn • Boston • Johannesburg • Madrid • Melbourne • Mexico City • New York • Paris
Singapore • Tokyo • Toronto • Albany, NY • Belmont, CA • Cincinnati, OH • Detroit, MI

The Open University, Walton Hall, Milton Keynes, MK7 6AA

First published by International Thomson Business Press, 1996

Edited, designed and typeset by the Open University

Printed in Spain by Mateu Cromo

ISBN 0 412 62840 6

This text forms part of an Open University Second Level Course. If you would like a copy of *Studying with the Open University*, please write to the Central Enquiry Service, PO Box 200, The Open University, Walton Hall, Milton Keynes, MK7 6YZ. If you have not already enrolled on the Course and would like to buy this or other Open University material, please write to Open University Educational Enterprises Ltd, 12 Cofferidge Close, Stony Stratford, Milton Keynes, MK11 1BY.

CONTENTS

PREFACE

Economics and Changing Economies is a new introductory economics text. One of our reasons for adding to this crowded field is that this text is especially written as an independent learning text for students working largely on their own. The book forms the core teaching of the Open University introductory economics course of the same title. More and more students in higher education are studying independently, whether as a result of expanding part-time and distance teaching or because large classes imply little individual attention. Economics principles texts originally designed for class use in the context of applied seminars and discussion can be very hard going for students without such support, and can provide a distinctly dry introduction to the subject. This text, by contrast, contains the kind of debate and reflection, and the mix of theory teaching with discussion of economic issues, which one might find in a seminar teaching format. Together with an interactive style of teaching drawn from the Open University's long experience of distance teaching, the text offers, we believe, an engaging introduction to an important social science.

Economics and Changing Economies reflects the Open University's approach to teaching in other ways too. Social science teaching at the Open University has a commitment to interdisciplinarity – to the active wearing down of the boundaries between disciplines and to learning from each other – which conflicts with the recurrent tendency of economists to retreat behind a narrow definition of economics. While our social scientist colleagues at the OU will doubtless feel the interdisciplinary content of this text is rather limited, we have nevertheless sought, as the Introduction explains, to recognize some influences on economics from broader social science. We have endeavoured to combine clear logical teaching of core economic theory with a sense of openness and debate: a sense, indeed, of economics as a product of its economic, political and intellectual context. This too gives the text a non-traditional feel, for those used to the 'principles' format.

Like all Open University courses, this book is a product of collective working. The course team, listed on p.ii, includes both Open University academics and outside contributors. The editors are particularly grateful to our external contributing authors for giving the considerable time required to this enterprise in a period when the university funding system offers few rewards for this type of writing. We also acknowledge their generosity in coping with the (sometimes shifting) demands of the editors as we sought to achieve both consistency of teaching and variety of style within the covers of this text.

An Open University course team also includes many essential contributors besides academic authors. The academic editors of this book are very appreciative of the hard work of the course managers, the secretarial staff, the publishing editors, the designers and artists who have put so much outstanding professional effort into producing this book. We would particularly like to thank the external assessor for the course as a whole, Malcolm Sawyer, who has been critic, supporter and adviser throughout the project, a role which has involved a truly enormous amount of work. A panel of Open University tutors put a great deal of effort into trying to ensure that the course content was appropriate for students; it is certainly not their fault if we did not always take their advice. Other academics outside the university were also generous with time and advice: our thanks go particularly to Marc Wuyts at the Institute of Social Studies in The Hague, and Ron Smith of Birkbeck College London; a similar caveat applies. Finally, Steve Reed of International Thomson Business Press has earned our appreciation for his energy and enthusiasm for this project.

AUGUST 1995

INTRODUCTION

Economics and Changing Economies, as the title suggests, combines an introduction to economic theory with an exploration of some major aspects of economic change in the international and national economies. You will therefore find two 'story lines' interwoven throughout the text. One is about economic analysis: the exposition of economic ideas and economic debates. The other story line is about economic change: how do economies change and what are the most important economic problems that arise?

Describing the two main strands of the text in this way acknowledges that they are closely related. We need economic concepts and ideas in order to understand economic change and to identify and analyse economic problems. But changing economic events also feed back upon and influence the ideas and preoccupations of economists.

In emphasizing the interaction of ideas and events, this book – like all texts in social science – is very much a child of its time and place. Written in Britain, in the West, and from within the Anglo-American tradition in economics, the text reflects a number of late twentieth-century uncertainties. This is perhaps most evident in the themes we have chosen for the 'changing economies' strand. They include the mid-1990s concerns about the re-emergence of chronic unemployment in Europe and North America, the environmental consequences of economic growth, economic success in East Asia, and the costs of economic restructuring in Eastern Europe and the former Soviet states. Reflecting the increasing integration of the world economy, the text explores aspects of economic change in Britain and Europe, and also in the wider international economy including Asia and North and South America.

Models and voices

In the 'economics' strand, too, *Economics and Changing Economies* reflects mid-1990s questioning, for example of the benefits and limits of both markets and government. The 1980s saw the high point of political confidence in the benefits of the unfettered market. Curiously, the disintegration of the Soviet Union, initially seen by many as a victory for the market system, has brought in its wake a new awareness of the difficulties of creating efficient markets, and of the ways in which market society is underpinned by non-market institutions. This context has strengthened a renewed interest among economists in economic institutions, reflected here in the discussions of market institutions and of the economics of policy and governing.

Over many years economics has been exploring the consequences of how markets go wrong, or 'fail' – a concern which has been rekindled by the current failure of Western market systems to re-employ all the unemployed. This text picks up this renewed concern with the imperfections of markets, treating markets that work imperfectly as the dominant case in analysing both the market system and the national economy.

There is a further sense in which the approach to economics in this text is clearly the product of its time. Economics is a social science, though one which makes considerable claims to precision and prediction. Recent social science more broadly has been marked by a systematic focus on what might be summarized as standpoint and language. There has been intensive questioning of whether there is necessarily a diversity of understanding of the social world structured by the points of view of those undertaking the theorizing. Related to this, there has been a renewed awareness of the importance of language and metaphor in social science.

These concerns with language and method in social science have until recently largely passed economics by. However, the last few years have seen a new interest among economists in the rhetoric of the subject, in the basis of its claims to knowledge about economies, and in its fundamental assumptions. In this text we have tried to reflect some of these concerns in our approach to teaching economics.

One of the main ways in which economists seek to understand economies is by constructing economic 'models'. These models are rather formal statements of how different elements of the economy interact: of what influences what and how. Economic models can be stated in words, visually in diagrams, or using mathematics. In an introductory text such as this, the main media are words and diagrams. Like all textbooks in economics, this book sets out to explain how economists construct models to try to understand the operation of economies. In the process – and this is less commonly found in economics texts – some of the authors reflect on the use of language and metaphor in these models, and the extent to which they embody different and partly competing ways of seeing the world.

Another activity encompassed within 'economics' is the examination of economic data, and the use of models and data together to explore economic change. This activity, its theory and practice, is the specialism of a branch of economics called econometrics. While this text does not teach econometrics, it recognizes that understanding economics requires some understanding of the excitements and difficulties of trying to confront models with data. There are two chapters on the use of data analysis for economics.

The moment we start to use data in economics, some problems emerge. We can – indeed must – try to collect data about economies that can refute our preconceived ideas. But the very categories in which we collect information are necessarily created by our existing economic ideas, and this can make it hard to challenge them. Indeed, it is difficult to design ways of testing many economic theories. The discussion of the role of data analysis in economics in this text reflects our awareness of the current interest in these problems of method in economics.

Finally, a word about styles of writing. Economists speak in many different 'voices', reflecting personalities, subject matter, aims and audiences. They write both to analyse and to persuade, and hence both in a cool and abstract tone and in emotive prose. Economics makes strong claims to clarity and exactitude while being a highly political subject: the stuff of public debate.

Unusually, this text contains some of this flavour of many voices. It is written by a variety of different authors, all professional economists, but with different specialisms and approaches to economics. The aim of the editors has been to ensure that the presentation of the theory and arguments proceeds logically through the text, but not to suppress differences in style and approach. Style and content are deeply interrelated, and we hope to provide a feel for the variety and range of what is called economics.

Using the text

This is a distance learning text. That is, it is designed to be studied independently, without requiring the use of other books or teaching materials, and it is written in a style addressed to you, the student. As a result, the text is also designed to be studied in the order in which the material is presented. The presentation builds up logically from Chapter 1, with cross-referencing between chapters throughout.

The text is divided into two books: Book 1, 'The Market System', and Book 2, 'Macroeconomics and Economic Policy'. Each of the books is further sub-divided into parts. The core of Book 1, as the title suggests, is an exploration of the different ways in which economists understand how markets work. But individual markets do not function independently. They are embedded in a market system which also involves governmental bodies that produce, regulate and (very important) issue money, and which is a system structured by national borders that influence trading and migration. Book 1 includes an exploration of some of these other aspects of the market system, including money, government, and European economic integration.

Book 1 starts with introductory chapters on the subject matter and scope of economics, and on the idea of economic modelling. Chapter 2 explains that an economic model is the basis of national economic accounting, and uses this model to provide a 'map' of the various aspects of the economy studied in Book 1. Part 2 introduces the two main types of private economic agents in an economy: households and firms. Parts 3 and 4 then go on to explore the different ways in which economists model the activity of firms within markets. This picks up the emphasis noted above on problems of market functioning, since it begins from what economists call 'imperfect' markets, and treats perfectly competitive markets as a special, though important, case.

Part 5 offers a pause: instead of new economic theory, the single chapter in this part (Chapter 9) addresses the use of basic descriptive statistics in economics, and in the process considers some of the problems of method referred to above. Part 6 returns to the institutional concerns of Part 2, and considers two other major institutions of the market system: money and government. Finally, the last two parts of Book 1 turn to the international economy: transnational firms, international markets, and European integration. The final chapter (Chapter 15) reflects on different ways of understanding the market system as a whole, in considering the huge transition to a market system that is underway in Eastern Europe and the former Soviet Union.

Book 2 turns from models of markets to models of national economies. This is the field of macroeconomics and, as the first chapter notes, macroeconomic theorizing is deeply involved with the shifting concerns of economic policy. Chapter 16 provides a historical perspective on the interaction at the macroeconomic level between economic ideas and economic change, which is a theme of the whole text, and provides a framework for Book 2.

Parts 10 and 11 introduce and explore macroeconomic theory. From the beginning, the text acknowledges the importance of the international economy to events and policy at the national level, and the economic theory teaching reflects this, treating the economy from the start as open to the international market. Each chapter links economic models to economic policy debates, and Chapter 20 employs the theory just taught to examine in more depth some aspects of twentieth-century economic history.

Part 12, which focuses on the labour market, is something of a turning point in Book 2. Debates about the labour market are key elements of many macroeconomic policy debates. But the labour market is also central to attempts to explain the distribution of poverty and wealth in an economy. Part 13 therefore turns to explanations of the distribution of income, and the extent to which governments can and should redistribute income and wealth.

It is a characteristic of all market economies that they fluctuate, with good times followed by periods of lower employment and slow growth. Part 14 considers explanations of these fluctuations, and the unemployment and inflation that accompanies them. Part 15 then offers, like Part 5, a pause for consideration of data analysis in economics, focused this time on using economic data to analyse change over time, and linking back to some of the problems raised in the previous two chapters.

The final part of the text turns to some important current developments and debates for the longer term: environmental constraints on growth, and the search for international co-ordination of economic policy.

Throughout the text, we have used a number of conventions to assist your studying. The main ones are the following:

Reflections

These indicate a place to stop and think. The reflections ask you to pause to summarize your learning so far, or to try and relate your own experience to the text, before moving on.

Questions

Again, you should stop and try to find an answer to these yourself before reading the commentary that follows in the text. They are designed to help you find out how well you have understood the preceding material, and to get you to pause and think for yourself.

Exercises

The exercises allow you to test your understanding of concepts and techniques by applying and practising them. The answers are at the back of the book. You should not give in to the temptation to skip these, since they are an important part of the teaching. Sometimes you will only understand the following section if you have worked through an earlier exercise.

Sections on technique

Finally, these sections, printed on a pink background, develop further technical aspects of the subject discussed in a chapter. These *are* sections that you can skip, if you wish, the first time you read the chapter. You can then go back to them later. Some are sections which you may not need at all if you know some maths, some provide numerical examples, and some are essential background for later work. They are separated out in this way to avoid breaking up the main line of argument in a chapter with what may seem like technical digressions.

Welcome to *Economics and Changing Economies*. We hope that you enjoy this invitation to what we regard as the fascinating subject of economics.

BOOK I

The Market System

PART 1

CHAPTER 1

by Maureen Mackintosh

ECONOMIC ISSUES AND ECONOMIC MODELS

ECONOMIC ISSUES

1 Introduction

Every era defines for itself its most pressing economic problems. They emerge from a complex public dialogue, involving ideas and experience, theories and political pressures. Economists influence and take part in that dialogue, but they certainly do not control it. At times, as in Britain in the 1980s under Margaret Thatcher's premiership, highly abstract economic theory becomes an overt tool of political debate. In Britain's case, the theory led to the promotion of free markets as the basis for government policy. At other times, although the role of economics in politics may be less overt, assumptions about what is economically possible and desirable still influence political behaviour. John Maynard Keynes, perhaps the twentieth century's most famous economist, wrote at the end of his best known book:

> the ideas of economists and political philosophers, both when
> they are right and when they are wrong, are more powerful than
> is commonly understood … Practical men, who believe
> themselves to be quite exempt from any intellectual influences,
> are usually the slaves of some defunct economist.
>
> *(Keynes, 1936, p.383)*

The tone may be rather self-congratulatory, but the point has as much force now as in the 1930s. Economic issues change, but economic ideas continue to matter. To introduce this book, I have therefore chosen several major economic issues which are both important in current debate, and which I believe to have a long shelf-life. They have been of recurrent concern – over centuries in some cases – and will be with us for a long time yet.

The economic issues introduced in the chapter are:

- the question of global economic leadership: the reasons for the rise and fall of dominant economic powers;
- the recurrent debate about unemployment and inflation in economies throughout the world; and
- the closely interlinked issues of poverty and environmental sustainability – global economic issues for the end of the twentieth century.

Each of these issues is explored at greater length in many of the chapters in this text.

In this chapter I link a discussion of a set of ideas in economic theory to each issue. In Section 2 the question of economic leadership leads into a discussion of theories about how economies grow and change over time. In

Section 3 the problems of unemployment and inflation provide the context for an introduction to differing economic conceptions of markets. Section 4 suggests that addressing poverty and sustainability has forced economists to look more closely at the nature and development of economic institutions. Overall, I hope that this chapter will provide an inviting, if very preliminary, answer to the question 'what is economics about?', and an introduction to some ideas that run through the text.

2 Winners and losers: growth and decline

2.1 Changing the leaders: the rise of Pacific Asia

In 1988 Paul Kennedy published a book which became a bestseller in the USA. Called *The Rise and Fall of the Great Powers*, it explores the links between economic change and military conflict in the post-Renaissance world. The book tells a compelling story of the interaction between technical and commercial success and military might in the rise of successive great powers: Spain, the Netherlands, France, Britain, the USA. But what particularly captured the imagination of people in the USA was the discussion of the characteristic dilemmas faced by great powers at their height. In the long run, Kennedy argued, economic and military strength appear closely connected; at the turning point, over-ambition and costly wars have reinforced a cumulative process of relative economic – and hence military – decline.

The parallels with public concerns in the USA were sharp and evident. The country was going through an acute fit of anxiety about its sliding economic strength relative to its chief economic rival, Japan. The resonance of these fears about loss of world hegemony was evident during the 1992 US presidential elections, which brought to power a president disposed to pursue more active industrial and trade policies than those of the Reagan/ Bush years, in order to try and regain US economic leadership.

There is no doubt that the USA does face an economic challenge. Kennedy's concept of economic leadership focused particularly on dominance in manufacturing and trade. The USA shares in world totals of both have been slipping since the Second World War. In the early 1950s, the USA was producing 45 per cent of world manufacturing production (Table 1.1). The next twenty years saw an unprecedented expansion: accumulated world industrial output in those years was comparable to that in the previous century and a half. The USA remained the single largest producer, but its relative output slid to one-third (Table 1.1), while the US share of world manufacturing *exports* dropped from about a third to 16 per cent (Armstrong *et al.*, 1984).

As Table 1.1 suggests, although much of US attention in these years was directed to the Cold War battle with the USSR, the major economic threat building up was from Japan. Shortly after Kennedy wrote his book, the Soviet Union broke up and the constituent countries began the struggle to establish market-based economic systems. But the end of the perceived Soviet threat and the apparent victory of capitalism has served to focus political attention on the capitalist challenge from East Asia. There, the very rapid growth of Japan is being emulated by South Korea and Taiwan. More broadly, economic growth seems to be slipping away from Europe and the

Table 1.1   **Shares of various countries and regions in world manufacturing production (%)**

Date	USA	Europe	UK	USSR	Japan	China	Brazil
1913	32.0	40.8	13.6	8.2	2.7	3.6	0.5
1938	31.4	37.3	10.7	9.0	5.2	3.1	0.6
1953	44.7	26.1	8.4	10.7	2.9	2.3	0.6
1963	35.1	26.5	6.4	14.2	5.1	3.5	0.8
1973	33.0	24.5	4.9	14.4	8.8	3.9	1.1
1980	31.5	22.9	4.0	14.8	9.1	5.0	1.4

Source: Bairoch (1982) p.304

eastern seaboard of the United States, towards the whole Pacific rim, including South East Asia, Australia and the high-tech industries of California. In the words of one specialist on the region, 'The centre of world economic gravity is shifting rapidly towards Asia and the Pacific, as the Pacific takes its place as one of the key centres of world economic power' (Drysdale, 1986, p.11). The twenty-first century, it now seems to many, is likely to be the 'Pacific century' (Linder, 1986), a new focus of economic and, perhaps later, military power.

In this story there are a number of important economic issues. What do these concepts of economic leadership and economic strength – used so casually in the newspapers – really mean? How can we measure changing relative economic power? And why do these huge long-term shifts occur? The rest of this section considers these questions.

Economic growth in Pacific Asia

There are several ways to measure the strength of an economy, for example by its size, the rate at which it is growing, or the success of its industries in out-competing those of competitor nations. Each of these indicators suggests that the Pacific Asian region is now economically important.

Consider size first. We can measure the size of an economy by its gross domestic product (GDP) or its gross national product (GNP). You will find a precise definition of these terms in Chapter 2. For my purpose here, GDP measures the total output of a country, including exports. By 'output' I mean *final* output, after subtracting goods (such as steel) which are immediately used to produce other goods (such as cars). Net income earned abroad by a country's residents is added to this total to give GNP.

On this basis it has been calculated that the share in world output of the whole Pacific basin, including Australia, New Zealand and the US Pacific states, rose from 16 per cent in 1960 to 22 per cent in 1980, or from just over a third to about one-half of the gross output of the Atlantic basin (Western Europe plus the US Atlantic States) (Linder, 1986). If we consider just the largest Pacific Asian countries by population or incomes per head – that is, Japan, China, South Korea, Taiwan, Hong Kong, Indonesia, Malaysia, Singapore, the Philippines and Thailand – then by 1991 their share alone of world GNP was 21.8 per cent, up from 10.2 per cent in 1969 (see Figure 1.1).

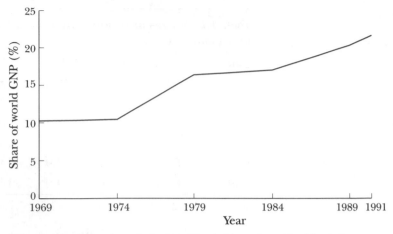

Figure 1.1 **The rise of the Pacific Asia region: Pacific Asia as a percentage of world GNP**

Source: *Europa World Year Book*, various years

Of all these countries, the most dramatic economic success story has been Japan. In 1957, after reconstructing a war-ravaged economy, Japan had average incomes per head only 13 per cent of US levels (Komiya, 1990). A country with few natural resources and a high population density, Japan began industrializing in earnest in the second half of the nineteenth century. The turning point in its history is often put at 1868, when the first emperor of the Meiji period ended the country's economic and social isolation from the rest of the world.

After that date, the country's infrastructure was rapidly improved, a central bank was established, a civilian government was elected, and Japan began to

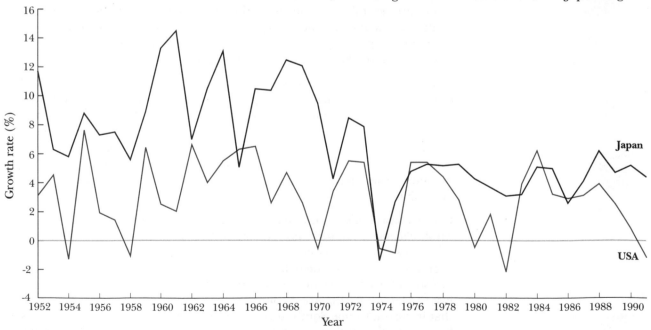

Figure 1.2 **Japan and USA: growth rates, 1952–1991**

Source: Japan Statistical Association (1987), OECD (1982), *OECD Economic Outlook* (1992), US Department of Commerce (1975)

build an empire. Foreign technology was actively sought. By the Second World War, Japan had changed from an agricultural to a light manufacturing economy, with rising exports. The country was to repeat the trick with heavy manufacturing and then electronics after 1950 (Ito, 1992).

By 1940, then, Japan was already growing rapidly. After the grim task of post-war reconstruction, the growth rate took off again. Figure 1.2 compares Japanese growth rates with those of the United States, and shows the enormously high rate of Japanese growth up to 1973. Between 1950 and 1973, the 'era of high speed growth' (Kosai, 1986), the Japanese economy grew at an average rate of 10 per cent per year, doubling in size every seven years.

Then came 1973, the year of the first 'oil crisis', when the Organization of Petroleum Exporting Countries (OPEC) quadrupled the international price of oil. Japan, wholly dependent on imports of oil, saw its growth slow down, but the economy still grew at a respectable average of 5 per cent per year between 1975 and 1980.

The implications of these growth rates was that Japan was catching up with USA – and with Europe – over the post-war period. This catching up was experienced most acutely by Europe and the USA in terms of industrial competition. Cars and electrical and electronic products are well-known examples. Figure 1.3 shows the sharp rise in car production in Japan, which caught up with US production levels in the late 1970s; the growth in production of the newer East Asian producers appears in the bottom right-hand corner. In both cars and electronics, Japan began by exporting, then moved production overseas to overcome resistance to rising Japanese imports in the European and US markets. Production by Japanese-owned firms came to dominate many markets. As another much-cited book on US decline expressed it, 'Americans invented the video camera and recorder and the fax; Europeans (the Dutch) invented the CD player. But measured in terms of sales, employment and profits, all three have become Japanese products' (Thurow, 1992, p.47).

By 1992 Japanese incomes per head were approaching US levels. What is worrying the USA is not only the historic catching up, but the trend. US official studies have concluded that the country looks particularly weak in some of the technologies of the future – the basis of the 'sunrise industries'

Figure 1.3 **Automobile production in selected Pacific rim countries**

Source: Nemetz (1990)

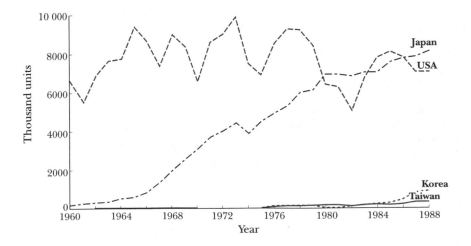

– such as robotics and many areas of electronics where Japan looks very strong, though the USA is still a leader in others, such as biotechnology (Thurow, 1992).

Meanwhile, the Japanese themselves are worrying about economic slowdown, and they too are looking over their shoulders – at the challenge from South Korea and Taiwan, and in the longer term from China. The rest of Pacific Asia is explicitly bent on emulating the Japanese success. South Korea has replicated in its own fashion Japan's progression from labour-intensive manufactured exports to higher-technology production, and like Japan has developed powerful companies that have moved into production overseas.

The newest economic competitor, however, is China. In the 1980s the Chinese economy grew at 9.5 per cent per year, much the same rate as South Korea, and as I write it shows no signs of slowing down. China contains 1.15 billion people, and may well be Asia's 'next economic giant' (Perkins, 1986).

Furthermore, the Pacific Asian countries support each other's growth: for example, they are important markets for each other's manufactures, and Japanese foreign investment is moving into China. Pacific Asia may be developing into a trading bloc to challenge others such as the European Union.

You will find much more on these issues of growth, competitiveness and trading blocs in this text, particularly in Chapters 12–14. I want now to stop for a moment and define some terms more carefully before I go on to relate these issues to some ideas from economic theory.

Understanding size and growth

So far I have used a number of economic terms rather casually: output, relative size, growth. These are all concepts involving measurement, and it will help to be more precise about these terms.

The relative size of economies is, as already suggested, a distinctly political issue. The question of the relative size of the USA and Japan will illustrate the problem nicely. To compare the output of the two countries, we need to translate output measured in dollars into output measured in yen. There are two ways to do this, using *exchange rates* or using measures of *purchasing power*. The two methods sometimes give remarkably different answers. First, look at the definition of exchange rates.

Definition

Exchange rates

The exchange rate between two currencies is the price at which one currency is traded for another. So, for example, the exchange rate between the Japanese yen and the US dollar on the day I am writing this is ¥108.3 to $1.

To compare levels of output or incomes in the two countries, we can add up the totals for each country, and translate them from one to the other using the current exchange rate. Figure 1.4 shows the relative size of the world's economies on an exchange rate basis. However, there is a problem with this. One thousand yen, once exchanged into dollars, may buy more goods in the USA than it does in Japan, since the yen is a strong currency in international markets. If so, measuring Japanese incomes by translating yen into dollars in this way may overstate how much Japanese people can really buy at home with their incomes, relative to US citizens. An alternative measure may therefore be better.

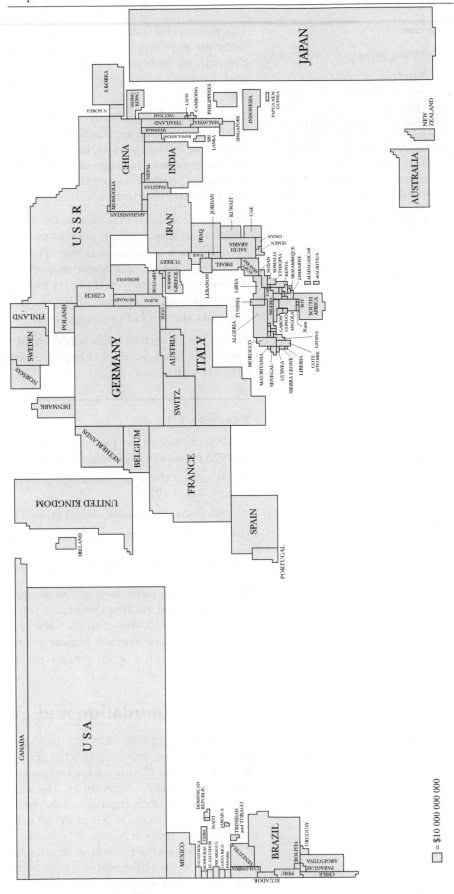

***Figure 1.4* The relative size of economies on an exchange rate basis, 1988**

Note: data for Germany combine figures from the then Federal and Democratic Republics

Source: Thomas *et al.* (1994)

Definition

Purchasing power of currencies

The purchasing power of a currency is the amount of goods it will purchase within its home economy. The purchasing power of currencies (PPC) conversion rate between dollars and yen, therefore, treats one dollar as equivalent to the amount of yen that will purchase in Japan the same goods as the dollar will purchase in the USA.

The second and increasingly common way to compare two economies is by using the purchasing power of currencies conversion rate. This allows us to compare incomes in two countries on the basis of the goods and services that the incomes will purchase at home. Look now at the definition of this.

The two measures give different answers to politically important questions. The Japanese economy was 60 per cent of the size of the US economy in 1991 using exchange rates, but only 43 per cent of the size using the purchasing power measure. If we look at average income per head, then on the exchange rate measure the Japanese were richer in 1991, while, on the PPC measure, they were not yet as rich.

The lesson of this is that there is no 'right' way to measure relative size; it depends on what we want to measure. The Japanese yen is strong – its exchange rate is higher than the PPC measure suggests that it should be – so Japanese purchasing power abroad is higher than it is at home. Americans, conversely, feel poorer in Japan than at home. Japanese tourism is thus (partially) explained! Chapter 11 discusses some of the factors that influence the level of exchange rates.

Earlier in this section I also talked about rates of growth of total output and output per head. Rates of change are used constantly in economics. Are you at home with them?

Exercise 1.1

In 1970 the size of the Japanese economy was measured at ¥152208 billion. In 1973 it was ¥185923 billion. On the basis of these figures alone,

1   What was the *total* percentage growth in the Japanese economy between 1970 and 1973?

2   What was the *annual average* growth rate over those three years?

Work out the answers if you can (but do not spend too long on them), then look them up at the end of the book.

If you got them right, then well done, growth rates clearly hold no mysteries. If you got them wrong, or if you were unsure how to start, then the final section of this chapter, 'Line graphs and growth rates', explains how to calculate and graph growth rates. You can turn to that section now and work through it before you go on, or you can read on below and return to this exercise later.

2.2   Accumulation and growth

Why do these great shifts in economic power and leadership happen? Or, to put the question another way, what are the driving forces behind economic growth, and what holds some countries back? These questions have interested thinkers for centuries. The eighteenth-century classic by Adam Smith which is often regarded as the founding document of economics as a distinct subject of study, has as its full title *An Inquiry into the Nature and Causes of the Wealth of Nations*. The book's central theme is an exploration of the conditions under which, as Smith writes in his introduction, 'the nation will be better or worse supplied with all the necessaries and conveniences for which it has occasion.'

Smith was writing at a time which historians identify in retrospect as an economic turning point: when the pace of economic change in Britain, the leading country in the Industrial Revolution, was beginning to quicken. However, the rate of economic growth in the eighteenth century was far slower than the rates described above for the mid twentieth century. There exist no economic statistics for this period of the type I used for recent economic growth in the USA and Japan – the systematic collection of national statistics developed as the complexity of both markets and government grew – but output in Britain appears to have grown at perhaps 0.6 per cent per year between 1700 and 1760, and at somewhere between 1 per cent and 1.2 per cent during the remainder of the century (Brown, 1992). Nevertheless, the manufacturing processes which were to transform the rate of economic growth were beginning to be created, and Smith was observing these changes.

Many of the elements which later economists have included in their understanding of growth and economic development were discussed by Smith. They include the organization of labour, the accumulation of capital stock, the size of the market open to producers, and the balance between agriculture and manufacturing.

Smith began his book with an influential discussion of the division of labour. He chose for his illustration a 'very trifling manufacture', pinmaking, and noted that the process of making a pin was 'divided into about eighteen distinct operations, which, in some manufactories, are all performed by distinct hands.' This, he said, allowed a group of workers to produce far more together than if each had produced one whole pin at a time.

> This great increase in the quantity of work which, in consequence of the division of labour, the same number of people are capable of performing, is owing to three different circumstances; first, to the increase of dexterity in every particular workman; secondly, to the saving of the time which is commonly lost in passing from one species of work to another, and lastly to the invention of a great number of machines which facilitate and abridge labour and enable one man to do the work of many.

> *(Smith, 1776, p.3)*

This was an argument with a long future ahead of it. The culmination of this approach to increasing the output per head of workers in manufacturing industry lay in the automated production line for the mass production of standard consumer goods. Its most famous exponent was Henry Ford, who first introduced the continuous moving assembly line in Detroit in 1914. The effect on output of the Model T Ford was dramatic: within three months the time needed to assemble one car had been reduced to one-tenth of that previously required (Braverman, 1974). This marked the end of artisanal car production except in a few curious corners such as the Morgan Motor Company.

Although there is a recurrent thread of interest in these issues in economics, the most influential theorists of the changing organization of production have been management experts, not economists. One of the best known was Frederick Winslow Taylor, who pioneered the 'scientific management' movement in the late nineteenth century; indeed, the use of production line technology to exert maximum management control over fragmented work processes is often called 'Taylorism'. Management theorists, influenced by the success of apparently rather different mass production methods in Japan, are now exploring the limitations of, and alternatives to, Taylorism, emphasizing its costs. They counterpose the benefits of teamwork, flexibility (a buzz-word of 1990s management theory) and multiskilling. Economists are becoming seriously interested again in the links between organization of production and economic success, a theme taken up in Chapters 4 and 12.

Adam Smith linked the division of labour to what we would now call technical change. Contemporary economists agree that the invention of new products and new ways of producing things are very important forces driving the growth of firms and economies. An influential study in the 1960s (Denison, 1967) concluded that 'advances in knowledge' appeared to account for between a quarter and a third of economic growth in North West Europe and the United States. A great deal of subsequent research has explored the link between such technical improvement and Smith's second main driver of economic growth: capital accumulation, or investment.

Smith noted in Book 2 of *The Wealth of Nations* that the expansion of production requires some part of incomes from production to be kept back from immediate consumption, and instead reinvested in the next round of productive activity. Investment serves to increase and improve the equipment in manufacturing, and hence to improve the productive capacity of firms and countries. This idea forms a central element of all economic models of growth. Contemporary debates on economic growth centre on the complex relations between the two processes of technical change and investment. How are they determined? Can they be separated out? How are they related? You will get a flavour of these debates in Chapter 14.

So if technical change and investment motor growth, what motivates investment and innovation? The most common answer within economics is: the expectation of making money out of it. Note the word 'expectation': you will meet it again. Investing in a new production process is a bet on the future – which may not come off. Potential investors can obtain as much information as possible to form their expectations – hence the importance of forecasting and the livelihood of many economists – but in the end they must take a risk in conditions of uncertainty. Taking this kind of risk is called *entrepreneurship,* and it is an important motor of economic change.

Sociologists have been particularly interested in understanding the conditions that produce entrepreneurs. Economists have not devoted a great deal of attention to this, but it is now also the focus of renewed interest. One of the best known theorists in this field was Joseph Schumpeter. In *The Theory of Economic Development* (1934) Schumpeter emphasized that economies do not simply expand by doing more of the same as before, but they change qualitatively in organization and output as they expand. Schumpeter called the agents of this qualitative change the entrepreneurs, who might be owners of firms or managers, so long as they were in a position to institute change. He then pointed out that the motivation of such entrepreneurs could not be pure personal gain, in the hedonistic sense. If it was, they would soon sit back and enjoy any wealth gained, and not continue to drive a company forward.

Instead, Schumpeter suggested several other motives: 'the dream and will to found a private kingdom', 'the will to conquer', and the 'joy of creating, of getting things done, or simply of exercising one's energy and ingenuity' (Schumpeter, 1934, p.93). Schumpeter's view of entrepreneurs was therefore of people who can break out of a rut, move parts of the world away from existing routines. Innovations in this sense include producing a new widget, but also include finding new markets for widgets, changing firms' organizational cultures to produce widgets in different ways, and finding new sources of widget inputs. Which cultures and which forms of organization of societies and companies best produce 'winners' in this sense has been a recurrent theme of social science investigation. Nineteenth- and early twentieth-century ideas linked capitalist entrepreneurship to Protestant ethics. Current debate recognizes that the organizational success of capitalism in Japan draws on different cultural roots (Dore, 1992).

Curiously, however, these big issues of long-term change have *not* been the central preoccupation of post-war economics. In the nineteenth and early twentieth centuries, growth seemed unstable, conflictual, problematic. This was the context in which David Ricardo – an eminent nineteenth-century economist – worried about the dangers of stagnation, and in which Karl Marx produced his influential vision of capitalism as an unstable system in which investment and technical change are driven by conflict: conflict between capitalists, and between capital and labour. This broad sweep of concern with 'dynamics' – change, especially large and discontinuous change, over historical time – has been replaced in recent years by a narrower focus on the workings of the market mechanism. Growth and stability for a while seemed to be taken for granted.

3   The workings of markets: order and disorder

3.1   Employment and unemployment in Europe

A man willing to work and unable to find work is perhaps the saddest sight that fortune's inequality exhibits under the sun.

(Thomas Carlyle, 1839)

Fear of unemployment is as old as the economic system whereby people need to sell their capacity to labour in return for income in order to survive. That is, it dates back to the development of a market in labour, to supply newly developing industries and services with 'hands'. In many countries the creation of a labour market coincided with that great movement of people, discussed by Adam Smith, off the land and into industries. In Britain this was driven in the later eighteenth century by the demand for labour in the mills. In other industrializing countries, for example in Asia and Latin America, the movement came later, but has been no less dramatic, creating a huge wave of movement to the cities.

The creation of a labour market was one of the most significant changes brought about by the economic system we call capitalism. True, there had been some buying and selling of labour before the Industrial Revolution, but the scale of the changes brought by industrial capitalism was enormous, as old social structures and allegiances were swept away, access to older forms of economic survival was destroyed, and markets were created in labour and goods which came to dominate economic life. In Europe and in Latin America there have been many observers of these changes who have thought them unsustainable. The social and economic costs and conflicts have seemed to them too great. Karl Marx, writing in mid-nineteenth-century Britain, argued that the system would tend to self-destruct under the weight of its internal contradictions. Karl Polanyi, another central European exile writing in Britain and the USA in the midst of the Second World War, looked back to the 1930s as an era which seemed to show that a system dominated by markets in everything, including labour, money and land, would come apart in chaos and authoritarianism (Polanyi, 1944).

Since then, Europe has been through a period of much greater optimism about the market system. East Asians, as I have suggested, tend to be optimistic that the system, duly adapted, suits their ambitions. Elsewhere, feelings are more mixed. The big countries in Latin America, such as Brazil, have had periods of growth almost as rapid as East Asia, and have been through social changes as extensive. But the costs in terms of unemployment and social instability have generally been much higher.

European labour markets

The labour market is now a pervasive influence in all our lives. Even in countries where industrialization has barely occurred, such as some African countries, people participate in the regional and global labour markets through patterns of long-distance migration. In the rural areas of West Africa I have met many people who have worked in Europe. In countries such as China and Russia, where people have long been subject to tight direction as to where they work, a more open labour market is now rapidly developing. And the rights of so-called 'economic migrants'– people seeking to move across international borders in search of work – have become an issue of political debate in Europe. Labour markets affect us all.

As a result, access to or exclusion from the labour market is a crucial economic issue for individuals. Position in the labour market is a central determinant of the quality of people's livelihoods. Furthermore, labour market experience is highly differentiated, the form indeed taken by 'fortune's inequality' in our times.

In Western Europe in the early post-war period, labour markets seemed to be working well. Unemployment was generally low, and school leavers found jobs fairly easily. Immigration into Europe rose to meet labour demand: for example, West Indian immigration to take up manual jobs in Britain was encouraged by the government.

Definitions

Unemployment and the labour force

An *unemployed* person is someone who is actively seeking work but unable to find it. The total of those working and seeking work constitute the *labour force*. The unemployment rate is therefore measured relative to the labour force.

The definitions opposite of unemployment and the labour force are by no means as straightforward as might appear. Here are two reasons why not: people who would like to work may be discouraged from seeking it by the evident absence of jobs in their locality, and people who are in fact looking for work may not be counted because they are not eligible for unemployment benefit. In countries without unemployment benefit systems, statistics of unemployment may be even shakier. You will find a discussion of unemployment data problems in Chapter 9.

Question

Look carefully at Figure 1.5, and summarize for yourself the main trends in unemployment in Europe, as compared with the USA and Japan.

Figure 1.5 shows the low unemployment rates of the 1960s in Western Europe and Japan. In these years, the scourge of unemployment, so well remembered from the 1930s, seemed finally to have been defeated. Rather, employers complained of the difficulty of recruitment. Looking back, some call the period a 'golden age' in Europe. Chapter 20 examines the period as a case study in things going right, economically speaking.

Figure 1.5 also shows the turnaround in Western European unemployment experience after 1970. In the UK, France and West Germany, unemployment climbed. For the USA and Japan, the turnaround was much less dramatic. Japan's unemployment rate has remained relatively low, while the US rate started higher but rose less. The US figures, however, somewhat understate the level of male joblessness, since unemployed men, ineligible for benefits, tend to drop out of the labour force. Europe has seen a sharp drop in

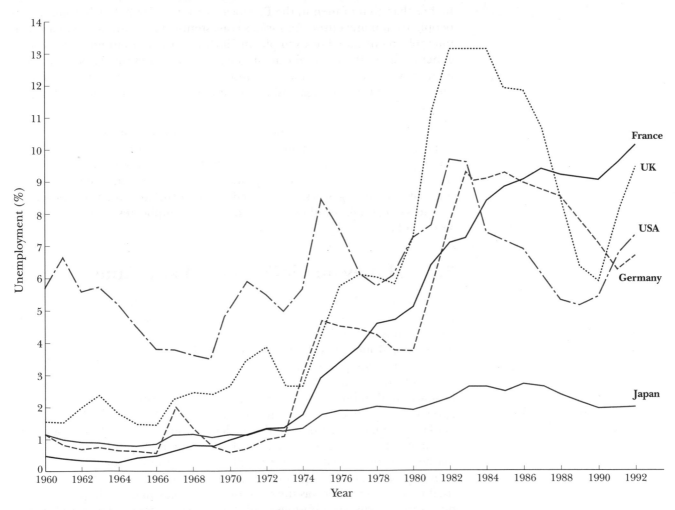

Figure 1.5   **Unemployment in Western Europe, the USA and Japan, 1960–1992**

Source: *Bulletin of Labour Statistics*, various years

demand for less skilled male manual labour in manufacturing, and rising long-term joblessness as a result.

Furthermore, the upward trend in European unemployment seems depressingly persistent. As anyone in employment or in business knows, market economies tend to fluctuate over time; they have good years and bad years. In bad years unemployment rises, and the general level of economic activity falls. In good years these trends are reversed. Economists call these short-term fluctuations *business cycles*, and they are discussed later in the text. The problem is that each cycle of good years has failed to reduce unemployment to its previous level, so there has been a 'ratchet' effect, with average unemployment climbing with each cycle.

European labour markets now, therefore, seem to be working rather badly and excluding large numbers of people. Furthermore, the probability of being excluded is heavily influenced by social factors, such as class, level of education and skill, gender and 'race'. The effects of these factors are complex. Throughout Europe in the last thirty years, many of the new manufacturing and service jobs have gone to women, but in some countries including Britain, much of this increase has been in part-time work. In spite of this, with the sole exception of Britain, women's unemployment rate was higher than that of men in the European Union in 1993. Furthermore, people from many ethnic minorities consistently have a higher than average unemployment rate. For example, in 1984, when UK unemployment was generally high, the unemployment rate for white males was 11 per cent; for men of West Indian or Guyanese ethnic origin it was 30 per cent, and for men of Pakistani or Bangladeshi descent it was 33 per cent (*Social Trends*, 1992).

Unemployment is not a problem limited to Europe, of course. The worst fear of unemployment is experienced in countries that are developing a labour market, but have little in the way of a social security safety net for the unemployed. In much of Latin America the difficulty of finding work is reflected in acute urban and rural poverty. At the same time, another market disorder complicates people's lives: severe inflation.

3.2   Money and inflation in Latin America

Money oils the wheels of commerce, and debt fuels growth in industrial capitalism. On these two generalizations economic historians are agreed. A complex market-based industrial economy cannot function without money and credit. Money provides flexibility in markets, allowing sellers to swap goods for general purchasing power, to be spent later. Credit allows firms to make investments from borrowed funds, to be repaid from returns to the business. Both money and banking seem as old as history: paper money appears to have been invented in eleventh-century China, and there was banking and money lending in the ancient world (Braudel, 1982). But it was the demands of industrial capitalism that created the complex money markets we know today. One great shift was to the widespread use of metal coinage, and then to the predominance of paper money which we are so used to today. Another was the creation of complex markets in paper claims on future returns from business and trade, such as stocks, shares and bonds: you will find more on these financial assets in Chapter 11.

Like labour markets, money and credit markets bring risks. Stock market speculative booms and subsequent collapses are a staple of newspaper headlines. In 1993, for example, the stock markets of the East Asian industrializing countries were booming, and a downturn was widely predicted. The eighteenth and nineteenth centuries saw a number of speculative booms, such as the South Sea Bubble, in which many investors lost their capital. Perhaps most famous of all, the 1930s depression was triggered by the Wall Street crash. But the most common risk lies in the devaluation of a currency through inflation.

One hundred per cent inflation means that prices have doubled in one year. This phenomenon is also as old as widespread monetized exchange, and is by no means limited to paper money systems. In seventeenth- and eighteenth-century France, for example, the 'base coinage' (copper coins) used for small purchases by the common people was constantly depreciating in value (Braudel, 1982).

The general level of prices can fall as well as rise, but such negative inflation has been unusual in the twentieth century. Some countries saw falling prices in the 1930s depression, but since 1945 the main industrialized countries have generally experienced moderate inflation. Inflation of 10 per cent per year is regarded as high, so when in 1975 the annual rate of inflation of UK consumer prices briefly exceeded 25 per cent, it was regarded with horror. However, countries undergoing sharp economic change tend to be more inflationary. South Korea averaged 12.2 per cent inflation over the whole period 1961–91. But by far the worst chronic inflation has been in Latin American countries, which, with the Caribbean, averaged 192 per cent inflation per year over the same period (World Bank, 1993).

Inflation in Brazil

Brazil reappears later in this chapter, so let me start with a little general background. Brazil is an extraordinarily diverse country of 150 million people. It is in many good and bad ways reminiscent of the USA of an earlier era (complete with murderous frontier). In the eighteenth and nineteenth centuries, fortunes were made in Brazil from gold and diamonds, from rubber plantations and from slave-worked coffee and sugar (Hewitt, 1992). Some of this cash was invested in creating cities and in early manufacturing industry. Like Japan, therefore, Brazil was already industrializing before the beginning of this century, but was a long way behind Europe and North America in 1950.

Since 1950, again like Japan, Brazil has had periods of very rapid growth. Brazil's so-called 'economic miracle' ran from the mid 1960s to the mid 1970s, when the country grew very much faster than Europe or North America. But Brazil's post-war economic development, unlike Japan's, has been immensely uneven and crisis-ridden.

The 'crisis' aspect of Brazilian growth has included instability in growth rates, chronic inflation, acute poverty and environmental problems. None of these problems is unique to Brazil, but it is precisely Brazil's relative success amid these problems – and the sheer underlying energy of the country – that makes this an interesting case study for my purposes.

Figure 1.6 shows Brazil's growth rate. One striking feature is that when the rest of the world, including Japan, slowed down after 1973, Brazil continued

Definition

Inflation

Inflation means a general rise in the price level in a country, as opposed to an increase in the price of any particular good.

to grow rapidly, despite being, like Japan, an oil importer. But it did so at the cost of rising international debt. All industrializing countries tend to incur foreign debt. They borrow overseas to invest in local production, with the intention of repaying the debt from growth and exports, just as a European firm might incur debt to a local bank. The problems start when the debt cannot be serviced – that is, when the cost of interest payments and repayments on the loans gets too high. This happened to Brazil – and to many other countries – in 1982, when international interest rates rose sharply. For several years, default by the large debtor countries – and Brazil was the largest – threatened to bring down some of the largest international banks, and thus to wreck the world trading system. This is what western governments and newspapers meant by the 'debt crisis', and you will find more about it in Chapter 20.

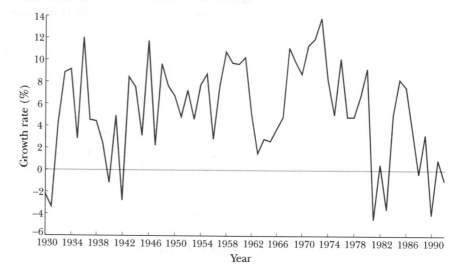

Figure 1.6 **Brazil's growth rate, 1930–1992**

Source: Dornbusch and Edwards (1991), *World Economic Outlook*, various years, *Anuário Estatístico do Brasil* (1987–88)

For Brazil, the immediate effect was dire. In 1983 GDP dropped sharply. Figure 1.6 shows the negative growth rates. Worse, the country was exporting large sums to pay some part of its debt obligations, so the incomes left for Brazilians fell even faster than GDP. In addition, the country's chronic inflation worsened.

The Brazilian economy seems to have a built-in inflationary bias. Figure 1.7 shows some of the inflationary history (note that on the vertical axis the scale for the first 250 per cent has been 'magnified' to allow you to see the variation in the lower inflation rates). Inflation after 1955 was not often below 20 per cent per year. Between 1983 and 1988, after the economic crisis set in, prices were rising at over 200 per cent per year on average. But worse was to come. In 1989-90, after a brief drop, inflation really took off: in March 1990 prices were 800 per cent higher than they had been in November 1989.

Very high rates of inflation of this order are called *hyperinflation*. They are relatively rare historically, and are frequently associated with acute economic and social upheaval. As a result, there have been a relatively high number of such inflationary upheavals in the twentieth century, sparked off by the aftermath of wars and/or the effects of major economic restructuring or debt arrears. These have included the German hyperinflation of 1922–23 (which had an average *monthly* inflation rate of 322 per cent); the Hungarian hyperinflation of 1945–46 (which was worse); and the Polish

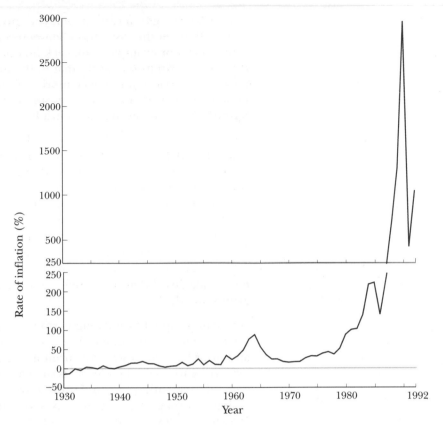

***Figure 1.7*   Brazil: rate of inflation, 1930–1992**

Source: Kiguel and Liviatan (1992), Parkin (1991), *World Economic Outlook*, various years, *Anuário Estatístico do Brasil* (1987–88)

inflation of 1989–90, which was nothing like as fast, but which saw prices quadruple in four months. In Latin America, Bolivia, Nicaragua and Peru all had very severe bouts of inflation in the 1980s (Sachs and Larrain, 1993).

Living with high and especially very variable inflation is not easy. It greatly increases the risks and uncertainty of day-to-day life; it makes ordinary economic transactions more complicated and often more costly; and it damages some groups of people relative to others. To explain this, I need to make a clear distinction between the definitions of real and nominal income

Definitions

Real and nominal income

Your *nominal* income is the cash you receive for your work (and as interest on your savings). Your *real* income, on the other hand, depends on the goods and services you can buy with that income: it is your purchasing power.

Question

Try this question to make sure you understand the definitions before you read on.

Suppose you had an income of £100 per week last year. This year your income has risen to £120 per week. At the same time prices rose by 10 per cent. What was the percentage increase in your nominal income? And how much did your real income rise over the year?

If you answered that there was a 20 per cent increase in nominal income and a 9.1 per cent increase in real income, then you clearly understand the two concepts. If your answer was 20 per cent and 10 per cent, then you have the right idea about the concepts, but need to work on the arithmetic. You will find a discussion of calculating percentage changes over time in the final section of this chapter, and exercises on calculating the relation between real and nominal data in Chapter 2. What is important here is to grasp that changes in cash incomes are not always what they seem. You will constantly meet the distinction between real and nominal magnitudes in economics. For example, look back now at Figures 1.2 and 1.6. Both of these are drawn in *real* terms: that is, the increase in output implies more goods and services, and hence more real income for people in the country. Otherwise the story I told above would not have made much sense: the 'growth' I was measuring might just have been price increases.

So back to life under inflation. If you live on a fixed *nominal* income, then price rises make life very uncomfortable. Suppose your wage is fixed for a year, then prices double. By the end of the year you are living on half your previous income. This is the more likely to happen to you, the less well organized your job is in trade union terms, or the less personally valuable you are to your employer. Typically, people in public sector jobs, and in low-paid and unorganized services, suffer particularly badly when inflation unexpectedly accelerates. So do pensioners living on income from savings. On the other hand, traders often do well, prospering from opportunities for money making. Inflation therefore redistributes income from some social groups to others.

Brazilians adapted over a long period to living with high inflation. High inflation implies that money in the bank rapidly loses its value, so people and firms learned to stay away from holding cash for long periods, preferring to hold tangible assets such as property, the prices of which generally rise with inflation. Furthermore, to keep real incomes from falling, most salaries, rents and tax allowances in Brazil between 1964 and 1986 were indexed to the rate of inflation; that is, they went up regularly in line with rising prices, so that continuing inflation was built into the system.

The worst problems do not arise from consistently high inflation, but when inflation suddenly accelerates. The combination of rising inflation and falling output in Brazil in the 1980s constituted a lethal mixture for the poor, who relied on tiny incomes. Very high and variable inflation make it even harder than usual for firms to predict their future incomes – to form expectations – and hence to know how and where to invest, and it undermines the useful role of cash in retail markets. So social divisions widen, and markets becomes less efficient. In 1990 and 1992, the years of dramatically high inflation, Brazilian economic growth was negative.

However, as the Brazilian story shows, persistent inflation is compatible with growth: compare Figures 1.6 and 1.7. As I write this in 1993, the Brazilian economy is growing rapidly again.

3.3   Markets and spontaneous order

I am now going to shift again from issues to theory. I have used this discussion of economic history to make two general points. First, as industrial capitalism has spread throughout the world, it has created a highly complex network of markets, including markets in labour and money. We depend on those markets for our livelihood, but (second point) they can work well or badly. They may seem well ordered, with high employment and low or at least predictable inflation. Or economic life may be more disordered, with dole queues and fears for the purchasing power of wages and savings.

Much of modern economics has been concerned with the attempt to understand how ordered markets function, and what can go wrong with them. I want therefore to take a first look here at how economists think about market order and disorder, to consider some of the assumptions and fundamental categories – the general cast of thought – that underlie the models and judgements you will meet in the rest of this text.

Spontaneous order

The most powerful *general* image economists have of 'things going right' in markets is the idea of 'spontaneous order'. Here is one of the most eloquent modern expressions of that old idea, by the economist Robert Sugden:

> Living things are marvellously intricate and elegant solutions to design problems; problems that are far beyond the grasp of human engineers. This used to be taken as evidence of a divine Designer. But we now know that living things are not the product of any designer; they are the unintended consequences of a blind process of evolution. The deepest insight of economics is that we depend for our survival on a network of exchange that in this respect is like a living thing or an eco-system: it is highly ordered, but no one has ordered it ... The idea of spontaneous order is fundamental to economics.
>
> *(Sugden, 1992, p.179)*

This is a striking image of the economy, 'a network of exchange that is ... like a living thing', an order that no one has designed.

Now here is a much older passage from Adam Smith on the same theme. Part of it may be familiar to you, since it was much quoted for political purposes in the 1980s, at least in Britain and the USA.

> ... man has almost constant occasion for the help of his brethren, and it is in vain for him to expect it from their benevolence only. He will be more likely to prevail if he can interest their self love in his favour, and show them that it is for their own advantage to do for them what he requires of them. Whoever offers to another a bargain of any kind, proposes to do this. Give me that which I want, and you shall have this which you want, is the meaning of every such offer; and it is in this manner that we obtain from one another the far greater part of those good offices which we stand in need of. It is not from the benevolence of the butcher, the brewer or the baker that we expect our dinner, but from their regard to their own interest. We address ourselves, not to their humanity but to their self love, and never talk to them of our own necessities, but of their advantages.
>
> *(Smith, 1776, p.13)*

Through trading, Smith argues in this section, there develops a division of labour in the whole economy to supply goods that others want. Work is parcelled out, and done more efficiently, without any 'human wisdom' which 'foresees and intends that general opulence to which it gives occasion'. Instead, 'It is the necessary, though very slow and gradual consequence of a certain propensity in human nature, which has in view no such extensive utility; the propensity to truck, barter and exchange one thing for another' (p.12).

Later in the book Smith formulates this idea of the unintended beneficial consequences of individual self-interested actions in his well-known metaphor of the 'invisible hand', which leads the merchant 'to promote an end which was no part of his intention' (p.400). This metaphor has been taken up by many others. Here is the economist and political thinker Friedrich Hayek, who used the idea of spontaneous order throughout a long writing life, commenting on Adam Smith and other intellectual predecessors:

> The chief concern of the great individualist writers was indeed to find a set of institutions by which man could be induced, by his own choice and from motives which determined his ordinary conduct, to contribute as much as possible to the needs of all others; and their discovery was that the system of private property did provide such inducements.
>
> *(Hayek, 1949, p.12)*

Question

Before you read on, make sure you have read these passages carefully. What do you think are the most important ideas put forward? Do you see anything striking about the style of writing of the three authors?

I think there are three important ideas developed by these three writers. All are central to much of the economic analysis of markets.

The first is the idea of *self-interest*. People's main objectives, for both Hayek and Smith, are seen to be self-interested ones. Hayek relates this to the concept of 'individualism'. Furthermore, there is an argument that this may be positively desirable: from the interaction of self-interest comes mutual benefit.

How does this interaction happen? This is the second idea: that a process of economic *exchange* acts as the expression of mutual benefit through self-interest. Sugden is the most general. His 'network of exchange' allows for different types of exchange, not only trading on a market. The other two writers explicitly envisage a *market* as the focus for mutually beneficial trading where people 'bargain', 'truck' and 'barter'.

Third, there is the idea of *unintended consequences*. All three writers focus on this point. Human survival, economic progress do not depend on anyone planning those outcomes. Instead, they are an unplanned effect of much narrower aims.

All three of these ideas are embedded in the concept of 'spontaneous order'. 'Spontaneous' here simply means unplanned, resulting from actions not consciously co-ordinated. 'Order' contains the idea, explicit in Smith and Hayek, of a beneficial outcome from anarchic or self-regarding actions; it also contains the idea made explicit by Sugden of an outcome which seems to have a logic of its own ('highly ordered'), although that logic has not been planned. Within this vision of the economy, economics consists of an attempt to lay bare the logic – the apparent rules – which structure the ordered system that we call the market. Many, indeed most, of the economic models you will encounter in the rest of this book form part of this general attempt.

Finally, I asked you whether you were struck by the writing style of these authors. There are many possible answers to this, but I had in mind two aspects: the use of *analogies*, and the importance of *psychological assumptions*.

Sugden uses the analogy of 'blind' evolution to describe spontaneous order, explicitly referring to Richard Dawkins' book on evolution, *The Blind Watchmaker* (1986). Biological analogies are common, though controversial, in economics, and indeed there have been cross-overs between the two subjects, with biologists using economic models. Sugden also uses an ecological system as an analogy for economic order. Hayek too, elsewhere in his writings, uses the analogy of a biological organism to explain spontaneous order.

These examples suggest that analogies are both useful and problematic: try to think critically about them when you meet them again. In Chapter 2 Grahame Thompson describes a different analogy, a mechanical one, whereby the economy can be thought of as a machine, rather than a living thing; indeed, machines have been built to model it.

The Smith passage seems to contain ideas about the psychology of individuals. Smith's phrase about a 'propensity in human nature' suggests that he sees trading as an activity that comes naturally to people. You will meet 'propensities' again in economics: this is a word economists have often used to mark essentially psychological assumptions about human behaviour which underpin their models. When you meet such assumptions, try to reflect on their realism and the reasons why the assumptions are made.

3.4   Disorder in markets

The images I have just been discussing, of mutually beneficial trading, have underpinned many arguments for free trade, from Adam Smith onwards. You will meet a number of powerful arguments along these lines in this book, for example in Chapters 7 and 13. Images of free and efficient markets are frequently used in economics as a benchmark against which to judge less satisfactory situations.

Markets can work badly too, for many different reasons which theoreticians have painstakingly unpicked. Markets, in other words, can exhibit disorder, and I have chosen inflation and unemployment as two forms of apparent disorder which cause anxiety for both economists and citizens. Theoretical debates in economics about inflation and unemployment also serve to illustrate some broad divisions of ideas in economics about why markets may 'go wrong'.

Consider unemployment first. It was J.M. Keynes's theorizing about the causes of unemployment that established his fame as an economist with a strong influence on policy. You may have heard the phrase 'Keynesianism' used to describe a particular school of economic thinking. Keynes was a Cambridge economist who also worked for the British Treasury, and he came to have a wide-ranging impact on Britain's economic policy in his lifetime. But his single most famous intervention was his argument that persistent unemployment in the 1930s demanded government intervention: that market forces alone would not remove it.

Here is a passage from Keynes's most famous book, *The General Theory of Employment, Interest and Money,* first published in 1936. I should point out that the tone of this extract does not reflect that of the rest of the book, which is largely a dense theoretical argument, but it certainly does capture the style of many of Keynes's pronouncements on policy issues: he had a considerable gift for polemic.

> If the Treasury were to fill old bottles with banknotes, bury them at suitable depths in disused coalmines which are then filled up to the surface with town rubbish, and leave it to private enterprise on well-tried principles of *laissez faire* to dig up the notes again there need be no more unemployment ... It would indeed be more sensible to build houses and the like, but if there are political and practical difficulties in the way of this, the above would be better than nothing.
>
> *(Keynes, 1936, p.129)*

This view that the market system in an individual country could get 'stuck' at a level below full employment was a reversal of all orthodox economic thinking in the 1930s, and provoked a very sharp reaction. Subsequently, it became an influential view: an orthodoxy in itself which others attacked. If your reaction on reading it was, 'it's not as simple as that', well that is of course the case, and Keynes, were he alive today, would no doubt agree. There are many causes of the scourge of unemployment, and Book 2 explores the debate in more detail.

For my purpose here, however, Keynes's polemic is just one example of a particular approach to market disorder in economics: the view that there are many circumstances in which markets, however freely operating, will not function well and that external intervention, for example by government, is needed to put the market's failures right.

Question

From your own general knowledge, can you think of politicians and economists who strongly disagree with this broad point of view?

Political debates in the 1980s offer a long list! One eminent exemplar is the US economist Milton Friedman, who set out in the post-war period to overturn 'Keynesian' views of economics and economic policy, much as Keynes had pursued a comparable crusade in the 1930s. Friedman is a polemicist too:

> The United States has continued to progress, its citizens have become better fed, better clothed, better housed ... All this has been the product of the initiative and drive of individuals co-operating through the free market. Government measures have hampered, not helped, this development.
>
> *(Friedman, 1962, pp.199–200)*

Like Keynes, Friedman has behind these pronouncements a closely reasoned theoretical argument which has been both highly influential and highly controversial. Economists of Friedman's general theoretical persuasion tend to argue that government intervention in markets is almost always worse than non-intervention, a view that has had considerable influence on recent economic policy. They therefore tend to recommend that government provide a stable context for markets, but not otherwise intervene.

The distinction is well illustrated by the European debate on the unemployment problem. Those who see government intervention as the main problem, focus on the perceived 'inflexibility' of the European labour markets. European governments, they argue, over-regulate their markets, preventing the growth in low-paid service jobs that has raised employment in the USA. Those seeing disorder as often inherent in markets note that much European unemployment is concentrated among lower-skilled workers. They suggest that unemployment is rooted in too low a level of skills and education in the European workforce, as compared with the Japanese. Hence, they argue, government should intervene to create a higher-skilled workforce capable of filling more demanding jobs.

A similar debate can be identified on inflation. Both Friedman and Keynes specialized in the economics of money. Economists persuaded at least in part by Friedman's arguments tend to see inflation as generated by government policy mistakes in the management of the central banking and financial system. Others believe some inflation is a necessary and not very serious cost of a high-employment economy. Hence, economists debate whether moderate inflation is a market disorder at all. There is further discussion of this in Book 2.

We can understand the distinction between internally and externally generated market disorders as a difference between two 'ways of seeing' the economy. Economists whose vision of the economy is essentially of freely functioning efficient markets impeded from 'outside' – by governments, trade unions or other awkward social institutions – tend to see efficient free markets as the benchmark for analysis. Actual, imperfect markets are judged by their distance from the benchmark. This has been a strong and productive line of reasoning within economic theory, and you will find many examples of it in this text.

Conversely, those who tend to see markets as containing inherent problems within their own functioning have a different theoretical cast of mind. For them the freely functioning efficient market is a 'special case'. More problematic, 'imperfect' markets are the norm or the 'general' case.

Economic theory is increasingly being reformulated to encompass the recognition that markets which function problematically seem to be the 'general case' in the real world. This text is deliberately structured to give you a feel for these current directions of thought in economics. Our presentation of the economics of firms and markets in Chapters 5–8 starts from the vision of markets as imperfectly functioning institutions, and works towards the benchmark of the efficient free market as a special, though highly important, case. In this way, we hope to give you a feel for these debates, while covering the material you need to espouse either of these alternative world views.

The recognition of the general imperfection of markets does not imply, however, that governments can necessarily do better. Economics has recognized that governments are also imperfect institutions, and that such imperfect institutions need to be understood. This is my final theme in this chapter.

4   Economics and institutions

4.1   Poverty and sustainability: global issues

In the late 1980s there was an explosion of international political debate – and of new work in economics – on the subject of the 'sustainability' of economic growth. The report of the Bruntland Commission on environment and development, set up by the United Nations, defined this idea: 'Humanity has the ability to make development sustainable – to ensure that it meets the needs of the present without compromising the ability of future generations to meet their own needs' (World Commission on Environment and Development, 1987, p.8).

Worries about the impact of economic development on the environment are far from new, but a significant feature of the recent debate has been the recognition that the issue is a global one: that sustainable development implied international co-operation. That recognition in turn linked the problem of sustainability to the issues of inequality and division in the international economy. Much of the current environmental degradation is generated by industrialized countries, while many of the resources people are now anxious to conserve lie in the less industrialized world, where people want economic growth. Furthermore, some environmental degradation is driven by poverty. Brazil again provides an example of some of these dilemmas.

Poverty and environment in Brazil

By the early 1990s the Brazilian economy had shaken off the worst impact of the debt crisis, and was into another of its spurts of rapid growth. If you came across Brazil in the newspapers in the early 1990s, it is most likely to have been in the context of the deforestation of the Amazon. Images of generalized economic crisis were being replaced by images of burning trees, aggressive ranching, do-it-yourself gold-mining, and collapsing indigenous communities. The symbolism became particularly stark when Brazil hosted the United Nations Conference on Environment and Development (UNCED) in June 1992. At that time photographic essays showed side-by-side the razzmatazz of the conference, the security measures which protected delegates from the crime and social divisions of Rio de Janeiro, and the destruction of the rain forests (see Figure 1.8).

The Brazilians are not alone in clearing forests. As the Brazilian government is quick to point out, the industrialized temperate-zone countries destroyed their forests in the process of economic development, and many are still chopping down or poisoning the remains. The Pacific Asian countries are also rapidly clearing their tropical forests, and indeed the rate of clearance in Asia is more rapid than in Latin America (Figure 1.9). Similarly, the acute poverty found in Brazil can be matched elsewhere in the world, for example in South Asia . I am simply using Brazil as my example because its acute contrasts – and its international economic influence – point up sharply the two economic issues addressed in this final section of the chapter.

Figure 1.8 Social division in Rio de Janeiro (*top*) and the burning of rain forest to enlarge a cattle ranch in the Amazon basin (*bottom*); this land remains fertile for only a few years, after which more forest is cleared

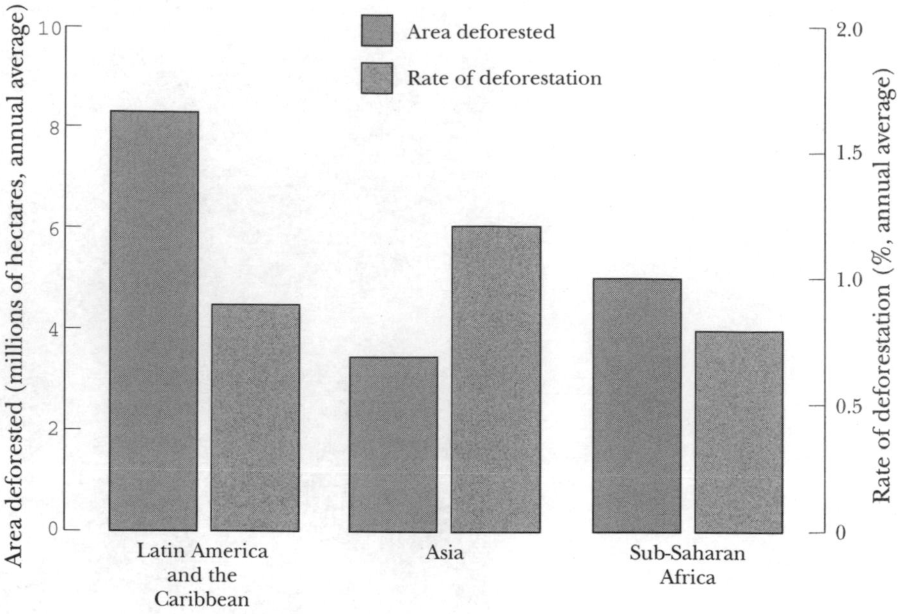

Figure 1.9 **Loss of tropical forests in developing regions, 1980–90**

Source: *World Development Report* (1992), based on Food and Agricultural Organization data

Why does the destruction of tropical rain forests matter? Some people in fact think it does not matter. Others – in a majority – cite two major concerns: the contribution to global warming, and the loss of biodiversity. Both are potential matters of concern in their own right, and both have potential economic costs which may be large but which are extremely hard to quantify. They include the costs of adapting to higher temperatures and possibly more extreme weather. They also include the difficulties of coping with future problems in a world agricultural system of low genetic diversity, without the reserves of genetic material now being lost through deforestation. There seems to be reasonable scientific agreement that some global warming is occurring (Solow, 1989), and that biodiversity is declining, but no scientific or economic agreement on the implications.

In Brazil, the issues of poverty and Amazonian deforestation are interrelated in complex ways. Brazil is a country where considerable wealth lives unusually close beside extreme poverty. In other words, Brazil has a highly unequal income distribution.

One way of measuring income distribution is shown in Table 1.2, which shows the proportion of total incomes in the hands of different fractions of the population.

Definitions

Poverty and income distribution

To be in *poverty* means to have too little income to achieve what is regarded in your own society as a decent minimum standard of living. The *income distribution*, on the other hand, refers to the division of incomes among rich and poor.

Table 1.2 **Income distribution in various countries: shares of the poorest 20%, richest 20% and richest 10% in total incomes**

Country	Date	Poorest 20%	Richest 20%	Richest 10%
Brazil	1989	2.1	67.5	51.3
Japan	1979	8.7	37.5	22.4
South Korea	1976	5.7	45.3	27.5
USA	1985	4.7	41.9	25.0
UK	1979	5.8	39.5	23.3

Source: *World Development Report* (1988, 1993)

Question

Before you read on, look carefully at Table 1.2. How does the income distribution in Brazil compare with that in Japan and South Korea?

Brazil is a far more unequal society, where the richest 20 per cent, and even more strikingly the richest 10 per cent, have a far higher proportion of total incomes than they do in Japan or South Korea, and the poorest have proportionately less. Economic history suggests that as countries industrialize, the income distribution tends first to worsen and then to improve over time, but it also shows that the pattern is very varied. The East Asian pattern of industrialization has tended to be more egalitarian than that of Latin America (World Bank, 1993). Other indicators bear out this impression: for example, life expectancy at birth, always a good barometer of conditions in a country, is much lower in Brazil than in Japan or in South Korea.

To understand the particular pattern of Amazonian deforestation, we have to understand how Brazilian poverty and inequality have interacted with the broader economic pressures of growth and inflation. The Amazon basin contains more than one-third of the world's remaining tropical rain forest, and 60 per cent of the forest is in Brazil, an area of about 3.8 million square kilometres. It contains an estimated one million plants and animal species. The rate of deforestation increased rapidly after the early 1970s, and in 1988, a peak year, an area the size of Belgium was cleared. The consequences for the Amazon's previous long-term inhabitants – Brazil's remaining ethnic Indians, of whom two-thirds live in the Amazon, and the 500 000 Amazonian rubber tappers – have been dire.

During the drive for growth in the 1960s and 1970s, the Brazilian government actively encouraged Amazonian exploration and settlement, by building roads and subsidizing ranchers, mining companies and other firms moving to the area. Called 'Operation Amazonia', this deliberate colonization was driven by strategic considerations, and by hopes of extensive mineral finds. It was part of a growth policy of a highly authoritarian military regime, which one social scientist working in the extremely poor Brazilian north east at the end of the 1970s called 'one of the most inhumane administrations anywhere in the world' (Mitchell, 1981, p.8).

Other aspects of Brazilian society have contributed to Amazonian colonization. Brazil has a very unequal land distribution. One per cent of landowners hold 43 per cent of the total land, in farms over 2500 acres. Big ranchers carry a lot of political weight, and have been responsible for a large element of Amazon clearances, driving them forward by the ruthless use of violence. In an inflationary economy, land is a good speculation, especially where supported by government subsidy.

At the other end of the scale, half of the farms in Brazil are squeezed into 3 per cent of the total land available, and mechanization has driven many tenants and labourers off large farms. Many of these migrated to the western Amazon in the late 1970s, where there was an active colonization policy along the TransAmazon highway, and land title was to be had for cleared ('improved') land. Small-scale gold-mining was another lure.

There is a sense, then, in which Amazonian clearance has acted as a safety valve for the acute strains of an economically divided society in Brazil. Amazonia lies next door to the impoverished and land-short Brazilian north east. Once it was opened up, it was bound to attract both poor and rich. The irony is that little of the colonization has shown itself economically viable. The tropical soils rapidly erode without tree cover, and crop yields decline. They form poor pasture land, and the ranches are generally uneconomic without subsidy (Mahar, 1989). Apart from iron ore and some gold, mineral exploration has also been generally disappointing.

Because of the ecological issues set out above, this cycle of destitution and deforestation is of more than local Brazilian concern. It has become instead a matter for international bargaining, and a symbol of a number of global economic issues facing us at the end of the twentieth century. Democracy has returned to Brazil, and the Brazilian government has been understandably resistant to overseas interference in its economic policy – particularly given its experience of external pressure during the debt negotiations of the 1980s. Along with the governments of a number of other developing countries, notably including India, Brazil has argued that developed countries must pay a price for the preservation of the rain forests. Industrialized countries, they point out, emit the bulk of the gases that produce global warming, deforestation adding a significant, but not dominant, contribution. Furthermore, poverty is a factor driving deforestation across the less developed countries. Hence, stopping environmental degradation implies transfers from richer to poorer countries. As yet, the governments of the North generally appear unwilling to pay.

The Amazonia story is just one example of a growing recognition that both poverty and environmental degradation are economic issues that cross national boundaries. Because of the international nature of markets, and because pollution and global warming respect no international borders, the need for international negotiations and co-operation is evident, yet has been found to be extremely difficult. Chapter 27 returns to these big economic issues.

4.2 The economics of institutions

The issues of poverty and sustainability raise important questions about government intervention in markets, and about non-market economic institutions such as governments and inter-governmental co-operation. If you look back at Section 3.4, you will see that government intervention was treated there as either a source of, or a solution to, market disorder. That discussion falls within a tradition in economics which treats *markets* as the main focus of economic analysis, and governments rather as outside forces which operate on economies, for good or ill. Robert Sugden, whose views on spontaneous order you have already met, calls this the 'US Cavalry' approach to economic policy: the government rides to the rescue (or tries to, at least) (Sugden, 1986, p.3).

Current economic thinking has been moving away from this approach. There is a growing recognition in economics that institutions matter, and there has been a move towards applying economic analysis to institutions such as governments themselves, allowing us to ask, for example, *why* governments behave as they do. A fascinating debate has developed about how economic institutions are to be understood. The importance of the debate was recognized in 1993 by the award of the Nobel prize to two economic historians, one of whom, Douglas North, has done very influential work on this topic.

What do I mean by institutions here? When we think of an 'institution', organizations and public buildings tend to come to mind. In economics, as you can see from the definition opposite, the word has developed a broader meaning.

Not all economists who analyse institutions would accept a definition quite as broad as the one given here, but I think most current definitions fall within it.

Within economics there are two broad approaches to analysing economic institutions. The first views the economic world as a collection of self-interested individuals. From this perspective, economists try to work out under what circumstances certain institutions – such as co-operation among individuals, or agreed social norms of behaviour on markets – will emerge. Individual competitive and self-seeking behaviour is seen as the norm. Co-operation, formal organizations and ethical norms can emerge when they are cumulatively seen to be in everyone's interests, but they are predicted to be fragile and hard to maintain. Economists use a technique called game theory – which you will encounter a number of times in this text – to study institutional problems of this kind.

The second perspective on economic institutions regards them as having a certain life of their own, once established. Social norms, particular patterns of property ownership, or the culture of particular organizations constrain and shape – but of course do not wholly determine – the behaviour of individuals. In this sense, history matters: the past institutional development in the economy shapes the present perception of what is 'done' and what is possible. Economists call that process 'path dependence': the path you have been following constrains the future possible paths, or, to put it more positively, established norms can make certain future paths possible to you but not to others.

This renewed debate on institutions is another feature of contemporary economic research reflected both here and in Book 2. This book recognizes that markets are influenced by the institutions which trade on them, i.e. households, firms and governments, all of which have very diverse characteristics. Chapters 3, 4 and 10 consider these main types of economic institution in turn. This chapter ends by considering briefly some institutional questions brought out in the Brazilian case study above.

Property rights and co-operation

One of the fundamental institutions in any society is the set of property rights: the rules, laws and social concepts that establish ownership of, and access to, property, and then protect (or at times fail to protect) the pattern of ownership. The establishment of private property rights and an associated law of contract – allowing the transfer of these rights – has been crucial in the development of market economies. Thus in the early 1990s the countries of the former Soviet Union and Eastern Europe were struggling to put together, very rapidly, new legal and social frameworks for the operation of private markets (for more on this see Chapter 15).

Definition

Institutions

The definition of an institution is currently much debated within economics. Institutions can be understood to include:

1   Organizations whose behaviour strongly influences economies and economic change: for instance companies, households, public service organizations, and government bureaucracies;

2   Social norms, rules, habits, customs and routines – that is, stable, shared and understood patterns of behaviour with economic implications;

3   Legal frameworks and constraints, such as the laws of property and contract, together with the pattern of property rights they protect.

One way of seeing the problems of international co-operation to protect the environment, discussed in the Brazilian case in Section 4.1, is to note that there are large parts of the global environment which no one owns, for example the atmosphere and climate which make life possible. Hence, people and governments are free to use such global resources as 'sinks' into which to pour waste from economic processes (such as cutting down trees). There is no owner to seek compensation.

There are also property rights issues affecting Amazonia itself. As ownership of Amazonian land has shifted, *de facto*, to new colonists, the use of the land has changed. Many of those affected by global warming or the loss of biodiversity have no 'shares' in Amazonia, and therefore no way of influencing the outcome, while the earlier forest dwellers, with no land title, have seen their livelihoods and lives threatened.

In other words, the structure of property rights affects the economic outcomes of market processes. When those outcomes are damaging, it is necessary to consider what can and should be done. Theorists argue that, in some cases, new property rights will be created under economic pressure to solve these problems. In other cases there seems no solution possible but co-operation in managing common resources: the air we breathe cannot be divided up. Economists debate how difficult this is likely to be, and what facilitates co-operation (see Chapter 10).

Distribution and ethics

The Brazilian case study in Section 4.1 also raised a number of complicated distributional questions, many of which have an institutional aspect. The Amazonian story can be read as a case study in the way the operation of legislation on land ownership, the inequality of distribution of existing land, the market for land, and the exercise of local political and coercive power in the service of the already powerful, combined to reproduce in Amazonia the acute inequalities of Brazilian society. Acute inequality – and resultant poverty – can be depressingly self-perpetuating in this fashion, a cycle hard to break without some institutional change.

To reinforce the point, here is a commentary on Brazilian growth from an influential book called *Hunger and Public Action*, by Jean Drèze and Amartya Sen, which discusses the implications of 'the indiscriminate pursuit of economic expansion':

> A particularly crude approach, which is not in fact uncommon, consists of attempting to *maximize* economic growth without paying any direct attention to the transformation of greater opulence into better living conditions …[This] is a roundabout, undependable and wasteful way of improving the living standards of the poor. In countries like Brazil, where the poorest quintile of the population have to get by with as little as two per cent of national income, exclusively relying on [this approach] would amount to accepting the need for generating 50 units of income for one unit that would go to the poor.
>
> *(Drèze and Sen, 1989, p.188)*

This argument is a salutary corrective to any tendency – which I may have fed in Section 2 – to see economic growth as an achievement. We may find countries where economic growth is happening, and markets seem to be working with reasonable efficiency, and yet where little of the country's increasing wealth is 'trickling down' to the poor.

That, then, is one problem of inequality in Brazil. Some redistribution of wealth and power seems essential to a more environmentally sustainable development. Another 'distributional' problem is the international one already alluded to: developing countries will seek to extract a price for more sustainable development paths, which those in wealthier countries are by no means certain to be willing to pay. The third problem is the distribution of resources between one generation and the next. The definition of sustainability at the beginning of Section 4.1 raises this problem explicitly. Will current generations be prepared to pay the price of creating an economic growth path which does not degrade the opportunities for future generations?

There are a number of different institutional issues embedded in these 'distributional' problems. I want to focus on just one: the difficult issue of ethics and equity which underpin these mechanisms.

The tone of the passage from Drèze and Sen is explicitly ethical, for good reason. The acceptability of particular levels of poverty is an ethical issue, and one on which people, acting through a variety of organizations, do take a view. Similarly, the distribution of resources between generations – or to put it differently, the weight given to the needs of different generations – is a moral issue. So the evidence to the Bruntland Commission (see Section 4.1) also had a strong ethical tone: contributors talked of a 'new ethic', and a 'new ethos ... for building understanding among people'.

Amartya Sen, the eminent development economist quoted above, has pointed out that the concern with ethics in economic systems can be traced back, like so much else in economics, to Adam Smith. He argues that many citations of Smith's work are unbalanced in focusing on self-interest. Smith's defence of self-interested behaviour comes in the specific context of trading on markets. Smith was opposed to the suppression of trade through bureaucratic barriers but took a broader view of proper behaviour in economy and society as a whole. Sen notes that Smith, in his other major book, *The Theory of Moral Sentiments* (1790), stresses the importance of sympathy and the role of ethical considerations in human behaviour. Smith seems to have understood self-interest only as being 'of all virtues that which is most helpful to the individual', while 'humanity, justice, generosity and public spirit, are the qualities most useful to others' (Smith, 1790, quoted in Sen, 1987, p.23). If the economy cannot be reduced to market trading – if wider institutions matter – then economic sentiment cannot be reduced to self-interest.

Distributional questions imply winners and losers, hence the need for explicit decisions about ethics and equity. We can think of shared ideas about proper levels of equity as a 'social norm' – an institution, in fact. The Brazilian case study illustrates one strand of thought in recent economic literature: neither citizens' ethical views, nor the actions of the state can be expected to be independent of the current distribution of property in society. Institutional structures – involving mutually supporting organizations and ideas – are therefore hard to overturn. As Douglas North has put it, 'ideas matter' in explaining economic change (North, 1993). Problems of distribution are discussed further in Book 2.

5   Conclusion

The range of this chapter has been very wide, both in examples and ideas. In case you feel rather overwhelmed, note that the chapter is intended as a true introduction to the text. That is, there are no major ideas and issues in it that you will not meet again.

In Section 1, I listed the main themes of this chapter, and you may now like to look back at it. You may have been struck by the fact that I have presented each set of ideas – growth, markets and institutions – in the form of a *debate* between differing points of view. You may have found this annoying and over-complicated, or (as of course I hope) stimulating.

This presentation of theory as debate carries the most general message of this chapter, namely that economic theory is not a fixed body of knowledge, but, like all social science, an arena of research and dispute. Economists, like other social scientists, develop differing and distinctive 'ways of seeing' the world, or broad conceputalizations within which they work. These different visions of the world are influenced by the issues which they regard as important. In other words, how economists think depends in part on what they think about.

Hence, as economies change, so does economics. I hope you will enjoy your exploration of this endlessly debateable subject.

Appendix

Line graphs and growth rates

This is the first of the series of more technical sections that you will find running through this book. It is intended to support your understanding of the exercises and technical points in the chapter.

Understanding growth rates

My objective here is to make sure that you are happy with calculating and interpreting growth rates.

A growth rate is a *percentage* expansion in some total, for example in a country's GDP. A percentage, in turn, is a proportion or fraction expressed as a share of 100. So, for example:

$$20\% = \frac{20}{100} = \text{one-fifth} = 0.2$$

$$5\% = \frac{5}{100} = \text{one-twentieth} = 0.05$$

To find a percentage of a number, divide that number by 100, and multiply by the percentage figure. So 15% of $3000 = \frac{3000}{100} \times 15 = 450$.

Exercise 1.2

If you want to check your understanding of percentages, write out 1%, 7%, 50%, 55%, 120%, 250% in the above format. Then find 12%, 70% and 135% of 4000.

One of the most common uses of percentages in economics is to calculate the percentage growth (or decline) between two dates. Exercise 1.1 in Section 2 asked you to do this. If you had any trouble, here is the principle.

The Japanese economy was measured at ¥152 208 billion in 1970, and ¥185 923 billion three years later. To calculate the total growth over the period, you need to express ¥185 923 as a percentage of ¥152 208 (ignoring the billions). Divide one by the other (to give you the relevant fractional relationship) and then multiply by 100 (to turn it into a percentage):

$$\frac{185\,923}{152\,208} \times 100 = 122.1506\%$$

So real incomes per head have gone up by about 22.15 per cent over the *whole* period (*not* each year – we come back in a moment to the second part of the exercise).

I now want to introduce a little algebra, to help clarify how growth rates work over time. Let me call a country's total income in the first year Y_1 (you will become used to this notation) and the growth rate of that income r. The growth rate r is a percentage, such as 5 per cent. Income Y is growing at r, so in the second year, Y will be larger. Let me call this second-year income Y_2. This means that $Y_2 = Y_1 + Y_1r$, since r is the percentage growth over the year. I can rewrite this as:

$$Y_2 = Y_1 + Y_1r = Y_1(1 + r)$$

Now consider year three. Growth continues at r. But this time the growth rate applies to the whole previous year's income, *including the growth achieved last time.* The formula illustrates how this happens. Let's call year three Y_3. Now,

$$Y_3 = Y_2 + Y_2r = Y_2(1 + r)$$

But we have a formula for Y_2 above, so:

$$Y_3 = Y_2(1 + r) = Y_1(1 + r)(1 + r) = Y_1(1 + r)^2$$

This is a very useful formula which can be generalized to any number of years. Therefore, in year 10, if growth is a steady r per cent,

$$Y_{10} = Y_1(1 + r)^9$$

This formula displays succinctly an important principle, called *compounding*, which is a major source of divergences in wealth between people and countries. (Compound interest, for example on a bank savings account, works in just the same way.)

Exercise 1.3

Suppose a country's GDP per head is $12 000, and this is growing at 3 per cent per annum. In five years' time, what will be the GDP per head?

Figure 1.10 illustrates the way in which slightly different growth rates can produce huge divergences in income over time through compounding. It shows three imaginary countries, each beginning with a real income per head of $300. Incomes per head in country A grow at 0.5 per cent per year, in country B at 3.6 per cent, and in country C at 7.8 per cent. These happen to be the relevant growth rates in Brazil, Japan and China for the period 1980–91 (*World Development Report*, 1993).

Question

Take a few minutes to look at Figure 1.10. What strikes you?

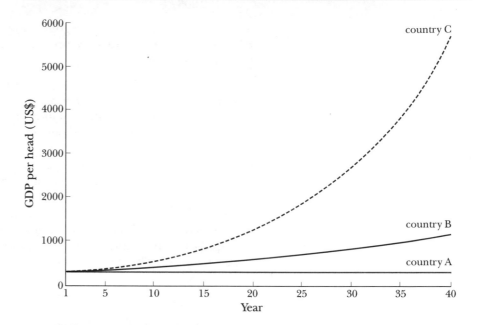

Figure 1.10   **Compounding**

The most striking aspect to me is the rapid divergence of the fast growing country. Country C is growing rather more than twice as fast as country B, but after 40 years it is a lot more than twice as well off. The compounding effect of constant growth rates causes divergences between the countries to increase over time.

Question

Now look at Figure 1.11, which shows Japanese total real incomes in the period 1965–84. How steady were growth rates over this period? If they changed, when were the faster rates of growth – earlier or later?

Did you think there was fairly steady growth? Or couldn't you tell? Or did you think that growth was dropping? If your answer was one of the first two, look again at Figure 1.11. If growth rates had been constant, income would have been accelerating, for the reason just explained: compounding. In fact Japan has been slowing down, as Section 2 explained. Figure 1.12, based on exactly the same data, but this time

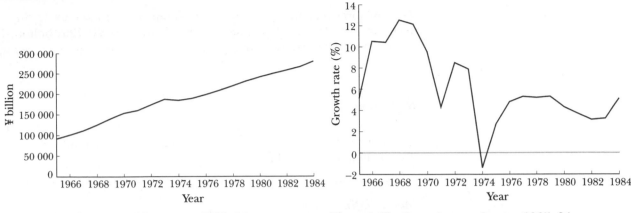

Figure 1.11   Japan: real incomes, 1965–84

Source: Japan Statistical Association (1987)

Figure 1.12   Japan's growth rate, 1965–84

Source: Japan Statistical Association (1987)

turned into annual growth rates, demonstrates the effect. This graph also shows that growth has not been particularly steady, but has fluctuated, especially in the 1970s. There is a final lesson from this comparison: use the right graph for the question you want to answer. If your interest is in growth rates, then transform your data into percentage growth rates in each year, and graph those.

In Figures 1.10 and 1.12 I have graphed growth rates in two different ways: a (hypothetical) constant growth rate over time, and an (actual) set of growth rates per year, which are different in each year. Figure 1.10 showed what would have happened if Japan and Brazil had started at the same level of incomes per head and grown at different constant rates. The World Bank data from which I drew the growth rates were in fact *annual average* growth rates for those countries' incomes per head in the period 1980–91.

How are these annual average growth rates calculated? There are, in fact, a variety of ways, and here is one. Consider two dates, three years apart. If we know the incomes per head of a country in those two years, how can we calculate the average growth rate? We can use the formula already learned, but in reverse. If the income in the first year, Y_1, is 4000, and three years later, Y_4, is 4500, then what is r?

$$Y_4 = Y_1 (1 + r)^3$$

That is:

$$4500 = 4000 (1 + r)^3$$

Or, dividing by 4000:

$$\frac{4500}{4000} = 1.125 = (1 + r)^3$$

This is annoying, because we want to find r, but it is stuck in a bracket and seems hard to extract. We therefore take the cube root of both sides. This gives:

$$1.04 = 1 + r, \text{ or}$$

$$r = 0.04$$

The average annual growth rate is therefore about 4 per cent.

You can apply the same method to the second part of Exercise 1.1 in Section 2. The (actual) Japanese data there give: Y_1 = ¥152 208 billion, Y_4 = ¥185 923 billion. Applying the same approach as above gives an average annual growth rate of 6.90 per cent.

Reflection

Check that you understand why you cannot just divide the total growth rate over the three years by three. If you are not sure, re-read the discussion of compounding.

Manipulating line graphs

Finally, I want to say a few words about graphs. All the graphs I have drawn in this chapter have been line graphs. That is, they are drawn by plotting a series of points in a graph, and then joining up the points with a line. All the graphs have also been times series graphs; that is, they have time (years) along the bottom (horizontal) axis, and a value such as a growth rate or an income level on the left-hand side (the vertical axis). They therefore track the change in growth or income over time.

It is important to look carefully at the numbering on the axes of these graphs. It is remarkably easy to change the impression given by a single set of data by changing the way the data are displayed. Indeed, it is a way of manipulating data well known to politicians. Consider the various illustrations in Figure 1.13. These are all drawn from the same Brazilian data. Figure 1.13(a) suggests steady growth with a problem in the early 1980s. Figure 1.13(b) is the kind of graph a politician coming to power in 1983 might favour to suggest economic turnaround. Note that the vertical axis does not start from zero. In Figure 1.13(c) the problem in the early 1980s has been mislaid by some judicious choice of illustrative years. A politician in power for ten years and fighting an election in 1987 might like this one; note that some years have vanished from the horizontal axis. So look very carefully at the graphs shown in newspapers and on television!

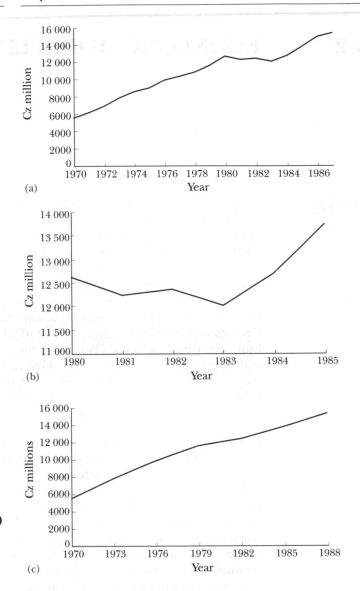

Figure 1.13   **Brazil's GDP (1980 prices)**

Source: *Anuário Estatístico do Brasil* (1987-88)

CHAPTER 2   ECONOMIC MODELLING

by Grahame F. Thompson

1   Introduction

According to International Monetary Fund data, in 1991 the yearly income per person in Finland was equivalent to US$24784, while for those living in Tanzania it was only US$104 (income measured as gross national product, GNP – see Section 3.4 below). These national income figures are a measure of the 'standard of living' or 'welfare' of the populations in each country. The enormous difference in per capita GNP between the two countries is indicative of the inequalities that typify the international economy of the late twentieth century, as discussed in a preliminary way in Chapter 1. The USA alone accounted for 26.2 per cent of global GNP in 1991, while the European Community was responsible for another 27.6 per cent, and Japan a further 15.4 per cent. Thus these three country groupings accounted for a staggering 69.2 per cent of the entire global GNP (estimated at US$21671 billion in 1991), whereas they accounted for only about 13.4 per cent of total world population at the time.

One of the main tasks economists have set themselves is to explain these levels and differences. This is no easy matter, but a start can be made by examining the notion of a 'national income' and how it might be modelled. This chapter introduces these two features of economic analysis: it examines the various measures of national income so that we can take an informed view of exactly what constitutes national income, and it discusses how we can systematically understand its origin and growth by developing a preliminary 'model' of its determination. We do not have to venture far into the study of economics before we come across the notion of a model: professional economists continually use models to investigate the nature of economic processes and relationships – indeed, the task of building economic models and using them probably constitutes the main activity for most economists.

Models in economics take a number of forms. Some models are simple affairs, with perhaps only two variables making up the model, while others are very large models that simulate a complete economy comprising a number of interacting markets, and perhaps involving several hundred variables expressed in many equations.

This chapter examines how models function in economic argument, and illustrates this by use of the circular flow of income model. The chapter approaches economic analysis as an intellectual activity that involves constructing arguments about the nature of the economy: how it functions, what are its key variables, how these variables are related to one another, and what are the consequences of various policy moves. There is a very complex process by which particular models and images of the economy come to be taken seriously (while others are not), and it is this process in part that informs the analysis here. Thus the objective is to place the notion of an economic model into a particular intellectual framework – to step back a little from the actual building and use of models in order to explore the place that this exercise occupies within a wider set of methodological considerations.

At the same time this chapter introduces some preliminary economic concepts and analysis. The key issues discussed in this respect are <u>national income, aggregate expenditure, and functional relationships involving investment and growth</u>. These are closely related to the circular flow of income model, so they follow immediately from it and contribute to bridging the two substantive concerns of the chapter.

I shall start by looking at what we mean by a 'model'. At this point I want to give a working definition that can subsequently be refined and assessed.

2   The notion of an economic model

<u>What is an economic model?</u> One straightforward approach is to treat a model simply as a mapping device, with the aid of which we can chart our way through the organizational complexity of the modern economy. Such an approach would stress the notion of abstraction from the detail of empirical reality: it represents the bare bones or framework for the richness of the elements of the economy that it is elucidating. If the model can be considered analogously to a torch that emits a beam of light, then in shining our model/torch on the complexity of economic existence, we would only expect it to highlight *some* of that complexity. Thus models or maps differ in the degree of detail they give and the elements on which they focus.

For some economists the above description would be taken as an example of the classical *positivist* notion of models. Positivism stresses the importance of facts and the observation of reality for the generation of knowledge and the construction of the laws of science and social organization. It has traditionally been associated with the notion of *empiricism*, which is an approach that holds experience as the key source of knowledge: ideas and concepts are derived from experience; we come to know something via the use of our senses, and it is these senses that help in the formulation of the facts.

For both these linked approaches it is empirical reality that acts as the basis for the construction of models designed to analyse that reality. This in turn links them to another, perhaps underlying, methodological approach known as *realism*. For realism the facts or experiences registered through our senses are themselves dependent upon a real material objective existence that operates externally to us or our senses and which in turn provides the material basis for those experiences and facts. Thus external reality acts as the touchstone for the maps we use to organize our understanding of the world. We first need to engage with the reality of economic relationships and data and then abstract the most important features of those relationships and data. Putting these abstract features together into some kind of consistent order or framework constitutes a 'model' of that reality. We can then use this model to highlight the important features of the real world, to try to understand what happens to those important features if something changes, or use it to help highlight other situations or similar circumstances which seem to compare with the original one modelled.

Against such a 'realist' notion of model building and use could be contrasted a more overtly 'theoretical' approach to models, based on the model-building activity of mathematics, for instance. In this case it would be formal and abstract thought experiments that would be the most important activity for model building. This is sometimes associated with *rationalism*: stressing the role and power of *a priori* (deductive) reasoning in grasping truths and generating knowledge about the world. This approach emphasizes the role of theory in organizing our thoughts about the world and our analysis of it. Models in this sense are not so much detailed maps of an already existing external reality, but more like a set of tools and techniques with which we begin to build a mental image of the economy. These tools and techniques could be linguistic (words, sentences) or they may be symbolic (algebraic or mathematical notation). What is highlighted as 'reality' in this case is a consequence of the theoretical tools (or models) we bring to bear in organizing our thoughts and understanding of it. We do not uncover models of reality; we impose an order of models on that reality and thereby construct an image of it. In contrast to the realist notion of a model outlined above, this vision of a model is sometimes called a *nominalist* one. As opposed to a pre-existing reality being the main underlying support for model building, it is the symbolic 'naming' or 'indication' of the features of the model on the basis of our thoughts about the real world that constitutes the key to an understanding of reality.

To sum up, we can say that there are two basic approaches to model building illustrated below. The first relies on generating a model from a thorough understanding of the empirical reality of the economy. It stresses data analysis and the establishment of empirical relationships. The second broad approach stresses the importance of abstraction, *a priori* thinking, and the formulation of conceptual tools and techniques.

The continuing debate between these two conflicting images of models (and a good many variations in between) is the subject of a great deal of methodological dispute in the social sciences. The argument below is that neither can be said to be the most appropriate, since it is not a straightforward question of a choice between them; there is no single correct approach. Ultimately the most appropriate attitude is probably one of agnosticism. A preparedness to take insights from both approaches seems sensible if we are called upon to justify the use of models in economic analysis. Models are a convenient device for organizing an analysis of economic life that at least has some claim to intellectual rigour. Clearly, we have to take evidence and data for theories seriously, but the extent to which the evidence/data exists independently of theory is the focus of dispute; this issue is explored in more detail in Chapter 9.

3 The circular flow model

I shall begin to illustrate the notion of a model in economics by using the example of what is termed the *circular flow of income* model. First, we need to examine what is being modelled, in this case the 'national income'. Then we need to look at the phrase 'circular flow of income' as a whole. After that we explore the key terms in this phrase separately. Finally, we return to the phrase as a whole to look at its central features more closely.

3.1 Why is national income important?

The circular flow of income model is designed to say something about an economy's aggregate output and how that output is produced. It forms the basis for the notion of a *national income*.

The importance of national income is that it represents a summary measure of a country's standard of living. It gives us an indication of how well-off we are in terms of what we can buy and our general welfare, and when compared to the national income of other countries it provides a quick comparative statistic of the relative standards of living between different countries. It is also linked to economic growth, since this is measured as a change in national income from one year to the next. As an economy grows, the national income expands. Because national income is such an important economic indicator, we need to be as precise as possible in measuring it. As we shall see, it is also a sensitive measure; it is based on a number of particular assumptions, which means that its calculation is controversial as well as complex. A country's national income can be measured in a number of different ways.

Consider the first two rows of data given in Table 2.1. These show a comparative analysis of per capita GNP for a range of countries, including Finland and Tanzania, which I mentioned in the introduction. The GNP figures are calculated using market rates of exchange to convert national currencies into their US dollar equivalents. Per capita figures are calculated by dividing the total national GNP by the population of the country.

Table 2.1   **National income and income per head for a number of countries in 1991 (at current market prices and exchange rates)**

	UK	Germany	Finland	Brazil	Tanzania	Austria
GNP (US$bn)	1015.7	1585.5	124.7	394.9	3.0	163.5
GNP per head (US$ exchange rate conversion)	17618	24721	24784	2576	104	
GDP per head (US$ PPC conversion)	16340	19770	16130	5240	570	17690

Source: *International Financial Statistics Yearbook* (1993) country tables; *World Development Report* (1993) Table 30

Exercise 2.1

Given that the population of Austria was approximately 7.8 million in 1991, what was its per capita GNP? Fill in the missing figure in Table 2.1.

One problem with the GNP figures is that it is unlikely that Tanzanians, for instance, could actually have lived on US$104 a year in 1991. But apparently they did! What these GNP figures do not take into account is the 'cost of living' in the various countries Prices in Tanzania in 1991 were likely to have been much lower than comparable prices in the USA, especially for things produced mainly with cheap local labour, from housing to haircuts. The figures do not therefore provide a proper comparative analysis of the domestic 'purchasing power' of the incomes. As suggested in Chapter 1, a proper comparative analysis of the standard of living requires an adjustment of the figures on the basis of the cost of living or the 'purchasing power of currencies' (PPC) rate of exchange between the countries' currencies, rather than comparing them on the basis of official exchange rates. The third row in Table 2.1 gives figures for income per head adjusted to take account of the different purchasing power of currencies in these countries. For reasons of data availability, the figures are based on gross domestic product (GDP). This is slightly different from GNP, and the differences are explored later in the chapter (see Sections 3.3 and 3.4). As can be seen, in general this conversion has the effect of decreasing the income per head in the advanced countries relative to that in the less developed economies. There are a number of conceptual and practical problems in compiling these figures, and I return to these in Section 7 below.

Here it is worth mentioning a further estimating complication that arises in connection with the figures in Table 2.1. These data should all be taken as approximate. All the original GNP and GDP totals were themselves estimates, and the GNP and GDP were converted into per capita figures on the basis of estimates of the populations at the time. These figures were then converted into US dollar equivalents to make an international comparison possible. The conversion of the GNP figures in the first two rows of Table 2.1 was done on the basis of the *average* official exchange rate between the home country currency and the US dollar for the period (year) in question.

However, other market exchange rates could have been used in this conversion which would have given a different impression of GNP and per capita equivalents. Take the case of Brazil, for instance, where the domestic currency (the cruzeiro) was depreciating very rapidly against the US dollar during 1991, largely because of the rate of inflation at the time (see Figure 1.7 in Chapter 1). The depreciation of the cruzeiro meant that many more of them were needed to buy an equivalent number of dollars at the end of the year than at the beginning. If the exchange rate at the end of the year had been used in the conversion, then Brazilian GNP would have been equivalent to US$170.1 billion, not US$394.9 billion as in Table 2.1: over half of Brazilian GNP would have disappeared! However, given that inflation was likely to have been continual throughout the year, the average exchange rate as used in the table is the more sensible one.

This question of the changes in the price level and how it might affect our judgement of national income and the movement of it from one year to the next, is taken up below. Where there is very rapid inflation, as in the case of Brazil, these issues arise within the year. Having taken a preliminary look at the measurement of what we are trying to model, we can move on to developing the model as a whole.

3.2   The circular flow of income: the phrase as a whole

This section examines how the various measures and estimates of national income shown in Table 2.1 are generated. One possibility is illustrated in Figure 2.1, which forms the basis of all economic models of the circular flow of income variety. For the purposes of this analysis the economy is divided into two sets of institutions, *households* and *firms*, and the figure shows the relationships between them. In fact there are two circular flows here: one is a 'physical' flow and the other is a 'monetary' flow. The physical flow (shown as a solid line in Figure 2.1) goes in a clockwise direction and involves the exchanges of real resources, goods and services. The monetary

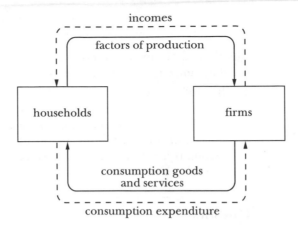

incomes

factors of production

households

firms

consumption goods
and services

consumption expenditure

Figure 2.1   **Simple circular flow of income**

flow (shown as a dashed line in Figure 2.1) goes in an anti-clockwise direction and represents transactions in monetary terms only.

Households and firms represent what economists call *economic agents*. Economic agents are the 'actors' of the economy: they embody behaviours and make decisions. In principle there could be many types of agent. For instance, as well as households and firms, *individuals* and the *government* could also be considered as economic agents. (There is further discussion of economic agents in Section 5.)

For the purposes of this analysis we assume that it is households who own all the factors of production (*capital services* and *labour services*), and who purchase all the final consumption goods and services produced by the firms, spending all their incomes as they do so.

In the main we refer to capital and labour only in this chapter. Firms in this model are assumed to own no factors of production, but rather they 'hire' these from households, to whom they sell all the consumption goods and services they produce, and to whom they pay all their net cash income in the form of either dividends or wages. Clearly, this is a very simple and formal model since it abstracts from the richness and detail of economic reality. It is designed to capture a few essential but key relationships. It can be made more complicated and realistic later.

Tracing, first, the flows of the 'physical' elements around the circuit, households provide their labour and capital services to the firms. The firms combine these and use them in turn to produce an output, which provides final consumption goods and services to the households. *Final consumption goods* would be items like food, washing machines, clothing, etc., while *consumption services* are items like bus-rides, haircuts and restaurant meals. *Labour services* are the effort and skill exerted in the work performed for employers, while *capital* in this case would be in the physical form of the services offered by factories, machines and tools. The term capital *services* is used to indicate that only part of the physical nature of factories, machines and tools would be used up in each round of this circuit, which would be commonly expressed as a measure of their physical deterioration or depletion.

Turning our attention to the monetary aspects of the circuit, it can be seen that these are the obverse of the physical flows. As households own the factors of production and 'let' these to firms, this produces household incomes (in the form of wages and dividends). These incomes then enable the households to make their consumption claims on the output of goods

Definition

Factors of production

Factors of production are the resources used by economic agents as inputs in producing a good or service. These can be of three broad types: the services provided by natural resources, capital and labour.

and services offered by firms. The realization of these claims constitutes household spending, and this then appears as revenue to the firms.

There are a number of important properties to this model, as indicated in the diagram, which are worth drawing attention to at this stage.

1   It is fully self-contained: everything matches, with the flows one way being exactly offset by flows the other way. Thus the system outlined could be said to be in *equilibrium*. As far as it goes, there is no reason for it to be disturbed, or for it to disturb itself. It is in a balance between the elements involved. Once established, there is no incentive for any changes to the system overall.

Question

Can you think of a qualification to this point?

Capital services might eventually all get used up if they were not replaced by the households who own them. This question of 'investment' is dealt with in Section 5.1. In addition, people need to be able to reproduce themselves so that further labour services can be supplied – this particular issue is taken up in Chapter 3.

2   This system is dynamic but timeless. It is not a static system at rest because it involves flows. It implies a 'period' over which these flows take place. A subsequent step, then, would be to designate a period over which we would measure the magnitude of the flows involved. All measurement in economics requires a periodization of time; that is, economic time emerges as a series of periods marked out by how we decide to split up the temporal order. Of course, in principle these periods could be of any length, but it is usual to measure them according to the normal conventions of clock time. National income, for instance, can be reported monthly, quarterly and yearly.

3   The key economic consequence of the system outlined here is that it establishes the nature of a relationship between the value of output, income and expenditure, namely that they are all equal to one another. If we were to designate aggregate output by the letter Q, consumer or consumption expenditure by the letter C, and incomes by the letter Y, then in Figure 2.1 by definition $Q = C = Y$. Note that all of these are now measures made in money terms. This is an important result, so it is worth reiterating. You might like to think of the economic processes as another kind of circuit, with three different stages through which anything passes: first things are produced (output), which when sold provides an income to the producers for their factor services. In purchasing the output with their incomes the consumers (who in aggregate are also the producers, of course) are merely undertaking an equal amount of expenditure. We are assuming at this stage that there are no savings or waste. After this stage we are back to where we started, and the circuit can begin again. Such a circuit is illustrated in Figure 2.2, which shows the three equivalent phases, Q, C and Y, through which economic activity moves. (Note that this is *not* a form of the circular flow diagram, though it is obviously linked to it.)

4   We have established both a relationship, and therefore a difference, between money measures and physical or 'real' measures. Economics is imbued with this distinction. As it stands in the above simple analysis, there

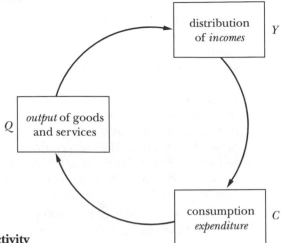

Figure 2.2   **Phases of economic activity**

is a direct congruence between the money realm and the physical realm. We can designate the physical elements in money terms by measuring them directly; the value of the output links the two. It is when we get an *in*congruence between the realm of money and the realm of physical goods and services that problems begin to arise. This would happen, for instance, when money values grow at a different rate than physical measures of output or services. If money values were to grow at a faster rate than physical values, this would be commonly designated as *inflation*; the 'real' value of money – money expressed in terms of the goods and services it could purchase – would be declining. This was just the point that arose in the case of Brazil mentioned above, and which led to the difficulty of converting Brazilian output into a common international measure of money value. In the case of the analysis in Figure 2.1, however, inflation is not possible: there is no growth or change in the magnitudes involved, though we can integrate changes into it, as analysed later.

Deflating data and the calculation of real income

This raises the question of how to deal with the change in a country's national income through time if there were inflation in that country's currency. Inflation would then imply that there was a difference between monetary national income measured in current prices, and real national income measured in constant prices. The way this is dealt with can be illustrated with the aid of the UK national income accounts, which express the national income of the UK both in current price terms and in terms of constant 1985 prices, as shown in Table 2.2. Note that the differences between GNP and GDP are discussed in Section 3.4.

Table 2.2   **UK gross domestic product (GDP) in current price terms and in constant price terms, 1971–91 (£m)[1]**

	1971	1981	1985	1991
GDP at current prices	57 740	254 851	357 268	574 146
GDP at constant 1985 prices	272 321	319 193	357 268	408 565

[1] All measured at market prices.

Source: *Key Data* (1992) Table 4.1

The only figures common between the two rows are those for 1985. The figures in the top row – GDP measured in the prices current in the years in question – have all been adjusted for inflation in the bottom row, taking 1985 prices as the 'base year' for the adjustment. They have been recalculated using a series of 'deflators' expressing purely the change in monetary values of national income. Hence the recalculation is called 'deflating' the data. Let us see how the calculation of real income works by taking a hypothetical example. Suppose that money GDP at market prices for Utopia in 1985 was equivalent to £400 million and it increased to £430 million in 1986. However, at the same time the inflation rate between 1985 and 1986 was 5 per cent. What was Utopia's real income in 1986 expressed in terms of 1985 prices? This can be calculated as follows:

1   First we can think of the 1985 prices as equivalent to 100. These are the 'base year' prices. In effect we are making 1985 income 100 per cent and then thinking of any change from one year to the next as a percentage change. To do this we derive an index of inflation between 1985 and 1986 expressed in terms of this figure of 100. With 5 per cent inflation the price index for 1986 will be 105.

2   We then need to deflate the 1986 money GDP of £430 million by using the inflation index. This is done by dividing 430 by 105 and then multiplying the result by 100. Thus,

$$\frac{430}{105} \times 100 = 409.5 \text{ (to one decimal place).}$$

This result is equivalent to dividing 430 by 1.05.

The real value of 1986 GDP is therefore £409.5 million, which is considerably less than the nominal GDP of £430 million.

Exercise 2.2

Suppose the inflation rate had been 7.5 per cent between 1985 and 1986. What would have been the real GDP of Utopia in 1986?

The figures in the bottom row of Table 2.2 have been recalculated using basically this method to provide 'real' values expressed in terms of 1985 prices. Clearly, the figures for those years before 1985 have been recalculated to 'inflate' them forward to 1985 prices, but the same principles apply. In fact the UK national income accounts provide a quick way to calculate these real changes in the national income totals by the use of the 'GDP deflator'. The GDP deflator expresses the ratio of GDP at current prices to GDP at constant prices:

$$\text{GDP deflator} = \frac{\text{GDP at current prices}}{\text{GDP at constant prices}} \times 100$$

Data for this ratio are shown in Table 2.3.

Table 2.3   **GDP deflator (1985 = 100), UK national accounts 1971, 1981, 1985 and 1991**

	1971	1981	1985	1991
GDP deflator	21.2	79.8	100.0	140.5

Source: *Key Data* (1992) Table 4.1

Once we have the GDP deflators, we can calculate real GDP according to the following formula:

$$\text{real GDP} = \frac{\text{money GDP}}{\text{GDP deflator}} \times 100$$

which is a reorganization of the above definition of the GDP deflator.

Exercise 2.3

You can check the way this is done by taking the figure for 1991 UK money GDP at market prices from the top row of Table 2.2 and calculating the real GDP for 1991 with the use of the GDP deflator from Table 2.3. Your answer should then coincide with the 1991 figure for real GDP at 1985 market prices as shown in the bottom row of Table 2.2. Have a go at this calculation now.

3.3   The key terms: flows and incomes

So much for the properties of the circuits or flows as a whole for the moment. Let us now move on to the key economic terms in the model of the circular flow of income. The two most important terms are *flow* and *income*.

Flows

In economics it is important to make a distinction between flows and stocks Only then can we properly understand the model of national income generation outlined so far.

In the analysis of Figure 2.1, both income and expenditure are flow measures since they take place through a period of time. An example of a stock would be the physical capital (e.g. machinery) in existence at any point in time. Remember that above we talked about *capital services*, which is a flow. In fact all the concepts explored in connection with Figure 2.1 are flows – hence the idea of the flow of income model.

We can explore the relationship between stocks and flows a little more in connection with the idea of capital. Suppose you owned a factory which was valued at £2 million on 31 December 1994. This constitutes your stock of capital at that point in time. During the year 1995 you invest in the physical plant of that factory to the tune of half a million pounds. This investment of £500 000 is a flow. Other things being equal (economists adopt the Latin phrase *ceteris paribus*, meaning literally 'everything else remaining the same', to express this crucial concept), the value of your capital at the end of 1985 would be £2.5 million. But other things are unlikely to remain the same. For instance, there is likely to be some physical deterioration of your original plant even if it stands idle and is not used. If it is used, then there will also have been some capital services used up. Conventional accounting describes this combination of natural deterioration and depletion of value due to use as depreciation. Thus if investment is a flow into your capital account, depreciation is a flow out of it.

You might think of your capital held in the form of a factory as analogous to a reservoir or water tank. The tap of investment adds to that reservoir, while the drain of depreciation depletes it. If depreciation is £300 000 over

Definition

Flows and stocks

These definitions relate to the way we break up time into discrete periods. We would normally measure a flow over some designated period and then measure the stock of something when we temporarily 'stop' time to indicate the transition from one period to another. So *flows* are economic activities or services that take place through time. *Stocks* are economic aggregates at a particular point in time.

Definition

Depreciation

Depreciation is a decline in capital values arising because of the obsolescence, natural deterioration, or use of capital equipment. Depreciation is thus a flow from a capital stock.

the year, then while your stock of *gross capital* at the end of the year is £2.5 million, your stock of *net capital* is less, at £2.2 million (£2m + £0.5m − £0.3m = £2.2m). Similarly, the flow of *gross investment* was £0.5 million, while the flow of *net investment* was only £0.2 million (£0.5m − £0.3m = £0.2m). In any economic analysis it is important to try not to mix up stocks and flows within a single analytical schema.

Exercise 2.4

In fact we have already had to do this in some of the analysis conducted above. Think back to the calculation of per capita incomes, which involved dividing national *income* by the population *stock*. What is the problem here in terms of flows and stocks?

So much for the difference between stocks and flows. We can now look more closely at the concept of *income*. Up to now we have been concentrating on the *measurement* of this without enquiring into the various definitions of the quantities involved.

Income

As we have seen, the circular flow model is designed to measure or estimate national income. You have already encountered the two main notions of national income, namely *gross domestic product* (GDP) and *gross national product* (GNP). In this section and in Section 3.4 we explore the relationship between these two basic measures, beginning here with GDP. As an aid to this discussion the main divisions in the UK national income statistics are shown in Table 2.4, and the following discussion refers to this table.

Table 2.4   **UK national income and domestic product, 1971, 1981, 1985 and 1991, at market prices and at factor cost (£m)**

At current prices	1971	1981	1985	1991
At market prices				
Gross domestic product at market prices ('money GDP')	57 740	254 851	357 268	574 146
Net property income from abroad	553	1 251	2 560	328
Gross national product at market prices	58 293	256 102	359 828	574 474
At factor cost				
Gross domestic product at market prices	57 740	254 851	357 268	574 146
Adjustment to factor cost	−7 714	−36 096	−49 367	−77 145
Gross domestic product at factor cost	50 026	218 755	307 901	497 001
Net property income from abroad	553	1 251	2 560	328
Gross national product at factor cost	50 579	220 006	310 461	497 329
less Capital consumption	−5 330	−31 641	−41 883	−63 968
Net national product at factor cost ('national income')	45 249	188 365	268 578	433 361

Source: *Key Data* (1992) Table 4.1

If we were to add up all the final output from the individual firms in the economy, the aggregate would be a measure of its GDP. Note that this is designated in terms of *final output.* In any real economy some output from some firms is likely to be an *intermediate output*: it would constitute an input into other firms' output rather than appearing as a final output going to consumers. Thus to avoid *double counting,* all this intermediate activity would need to be eliminated to find the true final output.

Definition

Value added

Value added is the incremental output added at each stage in the production process.

The way this is done in practice is to concentrate on the value added at each stage in the total production chain. If we look, for example, at the output of the shoe industry, the value of the leather or rubber used to help make shoes constitutes an output of these other supplier industries. The value added in the shoe industry is the value of its own output minus the cost of the inputs of rubber and leather bought from firms working in the other supplier industries (and any other input costs except labour). Tracing back the relationships in this way – isolating at each stage the value added at that particular stage – and then totalling these up gives the national product for that particular set of activities. Aggregating across activities gives a total measure of GDP.

Another point to note is that in this case the GDP is valued at *market prices.* For the purposes of national income accounting, market prices include all indirect taxes, i.e. those taxes levied on goods and services rather than on incomes. Taxes on incomes are mainly designated *direct taxes*, for example income tax, national insurance contributions and corporation tax. *Indirect taxes* are thus made up of revenues from purchase taxes, value-added tax (VAT), customs and excise duties, etc., which are levied on expenditures. Although these taxes are (formally at least) paid by final consumers, they do not form part of the income going to producers or the owners of the factors of production – they constitute an income to the government. In contrast, subsidies are an additional income to the factor activity (they are a 'transfer' to factors of production). The price net of indirect taxes but including subsidies is described as being *at factor cost.* GDP is reported 'at factor cost' as well as 'at market prices', as shown in Table 2.4.

Exercise 2.5

Look back at Table 2.4 and find the figure for 1991 GDP at market prices. For that year subsidies were £5878 million and taxes on expenditure £83023 million. What was GDP at factor cost?

You can check that all the other figures given in the table 'at factor cost' for both GDP and GNP have been adjusted in the same way from their 'at market price' equivalents.

Finally, the GDP figures also refer to *current production* only. Thus they exclude the value of transactions in already existing commodities like used cars or old houses. Note, however, that the value of current services provided by estate agents or used-car dealers in selling these items would be included because this is a current item.

3.4   GNP, GDP and NNP

So far we have been defining and refining the measure of GDP. Turning to *gross national product* (GNP), this refers to the final output of goods and services produced by *domestically owned* factors of production regardless of where that production actually takes place. Quite a lot of the actual production of value might be located abroad. Subtracting that part of GNP earned abroad gives us the measure of gross domestic product that we have been using above. Thus GDP is a measure of final production produced within the confines of the territory of the country, irrespective of who owns the factors of production undertaking that value-adding activity. If you are a British citizen but are temporarily working abroad, your income is part of UK GNP, but it is not part of its GDP because it is earned abroad. Similarly, that part of the profits that Nissan Motor Corporation earns by way of its production operations in the UK and which it repatriates back to Japan is part of UK GDP but is not part of UK GNP. The profit provides an income to Japanese nationals and is thus part of Japanese GNP.

The differences between GNP and GDP show the position when all the overseas earnings differences are netted out between countries. These earnings are made up of net interest, profits and dividends. As can be seen from Table 2.4, if you begin with GDP, GNP is derived by *adding* the 'net property income from abroad' to this. Clearly, if we begin with GNP and want to derive the GDP, then we simply *subtract* this item.

Exercise 2.6

1   In 1991 the UK earned £77 668 million in interest, profits and dividends from abroad, but it paid £77 340 million equivalent to foreign countries. The UK's GNP at factor cost was £497 329 million. What was its GDP at factor cost?

2   The net property earnings from abroad were therefore £328 million (hence GNP was greater than GDP). What does this indicate about the overseas earnings of UK nationals as against the local earnings of foreign nationals?

Finally, we should remember that GNP and GDP refer to *gross* measures of production. No reduction is made for the losses from the wear and tear of existing capital that would normally be a part of any production system – what was referred to above as the depreciation of the capital stock. In the table of accounts given above this is termed 'capital consumption'. If we subtract this item from the gross measure of national income, we would have a measure of the *net national product* (NNP). Thus NNP is GNP minus any capital consumption (similarly with NDP in relation to GDP). This would give us a measure of the long-term productive potential of the economy, and this is what is termed 'national income' in the accounts shown in Table 2.4.

3.5   Output, income and expenditure once again

Up to now we have been working mainly with a production/output basis for measuring 'national income'. But you will recall that within the circular flow model (Figure 2.1) output/production *equals* expenditure/consumption *equals* factor incomes: $Q = C = Y$.

Thus in principle we could work in terms of consumer expenditures or in terms of factor incomes, as well as in terms of production outputs, to measure and calculate the national income quantities indicated above. There are thus three equivalent approaches to measuring the same thing – what we have termed 'national income' – all of which should in principle give us exactly the same result.

I have already described the *output approach* at some length, so it is not necessary to go over this again in any detail. It involves collecting data, via surveys of business activity (production and sales), on the value added in each sector or industry, and then aggregating these in a way that avoids double counting. The advantage of this method is that it can also give a breakdown of the output value of each sector or industry in the economy separately, a useful statistic for disaggregated analysis of trends and problems in the economy.

As its name implies, the *expenditure method* relies on surveys and data collection centred on the final expenditures of various agents in the economy: households via the Household Expenditure Survey; the government via its accounts; firms in terms of their investment expenditures and stock holdings; and the 'overseas sector' (something we have not yet integrated into the analysis but will do in Section 5.3) via firms' and individuals' sales and purchases of imports and exports as registered in the international trade flows statistics. Adding all these final expenditures together, but eliminating net indirect taxes as mentioned in Section 3.3, gives another measure of aggregate national income at factor cost. The advantage of this method is that it provides estimates of the components of aggregate expenditures in the economy, which have been useful for economic policy purposes.

Table 2.5 shows an example of this method's results in terms of the UK's accounts over the period 1981 to 1991, expressed in current price terms only.

The *factor income approach* tries to measure incomes directly from the returns lodged with the tax-collecting branch of the government – in the UK, the Inland Revenue. If everything was reported correctly, this method would give an estimate of national income at factor cost. The advantage of this approach would be that it could provide statistics on the 'distribution' of incomes as between different social groups, or between the different aggregate 'factors of production' in the context of viewing the distribution between them across the whole economy.

Table 2.6 shows the figures for the UK accounts for the period 1981 to 1991, couched in terms of the factor income approach. For reasons already mentioned, these are given at factor cost only.

The history of national income accounting since the 1930s (when the current system was gradually introduced), particularly its early years, is littered with disputes between proponents of these three methods

Table 2.5   **UK national accounts by category of expenditure, 1981, 1985 and 1991 (£m)**

At current market prices	1981	1985	1991
Consumers' expenditure	155 412	218 947	367 853
General government final consumption	55 374	73 805	121 899
of which:			
Central government	33 879	45 879	74 442
Local authorities	21 495	27 926	47 457
Gross domestic fixed capital formation	41 304	60 353	95 442
Value of physical increase in stocks and work in progress	−2 768	821	−5 303
Total domestic expenditure	249 322	353 926	579 891
Exports of goods and services	67 432	102 208	135 115
of which:			
Goods	50 668	77 991	103 413
Services	16 764	24 217	31 702
Total final expenditure	316 754	456 134	715 006
less Imports of goods and services	−60 388	−98 866	−140 415
of which:			
Goods	−47 416	−81 336	−113 703
Services	−12 972	−17 530	−26 712
Statistical discrepancy (expenditure adjustment)	−1 515	−	−445
Gross domestic product	254 851	357 268	574 146
Net property income from abroad	1 251	2 560	328
Gross national product	256 102	359 828	574 474

Source: *Key Data* (1992) Table 4.2

Table 2.6   **UK national income accounts by category of income, 1981, 1985 and 1991 (£m)**

Factor incomes	1981	1985	1991
Income from employment	149 737	196 858	329 808
Income from self-employment	19 980	30 404	57 507
Gross trading profits of companies	27 341	51 287	60 674
Gross trading surplus of public corporations	7 974	7 120	3 119
Gross trading surplus of general government enterprises	236	265	119
Rent	16 366	21 875	44 092
Imputed charge for consumption of non-trading capital	2 351	2 830	4 490
Total domestic income	223 985	310 639	499 809
less Stock appreciation	−5 974	−2 738	−2 825
Statistical discrepancy (income adjustment)	744	—	17
Gross domestic product at factor cost	218 755	307 901	497 001

Source: *Key Data* (1992), derived from Table 4.3

(Stone, 1951; Studenski, 1958; Kendrick, 1970; Carson, 1975). As demonstrated above, the published accounts include measures based upon all three methods, though the consensus approach is with the expenditure method, and this is the one developed further below.

However, let us first return to examine the model that lies behind these practical estimating issues.

4   The model as a whole

This section raises some issues that are not often highlighted in discussions of the circular flow of income model. These issues relate first to the *language* in which the model is discussed, and second to the *style of reasoning* that this language embodies. Some of these points may seem obvious, but it is their very obviousness that makes them interesting and important, and which often leads to them being ignored. They are important because they say something about how we come to know the economy in the way that we do via this model, and therefore they also say something about the very nature of model building and of economics. In addition, this provides an opportunity to look briefly at the history of national income accounting in which the circular flow of income model has operated.

4.1   Models and language

Question

What do you think is particularly distinctive about the language that has been used so far to describe the national income model?

The distinctive feature of the language is its use of imagery: we have talked of the notion of a 'flow' around a system. Whilst this might seem a very ordinary image, it is this very ordinariness that makes it such a powerful one. Part of the reason why the circular flow model can be found described in much the same way in all introductory textbooks on economics is that this imagery is convenient, attractive and powerful.

Note that in discussing investment in Section 3.3 I referred to a tank or reservoir, with taps into it and a drain out of it that established the flows – a very homely analogy, you might think. That, of course, is the point. The description used a series of analogies and metaphors: *flows* (of a *liquid*) around an integrated *system* that involves something like a *tank* or *reservoir* with a *tap* leading into it and a *drain* leading out of it (the terms italicized being the analogies and the entire image being the metaphor). Indeed, this is exactly what a model is – a series of analogies and a metaphor. A model is a *representation*: that is, it both represents something else and is something in its own right which is different from and independent of that which it is supposed to be representing. The effect of a representation, then, is in part to obscure, or render invisible, that which it represents, while at the same time seeking to illuminate it. A model, then, is a *tool* (another analogy) or an *instrument* (another analogy) by which we begin to make some sense of the way an economy might operate. Remember how in Section 2 I spoke about a model as a *map* (another analogy) and a *torch* (another analogy), and in terms of the metaphor of shining the torch on that aspect of the economy under investigation to illuminate it? You can see how difficult (if not impossible) it becomes to talk about what the model does without speaking in terms of analogies and metaphors (McCloskey, 1986, 1990).

The way models perform is precisely by substituting themselves in the place of the thing they are supposed to represent. It is through the operation of the language of models that we can begin to understand exactly how they might function. Thus the terms of linguistic expression are just as important to an economic analysis as the forms of the economic analysis itself. Indeed, the one is rendered with respect to the other, because the discourse of economic analysis is conducted in terms of a 'language', even if that language is mathematical, algebraic or diagrammatic in form – see Section 8.2.

A way of making this discussion more concrete is to refer to one of the most famous examples of a circular flow of income model. In the early 1950s, A. W. Phillips, an engineer turned economist, constructed a physical model of the economy (Figure 2.3). This, then, is a literal model of the economy, and it is clearly not the same as the economy. In this case it is a physical

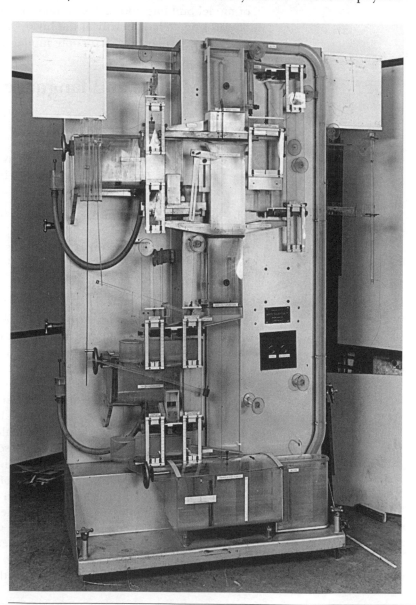

Figure 2.3   **The Phillips machine during renovation**

representation of it. The model (a working version of which is displayed at the London School of Economics) operates as a true 'flow diagram' (though it is not quite a full *circular* flow). It simulates the economy via the movement of coloured water through a complex system of tubes, taps, valves and tanks. The machine is operated by pulleys, pumps and the forces of gravity, and the magnitude of changes in the key variables are registered by graphs linked to moving valves in the tanks. The principles and economic analysis associated with the Phillips machine are discussed in Phillips (1950) and Newlyn (1950). These were developed mainly in mathematical terms by Phillips. There are other (non-working) machines in Leeds and Chicago, and there is at least one further working model in New Zealand (Barr, 1988). Note that this model displays well developed government and external sectors, which we shall look at in Sections 5.2 and 5.3 respectively.

Although we are not concerned with the detail of how the Phillips machine worked, its general characteristics are shown in Figure 2.4. Beginning at the

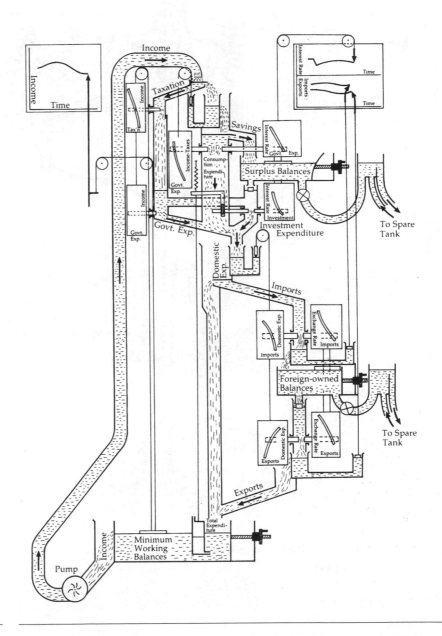

Figure 2.4 **The Phillips machine in more detail**

Source: Barr (1988) Figure 2

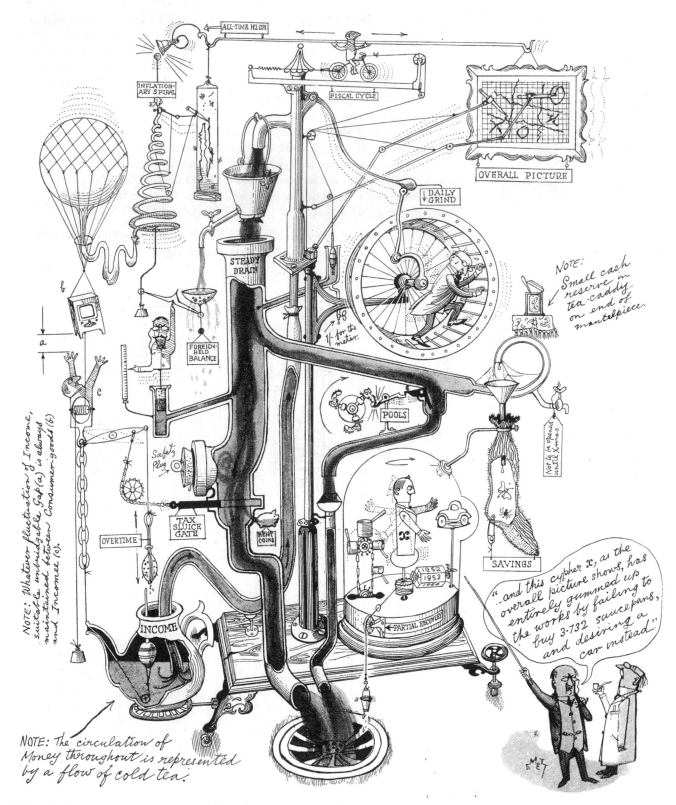

Figure 2.5   Cartoon of the Phillips machine

Source: *Punch*, 15 April 1953

bottom, a tank of water represents money balances, which are pumped to the top of the machine to become the basis of income flows. This income then goes through a complicated set of tubes, valves and sub-tanks which represent taxation by the government and its expenditure, savings by the public, investment, and domestic consumer expenditures. There is also an international account mechanism, which simulates the flows of imports and exports and the money balances held by foreigners. Expenditure flows return to the bottom of the model to begin the process again, though with some siphoning off into an idle money balances tank and an overseas money holdings account. You can see that this model is more complicated than the very simple circular flow shown in Figure 2.1. It has more components and constituent elements. We explore these added elements in greater detail in Section 5.

As Figure 2.5 shows, this model was subject to some ribald comment at the time (note the emphasis on the drain in this cartoon, which is not a strong feature of the actual machine)!

Part of the problem with economic models is understanding why one particular model becomes more popular than another, even to the point of totally displacing or discrediting the other. This raises major issues of economic methodology and how economics explains itself. Donald McCloskey, who has been instrumental in bringing these issues to the fore within economics, argues that there is a criterion of 'rightness' in the way some metaphors seem to be the most appropriate in analysing a particular problem or situation. For him it is not so much a matter of whether they are 'true' or 'correct' in an absolute sense, but whether they have 'force' and seem to 'fit'. Clearly, some metaphors are better than others; they seem more apt or more right because they explain more (McCloskey, 1990, pp.64–6). These metaphors provide a means by which economists can argue with and persuade one another. But a further point to make here is that the terms of language (the effectiveness and power of one set of analogies and metaphors as opposed to another, for instance), while providing part of the answer as to why one model is favoured over another, obviously do not provide a total picture. The *institutionalized nature* of economics is itself a powerful element in this picture, and I turn to this now.

4.2   The style of economic reasoning

This can be introduced through a consideration of the history of the circular flow model, which in turn raises questions of the intelligibility of economics in terms of its style of reasoning.

The eighteenth-century French economists of the Physiocratic School are generally credited with having founded the notion of a discrete 'national income'. They were concerned with the production of a surplus product in an economy that involved the relationships between various collective economic agents: those engaged in agriculture, those engaged in industry, and those engaged in trade. These groups variously contributed to the production of total national product or wealth, though for the Physiocrats it was the agricultural sector that contributed the key share of this.

An interesting feature of the Physiocratic system was that by the beginning of the twentieth century in France their approach had been rendered into a circular flow format, as shown in Figure 2.6. In fact, this was well before the

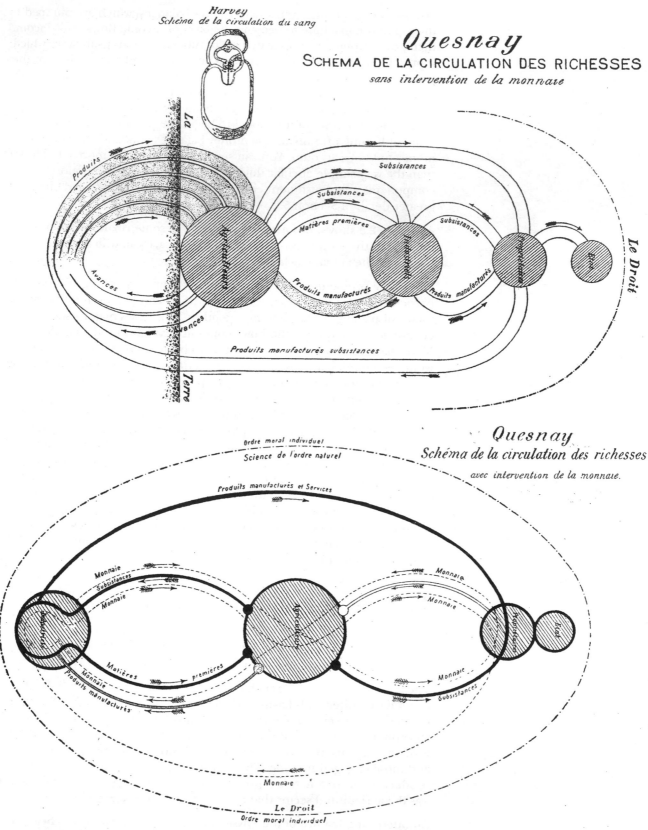

Figure 2.6   Some early circular flow diagrams based on Quesnay's 'Tableau Economique'

Source: *Denis* (1904)

advent of modern macroeconomic analysis in the 1930s and early 1940s, i.e. the systematic attempt to develop a coherent structure of national income accounting. Such developments are usually associated with John Maynard Keynes's development of modern macroeconomics from the 1930s onwards. Thus the circular flow analogy pre-dated its deployment in a Keynesian theoretical framework by at least thirty years, though it is this Keynesian theoretical framework that is often thought to have provided the stimulus for the development of the circular flow.

A key feature for understanding the way this circular flow format developed and took hold can be seen in the top left-hand corner of Figure 2.6. The whole schema is predicated on the analogy of the circulation of blood (*sang*) around the metaphor of a physiological body. The top part of the figure illustrates economic circulation without money – equivalent to the 'physical circuit' discussed above in relation to Figure 2.1 – while the bottom part of Figure 2.6 introduces money, which is the equivalent of the 'monetary circuit' in Figure 2.1. In the top part you can see the important position occupied by *la terre* (the earth) and agriculture in the Physiocratic schema, and similarly the central position it occupies in the lower, monetary diagram.

What happened in the two hundred years or so between the Physiocrats' original economic analysis and the diagrams representing it at the beginning of the twentieth century was that economics became institutionalized around the grand model of theoretical endeavour provided by the attempt to match the scientific approach of the physical sciences. In the case of Figure 2.6 this was provided by the physiological sciences, particularly by the biology of the nineteenth century (though one of the founders of the Physiocratic School, François Quesnay, was himself a medical practitioner, which probably accounts for the blood circulation analogy). Most of our current notions of economic systems and the most appropriate models designed to represent these still rely on a combination of the 'organicist' or 'mechanical' notion of physics and biology that was current at the time when economics was first institutionalized in the nineteenth century. Economics borrowed its model-building strategy extensively from these sciences, and they still live to haunt it, for good or ill. The Phillips machine is a classic example of the mechanical aspect of these dual defining features of much economic analysis. Indeed, the rhetorical strength of the circular flow model is that it combines both these analogies in a single schema; it is both 'organic' and 'mechanical', which legitimizes and strengthens a particular view of its scientific credentials.

The above discussion is designed to indicate the complex notion of economic model building with which we need to grapple in economics, and also the significance of some of the less discussed aspects of these processes. However, the way different intellectual traditions 'borrow' from each other, and whether these particular borrowings by economics are appropriate, remains an area of intense dispute among economic methodologists (Mirowski, 1989, is a recent example).

5   Extensions to the circular flow model

In this section we will be making our circular flow model in Figure 2.1 successively more realistic (and therefore more complicated), first by expanding the type of economic activity agents are involved in, and second by expanding the range of economic agents themselves. We do this in connection with the consumption/expenditure approach to estimating national income mentioned above.

We have already introduced the idea of *investment flows* into our model verbally, so we now need to make this a little more formal.

5.1   Investment and saving

The first thing to note is that for investment to take place in this still simple world there would first need to be *savings*. Householders do not typically spend all their income; they save some of it. But what do they do with their savings? Assuming they do not simply keep these at home in the form of idle cash balances, they deposit them in a financial institution.

But note that depositing household savings in the bank, while often called investment, is not the same as physical investment – the investment in directly productive assets. Financial institutions play a crucial role in collecting up savings, consolidating them and then lending these on to firms to help finance physical investment. Thus there is a difference between financial investment and physical investment. Financial institutions act as intermediaries between savings and investment.

On our circular flow diagram, savings by households have the effect of reducing consumers' expenditure below their incomes. Savings can therefore be envisaged as a 'drain' or leakage out of household spending (as shown in Figure 2.7), creating a potential imbalance between the flows of money and the flows of goods and services around the system. Savings (*S*) therefore allow the production of consumption goods and services to be less than total production. In addition to producing consumer goods, firms can produce some final capital goods, such as new machinery to purchase from each other. We can schematically picture two kinds of firms, one producing consumption goods, and the other producing capital or investment goods.

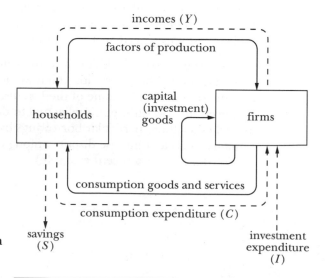

Figure 2.7   **The circular flow with savings and investment**

This is shown by the small capital goods circuit in Figure 2.7; the firms sector as a whole purchases capital goods from itself. Finally, the monetary flows 'injected' into the system when firms purchase capital goods from each other are shown by the investment expenditure (I) in Figure 2.7. Remember that the dashed lines are monetary flows, and the solid lines show flows of real goods and services.

Our circular flow model has now become more complicated, but it is still an enclosed and balanced world. Figure 2.7 shows a circuit with two kinds of production: production for consumption and production for investment. The expenditure approach to national income estimation has therefore been broadened to differentiate consumers' expenditure from investment expenditure. If we call consumption expenditure C and investment expenditure I, then

$$Y = C + I$$

This equation refers to expenditure on firms' output. On the household side, the incomes coming into the households, which by definition are equal to the value of total output, are either consumed (C) or form additions to savings (S). Hence, on the income side,

$$Y = C + S$$

The implication of this is that, in our simple model, *by definition*,

$$I = S$$

These are accounting identities. The same value of output is divided as income between consumption and savings, and as production between consumption and investment. Any unsold goods are accumulated as stocks and included in the investment total. At the end of our accounting period, the accounts on the expenditure and income side balance by definition. How this balance relates to what firms and households have *planned* to do, and how plans and expectations may be frustrated, are matters you will study later in Book 2.

For now the crucial thing to note about investment expenditure is that it can produce *additional* national income. We save now, and reduce our current potential expenditures, and firms use these resources to invest in the expectation that this will produce more for us later. Investment raises the issue of the *growth* in national income, as measured in real terms through time. This is explored further in Section 8 below.

5.2   The government sector

We can now make our flow diagram even more realistic by including the government sector within it. For this purpose we assume that the government is really a single agent, which receives an income in terms of taxes on households, and conducts current expenditures by buying goods and services from firms. A schematic representation of this extended circuit is shown in Figure 2.8. This has been simplified by showing only monetary flows.

Under the circumstances of Figure 2.8, households dispose of their incomes in three ways: they buy consumer goods, they save, or they pay taxes (T) to the government. Firms, on the other hand, receive income from consumer expenditure, from investment spending by other firms, and also from the

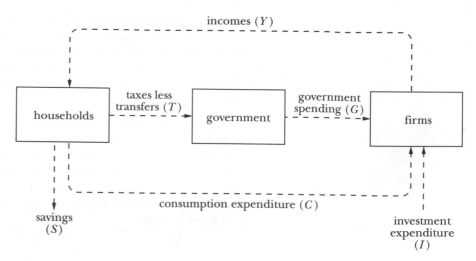

***Figure 2.8*   The circular flow with a government sector**

expenditure of the government on their goods and services (*G*). Clearly, in practice, some of the government's tax revenue would simply be transferred back to households, but this element is netted out of the tax payment *T,* as shown in the figure. Those elements of government expenditure known as *transfer payments* – unemployment benefit, housing subsidy benefit, income support benefit, and the like – while financed out of taxes are not part of the government's call on consumption resources, since they are actually spent by the households receiving the transfers. Thus they would appear under the heading of *C,* not *G*. The heading *T* represents only net taxes (total taxes minus transfer payments and other subsidies), which also applies to *G*, the government's own net claim on goods and services.

Under these circumstances, from the firms' point of view, or from the expenditure side, national income

$$Y = C + I + G$$

From the households' point of view, or from the income side,

$$Y = C + S + T$$

Since *C* is the same on both sides of the account, this implies that

$$I + G = S + T$$

If the government were to run a budget deficit, $T < G$, then this implies $I < S$, with household savings being greater than investment and the government having to borrow to finance some of its spending. (Note that $<$ means 'less than' and $>$ means 'greater than'.) The converse is true too, by definition: if the government has a budget surplus ($T > G$), then firms and households together, i.e. the private sector, must be running a financial deficit ($I > S$).

5.3   The international connection

Up to now in this formal analysis we have been considering a purely domestic economy. A more realistic picture introduces connections from the domestic economy to the rest of the world. We have already done this in our earlier discussion of the measurement of national income, i.e. in pointing out the difference between GDP and GNP, but the task now is to integrate the international sector more formally into the model.

For the purposes of the analysis we assume that both firms and households are involved in international economic exchanges: firms export goods and services, and households consume imports. Clearly, in practice this is not strictly the case, since firms are the intermediaries in international trade, importing goods and services for sale to households. But since we are concerned with final use of goods and services, we can treat households as the importers without losing any important insights.

The substance of the addition of the rest of the world to the circular flow model can be seen in Figure 2.9. Again, the diagram has been simplified to show only the monetary flows.

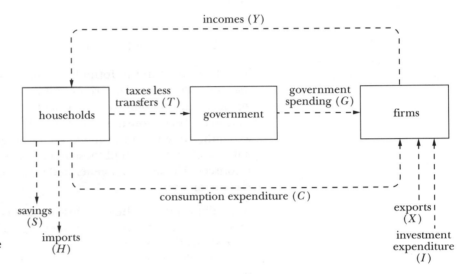

Figure 2.9   **The circular flow: the domestic economy and the rest of the world**

In Figure 2.9, exports give rise to a receipt (X) by the firms engaged in exporting. Imports give rise to payments abroad (H) ultimately by the households consuming the imports. The net payments ($X - H$) are a monetary measure of the *balance of trade* on the international account. There is no particular need or reason why X and H should balance in any period, so there may be a trade surplus ($X > H$) or a trade deficit ($X < H$). But overall, in any period, income must equal expenditure in the whole circular flow, with leakages such as savings, taxes and imports balancing injections such as investment, government spending and exports.

Note that the trade balance ($X - H$) captured in our circular flow model forms in practice just one part of a country's overall *balance of payments*. This balance of payments is made up of two main elements: (a) the *balance of trade* just discussed, and (b) the balance on the *capital account*. Outside our simple model, if there is an imbalance on the trade account there may be some compensating movement on the capital account, so that the overall accounts move towards balance. As its name implies, the capital account comprises movements of financial investment flows into and out of a country. If, for instance, the UK's balance of trade were positive, this would mean that it was earning more from its exports than it was paying for its imports. Under these circumstances it might use this additional overseas income to build up its overseas assets, or to pay off some of its accumulated debts to foreigners. Both of these would appear as negative flows on the capital account because the UK would either be buying capital assets abroad or paying off the foreign holders of UK debts. The reverse is the case if the balance of trade were negative; the UK would be spending more abroad than it was earning. To finance this net expenditure the options are either borrowing from abroad, or selling off some of its accumulated assets, both of which would appear as positive flows into the country on the capital account. None of these financial issues is captured in the circular flow model.

6   Aggregate expenditure

On the basis of Figure 2.9 we are in a position to look at the overall nature of the national income accounts, since we have now introduced all the main adjustments that bring the picture into a more realistic (though still abstract) focus. So far we have national income, $Y = C + I + G$. Adding on the value of the net trade flow gives us:

$$Y = C + I + G + (X - H)$$

The items listed in this formula are also known as the components of *aggregate expenditure*. They represent the net expenditure made by different agents in an economy in any particular period. Aggregate expenditure is thus made up of consumption expenditure, investment expenditure, the net expenditure of the government sector on goods and services, and the balance of trade. Each of these items represents a real claim on national resources. All have been generated with the aid of the circular flow of income model.

As an illustration of the way these elements of aggregate expenditure add up to the national income, consider the data presented in Table 2.7. This table shows the components of aggregate expenditure for five of the six countries shown in Table 2.2. (Note that total investment (I) is made up of investment in factories, machines, etc. (I'), plus any addition to stocks (I'') which refers to current production that is accumulated now for use later, and that net exports are the difference between total exports (X) and total imports (H).)

Table 2.7   **The components of aggregate expenditure for a range of countries, 1991 (US$bn)**

	UK	Germany	Finland	Brazil	Tanzania	Austria
C	650.53	856.10	68.65	262.44	2.40	
$+I'$	169.32	340.52	27.55	76.67	1.20	
$+I''$	−9.15	−5.18	−0.59	—	+0.09	
$+G$	215.80	282.07	29.83	58.56	0.40	
$+X$	238.81	610.55	27.05	34.53	0.60	
$−H$	−248.61	−498.46	−27.83	−26.44	−1.52	
$(X − H)$	(−9.8)	(+112.09)	(−0.78)	(+8.09)	(−0.92)	
Statistical discrepancy	+0.11	−0.06	+0.01	+0.01	−0.02	
Y (GDP)	1016.81	1585.54[1]	124.67	405.77	3.15	

[1] GNP

Notes: C = private final consumption expenditure; I' = gross fixed capital formation; I'' = increase (+) or decrease (−) in stocks; G = government final consumption expenditure; X = exports of goods and services; H = imports of goods and services.

Source: *International Financial Statistics Year Book* (1993) country tables

Exercise 2.7

The figures for Austria are not included in Table 2.7. Given that its GDP (in US$ billion) was 165.46, total investment 43.45, net exports 1.48, private final consumption expenditure 90.76, imports 66.15, government expenditures 29.77, and addition to stocks 1.91, fill in the completed breakdown for Austrian aggregate expenditure in 1991.

7   Issues and problems in measuring national income

As we have seen, the actual measurement of national income is no easy matter at the best of times, even with the aid of our model of the circular flow. But it is important to recognize a set of other conceptual and practical problems that have not so far been covered in the analysis, or that arise out of it. By and large these refer to estimation problems.

The output measured by all the national income accounting approaches is that which is registered through the market place. It is valued via its market price, either 'at market prices' or 'at factor cost', and these market prices are taken as a proxy measure of the welfare gained. But not all output, let alone all welfare, is registered simply by market transactions.

Question

Can you think of any economic activity that adds to our welfare but which might not be registered in the national income accounts because it is not subject to market-based transactions?

One example of non-market output would be that provided by domestic activity around the house. It is often argued that housework or gardening – while genuine work – is not properly registered in the national income accounts. Clearly, inasmuch as this type of work is remunerated in the form of the wages paid to domestic servants or gardeners, it does register in the national income accounts (as long as it is declared to the tax authorities). But this serves to make the point that all those domestic tasks fulfilled but not paid for escape the net of 'welfare benefits'. Since it is often women's work that appears under these categories of 'work performed without reward', this imparts a potential bias into the national income accounts and our measures of overall society welfare. The bulk of women's work may not be valued at market prices, and thus the output produced by 'work performed without reward' does not appear in the accounts as part of our social welfare.

Another instance of this point would be the 'underground economy'. All economic activity that is performed surreptitiously – in the form of 'moonlighting' or illegally because payment for it is deliberately concealed – escapes its representation via the national income accounts. How important is this? Estimates of the extent of the underground economy have varied from between 2–3 per cent of national income to as much as 12–15 per cent, even for a developed country like the UK, which has a sophisticated monitoring system.

Aligned to the issue of the underground economy is that of the 'secondary' or 'informal' economy. In many developing countries a good deal of real economic activity is unregistered or untaxed, though it is conducted in market terms. In this case it is performed in the so-called secondary or informal sector. Where this type of activity is widespread and large in scale it could seriously distort the measure of national income. In addition there is the issue of subsistence farming, where farmers produce for themselves and therefore do not have to resort to the market for all of their demands. There are usually estimates of this type of activity in the national accounts, but it could be wide of its true value. These, then, represent additional reasons (recall Section 3.1) why the national income of a country like Tanzania might be significantly underestimated by the techniques discussed so far in this chapter.

An additional problem would arise if there were significant barter exchanges of goods and services in an economy. Barter exchanges are not registered in market prices. In some societies barter is still practised, but if it becomes quantitatively significant then it can be estimated and included rather like subsistence activity. Barter only becomes really widespread where there is hyperinflation, and confidence in the market system and prices completely break down. This can afflict developed as well as developing countries.

But what about that type of economic activity in our society which, while registered positively and properly in the national income accounts, might still be considered detrimental to our overall welfare? A good deal of legitimate economic activity causes environmental damage, for instance, but is that activity necessarily a 'good'?

Question

Can you think of examples of activity along these lines that might appear as an addition to national income in the accounts, but which we might consider to be a negative item?

Considerable attention has been directed towards the output of the energy industries as potential pollutants – their waste products can produce 'acid rain', for instance. Is the production of CFC gases really an added benefit to our welfare when it seems to be partly responsible for the depletion of the ozone layer? We might also consider the output of the tobacco industry a 'bad' because it adversely affects our health, though as it stands at the moment this is an addition to our welfare as measured by the national income accounts.

Many of these issues involve what are called 'value judgements'. We are bringing subjective and ethical concerns explicitly into economic analysis. From some points of view this is frowned upon, since it is thought that economics should be an ethically neutral and thereby a 'positive' science, dealing only with uncovering how things operate, i.e. with what 'is' rather than with what 'ought to be'. But increasingly it is recognized that the unfettered operation of the market is not itself ethically free. It involves its own implicit value judgements, for instance about the overriding worth of individualized decision making within markets.

One way of dealing with some of these dilemmas would be to develop different forms of accounting, such as a system of social accounting which registered the 'bads' as well as the 'goods' of national output. However, as yet this kind of accounting in a national income framework has not progressed very far, though it is one area of considerable contemporary work and interest.

On a slightly different note, the national income accounts represent market measures of value-added output. But some sectors of the economy do not register an 'output' as such. What, for instance, is the output of the armed forces? How could this be measured in market terms? A lot of government-controlled activity in particular has no obvious market value, but it still has to be registered in the accounts. In fact this is done in terms of its *input costs.*

This raises its own problems. Suppose the 'productivity' of the army rises, so that it can perform its duties with fewer personnel and less equipment. If the input cost of the army declines as a result, as measured in terms of the accounts, then so would national income. Thus increases in productivity decrease the national income in this case.

Question

Can you suggest other types of government activity that may present similar problems?

Some examples are the police and the fire service, the health service in its preventative capacity, and even some parts of the education system. What, for example, is a sensible measure of the output of nursery education?

Clearly, one way round this would be to 'marketize' these kinds of services in various ways. They can then be bought and sold at a price and easily included in the national accounts. Such would also be the case for some of the environmental damage wrought by the discharge of waste products. If the environment could be properly valued, its destruction could then be indicated in the accounts.

This relates to a more general difficulty in GNP estimation. The *quality* of output can change dramatically over time. Thus whilst the price paid for goods and services may remain the same (or even fall), the 'welfare' they produce when they are consumed could have increased. The national income accounts develop elaborate adjustment mechanisms to try to measure quality changes in the output of goods and services, but if a major innovation is introduced, comparisons with a past but similar output combination become increasingly difficult. Thus the longer the period over which national income comparisons are made, the more severe are the uncertainties as to whether real changes have been picked up.

What these difficulties associated with national income estimation all raise is problems of measuring changes over time. Suppose that, in the case of a society like Tanzania, there is a sudden registration of the output of the secondary economy and any remaining subsistence farming is eliminated. This could increase at a stroke the national income as measured in the accounts without there necessarily being any real improvement in the underlying standard of living. Similarly, suppose that the extent of the underground economy in a country like Germany (or the UK) varied as the cycle of economic activity in the economy overall varied, so that it was more extensive in periods of recession than in periods of boom. In this case there would be a variation in the national income accounts due solely to the way this type of activity moved into and out of the formal economy. Again, suppose a great deal of traditional government activity is privatized, then national income could rise as the 'productivity' improvements were registered in these spheres due solely to measurement reasons, and not because of any underlying 'real' increase in their productivity. As we have seen, all these issues arise in addition to questions of comparisons over time which result from the changing value of money itself (and over space in terms of societies with radically different economic characteristics).

8   Change and growth

In the previous section I began to talk about the way changes in national income are measured over time. This raises the question of how such change can be understood and analysed. In this section I introduce some very preliminary ways in which economists have gone about modelling change, particularly in investment expenditures and incomes. The key concept here is that of the *investment function*.

8.1   The idea of a function

Let us first talk about the notion of a 'function'. When using this term we mean that one particular thing is in some way dependent upon something else. In the case of economics we would say 'one economic variable is dependent on some other variable'. Sometimes this is expressed as the behaviour of one economic variable being dependent upon the behaviour of another. While we are generally dealing here with the relationship among economic variables, it is possible for the behaviour of an economic variable to be dependent on a non-economic variable, such as when the output of a commodity is dependent on the weather. Functional relationships are just another form of an economic model, so when developing a functional relationship between variables we are developing a model of that relationship.

8.2   The investment function

One such functional relationship is known as the *investment function*. This links the expenditure on investment goods to the likely determinants of this. Clearly, there are a lot of things that are going to affect investment expenditure, so for the purposes of modelling this we want to concentrate on the most significant.

Investment is an important variable in economics because it is linked to the ability of a firm or economy to grow by increasing its output; it may be a key variable in growth theory. As we have seen, investment requires that an amount of current consumption be forgone – appearing in the form of savings – to release the resources to finance it. These resources are used to generate capital accumulation, which itself can lead to growth in the total productive output of an economy. Investment and growth are thus linked through the notion of *expanded reproduction*. The economic system reproduces itself, but it does so in an extended form, i.e. it grows.

There are two types of capital accumulation associated with investment. One occurs when the amount or extent of capital simply expands without changes in its character. Since there is more of it, output can be increased as a result. The other changes the form of capital in that it raises its *productivity*. That is, any given quantity of capital can produce more output. Here the possibility of increasing output occurs through productivity changes. Most actual investment involves a combination of these two basic types of capital accumulation.

But what determines investment expenditure in terms of the framework of the circular flow model? The first thing to note is that 'investment' as used here involves the purchase of a capital good. It is not the same as the term 'investment' used to indicate the purchase of a financial asset like a share or a bond. The latter is 'financial investment', and although these may be linked (i.e. a financial investment can provide the financial resources with which to purchase a capital good) they need to be distinguished. A capital good is a durable piece of physical equipment or plant that provides its services over a number of years. Thus investment represents an addition to the stock of capital or a replacement of depreciated capital; it is a flow that augments or replenishes the capital stock.

What about the functional relationship involving investment? What is going to determine investment?

The decision to invest

Question

Think about the decision to invest. Suppose that we know how much financial return will be produced by various investments. What main consideration will influence the investment decision?

I think the main issue will be the *cost of investment*. There are other considerations such as the judgement about future uncertainty of returns, but the important issue considered here is the cost of investment.

We now need to put these thoughts into some kind of a formal framework, i.e. to build a model.

What is the cost of investment? One way of expressing this is as the rate of interest. If you borrow money to invest in your house or to buy a new car, you will pay a rate of interest on the capital you borrow. But here we are dealing with firms, and their cost of capital is going to be a more complex variable. Firms have a number of different ways in which they can raise money to finance their investment: they can borrow from a bank, they can raise it on the stock exchange through the issue of stocks and shares, or they can in effect borrow it from themselves by using their internally retained surpluses (their retained profits and depreciation allowances) to purchase capital goods. Each of these different means of raising finance has a slightly different cost associated with it. Thus their overall cost of capital is going to be a combination of the individual costs associated with each of these methods; it will be a weighted average of these costs – weighted according to the proportions each type of finance the firms normally employ in financing their capital purchases. However, for simplicity we can concentrate here just on the rate of interest, since this will strongly influence the overall cost of capital. Let us call this rate of interest r.

The question now is exactly how real investment I is related to r. I am considering both investment and investment costs in real terms, after getting rid of the effects of inflation, since it is real returns which the firms themselves will be interested in.

Question

What is going to be the relationship between *I* and *r*?

We would expect that as *r increases*, investment would *decrease*, and vice versa – other things remaining equal (*ceteris paribus*). As the cost of capital increases you would be less willing to borrow to make additional investments, while as the cost of capital decreases you would be expected to increase your investment level. Thus there is going to be an *inverse* relationship between *I* and *r*. With a *higher interest rate* we would expect relatively *low levels of investment expenditure*, while with a *lower interest rate* we would anticipate relatively *higher levels* of such expenditures. We can now draw this on a diagram.

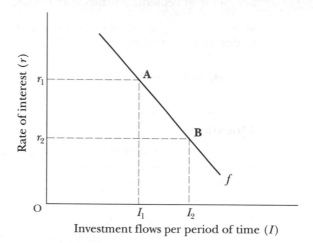

Figure 2.10   The investment function

The horizontal axis in Figure 2.10 shows the levels of investment – a movement along this being a measure of greater or lesser amounts of investment – while the vertical axis shows the rate of interest.

With this model the *determining* variable is the rate of interest (*r*) and the *determined* variable is investment (*I*), i.e. it is the rate of interest that determines investment. This is just another way of saying that, for the purposes of this model, we are assuming that variations in the levels of investment are *caused by* variations in the rate of interest. Another way to express these relationships is to say that *r* is the *exogenous* variable while *I* is the *endogenous* variable. Exogenous means 'determined outside' the confines of this particular model and endogenous means 'determined within' the confines of the model. Yet another way this is sometimes expressed is to say that *r* is the *independent* variable and *I* is the *dependent* one.

The line labelled *f* in Figure 2.10 is the investment function. It slopes downwards from left to right, indicating that as the interest rate falls the level of investment will rise, and vice versa. Thus if we were at point A on the investment function *f* with interest rate r_1 and investment I_1, then a reduction in the rate of interest to r_2 would mean an increase in investment to I_2 so that we move down the investment function to point *B*.

As well as drawing an investment function on a diagram, it can be expressed in symbolic terms. If we write '*f*' to designate 'function of', we can write the investment functional relationships as:

$$I = f(r)$$

which simply says that 'real investment is a function of the real interest rate'. This is the beginning of a type of model which we will develop further in later chapters.

Finally, a different way of expressing the investment function would be as an *equation*. This would convert the functional relationship into a mathematical one. The mathematical expression of the investment function is a way of giving it a formal definition that allows its estimation as a quantitative relationship between the variables involved. In Chapter 3, you will find just such a mathematical expression of a functional relationship – in that case between consumption and income.

I have argued, then, that in principle we can express the investment function model in four equivalent but different 'languages':

1   in words;

2   in graphical form;

3   in symbolic terms; and

4   in mathematical terms as an equation, which I have not developed here. (Since mathematics is nothing but the manipulation of symbols we could in fact reduce this to just three 'languages'.)

Finally, in linking investment to growth it is not being suggested that any growth in national income is entirely due to changes in the levels of investment. The point of this analysis is merely to indicate *one* of the constituent elements of the way growth can be understood. In practice, it is a very difficult empirical matter to isolate exactly what the contribution of investment is to overall growth in national income, though most economists would argue that it is a very important element. Remember also that there can be periods of negative growth (as between 1990 and 1991 in the UK). This issue of the possible reasons for economic growth (and decline) are examined later in this text.

9   Conclusion

We began this chapter with a discussion of the nature of model building in economics. Subsequently we developed various types of model, the basic circular flow analysis, the Phillips machine and the investment function being the main examples. In Section 2 it was suggested that model building could be of two broad types. The first relied on generating a model from a thorough understanding of the empirical reality of the economy. It stressed data analysis and the establishment of empirical relationships. We developed this type of approach in the context of looking at the levels and constituent parts of national income for a range of countries.

The second broad approach stressed the importance of abstraction and the formulation of conceptual tools and techniques. We developed this later in the chapter, first by elaborating the circular flow and then in the context of the investment function. These relied in the first instance more upon thought experiments to generate the models. Thus in this chapter we have employed both approaches in combination, and that is just the way economists generally go about their model building.

The economy-wide circular flow model is a combined production, income and expenditure model. It can be expressed as three main phases, summed up in Figure 2.2: production, distribution and then expenditure. When this sequence is viewed through time, after successive rounds of consumption, distribution and investment, the issue of growth in the national income emerges. Additional investment increases productive capacity and expands the scale of the circular flow of income over time: the flows become larger and the totals bigger.

This chapter has stressed the different forms that models can take. They can be expressed in words, in diagrammatic form, in symbolic form, and in mathematical form. All these are their own languages, and it is important to note exactly which words, expressions and images we use to describe models and the economy. Thus metaphor and analogy are central to our understanding and ability to make sense of the economy. But models also exist in an institutional setting. The institutional setting is important for what can be 'said' and what cannot be 'said' in terms of models, economic analysis, etc., because it defines the parameters of what is considered to be proper scientific endeavour. This means that economic analysis is not so innocent as it might at first seem. It is not neutral in respect of very important methodological considerations.

Exercise 2.8

Finally, here is an exercise to test your ability to deal with the national income accounts and to confirm that the income-expenditure approach adopted in this chapter actually works (i.e. that expenditure = income). Table 2.8 presents the two sides of the account. Using the data in Tables 2.4, 2.5 and 2.6, fill in the components in Table 2.8, and check that GDP at factor cost for 1991 was £497 billion in both cases, i.e. that the accounts balance. (Note that numbers may not add up exactly because of rounding.)

Table 2.8   **UK national income accounts, 1991 (£m)**

Expenditure		Income	
Consumers' expenditure		Income from employment	
General government final consumption		Income from self-employment	
Gross domestic fixed capital formation		Gross trading profits of companies	
Value of physical increases in stocks		Gross trading surplus of public corporations	
Total domestic expenditures		Gross trading surplus of government enterprises	
Exports of goods and services		Rent	
less Imports of goods and services		Imputed change for consumption of non-trading capital	
Statistical discrepancy		Total domestic income	
GDP at market prices		*less* Stock appreciation	
Adjustment to factor cost		Statistical discrepancy	
GDP at factor cost		GDP at factor cost	

PART 2
CHAPTER 3

ECONOMIC AGENCY
PEOPLE AND HOUSEHOLDS AS ECONOMIC AGENTS

by Jane Wheelock

1   Introduction

This chapter looks at how people, and the households they live in, behave as economic agents. The focus is on what we do to live on a day-to-day basis: what economists call 'consumption'. The household is a very important economic institution because it links significant economic activities – consumption, production and distribution – through the activities of its members. Indeed, the model introduced in Chapter 2 highlighted households as crucial agents in the circular flow process of the national economy (see Figure 3.1).

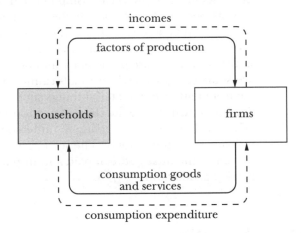

Figure 3.1 **Households in the simple circular flow of income**

It is people in households who make decisions about whether to take work in the labour market or to do unpaid work in the home or elsewhere. Paid work may involve the production of commodities which are sold on the market. Work in the home also maintains women and men in the current workforce. Bringing up children to reproduce a future labour force is work. Decisions about spending are also made by the members of a household; this involves decisions about who is going to get what, and therefore about distribution. The household is thus a significant economic institution whose activities require investigation.

This chapter will look at how people and households behave in individual markets: for example, when they make decisions about buying leaded or unleaded petrol. This is what economists call *micro* level behaviour.

Economists are also interested to see how household behaviour affects activity in the economy in general, at the *macro* level, for example in terms of the total amount of money that is saved or spent in the country.

How people live together in households can vary a lot. For example, the form that the household takes may be culturally specific, and depends on whether the household is in an urban or a rural setting. The form of the household has also changed over the course of history. Furthermore, households have different structures: for example, they may be single-person households or made up of a family with one or two parents, or a group of unrelated people, as with a student household. Households may also have different social characteristics, such as the class, race, gender or generation to which members of the household belong. The economic characteristics of households are what interest economists most: whether the household is rich, poor, in work, retired, unemployed, and so on.

Consumption, and the purchasing power of people in households, depends above all on levels of income. A recurring theme of this chapter is the relationship between spending and the demand for goods and services, and how rich or poor households are. But as I shall try to show throughout this chapter, consumption is a social as well as an economic process. The effects of cigarette advertising on encouraging children to smoke, or the urge to 'keep up with the Joneses' are just two examples of this.

The structure of the chapter is as follows. Section 2 looks at the (macro) behaviour of people and households in the economy as a whole, to gain an understanding of the relationship between income, expenditure and savings. Section 3 then asks whether there is any regular pattern in the relationship between income and expenditure for households in the economy as a whole. Section 4 moves to the micro level, asking why households purchase particular commodities, bearing in mind that there are some things which individuals cannot buy on the market, like a clean environment or non-material things such as spiritual fulfilment. Finally, Section 5 turns to the question of economic agency. Who actually spends? Whose behaviour are we trying to understand? Should we be talking about individuals or households? The section looks inside the household and considers the links between paid and unpaid work, and market and non-market production.

2   The personal sector of the economy: income, expenditure and savings

2.1   The personal sector

In this section I want to examine the behaviour of people and households in the economy as a whole, to gain an understanding of their importance for the macro economy. A useful way to start doing this is by looking at what those concerned with measuring the macro economy call the personal sector, to see its role in economic terms. Chapter 2 has already introduced you to the idea of national income accounting. In national income accounting terms, a sector is an aggregate of economic agents. When we talk about economic agents, the group that most often springs to mind is firms and other organizations which aim to make a profit. What is special about the personal sector is that the households which constitute the overwhelming bulk of the sector are by and large family units. Family units are not primarily formed to make a profit, and so it is often said that their purpose is fundamentally non-economic. This difference in micro-level behaviour is the basis for putting households in a separate sector.

In the national accounts, the personal sector is a complicated aggregate of economic transactors; it is essentially a non-government, non-firm rag-bag. In this section I shall focus on households as by far the most important part of the personal sector. Following on from Chapter 2's discussion of national income accounting, the easiest way to understand what the personal sector does in economic terms is to take an overview of the sector as a series of accounts, starting with an income and expenditure account, then looking at the capital account. Table 3.1 does this for the UK. The income and expenditure account tracks where household incomes come from and what they are spent on. The focus here is on consumption.

Table 3.1   **The personal sector in the UK: income, expenditure and savings, 1991 (£m)**

(a) Personal sector income and expenditure account

Income before deduction of tax

Income from employment	329 808
Income from self-employment	57 507
Rent, dividends, net interest	56 874
State benefits	71 767
Transfers from overseas, etc.	2 788
Total income	518 744

Expenditure

Consumers' expenditure	367 853
UK taxes on income including social security contributions	111 098
Total current expenditure	478 951

(Unmeasured: social consumption, consumption of the environment)

Balance on income and expenditure account: savings	39 793

(b) Personal sector capital account

Receipts

Gross savings (from income and expenditure account)	39 793
Capital transfers	3 966

Expenditure

Physical assets, predominantly houses	26 195
Acquisition of financial assets	17 564

Source: *United Kingdom National Accounts* (1992) Tables 3.1, 4.1, 4.2

When we look at the aggregate behaviour of households, we see that a relatively large proportion of income is not spent, so there is a substantial flow of savings as a balance on the income and expenditure account. It is this flow of savings that is the main source of receipts for the capital account – that is, the 'adding to wealth' account of households. Personal sector savings distribute purchasing power over time through the purchase of physical and financial assets. Housing, superannuation and life assurance are respectively the most significant of these; they are shown as expenditure on the capital account.

Households in the personal sector must have an income before they can spend it, and Table 3.1 indicates that there are two types of source. First, members of households sell productive services in the market. Some receive wages and salaries from selling their power to work, whether with their manual or intellectual skills; others gain income from self-employment, or from rents, dividends or interest through ownership of property or money capital in whatever form. The largest tranche of household income, 64 per cent in 1991, derives from employment; 11 per cent came from self-employment and 11 per cent from rents, dividends and net interest. The remaining 14 per cent came from the second type of source: transfer payments. These are paid by government as part of the welfare state, and are seen as 'unrequited' payments in that they are not made in respect of an immediate service rendered.

Question

In 1972 wages and salaries made up 69 per cent of household income, income from self-employment 10 per cent, income from rent dividends and interest 10 per cent, and state benefits 11 per cent (*UK National Accounts*, 1980, Table 4.1). Compare these with the 1991 proportions. What do you think are the reasons for the changes in the different sources of household income over these twenty years?

First, unemployment has risen substantially, so wage income has fallen relatively. This also means that more is paid out in state benefits. Furthermore, the post-war downward trend in self-employment has been reversed, at least partly due to the pressure of unemployment.

2.2   Personal sector expenditure

As Table 3.1 indicates, there are three main ways in which households use their incomes. Consumer expenditure for day-to-day living uses up by far the largest part – more than two-thirds of income. Economically this is very important because it ensures that people are in a fit state to produce what the economy needs. Of course, day-to-day living may mean very different things to different households, and Section 3.2 below looks at how consumption behaviour is affected by level of income.

Households in aggregate live within their means, so that as well as consuming goods here and now, the personal sector also distributes its purchasing power over time through savings. Once we start looking at what households do with their savings, we have moved on to the capital account. Households put savings to two main uses in adding to their wealth. First, they provide security for the family in the future. In this case savings are used to buy financial assets, particularly superannuation or private pension contributions. The other main use for savings is to provide shelter, and here physical assets are purchased, notably houses. The capital account as an adding-to-wealth account is concerned with the stream of future benefits to be obtained from these financial and physical assets.

The third major element in household spending is tax. Only taxes on income – income tax and national insurance payments – show up in the personal sector income and expenditure account. Nowadays, an increasing proportion of tax in the UK is levied on expenditure, mainly Value Added Tax (VAT). However, since VAT is a tax on consumers' expenditure, it is not a separate item in the personal sector accounts.

Essentially, tax is used by governments in two main ways. Governments use taxes to pay for social consumption, such as education, health, defence and roads, on behalf of households. Social consumption provides goods and services on a collective basis, in part because of the difficulties of making them available through the market mechanism. In addition to their money income, households thus receive an income in kind, sometimes known as the 'social wage'. The other main way in which tax can be used is to redistribute purchasing power between households. Tax is thus a rather special form of household spending in that people have no legal choice but to pay it.

Consumer expenditure

Let us now look in more detail at consumption expenditure. Table 3.2 gives a breakdown of the different elements of consumer expenditure in selected countries of the European Community (now the European Union) for 1989. You can see that food (with beverages and tobacco) and housing (including expenditure on fuel and power) make up the single largest parts of the broad categories of expenditure listed in the table. It is interesting to note that the proportion of household expenditure which went on food, beverages and tobacco varied quite substantially within Western Europe, from a low of 16.6 per cent in what was then the Federal Republic of Germany to nearly 40 per cent in the Republic of Ireland. There are also fairly large differences in proportional expenditure on housing.

Question

Why do you think there are such variations in the proportion of expenditure on food, beverages and tobacco in different European countries?

Table 3.2   **Percentage of household expenditure on selected commodities in selected European countries, 1989**

	Food, beverages, tobacco	Clothing and footwear	Rent, fuel and power	Furniture, furnishings, household equipment	Transport and communication	Recreation, entertainment, education, culture	Miscellaneous goods and services	Total
UK	21.1	6.2	19.5	6.9	17.7	9.5	19.1	100
France	19.4	6.9	18.9	8.1	16.8	7.3	23.1	100
Germany (Federal Republic)	16.6	7.7	18.4	8.8	15.1	9.0	24.5	100
Irish Republic	39.0	6.9	10.9	7.0	12.6	11.1	12.6	100
Italy	21.7	9.6	14.3	8.9	12.9	9.1	23.6	100
Spain	22.0	9.1	12.6	6.6	15.7	6.5	27.6	100

Source: *Social Trends*, no.22 (1992)

It is well known that poor households spend a greater proportion of their income on basic items like food. The Republic of Ireland and Spain are the poorest nations in Table 3.2, while Germany has the highest income per head. Like individual households, less well-off nations spend proportionately more on basics than the better-off.

2.3   Food for thought: some anomalies of definition

Before leaving this overview of personal sector expenditure, it is worth pointing out some anomalies in the way the personal sector accounts are drawn up. These anomalies have rather important economic implications.

Consumption, or investment in people?   This anomaly relates to the difficulty of making hard-and-fast distinctions between consumption and 'adding to wealth', or production. As already suggested, at its simplest consumption expenditure is eating in order to live. But it is living people who undertake productive work in the economy, so expenditure on consumption can also be viewed as maintaining the working people and the domestic carers who are essential to the productive functioning of the economy. In developed countries it is usually taken for granted that the workforce is in a fit state to work. Yet back at the turn of the century, the British establishment was horrified to discover that many of the working-class men who were recruited for the Boer War were too unfit to join the army. With substantial proportions of the populations of Third World countries suffering from malnutrition, many commentators argue that these countries do not so much need investment in capital resources requiring savings, but in people, requiring consumption expenditure. Under-nourished people cannot work as hard, and so add less to value. If incomes were redistributed to the poorest groups, households would have more to spend on food, and so would be fit enough to produce more in agriculture and in other sectors of the economy. There is therefore a sense in which consumer expenditure adds to wealth, the wealth incorporated in human beings, where people provide a stream of services throughout their working life.

Consuming the environment   It must be remembered that households, in the process of using what they have purchased, in the process of consuming, are also using up the environment. Cars pollute the air, rubbish uses up landfill sites, roads use open land, and so on. Degradation of the environment is generally not paid for by consumers out of their income, and so is not included in the accounting process. People are therefore made even less aware of it than they are of the social wage. However, just as a mortgage on your house is a debt to a bank or other lender, so degradation of the environment can be seen as a debt owed to future generations. Environmental degradation is a liability which the present generation is leaving to others to deal with.

In summary, then, the personal sector accounts show households dividing their income between expenditure and savings. Indeed, people could be pictured as going through a two-stage budgeting process: deciding how much to save and then deciding how the remainder should be spent. But as with every accounting convention, there are anomalies in the definitions used which have considerable economic significance.

3 The consumption function

Is there any regular pattern in the relation between income and expenditure? If so, can we develop a model for this? This section turns to beliefs and theories about how people and households behave over consumption. Common sense tells us that consumption will depend on levels of income, and this can be tested from two directions. Since the Second World War, national incomes in the developed capitalist countries grouped in the Organization for Economic Co-operation and Development (OECD) have generally risen, so we can look at what has happened to consumption by households in the aggregate as incomes have gone up over time. At any given moment in time, it is also possible to compare how consumer expenditure differs between households which have different levels of income. Asking whether the relationship between income and consumption is a relationship over time or a cross-sectional one between households gives the opportunity to analyse some data.

3.1   Aggregate household consumption behaviour over time

Table 3.A1 in the Appendix to this chapter gives some long-run data on total personal income (column 1) and consumers' expenditure (column 2) since 1950. (Don't worry about the other columns for the moment: they are explained later.) Notice that the income data in column 1 of this table is real disposable income; make sure that you understand the definition of this before continuing.

Since tax rates and the general level of prices vary from year to year, using data based on the real (inflation-adjusted) income that people have to dispose of (after taxes) eliminates these variables from the picture, and allows us to concentrate on the relationship between income and consumption without further complications. Figure 3.2 therefore takes real disposable income (column 1 in Table 3.A1) and real consumers' expenditure (column 2) and shows consumers' expenditure as a proportion of disposable income since 1950. The figure shows that there is indeed some regularity in this proportion, usually referred to by economists as the average propensity to consume (APC).

Definition

Real disposable income

This is the income available to all the households in the economy, once direct (income) taxes have been deducted, adjusted to take account of inflation.

Definition

The average propensity to consume

The average propensity to consume is the ratio between total consumers' expenditure and total disposable income.

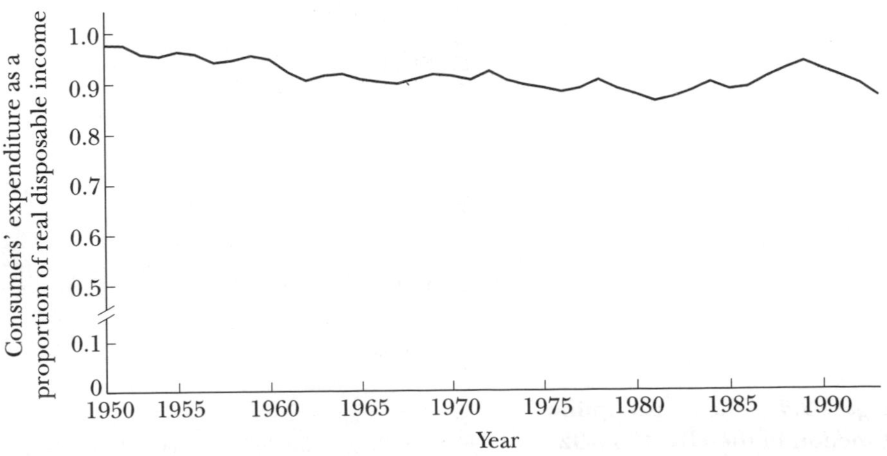

Figure 3.2   **The relationship between consumers' expenditure and real disposable income, 1950–92**

Source: Central Statistical Office

From the definition you can see that for any year the APC can be calculated by dividing consumers' expenditure (column 2 in Table 3.A1) by total disposable income (column 1) to give column 3, the APC. Figure 3.2 shows that in the UK the average propensity to consume did not change much from year to year between 1950 and 1992, though it generally declined slowly until the start of the 1980s, after which there was a rise and then a renewed decline. What can be used to explain these regularities? I have already suggested that a relationship between levels of disposable income and of consumers' expenditure makes intuitive sense.

A functional relationship between consumption and income

We can express such a relationship more technically by saying that consumers' expenditure is a function of income. Chapter 2 introduced you to the idea of a functional relationship. The standard notation for consumer expenditure is C, and for income Y, so this functional relationship can be written in the form:

$$C = f(Y)$$

This simply means that the variable on the left-hand side of the equation (in this case C) is dependent on, or influenced in identifiable ways by, the variable on the right-hand side of the equation (in this case Y). The equation is telling us that the amount of consumers' expenditure (the dependent variable) depends on, or is a function of, income, which is the independent variable.

How can we explore this functional relationship and create a model of it? The most obvious way to start is to examine the data just introduced. Figure 3.3 plots real disposable income against consumers' expenditure for each of the years between 1950 and 1992, using the data from Table 3.A1 in the Appendix. As you can see, there is considerable regularity in the pattern formed. Indeed, the points all fall along a fairly straight line, and a straight line has been drawn through these points, known as a 'line of best fit'. (The way in which such a line is derived will be explained later in this text.) You

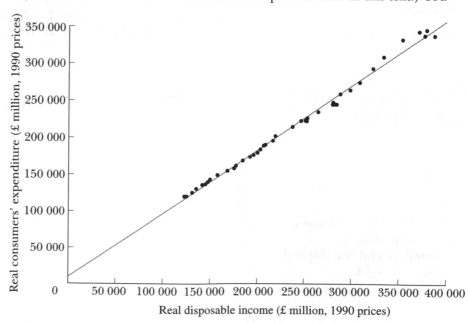

Figure 3.3 **The consumption function in the UK, 1950–92**

Source: Central Statistical Office

can see that the line fits rather less well in the later years (with higher incomes in the 1980s) than in the earlier years. This line of best fit gives an indication of the form of the 'consumption function'.

Let us explore the nature of this function further. To do this it will help to draw a diagram representing the general type of functional relationship between consumption expenditure and income, of which Figure 3.3 provided a specific UK example. This is done in Figure 3.4.

Figure 3.4 shows the consumption function in diagram form. It provides a general model of the type of relationship we have just found in the data for the post-war years. Consumers' expenditure, as the dependent variable, is plotted on the vertical axis of the graph, with disposable income, the independent variable, on the horizontal axis. Disposable income is labelled Y_d to remind us that this is not the same as total personal sector income before tax. With a little algebra, the general functional relationship we have been talking about and which is shown in Figure 3.4 can be expressed in a form which then allows it to be specified more precisely for our data, i.e. to be estimated. According to the data in Figure 3.3, as modelled in Figure 3.4, the relationship between consumers' expenditure and personal sector income takes the form of a straight line graph, where the function is:

$$C = a + b (Y_d)$$

The symbols a and b are *constants*, or *parameters*, of the relationship between the dependent variable and the independent variable. These parameters express a relationship between consumers' expenditure and personal sector disposable income, which, as Table 3.A1 shows, both change from year to year in our UK example. What exactly is the meaning of this relationship?

Note first that in Figure 3.4 the line representing the relationship starts above the origin (O) as determined by the constant a. This tells us that consumer expenditure in the aggregate will be greater than zero even when income is zero, which is scarcely surprising given that at the very least people need to eat to live.

It is a little more complicated to grasp the parameter b, but it is well worth the effort since it introduces another essential economic concept, the marginal propensity to consume. In the case of a linear consumption function represented in Figure 3.4, b gives us the slope of the line, or how steeply it rises. Translating this algebraic and graphical terminology back

Definition

The marginal propensity to consume

The slope of the consumption function (b) is called the marginal propensity to consume because it tells us the extent to which an incremental or marginal change in disposable income will be associated with a corresponding incremental or marginal change in consumption.

Figure 3.4 **The consumption function, showing the derivation of the marginal propensity to consume**

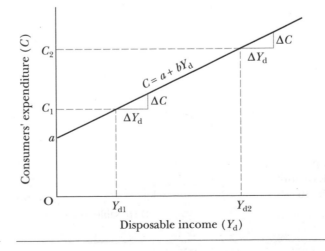

into everyday language, what does the steepness of the consumption function tell us? This slope shows the extent to which consumption increases (the extent of the vertical rise of the line) with respect to an increase in income (the horizontal movement).

The marginal propensity to consume therefore tells us how households' spending habits in the economy as a whole respond to increases or falls in real income. Returning to the algebraic formulations, the Greek capital letter for delta, written as Δ, is used to denote change in a variable. The slope of the consumption function in Figure 3.4, or the marginal propensity to consume, can therefore be expressed as:

$$b = \frac{\text{increase in consumption}}{\text{increase in disposable income}} = \frac{\Delta C}{\Delta Y_{d}}$$

The marginal propensity to consume is usually abbreviated to MPC, so its definition becomes:

$$\text{MPC} = \frac{\Delta C}{\Delta Y_{d}}$$

To complete your understanding of the general form of the consumption function, let us return for a moment to the average propensity to consume (defined at the start of this section), relating it to our model diagram, repeated in Figure 3.5. To remind you, the average propensity to consume is the relationship between *total* consumption and *total* disposable income, unlike the marginal propensity to consume, which relates only to relatively small *changes* in income and expenditure. Thus the average propensity to consume (APC) is given on our model diagram by:

$$\text{APC} = \frac{C}{Y_{d}}$$

If you were to calculate the average propensity to consume in Figure 3.5 for income level Y_{d1}, it would therefore be C_1/Y_{d1}. This is the same as the slope of the dashed line from the origin (O) to the point labelled 1 on the consumption function. For income level Y_{d2}, the APC is C_2/Y_{d2}. It can be seen that the slope of the dashed line from the origin is less steep when income has risen to Y_{d2}. This indicates that although the average propensity to consume is reasonably stable in the short run, over the long run it will gradually decline if our model is correct.

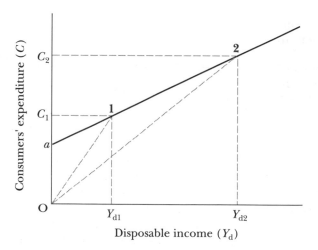

Figure 3.5   **The consumption function, showing the derivation of the average propensity to consume**

Consolidating what you know and estimating the model

Before returning to the data, here is an exercise for you to check that you understand the relationships I have just been explaining.

Exercise 3.1

If the constant $a = 1\,000\,000$, and the marginal propensity to consume is 0.5, and if we have personal disposable income values of £40 000 million, £60 000 million and £80 000 million in three different years, calculate the corresponding amounts of consumers' expenditure. Use the formula $C = a + \text{MPC}\,(Y_d)$. Go back to the definitions of a functional relationship and the marginal propensity to consume if you need reminding what the equation means.

Now let us return to the real world data of the post-war years, provided in Appendix Table 3.A1. The marginal propensity to consume over the years between 1950 and 1992 is given in column 6. Notice that it is calculated by dividing column 5, which is the change in consumer expenditure over the previous year, by column 4, the change in total personal disposable income over the previous year. You will see that the marginal propensity to consume from real disposable income in fact fluctuates a lot from year to year. Since inflation is unpredictable, people may under- or overestimate the increase in real income they will have in any year, and then correct for their mistakes the next. The model just described averages out these fluctuations from year to year by drawing a straight line with a constant MPC. Column 3, the average propensity to consume, shows considerably more stability than the marginal propensity to consume over the short run, but shows the long-run decline already noted from 1950 to the end of the 1970s. The unanticipated rise of the APC in the 1980s is discussed in Section 3.3 below.

Finally, let us consider how the model of the consumption function that we have been developing corresponds to the reality of the aggregate behaviour of UK households since 1950. Plotting personal disposable income against consumers' expenditure over the post-war years allowed us to draw a straight line of best fit in Figure 3.3. This is the line which can be described by a diagrammatic and algebraic model in the way I have just discussed. It takes the general form:

$$C = a + \text{MPC}\,(Y_d)$$

For this data, the line of best fit falls where the value of a is 9425.855, and the marginal propensity to consume is 0.87. The post-war UK consumption function is therefore

$$C = 9425.855 + 0.87Y_d$$

So it seems that we can indeed model the regularities in the way households behave with respect to consumption expenditure. It is important to be aware that full confirmation of the model relies on many technicalities which are too complex to enter into here. If you can take it on trust that such technicalities can be dealt with, then you can see that the data from the UK economy since 1950 have been used to estimate the consumption function model. This means that we can use the model to make predictions, though Section 3.3 below gives some indications of factors that this relatively simple model does not take into account.

3.2   The consumption behaviour of households with different incomes

Using *time series* analysis of aggregate consumers' expenditure – in other words, with data from a run of different years – the previous section has estimated an aggregate consumption function. This, one can presume, is the result of household decisions about whether to spend or save their incomes. Let us now turn to whether there are similar patterns in how different groups of households make these kinds of decisions during the same period. Table 3.3, taken from the UK *Family Expenditure Survey* for 1991, bands households according to income, with the poorest group of households consisting of those earning less than £60 a week, and the wealthiest group those earning over £800. This gives what is known as *cross-section* data for households, rather than the time series presented in the last section. Column 1 shows the average *gross* weekly income per household in each income group, i.e. income before tax. Column 2 shows the average weekly consumption expenditure. Note that < means 'less than', so '60 < 80' is read as 'at least £60 and less than £80 per week'.

Table 3.3   **Weekly income and expenditure per household in the UK, 1991 (£)**

Income bracket: gross normal weekly income	Average gross normal weekly income per household	Average weekly consumption expenditure per household
< 60	51	59
60 < 80	70	74
80 < 100	89	95
100 < 125	111	117
125 < 150	137	138
150 < 175	161	148
175 < 225	199	182
225 < 275	249	203
275 < 325	299	228
325 < 375	350	251
375 < 425	400	272
425 < 475	455	281
475 < 550	504	336
550 < 650	596	363
650 < 800	709	411
800+	1123	560

Source: *Family Expenditure Survey* (1992)

Table 3.3 shows that there is a consistent decline in the average propensity to consume out of gross income across income groups, and that the poorer people are, the more of their income they spend. Indeed, in the lowest income groups, consumption expenditure exceeds gross income. This is because the elderly and retired predominate in these groups, and they are withdrawing from their savings to make up the difference. As we saw in Section 1, the definition of income excludes withdrawals from savings. Another way in which

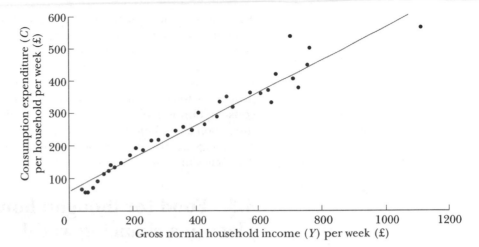

Figure 3.6 **The cross-section household consumption function in the UK, 1991**

Source: *Family Expenditure Survey* (1992)

households may be able to spend more than their income is through debt. The Policy Studies Institute, in a major study undertaken in 1989 of the debt held by British households, found that of more than 2.5 million households in debt, most were in difficulty as a result of low incomes, with the most prone to debt being those on benefits or low pay (Policy Studies Institute, 1992).

Figure 3.6 plots in graphical form the more disaggregated data from which Table 3.3 was constructed, and shows the cross-section consumption function for 1991. The estimated equation for the best fit line for these cross-section data is:

$$C = 67.8 + 0.49Y$$

The number for *a*, the intercept, is much smaller than that for Figure 3.3 because here we are working in £ per week. Furthermore, the estimate of *b*, the MPC, is also considerably lower, because the income figures being used here are gross, not disposable income. (That is the form in which these data are available.) So tax takes a bite of increased income before it can be spent. It may also be that lower-income households are more likely to use their savings to supplement income. Furthermore, households at the top end of the scale may take time to adjust their spending upwards, while those at the bottom find it hard to adjust theirs downwards, as indicated by the debt burden of low-income households just discussed.

Consolidating what you know: some broader implications

It was J.M. Keynes, the renowned academic economist, economic adviser to the British government during the Second World War, and architect of the post-war international financial institutions, who coined the phrase 'propensity to consume'. The word propensity implies that household consumer behaviour follows innate psychological laws. I have suggested that at its most basic, consumption behaviour depends on the physiological need for food and shelter. But the desire to consume TV sets or video recorders can hardly be explained in either physiological or psychological terms. Instead, household decisions on the ratio of consumption and savings to income will be determined by society's attitudes, ideologies and institutions, as well as by family background, and perhaps particularly by the volume of advertisements. Television, for example, has played an enormous role in raising material expectations among people in the Third World, and also in the former Soviet Union and Eastern Europe prior to the overthrow of communism.

Nevertheless, the objective social facts of how income is distributed are far more important. Even with the same social attitude, the low-paid single-parent family or the shanty town household will behave very differently from the household of the property tycoon or the business executive. Low-income households throughout the world will tend to have a high marginal propensity to consume, so if governments tax the rich and give to the poor, consumption is likely to rise. In other words, the propensity to consume for the nation as a whole depends on just two things: first, household consumer psychology determined by social conditioning, and second on how society distributes income.

3.3   Food for thought: household consumer plans in a changing world

Let us take a look at a few complicating factors as they affect households in an economy that has seen dramatic changes since the 1970s. A case study of the UK housing market illustrates how changes in institutional arrangements and the availability of credit, the influence of levels of physical wealth, fears of being made redundant or becoming unemployed, and the influence of inflation can all affect consumption behaviour. At the end of the section I will give a very brief introduction to some theories of the consumption function which try to develop the basic model to account for some of the effects of these changes.

A salutary example: the UK housing market

A whole raft of changes have interacted to bring about major difficulties in the housing market since the mid 1980s in Britain. They include: inflation; increases in the demand for, and supply of, credit; government policies encouraging owner-occupation; and growth policies relying on property development. Given the substantial and growing proportion of households who are owner-occupiers, problems in the housing market have also had knock-on effects on the labour market, because they have limited the mobility of households.

In the early 1980s many factors combined to encourage households to take out mortgages. Inflation was relatively high, so people chose to use money to buy physical assets, rather than face falling real values of money savings. Credit was increasingly available: thanks to the deregulation of financial markets, financial institutions were competing to loan money to house buyers. There were drastic cuts in the subsidies to public sector rented housing, together with tax concessions for owner-occupiers and subsidies for council house buyers. Not surprisingly, house prices rose, by even more than inflation. Between 1984 and 1988 the average price of an inter-war semi-detached house rose by 135 per cent. In London and the south east, house prices rose particularly dramatically, partly because unemployment was low in comparison with other parts of the country, and therefore households could afford to buy. There was also a shortage of accommodation, as people moved to the south east from other parts of the country because of the better chances of employment. By 1989 a Londoner who had bought an average priced house in 1984 had a tax-free capital gain of £60000, which was roughly equal to the average salary that would have been earned in that same five-year period.

Rising house prices seemed to be a virtuous circle for increasingly fortunate owner-occupiers. The result was a marked change in households' consumption behaviour, which had not been anticipated by economic forecasters. With little thought for the possibility that the boom might collapse, households were committing a higher and higher proportion of their income to mortgage repayments. (The long-run average ratio of house price to earnings is 3.3 times average earnings, and it peaked at 4.7 in June 1989.) After all, the present sacrifice would prove worthwhile when people sold their house at a higher price in a few years time! In addition, households who had bought their houses some years previously at much lower prices found that the financial institutions were happy to remortgage at current higher valuations, and households could use the additional credit for additional expenditure on holidays, consumer durables, or whatever. Rising house prices were causing a rising propensity to consume other things (on credit) as well. In 1988 mortgage holders were, on average, spending nearly twice as much on discretionary spending as non-mortgage holders. At the same time, the big differentials in house prices between north and south meant that the unemployed in the north could not afford to move to jobs in the south.

The boom in house prices came to an abrupt end at the start of the 1990s because of a combination of factors. First, interest rates rose, so households already stretched with high levels of mortgage repayments faced yet higher repayments with the rise in interest payments. Some could not afford these on the wages coming in. Young households too could no longer afford to purchase. In addition, the economic recession was affecting service as well as manufacturing employment; this was pushing up unemployment rates throughout the country, and not just in the north and west as with the recession at the start of the 1980s. Many households therefore had members who were made redundant. In some areas house prices fell by as much as 30 per cent between 1989 and 1993. Heavily mortgaged households were forced to sell their homes when jobs were lost, or found themselves facing a situation of 'negative equity': in other words, they owed more to the financial institutions than the value of their house. By 1993 it was estimated that some 1.7 million households, or 17 per cent of mortgage holders, were affected.

Once the collapse occurred, heavily indebted households began to behave quite differently. There was another marked change in consumption behaviour, again not anticipated by economic forecasters. Households with unemployed members became anxious to reduce their debts. The same was true of the many households who were afraid that they might lose jobs. Consumer expenditure was suddenly drastically reduced, at the same time as house prices fell. Very painfully for them, many households could not keep up their payments on the things they had already bought. House repossessions by mortgage and finance companies rose, as did repossessions of other consumer durables like cars.

Some theories of the consumption function in a changing world

The dramatic changes in consumer behaviour just described mean that the model of the consumption function needs adapting to take account of some of the many other factors besides real incomes which influence consumption behaviour. The two theories that I am going to introduce very briefly here differ from Keynes in moving away from aggregate theories of consumption and paying more attention to the microeconomics of individual household consumer behaviour. You will notice that the theories pick up on aspects of what affects consumption expenditure in a changing real world. They make modifications to the basic Keynesian model of the consumption function, to try and explain more aspects of consumers' expenditure data.

The first theory argues very plausibly that household consumption behaviour is relative, and thus socially determined. First, it is relative to the household's own previous income, rather than to what the household is earning now. I have already suggested that poor households go into debt to maintain essential living standards, for example. Second, consumption is relative to other households' incomes. Here the 'relative income hypothesis' argues that consumption expenditure is influenced by the demonstration effect or 'keeping up with the Joneses'. The 1980s case study seems to offer an example of this effect, with people copying their neighbours by going more deeply into debt. The consumption function is therefore not just dependent on current income.

A second theory suggests that households plan their consumption on the basis of the income they expect to get over their whole lifetime, rather than on their income here and now. In both youth and old age, incomes tend to be low. These are times when people will respectively borrow or draw on savings. Consumption will make up a high proportion of income at these stages of the life cycle. In contrast, in middle age income is relatively high but a smaller proportion is consumed. Not surprisingly this is known as the 'life-cycle hypothesis'. If people can borrow and lend freely, then consumption need not be very closely tied to income. There is then only an ultimate constraint on consumption determined by the wealth available to the household, and its future income from labour.

3.4   Savings behaviour since the Second World War

Since economists define the disposable income left after tax has been taken off as being divided between consumption and savings, how people behave with regard to savings is in many ways the mirror image of consumption behaviour. It is therefore interesting and useful to round off our consideration of the macro behaviour of households by looking at how the savings ratio in the personal sector as a whole has changed over the last half century in the UK, and to examine the explanations put forward.

Figure 3.7 (using figures from Appendix Table 3.A1, column 7) shows the personal savings ratio in the UK from 1950 to 1992. A glance at this shows how much it has varied. There has been a long-run upward trend in the proportion of income saved, which is to be expected with rising incomes, but closer examination suggests that there is much more to be explained. Dividing the half century into four periods helps with the analysis. From the end of the Second World War to 1960, the savings ratio rose from an exceptionally low level (though this is not shown, it was only 0.9 per cent in 1948, for example) to what was then considered a more normal level of 7.4 per cent in 1960. During the war years people had postponed consumption, so that afterwards they were catching up; consequently the savings ratio was exceptionally low, and only gradually returned to normality.

Definition

The savings ratio

The savings ratio is calculated as personal savings as a percentage of disposable income. The definition of the average propensity to consume implies that, since all disposable income is either spent or saved, a rise in the savings ratio must mean a fall in the average propensity to consume, and vice versa.

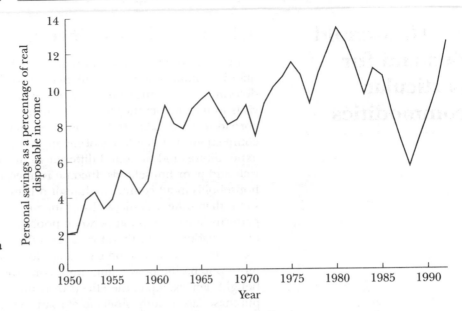

Figure 3.7 **Personal savings as a percentage of real disposable income in the UK, 1950–92**

Source: Central Statistical Office

Throughout the 1960s, and until 1971, there was no clear upward trend, and the savings ratio fluctuated around the 8–9 per cent level. However, there was a cyclical tendency for the savings ratio to fall when the economy slowed down, and rise when it accelerated. The decade from the early 1970s to the early 1980s saw a return to the upward trend in the savings ratio, peaking at 13.4 per cent in 1980. This was an unpredicted rise, and all the more surprising given that the high and accelerating rates of inflation characteristic of the period should discourage savings, as I explained in the case study of the housing market and its wider implications.

The 1980s saw a dramatic fall in the savings ratio – by 1988, at 5.7 per cent, it was lower than at any time since 1959. This, of course, meant that the average propensity to consume rose, and confirms perceptions of the 1980s as a decade dominated by a materially minded, consumer mentality. Indeed, the amount that consumers spent in the shops grew much faster than expected over the period. The case study of the housing market has indicated some of the reasons why this happened. The economic models in use assumed that spending depended on incomes and financial wealth, but did not include physical wealth such as housing, and nor, therefore, the effects of dramatically rising house prices. Combined with the greater availability of credit, British households were able to go on an unprecedented spending spree. This came to an end in 1989. Belatedly – or as economists would say, in a lagged response to indebtedness and fear of joblessness – by 1992 the savings ratio was back up to the 1981 level.

In conclusion, this section has looked at two important macroeconomic variables: consumption and saving. Time series and cross-sectional data sources both show that consumers' expenditure is a function of income. The propensity to consume for the nation as a whole depends on household consumption psychology determined by social conditioning, and on how society distributes income. However, the case study of substantial changes in the real world economy since the 1970s suggests that the microeconomics of household consumption behaviour may also have a role to play in understanding the consumption function.

4   Household demand for particular commodities

4.1   Demand and income

I now want to turn to how households behave as economic agents in the micro economy – that is, in the market for individual commodities. What determines how much butter or petrol households will buy, or how many visits to the cinema they will make, haircuts they will have, or holidays abroad they will take? In Section 3 we spent some time looking at the connections between levels of income and aggregate consumer expenditure, and we found differences in macroeconomic actions between rich and poor households. Income is unequally distributed between households in all countries, though it is more unequally distributed in some than others. A hierarchy of income distribution means a hierarchy of patterns of consumption between poor and rich. The unequal distribution of purchasing power therefore affects the market for individual products. If a country's national income goes up, its households in the aggregate have more purchasing power, and more commodities of most types will be bought. For example, the effects of rising national income on car purchases are readily observable: roads become more crowded, cities become more polluted, rush hours extend. But it can still be noticeably easier to find parking spaces in poorer residential districts than in rich ones. This gives us the first rule about the relationship between level of income and what economists call the demand (or amount purchased) for different sorts of goods: *those with higher incomes will purchase more of most commodities.*

Table 3.4 shows how the amount spent on alcoholic drink, tobacco, clothing and footwear and on leisure services goes up (with one or two small 'blips' – a non-technical term widely used by finance ministers) across the income brackets that were used in the last section to look at aggregate consumption expenditure.

Studies of households in poverty show their very limited purchases. There are some products, such as basic foodstuffs, or black and white television sets, where fewer items will be purchased as income rises. For example, as poor households in the Third World get richer, they will be able to substitute beans, meat or fish for part of their basic grain diet of rice, maize or millet. Less rice will therefore be purchased. The same goes for black and white television sets in a country like Britain, where incomes are now high enough for most households to purchase a colour television instead. When less of a commodity is purchased as incomes go up, they are called inferior goods. This gives us our second relationship between income and demand, qualifying the first one: *the rich and the poor may buy different sorts of things, so that in the case of so-called inferior goods, those with higher incomes actually buy less of them.*

Exercise 3.2

Draw up two columns, one of commodities that you think would be 'inferior goods' in the rich economies of the developed world, the other of inferior goods in a poor Third World economy.

Table 3.4   **Weekly income and expenditure on selected items per household, UK, 1991 (£)**

Gross normal weekly income	Alcoholic drink	Tobacco	Clothing & footwear	Leisure services
< 60	2.57	2.47	2.39	3.23
60 < 80	2.42	2.96	3.67	4.37
80 < 100	3.24	3.77	4.67	5.17
100 < 125	3.91	3.95	5.93	6.74
125 < 150	3.94	4.53	7.78	8.28
150 < 175	4.85	4.78	7.86	8.48
175 < 225	6.97	5.38	9.59	11.27
225 < 275	9.32	6.06	13.21	15.15
275 < 325	10.46	6.00	14.26	15.23
325 < 375	10.82	5.30	15.84	24.36
375 < 425	13.44	5.55	20.57	21.11
425 < 475	13.16	6.57	19.66	21.18
475 < 550	15.73	6.34	22.84	29.17
550 < 650	17.31	6.10	27.24	38.57
650 < 800	18.95	5.71	30.46	43.65
800+	27.99	5.24	36.77	82.07
All	10.83	5.15	15.80	22.20

Source: *Family Expenditure Survey* (1992)

4.2   Food for thought: some insights from socio-economics on other influences on demand

Being less easy to quantify than income or price (I deal with price in Section 4.3 below), what might be called the socio-economic influences on demand are often forgotten by economists. Let me provide some examples of such influences.

What is available on the market?   What we buy is inevitably influenced by what is available for purchase. This may seem rather a curious thing to say in the post-yuppie era of the 1990s. Isn't anything available on the market today? True, I may be able to buy all sorts of gadgets and gizmos, but it is not possible to live in a city and purchase clean air, or even clean streets. As touched upon in Section 1, there is frequently no market for environmental goods, and therefore need cannot be expressed in the form of market demand. Indeed, Joan Robinson, one of the few prominent women economists, once asked where it was possible to find the pricing system that offers consumers a fair choice between air to breathe and cars to drive around in (Robinson, 1978).

It is also interesting that with hindsight we realize that the restrictions of wartime rationing of food in Britain gave rise to healthier patterns of eating! Indeed, an increase in availability can actually have an undesirable effect. Food aid to Third World countries has brought about shifts in households' tastes from foods based on local whole grains, such as sorghum or millet, to processed wheat-based products like white bread. This then has a knock-on effect on local farmers who find it more difficult to sell their grains.

The influence of technology   It may seem simple enough to say that everyone has a need for clean clothes, for example, but the socio-economist Jonathan Gershuny (1978) has shown that the connection between psychological need and economic demand is not a direct one – it is one that is mediated by technology. How do we actually clean our clothes? Back in the 1950s, working-class households in Scottish cities went to the 'steamie' or municipal public wash-houses, where hot running water and washboards were available for women to do the week's wash (and where you could also get a bath if you were one of the many households without a bathroom). During the 1960s, innovatory automatic washing machines became available in privately run launderettes, and the steamie slipped out of use as more and more households also got their own bathrooms. Then family incomes rose and the technology used in automatic washers became cheaper. Household investment in automatic washing machines replaced private investment in launderettes, and nowadays people do not even use their section of the drying green for each tenement, but another consumer durable, the electric dryer.

This is just one example of how the means of satisfying a need changes. An important part of this is the response to technological change in its broader sense. Thus, technology in this example includes the institutional framework of publicly owned steamie, privately owned launderette, or household-owned washing machine, and a mass market of consumer durables, as well as the innovation of the automatic washing machine.

Gershuny calls this a socio-technical innovation, when the means by which a need is satisfied changes. A socio-technical innovation like a video-recorder, as a means of providing entertainment, can also lead to changes in the structure of household demand: not only do households purchase video-recorders, but families may stay in to watch hired videos instead of going out to the cinema.

There is an interesting further dimension to the process of socio-technical innovation, for the purchase of more consumer durables means that the work of using them is being undertaken by household members in their unpaid capacity. If you buy a car to go to work, rather than using public transport, then the work of driving the car becomes the private, unpaid responsibility of each commuter, instead of being the paid work of the bus driver. Gershuny calls this the self-service economy, where households service themselves using their own consumer durables, rather than buying the service on the market. As we shall see in the final section of this chapter, socio-technical innovations raise some interesting gender issues. Who within the household undertakes the work and/or enjoys the fruits of such innovations?

Reflection

Before you read on, consider what has been the impact of socio-technical innovations in food provision, entertainment or transport on the structure of household demand in your own household.

Social influences   Commentators from a number of disciplines have examined aspects of the socio-economic impact of advertising on demand, from a number of different perspectives. J.S. Duesenberry, an American economist, suggested that demand for particular commodities, as well as consumption expenditure in general, is affected by a 'demonstration effect', where people feel social pressures to purchase what others have. J.K. Galbraith, another North American economist, talks of a dependence effect, where wants are dependent on the very process by which they are satisfied, as producers use advertisements and salesmanship to persuade us to purchase what they are making. There is a feedback loop here.

Back at the turn of the century, Thorstein Veblen, the American institutional economist, paid much attention to the cultural influences on consumption. His ideas remain highly pertinent today. He argued (Veblen, 1912) that at every phase of culture, consumption behaviour has related on the one hand to a system of work and livelihood, and on the other to what he called a system of exploit, status and ceremonial adequacy. He therefore made a distinction between two sorts of consumption: instrumental, and ceremonial or wasteful consumption. In the latter case, possession of wealth becomes honourable in itself and so it becomes important to show off your wealth by means of conspicuous consumption. The rich therefore pursue a high-profile lifestyle, with demand for what in 1980s Britain were called 'yuppie products'.

4.3   Demand and price

I turn now to the final major influence on how much of a particular commodity will be purchased by individuals and households in an economy, namely its price. Price is generally considered by economists as one of the most important variables.

Perhaps the greatest virtue of the market system is that it allows people choice in terms of the price they are prepared to pay for individual items. The responsible consumer-cum-citizen in a market economy shops around for the cheapest bargain in meat, which incidentally may mean that there is still enough money left to buy an additional vegetable for the meal. If the price of meat falls, then the household may choose to have a meat meal more often, and more meat is purchased; if the price rises, they may decide to eat more fish and buy less meat. Of course, as we saw in Section 4.1, income is also a constraint on demand. It is sometimes argued (particularly on the right of the political spectrum) that the distribution of income is something that a market economy should not do anything about. If your household has a lower income, then you may choose to become a vegetarian, still enjoying a healthy diet, but avoiding expensive foods like meat, and instead buying cheaper pulses and vegetables. However, as we saw in Section 4.2, social influences may also affect demand: concern for heart disease may mean that some people cut back on their purchases of fatty meat in particular.

Let us, for the moment, concentrate on the effects of price, abstracting from the other things that influence demand. The relationship between demand and price can be represented in the form of a diagram, known as a demand curve. The market demand curve (which may in practice be a straight or a curved line) for a commodity like milk depicts buyers' willingness to purchase milk, depending on its price. The amount of milk purchased in an economy is not necessarily the amount that people need,

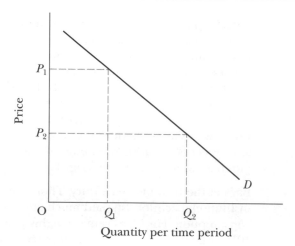

Figure 3.8 **A demand curve for commodity** x

but what they are willing and able to purchase. (Free milk was provided to children in British schools with the introduction of the welfare state after the Second World War, partly because it was thought that some households would not be able to afford it, but also because it was thought that the nation needed healthy children.) Figure 3.8 shows the relationship between market demand and price, based on the intuitively acceptable assumption that if the price falls – say from P_1 to P_2 – it will mean that (other things remaining equal) more is purchased – Q_2 rather than Q_1. It is important to remember to specify a time period within which the amount is purchased.

This inverse relationship between the price of a commodity and the quantity demanded (shown by the demand curve sloping downwards and to the right) is known as the 'law of demand'. However, our earlier discussion may have alerted you to some exceptions to this law.

If we follow Veblen in making a distinction between instrumental and wasteful consumption, then conspicuous consumption is a means of showing off wealth. This means that luxury items like exclusive jewellery, cars or designer clothes may be in greater demand at higher prices. Luxury items whose demand behaves in this way are known as *Veblen goods*.

At the lower end of the scale, consumers in very poor countries may actually spend less on an inferior good like rice when its price falls. This is because they can use the spending power released by the fall in the price of the basic foodstuff to purchase a greater variety. Such goods are called *Giffen goods* because the influential economist Alfred Marshall, apparently in error, gave Sir Robert Giffen credit for this exception to the general law of demand.

Let me now return to the example of what determines the demand for meat that I gave at the start of this section, because demand depends on a number of variables and not just the price.

Exercise 3.3

You were introduced to the terms 'dependent' variable and 'independent' variable in Section 3.1, when I argued that aggregate consumption was dependent on income. Make a list of how many independent variables were mentioned in discussing how much meat will be purchased by a particular household in a particular week.

Just as in Section 3.1 we derived a consumption function which showed the relationship between aggregate income and consumers' expenditure, we can also propose a market demand function for an individual commodity like meat, showing the factors affecting how much will be purchased in a given time period. The market demand for good *x* is the sum of all the individuals' or households' demands in the economy. Since we are taking demand as the dependent variable, we put it on the left-hand side of the demand function equation, while the independent variables go on the right.

Since we are particularly interested in the relationship between demand and price, let us start with a simple model, by supposing that we can hold all the other influencing factors constant besides the price of *x*. The demand for *x* is written D_x, and the price of *x* is written P_x. Latin has long been used by professionals to mystify outsiders, and economists are no exception, so 'other things remaining equal' becomes *ceteris paribus* (as you may recall from Chapter 2). The demand function is then:

$$D_x = f(P_x), \textit{ ceteris paribus}$$

This simplified version of the demand function spells out in a general algebraic form a relationship represented in a more specific graphical form as the demand curve in Figure 3.8. The graphical form of the demand curve is more specific in that it specifies a *negative* relationship between demand and price: a higher price for good *x* implies a lower demand (*ceteris paribus*).

What about the other independent variables that you have just listed in the case of meat? Income is obviously one, and in the case of all households this can be represented by *Y*, income. Demand for *x* also depends on how much other, related commodities cost – for example, how much a substitute food like fish or beans costs in relation to meat. Let us use P_r (the price of related goods) for this variable. Then there are the socio-economic factors mentioned in Section 4.2 which we could label *Z*. Finally, let us not forget that expectations about future prices may affect demand; as we saw in the case study of the housing market, people may want to buy now because they think that prices will be higher in the future, and vice versa (P_f stands for future prices).

We can now write the demand function for commodity *x* in the following form:

$$D_x = f(Y, P_x, P_r, P_f, Z)$$

The number of variables on the right-hand side of the equation shows that the complete demand function is quite complex.

Movements along the demand curve and shifts of the demand curve

We have so far been looking at the market demand curve on the assumption that other things remain equal. What happens if we relax the *ceteris paribus* assumption? Figure 3.9 shows a hypothetical British market demand curve for a seasonal product, strawberries, whose price varies at different times of the year. It shows that at the height of the British strawberry season, when prices are as low as £1.20 a kilo, six million kilos are purchased (point A). In early May, prices are higher at, say, £2.40 a kilo, since strawberries are being imported from southern Europe, with higher handling costs implied. *Ceteris paribus*, we can find out how many strawberries will be purchased by moving along the demand curve to point B, where the quantity demanded will be four million kilos. Around the new year, strawberries cost £4 a kilo, and people only buy small quantities to add colour to a fruit salad. We move along the demand curve to point C, and see that one and a third million kilos are purchased.

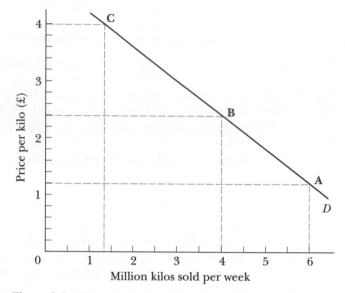

Figure 3.9   Hypothetical market demand curve for strawberries, showing movements along the demand curve

Returning again to point A on the demand curve, let us suppose that one of the other influencing factors changes. If real national income falls, one would expect everyone to spend less on all goods. The market demand for strawberries will therefore decrease at all prices. This means that we now have a new relationship between quantity demanded and price, and this is shown by the new demand curve, D_1, in Figure 3.10, lying to the left of the original one, *D*. A change in any of the variables other than price causes a *shift* in the whole demand curve, because the *ceteris paribus* assumption has been dropped. The shift may be to the left or right, depending on the cause of the change. However, if all other variables remain the same and it is price alone that changes, then there is movement *along* the given demand curve.

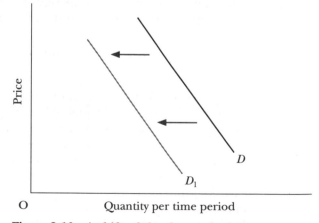

Figure 3.10   A shift of the demand curve

Here is an exercise to help you think about demand curve shifts.

Exercise 3.4

Think for a few minutes about how other things besides price may *not* remain equal in the market for strawberries. Work out what effect each will have on the demand curve. Then see if you can complete Table 3.5 below.

Table 3.5 **Shifts in the demand curve for strawberries**

Change in variable	Effect on demand curve
Decrease in national income.	Decrease in demand for strawberries at all prices. Demand curve shifts to the left.
Increase in national income.	
Rise in price of substitute goods (e.g. raspberries, or cherries).	
Fall in price of substitute goods.	
Rise in price of complementary goods (e.g. cream).	
Fall in price of complementary goods.	
Change in socio-economic preferences in favour of strawberries (e.g. advertising campaign).	
Change in socio-economic preferences away from strawberries (e.g. due to pollution of crops).	

I hope that you now understand the difference in principle between a shift along the demand curve and a shift of the curve itself, though you should realize that in practice it is not so easy to disentangle the variables.

Exercise 3.5

To check your understanding of the factors that affect demand, go back to the case study of the housing market in Section 3.3. Draw up a list of the factors that led to an increase in the demand for owner-occupied housing during the 1980s. Notice that demand increased despite large increases in prices. This means that the demand curve for owner-occupied houses was shifting to the right. Then list the factors that led to a decline in the demand once the boom ended at the start of the 1990s. Again, notice the fall in demand, despite falling prices. The demand curve for owner-occupied housing was shifting back to the left.

5   The economic agents: people or households?

5.1   The consumer's home, her castle: no entry to economists?

I want to round off this chapter by raising some fundamental issues about who economic agents actually are and how they behave. Once we start to ask such questions, it also becomes clear that the behaviour on which this chapter has focused – consumption – is not as straightforward as it might appear. Economics often speaks of the household as a significant and important economic agent, examines how the household behaves, and then in the next breath talks about the motivation for behaviour in terms of the rational individual who seeks to maximize his or her economic advantage. Economics is then defined as the science of choice (you will find more on this idea in Chapter 7). So are economists asking about individuals or about groups of individuals in households?

When the statistics are examined in developed industrial or post-industrial economies, it is increasingly found that the individual and the household are one and the same. Households are of many different sorts, and for example in Britain, official data in *Social Trends* show the proportions of households of different structures. This reveals that the 'typical family' of husband, wife and two children is not by any means the most common. One-person households constitute as many as 28 per cent of all households. However, the largest group is that of two-adult households without children, making up 34 per cent. The stereotypical family unit of male breadwinner, non-working wife and two children make up only 15 per cent of all households. Single-parent families are not far behind in terms of their importance at 10 per cent of all households. This variety in the household form even within Britain shows the need for further clarification of what is meant by both 'individual' and 'household'. Who is the economic agent? Whose behaviour are we trying to understand?

But the questions go further than this. What is the behaviour that we want to understand? In the introduction to the chapter, I pointed out that consumption is not simply an economic, but also a social process. So far I have generally been discussing consumption as though it is just a matter of purchase in the economic market-place. However, consumption is also the work we do in order to live. When we buy meat or pulses, they have to be cooked; when we buy a television or a video recorder it has to be tuned in to the right frequency. And, of course, we need to get to the shops in the first place, as well as finding out where we will get the best price, particularly for expensive items like consumer durables. Consumption is often presented as trouble-free enjoyment, but both the public image and the economic model are out of line with the real world. Consumption usually involves work as well, and this work is often unpaid work within the household. Who undertakes this work? It is easy to think of the stereotypical images of African women carrying water pots on their heads, women shopping in the market or in the supermarket queue, men connecting up the electrical gadgets and repairing the car, and therefore to realize that gender is a significant issue here.

Historically, very few economists have shown themselves aware of the importance of gender to economic behaviour. There are a handful of notable exceptions. Thorstein Veblen argued that, at the turn of the century, middle- and upper-class wives were a symbol of conspicuous consumption for their husbands. (To remind yourself of what he meant by conspicuous consumption, turn back to Section 4.2.) The fact that you could afford to maintain a wife who undertook no work but lived a life of leisure, was a means of demonstrating your wealth. Indeed, it meant that domestic servants were employed to undertake the work of cooking, cleaning and looking after children, which was seen as inferior to leisure. The 1901 census shows that as many as 42 per cent of working women were domestic servants in Britain.

Galbraith, from the perspective of 1975, saw the disappearance of personal servants (in the developed world) and rising standards of personal consumption creating an urgent need for consumption to be managed. He argued convincingly that women had been converted into a crypto-servant class whose role was critical for the expansion of consumption in the modern economy. The household then becomes a disguise for the role of women.

Reflection

Think of examples where 'consuming' a commodity that has been purchased involves work before it can actually be used or enjoyed: for example, loading the software on a personal computer can involve hours of frustrating work; and shopping itself involves work. Who in your household does this work?

Traditionally, what goes on behind the lace curtains is private, non-market activity and therefore non-economic. The household is conceptualized as an individual, or else as a black box, obviating the need to enquire further about differences between individuals. But the final quarter of the twentieth century has brought changing views on this, and there is growing awareness of the importance of the unpaid activities which bridge the generally hard-and-fast conceptual distinction between consumption and production. This also brings gender into focus as an issue for economists.

5.2   Food for thought: the significance of unpaid work

Let us take a look at some examples of the empirical significance of unpaid, non-market activities in various parts of the world.

Appropriate technology: cooking stoves in Africa

Those who argue for the use of appropriate technology are advocating a system of self-care as a means of support, rather than sole reliance on a market system. Self-help is therefore an important theme for appropriate technology schemes, with people and their needs as a point of departure, rather than purchased goods (McRobie, 1981). This case study of charcoal- and wood-burning stoves for use in Africa indicates the importance of noticing the technologies used by women in their consumption work. The context is that cutting trees for cooking fuel is a major cause of deforestation. Collecting wood is women's work and can take up to an hour a day or more. Women also do 70 per cent of the work of producing food crops. Finally, in cities and towns, poor families spend between 20 and 30 per cent of their income on wood and charcoal. Better stoves therefore reduce the burden on women, ease labour shortages in food production, and improve living standards of the poor in cities, as well as slowing forest destruction and soil erosion.

The major problems with improved stoves is that they have to have an acceptable design, and they need mass distribution and promotion. Improved charcoal-burning stoves, or *jikos,* have achieved this in Kenya. Though two to three times the cost of the old *jiko,* the improved stove lasts twice as long and burns on a third to a half less fuel. This means that with the average expenditure of a Nairobi family on charcoal, the stove can pay for itself in two months. By 1987, the programme had achieved enormous success, with 100000 stoves in use.

However, charcoal is produced very inefficiently in many parts of Africa, preserving only 12 per cent of the wood's original heat value. Burkina Faso developed a clay wood-burning stove which could be made by women themselves from local materials – three stones and a surround of local cement made from clay, millet chaff, dung and water – to fit a cooking pot. Though there was no cash involved, the costs and benefits can be calculated in labour time. The training to make the stove and making the stove itself each take half a day, or eight hours in all. The stove saves 35 to 75 per cent in fuel. Since women spend an average of seven hours a week collecting fuel, the stove saves between two and a half and five hours work a week, and the labour invested is recouped in two to four weeks (Harrison, 1987, pp.40–3).

House building and subsistence activities in Hungary

The process of economic transformation in the Hungarian economy since the fall of communism provides a context for examining how changing household combinations of paid and unpaid work may provide a buffer against the problems of transition to a market economy in both urban and rural localities. Under socialism in Hungary, there was already considerable dependence on unpaid economic activity in food production and house building. This was possible because of a deliberate policy of under-urbanization. Industrial development was subsidized by low investment in social capital and housing, and in agriculture. This meant that many of those working in industry in towns lived in rural areas.

By the end of the 1980s, three million people, or 60 per cent of Hungarian households, were directly involved in the Hungarian food economy, growing fruit and vegetables on ancillary household plots. Two-thirds of these did not work formally in agriculture. The non-agricultural population was using small-scale food production as a strategy of security through a combination of self-provisioning and commodity production. Commentators point out that the importance of this unpaid complementary economy for urban society has not been diminished in any way by entry into a market economy. Indeed, continued access to the auxiliary household plot is likely to be of considerable importance to the future stability of urban society.

The other aspect of under-investment is the severe housing shortage in both urban and rural areas in Hungary, combined with shortages of land and building materials. In rural areas there is also a shortage of labour, since skilled rural labour can readily find employment in city construction gangs. It is therefore very common in rural areas for households who need a new house to call upon informal networks of family and friends to build it. The work is undertaken on a reciprocal basis: whilst it is unpaid, it creates the obligation to do the same for others in the future. There is evidence that the growing problems of the communist economy, followed by the difficulties of transition to a market economy, have increased the importance of this type of arrangement. In 1977, about a quarter of residential construction in Hungary was self-built; by 1987 this had risen to 43 per cent, and by 1991 it was as high as 56 per cent (Sik, 1992; Symes, 1992).

Reflection

Think of other examples where unpaid work may be economically significant in either the developed or the developing world or in Eastern Europe. In what ways is it significant?

5.3   Towards an economics of gender

These examples give some flavour of the importance of unpaid economic activity, even in sectors where, from a British cultural perspective, economists may be accustomed to think in terms of purely market provision for consumption needs. It is significant that there is now a growing number of empirical studies of such activities. Equally significant is the growing awareness of the impact that the unpaid work going on within and between households has on the formal, market economy. There are two important insights that have particular relevance for a broader theoretical understanding of consumption. Both have strong gender implications. The insights also show that you can take neither the individual nor the household as the economic agent without further enquiry into roles and power relations.

The first is that unpaid work is *complementary* to production in the formal, market economy and is actually required before consumption can take place. The domestic tasks of shopping, cooking, washing up, cleaning and washing and ironing clothes, naming but six of the major domestic tasks that are undertaken within the household, are essential if the process of consumption is to be completed. So too are the responsibility functions of managing the household and budgeting.

Time budget studies, which ask people to keep diaries of time spent on different activities, have been used as the most accurate method of determining who does what inside the household. In a time budget study which looked at twelve countries with urban populations beyond the minimum level of industrialization, Robinson *et al.* (1972) found that the time devoted to work was very nearly doubled when housework and family care were added to formal paid work. Whilst men contributed 68 per cent of formal work time, they contributed only 22 per cent of housework time. Employed women spent half as much time on housework as their housewife sisters, but most striking were the work patterns for employed women on weekends. Whilst the employed man had leisure, and the housewife reduced her housework by 50 per cent, the employed woman doubled her time on housework on her day off. The sum of employed women's socio-economic obligations, including formal work, household tasks and travel, was greater than that of employed men both on workdays (49 per cent of a 24-hour day as against 43 per cent for men) and on days off (26 per cent for women, 16 per cent for men). Employed women also worked more than housewives through the week, but they did the same amount of work on a Sunday.

There is, then, a strong gender dimension to who does the unpaid work within the household, although it is also important to be aware of differentials between employed and non-employed women. In view of this strong gender imbalance, it is interesting to recall from Chapter 2 that unpaid economic activities are generally not measured in national accounts, nor are they recorded in labour statistics. True, there are technical issues that need to be addressed before an international comparable measure can be developed, but the same could be said of national income accounting techniques half a century ago (see Waring, 1989; Goldschmidt-Clermont, 1987). Estimates of the value of unpaid work undertaken within the domestic economy put it at a minimum of 40 per cent of national income in a developed economy like Britain. Figures for national income as they stand at present therefore gravely underestimate the economic contribution of women. Interestingly, insurance companies are developing techniques for quantifying the unpaid work that women undertake because of the potential market for insuring against the death or injury of the housewife and mother in the household. They make comparisons with how much it would cost to employ a nanny, a cook, a cleaner, etc. for the relevant number of hours.

The second way in which unpaid work is of significance to consumption has already been touched on at various stages in this chapter: the very process of consumption *produces* the current and the next generation of the labour force, and maintains the generation that has already retired. The economic significance of this cannot be underestimated. Nor can the gender imbalance in the specifically caring and nurturing dimension of the unpaid work that goes toward the reproduction of people. The fact that it is usually women who undertake the majority of child care is now generally well understood and documented. Indeed, this is an area where value judgements are common, with some social scientists maintaining that women should take on a major part of the child-care role, while others think it important that men should take a far greater proportion than they do at present. Perhaps the most interesting empirical work here is based on a concern to find out the circumstances under which traditional gender roles are changing, and the processes involved (Pleck, 1979). Recently, there has also been a growth in the empirical study of who does what in the way of caring for the elderly. Whilst there is also a gender imbalance here, there is some evidence that it is not as marked as in the case of caring for children.

5.4 Concluding thoughts: economic agency, consumption and the interrelations between paid and unpaid work

If we are to understand economic agency, we must recognize that economic behaviour is not that of a single type of individual. What is more, the activity of the economic agent is not as clear-cut as an initial definition might suggest. If we are looking at who undertakes consumption activities, we find that gender can be particularly significant in determining both the nature of the activity and the person who does it. These issues can be represented in a production, reproduction and consumption cloverleaf, as in Figure 3.11. The diagram visualizes the household and the individuals in it at the centre of the three production circuits that are essential for the functioning of any economy: market production, non-market production and state production. Households survive on the basis of inputs from each of the three circuits: purchased goods and services from the market circuit, services and goods from the state circuit, and unpriced goods and services from the domestic circuit, usually produced within the household itself. Each circuit also requires inputs of labour from the household, but each individual may provide different sorts and amounts of labour input to the three circuits.

This cloverleaf diagram is an expository tool which represents the importance of labour in the economy, by seeing the household as central to the different types of work undertaken in the economy. It therefore illustrates the crucial socio-economic role of the household in providing different kinds of labour to the economy. It is important to realize that this diagram is not of the circular flow type to which you were introduced in Chapter 2, for the lines are not balanced circular flows; nor, for example, is investment included. Instead the cloverleaf diagram shows three production circuits, the lines of which represent flows of labour within and outside the household, and a corresponding flow of goods and services back to the household, produced

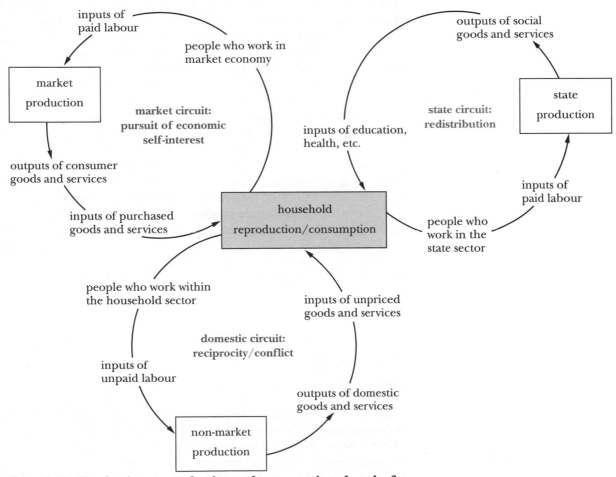

Figure 3.11   **Production, reproduction and consumption cloverleaf**

by the different kinds of labour contributed from the household. The diagram also emphasizes the variety of the types of labour that are used to produce marketed goods and services, and non-marketed government services. Although you will not find such a diagram in other economic texts, I hope you find it a useful representation of some important economic relationships.

The diagram also provides a reminder that the motivation for the behaviour of individuals active in each circuit may be different. In the market circuit, economic agents are frequently assumed to behave in such a way as to maximize their economic benefits. In that model, the conflicting interests of self-seeking individuals are considered to be harmonized through the market mechanism, in the manner outlined in Chapter 1. In the domestic circuit, where economic agents are living together in households, actions are more likely to be based on some form of co-operation. Economic anthropologists call this *reciprocity*, where the obligation to give, receive and return is a mode of integrating the inherent opposition between the self and the other. There may, however, also be conflict! Finally, in the state circuit, one motivation may be that public services and goods should be redistributed between households and individuals in line with need, although other motivations will be relevant too.

Representing economic activity in this cloverleaf form highlights the fact that economic agents within the household are wearing a number of different hats in turn, and that for the household to survive and prosper, all three circuits are necessary. In 1920, in his classic text *The Economics of Welfare*, A.C. Pigou pointed out that if a man married his housekeeper, this would reduce national income, because as a wife she would not be paid a wage. This is a rather trivial and dated illustration of an important principle that the cloverleaf diagram also shows. It is possible that production activities can shift between one circuit and another. Remind yourself of Gershuny's ideas of a self-service economy, for example (Section 4.2). Here, households purchase consumer durables from the market circuit, and substitute unpaid work using these household investment goods for purchased services. Ideas of Fordist mass consumption as a parallel to Fordist mass production (referred to in Chapter 1), involves a shift in the opposite direction. Busy households where both partners go out to work in the labour market substitute purchased convenience foods, or meals out, for home-made meals, in a process of 'commoditization'. The privatization of state services spearheaded by right-wing governments, and now pursued in many countries throughout the world, shifts parts of education or health to the market circuit and subjects them to market principles. The same shift is going on with the re-privatization process in former communist countries, sometimes dubbed 'marketization'. Despite these possibilities for substitution, it remains important that the circuits are also complementary to each other: all three are required to provide for the consumption needs of the household.

Shifts from one circuit to another have important implications for the structure of an economy, and it is worth being aware of changes in the relative weight of different sectors if we are to understand fully the idea of economic agency. For there is not just the possibility of macroeconomic shifts between circuits; individuals within households may also move between circuits. Indeed, changes in the economic structure may in turn influence what individuals do. For example, when men become unemployed, they may take on more domestic and child-care responsibilities, relieving their employed wives of some of these tasks (Wheelock, 1990).

The household in particular, and the economically unmeasured sector in general, are not an alternative society. They enact a set of activities which are complementary to the market, money economy. Household work strategies provide the interface between the market and the domestic circuits. The household, as the unit of reproduction, must apply its working activities to earning on the one hand, and to directly supplying goods and services on the other. The individuals within a household negotiate or otherwise decide a balance between work for income and for self-consumption.

Decisions over the gender divisions of labour within and outside the household are based on the interaction between different motivations: tradition and patriarchy, pursuit of economic interest and co-operation or reciprocity. Differences in power between generations and sexes can be significant too. The stage of the household life cycle – with or without children, their age, retired, etc. – may be influential. These decisions are also made in the light of social and economic changes brought about by economic restructuring, which may alter the gender divisions of labour within the household (Wheelock, 1990).

Reflection

Think about the decisions made in your household on consumption, distribution of incomes, and paid and unpaid work. Have there been any major changes in recent years; if so, why?

In conclusion, Section 5 has argued that once we are aware that production and consumption cannot readily be separated, gender becomes an important part of economic analysis. So the issue of economic agency can best be understood by placing the household and the persons in it at the centre of the three production circuits essential for the functioning of any economy: market production, non-market production and state production. This argument provides a context for the earlier parts of this chapter which investigated consumption mainly as a market-based activity, undertaken by the purchase of goods and services. The link I have made in this final section between consumption and production leads us into Chapter 4, which focuses on another major aspect of economic agency, market production.

Appendix

Table 3.A1   **Personal sector income and consumers' expenditure in the UK, constant prices, 1950–92**

	Total real disposable income (1990 prices) (£m)	Total real consumers' expenditure (1990 prices) (£m)	Average propensity to consume	Change in disposable income on previous year	Change in consumer expenditure on previous year	Marginal propensity to consume	Personal savings ratio
	(1)	(2)	(3)	(4)	(5)	(6)	(7)
1950	125 185	122 649	0.980				2.0
1951	123 608	121 042	0.979	−1 577	−1 607	1.019	2.1
1952	126 062	121 088	0.961	2 454	46	0.019	3.9
1953	132 016	126 362	0.957	5 954	5 274	0.886	4.3
1954	136 286	131 587	0.966	4 270	5 225	1.224	3.4
1955	142 664	137 136	0.961	6 378	5 549	0.870	3.9
1956	146 143	138 105	0.945	3 479	969	0.279	5.5
1957	148 510	141 004	0.949	2 367	2 899	1.225	5.1
1958	150 973	144 614	0.958	2 463	3 610	1.466	4.2
1959	158 738	150 913	0.951	7 765	6 299	0.811	4.9
1960	169 199	156 735	0.926	10 461	5 822	0.557	7.4
1961	176 256	160 199	0.909	7 057	3 464	0.490	9.1
1962	178 286	163 925	0.919	2 030	3 726	1.835	8.1
1963	185 426	170 874	0.922	7 140	6 949	0.973	7.8
1964	193 247	176 044	0.911	7 821	5 170	0.661	8.9
1965	196 998	178 493	0.906	3 751	2 449	0.653	9.4
1966	201 207	181 550	0.902	4 209	3 057	0.726	9.8
1967	204 171	185 985	0.911	2 964	4 435	1.496	8.9
1968	207 772	191 209	0.920	3 601	5 224	1.451	8.0
1969	209 684	192 366	0.917	1 912	1 157	0.605	8.3
1970	217 675	197 873	0.909	7 991	5 507	0.689	9.1
1971	220 344	204 139	0.926	2 669	6 266	2.348	7.4
1972	238 744	216 752	0.908	18 400	12 613	0.685	9.2
1973	254 329	228 615	0.899	15 585	11 863	0.761	10.1
1974	252 360	225 317	0.893	−1 969	−3 298	1.675	10.7
1975	253 814	224 580	0.885	1 454	−737	−0.507	11.5
1976	253 012	225 666	0.892	−802	1 086	−1.354	10.8
1977	247 695	224 892	0.908	−5 317	−774	0.146	9.2
1978	265 925	236 909	0.891	18 230	12 017	0.659	10.9
1979	281 084	247 212	0.879	15 159	10 303	0.680	12.1
1980	285 411	247 185	0.866	4 327	−27	−0.006	13.4
1981	283 176	247 402	0.874	−2 235	217	−0.097	12.6
1982	281 722	249 852	0.887	−1 454	2 450	−1.685	11.3
1983	289 204	261 200	0.903	7 482	11 348	1.517	9.7
1984	299 756	266 486	0.889	10 552	5 286	0.501	11.1
1985	309 821	276 742	0.893	10 065	10 256	1.019	10.7
1986	323 742	295 622	0.913	13 921	18 880	1.356	8.7
1987	334 881	311 234	0.929	11 139	15 612	1.402	7.1
1988	354 929	334 591	0.943	20 048	23 357	1.165	5.7
1989	372 356	345 406	0.928	17 427	10 815	0.621	7.2
1990	380 092	347 527	0.914	7 736	2 121	0.274	8.6
1991	378 189	339 993	0.899	−1 903	−7 534	3.959	10.1
1992	388 563	339 610	0.874	10 374	−383	−0.037	12.6

Source: data supplied by Central Statistical Office

CHAPTER 4   ORGANIZATIONS AS ECONOMIC AGENTS

by Neil Costello

1   Introduction

Chapter 3 considered the activities of households as economic agents in the economy, focusing particularly on consumption but also acknowledging the household as a site of productive activity. This chapter explores production more explicitly by concentrating on the other main set of economic agents in the circular flow model, namely firms (see Figure 4.1).

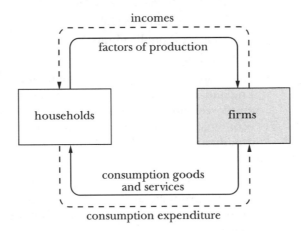

Figure 4.1 **Firms in the simple circular flow of income**

My objective in this chapter is to develop several models of firms as producing organizations in an effort to understand how firms operate in the economy. From an economic point of view, perhaps the single most important fact about firms is that they are formal organizations. They have defined organizational structures, often hierarchical, and they usually have a legal identity and status. The relationships *within* firms are rarely market relations but rather relations of command and/or co-operation. Just as economic analysis has shifted between, on the one hand, treating the household as an unproblematic consuming unit, and, on the other, exploring relations within households, so economists have shifted between treating firms as unproblematic profit-seeking units, and exploring the economic relationships within them. At present there is a renewed interest among economists in the internal culture and organization of firms.

Before looking at firms in detail, however, I want to emphasize that not all production takes place in private firms. As you know, some takes place in households, while other formal organizations also produce goods and services and play an influential role as economic agents: their activity influences the development of the economy.

Question

Try to think of formal organizations, other than private firms, which produce goods and services and therefore exercise an influence on economic life.

It's not difficult to come up with a list, but where do you stop? Which are important? Did you include any of the organizations in the list below? If you did, think briefly about why. If you did not include them, pause for a moment and consider whether or not they could constitute economic agents.

The Church of England

The Open University

The parks and recreation department of your local authority

Save the Children Fund

Voluntary helping organizations at your local hospital

The parent-teacher association (PTA) at your local school

The local athletics club

Your local public library

Pension funds

Some of these are large and influential producers of services. The Church of England, through its extensive investments, the salaries it pays to its employees, and the day-to-day upkeep of its buildings, is clearly an economic agent in a very full sense, though it might not be the first organization we think of when we are trying to work out how the economy works.

The Open University, with budgets of well over £120 million in 1993, is also a service producer and an economic agent. Its objectives are different from those of, say, major grocery chains, but it is certainly significant in economic terms.

What about the four voluntary organizations in the list: Save the Children Fund, helpers in a hospital, the local PTA and the local sports club? This is more difficult. All of them expend money, and whilst the latter three are certainly not major players, the economy could not function well without them in the sense of providing variety and services which people value. Save the Children Fund, on the other hand, is a sizeable economic agent. In 1990–91 it was the sixth largest charity in the UK, with a total voluntary income of nearly £39 million. In that year the total income of the 171434 charities registered in England and Wales was £16.18 billion or 3.4 per cent of GDP (Posnett, 1992).

Pension funds control an enormous proportion of financial investments in capitalist economies. For example, in the UK in 1991, 31 per cent of equities – that is, shareholdings in private companies – were held by pension funds (Dibben, 1993). But pension funds have different overriding objectives from, say, a typical small business such as a computer software company, because their horizons are very long-term.

If we are to make sense of the economy, we have to examine the nature of the economic agents that make up the economy. Their diversity is enormous: from the local corner shop to vast enterprises like the Pentagon (the US defence establishment); international corporations producing, for example, motor vehicles or pharmaceuticals; major multi-product organizations which are bigger on most measures of size than many nation states; universities and hospitals; small high-tech companies at the forefront of technology; market traders selling vegetables or cheap clothing. The list is potentially endless and extraordinarily diverse. How can we begin to make sense of an array of institutions like this?

One way is to consider formal organizations as institutions which have histories. Their evolution is driven both by their interactions and by changes in the social world. Their interactions are governed partly by socially defined rules. For example, there are clear, formally defined legal obligations which public companies in the UK must follow in their financial accounts, and the laws of contract prescribe the required behaviour in many activities related to buying and selling goods and services. More important in many respects, these institutions adhere to informal rules in relation to other firms or individuals such as customers, employees or suppliers. Wherever organizations sit in the spectrum of size or influence, they are, like the households you considered in Chapter 3, socially constructed.

Economists therefore try to understand the socially constructed rules that influence firms' behaviour. Later chapters focus on the relationships between economic agents and in particular how those relationships are managed through one form of social institution with its own set of informal rules – the market. This chapter, by contrast, considers the nature of the institutions themselves. As you will see, this cannot be separated from the organization's environment, but my focus will be on the organization. This will enable you to understand a good deal more about such organizations and give a background on which to base your subsequent analysis of such issues as inter-firm rivalry and market behaviour.

Most of the chapter concentrates on private firms. These have an existence which is in many respects independent of other social institutions, and they have been extraordinarily successful at creating wealth and a range of products undreamt of in our grandparents' generation. At the same time they are seen by some people as sources of divisiveness and inequality in society. They are seen to possess power greater than that of many national governments and, it is claimed, to ride roughshod over social and personal needs. For some they are the crowning glory of modern civilization; for others they are the source of exploitation and discontent. They are controversial, important, and a fascinating part of any attempt to understand economic behaviour.

1.1   Markets and firms

One question that economists have repeatedly asked is, why are some activities carried out within one firm which in other circumstances might be carried out via market transactions? For example, my employer has its own finance department with accountants and other financial experts. At one time I ran a small consultancy, but all my financial dealings were carried out using an accountancy firm whose time and expertise I hired through the market. So why does my employer organize its accounts internally rather than using the market? The same question can be asked of virtually every function carried out by any organization.

One answer relates to the cost of transacting through the market compared with the cost of the same transaction within the firm. If the market is cheaper and I am a profit-seeking firm, I will use the market rather than carry out the transaction myself. However, the issue is not entirely straightforward. Why don't we carry out all transactions through the market, or conversely why do markets exist when many activities are planned and co-ordinated within firms more effectively than they could be through the market? Why in particular do both systems coexist – why does my employer employ accountants, whereas it was more efficient for me to use market transactions?

This is an area of current economic controversy. Potential answers relate to such things as the 'lumpiness' of the activity: for example, I had no need for a full-time accountant but my employer has sufficient work for several. Furthermore, accountants use knowledge of their employer's business which is acquired over time. There are issues about the certainty that someone will be available when needed to carry out the work, and possibly questions of confidentiality. So cost, knowledge and security of supply influence the 'make or buy' decision, and this differs for organizations which have different objectives.

In addition, market transactions also differ, and companies use the market in different ways. For example, I recently discussed company strategy with the Morgan Motor Company, the UK specialist sports car manufacturer. The company prefers to build long-term relationships with its suppliers but is aware that not all suppliers are prepared to develop such an approach. Consequently the company buys some supplies from a variety of sources, but is prepared to limit itself to a single source for other materials. In the former case the market provides an immediate and relatively impersonal source; in the latter, it is an institution within which to develop trust and to avoid taking advantage of short-term opportunities. Such varied behaviour is typical of a wide range of firms and other organizations. Sometimes market transactions are replaced by firms' internal processes – that is, firms and their suppliers merge when the objective of the firms and the cost conditions they face make that an appropriate action.

Chapter 1 has already touched on Fordism and the desire of employers to exercise control over the production process (Chapter 1, Section 2.2). Control is generally easier to exercise within the organization than outside it. These arguments are also relevant to the discussion about the use of markets or internal structures.

1.2   Economics of organization

Economists have recently recognized anew the importance of considering the institutional structures of firms. Firms are not homogeneous black boxes which we need never look inside. The internal organization of firms, the ways in which their objectives are determined, and a recognition of their complexity have returned to prominence. It has become clear that firms cannot be considered simply as efficient organizers of production – a model discussed in Section 4. As Chapter 1 described, European and US firms have been outcompeted by Asian firms, and Asian cultures and organizational features are different from those of the West. Is there a particular kind of organizational structure towards which all firms should strive? An answer depends on the nature of the organization we are considering and the kind of environment in which it finds itself. These issues are taken up in Section 5.

In looking at such questions a helpful distinction is sometimes made between the passive and active behaviour of firms (Hay and Morris, 1991). Passive behaviour begins with constraints facing the firm, for example particular cost conditions, and then assumes that the firm will try to fulfil its objectives within those constraints. Active behaviour, conversely, would be that engaged in by the firm in order to try to change the constraints it faced. This might include merger with a competitor, or research and development in an attempt to reduce costs. Passive and active behaviour are frequently complementary, but they highlight a major difference in approaches to economic policy. A view that firms are largely passive tends to be associated with a belief in the efficacy of markets to achieve policy goals. A perspective that emphasizes the active role of firms will be associated with a tendency to downgrade the importance of industrial structure and to concentrate on the economic power of the corporate sector. The approaches adopted in Sections 4 and 5 can model both active and passive behaviour.

Before that, in Section 3, I shall consider a financial model of firms' behaviour which is neither active nor passive but primarily descriptive. As Section 3 shows, the description depends on assumptions about the nature of the firm and its relationships with other actors in the economy.

However, I shall begin in Section 2 with an empirical focus, in order to provide background material for you to get a sense of the place of firms in the economy and to provide us with some material that will be valuable later in the chapter.

2   Firms: a background

I am going to start with the story of one real-life firm, Protoscan Software Services Ltd. Protoscan is a firm of its time. It is almost a parable for the 1980s and 1990s. It is a high-tech company, based in the UK, which thrived and was subsequently taken over by a Japanese conglomerate. The case study includes some of the complexity of the real world and gives us a flavour of the issues and priorities facing firms during the 1990s. It tries to capture some of the excitement involved in running a firm, as well as the extent to which the firm is at the mercy of its environment – the passive view – or is able to control and change events – the active view. The case study is included here to exemplify some of the issues raised in the last section and as a resource for examples in subsequent sections.

Questions

As you read through Protoscan's story, try to assess the primary constraints it faced and those things that were major influences on its behaviour. For later consideration try also to pick out its major goals and think about the way in which it approached its business. You should also consider how the people who ran Protoscan related to each other – for example, did they see themselves in hierarchical terms or perhaps as a team of equals?

2.1   The Protoscan story

Protoscan was set up by Mike Hall and Andy Eltis in November 1987. It showed spectacular growth. At the end of its first year it employed six people. In March 1992 it employed 35 professional staff and 60 unskilled, casual staff. During the first three years sales turnover virtually tripled, from £1.2 million in 1988 to £3.4 million in 1990.

Mike Hall has a sales, marketing and general management background. Andy Eltis is a highly skilled computing expert. The combination of Andy's exceptional technical talents and Mike's business experience has been a fundamental strength in the development of their company. They initially developed proposals for a new business venture in their previous company but were turned down. Ultimately they decided to go it alone, and on 1 November 1987 they set themselves up as Protoscan in the back room of Mike's house.

The early weeks were characterized by many of the features reported by other high-tech start-ups. A very rapid response rate for customers was a way in which they could establish themselves in the market-place, and they found themselves working a shift system, four hours on and four hours off. Mike spent much of his time following up contacts and knocking on doors. Equipment was borrowed because of their severely limited financial resources.

But then the story begins to change. Unlike many first-generation high-tech companies, Protoscan did not involve a technical breakthrough looking for a market. It had been conceived as a result of an awareness of a gap in the market and from the beginning organized itself around the needs of its customers, not around the technical virtuosity of its product. Its product was technically advanced, but that was not the reason for the company's existence. In addition, Mike Hall's business experience plus the business plan they had developed meant that commercial disciplines were already at the forefront of their thinking.

They took advice from local contacts and sought support from the major high street banks. At this time they wanted to retain total control of the company but had no assets apart from their houses plus limited savings. The local bank was impressed and decided to support them.

There followed two years of very rapid growth. The company's product was a technical service. Mike Hall realized that turning round a simple product very quickly was not enough. The company had to offer potential customers something their competitors did not. Fortuitously 16-bit computers hit Europe at the time Protoscan was developing. Such machines require far more complex and costly programming than the simple 8-bit machines they replaced and, in addition, the computer games market was becoming very sophisticated. Games suppliers would pay thousands of dollars for the licence to produce a game based on, for example, a popular TV programme. Mike describes their entry into this market as partly accidental: 'We didn't deliberately go into the leisure market ... but because of what Andy did we were dragged into it'. Basically Andy devised 'Protec', a system for protecting disks. It is impossible to produce a foolproof protection system, since expert hackers can always take out the protective code. However, 'Protec' protected disks from easy copying by end-users. Protoscan thus provided a protection for disks as well as a copying service, and had moved into a mass market rather than simply a small, specialized technical market.

Early in 1990 Protoscan expanded further. It bought out a competitor to become Protoscan Europe plc. Protoscan's portfolio was expanded and the amount of equipment at their disposal significantly increased. Expansion brought with it difficulties. Profits had been ploughed back and the basic company was very healthy, but their dramatic growth rate, effectively doubling every year, created cash flow problems and a severe risk of over-trading – that is, essentially, a risk of taking on more business than they had the capacity to provide. Mike Hall tried to slow down the company's expansion, though this was difficult. With the help of Lloyd's Bank and Coopers & Lybrand he produced a three-year business plan with the aim of attracting venture capital from the City. He had spent over three months developing this strategy when Protoscan received a cold call from a major Japanese corporation with interests in the disk-copying market, Kao Corporation.

Kao Corporation is a large Japanese conglomerate. Their interests are primarily in chemicals, but a by-product of their operations provides the raw materials for manufacturing computer disks. They had set up major operations in Europe during the 1980s, and they also had extensive facilities in California. Kao had realized, like Protoscan, that only low margins are possible on disks, so that to make significant returns it was necessary to find some way of adding value. Kao were also keen to establish a sizeable base in Europe in anticipation (subsequently realized) of restrictive trade arrangements from the European Community's anti-dumping laws. Kao's manufacturing base in Barcelona could provide a European duplicating company with its disk requirements, and it seemed to Kao that potential synergies existed between themselves and European duplicators. Kao had reviewed the 24 companies then competing in the trade duplicating market in Europe, and Protoscan had come out at the top of the list.

It was clear that Kao were not prepared to take a minor stake in Protoscan. Given the size of Kao, the original owners could not hope to match the investment that Kao were proposing and the deal became very clear: sell the company or go it alone. Negotiations were protracted, as is the Japanese style, and eventually an offer was put to Protoscan which Kao believed would allow all the parties concerned to feel satisfied. However, for Andy the offer was too low. Mike believed it to be acceptable, but his respect for Andy and the nature of their working relationship meant that, after discussion, the proposal was rejected.

The Japanese negotiators were completely floored. It was outside their experience for negotiations to fall at the last hurdle. They had sensed the acceptability of their proposed solution inaccurately and were now in disarray. Protoscan worked hard to maintain contact and eventually an alternative arrangement was struck in July 1990. Until the end of March 1993 Protoscan was to become Kao Protoscan Software Services. Mike and Andy received a financial consideration and had three years to provide themselves with a significant return. Kao did not interfere during this period. (Such arrangements are often referred to as an 'earn-out'.) The recession of the early 1990s affected Protoscan's profitability, but at the end of the earn-out Mike and Andy finished with a good return, though less than they had originally hoped for.

2.2   Interpreting the case

The Protoscan story includes the messy detail of the real world, and it is not completely straightforward to work out answers to the questions that were suggested to you.

The major constraints faced by Protoscan were primarily financial. The company had to convince the banks early on that it was a worthwhile investment. Then, as expansion took place, the company, like many innovative small firms, found itself in a position where its short- to medium-term cash flow problems were a major hurdle in achieving its longer-term potential. Help was sought in the City, and Kao's provision of a solution to these problems was unexpected. Other major influences include the histories and the skills, in technical and managerial terms, of the two principals. In the external environment the rapidly changing nature of the high-tech world was also influential, in particular the change in the complexity of computers to 16-bit machines and the growth of the games market. These features significantly affected Protoscan's market in technical terms and in size.

The major goals of the company are not at all obvious. Much of the founders' motivation was implicitly to determine their own life chances. A certain amount of financial return was clearly required, but that did not appear to be the only or even the primary motive. Profit was a major motivating factor but does not appear to be *the* prime mover in this case. In cases like this firms are producing satisfactory rather than maximum profits. Such an objective is usually referred to as *satisficing*.

Protoscan was a small entrepreneurial company. Like many organizations with this structure, it approached its business by responding quickly to environmental change and was itself able to generate changes in the environment in the way it responded to challenges. It was flexible and sought out new opportunities. This is particularly evident in the way it responded to the opportunity presented by the games market.

Mike and Andy clearly saw themselves as a team. They each played a different role in the company and for them the combination of their skills was successful. This was partly the reason for their ability to respond effectively to change such as that presented by the games market and ultimately by Kao. Particularly in large organizations, such structures are sometimes considered to be unstable and less easy to control, but they can be very effective, as this case shows.

What is confirmed by the Protoscan example is the importance of recognizing the complexity of the real world and the need to look at a wide range of phenomena if we are to undertake a rich, detailed analysis. However, there are many features that apply to many cases. In looking at those general features we move away from the rich detail but give ourselves the opportunity to make broader and tentative generalizations. We shall come back to Protoscan. Now we need to explore some more empirical background on firms.

2.3   Background: the place of firms in the economy

Let us look at some evidence on the place of firms in the economy, taking the UK first. Table 4.1 shows the proportion of UK gross domestic product (GDP) contributed by different industrial sectors. Manufacturing (which in 1990 included Protoscan) is an important sector, though the growth of service industries, which include transport, communication, banking and finance, health and education – basically anything which cannot be dropped on your foot – is a feature of modern, advanced, western economies.

Table 4.1   **Industry output as a percentage of UK gross domestic product, 1980, 1985 and 1990**

	1980	1985	1990
Agriculture, forestry and fishing	2.1	1.9	1.5
Energy and water supply	9.7	10.7	5.1
Manufacturing	26.7	24.0	22.4
Construction	6.1	5.8	7.6
Service industries	55.1	57.7	63.4

Source: *Great Britain Annual Abstract of Statistics* (1992) Table 14.7

An examination of manufacturing is revealing, however, and detailed data are available on that. The *Census of Production*, produced by the Central Statistical Office, is a major source of data on firms in the UK. The most recent census, carried out in 1990, breaks up the manufacturing sector by size of firm, and Table 4.2 summarizes those findings.

Table 4.2 is a simplified version of the census data. I have also added three columns of percentages which I hope make the data easier to interpret. The table indicates a number of interesting features of the manufacturing sector.

Question

Examine Table 4.2 yourself before you read my commentary. Pick out what you see as the most important features.

Table 4.2   **Numbers of enterprises according to numbers employed, their employment totals and contribution to net output, United Kingdom manufacturing sector, 1990**

Size by total employment	Number of enterprises	Percentage of enterprises	Employment (thousands)	Percentage of employment	Net output (£ million)	Percentage of net output
1–99	127 998	96.28	1 203.7	25.0	26 682.2	19.2
100–999	4 362	3.28	1 156.6	24.0	30 545.5	22.0
1000–4999	469	0.35	944.7	19.7	29 201.6	21.0
5000–49 999	107	0.08	1 192.4	24.8	42 133.9	30.3
50 000 and over	4	0.003	311.3	6.5	10 420.3	7.5

Source: based on Central Statistical Office (1992) Table 12

By far and away the largest number of enterprises are small firms – 96.28 per cent – and they employ a quarter of the manufacturing workforce. Protoscan was one of these firms in 1990. In contrast, larger firms provide the greater part of total output. I added firm sizes together so that each size band (except the biggest) represents around a fifth to a quarter of total employment. As you can see, for firms with up to 5000 employees, each of the bands produces around one-fifth of net output. The largest firms, only three one-thousandths of 1 per cent of the total number of firms, employ over 6 per cent of manufacturing workers and produce 7.5 per cent of net output. Clearly, big firms are more important in terms of total output than they are collectively in terms of employment, and much more important than would be indicated by their proportion of all firms. On the other side of the coin, it is perhaps surprising, in a world which sometimes seems to be dominated by huge impersonal bureaucracies, to see the significance of firms that employ less than 100 people. With 25 per cent of employment and 19.2 per cent of net output, small firms made a sizeable contribution to the economy. Remember these data refer to manufacturing – they do not include the local corner shop or hairdressing salon.

The figures in this table refer to *enterprises*. The census also gives figures for *businesses*. In census terms enterprises refer to ownership. One enterprise can own several businesses. When analysed using an enterprise base, the figures for the number of businesses show an increasing concentration as we move from smaller to larger enterprises. For small firms the number of enterprises and businesses is roughly the same – in other words each business is a separate enterprise. However, as we move to bigger and bigger enterprises the position changes. The 4 enterprises that employ over 50000 people – the really large part of the manufacturing sector – own 135 separate businesses.

The census does not reveal information about individual companies, in order to avoid compromising their competitive position, so it is not possible to discover who those four enterprises are. However, we can obtain information about the world's largest companies from other sources; the figures for Europe in the same year as the UK census are given in Table 4.3.

Table 4.3   **Top European companies 1990 (ranked by turnover, £m)**

Company	Country of origin	Turnover
1 Royal Dutch Shell Petroleum Company	Netherlands	38867.0
2 British Petroleum	United Kingdom	37394.0
3 Daimler Benz AG	Germany	26245.7
4 Shell Transport and Trading	United Kingdom	25912.0
5 Fiat SpA	Italy	24377.8
6 IRI (state holding company)	Italy	23064.8
7 Volkswagen AG	Germany	22452.7
8 Siemens AG	Germany	21001.5
9 Nestlé SA	Switzerland	19447.0
10 Deutsche Bundespost	Germany	18038.6

Source: based on Allen (1990)

According to the *Census of Production*, in 1990 the gross output of all UK production enterprises was roughly £380 billion. As you can see from Table 4.3, the turnover figures for Royal Dutch Shell Petroleum and BP are each around £38 billion, or the rough equivalent of 10 per cent of the gross production of UK production enterprises. (Production in this context means energy and manufacturing. The census definition uses a standard convention adopted in official statistics about the economy and does not include primary products such as agriculture, fishing or mining nor services under the heading of 'production'.) The turnover of these companies is not generated totally within the UK, and gross output is not quite the same thing as turnover – turnover is essentially sales – but the comparative size indicated by such figures is revealing.

Protoscan could never have reached such a size as a producer of a specialized technical product, as the demand for its product is simply too small. Large and small firms are therefore likely to coexist. However, as with Kao and Protoscan, when potential synergies are seen to exist, one firm, in this case Kao, preferred to incorporate the smaller firm into its own organization rather than continue to operate through markets; Kao was in a sufficiently powerful position to put this preference into practice. As the census shows, many small firms are owned by major corporations, and the potential power of these corporations on an international scale is enormous.

Firms therefore have an almost infinite variety, from the small high-tech world of a firm like Protoscan to massive organizations such as Royal Dutch Shell which cross national boundaries and are by any standard immense.

3   Firms and finance

We now turn to some different perspectives on firms, which provide different ways of modelling them. The model that is most commonly used in day-to-day conversation to explain firms' behaviour is that based on accounting conventions. The primary focus of this model is the firm as a money processor. The firm uses its money to buy materials and labour which enable it to make more money. This model is important for firms in both the public and private sectors, since without finance they would not exist. The model is also valuable because it simplifies our view of the firm: instead of the firm being a complex organization, it becomes a vehicle for processing money.

In order to operate, the firm has to be able to raise finance. In the case of Protoscan finance was a major constraint throughout its existence. The two partners borrowed from one of the commercial banks using their houses as security and made use of their limited savings. This is a very common way for firms to get started.

However, it is unusual for a firm of any scale to have access to sufficient funds simply through reinvestment of profits or bank loans. Large firms are, therefore, frequently *joint stock companies*, which enables them to raise funds by selling shares to the public or borrowing through the sale of bonds. The establishment of joint stock companies in England in the middle of the nineteenth century (primarily to provide sufficient financial resources for the large industrial developments of the day, in particular the growth of railways) represents a major step in the history of private enterprise. The significant feature of a joint stock company is that it is regarded, in law, as a separate entity from the individuals who own it. It can enter into debt, issue contracts, own property, sue and be sued in its own right. It is the company, not its owners, that incurs legal obligations. The owners' responsibilities are limited to the amount of money they have invested in the company through purchasing shares. The owners will not be liable to lose their personal assets in order to meet the liabilities of the company. This is the concept of *limited liability* (in the UK this is the reason for the 'limited' descriptor in plc, public limited company). It means that share ownership can be undertaken by literally millions of small investors and that they will have complete knowledge of the maximum risks they are taking – namely the loss of money they have invested, and no more. Funds raised through the sale of shares are usually referred to as *equity*. Equity does not have to be repaid. Equity holders invest their money in order to share in the firm's profits. For the large firms described in Section 2.3, raising funds in this way can be a major preoccupation, though the companies in Table 4.3 also include organizations which are (or have recently been) funded by national governments, for example IRI, and one which is privately funded, Nestlé.

Borrowing through debenture capital or bonds is also possible for joint stock companies. The people who purchase bonds are not owners of the firm, they are creditors. The firm promises to pay interest on the loan each year and to repay the loan at some stated future date. These sums must be paid by law whether or not the firm makes a profit, and bondholders have first call on the company's assets if it is unable to pay. They can force the firm into liquidation; that is, they can require the firm to make its assets liquid – to sell them off – in order to pay its creditors. For the firm, therefore, bonds can be less attractive than equity, since they require payment and can sometimes force firms which are in only temporary difficulty into liquidation. On the other hand equity dilutes the amount of control that any one individual can exert, since shareholders have rights over the company's activities through shareholders' meetings and the opportunity to appoint directors.

The consequences of widespread share ownership are profound. In particular there is frequently a *separation of ownership from control*. Control is commonly exercised by the company's managers or its technostructure (this is a term sometimes used to describe the skilled managers and professionals who work for the company and are knowledgeable about its markets and other aspects of its environment in a way that a single shareholder could never hope to be).

Question

Think about organizations familiar to you in which ownership of the organization is separated from control. What do you think are the implications of this separation of ownership and control?

In these circumstances the owners' interests become only one feature of the firm's objective function. Managers can try to exert control in their own interests but must maintain sufficient return to equity to keep shareholders satisfied – remember this is called satisficing. When ownership and control are separated, it is possible for many groups to exert an influence subject to the owners being satisfied. Such groups are often called *stakeholders*.

One limitation on the ability of the company's technostructure to do whatever it wishes is the legal requirement to maintain adequate accounts. In order for any organization to function efficiently it must maintain adequate records. Without a system that provides for the maintenance of such records, the stakeholders will have, at best, incomplete information. Owners will not receive satisfactory summaries of the company's activities, and managers will be unable to take effective decisions as a result of the lack of relevant information. But the people who may have an interest in accounting information are not limited to the obvious categories of owners and managers. Other people and institutions have a genuine interest too.

Government needs information about the economy as a whole, and such information can only be accumulated by organizations contributing their own individual pieces of the jigsaw. The tax authorities also require information for taxation purposes.

Creditors require information on which the level of creditworthiness may be judged. The company's accounts are the basis for such judgements.

The information needs of employees have also become more widely recognized. Many companies now recognize their employees' rights to know about the viability of the organization they work for, particularly those which include share options of various kinds in their remuneration packages.

There are a number of other groups which have interests but which at present are not normally included in the formal reporting processes. These include the customers of the organization and the local community in which it functions. Their information needs may be linked with social and economic issues, or with environmental concerns, for example. At present such groups are not formally included in accounting procedures, though they can get access to the accounts of public companies since such accounts have to be made publicly available. It is important to recognize that different people have different opportunities to pick up issues, and their interests will be dealt with in different ways depending on their position in relation to the firm. The items that are included in accounts, and those that are excluded, reflect the interests which are seen as most important by the firm, the accounting professions and the legal authorities, and this in itself raises interesting issues about the appropriate spread of interests and property rights. These stakeholders are effectively determining the way in which the company is seen by defining those items that are seen as important and those that are not.

The picture of a firm that is drawn via its accounts is displayed basically in three main statements which are available for economists to scrutinize: the balance sheet, the profit statement, and the funds flow statement.

The structure of company accounts

The balance sheet

The balance sheet depicts the financial position of an organization at a particular moment, for example at the year end, by listing and attributing values to items owned (assets) and amounts owed (liabilities). The balance sheet will not normally show the economic value of assets and liabilities – what something is 'worth' in economic terms. It simply shows the values of the assets and liabilities as shown in the records of the organization. Here is an example.

OPEN ENTERPRISES

Balance Sheet

31 December 1995

Assets	£	Liabilities	£
Cash	80 000	Accounts payable	180 000
Accounts receivable	140 000	Salaries payable	100 000
Inventories	100 000	Mortgage	150 000
Buildings (original value £250 000)	200 000	Bank loan	80 000
Other equipment	220 000		510 000
		Net worth	230 000
	740 000		740 000

Assets are what the firm owns. They are shown on the left. Open Enterprises has some cash in the bank. It is also owed money, called 'accounts receivable', by customers and has large inventories in its warehouses. In addition it owns buildings which originally cost £250 000 but are now worth only £200 000 because of depreciation. Its other equipment has also depreciated and is now worth £220 000. The total value of Open Enterprises' assets is £740 000.

Liabilities are what a firm owes. They are shown on the right. They include unpaid bills and salaries, the mortgage, and a bank loan for short-term cash needs. The total value of debts is £510 000. The net worth of Open Enterprises is £230 000 – in other words, this is the excess of its assets over its liabilities.

Net worth is shown on the liabilities side. The firm is owned by the shareholders and the net worth is one of the resources to which the firm, as an organization, has access. But the net worth does not belong to the firm; it belongs to the shareholders. It is therefore a liability of the firm to the shareholders.

The profit statement

The profit statement (sometimes called an income statement or profit-and-loss account) tells us about the flow of money during a given year. The profit statement shows how the profit for a particular period has been determined by listing revenues and expenses. It does not just measure the difference between cash received and cash expended. It measures the difference between monetary values earned for providing goods or services and the monetary values incurred in generating such earnings. This is an important distinction in accounting. For example, in the consultancy firm with which I was involved, our accounting year ended on 31 March. If we carried out activities for a client in March and billed the client in the same month, we would not expect to receive payment until May or June of our next accounting year. However, the fact that the cash would not be received until the next accounting year would not stop us from including the relevant earnings on the profit statement relating to the year in which the money was earned. The profit statement is not measuring cash received or cash paid out. It is measuring economic values earned and the economic values associated with the generation of such earnings.

UNIVERSAL SECURITY SERVICES Profit statement Year ending 31 March 1995		
Revenue (£)		2 000 000
Expenses (£)		
Wages	1 400 000	
Rent	100 000	
Advertising	100 000	
Other expenses	200 000	
		1 800 000
Profits before tax		200 000
Taxes paid		50 000
Profits after tax		150 000

Universal Security Services (USS) is a firm that provides security personnel to other organizations. It charges £20 per hour for each security officer and pays each officer £14 per hour. During 1995 it provided 100 000 hours worth of security services and thus spent £1 400 000 on wages. Business expenses came to £400 000. All expenses therefore came to £1 800 000. Profits equal revenue minus costs, so taking costs from revenue gives a profit before tax of £200 000.

The funds flow statement

The funds flow statement shows where and how funds have come into an organization during a period, and what has happened to those funds. This statement would show the earnings in my consultancy firm mentioned above for March as flowing into the firm in May or June.

In the case of USS at the end of 1995, we can expect that it has not yet been paid for all the services it provided during the year. There will also be bills it owes which have not been paid. This will have implications for the firm's cash flow (which would be shown on the funds flow statement). Cash flow is the net amount of money actually received during the period. Profitable firms may have a poor cash flow when customers are slow to pay their bills or when new equipment has been purchased.

Depreciation was discussed in relation to national accounts in Chapter 2. Essentially the same rules apply to private firms. The basic idea is that the cost of *using* rather than buying a piece of capital equipment should be treated as costs within the year. When a piece of equipment is first acquired there is a large cash outflow, which is larger than the depreciation cost of using the equipment during its first year. Profits may be high but cash flow low. In subsequent years no further cash outlay is required, but depreciation is still calculated as an economic cost since the resale value of the equipment will decline each year. Cash flow will now be higher than profit (assuming unpaid bills remain much the same).

4   Production, costs and profits

The conventional approach adopted by economists is not to model the firm as a money processor, though that is clearly an important perspective, but to regard firms fundamentally as producers of goods and services. This has similarities to the previous model. It uses related categories, but here the *expenses* (which appeared in the USS profit statement) are called *costs* and are looked at in a rather different way. The analytical framework set out below is logically consistent and internally coherent and can be applied to *all* firms. A theory that applies to all firms in general is unlikely to be able to explain the detailed day-to-day behaviour and strategic development of a particular company, but in abstracting from that detail it provides powerful results which have been very insightful.

The starting point for this basic approach is to emphasize the firm as an efficient organizer of inputs – that is, an organization which always tries to minimize costs of production. It may have other objectives too, but provided it is concerned to minimize costs the analysis will hold.

I shall also assume that the firm can purchase all the inputs it needs from the relevant 'factor' markets (a factor market is simply the place where the inputs required for production are bought and sold). The market for labour is a factor market, and has many subsets, of course. Thus there is a market for different kinds of skilled labour, for strategic planners and for cleaners. From each of these the firm can buy just the amount of each kind of labour necessary for it to produce efficiently. Similarly it can enter the market for capital equipment and will invest in whatever machinery it requires; it can enter the market for land and raw materials and buy the relevant quantities there, and so on.

4.1   The production function

The production function summarizes the most efficient relationship between inputs and outputs, i.e. between the amount of product the firm wishes to produce and the factors of production it requires to produce that output. The production function is defined for a given state of technology.

For example, a restaurateur needs premises and raw materials (food), up-to-date capital equipment (good ovens, mixers, microwaves, and so on), skilled labour (the chef and chief waiter), plus various other forms of semi-skilled and unskilled labour (cleaners, kitchen porters, etc.). The restaurateur will buy amounts of these factors so that the required output – the number of meals per day – can be produced.

We can express this production function in an algebraic form of the kind you met in Chapters 2 and 3:

$$Q = f(F_1, F_2, \ldots F_n)$$

This means that Q is a function of $F_1, F_2 \ldots F_n$ (where Q is the quantity of meals required and the Fs refer to the factors of production; there are up to 'n' of them and the size of 'n' will vary, depending on the particular production process under consideration.) In other words the number of meals of a given quality that a restaurant can produce depends on the different factors of production that the restaurant possesses.

The factors can be combined in different ways. If we had more skilled chefs we might need fewer raw materials because they would waste less, or we might need a different kind of equipment. In general each of the *F*s can be combined in many different ways with each of the other *F*s. The limitation to this is the current state of technological knowledge. The production function is only concerned with efficient processes, however – that is, processes which will use more of one factor only if they use less of a second factor. This is known as technical efficiency. The production function is not concerned with processes that use more of all factors.

If technological improvements take place, then we would find that for any given *Q* we would need fewer *F*s – fewer people to make the same number of meals, for example, or we might combine the *F*s in rather different ways. When microwave ovens were invented it became possible to prepare more food prior to the time of consumption and to heat it up quickly in the microwave. This meant that skilled chefs could be used more effectively and perhaps less skilled people would carry out the reheating.

In this example, different people are doing different things – another example of the division of labour discussed in Chapter 1. You will remember from Section 2.2 of that chapter the reference to Smith's pin factory and the way that idea was extended by Taylor into 'scientific management'.

Different states of technology allow labour to be divided up to a greater or lesser extent. For example, in the case of motor vehicle production, the original motor vehicles produced by Gottlieb Daimler at the end of the nineteenth century were manufactured by small groups of skilled workers who hand-crafted every component. Those small teams could produce more vehicles per month than would have been the case if every single component had been made by the same person, but their output levels were completely outstripped by the mass-production methods introduced by Henry Ford in the 1920s, when each worker took on only a small part of the total production process. Using the division of labour in this way was seen as more efficient. Greater output could be produced with the same resources, and the limits to the division of labour were seen to be primarily the demand for the firm's product. These are powerful arguments and they begin to touch on issues relating directly to the organization of firms which we shall come to in Section 5.

The short and the long run

The dividing up of work in this way is something that is very familiar to us. The flexibility that is possible with such work organization will be different depending on the time scale. In the short run the firm is unable to build new factories or bring new machinery on line, and so the division of labour is limited to dividing workers up between the different processes in the existing workplaces and with existing equipment. In the long run new investment can take place and new buildings can be acquired. The range of options thus available is significantly greater, and completely new ways of working can be adopted.

To express this more generally, we would say that in the short run the firm's land and capital are fixed – they are fixed factors of production – whilst labour is variable. In the long run all factors are variable.

The short run and the long run will be different lengths of time depending on the particular processes we are talking about. Steelworks, for example, take much longer to set up than sandwich shops. It takes over five years to

---

Definition

Technical efficiency

A production process is technically efficient if it is not possible to produce a given quantity of goods or services with less of one factor of production without using more of another factor of production.

Definitions

Short run and long run

In the short run the firm is unable to vary its use of at least one of its factors of production.

In the long run the use of all factors of production is variable.

build a modern steelworks, so for steel the short run lasts five years. Its capital is fixed for five years. For a sandwich shop the short run is only a few weeks.

Exercise 4.1

To check your understanding try to answer the following questions without skipping forward to the answers and, if possible, without going back to the earlier text. Much of this material is basic to the theories and ideas introduced in later chapters, so it is important to make sure you have grasped its essentials now.

1   What is the production function?

2   Define the phrase 'division of labour'.

3   What is meant by 'the short run'?

4.2   The cost function

The cost function shows the relationship between output and costs. More specifically it shows the cost associated with any particular output level, assuming the method of production chosen is the lowest-cost method available. It relates to the production function since it identifies the least-cost method available from all the efficient options indicated by the production function.

Long-run costs

Let us look first at long-run costs. Remember that in the long run all factors are variable, so they can be combined in the least-cost way possible.

Question

Suppose for the moment that the firm can obtain all the *F*s it needs at current factor prices. How will its total costs change as it increases its output? Another way of asking this question is to say, 'What will its cost function look like?'.

We can say with absolute confidence that the firm's total costs will rise. Every time it increases output by one unit it will need to buy extra raw materials and labour hours, and so it will incur extra costs. The total costs it incurs get bigger.

Question

If output increases, total costs will rise, but will they rise exactly in proportion with the increase in output? Try to think through what this means. Is it necessary for costs to rise by exactly the same amount every time output increases by one unit?

The answer to this question is no, but why? The explanation lies in something with which we are very familiar. I think many people take it for granted that when a firm produces more of any product its costs per unit

Definitions

Average costs

Average costs are costs per unit – that is, total costs divided by the number of units produced.

Economies of scale

Economies of scale are reductions in average costs associated with expansion in output in the long run. Internal economies of scale are those which arise within the firm, as a result, for example, of taking advantage of opportunities for division of labour; external economies of scale are those which the firm gains because of the expansion of its industry.

fall in the long run. The example of Ford is instructive again. When Henry Ford was able to expand to a scale that enabled him to employ mass production methods, his costs per unit fell significantly. By using the potential of the division of labour he could reduce the costs he incurred from increasing output and thus make cheaper cars. Even though his *total costs* were rising, his average costs were falling.

This phenomenon – unit or average costs falling as output expands – is often referred to as the effect of economies of scale.

Some are called *internal* economies of scale because they are internal to the firm. An important internal economy is the potential of the division of labour which Henry Ford used so effectively. A second internal economy of scale arises because of a simple geometric relationship. The best example is that of the storage tank. The cost of a storage tank is largely determined by the area of the material used to construct its sides. If the sides of a tank are doubled in length, say from 2 metres to 4 metres, and each square metre of material costs £10, then this doubling in its dimensions increases costs from £40 per side ($2 \times 2 \times £10$) or £240 for the tank since the tank has 6 sides, to £160 per side ($4 \times 4 \times £10$) or £960 for the tank. That is a large increase: costs have quadrupled. However, the volume of the tank has increased from 8 cubic metres ($2 \times 2 \times 2$) to 64 cubic metres ($4 \times 4 \times 4$); there has thus been an eightfold increase in capacity (see Figure 4.2).

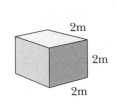

Figure 4.2   Technical economies of scale

volume = 8 cu. metres   volume = 64 cu. metres

There are, therefore, substantial economies of scale available in such circumstances since capacity is increasing twice as quickly as costs. It is this simple relationship that results in enormous oil tankers which have to manoeuvre for port hundreds of miles out to sea, and the same relationship creates the pressure to allow increasingly large lorries on our roads.

External economies of scale also exist. These are the reductions in costs which a firm experiences as a result of the expansion of the industry. For example, Protoscan almost certainly gained some external economies by being located in Huntingdon, close to Cambridge. The 'Cambridge phenomenon' – the concentration of numerous innovative high-tech companies in the Cambridge area – undoubtedly led to some factors relevant to such firms being available more cheaply and easily than for companies elsewhere (Segal, 1987).

There is a limit to economies of scale. Even Henry Ford eventually found that there was a level of output after which the extra cost of one more unit was pretty much the same as the costs incurred on the previous unit. This level of output is often referred to as the *minimum efficient scale* because it is the size or scale of the production process at which all economies of scale have been taken up. In terms of average costs it means that average costs are constant – total costs are still rising but the average cost per unit remains the same. These are likely to be the circumstances which prevail for most firms. In the long run most firms experience constant average costs for significant ranges of output.

The possibility that average costs rise as output increases beyond a certain point does not seem likely in many industries, except perhaps at a massive scale. What this means is that if we assume that the firm can obtain all the factors it wants at existing prices, it will not find that its costs per unit increase as it expands until it reaches a very large scale indeed. We can, however, envisage limits to expansion in organizational terms if no others: eventually a firm can become so cumbersome that it starts to cost increasingly large amounts to manage effectively. The break-up of ICI into ICI and Zenica in 1993 is a good example of this kind of behaviour.

We can draw the relationship between output and cost per unit in the long run as a graph which will look something like Figure 4.3.

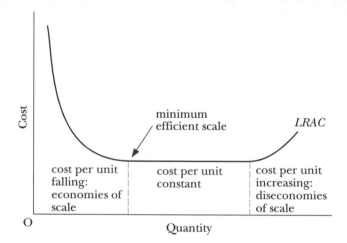

Figure 4.3   **Long-run average cost (*LRAC*) curve**

Note how the curve falls, showing average costs falling until minimum efficient scale is reached. There is then a flat section of constant average costs and the possibility that average costs rise at very high output levels. In the rest of this text you will find that we often draw long-run average cost curves 'L' shaped, ignoring the occasions when they may rise at high levels of output.

Short-run costs

In the short run, remember, the supply of some factors is fixed, so that the firm cannot increase its use of all factors as it expands. Realistically a firm will be unable to buy and install new plant and equipment except over a substantial period of time. In the short run, therefore, it is realistic to consider the firm having a *fixed* stock of plant, machinery, premises and equipment, but that it is able to *vary* the amount of labour it uses relatively easily either through overtime or through employing more staff.

Question

What happens to its costs in these circumstances as output changes?

The lowest cost level it can reach at any output level is that represented by the long-run cost curve. The long-run cost curve shows what we might call

Definition

Economic efficiency

A firm is economically efficient if it is working at a point on its long-run average cost curve.

the optimum combination of factors. This is often referred to as economic efficiency. It is, of course, possible for the firm to produce at a point above its long-run cost curve, but at that point it would be using factors inefficiently and would be able to reduce costs by becoming more economically efficient. (The firm may be combining factors in a way that is *technically* efficient but still be inefficient economically. This would arise if it was using large amounts of expensive factors and small amounts of cheaper factors. It would be more economically efficient to switch to a technique which used fewer expensive factors and more cheap factors. I shall come back to this point in a moment.) However, if the firm wishes to expand in the short run, it must do so without being able to obtain more of its fixed factors. It can vary only its labour input.

Think about Protoscan again. In the first few months of its existence it was housed in the back room of Mike Hall's house. The company copied disks using a shift system. There was very little equipment available and that equipment was the major determinant of output. At first the addition of labour to this fixed piece of equipment would enable output to rise and average costs to fall, as say eight hours' labour was increased to ten. The equipment costs would remain virtually the same – the same rental, insurance and maintenance – but for a little extra electricity, more blank disks and two hours' extra labour, the output of the machine would rise by 25 per cent (two hours' additional output to the eight already worked).

Eventually the machine worked 24 hours a day (less whatever time was necessary for routine checking and maintenance). The addition of extra labour then would still increase output a little: the disks could be sorted and boxed more quickly and efficiently; the distribution to customers could be faster; and more time could be spent with customers checking their needs. All this could be enhanced by increasing the amount of labour working alongside the limited equipment available. However, the cost per unit – the average cost – would now be increasing quite fast as the extra labour costs were borne by an output level which was very close to the maximum possible – determined by the continuous operation of the machine and its maximum output. This relationship – output increasing but by smaller increments each time more of the variable factor is added – is referred to as *diminishing returns* to the variable factor of production.

The short-run average cost curve which illustrates what is happening in these circumstances is shown in Figure 4.4.

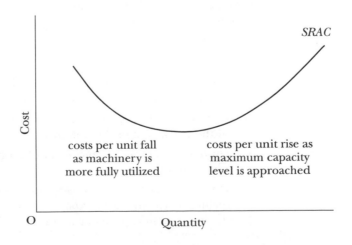

Figure 4.4   Short-run average cost (*SRAC*) curve

In such circumstances we can envisage a number of short-run average cost curves contained in the long-run average cost curve. Each short-run curve represents a particular size or combination of equipment and premises which is fixed in the short term. Figure 4.5 illustrates this point. In the circumstances in which a firm finds itself working on the rising part of the short-run average cost curve ($SRAC_1$), such as output level Q, for any significant period of time it will wish to invest in new equipment in order to expand its operation to the new economically efficient level, shown by a move from $SRAC_1$ to $SRAC_2$. Conversely, in periods of decline it may wish to scrap equipment or sell it to other companies in order to avoid incurring the maintenance and other charges associated with it. Each of the short-run curves is tangential to the long-run curve – they do not cross it. If they did, that would imply that costs in the short run could be lower than the optimum long-run position, which is impossible by definition. Note, furthermore, that while I have drawn the $SRAC$ curves as 'U' shaped, they may not take that precise form; they may have a flat bottom section where average costs per unit level out before output starts to approach the capacity of the equipment.

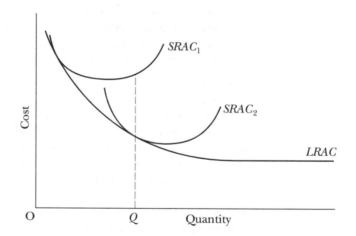

Figure 4.5 **The relationship between long-run and short-run average cost curves**

A summary of the differences between some technical terms

I have been using a number of terms which appear to be very similar but mean different things. Sometimes the differences are subtle, sometimes wider, and I would like to pause at this stage to clarify the different usages.

- *Economies of scale* are the *reductions* in costs associated with expansion in output in the long run.

- *Internal economies of scale* are those which arise within the firm, through such things as the division of labour.

- *External economies of scale* are economies which the *firm* gains as a result of the expansion of the *industry.*

- *Diseconomies of scale* are *increases* in cost associated with expansion of output in the long run.

- *Returns to scale* can be *increasing, constant* or *decreasing.* They reflect the technological effects of expansion or contraction in the long run. So the increase in capacity brought about by expanding the size of an oil tanker exhibits increasing returns to scale, as illustrated in Figure 4.2. If such expansion brings about a big increase in the price of the metal used in oil tanker construction, it might be that bigger oil tankers actually cost the oil companies more per litre of oil carried than before the expansion took place. But the process still exhibits increasing returns to scale.

Constant returns to scale implies that expansion or contraction does not have a technological effect on the cost per unit. Decreasing returns occur when the technological implications of expansion produce an increase in the cost per unit.

- *Diminishing returns* are not the same as decreasing returns to scale. Diminishing returns are a *short-run* phenomenon. As more of the variable factor (usually labour) is added to the fixed factor(s) (usually capital or land), the increase in output for every extra increment of the variable factor gets smaller. Diminishing returns to the variable factors set in on all pieces of equipment eventually, and prompt growing firms to invest in new capacity so that they can move to a more economically efficient plant in the long run. This is illustrated in Figure 4.5.

Variable factor prices

To simplify matters I have not yet considered what happens when factor prices change. If you recall the Protoscan case, it is unlikely that its initial recruitment of labour had any impact on the going rate for the job. However, when it expanded, it is possible that it may have been unable to recruit at its original rate. It was established then in a small town, Huntingdon, and may well have had to attract workers with the relevant skills from other companies and nearby towns. In those circumstances it would probably offer higher rates and would not have been able to satisfy its needs for labour at the pre-existing rate.

What will happen in such circumstances, when firms face an increase in their factor prices?

Question

What do you think will happen? Think about the behaviour of organizations with which you are familiar. The answer is straightforward, but now we can describe it in terms of cost curves. What would you expect to happen to the cost curves?

The first answer is that if factor prices go up, then total costs go up. The average cost curve would shifts upwards at any given output level to reflect a general increase in costs (shown in Figure 4.6). I expect your answer is clear on that.

But we need to consider a wider range of possibilities than an across-the-board increase in factor costs. What if the price of only one factor goes up? The outcome then depends on the production function and the extent to which it is possible to substitute one factor for another. If factors have to be used in fixed proportions, for example each pan needs a lid and each chef needs a grill, then an increase in the price of one factor has a similar effect as an across-the-board increase. However, factors do not usually need to be

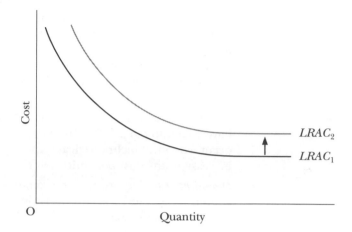

Figure 4.6   **Upward shift of the long-run average cost curve**

combined in such fixed ways. Pans can share lids, plates can double up as lids, and chefs can share grills. In such circumstances firms will use more of the factor which has not increased in price and less of the factor which is now more expensive. This is known as *factor substitution*.

The long-run average cost curve will then have changed so that each point on it, which remember is an optimal point, will represent a factor combination using less of the relatively expensive factor and more of those factors that can be substituted for it. The curve will be higher than the original curve, since costs have increased, but not so high as in the circumstances where factor proportions are fixed.

Marginal costs

There is one more concept in relation to costs that is used a great deal by economists. It is known as marginal cost. You need to be clear about this and then you are all set: you will have the basic armoury of cost concepts that you need to undertake this kind of economic analysis.

Marginal cost is one of those concepts that is simple when you know what it is but can be a bit of a struggle to get the hang of. It is essentially the cost of the additional unit produced. If average costs are constant, then the extra cost incurred by producing one more unit is the same as the average cost. If average costs are falling, however, the cost of the last unit must be less than the average. In effect the firm is still moving down its average cost curve and reaping the benefits of expansion. The extra cost of one more unit in these circumstances is less than the extra cost incurred by the unit before it. Conversely, if average costs are rising, marginal costs will be above average costs. The relationship between average costs and marginal costs is shown in Figure 4.7.

The concept can probably be understood more easily if we use a numerical example. The example in Table 4.4 shows the change in cost as the firm expands its output from one unit per day to four units per day. The total cost of the first unit is £100. Since only one unit is produced, the cost of the last unit – the marginal cost – is also £100 and the average cost, i.e. total cost divided by number of units produced, is also £100.

To expand output by one unit the firm has to employ more labour, buy in extra raw materials, and perhaps incur bigger maintenance charges, but some costs do not increase, for example building rental. Expanding from

Definition

Marginal cost

Marginal cost is the change in total costs incurred by changing production by one unit. It reflects the extra amount of resources that the firm must lay out as it expands, or the resources saved as it contracts, and is the specific cost associated with changing output by one unit. It does not include overheads or other costs which are incurred whatever the level of output.

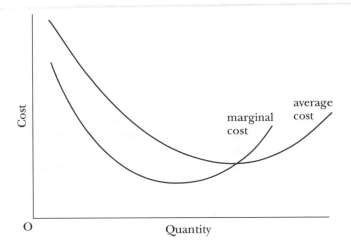

Figure 4.7   Average costs and marginal costs

Table 4.4

Level of output (no. of units per day)	Total cost (£)	Average cost (£)	Marginal cost (£)
1	100	100	100
2	180	90	80
3	240	80	60
4	300	75	60

one to two units a day is, nevertheless, a significant expansion, and the extra cost incurred is £80. This is the marginal cost. The total cost is £180, and the average cost £90 per unit.

A further expansion to three units per day can be undertaken without taking on more labour. The existing workforce has to work longer hours, but many costs do not change. The extra unit costs £60 to produce. Total costs are now £240 and average costs are £80 per unit.

Expansion from three to four units costs just as much as the previous expansion. More overtime has to be worked at the same rate as before and the marginal cost is £60 again. Total costs are still rising, of course, but the average cost per unit is still falling and is now £75.

Question

What will happen to the average cost per unit if the firm expands to five units per day and can still finance the expansion simply by extending overtime?

I hope you found this easy. The fifth unit would cost an additional £60, so the marginal cost is £60. Total costs are now £360, so the average cost per unit will be £72.

As you can see, average costs are falling but by a smaller amount each time as they get nearer to the marginal cost. At some point we would expect marginal costs to rise. The firm is unlikely to be able to expand solely by increasing overtime. It will probably have to take on extra staff, even if only part time. The firm may also find that it is becoming somewhat cramped in its premises, even though it may have moved equipment around and created storage areas. Let's say the sixth unit costs the company an additional £72 to produce. Total costs are thus £432 and average costs remain at £72. Average costs and marginal costs are now equal. If we carried on with this numerical example we would find that extra units begin to cost the company increasingly large amounts as it squeezes more labour into its premises and works the limited amount of equipment continuously. In other words, marginal costs would be rising rapidly. Average costs would also be rising but would not be as high as marginal costs. If you sketch this numerical example, you will see that the marginal cost curve turns up, to cut the average cost curve at the minimum level of average costs.

A note on smooth curves

You will notice that whenever I draw cost curves I have drawn them as smooth curves. In general, curves are drawn in this way in economics. But in doing that we must bear in mind a number of issues, so that we are clear about the implications of what we are doing:

- If I graphed the marginal and average cost curves from the *actual* costs incurred by a specific firm – as I have just suggested you do for the numerical example above – they would not come out as smooth curves, but would have lots of corners in them. The data would be in discrete amounts and the cost curve would simply join up the relevant points.

- However, smoothing them out is not just to make them look pretty. The smooth curves used in much theoretical work in economics imply that output or cost or whatever we are graphing is infinitely variable – that is, it can be changed by infinitesimally small amounts so that all the corners – the lumpiness – of realistic discrete changes disappear. In a theoretical model this has the major advantage of making it amenable to a range of powerful mathematical techniques, in particular differential calculus. We don't use those techniques in this text, but they are used a good deal in advanced economic theory and occur frequently in the economic literature.

- *Estimated* curves, based on an examination of actual data, also look smooth but these are drawn as a line of best fit through identified points. They are smoothed out by statistical techniques. You need to recognize the difference between theoretical smooth curves and the estimated curves calculated by economic statisticians.

You have already met all of these types of curves in this text. The line graphs in Chapter 1 were of the join-up-the-dots type. The cost curves in this chapter are smooth curves of the second type, while in Chapter 3 you saw an estimated line drawn through points to plot the consumption function. You will find more on estimation in Chapters 9 and 26.

Marginal costs are important for the firm because they measure the precise impact on the firm's costs of producing one extra item. If a firm knows what its marginal costs are, it is in a strong position to maximize its profits. Overall, however, if it is to remain profitable the firm must cover its total costs; that is, it must receive revenue per unit which is at least equal to cost per unit (or average cost). We shall be referring to this in much more detail in subsequent chapters. For now it is important that you feel comfortable with the cost concepts discussed so far. Have a go at the following exercise.

Exercise 4.2

Attempt the following questions in order to check your understanding of the important concepts we have just discussed.

1   Draw a long-run average cost curve. What does it show?

2   Why do short-run average costs differ from long-run average costs?

3   Draw the relationship between the long-run average cost curve and short-run average cost curves.

4   What happens to long-run average costs if the price of a factor rises and factors are substitutable for each other?

5   Complete the figures in Table 4.5.

Table 4.5

Level of output (no. of units per day)	Total cost (£)	Average cost (£)	Marginal cost (£)
1			50
2	90		
3		50	
4			70

5   Organizational structures, cultures and goals

5.1   Firms' objectives

Models of firms as essentially producers of goods and services or as processors of money provide a sound framework, but in abstracting from the complexity of *social* institutions, what is missing are the human dimensions and the sense of excitement and uniqueness, evident for example in the Protoscan case. Furthermore, in emphasizing impersonal features, the histories of firms and the sense of them as institutions are pushed to one side as if irrelevant to the structures under analysis. The problem is that if we concentrate on the detail, the task of explaining changes and relationships can become so large that we finish up with a series of case studies but no overall sense of the dynamics driving firms and other organizations. But it is important to tackle this level of analysis. It is possible to identify categories and trends that enable us to flesh out the broader theories and which give us major insights into the behaviour of particular market relationships or particular companies. If we wish to have a deep understanding of the organizations which act as economic agents, we have to tackle their complexity and not just abstract from it.

Question

Firms' objectives are an important part of the analysis. After all, if we can identify objectives, then, in principle, we can devise methods by which they can be achieved. What would you expect to be the primary objectives of firms?

Once we get inside the organization we find that it can be intensely difficult to understand. It may not be easy to identify the firm's objectives. Whilst it is true that there may be an underlying acceptance of the simple objective of minimizing costs, that will be a means to achieving other goals and not the prime motivator in its own right. Liebenstein (1966) indicates that firms usually work above their long-run average cost curves unless forced down to the cost curve by their environments. Important features of the environment relate to internal motivation, he argues, not just external pressures. This accords with our observation of the world around us, that neither individuals nor firms always work as hard as they could, but this may be a legitimate objective for the organization and may be compatible with other long-term goals. So even something as simple as cost minimization may be an aspiration rather than a measurable standard to be achieved.

As part of the objective function (the interrelated set of objectives of a firm) there will frequently be some kind of *profit constraint* – a minimum level of profit that is acceptable to the organization's owners, the *satisficing* level – but alongside this, other objectives appear. Some organizations regard *sales volumes* as a major objective. Others appear to see *growth* as their major objective.

Many Japanese firms appear to value growth highly. Conversely, other firms claim to eschew profits except as a way of maintaining their business. For example, BUPA (a private health services company) claims that all their profits are reinvested into health care. But it is misleading to concentrate on a single objective for most companies. Their objectives will change as the environment changes. If the environment becomes very tough, survival may become the sole concern. On the other hand, in an easier environment other priorities may appear. One priority can be the wish to gain some control over the environment in order to provide opportunities for more discretion in the way the firm can actively engage with it. In many organizations different parts will have different priorities, and the organization's behaviour will be centred around some kind of *coalition* which may vary over time. Thus we find that the company will be attempting to achieve several objectives simultaneously and from time to time may have to trade off one objective against another.

A number of economic models have been devised using, for example, sales or revenue as the major objective, but the objective that is usually assumed in economics is profit. Firms are assumed to be *profit maximizers,* though even in this case the concept is not unambiguous since short-run profit maximization – screwing as much as possible out of the immediate situation – may be incompatible with long-run profit maximization when the maintenance of a loyal customer base may be more important. Nevertheless, in analysis using the kinds of models set out in Section 4, profit maximization is frequently assumed in order to clarify its implications for a firm's decision making. Profit is likely to be an important feature of all private firms' objective function, but, as I've argued earlier, it is unlikely to be the sole objective.

5.2   Organizational cultures

In order to understand the ways in which multiple objectives are determined, as well as to gain insight into the internal complexity of organizations and thus the ways in which those objectives might be fulfilled, it is valuable to consider organizational culture. Internal structures are often pictured using a simple mechanical analogy which assumes that, like simple mechanical devices, if one bit of the machine is moved, a second piece will move until an inevitable and easily predictable outcome is reached. In practice I think you will know that most, if not all, organizations do not react like that. There are frequently features that appear to be mechanical, but these are usually combined with much more complex forms reflecting the kinds of people employed by the organization, their own personal goals and values, power systems, information processing limitations, and much more.

Different cultures will have different taken-for-granted assumptions about the world and will respond in different ways to environmental stimuli, depending on the meanings perceived by actors within the organization, and to the importance of the culture of the organization and the symbols that are used as part of that culture. Non-cultural features are vital, of course – for example the context, the objective conditions faced by the organization, the knowledge and understanding of the organization's members, and the network of potential and actual collaborators – but the culture of the organization will interpret these in different ways. Different outcomes will arise depending on the balance of features. The organization's *history* bears heavily on its interpretation of events. The organization will have *developed ideologies* and possess particular *organizational structures* and distinctive *competences*. Thus the way in which any organization responds to changes in its environment, such as changes in competitors' behaviour or newly perceived opportunities, will be determined by a complex web of cultural features which interpret the new environment and indicate appropriate directions in which the organization might move.

For example, Cadbury, the chocolate manufacturer, has a long tradition of concern for the welfare and community-related aspects of its work. This dates back to the company's origins as a Quaker family firm. More recently the company has undergone a number of significant changes, and its founding values have been important:

> Cadburyism remained a strong ideology in the consciousness of family members, managers and workers, who all perpetuated it. It appears to have been both a benchmark for change and a force mediating that change. As a benchmark it provoked key change agents deliberately to set out their case against the fundamentals of the tradition. For example, the Cadbury (later group) technical director twice put up proposals to evacuate production out of Bournville, the centre and very essence of the Cadbury tradition. He argued that Bournville was too large and too institutionalized. He claimed that his intention on the second occasion was to spur the two leading family directors into a commitment to radical change ... At the same time, the company was able to invoke elements of the ideology and remould these in different circumstances ... In short, a dominant traditional corporate ideology should not necessarily be seen merely as an obstacle to transformation. For many it may encourage a clearer

articulation of alternatives the more highly developed it is, and if reshaped or re-applied flexibly it may provide an important legitimatory bridge for the transition from one organizational policy/configuration to another.

(Child and Smith, 1987, pp.584–5)

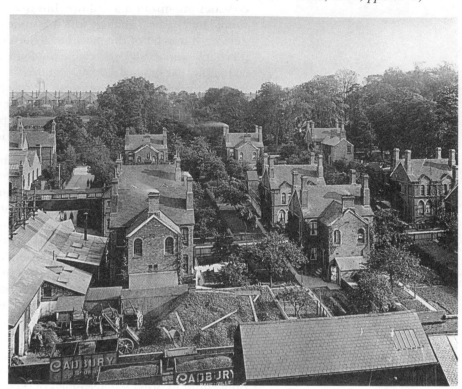

Figure 4.8 **The Bournville estate: Cadbury's concern for the welfare of the community in operation**

What this amounts to is that to understand how firms react to changes we need to have a full analysis of the kind of organization we are dealing with, including a knowledge of its history and its interpretation of the objective conditions that it faces, as well as an understanding of the many competencies the firm may have. A decision to move from Bournville in order to maintain competitive strengths involved fundamental discussions about the nature of the company, and was connected to the existence of multiple objectives, including concerns about community values. At any given time Cadbury's goals were a kind of negotiated consensus in which ideas about the nature of the company and its history were influential.

Organizations, like Cadbury, also engage actively with their environments. In many respects they create or 'enact' their own environments (Weick, 1979). The idea of enactment questions the assumption that we can think of an organization and its environment as two quite separate things. It makes the point that a firm that is operating in a particular market is able to influence that market by the way in which it responds to market changes or tries to initiate changes itself – the extent to which it is active or passive. Many firms are important players in their own markets. Some firms will have more impact on the environment than others, but all will influence it, so that sometimes it is difficult to say precisely where the organization ends and the environment begins.

5.3   Organizational configurations

We can make connections between the firm, its cultural features and its environment, though these will change as the environment and culture change and interact. What we are considering here is a framework for understanding firms in a changing or dynamic world, not simply the static picture of Section 4. Firms are likely to be attempting to minimize costs alongside other (sometimes incompatible) objectives. In a changing world the minimization of costs *now* may be less important than a longer-term objective and the need to create an organizational structure flexible enough to cope with expectations about change. Much of this is indeterminate.

Firms' organizational structures can be categorized in different ways. The main distinction in industrial economics has been between the U form and the M form. The U, for unitary, form refers to the archetypal form of business organization with a hierarchical structure in which different divisions report to a chief executive officer (CEO) or managing director. The M, or multi-divisional, form is generally larger and has a central office to which several operating divisions report, each of which has a structure like the U form and each of which is likely to have its own CEO. During the last century there has been a move first to large U form organizations, and then to M form organizations as the unitary structure became difficult to manage. This distinction highlights an important feature of recent economic history, namely the growth of firms into massive institutions. In looking at the complexity of firms it is useful to break down these distinctions further and to relate them to the kinds of environments in which they might thrive and the kinds of cultures which seem suited to particular configurations (Mintzberg, 1989). Firms move between configurations as their environments and cultures change and interact, but I shall set out different configurations for consideration separately for ease of exposition.

Firms usually begin their lives as *entrepreneurial organizations*. They are simple small units which can be flexible and responsive. They are in many ways the models for the firms analysed by the more abstract forms of economic theory in Section 4. They are vulnerable in a dynamic economy because they rely on the expertise of a few individuals and do not have easy access to substantial financial resources. Protoscan was a company of this kind. Through its takeover by Kao it became part of a *machine organization* or *bureaucracy*. In this configuration jobs are specialized and standardized, the organization has elaborate administrative structures, and it is frequently controlled by a technostructure of experts. The expertise of the technostructure gives it a good deal of informal and formal power because it possesses the skill and information necessary to the organization's success. These machine organizations are essentially the U form. In the West, their cultures are typically Fordist and they tend to thrive in circumstances where the product is *standardized* and the environment is *stable*. In Japan their cultures seem to be more flexible (Best, 1990).

When the environment becomes *complex*, standardized procedures may not respond adequately and a more appropriate configuration may be the *professional organization*. This is made up of individuals who are highly skilled. They frequently work independently and autonomously. Their expertise is regulated through professional bodies. They are expensive in comparison with the standardized workers in the bureaucratic form, and they are supported by an administration which is itself professional. 'Scientific management' is not appropriate in such circumstances. Project-based firms in relatively stable environments, such as engineering consultancies, take this form, and hospitals and universities are organizations of this type. Such organizations are typically small autonomous units working within a more bureaucratic framework. They will respond to environmental changes and try to enact environmental changes in a very different manner from, say, the world of the entrepreneurial firm.

The organizational forms discussed so far find it difficult to respond to complexity *and* instability. In these circumstances the *innovative organization* or *'adhocracy'* is important. Such organizations are typified by team working and project groups which break up and re-form according to the particular needs of the moment. Aerospace, many forms of computing, consulting, and 'creative' occupations such as film-making usually take on this organizational form. Protoscan had elements of this form. Adhocracy is typically an organic structure relying on extensive liaison and co-ordination. The term *matrix organization* is sometimes used for this kind of structure. Environments that are complex and dynamic, requiring sophisticated innovative activity which calls for the co-operative effort of many different experts, are ones in which adhocracies flourish. They tend to be small or part of bigger *diversified organizations*.

Diversified organizations are typical of the world's largest organizations and are usually a loose coupling of other organizational forms under a broad umbrella. In essence this is the M form. The headquarters of such organizations rely on performance control systems to try to ensure that each part of the diversified form plays its role effectively. Because they are so large, such organizations can be fascinating in their own right. Table 4.6 gives some background information on the world's biggest industrial groupings. It is based on *The Times 1000*, which is one of an increasing number of publications that list the world's biggest companies by various measures of size.

Table 4.6   **The world's top ten industrial groupings in 1990**

Company	Headquarters	Main activity	Sales (£m)
1 Sumitomo	Japan	Sogo shosha	80 520.7
2 C Itoh	Japan	Sogo shosha	77 244.5
3 Mitsui & Co.	Japan	Sogo shosha	76 369.2
4 General Motors	USA	Vehicle manufacturer	71 571.4
5 Marubeni	Japan	Sogo shosha	68 650.2
6 Mitsubishi	Japan	Sogo shosha	62 502.2
7 Nissho Iwai	Japan	Sogo shosha	56 608.9
8 Ford	USA	Vehicle manufacturer	54 212.5
9 Exxon Corporation	USA	Oil and natural gas	54 173.1
10 Royal Dutch/Shell Group	Netherlands/UK	Oil industry	44 003.0

Source: Allen (1990)

As you can see, the top ten is dominated by Japanese companies, thus confirming the importance of Asian companies first noted in Chapter 1. *Sogo shoshas* are vast umbrella organizations providing integrated services to member companies. Until quite recently they were unique to Japan, but they are now developing in other Asian countries. The scale of these companies is truly enormous. Sumitomo's £80 500 million worth of sales, or roughly $140 billion, is bigger, for example, than the GNP of one of Europe's wealthiest nations, Denmark, which had a GNP of $113.5 billion in 1990. GNP and sales are not the same thing, but organizations of such scale are potentially enormously powerful. It is not surprising that many industrial economists are fascinated by this configuration. Kao's takeover of Protoscan is part of the trend highlighted by this table. It represents a shift towards Pacific rim economies and change in the institutional and cultural forms that firms take.

If we wish to understand better the behaviour of particular companies, the use of such organizational configurations can be helpful. We no longer assume that all companies respond in the same way, but try to analyse their heterogeneity. An entrepreneurial organization will respond to changes differently from a large diversified company (whose preoccupation will sometimes be trying to hold the disparate parts together and to deal with their differing objectives) and different again from an innovative organization. We can also see that different cultures will thrive better in different environments and that these are linked to the kind of configuration adopted. These will change as the environment changes and the culture shifts.

6   Conclusion

This chapter has started from the position that firms are complex social institutions. In trying to understand their behaviour a number of strategies are open to us. We can abstract from the detail and concentrate on particular features, as do the financial models and the abstract theoretical models. Such models produce powerful insights which enable us to make general statements about firms' behaviour. The nature of firms as institutions cannot be ignored, however. It raises questions about the nature of the market itself – whether markets or firms are the most appropriate way to organize production – and it forces us to recognize the heterogeneity of firms and to consider the richness of the detail. There is no right or wrong way to approach these issues. Our approach depends on the level of analysis appropriate to the questions we are asking. However, it is important to recognize the significance of each of the different approaches adopted here to the full understanding of the behaviour of organizations as economic agents.

So far we have been considering firms largely as independent entities. Chapter 5 now goes on to study the *interdependence* of firms within markets and the impact this may have on their behaviour.

PART 3

CHAPTER 5

by Vivienne Brown

COMPETITION AND MARKET POWER
STRATEGIC COMPETITION

1 Introduction: fierce competition and 'dirty tricks'

On 12 January 1993 the *Financial Times* ran a headline story on the near-record libel damages won by Richard Branson and his Virgin Atlantic Airways against British Airways. BA apologized unreservedly to Richard Branson for alleging that Virgin Atlantic Airways was only seeking publicity in its claim that a 'dirty tricks' campaign was being waged against it by BA. In addition, BA was to pay Virgin £610 000 plus about £3 million in legal costs. This was an extraordinary event in the world of high corporate rivalry. In the words of the *Financial Times* reporter:

> In scenes of high theatre outside the High Court, Mr Branson claimed 'complete and total vindication' for his company which had accused BA of trying to put it out of business.
> In charging BA with going 'beyond any limits of commercially acceptable practice,' Mr Branson listed details of his rival's campaign to discredit Virgin.
>
> *(Financial Times, 12 January 1993, p.1)*

The rivalry between BA and Virgin was that between a large operator supplying a substantial proportion of the market and a new operator trying to establish a profitable niche for itself. In challenging the supremacy of the large firm, Virgin emphasized its competitive drive in offering its passengers a better service at lower prices. But Virgin claimed that BA was trying to bolster its own powerful position in the market by deliberately trying to drive Virgin out of business, not by fair competitive means, but by unfair and even illegal ones. Virgin claimed that BA had poached passengers by posing as its own staff, and that it had spread false rumours about Virgin. At the time of writing this chapter, Virgin and British Airways had still not come to an agreement concerning damages, and it was not clear whether Virgin would pursue this further through the courts. British Airways had offered £9 million in compensation, but Virgin claimed that this included unacceptable constraints on its freedom to refer to the affair in future.

One fundamental aspect of this headline rivalry between British Airways and Virgin Atlantic Airways, is that each company was able to identify the other as a significant competitor. Each recognized the presence of the other firm as part of the market environment and that this had implications for its own competitive policies. In this particular case, the recognition of mutual competition was made more intense by the personal rivalry of Richard Branson, the flamboyant owner of Virgin, and Lord King, then chairman of

BA. But whether there is this personal element or not, the crucial feature from an economic point of view is that the two firms recognized each other as competitors.

Thus the international airline carrier market is characterized by a recognized mutual interdependence between a small number of clearly identified firms. This implies that a firm will need to take into account the responses of its rivals when formulating its own policy. If a new competitive policy introduced by one firm results in sparking off countermeasures by its rivals, then this expected response will need to be considered in advance by the firm in order to determine its most advantageous policy. This kind of market structure where firms recognize their mutual interdependence is known as *oligopoly* and is the subject of this chapter. In Section 2 we will look at some examples of oligopoly markets, and Section 3 will introduce *game theory* to look at one kind of interdependence that is found in such markets. Section 4 will extend this analysis of interdependence by examining the *prisoners' dilemma* game in relation to collusion and strategic alliances. Finally, Section 5 will develop some links between this analysis and that of Chapters 3 and 4 by constructing a demand curve facing a profit-maximizing firm operating within an oligopolistic market.

2   Oligopoly and market structure

Definitions

Oligopoly

An oligopoly is a market with such a small number of rival firms that there is a recognized mutual interdependence between them. A firm operating in such an environment is known as an *oligopolist*. If there are only two such firms, this market structure is known as a *duopoly*, and the two firms are *duopolists*.

Strategic interdependence

Interdependence between firms means that a firm has to take into account the expected reaction of rival firms when deciding on its own strategy.

Oligopoly is generally recognized to be the most significant market form in advanced economies. As we have seen, oligopolies occur where there are so few competitors that there is an important element of mutual strategic interdependence between them. This interdependence can make corporate decision making very complicated for a firm which tries to outguess the expected reaction of its rivals when considering changes in its own policies.

Oligopoly tends to be a feature of those markets which are dominated by a small number of clearly identifiable firms producing similar goods. This may be found at the level of the local neighbourhood, at the level of the national economy, or at a global level where firms compete for customers across national boundaries. In these markets competing firms tend to recognize each other as rivals. This holds for markets where the number of competing firms is not large, or where the brand name or maker's 'marque' provides each firm's product with a distinct identity. In such markets, it is possible to identify the percentage share of total sales accruing to each oligopolist, and this information is eagerly sought by rival firms. Some oligopolists set up their own market research department to provide them with up-to-date information on market shares. In addition, market research and marketing agencies specialize in producing this information and selling it to clients. Thus it is a characteristic feature of oligopoly markets that each firm watches market shares closely, and knows that rival firms do so too.

Consider the case of the airline carrier market, and the intense rivalry between British Airways and Virgin Atlantic. In 1991, British Airways had a 35.6 per cent share of the UK international scheduled air traffic and Virgin Atlantic had only 1.9 per cent (*Airlines*, 1993, p.39). But Virgin had chosen to compete with BA only on selected routes over the North Atlantic which were particularly profitable, and this led to BA's accusation that Virgin's competitive strategy amounted to 'cherry picking' the most lucrative routes. In the North Atlantic market, Virgin's market share amounted to 10 per cent while British Airways' share was 40 per cent, according to a Reuters survey in 1992 (*Financial Times*, 11 May 1992). The international airline carrier market is characterized by growing competition as the national flag carriers have had to face the increased competition of a deregulated era, and where the different airlines have become fully aware of the changes in price and service offered by their rivals. In such a context, the threat of a small but growing independent airline such as Virgin Atlantic, which deliberately sets itself the task of offering a more competitive product than its large rival, is disproportionate to its actual size.

The motor vehicle market is another example of oligopoly. Each company watches the moves made by rival firms over model development, fuel consumption, safety, price and service. Each firm watches its own market share. In the early 1990s there were six major manufacturers in Western Europe – Volkswagen (16.7 %), General Motors (12.8%), PSA (12.0%), Fiat (11.4 %), Ford (11.3%) and Renault (10.6%) – but the companies with small market shares were by no means insignificant and included Nissan (3.5%), BMW (3.3%), Mercedez-Benz (2.8%), Toyota and Rover (both 2.7%), Mazda (1.8%), Volvo and Honda (both 1.4%) and Mitsubishi (1.3 %). (*UK Motor Industry,*1993, p.27; data for January to July 1993.)

For both the airline carrier market and the motor vehicle market, the early 1990s were a time of great change. Recession in Europe and Japan but buoyant markets in the USA, Asia and China held out both the threat of economic failure and the lure of economic success. Competition was becoming increasingly 'global'; successful companies were those that were able to innovate and keep ahead of international competitors while also steadily reducing costs, and this had implications for research and development, labour relations, purchasing and marketing on a global scale. It is in this dynamic and global context that many oligopoly markets must be understood. As each firm prepares its strategy, it has to bear in mind that rival firms are also preparing theirs: it must anticipate other firms' plans as well as their reactions to its own plans.

So far I have mentioned just two cases of oligopoly markets, but there are many other examples. Some will have a global reach, but others will be nationally or locally based.

Question

Try to think of other examples of oligopolies. Consider some goods or services that your have purchased recently. Perhaps your own neighbourhood shopping centre provides some examples?

The following examples seem to me to provide good examples of oligopolies:

- disposable nappies
- breakfast cereals
- domestic appliances (cookers, refrigerators, washing machines and dishwashers)
- instant coffee
- carbonated drinks
- cigarettes
- confectionery
- detergents
- petrol
- high street banks
- supermarket chains

Even this relatively short list shows how pervasive oligopoly is.

Some instances of oligopoly may occur where there are large economies of scale in production. As explained in Chapter 4, economies of scale exist where the cost of producing a unit of output is lower at higher rates of output. The minimum efficient size may represent a large proportion of the domestic market, so that any individual domestic market may be fully supplied by a small number of firms. The motor vehicle market and the domestic appliance market are examples. Looking only at the domestic market, however, may be misleading if the product is traded internationally and there is fierce international competition.

Sometimes oligopolies are associated with products where the brand image or 'marque' is important in selling the product. There may be a few famous brands that are household names and which dominate the market even though there may not be significant economies of scale in production. Goods such as confectionery, instant coffee, carbonated drinks, detergents, cigarettes and breakfast cereals come into this category.

Neighbourhood oligopolies in the retailing of goods and services are quite common. A neighbourhood with two or three supermarkets or corner stores or hairdressers would be an example. A busy road junction or roundabout with two petrol filling stations facing each other would be an example of a local duopoly. Similarly, the presence of two or three high street banks trading in the same neighbourhood would be another example. These neighbourhood oligopolies in retailing are also evident at the national level where, for example, a small number of supermarket or banking chains dominate the retailing of those goods and services throughout the national market.

Even from this brief overview, it is clear that there are different kinds of oligopolies relating to different kinds of products, different kinds of branded goods and different degrees of local, national or international competition. What they all have in common is the competitive rivalry that takes place between a relatively small number of identifiable firms which inevitably come to recognize their mutual interdependence.

3   Oligopoly and interdependence

3.1   Introducing game theory

It was argued above that the distinguishing characteristic of an oligopolist is that it recognizes the mutual interdependence existing between itself and its rivals. This means that it has to anticipate the strategic plans of rival firms as well as their reactions to its own policy. As you can imagine, this is not at all straightforward and will involve a firm in trying to outguess the tactics and objectives of its rivals, together with their reactions to events taking place in the market. The success of any firm's strategy depends partly on the extent to which it can correctly estimate the future moves of its competitors.

In trying to understand the possible outcomes in any situation, economists have been helped enormously by the insights of *game theory* which is expressly directed at analysing strategic responses in situations of mutual interdependence between a small number of players.

Game theory

Game theory analyses the range of 'best moves' available in a situation of mutual interdependence. A *game* is a situation where decision-makers recognize this mutual interdependence. The decision-makers in a game are known as players. The plan of action adopted by a player is known as a *strategy*, and decisions which recognize this mutual interdependence are known as *strategic decisions*. Thus *game theory is the study of strategic decision making*.

Game theory assumes that players are self-interested in that they try to maximize their own *pay-off* from the game. In economic games, the pay-off is usually taken to be profits, output or sales, but there is no restriction on the form the pay-off can take. A game may be a one-off game that is played just once, or it may be a repeated game that is played again and again.

The behavioural assumptions of game theory are:

1   *individualistic* – in that the pay-off is calculated individually for each player without recourse to wider notions of collective well-being, and

2   *rationalistic* – in that players are deemed able to calculate pay-offs correctly and then select the one that will maximize individual pay-off.

In presenting a game, the range of potential pay-offs are presented in a *pay-off matrix*, which is a tabular array showing all the various possible outcomes on the basis of which the players individually select their own preferred strategy. The actual values of the pay-offs are normally selected arbitrarily to illustrate particular outcomes of a game and are not intended to represent realistic values for actual games played out in real situations. This means that it is the structure of pay-offs that is important rather than their absolute levels.

The results of game theory are of wide application including situations of war, politics, business, personal and family relations, as well as economics. In an introductory book on game theory entitled *Thinking Strategically: the Competitive Edge in Business, Politics, and Everyday Life*, Avinish Dixit and Barry Nalebuff argue that life is itself a game, and that strategic thinking is required in just about all aspects of life. They write:

> … think of the difference between the decisions of a lumberjack and those of a general. When the lumberjack decides how to chop wood, he does not expect the wood to fight back; his environment is neutral. But when the general tries to cut down the enemy's army, he must anticipate and overcome resistance to his plans. Like the general, you must recognize that your business rivals, prospective spouse, and even your child are intelligent and purposive people. Their aims often conflict with yours, but they include some potential allies. Your own choice must allow for the conflict, and utilize the cooperation. Such interactive decisions are called strategic, and the plan of action appropriate to them is called a strategy.
>
> *(Dixit and Nalebuff, 1991, pp.1–2)*

Dixit and Nalebuff are emphasizing the interactive nature of strategic decisions where the environment is not neutral. Economists have also come to realize that the environment facing many firms is not neutral, and that firms' own actions produce feedback effects that they have to take into account. This is what differentiates oligopolists from other kinds of firms and makes game theory an important part of the study of oligopoly.

Consider what it might mean to say that strategic decision making implies that a firm's environment is not neutral. If a firm is faced with the choice between decision A and decision B, and it knows that other firms will react differently to A than to B, then a smart firm will take those other firms' reactions into account. Indeed, a really smart firm will deliberately try to manipulate those other firms into reacting in a way that benefits itself. In this manner, a firm can try actively to affect its own market environment by anticipating the strategic consequences of its own actions. For this reason, theories of oligopoly emphasize that the environment in which firms operate is not simply given to them as a natural part of the landscape, but is to a significant degree constructed by their own actions. From this point of view, 'market structure' is not entirely external to firms, but is to some degree the outcome of past behaviour.

Notice, too, the behavioural presuppositions in the passage which are both individualistic and rationalistic. Dixit and Nalebuff take it for granted that we relate to our business rivals, prospective spouse and even our children in some measure just as a general might relate to his enemies. Just as the general rationally and self-interestedly calculates his own best strategy vis-à-vis the enemy, so may business rivals, spouses and parents calculate their best interest. Notice, too, how Dixit and Nalebuff incorporate both conflict and co-operation in the passage. They recognize that players in the game will not always have aims that conflict, and so they advise players to utilize the co-operation as well as allowing for the conflict. But, given the self-interested premises of the game, co-operation is restricted here to functioning as another weapon that a smart player can use to secure the appropriate individual pay-off. Co-operation is not regarded as an alternative behavioural mode with its own norms, but as an instrument for achieving individual objectives. I shall return to this issue of conflict and co-operation in Section 4.

Game theory has been enormously influential in recent years in analysis of market situations of mutual interdependence. As with any other metaphor or theoretical framework, however, seeing competitive behaviour as a particular kind of game brings with it certain presuppositions. These suppositions help to give the approach its power in addressing technical issues and in reformulating old problems, but these presuppositions may also remain relatively unquestioned. In this case, a point at issue is whether self-interested decision making is appropriate in situations of significant interdependence, as it is in just these cases that any player's decision most affects other players.

For the moment, I will continue by using game theory to explore market interdependence amongst a small group of competing firms, starting with the case of price competition.

3.2   Price competition

In the course of this chapter, we will consider a number of possible strategies available to an oligopolist which wants to increase profits. One possible strategy involves competing with other firms on the basis of changing the price charged for the product. In price competition, the oligopolist may reduce price in the attempt to generate more sales and increase its market share. Alternatively, the oligopolist may increase price in the hope that the higher price more than compensates for some reduction in sales caused by the higher price.

Given the high degree of interdependence, the oligopolist would have to consider the possible reactions of its rivals if it changes the price of its product. One possible outcome is that rival firms would take no action at all but would carry on exactly as before. But the oligopolist may well decide that this is not the most likely outcome. If it generates more sales as a result of its price reduction, then the sales of rival firms must fall. In this case, is it reasonable to expect that rival firms would sit by and do nothing but watch their own sales decline?

The oligopolist may think such inaction unlikely. In this case, it is more likely that rival firms would also reduce price in order to reclaim lost customers. They might reduce price by a small amount just to limit the extent of lost sales. Or they might exactly match the first firm's price reduction in order to establish the original relative market shares between them. In the latter case, the relative position of the firms would be the same as before the price reduction, although each would have lower profits. On the other hand, the rival firms may not be content with simply restoring the original relative situation, but might be provoked into a more aggressive stance; they might reduce price by an even greater amount in order to undercut the first firm's price reduction. The first oligopolist should then take this possibility into account in deciding whether to reduce its price. Does it really want to start off the possibility of a ruinous price war with its rivals, pushing the price down lower and lower until they all regret that it ever started in the first place? Does it expect that rivals will respond aggressively, or are they likely to settle for a quiet life if their market share is not reduced by too great an amount? In considering these issues, the oligopolist is likely to take into account many factors – including the past history of relations between the firms, whether rivals have been aggressive in the past, and whether the total market is capable of much overall expansion if all firms are cutting price.

Similarly, in considering a possible price increase, a firm will consider how rival oligopolists are likely to respond. If the rivals take no action, then the first firm would lose sales to them. Does it really want to let this happen and allow rival firms to gain a larger share of the market at the original price? Alternatively, if rival firms follow and increase their price, then the relative position of firms is preserved, but they may well have to be content with sharing a smaller market between them.

An implication of the oligopolist's recognition of interdependence is that the number of possible outcomes has increased. If the oligopolist could ignore the issue of possible retaliation, then there would be only two possible outcomes to compare with the existing state of affairs: I will label them outcome B with a lower price and a higher rate of sales, and outcome C with a higher price and a lower rate of sales. Once the possibility of retaliation is included, however, there are four possible outcomes, since each of B and C is now associated with two possibilities depending on whether rivals firms react or not. These four possible outcomes can be presented in a 2×2 tabular array or matrix as shown in Figure 5.1.

In the first row in Figure 5.1, the two possible outcomes if firm 1 reduces price are labelled B_1 and B_2; in the second row, C_1 and C_2 are the outcomes if it decides to increase price. The columns of Figure 5.1 show that the outcome of firm 1's strategy is dependent on the reaction of other firms. If it is expected that other firms will not react, then the outcomes for firm 1 are the cells in the first column marked as B_1 and C_1. If, however, it is expected that they will take action, then the outcomes for firm 1 are those shown in the second column as B_2 and C_2.

Firm 1 \ Rival firms	no reaction	reaction
reduce price	B_1	B_2
increase price	C_1	C_2

Figure 5.1   **Firm 1's possible strategies**

Question

Which of these four cells represent the best possible outcomes for firm 1, and which represent the worst possible outcomes?

In the case of a price reduction, the best outcome for firm 1 arises when it is able to take sales away from rival firms. Therefore, cell B_1 is unambiguously better for firm 1 than B_2. In the case of the price increase, the best outcome arises for firm 1 if rivals do react. Therefore, cell C_2 is unambiguously better for firm 1 than C_1. Thus, the best strategy for firm 1 is asymmetric with respect to rival firms' responses: in the case of a price reduction, firm 1 would prefer other firms not to follow its action, but in the case of a price increase, firm 1 would prefer it if they followed suit. This is represented in Figure 5.2 by deleting the cells which firm 1 would least prefer in order to show its most preferred options.

Firm 1 \ Rival firms	no reaction	reaction
reduce price	B_1	—
increase price	—	C_2

Figure 5.2   **Firm 1's preferred strategies**

In Figure 5.2, cells B_2 and C_1 have been erased to highlight the most advantageous strategies for firm 1. Without knowing further details of the firm's demand curve (and cost curves), it is not possible to know whether cell B_1 or C_2 is more advantageous for firm 1. Note, however, that the best strategy for firm 1 is dependent on rival firms' expected reaction. In the language of game theory, we say that there is no dominant strategy for firm 1 in this game. This means that the actual strategy chosen by firm 1 depends crucially on how it expects rival firms to react.

Definition

Dominant strategy

A dominant strategy is one that is preferred by a player irrespective of the strategy chosen by the other player.

Question

With this in mind, how do you think firm 1 should expect rival firms to react? The crucial issue here is whether other firms are equally likely to respond to a price cut as to a price increase. What would you expect?

Some economists have argued that oligopolists expect that rival firms are more likely to react to a price reduction than to a price increase. If price is reduced by firm 1, then the result will be to take sales away from rivals; in this case, the rivals are worse off as a result of the strategy of firm 1 and so may well feel that they have to retaliate. If firm 1 increases its price, however, it will lose sales to rival firms; in this case, they gain from firm 1's strategy without doing anything. Thus, rivals have more of an incentive to retaliate in the case of a price reduction than a price increase.

With this result in mind, we can return to the matrix summarizing firm 1's possible strategies and delete the cells that are least likely to occur. This means deleting cells B_1 and C_2 as shown in Figure 5.3.

In Figure 5.3, cells B_1 and C_2 have been deleted as these represent rival firms' least likely strategies. This means that if firm 1 correctly anticipates rival reactions, it knows that the strategies actually available to it are those as shown by cells B_2 and C_1.

Rival firms Firm 1	no reaction	reaction
reduce price	—	B_2
increase price	C_1	—

Figure 5.3 **Firm 1's available strategies**

Question

Examine firm 1's available strategies in Figure 5.3 and compare these with firm 1's preferred strategies in Figure 5.2. On the basis of this comparison, outline the best pricing policy for firm 1.

I wonder if you found anything surprising in your result. Out of the four possible cells, the two cells that are preferred by firm 1 are B_1 and C_2, the two cells that are least likely to occur given the expected strategies of rival firms. Similarly, the two cells that are most likely to be available as strategies for firm 1 are B_2 and C_1, the two cells that are least preferred by that firm. What can we conclude from this? The conclusion, I think, is that the oligopolist is less likely to choose either to increase or reduce its current price once it takes into account the possible reactions of its rivals.

This example shows that taking into account other firms' likely reactions will materially affect an oligopolist's decisions. But this interdependent decision-making process is extraordinarily difficult to model, as we shall see later. One problem is that firms don't know other firms' policies. This means that a firm will have to make informed guesses about the output or price decisions of other firms, and their investment or marketing plans. Similarly, one oligopolist does not know another firm's objectives. The previous section noted that in game theory it is normally assumed that players are rational in the sense that they try to maximize their pay-off. It is therefore rational for a firm which is itself a profit maximizer to assume that this is also what other firms try to achieve. As you know from Chapter 4, however, this assumption is controversial, since some economists argue that firms do not try to maximize profits but have other objectives such as a target rate of growth or satisficing, or even multiple objectives which are traded off against each other.

Non-price competition

One implication of this particular model of oligopolistic interdependence is that firms may be cautious about the effects of price changes on their rivals. This suggests in turn that oligopolists will often look for non-price forms of competition which are less risky and less likely to prove ruinous once enacted. Non-price competition can take many forms depending on the characteristics of the market. Sometimes it takes the form of product improvement, or introduction of new products altogether, although the dividing line between product improvement and new products can sometimes become fuzzy. The motor vehicle market is characterized by continuous product improvement in terms of styling, safety, fuel consumption and so on. In the early 1990s the MPV or multi-purpose vehicle was developed as a cross between a minivan and an estate car, but should the MPV be regarded as a new product or as an improvement of an old one?

Similarly, many firms try to improve services as a form of non-price competition, but again the dividing line between the product and the service is often fuzzy. For example, although competition between rival international airlines does include recurrent price cutting and discounts, great emphasis is also placed on improved service as a means of luring customers away from rival airlines. So the business traveller is offered better in-flight meals and service, bigger seats, on-board massages, free gifts, executive lounges with office machines, and so on. Classic airline policy has been to offer improved services to the front-of-cabin passengers who provide most of the revenue, and reserve price cutting for the leisure travellers at the back of the plane, although one of the main problems for airlines in the recession of the early 1990s was that many business passengers were switching to the cheaper tickets.

The development of new products, new product variants and improved service are aspects of the overriding importance of constant innovation in both products and processes. In pursuit of innovation, firms have to determine appropriate investment strategies that will provide them with the necessary new ideas, equipment, technical know-how or specialized personnel. Thus, particular investment strategies undertaken by firms also constitute another form of non-price competition.

Non-price competition in oligopoly markets also includes increased inducements to consumers to purchase a largely unchanged product. These forms of competition include advertising to promote brand loyalty, free gifts, stamps or coupons that can be collected in exchange for gifts, or extra volume (e.g. 10 per cent extra in the packaging). Products such as detergents, confectionery, cigarettes and soft drinks are subject to extensive advertising. Competition between filling stations where there is relatively little scope for product improvement sometimes takes the form of free gifts. Competition between rival supermarkets takes many forms including price competition over selected items, and non-price forms of competition relating to quality of service, such as width of shopping aisles, speed of check-out and free car parking. Very often an oligopolist has a package of competitive responses, and the mix of policies is varied according to circumstances and changing expectations about other firms.

Finally, this model of interdependence also implies that firms would be reluctant to change prices in response to small changes in costs for fear of setting off the unfavourable reactions of its rivals. An oligopolist may decide to absorb a cost increase rather than be the only firm to put up prices. Similarly, an oligopolist may achieve a reduction in costs but, fearing a price war, it may pass this on to the consumer in the form of an improved product.

So what happens if there is a general increase in costs? If a firm puts up its own price and discovers that all other firms have put up theirs, then that should suggest to it that cell C_2 is a possibility after all, and that it was mistaken in thinking otherwise. On the other hand, if the firm can distinguish between a general increase in costs and a specific increase affecting only itself, then it could pass on a general increase in costs but not its own increases. However, it is extremely difficult in an uncertain world for a firm to distinguish between a change in market prices resulting from a change in market demand, a change in other firms' costs, or from other firms' aggressive pricing policy. In any real world situation, a firm may well be using a mix of competitive policies and cost responses. Although our simple model may pick up on some aspects of this mix, it cannot do justice to the complexity of an oligopolist's overall competitive strategy.

3.3   Price wars

The analysis of the previous section helps to explain why price cutting is not more widespread and why it is that various forms of non-price competition are sometimes important in oligopoly markets. According to this analysis, oligopolists come to learn that there exists a certain price for the product which maximizes profits, and that deviations from this price result in lower profits. Oligopolists may discover this price by way of a learning process in the market. In the case of a price reduction, the oligopolist learns that the expected profit increase vanishes when other firms also reduce price. In the case of a price increase, it learns that the expected increase in profit does not materialize.

But price cutting does occur and so it is worth pausing to consider why this happens. Extra sales can come from a general increase in the quantity demanded as new consumers move into the market, or an individual oligopolist can benefit at the expense of other firms if it can poach their customers. If a single oligopolist reduces its price, it will hope to benefit from both sources of extra sales. If all firms reduce price by an equal amount, then there is only the first source of increased sales for any individual firm. Thus, if the firms expect the market demand to be sensitive to price cuts, then it is possible for them all to derive some benefit from a price reduction, even though any individual oligopolist would benefit less than would be the case if it were the only one to reduce price.

Questions

How would the analysis of this section help you to account for recent examples of competitive price cutting?

What was the outcome of the price war for the firms involved?

There is some evidence to suggest that price cutting is linked to the cyclical state of the economy; if the economy is in recession and sales are depressed, then there may be more of an incentive for all firms in an industry to reduce price. This may have been associated with the wave of price cutting in British supermarkets in early 1993 during a recession. Tesco supermarkets reduced prices on selected items, and some other supermarkets followed with similar specific cuts. Note, though, that by restricting the price reductions to specific items, the harmful effects of the price cuts were minimized for the price-cutting stores. Similarly, if an economy is expected shortly to be coming out of a recession, then firms may cut price as an aggressive policy to try to improve market shares and establish new customer loyalties in preparation for the coming upturn. This may explain to some degree the wave of price cutting in 1992–93 in transatlantic air fares.

Another factor accounting for price wars is that different firms may not be able to offer the same degree of price cuts. If different firms have different costs, then those firms that have the lowest costs will be able to offer the greatest price reductions to its customers, and so may be able to attract a disproportionate amount of sales. Thus, a price war may be started by a firm that believes that it has lower costs than other firms. In terms of Figure 5.3, this means that the firm initiating the price cuts thinks that cell B_1 is available to it as a strategy after all. An example of this is provided by the price war started in the UK in the early 1990s by Superdrug, the fast-growing discount drugstore company, against Boots which was the largest chemists chain in the UK. First of all, Superdrug reduced the price of perfumes by up to 30 per cent at 42 of its 680 stores. It then followed this by cutting branded suncare products by 25 per cent. Analysts were agreed that the main target of Superdrug's actions was the Boots chain. Boots' response to the perfume price cuts was fairly measured, gradually reducing perfume prices and only in those stores located near the discounted Superdrug stores. In the case of the suncare price battle, however, Boots reacted immediately by cutting prices by 30 per cent in all its 1000 stores. According to Boots company statements at the time, the more determined response to the suncare price cut was a deliberate strategy employed to send a particular message to Superdrug: 'One reason we have taken a high profile this time is to send a clear signal that we care about our market share', Gordon Hourston, Managing Director of Boots, is reported to have said (*Financial Times*, 12 May 1993). Here, Boots is sending a clear message to Superdrug that they would react to price cuts by cutting prices still further, and that they would not stand idly by while their market shares were eroded.

Another element in the price-cutting game is that firms are sometimes under pressure to reduce costs. A number of firms have instituted schemes for encouraging a constant flow of suggestions for cutting costs, both from employees and from suppliers. In many Japanese customer-supplier relationships, it is expected that suppliers' prices will be reduced in the course of time, and Japanese business methods have popularized the idea of constant cost-cutting in order to produce leaner and more competitive enterprises. In such an environment, the issue of price-cutting is transformed from the question of whether other firms might follow suit and destroy the advantage of being the only firm to reduce price, to that of the necessity of reducing price in order not to be the only firm that does not reduce price. In this case, cell B_1 has to be reinterpreted. Figures 5.1 to 5.3 were drawn on the assumption of *ceteris paribus*, which includes the assumption that costs remain unchanged. In a period of rapid cost-cutting where price reductions (relative to product quality) are the norm, a price war would take place when prices were reduced relatively to the falling costs.

As in the conduct of many wars, some moves in these price wars are exploratory, testing the other side to see the kinds of response that might be offered, and testing the market, too, to see how responsive the consumer is to price and quality changes. In these cases, the price cuts are part of the learning process for firms who are exploring the limits of their rivals' responses. In addition, some firms may take a long-term view of these skirmishes, hoping to drive out the weaker rivals by an ostentatious show of strength in the short term. In these circumstances, a firm may temporarily reduce prices to the absolute minimum in order to drive out weaker or smaller firms which it thinks will be unable to bear the short-term losses caused by this. If the price is reduced even below costs, this is known as 'predatory pricing' as the objective is to force the weaker firms out of the industry, and then afterwards to increase price and take advantage of the reduced competition in the future. In many countries, predatory pricing is illegal.

Section 3 has argued that an oligopolist's strategies are fundamentally affected by the reactions that it expects from its rivals in an uncertain world. But if this is the case, then perhaps an oligopolist would earn greater profits if it could come to some sort of agreement with other firms. Given the highly interdependent nature of oligopoly markets, perhaps it would be in the interests of all oligopolists to agree on strategy together? This is considered in the following section.

4   Competition, collusion and co-operation

4.1   Introduction: individualism and co-operation

In Section 3.1, I argued that a paradox for game theory is the tension between an individualistic approach and the interdependence between the outcomes for the players. This paradox is illustrated by a game known as the *prisoners' dilemma*. This is set up as a game involving two prisoners who are faced with the decision as to whether they should confess or deny having committed a crime which they are alleged to have undertaken together. The structure of pay-offs in this game illustrates how decisions taken independently can lead to an inferior outcome for the two prisoners compared with the situation where the decision is taken jointly.

Note again that the behavioural assumptions are individualistic and rationalistic. The pay-offs for the prisoners take the form of years of imprisonment, and the single objective of each prisoner is to minimize the individual period of imprisonment. The issue of their guilt or innocence is beside the point, as is the question of any moral reflection on their alleged crime, the purpose of their imprisonment, their loyalty to each other, or the impact of their decision on the wider society.

In the prisoners' dilemma game, the best solution for the prisoners would be to agree jointly to deny having committed the crime, since this will minimize their individual periods of imprisonment. When they are interrogated separately, however, it turns out that the best option for each individually is to confess, and this holds whatever each assumes about the behaviour of the other prisoner. But, if both prisoners do confess, this results in the worst possible outcome for the prisoners since this entails the longest period of imprisonment. Thus, the best option is the collective decision but this is ruled out when the decision is taken individually, and the individual option turns out to be the worst possible when both prisoners' decisions are considered together. The significance of this result in game theory is that it shows how individual decision making can in certain circumstances lead to inferior results for the players of the game.

The prisoners' dilemma

In this game the outcomes for two prisoners are compared on the basis that each prisoner chooses whether to deny or confess. As each prisoner has the choice of two courses of action, there are $2 \times 2 = 4$ possible outcomes altogether. These four possible outcomes are presented in a 2×2 pay-off matrix where the pay-offs are denominated in terms of years of imprisonment. The numerical structure of the pay-off matrix shows how individual decision making leads to an inferior outcome (for the prisoners) compared with collective decision making, but the actual values selected to illustrate this are chosen arbitrarily.

The two prisoners are kept in separate cells. Each one knows that, if both confess, each will receive four years' imprisonment but that, if they both deny, each will receive only two years' imprisonment. They also know that, if one confesses and the other denies, then the confessing prisoner receives one year and the denying prisoner receives five years. These possibilities are laid out in the pay-off matrix in Figure 5.4. Note again that it is the structure of pay-offs that determines the apparently paradoxical result, while the illustrative numbers chosen are arbitrary as long as they are consistent with this structure.

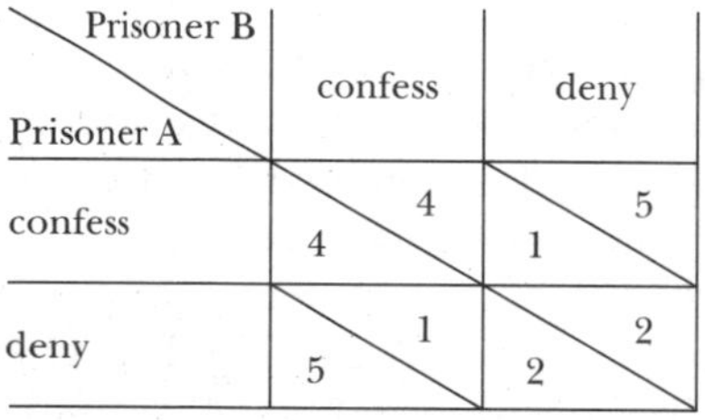

Consider A's situation shown in the lower left-hand triangle within each of the four cells of the matrix; here the cells are read vertically. If B confesses, it is better for A to confess (i.e. four years as against five years) and if B denies, it is also better for A to confess (i.e. one year as against two years). Whatever B does, it is in A's self-interest to confess. Thus, confessing is a dominant strategy for A since it is preferred by A no matter which decision is taken by B.

Similarly, whatever A does, it is in B's interest to confess: four years as against five years if A confesses, and one as against two years if A denies. Again, confessing is a dominant strategy for B. Prisoner B is shown in the right-hand triangles; here the cells are read horizontally.

Therefore, both A and B confess and each receives four years, even though had they both denied, they would each have received two years.

The outcome is unaffected by each prisoner believing that the other will keep to a collective decision. Even if a prisoner does believe that the other will adhere to a collective agreement and deny the crime, it is still in the best interest of that prisoner to confess. The problem does not lie in a lack of trust in the other, but in the lack of commitment to the collective decision in the face of the apparently superior pay-off to the individual decision.

Figure 5.4 **Pay-off matrix showing prisoners' dilemma**

Exercise 5.1

It was emphasized above that it is the structure of pay-offs, not their absolute level, that is significant. Bearing this in mind, try constructing your own version of the prisoners' dilemma game. Try working out a situation where this game would be appropriate, and then illustrate it using numbers of your own choice.

The answer to this exercise presents a general form of the pay-off structure for the prisoners' dilemma game which you can use to check that your own numerical values have the right structure.

The importance of the prisoners' dilemma game lies in showing how independent decision making can lead to inferior results for the players. In such cases, collective decisions are more efficient from the point of view of the players. The applications of this game are extraordinarily wide-ranging and can be applied to many areas of business, politics and public policy making. Because it starkly demonstrates the suboptimal consequences for individual agents of their own individual self-interested decision making, it has been used to provide arguments for a number of different types of public policy interventions or contractual/institutional frameworks.

In the case of the prisoners, the institutional context of separate interrogation may be justified by the argument that it prevents prisoners from jointly fabricating evidence in their favour. In other cases, individual decision making may be viewed as having less social justification. Consider, for example, the case of the need to preserve the ozone layer. Is it worthwhile for an individual consumer to pay extra in order to buy an ozone-friendly refrigerator? Whether or not others buy such a refrigerator, self-interested behaviour will dictate that such a purchase is not worthwhile because one single purchase will not have any discernible effect on a better environment. But, if everyone thinks in this way, then no one will buy an ozone-friendly refrigerator, even if everyone's preferred option is that everyone should. One solution is for there to be an external agency in the form of government to impose the collective solution, for example by obliging manufacturers to meet certain product specifications.

The prisoners' dilemma has been used to show how individual decision making may lead to inferior results compared with collective decision making, even where the outcomes are assessed in terms of individual preferences. Thus the game is consistent with the individualistic and rationalistic premises of game theory. Indeed, the strength of the paradox is heightened by the fact that a collective decision-making procedure is found to be superior even when measured in terms of self-interested individual preferences. In Section 4.2 I shall show how this game can be applied to cases of cartels and in Section 4.3 I shall examine its relevance for strategic alliances.

4.2   Collusion

If oligopolists get together and agree on their strategy, then surely each one could do better than competing against the others and having to outguess their strategy? The advantages of collusion to the oligopolists seem straightforward, and so do their disadvantages to the paying public. Most countries have enacted legislation against collusion, but one policy problem is that collusion can be difficult to trace. Collusion may be explicit, with written or spoken forms of agreement, or it may be implicit without any such forms. Many collusive agreements take the form of secret or tacit agreements between firms and are difficult to discover. For example, if firms tend to have similar prices over a period of time, is this evidence of an agreement not to compete over price, or is it evidence that the firms are independently facing similar cost conditions?

There is also a problem from the point of view of the firms' interests: collusion is a risky business because cartels can be unstable. Consider a case where two duopolists collude to restrict output and so to drive up the price. They calculate that if each firm keeps to the agreement and restricts output as agreed, then both firms will gain increased profits. In this case, the strategic variable is the quantity produced, and the firms accept the price as given by the market. Note that this is the opposite of the case discussed above where firms decide on price and then sell what they can at that price. But why should the firms keep to their agreement? What are the incentives and penalties for reneging on the agreement?

If both firms adhere to the terms of the agreement on restricting output, then each firm will increase profits. But consider what happens if one firm reneges on the agreement and increases its output. Then, the extent of the anticipated price increase is reduced but, since the defaulting firm is selling more than allowed for under the agreement, it calculates that its profits will increase by an even greater amount. The other firm, however, finds that, as the price increase is not as high as expected, its profits increase less than expected. The result is that the defaulting firm makes even greater profits at the expense of the other firm. Thus, each firm has an incentive to default, but, if both do so, breaking the agreement and producing more than agreed, then each firm's profits increase less than if they had jointly restricted output.

This situation can be depicted on a 2 × 2 pay-off matrix. Each firm can choose one of two strategies, to keep to the agreement or to break it, so this makes four possible outcomes overall. These strategic choices are shown in the pay-off matrix in Figure 5.5 using illustrative numbers.

In Figure 5.5, firm A's possible decisions are shown in the left-hand triangle and firm B's in the right-hand triangle in each of the four cells of the matrix. If both firms keep to the agreement, profits increase by £100 for each firm as shown in the bottom right cell. If, however, one firm defaults and the other plays fair, then the outcome is that the defaulting firm receives £150 more profits and the other firm receives only £10 more. These two outcomes are shown in the bottom left and top right cells. If both firms default, they each earn £50 more profits as shown in the top left cell.

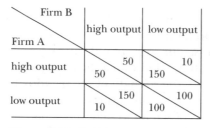

Figure 5.5   **Collusion to restrict output**

Question

Which of the four cells do you think represents the most likely final outcome for firm A and firm B?

Consider firm A. It has the choice of keeping to the agreement or not. If it keeps to the agreement and produces a low output as shown in the bottom row, it will receive either £10 or £100 more depending on whether firm B defaults or not. If firm A produces more output than agreed, it will receive either £50 or £150 depending on firm B's action. So whatever firm B does, it is in firm A's interest to produce more than agreed. In this case, there is a dominant strategy for firm A as its best course of action is independent of firm B's decision. The same reasoning applies to firm B; its best course of action is to default, and this holds whatever firm A decides to do. The outcome, therefore, is that both firms overproduce and the solution is represented by the top left cell in which each firm earns £50 more profit. But if they had both kept to the agreement, each would have received £100 more profits. Hence, although the overall best solution for the firms (not the consumers!) is that both should keep to the agreement and earn £100 more profit each, taking the strategic decision separately means that each firm finds that it is in its best interest to default; in this case each firm earns only £50 more profit.

This example of collusion to restrict output provides therefore another example of a prisoners' dilemma game. From the point of view of the colluding firms, the best outcome requires that each firm adheres to the agreement, but it is in the interest of each firm to break the agreement, and this holds irrespective of whether it expects that the other firm will renege. It is for this reason that the pay-off structure in Figure 5.5 corresponds to the pay-off structure in the prisoners' dilemma game, as shown in the answer to Exercise 5.1 above.

We can apply this result to the case of collusion amongst oligopolists. There are strong incentives for individual firms to default, even though it would be in the best interests of all the firms taken together to adhere to the agreement. For this reason, cartels and collusive agreements have a tendency to be unstable. This application of the prisoners' dilemma game shows how decisions taken independently can lead to an inferior outcome for the players than a decision taken jointly. In the case of cartels it can be used to explain the inherent instability of agreements to restrict output in order to maintain an increased price. Whatever the other members of the cartel actually do, it is always in the interest of an individual member to break the agreement and produce a little extra. In this way it will have the benefit of both the higher price and the extra sales. If just one or two small firms do this, the cartel may yet survive but, as soon as this behaviour becomes widespread, the cartel will collapse because the increased rate of output will drive down the price.

Cartels among primary commodity producers – of which the most famous is OPEC, the Organization of Petroleum Exporting Countries – have often found it hard to maintain their unity, for this among other reasons. If just one small member country breaks its output quota, the effect on the price is hardly significant, but if a number of countries keep doing this, eventually the quota system breaks down, output rises sharply and the cartel collapses.

Cartels often find it hard to detect, prevent or punish firms which break the agreement. Detection requires information about rival behaviour and this may be more easily available if the number of sellers is small and sales are relatively frequent. Open information on price, however, may tend to promote the stability of collusion, by making it easier for the colluding firms to police their own members. Paradoxically, therefore, open price lists may actually promote stable collusion whereas secret price-setting may undermine it. This provides another example of the ways in which the institutional framework can produce particular outcomes in the prisoners' dilemma game.

Threats of punishment may be used to deter defaulting, but to be effective, such threats have to be 'credible', that is, it must be believed that the threat will in fact be carried out. Otherwise the threat becomes incredible and so loses its force. For example, one firm could threaten to flood the market with increased output and drive down the price if any other firm breaks the agreement and increases output. But although this threat would, if carried out, reduce the defaulting firm's profit, it would also reduce the profits of the firm administering the punishment. For this reason, the threat loses its credibility, and hence its effectiveness as a threat.

One way to establish credibility is through 'precommitment': that is, the punishing firm is precommitted in some way to imposing the punishment and cannot default on this. This precommitment is recognized by all the firms who are therefore discouraged from cheating. The success of a credible threat is that it does not have to be carried out.

Some contractual and marketing arrangements have binding effects which establish precommitment and hence constitute credible threats. For example, some contracts include a 'meet competition' clause. A buyer is assured that if another seller can offer the good at a lower price, then the first seller is obliged to sell at that price too. Some retail stores have this policy. If buyers can provide evidence that another store is selling the same goods at a lower price, the store will refund the difference. Buyers generally see this commitment as a sign of intense competition but it can also be seen as a form of precommitment in a strategic game. The 'meet competition' obligation functions as a precommitment that any price-cutting behaviour by a rogue store will be matched by the other stores; as a precommitment to punish default by matching it, the 'meet competition' agreement has the effect of deterring that default. This strategy may be analysed in the form of a prisoners' dilemma game using Figure 5.6.

Firm B → Firm A ↓	high price	low price
high price	5 5	8 0
low price	0 8	2 2

Figure 5.6 **Pay-off matrix for analysis of 'meet competition' as a form of precommitment**

Question

Explain how the pay-off matrix in Figure 5.6 corresponds to the prisoners' dilemma. How would the introduction of a 'meet competition' clause affect the outcome?

In this situation, each firm would end up selling at a low price because that is the dominant strategy for each firm. Whether firm B priced high or low, it would still be in firm A's interest to price low since that would give higher profits (£8 as opposed to £5 in the case of B's high price, and £2 as against £0 in the case of B's low price). Similarly for firm B, which would price low irrespective of A's pricing policy (£8 as against £5 if A prices high, and £2 as opposed to £0 if A prices low). If a 'meet competition' clause is introduced, however, this implies that price cuts by one firm have to be met by the other. This means that the two high-price/low-price combinations in the top right and bottom left cells are eliminated as possible outcomes. Faced with the two remaining cells of high/high and low/low, both firms would choose to price high.

This 'meet competition' example provides another instance of where institutional arrangements influence outcomes: contractual arrangements provide a form of precommitment that enables firms to escape from the prisoners' dilemma and enforce the more profitable collective solution. Competition policy, discussed in Chapter 8, tries to put an end to such collusive pricing agreements, but the analysis in this section underlines just how difficult this can be in practice. Without taking account of the strategic implications, it would readily be inferred that commitments such as open price lists and 'meet competition' agreements enhance competition by ensuring that all firms price competitively. Certainly, these policies are held out to customers as evidence of healthy competition at work. If in fact this is not always the case, and if such arrangements sometimes work to the detriment of price competition, then commonsense intuitions about competition may be turned upside down.

4.3 Strategic alliances

The collusive practices discussed in the previous section involve a minimal level of joint decision making. In recent years, many firms have begun to experiment with closer forms of co-operation in the form of strategic alliances. Faced with the rising costs of developing new technologies and making new products on a global basis, many large corporations are experimenting with strategic alliances. Many new projects are extremely capital intensive, requiring such large outlays that they are beyond the resources of a single firm; sharing the costs of development provides a way of sharing the risks involved. Strategic alliances also provide entry into new markets and into a more specialized technological base.

Strategic alliances involve transforming old rivals into new partners. Even where the partners are competing directly in the same market, complementary skills, facilities or access to new market possibilities may provide the basis for an alliance. Where the partners are not directly competing, mutually beneficial co-operation may come from technology licensing, supply arrangements, joint ventures, research agreements, mutual training schemes or just a cross-fertilization of people and ideas.

The idea of strategic alliances has been pioneered by Japanese firms with their greater commitment to relations of trust between trading firms, but the basic idea is now increasingly being adopted by others. Toshiba Corporation is one of these pioneering firms and has advertised its commitment to strategic alliances as a way of securing global growth by sharing the costs and the risks with other firms. Fumio Sato, President of Toshiba, argued that there is no contradiction between competition and strategic alliances.

> When you consider the severe economic environment today in Japan and the unsettled nature of most major overseas markets, you can understand our desire to try to turn yesterday's competitors into tomorrow's partners. We still compete with most of the companies with whom we have formed alliances. But we have found that co-operation is often more sensible in certain markets where it involves creating a new business opportunity.
>
> *(Fortune International, 23 August 1993, p.S.5)*

According to this view of strategic alliances, their main function is to promote competition rather than restrain it. By allowing the partners to develop into areas that would otherwise have been impossible, it is argued that strategic alliances facilitate an intensification of global competition rather than eroding it through collusion.

One reason for the different approach to the competitive implications of co-operative agreement between firms relates to the context in which they are seen as operating. The context for strategic alliances is that of a dynamic and global competition in which the most innovative and efficient firms are the ones which prosper. This view sees market competition as a journey into unknown territory, but a journey which is becoming increasingly specialized and expensive, and where travellers are ill-advised to venture alone.

This raises the question of the kind of collective decision making that takes place in such alliances. In the prisoners' dilemma game we saw that collective decision making may be more efficient than individual decision making in that it furthers individual self-interest more effectively. Hence, strategic alliances may be more effective in furthering the interests of the individual firms involved as they substitute joint for individual decision making. Here, precommitment is achieved by inter-firm shareholding and by reciprocal trading. In this way, minimal contractual obligations provide an institutional solution to the need for precommitment to the co-operative outcome.

But strategic alliances also raise the question of the cultural context in which such partnerships are viable. Do these commitments go beyond the furtherance of individual interests and minimal contractual obligations, to constitute a mutuality of interests in which different norms prevail? The prisoners' dilemma game precludes mutual trust between the players, but the successful operation of strategic alliances possibly does require background assumptions of basic levels of trust and reciprocity. If so, the commitment becomes more open-ended and subject to 'goodwill trust' which precludes opportunistic behaviour at the expense of the other partner. This in turn requires a different conception of business ethics and inter-firm relations. This issue has been the subject of considerable interest recently among economists as well as European and American firms seeking to learn from Japanese business practices (see for example Kay, 1993).

5   Models of the profit-maximizing oligopolist

5.1   Models of oligopoly

In this chapter we have covered a number of different approaches to strategic behaviour among oligopolists. In looking for a general principle to guide us, we could say that the diversity of actual situations in any economy means that it is not possible to have general laws which will predict what oligopolists will do in all circumstances. Rather, economists have developed a large number of different models of oligopoly which are then available to be applied in the complexity and diversity of real world situations. Game theory and oligopoly theory have been growth areas in economics in recent years and so the number of these models has proliferated. This is evidenced by state-of-the-art surveys summarizing findings for other economists (e.g. Schmalensee and Willig, 1989). One economist concluded such a survey of theories of oligopoly behaviour by describing these diverse theories as a 'bag of tools' which economists can apply to real oligopolies:

> Here is where the 'bag of tools' analogy applies. After learning the basic facts about an industry, the analyst with a working understanding of oligopoly theory should be able to use these tools to identify the main strategic aspects present in that industry. One industry may be competitive because rapid expansions in capacity are possible in short order and consumers are willing to switch suppliers in response to small price differentials. In another industry, advertising may serve a key strategic role, since brand loyalty is significant. Yet another industry may succeed in achieving a tacitly collusive outcome because secret price-cutting is impossible. And so on. Hopefully, as further progress is made, we will learn about additional modes of strategic behaviour and understand more fully the strategies already identified.

(Shapiro, 1989, p.409)

Carl Shapiro's emphasis is on the diversity of oligopoly responses, a diversity which game theoretic modelling has accentuated. Shapiro acknowledges that there is still much more to learn and that the theory of oligopoly is still far from complete.

We can see links here with the treatment of models in Chapter 2, where it was argued that the insights which any particular model can provide depend to a large degree on the kind of model that we build and the kinds of questions that we ask of it. In this chapter we have looked at the strategic consequences of firms' interdependence, and have drawn on game theory in order to do this. I have also raised some questions about the assumptions of game theory as a means of modelling inter-firm relations.

In this final section of the chapter, I shall pursue this issue of different kinds of modelling by linking these strategic aspects of oligopoly with the demand curve which you met in Chapter 3 and the concept of profit maximization you met in Chapter 4. In order to do this I shall derive a demand curve for the oligopolist, and I shall combine this with an examination of the implications for profit maximization.

5.2   The oligopolist's demand curve

In Section 3 we examined the case of an oligopolist which has to take into account the expected reactions of rival firms in deciding whether to change price. We considered the reasons why an oligopolist may expect an asymmetry of response from rivals, where price increases would not be followed by rival firms whereas price reductions would, and why, in this situation, the oligopolist would be unlikely to change price as a purposive competitive strategy.

Further, we also noted the circumstances in which an oligopolist would hold the opposite expectations. For example, if costs were increasing for the industry as a whole, the oligopolist might expect all firms to raise price. And if a firm faced lower costs than other firms, it might expect that its own price reductions would not be followed by rival firms.

Any firm's estimate of the demand curve it faces depends on its knowledge and expectations of the market that it supplies. Many firms employ market research consultants or econometricians to estimate the demand curve for their products. Ideally, then, firms have a working understanding of the demand conditions that they face but, in practice, these estimated demand relationships provide approximate and incomplete information. In addition, estimated demand relationships are uncertain because they are based on past data, whereas the firm really needs to know its demand curve for the current and subsequent periods.

In the case of an oligopolist, however, we have identified yet another source of uncertainty. The oligopolist's demand curve also depends on the reactions of its rivals. This information cannot be known with certainty and is not susceptible to market research enquiries. Any oligopolist over a period of time will have come to form certain expectations about the reactions of its rivals, and these expectations may perhaps be based on a previous process of experimentation with price changes to observe market reactions. For example, Superdrug learnt that if it cut the price of suntan lotion then Boots would repay in kind.

If the oligopolist expects that rivals are unlikely to follow an increase in price, then it would expect that a price increase would be accompanied by a relatively large fall in sales. In this case, the portion of the firm's demand curve above the existing price/quantity point would be relatively flat. Conversely, if the oligopolist expects that rivals would be likely to follow price reductions, then a price reduction would be expected to produce only a relatively small increase in sales. In this case, the portion of the firm's demand curve below the given price/quantity point would be relatively steep. This implies that the firm's demand curve is not a straight line or a smooth curve but instead has a 'kink' at the existing price/quantity point.

This demand curve is thus very different from the one you met in Chapter 3. That demand curve showed the market demand for the good in question. The oligopolist's demand curve, however, is a demand curve facing a single firm, not a market demand curve. Furthermore, the oligopolist's demand curve depends crucially on the prices being charged by rival firms; this is because the quantity demanded of its own product at any price must depend on the prices of rival products. Hence, the working demand curve for an oligopolist is a hypothetical demand curve based on its expectations about the behaviour of rival firms.

An illustration of this hypothetical kinked demand curve is shown in Figure 5.7 as *D*. The kink is found at the existing price *P,* and the existing output *Q.* For increases in price above *P,* the oligopolist expects that other firms will tend not to respond with price increases of their own. The oligopolist's demand curve above *P* is therefore relatively flat. An increase in price is expected to result in a relatively large reduction in the quantity demanded of the oligopolist's produce. For reductions in price below *P,* the oligopolist expects that other firms will tend to retaliate by reducing price in order not to lose market shares. The demand curve below *P* is therefore relatively steep. A reduction in price is not expected to increase sales very much.

Another way of understanding the kinked demand curve is to think of it as a combination of two separate demand curves based on different expectations about rival behaviour. One demand curve is based on the assumption that other firms will not react to changes in price. The other demand curve is based on the expectation that other firms will react to changes in price by following suit; this demand curve would be steeper than the former as sales

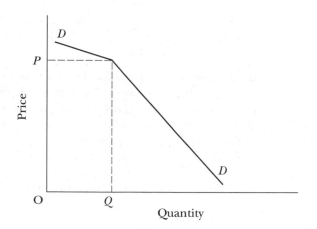

Figure 5.7 **An oligopolist's kinked demand curve**

are less responsive to changes in price. These two demand curves intersect at the existing price/quantity combination as shown in Figure 5.8.

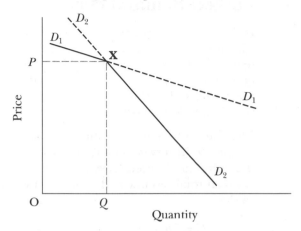

Figure 5.8   **Another look at the kinked demand curve**

The demand curve labelled D_1 is the one based on the expectation that other firms do not follow and so is flatter than D_2 which assumes that other firms do follow. If the oligopolist is at point X, the point of intersection, then it faces four possibilities corresponding to the four different portions of the demand curves. These are the same as the four different outcomes which we studied in Section 3.2 and which we categorized in the 2 × 2 array in Figure 5.1

Question

Which of the outcomes in Figure 5.1 (reproduced here) correspond to the four different portions of the demand curves in Figure 5.8?

Figure 5.1 is reproduced here so that you can insert those parts of the demand curves that fit into the corresponding cell of the matrix. Note that the price increases and reductions are from the existing price P in Figure 5.8.

Rival firms / Firm 1	no reaction	reaction
reduce price	B_1	B_2
increase price	C_1	C_2

Figure 5.1   **Firm 1's possible strategies**

The cells in Figure 5.1 which correspond to no reaction for the rival firms are cells B_1 and C_1. This means that cell B_1 corresponds to the lower portion of D_1 and cell C_1 to the upper part of D_1. Similarly, the cells B_2 and C_2 correspond to the case where the firms do react; this implies that cell B_2 corresponds to the lower part of D_2 and cell C_2 corresponds to the upper part of D_2.

We found in Section 3.2 that the cells which were most advantageous for the oligopolist were the ones that it could not expect to happen. For this reason, we deleted cells B_1 and C_2 in Figure 5.3. For the same reason in the diagram showing the two demand curves, we have to erase the upper portion of D_2 and the lower portion of D_1. What remains is the kinked demand curve corresponding to cells B_2 and C_1 as shown in Figure 5.3 above.

We have now established the rationale for the kinked demand curve which illustrates how an oligopolist may hold asymmetric expectations about the responses of rivals to price changes in its own product. We have, therefore, derived an oligopolist's version of the market demand curve which you met in Chapter 3.

5.3   Profit maximization in the case of the kinked demand curve

Is the firm doing the best it can if it is on the kink of this demand curve? The answer to this question will depend on the firm's objectives. As you learnt in Chapter 4, a firm may have a number of objectives, but in economic analysis it is usually accepted that the firm's primary objective is to maximize profits. If this is so, then the question we have to ask is whether the oligopolist is maximizing profits when it is on the kink.

There are different accounting notions of profits but, as you learnt in Chapter 4, in very general terms we can say that a firm's profits are given by the difference between revenues and costs. Total profits are the difference between total revenue and total cost. I will use the Greek letter Π for profit, so that

$$\Pi = TR - TC$$

where $\Pi = TR - TC$

TR = total revenue

TC = total costs

If total revenue is greater than total cost, then profit is positive. If total revenue is less than total cost then profit is negative and losses are being incurred.

Profit maximization implies that the difference between total revenue and total cost is maximized. To get an intuitive grasp of this idea, consider the conditions under which a firm could increase profits by increasing output in the short run. The basic question here is whether extra units of output would add more to revenue than to cost. If extra units add more to revenue than to cost, then the firm would increase profits by expanding output. Conversely, if successively more units of output add more to costs than to revenues, then the firm would increase profits by reducing output. This implies that the profit-maximizing output is at that level where one more unit of output adds only the same amount to revenues as it does to costs.

Note that this account of profit maximizing depends on what is happening to revenues and costs as the firm produces one more or one less unit of output. In other words, what is important are the *marginal* changes in revenues and costs.

In Chapter 4 you met the notion of marginal cost as the change in total cost arising from the production of one more unit of output. This may be written as

$$MC = \frac{\Delta TC}{\Delta Q}$$

where MC is marginal cost

ΔTC is change in total cost

ΔQ is change in output

Similarly, we can define marginal revenue as the change in total revenue arising from the sale of one more unit of output. This may be written as

$$MR = \frac{\Delta TR}{\Delta Q}$$

where MR is marginal revenue

ΔTR is change in total revenue

ΔQ is change in output

If profit is maximized when one more unit of output adds the same amount to cost as it does to revenue, this is equivalent to saying that profit is maximized when marginal cost equals marginal revenue. Or, profit is maximized when

$MC = MR$

The condition that profit is maximized when marginal cost equals marginal revenue is a general result and you will be meeting it again many times.

If extra units add more to cost than to revenue, then the firm would increase profit by reducing output. In other words, if MC is greater than MR for each extra unit, then the firm will increase profit by reducing output, i.e.

if $MC > MR$, the firm should reduce output.

Similarly, if the last unit produced adds less to cost than to revenue, then the firm should increase production in order to increase profit. In other words, if MC is less than MR for each extra unit, then the firm will increase profit by increasing output, i.e.

if $MC < MR$, the firm should increase output.

In order to consider whether the oligopolist facing a kinked demand curve is maximizing profits, we need to know marginal cost and marginal revenue. In the rest of this chapter, I shall take it that output can be expanded at constant marginal cost. If this is the case, then the short-run marginal cost curve is drawn as a horizontal line. This simplifies the diagram without losing anything important from the analysis of the oligopolist's profit maximization.

Marginal revenue, which is derived from a firm's demand curve, has not yet been explained in this text. A firm's marginal revenue depends on the structure of the market in which it is operating. For this reason, the marginal revenue curve corresponding to the kinked demand curve is specific to oligopoly. In later chapters of this text, you will learn about the marginal revenue curves for other market structures.

Consider what the oligopolist expects as the price of a good begins to fall. As the price falls, the oligopolist expects a small increase in sales. But if price is falling, the marginal revenue must be falling even faster. This is because extra sales are possible only if all the units are sold at the lower price, including those that were previously being sold at the higher price. This means that the net addition to total revenue must be less than the price at which the last or marginal unit is sold. Marginal revenue is therefore less than price and falls faster than price as sales increase.

In diagrammatic terms this implies that the marginal revenue curve lies below the demand curve and has a steeper slope. As the demand curve is kinked, the marginal revenue curve reflects this shape, as shown in Figure 5.9.

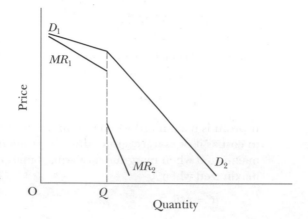

Figure 5.9 **The kinked demand curve and the marginal revenue curve**

Figure 5.9 shows a kinked demand curve together with the corresponding marginal revenue curve. The demand curve lies above the marginal revenue curve at all points and is falling less steeply. Note too a characteristic feature of this marginal revenue curve: it has a discontinuity at the rate of output corresponding to the kink.

The kinked demand curve and its marginal revenue curve

If you feel that working through an arithmetic exercise helps you to understand the economic analysis, you might like to work through the following arithmetic example of the relation between the kinked demand curve and the marginal revenue curve. The numbers are purely illustrative and are not meant to represent a real situation.

Consider the case where 100 units of a good are sold at £5 each. This price/output combination gives the position of the kink in the demand curve. Consider what the oligopolist expects to happen (a) in the case of a putative price fall, and (b) in the case of a putative price rise.

In case (a), if price falls to £4.98, the oligopolist expects that sales will increase to 101 units. The total revenue would increase from £500 to £502.98, which means that marginal revenue would be £2.98 at an output of 101. Marginal revenue is here less than the price. This is shown in Table 5.1a. Similarly, the oligopolist expects sales to increase to 102 units if the price falls to £4.96, so that total revenue is expected to rise to £505.92. In this case, marginal revenue would be £2.94. As price falls, so does marginal revenue, but marginal revenue is less than price and it also falls faster than price.

Table 5.1a   **Deriving an oligopolist's marginal revenue: case (a)**

Price	Expected quantity demanded	TR	MR
£5.00	100	£500.00	—
£4.98	101	£502.98	£2.98
£4.96	102	£505.92	£2.94
£4.94	103		
£4.92	104		
£4.90	105		

Exercise 5.2

Table 5.1a provides data on quantity demanded for some putative price reductions. Try completing the columns showing total revenue and marginal revenue.

You should have discovered that this oligopolist expects marginal revenue to fall from £2.98 (when price is reduced from £5.00 to £4.98) to £2.82 (when price is reduced from £4.92 to £4.90). Thus, marginal revenue is less than price and it also falls at a faster rate; price is falling by 2p but marginal revenue is falling by 4p for each unit increase in sales. Note too that marginal revenue is not defined at the current price as it can be calculated only for changes in price.

We now have the demand curve and marginal revenue for one half of the kinked demand curve, where the oligopolist is considering the effect on sales of *reducing* the price. We now need to consider case (b), the other section of the kinked demand curve where the oligopolist is considering whether to *increase* the price. Here it is expected that an increase in price from £5.00 to £5.01 will reduce sales from 100 to 99 units. Total revenue falls. The marginal revenue is the change in *TR* (−4.01) divided by the change in sales (−1), hence the *MR* is £4.01 and is less than price. Table 5.1b adds more price and quantity data.

Table 5.1b **Deriving an oligopolist's marginal revenue: case (b)**

Price	Expected quantity demanded	TR	MR
£5.00	100	£500	—
£5.01	99	£495.99	£4.01
£5.02	98		
£5.03	97		
£5.04	96		
£5.05	95		

Exercise 5.3

Try filling in the missing values for total revenue and marginal revenue in Table 5.1b for the putative price increases.

You should find that marginal revenue (the drop in total revenue per unit of sales lost) is expected to get larger, from £4.01 to £4.09, as the oligopolist considers increasing the price of the good from £5.00 through to £5.05. Note again that marginal revenue is undefined at the current price.

Taking Tables 5.1a and 5.1b together, you can see how the marginal revenue curve is related to the kinked demand curve. The marginal revenue curve is steeper than the demand curve and lies below it at all points. In addition, there is a discontinuity in the marginal revenue curve corresponding to the kink in the demand curve. The reason for this is that, at the kink, the oligopolist can be thought of as switching from one demand curve to another. This implies that it is also switching from one marginal revenue curve to another but, as the marginal revenue curves have different values at this point, the switch implies a discontinuity. (Interested readers will find in the Appendix the complete marginal revenue schedules corresponding to the two complete demand curves D_1 and D_2.)

We are now ready to consider whether the oligopolist is maximizing profits at the level of output shown by the kink. In order to do this we need to compare marginal revenue and marginal cost. The marginal revenue curve has been shown in Figure 5.9 with its discontinuity at the rate of output corresponding to the kink. The profit-maximizing condition states that if marginal cost is less than marginal revenue, then output should be higher, and that if marginal cost is greater than marginal revenue then output should be lower.

This means that the oligopolist is maximizing profits at the point of the kink in the demand curve – that is, at the existing rate of output – if the marginal cost curve passes through the discontinuity in the marginal revenue curve as shown in Figure 5.10.

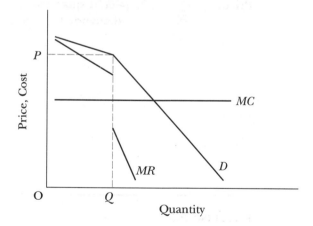

Figure 5.10   **Profit maximizing and the kinked demand curve**

Question

To help you see that this is so, consider Figure 5.11. The oligopolist is producing quantity Q. Explain what would happen to profits if the oligopolist

1   increased output to Q_1 at a lower price, or

2   reduced output to Q_2 at a higher price.

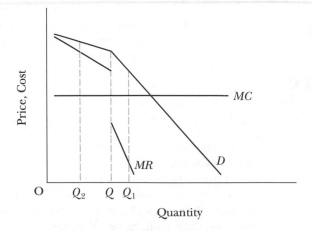

Figure 5.11 **The profit-maximizing oligopolist**

If the oligopolist increased output to Q_1 at a lower price, then marginal cost would exceed marginal revenue. So profits would be higher if output remained at Q. If the oligopolist were to reduce output to Q_2 at a higher price, then the drop in total revenue (marginal revenue) would exceed the savings in cost (marginal cost). Thus profits would be reduced. If increasing output above Q reduces profits, and reducing output below Q does likewise, then an output of Q at the kink must maximize profits.

Note that one implication of this profit-maximizing analysis of the oligopolist is that prices will tend to be stable. Not only do oligopolists have little incentive to change price as a competitive strategy against other firms, but marginal costs can change to some degree without there being any change in the price charged. In Figure 5.10, marginal cost may fluctuate by a certain amount without changing the price; as long as the fluctuation is contained within the gap, there will be no change in the profit-maximizing price or quantity. Some economists have wondered whether this explains why some prices seem to be relatively stable. (Sometimes these stable prices are referred to as 'fix-prices' or 'sticky prices'.) The kinked demand curve analysis was first developed during the 1930s in order to explain what was thought to be the relative stability of prices at that time in spite of widespread unemployment and depressed trading conditions. Since that period, most economies have been characterized by inflation rather than stable prices, but the issue of the flexibility of prices in response to conditions of boom or recession still remains and is discussed in Book 2. The claim that oligopoly prices tend to be relatively stable has been subject to considerable debate and the empirical evidence is not clear cut (Reid, 1981, surveys the debate.) Recent developments in advanced game theory, however, have reinforced the kinked demand curve analysis, emphasizing firms' fear of losing market share by increasing prices even during booms (Maskin and Tirole, 1988).

This conclusion returns us to the point made in the introduction to this section, that different models will yield different kinds of insights. Given the complexity of economic events, it is often the case that there is no one single best model. Economists have to bear in mind the particular circumstances of the situation, and the relevant institutional or historical context, and then make a judgment about the right sort of model to use. As Carl Shapiro said in the passage quoted above, economic theory is like a bag of tools from which the economist must select according to circumstances. Part of the economist's skill lies in knowing how to make a judgment about the best available tool to use.

6   Conclusion: strategic interdependence

This chapter has examined a number of different models of oligopoly. The emphasis of the chapter has been on the diversity of such models and the difficulty of providing undisputed or clear-cut laws that can be applied across the board. An implication of this is to underline the importance of careful individual industry studies which try to understand the features that are specific to that market as well as the general features of oligopoly markets which are common to a number of different oligopolists.

This chapter has also emphasized the importance of strategic decision making for oligopolists. As we have seen, this implies having a view as to how other oligopolists are going to react. One response to this situation is to form a strategic alliance with another firm, where there can be some pooling of strategies based on goodwill trust. Alternatively, firms try to outguess their rivals as best they can, and here the role of information is crucial. This chapter has noted on a number of occasions that this is a world of imperfect information and uncertainty. Economists are particularly interested in the ways that firms in different market contexts respond to different kinds of information signals including price changes.

But strategic decision making also implies that oligopolists may have an unhealthy interest in soliciting information about rivals' plans and objectives, and that fierce inter-firm rivalry may sometimes cross the boundary between legitimate competitive practices and illegitimate ones. On this more speculative note concerning business ethics, I shall leave you with the case with which I began. This is the *Financial Times* leading article on the 'dirty tricks' campaign waged by British Airways against Virgin Atlantic Airways.

> The rout of British Airways in its legal battle with Virgin Atlantic raises some curious questions of business morality. By its own tacit admission, BA employed some very dubious tactics in trying to overwhelm a smaller competitor. Are we to suppose that such behaviour is general in the corporate world? Again, BA technically came to grief not over dirty tricks, but because it had libelled Mr Branson. Suppose the rest of its behaviour were within the law. Does that make it acceptable?
> The answer to the first question is not wholly simple. The principal charge against BA boils down to the fact that it sought to divert business from a competitor. In itself, that is commonplace. If an engineering company hears a competitor is about to land an order, it will call the customer and try to change his mind. It is less usual in consumer markets: we might be surprised, on buying a tin of beans in a supermarket, to find another bean-maker pressing his own wares upon us at a discount. But that would not be illegal, simply uncommercial in the context of the price of a tin of beans. A first-class air ticket might be another matter.
> BA's position, in fact, was in many ways exceptional. Despite its apparent market dominance, it found Mr Branson able to make surprisingly rapid inroads into some of its most lucrative routes. The airline market is also unusual in that competitors routinely take on each other's customers and that their order books are relatively transparent. BA may have been guilty of arrogance or stupidity in allowing itself to be needled by Mr Branson, who

comes out of the affair as much the better tactician. But perhaps not every company in BA's position, possessing both the motive and the means, would have behaved much better.

The second charge against BA is that it sought to blacken Virgin's name through the press. As any journalist who has covered a contested takeover can attest, this is not unprecedented behaviour either. In both cases, the question is not so much what is done as what means are employed to do it. If a company can be shown to have broken the Data Protection Act, or abused its market dominance in suppressing competition, or made slanderous allegations, it can be prosecuted accordingly. But that brings us back to our second question. Suppose none of these things happened. Does that make it all right?

The answer, obviously, is no. It is not even necessary here to appeal to business ethics. The point can be made on practical grounds. If BA has offended the sense of natural justice in the world at large, its business will suffer. Its customers may, at the margin, take their business elsewhere. If it has compromised its reputation for straight dealing in the eyes of governments, it may find its global ambitions harder to pursue. The message of the affair, in short, is that dirty tricks have a price of their own.

(Financial Times, 12 January 1993)

Appendix

Completed marginal revenue schedules

Completed marginal revenue schedules are shown in Tables 5.A1 and 5.A2 below, corresponding to the two complete demand curves, from which the oligopolist's kinked demand curve can be derived.

Table 5.A1   **The schedules corresponding to the case of price reductions (D_2 in Figure 5.8)**

Price	Expected quantity demanded	TR	MR
£5.10	95	£484.50	–
£5.08	96	£487.68	£3.18
£5.06	97	£490.82	£3.14
£5.04	98	£493.92	£3.10
£5.02	99	£496.98	£3.06
£5.00	100	£500.00	£3.02
£4.98	101	£502.98	£2.98
£4.96	102	£505.92	£2.94
£4.94	103	£508.82	£2.90
£4.92	104	£511.68	£2.86
£4.90	105	£514.50	£2.82

Table 5.A2   **The schedules corresponding to the case of price increases**
(D_1 in Figure 5.8)

Price	Expected quantity demanded	TR	MR
£4.95	105	£519.75	–
£4.96	104	£515.84	£3.91
£4.97	103	£511.91	£3.93
£4.98	102	£507.96	£3.95
£4.99	101	£503.99	£3.97
£5.00	100	£500.00	£3.99
£5.01	99	£495.99	£4.01
£5.02	98	£491.96	£4.03
£5.03	97	£487.91	£4.05
£5.04	96	£483.84	£4.07
£5.05	95	£479.75	£4.09

Note that at the price/quantity combination £5.00/100, the two marginal revenue
curves have different values. It is this that accounts for the discontinuity of the
oligopolist's marginal revenue curve at the kink.

CHAPTER 6   MONOPOLY POWER

by Andrew B. Trigg

1   Introduction

As the chill autumn winds begin to sweep across Lake Washington near America's north-western seaboard, workmen pick their way around a clump of low buildings on the hillside by the shore. You would not know it from the outside, but this is soon to be the palatial home and playground of Bill Gates, one of the century's most successful entrepreneurs. But this year, it sits beneath an unseasonably gloomy cloud.

The $35m (£23m) mansion was first conceived when Mr Gates, the chairman, chief executive and founder of Microsoft, was on the up and up. He wanted it to be more than just a home with a private beach, cinema, conference hall, and swimming pool. When complete, guests will be able to use a computer database to summon up famous works of art on the big TV screens around the walls, or watch video images of what it's like to be on top of Mount Everest.

The complex will also explore the computer technology of the future. But what role does the future hold for its owner? At 37, Bill Gates is America's youngest-ever multi-billionaire. But – for the first time in his charmed life – the going has got a little tough.

This month, the European Commission announced it was investigating allegations that Microsoft, the world's biggest computer software company, has been involved in anti-competitive practices. Shortly before, the US Justice Department said it was launching a similar inquiry, after a three-and-a-half year probe into Microsoft by the US Federal Trade Commission ended in deadlock. There are mutterings that Mr Gates may be forced to split up his empire.

(Independent on Sunday, 26 September 1993)

Bill Gates and his Microsoft company are accused of exercising monopoly power. The company's most successful product, *Windows* software, is crucial to the basic operation of many of the functions which computers now perform. Take, for example, the widely used word processing package, *Word for Windows*. Users must have access to *Windows* software to use this package and *Windows* can only be purchased from one producer, Microsoft. It follows that Microsoft is in an extremely powerful position, with its exclusive trading right for the production of *Windows* software.

This exclusive trading right is defined by economists as a position of monopoly power. As the sole or 'mono' producer of a product the firm is in a powerful position relative to other firms. This situation can be said to be anti-competitive because in pursuing its objectives the firm does not have to take into consideration the behaviour of other firms. Competition –

the pursuit by more than one firm of similar objectives – cannot take place. Whether a firm seeks to maximize profits, technological advancement or any other objective, as a monopolist it will not have to compete with other firms pursuing the same objective.

Governments have for many years tried to prevent firms from wielding monopoly power. As far back as 1890, the US government stated that 'every person who shall monopolise, or attempt to monopolise, or combine to conspire with any other person or persons to monopolise any part of the trade or commerce among the several States, or within foreign nations, shall be guilty of misdemeanor ... ' (Burke *et al.*, 1988, p.140). In the past a number of US companies have been broken up because they were thought to wield too much monopoly power. The oil industry in 1911 is a notable example, with the giant Standard Oil company split up into Esso, Mobil and others by the US government. As I write, in early 1994, Microsoft faces a similar fate.

It is of great interest to economists to be able to analyse the behaviour of firms which wield monopoly power, and to that end economic theories have been developed which help to understand and predict the behaviour of the monopolist. These theories also serve as the basis for a discussion of the likely advantages and disadvantages that are associated with monopoly power. In this chapter I shall introduce these theories of monopoly power and identify a number of problems associated with them.

You will find that there is some similarity between the various theories of monopoly and the theories of oligopoly introduced in the previous chapter. This similarity arises not just because the theories can make use of similar techniques, but also because they can be used to look at similar markets. The objectives of this chapter, however, are somewhat different from Chapter 5. Instead of looking at interdependence between firms, which is the focus of theories of oligopoly, this chapter will concentrate on the behaviour of firms which pursue monopoly power.

There are a number of questions which need to be asked.

- How prevalent is monopoly power in real world markets?
- What are the origins of monopoly power?
- What are the advantages and disadvantages of monopoly power?

The objectives of the chapter are geared towards addressing these questions. The first objective, addressed in Section 2, is to examine the magnitude of the problem – to find out the extent to which firms exercise monopoly power in real world markets. The advantages and disadvantages of monopoly power cannot be properly discussed until we have looked at how economists measure it. The second objective, covered in Section 3, is to examine the origins of monopoly power. If we can understand why monopolies come about, this will influence our decision as to whether they are formed for good reasons. Finally in Section 4, I introduce the various theories which economists have developed in order to explain the behaviour of firms which enjoy monopoly power. It will be shown that different schools of thought have taken conflicting positions on the advantages and disadvantages of monopoly power because they look at the behaviour of firms through different theoretical spectacles.

2   Measuring the extent of monopoly power

One of the main ways in which economists measure monopoly power is by looking at the levels of concentration of firms in markets. In the extreme, if most of the output of a particular good is concentrated in the hands of one firm then it could be said to have a high degree of monopoly power. For example, in 1992 British Telecom provided about 90 per cent of telephone service provision in the UK (*Financial Times*, 15 October 1992). In other parts of Europe such as France and Germany nationalized telecommunications companies controlled 100 per cent of the provision. It can be argued that such a concentration of output in the hands of one company enables it to choose the price it wishes to set for its product. The *Financial Times* observed that 'a three-minute call from Brussels to London, a distance of 200 miles, costs $2.32. Yet Americans can make a three-minute, 2,500-mile call from New York to San Francisco for as little as 30 cents' (21 June 1992, p.5). The argument here is that the more competitive nature of the telecommunications industry in the USA, with many firms instead of one main firm, leads to lower prices than in Europe. The high concentration of output enjoyed by European telecommunications companies leads to monopoly power.

The telecommunications industry is of course an extreme. The European Commission describes telecommunications as 'the most concentrated service sector in the member states – there is only one firm' (Commission of the European Communities, 1993). In most industries, however, there are a number of firms producing, and some sort of indicator of the degree of concentration is needed.

There are two types of indicators of concentration which I will consider in this part of the chapter. First, the concentration of the largest firms in manufacturing as a whole can be considered for a particular country or group of countries. Second, the concentration in a particular sector, such as telecommunications, can be measured.

Measures of concentration in manufacturing as a whole are useful for cross-country comparisons. In 1986, for example, the 40 largest firms in manufacturing industry in the then European Community (EC) produced 23 per cent of the output. This indicates the degree of concentration of manufacturing output in the hands of these large firms, and is particularly striking if we note that these 40 firms made up less than 0.5 per cent of the total number of manufacturing firms in Europe. Figure 6.1 demonstrates that whilst the concentration of manufacturing output in the largest 40 firms is similar in Japan and Europe, in the USA it is significantly higher.

Figure 6.1   **Share of the largest 40 firms in the output of manufacturing industry in the EC, USA and Japan, 1986**

Source: Jacquemin *et al.* (1989) p.40

In the USA the 40 largest firms controlled over a third of manufacturing output. It can therefore be argued that more output was concentrated in the hands of a small number of large firms in the manufacturing sector in the USA than is the case in Europe and Japan. If, for instance, we wanted to

Definition

Concentration ratio

The 5-firm concentration ratio measures the proportion of total output produced by the five largest firms in an industrial sector. A 40-firm concentration ratio measures the proportion of total output produced by the 40 largest firms in a sector.

compare the effects of anti-monopoly laws in these parts of the world economy, then this type of comparison between levels of firm concentration would be necessary.

Measures of concentration are defined in economics as concentration ratios and can be defined for any number of firms. I shall now introduce the concentration ratio for the purpose of comparing specific industrial sectors in the UK. There are approximately 100 industrial sectors which make up manufacturing in the UK. The above example dealt with the largest 40 firms in the manufacturing sector but in the *Census of Production*, a survey of industrial activity in the UK, the five largest firms in each industrial sector are considered.

Assume that there are 15 firms in the shoe manufacturing sector. Assume also that the largest firm produces 50 per cent of total sales, and that 10 per cent is produced by each of the next four largest firms. The 5-firm concentration ratio for this industry is

$$50 + 10 + 10 + 10 + 10 = 90 \text{ per cent}$$

In another industry in which 15 firms produce textiles, assume that the top five firms produce 10 per cent each of total sales. The 5-firm concentration ratio for this industry is

$$10 + 10 + 10 + 10 + 10 = 50 \text{ per cent}$$

The share of total sales of the top five companies in the textile industry (50 per cent) is less than in the shoe industry (90 per cent). This comparison could be used to argue that firms in the textile industry would be less likely to exercise monopoly power than firms in the shoe industry. The more concentrated the share of output by the big firms in an industry, the more monopoly power they are likely to wield.

Exercise 6.1

Table 6.1 shows the shares in industrial output of firms producing in an industry in which ten firms operate.

Calculate the 5-firm concentration ratio for this industry.

Table 6.1

	Share of total sales (%)
Firm 1	40
Firm 2	20
Firm 3	10
Firm 4	5
Firm 5	5
Firm 6	5
Firm 7	5
Firm 8	4
Firm 9	4
Firm 10	2

A selection of 5-firm concentration ratios in the UK is shown in Table 6.2. The table shows that the shares of the top five companies vary considerably among industries. For example, the top five companies in the tobacco industry produce 99.1 per cent of total sales. This would suggest that the large tobacco companies could enjoy considerable monopoly power. At the other extreme, in the processing of plastics industry, the top five companies only produce 9.6 per cent of total sales. This could paint the picture of numerous plastics companies engaging in a competitive environment.

Table 6.2   **Concentration ratios for the five largest enterprises in a selection of UK industrial sectors, 1990**

Census of Production code no.	**Industry**	**5-firm concentration index (%)**
429	Tobacco industry	99.1
221	Iron and steel	94.8
244	Asbestos goods	87.4
351	Motor vehicles and engineering	87.3
364	Aerospace equipment	77.1
329	Ordnance, small arms and ammunition	75.8
321	Agricultural machinery and tractors	75.1
258	Soap and toilet preparations	56.3
427	Brewing and malting	45.1
344	Telecommunications equipment	33.1
243	Building products	31.0
431	Woollen and worsted industry	27.7
256	Specialized chemicals	27.6
312	Forging, pressing and stamping	19.7
464	Wooden containers	17.3
453	Clothing, hats and gloves	16.4
467	Wooden and upholsterous furniture	14.5
316	Hand tools and finished metal goods	10.7
483	Processing of plastics	9.6

Source: Central Statistical Office (1992)

Concentration ratios provide an important function for policy makers. Whether or not a firm's activities should be considered for investigation by government for alleged monopoly practices usually depends partly on the size of the concentration ratio in the respective sector. In Chapter 8, George Yarrow provides a discussion of this type of industrial intervention by governments.

There are, however, some problems associated with concentration ratios. In choosing a particular industry and looking at the degree of firm concentration, the assumption is made that this will to some extent reflect the degree of monopoly power in an industry. A key problem, however, is that the information is not collected for this purpose. Industries are put into categories such as those shown in Table 6.2 using criteria which often have nothing to do with monopoly power.

A classic example is that of metal and plastic buckets. In Table 6.2 metal buckets are produced in industry 316 (hand tools and finished metal goods) whilst plastic buckets are produced in industry 483 (processing of plastics). The problem is that we might observe from our visits to the local hardware store that the two products are in competition with each other. If metal buckets are priced too high we might buy a plastic bucket instead, and vice versa. Despite this intuitive observation, the industrial classification in Table 6.2 classifies these products as being produced in separate markets. The reason for this anomaly is that one of the main criteria used to construct the industry classifications in surveys such as the *Census of Production* is the nature of the raw material inputs used by the industries concerned. The boundaries of industrial sectors are defined according to the raw materials – metal and plastic – used to make the buckets, whereas the existence or non-existence of competition has to do with the boundaries of markets.

Conversely, this organization of firms into industries according to their use of raw materials may also vastly underestimate the degree of concentration. Firms in an industry may be producing goods made from the same materials but there may be no competition between them. For example, in industry 364 (aerospace equipment) some firms may be producing equipment for war planes and others for civil purposes. The degree of concentration for the production of war plane equipment may be much higher than the broad figure for aerospace equipment suggests. Since the industry groups are so broad they may underestimate the extent to which firms can monopolize the production of particular products.

An additional problem with concentration ratios is that they are calculated within the national boundaries of countries. A firm may have a high concentration of total output within the national boundaries of a country, and it may thus appear that the firm can exercise monopoly power. If, however, the firm faces fierce competition from overseas then it may be wrong to deduce from the concentration ratio that the firm is a monopolist. In Chapter 12, Paul Auerbach will look into the role of the firm in the international economy.

This section has introduced the concentration ratio, and considered some of the problems associated with concentration ratios as indicators of monopoly power. The extent to which firms wield monopoly power in real world markets is a matter for discussion, depending both on our interpretation of concentration ratios and the judgements we make of their accuracy.

In the next section I shall concentrate on the origins of monopoly power.

3   The origins of monopoly power

Economists have put forward two main explanations for the origins of monopoly power. The first is the tendency for firms to engage in mergers and acquisitions; the second is the ability of firms to put up barriers to entry. These two explanations will be considered separately in this section.

3.1   Mergers and acquisitions

The most direct way for a firm to obtain a position of monopoly power is to take over the operations of another firm operating in the market. As far back as the last century Karl Marx observed that 'one capitalist always kills many', which leads to a 'constantly diminishing number of the magnates of capital, who usurp and monopolise all advantages of the process of transformation' (Marx, 1867, p.836). Whether this process is called a merger or an acquisition depends on the party concerned. As Townsend (1968, p.48) has noted, 'directors of one company are apt to talk of "acquisition" amongst themselves whilst talking of "merger" to the directors of the company they aspire to control'.

There are three main types of merger: diversified, vertical, and horizontal. A diversified merger occurs when a firm fuses with another firm engaged in a different type of activity. If an aircraft company merged with a car producer, for example, this would be a diversified merger. The aircraft company would be diversifying into an additional activity. A vertical merger arises when a firm amalgamates with firms which operate at different stages of production of the same good. A firm which brews beer, for example, could either acquire interests in farms which grow the original hops (backward vertical), or it could reach out to the ownership of pubs which sell the final product (forward vertical). In contrast, a horizontal merger concerns the combination of firms at the same stage of production – one brewer acquires interests in another brewer. Figure 6.2 provides an example of the horizontal mergers which took place to form the electrical engineering firm GEC in the 1960s.

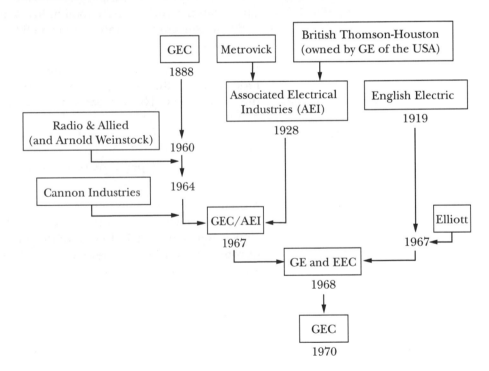

Figure 6.2   **The history of the General Electrical Company (GEC)**

Source: Cowling (1982) p.75

This particular series of mergers was part of a wave of horizontal mergers which took place in the UK during the 1960s. The number of acquisitions per year increased from 58 in 1957 to 96 in 1967 and 133 in the peak year of 1968 (Cowling, 1982).

A study by Hannah and Kay (1977) found that many of the changes in firm concentration in the UK over this period could be explained by mergers. Changes in the 10-firm concentration ratio and the percentage change due to merger are shown in Table 6.3.

Table 6.3   **The effect of the 1960s merger wave on UK firm concentration**

Industry	10-firm concentration ratio		% of change due to merger
	1957	1969	
Food	62.1	80.5	70.1
Drink	40.8	87.2	76.3
Tobacco	100.0	100.0	—
Chemicals	80.6	86.4	31.2
Non-electrical engineering	39.0	32.1	—
Shipbuilding	80.3	93.3	80.8
Vehicles and aircraft	57.2	85.8	70.6
Building materials	71.2	65.0	—
Miscellaneous	58.3	65.6	95.9

Source: Hannah and Kay (1977); Cowling (1982) p.78

The first two columns of figures in Table 6.3 show the concentration ratios for various industries. In the food industry, for example, between 1957 and 1969 the concentration ratio rose from 62.1 to 80.5 per cent, a change of +18.4 percentage points.

Hannah and Kay found, by carrying out a survey of the firms in the food industry, that 70.1 per cent of the change in concentration was due to mergers. The increases in concentration not explained by mergers can be explained by other factors such as the growth of large firms relative to small firms. In the chemicals industry, for example, only 31.2 per cent of the increase in concentration is explained by mergers – so 68.8 per cent of the change must be explained by other factors.

A similar merger wave to that of the 1960s took place in the UK during the late 1980s. During 1987, at the peak of the late 1980s boom, there were 1528 mergers in the UK. In view of the UK's increasing integration into Europe, however, this merger wave must be placed in the European context. *The Economist* observed that:

> Once businessmen decided that the European Community's ambitious programme to create a single internal market was going to succeed, they scrambled to get ready by merging, acquiring and bidding for other firms on an unprecedented scale, even before the continent's maze of national barriers had come down.

> *(The Economist, 4 July 1992)*

The number of mergers and acquisitions in the European Community (now the European Union) and in the UK is shown in Figure 6.3. The implications of this merger wave for the degree of concentration is still to be fully assessed by economists. Indeed, such an assessment is more complex than the analysis of the 1960s UK merger wave. The world has changed so markedly since the 1960s, with the integration of the UK into Europe, that an analysis of the effect of the 1980s merger wave on UK concentration

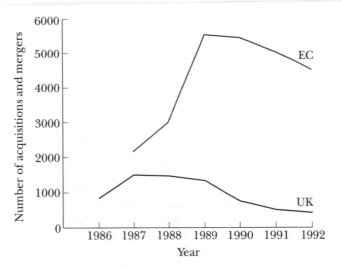

Figure 6.3 **Number of acquisitions and mergers in the European Community and the UK, 1986–92**

Source: for the UK: *Financial Statistics* (July 1993, July 1992, July 1991) Table 8.8; for the EC: Commission of the European Communities (1993)

ratios would be too limited. The UK can no longer be seen as a market separated from the rest of Europe.

3.2 Barriers to entry

Whilst mergers seem to be a very important explanation of changes in concentration, we have seen that there are other factors which need to be considered. We have also seen that concentration itself does not provide a complete determinant of monopoly power. Firms can use barriers to entry to prevent competition from other firms. The more a firm can prevent other firms from entering a market, the more freedom it will have to exercise monopoly power.

Question

If you were setting up your own business, which of the following ideas would you consider to be the most viable? Rank them in order of preference, and then for each note down one barrier you would face in such an undertaking.

- A sandwich stall
- Operating an oil tanker
- Ferret training
- Brain surgery
- Manufacturing perfume

There are a number of responses you could have given to each business idea. Here are some of my own suggestions. You will recall from Chapter 4 that the oil tanker was used to illustrate economies of scale. Oil tends to be transported in huge tankers because this reduces average costs – the costs per unit of oil transported. There are economies to be made from the large scale of the operation. For this reason I would guess that you did not choose the oil tanker option for your most attractive business venture. Economies of scale provide a barrier to entry. The huge scale of operations in the oil transport industry would make it impossible for most of us to consider setting up in this line of business.

There are, of course, other barriers to entry into markets. Manufacturing your own brand of perfume would be very difficult without some form of bottle to package the product. The local chemist tends to buy brands which are packaged in a certain way. The need to package your product therefore provides one barrier to entry. It may also be very difficult to set up a sandwich stall without the relevant licence – there are legal restrictions to entry in many markets. In addition, it may be the case that you do not have the necessary skills to operate in some sectors of the economy. Brain surgery is an obvious example, although I am told that ferret training also requires great skill.

Whilst these additional barriers to entry are important, economists have focused much of their attention on economies of scale. To look at economies of scale in a formal way I shall have to look at the cost conditions in which a firm operates. Economies of scale are shown formally by using the long-run average cost ($LRAC$) curve. You will recall from Chapter 4 that economists often assume that the long-run average cost curve is L-shaped over relevant ranges of output. As the scale of a firm's operations is increased, costs per unit will fall until the point of minimum efficient scale is reached. Costs per unit of output are then constant as output moves beyond this point. The point of minimum efficient scale in Figure 6.4 is output level Q_1. At levels of output below (to the left of) Q_1 the firm enjoys economies of scale as output is increased. At levels of output above (to the right of) Q_1 the firm enjoys constant average costs – as output is increased the costs per unit of output are constant.

Economies of scale can become important when the cost of a firm's product is related to the demand for the product in the market. Assume that there is limited market demand for the firm's product such that at the price level P_1 in Figure 6.4 consumers only require Q_1 of the good. This is shown by drawing a downward sloping demand market curve (D) in Figure 6.4. You will recall from Chapter 3 that economists generally assume that the demand curve is downward sloping since as the price of a good falls, demand for the good will usually increase.

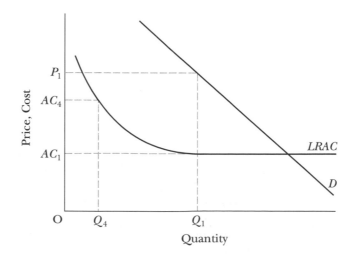

Figure 6.4 **Barriers to entry under economies of scale**

It follows from these assumptions that in the situation illustrated in Figure 6.4 it would make sense for the firm to satisfy all the demand in the economy for the good in question. Figure 6.4 compares the market demand curve (D) with the long-run average cost ($LRAC$) curve for one particular firm. If the price level is set at P_1 this firm can satisfy all of the available demand in the market (Q_1) at its point of minimum efficient scale – the minimum of the $LRAC$ curve. The logical conclusion is that the economies of scale for this firm create a situation in which there is only room for one firm in the market. This situation is called a natural monopoly. The firm has a monopoly over the production of a good because the conditions of production mean that there is room for only one firm to produce at the most efficient level.

If we assume that all firms have access to the same shaped cost curves, it follows that any firm that tried to enter the market would have to take a slice of the market demand at a higher level of long-run average costs than the minimum of the $LRAC$ curve. Returning to the example of the oil tanker business, assume that there is only one tanker which takes oil to the Falkland Islands. There are technical economies of scale associated with using one large container. If another firm tries to muscle in on the market then it may, for example, try to obtain a quarter of the trade in oil to the Falklands. In Figure 6.4 it can be seen that at a quarter of the available demand (Q_4) the average costs are considerably higher (AC_4) than those associated with the established tanker (AC_1). This provides a cost barrier to entry because the costs per unit of output for any new firm are likely to be formidable. The point to be stressed is that if economies of scale exist up to a high level of output, this can provide a barrier to the entry of new firms.

It should also be stressed that the case of natural monopoly depends crucially on the shape of the $LRAC$ curve. There is a barrier to entry in Figure 6.4 because at the new firm's entry level of output (Q_4) average costs are higher than at the existing firm's level of output (Q_1). The downward sloping part of the average cost curve provides the deterrent to entry by the new firm. Recall that the assumption on which this downward sloping part of the $LRAC$ curve is drawn is that of economies of scale. As the scale of output is increased costs per unit (average costs) fall because of economies of scale.

Definition

Natural monopoly

A natural monopoly exists in an industry when the minimum efficient scale is sufficiently large that there is room for only one producer in the market.

Question

Study Figure 6.5. Assume that firm A produces at output level Q_1. What would be the (cost) entry conditions for firm B if it operated at Q_4? Would firm B be operating under better/worse/the same cost conditions as firm A?

Under constant returns to scale the same level of average cost is associated with each level of the firm's output. The average cost curve is a horizontal line. In Figure 6.5 constant average costs are assumed at every level of output. On this assumption there is no cost disincentive for a new firm to enter the market. Although the original firm in the market produces at Q_1, the new entrant may produce at any scale of output, however small, for the same average cost.

It follows that the shape of cost curves is important in trying to explain the origins of monopoly power. There will always be some sectors of the economy, such as the oil industry, where substantial economies of scale

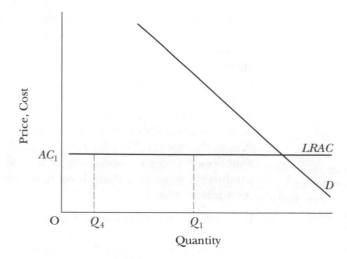

Figure 6.5 **Barriers to entry under constant average costs?**

generate the necessary conditions for a natural monopoly to exist. You may recall at this juncture (from Chapter 4) that there is a difference between returns to scale and economies of scale. Returns to scale refer to the technical economies, such as those associated with the oil tanker. Economies of scale in general encompass all technical economies plus any wider economies of scale which may reduce costs. A large firm may, for example, be better placed to negotiate prices of inputs to production than a smaller firm – this would also be classified as a scale economy.

Having established that economies of scale may explain how a firm can attain monopoly power, some empirical evidence can briefly be considered. There is some evidence that returns to scale or technical economies of scale help to explain variations in firm concentration between industries. Scherer (1975) calculated the points of minimum efficient scale in a technical sense (the point where increasing returns stop and constant or decreasing returns set in) for a number of industries. He compared the size of the market with the minimum efficient scale in this sense for the USA, Canada and Sweden. An indicator is devised (*NE*) to show the number of plants which could operate at the minimum efficient scale. For example, if the market demands say $100 000 worth of goods and the minimum efficient scale is $25 000, then four plants could operate at the minimum efficient scale: *NE* is equal to 4. In Table 6.4 this indicator is compared with 3-firm concentration ratios for each industry (showing the market share of the top three firms).

Table 6.4   **A comparison of minimum efficient scale and concentration ratios**

		Cigarettes	Steel	Weaving	Shoes
USA	*NE*	16	35	447	493
	CR_3 (%)	68	42	30	17
Canada	*NE*	1	3	12	48
	CR_3 (%)	90	80	67	18
Sweden	*NE*	1	1	6	13
	CR_3 (%)	100	63	50	37

Note: *NE* = maximum number of firms which can operate at minimum efficient scale and CR_3 = 3-firm concentration ratio.

Source: Scherer (1975) Appendix Table 3.7

For all three countries considered there is a direct relationship between technical economies of scale and firm concentration. In Canada, for example, there is only room for three firms producing at the minimum efficient scale in the steel industry; and the top three firms have 80 per cent of the market share. Conversely, in the industry producing shoes there is room for 48 firms and the concentration ratio is only 18 per cent – the top three firms have only 18 per cent of the market share. This pattern is broadly followed across industries in all three countries. Economies of scale can be an important factor in explaining variations in firm concentration between industries.

I have now explained how economists measure monopoly power, using concentration ratios, and how they explain its origins. There is evidence to suggest that both mergers and acquisitions, and barriers to entry are important explanations for the origins of monopoly power.

I shall now consider two types of theories which economists have developed to explain the behaviour of firms which wield monopoly power. The first type is static. Firms are looked at in positions of equilibrium where they settle for the level of output which maximizes their profits. The second type of theory to be considered is dynamic. In this theory, monopoly power is seen as part of an ongoing process of growth and innovation. There are two main variants of the static theory of monopoly: the theory of pure monopoly and the theory of monopolistic competition. Both these theories generate conclusions which point to the disadvantages of monopoly power, both for consumers and the economy as a whole.

4   Static theories of monopoly

Definition

Pure monopolist

A pure monopolist is a seller which controls the entire output in a particular market.

4.1   Pure monopoly

The model of pure monopoly focuses on the case in which there is only one firm in an industry – the 1-firm concentration ratio is 100 per cent. There are, as we have seen, some industries in which there is only one firm, but in the exposition that follows this case is also seen as a theoretical extreme.

In order to explain the behaviour of the pure monopolist it will be necessary to compare the costs and revenues associated with different levels of output. You have seen in the previous chapter that the usual assumption which economists make is that of profit maximization. Firms are assumed to maximize profits, that is they maximize the difference between costs and revenues. The model of pure monopoly uses the assumption of profit maximization to explain the behaviour of the pure monopolist.

Consider the simple example of the market for children's computer games. Assume that by a process of mergers and takeovers an imaginary firm, the Segtendo Corporation, has gained complete control of the market for these games. Since there are no other producers of these computer games the Segtendo Corporation can be said to enjoy a pure monopoly.

This situation generates some obvious advantages for the Segtendo Corporation. In particular, it can choose with complete freedom either the level of output or the price of the computer games it sells. Unlike oligopolists (considered in Chapter 5) the firm does not have to take into account the reactions of other firms. There are, in fact, no close substitutes for the product which the pure monopolist is producing. The only

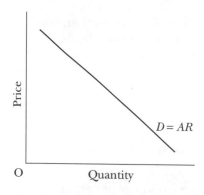

Figure 6.6 **The demand (average revenue) curve faced by the pure monopolist**

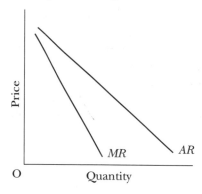

Figure 6.7 **The average revenue (AR) and marginal revenue (MR) curves for a pure monopolist**

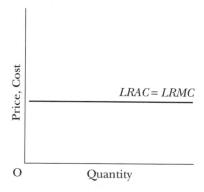

Figure 6.8 **Constant long-run average and marginal costs**

constraint in this extreme situation is the demand for the product in the market. Although computer games are very popular, there is a limit to the amount of income which consumers are prepared to spend on them. In addition the amount spent will depend on the price at which the product is sold. The Segtendo Corporation is therefore faced with a downward sloping demand curve for its computer games (Figure 6.6).

It can be seen that at high price levels output demanded is low and at low price levels output demanded is relatively high. Note that these levels of price and output are represented on one demand curve. In the previous chapter the oligopolist was faced with two hypothetical demand curves, each depending on the reactions of other firms to any price decisions (the kinked demand curve). Since for the case of the pure monopolist there are no other firms to consider, this means that there is only one demand curve.

Note also that this demand curve, indicated by the label D, can also be interpreted as an average revenue (AR) curve. Average revenue is the total revenue per unit of output sold. For example, at a certain level of sales the revenue per unit sold might be five. Each unit sells at a price of five and this is the same as the average revenue that the firm receives for each unit.

In addition to the average revenue curve, a marginal revenue (MR) curve can be drawn for the Segtendo Corporation (Figure 6.7).

You may recall from Chapter 5 that marginal revenue is the total additional revenue a firm receives when it sells an extra unit of output. It can be seen in Figure 6.7 that as average revenue falls, marginal revenue is always less than average revenue and falls more rapidly. It was explained in the previous chapter that with a downward sloping demand curve, the marginal changes in total revenue from selling an extra unit of output must be less than the price (average revenue) since the price of all the units needs to be reduced in order to sell the extra unit.

Having introduced the shape of the revenue curves for the Segtendo Corporation, under the assumption that the firm has a pure monopoly, we must look at the price which the firm will decide to charge for its computer games. Assume that the firm chooses the price level which generates the maximum level of profits. Since profits are the difference between revenue and costs, some consideration needs to be given to the costs which Segtendo incurs at different levels of output.

In Chapter 4 the concepts of average and marginal cost were introduced. Average cost is the cost per unit of output and marginal cost is the additional cost associated with each extra unit of output. For simplicity, I will assume that average and marginal costs are constant for the Segtendo Corporation. This means that average and marginal costs are the same at each level of output: there is a horizontal cost curve at which average cost = marginal cost (see Figure 6.8).

Note that Figure 6.8 shows a long-run cost curve. The horizontal line represents both long-run average costs ($LRAC$) and long-run marginal costs ($LRMC$). The reason why long-run costs are considered here is that the pure monopolist faces no threat from any other firms in the long term. The Segtendo Corporation is assumed to control the entire output of the computer games market because no firms are allowed to enter the market at any time. You will see later in this chapter that sometimes the firm is only capable of holding a position of monopoly in the short run, when the quantities of only some factors of production such as labour and raw materials can be varied. The model of the pure monopolist, however, assumes that a monopoly position can be maintained even in the long run, when all factors can be varied.

I have now established three curves or schedules for the Segtendo Corporation: average revenue (Figure 6.6), marginal revenue (Figure 6.7) and average/marginal costs (Figure 6.8).

Reflection

For purposes of revision, briefly explain to yourself the concepts used in Figures 6.6, 6.7 and 6.8. You might need to refer back to Chapters 4 and 5.

These curves can now be put together to determine the level of price chosen by the pure monopolist. To do this the profit-maximization rule introduced in Chapter 5 is used. In order to maximize profits a firm will always set marginal cost equal to marginal revenue. If marginal cost were below marginal revenue then the firm could increase profits by raising output, since more revenue than cost is associated with the additional sales. Conversely, if marginal revenue were below marginal cost the firm would save money by reducing output. The point of profit maximization is where marginal revenue is equal to marginal cost.

This point of profit maximization for the pure monopolist is shown in Figure 6.9.

The pure monopolist chooses to produce at output level *Q*, where *LRMC* = *MR*. This is the firm's profit-maximizing point. The demand curve (*AR*) shows that it will have to set a price *P* in order to sell that output (follow the vertical dashed line up from the horizontal axis at *Q* through point C).

For Segtendo to sell its profit-maximizing level of output it must choose the appropriate price level *P*. If it chooses too high a price then consumers will be dissuaded from buying the product; if it chooses too low a price then costs exceed revenues for the marginal goods sold. This is a nice problem

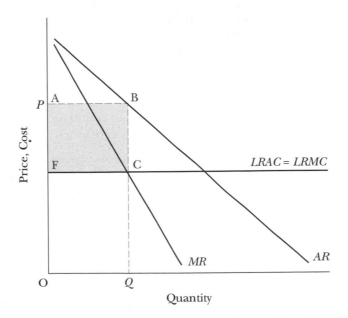

Figure 6.9 **The point of profit maximization for the pure monopolist**

Definitions

Price maker

A price maker is a firm with sufficient monopoly power to choose the price it wishes to charge for its product.

Normal profit

Normal profit is a profit which is just sufficient to induce the firm to remain in business.

Supernormal profit

Supernormal profit is a profit over and above normal profit.

for the firm to have, however, since it is the firm alone that sets the price. As a pure monopolist the firm is a price maker

This situation contrasts with the behaviour of firms in oligopolistic markets considered in the previous chapter. An oligopolist sets a price, but each price decision must take into account the reactions of other firms. The pure monopolist does not have to deal with such inconveniences.

This position of total dominance brings with it some obvious rewards. The profits which the monopolist is able to maximize can be huge. These profits are often referred to as supernormal profits, that is they are higher than the normal profits which would be earned if there were many firms in a market. If many firms could enter a market then it is plausible to suggest that the price would be lower than if there were only one firm in the market. If the Segtendo Corporation were the only seller of computer games then the price is likely to be higher than if, say, 50 different firms sold computer games. If each firm tried to undercut the prices charged by other firms (in order to compete for market shares) then the prices charged would almost certainly be less than the price charged by a pure monopolist. Indeed, as Section 4.3 will show, price would be driven down to equal the long-run average cost of production. At this price firms would gain just enough profits to prevent them from leaving the market.

How then, you might ask, can profit be considered to be a cost? The reason is that when a firm decides to invest its capital in a particular business activity it has to consider the return which could have been made on its capital from an alternative activity. By investing in, say, the computer business, the firm incurs a cost in terms of what it could have made in, for example, property development. This cost is referred to in economics as the *opportunity cost* – the amount of money a firm could have made from an alternative activity, but which has been forgone by carrying out its current activity. These opportunity costs are an integral part of the average cost curve.

The pure monopolist does not have to be content merely with normal profits. As we have seen, with a position of total monopoly power a price level higher than average costs can be charged. Assume, for example, that the Segtendo Corporation sells a million computer games at a price of 40 per game. If the average cost (including normal profit) of producing each game is 30, then a supernormal profit margin of 10 is made from each game. A total volume of supernormal profits of 10 million would be made from the million copies sold. If, on the other hand, there were 50 firms' selling computer games they may, through price competition, have to charge a price of 30 per game, so that no supernormal profits would be earned. Only the normal profits embodied in the average cost of 30 would be earned by each firm concerned.

In Figure 6.9 the volume of supernormal profits made by the pure monopolist is represented by the shaded area ABCF. The vertical distance between A and F (or between B and C) represents the profit margin, the difference between the price and average cost. The horizontal distance between A and B (or between F and C) represents the quantity of output produced. As shown in the computer games example, total supernormal profits are calculated by multiplying the profit margin by the total quantity of output. On the diagram this is the same as multiplying the distance AF by the distance AB to get the area of the rectangle ABCF. This area represents the total volume of supernormal profits earned by the pure monopolist.

Exercise 6.2

A pure monopolist produces 5 units of output at a price of 10 per unit. The average cost is 1 per unit. How much supernormal profit will the firm make? Illustrate your answer on a diagram under the assumption that the firm maximizes profits.

The next part of the chapter looks at the profit-maximizing behaviour of the monopolist in more detail by developing the concept of the price elasticity.

4.2   Elasticity and demand

Definition

Price elasticity of demand

The price elasticity of demand measures the responsiveness of the quantity demanded of a product to changes in its price.

An additional concept which is useful in understanding the behaviour of the monopolist is the price elasticity of demand. The monopolist will be interested in the responsiveness of consumers to changes in the price of its product.

The price elasticity is constructed, for a given price change, by comparing the proportion in which quantity demanded changes to the proportionate change in price. It has the following formula:

$$\text{price elasticity} = \frac{\text{proportionate change in quantity demanded}}{\text{proportionate change in price}}$$

The proportions are often expressed as percentages. Consider the case, for example, in which the price falls by 10 per cent and the quantity demanded increases by 100 per cent. To calculate the price elasticity, all that is required is to divide the proportionate change in quantity (100%) by the proportionate change in price (−10%). The price elasticity for this example is −10. Price elasticities of demand are generally negative because the price and demand changes move in opposite directions. In practice we compare the size of elasticities by just looking at the number, and ignoring the minus sign. We might say, for example, that an elasticity of −4 is greater or stronger than an elasticity of −1. This simply means that the number 4 is larger in magnitude than the number 1.

An analogy can be made between the strength of an elastic band and the size of an elasticity. If you pull a taut elastic band it will react sharply. Similarly, for a strong elasticity the reaction of the quantity demanded to a change in price will be pronounced.

There are two important things to note about the strength of the price elasticity and the behaviour of the monopolist. First, the monopolist will always prefer to produce a product which has a weak price elasticity. If the elasticity is weak (low) then the monopolist can increase the price and incur only a small proportionate reduction in quantity demanded. If the demand for the product is not completely choked off by the price rise then supernormal profits can be reaped. This point will be explained in more detail later in the chapter.

The second point to note is that the strength of the elasticity varies between points on the demand curve. These variations in the elasticity have an important bearing on the pricing decision of the monopolist, as will be made clear in the following more detailed explanation of the price elasticity.

Calculating the price elasticity

The formula for calculating the price elasticity can be investigated in more detail by defining some additional terms. First, let ΔP be the change in price and ΔQ the consequent change in quantity. The price elasticity will be represented by the Greek letter ε, and the price elasticity of demand by ε_D. With P representing the price level and Q the quantity demanded, the formula for the price elasticity can be expressed as

$$\varepsilon = \frac{\dfrac{\Delta Q}{Q}}{\dfrac{\Delta P}{P}}$$

The numerator represents the proportionate change in quantity $\dfrac{\Delta Q}{Q}$ whilst the denominator represents the proportionate change in price $\dfrac{\Delta P}{P}$.

I am now going to show how this elasticity can be calculated in terms of the slope of the demand curve. The price elasticity of demand (ε_D) will be calculated. This needs a bit of algebra, but I shall take you through this step by step.

The rule of thumb for manipulating fractions is that if any change is made to the numerator (the top part) this must also be carried out for the denominator (the bottom part). If both parts of the elasticity formula are multiplied by $\dfrac{P}{\Delta P}$ we have the expression

$$\varepsilon_D = \frac{\dfrac{\Delta Q}{Q}}{\dfrac{\Delta P}{P}} \cdot \frac{\dfrac{P}{\Delta P}}{\dfrac{P}{\Delta P}} = \frac{\Delta Q}{Q} \cdot \frac{P}{\Delta P}$$

Note that . here means 'multiplied by'. The P and ΔP terms in the bottom part of the elasticity cancel out such that only the top part is left. This amounts to flipping the term $\dfrac{\Delta P}{P}$ up into the numerator of the equation by inverting it to $\dfrac{P}{\Delta P}$. (Note that this rule of thumb for fractions only applies to the multiplication of terms in the numerator and denominator, and not to the addition and subtraction of terms.) Rearranging the terms, the elasticity can be presented in the form

$$\varepsilon_D = \frac{\Delta Q}{\Delta P} \cdot \frac{P}{Q}$$

A further expression can be derived by using the same process again to flip the term $\dfrac{\Delta Q}{\Delta P}$ to the denominator of the elasticity equation such that

$$\varepsilon_D = \frac{\dfrac{P}{Q}}{\dfrac{\Delta P}{\Delta Q}}$$

Note that the denominator here is the slope $\left(\dfrac{\Delta P}{\Delta Q}\right)$ of the demand curve.

This is illustrated in Figure 6.10a where for a change in P by -1 there is a change in Q of 1.

This means that the slope of the demand curve in Figure 6.10a is

$$\text{slope} = \frac{\Delta P}{\Delta Q} = \frac{-1}{1} = -1$$

The formula for the elasticity can therefore be represented as

$$\varepsilon_D = \frac{\dfrac{P}{Q}}{\text{slope}}$$

To calculate the price elasticity of demand (ε_D) at a point on a demand curve all that is needed, therefore, is the slope of the demand curve and the proportion $\dfrac{P}{Q}$. This calculation can be illustrated by calculating some price elasticities for different points on the same demand curve. These points are shown in Figure 6.10b. At point A the price of £8 per unit of output generates 2 units of demand. At point B a price of £5 generates 5 units of demand.

Since the value of P at point A is 8 and the value of Q is 2, it follows that the price elasticity of demand at A is

$$\varepsilon_D = \frac{\dfrac{P}{Q}}{\text{slope}} = \frac{\dfrac{8}{2}}{-1} = \frac{4}{-1} = -4$$

Therefore by entering these elements into the formula for the price elasticity an estimate of -4 is calculated.

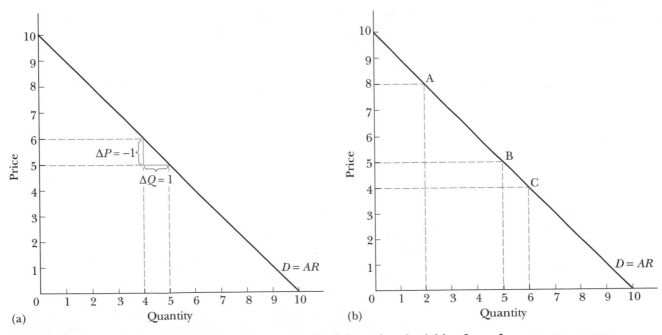

Figure 6.10   **(a) The slope of the demand curve. (b) Deriving price elasticities from the average revenue (demand) curve**

Question

What is the price elasticity for the demand for computer games at point B in Figure 6.10b? We know that the slope of the demand curve is −1 from Figure 6.10a. You need to read off the values for Q and P from the diagram and plug these terms, together with the slope, into the elasticity formula.

The price elasticities at each of the three points on Figure 6.10b are shown in Table 6.5.

Table 6.5

Point in Figure 6.10b	P	Q	$\dfrac{P}{Q}$	Slope $\left(\dfrac{\Delta P}{\Delta Q}\right)$	Elasticity $\left(\dfrac{\frac{P}{Q}}{\text{slope}}\right)$
A	8	2	4	−1	−4
B	5	5	1	−1	−1
C	4	6	$\dfrac{2}{3}$	−1	$-\dfrac{2}{3}$

Notice that the strength of the elasticity falls as we move along the demand curve from A to C in Table 6.5. At point A a change in price has a strong proportionate effect on demand, resulting in a price elasticity of −4. On the other hand at point C the price elasticity is much weaker with a value of only $-\dfrac{2}{3}$. Point B, with an elasticity of −1, provides an important watershed between the two extremes. Points A to C represent three different values of elasticities: the elasticity at point A is characterized as elastic, the elasticity at point B as unit elastic, and the elasticity at point C as inelastic.

Notice therefore that the demand curve in Figure 6.10a and b is a straight line with a constant slope $\left(\dfrac{\Delta P}{\Delta Q} = -1\right)$ but nevertheless has varying elasticity along its length.

In addition to explaining the nature of demand for different goods, elasticities are important because they define the different segments of the demand curve. On the region of the demand curve to the right of point B in Figure 6.10b demand is inelastic. Under the assumption of profit-maximization the Segtendo Corporation will only be interested in selling its product at a price which corresponds to the elastic part of the demand curve. This is because at a price corresponding to the inelastic part of the demand curve marginal revenue is negative – there is a loss in terms of additional revenue from lowering the price of the good, though the extra output still incurs positive marginal costs.

Why is this so? If demand is inelastic, the proportionate change in quantity is less than the proportionate change in price – elasticity is less than 1. So if price falls say by 10 per cent, quantity demanded will rise by less than 10 per cent. Hence total revenue will be reduced. It also follows that when there is a unit elasticity the marginal revenue is zero (point B in Figure 6.10b). So a wise monopolist will choose its output only on the elastic part of the demand curve – to the left of point B in Figure 6.10b, where marginal revenue is positive.

Definitions

Elastic demand

The demand is elastic if $\varepsilon_D > 1$ (the proportionate change in quantity demanded is greater than the proportionate change in price).

Unit elastic demand

The demand is unit elastic if $\varepsilon_D = 1$ (the proportionate change in quantity demanded is the same as the proportionate change in price).

Inelastic demand

The demand is inelastic if $\varepsilon_D < 1$ (the proportionate change in quantity demanded is less than the proportionate change in price).

(Note that these definitions ignore the minus sign.)

How can the behaviour of a pure monopolist be characterized? Write your own note, using the following key words in your exposition: marginal revenue, marginal cost, price maker, price elasticity, supernormal profits.

4.3   Monopolistic competition

Since pure monopoly is very much a limiting case, a more general theory of monopoly power has been developed in which there are many firms in a market. Competition between firms is therefore present but each firm also retains some monopoly power – hence the term monopolistic competition. The key characteristic which allows these firms to retain some monopoly power is *product differentiation*. Each firm develops a specific profile or brand for its product which makes it slightly different from the products of other firms – it can be differentiated from other products.

McDonald's, for example, sells hamburgers but its product is promoted as distinctively different from the hamburgers sold by other chains. McDonald's can be said to have monopoly power because it can to some extent choose the price of its hamburgers. Even if it doubled its prices there are some particularly spoilt children who would demand a McDonald's, and there are some particularly weak parents who would buy it. McDonald's has a monopoly over the production of McDonald's hamburgers.

There are similarities between the types of markets to which the theory of monopolistic competition applies and those to which the theory of oligopoly, discussed in the previous chapter, applies. Both theories apply to markets in which there is more than one firm competing. The best way to understand these theories is to view them as different 'ways of seeing' markets in which there is more than one firm with monopoly power. In the model of oligopoly, each firm engages in a game of moves and counter moves, and oligopoly theory tries to determine the outcome. Under monopolistic competition the main difference between firms focuses on the extent to which they can differentiate their products from each other. As will be explained, this product differentiation provides the means by which firms can charge higher prices than if they all produced the same product.

This ability to choose or make the price of the product means that each firm under monopolistic competition faces a downward sloping demand curve. If a firm charges a high price for its particular brand of product, the demand will be less than if it charged a lower price. Suppose that initially a firm has developed a distinctive product which allows it to choose its price so as to make supernormal profits. In Figure 6.11 the firm makes the most of its monopoly power to force up price and restrict output at Q_2. At this stage the firm is behaving exactly like the monopolist just studied.

Note that unlike the case of pure monopoly, under monopolistic competition the firms cannot prevent the entry of other firms into the market. To enter the market these firms will need to employ new factors of production, which requires us to look at their long-run cost curves.

It should also be noted that the long-run average cost ($LRAC$) curve drawn in Figure 6.11 is L-shaped, in contrast to the case of pure monopoly where,

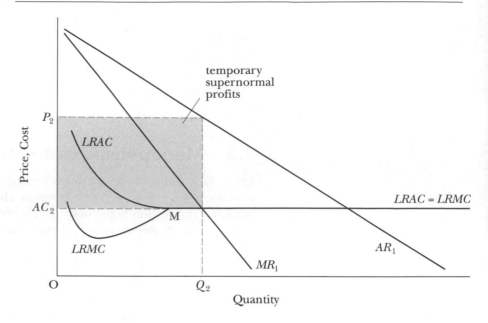

Figure 6.11 A temporary monopoly position under monopolistic competition

for simplicity, a horizontal line was assumed. The precise shape of this curve is a matter of some dispute in economics, but following Neil Costello's discussion in Chapter 4 I will assume an L-shaped *LRAC* curve in this chapter. To the left of point M (the point of minimum efficient scale) the long-run marginal cost (*LRMC*) curve is below the long-run average cost (*LRAC*) curve. To the right of point M the equality *LRAC* = *LRMC* holds. Note also that since other firms are allowed to enter the market the demand curve faced by the firm is not the same as the demand curve for the whole market. In the case of pure monopoly there was only one firm so the demand curve faced by the firm was the market demand curve. Once there is more than one firm producing in a market we have to focus on the demand curve faced by the individual firm, since this is not the same as the market demand curve. This individual firm is often referred to as the representative firm, since it represents the behaviour of a typical firm in the market.

In the first instance (in Figure 6.11) the firm equalizes marginal cost with marginal revenue at output level Q_2. A price level P_2 is charged and, in view of the margin between this price and average costs (AC_2), supernormal profits are made by the firm. The supernormal profits which the firm makes are shown by the shaded area. In the short run new firms will not be able to enter the market. There will be no time for them to buy the new equipment and premises necessary to engage in competition. Just after the fall of the Berlin Wall, for example, McDonald's set up a new shop in Moscow. The demand for McDonald's hamburgers was so considerable that it probably made supernormal profits in the short run. In the long run, however, other burger chains will move to Moscow as Russia becomes more open and the supernormal profits which McDonald's first made will be bid down by the competition.

In the second stage other firms are attracted into the market by the volume of supernormal profits made by the firm. This reduces the demand for the representative firm's product and its own demand curve shifts to the left. For each price level, consumers demand less of the firm's product than before the new firms entered the market. This shift in the demand (average revenue) curve is shown in Figure 6.12.

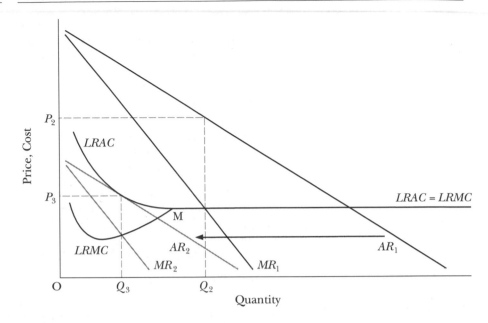

Figure 6.12 **The long-run equilibrium position under monopolistic competition**

The firm's demand curve therefore moves from AR_1 to AR_2. The curve AR_2 is the result of a process in which the demand curve moves to the left until all supernormal profits are eaten away. A new marginal revenue curve (MR_2) is drawn underneath the new demand curve such that the firm now maximizes profits (hence $MR_2 = LRMC$) at output level Q_3. The new price level charged by the firm is P_3, which is the same as the long-run average cost of producing Q_3. Since price is now equal to average cost the firm no longer makes any supernormal profits.

A good example of monopolistic competition is the market for up-market four-wheel drive road vehicles. The Range Rover, introduced in the early 1970s, pioneered a new niche in the world car market: a trendy and more comfortable alternative to the more established Land Rover. It became fashionable for well-to-do mothers to use four-wheel drive vehicles for visits to the supermarket, with their children safely strapped in the back seat. In the short run, Rover were able to make supernormal profits on this innovatory product. In the long run, however, the Range Rover has faced competition from the Toyota Landcruiser, the Mitsubishi Shogun, the Vauxhall Frontera and several other alternative four-wheel drive vehicles. This has eaten away the initial supernormal profits made by Rover. Due to product differentiation some consumers will still demand Range Rovers, but many will be attracted by alternative brands.

It could be argued, of course, that the car market is also oligopolistic in the sense that the major car producers will engage in interdependent (perhaps game theoretic) behaviour. The point to be made is that both monopolistic competition and oligopoly are different ways of seeing this type of market.

Question

List both the similarities and the differences between the theory of pure monopoly and the theory of monopolistic competition.

Under both pure monopoly and monopolistic competition the firm is a price maker – it faces a demand curve for its product for which a price level must be chosen. Under both theories the firm is also usually assumed to maximize profits such that marginal revenue is equal to marginal cost. The difference between the theories arises because the pure monopolist can restrict the entry by other firms into the market. It makes supernormal profits and these can be maintained in the long run in the absence of any entry by other firms. Under monopolistic competition, however, supernormal profits can only be made in the short run. In the long run other firms will enter the market, thereby reducing demand and eating away the short-run profits earned by the firm.

In the discussion that follows, these theories are used to assess the disadvantages of monopoly power.

4.4   The disadvantages of monopoly

I shall now turn to a common theme which characterizes both the theory of pure monopoly and the theory of monopolistic competition. Monopoly power generates restrictions in output which result in high prices. Under certain assumptions in both these theories of monopoly firms could have also produced their products at a lower level of costs. In view of their monopoly power, however, they can be tempted to produce at a higher level of costs than the minimum of the average cost curve. For the firm, the key consideration is the level of profits not the level of costs – the firm in these models monitors the difference between price and costs. Since a restriction of output forces up the price level, firms are prepared to produce at a higher level of cost and at an even higher level of price.

There are three main disadvantages of monopoly power which flow from this scenario.

High costs

One of the consequences of monopoly power is that firms do not always produce at their point of minimum efficient scale. Consider the behaviour of the firm engaged in monopolistic competition in Figure 6.12. The firm produces at a long-run level of output of Q_3. This firm is not minimizing average costs. If it produced at point M or anywhere to the right of point M, average costs would be lower than at Q_3.

The point to be made is that for a firm with monopoly power cost minimization is not its main objective. Its main objective is the pursuit of profit maximization, and this can result in levels of output which are not at the point of minimum efficient scale. The reason for this outcome is that firms which enjoy monopoly power tend to restrict output in order to charge a high profit-maximizing price for their product. The conclusion to be drawn is that monopoly power leads to a high cost, high price product.

Stagnation

The restriction of output levels by firms which enjoy monopoly power has knock-on effects on the economy as a whole. For some economists this behaviour is now considered to be prevalent throughout the world economy, and is the key reason why unemployment is so high in most countries. These economists are part of the monopoly capitalism school of thought, a tradition which has its roots at the start of the twentieth century.

The organizing theme of this tradition is that monopoly power has steadily grown over the last hundred or so years (see for example, Cowling, 1982). Evidence for this growth is provided by the steady increase over time of firm concentration ratios. Whilst there are problems with concentration ratios as indicators of monopoly power, as we have seen, these problems are not considered to be so serious by members of the school of monopoly capitalism as to make them useless. They regard the evidence for a long-run increase in monopoly power as compelling.

There are a number of variants of the stagnation model but in the exposition that follows I shall concentrate on the restrictions of output associated with increases in monopoly power for individual firms. This is shown in Figure 6.13, where a representative firm is initially producing at Q_1. At this initial position the firm does not enjoy any monopoly power. (The behaviour of firms without monopoly power is discussed in the next chapter.)

Assume that the firm gains some monopoly power and restricts output to Q_2 in order to force up the price to P_2. The firm gains supernormal profits equivalent to the area ABCF.

The problem with this outcome is that the firm and the market in which it operates are considered in isolation from other firms in other markets. If the increase in monopoly power were to happen for a selection of firms in various markets then the impacts of restrictions in output for all these firms must be accounted for. These impacts work via the consumption function, which was introduced in Chapter 3. Recall that the consumption function measures the relationship between consumption and income:

consumption = f(income)

If all the firms which gain monopoly power restrict their output, then it follows that each firm will employ fewer workers. Workers who lose their jobs will also lose their income, at least whilst they remain unemployed. Since they receive less income they will also, as the consumption function indicates, spend less money in the market-place. In short the increase in

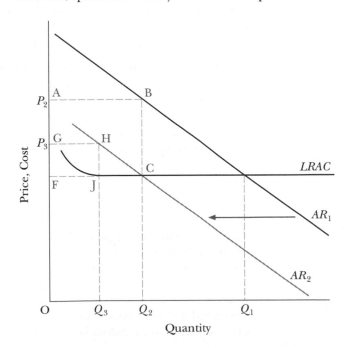

Figure 6.13   **The indirect effect of monopoly power on demand**

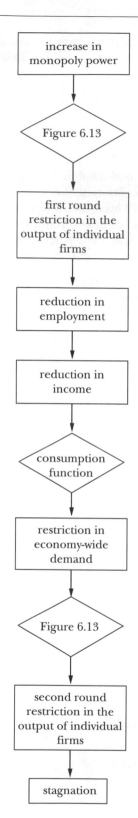

Figure 6.14 **A flow diagram of the stagnation model**

monopoly power throughout the economy reduces the level of consumer demand in the economy. Monopolists restrict output, sack workers, and these workers demand fewer goods and services.

The problem is that the monopolists sell goods and services to workers. For each individual firm the impact of sacking its workers on the demand for its own product will be small. However, when the expenditure of workers sacked by each firm is added up for the economy as a whole, the effect on demand can be considerable. Since each firm sells its product to workers throughout the economy, each firm can face a reduction in demand for its product. This reduction is represented in Figure 6.13 by the leftward shift of the demand curve. It can be seen that whilst the firm was quite right in its own terms to restrict output to Q_2 in order to make supernormal profits (ABCF), the eventual outcome is a further restriction in output and a reduced level of supernormal profits (FGHJ).

The result of this scenario is that output undergoes a twofold reduction (see Figure 6.14). In the first round the increase in monopoly power effects a restriction in the output of the individual firm. In the second round this restriction effects a cut in consumer demand, based on the knock-on effects of less employment and less income. The cut in consumer demand restricts the level of economy-wide demand, and this means that the demand for each individual firm's product is reduced. There is, therefore, a second-round restriction of the output of the individual firm.

The consequence of these reductions in output as a result of monopoly power is that for the economy as a whole there is stagnation. The individual firms do not receive the supernormal profits they expected from obtaining their monopoly power, and their output is severely restricted. When output is restricted over a long period of time – which it will be if monopoly power increases over time – this can be characterized as a situation in which there is stagnation. The demand in the economy and the level of output are so low that not enough workers are employed in the economy to prevent widespread unemployment. For proponents of the school of monopoly capitalism the high level of monopoly power means that capitalist economies are now permanently burdened with high levels of unemployment – they are permanently stagnating.

It could be argued that although worker consumption is reduced by the increase in monopoly power, there could be a counterbalancing increase in consumption out of profits. If the increase in monopoly power generates more potential profits for the firms in question, then the recipients of these profits – the shareholders in the firms – may increase their consumption of goods and services. The problem with this argument is that shareholders tend to be drawn from high income groups and their propensities to consume goods and services will tend to be less than the consumption propensities of the sacked workers. The redistribution from workers to shareholders will almost certainly have a detrimental impact on consumer demand.

Another criticism of the theory is that firms are behaving irrationally if they deliberately generate a reduction in economy-wide demand. If the knock-on effects of a restriction in output on consumer demand and the consequent effect on profits are so evident, why do firms behave in this way? A possible defence against this argument is that there are unintended consequences associated with individual actions. Firms do not have the ability to predict the economy-wide consequences of their behaviour. Recall that in Chapter 5 the prisoners' dilemma showed that the consequence of each firm pursuing profit maximization may turn out to be adverse for firms in total. The extent to which firms can predict these indirect consequences is a matter for discussion.

Before moving on to some additional disadvantages of monopoly power, it should be emphasized that the stagnation model is a different type of theory from the static theories of monopoly introduced in the rest of Section 4. The main difference is that it looks at the economy as a whole and not just at the behaviour of individual firms. The consumption function establishes relationships between different monopolists and consumers which are not considered in the static theory of monopoly. You may recall from Section 2 of this chapter that economists either look at monopoly power for specific industries or for the economy as a whole. The stagnation model falls into the latter category. This type of economy-wide analysis will be looked at in much greater detail in Book 2 of this text.

It should also be mentioned that this exposition of the stagnation model forms only part of the literature associated with the school of monopoly capitalism. Questions such as the relationship between monopoly power, investment and technical progress, which form important areas of interest for this school, have not been considered.

Advertising

We have seen that under monopolistic competition firms undertake product differentiation. McDonald's seek to differentiate their hamburgers from those produced by other chains. One of the ways in which this is accomplished is through advertising. Advertisements on television, radio and posters create an image with consumers of a particular product. This has become an important part of the activities of firms. Figure 6.15 shows the amount of money (at constant prices) spent on advertising expenditure in the UK since 1938. These figures include advertising which firms use to sell goods to other firms as well as advertising to attract consumers.

Apart from a blip in the 1940s, there has been a steady increase in the volume of UK advertising expenditure since the Second World War. The latest figure of about £5 billion in 1992 represents a considerable

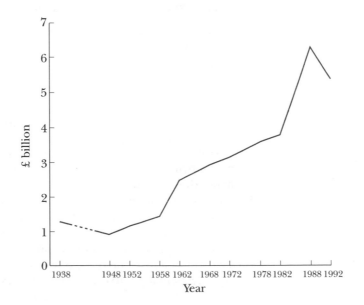

Figure 6.15 **UK total advertising expenditure (constant 1985 prices)**

Source: The UK Advertising Association

proportion of the economy's resources. By way of comparison, the UK Department of Transport planned to spend £5.9 billion on all its various responsibilities during the period 1993–94 (HM Treasury, 1993). This means that advertising expenditure in the UK is equivalent to the expenditure of a major government department. All the money spent on posters and television advertisements, etc. is equivalent to the amount spent in the public sector on the UK transport network.

A question to be asked, in view of the amount of money spent on it, is whether advertising expenditure is useful to society. Advertising is used to build up the loyalty of consumers to a product by associating that product with particular characteristics which are found to be pleasing. For Green and Sutcliffe (1987) these characteristics are often not inherent in the product itself – they are used merely to distinguish the product from other brands:

> Thus a particular item of clothing (as worn by such and such a princess) may seem to fulfil a desire for social advancement, a particular model of motor car (draped with near-naked young women) to be a passport to sexual fulfilment for heterosexual men, a particular brand of fast-acting floor cleaner to look like the way to better motherhood, or a make of cigarette to give you that cool, masculine image (without, of course, troubling you with the associated health risks).

(Green and Sutcliffe, 1987, p.67)

The main disadvantage of advertising, therefore, is that it can represent a waste of resources. It also creates wants in consumers for products which they would not have bought without such manipulation. You will recall from Chapter 3 that wants in consumers can be created according to the so-called 'demonstration effect' whereby consumers are influenced by the consumption of other agents. The problem with this concept, originating in the work of the economist J.S. Duesenberry, is that it does not successfully identify the original source of consumption. Duesenberry weakly asserted that the 'basic source of the drive toward higher consumption is to be found in the character of our culture' (Cowling, 1982, p.62). This gap in the theory can be filled by advertising, which can provide an initial source for consumer expenditure which influences the behaviour of other consumers.

The effect of advertising on consumer behaviour can be formalized by looking at an individual firm's demand curve (see Figure 6.16). Each firm takes an interest in the slope of the demand curve for its product.

Assume that a new advertising campaign changes the shape of the demand curve. The original curve AR_1 is replaced by a new and steeper curve (AR_2). Advertising makes the demand curve steeper by increasing the loyalty of consumers to the firm's product. This can be shown in Figure 6.16 by comparing the magnitudes of changes in price (ΔP) and quantity (ΔQ). Since the firm is always interested in the effects of an increase in its price on demand, these terms can be compared for the original demand curve AR_1. It can be seen that an increase in price of one unit ($\Delta P=1$) between points A and B will generate a fall in quantity demanded of two units ($\Delta Q=-2$). The firm would have to take note of this loss in demand for its product if it increased the price level. After the advertising campaign, however, the effect on demand of a price increase is less pronounced. Between points C and F on the new demand curve the same increase in price ($\Delta P=1$) generates a

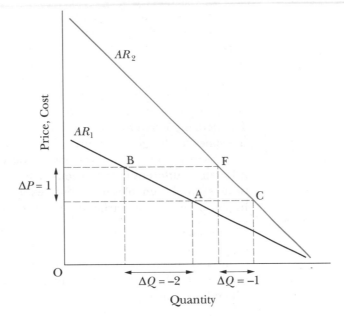

Figure 6.16 **The effect of advertising on price elasticities**

fall in demand of only one unit ($\Delta Q = -1$). After the advertising campaign the firm is in a better position to increase price, and reap the rewards in terms of higher profits.

Advertising and the price elasticity

This effect of advertising on the shape of the demand curve can be interpreted in terms of the size of the price elasticity. Recall that the formula for the price elasticity is

$$\frac{\dfrac{P}{Q}}{\text{slope}}$$

where the slope is equal to $\dfrac{\Delta P}{\Delta Q}$. For the first demand curve (AR_1) in Figure 6.16 $\Delta P = 1$ and $\Delta Q = -2$; which means that

$$\frac{\Delta P}{\Delta Q} = -\frac{1}{2}$$

On the other hand, for the second demand curve $\Delta P = 1$ and $\Delta Q = -1$, so it follows that

$$\frac{\Delta P}{\Delta Q} = -1$$

On examining the formula for the price elasticity this means that the price elasticity of the first demand curve in Figure 6.16 is greater in magnitude than the price elasticity of the second. Since for any given price level the slope of AR_1 is less than the slope of AR_2, it follows that the price elasticity

$$\frac{\dfrac{P}{Q}}{\text{slope}}$$

for AR_1 will at each price level be greater than the price elasticity of AR_2.

A steeper demand curve, such as AR_2, can be described as more inelastic than the original demand curve AR_1. The more inelastic is the demand curve the more the firm is able to charge a high price. An example of this is provided in the early 1990s by certain brands of sports shoes that children of a certain age like to wear. Since the wants of these young consumers are so strong, built up through advertising and the 'demonstration effect', they (or their parents) are prepared to buy the shoes for a considerable price. The demand curve for this product is sufficiently inelastic for the sellers of the shoes to charge a high price. The argument against advertising in this instance is not only that it represents wasted expenditure – there is nothing inherently different in the expensive equipment from that of less expensive brands – it also enables the firm to exercise monopoly power and charge a higher price, to the detriment of the consumer.

At this stage I have, of course, only presented one side of the argument – the disadvantages of advertising which follow from the static theory of monopoly. There are important advantages associated with advertising and these will be discussed in the context of dynamic theories of monopoly to which I now turn.

5   The dynamic theory of monopoly

The main proponents of the dynamic theory of monopoly have been the economists, Joseph Schumpeter and Ludwig Hayek. Since they were both Austrian and both criticized the static theory of monopoly I shall refer to their dynamic approach as the Austrian critique.

5.1   The Austrian critique

The theories of pure monopoly and monopolistic competition are both characterized by their static nature. Firms are captured at a particular point in time in which profits are maximized and decisions made about price and output. An equilibrium is formed where the firm settles at its most profitable level of output. This equilibrium can be said to result in high costs and prices, and low levels of output. Any theory which uses the notion of equilibrium is static because there is no motion – the demand curve and the cost curves are fixed. There is some motion associated with monopolistic competition, of course, since the firm can only make supernormal profits in the short run. The firm moves from its short-run equilibrium to its long-run equilibrium. Nevertheless the theory is still static because any motion is merely displayed as movements between two forms of static equilibrium. This mode of analysis is often referred to as *comparative statics*.

A different perspective is taken by a set of writers known as the Austrian school. For them monopoly power must be set in a dynamic context – a context in which the dominant economic forces are never in equilibrium. Joseph Schumpeter, one of the Austrian school's most notable exponents, has been a major critic of those economists who use static theories to explain monopolistic behaviour. For these economists, big firms 'seem to aim at nothing but high prices and restrictions of output'. Yet they 'accept the data of the momentary situation as if there were no past or future to it and think that they have understood what there is to understand if they interpret the behaviour of those firms by means of the principle of maximizing profits with reference to those data' (Schumpeter, 1942, p.84).

For Schumpeter the past and future are central to an understanding of any firm's activities. The snapshot provided by static theories of equilibrium does not provide a full picture of whether the firm's activities are beneficial or detrimental to society.

In Schumpeter's view capitalism develops through a process of creative destruction. Firms do not merely compete with each other using prices. For Schumpeter (1942, p.84) 'in capitalist reality as distinguished from its textbook picture, it is not that kind of competition which counts but the competition from the new commodity, the new technology … '. Firms continually develop new techniques of production and new products which can completely replace the products produced by their rivals. The motor car replaces the horse and cart, the railways replace the canals, such that whole sections of the economy are destroyed by new innovations. This destruction is creative because it is part of the motor of capitalist development – capitalism grows through innovation and the destruction of old methods.

Once the behaviour of the firm is set in this context, no firm can hold a position of monopoly power for any length of time. The canal companies come under threat from the railways and the railways from the motor car. No firm can rest from the threat of new innovations and new products. For Schumpeter, one of the distinguishing features of the growth of capitalism since its inception has been the increase in the quality of goods and services which firms provide. This drive towards new and better quality products is something to which all firms must respond.

Figure 6.17 provides an example of how this process of creative destruction might work. In Period 1 there are three firms competing in a particular market. It is assumed that firm 3 introduces a new innovation which completely destroys the competition of the other two firms. Firms 1 and 2, accordingly, go out of business and in the second period firm 3 becomes a pure monopolist – the only producer in the market. The point to be made, however, is that this process of destruction has been creative because a new innovation has been introduced which will be beneficial to society. The

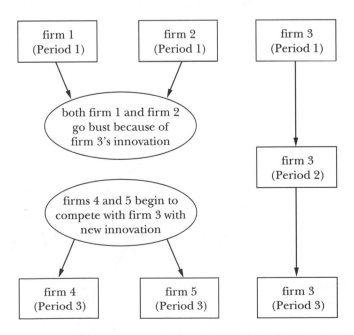

Figure 6.17 **A three period example of creative destruction**

position of monopoly power which firm 3 attains in the second period provides the incentive for this innovation. Moreover, this position of monopoly power provides the incentive in the third period for two additional firms – firms 4 and 5 – to enter the market with their own innovations in an attempt to destroy firm 3.

Monopoly power is therefore not considered to be a problem by the Austrian school because of its temporary role in the process of creative destruction. A static view of Period 2 in the example would cause all sorts of alarm bells to ring; but once a firm's behaviour is set in a dynamic context there are benefits to be gained by society from a temporary position of monopoly power.

5.2   The advantages of monopoly power

I shall outline several advantages which can be associated with monopoly power under an Austrian perspective.

Innovation

The attraction of monopoly power to firms is the possibility of making supernormal profits. Schumpeter argued that this can be beneficial to the process of creative destruction. Firms which are engaged in risky innovations may not be able to obtain financial backing from banks for the research and development stage of the production process. A flow of supernormal profits can provide the funding for such purposes. Smaller firms operating in more competitive environments may not be able to invest the same resources in the development of new innovations.

If monopolistic firms can invest more resources into innovations this will enable the firm to produce at lower cost levels. Costs may be so low for firms with monopoly power that the overall production of society is economically more efficient than if there was more competition. Figure 6.18 uses the static model to illustrate this point by showing a monopolist producing an output Q_1 at an average cost per unit of AC_1 and a price per unit of P_1.

The introduction of an innovation in the method of production shifts the cost curve downwards since the quantity produced can be produced at a

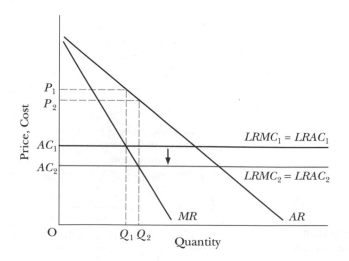

Figure 6.18 **The effect of a monopolist's innovation on price and costs**

lower cost per unit. The firm maximizes profits such that marginal cost is equalized with marginal revenue at a new level of output Q_2. At this new level of output both the average cost (AC_2) and the price (P_2) are lower than before the innovation.

In simple terms the firm's monopoly power enables it to invest in cost-reducing innovations and this enables it to charge a lower price level than if it faced more competition. In the process of creative destruction, which Schumpeter envisaged, firms can use their monopoly power to invest in new innovations; and this leads to industrial growth and a provision of cheaper products.

Evidence on the extent to which firms that enjoy monopoly power engage in innovations can be provided by looking at the amount spent on research and development for firms of different sizes. We know, of course, that large firms do not necessarily enjoy monopoly power – this depends on the size of the market in question. However, we also know that the necessary conditions for monopoly power are often gained via mergers with other firms or via economies of scale. Both these origins of monopoly power tend to increase the size of the firm.

On the face of it there is a relationship between the size of the firm and innovation. In the USA, for example, 89 per cent of all industrial research and development (R&D) in 1978 was performed by firms with more than 5000 employees (Freeman, 1982). Similarly, in Japan, firms employing more than 3000 employees conducted about two-thirds of all R&D. It would, however, be crude to deduce simply from this evidence that big firms are more innovative than small firms. The amount of money spent on R&D is not the same thing as the output which comes from it. There can be research and development which does not result in any innovations.

One possible way of finding the output of R&D is to look at the number of patents. Firms often put patents on new innovations which prevent their competitors from stealing them. The number of patents secured by different sized firms can therefore provide an indication of their propensity to innovate. Soete (1979) looked at both R&D expenditure and the number of patents for a sample of the largest firms in the USA (Table 6.6).

Table 6.6 **Firm size, patents, and research and development in the USA, 1976**

Number of firms	Number of patents per $ billion of sales	R&D as % of sales
Largest 4	11.86	2.69
Largest 8	17.98	2.94
Largest 12	20.17	2.90
Largest 16	20.06	2.50
Largest 20	21.41	2.44
Largest 30	24.47	2.50
Largest 40	23.03	2.34
Largest 50	23.55	2.32
Largest 75	23.17	2.14
Largest 100	22.99	2.02

Source: Soete (1979) reproduced in Freeman (1982) p.135

The results are somewhat conflicting. The evidence that R&D increases with firm size is confirmed. The largest eight firms in the group spend 2.94 per cent of their sales on R&D compared to only 2.02 per cent for the largest 100. On the other hand, the ratio of patents secured to sales by firms falls as they increase in size. The largest 100 companies secure 22.99 patents per billion dollars of sales, compared to only 11.86 patents for the largest four firms.

Small firms may, however, be more likely to secure patents than large firms because there is an incentive to sell their ideas to others. The high number of patents for small firms may not mean that they are more innovative than large firms. This factor can be analysed by distinguishing between inventions and development. For a new innovation to come into play there must be an initial invention and a process of development in which the invention is tailored to the needs of the market. It may be that small firms are more likely to introduce inventions but they are more likely to be developed by larger firms. The extent to which this is true depends on the industry in question. Freeman (1982, p.137) writes, 'In the chemical industry, where both research and development work are often very expensive, large firms predominate in both invention and innovation. In the mechanical engineering industry, inexpensive ingenuity can play a greater part and small firms or private inventors make a larger contribution.' For some industries the small organization can enable it to undertake innovations which leave the larger firms lagging behind.

Stability

A classic argument in favour of monopolistic practices is that they provide stability. For Schumpeter firms which are undermined by the process of creative destruction can be given some temporary protection from monopoly power which will slow down their demise. Some firms may even be given time to adapt to new innovations and hence survive the process of creative destruction. Schumpeter (1942, p.90) states that 'there is certainly no point in trying to conserve obsolescent industries indefinitely; but there is a point in trying to avoid their coming down with a crash and in attempting to turn a rout, which may become a canter of cumulative depressive effects, into orderly retreat.' Similarly, there is a case for firms which are advancing their position making an 'orderly advance'. It can be argued that the process of creative destruction can produce a more steady expansion of output if firms are able to protect themselves from the full blown gale of competition.

Information

We saw, in our run through the disadvantages of monopoly power, that the degree of advertising associated with monopolistic competition is considered by some commentators to be a problem. From an Austrian perspective advertising can be considered to be an integral part of economic growth. For Hayek (1937) the distinguishing feature of a market economy is that all transactions are voluntary. Consumers decide on which transactions to make according to all the available information. Advertising provides a major part of this information – it acts as a tool which enables the market to function. If a particular advertisement is inappropriate or inefficient then in the long run consumers will not buy the product which is being advertised. It follows that in the long run advertising is an efficient part of the process by which firms operate.

A good example of the possible advantages of advertising is in the provision of legal services. Historically the legal profession has not been allowed to advertise its services, although there have been some changes in both the UK and USA in recent years. This has meant that consumers have not been able to find out about the various legal services which are available. Indeed, it could be argued that since lawyers have not been allowed to advertise the price of their services, this has led to high prices. With a ban on advertising consumers cannot easily find out the prices which different lawyers charge for their services. From a Hayekian perspective advertising provides information to consumers, allowing them to choose the best product, thereby rewarding the best producers in the market.

Reflection

Look back through the chapter and list the advantages and disadvantages of monopoly power.

6   Conclusion

You have learnt a number of new skills in this chapter which should enable you to discuss the case for and against monopoly power. There are two extreme positions which you could take.

You could use the material in this chapter to argue that monopoly power is a major problem which policy makers should use all their energy to tackle. Using concentration ratios you could show that monopoly power is a widespread phenomenon in the world economy. In addition, it has been shown that much of the increase in concentration has no explanation other than the merging of firms in pursuit of supernormal profits. These profits are made at the expense of the consumer who has to pay high prices. Furthermore, monopolists force up prices by cutting output and this generates stagnation in the economy as a whole.

At the other extreme you could attack these arguments and argue that monopoly power is not really a problem at all. You could argue that the concentration ratios which economists use are virtually meaningless. It may even be the case that with the opening up of markets competition has actually increased. Taking a long-run Austrian perspective, firms are forever competing over the provision of new products of increasing quality. In this context firms can only enjoy monopoly power over short periods of time. In those cases in which particular firms hold on to monopoly power there may be some very good technical reasons which cannot be avoided. Even if there is monopoly power this may provide extra resources for investment and stability.

These two extreme positions miss out many other factors which we have considered, but they do illustrate the way in which the material in this chapter can be used to discuss monopoly power. There is no need, of course, to take either of these extreme positions. Monopoly power could be argued to be advantageous in some circumstances and disadvantageous in others. The point to be made is that there is a dispute between economists over monopoly power which the skills acquired in this chapter can be used to debate.

PART 4
CHAPTER 7

EVALUATING COMPETITION
THE PERFECTLY COMPETITIVE MARKET

by Catherine Price

1 Introduction

> The primary objective of the Government's privatization programme is to reduce the power of the monopolist and to encourage competition. The long term success of the privatization programme will stand or fall by the extent to which it maximises competition. If competition cannot be achieved, an historic opportunity will have been lost. Competition is an extraordinarily efficient mechanism.
>
> *(John Moore quoted in Kay et al. (eds), 1986)*

In this way, John Moore, then Secretary to the Treasury, justified the UK privatization programme in 1983. His arguments mirror the concern about monopolies expressed in the previous chapter, and provide a useful link to the theme of this chapter. How do competitive firms and industries behave, and in what sense are they 'extraordinarily efficient'?

This chapter explains that a very particular set of economic ideas about competition lies behind statements such as the one above. The way of seeing competition discussed in this chapter sharply counterposes competition and monopoly. Less monopoly power, as John Moore suggests, implies more competition. Competitive markets in this view are markets where firms and consumers lack monopoly power.

The central objective of this chapter is to examine this view of competition. I start by considering what it might mean for firms to have no monopoly power. In contrast to the firms discussed in Chapter 6, competitive firms in this sense must be small relative to the market, and able to exercise little or no influence over the price at which they sell their product. Many markets exhibit these characteristics to some extent as Section 2 demonstrates. For example, a 'competitive fringe' of firms competing with a dominant supplier in a market may have little influence over the price of their products.

Sections 3 and 4 discuss a model of competition built upon this assumption of absence of monopoly power. This model of 'perfect competition' is an important model within economics, for several reasons which this chapter explains. In addition to capturing some aspects of how competition functions in observed markets, the model also generates some strong conclusions concerning the superior efficiency of competitive over monopolized markets. As the quotation from John Moore suggests, these conclusions have influenced government policy, from privatization in Britain to economic reform in Eastern Europe.

Sections 5 and 6 then show that in order for the model of perfect competition to play this evaluative role, it is necessary to extend the idea of maximization from firms to consumers. Not only do firms maximize profits in this model, but consumers spend their limited incomes to get maximum satisfaction from their purchases. This view of consumption is sometimes called 'rational choice', and it contrasts with the emphasis put by Jane Wheelock in Chapter 3 on consumption as a social process. On rational choice assumptions, the perfect competition model generates strong conclusions about the efficiency of competitive markets.

These conclusions have resulted in an important role for perfect competition as a benchmark in economic theory and policy. So the model will reappear quite frequently in the chapters which follow, starting in Chapter 8 where George Yarrow reflects on its uses and limitations in the kind of industrial policies referred to by John Moore.

2   Competitive markets

2.1   Small firms

Family values

Among the odder sights to be seen on the streets of Milan are crowds of otherwise chic Italians wearing drab, sage-coloured jackets made of oiled cotton. Originally designed for fishermen and farmers almost a century ago, Barbour jackets are now high fashion throughout Western Europe – almost despite the efforts of the small British firm that makes them. ...
The success of anachronistic, eccentric or nostalgic British products seems to be behind the prosperity of a number of small family-owned firms. ...
What links all these firms is that they ought not to exist. All face fierce competition, usually from bigger and richer rivals, and many have spawned copycat products. ...Most sell in markets where new products arrive every few months, yet they measure their own product introductions by the decade. ...
Still owned by the Barbour family the company is expanding cautiously.
The foundation of Barbour's success is a single minded dedication to its traditional customers – farmers, fishermen and other outdoor workers. The firm chooses its retailers carefully, relying on them for feedback from customers. Owners of its thornproof and waterproof jackets are urged to send their garment back to the factory when it needs repair, rather than to buy a new one. At farming exhibitions, the company offers on-the-spot refurbishment for free.
This close relationship with customers provides Barbour with detailed information about the performance of its products (which also include bags, shoes, sweaters and shirts), helping the firm constantly to refine its manufacturing skills. ... productivity ... is high by clothing industry standards. Quality control, the responsibility of each worker, is high by any standards.

(The Economist, 25 December 1993 – 7 January 1994)

The last chapter concentrated on large firms, their behaviour, and the policy implications. This chapter looks at the converse situation, where every producer and purchaser is very small relative to the market. An industry composed of a large number of relatively small firms is likely to have a low concentration ratio.

Table 6.1 in the previous chapter showed an extraordinary variety in the five-firm concentration index in the UK; industries with low ratios (hand tools, furniture, clothing) probably contain many small firms. The extract from *The Economist* describes one such company. Though it is not strictly small by the usual definition of small firms as those with less than 200 employees, it is small relative to total sales in the clothing industry.

Why do firms remain small, when the previous two chapters have discussed the benefits of growth and economies of scale? Big firms are more likely to hit the headlines, but small firms as Chapter 4 noted play a surprisingly significant role in the economy. They make up in numbers what they lack in individual size. Figure 7.1 shows that more than two-thirds of UK businesses in 1989 employed one or two people. The number of small businesses in the UK has grown recently, after a continuous decline from the 1920s to the late 1960s. Net growth in the 1980s was particularly dramatic, and, though many small businesses fail, these failures have been outstripped by the establishment of new companies during that decade.

In some other countries small firms provide an even higher proportion of employment than in the UK. In Switzerland, Norway and Japan more than half the manufacturing employment is provided by small firms, compared with about a quarter in the UK (Ganguly, 1985).

Because of their importance in providing employment, such firms are often actively encouraged by governments. In newly developing markets such as those of Eastern Europe they are seen as a major way of encouraging growth; in less developed countries (LDCs) this strategy contrasts with earlier policies to support large and prestigious projects and industries, which were often unsuccessful.

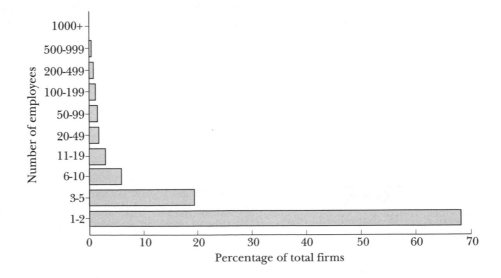

Figure 7.1 **Percentage of firms in the UK by employment size, 1989**

Source: *Daly and McCann* (1992)

Question

So why do small businesses persist?

The special characteristics of small firms tend to provide both their initial momentum and the limit to their growth. They are often newly founded by an enthusiastic entrepreneur. Other advantages come from benefits of geographical proximity and a small workforce. The firm can be located close to the market and therefore avoids transportation costs, both to and from markets and between dispersed plants. Management can be informal and flexible, reacting quickly to changing market conditions. Morale can be maintained through personal contact. Working hours may offer flexibility to the benefit of both business and employees, though working conditions in small firms can also be very poor. Objectives are likely to be clear, with an owner-manager taking a personal interest in the business.

The ability to respond to changing market conditions is particularly important. One small light-fitting importer spotted the potential market in importing skateboards from Germany to the UK in the 1970s and was able to increase profits dramatically. A tour operator started a low-price travel company based on his experience of selling tickets to travel in the truck he was obliged to drive from Kabul in Afghanistan to Delhi (Binks and Coyne, 1983). Taking advantage of such opportunities often lies at the heart of successful small businesses, which rely heavily on the owner-entrepreneur.

However, the very characteristics which favour small firms are also limitations. It may be difficult to encompass all the necessary management skills in one entrepreneur. Growth may be limited by bureaucratic requirements and tax and employment laws. The small firm is much more vulnerable to cost or marketing disasters than is a larger firm. Information on costs is often sparse, and the firm may not detect potential problems before financial difficulties are well advanced and creditors such as banks intervene. For these reasons there is a high attrition rate amongst such firms – many deaths as well as births.

Some industries remain atomistic over long periods: that is, despite attrition, small firms tend to persist in these industries. This suggests that the minimum efficient scale in those industries is small relative to the size of the market, and that economies of scale are limited. Otherwise a dominant firm would be likely to emerge. Of course some small firms may be merely 'infants' on their way to becoming larger companies, and one problem with examining a snapshot is that it will include some high-growth firms and some which are declining and dying. Nevertheless, some sectors do contain a high proportion of small firms which seem to operate best at a small scale.

If there are binding limits to the growth of small firms in some industries, then we can model the competitive firm as one which has a 'U'-shaped long-run average cost curve (Figure 7.2). Furthermore the diseconomies of scale – the upward turning portion of the *LRAC* curve – must set in at a scale which is small relative to the size of the market.

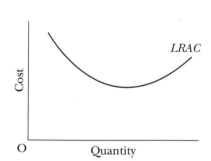

Figure 7.2 **'U'-shaped long-run average cost curve**

2.2   Firms as price takers

The competitive market, as modelled in the next three sections, is therefore conceptualized as an industry in which all the firms and consumers are small relative to the market.

The relation of the firm's size to the market is crucial: a 'small' firm in this context may have a very large turnover, but still count as 'small' if it is not influential in the market. For example, a city may support many large grocery stores but only one small seller of specialist Icelandic food. The latter is large relative to the local market for such specialized tastes (a monopolist in the local market) while the general stores compete with each other despite their greater size. Similarly, a large steel firm may be small compared with the world market for the product.

In this situation, each firm is likely to have little monopoly power. What precisely does this mean? One way to model it is to suppose that the firms' impact on their market is too small to influence the market price. While a monopolist has to reduce price to sell more, a competitive firm in this sense knows it can sell as much as it likes at the market price. It is so small relative to the market that price reductions are unnecessary even for quantities that seem large by the firm's standards. Such a firm is described as a price taker

If the firms face this situation, they can choose only how much to buy and sell, rather than being able to choose among a number of combinations of quantity and price. Being a price taker in this way is familiar for a consumer; most consumers have such a small demand relative to the entire market (for clothes, carrots or washing machines) that they are used to taking the market price as a 'given'. Many firms are also so small in their market that they must sell what they produce at the 'going rate'.

Definition

Price taker

A price taker is a firm or consumer whose output or demand is so small relative to the market that it has no effect on the market price. Such a firm or consumer can each sell or buy as much as they wish at the market price.

Question

What examples can you identify where firms sell their goods at a price determined by the market?

Many markets contain some firms that are price takers. Agricultural markets often have small independent farmers and suppliers whose revenue is determined by market conditions. Individual operators on the foreign exchanges sell pounds for dollars and other currencies at a price dictated by overall market conditions. The clothing industry, as the quotation from *The Economist* suggested, also contains many small producers, who can exercise little individual influence on market prices.

This chapter analyses a model of a market which is composed entirely of such small 'actors' with no dominant operators. In the examples mentioned above there are sometimes dominant firms (in agriculture, foreign exchange and clothing) or regulation by government which affects prices, output or entry to the market. But it is helpful to consider the special characteristics of a market without any such dominant actors.

How is this role of 'price taker' reflected in the demand curve facing the firm? Chapter 3 discussed the nature of market demand, showing the market demand curve sloping downward. This indicates that a lower price is required to sell a greater quantity of goods. It remains true that the demand curve for the whole market slopes downward whatever the structure of the firms within that market.

But for a firm operating in the market, the shape of the demand curve for its own product depends crucially on the market's structure. The shape of the demand curve facing a price-taking firm looks different from the market demand curve.

The previous chapter discussed the responsiveness of demand to price changes, summing this idea up in the concept of the price elasticity of demand.

Question

How do you think increased competition affects the responsiveness of a firm's demand to changes in the prices it charges?

The more choice the consumer has between competing suppliers, the more sensitive a firm's demand will be to changes in the price of its own product. A firm raising its price when its competitors do not raise theirs can expect to lose customers to its competitors and so its demand curve will be quite flat. (A similar argument was made for the flatter 'upper part' of the kinked demand curve in Chapter 5.)

We can conclude that the price responsiveness of the firm's demand curve tends to increase with the degree of competition, because consumers have alternative sources of supply if the price is raised. In the extreme case the firm is left with no discretion about price at all. If it raises its own price above the market price, all sales are lost to competitors; there is no point in lowering its own price because it can sell all it wants to at the market price, and need not reduce price to sell more. In such a case the firm observes the prevailing market price, and then decides how much to produce. This decision will depend on the firm's costs, as discussed below.

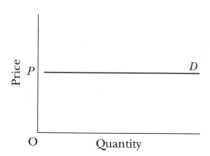

Figure 7.3 **Horizontal demand curve facing a price-taking firm**

In diagrammatic terms, the demand curve gets flatter and flatter as more competition is introduced. The limiting case is reached when the firm has no influence on price at all. The firm's demand curve is then completely horizontal (Figure 7.3). The firm has no discretion about what price to charge, and becomes a price taker.

What is the price elasticity of a horizontal demand curve? Recall that its definition is: the elasticity of demand (ε_D) = proportionate change in quantity demanded divided by the proportionate change in price. As the demand curve gets flatter and flatter, the top part of the equation increases enormously. The proportionate change in quantity demanded becomes very large, for a small proportionate change in price. In the limiting case of a horizontal demand curve, ε_D becomes infinitely large, and the firm's demand curve is said to be infinitely elastic.

The firm acting in such a market sees that its actions are too insignificant to affect the price. The market itself determines at what price the product or service should be traded, and the firm determines only how much to sell. Because the individual firm is so small relative to the market, it can sell as little or as much as it likes without affecting market price. But remember that the horizontal demand curve is the demand curve facing the price-taking *firm*. The demand curve for the output of the industry as a whole will still be downward sloping.

2.3   Information and market access

If firms are to be prevented from exercising monopoly power, there are some other conditions which must hold, besides small relative size. One is that all those undertaking transactions, and potential participants in the market, must be well informed.

Beer supping reform comes to successful head

The Government's plan to deregulate the creamy-headed Northern pint of beer was acknowledged, unemotionally, as ordinary common sense at the Albert in the West Yorkshire town of Yeadon last night.
Sam Windmill, who recently moved from the Babes in the Wood at Dewsbury to take over the old Victorian local, does not look the type to make a few sly pennies through short measures. And anyway, as regular Len Towers pointed out over a slow evening Tetley's, there were pure, Tory market-forces reasons to stop him or any other Yeadon landlord trying.
'I cannot see anyone getting away with it here' said Mr Towers, a computer operator with an encyclopaedic knowledge of the town's pubs. 'People would just try somewhere else: the New Inn round the corner, the Swan up the road, the Clothiers opposite and two or three more just down the High Street'...

(The Guardian, 20 January 1994)

The ability of buyers to 'shop around' if firms sell at different prices depends on their knowledge of the market. The significance of this condition, like many in economics, is best illustrated by considering what might happen if it were *not* true. If buyers have no access to information about other offers they have no way of judging the reasonableness of the price offered, and sellers therefore have considerable discretion. The commentary on the British government's decision to remove regulations about the 'head' on a pint of beer similarly suggests how important the customer's knowledge is in preventing exploitation by the seller, in this case in the form of short measures.

So, if consumers are not well informed about other possible bargains, firms will be able to raise their prices. Local fruit and vegetable markets are often regarded as highly competitive, and they fit the information requirement very well because of the ease of price comparisons. By wandering round the stalls, buyers can discover quickly the different prices and qualities on offer; loud calls of 'only fifty pence for half a pound of mushrooms' provides even more information. It is important that information is not only available but reasonably easy to obtain. For, if it is very difficult to find the price which different suppliers might charge (e.g. for a non-standard car repair), then information gathering becomes costly (taking it to different garages for estimates) and consumers may not be prepared to pay this cost. Advertising is one way to increase information, though the advertiser may not want to impart 'the truth, the whole truth and nothing but the truth'. However, as Chapter 6 explained, advertising may also be a source of monopoly power.

Government regulation of the minimum quality of goods, and the provision of information, for example about hazards of certain goods, can improve consumers' information. Where firms are the buyers – for example of inputs – we might expect them to be well informed about their suppliers.

Shopping around becomes more effective the closer to identical are the products of the various firms. If one garage's repairs are as good as another, and one apple indistinguishable from another, then individual suppliers have little leverage. Conversely, if I believe that MR Motor Repairs are more reliable than Kowboyfix, MR will be able to charge me more for work done, and are not price takers in the way this has been defined. 'Homogeneity' or similarity of the product is significant in so far as it affects consumers' perceptions. European Union regulations which seek to define an 'ice cream', though they can seem risible, are directed at increasing European-wide competition by establishing greater homogeneity within product categories. And the lower transport costs become, the wider is the market for such interchangeable products.

Finally, as Chapter 6 has argued, barriers to entry are crucial to the establishment of monopoly power. Conversely, then, firms without monopoly power must face low barriers to entry by competitors. Firms must be able to enter and leave the competitive industry at low cost. Where the minimum efficient scale is small, set-up costs are likely to be relatively low, and economies of scale do not pose an entry barrier. And similarly, it is harder for incumbent firms to create 'unnatural' or artificial barriers to entry to exclude new entrants.

In summary, there is a variety of real-world examples of markets where monopoly power is slight. So a model of competitive markets, built on the assumptions of price taking firms exercising no monopoly power, can provide some real insights into the competitive process. The next two sections of this chapter build up such a model of the behaviour of a competitive firm and industry. This model, of 'perfect competition', involves a considerable abstraction from reality. But the influence the model has had, for example, on industrial policy – as the quotation from John Moore suggested – illustrates the way analysis of a pure or extreme case is often influential in debates on policy.

Figure 7.4 **Price comparisons are easily made in fruit and vegetable markets**

3   The firm in perfect competition

This section and the next construct a model of an industry where no firms have monopoly power. Specifically, the model of perfect competition assumes a large number of relatively small price-taking firms, selling a homogenous product, perfectly informed themselves and facing perfectly informed buyers not restricted by transport costs, and coping with numerous competitors unrestricted by entry barriers to the industry.

The distinction between the economic behaviour of firm and industry is important to understanding the model. Many industries see quite rapid entry and exit of firms as ruling market prices change. So the model will be built up in two stages, starting with the output decisions of the firm, and then discussing the changes in the conditions in the industry as firms open up and close down.

3.1   The firm's output decision

Like the firms in the models in Chapters 5 and 6, firms in perfect competition are assumed to maximize profits. What determines the quantity of hard disks, apples or fish or wheat marketed by each company, stall or farmer, given that they can sell as much as they wish at the going price?

Like firms with some monopoly power, competitive firms will expand output so long as the benefits from doing so (the revenue) exceed the marginal costs. They will stop expansion when the extra revenue is exactly balanced by the extra costs. But the competitive firm can choose its output only, not the price at which it sells.

The horizontal demand curve revisited

Question

Look back at Figure 7.3. Can you draw in the marginal revenue curve for the firm facing a horizontal demand curve?

The relation between demand and marginal revenue looks different for the perfectly competitive firm. The last two chapters showed that a firm with monopoly power (or 'market power' as this is sometimes called), faces a downward-sloping demand curve. It will therefore find that its marginal revenue (that is, the increase in total revenue which the firm receives from selling one more unit) will be below the demand curve, because to sell more, the firm not only has to lower the price of *that* unit but of all the other units which could otherwise have been sold at a higher price.

However, with a horizontal demand curve, the price is dictated by the market. The firm can sell as many units as it likes at that price, and therefore the extra revenue from selling one more unit is simply the price for that unit. Marginal revenue does not change as output expands. We can now add the marginal revenue curve to the previous diagram. As Figure 7.5 shows, in perfect competition a single horizontal line represents the demand and marginal revenue (*MR*) curves. Remember from Chapter 6 that the demand curve traces the firm's average revenue (*AR*) at each level

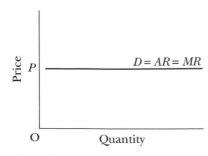

Figure 7.5 **Demand and marginal revenue of the firm in perfect competition**

of output. Since the firm faces a given market price (P) we have our first conclusion from the model. In perfect competition:

$$AR = MR = P$$

These equalities have important implications for evaluating competitive markets, as Sections 5 and 6 show.

The profit-maximizing output

We can now identify the output which will produce maximum profit for the firm.

Intuitively the argument is as follows. For a given market price, the firm should produce the output at which the marginal cost of production is equal to marginal revenue. This is the same profit-maximizing condition as for the firms with market power discussed in Chapters 5 and 6:

$$MC = MR$$

If marginal revenue is above marginal cost, the firm will raise profits by producing and selling more output. Conversely, if marginal revenue is below marginal cost, profit can be increased by reducing output.

But, as just noted, for a competitive price-taking firm, marginal revenue is equal to the market price at all levels of output. So for the competitive firm, the condition for profit maximizing reduces to

$$MC = P \text{ (market price)}$$

This condition is illustrated on Figure 7.6. Q is the profit-maximizing output. This output level is an equilibrium because the firm has no incentive to change its output. At Q_1, the marginal revenue is above marginal cost, so output should be raised. Q_2 conversely is too high an output: marginal cost exceeds marginal revenue. The profit-maximizing output Q occurs where $MC = MR = P$ (market price).

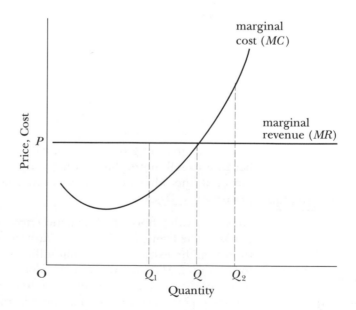

Figure 7.6 **Profit-maximizing output of a firm in perfect competition**

Profit-maximization in perfect competition: a numerical example

If it helps to work through a numerical example, here is an illustrative exercise, which is referred to again below. Suppose that the firm is a small owner-managed shirt manufacturer operating in a perfectly competitive market. The owner incurs £12 per day fixed costs for renting premises and equipment; these are not avoidable in the short run. In addition she must pay variable costs of employing labour, materials and maintenance of equipment which depend on the quantity of shirts made. Table 7.1 shows these variable costs at different levels of production.

Table 7.1

Output shirts/day	Total variable cost	Total cost
0	0	12
1	5	17
2	8	20
3	9	21
4	12	24
5	17	29
6	24	36
7	33	45
8	44	56

From these figures you can derive average variable cost, average total cost and marginal costs for the different levels of output shown. All of these are significant in the short-run output decision. Marginal cost enables the profit-maximizing output to be identified, and the average cost columns will later be used to determine the size of those maximum profits.

Exercise 7.1

(a) Derive the marginal, average variable and average total costs from the data in Table 7.1.

(b) If the market price is £7, what output of shirts maximizes the firm's profits?

Exercises like this are not of course meant to suggest that firms think in terms of marginal revenue and marginal cost curves. The marginal revenue and cost curves are the economist's apparatus for modelling decisions. Perhaps it is helpful to imagine a discussion at a board meeting between the marketing director and the production controller along these lines. If the marketing director believes that the value of increased sales will be more than the extra costs which the production manager says would be incurred, the firm will produce more; if the extra sales are less than extra costs they would do better not to increase output. It is the same *process* as the argument presented in terms of marginal revenue and marginal cost curves, but not framed in these terms.

3.2   The supply curves of the competitive firm

Section 3.1 concluded that under perfect competition, the firm will produce where price is equal to marginal cost.

$$MC = P$$

With a little more analysis of a firm's decision making we can use this information to derive a supply curve for the firm.

Definition

Supply curve

The supply curve of a firm indicates how much it will supply at each market price.

The supply curve is analogous to the demand curve, in that it provides information about how much the firm will supply at each price, just as the demand curve shows how much consumers buy at each price. The marginal cost curve of the perfectly competitive firm traces out the firm's supply decisions as prices change.

Figure 7.7 shows the profit-maximizing outputs, Q_1 and Q_2, for a perfectly competitive firm facing two different market price levels, P_1 and P_2. When the price rises, output increases, and the extent of the increase is determined by the shape of the marginal cost curve. To complete this analysis of supply, we now need to consider the firm's cost curves more carefully.

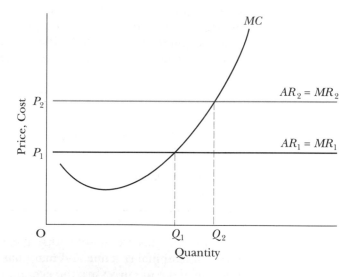

Figure 7.7 **The supply decisions of the perfectly competitive firm as prices change**

Short-run supply

Figure 7.8 shows the cost curves of the perfectly competitive firm in the short run. I have distinguished between the short-run average cost (*SRAC*) which is the average of the *total* costs of the firm per unit produced, and the average of the short-run *variable* costs (*SRAVC*) alone. The two curves converge because a fixed overhead cost is averaged over a larger number of units as output rises. At a market price of P_1 the output level at which marginal cost equals price is Q_1.

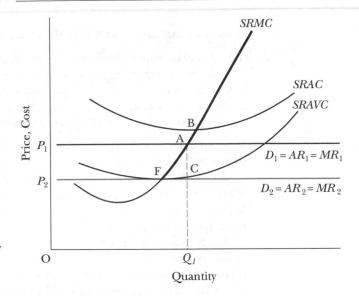

Figure 7.8   The short-run supply curve of the perfectly competitive firm

Question

At price P_1, $MC = MR$ at point A, with output Q_1. Will the firm in fact choose to produce Q_1, or will it prefer not to produce at all?

The firm's decision to produce or not to produce depends on the comparison of costs and revenues. At Q_1, the price the firm receives for its goods, P_1, is high enough to cover its average variable costs at that output (point C). P_1 is not however high enough to cover its average total costs ($SRAC$) at any output. But each unit sold is making a contribution equivalent to the distance AC on Figure 7.8, to its fixed costs or overheads.

The firm is therefore making a loss: it is not covering total costs. But its fixed costs are unavoidable in the short run. So in the short run as long as the price is above average variable costs the firm is better off continuing to produce. Q_1 is the loss-minimizing output and the best the firm can do in the short run. The excess of price over the variable costs makes some contribution to the fixed costs.

Definition

Short-run supply curve

The short-run supply curve of the perfectly competitive firm is that part of the short-run marginal cost curve above the short-run average variable cost curve.

These considerations allow us to complete the short-run supply curve of the perfectly competitive firm. The short-run marginal cost curve on Figure 7.8 cuts the short-run average variable cost curve at its minimum point F. If the market price falls below price P_2, then the firm is not covering even its average variable costs. This creates a loss which can be avoided if the firm stops producing altogether. At any point on the marginal cost curve between F and B (where B is the point of minimum average total costs) the firm will continue to produce in the short run despite an overall loss. At any point above B, price is above average total costs and the firm will be making supernormal profits.

We can conclude from this argument that the emphasized part of the firm's short-run marginal cost curve, above point F in Figure 7.8, is also its supply curve.

Short-run supply: a numerical example

The short-run supply curve can be illustrated from the clothing manufacturer example. Look again at the marginal cost data which you calculated from Table 7.1. At each price, the firm will supply the quantity at which price equals marginal cost. If the market price is £7, six shirts will be produced per day; if £9, seven shirts.

You can also use your answer to Exercise 7.2 to check the minimum point of average variable costs, below which the clothing manufacturers will cease production. When the price is £5 per shirt the manufacturer will make five shirts per day; average variable cost at this output is £3.4/shirt, leaving a contribution of £1.6 per shirt to fixed costs. So the firm will continue to produce in the short run. As prices fall, the firm will cease production once the revenue from output does not cover the variable costs. For example, at a price of £1, the best the firm can do is by producing three shirts, but to do so it incurs variable costs of £3/shirt. It will be better to produce nothing, forgoing £1/shirt revenue but saving £3/shirt in variable costs. In the short run the minimum price which covers average variable costs is £3. At prices lower than this the firm stops production.

Long-run supply

The analysis of short-run supply has identified the firm's decisions when the fixed costs are unavoidable. In the long run the firm has more choices.

Question

What distinguishes the long-run and short-run cost curves of firms?

In the long run, the firm is able to vary all its inputs. There are no fixed costs. Chapter 4 showed that the long-run average cost curve is a flatter 'envelope' of the short-run curves (Figure 4.10). But, as noted in Section 2, a firm in an atomized competitive industry must face diseconomies of scale at relatively low output levels. So the long-run average cost curve ($LRAC$) is 'U' shaped (Figure 7.2).

We can now derive the long-run supply curve of the perfectly competitive firm just as we did for the short run. The long-run marginal cost curve ($LRMC$), like the $LRAC$ curve, is flatter than the short run curves, since average costs can be lowered in the long run by adjusting capacity. The firm will produce where price equals long-run marginal cost, so long as price is not below long-run average costs. So the *long-run supply curve* is the output levels traced by the $LRMC$ curve above minimum average costs: the emphasized part of the $LRMC$ curve on Figure 7.9.

In summary, firms in perfect competition base their output decisions on two factors: the relation between price and marginal cost, and the relation between price and average costs. A firm already committed to incurring fixed costs will produce in the short run so long as price exceeds average short-run variable costs, and in the long run will remain in the industry so long as the price covers all long-run average costs.

Because competitive firms have no discretion over market price – which they take as given – they produce where price equals marginal cost. This has

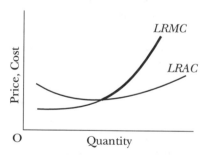

Figure 7.9 **The long-run supply curve of the perfectly competitive firm**

allowed us to draw a supply curve for the firm in both the short and the long run, showing the output level of the firm at each market price. Such a supply curve is unique to perfect competition, because it depends on the characteristic that each firm is a price taker. We could not draw a supply curve of this kind for the monopolist analysed in the last chapter, because monopolists have discretion over price: they choose their preferred price/ quantity mix according to market conditions.

Finally, it is worth noting the assumptions we have made. We have assumed that the firm is endowed with considerable knowledge about its own costs and the market. Uncertainty about the price of shirts and the quantities which will actually be made have been ignored; so have any unexpected cost changes. These factors are omitted not because they are unimportant, but because they allow the simplest version of the perfect competition model to be examined.

Within these limitations the model has provided answers to three questions posed for the firm: how much to produce, whether to produce in the short run, and whether in the long run to remain in the industry.

4   The perfectly competitive industry

The softening of software

It had to happen. After two years in which the cost of personal computers has fallen by more than half, the price of the applications software used in those PCs – spreadsheets, word processors, data bases and the like – is being dragged down too. In 1993 alone the price of applications software probably fell by about a quarter in America and more than a third in Europe. Such software accounts for some $20 billion of the world's $60 billion off-the-shelf software market, and remains, in unit sales, the fastest-growing part of the industry.
Falling prices and soaring costs are starting to bite. In the quarter to September 1993, Borland's net profit margin shrank to 2.6% of sales, down from 4.2% a year earlier; at Lotus the figure dipped to 7.6% from 14.6% a year earlier; even Microsoft's margins slipped a little. … In the long run Mr Gates reckons his firm's net margin will fall to around 15% – mostly because of collapsing profits from applications software. …
These flagging profits explain the hunt for new markets. Nearly two years after PC makers such as Compaq, Packard Bell and Gateway 2000 started trying to sell to domestic – rather than business – computer users, the software industry is doing the same. …
Microsoft took the plunge into this enticing new market late last year with the launch of its Home brand of PC software, as did WordPerfect with its Main Street software. Microsoft expects to release about 100 Home products over the next year or so, ranging from multimedia games to what it describes as 'personal productivity software'.

(The Economist, 8 January 1994)

Although Microsoft was one of Andrew Trigg's examples in Chapter 6 of a firm with monopoly power, nevertheless many smaller software firms are forced to act like price takers in the highly competitive computing industry. And as the quotation suggests, it is profit margins which drive firms to leave some markets and to enter others.

So when we turn our attention from the competitive *firm* to the perfectly competitive *industry* as a whole, we have to add to the model the entry and exit of firms. The perfectly competitive industry consists of a large number of firms, each very small relative to the industry's size. Although each is too small to influence the market individually, the sum of their separate actions constitute the characteristics of the industry which then feed back upon the firms. This effect is often claimed to illustrate Adam Smith's reference (cited in Chapter 1) to an individual being 'led by an invisible hand to promote an end which was no part of his intention' and we shall return to this in assessing the model.

Supply in a competitive industry is determined by two factors: the supply decisions of each firm within the industry, and whether there are new entrants or leavers. In the short run there are a fixed number of firms in the industry, each deciding on a short-term basis how much to produce according to their marginal costs and the market price. Thus at each market price we can deduce how much each firm will produce and sell, and we can add these up to find the total supplied.

Figure 7.10 illustrates this idea. The short run supply curves $SRMC_1$ and $SRMC_2$ of two firms are added up horizontally to create an industry supply curve (S). (Note that this addition assumes that the simultaneous expansion of all the firms does not drive up their input costs.)

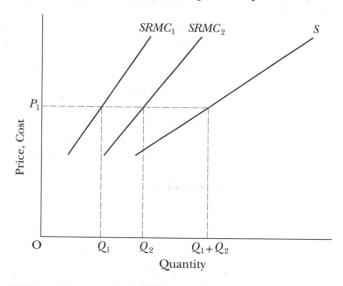

Figure 7.10 **Deriving the short-run supply curve of a competitive industry**

The horizontal addition of supply curves

Here is a numerical example of this 'adding up'. Table 7.2 shows the short run marginal costs of two shirtmakers, for several different rates of output (shirts per day).

Table 7.2 **Marginal costs of two shirt manufacturers**

Quantity made/day	*MC* of manufacturer 1	*MC* of manufacturer 2
	£	£
5	5	3
6	7	5
7	9	7
8	11	9

Exercise 7.3

How much will be supplied altogether at prices of £5, £7 and £9 per shirt? Complete Table 7.3 and then graph your results in the format shown in Figure 7.9. Assume that the prices are sufficient to cover average variable costs.

Table 7.3   **Short-run industry supply: shirts per day**

Price (£)	Manufacturer 1	Manufacturer 2	Total
5			
7			
9			

This is a short-run analysis, in which the number of firms in the industry and some of their costs are fixed. The firms' marginal cost curves, and therefore the industry short-run supply curve, will be relatively steep, since some of the factors of production are fixed (the manufacturers can increase output only by more intensive use of the existing capital equipment). In the longer run, existing firms can change the scale of their operation, moving along their long-run average cost curve, and firms may enter or leave the industry.

Consider the situation where the market price in a perfectly competitive industry has recently risen sharply. Perhaps the product has suddenly become fashionable. Then in the short run, the firms in the industry are making supernormal profits, as depicted in Figure 7.11.

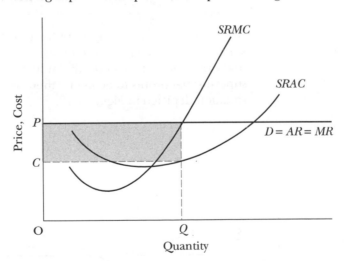

Figure 7.11   **Short-run supernormal profits of a perfectly competitive firm**

Recall from Chapter 6 that *normal profit* is that level of profit just sufficient to keep the firm in the industry. The normal profit is included in the average cost curves. The firm depicted in Figure 7.11 will produce output *Q* at the ruling market price *P*. It is making supernormal profits equivalent to the shaded area: that is, the difference between price *P* and average total cost *C*, multiplied by the number of units of output produced *Q*.

Question

What effect will high profits have on firms within the industry and those outside it? Recall that one of the assumptions of the perfectly competitive model is perfectly informed firms and consumers, so the profitability of firms and their costs and market conditions are common knowledge.

Such profitability will have two effects. Incumbent firms may choose to expand in the long run when all factors can be adjusted, including those fixed in the short run. And other firms, who know about the profits made in the industry, will be attracted into it. Remember that perfect competition assumes no barriers to entry by new firms, though in practice some entry barriers always exist, if only the investment of the owner's time. If the industry makes its products from readily available and unspecialized inputs (e.g. materials and unskilled labour) then new firms may be able to reproduce the conditions of the existing firms at the same cost levels.

One example of such entry occurred in firms to service the City of London stock market when the entry rules were relaxed in 1986. Many firms were attracted into the industry, and many then left after the profitability was adversely affected by the stock market collapse a year later. Similarly, there was a huge expansion in the number of firms offering sunbeds in many European countries in the mid-eighties. The entry costs were relatively low, and many responded to the new opportunities which an expanded market and new technology offered.

Question

What will happen to market price as new firms enter the industry?

As new firms come in, prices are likely to be bid downwards. The supernormal profits pictured on Figure 7.11 will be squeezed. If we assume that firms continue to enter the industry until there are no more supernormal profits to be made, then prices will fall until firms are in the situation depicted in Figure 7.12.

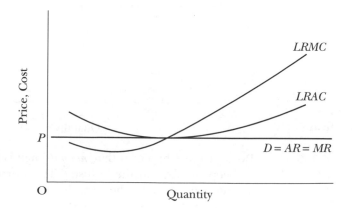

Figure 7.12 **The perfectly competitive firm in long-run equilibrium**

It is possible of course for the falling prices to have dramatic effects on the industry.

Seagate's watershed

Managing the boom-to-bust business of making personal computers is hard enough. But it is a pushover compared with trying to earn a living from supplying hard-bargaining computer companies with components – especially such tricky devices as hard disk drives, the spinning magnetic disks that store megabytes of data inside computers. With personal computer prices down by almost half in the past two years, makers of hard-disk drives have been forced to shave their margins to the bone. Of the 100 or more firms that tried their hand at the business over the past decade, fewer than a dozen remain. Fewer still are profitable. ...

(The Economist, 13 November 1993)

If eager entrants find they have together driven prices below long-run average costs, many firms will fail. This may allow prices to rise again until the remaining firms can cover costs.

Figure 7.12 supposes that the firm pictured is somehow 'typical' of the whole industry. However, if all the firms in the industry were exactly identical, with the same cost curves, we would have an 'all or nothing' situation in which all firms would leave the industry when price was below the minimum average cost, or all enter for prices above this cost level. This does not seem realistic, and it is perhaps more reasonable to consider our firm the *marginal* firm in the industry. Its normal profits represent the best new entrants can expect though some older firms may be doing rather better.

So what shape is the industry supply curve in the long run? Industry supply is likely to be more price elastic in the long run than in the short run (Figure 7.13). If prices rise from P_1 to P_2, supply available at P_2 will increase in the long run from Q_2 to Q_3 as new firms come in. The long-run supply curve (S_L) however is still likely to be upward sloping. New firms may be less efficient than older firms and the industry as a whole may experience cost constraints on expansion. For example, labour available for clothing manufacture may not be attracted away from other industries except at increased wages. The industry supply curve slopes upward, showing the higher price needed to coax additional supplies from an industry in which costs rise with total output (Figure 7.13).

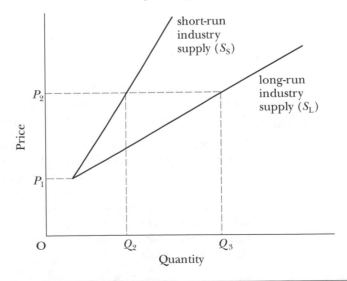

Figure 7.13 **The short-run and long-run supply curves of a perfectly competitive industry**

In summary, the model of perfect competition allows us to construct short- and long-run supply curves for the perfectly competitive industry. We can draw these supply curves independently of the particular demand conditions obtaining at any moment in the market as a whole.

That completes this chapter's analysis of supply. The next section considers market demand and supply together. The analysis in the chapter is then used to reflect on the reasons why the model of the perfectly competitive market has such important benchmark properties within economic analysis as a whole.

5   Market demand, supply and equilibrium

5.1   Demand revisited

Chill in eastern US heats hogs, gas futures

… Arctic cold gripping the eastern half of the United States drove up prices of commodities ranging from hogs to natural gas yesterday, while orange juice prices plunged after Florida's groves were untouched by the cold wave.

Fewer hogs were shipped to the US markets because of the bitter cold, and traders anticipated a bullish report at midweek that will show the United States has fewer pigs than a year ago…

… hogs rose 0.2 cents to 45.4 cents (US) a pound at the Chicago Mercantile Exchange …

The US cold wave lifted sluggish demand for natural gas and heating oil needed to heat homes and businesses, although some traders were sceptical of the steep rise in gas prices. …

The orange juice market stumbled lower when traders sold contracts that they had bought, betting that freezing temperatures would reach Florida's groves. The bet turned out to be a bad one.

'There was some disappointment that there was no damaging cold weather over the Christmas weekend' one trader said. … orange juice lost 2.15 cents to end at 105.75 cents a pound at the New York Cotton Exchange.

(Toronto Globe and Mail, 28 December 1993)

In market economies, prices of goods and services shift frequently, and people react to price changes – none faster than traders who make their living on commodity exchanges. On such exchanges, there may be dominant traders, who handle large enough volumes to influence prices by their purchases and sales. And there may be many small players who individually take the market price as given, though together they too may shift the market if they all move in the same direction at once.

The model of the perfectly competitive market assumes that buyers as well as sellers are price takers. Individual consumers make their buying decisions in response to a ruling market price. Market demand is the sum of their decisions. For the market as a whole the demand curve is downward sloping implying, as Chapter 3 explained, larger total purchases at lower prices. This section brings together market demand and the market supply curve, to show how the 'insignificant' individual players and the market interact.

First, some revision of demand, from Chapter 3.

Question

The *Globe and Mail* quotation refers to a rise in demand for natural gas and heating oil. Is this an example of a movement along a demand curve, or a shift in a demand curve?

A movement along a demand curve is caused by a change in price (since the curve defines the relation between price and quantity demanded). A shift is caused by changes in other factors such as income or advertising. The *Globe and Mail* article shows the effect of a cold snap on the price of various commodities. The demand for natural gas and oil rose (at the prevailing price); and so the demand curve shifted to the right (Figure 7.14). Quantity demanded at the original price rose from Q_1 to Q_2.

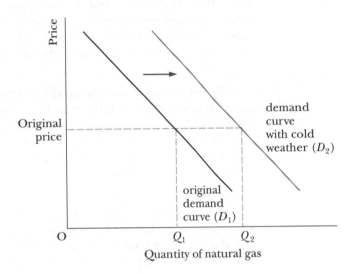

Figure 7.14   **A shift to the right in the demand curve for natural gas**

Many factors can shift the demand curve, by changing the relationship between demand and price. For example, if eggs are suddenly subject to concerns about food poisoning, shoppers will buy fewer eggs at any given price. Similarly, demand for many products falls in a recession, as people's incomes fall and expectations are low; at any particular price shoppers will tend to buy less and hence the demand curve would shift to the left.

Reinterpreting demand

The downward sloping market demand curve can be thought of as the sum of many individual demand curves for an industry's product. As Chapter 3 noted, *ceteris paribus* (all other things being held constant) people can be expected to buy less of a product as its price rises. If we take the *ceteris paribus* qualification seriously, and abstract from the many social and economic influences on consumption discussed in Chapter 3, then we can interpret the demand curve in a way which will be useful for evaluating perfect competition in the final section of this chapter.

We can consider each consumer as an independent decision maker, and make similar assumptions about self-interest as were made for firms. Just as firms are supposed to be 'self-seeking' in maximizing profits, so consumers are expected to pursue their own best interests in making purchases to maximize their satisfaction. They are assumed to know what is in their own best interests and to make consistent choices given their preferences and their incomes. Within such a framework we can analyse how a consumer will choose purchases of different products and it quickly becomes clear that it is purchases at the *margin,* that is, the last apple or kilo of rice bought, that are particularly important in influencing market prices. This is similar to the earlier analysis of the firm where it is the cost of the *marginal* unit, that is, of the last unit produced, which is relevant to the decision on how much to produce.

Like the firm, the consumer in a perfectly competitive market is a price taker, facing market prices over which she has no control. To allocate her income so that satisfaction is maximized, she must spend it in such a way that the last pound's worth of each product provides her with equal satisfaction. If that were not so, the consumer could still transfer a pound from a product which provides less satisfaction, to one which provides more. This would increase total satisfaction, so without such adjustment she would not be acting in the rational way which this analysis of demand requires.

In other words, the consumer in this interpretation of demand thinks carefully about choices at the margin. Would a little more spent on food bring more satisfaction than the same money spent on drink, or clothing, or a child's toy? If so, the food budget should be increased a bit, relative to expenditure on the other items. For this reason, this model of demand is often called 'rational choice'.

The implication of this line of thought is that, in allocating an income amongst the competing possible purchases, the consumer will adjust consumption so that the extra benefit from the last or marginal purchase is equal to the price paid. So for example if an extra holiday – say, a weekend trip – costs twice as much as the cost of the last improvement made to your home, then it must have been worth twice as much to you. Otherwise you could have maximized your satisfaction from consumption by fewer (or less expensive) trips and more domestic improvements.

There are two assumptions which are important to this analysis of demand. One is that more consumption increases satisfaction. The other is that, the more we buy of something, the less the last or marginal unit is worth. So as we buy more, the price we are willing to pay falls. If we can accept these two ideas, then this approach enables us to interpret the demand curve in a new way. The demand curve is not only a description of how much is bought at each price, but for each individual represents the *willingness to pay for the last unit of each good bought.*

Price-taking consumers therefore simultaneously contribute to total market demand and determine their own demand from the given market price. Like market supply, market demand for a good can be thought of as the horizontal sum of individual demand curves for the product (Figure 7.15).

How then is this market price determined? We need to bring the information about supply and demand characteristics together.

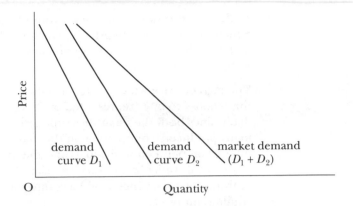

Figure 7.15 **Horizontal addition of demand curves**

5.2   Market equilibrium

We can bring together the firm, the individual consumer and the industry in a three part diagram, as in Figure 7.16.

The diagram on the left (7.16a) shows a typical individual consumer, with a downward-sloping demand curve. This curve shows how much he will buy at each price. Since market demand is the horizontal addition of individual demand, if there are a million such consumers, the total demand will be one million times that quantity at each price. This aggregate demand is the market demand curve in (b), and the units on the horizontal axis of (b) are much larger than those on (a) (or (c)).

Similarly, the right hand diagram (c) shows the marginal cost curve of a typical firm; the firm maximizes profit at the point where (horizontal) marginal revenue is equal to marginal cost, so at levels of marginal cost above minimum average costs, this becomes the supply curve. If there are 500 such firms, the supply for the market will be 500 times that which each individual producer will make. Again, the market supply is the horizontal addition of the individual supply curves and is shown in (c). These diagrams (a) and (c) represent the equilibrium for each consumer and producer, i.e. the best position they can achieve given the market price.

Diagram (b) shows how the individual decisions of consumers and producers come together in the market to determine an equilibrium price,

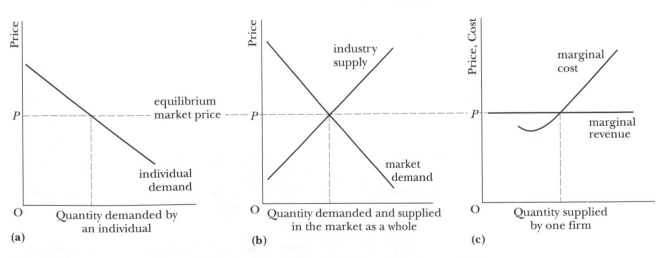

Figure 7.16 **Consumer's demand (a), market equilibrium (b) and firm's supply (c)**

P, which in turn informs the decisions of the individual participants. The equilibrium price is the price at which market supply and demand are equal. At this point there is no pressure for change from within the market, so this is a *market equilibrium.*

The market price which each consumer observes determines the amount they choose to buy (represented by their demand curves); and the price also determines both the quantities supplied by individual producers and how many producers choose to be in the market. There is thus a constant interaction between individuals and the market, where the market sends price signals which are in turn translated into quantity decisions by individual actors, which feed back into the market to determine the equilibrium price.

Changes in market conditions

We know from earlier analysis that the slope of the supply curve depends on whether we are considering the short or long run. Similarly, consumers will be able to make a fuller response to price changes (e.g. changing the type of boiler if the price of a fuel changes) over a longer period. Once the time period is established, supply can be analysed in the same way as demand. The same distinction between shifts in the curves and movement along them is valid.

Question

Which types of changes would cause a shift in a supply curve, and which a movement along it?

The important distinction, again, is between responses to price changes (movements along the supply curve) and to changes in other factors (shifts of the curve). Factors which affect the amount a firm is prepared to supply at a particular price are incorporated in the marginal cost curves from which the supply curve is derived. Changes in them therefore cause the supply curve to shift. An increase in the costs of a significant input, or a technological breakthrough, for example would change the costs of a company, and therefore its supply curve. The effect on the industry supply depends on whether the cost changes are particular to the firm or more generally experienced.

Question

In the *Globe and Mail* article about the cold weather, what shifts in supply were identified?

The supply of hogs was cut by the cold weather, shifting the short-run supply curve to the left (Figure 7.17).

The decline in the number of pigs has reduced supply at each price, shifting the supply curve from S_1 to S_2. At the old equilibrium price, P_1, there is now *excess demand*. At P_1, people still wish to buy Q_1, but only Q_3 is now on offer. The price will have to rise to P_2 before the supply and demand for hogs is back in balance at output Q_2.

The orange juice case is more complicated. Traders had been betting that orange juice supplies would go the same way as hogs. Prices had risen in

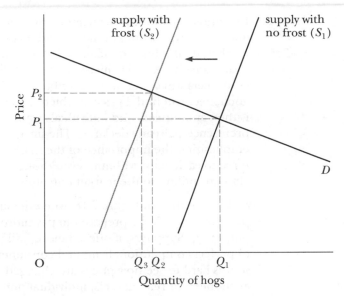

Figure 7.17   A shift in the supply curve for hogs

anticipation of frosted orange groves (that is, an expected supply shift to the left). But the cold missed Florida, supply did not shift, and orange juice prices dropped back.

A shift in supply like a shift in demand therefore produces a new equilibrium market price. Consider again the increase in demand for gas and oil created by the cold snap in 1993. Figure 7.18 adds a supply curve to Figure 7.14, assuming for a moment that gas is supplied in a perfectly competitive market. When the cold weather hits, demand rises and there is excess demand at P_1, equal to $Q_3 - Q_1$. Price will have to rise to P_2 to clear the market at a new equilibrium between supply and demand.

This analysis has identified the characteristics of market equilibrium, rather than the process by which the market moves from one equilibrium to another. It is therefore a *comparative static* approach, comparing two equilibrium positions rather than a dynamic model of how change occurs.

The model is rather evasive on the mechanism of achieving equilibrium. A nineteenth century economist, Léon Walras, suggested the image of an auctioneer, helping the market to move from one equilibrium to another in rapid succession. Potential buyers and sellers tell the auctioneer their bids

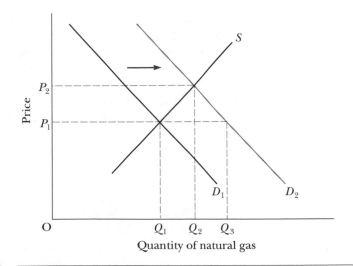

Figure 7.18   A higher equilibrium price for gas in a cold snap

for various quantities (determined by their own interests) and the auctioneer works out at what price demand and supply will balance in the market. While this is done, time is suspended, so the adjustment appears instantaneous. As price increases, firms will offer greater quantities, and consumers will generally want to buy less. It is therefore very likely that the auctioneer will find a price at which demand and supply balance. The price is then announced, and individuals trade according to their own preferences, already declared. The image of the auctioneer is useful in emphasizing the importance of the market as an outside and impersonal force to each actor within it, even though each individual contributes (imperceptibly) to the market outcome.

So for example, in Figure 7.18, when demand shifts to D_2, potential purchasers would be prepared to pay more than the going price P_1 for output Q_1. Suppliers, if offered more, will produce more. But in the model of perfect competition, firms and consumers are assumed to be price takers, so it is hard to see how prices are changed without the useful fiction of the auctioneer. In real markets, individual purchasers may offer more, and suppliers respond by moving along their supply curves as prices are shifted up, so expanding total supply. The model just tells us that P_2 and Q_2 are the new equilibrium price and quantity.

Exercise 7.4

Suppose that unexpectedly warm weather increases the supply of orange juice. What will happen to the equilibrium price? Illustrate your answer with a diagram, and comment on the way in which the market might shift from the old equilibrium to the new one.

The market model developed here then is a comparative static model: it compares equilibrium points and their characteristics, rather than analysing the movement between equilibrium points. The examples of changes in equilibrium illustrate the difference between shifts in and movements along the market supply and demand curves. In each example the initial disturbance was caused by a shift in the demand or supply curve. The new equilibrium was found at another point along the curve which did not shift. Of course, in practice, there are continuous shifts in both demand and supply so that long-run equilibrium really does seem like the horizon – always in sight but never reached. The impracticability of keeping everything else constant while one adjustment is acted out through the market mechanism is one obvious difference between economics and an experimental science, and is an important factor in some of the debates about whether or not economics can be classified as a science. Though the concept of equilibrium is borrowed from the mechanical sciences, it cannot be tested realistically in controlled situations.

6   Assessment of perfect competition

The perfectly competitive model holds a special place in economic analysis; the very adjective 'perfect' carries positive connotations. This arises not from its realism, for we have already encountered the model's restrictive assumptions.

Reflection

Recall the main assumptions underlying the model of perfect competition, and then check your response with the summary at the beginning of Section 3.

The model is valuable in two important ways. First, it analyses an extreme case of competition where firms are price takers; this can be contrasted with the other extreme, monopoly, to provide insight into the competitive process, and the effects of changes which introduce more (or less) competition. Chapter 8 discusses this use of the perfect competition model in industrial policy.

The perfectly competitive market model is also important because it enables us to identify a concept of economic efficiency which is widely used as a benchmark in economic analysis. If we understand the model, as described in Section 5, as a framework for analysing the interaction of consumers and firms, each acting in their own best interests, then the perfectly competitive market can be shown to be, in a strong sense, an *efficient* market.

This section explores this ambitious move from describing how an economic model works to assessing *how well* it works. The argument is based on the idea, introduced in Section 5, that consumers can be modelled as individuals seeking to maximize their own satisfaction, given their preferences and their incomes. On this basis, we can make some judgements about which economic situations are 'better' or 'worse' than others. Such judgements can be called 'normative', as compared with a 'positive' description of how markets work. Normative analysis involves judgements about economic welfare.

6.1   Scarcity and economic welfare

An efficient economy, in the sense of efficiency used in the rest of this chapter, is an economy which maximizes economic welfare in given circumstances. The qualification, 'given circumstances' is important. Underlying this idea of efficiency is an assumption that the external environment is one of scarcity relative to people's wants. Wants are seen as virtually insatiable, and certainly greater than can be satisfied from within existing production capabilities. Some economists have defined the problem of how to allocate resources in such a situation of scarcity as the economic problem

This concept of economic scarcity faced by infinite wants may seem a good reflection of modern western experience, but other cultures and economies have made different assumptions.

> ... a young Modoc named Kintpuash was coming to manhood and could not understand why Modocs and white people could not live together without trying to kill each other. The Tule Lake country was limitless as the sky, with enough deer, antelope,

Definitions

Welfare

The welfare of an individual or community is the well-being or satisfaction each enjoys.

Economic welfare

Economic welfare is the part of that well-being which is related to economic transactions.

Definition

The economic problem

The economic problem is sometimes defined as the problem of how best to allocate scarce resources among competing ends.

ducks, geese, fish and camas roots for everybody ...
The earth was created by the assistance of the sun, and it should
be left as it was ... . The country was made without lines of
demarcation, and it is no man's business to divide it ... . I see the
whites all over the country gaining wealth, and see their desire to
give us lands which are worthless ... . The earth and myself are of
one mind. The measure of the land and the measure of our
bodies are the same. Say to us if you can say it, that you were sent
by the Creative Power to talk to us. Perhaps you think the
Creator sent you here to dispose of us as you see fit. If I thought
you were sent by the Creator I might be induced to think you
had a right to dispose of me. Do not misunderstand me, but
understand me fully with reference to my affection for the land. I
never said the land was mine to do with it as I chose. The one
who has the right to dispose of it is the one who has created it. I
claim a right to live on my land, and accord you the privilege to
live on yours.

(Henmot Tooyalaket of the Nez Percés, from Bury My Heart at Wounded
Knee by Dee Brown, pp.178, 249–50)

These quotations about the ideas of nineteenth-century native Americans
show very different attitudes to scarcity and property ownership from the
orthodox western economic stance which lies behind the concept of 'the
economic problem' just described. The analysis which follows would seem
quite alien in such a culture.

So long as consumers do want in total more than can be provided from the
resources available, some way of rationing the output must be found. This in
turn raises the questions of which goods and services should be made from
scarce primary resources, how they should be produced, and who should
enjoy them. This section examines how well the perfectly competitive
economy achieves such an allocation.

6.2   The concept of Pareto efficiency

To analyse the efficiency of competitive markets we need a precise
definition of 'efficient'. We owe the concept of efficiency used in this
section to Vilfredo Pareto, an Italian economist working at the end of the
nineteenth century and beginning of the twentieth century. Pareto
developed a definition of efficiency which relied only on individual
consumers' judgements of their own welfare. He argued that on this basis,
an economic change was an improvement only if it benefited some people
(on their own judgement) without harming anyone. Hence, an economic
situation is Pareto efficient only if no more improvements of this type are
available.

Note that 'better off' and 'worse off' in this definition refer only to
individuals' own judgements of their own welfare. Because Pareto
demonstrated the conclusions about general economic welfare which could
be drawn from these individualist premises, he is regarded as the founder
of modern welfare economics.

This question of whether a rearrangement of resources can improve a
situation is therefore crucial to Pareto efficiency. We can illustrate this idea
by beginning from the example of a fixed government budget:

Definition

Pareto efficient

An economic situation is Pareto
efficient if and only if there are
no changes possible which make
at least one person better off
without making any person
worse off.

The basic issue

A report [on education] … argues persuasively, for … new initiatives.

The first, and most urgent, is to expand the provision of nursery education, starting with disadvantaged children. Britain offers publicly-financed nursery education to fewer than 50% of its 3–5 year olds, compared with 77% in Germany, 85% in Denmark and Italy, and 95% in France. Yet Britain has more working mothers and broken families than any other Western European country.

…

How to pay for it? The best way to pay for new nursery schools would be to spend less on University students. The Government currently pays their fees and helps with their living expenses. This is regressive (students are mainly middle class by social origin) and restrictive (the number of students is limited by Treasury fiat rather than by demand). …

(The Economist, 20 November 1993)

The quotation from *The Economist* illustrates the choices to be made in a situation where the resources for education are limited. In spending more on nursery provision, the government has less available from a fixed budget for university students. We can illustrate the fixed budget and the choice between nursery and university places as in Figure 7.19.

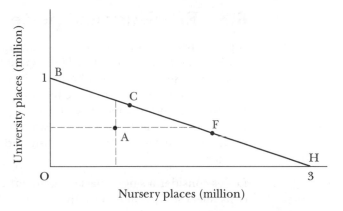

Figure 7.19 **Allocation of the education budget**

Suppose that university places cost £6000 per annum and each nursery place £2000, and the total budget for both is £6000 million. The government could provide one million university places or three million nursery places, or any combination in between. This is shown by the straight line BH in Figure 7.19.

BH represents the frontier between what it is possible to provide within the budget and what is outside the budget. Within this frontier (a point such as A) the government can buy more of one or other type of education within the funds provided. In terms of Pareto's criterion, A is not an efficient point since the government can provide more of one kind of education without sacrificing the other. Points such as C on the frontier are an improvement over A on Pareto's criterion because more of both places is provided.

Once on BH however, there may be little room for further improvement. Suppose that the citizens divide into one set of people wanting more university places and another set wanting more nurseries. Then all the

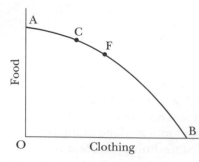

Figure 7.20 **A production possibility frontier**

Definition

Productively efficient

An economy is productively efficient when it cannot produce more of one good without producing less of another.

points along BH are Pareto efficient, since a move from say point B, one million university places, towards C, providing a mix, will always harm those who want more university places.

In more general terms, we might think of an economy as producing two goods, say, food and clothing. Then we could draw a production possibility frontier (Figure 7.20) which traces out the different maximum mixes of food and clothes which can be achieved with the resources available. This frontier may not necessarily be a straight line.

At any point along the production possibility frontier AB, the economy is productively efficient.

However, not all of the points along the production possibility frontier are necessarily Pareto efficient, because Pareto efficiency depends not just on the outputs but also on people's preferences. Imagine a situation where the economy produced all food and no clothing at all. Then it is quite possible that *everyone* would be made better off by moving away from point A towards, say, point C, because everyone would prefer a mixture of goods including some clothing.

In other words, productive efficiency is a necessary condition for Pareto efficiency. A Pareto-efficient economy must be on its production possibility frontier. But productive efficiency may not be enough. Pareto efficiency also depends on people's wants.

6.3 Efficiency and perfect competition

A perfectly competitive economy satisfying all the assumptions set out above is a Pareto-efficient economy. The argument supporting this statement is too complex to set out in detail here, but it is possible to gain from the following argument an intuitive feel for why perfect competition produces a Pareto-efficient outcome. The efficiency properties of the perfectly competitive model are the main reason for the influence of this model on economic policy – an influence illustrated in a number of later chapters in this text.

Let us consider a single market again, and begin with consumers. The consumers seek to maximize their benefit from their incomes. Economists often refer to the benefits from consumption as *utility*. Consumers are assumed to gain utility from consumption, and to seek to maximize their utility from their incomes. 'Utility' here is a more technical term for the 'satisfaction' from consumption discussed in Section 5.

The concept of utility has its roots in a philosophical tradition called utilitarianism, associated particularly with the nineteenth-century thinker Jeremy Bentham. Pareto's approach was to treat utility (he preferred to call it 'ophelimity') as something personal and non-comparable between people. I can say, this purchase gives me more utility than that purchase. But we cannot say, you get more utility from this purchase than I do, since there is no way of comparing your satisfaction with mine.

It was argued in Section 5 that a consumer who maximizes his satisfaction (or utility) will alter his purchases at the margin until he gets the same amount of satisfaction (utility) from the last pound spent on each good. In other words, the *marginal utility* – the satisfaction from the last item – of each good bought is in a sense equal to the price. If the marginal utility from a good was less than the price, it would be worth too little to the consumer and the last item would not be bought. So price equals marginal utility.

Now consider the production side. The earlier sections of this chapter established that under perfect competition the firm will produce where $MR = P = MC$. This indeed is the main distinction drawn between perfect competition and the models of market power in Chapter 6. Because the firm is a price taker it maximizes profits where price equals marginal cost.

The implication is that, under perfect competition, the common price taken by firms and consumers becomes a mediator which ensures that the worth to the consumer of the last item of each good bought is equal to the marginal cost of producing it. Marginal utility equals price equals marginal cost.

Once the perfectly competitive market has settled at an equilibrium where these equalities hold, no further improvement is possible by expanding or contracting output. Since marginal costs are assumed to rise, and consumers' willingness to pay falls, as output increases, a production increase will mean that consumers value the last unit below its marginal cost to society. And conversely, lower output means marginal benefit above marginal cost, suggesting that the economy should produce more.

An example of a choice between two goods may help to show that a competitive equilibrium is Pareto efficient.

Question

Suppose that the equality of marginal benefits with marginal costs does not hold. On the contrary, a consumer values the last meal at twice the last pair of socks, but the last meal costs three times as much to produce. Could production and consumption be rearranged to give more total benefit?

We could certainly extract more benefit here. The consumer could sacrifice a meal and be compensated fully with two pairs of socks. But the resources released allow three pairs of socks to be produced. So either the consumer, or someone else, is better off to the tune of one pair of socks. Or the spare resources from one pair of socks can be used for some other beneficial purpose.

Hence, when the equivalence of marginal benefit and marginal cost does not hold, there is scope for a Pareto improvement. In the above example the ratios of the marginal costs of socks and meals (the rate at which one could be replaced with the other at the margin) did not equal the ratios of the marginal benefits to the consumer. Thus rearrangement improved welfare. Once marginal costs are equated to marginal benefits, there is no scope left for this kind of rearrangement.

In this way perfectly competitive markets lead to a Pareto-efficient outcome. In equilibrium in a perfectly competitive market there are no benefits in further adjusting consumption/production, because the value lost to the consumer if a good is not bought is exactly balanced by the marginal cost saved. In maximizing their own welfare, consumers and producers make choices at the margin which ensure that there is no better outcome for one participant except at a cost to another. Such a situation is Pareto efficient.

This intuitive explanation has referred to product markets and to two-good economies. It can however be extended to more complex economies as a whole, with markets for factors of production as well as goods and services. It can be shown quite generally that if all markets are perfectly competitive, then the equilibrium for the economy as a whole is Pareto efficient. Another way of saying this is that a perfectly competitive economy is *allocatively efficient*: resources could not be reallocated to improve anyone's welfare without reducing the welfare of another.

This efficiency property of perfect competition has constituted a powerful argument for free markets. But you should note how strong the conditions are. All producers and consumers in product and factor markets must be perfectly informed price takers. The essence of efficiency in perfect competition lies in the choices which producers and consumers make – between factors of production, in how much to produce, and in the allocation of incomes between goods. Unless the prices of all products reflect marginal costs, consumers' choices will be based on misleading information, and analogous conditions apply to factor markets and production.

Hence, to achieve Pareto efficiency the entire economy must operate under conditions of perfect competition, a condition which is likely to be impracticable in real life. It requires only one monopolist or firm operating strategically in oligopoly to put price above marginal cost (which, as we have seen in previous units, they will do to maximize their profits) for these efficiency characteristics in the rest of the economy to be lost. Indeed Lipsey and Lancaster (1956) in their 'theory of the second best' showed that in such circumstances it might be better for even those markets which could achieve marginal-cost pricing to abandon it (though it is difficult to identify just what their prices should be under such circumstances). This dependence for efficiency on universal applicability throughout the economy is a harsh blow to the practical use of perfectly competitive models as a basis for policy.

Perfect competition then achieves Pareto efficiency only under restrictive assumptions. Some more of these restrictions – and some possible solutions – are discussed in later chapters. This chapter ends, however, with a discussion of one other very important qualification to the positive assessment of the outcome from perfectly competitive markets: its apparent omission of any consideration of how resources are distributed among different people in the market.

6.4 Efficiency and distribution

The Pareto criterion for efficiency is constructed only upon each consumer's definition of their own welfare. Because the utility of people cannot be compared, the criterion offers no guidance on how to make judgements on changes in the distribution of resources among individuals.

Thus Figure 7.19, drawn on the assumption of unsatisfied desire for both university and nursery places, defines the efficient choices within education expenditure, but it provides no guidance on the appropriate mix between the two groups of users. More university places can be purchased along the frontier only at the cost of lower nursery provision, and the consequent loss entailed by young families precludes a choice based on Pareto's criterion. This builds inertia into the situation by providing a veto to anyone who would be adversely affected by moving away from the *status quo*.

A separation between criteria for efficiency, and questions of distribution (or equity), appears attractive because it seems to provide an ethically neutral definition of efficiency. Views on the distribution of wealth and income are often overtly political and difficult to resolve. There is a temptation to 'shelve' them, not because they are thought to be unimportant, but so that they shall not impede understanding of efficiency. While this is a useful mechanism to explore efficiency, it carries with it the inherent danger of ignoring equity issues so that they remain 'on the shelf' indefinitely.

Income distribution however lies behind much of the analysis of market efficiency just conducted. For example, Chapter 3 explained the significance of income in determining demand for any product. An individual whose income is high may be prepared to pay much more for a product than if she had a low income, simply because there is more money available to 'bid' for the product. Thus the willingness to pay reflects both the strength of 'wanting' (intrinsic value or utility) and the available income. One particularly stark illustration occurs in famines, and is illustrated by Sen's analysis of hunger and famine.

> Hunger is not a recent phenomenon. Nor is famine. Life has been short and hard in much of the world, most of the time. Both chronic under-nourishment and recurrent famines have been among the causal antecedents of the brutishness and brevity of human life in history.
>
> Hunger in the modern world is more intolerable than past hunger not because it is typically more intense, but because it is now so unnecessary. The enormous expansion of productive power that has taken place over the last few centuries has made it possible, for the first time in history, to guarantee adequate food for all … . When millions of people suddenly die in a famine, it is hard to avoid the thought that there must have been a major decline in the output and availability of food in the economy. But while that is sometimes the case, there have frequently been famines in which food output and availability have remained high and undiminished. Indeed some famines have occurred in periods of peak food availability for the economy as a whole (e.g. the Bangladesh famine of 1974).
>
> The real issue is not primarily over-all availability of food, but its acquirement by individuals and families. If a person lacks the means to acquire food, the presence of food in the market is not much consolation. To understand hunger, we have to look at people's entitlements, i.e. … what commodity bundles (including food) they can make their own. The entitlement approach to hunger concentrates on the determination of command over commodities, including food. Famines are seen as the result of entitlement failures of large groups, often belonging to some specific occupations (e.g. landless rural labourers, pastoralists).

(Sen, 1987, pp.5, 7–8)

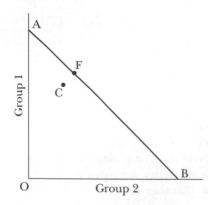

Figure 7.21 **Allocation of food between two competing groups**

The fact that famines can occur in the presence of plentiful supplies of food shows how the entitlements of some may be inadequate; in such a situation there is a very unequal distribution of income (and therefore food) between different groups and people in society. All the resources go to one group, and in diagrammatic terms we are right at one end of the efficiency frontier, at a point such as A in Figure 7.21. Note that here the frontier represents allocations of one good between groups, not a mix of two products. The distribution at point A is no less efficient than other points on the frontier such as F, but it is very inequitable and indeed disastrous for one group.

Effective demand for goods by individuals therefore depends on their income, and the market demand depends on the distribution of income within society. A very unequal distribution means high demand for luxury items; a more equitable distribution will result in less demand for luxury goods and more for 'middle income' products. The pattern of demand depends on the income distribution.

The implication is that for a given quantity of scarce resources, a perfectly competitive economy may be in equilibrium at different points on its production possibility frontier. It is the initial distribution of resources among people – the income distribution – which determines *where* on the frontier the economy will produce (that is, which products are produced) as well as who gets what. Hence underlying each alternative Pareto-efficient position is a different income distribution. Distribution cannot be divorced from efficiency as easily as first appeared.

Nor does growth solve the problem. For example, the article on education choices quoted earlier continued to make another suggestion.

> The Commission argues, as has this newspaper, that universities should be allowed to charge fees to students and offer them loans. Some would be able to pay for their education up-front, at a discount. Most would rely on state loans to cover fees and maintenance, repayable once they were in a job and as their incomes allowed. Pioneered in Australia, this system allows universities to expand and, at the same time, ensures that those who reap the benefits bear most of the costs.
>
> *(The Economist, 20 November 1993)*

This argues for a reorganization of university funding to enable more of both nursery school and university places. It moves the frontier out by changing the way in which university places are funded, so that more can be obtained from the same budget. This is rather like a technical change (such as a change in teaching method) which can move out a production possibility frontier, enabling more of both goods to be produced. However, in the education budget case, as in many experiences of economic growth, there are losers: those young people who would have to pay for their presently subsidized education. The Pareto criterion could not therefore be used to judge whether the reform was an improvement, since some members of society are worse off. Only by using a compensation principle could such a judgement be made. Is the gain to those who now have greater access to university and nursery places sufficient to compensate those who would otherwise have had their college life subsidized?

To circumvent the restrictiveness of the Pareto criterion and to make judgements about changes which involve some losers, such compensation principles have been proposed. These are based on whether the 'winners' from a change had sufficient gains from the change to compensate the 'losers' for their loss. While this is an appealing idea, it is fraught with practical difficulties, including the problem of comparing one person's gain with another's loss and the question of whether the compensation must actually be paid. Comparisons of the welfare of different individuals cannot be avoided once questions of income distribution become important.

The implication of the famine example, quoted above, is that it is quite possible to judge an economy to be both efficient and unacceptable. If we do not approve of starvation, we might reasonably prefer an inefficient point where some food has been wasted, say C, on Figure 7.21, to A (though F would still be preferable to C).

The demonstration that perfectly competitive economies are Pareto-efficient forms an important element of a tradition of analysis of economic welfare which seeks to base judgements on individual utilities, without controversial interpersonal comparisons of welfare. But there has also been considerable debate in modern economics about the ways in which societies or governments make distributional judgements. It has already been noted that the choice of a Pareto-efficient outcome under perfect competition is not 'value free' since it results from an underlying income distribution, of which we may or may not approve. In a given, efficient situation the Pareto criterion is restrictive in that it gives, in effect, each member of society a veto on any change they consider detrimental. Hence it gives tremendous power to the *status quo*. A concern with Pareto efficiency alone would block any redistribution from the rich to the poor, and hence would protect those who were rich from any reform which would encroach on their wealth.

The counter argument to this charge that the Pareto criterion is inherently conservative is that it is appropriate to separate equity from efficiency so that they can be dealt with individually. The efficiency could be pursued for example through policies to promote competition, while equity could be subject to separate policies, perhaps being dealt with through the tax and benefit system. In practice, however, efficiency and distribution are very hard to separate in this way. Distributional issues are discussed in more depth in Book 2.

Conclusion

The link between perfect competition and Pareto efficiency is strong theoretically and provides the model of perfect competition with some powerful properties. It is a model which sheds light on the competitive process and how it can lead to efficient price-setting. However, this power must be balanced with the model's limitations, both in terms of realism and the self-imposed boundaries of the analysis.

This chapter has dealt with one of the most extreme and abstract models of economic markets, showing how buyers and sellers react, and market equilibrium is established, when each actor is insignificant relative to the size of the market. Supply curves of individual firms and for the market as a whole were derived on the basis that firms are 'price takers' under perfect competition. Similarly, the market demand was reinterpreted as the sum of individual demand curves, each based on consumers spending their budgets to their own best advantage. Market equilibrium was then examined as the culmination of these individual 'rational choices' to determine the market-clearing price, which in turn became the price 'taken' by each firm and consumer in determining their own decisions about how much to sell or buy.

The final section of the chapter identified some important efficiency properties of the perfectly competitive equilibrium. In its pure form perfect competition achieves Pareto efficiency. This model underpins the arguments for free market policies such as the UK government's drive for competition quoted at the beginning of the chapter. But the assumptions of the model are restrictive and there are many obstacles to a desirable economic outcome, not least the model's own exclusion of issues of equity. Perfect competition thus remains an important but limited framework of analysis. The next chapter examines some of its applications to important policy issues.

CHAPTER 8

COMPETITION POLICIES AND INDUSTRIAL POLICIES

by George Yarrow

1 Introduction

Adam Smith was in no doubt about the pitfalls of monopoly as a form of industrial organization. In *The Wealth of Nations* he wrote:

> By a perpetual monopoly, all the other subjects of the state are taxed very absurdly in two different ways; first, by the high price of goods, which, in the case of a free trade, they could buy much cheaper; and, secondly, by their total exclusion from a branch of business, which it might be both convenient and profitable for many of them to carry on. It is for the most worthless of all purposes too that they are taxed in this manner. It is merely to enable the company to support the negligence, profusion, and malversion of their own servants, whose disorderly conduct seldom allows the dividend of the company to exceed the ordinary rate of profit in trades which are altogether free, and very frequently makes it all even a good deal short of that rate.
>
> *(Smith, 1776; 1976 edn, vol. 2, p.755)*

Smith's critique of monopoly is particularly directed at what are called statutory monopolies, where the state grants monopoly rights to individual firms. Such firms are fully protected from competition or the threat of competition, and the economist's traditional model of monopoly, set out in Chapter 6, can be applied.

Problems of analysis multiply, however, once we leave the world of fully protected monopoly. It is relatively rare to find that all the output in an industry is accounted for by one firm; and even when there is only one supplier, decisions may be affected by the fear that rival firms could enter the market. In practice, then, public policy has to operate in economic contexts where there is likely to be a mix of monopolistic and competitive elements. Principles therefore have to be developed to cope with an often untidy reality.

As explained in Chapter 5, oligopoly theory provides a first basis for thinking systematically about these issues of monopoly and competition. What quickly becomes clear from the analysis is that it is very difficult to quantify the extent to which particular industries are more or less monopolistic/competitive. Thus, while it might be argued that monopoly is, in general, a bad thing and that increasing competition is, in general, a good thing, the problem with this position is not so much that it is obviously wrong but rather that it offers little practical guidance for policy once we move away from situations of extreme market power such as statutory monopoly.

Putting this another way, it is not helpful to think of different types of markets being ranked in a simple, one-dimensional continuum with perfect competition and monopoly at its end points. Things are more complex than this, and while economic analysis necessarily attempts to simplify reality in order to understand it better, the competition/monopoly area is an example of a case where over-simplification can be positively misleading.

In this chapter I will look both at government actions aimed at changing the balance of competitive and monopolistic elements within markets, and at the economic factors underlying these actions. When the interventions are guided by general rules that apply across a wide range of economic activities, they are usually referred to as *competition policies*; when they are more specific, and are targeted on particular sectors or activities, they tend to be called *industrial policies*. As will be seen, however, there is no hard-and-fast boundary between the two.

The structure of the chapter is as follows. Section 2 will outline the main aspects of the economic critique of monopoly as a form of industrial organization, while Section 3 will provide a framework for evaluating different types of policy response to the monopoly problem. Section 4 will introduce the key concept of market dominance, which underpins much implicit and explicit theorizing about competition and monopoly, and will explore its ambiguities. Sections 5, 6 and 7 will then consider three specific sets of policy issues, concerning collusion, vertical supply arrangements and mergers respectively. In each case the discussion will explore the links (or lack of links) between policy conduct and economic principles. In Section 8 we will take a brief look at problems of monopoly and competition associated with the privatization of major utilities such as telecommunications, gas and electricity. Finally, Section 9 will examine aspects of government policy towards industries that compete in international markets in which there exist substantial monopolistic elements.

2   Market power and its problems

A number of the potential disadvantages of monopoly have been discussed in Chapter 6, and these arguments carry over into cases where firms or groups of firms have substantial market power – that is, the power substantially to affect market conditions, including the market price, independently of rivals or potential rivals.

2.1   Static efficiency losses

The most basic potential disadvantage of market power is that, by restricting their output, firms prevent the achievement of potential gains from trade. The result is inefficiency in resource allocation, as illustrated in Figure 8.1.

This figure shows an industry where firms have market power. In general, the effect of market power is to allow firms to restrict output and push up prices in an attempt to extract supernormal profits. Chapter 6, Section 4.1, explained the ability of a pure monopolist to hold prices above average costs. Chapter 5, Section 4.2, noted that oligopolists have an incentive to collude to restrict output and to share out the resultant profits. In general, static models of monopoly power suggest that markets where firms have

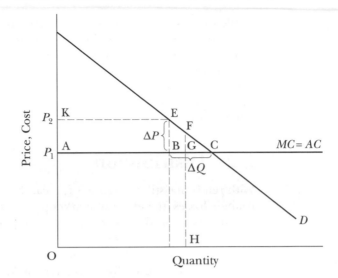

Figure 8.1   Efficiency losses arising from monopoly power

some market power will tend to display higher prices and lower output than would be the case if the market was perfectly competitive.

In Figure 8.1, *D* is the industry demand curve. We assume for simplicity that firms' average costs are constant (and identical), so *MC = AC* shows average costs as industry output expands. If the industry was perfectly competitive, this would be the industry supply curve. Point C therefore indicates the perfectly competitive market equilibrium at price P_1.

An imperfectly competitive industry – where firms have market power – will tend to produce at a point on the demand curve to the left of C, such as E, with higher price P_2 and lower output. On the demand curve to the right of E are a series of points such as F where consumers would be willing to pay more for extra units of output than it would cost to produce those units. Thus at F, the value of an extra unit of output is FH, whereas the cost of producing an extra unit is GH. If, therefore, the extra unit were produced and sold at a price equal to its marginal cost, there would be a net gain to the consumer of FG, equal to the value put on the good by the consumer less the price paid. This gain is called the consumer surplus.

Definition

Consumer surplus

Consumer surplus is the difference between what a consumer is willing to pay for a good and the amount actually paid for it. It is a measure of the benefits to a consumer of trading in the market.

Potential benefits that could be achieved by expanding output exist at all points along the demand curve between E and C (to the right of C the cost of producing extra output exceeds its value to consumers). If, therefore, output were expanded up to the point where the demand curve cuts the marginal cost curve (i.e. point C), the overall increase in economic welfare would be given by the area of the triangle BCE. The triangle BCE can therefore be interpreted as a *measure of the inefficiency of market power*.

Empirical estimates of the 'triangle' losses attributable to market power have tended to produce what are generally regarded as low values. The reason for this can be seen by noting that the area of the triangle is approximately $0.5 \times \Delta P \Delta Q$ (the approximation is exact if the demand curve is a straight line). Suppose, for example, that the effect of market power is to increase prices by 5 per cent and to reduce output by 10 per cent (i.e. the price elasticity of market demand is 2). Then, using the formula $0.5 \times \Delta P \Delta Q$, the inefficiency attributable to market power would be one-quarter of one per cent (= $0.5 \times 0.05 \times 0.1 \times 100$) of the value of sales at the competitive equilibrium (i.e. at point C in Figure 8.1).

While the resulting number may be far from negligible – £25 million for a £10 billion industry – it is also not so large as to create great excitement. For example, if the industry were growing by 3 per cent per year, it would be equivalent to one month's growth. Though this would certainly be worth having, it is open to question whether the problem is sufficiently serious as to warrant the development of a whole strand of public policy with its own attendant costs.

2.2   Distribution

With reference still to Figure 8.1, it can be seen that, in addition to the triangle losses, the effect of market power is to redistribute income from consumers to producers by an amount equal to the area of the rectangle ABEK. That is, at a traded volume measured by the length of the line KE, the increase in price due to monopoly power ($=AK = P_2 - P_1$) means an increased expenditure for consumers of ABEK, and an equivalent increase in the profits of the firm. The overall effects associated with a shift in equilibrium from C to E are therefore:

Loss to consumers: rectangle ABEK plus triangle BCE;

Gain to producers: rectangle ABEK.

A crucial point which I can demonstrate at this stage is that the area of ABEK is likely to be much greater than the area of triangle BCE.

Exercise 8.1

Suppose again that prices rise by 5 per cent and output falls by 10 per cent when the industry moves from C to E. How big is the rectangle ABEK as a percentage of industry sales at the competitive equilibrium C?

The calculation, explained in the answer to the exercise, gives a value of 4.5 per cent of the sales value at C, or eighteen times larger than the efficiency loss of 0.25 per cent from triangle BCE. This is an illustration of the point that, in quantitative terms, *the distributional effects of market power are likely to be much greater than its short-term effect on efficiency* (i.e. than the triangle losses). There is, therefore, potentially a lot at stake for the major interest groups, and even if competition policy does not add much to the sum total of economic efficiency, there may be strong political pressures for (and against) such a policy emanating from those groups.

Question

For a given price increase, can you work out from Figure 8.1 how the magnitudes of the efficiency and distributional changes are affected by the price elasticity of demand? Start from point C in Figure 8.1, and take ΔP as given. How will the demand elasticity affect the value of ΔQ? And how will this in turn affect ABEK and BCE?

As the elasticity of demand increases, the decline in demand increases. So KE = AB becomes shorter. Hence the rectangle ABEK, the distributional effect, is reduced. On the other hand, BC becomes larger, so the triangle loss increases.

Exercise 8.2

Can you use algebra to demonstrate these relationships between the elasticity of demand and the efficiency and distributional losses? Start from the definition of the price elasticity of demand (Chapter 6) and try to establish the relationship between ε_D and ΔQ.

A good illustration of the importance of distributive issues in competition policy is the price of motor cars in the European Union, a matter that has received considerable attention from both the UK Monopolies and Mergers Commission and the EU competition authorities. Consumer groups in the UK have complained vociferously that there has been a persistent tendency for new car prices to be higher in the UK than in most other EU member states. Although this has been disputed by the manufacturers, let us suppose for the sake of argument that the consumer groups' complaints are broadly correct. On this basis, the variation in car prices among EU member states would be an example of *price discrimination* (selling similar goods at different prices to different customers).

Suppose next that price discrimination were prohibited (and it can be noted that the European Commission does have a policy that price differentials should not move out of permissible bands). It is not clear whether the efficiency of resource allocation would rise or fall in the European Union. Prices might fall in some member states, thus stimulating a greater volume of trade in those countries, but rise in other member states, thus depressing volumes there. It is unlikely, therefore, that even if positive, any increase in efficiency would be large. Nevertheless, the matter will not be one of indifference to UK consumers, who could be expected to take a fairly dim view of arguments that efficiency considerations mean there is no call for policy intervention in the given circumstances – that is, of price discrimination that redistributes income away from UK consumers.

2.3   Cost levels and dynamic efficiency

The economic analysis in the discussion so far has been based on the assumption that cost conditions in an industry are not dependent on the state of competition in that market. In Figure 8.1, for example, it is assumed that when price increases as a consequence of market power, there will be no corresponding effect on costs. In practice this may be unrealistic; if market power does affect costs, its consequences for efficiency can be substantially greater than is suggested by the arguments in Section 2.1. Put another way, dynamic efficiency effects such as those discussed in Chapter 6 may be very important aspects of economic performance.

The existence or prospect of monopoly profits gives firms incentives to devote resources to the maintenance or development of market power. To illustrate this, in the situation represented by equilibrium at point E in Figure 8.1, market power has a value equal to ABEK to firms operating in the industry. It would, therefore, be worth firms' spending up to this amount to protect themselves against a shift to the competitive equilibrium at C. Firms might, for example, engage in excessive advertising in order to

Definition

Dynamic efficiency effects

Dynamic efficiency effects are those changes in economic efficiency that arise from the discovery and introduction of new production techniques and new products.

raise barriers to entry into the industry. More generally, the potential profit benefits of market power might be dissipated in a whole range of inefficiencies in the ways in which firms make use of their economic inputs. Not least among these is inefficiency in the use of management resources, a problem summarized in the concept of the 'sleepy monopolist'.

When all or part of the potential profit benefit of market power is converted into extra costs, the process is known as *rent transformation*. The concept derives from the idea of *economic rent*: that is, the additional benefit to factors of production – in this case to the owners of the capital invested in the firm – over and above the minimum payment needed to keep them in the business. The benefits of market power are a form of economic rent which may be transformed into higher costs. Sometimes rent transformation is good for economic performance, as when the prospect of monopoly profits provides incentives for innovation. This is the rationale of the patent system, which grants monopoly rights in inventions precisely so as to provide incentives for invention. On the other hand, sometimes rent transformation is bad for economic performance, as when the expenditures involve misleading advertising (the effects of which are discussed in Chapter 6). Distinguishing the two cases is therefore clearly an exercise of some importance.

An example of a situation where rent transformation is bad for economic efficiency is when market prices are governed by a cartel agreement, but firms are able to enter and exit the industry freely. This is illustrated in Figure 8.2, where the line AF is the market demand curve and the line labelled *LRAC* shows long-run average costs (assumed identical for all firms). With only one firm in the market, the existence of monopoly profit will lead to new entry. Assuming firms agree to share the market at a common price, the demand for each firm will be represented by demand curves such as AB. For example, with three firms sharing the market, the distance OB will be equal to one-third the distance OF.

Entry into the market will continue to occur until firms' demand curves are tangential to the average cost curve, as illustrated by point E (the argument here is identical to that in Chapter 6, Section 4.3). At the equilibrium point E, price is equal to average costs and there are no monopoly profits.

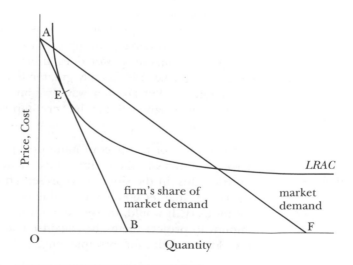

Figure 8.2 **A cartel equilibrium**

Nevertheless, both price and costs could be substantially reduced if cartelization were ended and concentration in the industry were increased. What has happened is that potential monopoly profits have been transformed into higher costs via a loss of scale economies. Moreover, since in this case there is no profit benefit to firms to be set against consumer losses from higher prices, the inefficiencies attributable to market power will tend to be much greater than under simple monopoly. Note also that ending cartelization and increasing price competition would lead to an *increase* in concentration in the industry, a point that will be taken up again in the next section.

Question

Who gains from the cartel equilibrium shown in Figure 8.2?

At first sight it appears that no one gains, since firms make only normal profits and consumers are worse off as a result of higher prices. The key to the answer is to distinguish between the short run and the long run. In the short run (when the capital input is given) firms would, on average, earn a less than normal return on capital if price competition were increased. In the long run, as they expanded capacity, average costs would fall for the firms remaining in the industry.

If it is fear of abnormally low profits that provides incentives for cartel formation, this suggests that cartelization will tend to occur more frequently in periods of depressed demand. It is certainly true, for example, that cartelization was rife in Europe in the depressed economic conditions of the 1930s and that cartels are often found when industries experience periods of excess capacity. This suggests that cartels may sometimes give rise to beneficial effects (e.g. maintaining employment), particularly if low demand is not expected to persist indefinitely and the cartel itself is temporary.

As already indicated, however, not all rent transformation is bad. If the prospect of monopoly profits leads to higher expenditures today on research and development, for example, these expenditures will be likely to have dynamic benefits in terms of lower cost levels (or improved products) tomorrow. Note, however, that such beneficial cases of rent transformation should not be interpreted as meaning that monopoly itself is a good thing. It is essential for the dynamic process that there be competition *for* monopoly profits. If that competition is itself weak, then the result may simply be a 'sleepy' monopoly, characterized by lack of dynamism.

Rent transformation illustrates a fundamental point about market economies, namely that dynamic efficiency depends on achieving effective blends of competition and monopoly. Thus, for example, it is quite possible for price competition sometimes to be too intense, for the simple reason that the prospect of cut-throat price competition may deter beneficial, longer-term investments in a market.

3   Policy approaches to issues of monoply and competition

In practice, a variety of different policy approaches to problems of monopoly and competition have been adopted in different countries at different times. A method of categorizing the principal (broadly defined) options is set out in the matrix shown in Figure 8.3, which shows two dimensions of choice. The first concerns the general type of policy (policy stance), and the second concerns the target of the policy (market structure or market conduct). These will be discussed in turn.

Target ⟍ Policy stance	Market conduct	Market structure
Laissez-faire		
Rule of reason		
Prohibition with exemption		
Per se		

Figure 8.3   **Policy stances and targets**

3.1   Policy options

Laissez-faire is the policy stance in which governments decline to intervene at all. It is not an option that is now generally adopted by governments, although competition policies are frequently framed in ways that exclude large parts of economic activity from their domains, as for example when industries are deemed sufficiently unconcentrated as to be of no concern to merger control authorities. The latter approach might be termed conditional *laissez-faire*.

At the other end of the spectrum lie *per se* policies, in which certain types of behaviour or certain types of industry structure are ruled to be illegal in and of themselves, irrespective of the existence or non-existence of strong arguments in defence of such behaviour or structures. That is, this type of policy is characterized by the strict application of *rules*, with little or no discretion given to public officials to allow exceptions. Examples include laws prohibiting predatory pricing or regulations preventing mergers that would increase industrial concentration above a specified value. The *per se* approach has been more popular in the USA than in Europe.

Rule of reason approaches, by contrast, allow for the *effects* of business practices or market structures in particular circumstances to be taken into account. The purest type of rule of reason approach simply grants discretion to the relevant competition agency to investigate particular problems and make recommendations or decisions as to whether or not any policy interventions are justified. There are no strict rules about what is allowed and what is not allowed. UK monopolies policy is of this form, with the Monopolies and Mergers Commission investigating companies and industries on a case-by-case basis.

EU competition law towards restrictive practices is based on a third approach, *prohibition with exemption*, which mixes *per se* and rule of reason elements (i.e. it mixes rules with discretion). Certain business practices, such as colluding to fix prices, are prohibited, but exemptions are allowed if it can be shown that there are substantial benefits from the practice. Here the burden of proof is somewhat different: it is up to the companies concerned to argue a convincing case for exemption, and since prohibited practices are illegal, unlike in the UK, in the absence of exemption companies can be fined and sued for damages by affected parties.

The second broad dimension of choice shown in Figure 8.3 is whether policy should be directed chiefly at influencing the behaviour (or conduct) of firms or at influencing the market structures in which companies operate. Of course, to put the issue in these terms is to oversimplify. Policies can, and do, rely on a mix of 'conduct' and 'structural' approaches. Nevertheless, there is a balance to be struck, and decisions can lie closer to one end of the spectrum than to the other.

Traditionally, UK and EU policies towards monopolies and cartels have focused chiefly on business conduct. In respect of monopolies and dominant firms, for example, both regimes take the position that there is nothing necessarily wrong with a company having a large market share, but abuses of market power must be prevented. The emphasis on the *abuse* of market power, rather than on its *existence*, represents a behavioural rather than a structural emphasis.

In the later 1980s and early 1990s, however, there was something of a swing to 'structuralist' views, particularly in the UK. In 1991 the then Secretary of State for Industry, Mr Peter Lilley, put the matter very clearly when he stated that he preferred to see clean structural remedies rather than behavioural remedies which involved long-term monitoring by the Office of Fair Trading.

More significantly, the emphasis on structure is visible in the following UK cases:

- In 1989 the Monopolies and Mergers Commission (MMC) recommended that major UK brewers be required to divest themselves of large numbers of public houses that they owned. The government later implemented a modified version of the proposal.

- In 1990, the electricity industry was restructured prior to privatization. In the name of creating a market environment in which competition could flourish, the Central Electricity Generating Board was split into four different companies: the National Grid company, National Power, PowerGen and Nuclear Electric (see Vickers and Yarrow, 1991).

- In 1993 the Monopolies and Mergers Commission recommended that British Gas be required to divest itself of its gas sales business, with the aim of preventing British Gas from using its control of pipelines and storage facilities to hinder competition from rivals in gas sales. In this case the government declined to accept the MMC's recommendation.

As yet, the European Commission has been much more cautious in adopting structuralist approaches to competition problems, but the issue remains a live and important one at the European level.

3.2   Structure vs. conduct

Let us now consider some of the arguments that address the extent to which competition policy should rely on a structuralist rather than a behavioural approach. Two important elements of market structure are *market concentration* and *barriers to entry*, and their effects are closely linked.

An implication of economic analysis which is worth stressing in this context is that entry barriers are necessary for the existence of market power. That is, in the absence of entry barriers, the level of concentration does not matter for economic performance. The extreme case of zero entry barriers – or, as it is sometimes called, ultra-free entry – has been modelled extensively in an area of economic analysis known as the theory of contestable markets.

If a market is contestable, then a potential entrant is economically equivalent to an incumbent firm. Since there is no substantive difference between established firms and potential entrants (there are no entry/exit barriers and costs are identical), established firms are effectively in competition with a very large number of rivals. In these circumstances, competitive pressures would be intense even if the market was highly concentrated.

As an example of reasoning in this area, consider Figure 8.4, which shows cost and demand conditions for an industry with extensive economies of scale. The industry illustrated is a *natural monopoly*, defined in Chapter 6 as an industry where demand can be met at least cost by a single firm. Suppose that initially a single firm supplies the market and is considering setting a price *P* to sell quantity *Q*. Since *P* is above average cost, if this were the price charged there would be an opportunity (on contestable market assumptions) for a rival firm immediately and costlessly to enter the market and undercut *P*, yet still make supernormal profits. The key assumption here is that entry can occur before the established firm has time to react by cutting its price. In this case, *P* cannot be an equilibrium price since it cannot be sustained in the face of entry competition.

The same reasoning applies to any other price above average costs. On the other hand, prices below average costs will lead to losses, in which case the firm would (costlessly) exit the market. Equilibrium can therefore only occur at point E, where, since price equals average cost, the incumbent firm can

Definition

Contestable markets

A contestable market is one in which (a) entry and exit are costless, and (b) all firms have identical cost functions.

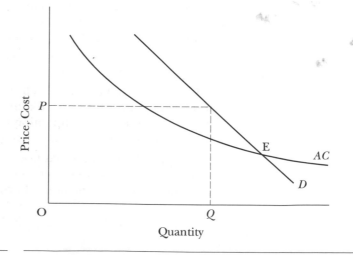

***Figure 8.4*   Opportunities for 'hit-and-run' entry?**

make normal profits and will not be undercut. Note that precisely because price competition is so effective, only one firm can survive in the market.

Question

Contestability of markets is often presented as a good thing because it leads to low prices. Returning to the closing point of Section 2, however, we may have some doubts about this. One of the reasons a firm will innovate is to reduce its costs below the costs of its rivals, but this would violate the conditions for contestability. Does this indicate, then, that contestability is incompatible with dynamic efficiency?

In general, the answer is yes. In practice, the conditions required for ultra-free entry will not be satisfied. Nevertheless, the more general implication of the analysis – that strong competition may lead to high concentration – is one that has wider application. Thus, in the cartel example discussed above, weak price competition led to excessive entry and was therefore associated with relatively *low* concentration.

This inverse relationship between concentration and the intensity of competition is sufficient to demonstrate the dangers of relying on what is called the *concentration doctrine* – that is, the notion that higher concentration is associated with weaker competition. Further, given that the links between concentration and competition are complex, it also serves as a warning against simplistic notions about the economic effects of policy-induced changes in concentration. It is quite possible, for example, that policies designed to achieve de-concentration as a means to increasing price competition could have exactly the opposite effect. The only way of achieving de-concentration might be to implement measures that, in effect, relax price competition.

Structuralist policies aimed at reducing entry barriers also have weaknesses. Particularly when dealing with issues of dynamic efficiency, there are cases where reducing entry barriers can have negative effects on economic performance. Patent protection, for example, is a source of entry barriers, but its elimination may reduce incentives to innovate. However, there is also a wide range of circumstances where reduction of entry barriers could be expected to have beneficial effects, and in these cases the difficulties in implementing structuralist policies are most frequently related to the practical problems of measuring entry barriers.

To illustrate this, consider the 1988 UK Monopolies and Mergers Commission report on the pricing behaviour of British Gas in industrial markets. The report found that there were a number of obstacles to entry into the market, including:

- British Gas's policy of price discrimination, which enabled the company to target price reductions on specific customers in the event that rivals sought to supply those customers;

- British Gas's stranglehold on gas supplies from the North Sea, which made it difficult for entrants to purchase gas for resale to final customers; and

- British Gas's behaviour with respect to terms and conditions available for rivals wishing to make use of existing pipeline and storage facilities.

The MMC made recommendations directed at each of these points, but did not at that stage recommend the separation of the transportation/storage and sales businesses of British Gas. When, in 1991, the Office of Fair Trading reviewed the effects of the 1988 measures, it concluded that substantial entry barriers remained.

The question of interest here is, how did the Office of Fair Trading (OFT) arrive at its conclusion that the behavioural remedies of the 1988 MMC report had been largely ineffective in reducing entry barriers? The answer seems to be that the OFT relied heavily on market share data. By 1991 rivals to British Gas had captured only a small share of the market potentially available to them, and this was taken as an indication that competition was largely absent.

As we have seen from Figure 8.4, however, this inference cannot be automatic, since large market shares are quite compatible with low entry barriers. Indeed, under conditions of economies of scale and low entry barriers, falling concentration could be a sign of weakening, not strengthening, competition.

These arguments do not imply that it is impossible to assess or measure entry barriers. In the gas case, for example, it would have been possible for the Office of Fair Trading to use evaluations of changes in British Gas's conduct and performance as another source of information. One relevant piece of evidence here would have been changes in British Gas's profit margins on industrial supplies, which fell significantly from 1988 onwards. The point is simply that the task is not a straightforward one, and there is plenty of scope for mistakes.

4 Market dominance

Competition policy is largely concerned with issues arising from situations in which a firm or a group of firms has the power substantially to affect market conditions, including the market price, independently of rivals or potential rivals. In the context of EU competition policy, this is referred to as a position of market dominance; in the UK context the term used is monopoly. The EU terminology is generally to be preferred, since it does not risk confusion with the technical, economic definition of monopoly (namely, single supplier).

Three principal concepts of market dominance can be found in the law and economics of competition policy:

- single-firm dominance;
- joint dominance without agreements; and
- joint dominance based on agreements (collusion).

The third of these, collusion, will be examined in Section 5.

4.1 Single-firm dominance

Article 86 of the (1957) Treaty of Rome, which established what is now the EU, renders it illegal to abuse a dominant position in any way which may affect trade between member states. Translating from legal jargon into economic jargon, this roughly means that it is illegal for a firm with substantial market power to behave in ways that have unacceptable efficiency or distributional consequences. The Article itself does not define what is meant by a dominant position, nor what constitutes abusive behaviour: these are left for the European Commission and the European Court of Justice to decide.

In practice, then, in each case there are three substantive stages of the policy process:

1   evaluations to determine whether a firm does nor does not enjoy a dominant position;

2   evaluations to determine whether dominance has or has not been abused; and

3   determination of remedies and/or penalties.

Evaluating dominance

On several occasions the European Commission and the Court of Justice have reaffirmed a basic definition of dominance as: 'the power to hinder effective competition in a substantial part of the market in question'.

This immediately poses the question of how 'the market in question' – usually referred to as the 'relevant market' – should be defined. Unfortunately, as Chapter 6 noted, the issue is far from easy to resolve. 'Markets', like 'industries', are economic abstractions, not institutions that can readily be identified. Clear breaks in the ease with which customers and producers can switch between one product or group of products and other products may not exist, and the definition of the boundary of a market may in consequence be rather arbitrary. For example, should bus transportation be regarded as a distinct market, or should rail transport be included as part of the same relevant market? And what about taxis, private cars, air transport, and bicycles?

The result of the requirement to define a relevant market has led to a number of interesting debates, in which defending firms typically argue for a wide market definition and the European Commission typically argues for a narrow market definition. The types of issue involved are illustrated by the *United Brands* (1978) case (Whish, 1993, contains further discussion of this and other cases cited). Here the question was, are bananas in the same relevant market as other fruit? In considering this issue the European Court said that this depended on whether the banana could be: 'singled out by such special features distinguishing it from other fruits that it is only to a limited extent interchangeable with them and is only exposed to their competition in a way that is hardly perceptible'.

Question

A small firm producing fountain pens claims that it is suffering from predatory behaviour by a large manufacturer that dominates the market. In its defence the large firm argues that it is not dominant because the relevant market includes all writing instruments: fountain pens, ballpoints, rollerballs, felt-tips, pencils, typewriters, word processors, crayons, chalk, etc. Which products do you think should be classified as being part of the relevant market?

There is no obviously right answer. We would need to know more about the degrees of substitutability among the products in the eyes of consumers, but even armed with such quantitative information, there is plenty of scope for disagreement about definitions. In this context the 'market' is a concept in search of a definition, not a place or an institution.

In terms of the underlying economics, the precise definition of the relevant market should not matter a great deal. The important thing is the intensity of the competitive pressures faced by the firm. In practice, the market definition stage is of some importance by virtue of the fact that market share statistics appear to be the most influential indicators of dominance. The European Commission uses a figure of around 40 per cent as a rough guide: market shares above this value are taken as fairly strong signals of the existence of single-firm dominance. It is, of course, more likely that a firm will find itself with more than 40 per cent of a narrowly defined market than of a widely defined market.

In focusing attention on market definition, then, there is a tendency to adopt what might be called a 'naive structuralist' position, based on the concentration doctrine. The market share of the allegedly dominant firm tends to be accorded a rather greater weight as an indicator of the state of competition than can usually be justified on the basis of the economic analysis of markets.

Unfortunately, there is no mechanistic way of reaching a quick and reliable resolution of the issues. The question 'does dominance exist?' can only be answered by a thorough appraisal of the competitive situation of the firm(s) concerned. Such an appraisal needs to take account of a large number of economic factors, including market shares, profit margins, entry conditions, the availability of substitute products, the market power of buyers, and the market power of suppliers.

In Britain the scope of policy towards dominant firms is defined explicitly by a market share test: cases may be referred to the MMC (by either the Office of Fair Trading or the minister of state) if the firm in question controls 25 per cent or more of the supply of some good or service. There is no presumption, however, that *all* such cases will be referred to the MMC, and in practice most are not.

The meaning of abuse

As with the concept of market dominance itself, there is no generally accepted, precise definition of what constitutes abuse of a dominant position. Article 86 of the Treaty of Rome simply sets out four *examples* of abusive conduct, but the list is not intended to be exhaustive. The practices cited are: the imposition of unfair trading conditions; limitations of production, markets or technical development; discriminatory behaviour in dealings with other firms; and tying practices.

Limited as it is, the list indicates that EU policy is concerned both with issues of efficiency (e.g. limitations of technical development) and with issues of distribution (e.g. imposition of unfair trading conditions). This, together with the open-ended nature of Article 86, means that what is and what is not considered acceptable as business conduct by a dominant firm is a matter that has come to be determined in large part by the evolution of case law in the relevant area.

Discriminatory or predatory pricing directed at weakening the competitive position of a rival is one type of behaviour that has been vigorously attacked by the EU authorities. A good example is the *Napier Brown/British Sugar* (1988) case. British Sugar refined and supplied beet sugar in bulk, and also sold its own sugar in packaged form for retailing in grocery shops and supermarkets. Napier Brown purchased bulk sugar, packaged it and sold it to retailers in competition with British Sugar. Through its control of both bulk and retail-packaged prices, British Sugar was held to have reduced the margin between these prices to a level designed to drive sugar merchants such as Napier Brown out of the market. The Commission concluded that this was an abuse of a dominant position (British Sugar is the leading UK refiner, with well over 40 per cent of the sales in the UK market), and in 1988 imposed a fine of three million ecu.

In contrast, the position in respect of price levels that are 'excessive' – which is the classic monopoly pricing problem – is less clear. Article 86 gives scope for attacking monopolistic pricing, but the EU authorities have been reluctant to press too far in this direction. Apart from the difficult question of establishing procedures for determining whether or not prices are excessive, there are good policy grounds for this reluctance. If the excessive pricing is made possible by other anti-competitive actions, such as strategic behaviour to increase entry barriers, it will be eroded by attacking the problem at its source. If, on the other hand, high prices are made possible by temporary competitive advantages gained by innovation and efficiency, then attacking those prices will damage the dynamic incentives of the market.

In the UK there has been a greater concern with the problem of excessive pricing, but the dynamic efficiency defence still carries some weight. Thus, in *Soluble Coffee* (1991) the MMC made no adverse finding against Nestlé, even though, through its Nescafé brands, the company accounted for over 50 per cent of the instant coffee market and had a return on tangible capital employed of 114 per cent in 1989. Among other things, the MMC examined the possible effects of high levels of advertising expenditures on entry conditions, but rejected the view that such expenditures led to major entry barriers in this case. The MMC found that advertising costs for soluble coffee were not particularly high in comparison with other branded grocery products, that there was no shortage in the supply of soluble coffee for import into the UK, and that a number of new entrants had built up niche market positions. The overall conclusion was that: 'Its [Nestlé's] profitability, in our view reflects its success in meeting consumers' preferences in an effectively competitive market'.

Remedies

Part of the difference between the EU and UK approaches to excess profits is attributable to differences in the powers of the relevant authorities, particularly in relation to remedies. At the European level, policy is administered by the Commission, which has powers both to investigate and decide particular cases (investigations are often triggered by complaints from the allegedly dominant firm's competitors). The Commission has powers to impose interim measures if it sees fit and, following a finding that abuse of dominance has occurred, can impose fines of up to 10 per cent of the worldwide sales revenue of the dominant firm attributable to the relevant products or services.

In the UK there is no equivalent power to fine firms for anti-competitive conduct. Remedies are frequently of a kind that require the firm in question to 'cease and desist' from certain forms of business conduct. On the other hand, more 'interventionist' remedies are available in the UK, including price controls and divestment (the requirement that a company sell, or otherwise dispose of, part of its business).

4.2   Joint dominance

Article 86 refers to abuses of dominance by one *or more* undertakings. It is, therefore, open to an interpretation which allows it to cover oligopolistic markets where no single firm is dominant, but where it is believed there is some failure of competition that is not the result of explicit or tacit agreements among firms. The European Commission has tried, over the years, to widen the scope of Article 86 to cover such 'oligopolistic' cases – to which the term 'joint dominance' is usually applied – but so far the European Court has resisted the extension, interpreting the plural terms in the Article as referring to enterprises which are part of the same corporate group or which are otherwise strongly linked.

There is no similar problem in the UK, where competition law allows the Monopolies and Mergers Commission to investigate what are called 'complex monopolies', defined as situations in which a number of firms behave in ways that prevent, restrict or distort competition and collectively control at least 25 per cent of the supply of the reference good. The market share test here is so weak that practically any industry could be caught by it. There is, therefore, virtually no restriction on the potential coverage of 'monopolies' investigations in the UK.

5   Collusion

When individual firms are not dominant they may nevertheless co-ordinate their behaviour in ways that materially affect market conditions. For example, firms may come together to fix prices or to establish trading arrangements that make it more difficult for new firms to enter the industry. The co-ordination of behaviour may be either by explicit agreement or by a tacit understanding among firms.

One distinction of great economic importance is between horizontal and vertical agreements. A horizontal agreement is one among firms engaged in activities at the same stage of production/distribution, such as a price-fixing or market-sharing arrangement among the manufacturers of a particular product. Vertical agreements are those between firms at successive stages of the production/distribution chain: an example would be an exclusive dealing arrangement whereby a retailer agrees to stock the products of only one supplier.

5.1   The pros and cons of horizontal agreements

Section 2 argued that horizontal price-fixing agreements may be particularly bad for economic welfare because they can lead to equilibria in which production structures are inefficient and unit costs are high. Hence, not surprisingly, there has been a strong anti-cartel strand to mainstream economic thinking. But is there anything to be said in favour of collusive behaviour?

If we replace the description 'collusion among firms' with the rather friendlier terminology 'co-operation among firms', it seems likely that there will indeed be situations in which such behaviour is not harmful. For we know in general that there are circumstances where co-operative behaviour produces better outcomes than competitive behaviour: that is the general message of games of the prisoners' dilemma type, which were analysed in Chapter 5. (See also the discussion of strategic alliances in that chapter.)

One *possible* source of benefit from collusion is the effect on employment. Abandonment of a collusive agreement may well lead to redundancies as price competition puts downward pressure on costs, and production is concentrated in fewer, larger units. In conditions of high unemployment this may be socially inefficient as well as being damaging to the individuals concerned.

Another significant argument in favour of horizontal agreements concerns the stability of the relevant industry. In conditions of depressed demand and excess capacity, firms will naturally tend to seek reductions in capacity by means of plant closures. In theory, market competition should ensure that higher-cost plant is closed first, and also that the overall level of capacity reduction properly takes into account the likelihood of increased demand at a later date. In practice, in the disturbed conditions of severe recession, firms (acting individualistically) may over-adjust, leading to a period of deficient capacity and high prices when recovery comes. Together with the employment argument, this provides a potential justification for tolerance of *distress* or *crisis* cartels.

5.2   Detecting horizontal agreements

The analysis of the collusive equilibrium in Section 2 indicated that price fixing sustains more firms in the market than would be the case under price competition, and that each firm only makes normal profits (a consequence of the free entry assumption). This combination of relatively low market concentration and normal profits clearly makes the equilibrium rather difficult to distinguish in practice from a competitive equilibrium. This suggests that a closer look at market conduct is required if collusion is to be detected.

One phenomenon that is often taken as a signal of explicit or tacit co-ordination among firms is *parallel pricing*. This occurs when, over time, the prices charged by firms are increased or decreased at the same time and by the same amount. Such a pattern of price movements is consistent with co-ordination of pricing decisions by firms. On the other hand, parallel pricing is also consistent with competition: if the products of different firms are homogeneous (as in perfect competition) or nearly homogeneous, then at a competitive equilibrium no firm will find it advantageous to charge a price significantly different from the prices of its rivals.

Question

What kind of patterns in the movement of retail petrol prices might indicate that there was an explicit or implicit agreement among suppliers?

It is relevant here that all suppliers have a common input, crude oil, which exhibits quite marked price variations. How, for example, would you expect retail petrol prices to change as crude oil prices rise and fall if the market were perfectly competitive?

In a perfectly competitive market there would be a close correlation between retail petrol prices and crude oil prices. This implies that there would be parallelism in prices at the petrol pump. It would, however, be much more suspicious if retail prices moved in parallel but were not highly correlated with crude oil prices (e.g. if retail prices increased together by a substantial amount in a period when the price of crude oil was stable).

The practical difficulties raised for policy enforcement by the problem of detection are well illustrated by one of the key European cases of recent years. In *Wood Pulp* (1985) the European Commission held that producers of wood pulp had been guilty of price fixing in the common market. There was no direct evidence of explicit price-fixing agreements, and the decision was based upon (a) parallel pricing conduct by suppliers between 1975 and 1981, and (b) the existence of direct and indirect exchanges of information about prices among suppliers. In addition, the Commission argued that its economic analysis of the market showed that this was not a case where parallel pricing would be expected in the absence of an agreement: there was some differentiation of products, cost structures were different, and suppliers were located in different countries.

This last piece of the jigsaw – to the effect that parallel pricing was inconsistent with price competition – is clearly a crucial step in the reasoning. The point to note is that, in the Commission's view, it is based on the economic analysis of a *hypothetical* situation (the situation that would have occurred in the absence of the alleged agreement). Guilt or innocence in such a case hangs, therefore, on the status accorded to an economic model!

In the event, the European Court did not uphold the Commission's position in *Wood Pulp*. Advocate General Damon (1992) concluded, among other things, that the Commission's decision was inadequately reasoned. He was sharply critical of the Commission's analysis of the wood pulp market and of the available evidence, making it clear that under EC competition law, firms were free to align themselves independently with the conduct of competitors where such alignment was a rational response to the existing or anticipated conduct of those competitors. For example, there is nothing illegal in failing to move prices out of line with competitors on the basis of expectations that upward movements will be unprofitable because they will *not* be followed, and downward movements will be unprofitable because they *will* be followed (as in the kinked demand curve analysis). Put more generally, the parallel conduct of producers does not in itself constitute proof of a concerted practice.

The implication of *Wood Pulp* is that, in cartel cases, the European Commission will continue to have to rely heavily on 'smoking gun' evidence, such as the existence of company documents which reveal explicit or implicit agreements with other firms. Clearly, then, powers to acquire such evidence are an important requirement for an effective anti-collusion policy.

5.3   UK and EU policies

Existing UK and EU policies towards horizontal agreements are based (more loosely in the UK case) on the prohibition with exemption approach outlined above. In the UK, the Restrictive Trade Practices Act 1976 requires that certain types of agreement be registered with the Director General of Fair Trading, who is required to refer registrable agreements to the Restrictive Practices Court for a decision as to whether or not they are contrary to the public interest. Agreements are initially presumed contrary to the public interest, so that, unlike in mergers cases (see below), the burden of proof lies with the firms concerned. Where companies do decide to defend an agreement, they can do so by arguing that the restrictions lead to public interest benefits falling under one or more headings, or 'gateways', that are specified in the legislation.

Each gateway specifies particular types of beneficial economic effect that, in specific circumstances, might possibly be associated with collusive behaviour. These include factors such as the effects of agreements on the balance of trade, on regional unemployment, and on consumer interests. Broadly speaking, they embody the notion that competitive markets may fail in a number of respects and that, where such failures occur, it is possible that restrictive agreements may help to alleviate the situation.

However, it is not sufficient for parties to an agreement to convince the Court that there are public interest benefits associated with an agreement that fall under one or more of the gateway headings. The Court must also be convinced that, looking at the effects of an agreement as a whole, the magnitude of the benefits is such as to more than counterbalance the likely detriments. Only if this is done will the agreement be allowed to stand.

In practice, few agreements have been allowed to stand, but outstanding exceptions include the *Net Book Agreement* (1962). The Net Book Agreement is still (in 1994) with us, despite vigorous attempts to have it struck down by interested parties such as the Dillons chain of bookshops. In 1962 the Restrictive Practices Court held that the agreement whereby book publishers agreed among themselves to fix the *retail* price of certain books, was in the public interest because it helped to maintain the number of stockholding booksellers, to keep down the price of most books, and to keep up the number of books published, in particular those of literary and scholastic merit.

Article 85 of the Treaty of Rome prohibits any agreements and concerted practices which may affect trade between member states and which have as their object or effect the prevention, restriction or distortion of competition. However, agreements or classes of agreement may be exempted where they are found to contribute to the production or distribution of goods, or to promote technical or economic progress, and providing that they allow consumers a fair share of the resulting benefits and are the least restrictive way of attaining these objectives.

For example, in *Synthetic Fibres* (1984) the Commission permitted, under Article 85(3), a three-year agreement by which firms collectively planned to reduce capacity in the industry by 18 per cent. This was the first restructuring agreement exempted in this way, and reflects the influence of the 'crisis cartel' arguments described above.

An example of a *block exemption* covering a whole class of horizontal agreements is provided by the treatment of certain types of arrangements concerning research and development. Provided that such agreements meet conditions set out in the relevant regulation, firms are free to enter into co-operative arrangements with one another in this area.

Since anti-competitive restrictive practices are illegal under EU legislation, it is possible for parties damaged by anti-competitive conduct themselves to take legal action against firms engaged in the practices. For example, if two or more firms agree to cut prices with the aim of driving other competitors out of the market, the firms that suffer can seek compensation in the courts. The European Commission can also impose fines on companies that are found to have digressed. Both types of sanction are absent from domestic UK law.

6   Vertical supply arrangements

Definitions

Substitutes and complements

Two products are said to be *substitutes* when a reduction in the price of one lowers the demand for the other, and are said to be *complements* when a reduction in the price of one increases the demand for the other.

At first sight it may appear that vertical arrangements are similar in their economic effects to their horizontal cousins. There is, however, a fundamental difference: the goods and services involved are generally complementary to one another, rather than substitutes.

Consider the market situation shown in Figure 8.5. Upstream firms U1 and U2 supply an input to downstream firms D1 and D2, which compete with each other to supply final consumers. Suppose D1 lowers its price. This is bad for firm D2 because it will lose revenue as at least some of its customers switch to D1 (the products are substitutes). On the other hand, it is *good* for U1 and U2 because the lower average price in the final market will tend to increase the total demand for the input they supply (the final product and the input are complements). Similarly, a price cut by U1 will tend to be bad news for U2 but good news for D1 and D2.

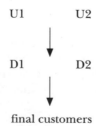

Figure 8.5   **Upstream and downstream firms**

When firms enter into agreements with each other, therefore, the agenda will tend to be very different according to whether the products concerned are substitutes or complements. When D1 talks to D2 there are good reasons to be suspicious: each would like the other to raise its price, to the detriment of final consumers. However, when D1 talks to U1 or U2, each would like the other to reduce its price, and in this case final consumers will tend to benefit from an agreement.

Furthermore, if U1 and D1 enter into a vertical agreement but U2 and D2 don't, the latter two firms will suffer as a result. Why? If U1 (selling to D1) and D1 both agree to lower prices, they will attract customers away from the other firms and damage the other firms' profits.

Question

This last argument suggests that one of the principal groups complaining against vertical links of various kinds will comprise firms which do not have such links. Should competition authorities pay much attention to such complaints?

In general, the effects on non-integrated firms should only be taken into account if the policy authorities are interested in the distribution of profits among firms. There might, however, be specific circumstances where there are also negative efficiency effects. These are more likely when at least one of U1 or D1 is a dominant firm.

Policy approaches to vertical supply agreements vary significantly from country to country. In Japan, for example, large manufacturing companies contract out substantial volumes of work to small suppliers, and the relationships between supplier and customer tend to be very close. Policy has generally encouraged rather than condemned these links, and it has also been tolerant of vertical links among many larger companies, including relationships deriving from factors such as common banking ties and cross-ownership: for example, each of companies A, B and C may own stock in the others, and one of the three might be a bank which, among other things, provides debt finance to the other two companies. Indeed, it can be argued that the ability of Japanese firms to extract benefits from vertical co-ordination of activities is one of the bases of their competitive success in international markets.

The benefits of vertical supply agreements are also recognized in EU competition policy. The recognition takes the form of a series of block exemptions to Article 85 that are granted to certain types of business practice, such as exclusive purchasing or exclusive distribution agreements, provided that certain specified conditions are satisfied. Franchise agreements also enjoy the benefits of block exemption, and there are special exemption arrangements for the beer, petrol and motor vehicle industries. Major reviews of the motor vehicle and beer exemptions are, however, scheduled for the mid 1990s.

It would nevertheless be wrong to conclude that vertical agreements are benign in all circumstances. Where there is market dominance in a particular market, such agreements *may* provide a means by which that dominance can be extended into other activities, and a number of recent UK monopolies cases have been very much concerned with this 'extension of market power' issue, including *Beer* (1989), *Petrol* (1990) and *Gas* (1993).

In both the supply of beer and of petrol in the UK there is widespread ownership of retail outlets by upstream suppliers. Some of these outlets are run directly by the owning companies, while others are made available to independent operators under tenancy and leasing agreements. In both cases a substantial share of retailing activity is also accounted for by outlets not owned by suppliers. Both industries are oligopolistic with similar levels of concentration, but in neither case is there a dominant firm, and the MMC found no evidence of collusive agreements. The two investigations were conducted under the complex monopoly provisions of UK competition policy.

Despite an absence of market dominance, the MMC found that various aspects of the supply arrangements in beer could be expected to operate against the public interest and, among other things, recommended the termination of existing exclusive supply arrangements in a substantial proportion of the public houses then owned by brewers. The government partially accepted the MMC's proposals and subsequently imposed a substantial programme of divestment of public houses by major brewers. This was completed in 1992, and was accompanied by substantial increases in real prices of beer (indicating the dangers of attacking vertical agreements entered into by non-dominant firms). In contrast, in the case of petrol the MMC concluded that the vertical supply arrangements between petrol companies and petrol station operators were one of the means by which the companies competed.

Two contrasting views of vertical agreements – as restrictions of competition and as methods of competing – are therefore to be found in MMC reports published within a year or so of each other. The discrepancies between them, together with the lack of a demonstrable track record of success for regulation introduced in the wake of such cases, serve as a warning of the limitations of competition policy as an instrument for fine-tuning behaviour in markets that are oligopolistic but not characterized by single-firm dominance or collusive behaviour.

7   Mergers

In both Britain and the EU there is no presumption that the existence of a dominant market position is in itself a bad thing. However, policies directed at horizontal agreements can be viewed as being aimed at a certain means of *acquiring* dominance, and mergers policy can be looked at in a similar light. The underlying point here is that the way in which firms acquire market power itself has significant implications for economic efficiency.

Suppose that a firm establishes a strong market position by dint of its innovative efforts (Nestlé in the soluble coffee market being a good example). Monopoly profits then serve as a reward for innovation, and the prospect of this reward provides incentives for technical progress. To prevent acquisition of dominance via this route would weaken the incentives for progress and indeed for competition via innovation. That is, competition for the monopoly position would be less intense and, since innovative effort has social value, economic efficiency could be impaired.

Thus, when considering the overall shape of mergers policy, what is required is a general view of the likely effects of mergers. On one side of the equation are the possible detrimental effects of increased market power, while on the other are the potential benefits such as improved cost efficiency that can arise from the amalgamation of two firms. This type of trade-off is illustrated in Figure 8.6. Assume that the initial equilibrium is at C, where price equals marginal cost (MC_1), and that the increase in market power associated with the merger leads to an increase in the market price of the relevant output from P_1 to P_2. Exactly as shown for Figure 8.1 above, this will lead to a loss in consumer surplus equal in magnitude to the area of triangle BCE. If there were no change in costs, this would be a measure of the net effect of the merger. If, however, the merger has the effect of reducing unit costs from MC_1 to MC_2 (= AC_2), there will be a gain equal to the reduction in total costs at the new output level. In the diagram this gain is represented by the area of the shaded rectangle ABFG, which is equal to the reduction in costs per unit multiplied by the number of units produced. If the area of the rectangle ABFG exceeds the area of the triangle BCE (i.e. if the cost savings outweigh the loss in consumer surplus), economic efficiency as a whole will be increased and, on this criterion, the merger is beneficial.

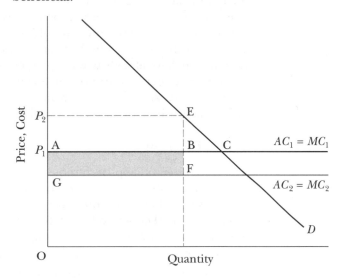

Figure 8.6   **Efficiency trade-offs for mergers**

Exercise 8.3

In Figure 8.6 merger increases the profitability of the merged enterprise, but what is the effect on the profits of rival firms? Would you expect your conclusion to be true in all merger situations? (Hint: is the higher, post-merger price a good or bad thing so far as rivals are concerned?)

One way of proceeding from this point is to try to define groups of circumstances where one or other of the effects is likely to dominate. For example, *conglomerate* mergers, which bring together firms operating in different product markets, can be expected normally not to have very substantial effects on market power. Similarly, in the absence of dominance at one or more horizontal market levels, *vertical* mergers between firms at successive stages of the chain of production/distribution will not generally be problematic. The chief focus of competition-based mergers policies will therefore tend to be *horizontal* amalgamations, where the relevant firms or businesses operate in the same product markets.

7.1   Policy options revisited

I begin the discussion of mergers policy by noting briefly the consequences of the various policy stances set out in Section 3 above (excluding *laissez-faire*).

The *per se* approach

A deceptively simple merger policy option would be to prevent or prohibit all prospective mergers that lead to industrial concentration levels above certain designated limits. For example, amalgamations could be disallowed if the combined shares of the firms in a relevant market exceeded, say, 50 per cent. Alternatively, the structural test could be generalized by prohibiting all mergers that would result in a position of market dominance.

Such thorough-going structuralism would seem to offer simplicity (hence cheapness) and a less uncertain policy environment (because non-discretionary). However, the difficulties of defining a market, and the complexity of assessing whether concentration will bring market dominance, have already been explained. Hence serious inefficiencies may result from either inappropriately formulated rules (more likely when the structural tests are simple), or from mistakes in the application of the rules (more likely when the tests are complicated).

Rule of reason

The rule of reason approach requires the competition policy authorities to engage in case-by-case evaluation of *all* mergers. This would be a costly and cumbersome affair, and would discourage small amalgamations with trivial impacts on market power. In practice, therefore, the rule of reason approach usually rests on a three-stage procedure:

1   Use of simple screening tests (such as market share) to weed out cases where the impact on competition is likely to be negligible.

2   More detailed investigation of non-trivial cases to test for likely market dominance.

3   Where substantial market power effects are anticipated, an overall assessment, without a *strong* presumption for or against, of the desirability of the merger, taking into account cost efficiency effects and any other factors relevant to policy objectives.

Prohibition with exemptions

Arguably, the approach just outlined leaves too much to the discretion of the relevant authorities, in particular in respect of the extent to which any anticipated anti-competitive effects of merger can be compensated for by other forms of benefit. A prohibition with exemption approach will differ from that just outlined, in according stage 2 greater importance. It would also prohibit mergers expected to lead to a dominant position, but with the possibility of exemption if significant counterbalancing efficiency gains could be shown to be likely.

7.2   Current policy

UK mergers policy operates on a rule of reason basis, taking into account a potentially large range of public interest issues, but with an initial screening test. Mergers are only examined if the combined post-merger market shares of the companies concerned are expected to exceed 25 per cent or if the value of the assets taken over exceeds £70 million (a figure that is periodically adjusted to reflect factors such as inflation). At present the main criterion for deciding whether the Secretary of State refers a particular merger to the Monopolies and Mergers Commission for investigation is the expected effect of the merger on competition.

When a merger is referred, the Monopolies and Mergers Commission is asked to report on whether or not, in its opinion, the amalgamation may be expected to operate against the public interest. Firms do not have to establish positive public interest benefits to gain clearance for the transaction: the burden of proof lies with those who might want to object to the merger. Even if the MMC does conclude that the merger may be expected to operate against the public interest, the Secretary of State is not required by law to prevent it. He or she may of course do so – and as a general rule the MMC's judgement *is* acted upon in this way – but there is also discretion to allow the merger to proceed unconditionally or subject to conditions.

A number of the difficulties involved in evaluations of mergers are illustrated in the *British Airways/British Caledonian* (BA/BCal) case of 1987. Among other things this involved an assessment of possible cost savings from the merger and of potential reductions in competition, particularly in respect of UK domestic routes. As in all merger cases, the assessments were complicated by the fact that the effects to be traded off were all prospective (rather than historical). In general, neither the future conduct of the firms concerned nor the future market conditions in which they will operate can be forecast with any great precision. This makes the assessment of cost savings particularly difficult, at least in cases where the merger is agreed between the two managements, since the investigating authority will generally have to depend on information supplied by the two firms, who clearly have an interest in shaping that information in ways favourable to their case.

In the BA/BCal case there was also the complicating factor that the smaller airline was in financial difficulties. The MMC was therefore faced with the question of what would happen if the merger was not allowed. Would BCal go bankrupt and, if so, what would happen next? In particular, what would happen to the routes it was allocated by the regulatory authorities in the airline industry? Alternatively, would BCal be taken over by some other company – the Scandinavian airline SAS had also made a bid – and, if so, would this damage BA's competitiveness in international markets? Simply to pose these questions is to show how speculative some of the reasoning on which mergers decisions are based must be, at least under the UK system as it currently operates. In the event, in this case the MMC allowed the merger to proceed.

At the EU level there was, until recently, no specific framework for dealing with mergers. In September 1990, however, a Merger Regulation was finally introduced which applies to mergers, acquisitions and (some) joint ventures which have a 'community dimension'.

The Regulation covers amalgamations where:

- the aggregate worldwide turnover of all parties to the transaction exceeds 5 billion ecu, and
- the aggregate EU turnover of at least two of the parties, taken individually, exceeds 250 million ecu;

unless each of the merging parties has over two-thirds of its EU turnover in one and the same member state.

The European Commission's investigations focus on possible anti-competitive effects of the merger, either by enhancing or by creating a dominant position. Of those mergers investigated in detail, most have been cleared rapidly, and, as in the UK, there has been a tendency to seek to impose negotiated conditions in cases where problems of competition are detected.

For example, in *Nestlé/Perrier* (1992), Nestlé SA sought to acquire the French bottled water group Source Perrier SA, a transaction which would have left the amalgamated company with a large share of the French market for bottled water. Anticipating the problem, Nestlé agreed to sell one of Perrier's brands, Volvic, to the French food company BSN. On this basis the acquisition would leave Nestlé with a 36.8 per cent share and BSN with a 30.9 per cent share. Nevertheless, the Commission was not satisfied with the proposal, arguing that it would leave Nestlé and BSN in a position of joint dominance. It therefore concluded that the acquisition should only proceed if Nestlé disposed of a number of lesser brands to a single purchaser (other than BSN).

The idea behind the specifics of the Commission's condition in *Nestlé/Perrier* – the sale of brands to a *single* purchaser – was to create a 'third force' in the French market. Hence the Commission's conditions for approving the acquisition were clearly meant to guide the market in a particular direction, rather than simply to prevent monopolization. In this case, therefore, the Commission's decision can be viewed, at least in part, as an exercise in industrial policy.

8   Privatization and regulation

In competition policy, the prohibition with exemption approach operates on the presumption that competition is generally a good thing but that there are specific circumstances where this presumption should be overturned. Usually, the exceptions are related to some inefficiency in the market, such as a failure in labour markets that leads to high levels of unemployment (see Section 5.1).

In market economies the existence of state-owned enterprises can be interpreted in a similar way: there has been a general presumption in favour of private ownership, but exceptional circumstances may lead to the introduction of public ownership to meet particular policy objectives. Sometimes the policy response is specific to a particular firm – as when Rolls Royce was taken into the UK public sector in the 1970s to avoid bankruptcy – and sometimes it involves the public ownership of whole industries or sectors (e.g. coal and railways).

The core of the public sector in developed, market economies has been in what might be termed the *network industries* (electricity, gas, telecommunications, water, railways, postal services, etc.), important parts of which are natural monopolies where standard arguments in favour of competitive markets do not necessarily apply. Governments have also typically used state ownership in these industries to implement explicit or implicit industrial policies. For example, domestic industries have been supported by public sector procurement policies. The trend to privatization of these industries, led by the UK in the 1980s, raises the question of how public policy is conducted within the new framework of private ownership.

An immediate policy problem is how to deal with the extreme forms of market dominance that are to be found in parts of the network industries. Encouraging competition in the supply of gas via a common pipeline network may be quite feasible, but, with current technology, it is difficult to see competition between different pipeline networks as holding much promise as a means of promoting efficiency and protecting consumers. Natural entry barriers would give plenty of scope for high prices and supernormal profits or the quiet life.

In the UK and other countries which now have privatized utilities, the most frequent policy response has been to set up industry-specific regulatory agencies. In Britain their principal tasks can be summarized as 'to promote competition where competition is feasible, and to impose price controls where monopoly is entrenched'. There has, however, been a strong tendency for regulators to get involved in a wide range of aspects of decision making in the industries concerned. In effect, regulators find themselves responsible for sectoral (industrial) policy decisions as well as for matters of competition and monopoly.

As an illustration of the nature of the regulatory problems to be tackled, consider the issue of price control. In Britain control is accomplished by means of price-caps (constraints on maximum prices) that are reviewed every four or five years; between reviews they are linked to the index of retail prices. When British Telecom was privatized in 1984, for example, it was required to increase prices in any year by no more than the percentage increase in the retail price index (RPI) in that year less three percentage points. Thus, if inflation was 5 per cent in a given year, BT would be allowed to raise prices by 2 per cent on average, whereas if inflation were 2 per cent BT would be required to reduce average prices by 1 per cent. The method is generally referred to as the 'RPI minus X (RPI–X) regulation', the value of X in this case being 3 per cent. Four years after privatization, when the formula was reviewed by the Director General of Telecommunications, X was increased to 4.5 per cent, meaning that telephone bills fell (on average and in real terms) more quickly from that point on.

The RPI–X approach was introduced to overcome incentive problems associated with *cost of service* regulation (also called *rate of return* regulation because of the inclusion in costs of a 'fair' rate of return on capital). Under this latter approach, price controls are reset each period to reflect changes in the cost to the utility of providing the regulated service. As a result, the regulated firm has little incentive to reduce costs; for if it were able to reduce unit costs by, say, 5 per cent, it would expect regulators to step in relatively quickly to reduce its allowable prices by an equivalent amount. The reward, in terms of higher profits, for reducing cost efficiency would therefore be relatively limited.

In contrast, under RPI–X regulation, allowable prices are predetermined for a period, during which the benefits of the cost reduction will feed through fully into higher profits, thereby giving the firm greater incentives to reduce costs.

Exercise 8.4

A regulated firm produces one billion units which it is allowed to sell at £1 per unit. Average cost (assumed equal to marginal cost) is 90p per unit, which could be reduced by 5p by a major cost-cutting campaign. The price elasticity of demand for the firm's product is 0.5. Calculate the profit gains if (a) the regulated price is unchanged as costs fall, and (b) a cost reduction of 5p would lead to a price reduction of 5p. How does the latter estimate vary with the price elasticity?

Hint: If the regulated price does not change, then neither does output. For part (a), therefore, it is sufficient to work out the change in costs at the initial output. For part (b) you need to allow for the fact that output will increase. In this case the additional profit will be the profit achieved on the incremental sales.

However, RPI–X has weaknesses of its own. First, the firm may seek to cut costs (and increase profits) by reducing the quality of its goods or services, knowing that this will not affect the price at which it can sell. Second, investors may be more reluctant to supply finance since, unlike under cost-of-service regulation, they are not given any guarantees that prices will be sufficiently high to cover capital costs. Among other things, investors may fear that their wealth would be damaged by a changed political climate that gave a high priority to keeping utility prices low.

To offset these potential biases in incentives arising from price controls, regulators tend to get involved in a wide range of issues involving service standards and investment in the industries concerned. For example, as well as setting prices, the regulator may determine certain minimum quality standards that have to be reached and specify certain investment targets that have to be met. At this point we are within the territory of industrial policy.

9   Sectoral policies

Industrial policies designed to alter the allocation of resources among industries and sectors of the economy are invariably discriminatory in some way or other. If, for example, the aim is to slow down the decline of a particular industry, there are a number of options available, including direct subsidy or taxation of substitute products, but all involve dissimilar treatment of industries or activities. Past and present UK examples of discriminatory policies include the taxation of heavy fuel oil to help increase the demand for domestically produced coal, and the levy on electricity generated from fossil fuels which is paid as a subsidy to Nuclear Electric.

The favouring of some domestic industries at the expense of other domestic industries will obviously be unpopular with those *not* favoured, and there is therefore a tendency for governments to try to keep the costs of state aids well hidden. When, however, the aim is to favour domestic industry over foreign industry, the views of the latter tend not to be so politically influential. Export subsidies and various forms of protection are therefore among the most commonly used instruments of industrial policy.

9.1   Sectoral trade policy

Consider, for example, a policy of protecting a domestic industry by raising barriers to overseas firms' entry into the domestic market. Under certain conditions it is possible that such a policy may actually improve the international competitiveness of the domestic industry. One mechanism for this effect is illustrated in Figure 8.7, which shows an industry with declining marginal costs (the greater the output, the lower the cost of producing additional units). For any given domestic market volume, say Q_1, the relevant marginal cost curve for exports is *MC*. It can be seen that expansions beyond Q_1 in the domestic volume of sales have the effect of reducing the marginal costs of exports and, other things being equal, of increasing the industry's competitiveness in international markets.

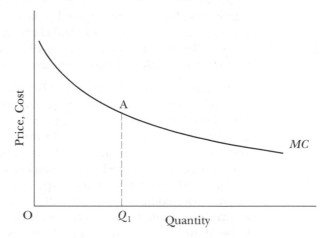

Figure 8.7   **Domestic sales and the marginal cost of exports**

However, the analysis on which this argument is based is highly incomplete. For example, when the cost curve itself can be affected by corporate decisions, as it will be in the longer term, there is a potential danger that the guarantee of a protected home market will reduce incentives for cost reduction and innovation (see the quotation from Adam Smith at the beginning of this chapter). The danger will obviously be greater, the less the future prospects of the firm depend on its own performance relative to that of international rivals. This in turn will depend on factors such as the size of the home market, whether the support given by the government is temporary or permanent, and whether the domestic market is itself competitive.

The last factor in this list is a particularly interesting one. Where there are several competing domestic firms, home demand will be spread more thinly and the costs of exports may be higher than if there were only one 'national champion'. On the other hand, the greater competitive pressures in the home market may mean that the cost curve as a whole is lower than it would be in the national champion case. The trade-off will be more severe, the smaller is the size of the domestic market and the greater are the economies of scale. A policy based on protection from international competition but encouragement of domestic competition will therefore tend, other things being equal, to be more effective when the domestic market is large. Aspects of Japanese industrial policy are sometimes claimed to fit this model.

Evidence of the effectiveness of sectoral trade policies is somewhat mixed. There exist examples, such as the Korean car industry, where domestic protection and support for exports appear to have stimulated the rapid growth of an industry that has subsequently been able to compete successfully in international markets. On the other hand, there are plenty of cases of industrial support where the firms concerned have failed to develop or have continued to decline inexorably, as was the case with British-owned car manufacturers.

9.2   State aids

Industrial policies are even more narrowly targeted, and therefore tend to be even more discriminatory, when they are directed at particular firms rather than whole sectors. Public ownership is one of the favoured frameworks for narrowly targeted policies, since discrimination is less transparent and less open to legal challenge. Thus, when British Leyland ran into financial difficulties in the 1970s, it was taken into state ownership in order to provide the necessary state support to keep it going.

By subsidizing British Leyland, the British government implicitly discriminated against rival car manufacturers based in the UK. The negative effects on the rival car manufacturers were offset, however, by an implicit policy of tolerating higher prices in the UK, underpinned by a willingness to restrict imports to some degree. Thus, although companies such as Ford would likely have enjoyed higher market shares in the event that British Leyland had been allowed to collapse, they were compensated in part by less intense price competition in the UK market. Over time, as the market share of British Leyland and its successors fell, rival companies were able gradually to build market share at favourable prices.

Since state aids and related policies tend to distort competition in the market concerned, they lead to very definite tensions with more general competition policies. One major source of increased tension here has been the continuing development of the European Union. A fundamental objective of the European venture has been the promotion of a single market, and this is harder to achieve in a situation where the governments of member states are engaged in activities that give their own firms competitive advantages over firms based in other member states. By distorting competition, national state aids tend to undermine the common market.

From the outset, therefore, the EU (as it now is) has been keen to constrain discriminatory state aids. Article 92(1) of the Treaty of Rome states that:

> Save as otherwise provided in this Treaty, any aid granted by a Member State or through state resources in any form whatsoever which distorts or threatens to distort competition by favouring certain undertakings or the production of certain goods shall, in so far as it affects trade between Member States, be incompatible with the Common Market.

As in Article 85, there are provisions for exceptions, but the general philosophy is clear.

Application of the policy involves the sometimes difficult question of identifying what is and what is not a state aid, particularly when public enterprise is involved. If, for example, a state-owned bank provides additional capital to an ailing firm or industry, is this a state aid? One question that the Commission asks in this context is whether a private investor would have conducted the same transaction in the same circumstances (the 'market economy investor principle'). If not, then the transaction constitutes a state aid.

If strictly applied, the market economy investor principle rules out national industrial policies based on state aid, for if a private sector investor would not be willing to take the same action, then the action is prohibited. On the other hand, if private investors would be willing to enter into equivalent transactions, then the public policy is effectively redundant: matters could be left to private investors.

In practice, however, the intention of EU policy is to prevent the more substantial forms of discrimination rather than to block national industrial policies altogether. For example, in 1992 the Commission found that capital injections of FF 4 billion by the French state into the French computer manufacturer Compagnie des Machines Bull (in which the government had a majority shareholding) would not provide a rate of return that would be acceptable to a private investor. Nevertheless, the Commission approved the aid on the grounds that it was a necessary part of a restructuring plan, involving substantial redundancies and a loss of market share, aimed at restoring profitability. That is, the aid was not intended to be permanent and was not directed at reducing the market shares of other producers in the then EC.

In general, EU policy condemns state aids not so much out of any belief in *laissez-faire*, but rather because, if used at the level of member states, their discriminatory effects tend to hinder the achievement of a common market (Waelbroeck, 1992).

At the level of the EU as a whole, however, no such problem arises, and it would appear that the Treaty of Rome does not prevent the development of EU-wide industrial policies. For example, the Commission has negotiated, on behalf of member states, various restrictions on imports of Japanese cars, with a view to providing some protection for the car manufacturing industry throughout the Community. There are also various EU programmes designed to support and encourage research and development, particularly in high-tech industries. Finally, the Commission is not likely to object when member states provide state aids to promote an activity of common European interest, as in the development of the consortium set up to manufacture the Airbus range of airplanes.

9.3   Strategic industrial policy

The Airbus case is a much studied example of 'strategic' industrial policy in which governments effectively enter into an international policy game with the aim of supporting their domestic firms and industries in oligopolistic competition in world markets. The general aim of governments in this kind of activity is to redistribute world economic resources in ways that are favourable to domestic interest groups.

Before the launch of Airbus, the international civil airliner industry was dominated by American companies, of which Boeing was much the largest (McDonnell Douglas and Lockheed being other major players). Boeing's established market position, coupled with the substantial costs that are involved in developing and manufacturing a new civil airliner, meant that it was difficult for new firms to enter the market (large amounts of start-up capital were required, and there was a clear prospect of a price war in the event of a challenge to Boeing).

However, by means of state aids and government pressures on European airlines to place initial orders, Airbus was able to establish itself in the market. Moreover, the fact that Airbus was backed by public funds must have discouraged Boeing and other US airlines from attempting to drive Airbus from the market by means of price discounting. Boeing would likely have reasoned that lower prices would simply have brought forth greater subsidies rather than exit from the market.

Clearly, the support given by European governments to Airbus was discriminatory, although it could be argued that, because competition in the world airline industry was already distorted by the dominance of Boeing, the intervention was actually pro-competitive. (It can also be argued that Boeing derived competitive advantage in the civil airliner business from its protected position as a supplier of military aircraft to the US government.) As a consequence it is possible that, over the longer term, European consumers (as well as European industry) will benefit from the new entry.

The greatest problem with strategic industrial policies is the fact that different governments, in the search for competitive advantage for their own firms, tend to negate the efforts of other governments. This is not always a bad thing: when, as in the case of R&D, there may be a market bias against the activity, state support may produce direct social benefits. In many cases, however, an increase in the relevant activity level will not have any particular value of its own. For example, the advantage gained by one country if it subsidizes exports will be lost if other countries pursue similar policies.

When such policy competition produces no net benefits, it is preferable for all governments to desist from implementing at least the more blatant types of discriminatory policies. Such a co-operative outcome may be difficult to achieve because of the incentives for individual countries to deviate from co-operation in the search for national advantage. Nevertheless, there is an increasing emphasis in international negotiations on trying to get such agreement, and the EU state aids policy described above is an example of an attempt to restrict damaging policy competition.

10   Conclusions

This chapter started with a quotation from Adam Smith, attacking monopoly and (implicitly) praising competition; it has ended with an example of potentially destructive competition (among governments) where co-operative behaviour would be preferable. In between, we have seen examples where increasing competition is likely to be beneficial (privatized utilities) and other examples where monopoly may be more efficient (patents). Similarly, sometimes co-operative behaviour among firms may be a bad thing (price-fixing cartels) and sometimes it may be a good thing (vertical supply agreements). Anyone who looks up the quotation from Smith will find that his attack on 'perpetual' monopoly comes immediately after a defence of 'temporary' monopoly.

Most markets exhibit both competitive and monopolistic elements, and good economic performance will depend on the existence of the right blend of the two. There is, however, no optimum mixture that holds across markets, simply because background economic conditions (technologies, input supplies, demands) vary from one product/service to another.

It follows that it is inappropriate to attempt to impose a single, uniform market structure across all industries, and effective competition policies will always need to take account of the circumstances of particular cases. As a corollary, it is difficult to draw a clear distinction between such policies and what have traditionally been referred to as industrial policies.

It is also very difficult to specify what is the most effective mix of competitive and monopolistic elements in particular markets. Economic models of competition, monopoly and oligopoly provide a framework for thinking about the issues, but do not deliver neat, easy solutions. The ability of governments to optimize the mix is also open to serious question – a point reinforced by the fact that pressures for government intervention most frequently derive from interest groups concerned more with the distribution of resources than with overall economic efficiency.

This is not to argue for *laissez-faire*, since markets can and do sometimes fail badly (and, given interest group pressures, *laissez-faire* is probably not a feasible option anyway). Rather, it is an argument against general attempts at government fine tuning of markets and an argument in favour of targeting policies only at those markets where the balance of monopoly and competition is clearly and demonstrably not working effectively.

PART 5

CHAPTER 9

DATA AND ECONOMIC MODELS

DATA ANALYSIS AND ECONOMIC MODELLING

by Wendy Olsen

1 Introduction

Understanding economies requires, as we hope the last eight chapters have shown, a mixture of theorizing and the use of evidence. We construct models of how we think firms, say, or consumers behave. And we look at evidence, which often takes the form of quantitative data. Chapter 3 of this text provided an early look at the links between theory and data. Jane Wheelock developed a theoretical model of the consumption function. She showed that the pattern predicted by the model could be found in UK data for consumers' expenditure and disposable income. And she then noted that the data could be used to estimate – or put a numerical value upon – the relationship of consumption to income proposed by the theory.

In this chapter, we pause to take a closer look at the use of data as part of economic reasoning. The chapter has two main objectives.

The first objective is to explore more carefully some of the relationships between data and economic theorizing. Chapter 2 noted that data and theory are not independent, since we use models to construct categories which then allow us to collect and interpret data. For example, the model of the circular flow of income identifies data categories for the national accounts. The same model in Chapter 2 was used to divide household incomes into income from capital services, from labour services, and from state benefits. Figure 9.1 shows those data for the UK in a bar chart of the kind you often see in a newspaper or textbook. The data presented are average incomes of households from different social classes. The social classes are those used by the UK government, usually termed the Registrar General's classification scheme. The height of each bar indicates the average income coming in from the three sources: wages, state benefits, and investment income. You can see that investment income, such as interest and profits, is relatively concentrated in the professional and managerial classes, while state benefits are a larger share of total income (on average) for working class people.

This bar chart seems a straightforward example of descriptive statistics. It is, however, problematic in several ways. We could ask, for example, where did the data come from and how did people get categorized in the way shown? Or we could query whether *average* income is a good way to compare the incomes of groups of people.

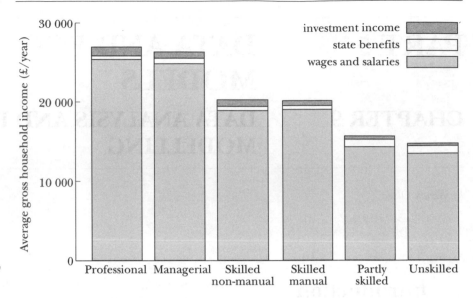

Figure 9.1   **Bar chart of average gross household income from three sources by social class, UK, 1991**

Source: *British Household Panel Survey* (1991)

Questions like these have shaped the content of this chapter. We begin by looking at the origins of data in Section 2. Section 3 then considers how to describe and summarize data. Finally, Section 4 discusses some ways of presenting and examining the relationship between two economic variables, such as income and social class as in Figure 9.1, or consumption and income as in Chapter 3.

As you work through the examples and exercises, I hope that the chapter will also meet its second objective: to give you confidence and practice in handling numerical data. Some people find that their eye tends to slide over parts of the text containing numbers. If that should be true of you, I hope this chapter will encourage you to look more confidently and critically at the use of data in economic reasoning.

2   Creating economic data

Numbers are a powerful medium. They seem to give a certain validity to statements that are made about them. For example, when you see a graph in the newspaper or on television, showing something moving upward, the claim made about that graph often seems to have additional force. Many people feel that numbers (data) will *prove* a point, because data appear as specific, apparently concrete evidence about a claim. This section looks at ways in which we should *question* numbers, and I hope the discussion will stimulate you to question the data and graphs that you come across in daily life.

2.1   Questioning data

An example might be the population Census. Every resident of the UK was legally bound to fill in a Census form in 1991, and as the results come out from these questionnaires they 'prove' that some cities are getting bigger, while others are losing people through out-migration. Census data are used for many purposes besides these basic descriptions of changes in the population, such as for planning local government financing, for setting the levels of local taxes, and for distributing funds to local health authorities.

If you were to look carefully at Census data, however, you might begin to worry about *non-response*. Several groups may be omitted from the Census figures: the homeless, people on holiday, new migrants who may be in temporary accommodation, people who travel around a lot, and some people who feel they need to hide their address from official databases. Residential university students are quite hard to catch, since they move between their home and their university lodgings and may not think they need to fill in the Census forms. Some people speak languages that are not the official language of government, and without interpreters may not fill in Census forms. The actual response rate for the Census (the proportion of those who should have responded who actually did so) will never be known, so one could begin to speculate about problems in the forecasts and plans that are based on it. For example, there may be disputes about local government funding with local councils claiming that under-reporting has left them under-funded. Similar disputes arise in many countries over the population census, and the problems of counting everyone are severe in some situations (e.g. during mass migration or war).

Most economic data have characteristics in common with the Census. Many data sets are collected through official agencies, including several government departments. Most data sets require responses from people (or firms or other institutions) of particular types, and whether the response is voluntary or not there may still be a certain percentage of non-response. In many cases the people responding may suspect the data collectors of having unspecified purposes that are materially important to the respondents, e.g. to pass information to the tax authorities. Therefore they may try to shape their response in ways that will work to their advantage — or they may avoid responding at all.

Thus the process of *data collection* is one which can be questioned. It could be called, instead, a process of *data creation*. Here are some examples of how economic data are created, each of which might raise questions about bias in the data:

- customs data on imports and exports
- income data taken from income tax returns
- data on unemployment taken from registrations for unemployment benefit
- opinion polls taken from magazine readers by voluntary response
- market research about consumers done by asking for voluntary completion of a questionnaire when registering a product by post after purchase
- records of currency flowing into and out of a country, taken from bank records of money transferred.

Question

What problems might there be with unrepresentativeness, bias in reporting from respondents, or response avoidance, in the case of telephone surveys of opinions regarding the management of the economy?

Opinion polls that use the telephone are biased away from people who do not have phones – 10 per cent of British individuals in 1991. Such surveys will tend to under-represent the opinions of poor and transient people. You may also be able to think of other problems with this type of survey.

In many economic data sets you could argue that there are hidden biases. A good example is the use of the unemployment register (people who are claiming benefits available to the unemployed) as a measure of unemployment. There are lots of people who would consider themselves unemployed, but who for various reasons are not claiming benefit. Two groups who are not allowed to claim benefit in the UK at the time of writing are students and people on training schemes. These people might like to have a job, and not be able to find one. They may be studying or in training *because* they could not find a job. Yet they are not included in the official unemployment figures. The resulting bias is toward an underestimate of the unemployment rate defined as the percentage of the 'working' population who are looking for paid work and unable to find it.

There are in fact two problems here. One is bias in the sense of unrepresentativeness: the people being counted as unemployed may not include all those who fall within the accepted definition of unemployment. The other problem is about different conceptual frameworks: those the government wishes to count as unemployed may not be the same group as those who believe themselves to be unemployed. These different frameworks can also lead to accusations of 'bias', especially if the chosen definitions appear to serve political ends.

Careful study of the process of data creation shows that data are always shaped by the conceptual frameworks and measurement methods of the people who create them. For instance, to continue the unemployment example, one estimate of the unemployment rate in the UK in 1991 averaged 8.1 per cent over the year (*Key Data*, 1992, p.17). This figure was calculated as the ratio:

$$\frac{\text{number of claimants of unemployment benefits}}{\text{economically active population}} = \frac{2288}{28\,337} = 0.081$$
(numbers measured in thousands).

Definitions

Sample

A sample is a selection of cases (e.g. people, households) from a defined population (e.g. all households in the UK, all households with telephones).

Random sample

A random sample is a sample in which every case in the population has an equal chance of being selected for the sample.

A different way to measure the unemployed would be to use a sample survey to count the number of people who said they were seeking work, but were either unemployed or temporarily out of a job. Several large-scale surveys try to achieve a truly random sample of the population.

One such survey in the UK, the *Family Expenditure Survey* for 1991, gives an unemployment rate of 11 per cent. The difference between the two figures is the net effect of several conceptual and empirical differences. The main conceptual difference is the use of people's own assessment of their employment status. There is no requirement here that the person be registered as a benefit claimant. The main empirical difference is that the unemployment estimate obtained from the *Family Expenditure Survey* is subject to possible bias in the survey sample. Unemployed people might be more (or perhaps less) likely to agree to be involved in a detailed study of their expenditures. This error arising from response bias is very hard to measure.

When we look at them closely, then, most data sets are revealed to be tools of analysis aimed at the intended purposes of their creators. In the above case, measures of unemployment vary, yet are consistent in measuring people's *paid* labour, not their unpaid work. People who work without pay, such as domestic workers and carers, are excluded from both parts of the ratio. They are also considered economically inactive in many economic analyses of labour market activity.

The unemployment example casts doubt on the idea that data are objective facts, and suggests that data are rather social artefacts: creations of people. The legitimacy and apparent accuracy of numbers and graphs now fades somewhat, and it becomes easier to question the 'hard data' that are used by economists, politicians and journalists. According to this view, data are just one part of argumentative strategies and research programmes. They need to be used with care, along with careful reasoning, theoretical model building, checks for consistency, and assessment of their reasonableness. In this context it is important both to search for bias and to question the conceptual frameworks structuring the data. This helps to establish the limitations of data and to allow them to be used effectively for exploratory, analytical, and rhetorical purposes.

The discussion above forms part of a major philosophical debate. These discussions of the origin, objectivity, and meaning of data are *epistemological debates*. Epistemology is the theory of the methods or foundations of knowledge. In economics there have repeatedly been debates of this kind, for example in disputes about the extent to which data can be used to test economic theories. The epistemology that underlies much official data collection is called *positivism*, a concept which you met in Chapter 2. In its strong form, positivism assumes that data are factual and objective. What this means is that data can in principle be collected which are independent of the subjective points of view (values, beliefs and prejudices) both of the investigators and of the agents whose actions are being studied. Excluding these influences, data collection can allow us to arrive at *positive* statements about society and the economy, emerging from stable patterns in the data.

This section has questioned positivism by arguing that data sets are socially constructed, shaped by the frameworks set up by data creators: many economists would question the strong form of positivism just outlined. But these reflections do not mean that we should give up on the use of surveys and data. A socially constructed data set is still revealing and interesting. Nor do they imply that bias does not matter: on the contrary, it is important to reflect critically on bias emerging from non-response or poorly constructed samples.

The rest of this chapter helps you to explore data, and to make the most of some economic data that are widely available.

Reflection

To consolidate this section, think about how different unemployment data would look if they were collected from each of the following sources:

- companies reporting redundancies
- workers through a random sample survey of individuals
- the population as a whole, through a random sample survey of households
- a survey of passers-by done regularly in major urban shopping centres
- trade unions.

Consider the biases in each of these methods. What are some of the conceptual and empirical differences between the methods?

2.2   Studying households or studying individuals?

Some of the conceptual issues underlying data collection can be illustrated by a problem which you have met in Chapter 3: whether to analyse the behaviour of households or of individuals. Much of economic theory is phrased as if it were about individual decision making. For instance, the theory of consumer behaviour introduced in Chapter 7 starts by considering an individual choosing things to buy with their (personal) income. However, data about these decisions are often collected at the level of the household, because that is seen as the unit of consumption and expenditure for families in Western societies. The household is often defined as a group of people living and eating together; the assumption is made that they also share their incomes and make decisions together about spending.

These assumptions have been questioned by two groups of people. First, social scientists working in the Third World have long pointed out that the household as defined above excludes major contributors to household income such as migrant workers. Furthermore, they say, family structure varies so much across classes and cultures that it is ethnocentric to assume a nuclear family household unit. Some families live in joint households with two or more hearths; others have adopted children or lodgers; some families share resources over a wide network of kin (the extended family). These examples suggest that the 'household' has limitations as a unit of analysis, arising from the huge diversity of human living arrangements.

The second group of social scientists questioning the use of the household as a consuming unit are those analysing gender. Throughout the world, people do not get equal shares within the household, of what is purchased. They do not have equal access to the cash incomes of those who earn. There may be, effectively, a dictator within the household making spending decisions; or there may be a consensus; or there is (more likely) a long-term, changing process of negotiation among family members who do not all have equal power in relation to decisions affecting them. There are several implications of these points for economic data on consumption and expenditure.

First, one should not simply divide household income by the number of people to get average income per head. Access to resources is not so equal. Studies in a number of societies have shown that girls systematically get less to eat, less health care, and less education, and yet have to do more household work than boys; partly as a result, girls are less likely to survive than boys in some societies. Adult women, widows, people with physical and mental disabilities, and people without children are sometimes similarly limited in their access to household resources. Their low status and limited power effectively constrains their access to resources in a way that is hidden by taking household income as a measure of economic welfare.

Second, since the above reflections imply conflict and competing claims among household members, 'the household' cannot be assumed to behave logically and consistently in the same way that an individual might. The theory of consumption called 'rational choice', introduced in Chapter 7, seems insecure if the theory is supposed to apply to household decision making. It is not clear that households do behave like individuals. (Chapter 4 raised the same query about the behaviour of firms.)

Third, the analysis of gender leads to some rich discussions of intra-household decision-making processes. Relationships between men and women, carers and those cared for, healthy and less healthy, old and young people all come under scrutiny. These social relationships also have economic and financial aspects. They affect the distribution of earned income and wealth; how each person spends their time on paid and unpaid work, and leisure; who consumes which items bought 'by the household'; and what transfers of money there are between household members (rent, keep, gifts, and so on). All these economic decisions are ignored if we simply take the household as a unit of analysis.

One way of dealing with this problem is to use the concept of the household for measuring some things, e.g. household size, size of the home, total income, number of consumer durables, etc., but to consider the individual the basic decision-making unit. For example, it would be odd to give the number of refrigerators per person; the number per household is more meaningful. Household-level information can be applied to each individual in that household, and becomes a characteristic of the individuals. We can then analyse women's behaviour separately from men's, and so on. This approach involves using both the household and the individual as *units of measurement*, while using the individual as the *unit of analysis*. This approach can be used in many societies with different living arrangements, without hiding the inner workings of the home. It raises another question about Figure 9.1. The figure assumes that the people within these households are all 'at' the average household income level. This does not allow for conflicts over money nor for an unequal allocation of money within the household.

Reflection

Think about your own family, and your household. Are the two the same, overlapping, or subsets of each other? Consider who earns money in your household. There are various systems of money management for households, including full and partial pooling of money into joint accounts or money jars; independent use of cash earned (presuming that each person has a cash income); and control of all cash by one person. Which one does your household use? Are there some people in your household who do not have much control over money? Does anyone get housekeeping money? Are there some people who have little control over their time? Who has the most leisure time? These questions lead to a more unequal and complex view of the household than that implied by some official data sets.

So another way of questioning Figure 9.1 is to ask about how people are classified. Class breakdowns like Figure 9.1 always have to be done either at the level of the household or of the individual, but social and cultural differences cause the concept of the 'household' to mean different things for subgroups within the population. These cultural, ethnic, and behavioural differences are rarely stressed in economic analysis, although it is possible to incorporate them. Beware of *masking* important social differences when taking averages and reporting aggregates.

2.3   The great debate about economic data

So far we have questioned some aspects of socio-economic data: its representativeness, objectivity, and accuracy, and whether it hides some aspects of society. Now we turn to considering how such data are used. Where do they belong in economic arguments? There are several possibilities:

- economic data suggest theories and models
- economic data are used to test theories and models
- economic data cannot be found for some theories and models
- economic data and economic theorizing interact.

The first possibility above suggests that data can be collected before a theory is posited. One would explore the data, and then come to some conclusions. This is called a process of *induction*. Inductive reasoning moves from the particular to the general. For instance, if we observed that many economies had both inflation and growth in their supply of money, we might conclude that the growth in the money supply caused the inflation. Induction is an interesting and an important stage in economic research. We learn from data; we explore data; we explore the economy by looking at data about it.

In contrast to inductive reasoning, the positivist tradition has been to use data to test theories that have been posited independently of the data. The theories may be deduced from simple assumptions about economic behaviour which seem incontrovertible: for example the assumption made in Chapter 7 that the more we buy of something, the less we are willing to pay for the last unit bought. This deductive approach to model building was labelled a 'rationalist' approach in Chapter 2. The model predicts an outcome: in this case that demand will tend to increase as price falls. Data collected about prices, and about quantities supplied and purchased, then allow us to test the model and to draw the conclusion that the data support or do not support the predictions. The tests lead one to support or modify the theory, or to declare it refuted. This approach to testing is in the positivist tradition.

There are some problems with both inductive and deductive-plus-testing approaches to the link between data and theory. Some economic concepts cannot in principle be measured directly: utility, introduced in Chapter 7, is an example. We can use utility theory to make predictions which may be testable, but cannot observe utility itself. Some other economic concepts are hard to measure, e.g. intensity of work or profitability of family farms. Consumption itself is hard to measure. It is very intrusive to weigh what people eat before they eat it! Measuring might put the respondents off eating the food. Data about food consumption, then, can only be related to theory in indirect and perhaps faulty ways, and, as is done later in the chapter, expenditure on food items is often used as a substitute for actual consumption of the items.

A more fundamental problem, however, with both induction and testing is the social construction of data, already discussed. One must have a theory, at least implicitly, in order to collect data in the first place. In practice, therefore, data collection and theorizing interact. Game theory (Chapter 5) is an example. Observation suggests ideas for models of the competitive interaction of firms using game theory; data are then gathered to see whether they bear out the particular model being tested. The model may then need modification to explain what has been observed. In other words, data can be used within a research process where theory affects data, which affects the development of theory, which leads to the gathering of new data, and so on. At the end of this process data can be used to illustrate and support the conclusions that have been reached. In economic research there is a rich tradition of using data in conjunction with theorizing. And there is always room for disagreement about how far data support or do not support theories.

Finally, economic data often play a persuasive role in arguments: they can be used for rhetorical and polemical purposes. For instance, a falling inflation rate may be used as evidence for a successful economic policy, even though the cause of the lower inflation might not be the government's actions but some external factor such as lower oil import prices. Beware of interpreters of data who 'massage' them in their own favour.

In this section, I have argued that data can be questioned in their own right, and that data are not objective facts as the positivist tradition might suggest. I have considered the need to distinguish units of measurement and units of analysis. And I have examined various uses of data within the process of economic reasoning. We now turn to techniques for analysing data.

3 Exploring economic data

In this section we begin analysing data. The section explains and examines a variety of *descriptive statistics*. These are different methods of summarizing and displaying data in order to draw conclusions from them.

We are first going to explore people's access to housing, using a fairly representative British data set. We might be doing this with a view to examining the production of homes (supply-side factors), or with an orientation toward the use of housing by people (demand-side factors). The two sets of factors both affect observed data, which therefore require careful interpretation.

We begin by analysing a single economic variable. There are numerical ways of representing variables (e.g. tables or summary statistics), and there are graphical ways. At the moment, you may feel more comfortable with one of these than the other, but I hope you will develop your skills in both areas as you progress through the chapter.

I should begin by explaining the term variable. A variable is created when we choose a word or a letter to represent a whole set of values of an economic concept such as income or expenditure. The values may be known or unknown, and they each represent the value of the variable for a particular 'case' – a person, a household, or whatever is the unit of analysis. In data sets the values are set out in a table or a computer, usually in a column, and we can imagine the variable name as the heading on the column. So the variable *gender* has the values *female* and *male*, for various people, with the values numbered, say, *1* and *2*. In theoretical work, as you

Definition

Variable

A variable is an economic concept to which we give a name (a letter or word) which represents all the possible values of the concept when measured.

have seen already in this text, a variable might be indicated by a letter, such as Q or P, and the values might be unknown or hypothetical.

3.1 Describing one variable

Definition

Frequency distribution

The frequency distribution of a variable shows the number of cases for each possible value of a variable.

A single variable can be described by its frequency distribution. The distribution can be shown in a table or in a frequency diagram such as a bar chart. Table 9.1 shows types of housing tenure for over 10 000 people in Britain. The source of these data is the *British Household Panel Survey*, or *BHPS*.

Table 9.1 Types of tenure, UK, 1991

Category	Value	Frequency
Owned outright	1	2301
Owned with mortgage	2	4918
Local authority rented	3	1843
Housing association rented	4	306
Rented from employer	5	111
Rented private unfurnished	6	392
Rented private furnished	7	355
Other rented	8	21
Data are missing	9	17
	Total	10 264

Source: *BHPS* (1991)

From a table like this we can either read off the number of cases (the frequency) or we can calculate the percentage of cases falling into each category. The percentage of British people in this sample survey living in homes that are owned outright was 22 per cent in 1991: $\frac{2301}{10\,264}$ expressed as a percentage.

The numbers in the table can be presented equally well in a bar chart of frequencies. The height of each bar, seen in the scale of Figure 9.2 on the vertical axis, measures the number of people living under each tenure type. The width of the bar is not relevant to the bar chart.

Definitions

Bar chart of frequencies

A bar chart of frequencies shows the distribution of a single variable. It has the values of a categorical variable (defined below) on the horizontal axis, and the height of each bar corresponds to the count of cases in each category.

Exercise 9.1

Use a calculator to convert the frequencies in Table 9.1 to percentages. What percentage of people in the British sample live in houses that they own? What percentage live in homes that they rent? Draw a bar chart of frequencies for the two values: home owners and renters.

Categorical variable

A categorical variable is one which takes two or more distinct categories as values.

Tenure in Figure 9.2 and Table 9.1 is an example of a categorical variable This means that the values of the variable are distinct, non-overlapping categories. In Table 9.1, values for tenure outside the range of 1–9 would reflect errors, since the categories are chosen to be exhaustive.

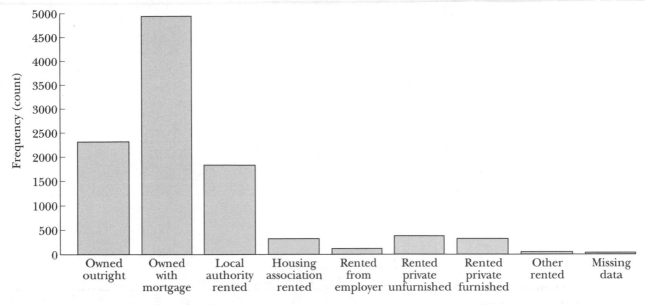

Figure 9.2   **Bar chart of frequencies of types of tenure, UK, 1991**

Source: *BHPS* (1991)

Exercise 9.2

Check that you are clear now about the difference between a *value* and a *frequency* for socio-economic data. Could 3.54 be a valid value? Could it be a valid frequency?

Definitions

Continuous variable

A continuous variable is one measured on a scale which is both exact and divisible.

Another type of variable is a *continuous* variable. A good example of a continuous variable is the value of houses. Measured in currency units such as francs or pounds sterling, the variable can take any amount from just above zero to values in the millions. To give any useful meaning to a frequency distribution for a variable of this type, values have to be grouped into intervals: for example, we could count how many houses are valued between £50 000 and £60 000, and between £60 000 and £70 000, but it makes little sense to count how many are valued at exactly £60 000. To represent such a distribution graphically, we draw an adaptation of a bar chart known as a histogram.

Histogram

A histogram shows the distribution of a single variable, with the variable's values in intervals on the horizontal axis; the area of each bar corresponds to the number of cases within the interval.

A histogram is an adaptation of a bar chart to the needs of numeric, continuous variables. In a bar chart, you have categories on the horizontal axis and frequencies on the vertical axis. Each bar's *height* shows frequency. In a histogram, the categories on the horizontal axis are inclusive ranges of values, such as 1–1000, 1001–2000. It is the combination of the height and the width of the bars which reflects the number of cases falling into each interval. To allow for intervals of different widths, the histogram is drawn so that the *area* of each bar reflects how many cases fall in that horizontal interval. The horizontal axis must have a numeric scale, and the author of the graph must specify the units for the variable. Then a computation is done so that the area of each bar corresponds to the frequency. The bar chart in Figure 9.2 and histogram in Figure 9.3 illustrate the appropriate use of the two types of graph: a bar chart for the frequencies of a categorical

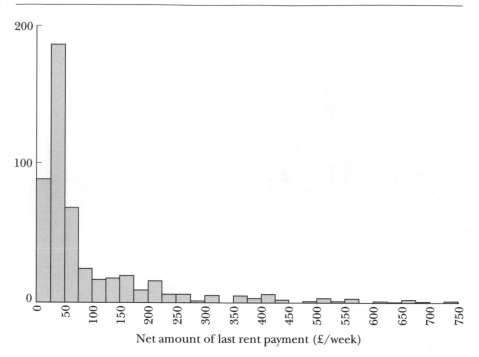

Figure 9.3 **Histogram showing net amount of last rent payment, UK, 1991**

variable, and a histogram for a continuous variable. In both histograms and bar charts the largest bar represents the largest number of cases.

In looking at these two figures, we see two frequency distributions. The bar chart for the categorical variable would look quite different if we re-ordered the categories, which we could easily do since their order is arbitrary. However for a continuous variable the scale would not make sense if you re-ordered the cases. If you look at Figure 9.3, you will see that you cannot swap the bars around. So the picture that results (the histogram) tells the viewer a lot about the variable displayed.

Making a histogram

To make a histogram, first label the horizontal axis with the range of values that the variable actually takes, e.g. from zero to its maximum. Then work out some intervals you wish to use for the graph, and record the widths in a table. The widths may vary. Copy the number of cases into the table for each bar, adding up as necessary if the data are given in a very detailed format. Here is a hypothetical example:

Interval start	Interval end	Width	Number of cases (area)	Height
0	1000	1000	5000	5
1001	2500	1500	12 000	8
2501	5000	2500	500	0.2

Given the number of cases, the height of the bar in the final column was calculated above using the formula:

$$\text{height} = \frac{\text{area}}{\text{width}}$$

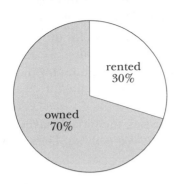

***Figure 9.4*   Pie chart of tenure types collapsed into owned and rented**

This is a restatement of the formula for area:

area = width × height

Once you have the height you can draw the histogram.

Exercise 9.3

Sketch the histogram from the above data.

Definition

Ordinal variable

An ordinal variable is one whose values can be ranked.

One more way to display a frequency distribution is in a pie chart. Figure 9.4 shows the categorical variable tenure in Table 9.1, collapsed into owned and rented as in the answer to Exercise 9.2, in a pie chart. The area of each segment as a percentage of the circle corresponds to the percentage of cases taking each value.

Some categorical variables have the special trait that the categories can be put in a rank order. This is always true of continuous variables, because numbers can be ordered, but it is also true of some category variables. These are called ordinal variables. For instance, performance in university degrees may be judged on an ordinal scale (First, Second, or Third Class). Preferences such as 'Like a Lot; Like; Don't Like; Very Much Dislike' can be ranked and put on an ordinal scale. These levels of 'liking' are rankings, not quantifiable degrees of liking. When you write down the values of an ordinal variable you may abbreviate them with numbers such as 4 = Strongly Agree, 3 = Agree, 2 = Disagree, 1 = Strongly Disagree. But these numbers do not measure in exact 'units' the *depth* of disagreement; they only show the level or rank of the person's response. The most widely used ordinal variable in economics is probably utility. This concept, as Chapter 7 explained, cannot be directly measured; but in theoretical models utility is a variable which is thought of as having ranked values: an individual may gain more or less utility from different purchases.

Definition

Discrete variable

A discrete variable is a numerical variable which can only take certain values, and not others in between those values.

Finally, there are other numerical variables besides continuous ones. For example, the number of bedrooms in a house or the number of children in a family can only take on whole number values. These are called discrete variables. Individuals cannot have 2.4 children, for example. It can be argued that all the numerical variables used in economics are really examples of discrete variables, since there is always a minimum unit of measurement below which one does not in practice go. However, economists often find it convenient to model economic data as continuous variables.

Summarizing, a variable may be measured: as categories; as ranked categories; or as numbers, which may be discrete or continuous. Occasionally you will come across a variable such as 'age' which can be measured in any of these ways. Age categories might be 'youth' and 'adult'. 'Age' in ranked categories might look like this: infant, child, teenager, adult, over-65; or like this: 0–20, 21–40, 41–65, 65+. Finally, age can be represented as a numerical variable and while, in theory, is a continuous variable, in practice is usually measured in discrete units of years, months or even days.

The phrase *level of measurement* refers to these three ways of measuring variables. Let us review the three levels of measurement:

- *categorical level of measurement*: there are several categories for the variable's values, but these cannot be ranked or compared,
- *ordinal level of measurement* (also called ranked): the categories for the variable's values can be ranked but not measured as meaningful quantities,
- *numerical level of measurement*: instead of categories, the variable takes values which are numbers which have meaning as quantities. These can be *continuous* or *discrete*.

Summary measures

We now turn to describing variables using summary statistics: the mode, median and mean. Each of these is a *measure of central tendency*, focusing on the most common, or average, value of the variable. These measures are useful summaries and we use them every day in statements like, 'most of the kids were 12 years old' and 'most of the stalls had tomatoes at around 80p per kilo'.

The mode is the value or group of values of the variable that has the highest frequency. We can see for example in Figure 9.2 that the mode for housing tenure in Britain is to live in a house that is owned with a mortgage. The mode can be seen either as the highest frequency in the list of numbers in Table 9.1; or as the highest bar in the bar chart in Figure 9.2. For a continuous variable, one would have to split its value into intervals, in order to find the modal or most frequent interval. In Figure 9.3 the modal interval is a rent of between £25 and £50 per week. Again it corresponds to the highest bar in the histogram. An easy way to remember is that 'modish' means fashionable or most popular.

The median is the 'middle' value among the cases of a variable, in the special sense that half of the cases have lower (or equal) values and half have higher (or equal) values. In order to have a median you have to be able to rank the values. The median does not make sense for housing tenure, because the categories of this variable cannot be ranked. In most university marking systems, the median does make sense as one measure of the average class of degree. For example, the median might be the II-ii (lower second) class of degree, or class 3 in the Open University degree system. A vertical line drawn at the median will cut a bar chart or histogram in two, so that half the area is to the left and half is to the right of the median.

The mean is the average of the set of values, in our most common sense of 'average'. It is found by summing up all the values and then dividing by the number of cases, so it can only be calculated for a numerical variable. It is not usually possible to see the mean from a figure such as Figure 9.3. Rather, it has to be calculated by dividing the total of the values (total rent payments in Figure 9.3) by the number of cases (total rent payers in that example). The mean for the data displayed in Figure 9.3 is in fact £81.90 per week.

Definitions

Mode

The mode is the most frequently occurring of the values of a variable.

Median

The median is the value of the middle case of a set of ranked cases of a variable.

Mean

The mean is the average of the set of values of a variable.

Formally, the calculation of the mean can be described by an algebraic expression:

$$\frac{\Sigma X_i}{n}$$

The interpretation of this is not complicated. X is the name of the variable. This variable has a number of cases: n stands for the number of cases with valid data. Each case has a value, so we write X_i as the value of case i, that is, of each case of the variable taken separately. The Greek letter sigma Σ tells us to add up all the different values: all the X_i. So you read out this algebraic expression as 'the sum of X_i for all i from 1 to n, divided by n'. For instance, if we recorded prices of £4, £3.90, and £3.10 for three sets of batteries, then the mean price would be

$$\frac{£4 + £3.90 + £3.10}{3} = \frac{£11}{3} = £3.67$$

Table 9.2 sets out the best ways of summarizing the *central tendency* of variables of each of the three types.

Table 9.2   Summary of appropriate measures of central tendency for different levels of measurement

Level of measurement of a variable	Appropriate measures of central tendency	Examples of such variables
Categorical	Mode only	Social class; type of housing tenure
Ordinal (ranked)	Mode and median	Preference scales; class of degrees
Numerical (discrete and continuous)	Mode, median and mean	Value of house; number of hours worked; numerical score in an exam

Exercise 9.4

Explain why you cannot take the mean of a categorical variable. Use the example of *gender* with 60 men and 40 women, and with men being recorded as the value 1 and women as 2. What graph would you use to show the frequencies of *gender*?

There is a final snag in calculating means. In some cases you will need to work out a *weighted average* of a set of numbers. You may find that you have data which is grouped, with a value for each group, but the data may still be for a numerical variable. Table 9.3 provides a simple example.

Table 9.3

House value in £000s	Number of houses
30	10
40	15
50	5

How in this example could you work out the average house value? To add together 30, 40 and 50 and divide by 3 would be misleading, since different numbers of houses in the example have each value. To find the true average you must weight the values by the frequencies. So you multiply each value by the number of houses having that value (30×10 and 40×15 and 50×5), then divide the sum of your results by the total number of houses (30). You should get 38.33. Interpret this in the units given (£ thousands) and you find that £38 333 is the average house value.

That concludes the discussion of the three *levels of measurement*: categorical, ordinal and numerical. Much data in economics are numerical and we can often do more with it than with other types of data. However, some socio-economic variables are inherently categorical or ordinal, so we will continue to give such variables some attention.

3.2   Describing distributions

The previous section defined three numeric measures of the central tendency of a distribution. I also introduced *visual* ways of seeing the variable's values. These visual representations help us to see the *dispersion* of a variable as well as the *central tendency*. Dispersion refers to the spread across low, medium and high values of a variable. Measures of dispersion are most important for numerical variables, and in fact do not apply easily to categorical and ordinal variables. Dispersion is low when all the values of a variable are near the average value. It is high when a lot of cases have very low or very high values relative to the central tendency. For instance, the food intake of adults ranges generally from around 1500 calories per day to 2000 or 3000. This dispersion is small compared with the wide range of weekly earnings of people which includes lots of 'zeroes', lots of low-paid people and part-time workers, and some highly-paid people such as executives, doctors and lawyers. The spread of the data in the first example is less *relative to the mean* than the spread in the second example.

Some variables, such as income, may have lots of small values and a few very large values which push the mean far above the mode and the median. Such distributions are called *skewed distributions*. A good example would be income in a village with a millionaire. (Many parts of the Third World have extreme inequality, and this is reflected in a skewed income distribution.)

Measures of dispersion have to take into account each value in the set of cases. Usually each one is compared with the mean. You can visualize this dispersion as the 'spread' in a histogram such as Figure 9.3, and there are also numeric measures that summarize how much spread there is. With these methods we can compare two distributions with different means and see whether all the cases in one are higher than those in another, or whether only some are. In Figure 9.1, where mean incomes for each social class were shown in the bar chart, dispersion was not depicted at all. It would be useful to see the spread of incomes within each class before concluding (for instance) that 'skilled non-manual households have higher gross income than skilled manual households' since this might well not be true for all households in each class. Thus, measuring dispersion helps us draw better conclusions about data.

The following three distributions show patterns of dispersion of distributions that are skewed and non-skewed.

First, look at the histogram of house values for British homeowners in 1991 in Figure 9.5. House values are on the horizontal axis. Notice that this distribution is skewed. The mean is £77 628.5, the median is £65 000, and there are 1298 cases ($n = 1298$). The mode is to the left of (below) the mean as is the median, an indication of a skewed distribution.

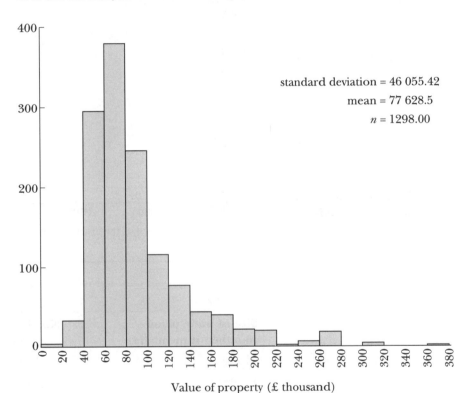

Figure 9.5   Histogram showing value of property for home owners, UK, 1991

Source: *BHPS* (1991)

Second, look back at the data in Chapter 4 on sizes of businesses in Table 4.2. In the UK in 1990, 90.5 per cent of all businesses had less than 100 employees: only 0.1 per cent had over 50 000 employees. The distribution of the variable *size of business* is so skewed toward smaller businesses that it would be very hard to represent it in a histogram.

Here is an exercise on drawing a histogram of skewed data. Again, the variable *size of trade union* is so skewed it is hard to represent graphically. However, by truncating (shortening) the last interval, as shown in the exercise, a manageable graph can be produced.

Exercise 9.5

Use the axes in Figure 9.6 to draw a histogram of the data in Table 9.4 for the variable *size of trade union* in the UK in 1989. Remember that, as described earlier, you can use a table to calculate the height of each bar, given that the area of each bar equals the product of its height and width. In order to be able to represent the top end of the graph, draw the final bar (> 10 000 members) as if these unions did not have more than 20 000 members. The break in the horizontal axis shows the existence of higher values.

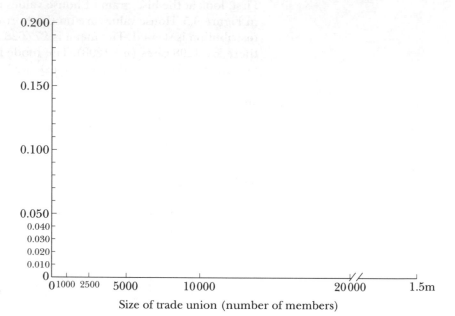

Figure 9.6 **Axes for histogram showing size of trade union, UK, 1989**

Size of trade union (number of members)

Table 9.4

Size of trade union (number of members)	Number of unions	Per cent of unions
<1000	140	45.90
1000–2499	49	16.07
2500–4999	27	8.85
5000–9999	18	5.90
10 000 to 1.5 million	71	23.28
Total	305	100

Source: Bird *et al.* (1991) p.338

My third example is a non-skewed distribution. The variable is the number of bedrooms reported in people's houses in Britain; the mode and median are both 3 and the mean is 2.73 bedrooms. The number of cases is 2030. You can see that the frequency distribution (shown here as a bar chart although a histogram would be equally acceptable) is not biased much toward left or right. It has a similar, though not exactly symmetrical, shape on either side.

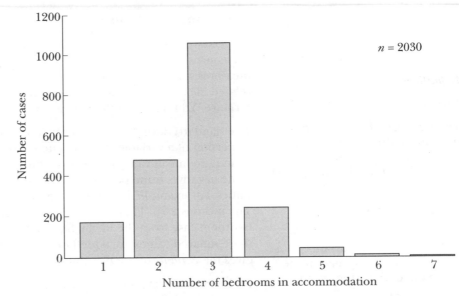

Figure 9.7 **Bar chart of number of bedrooms in accommodation, UK, 1991**

Source: *BHPS* (1991)

Other examples of non-skewed distributions in real life are heights of adult people; the yields of crops (per acre); and distribution of people's ages in some societies. In each case there is dispersion – short and tall; high-yield and low-yield; young and old – but there is no strong clumping of values at one end of the spectrum of possible values. In the last case mentioned, the distribution of *age*, an interesting contrast arises when we compare developing countries' age distribution with that in the industrialized countries. Figure 9.8 illustrates the two distributions. Income and wealth, by contrast, are generally very strongly skewed throughout the world.

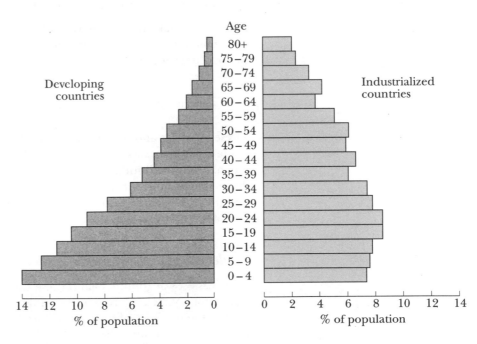

Figure 9.8 **Population distribution by age in developing and industrialized countries, 1980**

Source: Crow *et al.* (1983)

Measuring dispersion

Dispersion and skewness can be measured numerically. Economists use these measures in order to avoid having to scan graphs; the numerical measures summarize the information efficiently. We will look at two closely related measures of dispersion here, the standard deviation and the variance. You will meet these measures a number of times in this text.

The standard deviation is the most commonly used measure of the dispersion of a variable. To calculate it, you take each value, and subtract from it the mean value for the distribution. Then each of these differences – some negative, some positive – is squared in order to turn them into positive values. For example, in Figure 9.7 a two-bedroom house takes the value 2. The mean is 2.78. Therefore 2 – 2.78 = –0.78 is the deviation of the two-bedroom case from the mean. Squared, this is –0.78 × –0.78 = 0.61. Finally these squared values are added up and divided by the number of cases. This gives the *variance* of the distribution.

Building on the algebraic expression for the mean we can therefore write an expression for the variance. The only new symbol is $\overline{X}$ which is the mean of the values taken by X. The variance is then

$$\text{variance} = \frac{\Sigma\left(X_i - \overline{X}\right)^2}{n}$$

This formula takes each case's value, X_i, and subtracts from it the mean value $\overline{X}$. Each of these differences is squared, and then all the squared values are summed. The sum is divided by n, the number of cases, so the variance measure does not necessarily get bigger for large samples. The variance represents the spread, not the 'size', of the variable's distribution.

Finally, if we take the square root of the variance, we get the standard deviation. The units of the standard deviation are the same as the units of the original variable.

$$\text{standard deviation} = \sqrt{\text{variance}} = \sqrt{\frac{\Sigma\left(X_i - \overline{X}\right)^2}{n}}$$

These formulas and definitions are useful when summary statements are made about data sets. If the standard deviations are large relative to the mean, results or findings have to be stated cautiously; for example, if the dispersion around the mean income by class in Figure 9.1 was great, then one would be cautious about stating that one class in general had higher incomes than the other.

Definitions

Variance

The variance of a distribution is the sum of the square of each deviation of a value from the mean, divided by the number of cases.

Standard deviation

The standard deviation is the square root of the variance. It is a measure of the spread of the set of values from the mean.

Calculating the variance and standard deviation

The easiest way to understand these two concepts is to try calculating them for yourself. Here is an example of an income variable. Table 9.5 shows the incomes of four people, and space for you to do the calculations set out in Exercise 9.6.

Table 9.5 Example for the calculation of variance and standard deviation

Person	Income X_i	(Income – mean) $(X_i - \overline{X})$	Squared difference $(X_i - \overline{X})^2$
Jane	50		
Sunil	100		
Jim	40		
Arnold	110		
Sum			
Mean income			
Variance			
Standard deviation			

Exercise 9.6

Fill in the following calculations on Table 9.5.

1 Add up the incomes, and calculate the mean.

2 Subtract your figure for the mean from each income in turn, and fill in each result in the column headed $(X_i - \overline{X})$. Check that the sum of these four differences from the mean (some of which will be negative) is zero.

3 Square each difference, and put the results in the column headed $(X_i - \overline{X})^2$. Add up these squared differences.

4 Divide the sum of squared differences by the number of cases (people) and put in the result as the variance.

5 Take the square root of the variance (with a calculator) to get the standard deviation.

You should have found that the standard deviation is rather less than half the mean, which implies that the distribution is moderately dispersed. If you know the distribution is not skewed you can sketch the distribution from these two pieces of information. However, if the variable is also skewed then you would have to measure that separately. (We are not covering skewness measures in this text.)

Table 9.6 shows the mean, mode, median and standard deviation of five variables from the housing data set we have been using in this section.

Table 9.6   **Mean, mode, median and standard deviation for five variables**

Variable	Mean	Median	Mode	Standard deviation
Household income	£16 081	£13 533	(Note 1)	£12 056
Value of the home if owned[2]	£77 628.5	£65 000	£60 000 to £80 000	£46 055
Number of persons in the household	2.87	3	2	1.34
Number of bedrooms in the home	2.73	3	3	1.20
Number of rooms in the home	4.3	4	4	1.60

[1] A modal interval cannot be identified for this variable without drawing a histogram. £2546 is the most common single value of income. It equals the standard rate of state benefits at the time of the survey.

[2] Includes homes owned with a mortgage.

Source: *BHPS* (1991)

Question

Which of the distributions in Table 9.6 are the more dispersed? Which are skewed and which are not?

Household income is skewed: the mean is well above the median. The value of homes owned is quite skewed (the data are shown in Figure 9.5), and the number of persons in the household is slightly skewed. The other two are not skewed. Household income and home value are the most dispersed of the distributions: they have standard deviations of 75 and 60 per cent of their means, respectively, while the other three have standard deviations of less than half of their means.

Standard deviations, then, are used in economics to allow readers to grasp the amount of dispersion without having seen a graph. However, it is important to understand the main difference between skewed and non-skewed distributions. For the latter, the mean is a perfectly good measure of central tendency. But for skewed distributions, such as income or size of business, the mean is a long way from the mode and the median. Skewed distributions also tend to have a high standard deviation relative to the mean. A high standard deviation can simply mean a high dispersion, but it can also be a signal to look for skewness.

Finally, note that the mean and the standard deviation are measured in the original units of the variable itself. If the units of the variable change, then so do the mean and standard deviation. Keeping track of the units in which things are measured is very important.

4 Modelling economic relationships

We now turn from describing one variable to exploring relationships between two variables. Here we are back on the terrain of economic modelling, and I will explore further some economic relationships which you have already met.

4.1 Displaying relationships between variables

In this section we will look at how graphs can help us to understand the relationship between two variables. Always check whether graphs represent one or two variables. If one axis is labelled 'frequency' or 'per cent', the graph shows only one variable. But if there are two variable names then it is a *bivariate* graph. First I will explain which graphs can be used for representing two variables, and then I will explain how to construct and read a scatterplot.

An immediate example is the bar chart used to introduce this chapter (Figure 9.1). The variable *household income* is shown against the variable *social class of the household*. This bar chart is not a frequency distribution like the ones seen in Section 3.2. Rather, it is a *bar chart of means*. The height of each bar is the mean value of income for that social class. Dispersion of incomes within groups is not visible in the graph. What does show up is that people in working class households have lower mean incomes. The usual conditions for using a bar chart of means are:

1   a continuous variable on the vertical axis, and

2   a categorical or ranked variable on the horizontal axis.

If by contrast you have two categorical variables and you want to see how or whether they are related in any way, you should construct a cross-tabulation. For instance, one can examine the *social class of individuals* against the *social class of their household*. In Table 9.7 these two variables have been tabulated for a group of British women. Some women are not easy to classify because they do not have paid work; these have been left out of the table. The social class of a household has been defined here as the social class of the *head of the household*, who in turn is taken as the male spouse of a couple or the male or female single head of household. These are standard definitions that have been used in several British surveys although as we have seen in Chapter 3 they could be questioned.

The cross-tabulation in Table 9.7 shows many women differing from their 'household's' social class. In particular, look at the large group of women in the social class of 'skilled non-manual employees', often thought of as white-collar workers. These women often differ from the social class of their household head; in part this reflects the predominance of women in 'skilled non-manual' jobs, compared with the spread of men's work across various social classes. However, this finding would be hidden in a presentation of frequencies for 'household social class'.

You could work out the percentages of women who differ from their 'household' social class for people from particular classes by taking the ratio of the frequency in a table cell to the total frequency for that class, given at the right-hand side of the cross-tabulation. Cross-tabulations allow some findings to be derived even when data are only at the categorical level of measurement.

Table 9.7 **Cross-tabulation of social class of person (by present job) by social class of household head, women only (count)**

	Class of person (by job)	Class of household (by head of household): Professional occupation I	Managerial and technical II	Skilled non-manual III	Skilled manual IV	Partly skilled occupation V	Unskilled occupation VI	Row total number (%)
I	Professional occupation	4	2	1	1	1		9 (1.9)
II	Managerial and technical	9	85	16	18	6		134 (27.7)
III	Skilled non-manual	10	52	73	48	18		201 (41.6)
IV	Skilled manual	2	2	2	18	5	1	30 (6.2)
V	Partly skilled occupation	2	11	6	31	27	2	79 (16.3)
VI	Unskilled occupation		4	3	5	3	15	30 (6.2)
	Total number	27	156	101	121	60	18	483
	(Total percentage)	(5.6)	(32.3)	(20.9)	(25.1)	(12.4)	(3.7)	(100.0)

Source: *BHPS* (1991)

In economics, attempts are often made to measure variables on a numerical scale, whether continuous or discrete. Such variables take values which can be added and divided, and are easier to view and use than categorical variables.

Scatterplots are used to view relationships between two numerical (continuous or discrete) variables. In scatterplots of data the axes must be labelled in their numeric units, e.g. £20, £40, £60 if one variable was price, so that points can be identified in the plot's space. Every data point refers to a horizontal move of X_i units away from the origin (e.g. 20 kg if the other variable was quantity), and a vertical move that we might call Y_i (e.g. £10) away from the horizontal axis. In Figure 9.9 arrows show how to locate this data point in the plot space.

Most scatterplots show a lot of dots reflecting various actual combinations of the X variable and the Y variable. By convention X is used for the horizontal axis and Y for the vertical axis, unless there are more specific names such as Q and P for quantity and price.

For instance, Figure 3.6 in Chapter 3 was a scatterplot, using the two variables *household income* and *household expenditure.* The figure is reproduced here with one amendment, and I shall now discuss it in more detail (see Figure 9.10).

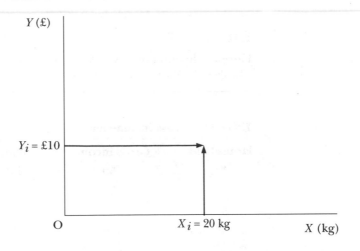

Figure 9.9   Creating a scatterplot

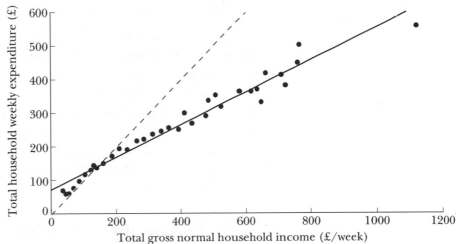

Figure 9.10   Consumption function for the UK, 1991

Source: Central Statistical Office *Family Expenditure Survey* (1992)

Definition

Line of best fit

A line of best fit is a line drawn through a set of points so that the squared vertical distances between the points and the line are minimized. It will look closer to the points than other lines one might draw.

Households with higher incomes have higher levels of expenditure, giving an upward scatter to the data as you move to the right. The line drawn through the points, called a line of best fit, represents this upward trend in summary form. (You will learn how to draw and interpret these lines of best fit in Chapter 26.) The line begins where income is zero and expenditure is about £70 a week. Then it moves upward to show rising expenditure for higher-income households.

In Figure 9.10, households on the lowest gross incomes had low expenditure levels, but their expenditures were higher than their income. If they had not been, they would have spent so little money that people might have starved. A red dashed diagonal line shows the points where *expenditure equals income*. The actual expenditures differ substantially from that line. (Often a diagonal line on a scatterplot shows the points where the X value equals the Y value. Check the axis labels carefully before you draw this conclusion, however.) At the highest income levels, total expenditure is considerably lower than total income. There are two main reasons for this difference:

1   taxation, which makes disposable income lower than gross income for these households, and

2   savings, which reduce expenditure.

Exercise 9.7

Here are hypothetical weekly income and savings data for five households (Table 9.8). Plot these points on a scattergram.

Table 9.8   **Gross income and savings (£/week)**

Household	Gross income	Savings
1	50	–50
2	150	0
3	200	25
4	450	75
5	800	150

To summarize the discussion so far, when we want to view the relation between two economic variables we use one of three types of charts:

• a *bar chart of means* – if one variable is categorical and the other is numerical (continuous or discrete)

• a *cross-tabulation* – if both variables are categorical

• a *scatterplot* – if both variables are numerical (continuous or discrete).

These ways of representing data are discussed further in *How to Lie With Statistics*, a classic by Huff (1991) and in the Open University's *The Good Study Guide* (Northedge, 1990).

4.2   Estimating relationships between variables

These charts *describe* the data, relating one variable to another. When we try to deduce economic patterns from data, we can go further than this and put a number on the relationship: that is, we can *estimate* it. For instance, in the consumption function a line of best fit through the points gave an idea of the trend in the relationship. The line that best fits the data in Figure 9.10 has a slope of 0.49. You have already learned in Chapters 3 and 6 how to calculate slopes. Let us revise it here. You can calculate the slope of a line as the 'rise' (upwards), divided by the 'run' (along), or in other words the vertical change divided by the horizontal change. In the case of Figure 9.10, this is calculated as

$$\frac{\text{the change in expenditure}}{\text{the change in income}}$$

You can calculate this by taking the ratio of the height to the width of a right-handed triangle drawn anywhere along the line; this ratio is the slope. Figure 9.11 illustrates this concept.

In Figure 9.11, each line has a triangle drawn on it with base 50. For the diagonal line in Figure 9.11a:

$$\text{slope} = \frac{\text{rise}}{\text{run}} = \frac{50}{50} = 1$$

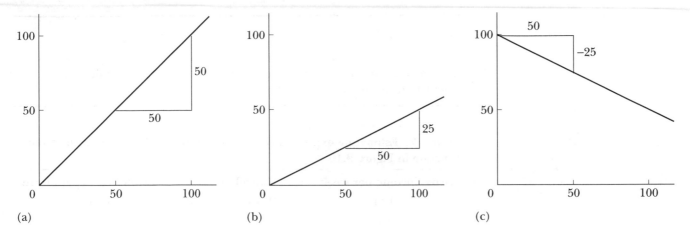

Figure 9.11   **Three slopes: visual and numeric representation. (a) Diagonal line: slope = 1, (b) less steep line: slope = 0.5, and (c) downward sloping line: slope = –0.5**

For the less steep line in Figure 9.11b:

$$\text{slope} = \frac{\text{rise}}{\text{run}} = \frac{25}{50} = 0.5$$

In other words, a less steep line has a smaller slope.

For the downward sloping line in Figure 9.11c:

$$\text{slope} = \frac{\text{rise}}{\text{run}} = \frac{-25}{50} = -0.5$$

Downward sloping lines have a negative slope: 'rise' here is negative (a fall).

Let us now look more closely at the line of best fit on Figure 9.10. This line can be described – as Chapter 3 noted – using just two values (called 'parameters'): the *slope*, and the *intercept*.

The slope of the line in Figure 9.10 is 0.49. For every extra £1 of gross income, 49p was spent on average in the UK in 1991. For every £100, £49 was spent. Of course this is not a fixed ratio in reality since the actual data are scattered around the line. But fitting a line to the data estimates a single ratio because straight lines have a single, constant slope. The intercept – where the line touches the vertical axis – is £67.81 in Figure 9.10.

This implies that consumption expenditure for households with zero gross income (if that were possible) would be estimated as £67.81. That is 67.81 + (0.49 × 0). In practical terms, this expenditure reflects:

1   the spending of state benefits;

2   dissaving, or borrowing;

3   spending of unreported income.

Putting these two pieces of information together, the line of Figure 9.10 is specified by the equation

$$\text{expenditure} = 67.81 + (0.49 \times \text{income})$$

This tells us the line starts at a value of £67.81 for spending at zero income and then rises with a slope of 0.49. Given the equation, we can estimate expenditure for a given income.

Exercise 9.8

Table 9.9 shows a calculation of estimated expenditure for a gross weekly income of £100, based on the above consumption function. Fill in the calculations for incomes of £200 and £300 per week.

Table 9.9   **Estimating expenditure from the equation for the consumption function in Figure 9.10**

Gross income per week	Calculation	Estimated expenditure
£100	$67.81 + (0.49 \times 100)$	£116.81
£200		
£300		

Calculations like these of course obscure variations resulting from such factors as the size of households, the role of state benefits in particular households' disposable income, and the regional distribution of spending. At the same time though, the equation 'expenditure = 67.81 + (0.49 × income)' is a succinct *summary* of a relationship and you will often see such equations in economics.

The lines estimated to fit through data points are not usually a perfect fit. You can see that the same line can represent different data sets, including those with more or less dispersion of the data. Figure 9.12 shows three scatterplots where the same line represents a range from a very good fit to a poor fit for 10 and more dispersed data points. You will find more about the dispersion of points around a line in Chapter 26.

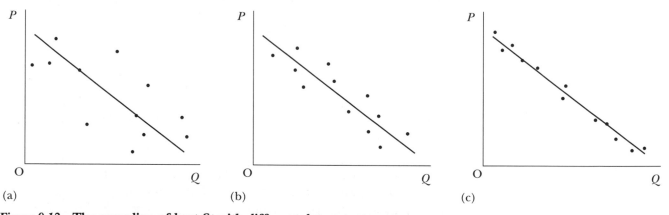

(a)   (b)   (c)

Figure 9.12   **The same line of best fit with different data sets**

Drawing lines from equations

Being able to plot points and draw lines from equations is a useful skill in economics. Here is some practice on this.

Exercise 9.9

Consider a demand curve (actually a straight line in this example) that is estimated as

$$P = 2000 - 15Q$$

Draw this demand curve using the axes in Figure 9.13. Notice that the variable Q goes on the horizontal axis here.

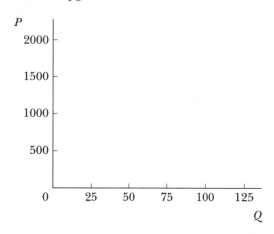

Figure 9.13   **Axes for graphing a demand curve**

Definitions

Dependent variable

In a relationship between two or more variables, the dependent variable is the one the model claims is determined by the other variables.

Independent variable

An independent variable has its values determined outside of or independently of the model.

How can we interpret the demand curve you have just graphed? A question facing consumers may be 'What quantity would you buy if the price was P per unit?' Q is called the dependent variable in this construction, and P is the independent variable. You could rewrite the estimated curve in Exercise 9.9 as

$$Q = \frac{2000 - P}{15}$$

putting the dependent variable on the left, as in the explanation of the demand function in Chapter 3. Economic graphs can be drawn with either P or Q on the vertical axis, but for the moment I have put P there in a way familiar to you from Chapter 7.

In the answer to Exercise 9.9, I described the points which I plotted as (0, 2000) and (100, 500). This is a typical way of giving *coordinates* of a point when making plots. Coordinates are written (x, y) where x is the horizontal axis variable and y is the vertical axis variable. The equation can also be thought of as taking the general form $y = a + bx$ where a and b are constants. Indeed $y = a + bx$ is the most common general way of describing a straight line.

One final example will illustrate this. It is a model of a person's weekly wage. They have a basic rate of £40 and a rate per hour of £3.00. Then earnings are:

gross earnings = 40 + 3.00 × hours

Plug in various figures for hours worked in different weeks, multiply by 3 and add 40 and you get the gross earnings in each week. In the sample equation the number 40, or a in the general formula for a line, is the y-intercept. The slope is b, or 3 in the sample equation.

Exercise 9.10

Draw a graph of this wage model. Which variable is the independent variable in the model?

Some problems in estimating economic relationships

The functional relationships just presented have been without the underlying economic data. Economic relationships are often specified exactly like this in theory. Real data are generally more messy. I now want to look a little more closely at the problematic relationship between data and theory, using the problems of measuring demand and supply relationships as my example. There are some serious problems in relating the *theory of demand* to *data about expenditure.* When we measure prices paid on a given day for one product, we generally get a wide range of quantities but a small range of prices. The data collected might look something like Figure 9.14a. By contrast, the theory of demand expects to see lines (demand curves) with a steeper slope and considerably more price variation, as in Figure 9.14b.

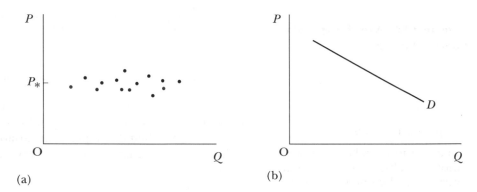

Figure 9.14 (a) Price/quantity data in expenditure survey, and (b) price/quantity relationship in theory of demand

Some of the problems here are problems of measurement. Goods at prices well below or above P_* may be of lower or higher quality than the particular commodity we want to examine. For instance, food prices fall as the product deteriorates, but this is not the kind of price variation meant to be shown by the demand curve. Demand curves are intended as a snapshot of buying intentions at a set time. They are not meant to represent changes over time. The demand curve also refers to a product with a fixed set of characteristics: standard quality, size, age, and so on.

The problems of relating data to theoretical curves is also a conceptual one. It is very hard to get data representing an entire demand curve. At the extremes we are considering hypothetical situations such as:

- if the price of this product were halved, how much would you buy?
- if the price of this product doubled, how much would you buy?

Such data are rarely collected, because there are doubts about the reliability and comparability of people's responses to hypothetical questions. Differences in price paid by individuals for similar goods often reflect quality differences, or packaging and marketing differences. Hence observed differences in demand respond to these factors as well as to price differences.

An additional conceptual problem for the collection of price–quantity data about the demand for a product is the continual shifting of both the supply curve and the demand curve noted in Chapter 7. While we travel around various markets or shops collecting data on purchases, other people are producing and delivering loads of the same goods. An example would be the arrival of fresh Spanish vegetables that compete with local vegetables on the UK market, pushing the price down. Supply shortages affect price, too, by shifting the supply curve. Furthermore, the demand curve may shift during the same period of time. If you went to collect prices of sun-tan lotion, but a heat-wave struck and tourism rose halfway through your survey, the increase in quantity demanded would be due to a shift outward, not a movement along, the demand curve. It is hard to separate these various effects on the price and quantity data you collect.

Recall that a shift rightwards in the demand curve means more would be demanded at each possible price. A movement along a demand curve, by contrast, means choosing different price–quantity combinations that would satisfy consumers.

Supply curve shifts refer to a change in the relationship between quantity supplied and price, which arises from a change in the conditions of supply such as new imports. Their graphical representation will be a new line showing increased quantities supplied at every price.

The problems of estimation which can arise above are illustrated in Figure 9.15. The left-hand graphs show how the curves shift and a new equilibrium price results from (a) a supply increase (Figure 9.15a); (b) an upward shift in demand (Figure 9.15b); and (c) a combination of both effects. The right-hand graphs show that the resulting 'data', if recorded in an economic survey, could be read as suggesting various slopes for the demand curve.

Figure 9.15 illustrates the difficulties of matching economic data to demand curves. Theoretically it is easy to imagine the price–quantity decisions and intentions of consumers as a demand curve. But empirically it is difficult to identify the curve.

The discipline of econometrics specializes in the statistical estimation of economic models using empirical data. The work of econometricians involves the collection and analysis of survey data and official data about economic behaviour. They use advanced statistical methods to try to identify and measure economic relationships that are of theoretical interest. The lesson to be drawn from the above example is that some theories lend themselves to measurement much more easily than others.

Now as a final example of estimating relationships from quite large data sets let us examine some consumption data in more detail. As usual, I will use expenditure data to represent consumption, and my source will be the *Family Expenditure Survey* (UK), 1991. The four figures, Figures 9.16, 9.17, 9.20 and 9.21, all have gross household income on the horizontal axes. Each one explores the effect of income on an expenditure variable. Figure 9.16 shows total household expenditure, and is therefore another estimate of the UK consumption function. Compare it with Figure 9.10, and *draw in the diagonal line* where income equals expenditure as we did earlier. (Remember that the line where income equals expenditure may not *look* diagonal if the axes are scaled differently.) The main difference between the two graphs is

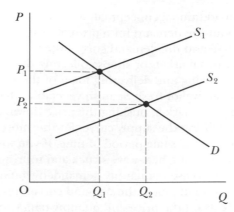

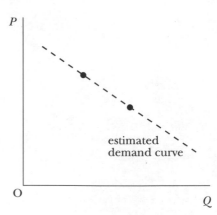

(a) Left: ideally shifts in the supply curve offer opportunities to measure changes in demand in response to price changes. Here more vegetables are bought at the new lower price after fresh imports arrive.

Right: a downward sloping demand curve could be estimated from these data.

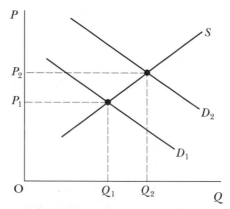

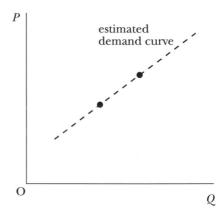

(b) Left: two price–quantity combinations for sun-tan lotion, before and after a heat-wave, as a result of a shift in the demand curve.

Right: the two price–quantity combinations could suggest an upward-sloping demand curve, but this would be the wrong induction to make.

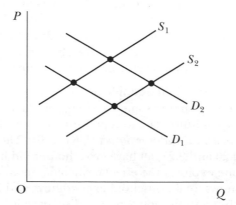

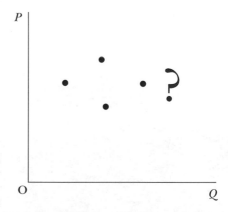

Figure 9.15 **Estimating demand curves while demand and supply curves shift**

(c) Left: demand and supply curves both shift.

Right: in the resulting price–quantity data, the two effects can be very hard to disentangle. Extreme values of P and Q are also rarely observed in empirical data.

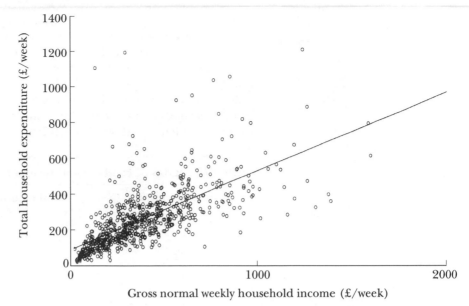

Figure 9.16 **Total household expenditure plotted against gross normal household income, UK, 1991**

Source: Central Statistical Office
Family Expenditure Survey (1992)

due to the aggregation within income groups in Figure 9.10: the data points are in fact averages for income groups, whereas the data in Figure 9.16 are disaggregated.

The equation for the line in Figure 9.16 is:

$$\text{expenditure} = 90 + 0.45 \times \text{income}$$

The slope is similar to the one obtained with 34 data points, but now there are 756 points. Each represents the income–expenditure combination of a single household.

There is considerable variation in the graph, by which I mean dispersion above and below the line itself. Other factors also affect consumption, such as the number of children in the home and the number of income earners. Two-dimensional graphs (those with two variables) rarely give a perfect linear relationship.

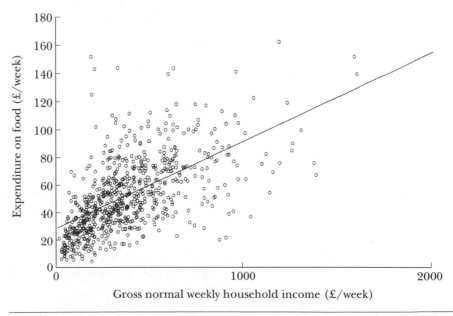

Figure 9.17 **Food expenditure plotted against gross normal household income, UK, 1991**

Source: Central Statistical Office
Family Expenditure Survey (1992)

In Figure 9.17, we move to the question of expenditure on food. Because food is a necessity, we might expect a falling *proportion* of income to be spent on it as income rises. Look carefully at the scales on this graph. Where would the diagonal line be placed? (Quite steeply rising from the corner.) Food expenditure does indeed follow our prediction. You can see this if you read two points from the line on the graph. Take the coordinates and work out the ratio of food expenditure to income at these points. Here are some examples which I read off (Table 9.10).

Table 9.10   **Ratio of food expenditure to total income in Figure 9.17**

Food expenditure	Total income	Ratio
29	0	—
35	100	0.35
41	200	0.205
89	1000	0.089

This calculation is much easier if you know the equation for the line, which is:

food expenditure = 29 + 0.06 × income

As income rises, people spend relatively less on necessities such as food and more on luxury goods as we shall see again later.

The lines on these two graphs can be used to calculate the income elasticity of demand. You have not yet met this concept of elasticity. Chapter 6 introduced the *price elasticity of demand*, which is the responsiveness of demand to price changes. Similarly, we can define the income elasticity of demand, as the responsiveness of demand to changes in one's income.

While you know that normally the former is negative, the income elasticity of demand is normally positive. As price rises, you buy less of that commodity, and your responsiveness to price is measured by the price elasticity. But as your income rises, you buy *more* of most goods, and this elasticity is therefore positive.

More formally, the income elasticity of demand is measured as the ratio:

$$\frac{\text{proportionate change in expenditure}}{\text{proportionate change in income}}$$

You will remember from the discussion of price elasticities (Chapter 6, Section 4.2) that elasticities, unlike slopes, change as you move along a straight line. However, calculating the slope is the first step in calculating an elasticity.

Let us start by drawing a simplified diagram of the expenditure functions (or consumption functions) from Figures 9.16 and 9.17. Figure 9.18 shows an expenditure function with slope *b*. This is another function of the general form which should now be increasingly familiar:

$EXP = a + (b \, . \, INC)$

where *EXP* represents expenditure, *INC* represents income, *a* is the intercept, and *b* is the slope (and the dot, you may recall, means 'multiply').

Definition

Income elasticity of demand

The income elasticity of demand measures the responsiveness of the quantity demanded to a change in income.

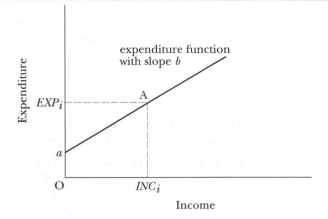

Figure 9.18   Measuring the income elasticity of demand

On Figure 9.18, at point A represented by the coordinates (INC_i, EXP_i) the income elasticity can be calculated according to the formula

$$\text{income elasticity of demand} = \text{slope} \cdot \frac{INC_i}{EXP_i} = b \cdot \frac{INC_i}{EXP_i}$$

Thus, the slope influences the income elasticity, but so does the total amount of income and expenditure at point A.

This formula is similar to – but not in precisely the same format as – the formula for calculating the price elasticity of demand.

Calculating the income elasticity of demand

Here is an explanation of the formula for the income elasticity, and of the way it differs from the price elasticity formula. Let the change in expenditure be ΔEXP and the change in income be ΔINC, and let INC and EXP be the values of income and expenditure at a point. Then the income elasticity of expenditure (or demand) can be written as

$$\frac{\text{proportionate change in expenditure}}{\text{proportionate change in income}} = \frac{\dfrac{\Delta EXP}{EXP}}{\dfrac{\Delta INC}{INC}}$$

which, with exactly the same manipulations as those explained in Chapter 6, can be rewritten as

$$\frac{\Delta EXP}{EXP} \cdot \frac{INC}{\Delta INC} = \frac{\Delta EXP}{\Delta INC} \cdot \frac{INC}{EXP}$$

$\dfrac{\Delta EXP}{\Delta INC}$ is the slope of the expenditure function, as you already know.
Therefore:

$$\text{income elasticity of demand} = \text{slope} \cdot \frac{INC}{EXP}$$

So how does this differ in form from the formula for the price elasticity of demand? In Chapter 6 the price elasticity of demand was calculated as

$$\varepsilon_D = \frac{\dfrac{P}{Q}}{\text{slope}}$$

The reason for the difference lies in the way the figures are drawn and hence the calculation of the slope.

Look at Figure 9.19. The price elasticity of demand at point A on Figure 9.19a tells us the responsiveness of demand (the dependent variable on the *horizontal* axis) to a change of price (on the *vertical* axis). In Figure 9.19b the income elasticity of demand at point B measures the responsiveness of expenditure (the dependent variable on the *vertical* axis) to income (on the *horizontal* axis). These are simply the conventional ways of drawing the two functions. However, the slope in each diagram is calculated as

$$\frac{\text{rise}}{\text{run}} = \frac{\text{change in variable on vertical axis}}{\text{change in variable on horizontal axis}}$$

The implication is that one elasticity formula is the *inverse* of the other. In (a), the price elasticity of demand can be written as

$$\frac{1}{\text{slope}} \cdot \frac{\text{vertical axis variable}}{\text{horizontal axis variable}}$$

In (b), the income elasticity can be written as

$$\text{slope} \cdot \frac{\text{horizontal axis variable}}{\text{vertical axis variable}}$$

The principle is exactly the same; the difference in the formula arises simply from the way the function is drawn.

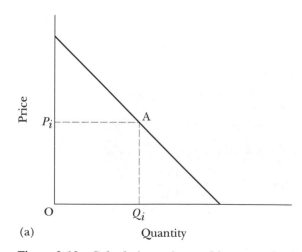

(a)

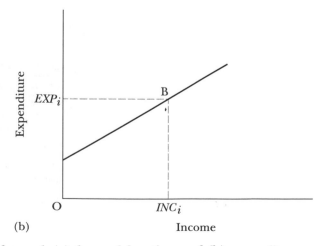

(b)

Figure 9.19   **Calculating price and income elasticities of demand: (a) demand function, and (b) expenditure function**

Lest you conclude that elasticities are merely a technical matter, consider a practical example. Some foods are very popular among the poor, but less so among the middle class and richer families. In Britain, potatoes and turnips are two such examples. As income rises for very poor families, more potatoes will be bought, reflecting higher calorie intake. But for middle class families, this increase is *smaller* (relative to a given percentage rise in income), and for rich families it is even smaller. This changing responsiveness of purchases to income in a cross-sectional sample is measured by income elasticities.

The next diagram (Figure 9.20) is aimed at illustrating a common problem with survey data on consumption. Here we have household expenditure on raw potatoes, one of the many goods comprising the category 'food expenditure'. The survey used two-week recall and diaries of expenditure. Among the 750 households presented here, only a couple of hundred actually bought raw potatoes during their reference period; many bought no potatoes. The figures need to be added up and averaged to get sensible results.

The line fitted to the potato data has a poor fit for the same reason. It is:

$$\text{potato expenditure} = 0.12 + 0.0007 \times \text{income}$$

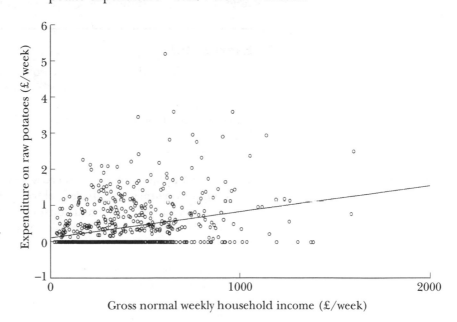

Figure 9.20 Expenditure on raw potatoes plotted against gross normal household income

Source: Central Statistical Office *Family Expenditure Survey* (1992)

Clearly, raw potatoes are a cheap good bought by a minority of British people in any one week. You may already have realized that the larger purchases at the top of the graph might represent several things:

- larger families
- preference for home cooking over pre-cooked meals
- buying in bulk for future weeks' use.

As a result, I would not place much confidence in the income elasticities that I could calculate from this line.

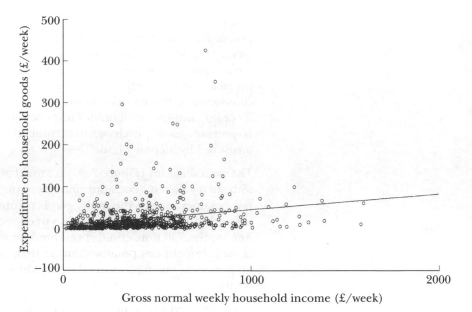

Figure 9.21   **Expenditure on household goods plotted against gross normal household income**

Source: Central Statistical Office *Family Expenditure Survey* (1992)

In Figure 9.21 we move back to an analysis of aggregated expenditure, this time spending on household goods (durables and non-durables).

Exercise 9.11

Can you work out the approximate equation for the line in Figure 9.21? Do so by reading the *y*-intercept (you will have to guess the exact number), and then using the 'triangle' method to get the slope. Use a right-angled triangle with a base from 0 to 1000 on the horizontal axis, and estimate its height.

In these examples, we have used cross-sectional data to examine consumption patterns. We have had to use total expenditure on product categories as a proxy for actual consumption or use, and we have seen considerable variation in household expenditure with some broad patterns emerging.

Beware, however, of assuming, because you find in data a relationship of the type we have traced, that there is necessarily a causal relationship between the variables. The relationship might be spurious: two variables may both increase over time without being related to each other. Or there may be an intervening variable which needs to be brought into your model. As a final example illustrating that caution should be used in interpreting scattergrams, look at Figure 9.22.

Can you see that a line (or better, a curve) would fit through these data? It would suggest a positive correlation of GNP per capita and average life expectancy. But in explaining this observation, we could not simply say that money makes you live longer. We would have to go into a multi-causal explanation of how higher incomes translate into better health (through food, medical care, education, and so on), which then causes longer life expectancies. We could also question the use of one 'dot' per country; some countries have huge populations and others very small populations, and inequality within countries varies considerably too.

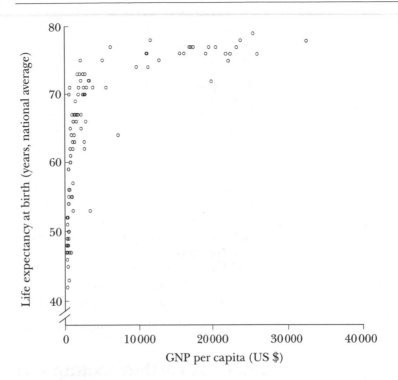

Figure 9.22 **Life expectancy at birth plotted against GNP per capita, 1989**

Source: World Bank (1992)

4.3   Time series data

In many books of economic statistics, you will see graphs with time measured in years on the horizontal axis. You saw such graphs in Chapter 1. For example, Figure 9.23 shows changes over time in the tenure of UK dwellings.

These graphs are called time series graphs. Normally a line is used to connect the available data points, so they can also be called line graphs. The actual data might be monthly, quarterly, or annual, but the gaps in the data are often hidden when the line is drawn. Time series data are very different

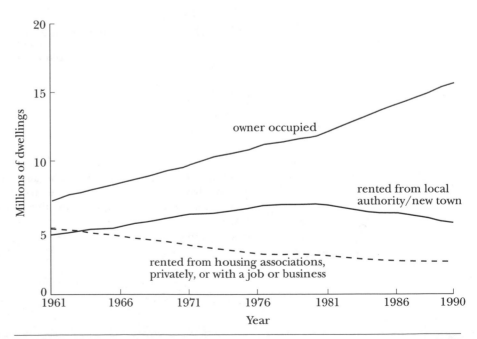

Figure 9.23 **Time series data on UK housing tenure**

Source: *Key Data* (1992) p.75, Fig. 17.1

from the kind of data we have looked at so far. Time series use *longitudinal* data, whereas our graphs so far have used *cross-sectional* data referring to a point in time.

We might conceptualize time series data by calling *time* a variable in its own right. The graph above is then seen as showing the relationships between two variables, in this case *housing tenure* and *time*. The units of measurement for time are for example years or months; the level of measurement is numerical and continuous.

Economists often analyse time series data with a view to forecasting trends beyond the present. To do this they begin with a graph of two variables and they might fit a line or curve representing the relationship $y = a + bt$ or $y = f(t)$, where y is on the vertical axis and y is a function of t, time. The notation $f(\ )$, which you have now seen a number of times, is used to represent any function – linear, curved, and so on. Frequently, economists build models using three or more variables, e.g. expenditure = f(income, time), and graphs (which are by their nature usually two-dimensional) are then used only at the final stage to illustrate the findings of the model.

Time series data are the subject of Chapter 26 of this text.

4.4   A further example of analysis of two variables: gender and pay

As further practice with the tools you have learnt up to now, let us look at the earnings of men and women separately. I will use several representations to show you the relationship between *earnings* (from waged work) and *gender*. However, one has to consider carefully what variable to use to measure pay. Average annual earnings of employed men and women from waged work are vastly different (in the UK men averaged £13 654 per year in 1991 and women £7157). An alternative measure would be hourly earnings, i.e. average wages per hour before tax. These data are presented in Table 9.11.

Table 9.11   **Average earnings, men and women, UK, 1991**

	Mean (£)	Standard deviation (£)	n[1]
Annual earnings of men	13 654	11 214	461
Annual earnings of women	7157	5819	416
Hourly earnings of men	6.88	4.27	340
Hourly earnings of women	4.82	2.75	357

[1]The number of cases used, n, varies because those who reported zero hours or zero earnings have been excluded in the calculations. Some people also could not report their 'hours worked', perhaps because they did piece-work and did not have hourly pay.

Source: *BHPS* (1991)

Exercise 9.12

Draw a bar chart of means for '*annual earnings* by *gender*' from Table 9.11. Draw another for '*hourly earnings* by *gender*'.

Question

Can you think of problems with the comparisons shown by your bar charts?

I would make three comments on this information. First, the bar charts you have drawn do not allow for the differences in types of work done; studies of pay rates usually compare like with like instead of averaging all workers together. Equal pay legislation, for instance, insists that women and men get equal pay for similar work, not for work in general. The research needed to examine pay differentials would be *multivariate*, not bivariate. Our graphs have only touched the surface of this issue.

Second, the dispersion in the two distributions has been hidden in the bar chart of means. There is considerable spread from low to high wages, as seen in the standard deviations which are over 50 per cent of the mean. Some *particular* women earn more than some men; however 'on average' women earn less. If you had more data it would be better to use two histograms to portray the spread of earnings for the two groups of people.

Third, because of the skewness in these distributions – most distributions of data on incomes are skewed – the 'mean' is not really a good measure of usual earnings.

The final exercise consolidates some of the techniques in this chapter, by considering these last two points further.

Exercise 9.13

1   Figure 9.24 shows the distribution of a variable, X, which is not skewed. The distribution is drawn as a smooth curve rather than using a histogram. Sketch this distribution as it might look with the same mean but a smaller standard deviation.

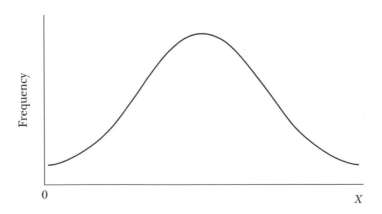

Figure 9.24 **A non-skewed distribution**

2 Suppose that there was no skewness in the distribution of average hourly earnings of men and women in the example in Table 9.11 and Exercise 9.12. Sketch the two distributions of this variable for men and women, again using smooth curves, as in Figure 9.24, not histograms.

3 Since there is considerable dispersion in each distribution, do your sketch graphs show an overlap in the distributions? If so, how do you interpret the overlap?

4 How would your sketched distributions be different if the hourly earnings distributions were skewed? What does your answer suggest about the use of the mean as the measure of usual earnings?

5 Conclusion

This chapter has taken you through some tools of analysis which will help you to display, describe and summarize data. Histograms, scattergrams, distributions and summary statistics will all be useful in your study of economics. In this discussion there has been one evident omission: although we have introduced and briefly defined a line of best fit, we have not explained how the line is drawn, nor defined any ideas about *how well* the line fits the data. These topics, hinging on the concept of correlation, are introduced in Chapter 26.

In addition to introducing descriptive data handling, the chapter has also explored a few of the issues which emerge when we try to relate theory to data. The chapter has shown that these problems are both conceptual and empirical. Neither theory nor data offer simple representations of the economy; on the contrary, data are shaped by theory, and in turn provide evidence which reshapes theories. Good data analysis and empirical modelling are key elements of economics.

PART 6
CHAPTER 10

MONEY AND GOVERNMENT
GOVERNMENT AND THE ECONOMY

by Maureen Mackintosh

1 Introduction: the economics of governing

1.1 State vs. market?

There is a tendency to think of the 'state' and the 'market' as in some sense opposed phenomena. The world-wide emphasis in the 1980s and early 1990s on privatization and 'rolling back the state' created a common-sense notion that more market meant less state and vice versa. But economic history demonstrates that matters are more complicated than that. The rise of industrial capitalism and the market economy brought with it an unprecedented increase in the scale and range of activities of governments. The spread of market exchange was matched by a proliferation of state intervention and regulation of markets, some examples of which you studied in Chapter 8. These regulations were annoying economic liberals in Europe long before the current protests about petty regulations within the European Union.

In nineteenth-century Britain, the industrial pioneer, the freeing of markets was enforced by the state, as the historian and political economist Karl Polanyi pointed out. 'The [eighteen] thirties and forties saw not only an outburst of legislation repealing restrictive regulations, but also an enormous increase in the administrative functions of the state, which was now being endowed with a central bureaucracy able to fulfil the tasks set by the adherents of liberalism … *Laissez-faire* was planned.' (Polanyi, 1944, pp.139–40.)

The road to the free market passed through complex legislative frameworks establishing the preconditions for market trading, such as the enclosure laws establishing property rights in land. Not long after began the rise in what the free trade proponents of that time denounced as restrictions on trade: administrative regulations such as controls on child labour, provisions for inspection of the quality of food and drink, local taxation for provision of local drainage, health and safety regulations, and enforced vaccination.

Throughout Europe, the rise in industrial capitalism and the associated sweeping urbanization brought an increase in municipal government in the late nineteenth and early twentieth century: sanitation, public utilities, roads, policing. Such 'collectivist' measures were the property of no one political tendency. Catholic politicians in Austria and Germany, anti-clericals in France, Conservatives and Liberals in Britain and Social Democrats in Germany enacted similar measures in response to common pressures.

Later in the twentieth century and particularly after the Second World War, the expansion of the state shifted to the national level throughout most of Europe. The provision of public services – notably health and education –

continued to expand. And social insurance and income support for the poor became an increasingly important function of national governments. As the Dutch sociologist Abram de Swaan notes, 'the contemporary state is very much the product of the collectivization of health care, education and income maintenance.' Furthermore, he adds, 'modern life in its most intimate and pervasive aspects, is shaped by this collectivizing process' (de Swaan, 1988, p.11).

These trends have not been limited to Europe. Japanese economic growth has also been associated with an active and interventionist state, and in recent years Japanese government spending, especially on social security, has risen rapidly. And other growing middle income countries have active and expanding states. There has also been a rise in international governmental institutions such as the European parliament and the Brussels-based European Commission, the United Nations, the World Bank and the International Monetary Fund (IMF).

Recently, however, as I noted above, the inevitability of this association between an expanding market and a growing state has been seriously challenged. Economic liberalism – the view that where possible economic activity should be left to individual initiative and free exchange – gained ground again. Governments were elected in many industrial countries – notably the UK, the USA, and New Zealand – promising to roll back the state. More recently, Western Europe, and most dramatically Eastern European countries, embarked on privatization programmes. Multilateral institutions such as the World Bank and the IMF took this message to industrializing countries, making privatization a condition of financial aid.

With industrial privatization also came a levelling off of the growth of state welfare activities in many countries. There developed by the early 1990s a widely held view which suggested that public services and welfare activities – social insurance, health, education – should increasingly be shifted out of the state, back to private initiative and charitable or 'voluntary' provision. The wheel seemed to have come full circle.

1.2   An economics of governing?

I quoted Abram de Swaan above using the word 'collectivizing' about state provision of social welfare. But do the ideas of 'collective' and 'state' coincide? The debates of the 1980s and 1990s have clarified for us (again) the importance of making a clear distinction between two questions.

1   Which economic activities should be undertaken collectively or co-operatively rather than by individuals?

and

2   Which economic activities should be undertaken by the state?

Question

Stop for a moment and think about these questions. How would you answer them?

The first question is very broad. There is an immense range of co-operative activity in any complex economy. You might have included any work which requires teamwork to plan and undertake projects. You may have included the examples already mentioned above: tax-financed public services such as education, or social security for the poor and unemployed. You might have included charitable activity. You might have mentioned co-operation within the household, discussed in Chapter 3. How long your list is will depend on your economic and political opinions. There are deep divisions of view on how much economic activity can and should be undertaken collectively, and the very word 'collective' carries a complex set of positive and negative associations.

The second question is clearly narrower. The list of activities which require co-operation is likely to be much longer than the list of state functions. This is because the state is not simply an expression of and servant to our collective wishes. On the contrary, it is an institution often beholden to particular sets of interests, and having a variety of specific interests of its own. Public services were able to grow, furthermore, only as the state developed the capacity to administer complex processes. The implication, as de Swaan notes, was: 'The emergence of a stratum of professional experts and administrators who depended on these collective arrangements for employment and advancement. These "new" middle classes represented a formidable array of interest groups for the promotion of the expansion of collective arrangements.' (de Swaan, 1988, p.225.)

The implied fear – that the state may operate in its own interests, or those of only a segment of the public it should be serving – is echoed in many people's experiences of unresponsive or invasive state officials. The state can present very different faces to the benefit recipient and the higher income taxpayer; to the long distance rail traveller and the inner city bus user; to the house owner with a (subsidized) mortgage and the municipal tenant needing (hard to find) rehousing. The concept of the state as serving the interests of particular social groups has been a political driving force behind an array of proposals to break up state monopolies of service provision, and to introduce competition, alternative providers and consumer rights. The idea of the 'mixed economy of welfare' has been taking over from the older social democratic concept – never wholly realized but for some an ideal – of universal state provision.

These debates about the proper economic boundaries of the state form part of what we might call the economics of 'governing': that is, the analysis of economic activities which are not conducted through individual market exchange. I call it 'governing' because issues of organization and control are central to this literature. It asks, how are non-market activities organized and to what pressures – if not market demand – do they respond? The phrase also points to the fact that this is not just the economics of the state – which we might understand as the institutions and activities which continue as governments change – but that the analysis is embedded in a wider understanding of the economics of consent and co-operation.

This is one of the most fascinating branches of economics – or so I hope to persuade you. My objectives in this chapter are the following.

Most generally, this chapter analyses an important economic agent introduced in the circular flow diagrams in Chapter 2, but not yet discussed in detail: the government (Figure 10.1). The chapter includes a discussion of the government accounts, paralleling the households' and firms' accounts in Chapters 3 and 4.

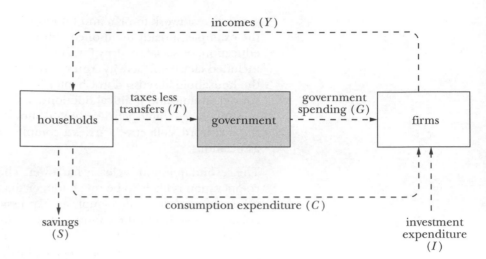

incomes (Y)

taxes less transfers (T)   government spending (G)

households   government   firms

savings (S)   consumption expenditure (C)   investment expenditure (I)

Figure 10.1 **Government in the simple circular flow of income**

More specifically, I hope to demonstrate that in the analysis of government, as in the study of firms and households, how we 'model' the institutions matters. There are two distinct ways of seeing the state and the government – as it were, through an individualist and a collectivist lens – and they have very different implications concerning the proper role of these institutions in the economy. This theme runs right through the chapter, and is introduced with the problem of 'governing the commons'.

In practice, much of the chapter explores the economic relations between states and markets. The chapter examines the argument that market failures justify the economic activities of government. And conversely, it considers the impact of government on markets, notably through taxation. Finally, this chapter provides some further practice in both game theory and the diagrammatic analysis of supply and demand.

2   Governing the commons

I want to start the analysis of the economics of governing with a famous problem which is also a very current one: how can we ensure that a common asset, such as common grazing land or the air we breathe, is efficiently used, and not degraded? As we shall see, the answer to this question depends on the assumptions we make: on how we model the problem.

2.1   The tragedy of the commons

In 1968, Garett Hardin published an influential article called 'The tragedy of the commons', which discussed this problem of the degradation of a common resource. He explained the problem in terms of the overgrazing of common pasture land. Envisage a situation where the carrying capacity of common land is limited, and local herdsmen are free to graze their herds. Each herdsman benefits from his own herd (in terms of the sale of cattle, meat and milk) and loses income when, beyond a certain number of animals on the land, overgrazing means each animal has less sustenance.

The problem as Hardin sees it arises because each herder gains the whole benefit from his own herd, and hence wishes to increase it. By increasing the herd beyond a certain point, he contributes to overgrazing. However, he suffers only a small part of the losses from overgrazing which expansion of his own herd beyond a certain point will cause: the rest of the losses fall on the other herdsmen. If all herdsmen pursue their own interests, worsening degradation of the land will occur.

Hardin's conclusion is infinitely gloomy: 'Each man is locked into a system which compels him to increase his herd without limit – in a world that is limited. Ruin is the destination towards which all men rush, each pursuing his own best interest in a society that believes in the freedom of the commons.' (Hardin, 1968, p.1244.) Hence the 'tragedy' of the commons.

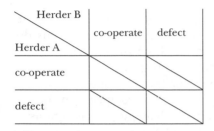

Figure 10.2 **Herders' blank pay-off matrix**

Exercise 10.1

You have seen an argument of this general abstract form before. Try to restate Hardin's argument, using the prisoners' dilemma game introduced in Chapter 5. Fill in the pay-off matrix in Figure 10.2 before you turn to the answer. Hint: consider two herders, A and B. Set a maximum pay-off from sharing the maximum carrying capacity of the land equally, and call that 'co-operate'. Then, consider what happens if each 'defects', that is increases their herd without limit.

The specific numbers which you chose to put in the matrix do not matter, so long as the following holds. The dominant strategy for each herder should be to 'defect', whatever the other does. Although the best collective outcome – the highest joint income – would arise if both co-operate, the logic of the game drives them to the worst joint outcome, where they have the lowest joint income.

The conclusion Hardin draws from his parable is that only the government can prevent disaster through regulation: or as he puts it, 'mutual coercion, mutually agreed upon' to restrain over-use. He was not the first to draw this moral. The classic statement of this argument for acceptable governmental coercion was made by Thomas Hobbes. He argued in *Leviathan*, published in the mid seventeenth century that, 'during the time when men live without a common power to keep them all in awe, they are in that condition which is called war' (Hobbes, 1651, p.143). Humanity's only hope of peace and progress was therefore to join together and submit themselves to a common sovereign power which could prevent mutual destruction.

However, others have pointed out that governments too cannot necessarily be relied upon to conserve common resources. Even democratically elected governments may pollute their own backyards against the wishes of their citizens. We return below to why that might be so. Meanwhile, are there other alternative modes of governing the commons? There are I suggest two broad possibilities, and they depend heavily on the assumptions which we make about the behaviour of people and communities.

2.2 The scope for co-operation

Question

Before you read on, think about the story of the commons again. It is a very gloomy one. What are the most important assumptions which are being made here?

I think there are three important assumptions.

1   People consider only their own self-interest.

2   People cannot co-operate in their shared interests: this assumption is made clear in the formulation of the prisoners' dilemma.

3   People lack information about the consequences of their own actions. This assumption is needed because otherwise, in Hardin's example, people would realize what was happening before the complete collapse of the commons, and stop in their *own* interests, before they themselves lost everything.

As the anthropologist Robert Wade (1987) points out, in his study of the use of common water resources by Indian villagers, these assumptions do not necessarily hold. In particular, they may not hold where the common resource is held by a small homogeneous group, and the return from co-operation is high. In such a small-scale society, people may be able to see that they have shared interests in co-operation, be able to perceive and demonstrate the results of their individual actions and be able to organize co-operation cheaply relative to the benefits. So, in this case, *voluntary co-operative action* is a possible solution to the dangers of tragedy.

Elinor Ostrom, in *Governing the Commons* (1990), offers an example of the management of common grazing land which appears to contradict Hardin's gloomy prediction. The case, drawn from a book called *Balancing on an Alp* (Netting, 1981) describes communally-owned alpine grazing meadows in the village of Torbel in Switzerland. Written documents on these meadows go back to the thirteenth century. An alp association of all cattle-owning villagers, dating from the fifteenth century, maintains the pastures and imposes fines for misuse, as well as distributing common outputs such as trees and cheese. The villagers are entirely familiar with private rights to land for their own gardens, grain fields and vineyards, but have chosen to continue to hold and manage the alpine pastures in common. The (fragile) land has maintained its productivity over centuries without degradation.

Question

If we were to model the Swiss pastures in the form of a game, which of Hardin's main assumptions would have to go?

The short answer seems to be, all three. People in this Swiss village understand the consequences of their actions for others. As a result, they can see past their immediate self-interest, and have the capacity to co-operate. This may be because they fit Wade's criteria for voluntary co-operation quite well (small scale, homogeneity, visible interdependence). They have chosen to formulate their co-operation in an association with appointed officials. Can we use the game theory to model this new situation? Clearly, the 'prisoners' dilemma' will no longer do: co-operation has to be possible. The co-operators understand the pay-offs from their actions and can act upon them in their individual or collective interest. One among a number of ways to express this in game theory is to allow the players to make binding agreements before the game is played. These binding agreements might take the form, as in the Swiss meadow, of agreed rules of use (maximum herd size) and fines to be paid for defection. This might change the pay-offs as in Figure 10.3.

Herder A \ Herder B	co-operate	defect
co-operate	(100–1) / (100–1)	(120–1–40) / (10–1)
defect	(10–1) / (120–1–40)	(20–1–40) / (20–1–40)

that is:

Herder A \ Herder B	co-operate	defect
co-operate	99 / 99	79 / 9
defect	9 / 79	–21 / –21

cost of administration = 1

fine for defection = 40

Figure 10.3 **Herders' pay-off matrix with agreed sanctions**

Definition

Externalities

An externality exists when the actions of one economic agent have effects on another agent which can be ignored by the first. The most important category of externalities in economic theory arises when economic behaviour in market systems has effects on others which do not pass through the market price mechanism. The resulting market outcome is then allocatively inefficient.

Here, the pay-offs in Figure 10.11 are altered by the assumptions that: (a) the costs of the association are one unit for each herdsman, and (b) 'defection' (over-use) is sanctioned by a fine of 40.

Question

What is now the dominant strategy?

Co-operation is now the dominant *individual* strategy, as well as being the best collective solution, because of the effect of the fines. Each herder will prefer co-operation, whatever the other herder decides. Make sure that you understand that statement.

Note that the same outcome could be achieved in principle by an outside authority imposing fines: Hardin's solution of state regulation. However, Ostrom suggests that in small-scale situations co-operation may be more efficient, since the users have better information than any outside authority, can 'vet' each other easily, share objectives, and can regulate the situation very cheaply.

2.3   Privatizing the commons

Let us now suppose that co-operation breaks down in the village and that the state cannot be relied upon. Is there a third possibility? An alternative solution which has been proposed is to divide up, or 'privatize' the commons. The common land is parcelled out into plots of grazing land for each herder. Why is this thought to be a solution?

To see this, we need a new economic concept, that of externalities

We can illustrate the idea of externalities from Hardin's original parable. Each herder, in this story, gained the full benefit from each increase in his own stock, but imposed part of the costs on the others who were also using the commons. This is an externality. In other words, no herder has to consider the full costs of his actions, hence the anti-social behaviour.

The effect of dividing the commons is then to create private property from common property. The aim of this is to *internalize the externality* and remove the problem of over-use. Whereas previously, each cattle owner considered only the costs of his actions which fell on him, now he suffers the whole costs of over-stocking his own land. Either all the costs of over-stocking fall upon the herder's own land, by denuding it, or they 'spill over' (for example, because of cattle breaking out in search of grass elsewhere) in which case the owner of the next-door plot will force him to pay penalties. The externality has vanished.

Note, further, the assumption that there are now *markets* where previously there was common land. Someone who wishes to cease being a herder, or to keep a smaller herd, can now sell the land to someone who wants to expand their cattle keeping. Someone affected by a neighbour can demand compensation. A price mechanism has appeared. How effective this price mechanism is likely to be in this case, is something I consider further below.

This type of solution to the tragedy of the commons has been proposed by economists to deal with a wide range of environmental (and other) problems which they analyse in this abstract form. The general approach is to try where possible to create *property rights* where there were none before. Economists who emphasize this approach argue that it is always preferable where possible to create property rights through privatization in order to deal with externalities, rather than rely on the state to deal with the problem. Part of the reason for this is that they see state property as suffering from precisely the same problems as common property: the lack of a true 'owner' means that it will be degraded and run inefficiently. More on this, too, below.

2.4   The economics of the commons

I used above the phrase 'a parable' to describe Hardin's tragedy of the commons. Hardin told a (classic) story in a form which turned it into an economic model of a problem. I have specified that model in terms of structure and assumptions, and shown that it takes the basic form of a model you have already met. But Hardin also told the story rather emotively, as the quotation above shows. This is what gives the model its 'parable' quality, and in this sense the simple model of the commons has been used, as Elinor Ostrom notes, as a *metaphor* for a much wider range of situations. The danger is that the force of the parable induces a sense of hopelessness about the problem.

That is why I have begun this chapter by suggesting that there are in principle three methods of coping with common resource problems of this type: co-operation; state action; or privatization and market creation. Which should be used when is likely to depend on specific circumstances. There are some very special features of communities which, in one form or another, 'balance on an alp'.

3   Market failures and public responses

I could restate Hardin's argument in Section 2 in the following general form. He described a situation where the market was not working, where there was indeed no market for common land. The solutions which emerged were either to *replace* the missing market by co-operation or state action, or to *construct* a market that would work. This general approach is the most common way in which economists think about public – state or collective – economic action. As one of the most eminent economic theorists, Kenneth Arrow, formulated it: 'I propose here the view that, when the market fails to achieve an optimal state, society will, to some extent at least, recognize the gap, and non-market social institutions will arise attempting to bridge it.' (Arrow, 1963, p.947.)

You met in Chapter 7 the idea of an 'optimal' market outcome. Here we look more closely at its converse: market failure.

3.1   Externalities

One of the major reasons why markets fail in principle to operate efficiently is because of the existence of externalities. I now want to explain and explore this concept in more detail, using some of the techniques of market analysis which you studied in Chapters 5–8.

The best way to grasp the idea of externalities is through another example. The environmental policy debates of the early 1990s provide some excellent ones. Acid rain, the pollution of rivers, the depletion of the ozone layer and global warming, these can all be understood as arising in part because they are external effects of market production – though that is not their *only* cause.

Acid rain results from the dissolving of sulphur oxides and nitrogen dioxide in cloud and rain, to create rainfall which is polluted with sulphuric and nitric acids. In most countries the bulk of these pollutants result from power generation from coal or oil with a high sulphur content. Acidity in rain is a major problem because it appears to damage forests and to kill fish in areas downwind of the power stations. Much of the political controversy over acid rain has arisen because many countries 'import' this pollution from elsewhere. For example, from a national point of view, 80% of acidity in British rain is self inflicted by British pollution, but over 90% of acidity in Norwegian rain appears to be imported (Pearce and Turner, 1990).

Those building power stations have no reason to take any of these acid rain effects into account, unless they are forced to do so by governmental or some other form of public action. They treat the atmosphere as a common resource, a sink into which pollution can be tipped. Hence the costs of particular types of power stations are lower than they would be if they included the full costs to society of their operation. Some costs – the forests and the fisheries – are *external* to the calculation.

This fact in turn means that the decisions of the firms are inefficient. Consider Figure 10.4. This shows the equilibrium in the market for power generation. Quite implausibly, in order to simplify argument and diagram, I am going to assume that the industry is perfectly competitive. The curve labelled *MPC* = *S* is the supply curve for the industry, which you will remember from Chapter 7 is derived from the marginal cost curves of the individual firms. But this marginal cost curve only includes those costs which each firm actually has to pay. Hence it is the marginal *private* cost (*MPC*) curve. The costs of the loss of livelihood of the Norwegian fishermen are paid by those fishermen, and perhaps by the Norwegian state if it pays unemployment benefit to them. So the marginal *social* costs (*MSC*), including those in Norway, are higher than the marginal private costs as shown by the gap between the *MSC* and the *MPC* curves in Figure 10.4.

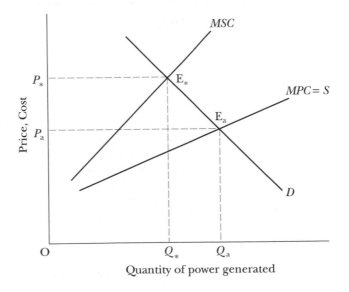

Figure 10.4 **The divergence between private and social costs of power generation**

So what are the market outcomes? If we assume this is a perfectly competitive industry, then the market equilibrium will be at E_a. But this is not an *efficient* equilibrium. The reason is that for an allocatively-efficient market outcome, the sum consumers are willing to pay for the last unit of power generation (indicated by the demand curve) should be equal to the marginal cost of generating that last unit. (Look back at Chapter 7 if you are not sure why this is so.) In Figure 10.4, this would be point E_*, where the marginal benefit is equal to the full marginal social cost. The market equilibrium produces too much power, Q_a rather than Q_*, and charges too low a price, P_a rather than P_*.

Notice several other points about this example. As it is designed, it does not support the idea that acid rain should be reduced to zero. On the contrary, the assumption underlying the diagram is that the effects of acid rain can be costed, and a price put upon them. Preventing acid rain has a cost, and the price put upon acidic pollution of the atmosphere should reflect the balance of people's desires to fish or walk in forests, on the one hand, and to heat their houses and power their industries on the other. Not everyone is happy with this way of posing the problems of environmental damage. You will find an extended discussion of some of these issues in Chapter 27.

Second, this simple model suggests a possible role for the non-market social institutions, state or co-operative, to make the polluters pay the marginal social cost. The 'polluter pays' principle has become one of the basic principles of environmental policy. In the acid rain case, it is very hard for voluntary action to work. Norwegian fishermen can exercise little leverage over British power stations. But state intervention could in principle exert effective influence. One method would be to impose a tax on polluting activity, to raise the costs of highly polluting forms of power generation relative to less polluting forms. This would raise the price to the consumer, and discourage both production of power in this form, and its consumption. A similar effect might be achieved by insisting on the installation by power generators of scrubbing equipment, which would reduce the acid content of emissions, and simultaneously raise the costs of generation. The way taxes affect the market is explored further in Section 5 of this chapter.

Exercise 10.2

Copy Figure 10.4. Now use this diagram to show the effect of a regulation requiring scrubbing equipment, of the type just described.

Note that the effect of regulation (the scrubbers in this case) is that both the producer and the consumer of the power pay the costs of reducing acid-causing emissions. The producer faces higher costs and lower demand, hence lower total profits. But the consumer also loses. Higher prices mean lower power consumption. So the intervention treats the 'polluter' who is to pay as both the producer and the user of power, which, when you think about it, seems fair. Previously, the consumers were paying too little for power, and some of the costs were falling upon others.

Finally, there are costs and problems with this proposal for intervention. First, there are administrative costs. Second, there are information costs and problems; it is hard to measure pollution levels, hard to calculate the true social costs, and difficult to calculate an appropriate tax or regulation to improve the situation. Third, the situation is complicated, as Chapter 7 noted, if the economy is not perfectly competitive. In such a situation, that is, if pollution is just one of many market failures, just correcting this externality will not produce an optimal market outcome, and may not improve allocative efficiency overall.

Fourth, and perhaps worse, in the case of environmental damage governments are often part of the problem. Some of the worst emitters of the pollution which produces acid rain are the state-owned power stations of the ex-Soviet Union and Eastern Europe. And in Britain, the offending power stations were until recently in the public sector. Why should the British state suddenly become an efficient regulator, when it was a polluting producer? Considerations like that might lead us to wonder whether Hardin's solution – creating property rights – might not work better instead.

3.2   Creating missing markets

I suggested above that Norwegian fishermen cannot influence the power stations. But why not? One answer to this is that – as for the grazing land – there is a *missing market*. The central problem, in this view, is that there is no market in air quality, hence in quality of rain. No one 'owns' the fresh air, and hence can impose a charge on those who pollute it. So could property rights be created?

It is hard to see how this trick could be achieved for air. The problem is that this is really not a case of *common property* – that is, the shared property of a group as in the 'commons' example – at all. Rather, it falls into the environmental economists' category of *global free access resources* such as air and the sea, that is, resources for which no identifiable community has ownership rights. These resources do not lend themselves to being divided up. Instead, they seem to demand some form of co-operation between states to control dumping of pollution. And this co-operation seems to be demanded in circumstances precisely opposite to those identified above as assisting co-operation: large areas, lack of social homogeneity and difficulty in establishing costs and benefits.

In the latter type of circumstances, economists expect co-operation to be hard to establish because – as in the failed cartels Vivienne Brown discussed in Chapter 5 – there is an incentive for individuals to cheat. The benefits from cheating are great, the transgressors hard to detect. Economists call this kind of cheating 'free riding', and it is analysed in more detail in Section 3.3. First, however, I want to consider market creation in circumstances where it seems feasible, by reverting one last time to the 'commons'.

Question

Where the commons can be divided and privatized, will the result be desirable? You could think about two issues here. First, will an allocatively-efficient market emerge, i.e. will the market failure be resolved? And second, are there any other reasons why you might not think the outcome better than the previous situation?

There are at least three important issues you might have thought of here.

1   Are the previous externalities now effectively internalized, in the sense that all the effects of individual activity remain within the individual's own property?

2   If they do not, i.e. where 'spillovers' remain, will a market emerge which forces people to pay the full costs of these spillovers?

3   Are there any distributional effects of the privatization which might be problematic, e.g. will some herders lose their livelihood?

In practice, it seems likely that spillover effects might remain. Where these occur, there are several interesting problems with a market process of settling disputes between neighbours. Consider our two herders one more time. Suppose that herder A grows feed using chemicals which pollute the land of herder B. Herder B objects. If there is private property, but no legal right to compensation if land is damaged by a neighbour, then the only option is for B to bribe A to reduce the chemicals. How much B is willing to pay depends on how strongly he feels about the damage. Figure 10.5 illustrates this idea. The MC (B) curve is the marginal cost of the pollution to B. The D (A) curve is A's 'demand for pollution': that is, A's benefits (in the form of more feed) from spreading chemical pollution around.

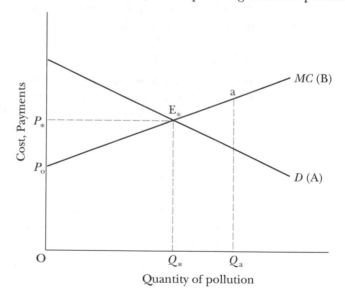

Figure 10.5   **Pollution and private property rights**

Suppose Q_a represents the current situation: the marginal cost to B outweighs the marginal advantage to A of the pollution. The efficient level of pollution would be Q_* where demand for pollution equals the marginal cost to the neighbour. Where there are no legal compensation rights, B would have to bribe A to move back towards Q_*. That is the allocatively-efficient market solution property rights theorists identify as possible without state intervention.

If there were to be a state backing-up the property rights with legal rights to compensation, then the situation might be different. In this case, B could demand compensation from A. If the current situation is that pollution is at Q_a then the compensation required is measured by the total cost of the pollution to B: this is the area under the marginal cost curve, represented by OP_oaQ_a. Think of this area as adding up the cost to B of each (marginal) additional bit of pollution.

However, it is likely that A will refuse to pay this much compensation. He will prefer to cut back his chemicals to reduce the pollution to Q_*. At that point, the marginal compensation cost to A will have fallen to the point where it just matches A's willingness to pay in order to pollute (that is, P_*). The same result in terms of a cut in pollution is achieved, but the *distributional* costs differ, depending upon the nature of the property rights, that is, upon whether property rights are backed up by legal rights to compensation. This distinction determines whether it is A or B who has to pay the external costs of A's pollution.

This is one kind of distributional effect of privatizing the commons. There may be others. The most evident is the difficult question of how the land will be divided up. Equally? If not, why not, and on what principles should it be divided?

Finally, there is one more problem. Markets, like states and associations, are expensive. The organizational costs involved in markets for pollution are considerable. They include the costs of bargaining, the time and effort involved, and they include the enforcement costs. What do you do if you pay the bribe and nothing happens, or you reduce pollution and the bribe remains unpaid? Even without a compensation law, some authority may be needed to enforce contracts. In other words, markets have *transactions costs*, and if they are high, the market may not be efficient after all. These costs are another and separate source of market failure.

Notice an interesting implication of this argument. The market if it is created is backed up – and influenced – by the role of the state. Some state entity is needed to guarantee the property rights. Furthermore, a government is needed to decide upon the land division and the compensation laws or their absence. Some form of political governance is needed even for the market solution. This takes us back to the historical point made at the beginning of the chapter: markets and states seem mutually dependent, tending to develop together.

3.3   Public goods

Both common and free access resources share the feature that use is unconstrained but capacity limited: after a certain point, more use by you has bad effects on me. My final category of market failures – cases where almost all economists agree some state action is needed – are situations where capacity is not limited. Public goods are a bit like perfect competition: an important concept in economics, and an extreme concept which helps to clarify theoretical relationships, but hard to identify in the real world.

Definition

Public goods

Public goods are goods which are *non-rival*: that is, more for me does not imply less for you. Furthermore, they are also *non-excludable*, that is, if I am consuming some, I cannot stop you from having some too.

Question

Can you think of any goods which fit the definition of public goods?

You may have found it easier to think of goods that are a bit like the definition, than goods which are completely described by those phrases. Here are some examples which get close.

1   National defence: the armed forces.

You might question whether they are 'goods' at all of course. A pacifist might wish to classify them as 'bads'. If you accept their desirability, you might still note that they exclude other countries' residents by definition, but within a country they seem to fit the definition quite well. Defence for one is defence for all, and you cannot decide to be undefended, thank you.

2   Lighthouses.

A much discussed example in economics. They cast their light on anyone who passes by (non-excludable) and many ships can see the light at once (non-rival).

3   Uncrowded country roads.

Quite a good example. You can hardly put a toll-gate on every farm lane, to allow you to exclude people. And if there are few cars around, your car does not reduce my space. (This is not of course the case in, for example, central London in the rush hour.)

4   Street lighting.

This has a localized effect, and I suppose there are limits to how many people can get under one lamppost. But locally, this also fits the definition fairly well.

5   Acid rain.

A 'public bad'? See further on.

Why are public goods a problem for economic theory? Because a private market cannot *in principle* allocate these goods efficiently. Perfect competition cannot work here, by definition. Why not? The essence of the problem is that one solution suggested above to market failure on the commons – divide up and privatize – is not available. We cannot, as just discussed, divide national defence up into bits and have a piece each.

This has effects on the demand and on the supply side. Let me give an example, starting with the supply side. If I supply country roads to farmer Bloggs, I am also providing the same network of country roads to farmer Jones. There is only one supply decision and only one supply curve.

On the demand side, life gets more complicated. Farmer Bloggs has a demand curve for country roads. She is prepared to pay a certain sum towards a new local road. Farmer Jones is meaner, he would rather leave the road network in more of a mess so he would offer less. If there are a number of farmers like these two, what is the market demand for country roads?

These farmers are expressing their willingness to pay for an increment of road. Since it is the *same* bit of road, we can add up these offers, or demands: the total of farmer Bloggs's willingness to pay for the road, plus farmer Jones's grudging contribution to the same stretch, and all others like them, gives the *total* willingness to pay for that bit of new road.

Fine, so far so good. So now how does the eager road builder get his or her hands on the cash? Here we meet another snag. How does the road builder find out what people are really willing to pay? In this situation, it will be in the interests of any one farmer to understate how much they are willing to pay. Because once the road is built, no one can be kept off it, certainly not the iconoclast who argued that they had no car and did not want the road anyway. So the best financial strategy (supposing you do not care what your neighbours think of you) is to keep your head down and hope others will build the road for you to use for free.

This behaviour involves riding on the backs of others, or 'free riding'. If people consult only their own interests, then it is likely to be a serious problem. If that is so, then this is an important market failure. There is no market here on which people have to reveal their preferences by making individual purchases. And the story implies that voluntary contributions will not work either, because everyone will calculate that they could get something for nothing. Hence, economists tend to say, compulsion is needed: enter the obligation to pay taxes. It is governments – usually local governments – which build country roads.

However, note the qualification above about not caring what the neighbours think. In the case just described, that is unlikely to be true for most farmers. Farmers in sparsely-populated country areas need to co-operate. A rural community of commercial farmers of the type I have just described seems to lie somewhere between the close-knit Swiss village and the impersonal city, so 'free riding' might be limited in practice. Furthermore, empirical research suggests that free-riding behaviour is in practice less common than economists tend to assume.

Less common among people, that is. National governments may be another matter. So what of acid rain? Can this be analysed in the same framework? We might think of air quality as having many of the characteristics of a public good. Good air is free for breathing, polluted air is likewise shared. Governments and voters have a certain willingness to pay to clean up the air. Then the problem is that of eliminating free riders: those governments which seek to conceal their true demand curve for clean air, in the hope that others will clean up the atmosphere for their benefit. There have been moments in the debates on acid rain when the British government has been accused of free riding, for example by installing high chimneys (which disperse the pollution nicely away from Britain to other recipients), while refusing to pay their share of a more general clean up in the hope that other countries will do it anyway. So this seems the moment to turn to a closer consideration of the behaviour of the state.

4   The public or the private state?

The arguments for collective action considered in the last two sections can be summed up as arguments about efficiency: how can allocative efficiency be achieved when markets fail? The argument was on a distinctly abstract level, and may have seemed a rather bloodless way of addressing as pervasive and complex an institution as the state. As Section 1 noted, the state has become a large and extremely important economic institution in its own right. It structures the operation of markets, provides or finances a very wide range of services and redistributes resources extensively between people and social groups. Abram de Swaan, quoted in Section 1, suggests that our private lives are deeply influenced by the 'collectivization' of social services via the state.

For a long time, however, the economic analysis of the operation of the state itself lagged behind the analysis of the behaviour of firms. There was a tendency within economic theory to treat the state as the *deus ex machina*: the god outside the machine of the market who put it right when it went wrong. (Economic advisers to governments, of course, have never really seen them in that light!) In the last 20 years, however, much greater attention has been paid to the analysis of the economic behaviour of the state itself. This section gives you a flavour of these debates. I am going to concentrate, here again, on issues about the efficiency of the state, leaving the very important range of issues about the redistributive activities of the state to Chapter 23, where you will get another chance to use many of the concepts developed here.

4.1   Public or private interests

Let me start with a deceptively specific question. Whose interests does the state serve?

Reflection

Before you read on, note down some of your instinctive reactions to this question.

You may have noted some of the following (partly conflicting) possibilities. You may think that the state chiefly serves the interests of the better off and influential. Or that it provides some security for the least well off. Or that it chiefly serves the interests of those who work for it. Or that different parts of the state serve different interests. You may have noted that the state 'should' operate in the general public interest, but I doubt, somehow, that you think that it always does.

Alternatively, you may have stopped short and asked, what do I mean by the state? You may in particular have wanted to draw some distinctions between government and state employees. We can think of the government as the political level: questions of constitution, political representation, principles of organization and policy seem properly to reside with government, whether centrally or locally. State employees may also fulfil explicitly political roles – as in the *cabinets* who come in with new French government ministers, or the US President's powers of political patronage. But the official story, so to speak, about most state employees is that their job is to serve the objectives of government and the needs of the users of their particular services (two tasks which may not of course always seem compatible).

Given these distinctions, we can formulate two polarized – and therefore highly simplified – sets of assumptions which underlie the alternative models of state economic behaviour.

The first, *public interest* view of the state, supposes that the government formulates a conception of the public interest which responds to the wishes of the citizen as it understands them, as expressed through the ballot box. And it supposes that state employees also seek, in that now old-fashioned phrase, to act as 'public servants' in the sense just described as the 'official story'.

The second, *private interest* view of the state, takes the opposite position. It considers both politicians and employees to be motivated solely by self-interest. So politicians respond, not only to those who vote, but to those who finance election campaigns and exert political pressure. And state employees also have interests of their own, which they pursue to their own advantage.

The second set of assumptions has been the basis for an explosion of economic modelling work on the state in recent years. It boils down to a view of the state as a collection of self-interested individuals: in other words, to models of the state based on the same assumptions which underlies most market models and game-theoretic models.

The plausibility of these models is reinforced by the fact that most people have met *some* public officials clearly pursuing their own private agenda. These 'private interest' models have been highly influential in recent economic policy debate concerning the size, role and organization of the state. In Britain, the assumptions behind these models have been widely referred to in order to justify sweeping public sector reforms, while the World Bank has used the ideas to underpin its public sector reform policies in the Third World. Here I consider two relevant debates, on the size and the internal organization of the state.

4.2   The Leviathan state?

Concern that the state had grown too large was a political theme which spread in the 1970s from the political right, across the political spectrum. It was suggested that states had grown inefficiently large by undertaking activities which could be done more efficiently by private individuals. Or that it had grown to the point where the freedom of the individual was threatened. Or merely that it had grown larger than its citizens truly wished. At the extreme, the state has been pictured as a monster, a 'predator' state, Hobbes's necessary autocrat gone out of control.

These images are powerful. The moral impetus which they gave to attempts to restrict the state interacted with the economic models built on private interest premises to produce a very compelling attack.

I want to consider these images from two angles. First, how much have states grown? And second, what different theories about that growth are generated by the two opposed perspectives on the behaviour of the state? To answer the first of these, however, requires a preliminary discussion of basic data: the government accounts.

Accounting for government

Table 10.1 presents a simplified set of British government accounts for 1991, showing revenue and expenditure. The general government accounts combine central and local government. They are income and expenditure (flow of funds) accounts; not the trading accounts and balance sheet presented by a firm. (The government does now draw up a public sector balance sheet, but accounting for public assets is still underdeveloped.) In addition to the income and expenditure accounts, the other important government accounts – not shown here – are the financial accounts, showing the management of government financial assets.

The most common way of measuring the size of the state is to look at the public expenditure total for any year. But this can be misleading for a number of reasons. First, there are two important categories within government expenditure: exhaustive expenditure and transfers, which have different economic implications.

Exhaustive expenditure is the simplest estimate of government production activity, the cost of the goods and services it produces. It includes both current government expenditure on goods and services, and the government's gross domestic fixed capital formation (gross investment), totalling £130.3 billion in 1991. The ratio of exhaustive expenditure to GDP, 22.7 per cent in 1991, gives a measure of the share of total domestic resources directly employed by the British state.

Definitions

Exhaustive expenditure

Exhaustive expenditure is government spending which uses up – or exhausts – resources. So it includes all purchases of goods and services, and the costs of directly employing people.

Transfers

Transfers are spending power which the government passes on from the government budget to other private agents.

Table 10.1   **British government accounts: general government, 1991 (£m)**

Expenditure		Income	
Current expenditure on goods and services[1]	118 009	Taxes on income	75 105
of which: defence[2]	24 410	Social security contributions	36 643
health[2]	29 812	Community charge	8 162
education[3]	21 835	Taxes on expenditure	83 023
Subsidies and grants	78 694	Gross trading surplus	119
Debt interest	17 097	Rent and royalties	4 302
		Interest and dividends	5 975
		Other	370
Current expenditure[1]	213 800	*Current receipts*	213 699
Gross domestic fixed capital formation[4]	12 324	Taxes on capital and capital receipts	3 542
Capital grants	6 769		
Capital expenditure	19 093	*Capital receipts*	3 542
Total expenditure	232 893	*Total receipts*	217 241
Balances: financial surplus	−15 652		

Note: elements may not add precisely to totals because of rounding.

[1] Excludes estimated capital consumption, hence 'current expenditure on goods and services' is not identical to 'general government final consumption' in Table 2.5.

[2] Central government only.

[3] Local government only.

[4] Includes value of physical increase in stocks.

Source: *United Kingdom National Accounts* (1992)

Transfers, covering all the other main spending categories, were almost as large at £102.6 billion including social security benefits, grants to individuals or companies, and debt interest. Including these in a ratio of public expenditure to GDP can be misleading, since it involves *double counting*: the transfers are counted twice, once when paid out by the government, and again when spent by the recipients. Nevertheless, the scale of transfers handled by the government is important because, along with exhaustive expenditure, they have to be financed through taxes, borrowing, asset sales, or charges.

Finally, a few warnings about interpreting government expenditure figures. The definition of the public expenditure totals is a convention which excludes a number of the state's economic activities. The total is also highly subject to political manipulation. As an ex-Treasury official explained:

> ... different definitions of public expenditure have been used over the years, and ... the choice of definition is anything but an academic question. It determines what comes within the government's expenditure limits, and ... time after time spending Ministers and Departments have fought to get round the limits by arguing that particular items should not count as public expenditure ...

> *(Pliatsky, 1982, p.156)*

Here then are some ways in which the UK government spending figures do not measure the whole activity of the state. The activity of public enterprises, which despite privatization still had a turnover of £30.6 billion in 1991, is entirely excluded, except for grants and subsidies provided to support their operation. The total also excludes tax expenditures, or 'tax breaks' such as the remaining tax relief on mortgage interest payments which was valued at £5.6 billion in 1991. These are subsidies under another name, which, if collected could be spent. Finally, the government treats as 'negative expenditure', and subtracts, fees and charges (totalling £6.8 billion in 1991) and asset sales (£3.15 billion in 1991), thus reducing the public expenditure total below actual spending. Privatization proceeds from the sale of shares in public companies (£9 billion in 1991) helped finance the expenditure total, reducing the taxation or borrowing required. For all these reasons, you should treat public spending measures and trends with caution.

Why does the state grow?

Now, armed with these definitions and caveats, look at Table 10.2 and answer the following questions.

Table 10.2   **Expenditure of selected OECD states**

(a) Government final consumption expenditure as a % of GDP

Country	1960	1968	1974	1980	1985	1990
USA	16.6	18.8	18.1	17.6	18.4	18.1
Japan	8.0	7.4	9.1	9.8	9.6	9.1
UK	16.4	17.6	20.0	21.2	20.8	19.9
France	14.2	14.8	15.4	18.1	19.4	18.0
Germany (Federal Republic)	13.4	15.5	19.3	20.2	20.1	18.4
Italy	12.0	13.6	13.8	14.7	16.4	17.3
Denmark	13.3	18.6	23.4	26.7	25.3	25.2
Spain	8.3	9.2	10.0	13.3	14.7	15.2
Greece	11.7	12.9	13.8	16.4	20.4	21.2
Portugal	10.5	13.1	14.1	14.5	15.5	16.7

(b) Social security transfers as a % of GDP

Country	1960	1968	1974	1980	1985	1990
USA	5.0	6.4	9.5	10.9	11.0	10.8[1]
Japan	3.8	4.5	6.2	10.1	10.9	11.5
UK	6.8	8.7	9.8	11.7	13.9	12.2
France	13.5	17.0	15.5	19.2	22.1	21.4
Germany (Federal Republic)	12.0	13.7	14.6	16.6	16.2	15.3
Italy	9.8	12.6	13.7	14.1	17.2	18.0
Denmark	7.4	10.8	12.0	16.6	16.3	18.4
Spain	2.3	8.1	9.5	14.2	16.0	15.3[1]
Greece	5.3	8.4	7.1	9.2	14.8	16.0
Portugal	2.9	3.1	5.3	10.6	10.8	12.1[1]

[1] Data for 1989 (USA and Portugal) or 1988 (Spain).

Source: OECD (1992)

Questions

1   Is there evidence in these data of an international squeeze on the growth of the state relative to GDP after the mid 1970s? If so, on which elements of public expenditure, and where?

2   The British government in the 1980s was a leading proponent of squeezing the state. Do these figures suggest Britain had an unusual problem with the growth of the state? It may help to graph the data in order to see the trends clearly.

There is a lot of information in this table. Here are some brief responses to compare with yours:

1   Government final consumption expenditure (the bulk of exhaustive expenditure) rose relative to GDP in the OECD countries up to 1974, but in most countries less rapidly than social security transfers. Final consumption expenditure then levelled off relative to GDP, and fell in a number of countries though by no means in all. Social security expenditure continued to grow through the 1980s relative to GDP in some countries, including some of the poorest European countries, and also, interestingly, in Japan.

2   There appears to be nothing special about trends in the UK, not even the squeeze on government final consumption spending relative to GDP in the 1980s. The government final consumption to GDP ratio is relatively high, and the social security transfers ratio conversely low. Overall, the British government does not stand out as a particularly high spender.

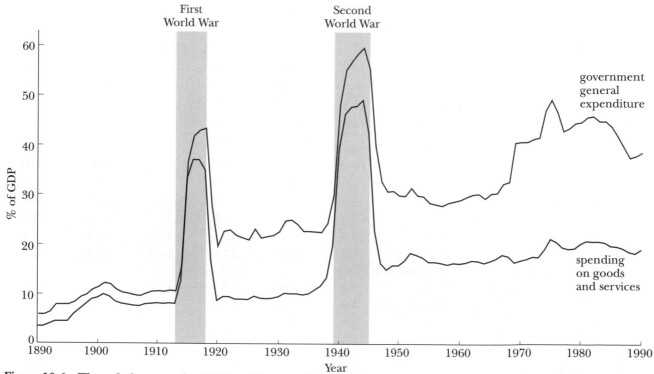

Figure 10.6   **The relative growth of UK public spending, 1890–1990 (data in current market prices)**

Source: Feinstein (1972), *United Kingdom National Accounts* (various years); based on Brown and Jackson (1990) Figure 6.1

With the important exception of low spending Japan, these data suggest a process of convergence in the last 30 years in the ratio of current exhaustive expenditure to GDP in industrialized countries. Over the long period, as Section 1 suggests, the growth in the absolute and relative size of the state in industrialized countries has been rather dramatic. Figure 10.6 illustrates the growth of total government expenditure and of spending on goods and services relative to UK GDP over a century. How would the competing views of the state understand this pattern of growth and slowdown?

The benefits of public spending ...

The public interest view of the state would emphasize the role of public demand in driving the increase in public expenditure. This assumes that a demand for public investment, public services and transfers, is expressed through the ballot box. The idea was first formulated by the nineteenth-century German economist Adolf Wagner in his 'law' of increasing state activity: 'That law is the result of empirical observation in progressive countries at least in our Western European civilisation; its explanation, justification and cause is the pressure for social progress and the resulting changes in the relative spheres of private and public economy, especially compulsory public economy.' (Wagner, 1883, p.8.)

In the early stages of industrialization, for example, economic historians have emphasized the importance of public investment, such as transport infrastructure and research, in supporting industrial growth. Public services such as education, too, can be a crucial underpinning to economic growth. While both Japan and South Korea began their industrialization with a low level of income, their industries drew on a labour force which was markedly better educated than that of their industrializing competitors. Indeed, it is now widely argued that one reason for the competitive difficulties of the US economy is the poor quality of its public education system. So public spending may respond to the needs of industrial competitiveness and economic growth.

Similarly, historians and economic theorists suggest that public spending is income elastic: people seek more public services relative to income, once basic needs are satisfied through private expenditure. Health services, housing improvements, better public transport might be examples of widely desired public services. Finally, redistributive expenditure, for example through the social security system can also be put, on these assumptions, into the same category: an important and desirable activity which societies typically institute when they are rich enough.

... are overstated?

The alternative, private interest view of the state takes the above arguments to be incorrect – indeed naïve. Public expenditure, they argue, has long passed the point where the benefits to the taxpayer justify the tax costs. Politicians respond to sectional interests, and public employees – 'bureaucrats' as they are typically called in this school of thought, with an intended derogatory edge – are both able and eager to expand the government sector. Or, in the words of the television programme, *Yes Minister*. 'The Civil Service does not make profits and losses. Ergo we measure success by the size of our staff and our budget. By definition a big department is more successful than a small one.' (*Yes Minister*, BBC, quoted in Likierman, 1988, p.16.)

X-inefficiency (sometimes called production inefficiency) occurs when the cost curves of a producer in the public or private sector are above their minimum level.

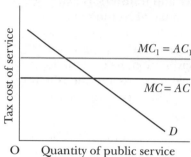

Figure 10.7 **X-inefficiency in the public sector**

Why are public officials (and 'spending Ministers' who also like empires) thought to be able to promote over-expansion? Private interest theory suggests that power is rooted in a monopoly of information. Officials and professionals employed by governments hold information about both costs and benefits of their activity not available to, say, the Finance Ministry which may be trying to control expenditure. Furthermore, they often have a monopoly of supply of a service.

This situation will, on the private interest assumptions about the behaviour of state officials, have two main effects. It will allow expenditure to be pushed up because the benefits can be overstated without challenge. And it will allow costs to be 'padded' to a level above the minimum which provides perks for employees. In the latter case, this creates what economists call X-inefficiency. You came across the idea, though not the phrase, in Chapter 4.

Figure 10.7 shows this effect for the public sector case. Here the demand curve D shows the demand for a public service at various tax costs to voters. The cost curve $MC = AC$ shows minimum costs for producing the service. But costs are artificially raised to $MC_1 = AC_1$. This upward shift in a cost curve displays X-inefficiency: private interest theorists expect the public sector to be highly X-inefficient.

Competing interpretations

To see how evidence can be interpreted in competing ways, look back at Figure 10.6. Peacock and Wiseman, in a study of the growth of UK public expenditure, noted that data of this type show that periods of economic and social upheaval, such as war, appear to have a ratchet effect on public spending, leaving it permanently higher than it otherwise would have been. You can trace this effect in Figure 10.6.

The authors' explanation is an interesting mixture of our two views. As they summed it up: 'governments like to spend more money, … citizens do not like to pay more taxes, and … governments need to pay some attention to the wishes of their citizens' (Peacock and Wiseman, 1961, p.xxiii). However, wars and other upheavals, they suggested, accustom taxpayers to a higher level of taxation, and after the event tax rates do not fall all the way back to old levels. Furthermore, social upheaval exposes both the scale of social problems and the possibilities of government action to deal with them. The two effects, the *displacement effect* on tax tolerance, and the *inspection effect* on knowledge of the benefits of public spending, combine to expand the state. Note that this argument does not challenge the benefits of public spending, only the willingness of citizens to pay for them. In that, it is itself a product of the British post-war social democratic consensus. The more radical challenge to the benefits from government came in the 1980s.

4.3   Reforming Leviathan

The private interest view of the state has been highly influential in the restructuring of the public sector which is under way in many industrialized and less developed countries. Public sector reform has been underpinned by the set of ideas about public production just discussed. Public provision is argued to be inefficient and over large because the 'providers' hold a monopoly (or at least semi-monopoly) of both provision and information about provision.

The proposed reforms follow directly from this argument. If public sector employees are presumed motivated by their own self-interest, then that self-interest needs to be overridden by the interests of those they are there to serve. In the private sector, it is argued, this is achieved through market demand and competition. If individuals do not like the service or price, they can go elsewhere. The private producer will see profits fall, and shareholders and managers will force a change in attitude. In the public sector, on the other hand, there is no equivalent force to market demand, since any employee motivation to serve the public is assumed away in this theoretical model.

The conclusion – and it has been an extremely influential one – is that the only solution to public sector inefficiency and lack of responsiveness to the public is to introduce, as far as is possible, markets and competition into the public sector. There have been two main elements of these reforms, privatization, and the introduction of 'internal markets' into the state. The two reforms are not entirely distinct, but shade into one another.

Privatization

Britain was something of a 'market leader' in privatization, if by this we mean the wholesale disposal of public production activities as going concerns. From 1983, an *ad hoc* idea gradually turned into a fixed government policy for the disposal of publicly-owned industries and utilities. By early 1994, as I write this, only the 'hard cases' of the railways – in the process of privatization – and the core postal services remain.

In the mid 1990s, privatization of this type is being pursued throughout Europe. Eastern European countries have been trying to create, via privatization and new starts, a private industrial sector. Germany, Italy, Japan are all in the process of restructuring public industrial or transport undertakings for sale. Privatization programmes – often slow to take effect – are also widespread in semi-industrialized countries such as Brazil, Argentina and Malaysia.

Concerns about these privatizations have centred on the implications of the terms of privatization (including the price paid and whether monopolies are broken up) for the consumer. Does the privatization in fact bring competition and responsiveness? What are the effects on quality, access and the environment? These questions are asked with particular intensity where the privatized industry produces a highly essential and sensitive product such as clean water.

Other forms of privatization also exist short of sell-off. These include 'contracting out': that is, putting publicly funded services out to tender by private firms. This allows previously public monopolies to be contested by private companies.

Internal markets

At this point, privatization overlaps with the creation of 'internal markets'. The idea here is to create a simulated market within the public sector itself, in order to generate the expected benefits of competition, notably lower costs. Contracting out creates the basis for this: services which remain in public hands have to be organized as trading organizations, in order to compete for and deliver contracts. This introduces internal trading within the public sector.

The mid-1990s public sector reforms have typically involved reorganizing public provision into competing autonomous units or agencies. The intention is generally to free the agencies from day to day political controls, and to force down costs through competitive bidding for contracts. Common objectives have been greater management control of professions, and forcing professional staff to take greater account of costs.

One large-scale creation of an internal public sector 'market' is the 1990s' reform of the British National Health Service. This very large organization, on which the government spent £28.26 billion in 1991, has been broken up into large numbers of autonomous 'provider' units (hospitals, ambulance services, community nursing services). The structure allows private providers to bid for contracts, and the providers to do privately paid work.

I put the word 'market' above in quotation marks, partly because the British government has hesitated in the sensitive case of health care to use the market language, and partly because it is not clear to what extent this is indeed a market. The main reason is that the buyer of services remains, not the patient, but government bodies (the health authorities) and to a smaller extent some primary doctors (general practitioners). Some commentators have called this a 'quasi-market' (Le Grand, 1991).

The structure would clearly be more 'market-like' if people purchased their own health care. This thought has generated proposals for a variety of types of 'vouchers', where people are given notional purchasing power to 'buy' health care, education or training. In health care, there is a particular problem with this: the need for health care is uncertain, hence some form of private or social insurance is required, with access based on professional judgement of need.

That last point raises an important general issue. Reintroducing market systems into public services can be a problem if market failures re-emerge. One important market failure, just referred to, is called by economists *asymmetric information*: the situation where one party to an exchange has more information than the other. Clearly, for markets to work well, customers have to know what they are buying. But this is not always the case. Consumers, far from being sovereign, seem potentially vulnerable in many markets. We rely on the reputation of certain stores, and on health and safety legislation, to reduce the risk of being sold substandard goods. And we eye second-hand cars with suspicion for good reason.

But even more at a disadvantage are the consumers of health care. Users of health services are often at their most vulnerable: ill, often frightened and lacking the information to judge the care on offer. The doctors, who supply the service, monopolize the relevant information. This causes the terms of the exchange to be potentially highly unequal, since one person cannot adequately decide upon their demand price for something they cannot assess. This problem exists potentially in *all* health care systems: going back to markets will not solve it. But a combination of public interest regulation and ethical behaviour by doctors can help.

Ethics, co-operation and public services

So what of professional ethics and public service? For many people, there is a satisfying cynicism about the private interest view of the state. There are clearly widespread inefficiencies in the public sector, and unresponsive bureaucrats most certainly exist world-wide. And those who suggest that the public sector should service the public interest often feel vulnerable to a charge of naïvety.

However, there is something over-simple about *both* the public interest and private interest accounts of the state – and the naïvety does seem to centre on the issue of work motivation. Neil Costello noted in Chapter 4 that it is increasingly recognized that organizational culture matters to the efficiency of *private* firms. Economics increasingly recognizes that people are not motivated at work by cash alone, nor, fortunately, do they always do the minimum they can get away with. How to create work motivation for those who are not closely supervised is a serious issue for economics as well as management theory, and the literature increasingly recognizes both individual incentives and other forms of motivation including trust and loyalty. The issue of work motivation is particularly important in services, public and private, where the quality of service in part simply consists in the relationship between provider and customer or client.

The private interest view, therefore, has provided a necessary and powerful counter to the idea that all public employees seek to serve the public. But in doing so it has gone to the other extreme. The danger of assuming that people are all motivated by self-interest is of course that one may create incentives which undermine public-spirited behaviour. Internal trading, furthermore, can be exceedingly expensive in paperwork and – yes – in bureaucrats. In reaction, a number of public service reformers have sought patterns of restructuring which might reinforce public service motivations rather than undermining them.

The most common approach is again decentralization: but for the purposes of trying to create common cause between provider and client, rather than to create trading units. The idea is rooted in those arguments about governing the commons considered in Section 2. You may remember that the successful co-operative groups cited were small scale and focused on *common*, rather than *free access* property. The strength of the small-scale co-operative arrangements seem to be that they effectively combine self-interest – because of the social costs of bad behaviour – and co-operative instincts – arising from a common culture and a shared sense of a common fate. Decentralization approaches to public service reform seek to reproduce in culturally appropriate ways this benign combination of shared interests and ethics. Whether this can work is a matter for debate.

5   Taxes and markets

I now want to turn in this final section to the question of financing the state. Some public finance comes from charges and from public borrowing (a matter of which you will hear much more in Book 2). But the bulk is financed from taxes.

It is said that nothing is inevitable except death and taxes. In fact, the latter point is not entirely correct. Some people avoid taxation rather successfully. Indeed in practice, societies can only be taxed effectively with their consent, and once tax evasion becomes widespread, it is very hard to reverse. If people do not see some link between tax and benefits, and do not trust the probity of the state, taxation becomes difficult. However, on an individual level, coercion and taxation do feel closely intertwined.

This section on taxation returns to the theme of the effects of the state on the market. It uses supply and demand analysis to show how taxes affect market equilibrium, and to demonstrate that taxes have economic costs. It shows that the elasticity of demand affects who pays a tax. And it completes the earlier discussion of pollution policy by analysing a tax to reduce power station pollution. First, a brief look at the structure of tax finance.

5.1   Financing government

Definition

Direct and indirect taxes

Broadly, direct taxes are taxes levied on individuals or firms. Indirect taxes are taxes levied on goods and services, and hence paid only when you buy the item. Income tax is therefore an example of a direct tax, and value added tax (VAT) an example of an indirect tax.

Look back at Table 10.1. As it shows, most of government revenue comes from taxes (but remember those netted-out charges and asset sales). The most important distinction on this side of the accounts is between direct and indirect taxes

You should be warned that this distinction, while widely used, is not as simple as it looks. This is because the person who effectively pays a tax may not be the person who apparently pays it. There is more on this issue of tax incidence later in this section.

In Britain, the main indirect taxes are value added tax (VAT), other customs and excise duties (mainly on drink, tobacco and petrol), motor vehicle taxation, and (since 1990) national business rates (property taxes). These are all included under 'taxes on expenditure' in Table 10.1, forming 38 per cent of total revenue. The largest direct tax, personal income tax, brought in £57.4 billion out of total taxes on income of £75.1 billion, or 26 per cent of total revenue. Social security contributions (£36.6 billion) are considerably lower than social security payments which were £63 billion: much of social security is financed out of general taxation. Income taxes are a relatively recent institution, made possible by the rise of an effective administration in the nineteenth century. They were deplored by many politicians of the day, including Gladstone, as encouraging public profligacy.

5.2   The market impact of taxation

It is not only market failures which have efficiency costs. Taxes too create inefficiencies in competitive markets. So the decision to try to correct a market failure via a tax-financed public sector activity poses, in its turn, its own costs to the economy. In this section, I examine some of the costs of taxes. I will concentrate on taxes on goods and services, which illustrate the main analytical issues. The important question of taxes on incomes is discussed in Chapter 23.

There are two main types of taxes on goods and services. One is a general sales tax of some kind; a turnover tax, or a value added tax (VAT). The other type is a specific tax on certain items, such as taxes on alcoholic drinks and cigarettes. In Britain these are called excise duties. What is the effect on equilibrium in a market of putting a tax on a good or service?

Consider Figure 10.8. The demand and supply curves, *D* and *S*, show, let us suppose, the demand and supply for petrol in a competitive market. The government has imposed an excise duty of a given cash sum (not a percentage of the price) on each litre of petrol. This has no effect on the demand curve. But from the point of view of the consumer, it shifts the supply curve upwards. S_1 is the supply curve the consumer faces. The vertical distance between the supply curve without the tax, *S*, and S_1 is the

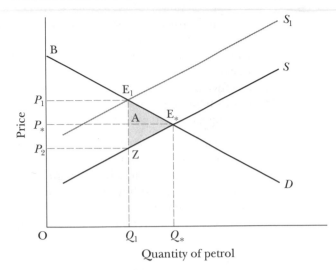

Figure 10.8   **The incidence of a specific tax on petrol**

tax. Since the tax is a fixed cash sum, price for each quantity supplied is increased by precisely that sum, so S and S_1 are parallel.

The market equilibrium with the tax is E_1 with the price to the consumer of P_1 and quantity produced and sold of Q_1. Note that the price to the consumer, P_1, is now greater than the price received by the producer, P_2. The government gets the difference $(P_1 - P_2)$ which equals the tax per litre (less collection costs).

Question

Who pays the tax?

The common-sense answers to this are either: the producers (because they hand the taxes over to the government); or, the consumers (because they pay to put the petrol in their cars). The right answer, however, is that both pay it. This is exactly comparable to the example of regulating pollution discussed in Section 3. Consider Figure 10.8 again, and compare E_* and E_1. Relative to the market equilibrium without the tax, the consumer pays more (P_1 is greater than P_*), and the producer receives less (P_2 is less than P_*) per litre of petrol. So the incidence of the tax is upon both producer and consumer.

In Figure 10.8, the tax paid by the producer is the rectangle P_2ZAP_*, or, to put the same thing another way $(P_* - P_2)Q_1$, that is the difference between the price the producer was receiving before and after the tax, times the new quantity produced. The tax paid by the consumer is the difference between the old price and the new higher price, times the new quantity bought: that is, the rectangle $P_*AE_1P_1$, or $(P_1 - P_*)Q_1$.

Taxation and allocative inefficiency

Chapter 7 introduced the concept of allocative efficiency. If we continue to work within the framework of competitive equilibrium set up in that chapter, then we can draw some further general conclusions about the impact of taxes.

Look back once again at Figure 10.8. I pointed out above that the effect of taxes is to drive a wedge between prices as perceived by producer and

Definition

Tax incidence

Tax incidence is defined by who pays the tax. *Statutory* tax incidence is upon the person legally liable (in my example, the producer, who, I was implicitly assuming, was also the seller). *Economic* tax incidence is upon the person who effectively pays once the new market equilibrium is established.

consumer: the consumer pays more than the producer receives. This has implications for allocative efficiency. As Catherine Price explained in Chapter 7, perfect competition produces an allocatively-efficient outcome because, if all markets are perfectly competitive, then all firms are operating as efficiently as possible in cost terms, and it is not possible – by reallocating goods from one use to another – to make someone better off without making someone else worse off.

This startlingly powerful result is based, as Chapter 7 explained, on some very strong requirements. One of them is that producers and consumers face the same relative prices between goods. Only if this is true will it be the case that, in market equilibrium, the marginal utility which consumers gain from good A as compared to good B will be equal to the rate at which – by reallocating resources at the margin – producers can replace production of good A with good B. To achieve a Pareto optimal market outcome, therefore, the prices to which producers equate marginal costs need to be the same as the prices which consumers face when considering the use of their cash.

Now consider a situation where there is an excise duty on petrol as in Figure 10.8 but not on bicycle tyres. The result is that the relative consumer price between bicycle tyres and petrol differ from the relative prices received by producers. Hence, there is a source of allocative inefficiency. In Figure 10.8, the market equilibrium without the tax is E_*; this, if all markets were perfectly competitive, would be the allocatively-efficient market outcome. Relative to this, the price consumers face, P_1, is too high, and the price the producer receives, P_2, is too low so too little petrol is being consumed. Consumers are reallocating their spending (inefficiently) towards other goods (as well as paying part of their income to the government). So the tax causes the consumption of too few car miles relative to bicycle miles.

Reflection

Can you think of a possible snag with the above example? Does it have anything to do with externalities? Think about this before you read on. You will find a discussion relating to this reflection later in this section.

The general result is that, in the context of a competitive equilibrium, taxes distort the market and create allocative inefficiency. But some taxes distort more than others. The extent to which taxes distort markets depends strongly on the elasticity of demand and supply. This provides one part of the answer to the following frequently asked question.

Why booze?

Every year, the Chancellor of the Exchequer (the British Finance Minister) raises the excise duties on alcoholic drink and cigarettes. When beer and spirits escaped in December 1993, it was a matter to be publicized. The same budget put 11p on a pack of cigarettes and 2p on a bottle of wine. Each year the increases are greeted with groans and protests. Why is booze a target?

There are a number of reasons. One, as for cigarettes, may be to try to reduce consumption of addictive substances. But there are economic reasons why taxing drinking is advantageous. Alcoholic drink tends to have a low price elasticity of demand. As a result, the efficiency costs of taxing

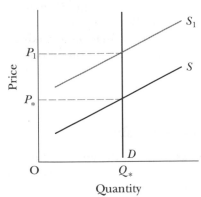

Figure 10.9   A specific tax on a good with inelastic demand

drinking are relatively low. This conclusion emerges from a general argument about taxation and elasticities which was developed in the 1920s by the eminent economist Frank Ramsey. The argument goes as follows. Consider Figure 10.9. This shows a specific tax on a good for which the demand is completely inelastic.

Question

In Figure 10.9, who pays the tax?

In this situation, unlike that in Figure 10.8, the tax is wholly paid by the consumer. The quantity bought remains the same, and the whole additional cost is paid by the consumer to the government. The producer loses nothing.

Furthermore, not only has the tax incidence shifted in Figure 10.9, there is also no net loss to the economy as a whole when demand is inelastic. To see this, look back again at Figure 10.8, and consider the original market equilibrium, E_*. In this situation, the total benefits of the good bought by consumers can be thought of as the area OBE_*Q_*. This represents the total of each unit purchased multiplied by the price consumers would have been willing to pay for it. This price – traced by the demand curve – indicates how consumers valued each successive unit purchased. But all the units were actually purchased at P_*, the market price. So the triangle BP_*E_* is called the *consumer surplus*. This was defined in Chapter 8 as the excess of what consumers would have been willing to pay for a certain quantity of goods over what they actually paid. Now consider the new after-tax equilibrium E_1.

Question

After tax, how big is the consumer surplus?

It has shrunk to BP_1E_1. The government has most of the rest: the rectangle $P_*AE_1P_1$, as already discussed. But there is an element of the old consumer surplus, the triangle AE_1E_* which has vanished. No one has this any more.

There is net loss from the producer side too. Previously the producers received P_* times Q_*, or the rectangle $OP_*E_*Q_*$. After tax they get P_2 times Q_1, or OP_2ZQ_1. The government gets some of the rest (the rectangle P_*AZP_2), and the firm saves its marginal costs of producing all the units between Q_1 and Q_* (the area $Q_1ZE_*Q_*$). But again there is a net loss: the triangle AZE_*.

The sum of the loss to producers and consumers, the whole shaded triangle ZE_1E_* is called the *deadweight loss* from taxation: the loss to producers and consumers which does not go to the government. This deadweight loss is a cost to the economy as a whole of raising taxes.

Question

Now look again at Figure 10.9. How big is the deadweight loss?

The deadweight loss is zero. Because quantity sold does not change, the producers lose nothing and the whole loss to consumers $(P_1 - P_*)Q_*$ goes to the government.

Of course, the demand for alcoholic drink is not wholly inelastic. (If it gets too expensive, some people start making their own.) But after a drop in purchases, after the budget, people do tend to return to their old drinking habits. This discussion is an illustration of two general conclusions about taxes. The more inelastic the demand for a good, the more of the tax is paid by consumers, and the less is the deadweight loss from the tax for the economy as a whole.

What about market failure? Taxes and externalities

I should emphasize that these results, strong as they are, depend on the assumption of perfect competition and no market failure. But we have been at pains to point out earlier in the text that markets are in fact highly imperfect, and much of this chapter has been about market failure. So how do the market failures affect the impact of taxation on markets?

Let me return to the tax on petrol. You may remember that I ended that discussion by saying that the effect of the tax was to cause an inefficiently low use of cars relative to bicycles? And that I then asked if you could think of a snag?

What I had in mind was the following. When you read that conclusion, you might have thought, wait a minute, cars create externalities in the form of exhaust fumes and the resultant health problems in cities, not to mention global warming. So there are market failures in car use. But bicycles seem to create relatively few problems for others. So maybe the tax is not so bad after all? If you did reflect on these issues, then you were quite right. If indeed petrol use, but not bicycle tyre use, generates negative externalities, then a tax on petrol, far from creating a distortion, may at least partly put one right.

Figure 10.10 illustrates the point. Very similar to the diagram which I used to illustrate the discussion of acid rain, this one illustrates the external costs of petrol consumption. A 'green' tax, if calculated correctly, could push consumption down to the efficient point E_*, where $MSC = D$. The tax $(P_* - P)$, goes to the government. There is no deadweight loss at all, since E_*, not E_a is the efficient market equilibrium to which the tax has moved us. If the market is inefficient, then a well-calculated tax can improve market

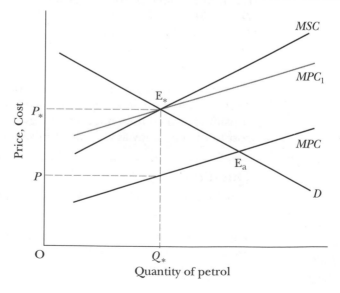

***Figure 10.10* A 'green' tax on petrol**

efficiency. Getting this calculation precisely right is of course very difficult. Getting the direction of change right may, however, be easier.

Taxes and private interests

Question

Pause now and consider: which of our two views of the state has been implicit in this discussion so far?

This whole discussion has been conducted implicitly on the public interest view of the state. Its unstated assumption was that the government will seek to tax efficiently and to correct externalities effectively. Even if it does not behave like this, however, we may still be interested in judging the efficiency of its actions. Private interest theorists have taken a close interest in the way tax and subsidy policy may be swayed by private lobbying, and the efficiency implications of such 'tax breaks'. This has been particularly a concern in the USA, where the lobbying industry has reached startling heights. Private interest analysis is further discussed in Chapter 23.

6   Conclusion: modelling government

This chapter has been concerned with different ways to construct economic models of government in its broadest sense. That is, it has looked at some ways of modelling non-market economic activity, and analysed some of the interactions between governments and markets.

One theme of the chapter has been, how far can we apply market analysis rather directly to government? That is, can we take the assumptions which economists make about economic agents in markets and apply them to decision makers within the state? I have tried to suggest some of the strengths and weaknesses of this influential idea. Alternatively, is there scope for making different economic assumptions in analysing governing: for assuming that people can co-operate voluntarily, or that they work in the public interest? Again, I have tried to give you a flavour of current debates on these issues in a rapidly expanding area of economic analysis.

A central issue in the economic modelling of government is how to incorporate politics into economics. Models of government cannot avoid this since, inevitably, political processes to some extent take the place of market demand in collective provision of services. It is hard to bring politics into economic models, and you may have found the two views of the state which I used to structure this chapter irritatingly polarized and over-simplified. There are certainly many important aspects of the political role of states which are largely absent from this chapter, notably the use of power, and discussion of autocratic and oppressive states beholden primarily to the rich and powerful. Both of the economic models I have been discussing are models of democratic states responding to rather widespread pressures and political demands.

Governments, then, are complex economic agents. Indeed, it is not clear that we should try to model states or governments as single economic agents at all. Nevertheless, I have treated government as a unitary economic agent in most of my discussion of the second main theme of the chapter: the interaction of government and markets. Within this theme, a good deal of the chapter examined the standard justification for government within economic analysis: responding to market failure. While there are many situations which require some form of non-market economic action, from voluntary co-operation to government enforcement, market failure alone is not a sufficient justification for state action. Governments too can be inefficient. Much of the debate today centres on the proper boundaries of state, co-operative and private action, and on the proper economic organization of the state itself, and these issues are far from resolved.

Within this second broad theme of the interaction of state and market, the chapter also examined some of the effects of taxation on markets for goods and services. Here, the general argument is that taxes have economic costs, and that this is one reason why the size of the state is a matter of economic concern. The state is, on any measure, a large economic agent or complex of agents, and its behaviour has widespread effects on the economy.

Finally, two comments on what the chapter does not discuss. First, all the modelling in this chapter of the impact of states on markets has been in a static framework. The concept of efficiency used was that of static allocative efficiency: the best use of resources at a moment in time. There has been no discussion of the important set of issues about dynamic efficiency: that is, the impact of the state on growth and change. Second, the discussion has been largely about government production of goods and services (exhaustive expenditure), and taxation of goods and services. There has been little on redistribution and the taxation of income and wealth. We return to both these important sets of issues later in this text.

CHAPTER 11

MONEY IN MARKET ECONOMIES

by Graham Dawson

1 Introduction: money in the economy

My main objective in this chapter is to enable you to understand the role of money in changing market economies. I want to focus on three aspects of monetary activity: first the use of money in markets for goods and services and then two different ways in which money is itself the object of market transactions, in the domestic money markets and in the foreign exchange markets.

So I start from the question, what functions does money perform in markets for goods and services? I will take up this question in Section 2, by looking briefly at some of the circumstances in which people rely on direct exchange or barter instead of monetary exchange. If we can understand why people sometimes cease to use money in exchanging goods and services, we should be able to clarify why it is that under normal circumstances most of us have no choice but to use it.

Next the chapter examines the domestic money markets where prices take the form of interest rates and the 'goods and services' exchanged are forms of money itself. These are best thought of as claims and promises – promises to pay and claims to be paid. Buying and selling money means taking out and making loans. A debtor exchanges a promise to pay for purchasing power now and is willing to pay, not only the amount borrowed, but interest too. The creditor sacrifices current spending for the sake of the interest to be earned until the loan is repaid. Time and expectations about the future – for example, about the risk that the debtor will be unable to repay the loan – therefore play a central role in these markets and are the sources of much of their complexity.

The money markets are examined in Sections 3, 4 and 5. Once again the supply and demand analysis which you have used in previous chapters provides the theoretical framework. Section 3 looks more closely at the nature of the 'goods and services' traded in money markets, that is to say, at the nature of money itself. Money is being constantly reinvented and financial innovation is a central concern of this section. In fact, it will become clear that it is not possible to draw a watertight distinction between money and non-money, and that it is better to think in terms of degrees of 'moneyness'.

In markets for money, prices take the form of rates of interest and Sections 4 and 5, on the demand for and supply of money, respectively, are linked by the common theme of the determination of interest rates. Are borrowers and lenders price takers? On the demand side, the speculative motive introduces uncertainty about the future into decisions about holding money. As for the supply of money, the question to ask is, is it under the control of the government or does it depend upon the actions of the commercial banks in responding to developments in the 'real' economy of output and jobs? The conclusion drawn is that the answer depends on the institutional structure of the financial sector of the particular economy under consideration. This has implications for one of the issues to be examined in Book 2 – inflation – and I will look ahead very briefly to Chapter 28 where the control of inflation is further discussed.

Many goods markets are international rather than domestic, buyers from one country purchasing goods from sellers in another. This gives rise to another set of markets, examined in Section 6, where money itself, this time in the shape of different national currencies, is bought and sold. The prices in this kind of market are exchange rates, an exchange rate being the price of one national currency measured in terms of another. In recent years there has been much turbulence on the foreign exchange markets and my account of them will develop the theme of monetary disorder in the international sphere. The concepts of supply and demand will be used to analyse exchange rate volatility and the way in which it disrupts the growth of 'the wealth of nations'. This will lead into some of the issues surrounding international trade which will be the subject of Chapters 12 –14.

The money markets, interest rates and exchange rates will be further investigated in Book 2 in connection with monetary policy and international macroeconomic policy co-ordination. For the moment I want to remind you of the place of money and financial institutions in the model of the economy set out in Chapter 2.

In the account of the circular flow of income in Chapter 2, it was explained that each flow of 'real' things such as goods or the services of factors of production is matched by a flow of money travelling in the opposite direction (Figure 11.1). Households exchange their services as factors of production for income paid to them by firms. And firms exchange the goods and services they produce for the money households, as consumers, spend on them. So here is one way in which money plays a part in a model of the economy.

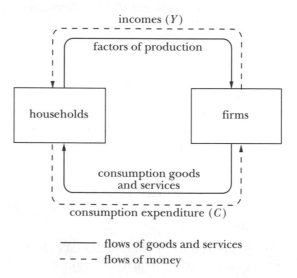

Figure 11.1 **Money in the simple circular flow of income**

——— flows of goods and services
– – – – flows of money

The circular flow model of the economy was made more complicated during the course of Chapter 2, Section 5.1, with the addition of injections into and leakages out of the circular flow. One of the leakages is saving by households, which typically takes the form of putting money into financial institutions such as banks, building societies, pension funds or insurance companies. So in everyday speech we sometimes talk of saving as investing, by which we mean, for example, putting a sum of money into a financial institution with the object of seeing it grow in value. This needs to be distinguished from physical investment which, you will recall, is investment in productive capacity, and is what economists mean when they talk of investment. Sometimes firms finance their investment in this sense by 'ploughing back' some of their own profits. On other occasions, they might approach financial institutions for a loan, in which case the savings of households are repackaged and lent to firms to finance their investment in capital equipment. It is in this sense that financial institutions act as intermediaries between financial investment by households (saving) and physical investment by firms.

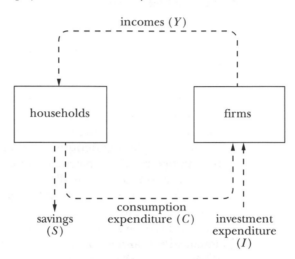

Figure 11.2 **Savings and investment in the circular flow of income**

2   Monetary exchange

2.1   Monetary exchange and barter

The most fundamental function of money is to act as a means of payment, or a medium of exchange, something which is acceptable in exchange for goods or services. In Germany's hyperinflation between 1922 and 1923 people rushed to buy goods as soon as they were paid, before the next leap in prices. Shopkeepers closed after only a few hours so that they could spend their takings before they became worthless – a self-defeating strategy if adopted universally! Eventually many people refused to accept marks – the national currency – in payment for goods and services and the lack of a universally acceptable medium of exchange brought business activity to a standstill, closed factories and threatened the population of some towns with starvation. Hyperinflation clearly rendered the mark unacceptable as a medium of exchange and so it ceased to perform the central function of money. The feverish spending of money as it was received contrasts with the widespread habit under normal, or low-inflationary, circumstances of saving up in order to buy something later. Here money is being used as a means of storing wealth. I want to look at these two functions of money in a little more detail.

A few years ago the French car maker, Renault, made a rather unusual deal with a Third World government, exchanging some of its cars not for money, for the country involved lacked hard currency, but for coffee. The fact that direct exchange without the use of money is still used occasionally in international trade, tells us something about the function of money as a medium of exchange. Barter is feasible in one-off deals often involving governments, where the size of the transaction makes the high transaction costs entailed by non-monetary exchange tolerable. The high cost of arranging a direct barter transaction of this kind arises from the 'double coincidence of wants' that such exchanges require. It is not enough to find a firm selling cars you want to buy; it must also be a firm that is willing to accept the commodity you have to exchange. The costs of searching for such a partner are obviously prohibitive for routine, small denomination transactions.

However, direct barter of this kind is not the only alternative to conventional forms of money. Read the following account of Local Exchange Trading Systems (LETS).

Twelve acorns for a haircut

What do you do when you have a product or a service to sell, but your customers have no money to buy? The answer is you shun sterling and accept 'bobbins', 'acorns', or 'beaks' instead. Recession has worked wonders for home-grown local currencies. Two years ago there were five. Now, nearly 200 towns and cities in the UK are busily buying and selling in their own units.

Businesses including dentists, solicitors, shops and cafes are finding that receiving payment in local barter currencies is a lot better than not trading at all.

The networks, known as Local Exchange Trading Systems, started as a way of helping the unemployed use their skills. Members open an account in the local currency with a central administrator and are issued with a cheque book.

When one member buys something from another, the cheque is sent on to the central administrator who acts as banker, debiting one account and crediting the other. No physical tokens are involved.

Members enter their products or skills for sale in a local directory, with many members offering a range of services. Paul Johnson of Tradelink in Wiltshire is fairly typical: he will program your computer or decorate your house. The founders of the scheme view money with strong suspicion and have a moral repugnance for the payment of interest. But LETS are now moving away from their hippy roots and businesses are beginning to accept payment in LETS units as part of a hard-nosed business strategy.

A solicitor in Stroud who accepts LETS payments does so because he recognises that it brings in customers who otherwise might not use a solicitor. Moreover, customers acquired in that way may be more likely to stay loyal.

'Initially we joined the scheme because we were new in the area and because we felt we couldn't say no,' says Carolyn Whitwell of the Bishopston Trading Company which runs five ethical clothing stores in the west country. 'But now we do it out of pure self interest. Recession has hit us very badly and this is a way of creating a market for people who have no money.' The shop accepts 25 per cent of the value of its goods in LETS units, but when it increased the proportion to 50 per cent during a recent sale, it was surprised at how sharply its turnover increased. […]

At Mills cafe in Stroud, meals and drinks can be bought via LETS and with the proceeds the proprietor is paying workers to till a nearby plot of land for her. Meanwhile, the owner of a market stall has earned enough LETS units to hire an architect to redesign his home.

As the idea of the schemes is to keep business within a community, they tend to work best in places where the spirit of the community is strong. Many of the people who are the keenest users like them because, unlike money, they make trading less impersonal.

'The years of Thatcherism have taken the humanity out of doing business,' says Harry Turner of Letslink UK, the national co-ordinating body. 'There are lots of people who prefer a more human way of doing things.' [...]

LETS keep tabs on how much each member of the scheme is trading and sends them regular statements. There are no credit limits: most feel that the local nature of the schemes as well as the types of products on offer will prevent people from spending a million bobbins and then doing a runner.

The Inland Revenue is watching the growth of LETS with interest. A spokeswoman said that if local currencies were used for occasional babysitting or gardening, the Revenue would turn a blind eye. But if businesses were using them, all amounts should be declared in the usual way.

'And we want tax paid in sterling. The chancellor will not appreciate having his lawn mowed,' she said.

(*Financial Times, 30 November 1993*)

Questions

What problem involved in direct barter is solved by LETS? In view of the success of LETS in solving this problem, why go on using conventional forms of money?

LETS appear to have overcome the problem of the double coincidence of wants. An accountant who wants her garden landscaped does not have to find a landscape gardener who needs a 'wall's worth' of work doing on his accounts; once she has earned enough acorns or whatever, any gardener in the scheme will do. The success of LETS in obviating the need for a double coincidence of wants forces us to think more carefully about the functions of money. What are LETS units such as bobbins if not forms of money?

I think that the answer is implicit in the title of LETS – *Local* Exchange Trading Systems. There are two aspects to the local nature of LETS. First, 'the idea of the schemes is to keep business within a community'. So they are most likely to flourish in villages or small towns or perhaps districts of cities with a strong sense of community. This makes transactions less impersonal, appealing to people 'who prefer a more human way of doing things'. Second, there is no need for credit limits because the local and hence personal nature of LETS means that members can be trusted not to spend 'a million bobbins and then doing a runner'.

By contrast, a currency, however local its origins, has the potential to develop a much wider sphere of use, typically the nation. Under LETS people who have performed services have to rely on the trustworthiness of other members who provide the services they want. Within the local community, this works. But a national system would be much more vulnerable to the risk of default. What makes money different is its impersonality; you do not need to know anything about potential buyers of your services if they are willing to exchange enough money. When you provide the service or hand over the goods you have made, you are not left with only a claim against other members of your local community. Instead you possess something which is guaranteed to be acceptable to every seller in your national economy, something which is therefore almost as good as – in the sense of being readily convertible into – goods themselves.

2.2   Money, time and interest

In a direct barter economy, goods are exchanged for goods. There is always an equilibrium between supply and demand, in that the decision to demand some goods is also a decision to supply other goods of an equivalent amount. But money opens up a gap between the goods you want and the goods you wish to get rid of; there are two transactions, the goods you exchange for money and then money for the goods you want. The seller is not necessarily also a buyer, demanding does not by definition involve supplying. You might decide to hold on to the money you have been paid in exchange for goods or services, perhaps in the expectation that the goods you want to buy will shortly fall in price.

The consequence is that instability is likely to be a feature of a money economy. On the one hand, if people save more than they have been accustomed to do, falling sales will persuade producers to cut output and jobs and unemployment will increase. On the other hand, people might decide to borrow more, bringing forward consumption plans and causing the economy to overheat in an inflationary boom.

The instability of a money economy arises from the fact that people can hold money instead of spending it, that is, from the fact that money can be used as a store of wealth as well as a medium of exchange. What lies behind this function is ultimately a lack of synchronization between receipts of income and items of expenditure. People are therefore faced with a choice as to how best to look after any transitory, or – if they are lucky or frugal – permanent, surplus of income over expenditure.

Other things being equal, it is reasonable for an individual to prefer consumption in the present to consumption in the future. For example, if you were given a choice between £100 now and £100 in twelve months' time, with no strings attached either way, I would expect you to opt for £100 now. I would. After all, who knows what might have happened in a year's time? Taking a cheerful view, you might have won so much money on the national lottery that you would not notice another £100. The downside is, as Keynes put it, 'in the long run we're all dead'. So it is reasonable to prefer £100 now to £100 in a year's time.

The implication is that people with more money than they need to spend now will nevertheless expect to be compensated for lending it to people whose expenditure outstrips their current income. And these would-be

Interest is, from the lender's perspective, the reward or compensation for sacrificing the ability to purchase now. From the borrower's perspective, it is the cost of borrowing, that is of being able to purchase now rather than having to wait.

borrowers will be willing to pay that compensation or reward. So the payment of interest on loans seems to reflect a principle of individual rational economic action – *positive time preference*. And positive time preference, the preference for payment or consumption in the present rather than in the future, in turn reflects uncertainty in the sense of the unknowability of the future.

It is often convenient in economics to talk about the rate of interest, as though there were a single rate of interest which applied to all loans. In fact there are many different rates of interest; for example, not only is 'the' mortgage rate different from the interest rate charged on bank loans for buying cars, different mortgage lenders charge slightly different rates. Different categories of loan attract different rates of interest. That is not terribly helpful until we know which categories attract high rates and which require only low rates.

The most reliable generalization about interest rates is that longer term loans attract higher rates than shorter term loans. The longer the period over which a loan is to be repaid, the longer the time during which consumption by the lender has to be postponed pending the repayment of the loan plus interest and the greater the uncertainty the lender faces. The fact that loans of different time periods attract different rates of interest is known as the *term structure of interest rates*.

Table 11.1   **Selected UK interest rates, June 1993**

	Access rules	**%**
Bank deposit account	Instant access	3.81
Bank deposit account	3 months	5.18
Treasury bills	3 months	5.19
Inter-bank loans	Overnight	5.13
Inter-bank loans	7 days	5.75
Inter-bank loans	1 month	5.91
Inter-bank loans	3 months	5.94
Government bonds		
Short dated	5 years	7.12
Medium dated	10 years	8.00
Long dated	20 years	8.46
Building society[1] mortgage	Variable, e.g. 25 years	8.01

[1] 'Building societies' are mutual societies: financial institutions owned by depositors, set up originally as mortgage lenders.

Source: *Financial Statistics* (1994) no.384, April, Tables 7.1E, p.118 and 7.1H, p.121

Questions

What evidence is there in Table 11.1 of the term structure of interest rates? What other factors might explain the pattern of interest rates shown in Table 11.1?

The term structure of interest rates is most clearly reflected in the rates on inter-bank loans, where the interest rate rises in line with the period of the loan (and there are no other differences to obscure the term structure). The other factors that seem to matter might be classified according to the risks associated with the loan or the standing of the borrower. Mortgage interest rates are relatively low despite the length of the repayment period because they are secured on the house being bought. Interest rates on loans to the public sector tend to be low. Such loans are attractive to risk-averse lenders because they are ultimately backed by the government, which can always as a last resort repay through raising taxes. The various financial assets in Table 11.1 are explained in more detail in Section 3 below.

So far, this all seems to be for the best in the best of all possible worlds. But we have already seen that there is a catch: inflation, especially hyperinflation, means that money can become, in effect, as perishable as apples. No one wants to store their wealth in a form which loses part of its value, or purchasing power, per month.

Of course, in a contemporary monetary economy, they do not have to, because money is usually held as a store of wealth in the form of deposits with a bank or building society. The bank, or other financial institution, pays interest on the money deposited with it. Provided the rate of interest (that is, the rate at which the sum of money deposited is increasing) is at least equal to the rate of inflation (the rate at which it is losing its value), the bank deposit will at least maintain its purchasing power. Hence, the depositor will be particularly interested in the real rate of interest on the deposit.

Definition

Real rate of interest

The real rate of interest is the money or nominal rate adjusted for the rate of inflation.

Calculating the real rate of interest

For example, suppose your deposit is earning 7% per year (the nominal rate of interest) and inflation is running at 3% per year. For low rates of both interest and inflation, simply subtracting the inflation rate from the nominal interest rate will give a rough approximation of the real rate: 4% in this case. However, the real rate of interest can be calculated accurately according to the formula

$$\text{real rate (\%)} = \left(\frac{\text{nominal rate (\%)} + 100}{\text{inflation rate (\%)} + 100} - 1 \right) \times 100$$

So, if r is the real interest rate:

$$r = \left(\frac{7 + 100}{3 + 100} - 1 \right) \times 100$$

$$r = \left(\frac{107}{103} - 1 \right) \times 100$$

$$r = 3.88$$

This might not strike you as a terribly significant improvement in accuracy but at higher rates it can make a big difference, especially if you are working out the interest on a loan of, say, £10 million. Remember the number of decimal places shown in Table 11.1!

Real interest rates are not always positive. In the 1970s inflation sometimes turned out to be considerably higher than expected, with the consequence that real interest rates, adjusted on the basis of past inflation, were sometimes negative.

Question

For example, at one time in the UK even with the nominal interest rate as high as 17%, inflation turned out higher at 22%. What was the real interest rate?

The real interest rate, calculated in the way demonstrated above, was −4.1%, or −4.098% if you want to be more precise. So bank or building society deposits 'growing' at 17% a year in nominal terms were in fact losing a little more than 4% of their value over a year.

There is one more function of money which I want to mention. If something is acceptable in exchange for goods of any kind, then it will be possible to compare the value of any pair of different goods in terms of this widely acceptable something – money. In a monetary economy, the obvious way of answering a question such as 'Is this newspaper worth more or less than this box of matches?' is to find out how much money is needed to buy each of those things. So money comes to be used as a unit of account or measurement.

Why do people want something to perform this accounting or measuring function? One reason of considerable historical importance is the desire of governments to tax their populations. The task of the civil servants who compiled the Domesday Book was made difficult by the limited usage of money in twelfth century England. Was someone who owned three geese, four pigs and a cow 'worth' more, and hence able to pay more tax, than someone who owned two cows, a goat and a sheep? The existence of money prices makes such a calculation simple.

Money facilitates much more than taxation. It was also in the twelfth century that Italian merchants began to draw up formal partnership agreements. An agreement between an investing partner and a travelling partner, who was frequently away buying the goods they would sell, would stipulate that the profits were to be divided equally. This commercial development transformed the role of money as a unit of account. From a unit for the simple recording of cash receipts and expenditures, it became the language of accountancy.

Exercise 11.1

List the three main functions of money outlined in this section.

3   Financial innovation

Having distinguished three main functions of money, I now want to discuss the range of financial assets which perform those functions in contemporary economies. This will be the first step towards understanding the domestic money markets; I will explore the nature of money here and then, in Sections 4 and 5, look at the demand for and supply of it.

3.1   The financial revolution of the 1980s

The idea of changing economies that underlies this text applies particularly forcefully to the monetary or financial sector. Some commentators describe the 1980s as a decade of financial revolution and argue that we will be living with its aftermath for the rest of the century.

This section is organized around the by now familiar ideas of demand and supply, starting with the demand side, with people as 'consumers', or users, of money services. Financial matters probably play a bigger part in most people's lives now than they did back in 1980 or so. Certainly this is the case in the UK economy. Many people who were council tenants in 1980 are repaying mortgages today and have had to cope with historically very high interest rates. As Chapter 3 noted, some existing home-owners borrowed against the increased value of their houses in the 1980s, using a bigger mortgage to buy consumer goods. So, in one way or another many people increased their debts substantially in the 1980s. The main consequence has been an increase in the volatility of the economy. The extra borrowing in the late 1980s fuelled the consumer boom and a rate of growth well above average for several years, which was then followed by the worst recession for 60 years.

A related effect is an increase in uncertainty. Some of those mortgages are endowment mortgages, for which the borrower enters into a savings contract for the period of the loan. Hence the value of the accumulated savings depends on the level of share prices at the end of the mortgage term. More people than ever before are contributing to private pensions and so depend for their standard of living in retirement on the level of share prices perhaps 20 years from now. So monetary phenomena – fluctuations in the price of financial assets and in interest rates – seem to have introduced a considerable degree of uncertainty into many people's lives.

Turning to the supply side, to the financial institutions such as banks and building societies, we can ask 'Where did all this new debt come from? How were the banks and building societies able to meet this demand for extra borrowing?' Well, government policy played a large part, deregulating the financial services industry in the early 1980s. This has blurred some of the hard and fast distinctions we used to be able to make. New products have been developed which combine characteristics that used to be incompatible. It is not so very long ago that UK bank deposits either paid no interest but allowed instant cash withdrawal, or paid interest but allowed cash withdrawal only after, say, seven days' notice. Competition between banks and building societies led to product innovation: the deposit that pays interest *and* allows instant access to cash. And the institutions themselves have become more alike, with banks offering mortgages and building societies loans for purposes other than house buying. One former building society, Abbey National, even turned itself into a bank. It does not end there: department stores such as Debenhams and Marks & Spencer are major financial institutions by virtue of their credit card operations, and Marks & Spencer now offers personal loans. This is a global phenomenon; for example, the third largest financial intermediary in the USA is a department store, Sears Roebuck.

Money is a social creation which is being constantly developed and refined, as financial institutions find new products to fulfil the role which money plays in the economy. I want to develop this line of thought by looking at the changing forms that money, and related assets, take.

3.2   The changing forms of money

It is probably best to think, not in terms of a clear and simple distinction between money and non-money, but instead in terms of a spectrum of assets. At either end we can find things that are unequivocally money or non-money, but in much of the middle section of this range of assets are things which are not unambiguously money or non-money. They share some, but not all, of the characteristics of those objects which everyone agrees are money.

The concept of liquidity enables us to organize these multifarious assets into a spectrum – a spectrum of liquidity. Cash occupies one end of the spectrum of liquidity, as the perfectly liquid asset in the sense that it is generally acceptable in exchange for goods and services. Within the limits of legal tender, its acceptance as a means of payment is even a legal requirement.

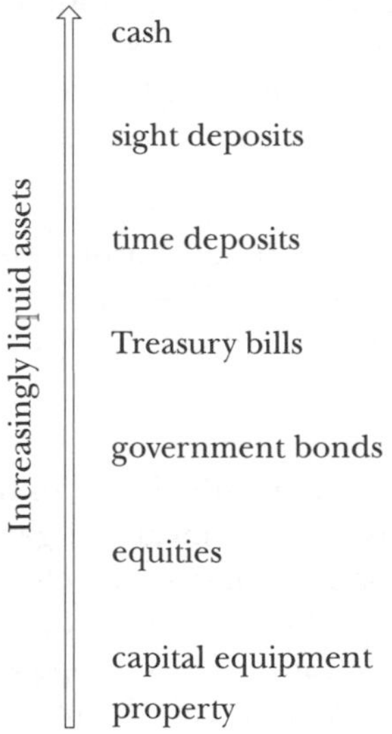

We can now begin to think in terms of degrees of liquidity as a means of classifying assets according to their 'distance' from cash as the paradigm case of a liquid asset. This distance has to be measured along two dimensions or in terms of two criteria. The first is time, how long it takes to convert one asset into another, and the second is probably best thought of as certainty, how certain we can be that the asset will maintain its value when converted into another. The point is that converting an asset into another quickly – selling it and buying something else with the proceeds – may involve having to accept a low price, lower possibly than the original purchase price.

What is happening is that the requirements of money as a medium of exchange and money as a store of wealth are pulling in opposite directions. A medium of exchange is not much use unless it is quickly accessible, while the whole point of a store of wealth is to keep its value intact. Liquidity is a composite notion, which qualifies degree of availability with some idea of the sacrifice, in terms of loss of value, which instant or at least rapid conversion into cash might entail (Figure 11.3).

Cash

Cash is perfectly liquid but inconvenient and in some circumstances dangerous to carry about in large quantities. So the introduction of credit cards in the early 1970s prompted the question, are we heading for 'the cashless society'? This question became topical again in the early 1990s, with the development of electronic funds transfer at point of sale (EFTPOS). Debit cards, as well as credit cards, could now be used in payment for goods.

Definition

Liquidity

The liquidity of an asset is the speed with which it can be converted into cash without loss of value.

Increasingly liquid assets

- cash
- sight deposits
- time deposits
- Treasury bills
- government bonds
- equities
- capital equipment property

Figure 11.3   **The spectrum of liquidity**

Question

Will we go on using cash?

There are two reasons for thinking we will. First, cash involves less time and trouble than 'plastic' for small denomination, everyday transactions such as bars of chocolate and bus fares – hence the 'five items or fewer cash only' checkout found in some supermarkets. Also, the anonymity of cash makes it attractive if you wish to avoid leaving any record of a transaction; for example, income can be earned tax-free in the 'cash-in-hand' economy. Furthermore, given that we might have reason for preferring to use cash, it is now easier than ever before to get hold of it. Another technological innovation, the 'hole in the wall' cash dispenser or automated teller machine (ATM) makes it possible to withdraw cash from your bank account at any time of the day or night.

Current account bank deposits

Traditional current account deposits (also known as sight deposits) allow instant cash withdrawal and are accessible by means of cheques, so they are only a little less liquid than cash. Bank deposits came to be used as a means of payment when depositors wrote to the bank instructing it to transfer money to the account of the person they wished to pay. These letters evolved into a standardized form – the cheque. Unlike bank notes, cheques are not themselves a form of money but rather an instruction issued by a depositor to his or her bank to transfer some of the money deposited with it to another person's account. It is the bank deposit that counts as money – a store of wealth which can also be used by means of cheques as a medium of exchange.

Reflection

Cash and bank deposits have been around for a long time. 'Plastic money' is a much more recent innovation. But, in the light of what I've just said about cheques, you might want to consider whether credit cards are really money at all.

In fact credit cards are not themselves included in any official definition of the money supply because they are regarded as another means of gaining – yes, I'm going to say it – *access* to money (a bank deposit), like cheques and, for that matter, cash dispensers. However, unlike a debit card, a credit card, while you have some unutilized credit on it, increases your potential spending power over and above the money you have in your bank account.

Question

Now that we have looked at current account bank deposits as well as cash, do you think it is cash that is threatened by the increasing use of debit and credit cards?

It looks as though we are heading for a chequeless rather than a cashless society. Once the technology is installed, electronic messages can be sent for a fraction of the £1 it costs to print and process each cheque you use. Bank

Definitions

Credit cards

Credit cards enable you to pay for goods in the shop and then settle your debt with the credit card company, usually by writing a cheque drawn on your bank account. If this is done within six or eight weeks no interest is charged.

Debit cards

Debit cards enable you to pay for goods in the shop by making a direct transfer of funds from your bank account to the shopkeeper's.

accounts will live on, accessed more efficiently by cash dispensers and debit cards. But those bank accounts themselves are changing, mainly because current accounts, offering no protection against rising prices, are unsatisfactory as a store of value.

Time deposits in banks and building societies

Finding something to fulfil that function takes us further along the liquidity spectrum into the section usually regarded as near-money, where we find traditional deposit account bank deposits (also known as time deposits) and building society deposits. They are protected against inflation by the interest they earn, the degree of protection depending on the extent to which inflation is anticipated. A deposit of this kind does not function as a medium of exchange, because it is not accessible by means of cheques.

Question

You might be wondering why I have twice used the word 'traditional' in referring to bank deposits. From your own experience of bank – and building society – deposits, does the distinction between current and deposit account deposits seem entirely valid these days?

In the UK the distinction is in practice becoming rather blurred, as a consequence of financial deregulation in the 1980s. Greater competition between banks and building societies, assisted by computer technology, has led to product innovation in the shape of deposits which try to give customers the best of both worlds – instant cash withdrawal and cheque facilities combined with interest on remaining balances. That is why this particular financial innovation is known as spectrum filling – filling in some of the gaps in the spectrum of liquidity.

3.3   Money and non-money

The next set of items along the liquidity spectrum are non-money ways of storing wealth. Bills and bonds are both ways of making loans to public or private institutions, which count as financial assets to the lender. The essential point is that lending money to someone is a way of storing wealth because it gives the lender, or creditor, a claim on the future income of the borrower, or debtor. If you were to lend me £1000 to be repaid in ten equal monthly instalments including 10 per cent interest on the whole loan, you would have a claim on £110 of my salary for each of the next ten months. So the loan is an *asset* to you, something of value which you own, in the sense that it is going to bring you a flow of income from me until it is repaid in full. The loan is a *liability* to me, because it places me under an obligation to hand over part of my salary to you for the next ten months. In return I have £1000 to spend – the cash is now my asset, the fact that I have to pay it back to you (plus interest) is your asset.

Short-term loans to the government

These are known as Treasury bills in the UK and the USA and are IOUs sold by the central bank on behalf of the government. You buy a Treasury bill with a face value of say £100 and a promise from the government to buy it back from you in three months (91 days to be precise). Bills do not earn any interest but they offer some safeguard against inflation – and the risk of default, admittedly negligible in the case of Treasury bills – through being sold at a discount. You might buy a £100 bill for £97, a discount rate of 3 per cent per quarter. Treasury bills are quite liquid because they can easily be sold without loss of value; you might keep a bill for one month before selling it at £98, still approximately a 3 per cent quarterly discount rate.

Private sector firms can issue commercial bills, while in the UK local authority bills are an important source of short-term finance for local government.

Bonds

Bonds are also a means of making loans but over a longer period of time, years rather than months, and, in the extreme case of perpetuities, they are never repurchased by the original seller. Buying at a discount to make money on repurchase obviously would not be possible, so perpetuities and indeed all bonds pay interest. For bonds other than perpetuities, their usefulness as a means of storing wealth depends on two things: the interest rate and the price at which they can be sold. A fundamental principle of the operation of asset markets is that the interest rate and the price of bonds vary inversely. Here is an example which explains why this is so.

Suppose that several years ago you bought a bond for £100 which pays £10 a year in interest, because the interest rate happened to be 10 per cent when you bought the bond. Regardless of how the interest rate changes during the life of your bond, it will go on paying £10 a year until maturity, when it is redeemed, or bought back, by the government. That is the way the system works: the sum of interest paid annually is calculated as a percentage (the interest rate when the bond was first issued and sold to you) of the face value.

Question

After a year or two, let's say, you need the cash and offer the bond for sale at £100, only to find that no one is remotely interested in taking it off your hands. When you turn to the financial pages of your newspaper you discover that the rate of interest has risen to 20 per cent. What should you do?

Who is going to hand over £100 to get £10 a year from your bond when they can buy a new £100 bond and receive £20 a year? You have no choice but to drop the asking price of your bond to £50, so that its £10 annual pay-out matches the current interest rate. So a rise in the rate of interest has caused a fall in the price of bonds.

The reverse can happen, too. A change in the demand for or supply of bonds, which changes their price, also changes the rate of interest. If you were not alone in wanting to sell bonds, there might be an excess of supply over demand, in which case the price of bonds would fall.

Question

Suppose a new investor can pick up an 'old' bond paying £10 a year for only, let's say, £40, a better deal than paying £100 for a new bond that's going to pay £20 a year (the current interest rate, remember, being 20 per cent). What do you think will happen next?

Now it is the government that has no choice but to offer a higher interest rate, 25 per cent, on new bonds if it wants to go on selling them. So a fall in the price of bonds has caused a rise in the rate of interest. Either way, the price of bonds and the rate of interest vary inversely.

In the UK, the term 'bond' is usually restricted to bonds issued by the government and hence they are also known as government securities or gilt-edged securities ('gilts', for short), the idea being that they are as good as gold, since the government cannot go bankrupt.

Equities

We can think of equities (also known as shares or stocks) as a way of short-circuiting the process of financial intermediation, in the sense that when you buy shares in a company you are putting money directly into it instead of depositing it with a financial institution which then lends it to the company. The share is simply a piece of paper which entitles you to receive a share of the company's profits each year, that is, a dividend. The dividend might turn out to be a better 'return' on your money than the interest it would have earned if placed on deposit. Then again, the company might make a loss and have to suspend dividend payments for a year. Worse still, it might go bankrupt, leaving you some worthless pieces of paper. So buying equities is a relatively high risk method of storing wealth. Since share prices can, as they say in the advertisements, 'go down as well as up' shares are not a very liquid store of wealth either, in that selling them quickly might incur a loss.

Real assets

It is not really possible to generalize very much about the reliability of real assets as a store of wealth; they might be anything from postage stamps to tracts of Scottish moorland. You have to rely on the advice of experts who might be able to accurately predict future price movements of the real asset whose market they know about, or you might play a hunch or use any specialist knowledge you happen to have. Still, some assets can be predicted to continue to be scarce in relation to demand and at times of inflation people buy such 'inflation hedges' precisely for their probable security as stores of wealth. If they increase in price at a faster rate than goods in general – at a faster rate than inflation – then your wealth will not merely be protected against inflation, it will actually appreciate.

3.4   Choosing a portfolio of assets

The spectrum of liquidity displays a range of ways of financing transactions and storing wealth: a range of monetary, near-monetary and non-monetary assets. A *portfolio* is a selection of those assets chosen by, or on behalf of, an agent – an individual, a household, a firm or a financial institution – which wishes to hold liquid money balances and less liquid wealth-storing assets in some satisfactory or perhaps optimal combination. So economic agents face a trade-off between the need to hold enough liquid assets to finance transactions while keeping as much wealth as possible in a form that is at least protected against inflation. However, in selecting a portfolio of assets, agents might be more ambitious, aiming to increase the real value of their wealth rather than merely inflation-proof it. If so, they are faced with another trade-off. There would be no problem if all of those assets which yielded a high return (in terms of interest, dividend or capital gain) also had a low risk attached to holding them. But life is not that simple. The high-performing assets, the ones that *on average* yield a high return, are precisely the ones that carry a high risk. Hence the second trade-off, the need to balance high-performing but high-risk assets with low-performing but low-risk ones.

What does economic theory have to say about portfolio balance decisions? How do economists try to explain the demand to hold money rather than other assets?

4 The demand for money

4.1 The transactions and precautionary motives

In *The General Theory of Employment, Interest and Money*, Keynes distinguished three motives for holding liquid assets, the precautionary and speculative motives, as well as the transactions demand. Economic agents have a minimum unavoidable demand for liquid assets, for cash and easily accessible bank deposits, which is known as the *transactions demand for money*. This demand relates to money's function as a medium of exchange. It therefore arises out of the fact that both households and firms find that the receipt of income and its expenditure are not perfectly synchronized. For example, a household might receive its income on one day of the week or month but spend it bit by bit over the whole period. If we think of the household as a single rational economic agent, it will want to minimize its holdings of money in order to earn interest from bank deposits. So we might imagine the household calculating how much money it needs to keep back for financing the transactions it expects to make until the next receipt of income. This will depend on two things: how many goods it intends to buy; and how much they will cost.

Aggregating this for all households, or the household sector of the economy, the transactions demand for money increases if there is an increase in either or both of (a) real output, the physical quantity of goods and services available for households to buy or (b) the general level of prices, or inflation.

Suppose that in Period 2 it intends to buy no more goods than it did in Period 1, so that it intends to engage in the same number of transactions. If the prices of the goods it intends to buy have on average increased between Periods 1 and 2 (if, in other words, each transaction is on average costing more), it will need more money for those transactions. The implication of this is that the transactions demand for money is a demand for *real money balances*, that is to say, nominal holdings of money adjusted to take account of inflation. What matters is the purchasing power of your holdings of money. So, when prices are rising, you need more nominal money if you are to have the same *real* money balances as before.

The *precautionary demand for money* arises out of a household's or a firm's belief that between now and the next receipt of income some unpredictable event might occur necessitating immediate expenditure out of liquid balances. For a firm, the unforeseen contingency might be a delay in receiving payment, a late payment. A household might face an unexpected bill for repairs to the car or washing machine. The precautionary motive, like the transactions demand, concerns money as a medium of exchange. It, too, depends on nominal income, because the greater a household's income, the more money it is likely to have left over after predicted transactions to set aside for precautionary purposes.

As I said, the transactions demand is a minimum unavoidable demand for liquid assets. Why worry about minimizing your holdings of money? Why not keep all your income in a highly liquid form?

When economists try to throw some light on the nature of choices such as this one, they rely ultimately on the concept of opportunity cost. Consider, for example, a consumer who is trying to decide which one of a number of goods to buy – a video of a favourite film, a water filter jug, a clock or a catflap, let's say. The consumer narrows the choice down to the video or the clock and buys the video. The opportunity cost is the benefit he or she would have enjoyed from owning the clock, which has been sacrificed in order to secure the benefit from the video.

So the answer to the question about not keeping all your assets in a highly liquid form is that you would incur an easily avoidable opportunity cost if you did so. Economic agents in a money economy face a trade-off between liquidity and the prospect of earning some extra income from interest. Cash is perfectly liquid but does not 'grow' because it does not earn interest and, if there is inflation, gradually loses its purchasing power, while a government bond pays interest but is not readily convertible into cash without loss of value. There is an opportunity cost involved in holding only highly liquid assets – the extra income you could have earned from the interest on less liquid assets such as bank and building society deposits which are not instantly accessible and government bonds. So it is not a good idea to hold all your assets in a liquid form; once you have decided on the minimum you need for transactions purposes, the rest, it seems, should be deposited to earn interest.

This means that the transactions motive for holding money – for, as Keynes put it, 'liquidity preference' – depends to some degree on the rate of interest: ' … as the rate of interest falls, it is likely … that more money will be absorbed by liquidity-preference due to the transactions motive. For … the cost of the convenience of plenty of ready cash in terms of loss of interest will be diminished' (Keynes, 1936, pp.171–2).

True, if you are already holding no more than what you think is the minimum amount of cash you need for transactions and precautionary purposes, you will have little scope to reduce it still further. And indeed Keynes noted that the transactions and precautionary motives were 'not very sensitive to changes in the rate of interest as such' (ibid.). Nevertheless, we must add the rate of interest to real output and inflation as determinants of the transactions and precautionary motives for holding money.

Definition

Opportunity cost

The opportunity cost of choosing *a* is the loss of the benefit which would have been gained if *b*, the next best alternative, had been chosen.

4.2   The speculative demand for money

The transactions and precautionary motives concern money as a medium of exchange and are not very sensitive to changes in the rate of interest. The speculative demand for money, by contrast, arises out of its function as a store of wealth and it is a little more complicated than the transactions and precautionary motives. The household or individual acting rationally in the way just discussed holds as much wealth as possible in the form of interest-earning assets such as time bank deposits, bills, bonds and equities – which I will follow Keynes in referring to simply as 'bonds' for short in the analysis which follows. But immediately there is a complication. The efficacy of storing wealth in the form of bonds (in this umbrella sense) rather than money, depends not only on the rate of interest but also on any capital gain or loss that might occur following a change in the price of bonds. Not too much of a complication perhaps, but as we saw above, the rate of interest and the price of bonds are not independent of one another but vary inversely.

What are the implications of this for decisions about holding money? Consider a large firm which has to decide what to do with the cash generated by the day's business. If the price of bonds is low and the rate of interest high, the firm puts all its money over and above transactions and precautionary balances into bonds. That way it earns high interest on the bonds until the interest rate falls and the price of bonds rises, when it sells all its bonds at a capital gain. If the price of bonds is high and the rate of interest low, the firm sells all its bonds and holds all its wealth in the form of money, for two reasons. The first is one we have already encountered: the opportunity cost of doing so – the rate of interest it could earn by holding bonds – is low, so there is nothing much to be lost by holding money. The second is the essence of the speculative motive: the firm wants to be in a position to buy bonds as soon as their price falls, so that it can hold them (earning a high rate of interest) until the next price rise, when it sells at another capital gain.

Notice that the speculative demand for money entails holding it, not as a source of any benefit at the time, nor because there are significant rewards actually accompanying the holding of money. No, the point is that the speculative demand involves holding money purely for the sake of being in a position, at some unknown time in the future, to buy something – bonds – with the object of selling them later at a capital gain. We are now in a position to see why Keynes believed that changes in the rate of interest could cause 'wide fluctuations in liquidity-preference due to the speculative-motive' (Keynes, 1936, p.171).

Question

Does the way in which firms (and other economic agents) switch from bonds to money and back again give rise to a systematic relationship between the rate of interest and the speculative demand for money?

The speculative demand for money varies inversely with the rate of interest. At a high rate of interest, firms and households buy bonds, their price being low, and so they do not hold any money except the minimum required for transactions and precautionary purposes. When the rate of interest is low, and the price of bonds high, they hold all their wealth as money in readiness for future opportunities to speculate in bonds.

I have now argued that the transactions and precautionary motives to a limited degree, and the speculative motive to a much greater degree, vary systematically with the rate of interest. This relationship can be depicted using a demand for money curve, putting the rate of interest on the vertical axis and the quantity of money demanded on the horizontal axis.

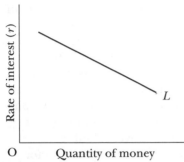

Figure 11.4   **The demand for money curve**

The demand for money curve labelled *L* for liquidity is downward sloping for two reasons. First, the opportunity cost of holding money for transactions purposes means that the demand for money responds to changes in the rate of interest, although only to a limited degree. In other words, the transactions demand for money is relatively inelastic with respect to the rate of interest and the curve therefore slopes downwards rather steeply. Second, the speculative demand is more elastic, which means that we should draw the demand for money curve as a whole, adding the speculative to the transactions (and precautionary) demands, with a relatively shallow slope.

It is worth thinking a little more about the speculative demand. A necessary condition of there being a speculative demand for money is uncertainty about the future course of the rate of interest. If everyone knows what the rate of interest is going to be at some future time, it is impossible for anyone to make money from speculation. Suppose you decide to sell bonds because they are paying what you regard as a rather low rate of interest and seem to you to be rather high in price. If you are right and the rate of interest subsequently rises while bond prices fall, you will have sufficient liquidity to buy back some cheap bonds in the expectation of a speculative gain from selling them as soon as they next rise in price. But what if everyone else thinks the same way? Well, you will not find anyone to buy the bonds you want to sell; they, too, will be trying to sell their bonds. So there cannot be a market in bonds at all unless there are people with different views about the future rate of interest and price of bonds. Otherwise, at any one time there would be people willing to buy but no one willing to sell, or vice versa.

In reality, of course, we can never know what the future holds and hence there is scope for a considerable range of expectations about the future rate of interest and price of bonds. It is these differences of opinion which give rise to sellers as well as buyers. The successful speculator is the person who has the right hunch today about the way the market will go tomorrow. In recent times the most spectacular example is from the foreign exchange market, where Mr George Soros made $1 billion by guessing correctly that sterling was going to be withdrawn from the Exchange Rate Mechanism (ERM) (see Section 6).

5   The supply of money

5.1   Narrow money, broad money and the economy

Since money performs several functions and different forms of money are more or less suitable as a medium of exchange or a store of wealth, it is not possible to identify a single measure which everyone will accept as 'the' money supply. Several distinct measures have been devised by putting figures on progressively wider slices of the first half or so of the spectrum of liquidity. The narrowest definition of money used in the UK is M0, comprising cash in circulation with the public and in the commercial banks' tills and cash balances held by the banks at the Bank of England. At the other extreme is M4, which includes a number of less liquid assets held as a store of wealth but in many cases almost immediately available for use as a medium of exchange. M4 comprises cash in circulation with the public plus sterling private sector sight and time deposits held at banks and building societies (minus building society deposits in banks to avoid double counting). So, provided a deposit is held in sterling by any private sector agent (individual, household or firm), it will be counted in M4, regardless of whether it is or is not accessible by cheque, or earns interest. M4 grew more rapidly than M0 throughout the 1980s (Figure 11.5), with implications to be discussed in Section 5.3.

The government is interested in controlling the quantity of money supplied at the intersection of the demand and supply curves in the money market – the quantity traded. One way of doing this is to operate on the demand side, which will involve changing interest rates because the demand for money is influenced by interest rates (Section 4). The alternative is to operate on the supply side.

In this section I want to examine two answers to a question about the supply side of the money market: who controls the supply of money to the money market – government or banks? I will also examine the implications of these two answers for the question of how the government can try to control the money supply in the sense of the quantity of money traded, the amount of

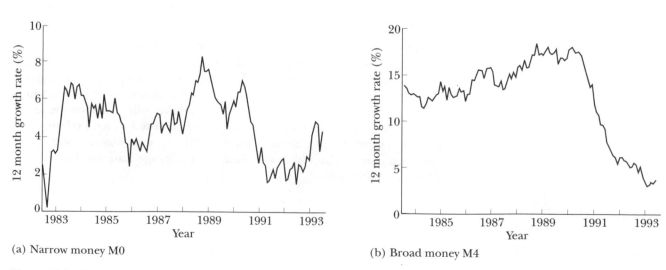

(a) Narrow money M0

(b) Broad money M4

Figure 11.5   **The growth rates of narrow money (M0) and broad money (M4) in the UK, 1982–93**

Source: *Economic Briefing* (1993) no.5, August

narrow money (M0) or broad money (M4) actually sloshing around the economy.

This leads into the last question to be raised in this section: why does the government wish to control the money supply? All I intend to do is to foreshadow the discussions of macroeconomic issues in Book 2, in particular Chapters 24, 25 and 28. My aim here is to indicate very briefly some of the ways in which events in the money market impinge upon the rest of the economy, with implications for inflation, economic growth and unemployment.

5.2   The government and the money supply

The first answer I want to consider is that it is the government which determines the supply of money to the money market by issuing a certain amount of cash to the commercial banks, which use it to create bank deposits in an almost mechanical way. But, first, what exactly does it mean to say that banks create bank deposits? So far I have discussed bank deposits as if they were all created by people going along to a bank with some cash and handing it over to the bank in return for interest. Now it is time to recognize that bank deposits are also created by the banks themselves. Suppose you go to a bank and ask for a loan. In deciding whether to grant you a loan, the bank is in fact deciding whether to create a deposit in your favour out of nothing, from scratch if you like, on the basis that you will repay, with interest, the money you spend from the deposit. Opening such a deposit is a way of lending you money, or granting you credit, so this process is known as *credit creation*. Credit creation therefore adds to the money supply, on all but its narrowest definition (M0).

The multiplier model of credit creation is based on the concept of *fractional reserve banking*, meaning that a bank holds a liquid asset such as cash in just sufficient quantities to cover expected withdrawals. Banks can use an increase in their liquid assets to generate a multiple expansion of their deposits. Suppose that the OU Bank is the only bank in a hypothetical economy and has deposits of £100 million, of which £10 million are kept as cash and £90 million are lent to customers. The bank is operating a 10 per cent *liquidity ratio*: only 10 per cent of its deposits are in a liquid form, cash, because the people who run the OU Bank have learned by experience that their customers, in the aggregate, never want to withdraw more than £10 million when deposits are £100 million. OU Bank now finds that its customers are depositing extra cash with them. The bankers soon realize that they have £1 million they do not need to meet expected withdrawals from existing deposits. So, in accordance with their customary 10 per cent liquidity ratio, they advance £9 million in new loans, knowing that the 'new' £1 million cash will service the expected demand for cash. As long as they are correct in their assumption that their new borrowers will never want to withdraw more than £1 million cash, the system works. A cash injection of only £1 million has enabled the OU Bank to create no less than £9 million of new money (or, since it takes the form of loans, credit).

In a more realistic economy with a number of banks, the net result is the same. Let us say there are 1000 banks of equal size. The OU Bank receives £1000 in new cash deposits. Unlike the time when it was the only bank in town, it cannot create £9000 of new deposits keeping the £1000 in reserve for expected withdrawals. If it were to allow applicants to open £9000 in new accounts against which they could write cheques, they would buy goods, paying by cheque. The sellers of the goods would pay the cheques into their own banks, which would be cleared by a transfer of cash from OU Bank. But OU Bank has only £1000 in reserve, so it would soon collapse, unable to meet demands for cash from the other banks.

In order to avoid this catastrophe, OU Bank, on receipt of the £1000 in cash, lends only £900, holding on to £100, thereby preserving its 10 per cent liquidity ratio. The other £900 eventually ends up with the other banks, once cheques drawn on the new OU Bank deposits have been cleared. These banks now have, in aggregate, an extra £900 in cash. Each one lends a percentage of its share of that cash, just as OU Bank did to set the process in motion, and cheques are drawn against the new deposits. These are paid into some of the banks and cash is transferred to them. And so the process begins another round. The banks continue to create new deposits by advancing loans to customers, the amount of money created each time round diminishing ultimately to nothing. At that point, the outcome is the same as in the single bank economy, because, although cash is lost to each bank at each stage of the process, none is lost to the banking system as a whole.

The formula for calculating the amount of new deposits created when the banking system receives a cash injection from the government is known as the money multiplier and, in the hypothetical economy I have described, is simply the inverse of the liquidity ratio. Remember that the liquidity ratio is the ratio of cash to total deposits. So, if the liquidity ratio is 10 per cent, the value of the money multiplier is 10, that is, the eventual increase in deposits is ten times the size of the initial cash injection.

$$\text{money multiplier} = \frac{1}{\text{liquidity ratio}}$$

Once we have worked out the value of the money multiplier, we can easily calculate the stock of money in the economy after the new deposits have been created. Because of its role in generating money (deposits), cash in circulation with the public or in the tills of the banks is known as *high-powered money* or the *monetary base*:

$$\text{money stock} = \text{money multiplier} \times \text{the monetary base}$$

The cash which comprises the monetary base may be in circulation with the public, in the tills of the commercial banks or held on deposit for the commercial banks by the central bank. How does an increase in the monetary base actually come about? Let us say that the government wishes to engineer a multiple expansion of the money supply by increasing the monetary base. There are two ways in which it can do this.

First, it can 'print money'. What happens is that the government issues some new bonds and sells them to the central bank, which pays for them by increasing the government's deposits with it. So the government has borrowed from the central bank, since the bonds will one day have to be redeemed. In the meantime the government can write cheques against the new deposits to finance any expenditure in excess of tax revenues it may wish to undertake. The commercial banks hold some of their liquid assets as cash deposited with the central bank – the government's bank. When the recipients of the government's cheques present them to the central bank for payment, it simply decreases the government's deposit and increases the

Definition

Open market operations

Open market operations are purchases or sales of bonds by the central bank on behalf of the government. Purchases of bonds can be used by the authorities to increase the money supply, because they increase the commercial banks' cash reserves and make possible a multiple expansion of bank deposits. Sales of bonds can be used by the authorities to try to reduce the money supply, because they decrease the commercial banks' cash reserves and may make necessary a multiple contraction of bank deposits.

commercial banks' deposits by the appropriate amount. These deposits are part of the monetary base, because they count as commercial banks' cash reserves.

Second, the government can instruct the central bank to engage in open market operations, in this case to buy bonds on its behalf from private individuals or institutions such as pension funds. The economic agents who sold the bonds to the government are now in receipt of cheques, which they pay into their deposits with the commercial banks. As before, the commercial banks present them to the central bank for payment and their cash deposits at the central bank are increased accordingly.

We can now start to draw a supply curve for money, relating money supply to the rate of interest. In this multiplier model of credit creation, the money supply curve is vertical because the money supply does not vary according to the rate of interest but is determined as a matter of policy by the monetary authorities (the government and/or the central bank). The money supply is said to be determined exogenously. That is, it is not a function of the level of national income but is the product of government policy. I want to consider very briefly the implications of this exogenously determined money supply for money market equilibrium and the interaction of the monetary and real sectors of the economy.

In Section 4 we saw that the demand for money curve is downward sloping, indicating an increasing willingness to hold money as interest rates fall. As with all demand curves, the demand for money curve is drawn on the assumption of other things being equal. Let us relax that assumption and see what happens when the demand for money curve shifts. Suppose that initially, the money supply is set by the government at M and the demand for money curve is at L_1, giving an equilibrium rate of interest of r_1 (Figure 11.6). Suppose that there is a change in the conditions of the demand for money, increasing people's willingness to hold money at each and every rate of interest and therefore shifting the curve to the right from L_1 to L_2. Think, for example, of the transactions demand for money. If the price level rose, people would want more money to engage in the accustomed number of transactions, or in other words, to maintain the real value or purchasing power of their money balances. So the demand for money curve shifts. At the initial interest rate, r_1, people sell bonds to increase their (nominal)

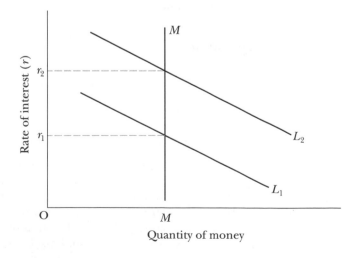

Figure 11.6   Money market equilibrium with exogenous money supply

money balances. This causes bond prices to fall, and hence the rate of interest to rise. Once it has risen from r_1 to r_2 the money market is back in equilibrium.

This rise in the rate of interest has important effects on the rest of the economy. The rate of interest has a dual significance as the cost of borrowing as well as the reward for surrendering liquidity. So credit creation slows down when the rate of interest rises. An increase in the cost of borrowing dissuades some people from going along to the bank to arrange a loan. They might be consumers who now have to shelve plans for credit-financed purchases, or firms which decide not to proceed with investment projects. There will be less demand for goods throughout the economy, curbing the inflation that disturbed the initial money market equilibrium in the example just given. So the exogenously determined money supply seems to provide the economy with a self-adjusting mechanism, causing in this case a rise in the rate of interest which chokes off any further inflation.

The multiplier model of credit creation discussed in this section, with its assumption that banks operate within a liquidity ratio constraint, is not universally applicable: ' ... in the UK at least, banks do not observe fixed ratios nor have they ever done so. In some countries the model can be defended by reference to legally imposed ratios (e.g. in Germany, the USA and Australia), but not in the UK' (Gowland, 1985, p.208).

5.3   Commercial banks and credit creation

The alternative approach to explaining the money supply sees money as determined *endogenously*, as a function of the level of national income. The commercial banks meet their customers' demand for loans and then take steps to acquire the necessary amount of liquid assets. In the UK, the central bank – the Bank of England – acts as 'lender of last resort' to the commercial banks, guaranteeing to lend them whatever liquid funds might be necessary to prevent even the remotest possibility of a collapse of the banking system through an unexpectedly large demand for cash withdrawal by the public. So in this model it is the government, through its agent, the Bank of England, that passively responds to the public's demand for credit. At any rate of interest, it effectively expands the money supply to accommodate whatever level of expenditure is generated by the level of national income.

Question

What is the implication of this view for the supply curve of money?

The money supply curve will be infinitely elastic, or horizontal, since the government is willing to supply whatever amount of money (liquid assets) the banks need to support their lending.

In order to add some detail to this picture, we need to examine the banks' balance sheet (Table 11.2). Assets are banks' claims on other economic agents and institutions, while liabilities are the claims of those institutions on banks. Every transaction creates both an asset and a liability. For example, depositing £100 in cash with a bank simultaneously constitutes £100 of assets – specifically, liquid assets which the bank can use to create money – and £100 of liabilities, namely the depositor's right to withdraw the cash (or write cheques which will eventually have the same effect). So total assets are always and necessarily balanced by total liabilities.

Table 11.2 **Banks in the UK: summary balance sheet, March 1994**

Assets (£m)		Liabilities (£m)	
Sterling		Sterling	
Cash	5 379	Sight deposits	204 779
Bills	169 842	Time deposits	287 089
Investments	49 257	CDs[1]	59 045
Advances	384 050		
Lending in other currencies	828 285	Deposits in other currencies	813 008
Miscellaneous assets	63 833	Miscellaneous liabilities	136 725
Total assets	1 500 646	Total liabilities	1 500 646

[1] Certificates of Deposit (CDs) are issued to firms which deposit money with a bank for a fixed period of time in return, of course, for the payment of interest. If the firm needs the money back, it can sell the CD.

Source: compiled from *Bank of England Quarterly Bulletin* (May, 1994)

In managing their portfolio of assets, banks face a trade-off similar to that encountered by other economic agents in deciding how best to store their wealth. This time the trade-off is between liquidity and profitability. A bank's revenue and hence its profits comes from the interest it charges borrowers, so liquid assets such as cash, which the bank does not lend but keeps in reserve, are not profitable. Households and firms are in general willing to pay higher rates of interest for longer term loans, which enable them to make purchases or undertake investment projects they would otherwise have to delay for several years. So the most profitable of a bank's assets are also its least liquid, in that the loans are not convertible into cash in full until the end of the term. In managing their assets, therefore, banks have to strike a balance between maintaining liquid assets at a level which is sufficient to meet demands for cash withdrawal and holding relatively illiquid but interest-bearing assets to earn satisfactory profits.

Let us now apply the profit maximizing model, already developed for firms in Chapter 4, to the behaviour of a bank. The bank's 'output' consists, perhaps somewhat intangibly, of loans to customers, since it is in the business of credit creation. This output could be measured in terms of the value of outstanding loans; I have shown it increasing along the horizontal axis of Figure 11.7. The bank's revenue is the interest it charges on those loans. The demand for money curve is downward sloping, as we have seen, so I can assume that the bank (not being perfectly competitive) faces a downward sloping *MR* curve (*MR*$_1$ in Figure 11.7). The increase in total revenue from interest each time the bank advances another loan to a customer declines because the rate of interest must fall to persuade people to borrow more money. The *MC* curve represents the increase in total costs which is incurred each time the bank induces another deposit of cash, these 'costs of production' comprising the interest paid to depositors plus administrative costs. I assume in Figure 11.7 that marginal costs are constant. The profit maximizing volume of credit is Q_*.

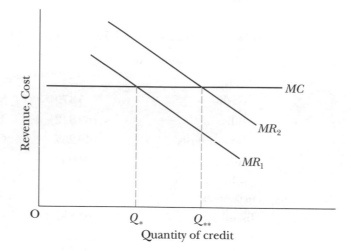

Figure 11.7   **The profit-maximizing model of credit creation by banks**

Question

How would an increase in the level of national income affect the equilibrium volume of credit?

The *MR* curve would shift to the right to MR_2 in Figure 11.7 because people are now better off and therefore need to hold more money to finance the greater number of transactions they can afford. This increase in the demand for credit at the prevailing rate of interest raises the bank's total revenue (and profits) at the new equilibrium volume of credit Q_{**}.

The essential insight of this model is that it is the commercial banks and ultimately the level of economic activity, not the government, that determine the money supply. In other words, the commercial banks will manage to supply whatever level of borrowing is demanded by credit-worthy customers, giving rise to a horizontal money supply curve M_1 in Figure 11.8.

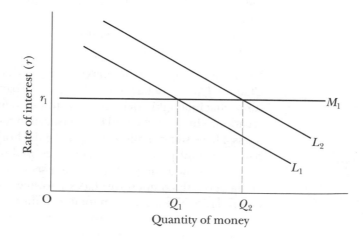

Figure 11.8   **Money market equilibrium with endogenous money supply**

In the early 1990s the UK government in effect acknowledged the reality of this situation and the limitations on the conduct of monetary policy it implies:

> Similarly monetary policy can never, at least in a world where money includes deposits with private sector banks, be simply a question of the authorities deciding on the quantity of money it will allow to circulate in the economy.
>
> *(Economic Briefing, 1993, no.5, August)*

What, then, can the monetary authorities – in the UK, the Treasury and the Bank of England – do if they believe that the money supply is too high or too low? The simple answer is that they can adjust interest rates (*Economic Briefing*, 1993, no.5, August).

Let us suppose, for example, that once again the initial equilibrium in the money market is disturbed by inflation (Figure 11.8). The increase in the demand for money for transactions purposes shifts the demand for money curve to the right, as before with an exogenous money supply. The difference is that the endogenous money supply curve is horizontal, which shows that the increase in the demand for money is met by the banks' expanding credit from Q_1 to Q_2 at the prevailing rate of interest r_1. So the money supply increases to accommodate the increase in demand, with the consequence that people can finance the accustomed number of transactions despite their higher average price. The inflation that started the process is unchecked; there is no self-adjusting mechanism in the money market to eliminate it.

The government could choose to intervene by raising the rate of interest. This would shift the money supply curve upwards from M_1 to M_2 in Figure 11.9 and return the money supply (in the sense of the quantity of money traded in the money market and hence available to finance transactions – the 'sloshing around the economy' sense) to Q_1. It is not unreasonable to interpret events in the UK economy in the late 1980s in this way. From 1982, the economy was expanding strongly and monetary growth was rapid as Figure 11.5 showed. Inflation accelerated in the late 1980s and the government responded by raising the rate of interest (Figure 11.10), with dramatic effects on monetary growth especially M4 (Figure 11.5b).

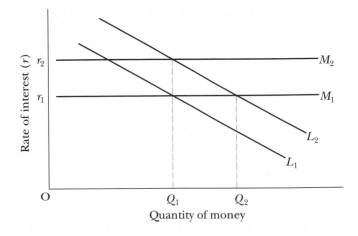

***Figure 11.9* Anti-inflationary monetary policy with endogenous money supply**

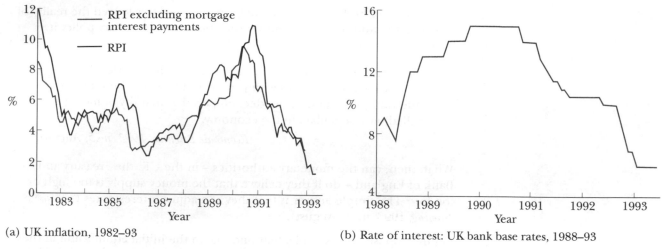

(a) UK inflation, 1982–93

(b) Rate of interest: UK bank base rates, 1988–93

Figure 11.10   UK inflation (Retail Price Index) and the rate of interest

Source: *Economic Briefing* (1993) no.5, August

6   International monetary disorder

Definitions

Bilateral exchange rate

The bilateral exchange rate is the number of units of foreign currency that exchange for one unit of the home currency. So if the exchange rate between sterling and the US dollar is £1 = $1.50, it takes $1.50 to buy £1.

Effective exchange rate

The effective exchange rate is the weighted average value of the home currency against a basket of foreign currencies, expressed as an index number.

6.1   The foreign exchange market

Monetary disorder can affect not only trade within a national economy, when hyperinflation makes its currency worthless, but also international trade when something goes wrong with the system for exchanging one national currency for another. The price of one currency in terms of another, that is, the exchange rate, is influenced by the forces of supply and demand, with governments frequently intervening to limit exchange rate movements or suppress them almost entirely in a fixed exchange rate system. This section will enable you to consolidate what you have learned about supply and demand in Chapter 7 and will at the same time introduce the issue of exchange rate volatility. Since the early 1970s exchange rate movements have at times been so rapid and on such a scale as to exemplify international monetary disorder. Policy responses to exchange rate instability will be discussed in Chapters 19 and 28.

There are several ways of measuring exchange rates, as the definitions show. The most commonly used is the bilateral exchange rate between two currencies. The effective exchange rate is a more general measure of a currency's price against others. The sterling effective exchange rate is the average value of the pound sterling against the currencies of the UK's major trading partners, each currency being weighted according to the amount of trade between its 'parent' nation and the UK. In March 1993 the sterling effective exchange rate was 77.3, indicating that sterling had then lost roughly a quarter of its value since the base year of 1985.

The foreign exchange market consists of dealers all over the world buying and selling currencies through telecommunications networks. It operates 24 hours every day of the year, in that if London or Frankfurt is closed, Hong Kong or Tokyo will be open. As in any other market, the equilibrium price is determined by supply and demand. Let us now consider who supplies currencies on the foreign exchange market and who buys them.

Question

List as many reasons as you can think of for buying a foreign currency – they might be the reasons which have actually led you to buy a foreign currency or they might be hypothetical. Why might firms and governments buy or sell currencies?

The only reason I've ever had for buying a foreign currency is to have some money to spend while travelling abroad. In a sense, firms have bought foreign currencies on my behalf, so that, for example, they could import the Japanese camera I bought a couple of years ago. For all I know, the pension fund I belong to has also bought foreign currency in the interests of future pensioners such as myself, so that it can buy foreign assets of some sort, such as shares in Toyota or US government securities. All these are straightforward trading reasons for buying foreign currency. Some relate to transactions under the current account (imported goods, services purchased abroad) or the capital account (foreign shares and government securities) of the balance of payments (the balance of payments is explained in Chapter 12, Section 2.1). These transactions give rise not only to a demand for foreign currencies but also to a supply of domestic currency, which is used to buy the foreign currency. Similar transactions abroad give rise to a demand for the domestic currency and a corresponding supply of various foreign currencies.

Figure 11.11 is essentially a conventional supply and demand diagram, with the 'price' on the vertical axis being the sterling exchange rate against the dollar and the quantity on the horizontal axis being the number of pounds sterling. The sterling demand curve slopes downwards. As you know, most demand curves do, but it is worth working out just why this one does. At a lower sterling exchange rate, the price in dollars of UK goods exported to the USA will be lower. This leads to an increase in the demand for UK goods and hence for pounds to purchase these goods.

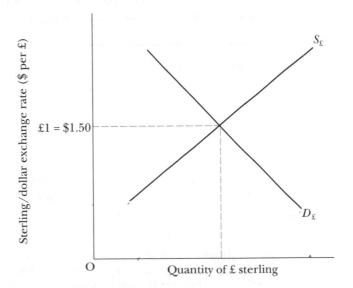

Figure 11.11   **The foreign exchange market for £ sterling**

Question

What assumption am I making about US residents' demand for UK goods?

I am assuming that US residents' demand for UK goods is not perfectly price inelastic, so that when the dollar price of UK goods falls, the demand for them increases.

The supply curve of sterling represents the desire of holders of sterling to sell sterling for dollars in order to buy US goods. It slopes upwards, indicating that a lower sterling exchange rate raises the price in pounds of US goods and hence reduces demand for them in the UK. If we assume that this demand, too, is relatively price elastic, the fall in demand will be greater in percentage terms than the price rise. So the demand for US dollars, and hence the supply of pounds sterling to buy these dollars, will fall.

The equilibrium exchange rate of £1 = $1.50 in Figure 11.11 changes whenever a change in the conditions of supply or demand shifts the relevant curve. For example, UK residents' demand for US goods increases when their real incomes increase.

Question

Yes, I'm making another assumption. What is it this time?

The assumption this time is about the income elasticity of demand for US goods. I am assuming that they are what economists call normal goods, that is, they have a positive income elasticity of demand.

Inflation also comes into the picture. If UK inflation is persistently and substantially higher than that in other industrial countries we would expect, other things being equal, to find US consumers switching to, say, German or Japanese goods or to domestic products. Some UK consumers will also switch to relatively cheaper US goods. Higher UK inflation will therefore have a double effect on the exchange rate.

Exercise 11.2

1   Draw a foreign exchange market diagram illustrating the effects on the sterling–dollar exchange rate of:

   (a) an increase in UK real incomes, and

   (b) higher inflation in the UK than in the USA.

2   You start selling your water-colours of European cities to the USA at a sterling price of £20 when the exchange rate is £1 = $1.50. You find you can sell 100 per quarter. Calculate:

   (a) the price in US dollars,

   (b) the dollar price after the exchange rate falls to £1 = $1.20, and

   (c) the change in the demand for pounds per quarter after the exchange rate decline on the assumption that the price elasticity of demand for your paintings is −1.75.

So far there does not seem to be anything very dramatic about the exchange rate movements likely to occur in response to changes in the conditions of supply and demand. Something is missing. Perhaps your list of reasons for buying a foreign currency included something like 'to sell it later at a profit'. That is what we must consider next: speculation.

6.2   Speculation and exchange rate instability

Speculation arises out of people's expectations about future movements in exchange rates. One of the capital account transactions which gives rise to foreign exchange deals is an international version of choosing the best place to 'store your wealth'. Instead of comparing the interest rates your money might earn in the different banks and building societies of your nearest town, you might look further afield, if the amount of money to be deposited warranted the extra time and trouble. Let us say you have £1000 to deposit and you discover that US interest rates are higher than those prevailing in the UK, perhaps 10 per cent against 5 per cent. Why not deposit your money there and have an extra £50 to spend?

One reason for caution is that your £50 profit could easily be wiped out by exchange rate movements. The total return on your investment is the product of both the interest rate differential and any capital loss or gain on the necessary currency transactions. Suppose the exchange rate when you bought the dollars to deposit in a US bank was £1 = $1.50, so that your £1000 gave you $1500. At the end of the year, you have made $150 in interest and decide to change the capital sum (the original $1500) plus interest ($150) back into pounds. You may be in for a surprise when you present your $1650.

Question

What is your $1650 worth in sterling if the exchange rate is now:

1   £1 = $1.20?

2   £1 = $1.60?

3   £1 = $2?

In Case 1 your $1650 becomes £1375, well in excess of the £1050 you would have had if you had deposited your £1000 with a UK bank. You would have a capital gain to add to the higher interest you earned by lending your money to a US bank, because when you exchanged your pounds for dollars at the start of the year you were switching from an asset that was about to lose value, or depreciate, to one that was about to appreciate. However, in Case 2 your $1650 yields only £1031, so, while you have still made a return on your £1000, you would have done better to stay with a UK bank. The 'nightmare scenario' is Case 3, where you end up with less than the £1000 you started with (£825 in fact).

The possibility of substantial gains from buying currencies before they appreciate encourages speculation. Speculation can have a stabilizing effect on the exchange rate, if speculators believe that its current trend will be reversed. They will, for example, sell a currency that is rising in value, thereby offsetting the factors that have increased the demand for it. If, on the other hand, speculators believe that an appreciating currency is likely to go on rising in value, they have every reason to buy it and, if enough speculators do so, the increase in demand will ensure that the currency's exchange rate does indeed continue to climb. <u>Equally, if enough speculators believe that a currency is overvalued and is set for a depreciation, their selling of it will so increase its supply that its exchange rate falls.</u> So speculation in this kind of situation is destabilizing and is a major factor in explaining exchange rate volatility.

<u>Exchange rate volatility</u> has been an important part of foreign exchange markets since the <u>collapse of the Bretton Woods system of fixed exchange rates in 1973</u> (see Chapters 19 and 28). The US dollar was particularly unstable in the 1980s, rising strongly to 1985 before falling back to finish the decade lower than it began. By contrast, the Japanese yen showed a remarkably strong appreciation throughout this period (Figure 11.12). One of the causes is the increasing integration of world financial markets and the ease with which funds can be transferred from, say, dollar deposits in New York to yen in Tokyo. Innovations in information and communications technology have contributed to this development. So, too, has the dismantling of foreign exchange controls, in the UK in 1979 and throughout the EU over the following decade. There are now no legal restrictions on the amount of foreign currency a person can buy or the purposes (trade or speculation) for which it can be used.

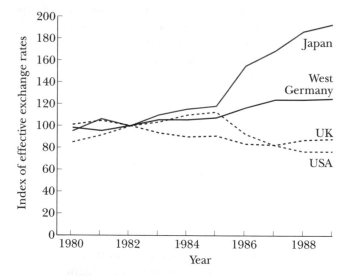

Figure 11.12   **Effective exchange rates, 1980–89 (1982 = 100)**

Source: based on Smithin (1990) Appendix to Chapter 5

The water-colour example illustrated, in microcosm, the sense in which exchange rate volatility is a form of monetary disorder. You would not know from one year to the next whether you can price your water-colours competitively in dollar terms and still earn pounds to cover your costs. This uncertainty makes investment in overseas distribution and service networks problematic, restricting the growth of international trade. National governments and the EU have sought to reinstate some stability into exchange rates through international agreements and the establishment of the Exchange Rate Mechanism (ERM). These will be discussed in Chapters 19 and 28.

7 Conclusion

I began this chapter by focusing on the functions of money and the difference it makes to economic activity, contrasting a money economy with barter. I moved on to discuss the changing nature of money and the institutions of money – the financial revolution of the 1980s – and then reviewed Keynes's insights into the demand for money. Then I looked ahead to later parts of the text, with an account of two theories of the supply of money. The growth and control of the money supply are important in connection with inflation and monetary policy and you will study these topics in some detail in Chapters 24, 25 and 28. I concluded with an introduction to the foreign exchange market. The issues of exchange rate determination, currency speculation and international policy co-ordination will be explored further in Chapters 19 and 28. The foreign exchange market is of more immediate relevance, because you will now be going on to study international trade in Chapters 12, 13 and 14.

PART 7

CHAPTER 12

INTERNATIONAL MARKETS

FIRMS, COMPETITIVENESS AND THE GLOBAL ECONOMY

by Paul Auerbach

1 Introduction

One of the most extraordinary aspects of economic life in the last several decades has been the way in which all nations, including the UK, have increasingly found themselves part of a global economy. To an ever increasing extent, the goods which we see on shelves and in shops, from soap and spaghetti to hi-fi and hoovers (a US company brand name!) are either produced abroad, or domestically in firms owned by foreign nationals. This profound change in everyday life underpins much of the political disputation we observe between nations, both within the European Union and world-wide.

This chapter, the first of two on international markets, begins with a discussion of this tendency in the direction of the 'globalization' of economic life. Economic life between nations has become so intimately intertwined in the contemporary world that it is difficult to recall that many of the developments leading to this level of intimacy are very recent. The chapter explores some of the major institutional and historical changes which lie behind globalization. It argues that a key explanation of this huge transformation in the international competitive environment is to be found in the changes that have taken place in the organization and behaviour of business. It is the volcanic eruption of giant firms in the twentieth century which has turned production into a more global activity and has driven the increasing integration of international markets.

This argument echoes a theme in Chapter 4, where Neil Costello noted that firms may actively reshape the markets in which they work. This chapter explores in more depth this perspective on the making of markets by disentangling two competing interpretations of that central concept in economics – *competition*. The chapter's main objective is to develop a perspective on competition which is *dynamic*, focusing on change and innovation. It argues that to understand the dynamics of competition, we need to start from the behaviour of firms themselves, and then to analyse market structure – the competitiveness of the market environment – as the outcome of firms' strategies. It is institutional changes and managerial decisions at the firm level which force changes in the competitive environment. Hence the emphasis on company strategy and organization in this chapter.

This view of competition builds on earlier discussions of firms' strategic behaviour and on 'Austrian' ideas about markets and competition, found in Chapters 5 and 6. It is contrasted with the more *static* view of competition embodied in traditional models of monopoly, monopolistic competition and perfect competition. These latter models take market structure – particularly, numbers of firms in the market – as determining firms' behaviour. Less concentrated markets are, almost by definition, more competitive markets. Chapter 8 showed that this view of competition has been highly influential, but also noted its limitations as a guide to policy for governments concerned with dynamic efficiency.

The transformation of the economic environment in the twentieth century has generated changes, not only in the competitive environment between firms, but also in the nature of economic rivalry between nations. Worrying about national 'competitiveness' has become another global activity. This chapter ends by applying the distinction between static and dynamic models of competition to this problem by considering what it takes for a nation to be competitive in the modern world.

Most economics textbooks, modelling themselves, consciously or unconsciously, on texts in physics, focus on the supposed eternal verities of the subject. This attitude has lent itself to an approach which involves starting from established, static models of the market, and then investigating loose ends later. Longer term change and dynamics are hard to model, and there is little consensus on how it should be done. But national economic policy concerns increasingly focus on how to cope with the dynamics of change in a highly competitive world. So this text has sought to give the much debated issues of competitive dynamics and institutional change a more prominent place than is usual, and this chapter forms part of that attempt.

2   Economic globalization

The interconnectedness of the present-day world economy has no precedent by both quantitative and qualitative measures. There are three key aspects of this growing interdependence, and this section considers each in turn. They are the growing importance of international trade, the expansion of overseas direct investment associated with the rise of the transnational firm, and finally the emergence, among these transnationals, of firms which 'think globally' about commercial strategy and organization.

Taken together, these trends form a process of internationalization of trade and production in the world economy. It is particularly the last of the three

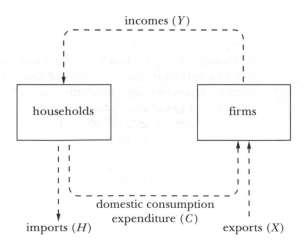

Figure 12.1   **The circular flow of income and the rest of the world**

– the 'global firm' – together with the increased speed of international communications, which has led some commentators to apply the label 'globalization' to these trends.

2.1 The growth in international trade

In focusing on international trade, this chapter and the next develop the last link in the circular flow diagram: the external sector (Figure 12.1).

A country's trade flows are registered in its balance of payments, which forms part of the national accounts. To complete your understanding of national accounts, let us start by looking briefly at the structure of the UK balance of payments.

Table 12.1 **UK balance of payments, 1991**

	£(m)
1 Current account	
Visible trade	
Export of goods	+103 413
Import of goods	−113 703
Visible trade balance	−10 290
Invisibles	
Exports of services	+31 702
Imports of services	−26 712
Net balance of services	+4990
Net balance of interest, profits and dividends	+328
Transfers balance	−1 349
Invisible balance	+3 969
Overall current account balance	−6 321
2 Capital account	
Transactions in UK external assets (capital exports)	−20 780
Transactions in UK external liabilities (capital imports)	+26 030
Capital account balance	+5 249
3 Sum of current + capital =	−1 072
4 Balancing item	+1 072
5 Overall balance	0

Note: numbers may not sum exactly to totals because of rounding.

Source: *Key Data* (1993) calculated from Tables 6.1 and 6.2, pp.28 and 29

The *current account* shows trade in goods, and in 'invisible' services such as tourism and insurance services. The *balance of trade* is the balance on goods and services taken together, which was −£5300m in 1991. In addition, the current 'invisibles' category includes profits, interest and dividends paid across UK borders, and transfers such as UK government payments to the European Union and the United Nations. The *capital account* tracks UK investment abroad, and overseas investment in the UK.

Question

Add up exports of goods and services in 1991 and compare this to UK 1991 GDP in Chapter 2. What percentage of UK GDP was exported?

At nearly a quarter of GDP (your answer should be 23.53%) exports are an important element of the UK economy. In other words the UK is a very 'open' economy. This has long been true. In the second half of the nineteenth century the British economy was about as open on this measure as it is now, reflecting the country's early lead in the industrial revolution and its long trading history. The trade to GDP ratio dropped sharply with the general decline in international trade as a result of the 1930s depression and the two world wars.

Since 1945, there has been a new world-wide trend to more open economies. The growth rate of output since the Second World War is, most probably, unprecedented in the history of capitalism, but the growth in international trade has been even more impressive.

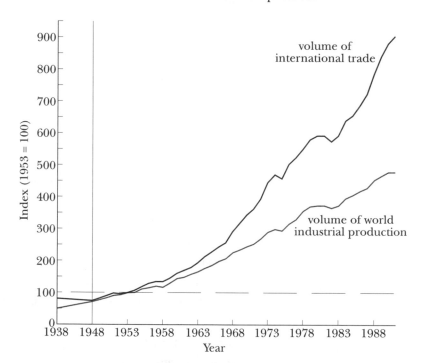

Figure 12.2   **Volume of international trade and of world industrial production, 1938, 1948, 1950–91**

Source: *International Trade* (various years)

Figure 12.2 thus provides a quantitative measure of internationalization, showing that world trade has grown much more quickly than industrial output. Clearly post-war improvements in transportation, such as the development of giant oil tankers and of 'containerization', which has reduced the costs of on- and off-loading goods at the docks, have been of major significance in promoting international trade. So have the remarkable developments in transnational communications with which we are all familiar. Much of this trade boom has been in trade among developed industrial economies, which, as a group have a much higher trade to output ratio than they had 50 or 100 years ago.

2.2 Foreign direct investment and the transnational firm

In addition to this quantitative change in trade ratios, a whole host of institutional changes in the world economy have increased its interconnectedness. In a qualitative sense, international involvement in nations' economies is also at an unprecedented level. This qualitative change is largely associated with the growth of foreign direct investment (FDI), that is, with the creation of transnational firms. Figure 12.3 shows a generally rising ratio of foreign direct investment to GNP for five major industrial economies, with a peak in the late 1980s.

Definition

Foreign direct investment (FDI)

Foreign direct investment is investment in the business or financial affairs of another country that involves a strong element of (potential or actual) direct control of these activities. An example would be the setting up of a subsidiary abroad by an existing company, as when Ford (UK) was created, and fully owned, by the US parent.

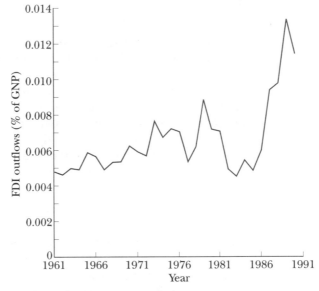

Figure 12.3 **FDI outflows as a percentage of GNP for the G-5 countries (USA, UK, Japan, Germany, France)**

Source: *National Westminster Bank Quarterly Review* (1992) Spring

Outward foreign direct investment is registered as acquisition of an overseas asset in the capital account of the balance of payments; inward FDI as a rise in liabilities to overseas owners. It is distinguished, within the capital account, from portfolio investment, which takes place when, for instance, a British subject purchases an American or Russian railway bond. There was an extraordinarily high level of overseas portfolio investment from Britain at the beginning of the century, showing that present developments are not entirely new.

However, portfolio investment is qualitatively different from the distinctive form of foreign involvement which has emerged in large measure since the Second World War, which has been FDI. There is no clear boundary line between portfolio investment and FDI, but the important step is from a passive activity such as the holding of the debt of a company, to a more active investor role. FDI carries with it the possibility of direct involvement in the economic affairs of a nation by foreign nationals.

Reflection

Can you think of examples of ways in which FDI may result in more 'intimate' economic or political relations between the nationals of different countries than is likely from trade relations or portfolio investment? Various aspects of this issue are addressed in the rest of this section.

The growing significance of FDI signals the increasing involvement of transnational (or multinational) firms in the domestic life of national economies. Such involvement can proceed in stages. An American firm may merely decide to open an office in London to supervise the marketing of its exports from the USA; it may produce goods in the USA and leave their final assembly to a plant in the UK; it may decide to have a complete production facility in the UK, with a full-fledged sub-division of the company there (e.g. Ford UK).

The problems of managing an operation such as Ford UK itself are formidable enough: the task of co-ordinating the activities of Ford UK with those in Europe and the rest of the world from Ford's headquarters in Detroit, Michigan, USA poses problems which would have seemed unimaginable to even the most sophisticated captains of industry from the turn of the century. A prerequisite for the successful spread of the modern day multinational was the turn of the century development of the techniques for the management of the giant firm in the context of the *domestic* US economy. This key development will be discussed in Section 3.

While these techniques for managing giant firms date, as will be shown, from the turn of the century, the multinational firm is largely a post-war phenomenon. An early burst of multinational investment from the USA in the 1920s collapsed after 1929 with the rest of international economic activity. As a result, most multinational activity continued to be identified with the international extraction of natural resources and raw materials, as in the case of the giant oil companies and the US tropical fruit firms which dominated the economies (and politics) of Central America.

The emergence of overwhelming US dominance in political, economic and cultural spheres in the immediate post-war world set the stage for the explosion of global economic activity, affecting both international trade and FDI from the USA. International trade was stimulated by the US initiation of the General Agreement on Tariffs and Trade (GATT) in 1947, which expressly sought to overcome the strategies of economic isolation pursued by many nations during the inter-war period (including the USA itself). Free trade and currency stabilization are policies often advocated by dominant and successful economic powers, such as Britain in the nineteenth century or the USA in the post-war period.

The post-war explosion of FDI had as an important prerequisite the re-establishment, for the first time since before the First World War, of stable rates of exchange between international currencies. This was a development of great significance, since US multinational investors, in the unstable post-war conditions, wished to have a sense of security that foreign currency earned from investing abroad would not lose its value in terms of the dollar. The overwhelming US dominance was used to implement the Bretton Woods system of international currency regulation, which was initiated in 1944. This *de facto* dollar-based regime brought about a period of relative exchange rate stability which lasted until 1971. The collapse of the Bretton Woods system at this time, however, did not dampen the long-term trend in the growth of FDI (Figure 12.3).

A further development that had been of significance was the move to full *convertibility* of most of the currencies of Western Europe about the time of the signing of the Treaty of Rome in 1957. US multinational investors not only wished to have fixed values between international currencies, but wanted to have the option of converting foreign currencies earned from investing abroad into dollars and repatriating these dollars to the USA. Lastly, the post-war development of 'political stability' in post-war Western Europe was important for US multinational investors. The US government played its part in discouraging the participation in government of radical and left-wing parties in many countries, including Italy and France (Kolko, 1968).

Reflection

Look back at this sub-section and note some institutional changes after 1945 which contributed to the expansion of the relative importance of international economic activity.

In the immediate post-war world, multinationals were overwhelmingly from the USA. As late as the mid 1960s, a famous book from France spoke of the 'American challenge' of US multinationals which were, it was feared, overwhelming their host country industries. Within a few years, however, it was clear that no such threat had existed. Multinational activity is no longer identified with FDI from the USA, as can be seen in Table 12.2.

Table 12.2 **Shares of FDI from different countries, 1960–90**

Country of origin	Percentage of world total of outward direct investment			
	1960	**1975**	**1985**	**1990**
USA	47.1	44.0	35.1	12.4
UK	18.3	13.1	14.7	7.7
Japan	0.7	5.7	11.7	20.5
West Germany	1.2	6.5	8.4	12.0
Switzerland	3.4	8.0	6.4	2.6
Netherlands	10.3	7.1	6.1	5.6
Canada	3.7	3.7	5.1	1.7
France	6.1	3.8	3.0	15.0
Italy	1.6	1.2	1.7	3.0
Sweden	0.6	1.7	1.3	6.0
Developed market economies	99.0	97.7	97.2	96.2
Developing market economies	1.0	2.3	2.7	3.8
World total	100.0	100.0	100.0	100.0

Note: numbers may not sum exactly to totals because of rounding.

Source: figures for 1960–85 from Dicken (1992) Table 3.2, p.53; figures for 1990 derived from OECD (1992a) Table 1, p.13, and UN (1993) Tables 1.3 and 1.4, p.16

Question

Summarize the trends identified in Table 12.2.

The most significant trend since 1960 is the decline in the relative importance of the USA as a source of FDI. It has been eclipsed by Japan, and to a lesser extent by Germany. France was very important in 1990, though this may be for temporary reasons (associated with the EU single market programme) and not a long-term trend. Also notable is the consistently dominant position of the 'developed market economies' as the source of FDI funds, though a few developing-economy investors are appearing.

For any *individual* firm, a decision between 'going multinational' or exporting is a strategic choice. For the international economic system as a whole, the atmosphere of early currency stabilization and continuing free trade in the post-war years has encouraged a vast expansion of *both* international trade and of FDI.

2.3 The 'global firm' and its impacts

Why should a firm 'go multinational' instead of exporting? Besides the obvious cases mentioned above, such as oil and tropical fruit, cases such as Kellogg's and Heinz are clear candidates: it makes little sense to ship such goods across the ocean. The major challenges to such expansion were the need for adequate vision and management expertise to organize such operations abroad, and the necessity for *creating markets* for such delicacies beyond the borders of the USA through advertising, marketing, and the customization of products to suit national tastes.

There are other reasons too for pursuing multinational activity instead of exporting. It may take place for political reasons: as a way of avoiding actual or potential barriers to trade, or in order to receive tax advantages or concessions from the host country to set up shop there. Japanese FDI in the USA and in the European Union has been largely motivated by such considerations.

Reflection

Consider a foreign owned firm known to you with a branch in your domestic economy. Why do you think it chose to locate there?

FDI may also take the form of a search for raw materials or cheap labour available in a foreign country. Up to the present day, however, most FDI seems to have been 'market driven' rather than being exclusively a search for cheap inputs. Thus, in the post-war world, Western Europe was the favoured venue for US multinationals because of the relatively high incomes and compatible consumption patterns there. Most FDI is still directed towards rich, high wage economies: in 1991, the stock of capital which had been invested abroad in developed countries was valued at $1369 billion, while that invested in developing countries was $338 billion (UN, 1993, p.17).

The ease and flexibility with which the modern transnational firm can shift its production between countries is, however, a fact of contemporary economic life, one which has its effects upon the relations between labour and capital everywhere. For example, a major motivation for support for the North American Free Trade Agreement (NAFTA) by US manufacturers was the desire of US multinationals to take advantage of the fact that wages and benefits of industrial workers in Mexico are a fraction of those in the USA – and half those of Taiwan, Singapore and South Korea (Baker *et al.*, 1993).

A final reason for pursuing multinational activity is perhaps the most nebulous and, at the same time, the most interesting. Management theorists and leaders of large companies now often speak about the need for a 'multinational vision' of their operations. What does this mean? At one level, it simply refers to the problems of international marketing and the search for cheap raw materials and labour inputs discussed above. But this multinational vision also seems to refer to the need, in the context of heightened international competition, to 'take the pulse' of the world-wide distribution of best practice techniques and technologies, and of changes in demand and fashion. Increasingly, some transnational firms develop their production and marketing on a truly global basis, as a case study of Asea Brown Boveri illustrates.

Asea Brown Boveri: an international production network

There are probably only a few TNCs [transnational corporations] in the world today which could be called truly global firms, and that own, organise and manage an international production network. Among those few firms is Asea Brown Boveri (ABB), which was formed in a 1987 merger of the Swedish firm Asea with the Swiss firm Brown Boveri. Following a massive restructuring, involving investments of some $3.6 billion in 60 newly-acquired or merged companies, ABB is now the world's leading supplier of power and railway equipment, with sales of $29 billion and 214,000 employees in 1991.

The structure and management practices of ABB place it among the few truly global corporations operating in the world economy; it comprises 1,300 companies located throughout the world, 130 of them in developing countries; its eight corporate board members are from five different countries; it has adopted an official language (English) for major transactions; and its 5,000 profit centres report all financial information in United States dollars to a single location, to allow for cross-border analysis. The firm is organized into a matrix structure, in which businesses are responsible to both a global leader as well as a national president. Leaders of the 50 Business Areas of ABB are based throughout the world and manage their operations on a global basis, devising overall strategies as regards exports, capacity and employee development; the leader of the power transmission business, for instance, is a Swede based in Germany, managing 25 factories in 16 countries. At the same time, the 1,300 individual companies ... must prove themselves competitive on a national basis. This structure, which the company's president and CEO [Chief Executive Officer] characterizes as 'multi-domestic', allows ABB to compete as if it were a national company in industries where local presence is important (such as locomotives), while at the same time drawing on the corporations' global resources in such areas as core technologies, design, component manufacturing, managerial expertise and finance. The management strategy of combining the advantages of globalization (economies of scale in both production and purchasing), along with the responsiveness of a national firm (ABB has companies in 140 countries), has led to the emergence of a globally integrated production and distribution system which involves extensive cross-border flows of goods and services, people, technology and know-how.

The operations of ABB reflect many of the trends of the new world economy, in which TNCs account for an increasing share of the world's trade, technology, financial and knowledge flows; in which economic distances are being shortened by new communication and information technologies; and in which regional integration is leading to the emergence of regional TNC-controlled production networks. … In North America, the combination of the emerging free trade area, relatively low United States wages and the specialized capabilities of United States-based affiliates of ABB will make the region an important export base for the company's global distribution network. In Europe, fewer production sites will serve larger markets to meet growing competition in the unified market … ABB has targeted the Asian region, which currently accounts for about 15 per cent of revenues, for major growth in the next few years. Selected developing countries, such as Brazil, are also emerging as important export bases for the global distribution network of ABB …

… A commercial bid by the power plant business segment for $136 million project in New Zealand illustrates the extent of intra-firm co-operation; ABB Project Finance raised finance for the proposal, ABB Credit arranged equipment leasing, ABB Credit B.V. procured interim financing, the World Treasury Center acted as lenders, while Sirius, another ABB company, provided credit risk insurance. ABB are at the forefront of a relatively small number of companies whose operations may be characterized as 'global'. To the extent to which other companies adopt similar strategies, they lay the foundation for a global production system, integrating both industrial as well as service activities.

(UN, 1992, pp.254–5)

While ABB is an extreme example of global thinking, it leads a continuing trend: the progressive internationalization of economic life. Transnational firms are both symptoms and promoters of an environment in which it is impossible to give exclusive consideration to economic policy at the level of the individual nation state. As the case study suggested, TNCs are increasingly integrating national economies through their own internal cross-border flows of goods and services, finance, personnel and technology.

One of the striking results has been the virtual disappearance of purely 'national' technologies. The multinational has been a key agent in this development, with its engendering of transnational co-operative research ventures (Bradshaw, 1993). It has promoted more rapid international diffusion of technology and thereby increased the level of competition in the international economy.

What are the effects of the explosion of multi-national activity for national economies? The multinational poses many new challenges for national economic policy makers. Exchange rate destabilization, often attributed to anonymous 'international speculators', is more likely due to the activities of the financial division of a multinational going about its 'normal' business of minimizing losses in international currency dealings.

Labour market conditions within a country are also likely to be influenced by multinationals' search for (other things equal) low wage rates, as well as pollution and health and safety regulations at the lowest levels available internationally, when deciding on sites for their activity. Under these conditions, a regulator desiring to set minimum standards for any of these factors within any *given* country is confronted with unprecedented difficulties.

Are the effects of multinational activity on host countries beneficial or pernicious? Broad generalizations are fraught with difficulty. In the developed countries of western Europe, at least, FDI from the USA had proved to be, on the whole, a mechanism for the development, rather than the destruction of domestic industries. As early as the 1920s, no more graphic demonstration of modern methods of car manufacture was available to domestic producers in the UK than the setting up of a full production plant there by Ford. While multinational investment may be better than none at all, many observers think that nationality still counts: foreign-owned multinationals usually pursue 'core' activities such as fundamental research and development at home, with the host country as an executant of the more mechanical and passive aspects of the business (Lorenz, 1994).

In some developing countries in the post-war world, such as the most rapid industrializers, it could be argued that beneficial effects have been present, though South Korea has kept the activities of multinationals at arm's length (Amsden, 1989). At the other extreme, it would be much more difficult to argue the case for the beneficent influence of the presence of the US multinational United Fruit (later United Brands) in Guatemala, given that firm's insidious interferences in the politics and domestic affairs of the nation over many decades (Pearce, 1981).

The nature of multinational activity has been changing since the early post-war years. The paradigmatic multinational in the post-war world was not only American, but was also largely internally self-sufficient: a giant firm making relatively little use of the host countries' business, financial and marketing resources. Since the early post-war years, however, much industrial activity in Europe and the rest of the world has equalled (or surpassed) US standards. As a result, the opportunity cost of high levels of self sufficiency (what will be referred to in Section 3 as 'vertical integration') for US and other multinationals has been rising: it has become too expensive for multinational firms to do everything for themselves when high quality inputs are available locally. It has, in many cases, become cheaper to purchase inputs abroad (though not necessarily in the host country) than to ship them from home.

We thus observe the emergence of available advertising, marketing, financial and other auxiliary services on an international basis. Alongside the global firm of the ABB type we now see the emergence of smaller, less self-sufficient multinationals, some of them from the Third World (Pearson *et al.*, 1993). As a result of these changes, the multinational is ceasing to be wholly identified with giant, self-sufficient firms, and is becoming progressively an unexceptional phenomenon – a varied, even ordinary, although extremely important, aspect of the progressive internationalization of economic life whose manifestations are all about us.

3 The emergence of the giant firm

3.1   The giant firm and the competitive environment

The globalization of economic life, therefore, did not just 'happen'. Furthermore, it was not simply caused by the emergence in the past century of the new technologies which have revolutionized transport and communications. Complementing, and often engendering, this technological revolution has been a transformation in the institutional arrangements within the capitalist market economy world-wide. In this section I take a closer look at this continuing process of change in the organization of large firms, before considering in Section 4 the implications of these changes for the nature of the competitive environment.

The notion of constant change is challenging for the idea that economics is a science. If economics is an attempt not only to systemize our understanding of events in the economic world, but to come up with scientific 'laws' to explain these events, then a world of constant change makes it especially difficult to formulate such laws. Mainstream approaches to economics have therefore tended to be resistant to the notion of constant change. There is a preference instead for modelling states of rest – equilibria – towards which an economic system naturally gravitates. This chapter suggests that the ways in which economic life has changed over the twentieth century have been of such a fundamental nature that they cause us to question some conventional methods of economic analysis.

If we examine how the industrial structure of Great Britain, Germany and the USA changed from the latter part of the nineteenth century to the middle of the twentieth century, the most striking fact is the emergence of the giant firm. At one level, this fact is unsurprising. The new technologies of the 'second industrial revolution' such as steel, chemicals and cars have far greater potential for the exploitation of economies of scale than did the earlier technologies surrounding such industries such as textiles. But the giant firm which emerged was not, as in a photograph, simply a blown-up version of the smaller firms of earlier times. It was a far more sophisticated entity, one designed to deal with a far more complex set of tasks than heretofore.

Is the giant firm a source of competition or a constraint upon it? You have seen in Chapters 6 and 8 that the answer can be different from a static and from a dynamic perspective on competition. The software giant Microsoft is both symbol and manifestation of a distinctive area of US success in maintaining its world-wide competitiveness: from a dynamic perspective, its creation of new products and processes (such as *Windows*) indicates that it is highly competitive in this sense. The high level of concentration enjoyed by Microsoft in the field of computer software, however, would indicate a low level of competition from a static perspective (and as a result has attracted the scrutiny of the anti-trust division of the US Justice Department).

This contradiction between the static and dynamic approaches to competition is evident in the early history of the emergence of giant firms. These new entities were simultaneously recognized as central factors for the promotion of 'modernization' and of the raising of national competitiveness, and at the same time were railed against as the creation of 'monopolies' against the public interest. An economic orthodoxy embodied in the static approach to competition helped to engender a still-influential myth that the emergence of the giant firm signified the replacement of a 'golden age' of competition with a new world of monopolies (see the discussion of monopoly capitalism in Chapter 6). Instead, I am proposing in this chapter that the giant firm promoted a new era of competition in the dynamic sense, with competitive *behaviour* at a level of intensity which had been unknown in former times.

3.2 The new structure of command

The expansion of the giant firm was often financed by the selling of limited liability shares to the public. In a great many of these companies, we then see the emergence of a remarkable development: these giant firms were often owned by a large number of anonymous shareholders, but they were under the control of a group of self-perpetuating professional managers whose link to the shareholders was often tenuous at best.

This is the phenomenon of 'the separation of ownership and control'. Most economists have viewed the emergence of this separation with horror: after all, if individuals are pursuing their self interest, there is no reason to believe that these professional managers will pursue the best interests of the firm (i.e. of its owners), rather than their own best interests. Reinforcing this negative approach was the attitude of the Austrian economist Joseph Schumpeter, who saw in this new phenomenon the death of the entrepreneurial spirit of capitalism and its replacement by a bureaucratic, uninnovative mentality.

However, as much of the great expansion of capitalism in the twentieth century has taken place in the context of firms dominated by professional managers, another approach to this phenomenon has developed. The business historian Alfred Dupont Chandler has suggested that this separation of ownership and control, far from sapping the entrepreneurial spirit of capitalism, has been an aspect of a necessary professionalization of the management of these giant firms. Chandler's argument is epitomized by the success of General Motors in the 1920s in displacing the Ford Motor Company from its dominant position in the US car industry. The owner-entrepreneur Henry Ford had been defeated by the thorough-going professionalism of the manager of General Motors, Alfred Sloan.

Professionalizing and systematizing the command structure and organization of the giant firm was a necessity. In the late nineteenth century, the first steps were taken in the USA by the railroads. Management tasks were split, in a military way, between staff (officers) who dealt with the broad planning and strategy for the organization, and line (non-commissioned officers), who dealt with day-by-day decisions and interacted with the railroads' workers.

Having freed the staff of the giant firm from having to make day-to-day decisions, the next task was to bring coherence to the organization of the staff headquarters. Instrumental in this development was the delineation of staff responsibilities into coherent divisions for the whole company such as finance, marketing, and general administration. Such a structure is often referred to as 'U (unitary) form' (see also Chapter 4, Section 5.3).

For many companies, further developments were necessary. General Motors after the First World War was a large, uncoordinated collection of ramshackle companies, including Chevrolet, Buick, Oldsmobile and Cadillac. The solution taken by Alfred Sloan and his colleagues was to give each of the subdivisions (Buick, Oldsmobile, etc.) its own integrity as a profit-making centre, with its own full staff and responsibilities. The general staff for the firm would only be concerned with those activities (e.g. long-term planning) relevant to the firm as a whole, and with monitoring and evaluating the success of the subdivisions. This solution, known as 'M (multi-divisional) form', is widespread in modern large firms. It is not, however, a magical solution to the problems of managing a large entity: the perpetual tension between 'centre' and 'division' is the very stuff of management theory.

While the shift from 'staff and line' management to U form to M form were key institutional changes, they should not be thought of as inspired, discontinuous reforms. An analogy with the history of technology may help here. In Britain and the USA, school children are taught about the great landmark inventions of the industrial revolution, such as the steam engine, the spinning jenny and the mule. It is thereby often implied that the key to the technological revolutions of the modern world is the discontinuous emergence of such 'inventions' from individual 'geniuses'. This disguises the slow improvements in the techniques of metal working and other practical skills from the late Middle Ages which were the real basis for the technological revolution (Bernal, 1965).

By analogy, the really critical events which made the efficient operation of the giant firm possible were not the discontinuous invention of new forms of command structure such as 'staff and line' management, or U form or M form. Rather they were the long-term development of the management techniques, including cost and management accounting, and the development of training and professionalization of the people administering these techniques. Such developments pioneered in the USA, were a necessity for the new forms of management. For a giant M form company to be run at a reasonable level of efficiency, it had to have a system of cost accounting which communicated to the centre sufficiently complete and accurate information about its subdivisions to allow rational decisions about the company's future. Similarly, in the absence of the systematic development of management education and the associated professional disciplines, it would be very difficult to fill the administrative posts of the subdivisions of an M form firm: semi-autonomy for subdivisions implies that the administrators there are competent to fulfil the tasks assigned to them from the centre without detailed guidance.

Question

Why has the 'new structure of command' been a prerequisite for the management of complex global operations such as ABB?

The multi-divisional firm, and the new management techniques, allowed the combining of coherent autonomous sub-divisions with continuing co-ordination from the centre. This permitted in turn the 'multi-domestic' structure of ABB. It is a short step from autonomous domestic sub-divisions to sub-divisions abroad. The groundwork for multi-national management was laid in the domestic economy.

3.3   Vertical integration and diversification

Definition

Vertical integration

The level of vertical integration of a firm increases when it takes in house activities needed for final production which were previously purchased from outside suppliers.

The emergent large firm was therefore not simply a smaller firm of earlier times 'writ large': the new entity adopted an innovative approach to the control of its activities. The scope of these activities also greatly expanded. One method of expansion was through a process of vertical integration, or, in Chandler's phrase, the substitution of the 'visible hand' of management for the 'invisible hand' of the market. Thus, among these great firms, it was common to engage in *backward integration* (e.g. through the purchase of a coal mine by a steel mill) or in *forward integration* (e.g. through a car maker's creation of retail outlets for the sale of its cars).

Question

What do you think are the advantages and disadvantages for the firm of vertical integration? Chapter 4 Sections 1 and 5 offer some pointers to this question.

For modern orthodox economic theorists such as Oliver Williamson, the main virtue of this process was that the 'transaction costs' of negotiation between independent companies (for instance, the need for the writing of complex contracts to deal with all possible contingencies) were avoided. As a result, the 'hierarchy' present within a vertically integrated organization was often more efficient than the market. To take a contemporary example, it may be easier and less costly to have an in-house cleaning staff in a hospital who can deal with whatever contingencies arise than to 'use the market' and hire outside cleaners, with the attendant need to write a contract covering every possible eventuality that might be faced by this cleaning staff.

For Chandler, vertical integration offered more positive benefits. According to him, it enhanced the ability of the firm to co-ordinate its different activities and to engage in long-term planning. For example, in recent times the remarkably rapid development of the CD player came about largely from in-house developments at the integrated multinationals Philips and Sony. Such rapid product evolution, with its co-ordination of so many disparate activities, would have been inconceivable on the basis of activities from a host of separate companies working at arm's length, co-ordinated by market contracts.

There are, however, also severe disadvantages associated with high levels of vertical integration. The extension of a firm's activities, as in the case of the Ford Motor Company in Henry Ford's day, from the ownership of the natural resources it used to the retailing of its products, can put great additional strain on the management of the firm. The increased complexity of the task of managing everything 'in house' can make the firm bureaucratically inefficient and slow to respond to new developments: the more the firm fulfils its needs from inside the organization, the more likely it is to have groups within the firm that turn inward and develop a negative, 'not invented here' syndrome about others' new product developments. Finally, vertical integration may add to the burden of the firm's fixed costs – a steel company may find itself paying financing charges on a coal mine it has previously purchased even when the coal is not needed for steel production due to depressed demand.

To many observers, it appeared obvious that there was an inexorable tendency with the emergence of giant firms for 'planning' to replace 'the market' through a continuous rise in vertical integration. Surprisingly, however, there appears to be *no* inexorable tendency for vertical integration to increase. The historical record in the USA is fairly unambiguous: vertical integration increased from the 1880s, when the giant firms emerged, and then appeared to level off from about 1929.

What may have taken place is the following: in the early years, with the emergence of large firms and their revolutionary forms of management and production technique, there were strong temptations within the large firms to 'do it yourself' rather than rely on services from more backward entities outside their perimeter. For example, in the 1920s, the Ford Motor Company owned its own steel mills and even rubber plantations. There is, however, a severe drain on the company's managerial resources if it attempts to do everything for itself. With the spread of modern techniques of production and management to smaller firms, the opportunity cost of performing activities which are peripheral to the large firm's core activities rose. Vertical integration stopped rising because the relative benefits of using the visible hand of administrative co-ordination came into balance with the invisible hand of 'the market', which consisted of the activities of these smaller firms. We have already seen in Section 2 a similar phenomenon now taking place internationally among multinationals.

There are constant swings in fashion among management theorists about the relative virtues of 'making' versus 'buying'. At present, the fashion is for firms to limit themselves to their 'core activities' and to purchase inputs on the market. In some cases, companies such as Toyota and Marks & Spencer have managed to have the best of all possible worlds (from their perspective) by having a large number of independently owned 'satellite' firms whose activities are carefully monitored and controlled by them. These companies thus receive much of the benefit of full vertical integration, but can avoid, for instance, having to accord the workers of these satellite firms all the employment benefits accruing to the workers of the dominant companies.

Diversification, or the expansion *horizontally* of a firm into activities unrelated to its 'core' pursuits is another important way in which the operation of the giant firm differs from traditional forms of business operation. A striking current example is the movement into the financial services industry by General Electric (US). In the extreme, diversification takes the form of a conglomerate such as Hanson Trust, which has no real core activities. Hanson is merely an umbrella for a collection of firms that work in ways utterly unrelated to each other.

Question

What motives might exist for a firm to diversify?

Given the fashion for firms to concentrate on their core activities, diversification seems problematic: the dangers of bureaucratic inefficiency are perhaps even more pronounced for a diversified than a vertically integrated firm. But even with the divestments of recent years, large firms at present have a far wider dispersion of activities than their predecessors. At the turn of the century, it was considered a bold act of diversification when US Steel started to produce products as diverse as steel rods and barbed wire. Now, in fields of rapid technological change such as telecommunications, firms narrow themselves to a particular segment of their industry at their peril, because one of the best ways to monitor developments in related activities is to participate in them.

A major reason why firms have diversified and have been able to do so has been the change in the conceptualization of the role of management. At the turn of the century, the manager of a steel firm was a 'steel man', devoted to and knowledgeable (only) about that industry. In 1993, on the contrary, the appointment of a new head of IBM from outside of the computer industry could pass with little comment. Indeed, some commentators have suggested that being an 'outsider' was an advantage. Thus, the task of the manager is now viewed as a relatively abstract one that can easily pass between industries. The manager, in the words of Alfred Sloan, is not in the business of making, for instance, cars, but of 'making money'.

It is possible that this trend in the Anglo-American world towards treating management as an abstract task, which can be pursued with little specialized knowledge of the industry in question, has been taken to irrational extremes: many German business people would suggest that this is so. It is, however, this very abstract and wide-ranging approach which has made giant firms a key aspect of globalization.

Reflection

Add to your notes on the last reflection some further ways in which the giant firm which emerged at the beginning of the century was not simply a traditional small firm 'writ large'.

4 Competition and competitiveness

4.1 Competition: static and dynamic approaches

I suggested at the beginning of Section 3 that the contradiction between the static and dynamic approaches to competition is embodied in reactions to the emergence of giant firms. The critique of these firms as 'monopolies' against the public interest, reflecting a static approach to competition, contrasted with recognition of their central role in the promotion of 'modernization'. The traditional static view urged that the emergence of the giant firm signified the replacement of a 'golden age' of competition with a new world of monopolies. In fact, I argue here, the giant firm promoted a new era of competition, dynamically conceived, with competitive *behaviour* at a new level of intensity.

Thus, the approach taken to competition will substantially affect the interpretation we impose upon these great events. For example, a study by

Elbaum and Lazonick (1986) contends that a major reason for the long-term decline of British competitiveness is the fact that many of its major industries were too 'competitive' as this concept is conventionally measured in static theory: that is, these industries contained too many firms. This section explores the relationship between the static and dynamic approaches to competition, in search of a reconciliation of this paradox.

The static analysis of competition

I can illustrate the static analysis of competition, still dominant in mainstream economic theory, by comparing pure monopoly, analysed in Chapter 6, with perfect competition (Chapter 7). Figure 12.4 brings the two ideas together on one diagram, and offers the classic illustration of the effects of monopoly in a static framework. I am going to discuss this diagram by imagining a 'controlled experiment' on the effect of monopolizing a potentially competitive market.

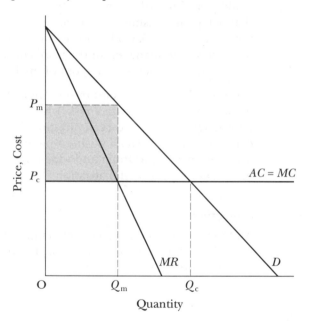

Figure 12.4 **Monopoly and competition compared in a static framework**

My imagined example is the shipping of tea to Boston harbour in the eighteenth century. *D* is the market demand curve, *MR* the monopolist's marginal revenue curve. The industry has a horizontal cost curve *AC = MC*, which is also the supply curve for the competitive industry.

This horizontal cost curve requires two assumptions. There must be no significant scale economies or diseconomies accruing to any individual entrepreneur from outfitting a large fleet of ships as compared with a single ship. If the amount of shipping doubles, so do total costs. The second assumption is that if the industry expands and the amount of shipping increases, there will be no change in the prices of factor inputs used by the industry, such as the wages of sailors or the prices of tea or ships. Thus, any changes in the market under consideration do not in this model cause collateral changes in *other* markets. This is the price we pay for doing *partial* equilibrium analysis (consideration of one market at a time), as opposed to *general* equilibrium analysis (consideration of all markets simultaneously), a topic to which we shall return below.

With a 'large' number of participants, the static model predicts that the price and quantity under such conditions will be P_c and Q_c respectively, the economic outcome in a perfectly competitive market. Now let us presume that the shipping of tea to Boston harbour becomes a monopoly as a result of a royal charter, with the 'fixed capital' of the industry (i.e. the ships which had produced output of Q_c) falling into the hand of the monopolist. The model predicts that price rises to P_m and quantity sold falls to Q_m (with the possible outcome that the tea will be dumped in the harbour). Monopoly profits are represented by the shaded rectangle. The key prediction is that price is higher, and quantity lower than in the competitive situation. Hence a once popular theoretical measure of monopoly power was:

$$\frac{P - MC}{P}$$

Called the 'degree of monopoly', this measures the extent of the mark-up on marginal cost created by monopoly.

Exercise 12.1

Suppose (a) price under monopoly (P_m) is 25, and marginal cost (MC) is 20; and (b) P_m is 45 and MC is 30. What is the 'degree of monopoly' in each case? Can you think of problems in using this measure as an indication of the presence of monopoly power in actual industries?

In this comparison, the only alteration in market conditions we have considered has been a change in the number of participants in the market from 'many' to one. We observe, as a result, a rise in profits and in the market price of tea, and a fall in the quantity sold. With a fixed capital stock, i.e. a given number of ships (of course, with its lower level of output, the monopolist will take some of these ships out of circulation), this model captures the essence of the contrast in the *short run* between regimes of monopoly and of competition.

Short-run statics vs. long-run dynamics

In the *long run*, however, in this model the capital stock is not fixed. Ship owners attracted by the monopoly profits can be expected to enter the industry with new ships. If the 'barriers to entry' (in this case the Royal Navy) were unable to prevent new competition, the long-run outcome would converge on the competitive solution. This distinction between short- and long-run outcomes is due to the economist Alfred Marshall, writing in the nineteenth and early twentieth centuries. I want to suggest that the distinction can be viewed as an ingenious attempt to reconcile two disparate and partially contradictory perspectives on the competitive process.

The short-run part of the theory is derived from a *static* view of competition which emerged in the late nineteenth century, often referred to as the neo-classical approach. Perhaps the most prominent exponent of this approach was Léon Walras. In the widely used model of *general* equilibrium derived from his pioneering work, the simultaneous equilibrium of supply and demand in all markets is considered, as opposed to Marshall's less rigorous, but more practical *partial* equilibrium approach, in which supply and demand equilibrium is considered one market at a time.

The imagery from the Walrasian model is that of a medieval fair. Little is said about how the goods were produced – they are brought to market. An independent auctioneer calls out bids experimentally until prices are found to create supply and demand equilibrium in every market simultaneously.

The focus in this model is on economic activity as *trade*. The market is competitive if there are sufficient participants in the market for a free auction to take place. With too few participants, the likelihood is that there will be monopolistic conspiracies in restraint of trade. Thus, in this static, neo-classical conception of the competitive process we can see two key aspects of the short-run part of the model of competition. First, the importance of the number of participants in the market-place, and second, the centrality of the level of prices as an indication of whether competition is 'working'.

The long-run part of the theory is derived from a *dynamic* view of competition which had emerged earlier, in the late eighteenth and early nineteenth centuries, often referred to as the classical approach. Its most important exponents were Adam Smith, David Ricardo and Karl Marx. For these economists, the focus for analysing the competitive process was the tendency for new capital to enter a sector in which high profits are being made, thereby tending to equalize returns between sectors.

In this context, the essential aspect of competition is not the number of participants in the market-place, as in the static model, but the *behaviour* of new entrants and existing participants as they actively pursue above normal profits in a given sector. The static model provides only for new entrants to compete by price cutting. In practice, however, there are a range of possible strategies that the new entrant might use, including the introduction of new and improved versions of the products.

Innovation is in fact a very common competitive strategy. We note here the distinction, often attributed to the economist Joseph Schumpeter, between *invention* and *innovation*. Invention is a technical concept, and involves the discovery of new scientific principles and technologies. Innovation, on the other hand, is an economic concept, and means the introduction of new products and processes to the economy, whether or not these innovations involve the creation of new technologies. Thus, the introduction in the mid 1980s by Alan Sugar's company Amstrad (Alan M. Sugar Trading Co.) of a self-contained word processor at a price competitive with a good typewriter was a highly successful innovation, but did not involve the invention of any new technologies.

Once we consider the long run, then, the assumptions of the static model are questioned. The nature of the product, the shape and position of the cost curves and the demand curve, all these can change along with the number of firms.

Reflection

Try to think of some more examples from your own general knowledge illustrating the economist's distinction between invention and innovation.

4.2   Market structure and competitive behaviour

The static approach

Figure 12.5   **The static model of competition**

Let me define 'market structure' initially as the level of concentration of firms in the industry. Then the static approach to competition derives the state of competition from the market structure. More concentrated markets imply less competitive behaviour (Figure 12.5).

In practice, industrial economists do use market concentration measures extensively to distinguish the competitiveness of markets. Chapter 6 noted some of the problems with this. There may, for instance, be no clear correspondence for a product (e.g. an electric room heater) between the industry, i.e. the *dynamic, long-run* competitive environment in which a firm exists (electrical appliances), and the market, i.e. the *short-run, static* competitive environment in which it sells and competes, which will include non-electric room heaters. While other factors, such as the level of entry barriers, are also of significance in static theory in determining the competitive situation, nevertheless the conception that less concentrated industries are more competitive has been highly influential in underpinning the 'structural' approach to competition policy (Chapter 8). The conception that the perfectly competitive market, with very low concentration, is closest to the ideal of a fully competitive environment still dominates text books and influences competition policy from San Francisco to Vladivostok.

Unfortunately, Chapter 8 noted this static formulation becomes unreliable as a guide to understanding and policy when we move away from pure monopoly and perfect competition towards the middle range of market structures. As you saw in Chapter 5, market outcomes under oligopoly will be contingent on the choices of strategic behaviour elected by the participants in the oligopolistic market. Thus, in the all important range of 'imperfect' market structures in between perfect competition and monopoly, market structure does not dictate the behaviour of firms even in the context of this static conceptualization of the competitive process. Can we then find a more satisfactory concept of competition which can capture the longer run?

The dynamic approach to competition

In modern times, the dynamic approach to competition has been upheld by the 'Austrian' school of economists (see Chapter 6), a school noted for its strong advocacy of the viability of unfettered capitalism. The economist whose work we shall be emphasizing here, Friedrich Hayek, is, fortuitously, Austrian (not all 'Austrian' economists are Austrian, and not all Austrian economists, such as Joseph Schumpeter are fully 'Austrian'). In Hayek's uncompromising attack on the static theory, he says that 'the theory of perfect competition ... has little claim to be called "competition" at all ... If the state of affairs assumed by the theory ... ever existed, it would not only deprive of their scope all the activities which the very verb "to compete" describes but would make them virtually impossible' (Hayek, 1948). Thus perfect competition paradoxically excludes all manifestations of agents actively *competing*: 'Advertising, undercutting, and improving ("differentiating") the goods and services are excluded by definition – "perfect competition" means the absence of all competitive activities'.

For Hayek, the crucial weakness of static theory is its by-passing of the question – and the problem – of the behaviour of firms. This aspect of his critique is central to any attempt to explore contemporary trends in the competitive environment. Hayek's approach to competition is closer to the strategic competition approach of Chapter 5 than to the static, market structure approach. But even in strategic conception, the 'playing field' for this strategic behaviour is taken as given: there is no real place for the role played by the behaviour (and changes in behaviour) of economic actors in the *shaping* of the economic environment.

Let me use as an example the world steel industry as it existed in the 1960s. Up to the 1960s, this industry was a series of national, relatively self-contained oligopolies. The Japanese industry descended upon this world like a shock. Japan was an unlikely candidate to create a revolution in this sector: not only was it without the requisite raw materials, but its low wage rates relative to other nations seemed to give it little incentive to install capital-intensive, 'best practice' technology. In fact the dramatic results from Japan's use of the latest technologies such as continuous casting and the oxygen process (both of which had been invented in Europe) were a blatant demonstration that the industry world-wide had not been operating on the frontier of its production function at all.

The decisive innovations from the Japanese steel industry that brought it to world dominance and revolutionized the industry world-wide were not technological, but were concerned with the resourceful organization of production and the assimilation of best practice technology developed abroad, the efficient use of material inputs, and the realization of hitherto under-exploited scale economies. These innovations were almost exclusively managerial: the Japanese firm itself – 'the machine that changed the world' (as it has been referred to in the context of the automobile industry) – and the managerial innovations associated with it have been the decisive aspect of Japanese economic success. The changes, often characterized as exogenous, which facilitated the development of the Japanese industry were to a great extent brought about by actions consciously taken by the Japanese themselves. Falling bulk transportation costs, for instance, were partially engendered by the industry's pioneering innovation of the giant bulk carrier for raw materials and the construction of steel plants in modern deep water port locations. Having established their industrial base, the Japanese then benefited from a 'virtuous circle' of development, by which the high growth rate in the economy as a whole and the government's long-term demand forecasts made the steel producers optimistic of continued increases in demand.

The competitive pressures and demonstration effects of Japanese success have subsequently led to dramatic changes in the behavioural patterns of steel producers (symbolized, but not exclusively associated with the rise of the mini-mills). This has occurred even in what had been the most notoriously laggard nations: thus, US firms are now in the forefront of current managerial innovation in the industry (Dickson, 1991). As producers in the steel industry world-wide have become more aggressive, they have sought out overseas markets. This development has been complemented by the increased tendency for purchasers of steel (e.g. in the car industry) to seek out the most economical sources in terms of cost, delivery times and quality, and not simply rely on local (i.e. national) producers.

In the orthodox static analysis, market structure determines firm behaviour. But here in the case of the world steel industry, an alternative line of causation may be observed, in which the behaviour of firms can shape and transform market structure: the new market structure may then feed back upon the behaviour of firms (Figure 12.6).

Figure 12.6 **The dynamic model of competition**

In the static model the emphasis on a simple form of rational behaviour dictates that all firms, even those in a perfectly competitive environment are 'monopolists at heart', always seeking to raise prices and restrict output. It is only the objective constraint of low market concentration that prevents firms in the perfectly competitive environment from operating in a monopolistic way. This short-term rationality is complemented by the presumption that firms are always on the frontiers of their production functions (upper boundaries of their production possibilities) and of their cost functions (lower boundaries of possible costs). This means that the firm is presumed to be always using the best available technology, given its scale of operation and the relative prices to which it is subject.

From Hayek's dynamic perspective, no such presumption is possible. The existence of minimum costs cannot be presumed, but requires 'constant struggle, absorbing the greater part of the energy of the manager' (Hayek, 1948a). Indeed, in the real world, the notion that producers at any moment are on a production or cost frontier seems highly inappropriate: one of the key aspects of the competitive advantage of Japanese steel producers over their international rivals was the far greater use which they made of world-wide best practice technology, little of which at that time had originated from Japan itself. Hayek's dynamic perspective on competition as a constant struggle for improvement therefore seems far more illuminating than the static paradigm for understanding Japanese competitiveness.

For Hayek, then, even markets with high concentration are (inherently) competitive in his dynamic sense of the term. Thus, he would suggest that the world market for aircraft engines has been highly competitive in spite of its history of high concentration (only three producers, General Electric (US), Pratt and Whitney, and Rolls-Royce, plus affiliates) since the behaviour of the small number of firms results in product differentiation to bring about better designs and new technologies. This example also illustrates, however, how hard it is to use evidence to adjudicate between economic models, since sophisticated industrial economists such as Scherer and Ross (1990), taking the market structure → behaviour approach, would suggest that the only problem with the static model in this case is the incomplete specification of the structural environment in the industry. 'Market structure' for them should include the inherent dynamism of the technology and the complexity of the product, all of which contribute to the industry's high level of competition.

But Hayek fails to see the other side of the coin, perhaps for ideological reasons. For instance, at the turn of the century we see in Britain an engineering industry which by any measure had a low level of market concentration and hence was competitive in the static sense. But the industry was falling behind international competition because the firms were failing to compete in a Hayekian sense. The participants in the industry were tradition-bound and idiosyncratic in their practices, at a time when 'best practice' world-wide was in the direction of standardization of parts so successfully exploited by Henry Ford. The behaviour in the industry was more one of 'live and let live' rather than the aggressive pursuit of profits which underlies both the orthodox static and the Hayekian approaches.

Here again, the dynamic approach seems to work better than the orthodox methodology. The sociology of the British engineering industry (e.g. the pride taken in the craftsmanship of the idiosyncratic engineering of these largely family-owned organizations) and the behaviour of participants in the industry dictated the market structure consisting of low concentration. Elbaum and Lazonick (1986) argue that the low level of concentration in this and other British industries in the early part of the century (in comparison with the USA and Germany), far from stimulating competitive behaviour, resulted in the unwillingness of any firms to invest in the latest technologies. The industry thereby failed to be competitive in the crucial area of technological dynamism *because* of its low concentration.

How could the industry have generated a higher level of competition in a dynamic sense? A change of behaviour by one, or more likely a consortium of participants in the industry in an aggressive, Ford-like direction of standardized mass production might have imposed standardization of specifications upon the industry. This could have paved the way, in turn, for more direct competition among participants. I should add that in this sense, and contrary to Hayek's presumption, there can be important insights offered by the parable of perfect competition: in this case, that the move towards 'homogeneity of product' through standardization can be crucial to the development of more competitive behaviour.

Note that this might well have resulted in much higher levels of market concentration. At an initial stage, the 'muscle' to impose uniform standards in the engineering industry may only be sufficient if the firms co-operating in the consortium actually decide to merge. Second, if the uniform specifications are indeed imposed, we would be likely to see a 'shake-out' of many of the small firms unable to compete in the new environment. Such was the case, for instance, with the emergence of Ford and a few other large car firms in the USA: at the beginning of the century there had been over 2000 car manufacturers. Thus, what is seen as a more competitive environment from a dynamic point of view would be decisively cast from a static perspective as an increase in concentration and monopoly power.

Implications for evaluating market competitiveness

Perceptions of trend in a competitive environment can therefore diverge sharply. The static model offers a strong presumption that firms are passive respondents to the market environment (e.g. levels of market concentration). Increases in market concentration will be decisively evaluated as a lowering of the level of competition in the market. In a dynamic evaluation of the competitive process, competitive behaviour and market structure interact with each other. Thus the aggressively competitive behaviour of Henry Ford helped to generate a more competitive environment than had previously existed in the US car industry, while at the same time sharp rises in market concentration were registered.

From a dynamic perspective then, there is a constant interaction between 'structure' and 'behaviour'. In the US car industry from the 1920s, the perpetuation of high levels of concentration *did* engender behavioural patterns which, from a dynamic point of view were clearly 'uncompetitive'. This uncompetitive behaviour then simplified the task of foreign competitors wanting to break into the US market, with a resultant sharp fall in levels of market concentration starting in the 1970s. In recent years, US car manufacturers seem in turn to have responded to their loss of a secure position in the US market by behaving more competitively.

In the British engineering industry at the turn of the century, the strategy suggested above for making the industry more dynamically competitive was the creation of a consortium to impose standards on the industry. Such a procedure would be an anathema to economists who identify a competitive environment with low concentration. But large firms sometimes inadvertently contribute in this way to the creation of a competitive environment. When Philips and Sony had developed the CD player, they issued a 'Red Book' of specifications for all manufacturers to follow for the making of CD players and discs, so that a broad unified market for these goods could be created and the potential economies of scale could be realized. Similar motivations influenced IBM when they did not attempt to make proprietary claim on the Intel microchip and the Microsoft operating system used in their new product, the IBM PC. In both industries, the search by large firms for industry standards resulted in highly competitive environments.

An alternative strategy in the British engineering case would be as antithetical to Hayek as the creation of the consortium is to the orthodox theorist. This strategy would call for the imposition of uniform standards by the government in order to create an environment in which true competition could exist. Contrary to the ideas of Hayek, in which the free market is always capable of generating a form of 'spontaneous order' in the absence of government interference, the history of the development of capitalism is coincident with the emergence of strong national governments. These governments imposed an order in which markets and competition could exist and then grow. The European Union's strenuous efforts at defining a sausage may at one level seem ludicrous, but are in fact linked in a coherent way to the principle suggested here: markets and competition can only work effectively in the context of an environment in which the 'rules of the game' have been laid out in a coherent and decisive manner.

4.3   National competitiveness – from foot race to warfare

During the early post-war era, economic rivalry between nations was conceptualized as if it were a foot race, with each nation running in its own 'lane'. Indeed, the biggest 'athletes' in this contest, the USA and the USSR, shared the characteristic of appearing exceptionally self-sufficient economically compared with other nations. Even then, however, the presumption of the economic self-sufficiency of these great nations may have been partially illusory. In recent decades, economic globalization and the decisive link, as in the case of Japan, between overall economic achievement and success in the international economic sphere has created a new image of nations, in the words of a popular book on economics cited in Chapter 1, facing each other 'Head to Head' in a form of economic warfare.

Recent history, then, has conflated in our minds overall economic success and international economic achievement. Overall economic success is usually identified with the growth rate in national income. 'Economic growth', as it is often termed (offering a rather dangerous analogy with 'natural', biological growth processes), is often seen as the solution to almost all a nation's problems. With sufficient growth, it is suggested, conflicts over the distribution of income will disappear and poverty will be automatically alleviated. While there are many reasons to be less than sanguine about the benefits of growth, not least on environmental grounds, the growth rate remains a central concern of policy makers, and the debate over the factors which determine the level of this growth in a nation remain among the most contentious and fundamental in economics.

As images of the growth process shift from foot race to battle, the growth problem is seen increasingly in terms of a struggle to compete. Hence the current concern with the state of a nation's 'competitiveness'

This concept is, at first glance, less straightforward than the competitiveness of firms. When we say that a firm is competitive in the sectors in which it functions, we are indicating a belief that it is able, over the long term, to sustain sufficient profitability in these sectors to survive. More simply, a firm is competitive if its long-run average costs are below the reigning prices in these sectors.

For a nation, however, there is no such unambiguous guidance from economic theory for defining competitiveness. Competitive success, in political and popular debate, is often judged by relative growth rates in real per capita income. Thus, Britain will be deemed competitive if it can maintain its target level of growth, or can maintain its present relative world ranking in real per capita income.

With the continuing process of economic globalization, the key to reaching these target levels of growth of real per capita income is often taken to be the trend in labour costs per unit output relative to other nations. Thus the most common measure used to identify international competitiveness is *relative unit labour cost* (RULC).

Definition

National competitiveness

A nation's competitiveness can be defined as the ability of that country to realize economic policy goals, especially the growth of incomes and high levels of employment, without running into balance of payment difficulties.

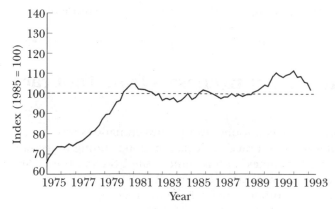

(a) Relative unit labour costs (in domestic currencies) against 15 major competitors

(b) Export cost competitiveness against 15 major competitors (RULC adjusted for exchange rate changes)

Figure 12.7   **Measures of UK international competitiveness, 1975–93. A fall means UK competitiveness has improved**

Source: HM Treasury (1993a) Chart 7, p.14, and Chart 8, p.15

Relative unit labour costs are measured by calculating the wage costs and the social costs of labour at current prices (social costs include items such as social security contributions), and dividing this by the gross product at current prices. This gives a measure of unit labour cost (ULC): costs per unit of output. To convert this to a measure of *relative* unit labour cost, these ULCs are in turn divided by the weighted average ULC for the country's trading partners (weighted by the importance of these partners in the country's trade). This gives a measure of RULC in domestic currencies. In addition, this measure of RULC can be further adjusted for exchange rate changes between the countries involved.

These measures are shown for the UK between 1975 and 1993 in Figure 12.7.

The general presumption is that rise in RULC will reduce a country's share of export markets and of inward FDI, undermine its balance of payments, and drag down the growth rate.

In principle, there are three reasons why RULC can increase and thus a country become relatively less competitive:

1   If wage costs and social costs increase faster in a country than in competitor countries, this will raise the average costs of a country's firms relative to international competitors.

2   If productivity (output per unit of labour) in the country increases at a slower rate than productivity elsewhere, then the gross product by which labour costs are divided in the above calculation increases more slowly than in other countries, leading to a relative increase in the RULC.

3   Finally, on the exchange rate-adjusted measure, a rise in the exchange rate will increase the country's RULC.

The reverse trends will tend to lead to a decrease in RULC and an improvement in a country's competitiveness.

Exercise 12.2

Outline the movements in the RULC indicated in Figure 12.7a and b. What do you think the reasons for the trends shown might be in terms of the three points mentioned above?

One of the great conundrums of this analysis is that while the UK had been improving its export cost competitiveness over much of the period since 1980, there does not seem to have been any sustained improvement in its balance of trade position, as might be expected if national competitiveness was improving.

The trade balance of the UK, along with the USA, Japan and Germany, is shown in Figure 12.8. This demonstrates that the UK was in a sustained trade deficit over the entire period shown from 1983 to 1992. A similar situation faced the USA. On the other hand Japan and Germany were in a generally sustained surplus, despite the latter country's difficulty with its unification programme. Yet on the exchange rate adjusted measure of competitiveness both Germany and Japan were becoming internationally more *uncompetitive* during the 1980s while the UK and the USA were both becoming more competitive.

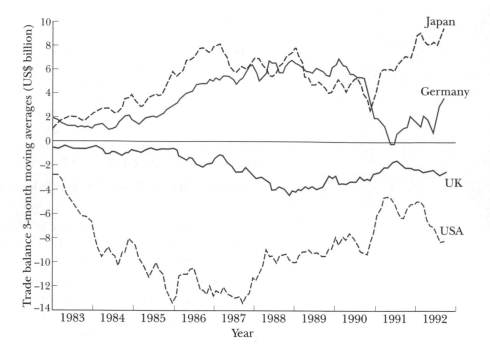

Figure 12.8 **Comparative trade balances: USA, UK, Germany and Japan**

Source: derived from *OECD Main Economic Indicators* (1993) January, p.24

It is seemingly perverse evidence of this kind that has led to a series of criticisms of the RULC approach to measuring international competitiveness, and indeed has led some economists to argue that it may no longer be cost competitiveness that adequately accounts for a successful national economic performance. Non-price factors include quality and design in manufacturing, delivery dates and after-sales service for durable goods, reliability and continuity of supply for non-durables. Along with effective marketing, these items drive non-price competitiveness.

The experiences of Japan between 1963 and 1975, with a rise in RULC and yet a rapidly expanded world market share and above average growth in national income, and Germany with a similar trend in RULC while broadly maintaining its international position, lends support to this view. Fagerberg's (1988) research suggests that Japan's performance is not anomalous: rather, technological advance and efficiency, and the ability to compete on delivery are more important to long-term international competitiveness than the ability to compete on price alone.

Policies for national competitiveness

In general, then, relative labour costs per unit output must be used with caution as a measure of competitiveness. In addition to their lack of apparent correlation with economic success, changes in the *composition* of output (e.g. a change in the tastes of the population in favour of goods which use relatively more labour and less capital) can affect the trend in labour costs per unit output in ways that have nothing to do with trends in the inherent efficiency of the economy.

However, if we accept that keeping down unit labour costs is relevant to international competitiveness, then the analysis above suggests three policies. One is to keep money wages and other labour costs down. Indeed, workers in many countries are constantly being urged by well-paid politicians and business people to control their wage demands.

Alternatively, if a nation is able to maintain suitable growth rates in labour productivity, then increases in money wages and other labour costs can be consistent with stable levels of labour costs per unit output. In general, long-term rises in labour productivity appear to be less related to employees working ever harder than to increases in the quantity and quality of the physical capital and, especially to improvements in the education and skills of the work-force (Marshall and Tucker, 1992). Thus, Flynn *et al.* (1994) note that Britain's relatively low wages have made it an attractive site for multinational investment, but that this attractive aspect has been partially negated by Britain's low ranking by multinationals (20 out of 22 developed nations) for its worker skill levels.

Finally, a currency devaluation can reduce relative labour costs. However, the laws of arithmetic dictate that this is a game that not every nation can play at once, and outbreaks of competitive devaluation between nations (sometimes called 'beggar thy neighbour' policies) can just generate instability. Furthermore, the beneficial impact of devaluation on international competitiveness may be at least partially negated by its inflationary effects in raising the cost of imported consumption goods (which may itself generate further wage demands), and in raising the cost of imported inputs for domestic business.

A final mechanism for attempting to maintain international competitiveness is to interfere with the free market. Frequent devices used here are tariffs and quotas on imported goods, as well as subsidies to key export sectors (see Chapter 13). Many of these kinds of practices are prohibited under the General Agreement on Tariffs and Trade and are violations of the principle of free trade (though all nations commit sins of this kind when it is in their interest). The extravagant success of South Korea in recent decades (an annual growth rate in national income of over 9 per cent from 1965 to 1988) while using such strategies cautions against a dogmatic rejection of such policies.

Question

Which of these approaches to maintaining a nation's international competitiveness seem most desirable?

Clearly, of the alternatives suggested above, the most attractive way to maintain competitiveness as measured by labour costs per unit output is for a society to generate a high growth rate in labour productivity. Indeed, as shown above, some nations such as Germany and Japan have for decades been functioning in a 'virtuous circle', in which a balance of payments surplus has been consistent with rising real wages *and* an upward trend in the international value of their currencies. The sustained increases in labour productivity in these countries have meant real wages could rise without a loss of competitiveness, with further benefits accruing to the work-force from the cheapening of imports through the revaluation of the currency.

Why have these nations been so successful at maintaining these high growth rates in labour productivity? As this is one of the central debates in current economics, a definitive answer cannot be given here. One clue seems to be embodied in a 'stylized fact': in the last several decades, those nations that have had greatest *overall* success in economic growth have also been relatively successful in the growth rates of their *industrial* sectors (*Industrial Policy in OECD Countries, Annual Review,* 1992).

For several reasons, this is a surprising fact. First, as discussed in Chapter 4, the industrial sector typically produces only a small share, perhaps a third, of the total value added of modern developed economies. In many economies, including the UK, this share has been declining. And economic theory seems to offer no obvious rationale for privileging industry over, say, the contribution of the service sector.

Question

The share of the labour force participating in industry has been declining even more rapidly than industry's share in the value added of the economy as a whole. Why might this be so?

This question points to one possible reason for a special status for industry. Unlike the service and primary sectors, the industrial sector seems to be the major site of activities with a potential for economies of scale. An economy which successfully expands its industrial sector may well be the beneficiary of the lower costs and the attendant increases in labour productivity from scale economies which are so desirable for competitiveness. Furthermore, the industrial sector, as compared to services and the primary sector is more open to rapid increases in labour productivity from the introduction of new technologies.

Furthermore, the industrial sector is much more likely to produce internationally tradable goods – goods available for export – than the other sectors of the economy. In the quest for competitiveness, therefore, the presence of a strong industrial sector is often seen as the key to a successful export strategy and as a way of discouraging domestic consumers from over-indulging in foreign imports. Thus, national economic strategists often put a priority on those industrial sectors which seem like good candidates for the development of a nation's exports.

The key to competitiveness, then, may seem very straightforward. All a nation has to do is to direct resources towards the industrial sector, with special emphasis on goods with high export potential. If only things were so simple.

In reality, they are not, as some prominent counter-examples show. The former Soviet Union, for instance, for many years focused resources on the industrial sector, at the expense of agriculture and services. What resulted was a lop-sided economy. It had an enormous body of heavy industry – the former Soviet Union was the world's greatest producer of raw steel and many other key commodities in the industrial sector – but one of the reasons for its profound inefficiency was the lack of a service sector (for instance, sophisticated financial and wholesaling services) to facilitate activities in the industrial sector. The underdevelopment of agriculture also greatly impinged on the quality of life and also prevented industrial development. (Workers spent an extraordinary share of their waking life queuing for food.)

What does seem to be characteristic among nations in the post-war world that have been successful in pursuing economic growth and competitiveness has been their maintenance and upgrading of their standards of education and training. Some nations, such as Germany, have continually maintained high standards in these areas. Perhaps even more notable has been the path pioneered by Japan, and then followed by South Korea, Taiwan and others. These nations have first pursued a low wage strategy to promote competitiveness and export led growth. But then through a significant commitment to education and training, they have been successfully making the transition to a high growth strategy based on a well paid, highly skilled work-force producing high quality goods (Marshall and Tucker, 1992; UN, 1993).

Thus, aside from the need for a population which is well educated and trained, there are few simple prescriptions for the generation of a high level of competitiveness for a nation. This should not be surprising: the issues confronted here are related to perhaps the fundamental question in economics – the nature and causes of the wealth of nations.

4.4 Competitiveness, competition and the wealth of nations

I want finally to draw some links between these approaches to competitiveness and economic growth and the earlier distinctions between static and dynamic approaches to competition.

In the static approach to competition it is assumed that all factors of production are being used optimally – on the upper bound of the firm's 'production function', or the lower bound of their cost functions. A production function is a 'cooking recipe' that relates the firm's maximum output to the inputs used. Orthodoxy asserts that all firms can (and do) follow this recipe successfully.

The usual approach to explaining the rate of economic growth of a whole nation has been rather similar. An aggregate production function for the whole economy, in which a series of economy-wide factors of production (for instance, the labour force and the capital stock) are envisaged as operating efficiently, is used to account for a national economy's growth.

The results from these statistical studies have been unconvincing. One might have expected that growth in per capita income would be largely accounted for by an increase in capital per head of the population, but surprisingly this was not confirmed. Instead there was a very large residual of unexplained growth (as large as 70 per cent of the total) which was dubbed 'technical change'. It was therefore widely suggested that at least two-thirds of all economic growth is due to technical change.

This story was never satisfactory. Technical change in this framework was 'exogenous' – it seemed to drop like manna from heaven. In recent years however, technical change has been made 'endogenous' in growth models by linking it to the nation's rate of investment. It is now argued that there are positive externalities or 'spillover effects' on society as a whole from technical change, hence that there is an extra *social* benefit from enhanced levels of real investment beyond the private benefits accruing to the individual firm. This new approach is discussed more fully in Chapter 14.

The implications of these developments in growth theory are quite startling. Britain in the late nineteenth and early twentieth centuries was investing substantial amounts of its financial capital in, for instance, American and Russian railway bonds. Critics of this practice, such as the MP Joseph Chamberlain, said that domestic industry was being run down. But advocates of the free market asserted that if the return on financial investment abroad was higher than that on domestic investment, to invest at home would be irrational.

The 'new growth theory' suggests, however, that in order to reap the external benefits accruing to society from technical change it might well be rational to ignore the signals of the free market. Domestic investment might be better for the national economy, even if the financial returns to investment abroad are higher. Such a conclusion strikes at the heart of the traditional free market approach to investment, and emerges from what is now mainstream growth theory.

But even this story has its problems. In the last 20 years especially, the existence of purely nationally-based technologies has given way to rapid world-wide diffusion of new techniques. The prize goes no longer solely (or even predominantly) to the nations engendering the new technologies, but to those capable of exploiting and adapting these technologies to commercial needs (Nelson and Wright, 1992), that is to say, to those capable of innovating as opposed to inventing. Furthermore, in recent decades, nations with strong records in invention (for example the USA) have not had outstanding rates of growth, while the pace setters in innovation and economic growth over the last several decades such as Japan and South Korea have not had outstanding records in invention.

The limitations of static economic theory are embodied in its assumptions. Because all factors are presumed to be used optimally in mainstream growth theory (as if hidden away were a world of static perfectly competitive equilibrium), growth itself must be accounted for by the specific *amount* of a factor available to a society.

But what if factors *are not* being used optimally in the first place? What if, instead of a world which we can take on 'first approximation' to be one in which resources in free market economies are being used more or less optimally, we actually have a situation better represented by the example of the steel industry described above? In this case, the great majority of producers world-wide are using resources sub-optimally and are not making use of available best practice technologies.

The prize went to the Japanese industry because of their superior organization of given resources and available technologies and their aggressive competitive *behaviour* identified in the context of a dynamic approach to competition. This dynamic approach to competition does not presuppose the optimal utilization of resources. Static theory has difficulties dealing with the central issues surrounding a nation's economic growth and its competitiveness for the same reasons that it cannot deal with real life competitive situations such as that in the steel industry: it has already assumed away many of the essential questions surrounding the issue of how best to organize resources by presuming that the competitive process has already done so optimally.

Because of the narrow perspective of mainstream theory, these issues are often confronted by writers outside the economics profession. The management consultant Michael Porter, for instance, observes that highly successful economies such as Japan are not uniformly excellent in every sector (Japan, for instance, has weak retail and agricultural sectors). He therefore advocates the creation of national economic strategies which involve the building up of competitiveness in core areas so that nations may gain 'competitive advantage' internationally (Porter, 1990). Whatever the merits of his specific recommendations, this argument for explicit decisions on the organization and allocation of resources is in sharp contrast to the passive approach to resource allocation to be found in free market orthodoxy.

5 Conclusion

This chapter has argued that giant firms are associated with a vast expansion of the business horizon, resulting in an acceleration of world-wide competition and a trend towards the globalization of economic life. In many nations, including Britain, foreign-owned firms now play central roles in the economy. This development, along with the long-term growth in almost every country of the share of economic activity associated with international trade, has led to an unprecedented 'openness' of the world economy.

Giant firms with modern management techniques have played, it has been argued, a central role in the growth of this 'openness' and in the increasingly competitive nature of the world economy. This view was contrasted with a perception, deriving from a static view of competition, that the giant firms engendered a new world of monopolies, displacing a previous 'golden age' of competition.

The static approach focuses on the level of market concentration, with highly concentrated markets viewed as relatively uncompetitive. The dynamic view of the competitive process puts the central emphasis, by contrast, on the behaviour of economic actors – on whether, for instance, firms are *acting* competitively by successfully innovating and producing new products.

The dynamic approach to competition appears the more useful for analysing national 'competitiveness'. The most commonly used indicator of a nation's competitiveness is the trend in its unit labour costs relative to other nations. However, in the real world of dynamic competition, it is not sufficient for a nation just to 'sell itself cheap' by keeping wages low. The ability of a nation to survive and prosper economically is intimately linked with the quality of the products it has to offer and the ability of the economy to assimilate new developments in technology and ways of doing business. These factors are in turn crucially dependent on the skill and dynamism with which enterprises are run, and the success of the society in developing the education, skills and innovative capacity of the population.

CHAPTER 13   INTERNATIONAL TRADE

by Anthony J. Venables

1   Introduction

International trade now comprises around one-quarter of the GDP of the UK: that is, the UK exports a quarter of all the goods and services that are produced, and imports a quarter of everything consumed and invested in the country. The share of trade in income has been on a steadily rising trend in the post-war period, after severe decline during the two world wars and in the interwar period. Around 60 per cent of the UK's trade is with partner countries in the EU, and 40 per cent with the rest of the world.

The trend of a rising share of trade in national income is not limited to the UK. Chapter 12 noted that, in the world economy as a whole, international trade has been growing faster than industrial production since 1950. In 1992, the value of total world exports was US$4640 billion, of which about 80 per cent was commodity trade (in primary commodities and manufactured goods) and the rest was trade in services. This rough division of 80 per cent commodity and 20 per cent service trade was the same as in 1970.

International trade therefore touches all of us as consumers, and most of us as 'producers'. As consumers, both the price and the variety of goods we are able to purchase are determined, either directly or indirectly, by international trade. Although some productive activities are not directly involved in international trade – the standard example being haircuts – most are. In many sectors of the economy the market conditions faced by firms are determined by competition on world markets. These market conditions in turn affect firms' employment levels and hence wages and incomes throughout the entire economy.

In recent decades there have been some significant shifts in the geographical pattern of world trade.

Question

Look at Table 13.1. What are the main patterns and trends in world trade demonstrated by these data?

The table indicates the continuing dominance of the developed market economies in world trade. North America, Europe and Japan together accounted for over 73 per cent of world trade in 1991, not much different to their position in 1970. But the importance of Japan has grown relative to the USA, whose share has declined. The small share of Eastern European and the then Soviet economies declined steadily over the period, while the

Table 13.1 **Shares in world trade 1970, 1980 and 1991 (per cent of total exports)**

	1970	1980	1991
Developed market economies	*72.1*	*63.7*	*73.2*
North America	19.9	15.2	16.3
Europe	45.6	41.7	47.5
Japan	6.5	6.8	9.3
Developing market economies	*17.0*	*29.7*	*23.7*
Oil-exporting	5.8	15.6	4.9
Non-oil-exporting	11.1	14.1	18.8
Eastern Europe and Soviet Union	*10.9*	*6.6*	*3.1*
Eastern Europe	6.6	3.6	1.7
Soviet Union	4.3	3.0	1.4
Total	**100.0**	**100.0**	**100.0**

Note: figures may not add up to totals because of rounding.

Source: *Economic Survey of Europe* (1993), calculated from Appendix Table C.1, p.279

relative position of the oil-exporting countries improved during the 1970s with the oil price boom, and then fell back by 1991. The rising share of the non-oil-exporting developing countries is noticeable, driven, as you already know, by the rise of some newly industrializing countries as manufacturing exporters, although in total, developing countries still accounted for less than 25 per cent of world trade in 1991.

International trade poses three types of questions for the economist. The first concerns the explanation of trade flows. What determines the size and pattern of trade flows? Part of the answer to this question is to be found in differences between countries. Some goods are produced relatively more cheaply in some countries than in others, and these differences create profitable opportunities for trade. Differences of this type are referred to as 'comparative advantage' and are explored in Sections 2 and 3 of this chapter. But it is not only differences between countries that generate trade. We also observe very high volumes of trade between similar countries – for example, between countries within the European Union at similar levels of development and with similar industrial structures. This trade is the natural outcome of competition between firms located in these countries. It often takes the form of 'intra-industry' trade – that is, the simultaneous import and export of similar goods. We study it in Section 5.

The second type of question is about the effects of trade on the economy. In particular, who gains and who loses from trade, and is trade beneficial for the economy as a whole? The existence of gains from trade, under a wide range of circumstances, is one of the most important conclusions from international trade theory, and we study it in Section 2. We also investigate the way in which trade may redistribute income within the economy.

The third set of questions concerns trade policy. What are the effects of deploying different trade policy instruments such as import tariffs or voluntary export restraints? Should a country follow a policy of free trade, or take a more protectionist stance? If trade restrictions are employed, who gains and who loses from such restrictions? These questions form the subject matter of Section 4 and parts of Section 5.

The method we follow to answer these questions is the usual one, of building models which illuminate the concerns we are interested in, while abstracting from other issues. The topic is potentially enormous, so it is essential that we focus on key issues and exclude other issues from our analysis. At the outset, two such exclusions should be noted. This chapter will deal neither with issues of the balance of payments nor of exchange rate determination. This is not so strange as it may seem. A balance of payments deficit occurs if, collectively, citizens of a country consume more than they produce (see Chapter 12). It can only be financed by running down previously held assets or by borrowing from citizens of other countries, and neither of these activities can continue indefinitely – people lend only if they expect to be repaid. What this means is that, on average through time, a country must be in balance on its balance of payments; a deficit and borrowing today must be associated with surplus and paying back at some other date. Since in this chapter we are concerned with long-run fundamentals rather than short-run fluctuations, it is proper for us to concentrate on situations in which the balance of trade is in balance. Similarly with exchange rate determination: we will be concerned with the relative prices of goods supplied by different countries, but only relative prices matter. We do not need to specify whether prices are denominated in dollars or deutschmarks. Our concern with the long run means that we do not need to develop the analysis in Chapter 11 of short-run exchange rate movements or inflation rates (for such a development, see Chapter 19).

2   Comparative advantage and the gains from trade

Our first task is to outline the basic forces that are at work in determining the pattern of trade, and to analyse the effects of trade on an economy. I shall follow tradition in developing an argument that goes back to David Ricardo, one of the founders of the discipline of economics, writing in 1817.

The simplest framework of thought – or model – in which we can operate is one in which there are only two countries (which I shall call 'home' and 'foreign') and two goods (which I shall call bicycles and coats). Each country can produce both goods, and, if there is no international trade, consumers are supplied by domestic production. What happens when there is trade? The answer is that the country that is relatively more productive at producing bicycles expands bicycle output and exports them, while the country that is relatively more productive in the coat industry expands production and exports coats.

This apparently obvious statement has some hidden depths. To bring them out we must first study the productive potential of each economy in more detail. We do this using the concept of a *production possibility frontier*, which you first encountered in Chapter 7. This describes how much of the two goods the country can produce. Figure 13.1 illustrates production possibility frontiers (from now on abbreviated to ppf) for the two countries, home and foreign. The vertical axis measures the number of coats produced and the horizontal axis the number of bicycles. Concentrate for the moment on the line HJ on the home Figure 13.1(a). This is the home country's ppf and the

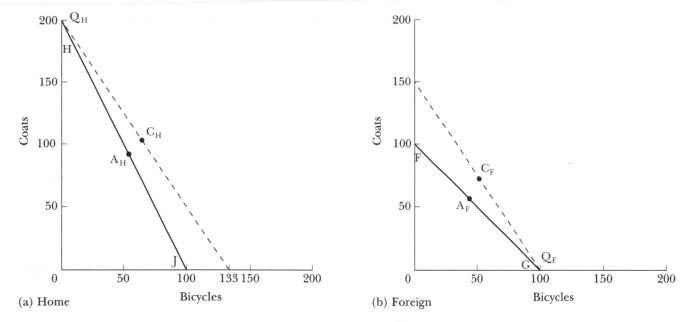

Figure 13.1   **Production possibility frontiers and the gains from trade**

points on it give the maximum output levels that the home country can achieve. Thus, if home produces no bicycles, we assume it can produce 200 coats . On the other hand, if it produces no coats it can produce 100 bicycles. Combinations of coats and bicycles are possible in the same ratio of 2 to 1, since the ppf is a straight line. So output mixtures such as 100 coats and 50 bicycles lie on the ppf.

The ppf is a rather general concept: it certainly need not be a straight line as illustrated, and can be generalized to handle many more than two goods. It is constructed assuming a given level of economic resources.

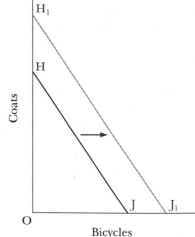

Figure 13.2   **A shift outwards in the production possibility frontier**

Question

Suppose the home country's resources increase. What will happen to the production possibility frontier?

An increase in home's resources would shift the production possibility frontier outwards (Figure 13.2). A decrease would have the opposite effect. Note too that HJ is a *frontier*, so it shows the combination of outputs potentially attainable when home's resources are used optimally. For present purposes we want to keep the shape of the ppf simple, and investigate what underlies the ppf in each country.

We will do this by developing a somewhat detailed numerical example. Look back again at Figure 13.1 (a). Suppose that home has 100 workers, each of whom can produce either 2 coats or 1 bicycle. The home ppf is constructed by observing that if all workers are employed in the coat industry, home can produce 200 coats; if all are employed in the bicycle industry, 100 bicycles are produced; by employing some workers in each industry different combinations of bicycles and coat output are possible, and these combinations are given by the ppf. Our example assumes full employment at all times.

The foreign ppf is line FG on Figure 13.1(b), and it is constructed in a similar way, but with different numbers. Let's assume that foreign has 200 workers, each of whom can produce either 0.5 coats or 0.5 bicycles. Thus, if all workers are employed in the coat industry, output is 100 coats and zero bicycles, and if they are all employed in the bicycle industry they produce 100 bicycles and zero coats. FG shows the maximum possible output combinations in between.

If there is no trade between home and foreign, then the level of production in each country is determined by consumer demand. Production might be, say, A_H in home, and A_F in foreign.

Question

Suppose that the home economy wants to consume one more bicycle. What is the cost to the home economy of this extra bicycle?

Although we usually measure the cost of something in terms of money, a more fundamental measure is given by what we have to give up in order to attain that thing. This is referred to as *opportunity cost*. You first met this concept in Chapter 11. Thus, the opportunity cost of a bigger house is the holiday you forgo; the opportunity cost of working another hour is leisure forgone. In our context, the opportunity cost of 1 extra bicycle in the home economy is 2 coats. This is because if home is to produce the extra bicycle, 1 worker has to be reallocated from the coat industry to the bicycle industry (assuming full employment), causing coat production to fall by 2 units. If we do the same thought experiment in the foreign country, we see that to produce 1 more bicycle requires reallocating 2 workers, thereby cutting output of coats by 1 unit. The opportunity cost of 1 bicycle in foreign is therefore 1 coat.

Now let's allow trade into our model. Suppose that the relative prices on the world market (on which our two countries are the only traders) are such that 1 bicycle costs 1.5 coats. We can think of this as the price of a bicycle being $300 and the price of a coat being $200, although, in fact, it is not necessary to specify these prices exactly – it is only their ratio, 1.5:1, that matters. How does this affect production and consumption in each economy? In home, production of each bicycle has an opportunity cost of 2 coats, but importing a bicycle only costs 1.5 coats. Home therefore contracts its bicycle industry, and specializes in production of coats at point Q_H on Figure 13.1(a) (200 coats). It can then purchase bicycles on the world market, and the combinations of bicycles and coats it can attain by producing at Q_H and then trading are given by the dashed line.

Question

Why does this dashed line strike the horizontal axis of home bicycle production at 133 bicycles?

If all its coat production were exported, it could import 133 units of bicycles (200 coats at price $200 can purchase 133 bicycles at price $300). But since consumers will want to consume both goods, home consumption will be likely to settle at a point such as C_H on this line.

In foreign we have the converse situation. Each bicycle produced has an opportunity cost of 1 coat, but exporting a bicycle finances the purchase of 1.5 coats. The bicycle industry expands, and the foreign economy ends up at point Q_F in Figure 13.1(b), specializing in bicycles (100 bicycles).

Question

If foreign exports all of its bicycle production, how many coats can it buy?

If foreign exported all of its bicycle production (100 units) it could afford to import 150 coats $\left(100 \times \dfrac{\$300}{\$200}\right)$. Again, this is the potential maximum supply of coats to foreign's market. But domestic demand for bicycles in foreign will mean that some are consumed at home and some exported, giving consumption at a point such as C_F.

Notice that the pattern of trade we have outlined is consistent in so far as each good is exported by one country and imported by the other. It must also be the case that the exact quantity exported by each country equals the quantity imported by the other (which just says that supply equals demand on world markets). The world prices of the two goods on competitive markets will adjust so that this is true.

I have spelled out this example in some detail as it allows us to draw some important conclusions. First, trade is determined by comparison of the opportunity costs of producing each good in each country. Bicycles are exported by the economy with the lower opportunity cost of producing bicycles (foreign) and imported by that with the higher opportunity cost (home). Because it is cheaper (in terms of opportunity cost) to produce bicycles relative to coats in foreign than it is in home, we say that foreign has a comparative advantage in bicycles, and home a comparative advantage in coats. It is comparative advantage that determines the pattern of trade.

Notice that our example has been constructed with home having an absolute advantage in the production of both goods: we assumed that home workers are more productive than foreign workers in the production of both bicycles and coats. Each home worker can produce 2 coats or 1 bike; each foreign worker can produce 0.5 coats or 0.5 bikes. But this does not mean that home exports both goods. That is obviously impossible, as it would be importing nothing in return, and foreign would not have the export revenue to finance its imports. Instead, each country specializes in the good in which it is *relatively* productive (i.e. has comparative advantage) and exports that good. This leads to a further observation. Every country has a comparative advantage in something. A country may be unproductive in every activity, but, compared to other countries, it will be relatively less unproductive in some activities than others – these are the ones in which it has comparative advantage.

Superficially, there is a paradox here. How can a country that is unproductive in all activities compete in world markets? The paradox is

Definitions

Comparative advantage

A country has a comparative advantage in the production of good *x* if the opportunity cost of producing a unit of *x*, in terms of other goods forgone, is lower in that country than abroad.

Absolute advantage

A country has an absolute advantage in the production of good *x* if it costs fewer resources to produce a unit of *x* in that country than abroad.

resolved by observing that wages will certainly be different across countries. To apply our simple example again, recall that labour is the only input (or resource) and that the price of a coat is $200. Each worker in home works in the coat industry and produces 2 coats; if markets are perfectly competitive, the worker therefore earns $400. At this wage the cost of producing a unit of output just equals the price it will fetch. Similarly in foreign: all workers are employed in the bicycle industry, each producing 0.5 of a unit of output which sells for $300, so giving a wage of $150. Absolute efficiency differences have therefore created wage differences between countries.

Table 13.2 pursues this line of reasoning and summarizes this model. The first two columns of the table give the labour inputs required to produce a bicycle and a coat in each country. If wages are as given in the third column, then unit costs of production of each good in each country are as described in columns four and five. Now compare these unit costs with world prices. World prices are, of course, the same for each country, and with free trade they also become the internal prices in each country. Now work out for yourself that the pattern of production and trade must be as predicted by comparative advantage. To do this, compare the unit costs of producers to world prices for each country.

Table 13.2   Wages, costs and prices in a simple trade model

	Labour units to produce 1 unit		Wage ($)	Unit cost of production ($)		World price ($)	
	bicycles	coats		bicycles	coats	bicycles	coats
Home	1	0.5	400	400	200	300	200
Foreign	2	2	150	300	300	300	200

Question

In each country, which type of producer (of coats or of bicycles) can break even, and which will make a loss?

Home firms can just break even in producing coats (unit cost = price = $200), but any firm attempting to produce bicycles would make a loss (unit cost being greater than price). Similarly, foreign firms break even producing bicycles (unit cost = price = $300), but any foreign firm producing coats would make a loss. So trade follows comparative advantage.

The second important conclusion we draw from this extended example is that each country *gains from trade*. Consider Figure 13.1 again. If there is no trade, then home consumption has to lie somewhere along the line HJ – that is, without trade you can only consume what you produce. Similarly, foreign consumption has to lie along FG. Trade increases the size of each economy's consumption possibilities, in the sense that each economy can now afford to consume more than it could in the absence of trade. Thus points C_H and C_F have higher consumption (of both goods) than do points A_H and A_F. There are two reasons for this welfare gain. First, trade allows countries to specialize according to comparative advantage, thus bringing about an efficient world allocation of production. Second, countries are no longer constrained to consume what they produce; they can exchange goods through world trade, and hence consume along the dashed lines in Figure 13.1.

This result, that *both* countries gain from trade, is extremely important, although some care needs to be taken in interpreting it. It is quite possible that trade creates gainers and losers within each country, and we shall see examples of this later in the chapter. Trade liberalization often encounters fierce opposition from vocal potential losers. However, what the theory tells us is that each country as a whole gains from trade in the sense that total gains exceed total losses; each country could therefore afford to compensate losers within the country, and still come out with net gains. Notice also that the gains-from-trade result does not say that both countries are equally well off, or that both gain equally. Indeed, in our example we saw a large wage gap between countries. What the result says is simply that both countries are better off with trade than they are without trade.

It is sometimes suggested that the principles of comparative advantage and gains from trade are the most important results in the whole of economics. They apply at the national, and also at the individual level. It may be that a doctor is better than a farmer both at practising medicine and at growing potatoes. It does not follow that the doctor should both practise medicine and grow potatoes. If each specializes in the activity in which they have *comparative* advantage, and then engage in trade, they are *both* better off than if each tries to be self-sufficient.

One of the first Nobel laureates in economics, Paul Samuelson, was once challenged by a distinguished mathematician to name one proposition in the social sciences that was both true and non-trivial. He had difficulty, or so the story goes. But some time afterwards he realized what he should have said – comparative advantage and gains from trade. To quote from Samuelson:

> That it is logically true need not be argued before a mathematician; that it is not trivial is attested by the thousands of important and intelligent men who have never been able to grasp the doctrine for themselves or to believe it after it was explained to them.
>
> *(Samuelson, 1969, p.9)*

3   Sources of comparative advantage

I have argued that comparative advantage determines the pattern of trade, but why does a country have a comparative advantage in a particular product or set of products? In the previous section I took the easy, but unsatisfactory, expedient of simply assuming that some economies were relatively more productive in some goods (as measured by the productivity of workers in each industry). In this section we look a little deeper into the determinants of comparative advantage.

Question

What do you think are the likely determinants of national comparative advantage?

The two main sources of comparative advantage are cross-country differences in technology, and in endowments – that is, the stocks of labour, capital and other resources in a country. We have seen the implications of cross-country differences in technology in the previous section. These differences may arise because of different intensities of research and development (R & D) activity, and different speeds of absorption of new technologies in different countries. The study of this takes us well beyond the scope of this chapter, and I will make just two remarks. First, in so far as technology is itself internationally tradable, it does not provide a basis for comparative advantage, since in principle all countries have access to that technology. It is only by being able continually to keep ahead in the technological race that technology can give a country a comparative advantage. Second, to say that technological leadership is a possible source of comparative advantage is not very insightful, unless we know what determines technological leadership. We must therefore push further back, to see what gives a country a comparative advantage in R & D. This depends, among other things, on the science base and supply of highly skilled labour in the economy.

This reflection suggests that we should focus attention on the second source of comparative advantage referred to above – international differences in endowments. Each economy contains within it quantities of natural resources, land of different types, labour of different skill levels, and physical capital of different sorts (machines, roads, houses, etc.). We refer to each of these human and physical resources as a separate *factor of production*. Collectively, we refer to the stock of factors of production as constituting the *endowment* of the economy. Endowments may change through time, as saving leads to accumulation of more capital, or education raises the skill level of the labour force. But at each point in time the endowment determines the productive potential of the economy, the relative productiveness of the economy in each good, and hence the comparative advantage of the economy.

The study of the relationship between an economy's endowment and its comparative advantage is the subject matter of the Heckscher–Ohlin theory of trade (Eli Heckscher and Bertil Ohlin were Swedish economists writing in the first part of this century). The theory is based on two observations. The first is that economies differ in the relative quantities of different factors of production with which they are endowed. For example, India is relatively abundantly endowed with unskilled labour, the USA with skilled labour, Germany with physical capital (machinery), and so on. The second observation is that production of different goods requires the use of factors of production in different proportions. Aircraft production, for example, makes intensive use of skilled labour, while assembly of electronics demands relatively more unskilled labour. Economists refer to this as differing *factor intensities* of production. Aircraft production is skilled-labour-intensive (and capital-intensive). Routine assembly work is unskilled-labour-intensive.

Putting these two observations together – differing endowments and differing factor intensities – the theory predicts that countries will have a comparative advantage in the production of goods that are relatively intensive users of factors of production with which they are relatively well endowed. Thus, the USA will have a comparative advantage in aircraft production using its abundant skilled labour, and India in goods which require lots of unskilled labour.

Reflection

Before you read on, study the last two paragraphs and make sure that you understand them. Try to summarize the Heckscher–Ohlin theory for yourself in a couple of sentences.

The theory accords well with common sense, although it has not been easy to find empirical support for it. In the first attempt to test the theory (published by W. Leontief in 1953) it was found that, contrary to expectations, the imports of the USA were more capital-intensive (that is, used more capital relative to labour) than its exports. This perverse finding was probably due to the fact that Leontief failed to distinguish between skilled and unskilled workers. We can think of skilled labour as 'human capital', the result of investing in people, and Leontief failed to capture the 'human capital' intensity of US exports. More recent studies have disaggregated countries' factor endowments (for example, a study by Bowen, Leamer and Sveikauskas (1987) looks at seven types of labour, three types of land, and physical capital) but they still find only weak support for the theory.

The Heckscher–Ohlin theory has more to offer than the observation that countries have a comparative advantage in (and hence will export) goods that are produced through the intensive use of factors of production with which they are relatively well endowed. The theory provides a structure within which we can investigate the effects of trade on the prices of different factors of production – that is, on wages, rents and the return to capital. Suppose that the foreign country is well endowed with unskilled labour, and home is relatively poorly endowed with unskilled labour. One would then expect the wage of unskilled labour to be relatively low in foreign (because there is a lot of it) and high in home (where it is relatively scarce). Now allow trade and consider the effects. Foreign will export goods intensive in unskilled labour. This will have the effect of raising demand for unskilled labour in foreign, and hence raising the wage. Home will therefore import goods intensive in unskilled labour, so reducing demand for home unskilled labour, and reducing the wage. This argument suggests two tentative conclusions: first, that we can identify the gainers and losers within each economy from trade, and second, that trade will tend to bring about convergence of factor prices across countries. Let's consider the link between these two conclusions.

The identification of gainers, and possible losers, is straightforward. Relatively abundant factors of production in a country will gain from trade, and relatively scarce ones may lose. For example, consider the enlargement of the North American Free Trade Area (NAFTA) to include Mexico.

Question

Which of the following are likely in principle to be in favour of the extension of NAFTA to Mexico: skilled labour in the USA; unskilled labour in the USA; unskilled labour in Mexico; the owners of capital in the USA?

It is to be expected that owners of capital, and skilled labour, in the USA will be in favour of the treaty, since capital and skilled labour are the factors that the USA is abundantly endowed with, relative to Mexico. So demand for their services – and hence their incomes – are likely to rise. At the same time it is to be expected that unskilled labour in the USA will be opposed to the treaty, since their position of relative scarcity is removed once there is free trade with Mexico. Mexico has an abundance of unskilled labour, so US unskilled labour may expect its wages to fall, while its Mexican counterparts expect better times. So unskilled wages may converge. Although we can predict gainers and losers, we must of course remember that there are also net gains from trade; each economy in this model still gains in aggregate from trade liberalization.

The prediction that trade will bring international convergence of factor prices has important implications, although it is controversial. It is evident that factor prices are not in fact the same in all countries, and the theory predicts that any barriers to trade or any international differences in technology will limit factor price convergence. (We saw in Section 2 that international differences in technology lead to differences in wages.) Despite these reservations, the idea that trade may lead to international convergence of factor prices is clearly of great importance in a number of contexts. For example, it suggests that openness to trade is a good policy for a less developed country that is seeking to raise the wages of its unskilled workers. A less developed country is likely to have a comparative advantage in unskilled-labour-intensive products; by exporting these it will raise demand for unskilled labour, and bid up their wages.

Another example concerns East–West trade. There are currently enormous differences between wages in eastern and western Europe, and the European Union is concerned about the possible flows of migrants from eastern Europe that this might engender. Trade theory suggests that this concern should lead the EU to have a liberal trade policy, permitting eastern Europe to export labour-intensive products to the West. This will raise demand for labour in the East, and contribute to narrowing the East–West gap. This argument can be put in starker terms. Existing East–West wage differentials are probably unsustainable; they can be narrowed either by workers from the East moving West to take jobs (migration) or by the development of labour-intensive industry in the East selling into the West (trade). The latter is probably politically preferable. Similar analysis can be applied in other contexts. For example, if NAFTA narrows the gap in wages between unskilled labour in Mexico and in the USA, then, in the long run, this may reduce Mexican immigration pressures on the USA.

4   Trade policy

Definition

Tariffs

Tariffs are taxes imposed on imports of commodities or services.

So far we have concentrated on two rather extreme situations – no trade and free trade. However, historically at least, free trade has been rather rare. Governments have employed a variety of trade policy measures both to restrict trade volumes, and, by taxing trade, to raise government revenue. The main instruments of these interventions have been import tariffs and quotas. A tariff is a tax imposed on imported goods, additional to the usual domestic taxes. A quota is a quantity limit on import volumes, typically administered by making importers obtain a licence, of which a fixed supply is available. Other instruments of trade policy have been used historically – for example, the creation of trade or shipping monopolies, giving particular companies (such as the Hudson Bay Company or Dutch East India company) exclusive trading

Definitions

Quotas

Quotas are quantitative limits placed on the volume of imports of specific commodities or services over a specified period.

Non-tariff barriers

Non-tariff barriers to trade are obstacles to trade other than quotas or tariffs. These can include legal restrictions and regulatory conditions.

rights in particular areas. Currently we see not only tariffs and quotas, but also the use of 'voluntary export restraints' (VERs), which are agreements with the exporting country that imports from that country should not exceed a certain level, and a variety of non-tariff barriers. Trade policy can be used on exports as well as imports. For example, OPEC members imposed an export tax on oil.

The effect of tariffs and other import restrictions is to offer home producers a measure of protection from international competitors. Figure 13.3 gives a summary of UK trade policy during the twentieth century. The figure displays an estimate of the average tariffs on all manufactured imports to the UK from 1920 to 1990. A liberal trade policy was inherited from the nineteenth century, but was rapidly eroded, and we see protection increasing dramatically through the 1920s and early 1930s. McKenna duties were introduced in 1915, and these were followed by the Safeguarding of Industry Act of 1921, which put duties of 33 per cent on selected industrial goods. Across-the-board protection came with the Import Duties Act of 1932, raising average tariffs on industrial goods to around 20 per cent, with tariffs on some goods up to 100 per cent. Similar policies were pursued elsewhere in the world, in particular in the USA where the notorious Smoot-Hawley Act of 1930 raised average US tariff rates to over 60 per cent. By 1933 exports of the main industrial nations had fallen by three-quarters, to 25 per cent of their 1929 levels.

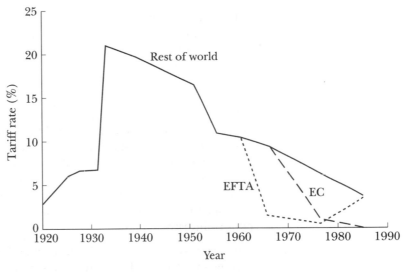

Figure 13.3 **Tariffs on manufactured imports to the UK, 1920–85**

Source: author's calculations from HM Customs and Excise data

The important thing to note from Figure 13.3 is not only the dramatic increase in protectionism in the 1930s, but also the remarkable progress made in removing this structure. In the second half of the 1930s tariff cutting took place in response to reciprocal foreign concessions. After the Second World War, responsibility for liberalizing world trade was taken up by GATT, the General Agreement on Tariffs and Trade. This body was set up by the western powers as part of the post-war settlement, along with the International Monetary Fund (IMF), and International Bank for Reconstruction and Development (IBRD), more popularly known as the World Bank. The GATT initiated negotiations to liberalize trade, and deep tariff cuts were made in the late 1940s and early 1950s. These were followed up by the Kennedy Round of trade negotiations in the 1960s, the Tokyo Round in the 1970s, and the Uruguay Round, which concluded in 1994. The success of these negotiations has been impressive, bringing tariff rates down to average levels of around 5 per cent.

We should note that within the overall picture, the UK has provided preferential treatment for imports from various sources: historically, the Empire and Commonwealth; then, from 1960, the European Free Trade Association (EFTA); and from 1973, what is now the European Union. The current position is that there are no tariffs on trade within the European Union. UK tariffs on imports from the rest of the world are set by the European Union, as part of the Union's Common External Tariff. The average level of tariffs is low, at less than 5 per cent.

4.1   The effects of trade policy

We turn now to analysis of the effects of trade policy. How does trade policy affect the economy? In order to study this problem we shall concentrate on a single good which is both imported and produced domestically, and consider the implications of putting a tariff on the good. We shall conduct the analysis in partial equilibrium terms – that is, by looking at supply and demand for the single good without looking at the repercussions of any changes for the rest of the economy. However, before going on to partial equilibrium analysis we must briefly note a few of the general equilibrium implications of a tariff, or in other words its effect on the wider economy.

A tariff will cut the volume of imports to the economy. I argued in the introduction that, in the long run, an economy's trade must be in balance. If a tariff cuts imports it must therefore, in the long run, also cut exports. The mechanism through which this is brought about is a change in the exchange rate. A lower volume of imports will improve the balance of trade. This will lead the exchange rate to be higher than it would otherwise be, since the supply of domestic currency offered for foreign currency (to purchase imports) will fall (see Chapter 11). This rise in the exchange rate will make exports more expensive abroad and so in turn will reduce exports. This negative effect of import policy on exports is sometimes overlooked, with dire consequences. Many less developed countries have followed policies of tight import controls, thus causing their exchange rates to be 'overvalued', and frustrating attempts to develop export industries.

Turning now to partial equilibrium analysis of the tariff, I demonstrate in this section that tariffs, like the taxes studied in Chapter 10, cause a net loss of welfare to the home economy. I also look at the distributional effects: the gainers and losers. The style of the argument should be familiar, but the diagrams will need careful study at first. Look at Figure 13.4. The horizontal axis measures production and consumption of the good under study, and the vertical axis measures the price of the good. The home economy's supply (S) and demand (D) curves are illustrated. If there is no trade, then the price would have to be P_a, i.e. the price at which home supply equals home demand.

Suppose now that the price of the good on world markets is P_w (expressed in domestic currency units). If there is free trade, then this must also be the price inside the home economy. At this lower price, home consumption is C_f and home production is only Q_f. The difference between domestic consumption and domestic production ($C_f - Q_f$) is met by imports.

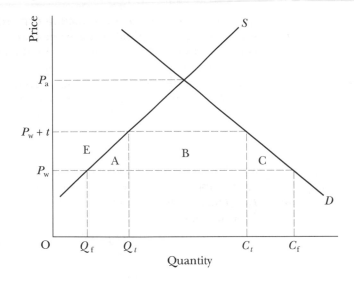

Figure 13.4 **The welfare effects of a tariff**

Exercise 13.1

Explain what would happen if P_w were above P_a. Illustrate your answer with a diagram.

Now consider the effects of a tariff at rate t per unit. This is added to the world price, giving a price (in the home economy) of $P_w + t$. You can see that consumption and production will be C_t and Q_t respectively. As would be expected, as prices rise, production rises and consumption falls. Imports therefore fall.

Question

Who are the gainers and losers from the tariff?

Notice first that government collects the tariff revenue. The value of this is the volume of imports with the tariff ($C_t - Q_t$) times the tariff rate, t, so is given by the rectangle labelled B. Consumers lose, since the price they pay for the good has increased by t per unit over the world price. The cost of the tariff to consumers can be analysed in the same way as the cost of taxes in Chapter 10. Consumers pay the price increase t times their new consumption level C_t, which is the area E + A + B in Figure 13.4. In addition, they lose their previous consumer surplus on the units they no longer consume because of higher prices – that is, area C. So the total cost to consumers is E + A + B + C.

Home producers, on the other hand, gain from the price rise. Their net gain is the area E: this is their total gain from the higher prices (t times the new level of output Q_t, or E + A), minus the increased marginal cost of supplying each additional unit above Q_f, that is area A. Subtracting losses from gains for the economy as a whole, we have *net loss*: that is, B − (E + A + B + C) + E = − (A + C). The tariff has therefore reduced welfare in the economy as a whole.

Intuitively this loss comes from two sources. Recall that the home supply curve also gives the home marginal cost of production, as a function of quantity produced. So as production expands from Q_f to Q_t, the economy is producing at marginal cost greater than P_w, the price at which the good could be imported. Evidently this is inefficient, and it costs the economy in total the area A. Similarly, on the demand side, the demand curve measures the marginal benefit of consuming each quantity. Cutting consumption from C_f to C_t means that consumers forgo consuming units of the good for which the marginal benefit (the height of the demand curve) exceeds the cost of supply (P_w), generating loss totalling the area C.

A number of remarks need to be made about this result that a tariff causes a welfare loss. The first is that the result is obviously closely related to the earlier discussion of the gains from trade. Experiment by moving the line $P_w + t$ up and down on Figure 13.4. You can see how welfare losses change (how the size of area A + C changes) as the level of the tariff, t, is varied from zero (free trade) at price P_w, to the prohibitive level at which trade goes to zero (where $P_w + t = P_a$).

Second, the analysis makes clear the gainers and losers from a tariff. Government gains revenue from the tariff. In societies with poorly developed tax systems this makes trade an attractive tax base for the government to use, and goes some way to explaining the historical importance of tariffs. Consumers lose from the tariff. Producers in the protected sector are better off. It is worth reflecting for a moment on who these 'producers' are. The beneficiaries will usually be the owners of factors of production that are used intensively in the protected sector. To take an example, a tariff (or other means of protection) on imports of agricultural produce will usually raise the price of land (a factor used intensively in agricultural production), thereby benefiting landowners. Of course, these landowners are also consumers, but not all consumers are landowners. Thus, it is usually the case that consumer losses are widely spread across the population, but may be small for each consumer. Producer benefits, on the other hand, affect fewer people, but are relatively large for each individual affected. It is often argued that this makes it easier to organize effective producer lobbies than consumer lobbies, and consequently may induce a protectionist bias to government policy. This is so even though the analysis tells us that the combined gains and losses (to government, consumers and 'producers') are negative, giving a net loss to society as a whole.

Definition

Voluntary export restraint (VER)

A VER is an agreement limiting the amount of a good or service exported to a particular country. It is a form of trade quota.

Third, we may briefly compare the effect of an import tariff with other forms of protection, such as an import quota or voluntary export restraint (VER). Consider a VER.

We can analyse this in Figure 13.4 as follows. The VER takes the form of foreign suppliers undertaking to supply no more than quantity $C_t - Q_t$ to the domestic market. How do they keep to this undertaking? Answer: by raising the price that they charge to a level equal to $P_w + t$. This gives an outcome which is similar to the tariff, in so far as the domestic price is the same as with the tariff, and domestic consumption and production are the same. But there are two important differences. First, the area B now goes not to the domestic government but to the foreign suppliers. This makes it clear that VERs can in fact be voluntary – foreign suppliers are invited to sell at a higher price, and they are happy to do so and take the profit. But this means that a VER is particularly damaging to the home economy as its cost is A + B + C, not just A + C. Second, VERs and quotas are less 'transparent' than tariffs, in the sense that it is less easy to establish how high a country's trade barriers are if these barriers take the form of a mixture of quotas, VERs and tariffs, than if they are tariffs alone. This has led the GATT to press for the removal of quotas (even if they are replaced by tariffs) in order to increase transparency and thereby facilitate negotiations on trade liberalization.

4.2   The optimal tariff

In the preceding sub-section I argued that protection reduced welfare. Are there circumstances in which this result can be overturned? The answer is in the affirmative in two quite distinct sets of circumstances. These circumstances go under the labels 'the optimal tariff argument' and 'second best tariffs'. We explore them in this and the following section.

In our analysis of tariffs we assumed that the world price of the product under study was constant, and unchanged by the tariff policy. However, this may not be the case since the effect of a tariff is to reduce demand for the product, and this may be expected to have an effect on the world price. In general, a fall in demand will tend to reduce the world price. If the world price is reduced as a result of the tariff, there will be some gain in welfare, which could offset the losses identified so far. Indeed, the effect of a tariff on world prices might be big enough for the tariff to generate a net gain to the economy, with lower import prices offsetting the other welfare losses. An optimal tariff is a tariff which maximizes this net gain.

Figure 13.5 illustrates this case. The left-hand part of the diagram is similar to Figure 13.4, and gives supply and demand curves in the home market for a particular good. The right-hand part looks not at the home market, but at the world market for the product, and has home country imports, $C - Q$, measured on the horizontal axis. Take a close look at the figure, and do not be put off by its apparent complexity. It contains nothing that is really new.

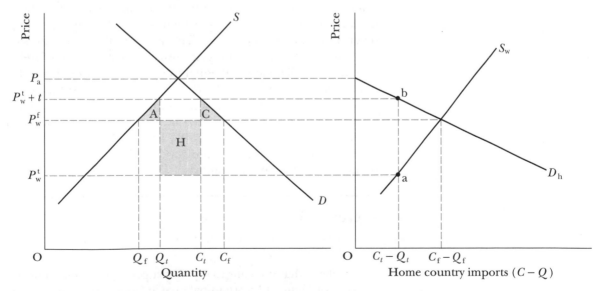

Figure 13.5 **Optimal tariffs and welfare**

The curve D_h is the home economy's demand curve for imports. It is constructed as the difference between the supply and demand curve in the home market. Thus, at P_a domestic demand and supply are equal, therefore import demand is zero, and D_h crosses the vertical axis. As the home price falls, the demand for imports grows and hence D_h traces the rising demand. Each point on it measures the difference between D and S in the home country.

The curve S_w is the foreign (or rest of the world) supply curve of exports of this good. The intersection of D_h and S_w determines the world price of the good, P_w. Previously we took P_w to be constant, but now this price adjusts to equate home demand for imports of the good to the supply of exports of this good from the rest of the world.

The free trade position is P_w^f (the world price with free trade), with home production Q_f and consumption C_f as before. What happens when a tariff of size t is imposed? The world price now falls to P_w^t, and the domestic price rises to $P_w^t + t$. This is the key point. The way to understand it is to see that domestic production, Q_t, consumption, C_t, and hence imports, are determined by domestic, i.e. tariff-inclusive, prices, $P_w^t + t$. However, foreign supply depends on the world price P_w^t (not including the tariff).

Question

Stop for a moment and work out for yourself the argument behind the last two sentences. Why is it only home consumers and producers who face the price $P_w^t + t$?

The tariff is on *imports*, so it raises the price of the good within the home country by the amount of the tax, t. The producers within the country get the higher price ($P_w^t + t$): the consumers pay it. Those exporting to the country get that price too, but out of it they have to pay the tariff t. So the price they receive is $(P_w^t + t) - t = P_w^t$.

Therefore if the world price is P_w^t, the home price is $P_w^t + t$, and home demand for imports is $C_t - Q_t$, which is given by point b on D_h. So what determines the world price P_w^t? This is where this case differs from the previous analysis. The world price must be just such that foreigners are prepared to sell an amount equal to the quantity of imports demanded. We must therefore slide down the S_w curve to point a. At this point quantities of imports demanded (point b) and supplied (point a) are equal, and there is a gap of t between the price faced by home demanders of imports ($P_w^t + t$) and foreign suppliers of exports P_w^t. The tariff has had the effect of reducing the world price for the good below the free trade price, P_w^f, by reducing the demand for imports.

Exercise 13.2

1   Explain in your own words how a tariff on imports can reduce the world price for a good.

2   Explain what it means to say that supply and demand in the right-hand part of Figure 13.5 are in balance at import quantity $(C_t - Q_t)$.

How does this impact on the world price change our welfare assessment? Changes in the welfare of consumers and producers and in government revenue can be identified in the same manner as before. The relevant comparison is between welfare at P_w^f, the free trade price, and the situation with the tariff. On exactly the same argument as before, the net loss as a result of the tariff includes A + C. But there is also a new offsetting element, a gain H. How do we interpret H? With the tariff, the economy is now importing $C_t - Q_t$. The tariff has caused the world price of home's imports to go down by an amount equal to $P_w^f - P_w^t$. The value of this reduction in the price of imports is the quantity imported times the price reduction, i.e. the area H. H is often referred to as a terms of trade gain. The terms of trade are a measure of the prices at which the economy is able to trade on world markets. By reducing the world price of imports, the tariff has improved the terms of trade of the home economy, and the value of this is the area H.

It is certainly possible that area H in Figure 13.5 is greater than areas A + C, which means that it is possible that welfare can be *increased* by a tariff. The value of the tariff that maximizes the gain is called the 'optimal tariff'. What is the relationship between this case and that analysed in the previous section? Look at Figure 13.5, and consider what would happen if the foreign export supply curve S_w were horizontal (i.e. infinitely elastic). In that case P_w would not change and the area H would disappear, so a tariff would reduce welfare.

Definition

Terms of trade

A country's terms of trade are the ratio of its export prices to its import prices. They can be measured as

$$\frac{\text{index of export prices}}{\text{index of import prices}} \times 100$$

Exercise 13.3

Try this for yourself. Draw Figure 13.5, but with a horizontal supply curve for imports, and show that area H vanishes.

The optimal tariff argument is therefore applicable if – and only if – the home country faces less than infinitely elastic supply curves for its imports from the rest of the world. If it does, it can change its terms of trade – the prices at which it purchases imports from or sells its exports to the rest of the world – by manipulating its tariffs.

These arguments demonstrate that, although there are gains from trade, there may also be further gains from trade policies designed to improve terms of trade. Does this provide a practical case for trade policy intervention? Answering this requires consideration of two points. First, can countries in fact influence their terms of trade in this way? This is an empirical matter, which turns essentially on how much of world demand (or supply) of a product a country controls. It is unlikely, for example, that Mauritius can affect the world price of oil by anything it does. But it is likely that if the USA were to raise the domestic price of oil significantly, this would reduce world demand by enough to cause a reduction in the world price, thereby improving the terms of trade of other oil-importing countries as well as its own.

The second consideration that must be taken into account is the effect of these policies on other countries. One country's terms of trade improvement is, necessarily, another country's terms of trade loss. A tariff that improves the terms of trade is therefore a 'beggar thy neighbour' policy. If one country employs them it may gain, at the expense of others. If all employ them, all are worse off. This is a standard prisoner's dilemma situation, as studied in Chapter 5. The message, of course, is that international co-ordination of behaviour is needed precisely to avoid mutually damaging trade wars. This is a major function of the GATT.

So far in this section I have talked about imports, but an exactly analogous argument holds for exports. The optimal import tariff argument is that a country may be able to drive down the price of its imports by importing less. Analogously, a country may be able to drive up the price of its exports by exporting less. This argument is familiar at the firm level, from monopoly theory: a firm raises price by restricting sales. At the country level it says that a country may be able to exploit monopoly power over the rest of the world by cutting exports, raising price, and thereby improving its terms of trade. At first it may seem a little surprising that a country may want to cut its exports, but the example of OPEC makes the point. By restricting oil exports in the 1970s and 1980s, OPEC was able to increase the world price of oil dramatically, and turn the terms of trade in favour of OPEC (and other oil-exporting countries) and against oil-importing countries (some of the effects were shown in Table 13.1 above). Many other groups of primary-commodity-producing countries have tried to emulate OPEC's initial success by forming export cartels to restrict exports and thereby raise price. However, single countries have not usually had sufficient monopoly power to be able to control world prices effectively, and cartels formed of a number of countries have frequently failed to agree on export limits, and hence have not succeeded in restricting exports and raising price.

4.3   Second best tariffs

A perfectly competitive economy leads to a Pareto-efficient allocation of resources, as was demonstrated in Chapter 7. That is, the signals given by prices work to equate the social marginal benefits and social marginal costs of different activities in the economy. However, the presence of 'imperfections' in the economy – externalities, monopoly power, and so on – means that price signals are no longer accurate measures of social marginal costs and benefits. When this happens there is a possibility that policy intervention can be employed to bring gains to the economy. The question we address in this section is, in the presence of such imperfections in the economy, what is the role of trade policy?

The answer to this question is that trade policy may have a *second best* policy role. Imperfections call for a policy response, and we define the *first best* policy to be that policy which is targeted directly on the imperfection. For example, if there is domestic monopoly, the first best policy is to regulate in such a way that the firm is forced to set price equal to marginal cost. However, if the first best policy cannot be implemented (for whatever reason), there *may* be a welfare gain from using some less well targeted policy instrument, this being referred to as a 'second best' policy response. Trade policy may be such an instrument. But, for imperfections in the home economy, international trade policy is *never* the first best policy.

The idea of policy targeting and the distinction between first best and second best policy is important because trade policy is sometimes advocated as an instrument for just about everything from curing unemployment to preserving national culture. The theory of policy targeting provides a systematic way of appraising these proposals. It says that given a policy proposal, one should first identify the problem and subject it to careful diagnosis. On the basis of this, a hierarchy of policies can be formulated in which the first best is a policy targeted directly at the problem that has been identified, the second best is less well targeted so may have some undesirable side effects of its own, the third best is even less focused, and so on.

The general theory of microeconomic policy formulation is well beyond the scope of this chapter. However, I shall endeavour to give a flavour of these arguments by using the example of a famous argument for protection, the 'infant industry' argument. The infant industry argument is that a new industry – which may be perfectly efficient and profitable in the long run – may need initial assistance to get started, and that this assistance can be provided by offering protection (an import tariff) in the early stages of development. In view of the theory of policy targeting, how should this argument for protection be assessed?

The starting point is the observation that (if there are no imperfections) the economy only wants the industry if it is profitable, in the sense that the present value of future profits is greater than present losses. But in this case, forward-looking entrepreneurs should be able to anticipate the future profits, and investment in the industry would in any case go ahead, without protection. This just says that in order to make the case for policy intervention, we need to identify the imperfections which prevent entrepreneurs from undertaking the investment. What might they be?

Clearly, the particular imperfections depend on the industry and country being studied. One sort of problem identified in the literature has to do with 'short termism'. This arises if there is a shortage of entrepreneurs, or if there are problems in the capital market which make it difficult to raise capital to finance current losses on the basis of expected future profits. In these circumstances there is a case for policy intervention – without it the economy might forgo profitable long-run projects. But first best policy is evidently in the capital market; markets for 'venture capital' need to be established to finance long-term projects. If this is impossible, then protection could be used to create strong enough incentives to attract even short-term investors. This ensures that the investment is undertaken. However, the policy is not properly targeted, and consequently has undesirable side-effects. For example, the tariff reduces consumer welfare (the loss of area C in Figure 13.4 in Section 4.1 above). The policy is therefore second best, and there is ambiguity about its overall desirability.

A second sort of imperfection is relevant to the infant industry argument as applied in the context of less developed countries (LDCs). In many LDCs, urban industrial wages are many times higher than wages in agriculture, this in turn leading to massive urban unemployment and the creation of large urban sectors of small-scale unremunerative self-employment. Relatively high urban wages discourage investment from coming in and soaking up this unemployment. The first best policy response is to subsidize modern sector urban employment, in order to make the wage paid by employers closer to the real supply price of labour in the economy. However, such a policy is probably unfeasible, since revenue for an employment subsidy is simply not available. An alternative policy is to set an import tariff and protect industry. Such a policy was widely followed in many LDCs, and had some initial success in expanding industrial employment. But the policy is certainly second best, so that in addition to its direct benefits it created other costs. For example, countries that followed these 'import-substituting' policies typically ended up with an industrial structure out of line with their comparative advantage. In particular, their industrial structure was relatively capital-intensive, and so failed to employ labour to the extent required. Tariffs and import substitution, as already noted, also damaged export industries, in some countries hitting agriculture in particular. Furthermore, because the new industries were not in line with comparative advantage, hopes that tariffs could be removed after the industries had 'grown up' proved to be false.

These examples confirm our theoretical expectations about the role of trade policy in acting as 'second best' policy to offset imperfections elsewhere in the economy. Second best tariffs have benefits – they may well enable a country to meet some objective, such as increasing employment in an 'infant' industry. But they also have costs, precisely because they are second best instruments, not targeted exactly on the initial distortion in the economy. Some of these costs can be easily anticipated – for example, the consumer welfare loss discussed in Figure 13.4. Other costs (such as the damage that import tariffs cause to export industries) are often not fully anticipated when the policy is originally introduced. The message is that second best policy will have implications throughout the economy; these may be difficult to quantify, and their costs might outweigh the intended benefits of the policy.

5   Trade and market structure

Definitions

Inter-industry trade

Inter-industry trade occurs when a country's imports are products of different industries from its exports.

Intra-industry trade

Intra-industry trade is the simultaneous export and import by a country of products of the same industry.

Throughout the discussion so far I have maintained two very strong assumptions. You may not have been fully aware of them, so let us now consider them carefully. The first assumption is that if a country imports a product, then it does not also export products of the same industry; that is, I have assumed that all trade is inter-industry trade. However, in reality a very high proportion of trade, particularly between similar countries such as trade within Europe, is intra-industry trade – that is, trade which involves a country both exporting and importing products of the same industry. The second assumption is that markets are perfectly competitive – I have so far largely ignored issues to do with market structure or firms' market power.

It turns out that these two assumptions are closely related, and in this section I shall relax them both. The argument will now allow for market structures that are less than perfectly competitive, and investigate the way in which this may generate both intra- and inter-industry trade. As will become apparent, relaxing these two assumptions requires extension, but not replacement, of the analytical framework and results we have so far derived.

5.1   The pattern of trade

As an example of the extent of intra-industry trade, consider the data given in Table 13.3, which shows the main exporters and importers of automotive products in 1992.

Table 13.3   **Ten leading importers and exporters of automotive products, 1992 (% share of world exports/imports)**

Exporters	Share in 1992 (%)	Importers	Share in 1992 (%)
Japan	21.7	United States	21.3
Germany	20.5	Germany	11.0
United States	11.2	Canada	6.9
Canada	8.5	France	6.1
France	8.0	Italy	5.9
Belgium	5.2	United Kingdom	5.8
United Kingdom	4.7	Belgium	5.2
Spain	4.3	Spain	3.5
Italy	3.5	Netherlands	2.4
Sweden	2.1	Mexico	2.1
Total of above 10	89.7	Total of above 10	70.2

Source: *International Trade: Statistics* (1993), extracted from Table 111.32, p.64

Question

What do these data tell you about the extent of intra-industry trade in the case of automotive products?

Of the twelve different countries appearing in this table, eight of them appear under both the exporting and the importing column, and these tend to be the important ones in each case. The eight (United States, Germany, Canada, France, Belgium, Italy, United Kingdom and Spain) accounted for 65.9 per cent of total world exports and 65.7 per cent of total world imports. The extent of intra-industry trade is thus very extensive in this industry. Note that Japan is conspicuous by its absence from the major importing nations, though it appeared just outside the top ten in 1992 (12th, with 1.7 per cent). The concentration of exports, and to a lesser extent of imports, in the top ten countries is also worth noting.

So why should a country both import and export products of the same industry? There are two very natural explanations. The first is based on variety. Within most industries output consists of production of differentiated products; different firms produce different varieties of product, designed to appeal to different sections of the market. If each variety on offer appeals to some consumers in each country, then we will expect to see intra-industry trade, with home varieties being exported and foreign varieties being imported.

The second explanation is based on the behaviour of firms in markets that are less than perfectly competitive. If markets are imperfectly competitive, then, even putting issues of product differentiation to one side, firms located in the home country will have an incentive to try and export to the foreign market. Foreign firms have the same incentive, so that the natural process of competition between firms will generate intra-industry trade.

Why is this so? Suppose market conditions are such that the price of the product under study is equal in the two countries, home and foreign. If there is perfect competition, then each firm is a price taker. It chooses the level of output at which marginal cost equals price, and firms do not care where their output is sold. Under these circumstances we would not observe two-way intra-industry trade in the same product. But if there is imperfect competition, firms will face downward-sloping demand curves in each market. They will also have separate marginal revenue schedules in the two markets. Even though price may be the same in both markets, marginal revenue may not be, and this generates incentives to sell in both markets. Putting the same point differently, firms with market power will form separate sales strategies in each different market, thus generating international trade. Of course, the precise form of the sales strategies – and hence marginal revenue curves and volumes of trade – will depend on the form of the competitive interaction between firms, a variety of which have been studied in Chapters 5 and 6.

How does the existence of large volumes of intra-industry trade fit in with our previous discussion (Sections 2 and 3) of the determinants of the pattern of trade? To combine these ideas we have to distinguish between gross and net trade flows. Gross trade flows are the total volumes of imports and exports in an industry, and net flows are the difference between them, so the UK has large gross imports and exports of motor vehicles but is a net importer of vehicles (as Table 13.3 suggests). We now have two complementary theories of international trade. Gross trade flows are determined by product differentiation and the interaction of firms in imperfectly competitive markets. Net trade flows depend on which country has relatively most of the industry's production, and this is determined by comparative advantage – the technological and factor endowment differences discussed in Section 3 above. So in the case of automotive products, Table 13.3 suggests that Japan has the largest comparative advantage of the main producers.

5.2   Gains from trade

The gains from trade that we have so far identified come from allowing production to locate according to comparative advantage. To this we now add two further potential sources of gain. The first is the product variety effect of trade: trade presents consumers with an increased range of varieties. Although this effect is difficult to quantify, few of us would deny that we would be impoverished if imported varieties of goods ceased to be available.

The second source of gain is the pro-competitive effect of trade. To see this, consider a monopolistically competitive industry of the type discussed in Chapter 6 in an initial position with no international trade. Production in the industry is subject to increasing returns to scale, and the number of firms is determined by the condition that there are, in the long run, no supernormal profits. The equilibrium of a single firm in the industry is illustrated in Figure 13.6. Increasing returns to scale mean that average costs, AC, are falling with output, so marginal cost is below average cost. The marginal revenue (MR) and average revenue (AR) curves are downward sloping, and the equilibrium is at point A, with output Q_a and price P_a. At this point, the firm chooses output to maximize profits (production is where

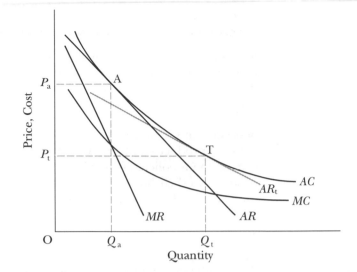

Figure 13.6   **Equilibrium of a firm in monopolistic competition before and after trade**

$MR = MC$), and the number of firms in the industry has adjusted, as explained in Chapter 6, to give only normal profits ($AR = AC$). The key point to note about the diagram is that AR is below AC everywhere except at point A, where it is tangent to it; in other words, the best that the firm can do is to make zero supernormal profits.

What is the effect of trade on such an industry? Let us do a thought experiment. Suppose that there are two identical economies, each containing the same number of firms in the industry. Reducing trade barriers between the economies causes intra-industry trade to occur, as each firm now exports as well as supplying its home market. Each market is now supplied by twice as many firms (both home and foreign). This increase in competition in each market will tend to squeeze price–cost margins and hence force some firms out of business, through bankruptcy or merger. Remaining firms become larger and, if there are increasing returns to scale, will have lower average costs. This is illustrated in Figure 13.6. Increased competition means that the demand (AR) curve facing each firm becomes flatter – if one firm increases price, it now leads to a larger loss of sales to rivals. The new AR schedule is labelled AR_t (this time meaning the demand curve with trade) in Figure 13.6. The equilibrium of the firm with trade, once the adjustments are over, is at point T, where AC is tangent to the new AR_t. The number of firms in the industry may have changed, and it must certainly be the case that each remaining firm's scale has increased, from Q_a (the quantity sold without trade) to Q_t (the quantity sold with trade). There are increasing returns to scale, so average cost and price are now lower, falling from P_a to P_t. This lower price, lower average cost, and increased exploitation of economies of scale together provide an additional source of gains from trade. To summarize, the effects of trade are: more firms supplying each market and hence more intense competition; fewer firms producing in each country, with remaining firms larger and operating at lower average cost. This reduction in average cost is a source of efficiency gain which we must add to comparative advantage gains and variety benefits.

Several further points need to be made about what we have labelled the pro-competitive effects of trade. First, the story above has the gains coming from increased competition driving firms down their average cost curves. It may also be the case that increased intensity of competition forces firms to improve their internal organization, thus reducing costs further. Such effects are well documented for some industries.

Second, it is possible that the potential pro-competitive effects of trade can be frustrated by what may appear to be rather small trade barriers. Part of the motivation for the Single Market Initiative of the European Union was the observation that, despite several decades of 'free trade' between member states, national borders were still acting to restrain competition between firms. Obstacles to trade such as frontier formalities, differing national product standards, and pro-domestic bias in government procurement policies, seemed to be allowing firms to retain dominant positions in their home markets. The Single Market Initiative sought to remove these barriers and thereby increase the intensity of cross-border competition, and release the pro-competitive gains from trade outlined above.

The third observation on the pro-competitive gains from trade is the qualification that – unlike gains from comparative advantage – it is not *necessarily* the case that all countries are gainers. This point is best made by modifying the previous example. In Figure 13.6 it was assumed that there were a large number of firms in the industry, so entry and exit reduced abnormal profits to zero. Now consider an industry that has extremely sharp increasing returns to scale – for example, one which has very high product development costs, such as the aircraft industry. Suppose that these returns to scale are large enough that, when trade barriers are high and there is no trade, each country has just a single firm which acts as a monopolist. This case is illustrated in Figure 13.7(a), which shows the firm's MC and AC curves, and the average and marginal revenue curves AR_a and MR_a faced by the firm before trade. The firm produces at Q_a and charges price P_a. Average cost at this level of output is AC_a. Since P_a exceeds AC_a, the firm makes abnormal profits, shown by the shaded area Π_a. However, these profits are not large enough to encourage entry of a second firm.

What happens if trade is liberalized? The firms in the two countries now compete, and this squeezes their profit margins. Figure 13.7(b) has the same cost curves as Figure 13.7(a), but the average and marginal revenue curves are those that would be faced by the firm if it became a duopolist competing in world markets with a foreign firm. These curves are labelled AR_d and MR_d. As discussed previously, increased competition makes the average revenue (demand) curve flatter (compare 13.7(a) with 13.7(b)). The example is constructed with AR_d below AC everywhere, illustrating that, once the monopoly becomes a duopoly, the firms are bound to make losses. The minimum attainable loss is area L. This means that one firm must exit the industry.

Figure 13.7(c) is drawn following the exit of one of the firms, so the remaining firm is a monopolist at the world level, and has average and marginal revenue curves AR_t and MR_t. This world monopolist sets price P_m, and makes profits given by area Π_t.

In this example, therefore, trade causes one firm to disappear and the other to become a world monopolist. Who are the gainers and losers from this? As before, increasing returns to scale means that average costs fall, so the world as a whole is getting the product more efficiently. But the country that is

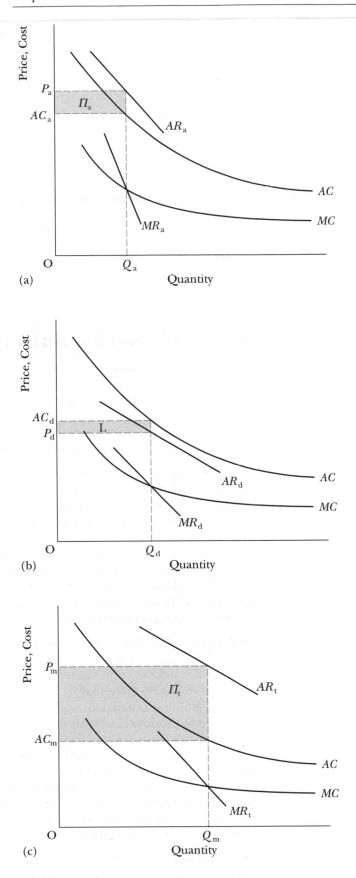

Figure 13.7 **Monopoly and trade: (a) monopoly before trade; (b) duopoly with trade; and (c) monopoly at a world level**

now importing the product has to pay the monopoly price P_m (Figure 13.7(c)), whereas before trade the resource cost to the country was AC_a (Figure 13.7(a)). This makes the importing economy as a whole worse off – the real cost per unit to the economy has gone up from AC_a to P_m. The loss comes from the disappearance of profits Π_a (Figure 13.7(a)) in the importing economy. That is, profits previously earned in the economy (Π_a) now form part of profits earned abroad (Π_t). Such arguments are often called the *profit-shifting* effects of trade. The remaining firm now, of course, makes larger profits – shown by area Π_t in Figure 13.7(c), rather than Π_a in Figure 13.7(a).

The points raised in this sub-section suggest that as we add consideration of intra-industry trade and market structure, it is likely that the gains from trade are many times larger than suggested by comparative advantage alone. However, once we add these considerations, a far richer range of possibilities arises. Large gains are likely, but it is certainly possible to construct examples where one economy loses from opening up to trade.

5.3   Trade and industrial policy

A good deal of international trade conflict arises in high technology industries, in which market structure is far from perfectly competitive. A few examples would include US/EU conflict over the use of subsidies to the aerospace industry; US/Japanese conflict over semiconductors; and EU/Japanese conflict over electrical and electronic goods. In this section we explore some of the policy issues that arise in high technology trade of this kind.

From the point of view of trade policy, high technology industries have perhaps two defining characteristics. First, they have large increasing returns to scale. This may be due to product development costs, or because of dynamic returns to scale. These arise if there are 'learning curves' in production, which mean that unit costs fall the more of the good has been produced over time. Second, there is a perception (real or imagined) that it is essential to maintain a technological lead in these industries, and that falling behind may be irreversible. This irreversibility may arise because of learning curves, or because of externalities between firms creating virtuous and vicious spirals in performance.

Analysis of trade policy in such industries is based on the principles we have outlined earlier: trade policy will bring benefits if it improves the terms of trade, or if it interacts with 'imperfections' in the economy. However, these issues are shown up quite sharply in a high technology industry. For example, holding a dominant position in a high technology industry may grant monopoly power, and this monopoly position may last for succeeding product generations in what may be a rapidly growing industry. Conversely, not being a leader in the industry may mean that the economy has to purchase the product – present and future generations of it, and perhaps also technologically related products – from a foreign monopolist. Clearly, the economy's terms of trade are better in the first circumstance than the second. What can policy do to try and capture potential monopoly profits (and terms of trade benefits) in the industry?

I will capture the flavour of policy arguments by developing the example set out in the preceding sub-section, this time using game theory. Suppose that

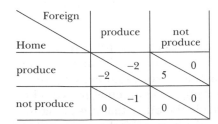

Foreign Home	produce	not produce
produce	−2 −2	5 0
not produce	0 5	0 0

Figure 13.8   Pay-off matrix 1

there are two countries (home and foreign), each with a single firm in the industry under study. The industry is one in which there are very significant economies of scale, so that with free trade the world market is big enough for only one firm to survive. This is as in Figure 13.7, and serves to illustrate the points that need to be made. We ignore dynamics (such as learning curve effects) and assume that the profits in the industry (when trade occurs) are as summarized in Figure 13.8, pay-off matrix 1. The row headings on the left-hand side give the strategy followed by the home firm, and the column headings across the top give that followed by the foreign firm. Pay-offs (profits) to the home and foreign firm are given by the lower left and upper right elements in the boxes respectively.

Firms have two strategies, produce or not produce (in which case they exit the industry). I shall write the strategies of firms in curly brackets, with the first element denoting the strategy of the first firm, and the second that of the second firm. Thus, if both produce, the strategy pair is {P, P}, where P just indicates 'produces'. In this case both firms make losses; these are the area L in Figure 13.7(b) for each firm, and they are assigned numbers (−2, −2). If neither firm produces, the strategies are {N, N}, where N indicates 'does not produce'. Then neither firm can make profit or loss (0, 0) in the lower right-hand quadrant. If the home firm produces and the foreign does not (strategy pair {P, N}), then the home firm takes monopoly profits equal to area Π_t of Figure 13.7(c), assigned the number 5, and the foreign firm gets nothing. The situation where the foreign firm produces and home does not, {N, P}, is symmetrical, giving pay-off (0, 5).

Unlike earlier games which you have seen, this game has two equilibria. One is when home produces and foreign does not, {P, N}. You can check that this is an equilibrium; if home chooses P, the best that foreign can do is choose N (giving foreign 0 as compared to −2 if it were to produce). If foreign chooses N, the best that home can do is choose P (giving home 5 as compared to 0). There is therefore no incentive for either firm to change its behaviour, so {P, N} is an equilibrium. The other equilibrium is symmetrical, with foreign producing and home not, {N, P}. So the question is, what determines which equilibrium is actually attained?

In the absence of policy, the outcome will depend on whether either firm has a *first mover advantage*. As an example of this, suppose it is the case that Boeing already produces aeroplanes and Airbus Industries does not. Then the equilibrium of this game is likely to be that in which Boeing produces, and Airbus does not.

How can policy change this? Home government policy can work in two different ways, either by damaging the foreign firm, or by assisting the home firm. In pay-off matrix 2 (Figure 13.9) we consider the case in which the home government can damage the foreign firm so badly that even in the case in which it is a monopoly – that is, the strategy pair {N, P} – it makes a loss. This effect is represented by changing the pay-offs in the case of equilibrium {N, P} from (0, 5) to (0, −1). The game now has a unique equilibrium in which home produces and foreign does not, {P, N}. The home government has succeeded in shifting the equilibrium to {P, N}, securing monopoly profits for the domestic firm.

Foreign Home	produce	not produce
produce	−2 −2	5 0
not produce	0 −1	0 0

Figure 13.9   Pay-off matrix 2

Exercise 13.4

Check that {*P, N*} is a unique equilibrium in pay-off matrix 2, by establishing that no other outcome will be chosen, given the pay-offs, and that neither firm has an incentive to move away from {*P, N*}.

It is difficult to imagine policies that would enable the home government to inflict as much damage on the foreign firm as would be required for this policy to work. Presumably the most severe sanction that the home government can employ is to close its market to imports, in which case the foreign firm could still be a monopolist in the foreign market. Furthermore, this policy is not credible. The home government might threaten that it would close its market to imports even if there were no domestic production (that is, strategy pair {*N, P*}), but the foreign firm would know that this was an empty threat. If it were actually the case that only the foreign firm was producing, then the home government would be under intense domestic pressure to change its mind and allow imports.

The alternative policy open to the home government is to assist the domestic firm. Notice that assisting the domestic firm in the event that it is a monopolist is of no use. If we change the elements of pay-off matrix 1 in outcome {*P, N*} from (5, 0) to (10, 0), then this has no effect in changing the outcome. The game still has two equilibria, {*P, N*} and {*N, P*}. What is needed is for home government to promise to subsidize the home firm in the case in which both firms produce, {*P, P*}. In this case the pay-off matrix is as described in pay-off matrix 3 (Figure 13.10). In this game the home firm has a dominant strategy; it wants to produce whatever the foreign firm does. But the foreign firm knows this, so the best it can do is not produce, giving equilibrium {*P, N*}.

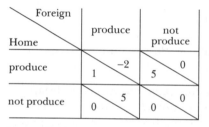

Figure 13.10   **Pay-off matrix 3**

Exercise 13.5

Given pay-off matrix 3, check that strategy {*P, N*} is a unique equilibrium.

It is interesting to note that in equilibrium {*P, N*}, the subsidy does not actually have to be paid since the foreign firm is not producing. An effective industrial policy has been operated, giving the home firm the monopoly position, without any cost whatsoever to public funds. The point is, of course, that the domestic government underwrote the domestic firm in the sense of *guaranteeing* that it would keep the firm in business. A *credible* guarantee of this sort is sufficient in this game to scare off the foreign firm, securing a costless victory.

This policy is an example of what is referred to as 'strategic trade policy'. Although extreme, this example is rather informative, and the main insight from it is applicable in a number of circumstances. For example, suppose that two firms, one from home and one foreign, are competing for sales in an export market. Each firm wants to persuade the other that it is going to act aggressively, supplying a lot, in the hope that this will induce the rival to sell less. However, each firm knows the other is bluffing. But suppose that home government now offers to subsidize the export sales of the home firm. The home firm's threat to act aggressively and sell a lot is no longer just a bluff – it really wants to do that in order to pick up the subsidy, which acts as an incentive. The foreign firm realizes this, and so cuts its sales (rather than see a large fall in price). It seems surprising that the home economy can gain from such a policy – after all, home taxpayers' money is being used to subsidize sales to foreigners. However, if the policy has a large enough strategic effect, persuading the foreign firm to give way to the home firm's sales, then the home economy can gain from the policy.

Strategic trade policy arguments of the sort sketched here have attracted a great deal of recent attention in both academic and policy circles. Do they provide a basis for an active trade and industrial policy? While it is undoubtedly the case that the arguments provide great insight into the way in which policy can be effectively used, two big reservations have to be raised over the desirability of using policies of this sort in practice.

The first reservation is that to operate these policies successfully in an industry requires a good deal of information about that industry: information about technology and demand, and also about the likely response of rival firms to changes in strategy. This information is hard to come by and, more fundamentally, the only people likely to have the information are people already in the industry. But people in the industry are unlikely to tell government the truth if they know that a possible government subsidy is riding on their answer – they are always likely to want a subsidy and thus give information to the government that will elicit this. In other words, design of these policies by governments is likely to be extremely difficult. Many governments that have tried to back high technology sectors have extremely poor records. Recent research (Beason and Weinstein, 1994) indicates that even in Japan, the policy of 'picking winners' has in fact ended up supporting slow-growing industries, not fast-growing ones.

The second reservation is one we have met previously. Policies of this type are likely to be beggar-thy-neighbour policies, and if pursued by all countries are unlikely to make all better off. For example, pay-off matrix 4 (Figure 13.11) modifies 3 by having both governments promising subsidies in the case {P, P}. Producing is then the dominant strategy for each firm, so {P, P} is the equilibrium. The outcome is then similar to Figure 13.7(b) – both firms produce and would make losses, were it not for government subsidies. Once again, then, international co-ordination – through the GATT or some expanded world trade and competitive authority – is needed to control such policies.

Figure 13.11   **Pay-off matrix 4**

Exercise 13.6

Check that {P, P} is the dominant strategy equilibrium in pay-off matrix 4.

6   Conclusion

It is likely that international trade will come to play an ever larger role in economic activity. This is partly because of the success of the GATT in reducing trade barriers; partly because of the development of regional trading arrangements such as the European Union and North American Free Trade Area; partly because many less developed countries are now pursuing more outward-looking economic policies; and also because technical change continues to reduce the cost of making international transactions. In this chapter we have explored the causes and effects of international trade. Undoubtedly trade poses many challenges, necessitating adjustment to new economic circumstances and, in the course of this adjustment, creating gainers and losers. However, the main message of the chapter is that there are great gains from participation in the trading system. Trade allows countries to consume at points outside their production possibility frontier; it permits specialization of production according to comparative advantage; it makes new varieties of product available; and it increases intensity of competition and enables firms to expand and exploit economies of scale.

PART 8

CHAPTER 14

ECONOMIC INTEGRATION AND TRANSFORMATION

EUROPEAN INTEGRATION AND ECONOMIC GROWTH

by L. Alan Winters

1   Introduction

With all the talk about the EU (European Union) and NAFTA (North American Free Trade Agreement), one could be forgiven for thinking that international economic integration is a modern idea; but it is not. For centuries statesmen have realized that integrating the economies of a region is a step towards integrating them in other ways and the latter is potentially a source of power and stability. Thus conquerors forced their monies on the conquered and instituted colonial trade, nation builders stressed not only political links but economic and economic policy links, and statesmen dreamed of international unity and co-operation. Pierre Dubois proposed a European confederation in the fourteenth century, William Penn called for European institutions in the seventeenth century and Proudhon foresaw and welcomed a process of federation at the end of the nineteenth century. Across the Atlantic, Alexander Hamilton made the case for economic and particularly for trade policy integration among the American states in the Federalist Papers, which contributed so much to the theory and practice of the US Constitution.

To be more concrete, Napoleon's Continental System imposed free trade within much of Europe as well as a degree of commonality in standards, practices and laws. Much of this benefit was lost after his fall and the growth of European nationalism. But the idea of integration took firm hold in the German *Zollverein*, a customs union between German states and principalities dating from 1833, which clearly contributed in some measure towards subsequent German unification and statehood.

While all this political or policy-driven integration was going on, 'natural' international economic integration – deriving from changes in communication technology – was also proceeding. As transport costs fell over the eighteenth and nineteenth centuries, nations naturally started to trade more with each other, so their economies became more complementary in the ways described in Chapter 13. By the beginning of the twentieth century a significant share of national output was traded internationally. Then it all began to fall apart. The First World War brought most commerce to a halt and the ensuing Treaty of Versailles perpetuated the economic fragmentation by creating many small nations, which typically used tariffs and other barriers to assert their independence. The slump of the 1930s and the protectionism it induced further reduced international trade and integration, and in the Second World War European integration plumbed the very depths.

At this point, however, a phoenix arose from the ashes. A spirit of internationalism pervaded the allies' thinking about the post-war world and many Europeans' plans for their own continent. This internationalism gave rise to global institutions such as the IMF and the GATT and also sowed the seeds for the gradual integration of the European economies and nations. It is important to realize that, although the destructive effects of economic disintegration were partly the cause of this revival of internationalism and the path of gradual economic integration was one of its main consequences, European integration was essentially a political-ideological phenomenon. It was not driven by the careful calculation of economic costs and benefits, but by a grand vision which had fortunate economic side effects.

This chapter is about European economic integration. We consider briefly its history and then ask how we may assess its economic effects. The chapter traces the steps from the removal of tariffs on intra-European trade, to the removal of other barriers to trade and to the harmonization of standards. The 'Single European Market' (SEM) initiative, also known as '1992', is the subject matter of Section 3. Sections 4 and 5 of the chapter then explore the consequences of economic integration for economic growth and technical progress. In doing so, they introduce some analysis of economic growth, which is arguably the most important sphere of economic theory and policy. First, however, we need to define integration a little more carefully.

2   The European Communities and economic integration

2.1   Degrees of integration

There are two ways of looking at international economic integration – as an outcome or as a policy. The former is what ultimately matters – whether economies become more closely integrated and hence better off – and that is what we measure. The latter definition views integration as a series of actions (policies) that governments might take, a view which then allows us to ask whether or not those policies are worthwhile. In order of increasing depth and commitment, the main types of international economic integration are:

Preference areas whereby countries agree to levy reduced, or preferential, tariffs on certain trade; for example the EU's Association Agreements with certain Mediterranean and developing countries.

Free trade areas whereby partners abolish tariffs on mutual trade, but each partner determines its own tariff on trade with non-partner countries. A potential problem here is that traders will try to import goods into the partner with the lowest external tariff and then re-export them to others tariff-free from there. To avoid this, complex rules of origin tend to govern intra-area trade to ensure that free trade refers only to partners' produce and not their imports.

Customs unions which involve intra-union free trade but also a common external tariff on all members' trade with non-members.

Common markets which are customs unions with additional provisions to encourage trade and integration through the free mobility of factors of production and the harmonization of trading standards and practices.

Economic union which adds further harmonization in the areas of general economic, legal and social policies, and the development of union-wide policies. Economic union may be supplemented by *monetary union*, which entails a common currency and monetary policy.

Political union which is the ultimate form of economic integration. It involves the submersion of separate national institutions. Even within this category, however, several degrees of integration exist. For example, in the USA the states have substantial powers of taxation, whereas UK local government has few such powers.

2.2   The early years

Modern economic integration in Western Europe began in 1944 with the formation of Benelux – a customs union comprising Belgium and Luxembourg (which already had some links) and the Netherlands. The next important step was the European Coal and Steel Community (ECSC), the origins of which were as much political as economic. Its purpose was to stimulate the recovery of heavy industries in (West) Germany while making it impossible for their output ever to be used to wage war again. The proposal – due to Jean Monnet and Robert Schuman – was that, by establishing a truly common European market in coal, iron and steel, countries would become so interdependent that war would be not only 'unthinkable, but materially impossible'. The customs union was to be supplemented by a 'High Authority', which had the power to dictate national output quotas, establish maximum and minimum prices, and enforce the laws of free competition (which outlawed subsidies).

The ECSC was created in 1951 by the Treaty of Paris. The members were the so-called 'Six' – Belgium, France, West Germany, Italy, Luxembourg and the Netherlands. The UK was invited to join but declined – ostensibly fearing to grant power over vital industries to a non-elected extra-parliamentary body like the High Authority. In fact, Britain resisted any measures of integration that contained elements of federalism, parliamentary or otherwise. The ECSC was a qualified success. The co-ordination of investment improved and tariffs were abolished, but other barriers were frequently permitted, such as subsidies to Belgian coal producers.

In 1955, plans were made for the formation of a general common market (the European Economic Community – EEC), and an atomic energy community (Euratom). These came to fruition in the Treaties of Rome in 1957, after a period of intense negotiation. Again, although taking part in the early negotiations, Britain remained aloof from the final agreements. In 1967 the three bodies were merged. Together they constituted the European Communities (EC), which has more recently evolved into the European Union (EU).

The constitutional structure of the European Union

The European Union is the successor to the European Communities. Under the Treaty of Maastricht, 1993, it is developing powers to make common political and foreign policies. Its governance is shared between a Commission, a Council, a Parliament and a Court.

The Commission (the 'European executive') comprises seventeen commissioners appointed by member states for four-year terms, two from each of the larger members and one from the others, plus a President appointed for two years by the Council. It initiates Community policy and executes it, but it cannot actually make policy – that falls to the *Council.* The Commission is explicitly supra-national, and is charged with preserving and promoting the European ideal. It represents the EU as a body in world trade negotiations and is increasingly influential in other fora.

The Council formally comprises the heads of government of all member states, although most business is conducted by the ministers concerned with specific issues, or by permanent officials. The Council shares executive power with the Commission. It may adopt the latter's policy proposals, in which case they become law, but it may not generally amend them.

The Court of Justice interprets Community law. Its findings are binding even on member governments. The judges are appointed by member states, but they are required to be quite independent of national interests and cannot be removed by member governments.

The European Parliament has a small but growing role in the Community. It must be consulted by the Commission and the Council before they decide many issues, and it has some power over the Community budget. Its greatest power is to dismiss the Commission *en masse*, although this is such an unwieldy weapon that it is of little practical use.

Dennis Swann (1992) provides more detail on EU institutions, which may change with the accession of new members.

Integration and enlargement

The EEC provided for a general common market among 'the Six'. The customs union covered trade in all goods; by 1968 all intra-EEC trade was duty free. Eventually, it was hoped, legal and administrative harmonization would allow the abolition of internal customs posts, but this has yet to occur even in 1994. The common external tariff was set at roughly the average of the rates of the partner countries, which involved tariff increases for West Germany and Benelux and decreases for France and Italy.

For most goods the EEC promoted competition and the free market, but for agriculture considerable intervention was envisaged to protect agricultural incomes and employment. Among the initial administrative and political successes of the EEC was the establishment of a Common Agricultural Policy (CAP). This involves high and guaranteed domestic prices (which are not in fact equal across the community), fierce protection against imports, and considerable surpluses of certain goods; it is a very costly and inefficient policy.

For years the EU's reluctance to reform the CAP prevented agriculture from entering the periodic rounds of trade liberalization that have been organized under the auspices of the GATT. In the most recent Round, the so-called Uruguay Round (1986–93), EU intransigence nearly derailed the talks several times, but in the end a mild degree of reform was achieved. Finally being able to cope – politically and emotionally – with a negotiated reform of the CAP shows that the EU is gradually achieving a degree of political maturity.

Britain did nothing to hinder integration among 'the Six', but it was shy of joining anything smacking of supra-nationality or federalism. Britain felt itself different from the other European countries, with stronger ties with America and the rest of the world and also had a much smaller and more efficient agricultural sector.

While Britain favoured intra-European free trade, it resisted the administrative and political structures of the EEC. The Scandinavian countries held similar suspicions. The Swiss constitution explicitly forbade their joining international political associations such as the EEC, and the powers of Eastern Europe objected to Austria joining. These countries, fearful that they would suffer as the EEC stimulated 'the Six's' economic growth, formed with Portugal a looser association in 1960 – the European Free Trade Association (EFTA). EFTA provided for mutual free trade in manufactured and a few primary goods between members. It made no effort to establish common external tariffs, however, nor to co-ordinate any other aspect of economic life.

Very soon after EFTA was initiated, the UK changed its mind and sought full membership of the EEC. After two rounds of failed negotiations, the issue was revived again in late 1968. Agreement was reached in 1971 for accession on 1 January 1973. Ireland, Denmark and Norway reached similar agreements, although at the last moment Norway withdrew its application after the electorate had voted in a referendum to stay out. Once Britain had decided to join, there was virtually no choice so far as the Irish and the Danes were concerned, since their high agricultural exports to the UK would have been decimated if they had stayed outside.

The terms reached for the enlargement were not broadly speaking very favourable to the new members. The EU's convention – probably correct from the point of view of political practicalities – is that new members have to accept all Community practices as they stand at the time of accession. Hence in this first enlargement, the CAP was hardly changed at all, and Britain assumed a substantial part of its financing costs. Although Britain accounted for only about 16 per cent of the EEC's GDP, it was initially expected to provide about 19 per cent of the EEC's total budget; and Commonwealth sugar, dairy products and meat suppliers lost heavily. EFTA carried on with its remaining five members. Significantly the EEC and EFTA signed a free trade agreement in manufactured goods. This has allowed a very high degree of integration between the two manufacturing sectors, with the result that several EFTA countries sold higher proportions of their output to the EU than did several EU member states.

2.3   The effects of integration: tariffs

For most of their existence, the most significant feature of the European Communities has been the removal of tariffs on all intra-EC trade. We now ask what effect that might have on international trade flows and, ultimately, on economic welfare. This is not necessarily a simple matter, because to analyse a free trade area or customs union we must recognize at least three (sorts of) countries – an active country (home), its partners in the integration scheme, and the rest of the world (non-partners). We also have to compare two situations in both of which tariffs are levied. The latter comparison puts us into a world of second best, in which simple policy rules can be misleading: see Chapter 13.

Given the analysis in Chapter 13, creating a free trade area (FTA) or a custom union (CU) might appear to be economically advantageous to the world as a whole because apparently it takes a step towards free trade; it removes tariffs from one set of trade flows. This is true if the common external tariff is set in a very particular way, but it is not certain otherwise. It may not even be beneficial to the integrating countries themselves, since it entails both welfare gains and losses. Removing the tariff from intra-CU trade is beneficial to CU producers and consumers since it stimulates trade between member countries. But that new trade may be at the expense of efficient producers in the rest of the world from which CU governments could previously collect tariff revenue. The balance of gains and losses emerging when a CU is created can be explored using Figure 14.1.

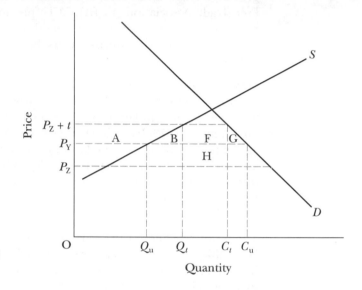

Figure 14.1 **The welfare effects of a customs union**

This figure refers to the home country X's market for a good. The horizontal axis measures production and consumption of the good in question, while the vertical axis measures the price of the good. It builds on Figure 13.4, showing the domestic demand curve (D), and the domestic supply curve (S) in country X. P_Y and P_Z are the prices at which countries Y and Z are willing to supply any quantity of the good to country X.

Suppose that country X initially levies tariff t on imports of the good from both Y and Z, but that it then forms a CU with Y, offering it free trade but continuing to impose t on Z. Suppose that Z is more competitive than Y. That is, P_Z is lower than P_Y so that initially all imports came from Z with border price P_Z. Adding the tariff, the internal price of imports was ($P_Z + t$) and since no domestic producer could sell above that price and none would sell below it, ($P_Z + t$) was also the domestic price. Domestic output was Q_t (the point along domestic supply curve S that corresponds to a price of $P_Z + t$) and consumption was C_t. Imports were ($C_t - Q_t$) and they generated tariff revenue equal to area (F + H).

After the creation of this customs union consumers in X shift to imports from Y rather Z, because, not facing the tariff, Y *appears* to be the cheaper source: i.e. $P_Y < (P_Z + t)$. The internal price falls to P_Y and domestic output and consumption change to Q_u and C_u respectively. Imports increase to ($C_u - Q_u$).

Question

Compared with an external tariff on imports from both Y and Z, is the customs union with Y beneficial? Identify on Figure 14.1 the cost and benefits for consumers, producers and the government from creating the customs union.

Some benefits accrue because the fall in the domestic price from $(P_Z + t)$ to P_Y generates net consumer gains of G and savings in domestic resources of B, just as in Figure 13.4. We refer to such increases in imports, which displace higher cost home production $(Q_t - Q_u)$ and which increase overall consumption $(C_u - C_t)$, as trade creation.

On the other hand, however, there is a loss, because the tariff revenue previously raised from imports from Z is lost. Part of the loss (area F) accrues to consumers who are now paying lower prices; hence it contributes an equivalent increase to their welfare and so has no effect on the balance. The other part (H), however, is completely lost because imports $(C_t - Q_t)$ which were previously imported from Z at a cost to the country of P_Z now come from Y at a higher price P_Y. We refer to this phenomenon as trade diversion: trade is diverted from the low cost non-partner supplier (Z) to the higher cost partner (Y), because the latter is exempt from the tariff.

The balance of the gains from trade creation (B + G) and the losses from trade diversion (H) determine whether or not the customs union is beneficial. This could clearly go either way according to which of the effects – displacing inefficient home production or displacing efficient non-partner imports – dominates. Understandably economists have devoted large amounts of effort to trying to work out the effects of European integration on trade flows and domestic consumption and production, and we turn now to look at some of their results. First, we take a long-term look at overall trade patterns in Western Europe, which certainly suggest that integration has affected trade. Then we look more closely at some recent data to consider EU production and trade together.

2.4   Trade integration in Western Europe

Both the EU and EFTA, as well as the relations between them, hinge around offering partner countries preferential market access, so we would expect trade to show some of the most marked effects of integration. The difficulty in measuring the effects of any policy change is to identify what the world would have been like in its absence: identifying the so-called *anti-monde* . One then compares the actual outcome with the *anti-monde* and attributes the difference to the policy. Clearly the estimate of integration effects is no better than the calculation of the *anti-monde*.

One approach to calculating the *anti-monde* is to assume that some critical variable would have remained unchanged or have continued to evolve according to some simple rule if no policy change had occurred. This is implicitly what we do when we compare 'before' and 'after' values of the statistic in question. Simple estimates of the effects of European integration adopt this approach. But we still have to decide what statistic to look at. In this sub-section we explore three possibilities, working with real data on aggregate Western European trade between 1928 and 1990. Each implies a different *anti-monde*. At least two things may be going on in these data. First, there may be 'natural integration' – the tendency for economies to grow closer together as their economic environments change. Second, starting from 1958 there may be 'policy-induced' integration – closeness induced by changes in policy – specifically the creation of the EEC and EFTA. By looking for changes in trends around 1960 we might hope to capture the latter effects statistically.

Trade shares

The first and most obvious *anti-monde* concerns the share of Western Europe's total exports that is directed to or comes from other Western European countries – the so-called 'intra-Western Europe', or 'intra-WE' trade share. To avoid confusion over whether we are referring to exports or imports we take their average, which we henceforward refer to as 'trade'. Having fallen during the 1930s and 1940s, the intra-WE share increases strongly thereafter. That is, from around 1955 WE trade increasingly comes from other WE countries. That is what our simple model above suggests, so we might conclude that policy-induced integration appears to matter.

Questions

What determines one country's share of another's trade? Must rising intra-WE shares be due to policy-induced integration within WE or could other factors be at work?

There is a problem with just looking at trade shares. The share of Western Europe's trade that occurs with any group of countries could increase either because there is a new bias towards that group or because that group's *total* trade has grown unusually rapidly. For example, as the four Asian Tigers (Hong Kong, Korea, Singapore and Taiwan) have leapt to prominence since the 1960s, they have accounted for an increasing share of Western Europe's trade even though Western Europe has accounted only for a static proportion of their trade. That is, if different partners start to account for different proportions of world trade, we might expect them to account for different shares of Western Europe's trade quite independently of any integration-induced effects. To identify any policy-induced effects, therefore, we need to compare the share of an area in Western Europe's trade with the share of that area in world trade. This is what the *trade intensity index* does.

A trade intensity index for Western Europe is the ratio of an area's share in WE's trade to its share in world trade. Dividing Western Europe's share of its own trade (the 'intra-WE' trade share) by Western Europe's share of world trade, we can calculate the 'intra-WE trade intensity' index. If the index exceeds one, Western European countries' exports and imports are biased towards other Western European countries: WE accounts for a larger share of WE's trade than it does of other countries' trade. We can repeat this sort of exercise to get Western Europe's 'extra-WE' trade intensity index: for all *non*-Western European countries' divide their share in Western Europe's trade by their share of world trade.

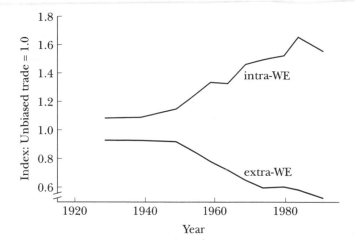

Figure 14.2   **Trade intensity indices for Western Europe**

Questions

Figure 14.2 presents the intra-WE and extra-WE trade intensity indices for WE trade. What do they tell us? Are they necessarily evidence of increasing WE integration? What *anti-monde* is implicit in looking at intensity indices through time?

Figure 14.2 suggests that post-war European integration has biased trade patterns towards intra-WE trade. The intra-WE index has been on a rising trend since 1940. It also suggests, however, that WE trade has always been biased towards itself (trade intensity exceeding one) and against non-WE trade. This is presumably because proximity stimulates mutual trade by reducing transactions and transportation costs. Observe that by looking at the evolution of trade intensity indices we are implicitly using an *anti-monde* which would hold trade intensity constant, i.e. which would have regions' shares of WE trade evolving exactly proportionately to their shares of world trade.

Trade intensity indices rely only on international trade data, but we have already seen that integration is likely to affect the trade-off between domestic and foreign goods as well. One way of examining the latter is to consider the share of GDP, rather than of trade, that is devoted to trade with particular partners. Such shares need to be adjusted for the partners' general willingness and ability to trade, for which we may use their shares of world trade as a proxy. The resulting measure is a *trade propensity*. We define this as follows for WE trade with non-WE partners, that is, the extra-WE trade propensity.

$$\text{extra-WE trade propensity} = \frac{\left(\dfrac{\text{extra-WE trade}}{\text{WE GDP}} \right)}{\left(\dfrac{\text{total non-WE trade}}{\text{total world trade}} \right)}$$

Thus the extra-WE propensity is the share of Western Europe's GDP devoted to extra-WE trade divided by the relative importance of non-Western European countries as a market. The implicit *anti-monde* here is that this propensity should be constant, i.e. the share of Western Europe's GDP devoted to trade with non-Western European economies should normally grow no faster or slower than the relative importance of those markets to world trade in general.

Exercise 14.1

Given this definition of extra-WE trade propensity, try to write out formally the definition of the analogous intra-WE trade propensity and explain in words what it means.

Question

Figure 14.3 gives an index of the intra-WE and extra-WE trade propensities just defined. What does this figure tell us about European integration since 1958?

On this measure, while Western European integration has shot ahead since 1958 (a rising intra-WE propensity index), integration with the rest of the world has declined modestly (see the extra-WE propensity index).

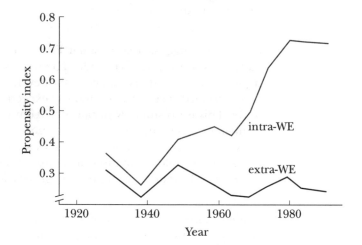

Figure 14.3   **Trade propensity indices for Western Europe**

Question

Comparing Figures 14.2 and 14.3, what can we conclude from observing that since 1958 WE's extra-WE trade intensity index has fallen rapidly, while its extra-WE trade propensity has fallen only a little?

The contrast between the two extra-WE trade indices suggests that the share of West European trade devoted to non-West European partners has fallen mainly because intra-WE trade has grown rapidly, rather than because a smaller share of Western European resources have been devoted to it.

Neither of these indices really addresses the issue of trade creation vs. trade diversion. But the trade propensities on Figure 14.3 do suggest that intra-WE trade has mainly displaced domestic non-traded output rather than extra-WE trade. This suggests WE integration has generated trade creation. We now look at some other data which address this issue more directly.

2.5   The trade effects of the European Communities

The calculations in the previous section concerned all of Western Europe and were essentially concerned with the shares of different partners in West European countries' international trade. Clearly we expect integration to raise the intra-European share, but it might do so either at the expense of non-European suppliers – trade diversion – or at the expense of domestic suppliers – trade creation. Since the distinction between trade creation and diversion is important in determining the welfare effects of a customs union, it is desirable to look a little more deeply into why the intra-European share of trade has increased. We do this now for the EU.

Consider the EU member countries' total use of a good, and distinguish between the shares provided by domestic producers (S_D), partner (i.e. other EU) producers (S_P) and non-partner producers (S_N). Shifts in these shares allow us approximately to identify three effects of a CU:

1   *trade creation* occurs when partner imports displace domestic sales: **higher S_P and lower S_D**.

2   *trade diversion* occurs when partner imports displace non-partner imports: **higher S_P and lower S_N**.

3   *external trade creation* occurs if non-partner imports displace domestic sales: **higher S_N and lower S_D**.

The last – which we have not met so far – arises for two possible reasons. First, the EU has reduced its tariffs against non-member countries through the periodic GATT rounds; this boosts S_N relative to both S_P and S_D; the former shift merely undoes some trade diversion, but the latter is a new and independent effect. Second, the economic effects of integration may shift EU demand towards non-EU goods; economists believe that this happened in the early years of the EEC, when the integration-induced investment boom on the Continent increased demand for UK and US investment goods.

Exercise 14.2

Imagine a good for which domestic sales are £1000, imports from partners are £400 and imports from non-partners £600. Calculate the shares S_D, S_P and S_N and, for each of the following changes, determine whether the trade creation, trade diversion or external trade creation has occurred.

(a) With fixed total sales, partner imports increase by £100 and home sales fall by £100.

(b) With fixed total sales, partner imports rise by £150 and non-partner imports fall by £150.

(c) With fixed total sales, partner imports increase by £100, non-partner imports by £50 and homes' sales fall by £150.

(d) Partner imports increase by £100, as do total sales.

The evidence for the EU is that trade creation has generally far exceeded trade diversion – suggesting that creating the EU has had net beneficial effects. For example, Edwin Truman (1975) suggested that, for manufacturing over the first ten years to 1968, trade creation totalled $7.2 billion, external creation $2.4 billion and diversion a mere $1.0 billion. Corresponding figures for EFTA were $0.9 billion, $3.0 billion and $0.3 billion respectively. Similarly, I suggested, in Winters (1987), that by 1979 UK accession had generated trade creation of around $10 billion, external creation of around $2 billion and diversion of $2 billion in the UK manufactures market alone.

I also found significant trade creation in EU markets as a result of UK accession, but concluded that accession had worsened the UK's balance of trade in manufacturing by perhaps $8 billion per year. This might appear to be bad news but in fact it was probably not, because it implies that UK consumers were able to obtain more (better and cheaper) manufactures than they had access to previously. Of course, the loss of demand for UK manufacturing will have caused some job loss in that sector, but just as labour once switched from agriculture to manufacturing, so it should now switch from manufactures to services in which the UK maintained its comparative advantage. If the job loss caused unemployment rather than relocation, this was a serious problem, but it was less one of integration than of labour market failure. Why were other sectors unable or unwilling to expand to take on extra labour?

Even if it brings economic benefits in aggregate, integration necessarily has both gainers and losers. The policy response to the latter's problems, however, should not be to eschew integration but to help the losers adjust to their new circumstances. The argument that UK accession to the EU caused losses by increasing manufacturing unemployment is essentially a statement that, while the British economy responded to integration by switching workers out of uncompetitive activities, it failed to exploit the benefits of doing so by switching them into competitive ones, i.e. into sectors such as services and finance.

The final piece of evidence we consider concerns the EC-9 – the original Six plus the 1973 accedents (UK, Denmark and Ireland). Table 14.1 presents more recent data, and distinguishes processed foods as a separate component of manufactured/processed output. It shows that even over the 1980s – at least eight years after enlargement – 'double' trade creation (internal and external) continued strongly for processed goods as a whole. Over 1980-91 the domestic supplier share fell by over ten percentage points. The stronger growth was on the partner share – i.e. regular trade creation – but external creation was also strongly positive. The latter probably reflected tariff reductions made in the Tokyo Round of GATT talks, the growth of manufacturing output elsewhere in the world – especially in the Far East – and continuing EC–EFTA integration.

The story for food, drink and tobacco in the right-hand half of Table 14.1 is quite different. The EU's Common Agricultural Policy (CAP) is mainly oriented towards crude agricultural goods – excluded from the table – but it also has significant effects on trade and production of processed foods. It is strongly trade diversionary with high barriers against non-EU suppliers and local production subsidies. As a consequence the extra-EU share of total consumption of processed foods fell over the 1980s, while that of intra-EU suppliers rose. This result emphasizes the costs of integration if the customs union maintains high external protection, because that increases trade diversion. The problem is not so much integration *per se*, but bad external trade policy. The CAP is an appallingly costly policy – costing EU consumers perhaps £800 per family per year – which should be reformed quite independently of the fact that it undermines some of the benefits of further economic integration.

Table 14.1   **Shares of EC-9 apparent consumption of processed products accounted for by three sources 1980–91 (%)**

	All processed products				Food, drink and tobacco			
Year	Domestic production	Intra-EC imports	Extra-EC imports	Total	Domestic production	Intra-EC imports	Extra-EC imports	Total
1980	66.7	19.1	14.2	100.0	82.1	11.1	6.7	100.0
1981	65.3	19.6	15.1	100.0	81.4	11.6	7.0	100.0
1982	64.3	20.5	15.2	100.0	81.1	12.0	6.9	100.0
1983	63.8	20.7	15.5	100.0	81.4	11.7	6.9	100.0
1984	61.6	21.5	16.9	100.0	80.6	12.1	7.3	100.0
1985	60.6	22.6	16.9	100.0	79.9	13.1	7.0	100.0
1986	61.2	22.6	16.2	100.0	81.1	12.9	6.1	100.0
1987	60.5	23.2	16.4	100.0	81.0	13.1	5.9	100.0
1988	58.8	23.5	17.7	100.0	80.0	13.8	6.2	100.0
1989	57.1	24.6	18.3	100.0	79.9	14.0	6.1	100.0
1990	57.4	24.5	18.1	100.0	80.5	13.7	5.8	100.0
1991	56.1	25.0	18.9	100.0	80.1	14.2	5.7	100.0

Source: Sapir (1992)

2.6   Integration and intra-industry trade

We must now consider the implications of intra-industry trade (see Chapter 13). Trade creation and diversion are perfectly possible in the presence of intra-industry trade: we merely need to consider Figure 14.1 as referring to one variety of a good (e.g. VW Polos) rather than to the whole market for that kind of good (cars). Trade creation and diversion then arise not from the total replacement of one source of supply by another, but through changes in market shares: as partner goods become cheaper because they no longer face trade barriers, they increase their market shares at the expense of domestic and non-partner suppliers.

One of the remarkable features of European integration right from the start was the growth of intra-industry trade (IIT). Indeed IIT was first seriously examined and defined in the context of European integration. Such trade appeared to be growing between all industrial countries, but it grew particularly fast between members of the EU and has now achieved quite remarkable levels. Table 14.2 shows the evolution and final levels of the intra-industry component of EU countries' intra-EU imports. Despite the fact that the post-1970 data refer to intra-EU trade among twelve rather than six countries we can still observe the strong growth of IIT. Levels of intra-industry trade appear to be positively related to the degree of industrial development; thus they are highest among the most industrialized EU members and lowest among the least. The strongest rates of growth appear among the middle range of countries – especially Spain and Ireland – as they integrate with the richer original 'Six'.

Table 14.2   **Share of intra-industry trade in intra-EC trade (%)**

Country	1958[1] (1)	1963[1] (2)	1970[1] (3)	1970[2] (4)	1980[2] (5)	1987[2] (6)
Belgium–Luxembourg	54	60	66	69	76	77
Denmark	–	–	–	41	52	57
France	61	68	73	76	83	83
Germany	47	57	67	73	78	76
Greece	–	–	–	22	24	31
Ireland	–	–	–	36	61	62
Italy	42	48	59	63	55	57
Netherlands	50	57	64	67	73	76
Portugal	–	–	–	23	32	37
Spain	–	–	–	35	57	64
UK	–	–	–	74	81	77

[1] Computed with EC-6 trade data.

[2] Computed with EC-12 trade data.

Sources: Sapir (1992), based on Balassa (1975) for columns (1) (2) and (3), and Buigues *et al.* (1990) for columns (4) (5) and (6)

One of the attractive features of the concentration of the trade effects of integration on intra-industry trade is that it probably reduces the adjustment costs faced by an individual EU member country: as its domestic sales of, say, cars are reduced by increased imports from partner countries its, exports of cars to those very same countries are increased as it penetrates their markets. Thus while the additional imports may require a response in terms of design, marketing, efficiency etc., one does not observe the wholesale collapse of industries as the result of integration. This makes it much easier to accommodate integration politically than it would be if the principal effects were on inter-industry trade.

3   Non-tariff barriers and the SEM

3.1   Deepening integration

European integration has always been a rather 'on and off' affair with periods of optimism and rapid advance followed by periods of doubt, retrenchment and even reverse. The former are, understandably, associated with economic booms and the latter with recessions. Thus the early 1980s found the EU very much down in the dumps. After the severe anti-inflationary policies at the beginning of the decade, the US and Japanese economies began to recover, but those of the EU seemed firmly stuck in the mire. Moreover, the rapid increase in intra-EU trade that had characterized the early stages of integration seemed to have halted or even gone into reverse. The cry was frequently heard that 'the steam had gone out of integration' and doubts were expressed about the viability of the EU as an institution, let alone any further progress.

The Commission's response to this situation was dramatic and imaginative. It had long been recognized that the actual integration of the EU economies fell short of the aspirations of the Treaty of Rome, and with the increasing focus on *national* policy and political difficulties there were signs that it was reversing. Recalling the stimulus that the initial creation of the EEC had induced, and following the prevailing trend towards economic liberalism, the European Commission pressed the case for a bold step towards complete economic integration. A new 'Single European Act' provided the political framework, while the economic and legislative programme were defined in a White Paper introduced by Commissioner Lord Cockfield in 1985 (Commission of the European Communities, *Completing the Internal Market,* Com (85), 310). The latter programme is known variously as Completing the Internal Market, the Single European Market (SEM) or as '1992', after the year at the end of which the programme was due to be completed.

The political skill with which the fractious and self-absorbed member governments were led to subscribe to such dramatic economic reform was of the highest order. The process of completion clearly involved a shift of sovereignty from national governments towards EU institutions, and yet it achieved sufficient momentum to carry along even the most doubtful of governments. This was mainly due to the Commission and its devoted and ambitious President, Jacques Delors, which, standing to gain considerable power from the process, was naturally the strongest advocate of completion. While not all the items in Cockfield's list were achieved by the end of 1992, other issues were added and sufficient progress was made overall that the final outcome has been a significant increase in integration relative to the 1980s.

3.2   Completing the European internal market

Completing the European internal market primarily entailed confirming the 'four freedoms of movement' within the EU that had been defined in the Treaty of Rome: those of goods, services, capital and persons. Free trade encourages efficiency in consumption and production, and, to the extent that some goods and services cannot be traded, the movement of capital, labour and technology can substitute. The movement of people is clearly related to the other movements, as well as being a *sine qua non* of an integrated society. The four freedoms were to be achieved essentially by removing the barriers existing to movement.

Question

What factors might hinder the ability to trade between, say, Italy and the UK, even though there are no tariffs or quantitative restrictions on trade between them?

Broadly speaking, in 1985 the remaining barriers to movement, and hence the reform agenda for the SEM comprised: restrictions on *market access* – through, for instance, customs formalities between EU member states, different national technical standards and foreign exchange controls; distortions of *competitive conditions* – for instance, indirect taxes, state aids (subsidies), biased public purchasing, merger regulations, and the airline cartel; and different national approaches to *market functioning* – as in, for example, trade marks, company law, the prudential regulation of banks and professional qualifications. The first two sets of barriers were to be treated by the elimination of the offending practices. The third entailed the *harmonization* of national regulations, although it also frequently entailed liberalization – i.e. harmonization to a less restrictive or interventionary level. It proceeded mostly through the mutual recognition by member states of each other's regulations, rather than the imposition of common regulations by Brussels.

Resisting the urge to write regulations centrally was part of Cockfield's smart politics: mutual recognition is much less threatening to national authorities than is 'interference by Brussels', even though it often entails the same thing. Other bits of smart politics included keeping clear of budgetary issues and all of the issues surrounding monetary union. The latter was pursued subsequently by the Commission, as part of the Maastricht Treaty, and has subsequently come to grief.

The White Paper gives primacy to the question of market access. There are, after all, traditions of negotiating over trade restrictions (e.g. in the GATT), and there is much greater agreement that trade restrictions are harmful than that domestic policy should be subject to international control. Moreover, once free market access is assured, it becomes much more difficult and expensive for governments to pursue other distortionary policies because they can be undermined by international trade. For example, if imports can move into the domestic market, a government finds it much harder to regulate its own firms.

A survey of 20 000 EU businesses in 1987 ranked the existing barriers to intra-EU trade in the following descending order of importance:

- technical standards and regulations
- administrative barriers
- frontier formalities
- freight transport regulations
- value added tax differences
- capital market controls
- government procurement (purchasing) restrictions

The SEM programme has certainly not yet attained uniform standards and regulations across the EU, but it has started the process and set up, in separate legislation, some means for continuing it. In addition, mutual recognition has removed many of the costs of differing standards. The reduction of administrative barriers and customs formalities is well underway, as are the removal of restrictions on intra-EU transportation and on intra-EU capital flows. The harmonization of value-added tax rates and coverage have proved very sensitive, but informal agreements seem to guarantee some progress by the end of the century; steps to liberalize government purchasing have been formally introduced but do not yet appear very effective. The effects of all these non-tariff barriers is three-fold: first, they waste real resources – e.g. lorries queuing at frontiers; second, they protect domestic producers from competition, just as tariffs do; and third, they segment national markets allowing producers to charge different prices in different markets. The last considerably enhances producers' market power and makes competition in EU markets less perfect.

3.3   The effects of the SEM: the EU version

After the SEM programme was agreed and well under way, the EU conducted a detailed assessment of its economic implications, *The Costs of Non-Europe*. (The ordering is not accidental. In the short run, politics is much easier if economists are not busy identifying winners and, more particularly, losers). It was a massive undertaking, with sixteen volumes of reports and papers, a full economic report (CEC, 1988) and a popular edition (Cecchini, 1988), referred to as the Cecchini report. The work has come under severe attack from some quarters since 1988, and its conclusion that the SEM programme will raise EU GNP by around five per cent has been strongly challenged. In fact, predicting the effects of something as broad as the SEM is very difficult, so that, while Cecchini's estimate is on the high side for the effects he considers, it is not beyond the bounds of plausibility.

Cecchini identified four broad areas of economic loss from the fragmentation of the EU market. The first was border frictions such as customs formalities, whose removal he estimated would offer welfare benefits of around ECU 9 billion (0.3 per cent of the EU's GDP). These estimates proceeded exactly parallel to our analysis of trade creation and diversion above, except that, whereas a tariff raises government revenue and hence transfers some welfare from consumers to taxpayers, customs formalities merely waste real resources – there are no transfers offsetting consumer losses. Second came restrictions on production rather than on inter-member trade. Since the value of production far exceeds that of trade the effect of these barriers is larger: ECU 71 billion (2.4 per cent of GDP). Excessive regulation on banks and other service providers figure most prominently in this category.

The third and fourth elements were essentially the pro-competitive effects of trade liberalization that you met in Chapter 13. An estimate was made of the effects of the economies of scale deriving from the restructuring of production (moving down the long- run average cost curve as the size of the market expanded) which yield resource savings and welfare gains, and of the reductions in monopoly rents as markets become more competitive.

The best estimate of gains from their combined effects was put at ECU 62 billion (2.1 per cent of GDP). Adding the four stages together suggested that the SEM would increase EU economic welfare by 4.8 per cent of GDP. As a summary measure, therefore, 5 per cent is not unfair to Cecchini.

3.4   Alternative views of the SEM

Critics of Cecchini's estimates are many. One worry is their undue reliance on scale economies. Most of Cecchini's information on economies of scale came from engineering studies of plant-level technical scale economies, and much referred to the 1960s, well before recent developments in computer-aided design and manufacture removed the need for long production runs in many sectors. Moreover, the evidence that EU firms were too small is actually rather weak (Geroski and Jacquemin, 1986). In many sectors, e.g. chemicals, EU firms are already of world size; thus their remaining unexploited economies of scale may have been overestimated. Furthermore, in an effort to meet the political imperative of making the SEM appear favourable, Cecchini pushed his estimates of the welfare benefits from industrial rationalization to their upper limit.

Another criticism of Cecchini is that he essentially considered each EU industry in isolation and then added up the results. The SEM boosts demand for most EU industries through its effects on trade creation and diversion, and if all could recruit additional labour – as Cecchini assumed – most would have the incentive to expand. But they cannot, because the EU labour force is approximately fixed. If industry A is to expand it must bid labour away from industry B. Under conditions of reasonably full employment the final outcome will depend on the *relative* incentives to expand, and will include higher returns for labour. Economists have long known about these effects, but exploiting them numerically to make predictions about the effects of international integration had to wait until the 1990s. Among the best of these so-called general equilibrium predictions are those by Haaland and Norman (1992), whose results are reported in Table 14.3.

Table 14.3 shows the effects of the SEM for industry groups producing goods which can be traded internationally ('tradeables'), taking account of their interrelationships through factor markets. The first column refers to the effects in the EU. It suggests modest but widespread increases in production: the general increases in efficiency allow most sectors to increase their output even if their inputs decline, but the biggest expansions occur in industries that were previously most afflicted by trade and other barriers and which operated in conditions of imperfect competition. These are the skill-intensive sectors. The metals processing industries, which were already relatively competitive, hence had less to gain from the SEM show an actual decline. The expansion of skill-intensive industries boosts total demand for skilled labour, whose price (i.e. wage), as a result, increases most as a result of the SEM. The rate of return to capital also increases with integration, which in turn will stimulate higher EU investment. The tabulated results do not allow for this, but it is a potentially important effect, which we discuss at length below.

The third feature to note from Table 14.3 is that the SEM apparently boosts EU real income (economic welfare) by only 1.9 per cent of final expenditure on tradeables, which translates into a slightly higher share of GDP. Tradeables are measured as a gross value – i.e. inclusive of material inputs – whereas GDP contains only value added (see Chapter 2). The gains are probably understated, because Haaland and Norman do not measure all the differences between EU member states that the SEM allows producers and traders to exploit, but it is a long way short of Cecchini's 5 per cent. In part, this reflects the latter's failure to recognize adequately the inter-connections between industries.

Haaland and Norman also estimated the effects of the SEM on other industrial economies. Those on the USA and Japan are minor, but those on EFTA, shown in Table 14.3, are significant.

Table 14.3   Effects on production, prices and welfare of '1992': percentage change from base position

	EU	EFTA
Production by industry		
Capital intensive		
Metals	−0.54	2.38
Chemical products	1.40	−0.30
Food products	1.00	0.80
Paper products	0.30	−0.20
Skill intensive		
Production machinery	1.30	−5.40
Office machinery	4.70	−0.70
Electrical goods	2.10	1.00
Transport equipment	4.50	−4.20
Labour intensive		
Metal products	0.30	0.02
Textiles, etc	0.05	0.00
Timber	0.40	−0.60
Plastics	0.70	0.70
Real factor prices		
Skilled labour	0.62	−0.18
Unskilled labour	0.50	−0.14
Capital	0.57	−0.04
Real income		
% of expenditures on tradeables	1.90	−0.40

Source: Haaland and Norman (1992)

Question

Why do you think the SEM affects the USA very little and EFTA much more?

As we noted before, EFTA firms rely very heavily on EU markets. The SEM makes the dominant suppliers in those markets – EU firms – more competitive by reducing their trade costs and increasing their scale and efficiency; this impacts heavily on EFTA sales and thus adversely affects their output. Note that the negative effects are largest on the skill-intensive sectors because that is where the SEM effects are greatest. Moreover, because these industries reduce their demand for factors of production as a result of the SEM, the competitive metals sector can expand in EFTA.

3.5   '1992': a tentative conclusion

All these effects are predictions and thus highly speculative. They are only very broad indicators of likely effects. Unfortunately we have no information yet with which to start discussing the actual effects of the SEM, for the programme is still far from complete even in 1994. We should observe, however, that the political success of the SEM programme led to a huge wave of optimism within Europe. In part this led to more and more ambitious plans for integration as embodied in the Treaty of Maastricht – e.g. monetary union and political co-ordination – which have since fallen under some doubt as the boom and the optimism evaporated. In part, the optimism also led to an investment boom. EU investment was very buoyant in the late 1980s, and it was notable how EFTA firms diverted their investment to the EU. In addition there was a considerable merger boom as European firms positioned themselves in their new market. While it is too early to tell definitely, one might also perceive an upturn in intra-EU manufacturing trade in 1991, which might also reflect the SEM. Thus while there is very little evidence to go on, there is at least some sign that the SEM is having the significant effects predicted for it.

4   Integration and economic growth

4.1   Introduction

Putting aside the creation of new nations such as the USA, Italy and Germany, the European Union has probably been the most successful example of international economic integration to date. It might seem, therefore, that, if even the best integration is worth only a few per cent of GDP, integration may be over-rated. Most politicians and economists, would respond that the problem is not integration *per se,* but the inadequate means we have to measure its effects. In particular they would argue that even if its immediate impact is small, integration has stronger long-run effects on an economy through stimulating confidence and enhancing economic growth. That is, it has strong *dynamic benefits.* This seems quite plausible if one observes the enthusiasm of most non-member countries to join the EU.

While economists may have long *believed* in the dynamic benefits of integration, they have until recently been quite unable to define or model them precisely and, as a result, neither have they been able to measure them. (If you don't know what a fish looks like, you can't say how big it is.) Recently, however, a novel application of an older piece of the theory of economic growth, coupled with some new developments, has opened up fresh ways of looking at the longer term effects of international economic integration. These are the subject of the rest of this chapter.

Nothing is for free, however. Before we can deal with integration we need to develop some pretty abstract tools for exploring economic growth. These are quite complex and will require you to read this part of the chapter slowly and carefully. The pay-off for doing so will be high, however, for there are some quite fascinating results to be uncovered along the way.

Among the most important of these is the surprising result that, except over a transitional period, *investment does nothing for economic growth!* At first sight this seems fantastic – aren't our politicians and businessmen always telling us to invest in order to grow – but, in fact, when one thinks about it analytically it is not such a shock. More investment allows us to accumulate more capital and this increases the *level* of output that a given labour force can produce. But because capital requires maintenance and replacement, we eventually arrive at a point at which all the extra output is absorbed by the extra maintenance and replacement required to keep the larger capital stock intact. At that point the stock of capital stops increasing (*net investment is zero*), output stabilizes and there is no more economic growth. Section 4 explores this result and looks at its implications for measuring the consequences of economic integration. Even if integration does not permanently increase the rate of economic growth, the fact that it encourages the accumulation of capital increases output and income above the levels we have described previously.

Section 5 then introduces two additional concepts which might further enhance the effects of integration. First, human capital. Like physical capital such as machinery, human capital makes workers more productive. It also requires building up through investment, but it represents another way of increasing output per worker and hence of eventually raising incomes and consumption.

The second additional concept is *economies of scale*. These increase output per unit input as the overall size of a firm, industry or economy rises, and hence mean that both integration and any resulting capital accumulation have a bigger effect on output than they would in a world of constant returns to scale. Neither of these factors overcomes the basic constraint that replacement eventually eats up all the extra investment, but they each mean that it takes longer for the constraint to bite.

If it is so simple to show that investment does not permanently stimulate growth, why does the result challenge our 'common sense' and everyday experience? In part, this is because in the real world the final benefits of accumulating extra capital emerge over several years of increasing GDP. This can *look* like a permanent improvement in growth even if, strictly speaking, it is not.

A second reason for believing that investment might affect growth is that it encourages technical advance. Most advances in production technique or in the quality of goods produced must be embodied either in physical equipment or in the skills of the workers. Thus, if there is a lot of investment, there is more scope for incorporating up-to-date technology, and hence for getting more output per unit of input. Even this process must come to an end, however, for eventually all equipment and skills will come to embody best-practice techniques. The only way of avoiding such an end point is if *technical progress itself is stimulated by investment*. If that is the case, it is conceivable that a positive external shock such as the SEM could establish

Definition

Human capital

Human capital is the level of knowledge and skills embodied in the work force through education and training.

a virtuous circle of perpetual growth. Research and development is essentially a fixed cost, and the larger the economy the greater the likely earnings from inventing something. Thus, as the economy grows the returns to research and development increase (higher earnings with fixed costs), so more is undertaken. As a result more technical progress occurs which in turn boosts income and sows the seeds for yet more research and development, and so on.

This story sounds extremely attractive. The problem is that, so far, it is not much more than a story, for it is extremely difficult to imagine that the conditions under which it occurs could be satisfied, and there is not yet that much evidence that economies do embark on perpetual virtuous circles. Thus, while the chapter concludes on a very favourable note, we should maintain a fair degree of caution in commenting on the real world. The issue for practical policy is not whether a virtuous circle *could* occur but whether it is *likely* to do so and what costs we might incur if we rely on it and are proved wrong.

4.2   The production function

Economic growth in the real world is a complex phenomenon, and, as we have already seen in other cases, in order to make any sense of it economists have to simplify matters drastically. We shall assume in this part that there is just one output – the level of which we shall term Y – which can be both consumed and invested. (Think of it as corn – which we can eat or replant – or as GDP). We shall also assume for now that it is produced by combining two inputs: labour, in amount L, which is a non-produced primary factor, and capital, in amount K, which is produced by investing some of Y. The relationship between output and inputs is a *production function*, not this time, as in Chapter 4, for a single firm, but for the whole economy. We write it as

$$Y = g(K,L)$$

where the notation $g(K,L)$ denotes a mathematical function that is applied to the *arguments* (factors) in the brackets.

We do not need to specify the function g completely but, to simplify, we shall assume that it displays two properties:

(a) constant returns to scale, so that an x per cent increase in both inputs generates an x per cent increase in output;

(b) positive, but diminishing, marginal productivities of each factor: that is, if the input of one factor is increased *holding the input of the other constant*, output still rises, but, as further units of the first factor are added, the increments to output become progressively smaller.

To make life even simpler we shall assume that the labour force in our economy is not growing at all. For analysing economic growth in Europe this is not an outrageous assumption, but it would not be suitable for analysing developing countries' experience.

If the labour force, L, is constant, output varies only with capital, so we can suppress L in the production function and just write

$$Y = f(K)$$

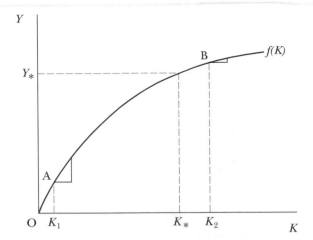

Figure 14.4   **The production function, showing diminishing returns to capital**

Diminishing marginal returns (condition (b) above) means that adding more capital, K, to a fixed labour supply will increase output, Y, but at a decreasing rate. So the relationship between output Y and capital inputs K (given L) can be represented by the line $f(K)$ in Figure 14.4: a rising but gradually flattening curve, along which the first few units of K are very productive but later units are less so.

Reflection

Stop here and look carefully at Figure 14.4. With capital input K_*, output is Y_*. From point A, with low capital input K_1, an additional unit of capital generates a larger increase in output Y than does an additional unit of capital input at B, with higher capital input K_2. Make sure you understand that before reading on.

It is the shape of this function, showing diminishing returns, which lies behind the assertion that investment cannot permanently increase the rate of economic growth.

4.3   Determining income

It turns out that the economy in Figure 14.4 will not grow, but, in exploring why, we can start to understand some of the basic ideas behind economic growth. To do so we need to recognise two further concepts. The first is *depreciation* (see Chapters 2 and 4). Capital equipment wears out, and to make life simple (again!) we shall assume that proportion δ (delta) of it wears out every year. That is, if we start the year (finish the previous year) with capital stock K, δK of it wears out by the end of this year. Hence if the economy is just to stand still it has to find δK of new capital per year – that is, it has to *invest* δK per year.

The second important concept is *saving*. In order to invest, our economy must save. A convenient assumption is that consumers save a fixed proportion *s* of income *Y*. So saving can be written *sY*. But we already know that $Y = f(K)$, as illustrated on Figure 14.4. So saving can be rewritten as

$$sY = sf(K)$$

In order for the economy to maintain its capital stock constant, in order to stand still, there must be saving to cover the investment. Hence:

$$\delta K = sf(K)$$

Savings, depreciation and growth

You may like to work through a more formal statement of that argument, and consolidate some ideas you have already learned. First, the production function (above) shows that

$$Y = f(K) \tag{1}$$

Second, if *I* is gross investment, then from the discussion of depreciation, in order to maintain the capital stock:

$$I = \delta K \tag{2}$$

Now, in the simple world we are considering here, income is either consumed (*C*) or saved (*S*), and output is either consumed (*C*) or invested (*I*) in new capital equipment (Chapter 2). Income for the whole economy is the same as the output that it produces, *Y*, so this implies that

$$Y = C + S = C + I \tag{3}$$

which in turn, implies that what is not consumed is saved and immediately invested

$$I = S \tag{4}$$

Savings are determined by people's incomes and by their preferences between current and future consumption. If consumers save a fixed proportion *s*, of their income, then

$$S = sY \tag{5}$$

Given $I = S$ (equation 4), and $I = \delta K$ (equation 2), and $S = sY$ (equation 5) we can see that in equilibrium,

$$sY = \delta K \tag{6}$$

which implies from (1)

$$sf(K) = \delta K \tag{7}$$

We can now develop Figure 14.4, to identify the point where the capital stock is constant. That point is an equilibrium, a position where the economy will settle and from which it will not move away. To show this we plot $sf(K)$ and δK on the same diagram (Figure 14.5).

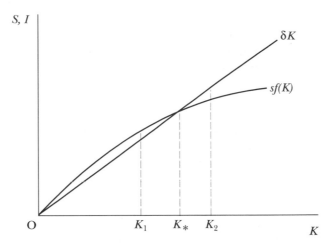

Figure 14.5   The economy in no-growth equilibrium

In Figure 14.5, $sf(K)$ is a scaled down version of $f(K)$ on Figure 14.4. So, for example, if $s = 0.1$ (10 per cent of income is saved), then for any level of K along the horizontal axis, $sf(K)$ on the vertical axis of Figure 14.5 is one tenth (10 per cent) of $f(K)$ as measured vertically on Figure 14.4. The straight line is δK: for any K measured horizontally, depreciation, or necessary investment (measured vertically) is δK. Where the two lines intersect, savings equal necessary investment and the economy is in equilibrium, with capital stock K_* on Figure 14.5. We can use this in Figure 14.4 to read off the resulting level of income Y_*.

The interesting thing about K_* and Y_* is that they are constant. There is no growth in Y. Given people's desire to save for the future, the savings rate s is determined. Investment must equal savings, and a given volume of investment can support only a certain capital stock according to the rate of depreciation. Given the capital stock, income is given.

Question

So why should the capital stock settle precisely at K_*? To answer this, consider what happens if it lies above at, say, K_2 on Figure 14.5.

With a capital stock of K_2, depreciation occurs at rate δK_2; this exceeds the rate of new investment, which equals savings $sf(K_2)$, and so the capital stock declines back towards K_*. A similar story pertains at points below K_* such as K_1. At K_1 depreciation is less than gross investment and so capital accumulates towards K_*. Thus, in fact, in this simplified world there are strong forces which return the capital stock and income to their equilibrium levels, K_* and Y_*.

4.4   Economic growth

What might change the level of income and hence induce economic growth? It is important to distinguish between changes in income from one constant level to another, genuine growth in which income continues to grow year on year, and finally changes in the rate of growth, whereby income increases through time but the rate at which it does so changes.

Question

How would the lines in Figure 14.5 have to shift to increase the equilibrium capital stock and income? What might cause those shifts?

We start by considering two shocks that change just the *level* of income. First, suppose that the capital stock suddenly became more durable, so that the rate of depreciation fell from δ to, say, δ'. The straight line in our figure would swivel downwards – see Figure 14.6: each unit of K would now require only δ' instead of δ of new investment per year to be replaced, and so a given rate of investment would support a higher capital stock. Starting from the initial level K_* gross investment would now exceed depreciation, so K would rise towards K'; as the capital stock rose, so would income and savings until full equilibrium was re-established at K' (with a correspondingly higher income which could be read off from Figure 14.4).

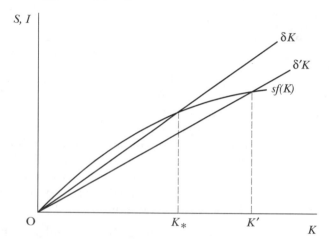

Figure 14.6 **The effect of a lower rate of depreciation on the equilibrium capital stock**

The second way of inducing a step change in income is if the savings rate increases: see Figure 14.7. Suppose that people become keener on future consumption and so save fraction s'' of their income rather than s. Now we have a new savings relationship $s''f(K)$, which, given the old investment relationship, implies a new higher capital stock K'' and (from Figure 14.4) a new higher level of income. More savings implies more investment which implies a higher stock of capital and consequently a higher income. Again, however, we must note that once the equilibrium K'' and the corresponding higher level of income have been established, no further change occurs.

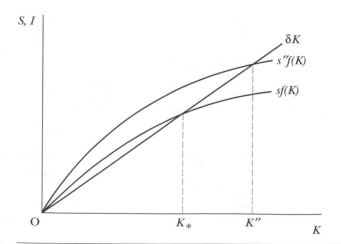

Figure 14.7 **The effect of a higher rate of saving on the equilibrium capital stock**

This example helps to establish that investment does not stimulate economic *growth*. The increase in savings generates an increase in investment, and while the economy evolves from K_* (and Y_*) to K'' with a higher Y, economic growth occurs. But, as soon as we reach the new equilibrium, the extra investment is entirely absorbed by the extra depreciation resulting from the higher capital stock ($\delta K''$ exceeds δK_*) and further progress ceases. *Income is higher, but it is not growing;* the growth rate is still zero just as it was before. Moreover the population is not necessarily better off at the higher income level, for although income is higher, savings are also higher, so *consumption* has not necessarily increased.

The previous paragraph is extremely important in the context of economic policy. Politicians often tell us that investment is necessary for economic growth, whereas this simple analysis suggests that, while increased investment will stimulate the economy to move from a lower to a higher level of income, it will do nothing for the underlying rate of growth, *except during that transitional period*. Eventually the extra investment will be entirely absorbed by the higher replacement demand resultant from the higher capital stock. We have discovered this result in the context of a model with zero growth, but it generalizes to simple models with constant growth rates. We now turn to economic growth proper.

If we refer back to Figure 14.7, it is plain that the cause of the increase in income is the expansion of savings which induces an expansion in investment. We increased the proportion of income saved s, but this clearly could not go on indefinitely since s could never exceed unity (100 per cent). We could envisage another cause of increased savings, which may be able to continue for ever: maybe $f(K)$ could be raised indefinitely. Then, even holding the savings *rate*, s, constant, total savings would increase and economic growth would occur.

What would increase $f(K)$, i.e. what would allow us to generate more income from a given capital stock? Three candidates present themselves. First, the labour force, L, could grow. We have assumed it constant so far, and hence have suppressed it in our notation, but since the marginal product of labour is positive (condition b) any increase in the labour force implies more output from a given capital stock – that is a new, higher, production function, $f'(K)$, which would lie everywhere above $f(K)$. If the labour force grew every year, $f(K)$ would expand every year and we would have continuing economic growth.

4.5   The medium-term growth effects of the SEM

The second, and more important cause of economic growth, is improvements in economic organization, which allows us to get more output from a given set of factor inputs. The first part of this chapter explored the benefits of European economic integration and showed that by removing barriers to trade, harmonizing standards and increasing competition we expected to increase the output and income available from a given set of inputs by up to 5 per cent. But in the terms of this part of the chapter, this process is none other than increasing $f(K)$ to $1.05f(K)$, and we now know that when $f(K)$ increases we get two effects: the 'impact' increase in output (here 5 per cent) at the initial capital stock K_*, and an 'induced' effect as the capital stock increases from K_* to its new equilibrium level, say K''. Figure 14.8 illustrates this.

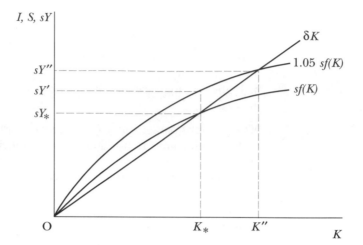

Figure 14.8 **The impact and induced effects of increased output from given inputs**

Figure 14.8, which is not drawn to scale, is very similar to Figure 14.7, but now the new savings relationship is written as $1.05sf(K)$, to denote that we save the same proportion, s, of a larger income $1.05f(K)$, and we have added the label sY to the vertical axis to remind us that, given total savings S and a fixed savings rate, s, total income Y is easily determined. If $S = sY$, then $Y = \dfrac{S}{s}$.

When economic integration shifts the production function from $f(K)$ to $1.05f(K)$ the impact effect calculated by Cecchini moves us from Y_* to Y' ($= 1.05Y_*$). But now savings exceeds required investment at K_* and so the capital stock starts to expand, giving a further 'induced' effect on income from Y' to Y''.

Richard Baldwin (1989), who first identified this effect of economic integration referred to the induced effect as the *medium-term growth bonus*. In a sense this is an unfortunate term, for as we have seen, it is not a permanent increase in economic growth, but an upward shift in the level of income which increases growth only over the medium-term transitional period as we move from K_* to K''. Thus, strictly it is best thought of as adding to the one-off benefits of the SEM identified by Cecchini. By assuming a particular form for the production function, in which a 1 per cent increase in capital stock generates approximately a 0.33 per cent increase in Y, Baldwin argues that the medium-term growth bonus is around 50 per cent of the impact effect. That is, if Cecchini's static estimate of the benefits of the SEM were correct, Baldwin argues that, allowing for the medium-term growth bonus, we should expect not a 5 per cent increase in income but about 7.5 per cent. In fact, Baldwin goes on to argue that the bonus is probably larger than this for reasons which we shall come to shortly.

Before leaving the medium-term growth bonus, two further points should be made. First, although the induced capital formation increases output, these increases are not free: they have to be paid for by increasing investment. Thus while Cecchini's static impact effect of integration is a pure gain in welfare, the medium-term bonus is not. In fact, it hardly represents a gain at all – merely a re-scheduling of consumption from now, when savings and investments rise, to the future when the investment starts to pay off. Baldwin (1993) very roughly estimates that the welfare bonus is smaller than the impact effect by at least a factor of ten.

Second, while the model we have used is just a parable – for example, it has only one output, two inputs, constant technology etc. – it does appear to capture some elements of reality. After Spain joined the EU in 1986, it experienced a huge investment boom (much of it from elsewhere in the EU); the boom in the EU in the late 1980s saw high levels of investment and substantial take-over activity as companies prepared for the SEM; and after the announcement of the SEM investors in the EFTA countries switched heavily from domestic investment to investment in the EU. These observations lend considerable plausibility to the existence of a medium-term growth bonus based on additional investment.

We now turn to the third cause of economic growth: technical progress proper.

5   Technical progress

Definition

Technical progress

Technical progress is not easy to define precisely, but there appear to be three key components:

1   More output can be produced with the same inputs.

2   Existing outputs undergo an improvement in quality.

3   Completely new goods or services become available.

5.1   What is technical progress?

Technical progress lies at the heart of economic growth and development. Life today is longer and more pleasant than in the Victorian age not just because we have more capital, nor because we have a better allocation of resources, but because we know how to do more with less: because, that is, of technical progress. Exactly how to generate technical progress is not clear, but it is clear that it is not generally free and that, in addition to having good ideas, one must implement them. In policy terms, these observations mean that resources – capital, energy and, above all, skilled labour – must be devoted to achieving technical progress, and that, for most countries most of the time, the important activity is not inventing new products or processes (including organizational and managerial processes), but adopting those that are already known elsewhere in the world.

The three aspects of technical progress listed in the definition appear to be straight-forward, but in fact raise serious issues of measurement when we come to apply them in practice. The difficulties include the phrase 'the same inputs': it is not often the case that inputs will remain identical, since technical progress usually has to be embodied in new capital equipment, new human skills or new intermediate products. A further implication of this difficulty is that there are therefore limits to the speed with which changes can occur, because new equipment comes on stream only at the rate of gross investment. Suppose new electricity generating methods allowed us to eliminate all pollutants (this is technical progress in the sense of getting more clean air out of the electricity industry), full implementation would still take around forty years. Although this is a fascinating subject for research, for our purposes we need merely note this *caveat* to our results and pass on.

The issue of quality is also difficult (see Chapter 2). Sometimes it entails getting more service out of a product – a good pair of shoes lasts longer than a poor one – in which case it is like getting more output. Usually, however, quality improvement is less measurable, and may not even be universally recognized, residing in factors such as design and ease of use. In these circumstances it is virtually never measured in aggregate output indicators, with the result that most official statistics probably understate true growth.

5.2   Technical progress and economic growth

To isolate the effects of technical progress, we introduce it explicitly into our model in a way that parallels the way in which we represented the SEM. We multiply the 'regular' production function, $f(K)$, by a factor A (greater than one) representing the ability to get more output per unit of input. That is, we now write the production function as

$$Y = Af(K)$$

where increases in the coefficient A capture technical progress. If A grows every year, so will Y and we shall have an economy exhibiting continuing economic growth. The situation will be like Figure 14.8 repeated year after year.

Anything that causes A to increase increases income. For a long time economists treated such technical progress as if it just arrived like manna from heaven, and were disconcerted to discover that, inexplicable as it was, it apparently accounted for much of the economic growth that occurred. With a little ingenuity, it is possible to measure increases in output and in the two inputs labour and capital. If we can approximate the effects of increases in L and K on Y, we can calculate how much actual growth is due to increased inputs and, by subtraction, how much remains to be explained by technical progress.

The impact of technical progress on growth

A good approximation for the proportionate effect of the growth of capital on output growth can be made using the share of capital in total costs of production: call that share α (alpha). The share of labour, the only other input, must be $(1 - \alpha)$. We can write technical progress (the rate of growth of A) as a; the growth of output (Y) as r; the growth of K as i, and of L as l.

Then we can approximate actual technical progress as

$$a = r - \alpha i - (1 - \alpha)\, l$$

That is, technical progress is measured as the proportionate change in output less the effects attributed to proportionate changes in inputs.

There is further discussion of this type of calculation in Chapter 20.

Table 14.4 breaks up economic growth into input and technical progress components for several industrial countries (technical progress is shown as the 'residual' in this table). It suggests that annual rates of technical progress range from around 1 per cent to 2 per cent and that they account for between one-third and one-half of total observed economic growth.

Table 14.4   **Contribution to growth of inputs and technical progress 1913–87 (average annual growth rates)**

Growth in:	France	Germany	Japan	Netherlands	UK	USA
GNP	2.8	3.0	5.1	3.0	2.0	3.0
Contribution of inputs	1.2	1.4	3.3	1.9	1.2	2.2
Residual	1.6	1.6	1.8	1.1	0.8	0.8

Note: An adjustment is made to account for the modernization of productive capital.

Source: Burda and Wyplosz (1993), based on Maddison (1991)

5.3   Human capital

The derived rates of technical progress in Table 14.4 are something of an embarrassment: they are, in a sense, indices of our ignorance. Hence, over the last decade, economists have put considerable effort into explaining them both in theory and numerically. An obvious candidate for explaining technical progress is human capital, defined above as the level of human skills and knowledge. This human capital is produced by investment, depreciates and requires replacement. In many respects human capital is a perfect parallel of physical capital (K above). We would expect that the higher a country's human capital, the higher will be its output and income per head. However, higher levels of human capital require higher levels of investment to be maintained.

Recognizing human capital H as a third factor of production we can write an extended production function as $Y = Ag(H, K, L)$. Because it is very difficult to measure the growth of human capital through time, not much use is made of this equation for explaining individual countries' growth histories. In a different dimension, however, it has proved immensely fruitful. Comparing economic performance across countries, differences in education appear to be very significant. Imagine that all countries had access to the same production technology $g(H, K, L)$ and that we sought to explain the differences in their outputs in terms of differences in their levels of inputs (H, K and L) and technical ability (A). If we work only with labour and physical capital, most of the differences between countries appear due to the inexplicable technical factor A. When we allow for human capital as well, however, differences in income relate much more closely to differences in inputs and the unexplained residual A is much smaller.

Figure 14.9 illustrates this result, at least indirectly. If every country has the same productive opportunities in this model, countries which start off a period with relatively low incomes per head (that is, with low *per capita* inputs of K and H) will grow more rapidly over the period as they converge to the levels achieved by the world leaders. In fact, however, crude post-war data relating growth to starting levels of income appear to belie this prediction; poor countries (e.g. those of Sub-Saharan Africa) have not caught up the OECD countries: if anything, they have fallen further behind.

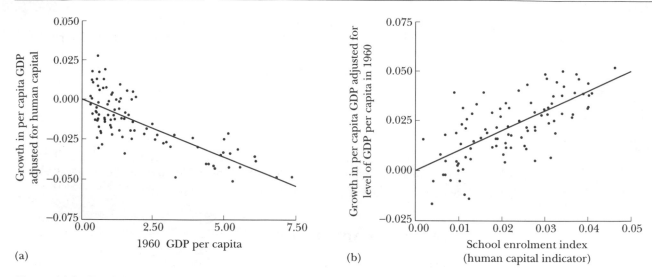

Figure 14.9 **Explaining economic growth 1960–85**
Source: Barro (1991), pp.415 and 417

Figure 14.9(a) shows, however, that once we allow for differences in levels of human capital, order is restored and the predicted negative relationship between growth and starting levels of income emerges. Alternatively, if we look at countries' growth rates taking account of their starting levels of income (and also of governmental and political factors), we find a strong positive relationship between growth and the stock of human capital (indicated by a school enrolment index). That is, higher levels of human capital help countries grow faster than one would expect from their other circumstances. This is illustrated in Figure 14.9(b).

In one sense, this excursion into human capital has been a bit of a detour – the European countries all have pretty high levels of human capital per head by world standards. However, the results remind us that, in policy terms, investment in and maintenance of the human capital stock is necessary for high levels of income. Moreover, if European integration is to boost incomes and if it is to foster convergence in income levels throughout the Union, human capital will be one of the crucial channels of causation.

The human capital story has another important implication for the analysis of the SEM. In discussing the medium-term growth bonus, Baldwin (1989) assumed that, based on their observed shares in total costs, the elasticities of output with respect to labour and capital were approximately $\frac{2}{3}$ and $\frac{1}{3}$ respectively. Elasticity here means the percentage change in output induced by a 1 per cent increase in the input.

Exercise 14.3

Given output elasticities of $\frac{2}{3}$ for the labour input and $\frac{1}{3}$ for the capital input, what would be the output consequences of (a) increasing labour input by 9 per cent, and (b) capital input by 15 per cent?

Looked at another way, Baldwin's assumption implied an elasticity of $\frac{2}{3}$ on the factor which was fixed in supply (labour) and of $\frac{1}{3}$ on the factor that could be accumulated through time (capital). Baldwin used this assumption to calculate that a change that induced a 1 per cent impact increase in output, holding K constant, would eventually increase output by 1.5 per cent once K had had time to increase in line with higher output, and this had then generated a further output increase. However, suppose we recognize that, out of the cost share of $\frac{2}{3}$ attributed to labour, about $\frac{1}{3}$ is due to crude labour and $\frac{1}{3}$ due to the human capital embodied in that labour. The human capital may be accumulated just like physical capital. Then the shares and elasticities become $\frac{1}{3}$ on the fixed factor and $\frac{2}{3}$ on the (two) factor(s) that can be accumulated (human and physical capital). In this case, Baldwin calculated that the medium term growth bonus increases from 1.5 to 3.0 times the original impact effect. The improvement arises from recognizing that, since human capital can be accumulated, inputs rise more than in the model which does not recognize human capital. The investment in human capital still has to be paid for, so welfare does not improve much from this, but output will be boosted more strongly than we previously imagined.

5.4   Economies of scale

One of the principal channels of benefit from the SEM and also one of the principal causes of economic growth is arguably economies of scale. The SEM allows firms to operate on a larger scale, and, if this reduces costs, economic welfare improves. Similarly, if something occurs that allows firms to reap economies of scale, they will derive more output per unit of input and economic growth will have occurred. In this section, we explore the implications of economies of scale for economic growth.

Economies of scale occur when an *x* per cent increase in *all* inputs generates a more than *x* per cent increase in output. That is, the output/input ratio improves. It is perfectly possible to have diminishing marginal returns when the input of one factor of production is increased individually, and yet still to have increasing returns when inputs of all are increased simultaneously.

Alfred Marshall, the great British economist working at the turn of the last century, distinguished between two sorts of economies of scale, both of which you have already encountered.

Internal economies of scale are those whereby, if a *firm* increases its scale, its output/input ratio improves or, equivalently, its unit costs fall. The benefits are internal to the firm: they refer to *its* inputs and *its* outputs. Clearly such economies of scale provide strong incentives for firms to expand and indeed typically lead to imperfectly competitive markets. It is they that lie behind the economies of scale and pro-competitive components of the estimated benefits of the SEM. A common source of economies of scale is a fixed cost to setting up production which is spread over more units as scale expands. For modern economies, one of the most important fixed costs is probably that of pre-production research and development.

The other source of economies of scale is *external economies*. These are economies that are external to the firm; they may be generated, for example, by rising scale of operation of the whole industry in which the firm operates. Under external economies, a firm benefits from the existence and/or expansion of certain other firms, which help it to reduce its own costs. Thus external economies are compatible with industries comprising very many small firms.

As well as working at industry level, external economies of scale may exist at the level of all manufacturing activity or even all industrial activity or total economic activity. They may also operate at the level of a geographical locality, a city, a region, a country or even globally. In contrast to such apparent ubiquity, external economies of scale are actually extremely difficult to pin down in practice. Indeed, debate still rages as to whether they exist, or more precisely, whether, given current firm and industry sizes, further external economies remain to be exploited by further expansion. We shall ask what happens if they do exist, but we should not be over-confident that they actually do.

Question

What phenomena might generate external economies of scale?

Adam Smith identified economies of scale as arising from the division of labour. Usually this will be within a firm – for example, through the introduction of an assembly line – but it can also occur between firms through the introduction of specialized marketed inputs.

If there are fixed costs to establishing a firm to make, say, car components, such firms will be created only when the demand from car producing firms is high enough. Thereafter, any further increase in the demand for parts from one car firm will benefit all the others by reducing average costs of parts. Similar effects may be felt via the training of labour: the establishment of specialized training facilities, or a well-stocked market for particular skills. The externality for inputs will normally be industry-based and may spread very widely geographically, even to the whole world market. That for skilled labour will frequently be localized (because workers are not very mobile) but based on several or even all industries, as, for example, for cost accountants or general engineers.

A second source of external economies is technological spill-overs. Some inventions can be patented but many can not be, e.g. organizational innovations. In the latter cases, they tend to leak between firms, and so a firm is a potential beneficiary of its rivals' endeavours. Again, in some cases, the externalities will operate in an industry-specific but geographically broad fashion, while others – for example, those that rely on face-to-face meetings or on poaching skilled labour – may be geographically constrained but industrially broad.

A third source of economies of scale – internal as well as external – is profit-motivated innovation. As an industry or the economy grows, the scope for exploiting new inventions increases because they can be applied more or less costlessly over a wider set of activities; as a result the potential returns to innovating rise. This in turn generates a larger flow of innovations, some of which boost the output of the firm which grew initially, but most of which are either located in or spill over to other firms. This effect, if it exists, could actually spark off a virtuous circle of growth and innovation, whereby each feeds off the other indefinitely. This possibility – which is far from proven yet – is known as *endogenous growth*, i.e. growth generated from inside the system. It transforms the way in which we look at the world; for example, countries' outputs per capita would no longer show any tendency to converge and a lucky accident could put a country on to a permanently higher growth path.

Do such external economies of scale exist? It is easy to see why they might, but, in order to prove that they do and are relevant at the level of the overall economy, we need empirical evidence. The matter is not settled beyond dispute, but there is at least some suggestive evidence. The idea is conceptually quite simple. First, we look at the effect of total manufacturing inputs on total manufacturing output. If this effect is more than proportional, we have evidence of economies of scale (more output per unit input as inputs grow) at the level of aggregate output. We do not, however, know whether they are internal or external economies: that is, whether the average industry's 'excess productivity' is related to its own inputs or to those of other firms. To discover this, we then look at the growth of individual industries, and subtract what can be attributed to their own increased inputs allowing for any internal economies of scale that might exist. Then, instead of immediately attributing all of the residual to technical progress, we ask whether it can be related statistically to growth in *total* manufacturing output. If so, we have identified external economies of scale.

Table 14.5 shows you some of the best estimates available at present. Cabellero and Lyons (1989 and 1990) find little evidence of internal economies, but evidence suggesting quite strong external economies. Thus, for example, an equally spread 1 per cent increase in all inputs into all German manufacturing industry appears to boost output by 1.22 per cent, all via external economies.

Table 14.5 **Estimates of economies of scale**

	% increase in total output from a 1% increase in total inputs
Belgium	1.42
France	1.59
Germany	1.22
UK	1.13
USA	1.36

Source: Baldwin (1989) based on Caballero and Lyons (1989 and 1990)

What effects do these economies of scale have? This can be envisaged in terms of the figures you have already studied. If the line $sf(K)$ is drawn assuming constant returns to scale, then the equivalent function under economies of scale will lie *above* it by an ever increasing amount as K, the capital input, increases. That is the new savings line, say $sf_*(K)$, will lie above $sf(K)$ and curve down less rapidly than it.

Copy Figure 14.6 and draw this in. You will see that :

(a) at either depreciation rate the new equilibrium capital stock and income are higher, and

(b) the effect of an exogenous shock – say the shift from δ to δ' – is greater with economies of scale than without.

The latter observation suggests that the effects of the SEM are likely to be even greater than predicted by a model with constant returns to scale.

It might seem that we should now revise our estimates of the effects of the SEM upward even more to take account of economies of scale. In fact this is not necessary, however, for the existing estimates of the effects of increasing capital on output arguably already allow them: if the world exhibits economies of scale, relating data on Y to those on K in order to calculate the effects of inputs on outputs will at least partially reflect these economies even if we are not looking for them explicitly. Hence these observations should not so much cause us to revise upwards our estimates of the effects of the SEM as to be more comfortable accepting the current relatively high figure.

5.6   Endogenous growth

Definition

Endogenous growth

Endogenous growth is growth that is generated *within* the normal workings of the economic system rather that being introduced from outside.

We now have the basis for analysing so-called endogenous growth. In terms of our analysis endogenous growth could arise from the virtuous circle of research and development generating a sufficient stimulus to income to make further research and development profitable. How does it fit into our model of economic growth? The economy settles down wherever the savings line $sf(K)$ cuts the investment line δK. If an economy were to continue growing indefinitely we should need to avoid this eventuality and have $sf(K)$ lying always above δK. This requires straightening $sf(K)$ out so that it never bends back to towards δK – that is, making $sf(K)$ a straight line, as in Figure 14.10.

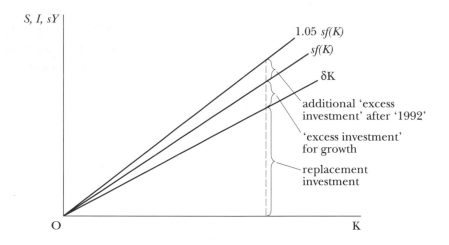

Figure 14.10   **Endogenous growth**

Taking $sf(K)$ as a straight line has a clear economic interpretation. Previously we assumed diminishing returns as we added more capital to a fixed labour force. This implies a flattening of $f(K)$, bending $sf(K)$ back towards δK. In other words it is diminishing returns that prevent indefinite growth, so that, if we can avoid these, we can avoid the growth constraint. With a straight line version of $sf(K)$, growth can continue for ever: savings always exceed investment requirements, so the capital stock, and hence income, expand for ever.

Clearly the results of this section are rather special. If output is proportionate to capital, constant growth is possible indefinitely. If it shows diminishing marginal returns, constant growth is impossible in the absence of a series of fortuitous external shocks. If output is more than proportionately sensitive to capital, $sf(K)$ will bend away from δK, the excess of savings over the investment requirement will grow as a proportion of K and both K and Y will accelerate towards infinitely rapid growth.

Not only is the last case implausible, but one suspects that if the world were actually like this, we should have noticed by now. Moreover, while there is some evidence that output is approximately proportionate to the capital stock, there is none that it is precisely so. Neither is there yet any evidence that integration stimulates economic growth over the long run. EC growth performance has been adequate since 1957, but hardly spectacular. It is difficult to accumulate more formal evidence on growth because it is so difficult to predict what growth would be in the absence of integration: see, for example, the spread of observations about the relationships given in Figure 14.9. If integration really mattered we would find members of the EU tending to lie above the lines in those figures, i.e. having higher growth than the average relationship would predict given their other circumstances, but, as De Melo and Panagariya (1993) show, we generally do not.

In a separate, forward-looking exercise, Baldwin (1989) re-examines the effects of the SEM on the assumption that endogenous growth is feasible. To understand the idea, look again at Figure 14.10. With the straight line $sf(K)$ on this figure, the economy is growing steadily, at a rate determined by the excess investment available over required investment. This excess investment is indicated by the gap between $sf(K)$ and δK. Baldwin assumes that the economy is already growing steadily in this way. When the SEM raises the productivity of the economy by 5 per cent, the savings line rotates upwards to $1.05\ sf(K)$. The permanent growth rate therefore increases, since additional 'excess investment' over replacement investment is now permanently available. Baldwin's estimates of plausible values for the model's paramaters would give us a growth rate of 1 per cent a year before the SEM, rising to 1.3 per cent per year afterwards.

An increased growth rate promises ever increasing future income. Allowing for the fact that future income is worth less than the equivalent income now (Chapter 11 called this 'positive time preference'), Baldwin argued that a permanent increase of 0.3 per cent on the annual growth rate is plausibly equivalent to a one-off (step) increase in GDP of about 7.5 per cent. Clearly these numbers are quite impressive and Baldwin argues that the permanent growth effect, which he calls the long-run growth bonus, may be worth rather more than we have suggested here. Even 7.5 per cent, however, is not to be sneezed at.

There is, however, an important caveat. The analyses underlying the medium term and long-term growth bonuses are mutually exclusive: if one applies, the other cannot. Either the economy exhibits endogenous growth, or the growth process converges as we assumed in Section 4. Thus accepting the standard static benefits of the SEM from the earlier part of this chapter and adding *one or other* of the bonuses that we have discovered in this later part, we get a range of benefits from the SEM stretching from about 4 per cent to 14 per cent of GDP. If, of course, the Cecchini estimates of the static effects are exaggerated, so too will be this range.

5.7   Human capital again

The discussion of both economies of scale and endogenous growth have stressed the role of human capital. While it was not explicit in the model we examined, a little reflection suggests that very highly skilled labour has at least two possible functions in an economy. First, it can combine with other inputs using known technology to produce goods and services. Thus, for example, the engineer who maintains a power station is involved in direct production and can through her presence render other labour and capital highly productive.

Second, however, highly skilled labour can be withdrawn from direct production and set to work trying to improve technology in one way or another. This generates no immediate output but promises, if only in probability, future benefits. Thus there is a trade off between the current level of output and future growth, and it is possible that policies that make it more desirable to devote human capital to production eventually detract from growth. For example, some poor countries restrict imports of spare parts for machinery either deliberately or through foreign exchange shortages. The ensuing shortages generate very high rewards for the engineer who can improvise her way around them and may divert her from thinking about longer-term issues such as the adaption of newer generations of technology to the country's needs. The parallel in industrial countries is military research and development. It is notable that among industrial countries, those devoting most resources to military research – the USA, the UK and France – grew much more slowly than those which devoted least – Germany and Japan.

When considering industrial country policies such as the SEM, it is important to ask how they affect the supplies of highly skilled labour to development activities. It is also important to consider the policies which produce skilled labour – education, training and migration. It is widely held that the UK economy is constrained by its poor supply and poor utilization of skilled labour. Similarly it is one of the more encouraging signs for the future growth of the transitional economies of Central and Eastern Europe that they apparently have more and better skilled labour than other economies with their levels of income per head (Hamilton and Winters 1992). In terms of the analysis above we argue that these countries have stocks of skilled labour that are currently under-used. When they get themselves better organized, rather than having to invest in skills in order to grow right from the start, they will initially be able to jump to higher levels of output very quickly.

Migration is a sensitive issue throughout the world and we can not deal with it fully here. It is worth noting, however, that while nearly all countries keep out unskilled workers from other countries, most are prepared to accept highly skilled workers with very little resistance. This suggests a practical, if not a theoretical, recognition of the role of human capital in growth and development.

The EU, of course, espouses the free movement of labour throughout its area, but in fact this is one of its least successful areas of policy. European labour seems geographically very immobile compared with US labour – for language and cultural reasons as well as for institutional reasons such as imperfections in housing markets. For highly skilled labour, a further difficulty is that either formally or informally many qualifications are not recognized outside the country in which they were granted. Correcting this was part of the SEM programme, and although some progress was made in that direction there is much further to go. When skilled labour is free to move to its region of highest productivity we might reasonably expect a significant boost to European income levels and even, perhaps, growth. There is a danger, however, that this may exacerbate regional disparities. If the key to productivity is externalities – bright people sparking off each other – and if these externalities are geographically restricted, we are likely to get isolated 'hot spots' of intense growth – like Silicon Valley in the USA – which attract skills from elsewhere, possibly reducing growth in the latter areas. All this is pretty speculative – again the issue is not whether it could happen, rather whether it is likely – but it serves to illustrate the possibly major impacts of international economic integration and the great significance of human capital in shaping its effects.

6 Conclusion

This chapter began by looking at the history of European integration and asking what economic impact this had upon the evolving European economy. In addressing that question, the chapter has brought together theory and evidence. The theory of customs unions was used to argue that the impact of early European integration was to create trade rather than to divert it. Later sections explored the theory of economic growth, including some very recent work. This theorizing was used in turn to consider the various empirical estimates of the effect of the Single European Market programme on European economic growth.

There are two types of conclusions you might draw from this chapter. The first concerns the size as well as the uncertainty of the possible economic benefits which Europeans may draw from European integration, and the importance of human capital to the realization of those benefits. The second type of conclusion which you might draw concerns the importance of careful theorizing to the evaluation of estimates like those made by Cecchini and Baldwin on the economic impact of European integration.

CHAPTER 15   THE MARKET SYSTEM

by Grahame F. Thompson

1   Introduction

We live in a society that has become accustomed to the idea of a 'market system'. Indeed, the celebration of the market system seems to have become almost ubiquitous since the mid 1970s. But what exactly does this term mean? The aim of this chapter is to take a step back from the detailed analysis in earlier chapters of the operation of individual markets, and to investigate the market process as a whole. The chapter develops two basic images or models of the market system as it has arisen historically – what are called here 'organized' and 'unorganized' capitalism. Thus in this chapter we return to the issue of model building in economics: from the historical experience of actual economic processes two stylized models are generated.

The implication of this approach to model building is that the models discussed here are less abstract than some of the models of markets in previous chapters. A central objective of this chapter is to consider the *institutionalized* nature of the market system, and the importance of the process of formation of market institutions for the subsequent conduct of economic activity. The analysis examines the way in which the historical dynamic of the economic process constrains current options for economic activity.

These issues are developed in part through a consideration of the *creation* of a market process in what used to be the centrally planned economies of Eastern Europe and the former Soviet Union. The period since the late 1980s has provided a unique 'experimental' opportunity for economists. The whirlwind of events in these economies represents an unprecedented transformative period for Eastern Europe and the former Soviet Union in which one system of resource allocation collapsed and the beginnings of a totally different one emerged. The rapidity of these events has propelled these societies to change radically and almost to re-invent their economies along the lines of market systems. This opportunity to analyse the creation of those market systems may also tell us something about existing systems, so those living in the industrialized market economies can also learn something from the experiences in Eastern Europe and the former Soviet Union (hereafter EE and the ex-SU).

The chapter begins by outlining the historical emergence of the two characteristic forms of the market system referred to above. Some of the implications of these two images are then raised. Subsequently the experience of EE and the ex-SU is assessed in the light of these features and issues. Finally, some insights to be gained from the 'experiment' in constructing a market system are highlighted.

2   Forms of the market system

It is important to remember that many of our present-day attitudes towards the market system were forged in the latter part of the nineteenth and the early years of the twentieth century (Tribe, 1994). Of particular importance in this evolutionary understanding was the rapid surge of industrial growth towards the end of the last century, occurring in the USA and Germany in particular and to a lesser extent in the UK. This was stimulated by a combination of factors – war and reconstruction, large reserves of indigenous and immigrant labour, concentrations of capital, new technologies, processes and products, and the development of extensive home markets. The dynamic growth at this time was accompanied by waves of mergers, which accelerated the growth of industrial concentration and led, as Chapter 12 noted, to a widespread concern about the 'process of monopolization', and to a new age of giant enterprises that seemed to herald the advent of the twentieth century.

Interestingly, the reaction to this common process was different in the USA and in Germany, the two newly emerging important economic powers of the time. In politically conservative Germany, protectionist sentiment was widespread. At the domestic level this manifested itself in the common restrictive practice of striking price and sales agreements between firms. These cartel agreements were notoriously fragile, however, since, as earlier chapters explained, an incentive always exists for the parties to break such agreements and to seek their own greater market share by price cutting and related competitive activity. However, in Germany cartel agreements were given protection in law by a landmark decision of the *Reichsgericht* (imperial court) in 1897. Cartel agreements became legally binding contracts, which if broken by any of the signatories rendered them liable to action by the remaining signatories. This arrangement gave German industrialists and financiers a large degree of stability that in some cases persisted until well into the mid twentieth century. It reflected a widespread attitude in Germany that accepted regulation and management of the market system and, perhaps more important, encouraged an institutional configuration to support it. Not only were large corporations tolerated and even officially fostered, but organized labour and governmental bodies were drawn into a more general accommodation towards 'organized capitalism'.

In the USA, by contrast, such cartels were viewed as inimical to the public welfare and against the public interest. They quickly became the object of judicial review. It was thought that market dominance by large corporations would eliminate the beneficial effects of free competition, such as product and process innovation, low and stable prices, and open labour and financial markets. Throughout the later part of the nineteenth and during the very early years of the twentieth century, what came to be known as the 'Trust Question' dominated public policy on these matters in the USA. The landmark public policy action was the 1890 Sherman Act, which was directed against inter-firm agreements restricting trade or seeking to monopolize inter-state commerce. Along with the Inter-State Commerce Commission (ICC) established in 1887, the Sherman Act defined a prevailing attitude and sentiment in the USA against 'big business', and a continuing commitment to the virtues of the free market.

Thus a sharp configurative difference was established in people's and government's understanding of the market system: the German form of 'organized', regulated and bureaucratically driven capitalism versus the

American system of 'unorganized', competitively based, free market capitalism. Each of these models demonstrated considerable durability and economic success. Both have performed well in the twentieth century, though at times with difficulty and subject to changing policy fashion. Thus, perhaps contrary to popular belief, the American (and UK) model of free markets and economic competition has not proved necessary to stimulate the essential dynamic properties of capitalist success. Capitalism based on a codified and regulated structure has performed just as well, and possibly better at times. But these two images have tended to dominate the ideological battles fought over the meaning of the market system that have haunted economic analysis ever since the turn of this century.

Reflection

Make some notes on the differences set out so far between 'organized' and 'unorganized' capitalism. How do economic actors understand the market system in each case, and what is their attitude towards the emergence of large corporations?

3   Interests and influences in the market system

3.1   Interest groups

The different ways in which the market system has been historically organized are associated with a big difference in the significance afforded to interest groups in the two systems. Consider first 'unorganized' capitalism. In this system interest groups are considered as similar to self-seeking individual agents who aim to maximize their own personal advantage. These interest groups are thus thought to seek either to maximize their collective interest at the expense of the majority, or to act as monopolists, extracting economic advantage by lowering output, forcing up price, and restricting competition.

Classic examples of interest groups conceived in this way are trade unions. These are analysed in the Anglo-American tradition as organizations that act as monopoly sellers by restricting the supply of labour and pushing its price above the competitive level. This implies that the way to deal with such interest groups is to ignore them, dismantle them, or even ruthlessly suppress them, and thus restore the benefits of a competitive process. In principle all organized interest groups can be conceived in this way – as seeking their own particular advantage – and in a society with a proliferation of such groups there is a problem in predicting the economic outcome.

An influential analysis of such general consequences for economic activity is provided by Mancur Olson (1982). What happens in a market system where interest groups are so embedded that they constitute the major constraint on adaptation and change? Olson argues that the social embeddedness of interest groups inhibits the domestic economy's response to any exogenous shocks; the economy is just not flexible enough to allow an adequate economic and social readjustment. In other words, the economy becomes inflexible because of the proliferation of interest groups which are only looking to protect their particular advantage; these groups become so mature, powerful and moribund that they fail the system just when it is faced with the need for rapid adjustment.

Olson stresses that collective action by interest groups can generate coalitions of economic agents whose struggle over distributional issues establishes a set of institutional rigidities, which then inhibit anything other than a narrow defensive response to unexpected exogenous shocks. Once such coalitions become established, they are very difficult to shift, and society as a whole suffers as a result. Countries with long traditions of plural government and continuity in social structure and cultural outlook become ossified, with a loss of dynamic energy for change. Such is the case in the USA, it is argued, with a resultant inability to respond effectively to a productivity slow-down occasioned by the impact of the oil price shocks in the 1970s (Olson, 1988). Long-term decline, it is claimed, is the inevitable result. On the other hand, those societies in which interest groups are less developed, or not so extensive, powerful or mature, retain their dynamic ability to respond innovatively to shocks and thus remain internationally competitive. In Olson's view, these national differences in the configuration of interest groups explain why some countries remain successful economically and socially while others do not.

A different view of the role of organized interest groups features in the analysis offered from within the 'organized' capitalism variant of the market system. As might be expected, an element in the organized nature of the social order in this case is an accommodation with social interest groups. Indeed, there is a presumption that these should be explicitly fostered if they do not already exist. For instance, in many continental European countries, the 'social partners', as they are known, continue to play a key role in the conduct of economic activity and its management. The main social partners are the labour organizations, those of employers (perhaps divided between large and small companies) and the governmental authorities, but in principle these might also encompass agricultural interests, consumers, and even environmentalists. These social partners bargain between themselves in various arenas, usually alongside the traditional channels of representative democracy, over economic objectives and the means to achieve them. This approach emphasizes co-operation between the social actors rather than competition between them in the conduct of economic activity. It is designed to reach a broad social consensus on economic objectives and the means to achieve them.

Reflection

Add to your previous notes a brief comparison of how interest groups are viewed within organized and unorganized market economies.

Neo-corporatism

This discussion of interest groups underpins a more general analysis of what are termed 'neo-corporatist' bargaining arrangements, and particularly the impact these have on the wage formation process and inflation in market systems. It is through the institutional organization of the labour market that neo-corporatism is thought to have its main impact. Broadly speaking we can draw a distinction between highly *centralized* bargaining (neo-corporatist arrangements) and *decentralized* bargaining (neo-liberal arrangements). Centralized bargaining of a neo-corporatist type implies that the peak organizations of labour and employers are brought together at a national or regional level, usually under government auspices, to decide systematically on wage levels, and often on other aspects of economic activity. Decentralized bargaining tends to leave individual employers and their workers to bargain over wages and conditions according to local conditions and circumstances, without the intervention of government. Thus no overall nationally considered outcome emerges (Flanagan *et al.*, 1993).

Question

What do you think would be the likely outcomes from these two different approaches to bargaining? Which one is the organized option, and which is the unorganized one?

The typical labour market outcome from these two approaches in the past has been that decentralized bargaining produces a level of (un)employment more sensitive to the variations in the real wage (the money wage adjusted for the level of inflation, which is taken as the main determinant of the incentive to work), but it has traditionally produced higher levels of overall unemployment over much of the post-war period up until the early 1980s. On the other hand, while centralized bargaining produces a less sensitive response of (un)employment to the level of the real wage, it tends to produce lower levels of overall unemployment (Soskice, 1991, pp.37–58; Layard *et al.*, 1991, pp.129–39; Henley and Tsakalotos, 1991, pp.433–9).

In addition, the authors cited above claim that there have been a number of other positive consequences for economic performance arising in countries with more centralized bargaining arrangements, including better investment, profitability and growth records. Henley and Tsakalotos sum up the evidence as follows:

> The first theme is the high growth and employment performance of those economies with a high degree of corporatism, such as the Scandinavian economies, the Netherlands and Austria. This has been noted by many other authors … It also emerges … that income and employment growth in corporatist economies have been relatively stable … We can clearly see on average the superior growth and investment performance of the strongly corporatist economies during the 1973–75 recession … The results show … that investment in the strong corporatism group is on average the least sensitive to short-run fluctuations in [corporate] income.
>
> *(Henley and Tsakalotos, 1991, pp.426-42)*

The authors cited claim that economies typified by neo-corporatist arrangements seemed able to out-perform their rivals under normal circumstances and to cope better with exogenous shocks. Economies like the UK, which have gone furthest down the route to decentralization and which are the most hostile to neo-corporatist forms of interest group governance, particularly labour market co-ordination, would thus be doubly disadvantaged if this analysis proved correct.

One other advantage claimed for neo-corporatism is that it enables *real* economic variables (employment, investment, output, training, etc.) to be targeted by governments, not just monetary ones (Rowthorn *et al.*, 1993). It provides a context in which explicit bargaining can in principle take place between the 'social partners' on a wide range of economic matters. For instance, trade unions in Germany have been closely involved in training, while they have been more or less systematically excluded from this role in the UK. Of course, neo-corporatism does not solve every economic problem, nor has it always been successful, but historically it is argued to have a proven record of economic achievement, at least in the European context. However, as the European economy integrates further, the specific role of the *individual* economies in the EU, whether they be neo-corporatist or not, will tend to lessen in the face of whatever new central mechanisms of regulation emerge at the European-wide level. Since there is no reason to assume that these common institutions of economic management will be neo-corporatist in nature, the 'organized' model may be on a long-term decline in Europe.

Summing up

We can now sum up this discussion of the role of interest groups. The proponents of the unorganized variant of the market system stress that interest groups are inimical to the proper conduct of economic business, and they should be ignored, dismantled or suppressed as a result. The proponents of the organized variant take the view that such groups are perfectly legitimate expressions of an interest, and that interest groups will emerge anyway, so they should be accommodated and built into the economic decision-making process in a positive way. The unorganized approach stresses the key role of competition in co-ordinating economic activity, while the organized variant stresses co-operation as the way to achieve the same result.

3.2   Consumers' and producers' preferences

Another difference between the organized and unorganized models of the market system is the latter's greater stress upon 'consumer preferences' as its most appropriate driving force, while the former is much more sensitive to the key role played by 'producer influence' in the economic mechanism.

For the proponents of the unorganized variant, the economy works in the interests of consumers. Producers (or workers) must adapt to the incentives provided for them by consumer preferences as registered through the market. But this defence of competition in the consumer interest should not be confused with its defence in the name of small manufacturing and retail businesses, which up until the 1920s and 1930s was the main rationale in practice for a defence of market competition against the threat of monopolization. Furthermore, even within unorganized capitalism, the regulation and public scrutiny of monopoly has focused particularly on the behaviour of firms rather than their relative size. Are they behaving in a manner that is inimical to the full operation of the market system by engaging in unfair competition or inhibiting the entry of new competitors? Even in the unorganized system, the growth of large firms in the name of efficiency has often been actively encouraged by the public authorities.

In the case of the organized variant of capitalist development, a greater tolerance can be seen of large, even monopoly firms and organizations. The organized economies, the best examples of which are Germany and Japan, have seen the emergence not only of cartel agreements, but also of integrated conglomerate-type holding companies of a strongly oligopolistic form. In Germany these were known as *Konzerns,* which were formally broken up after 1945, but still operate informally in many sectors. In Japan they were originally called *zaibatsu* and latterly *kaisha* (production companies) or *sogo shosha* (trading companies). Such organizations can also be seen in newer 'organized' industrializing economies such as South Korea, where they are known as *chaebols,* within a system of *Gyodo Jabon-Jui* – 'guided capitalism'.

The point of these examples is to stress the greater historical emphasis on 'producer interests' in these economies, often at the expense of an emphasis on consumers' interests and the role of consumption. Employees and employers are brought together in their 'peak organizations' to provide a regulatory structure for the economy which serves manufacturing and producer interests in the first instance. Again, co-operation rather than competition between employers and employees is stressed, though in some situations it is probably *coercion* that is more important in determining the 'co-operative' outcome.

Reflection

Complete your notes with a summary of the relationship between the two market system variants in their treatment of producer and consumer interests.

4   The importance of institutions and history

4.1   Path dependency

The above discussion stressed some broad institutional differences in the way the market system as a whole has been organized. In this section we look at this in a slightly different context, by examining the *path dependency* of economic change. Path dependency refers to a process of change 'in which important influences upon the eventual outcome can be exerted by temporarily remote events, including happenings dominated by chance elements rather than systematic forces' (David, 1985, p.332). Under these circumstances, what might be described as 'historical accidents' can take on an added importance, since the dynamic character of subsequent economic development becomes a thoroughly *historical* process, and one which is highly constrained institutionally.

As an example of the circumstances under which this might occur, David (1985) considers the case of the QWERTY typewriter keyboard, with the aid of which I am preparing this chapter. It is generally agreed that this is not the most efficient or healthy keyboard layout, particularly in an era of electronic word processing.

More rational and healthier alternatives to the traditional keyboard do exist, an example of which is shown in Figure 15.1. In this keyboard the arrangement of the letters follows the traditional QWERTY order, but the actual positioning of the keys is changed. There are other keyboards which change both the arrangement of the letters and the position of the keys.

Figure 15.1   **A reshaped keyboard designed to try to reduce Repetitive Strain Injury**

However, none of these alternatives has displaced the traditional QWERTY layout, which is effectively the only one in current use. This illustrates the fact that once something is firmly and 'institutionally' established (in that all keyboard makers and, perhaps more important, all keyboard users, have an inherited set of skills invested in that particular system), there are enormous incentives not to change it, and indeed it becomes quite commercially 'rational' not to do so. Present users are in the grip of long-forgotten events, and institutions are constrained in what it is now economically rational and efficient to do. In this case technological decisions and chance events in the 1890s stamped the present with its particular keyboard arrangement and irreversibly 'locked in' all the subsequent producers and users. Economic development and activity becomes generally 'path dependent' in this way: it depends upon and is constrained by decisions made in the past. We may have standardized on the 'wrong' system, but there is little that individuals can do now to change this (barring a wholesale revolution in the economic structure). Hence institutional aspects of economic systems can have a very significant impact on economic decisions.

This aspect of the market system is assumed away by the perfectly competitive model of a market system developed in Chapter 7. That model relies on a constant surveying of all possible alternatives in the present, and assumes optimal decision making based on this constant search. In this model, past decisions are 'bygones' that can in principle be ignored for the purposes of present decisions.

Reflection

Can you think of examples of economic decisions that involve a strong element of path dependency?

4.2   The location of economic activity

A further illustration of the importance of this style of analysis is offered by the impact of firms' past locational decisions on economic activity. Paul Krugman (1991, p.80) remarks that economic geography is unmistakably path dependent. It may have been a historical accident that first stimulated the clustering of US manufacturing within the central north-eastern regional industrial belts, but its persistence can only be explained by a cumulative process driven by economies of scale. Such economies of scale are both internal and external in character. Internal economies, once begun, tend to persist as long as the market continues to expand. External economies keep firms in an area because of the technological and other spillovers from other firms locating nearby.

Reflection

Can you think of other examples of such geographical clustering of related economic activity having persisted for a long period, perhaps in the UK and Europe?

I have argued in the last three sections that there are important elements of path dependency and institutional specificity in market systems. This analysis can now act as a backdrop to an investigation into the problems confronting those societies trying to construct a market system almost from scratch. I call these 'the economies in transformation', since this is exactly what they are experiencing: a transformation in their systems of resource allocation and distribution. This is an important terminology, since it is not expressed as a process of *transition*. A process of transition implies the movement from one already known system to another – from central planning to *the* market, for instance. The analysis here, however, suggests that path dependency and historical contingency are key to understanding this process. The 'historical accidents' of the past and the current processes of change in these economies are marking them with a particular dynamic, locking them into a unique institutionalization of the process of change, the precise nature and outcome of which cannot be predicted in advance. Thus these economies are best viewed as being genuinely transformed by this dynamic into something new, rather than being simply in a period of transition between already known states. However, as we shall see, there are elements of the organized and unorganized models being promoted as alternative images for this process.

5   Economic reform in Eastern Europe and the former Soviet Union

One way of summarizing the economic reforms of Eastern Europe and the former Soviet Union is to emphasize the following features (Fischer, 1991):

1   Price liberalization and the marketization of the economy.

2   Privatization and the construction of property rights.

3   Macroeconomic stabilization (for example, reducing inflation).

4   Removal of controls on cross-border financial transactions.

The first two features focus on the microeconomics of the process of adjustment, while the second two focus on the issues of national economic policy. There are clearly strong overlaps between all four areas. The overall process is seen as one of establishing a fully fledged market economy. Here I concentrate on the first two, picking up issues discussed in earlier chapters. Macroeconomic policy is analysed in Book 2 of this text.

The policy problem is perhaps best thought of as one of introducing packages of complementary reforms in the areas listed. The scale of economic reform is massive, and not exhausted just by these headings. For instance, consider the general issue of liberalizing (freeing) prices and 'marketization'.

Question

What do you think are the main requirements for creating a freely functioning price system?

The liberalization of prices requires not only the freeing from control of the distribution of goods and services, but also the de-monopolization and privatization of the means of production and the means of transportation and sale. It also implies the removal of quantitative restrictions on trading and producing, the reform of external tariffs and quotas, the reorganization of the labour market to allow hiring and firing of labour, the liberalization of wage bargaining, and the introduction of a properly functioning finance and banking system.

Institution building and structural reform, point 2 in the above list, equally involves a large-scale package of complementary reforms. Here legal reform is the most pressing, which redefines the whole nature of the state in these societies. Governments need to introduce a tax structure and budgetary and regulatory institutions. Unemployment insurance and other elements of a social welfare system are also required.

In the rest of the chapter we look closely at some of these components of the reform process, and discuss the problems that have emerged in the experiences of EE and the ex-SU as they have embarked on their reforms. The focus is on key issues rather than the specifics of any one country.

6 Price liberalization and marketization

Price liberalization and the marketization of economic activity are central to economic reforms. The old administered price system produced a general disequilibrium in the economies of EE and the ex-SU, and resulted in the misallocation of resources. The disequilibrium and misallocation were manifest in the well documented ills of their old economic systems. For example, these economies neglected infrastructure investment, and they faced an increasing technological gap with the West which helped to produce a relative decline in their growth rates. Consumers and producers faced increasing bottlenecks in the supply of goods and services, and these fuelled a growing 'monetary overhang', in the form of cash held by households and credit lines extended to enterprises and the state, that could not be absorbed by real productive activity or purchases (and thus created a situation of 'suppressed inflation'). As the official economy stagnated, the secondary, illegal economy expanded, bringing corruption in its wake. This in turn fed a general and increasing discordance between the officially sanctioned plans and norms and the actual conduct of economic activity by agents in the economy.

An obvious response when confronted by these problems is to resort to a thorough price liberalization and the marketization of the economy. This means loosening the administrative controls of central planning, and decentralizing decision making, thereby strengthening the forces of competition. Under these circumstances, however, it is often suggested that economic and political decentralization must go hand in hand.

Question

Why do you think economic and political decentralization should be considered together? What problems are likely to emerge in each case?

Whilst the model of economic decentralization is relatively well developed within economic analysis, the complementary process of political decentralization is more difficult for economic analysis to deal with. But even economic decentralization is not unproblematic in the context of the rapid transformation of Soviet-type economies. The following sub-sections deal with each in turn.

6.1   Economic decentralization

Any analysis of economic decentralization has to account for the 'creative destruction' which characterizes the dramatic transformations in the former Soviet-type economies as they 'marketize'. The neo-Austrian analysis discussed in Chapters 6 and 12 offers some insights into the situation in these countries, since economic decentralization allows and requires the emergence of entrepreneurs. However, the problem is that 'creative destruction' may simply remain as 'destruction'. There is no automatic guarantee of the emergence of a new entrepreneurial class. Indeed, a general economic disarray may thwart this by encouraging short-term speculative activity, black marketeering, and unfair trade which undermines longer-term investment (Kregel *et al.*, 1992).

Exchange and money

A generalized marketization of the economy inevitably raises questions about the role that money plays in a market system. As pointed out in Chapter 11, the market system is above all else an *exchange* system; this is the key to its successful allocation of resources. Exchange allows for decentralization and specialization in production, and it allows consumers to rearrange their endowments to obtain maximum benefits. Within this exchange system money has two central and closely interrelated roles: on the one hand it acts to represent wealth and value – we measure values in money terms in a market economy – and on the other it functions to bind the system of exchange together. Thus money both represents and functions. It lubricates the system of exchange via the functions of money described in Chapter 11 – acting as the standard of prices, the means of exchange, the unit of account, the means of deferred payment, and the measure of wealth. But while it lubricates, it also binds the system together, since someone's purchase is always someone else's sale.

By acting as a medium of exchange in this manner, money allows a spatial and a temporal separation of wants in the economy. The *spatial separation* takes the form of the movement of goods and services around the economy so that what is produced at one location can be purchased or consumed elsewhere. Without money the spatial separation of these two crucial economic functions would be much more difficult, and the division of labour and economic specialization would be highly constrained. In addition, the *temporal separation* of wants allows a time lag between production and consumption. Money balances in a market economy arise and are held (demanded) precisely because of this spatial and temporal separation of wants.

One important institutional consequence of this spatial and temporal separation of sales and purchases is that the market system requires there to be 'market makers' in the economic process. Such market makers comprise intermediaries and businesses that conduct wholesaling and retailing activities, and those that conduct the activity of financial intermediation. Financial intermediation can be of two basic types. The first involves the collection of small-scale surpluses and idle balances from a wide range of economic agents and the consolidation of these into larger amounts of 'capital' which can be lent on to those undertaking investment. The second, often complementary, type involves the conversion of short-term lending into long-term lending. When financial institutions collect up small-scale savings, these are often lent to them on a short-term basis, so that lenders can retrieve their savings at short notice without undue penalty. But borrowers often want to borrow for long-term reasons, for example to undertake investment. Financial institutions operate to facilitate this difference in the temporal perspective of lenders and borrowers.

Economic implications of decentralization

One problem, therefore, with price liberalization and marketization is the absence of existing and effective financial intermediaries that are able to create the necessary markets in investment funds. Enterprise financing in these economies was previously reliant on credit and subsidy from the state. If firms continue to remain heavily influenced by an 'employee mentality' – the idea that they are there to provide employment first and foremost – then their reaction to financial difficulties will be to seek further subsidy.

The resulting well-recognized danger is that price liberalization will trigger inflation. If prices increase – the expected outcome of price liberalization – workers will seek to raise wages. The orthodox remedy is to prevent this inflationary spiral by eliminating subsidies and forcing firms to work with limited financial resources. This is hard to achieve politically, since it threatens many firms with bankruptcy. An important objective, therefore, is to create effective financial intermediaries to undertake market-based lending. As Section 8 suggests, EE and ex-SU governments have a choice over the type of financial intermediaries they might create.

One further problem with price reform is the sheer number of prices that need to be changed. In the former Soviet Union alone there were in the region of 25 million different administered prices. What principles should guide the reformation of prices? One possibility is to use world prices. But this assumes the simultaneous opening of the domestic economy to foreign trade, so that world prices can actually influence domestic price changes. Without a general opening of the economy, domestic interest rates and asset prices will continue to diverge from world levels. In addition, world price levels only offer a 'rational' price reform for internationally traded goods.

Definition

Financial intermediation

Financial intermediation describes the function of financial institutions in a market economy. They 'mediate' between lenders and borrowers, consolidating small loans from individuals and organizations into larger batches of financial resources which can then be loaned onwards for investment.

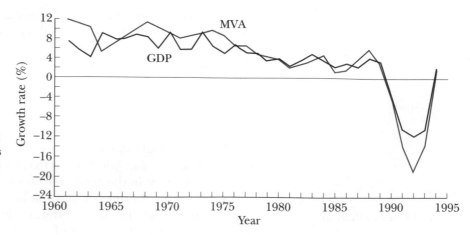

***Figure 15.2*   Growth rates of GDP and manufacturing value added (MVA) in Eastern Europe and the former USSR, 1961–94**

Note: Growth rates are computed using GDP and MVA data expressed in national currencies at 1980 prices and aggregated in terms of 1980 US dollar exchange rates. The data for 1994 are forecasts.

Source: UNIDO (1993)

Added to this is the fact that about half of the EE economies' trade was traditionally conducted with other Comecon or CEMA countries, and thus also traded in administered prices (Comecon and CEMA are names for the old trading area relationships between the centrally planned economies).

The rapid collapse in intra-Comecon trade in the early 1990s and the lack of its quick replacement by western trade was one of the major factors in the decline of GDP and the advent of recession in the Comecon countries (see Figure 15.2).

Question

Summarize for yourself the trends in GDP and MVA (value added in manufacturing) shown in Figure 15.2.

GDP and MVA had been moving closer together over the period. There was a long-term downward trend in the growth rates of both during the period up to the late 1980s, indicating the growing economic difficulties faced by those nations. Things took a dramatic turn for the worse as the old systems collapsed in the late 1980s and early 1990s. The economies experienced several years of negative growth. In 1993 there seemed to have been something of a revival in their growth prospects, with positive growth being achieved again, though growth rates were still at a historically low level.

6.2   Political decentralization

This brief discussion of the implications of 'decentralizing' economic decision making brings us back to the issue of political decentralization. Whether it is desirable or not, the break-up of the Soviet system has led not only to the undermining of the Comecon/CEMA system, but also to the break-up of many of the previously 'unified' states that comprised the national elements of that system. The outstanding example of this is the Soviet Union itself, but there are strong centrifugal tendencies in other countries of the system, notably in the Balkan area and in Czechoslovakia (which in June 1992 split into separate Czech and Slovak nations) and the Ukraine. Does this redefinition of political boundaries have any implications for the reform process and its possible success? The ex-SU countries are becoming more economically independent, increasingly developing their own currencies, implementing trade restrictions, and experimenting with import-substitution policies.

Question

Why should national boundaries matter for economic analysis?

Hogan (1991) has argued that the devolution of power to the individual sovereign states would very much complicate the transformation process. The substantial inter-regional division of labour within the old Comecon and SU areas was likely to unravel quickly, though without the means to create a new trade-based specialization between the now independent countries. The trade collapse inevitably hurt all the states concerned, particularly given the shortage of 'hard' (western convertible) currencies in which trade is now conducted.

Traditionally, economic theory has not considered national boundaries particularly important. This is because theory has often assumed complete mobility of factors of production across borders, and automatic adjustment mechanisms that quickly re-establish equilibrium across national boundaries. But reality is very different, especially in times of turmoil. The dissolution of the Austro-Hungarian empire after 1919 perhaps best represents the prospects for the Soviet Union in the early 1990s (Kregel *et al.*, 1992). In central southern Europe in the 1920s, tariffs, exchange controls and separate currencies were soon in place. What was crucial then was the break-up of a large free trade area with an effective political regime. The economic consequences in the 1920s were major inflation and a stagnation of growth in the countries concerned during much of the inter-war period, though not all of this can necessarily be attributed just to the dissolution of the Austro-Hungarian empire.

Borders matter in the ex-SU because of the previous extraordinary degree of political and economic centralization, the high level of monopolization of the productive structure, natural resources heavily concentrated in certain regions, and significant inter-regional and inter-republic trade. Similar comments, though less dramatic, could be made about the EE economies as well. Thus the central problem is to determine the form of the economic and political regulation that will evolve in the post-SU era within and between these countries. Economic activity is usually one of the first casualties when inter-republic or inter-ethnic strife breaks out in the wake of the undermining of effective political governance of the relations between national entities.

A summing up

The general implication of this discussion of liberalization and marketization, whether given an exclusively economic or wider political gloss, is that it is just not sufficient to 'loosen all the ties' and then expect the virtues of the market and competition to emerge spontaneously. Explicit and positive efforts are required to construct an adequate and effective market system – to create 'market makers', for instance, in trade and finance. Difficult choices must be made about the creation of the institutions of effective market governance and regulation, including the organization of trade among new states. We pursue these crucial institutional issues in the following sections.

7   Privatization and the construction of property rights

The discussion under this heading has obvious overlaps with Section 6. But here we concentrate explicitly on the privatization issue, and connect it to the legal framework in which the reformed economies are increasingly beginning to work.

7.1   Property rights and legal reform

Question

Why do property rights matter for the operation of a market system?

Most economists and even extreme economic libertarians recognize that for markets to work efficiently, there must be a well defined system of property rights, and that the costs of contracting between individuals need to be minimized in order to benefit from gains from trade. At the least this requires a legal order guaranteed by the state and the operation of the rule of law.

A number of different 'models' of privatization have either been proposed for the transformation in the former Soviet-type economies, or implemented during it. Broadly speaking they are as follows (Sadowski, 1991):

1   The restoration of the private rights over property for the previous owners of that property, or their descendants – sometimes known as re-privatization.

2   The wholesale and direct disposal of the firm and its effects to private individuals.

3   The sale of stocks and shares to private persons, providing property claims in the enterprise.

4   The transfer and distribution of property rights to private persons free of charge, via some kind of voucher system.

It is perhaps the second and third of these methods that have been the most widespread. The second has tended to be deployed in connection with small and medium-sized businesses, where family control can often be established relatively easily and quickly, since capital requirements are not great. The third and fourth methods have tended to be employed where large-scale firms are concerned. They rely on the generation (or distribution) of relatively large batches of capital.

The EE economies and the Soviet Union previously displayed one of the most highly concentrated productive structures in the world, with huge enterprises, so one of the tasks set for the privatization programme was to break up these enterprises, to try to avoid undesirable private monopoly outcomes. At the end of the 1990s in the Soviet Union, for instance, industrial enterprises with more than 1000 employees accounted for 73 per cent of total employment, while those with less than 100 employees accounted for only 2 per cent of employment. (Compare this with the data in Chapters 4 and 6.) Between 30 and 40 per cent of Soviet output was produced by organizations on single sites. Thus in some instances the process of privatization has taken a three-phased form; first the *corporatization* of the enterprises into autonomous firms still owned by the state, then their *restructuring* to attempt to eliminate potential monopolies, followed by their *privatization proper.*

Rather as in the case of price reform, a problem for rapid privatization was the sheer number of large state enterprises involved. At the beginning of the 1990s Hungary had about 2000 large state enterprises primed for privatization, and Poland 7500 (Fischer and Gelb, 1991, p.99). In the Ukraine alone, Hogan (1991, p.316) has estimated that in the early 1990s there were upwards of 30 000 state enterprises, including perhaps 15 000 employing over 1000 people, and 1000 enterprises employing over 3000 people. These numbers put a massive constraint on the speed of privatization and indicated a gradualist approach. Thus the objective might become the progressive reduction of state ownership and the fostering of the growth of private activity, not necessarily the total elimination of the state sector. The private sector would thus eventually make up the dominant share in national output, but a 'mixed economy' outcome is both expected and accepted (Sadowski, 1991, p.47). The unresolved question, however, is the legitimate extent of the public sector that is to continue in existence, and its exact constitutional and operational form.

Another often quoted form of privatization, but not one included in the list above despite the fact that it seems to have been widespread in practice, is so-called '*nomenklatura* privatization'. This involves the bureaucrats in the ministries and managers of state enterprises (the *nomenklatura*) illegally or surreptitiously converting public property into private property for themselves, or manoeuvring to position themselves so as to be able to take unfair advantage when the time for privatization arose. Thus not all the ownership reform in these economies followed the dictates of the economist's rational model of marketization. The creation of a market system can also be the result of corrupt practices.

To pause here for a moment, note that corruption can be a feature of any economic system, as the article quoted below recognizes. The important though uncomfortable point to recognize is that under some circumstances it can also be an 'effective' mechanism of economic allocation and distribution. We should not expect the arrival of a market system necessarily to reduce the extent of corruption in an economy; it may only change its character. In many ways the market system and corruption complement each other as economic co-ordination mechanisms.

University to offer course in corruption

Corruption is part of doing business in Argentina, a fact now recognised by the University of Buenos Aires, which will include a new course on 'perverse systems' in its MBA syllabus.
The course … will focus on the causes and nature of corruption, and discuss ways to combat it … it will be based on case studies of 100 episodes of corruption. Lecturers will include businessmen, judges and government officials, including the mayor of Buenos Aires … [President Carlos] Menem's free market policies have reduced corruption, through substantial deregulation packages and privatisations, but businessmen still complain that politicians and bureaucrats exploit every opportunity to demand bribes.

(Financial Times, 27 April 1993)

For this reason the privatization activity has been accompanied by the construction of a viable legal framework, intended to reduce the possibilities for corrupt practices. Property rights and a system of economic legality imply the progressive displacement of discretion (by 'bureaucrats') with the rule of law in economic matters. Classic Soviet-type planning, based on the administrative allocation of resources by the centre to the enterprises, relied on an extensive network of discretionary bargaining within and between the organizations involved. Thus continual discretionary adjustments to the plan were essential to the very feasibility of the planning mechanism. They relied on the existence of an elaborate network of personal contacts and 'fixers', employed by every enterprise and ministry, who undertook those adjustments. In this universe the monetary reward system played a very subordinate role in the overall incentive mechanism, and where it did operate it also worked in a discretionary manner, involving personal superior and subordinate relationships. By all accounts sometimes major (but more often petty) corruption was rife.

The image that is proposed to replace this is one of a 'contract-rich' market system. Discretion is eliminated, and replaced by a system of 'rational-legal' contracts. The coverage exerted by personal relationships is dissolved by a system that facilitates impersonal trade. At its extreme, this model envisages the possibility of rendering the whole of economic existence as reducible to a set of fully specified contracts, by investing near enough everything with property rights. Clearly one does not need to go quite this far to recognize that there is a requirement for the rule of law and an effective contract system in the former Soviet-type economies. But there is an additional and important caveat to this point which can be illustrated by recent Chinese economic reforms. There has been a rapid and largely successful commercialization and marketization of important sectors of the Chinese economy, but there has been no overall or radical reform of Chinese property law (Nolan, 1993). Thus the emphasis on the reform of property rights as the vital precondition for marketization and commercialization of economic activity can be exaggerated by western commentators. Uncertain or unclear, and therefore 'flexible', property relations (or sometimes none at all) can be just as conducive to the rapid development of market systems.

Furthermore, it is wrong to see complex contracts as impersonal and complete, even in developed and well functioning market systems. Indeed, in the more successful market systems there is an increasing space for some 'discretion' to be built back into economic relationships. Given the lack of complete information faced by participants in real world markets, and thus the possibility that some participants will take advantage of their superior knowledge, complex contracts need the support of personal credibility which creates the space for discretion. Economists call this economic discretion based on personal reputation a 'reputation effect', which reduces the impersonality of market transactions. It is precisely the commitment to a long-term relationship, which often cannot be reduced to a balance sheet or profit and loss item, that requires the institution of networks of personal contacts which lubricate economic relationships among 'market makers' within the market system. Not all of these relationships necessarily take a monetary form – they can be based on trust and loyalty, for instance.

There is a danger, then, that in their enthusiasm to dispense with a discredited and thoroughly corrupt system of economic management, the former Soviet-type economies will go too far towards the other extreme. The advocates of a fully contractualized economic universe, with only arms-length and impersonal competitive economic interactions allowed to characterize the system, are themselves speaking to an extreme vision of competitive capitalism, and one, it might be added, that is strictly speaking highly improbable.

7.2 Critical reflections on the privatization and marketization debate

The above critique of a certain type of economic analysis that has been imported into the debate about the introduction of property rights in the former Soviet-type economies allows us to conduct a rather more general critical assessment of the conventional ideas of privatization and marketization expressed so far in this section.

An interesting problem here is exactly what is to be 'privatized' to create a market system. To analyse this properly we must recall what the system of resource allocation and distribution amounted to under central planning. This comprised an administrative system of incredible hierarchical complexity. It was designed to gather information, disseminate instructions, co-ordinate interactions, manage change, and monitor and enforce command performance. Typically at its apex stood a Council of Ministers, with a vast array of central planning and control agencies below it responsible for translating the plans' objectives and policies, first into implementable assignments of resources and instructions on how to use them, and then into actual deployments of resources and goods and services (Ericson, 1991). This ministry/departmental structure was duplicated within each of the fifteen Soviet Republics ('Union-Republic Ministries').

Finally, at the base of this elaborate system were the organizations that carried out the actual production, construction, transportation, distribution and trading activities in the economy. In 1986 there were 46 000 industrial enterprises, 23 000 state farms, 27 000 collective farms, 17 500 interfarm and associated enterprises, 1000 agro-industrial associations, 17 000 construction organizations, and almost one million wholesale and retail trading organizations (Ericson, 1991, p.14). Alongside this huge organizational pyramid stood a large number of parallel monitoring and control hierarchies, exercising important powers of investigation and intervention to ensure that the intentions of the state planners were followed. Although less elaborate, this kind of structure could be found duplicated in all the Eastern European economies.

The reason for describing this hierarchical structure in some detail is to bring home the point that privatizing the bottom rung of this ladder, however difficult a task because of the number of establishments involved, is not of itself sufficient to create 'the market system'. Primary emphasis has been given to this task, though, with a relative neglect of what is to replace all the other elaborate institutionalized management mechanisms that made up the previous system, including the crucial role of market makers mentioned above. Thus, in a sense, what was needed was to privatize this elaborate administrative system itself. This is what comprised the *mechanism* that the market system was to replace. If the market was to substitute for this, it needed to 'mirror' it in some way. But clearly, no one would be willing to 'purchase' the administrative and managerial elements of such a system; it could not be 'privatized' in that sense, however necessary it might have been. The implication is that privatizing those tangible productive elements that could be corporatized, restructured and then sold off does not really amount to a marketization of productive activity. Indeed, in some ways this was of lesser importance for the task of the marketization than the creation of an alternative institutionalized regulatory structure to replace all the activity of those now defunct ministries and departments. They performed a massive co-ordination task akin to that of the market, however inefficiently.

The lack of a new market mechanism and the associated uncertainty over property rights were not, however, features of the situation in the former German Democratic Republic, which simply adopted (or had imposed) all the legal framework of the Federal Republic. Thus the institutional mechanisms of a market economy were instantly on hand, but in their specific German form – as an 'organized' market system. In principle this may have given the former GDR a major advantage compared to other similar economies in transition. In addition, the ex-GDR has had all the advantages of the massive economic assistance that the West German economy could offer. The portfolio of the firms created from the *Kombinate* (the ex-GDR conglomerate enterprises) were vested in the *Treuhandanstalt,* a public body charged with the responsibility for selling these to private interests. In some senses, the *Treuhandanstalt* acted in the manner of a substitute for the old planning system, if in an interim fashion. It met the need, discussed above, to find a surrogate mechanism for a fully operative central direction of economic resources before the market system proper could be installed.

This experience reinforces the argument I have been developing, that the market system has to be deliberately constructed and created on the basis of definite choices about the forms of contracts, the types of institutions and the conditions of their operation, the forms and levels of public intervention and involvement, and similar issues. In most cases this work still remains to be done in the economies in transformation.

One process that is underway in these economies is the installation of a necessary legal order and civil code. But although the Eastern European countries have expressed a strong interest in becoming associated with the European Union, the legal orders they have adopted do not seem to be compatible with those of the main EU countries, nor with the framework of the 1992 European integration process (Svejnar, 1991, p.132; see also Chapter 14). The creation of an entire legal system from nothing in these countries has resulted in an incomplete and at times inconsistent set of economic laws.

A further set of problems arises with the decision to restructure, but also often to liquidate, state-run firms. Such decisions have arisen as these organizations have been primed for privatization, since once exposed to an asset valuation based on market-determined (often international) prices, the organizations concerned exhibit negative financial net worth. In addition, a good many of the previous state-run enterprises have been drastically restructured to suit currently acceptable western notions of business success. This has meant breaking up what were often potentially viable productive combinations of assets and people in the face of immediate financial pressures of a balance-sheet type. Some of the state-run enterprises that were liquidated were potentially efficient producers, but unviable current financial entities. Little was done to address this problem in the rush to privatize as much and as quickly as possible. A good many opportunities were thereby lost to preserve technologically and organizationally modest enterprises that were potentially viable in the medium term in branches like construction, bakery, shoe manufacturing, and even some consumer-durable manufacturing, which were geared up for essentially regional or domestic production. (A case in point was the Ikarus bus enterprise in Hungary.)

8   Reform of the financial system

As the above discussion of financial intermediation suggested, another important area of reform, and one where the institutional conditions for the operation of the market involve definite choices, is the financial system. I include in this the creation or reform of the banking system, the nature of the central bank, and the general mechanisms of corporate finance and control. In many of the economies in transformation the existence of inter-enterprise credit (loans extended between different enterprises, sometimes taking the form of trade credit) had become one of the main ways of sustaining output and circumventing attempts to control enterprise deficits. But firms using such credit are often accused of erecting informational obstacles to a proper 'market rules' based assessment of individual firms' true creditworthiness. Balance sheets, it is argued, need to be 'cleansed' of these extraneous credit relationships before an effective scrutiny of efficient and inefficient borrowers can be conducted.

Again, however, the importance of tight budget and credit constraints on all economic activity for the successful conduct of that activity can be exaggerated. One of the reasons why actual market economies function successfully is that they *do not* have completely tight and comprehensively specified budget and credit constraints. There is a need for some flexibility to allow for the unexpected and the risks associated with market exchanges. Even at the economy-wide level, the central bank provides a 'lender of last resort' facility in market economies. A lender of last resort exists to provide liquidity to the market system and hence is able to prevent financial collapse when exogenous shocks hit it, or when endogenous developments lead to an unexpected lack of liquidity. A lender of last resort facility therefore offers, in effect, a credit line (or 'loose' constraint) which vitally lubricates the system in times of potential difficulty. What is the case for the market system overall is equally necessary for its individual parts, and hence all agents may from time to time need the flexibility of a loose budget or credit constraint.

There is also a question to be answered about the form of the institutional arrangement best suited to an effective scrutiny of both the worthy and the unworthy economic enterprises. As noted above, the privatization programmes in the economies in transformation have promoted the widespread dispersion of share ownership. But is the dispersion of share ownership – the creation of a 'share-owning democracy' – necessarily the best way of securing effective control and scrutiny of the newly privatized enterprises? As discussed below, the problem is that there may be little incentive for small and dispersed shareholders to participate in the control and restructuring of such firms. This is the issue of managerial versus ownership control, raised in Chapter 12, reappearing in the economies in transformation. Small shareholders will want to develop an extensive and liquid secondary market in shares, offering a low-risk and low-cost means of exchanging their rights to ownership. The existence of highly sophisticated stock markets is not necessarily a good sign of effective corporate control.

8.1   Institutions for marketized corporate control

This point can be further illustrated by a discussion of the differences in corporate control mechanisms that typify already well functioning marketized economies. By 'corporate control' I mean the mechanisms by which shareholders and other stakeholders in companies influence corporate decisions. Financial systems differ quite widely in Europe and elsewhere, and different systems carry implications for the efficient performance of the real economy. Enterprise financing is often thought to be an area for the sole prerogative of private managerial decision making, but it is likely to become increasingly an object of public policy in both the east and the west of Europe, because of the central importance of financial systems in the funding and regulation of manufacturing industry. The system of enterprise financing is fundamentally implicated in both competition policy and industrial policy.

Broadly speaking, there are two types of financial system current within market economies. On the one hand there is the 'Anglo-American' model typified by the UK and USA, where the stock market and a decentralized market-based approach predominate. This is associated with the unorganized model of the market system discussed above. On the other hand, there is the 'continental' model typified by Germany and Japan, and to a lesser extent in Europe by France and Spain, where the banks and a more centralized, administrative approach prevail. Here we have a model more closely corresponding to the organized market system. This distinction is most marked in terms of corporate control, but it also invades the general business of financial intermediation.

As soon as one draws such a stark distinction between two models it becomes clear, of course, that the actual practice of financial systems involves many common features and similar arrangements. Furthermore, these distinctions, while they might have been important in the past, may now be dissolving in western Europe in the face of the deregulationist neo-liberal policy programmes initiated by individual governments aided by the European Commission's own competition policy. However, enough significant differences remain for these to be important.

The characteristics of the two different models can be summed up under the title of 'insider' (organized) and 'outsider' (unorganized) systems, the typical properties of which are shown in Table 15.1.

The close involvement in corporate control of banks in the insider system takes a number of forms. In the first place, banks own equity in the industrial sector, some on their own account, some as custodians for private shareholders. Second, banks have representatives on the boards of these firms, often in the position of chairman of the Supervisory Board in German firms (Edwards and Fischer, 1991). This is not the case in the outsider system. Third, the banks can influence corporate activity more directly as a

Table 15.1   **Properties of insider and outsider systems of corporate control**

Insider systems (e.g. Germany and Japan)	Outsider systems (e.g. UK and USA)
Concentrated ownership and control	Dispersed ownership
Association of ownership with control	Separation of ownership and control
Control by interested parties (banks, related firms and employees)	Little incentive for outside investors to participate in corporate control
Absence of hostile takeovers	Hostile takeovers that are costly and antagonistic
Other stakeholders are represented	Interests of other stakeholders are not represented
Intervention by outside investors limited to periods of clear financial failure	Low commitment of outside investors to long-term strategies of firms
Insider systems may encourage collusion	Takeovers may create monopolies

Source: Corbett and Mayer (1991) Table 4, p.65

result of the previous two points. Sometimes this takes the form of leading in the rescue or restructuring of firms (e.g. in France and Spain). Fourth, banks often provide large amounts of corporate finance in the form of loans to their client firms, though contrary to popular belief this is not the case in Germany, where internally generated funds are the most important source (Edwards and Fisher, 1991). Internally generated funds take the form of depreciation allowances and retained earnings. They are made available for investment by the firm and are not distributed to outside investors. However, in insider systems banks do tend to provide the bulk of any external finance on a long-term loan basis, contrary to the outsider systems where funding is stock-market based. Fifth, even where bank ownership may be modest in insider systems, there is a greater reliance on the cross-holdings of equity (share) stakes between related companies. Finally, shareholding is concentrated in insider systems, whereas it is dispersed widely in outsider systems, and there is a much smaller number of quoted companies in insider than in outsider systems. All in all, it is important to note that the Anglo-American market-based outsider systems are the exception rather than the rule in Europe, and in the world as a whole.

8.2   Implications for economic performance

Question

What likely effects do you think these differences might have for the conduct and success of economic activity?

As might be expected, the effects these differences have on economic performance is the subject of fierce controversy. In principle, the competitive market-based system would seem to offer the most efficient and attractive method of corporate control – that is, self-regulation on the basis of the pursuit of an interest. But it has increasingly come under attack. In the first place, the mode of gaining control tends to be highly antagonistic.

Contested takeovers are common in outsider systems, whereas they are rare in insider ones. This can be costly and distracting, leading to all manner of pre-defensive strategies by managements to prevent takeovers. Furthermore, the form of corporate control represents only shareholder interests. The interests of other stakeholders (employees, customers, suppliers, the local community, the 'national interest' even) tend to be ignored. Outsider systems are also accused of leading to 'short-termism' – that is, to the inability of management to develop a long-term investment strategy, to devote enough resources to R & D and training, to think in terms of organic internal growth rather than external growth through merger or acquisition, and to take long-term decisions. It leads to a greater emphasis on competition for corporate control and a consequent relative neglect of competition in product markets. The insider system, by contrast, stresses long-term co-operation between producers and the providers of finance.

To support these accusations, those criticizing the emphasis on outsider 'financial engineering' point to the disappointing relative economic performance of the outsider system countries. For instance, previous rounds of merger activity in the UK do not appear to have led to a better company performance overall. The policy problem this poses for European integration and beyond is the likely form of the increasingly interdependent financial system as monetary and economic internationalization and globalization develop. Will liberalization and deregulation lead to the dominance of the Anglo-American over the continental model, even though the former has often proved to be less effective and efficient in the long run than the latter?

It is often suggested that Europe as a whole is moving more towards an Anglo-American style of system, with relaxed regulation and opportunistic adventures in acquisitions, which in the long run will tend to create a unified approach based on the City of London. The problem with this argument, however, is that national institutional differences still remain, despite some definite moves towards the liberalization and deregulation of EU financial markets. It is not clear, furthermore, that even national mergers are effective, let alone cross-border ones. UK conglomerates in particular have found great difficulties in buying businesses they know nothing about, and are increasingly faced with the 'unbundling' of their diversification strategies as profits and growth fail to appear. Even the expansion-by-buying strategies in the USA have presented considerable financial, managerial and operational strain, with ruinous effects on many British companies. Cross-border European liaisons have been plagued by dissension, trying to blend different business cultures, differing attitudes, and facing continued 'national political chauvinism'. Only rarely have large cross-European mergers in the same industry so far married partners with truly complementary strengths, most being marriages that combine different corporate cultures with similar industrial weaknesses.

There is also the problem of the continued antagonism within the EU between the dictates of its competition policy and the remnants of an industrial policy. Tensions remain between the ambition to strengthen European indigenous manufacturing capability and a mergers and acquisitions policy that takes a hands-off approach. The French, in particular, have been keen to veto certain potential mergers when these have either threatened French interests directly or undermined the possibility of creating Euro-champions. The French continue to favour subsidization of some industrial sectors and a continued strong state involvement in industrial affairs (even as they have embarked on their own privatization programme). Finally, while Germany has so far been instrumental in keeping 'industrial policy' considerations out of EU merger policy (after all, German industry is the strongest and most dynamic in Europe and faces few acquisition possibilities), that does not necessarily imply that it will allow its well established and demonstrably effective financial system to be undermined by a potentially poorly functioning Anglo-American one.

The fact is that up to now the advice being received by the Eastern European countries on the construction of their financial systems has tended to come from the USA and the UK, which have the most developed of the 'outsider' systems. But the choice needs to be posed. The crucial relationship between reform of the private banking system and the finance and control of corporate activity needs to be more closely identified and directed before the countries in transformation effectively opt for the potentially 'wrong' model of corporate funding and control.

8.3   Macroeconomic issues

As well as these issues associated with the reorganization of production and the financial system, the process of marketization involves financial issues of a more macroeconomic type. These include the macroeconomic stabilization of the domestic economy and the management of its relationship to the international economy. These aspects of economic policy are mainly addressed in Book 2 of this text, so only a couple of points are made here relating to the themes already developed in this chapter.

A central point concerns the liberalization of the capital account of the balance of payments. This involves the liberalization of inward investment as well as of outward capital movements, and has some serious implications for the control of productive activity. There are thus strong links between this issue and privatization policy. On this subject, the governments have been quite cautious. All have expressed the wish for some foreign ownership of their industries and capital. This has mainly proceeded in the form of the foreign purchase of the potentially profitable parts of the privatized state sector. In addition, there have been some joint ventures between overseas and local firms, and some 'green field' FDI (i.e. foreign direct investment setting up economic activity from scratch) undertaken by multinational companies. But there has yet to be a full capital account liberalization.

Discussion of the inward investment and the need to stabilize these economies raises the more general role of western financial aid to the economies in transformation. Although it is difficult to obtain accurate figures, Table 15.2 contains the best summary data available. Despite a rhetoric of official commitments to help in the restructuring of these economies, the figures show that there has been a *net outflow* of financial resources from these economies since their old orders crumbled in the late 1980s. This has mainly to do with high debt servicing charges on the official loans made to them, but it also indicates some capital flight on the part of those benefiting from the restructuring process.

Table 15.2   **Net transfer of resources to transitional market economies ($US billion)**

	1990	1991	1992
Bulgaria	0.5	0.1	−0.5
Czechoslovakia	0.6	−0.4	−0.2
Hungary	−0.7	−0.8	−0.8
Poland	−3.8	−0.5	−3.0
Romania	1.7	1.3	0.4
(ex) Soviet Union	−6.4	−3.8	n/a
Total	−8.1	−4.1	−4.1

Source: based on *World Economic Survey* (1994) Figure IV.7; *Economic Survey of Europe* (1992) Table 5.2.5

What, then, is the logic of the existing situation? For the majority of those involved in this dramatic transformation, the potential human misery and degradation should not be underestimated. But any process of transformation so deep and momentous as that being experienced in these countries cannot be completed without very significant hardship and sacrifice. There is likely to be a massive increase in inequality, for instance: all previous economic and political transformations of this significance have led to some people becoming very wealthy because of it, while others have lost out. There seems no reason to believe that this transformation will be any different.

9   Conclusion

This chapter has highlighted the differences between an 'organized' and an 'unorganized' form of the capitalist market system. Both of these are strong images, which pervade the ideological battles fought over the meaning and appropriateness of the market system. Both variants of the market system have been successful in organizing economic activity throughout the twentieth century. An appreciation of these differences contributes a further strand to our understanding of the complexities of economic policy towards industry. As Chapters 8 and 12 noted, firms may use restrictive agreements and concentration as tools of competition and growth. Insider systems have been able to build on some of the dynamic benefits of such firm behaviour, while the instinct of economists schooled in outsider systems is to insist that they are inimical to the operation of an effective market system. This difference of view is rooted in a different stance on the nature of capitalist exchange – organized versus unorganized notions of economic activity. It constitutes one more argument for the importance of paying close attention to institutions, including the way businesses organize for market success, in analysing market systems and prescribing market policies.

The second major issue at stake in the chapter is therefore the institutionalized nature of any market system. Market systems are not natural phenomena that simply emerge if permitted to do so, but are systems heavily imbued with the marks of historical contingency, economic process, dynamics, and 'path dependency': we cannot escape institutions. The historically established institutional configuration characterizing distinct national economies determines the manner in which they are currently able to conduct the 'business of economics'.

One of the great contemporary experiments in testing some of these experiences and ideas can be found in the 'economies in transformation'. This involves a process of constructing new market systems. In turn, this raises questions about the economic analysis of processes of integration and disintegration. The development of cartels, integrated manufacturing operations, and price commonalities over diverse geographical and operational areas, i.e. what could be considered anti-competitive behaviour, is absolutely central to economic integration and the construction of a wider 'national' (or semi-national in the EU sense) integrated market. Competition policy aimed at preventing or dismantling these processes can thus (perhaps unintentionally) hinder and inhibit the creation of an integrated market system. It may unwittingly foster further disintegration. Policy makers starting from the organized market system perspective might be less quick to prevent these forms of behaviour emerging, especially in the early stages of (re)integration of the transforming economies. The two images of the market system analysed at length in this chapter thus have implications for economic policy.

This chapter brings to an end Book 1 of this text. The chapter has sought, not in any way to summarize the various approaches to analysing markets developed in earlier chapters, but rather to suggest that market systems operate in practice in historically determined institutional contexts. These market institutions vary, with consequences for economic performance, and can be usefully understood through the two stylized models of organized/ unorganized, insider/outsider systems. The second half of this text now turns its attention to some of the national economic policy issues raised but not developed in this chapter, including questions of inflation, unemployment and the distribution of wealth.

BOOK 2

Macroeconomics and Economic Policy

PART 9

CHAPTER 16

CHANGING ECONOMIES AND ECONOMIC THEORY

ECONOMICS AND ECONOMIC POLICY

by Vivienne Brown

1 Introduction

In March 1994 an international 'Jobs Summit' was called by US President Clinton, and the main item on the agenda was the problem of unemployment and non-employment. At that time, about 35 million people were unemployed in the 24 countries belonging to the OECD, representing about 8.5 per cent of the labour force (OECD, 1994). The detailed statistics differed across countries. In 1993 unemployment rates in excess of 10 per cent were found in Australia, Canada, Denmark, Finland, France, Ireland, Italy, Spain and the UK, and relatively low rates (below 7 per cent) in Austria, Germany, Iceland, Japan, Luxembourg, Norway, Portugal, Switzerland and the USA. In addition, however, it was estimated that about another 15 million people in the OECD had either given up looking for work or had unwillingly accepted a part-time rather than a full-time job. Thus non-employment rates were also high, even in some countries where unemployment was relatively low.

For the first time in fifty years, comparisons were being made with the period of the 1930s when unemployment in some countries stood at record levels (see Figures 16.1 and 16.2). Those were the years of the hunger marches in the UK, when unemployed people marched on London to demonstrate their plight. Those were also the years that produced the great debate between the proponents of *laissez-faire*, who argued that the government should allow markets to resolve the problem of unemployment, and the proponents of intervention, who argued that the government should actively try to provide more jobs. It was during this period, too, that John Maynard Keynes published his book *The General Theory of Employment, Interest and Money* (1936), in which he developed a new kind of economic theory – macroeconomics – to back up the case for interventionist policies.

Looking at unemployment data for the UK in the twentieth century tells the story of the return of widespread unemployment. Figure 16.3, drawn from a longer run of data presented in Chapter 20, shows the percentage unemployment rate for the UK from 1921 to 1992, with a statistical break in the series for the Second World War. Looking at this graph, we can see the similarity in the two peaks of high unemployment in the 1930s and the 1980s and 1990s. In between these two peaks of high unemployment in the UK, there is a period of relatively low unemployment of 1–2 per cent in the period of the 1950s and 1960s. In those days, unemployment rates nudging up towards 2 per cent made the headline news! By the 1980s and 1990s

Figure 16.1   **Women hunger marchers arrive in London from Lancashire in October 1932**

Source: Hulton Deutsch Collection

Figure 16.2   **The return of high unemployment in the 1980s and 1990s: a Department of Social Security office in Marylebone, London**

Source: Network/Neil Libbert

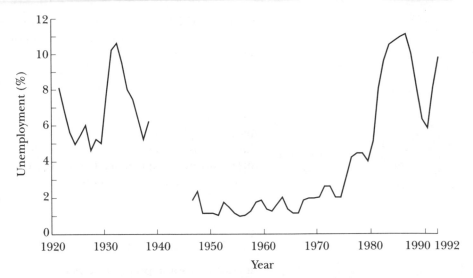

***Figure 16.3*   UK unemployment, 1921–92**

Source: Crafts and Woodward (1991) updated using *Economic Trends*

unemployment was around 10 per cent, and was also accompanied by an increase in those who had given up any hope of finding work and so were not even included in the count of the unemployed.

The inexorable increase in unemployment for western European countries was noted in Chapter 1, and it is shown in Figure 16.4 for the OECD area as a whole. Here again the 1950s and 1960s are marked by relatively low and stable unemployment levels, although note how even here the level seems to peak about every four years. At the time these peaks caused considerable consternation, but they have been dwarfed by the increases that have taken place since.

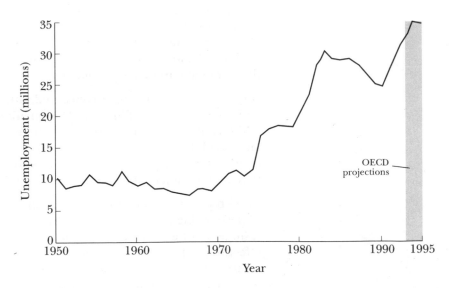

***Figure 16.4*   Unemployment in the OECD area, 1950–95**

Source: OECD (1994) p.9

Thus, half a century after the publication of one of the most influential books on unemployment and economic theory, some of the richest economies in the world were faced with an unemployment problem of similar, if not worse, dimensions than in the 1930s. Why was this? Were Keynes's ideas misguided? How had changes in the world economy contributed towards this increase in unemployment and non-employment?

Alongside rising unemployment and non-employment, the available evidence suggested that the distribution of income in a number of countries had become more unequal during the 1980s (OECD, 1993). This finding applied to Australia, Austria, Belgium, Canada, France, Japan, the Netherlands, Portugal, Spain, Sweden, the UK and the USA. In some countries the change was small, but in the UK and USA the increase in inequality was marked. Comparing the list of countries characterized by high unemployment with those for which inequality increased, we can see that there is no clear correlation. Countries with both high and low unemployment experienced an increase in inequality; the UK and USA had the greatest increases in inequality, but one had relatively high unemployment while the other did not. This suggests that the changes in the distribution of income were not simply the result of changes in unemployment, but were also influenced by changes in the functioning of the labour market and by differences in government policies.

In addition, some policy makers were becoming concerned about what they saw as the growth of a permanent 'underclass' – a class of people living at or well below the poverty line with no hope of a job that could pay enough to give them a decent standard of living. This growth of an underclass, it was claimed, was associated with all the traditional social and psychological problems of grinding poverty with no hope for the future – a vicious circle of material deprivation, poor educational standards, low expectations, and a high crime rate.

The leaders of the richest countries were therefore faced with questions concerning both employment and the distribution of income, and so were confronting not only an economic problem, but a social and political problem too. Following a decade or so dominated by the resurgence of economic liberalism, the unleashing of market forces, and the pruning of the welfare state, questions were beginning to surface in some quarters about the economic consequences, as well as the ethics and political wisdom, of allowing widening discrepancies in the life chances available to different sections of the population.

Book 2 of this text is largely concerned with such issues in macroeconomics and the distribution of income. This opening chapter of Book 2 will present a historical context to debates about these issues as an introduction to the analysis of the later chapters and to the current policy situation. In the course of this chapter I shall also review some of the main themes and issues that are the subject of later chapters in this book.

In Section 2, I examine Keynes's contribution to the theoretical understanding of unemployment. In Section 3, I present an account of the resurgence of economic liberalism, and the ways in which this posed an effective challenge to what had become the Keynesian orthodoxy. Section 4 returns to the current situation by outlining some of the main economic issues that face us now and which make these ongoing economic debates even more urgent and difficult. Section 5 concludes the chapter.

2   The Keynesian revolution

2.1   Introduction: a new theoretical approach

Before Keynes wrote *The General Theory*, unemployment was seen as the result of wages being too high. According to the demand and supply model of competitive markets which you met in Chapter 7, more of a good can be sold only if there is a reduction in its price. By analogy, if a person's labour is thought of as a good to be bought and sold on the labour market, then more can be sold only if its price – the wage rate – is reduced. The implication for policy is that the government needs to do nothing at all, except ensure that trade unions are not so powerful that they try to buck the market and end up pricing their own members out of a job.

The view that workers simply had to accept lower wages in order to reduce unemployment, was the reigning orthodoxy against which Keynes argued. An example of this orthodox 'classical' position is given by Professor Edwin Cannan's Presidential Address to the Annual Meeting of the Royal Economic Society in September 1932:

> But general unemployment is in reality to be explained almost in the same way as particular employment. In a particular employment, provided demand for its product is elastic, more persons can be employed if they will work for less remuneration. In all employments *taken together*, demand is indefinitely elastic, and consequently indefinite numbers can be employed if they do not ask for too high a remuneration. General unemployment appears when asking too much is a general phenomenon.
>
> *(Cannan, 1932, pp.367, original emphasis)*

Cannan is arguing that particular and general unemployment both have the same cause and can be analysed in the same way using competitive demand and supply analysis.

Keynes protested against this way of thinking. Particular unemployment was not at all the same as general unemployment, he argued. If a single group of unemployed workers accept a reduction in their rate of wages, then more of them will be employed because they are now cheaper to employ compared with other workers. This is the case of particular unemployment. But if *all* workers accept a reduction in their rate of wages, this will have effects right through the economy and must be analysed at an economy-wide level.

For this reason, Keynes argued that it is inappropriate when analysing the entire economy to use only the analysis of demand and supply based on a particular commodity. This was the core of the theoretical innovation of *The General Theory*, in which Keynes introduced a new theoretical apparatus for analysing the economy as a whole, or the 'aggregate economy'. This branch of economics is now known as macroeconomics. In particular, Keynes focused on the role of 'aggregate demand' – the total demand in the aggregate economy – as a key determinant of the level of unemployment. Aggregate demand is explained more fully in Chapter 17.

Economists are still wrestling with the implications of Keynes's original argument, as you will find out in later chapters. Keynes's theories have been the subject of an extensive debate among economists, who have not even agreed on what Keynes himself was trying to do with his new theoretical

Definition

Keynesian economics

Keynesian economics, or Keynesianism, stresses the importance of the role of aggregate demand in determining the rate of unemployment.

framework. That framework itself has been amended or criticized by many other economists who have formed themselves into distinct schools of thought. Adherents of Keynesian economics have tried to refine and improve on Keynes's work, while others have criticized it as being fundamentally erroneous.

Later chapters will introduce you to macroeconomic theory. In the following sections of this introductory chapter, I want to give you an overview of some of the big policy debates that have shaped thinking about the aggregate economy, and so I shall focus on the policy implications of Keynes's *General Theory*.

2.2   Do markets adjust automatically?

One of the main planks of pre-Keynesian thinking was that markets work automatically in a self-adjusting manner. As you learnt in Chapter 7, according to this way of thinking, the price mechanism works by allocating resources to where they are most needed. If a good is in short supply, then its price rises. When this happens, consumers become more sparing in their use of the good, and producers are encouraged to produce more of it. Similarly, if a good is in oversupply, then its price falls. The fall in price encourages consumers to use more of it and at the same time producers have less of an incentive to supply it. Inevitably, it was acknowledged, this process does not work perfectly or immediately, but in the absence of large-scale interference by governments, trade unions and monopolies, it will tend to work in the way just described.

In the case of labour, if there is widespread unemployment, this must be the result of wage rates being too high. In time, a free labour market would see a reduction in wages to the full employment level. If this does not happen, it must be the result of interference in the labour market – either from trade unions in keeping up the level of wages, or from government legislation which inhibits the untrammelled operation of market adjustment. Keynes argued that this view was wrong and that markets, including the labour market, are not able to adjust automatically to eliminate unemployment.

Thus Keynes argued against the view that markets are somehow self-adjusting. This was how he characterized the two positions in a BBC radio broadcast in 1934:

> I have said that we fall into two main groups. What is it that makes the cleavage which thus divides us? On the one side are those who believe that the existing economic system is, in the long run, a self-adjusting system, though with creaks and groans and jerks, and interrupted by time lags, outside interference and mistakes. ... On the other side of the gulf are those who reject the idea that the existing economic system is, in any significant sense, self-adjusting. They believe that the failure of effective demand to reach the full potentialities of supply, in spite of human psychological demand being immensely far from satisfied for the vast majority of individuals, is due to much more fundamental causes. ... The gulf between these two schools of thought is deeper, I believe, than most of those on either side of it are aware. On which side does the essential truth lie? That is the vital question for us to solve. ... I can scarcely begin here to

give you the reasons for what I believe to be the right answer. But I can tell you on which side of the gulf I myself stand ... Now *I* range myself with the heretics.

(Keynes, 1934, pp.486–9, original emphasis)

Keynes argued that the fault with the *laissez-faire* argument was that it ignored the relationship between employment and the aggregate economy. A position of widespread unemployment can emerge because there is an imbalance at the level of the aggregate economy, and it is this that prevents the labour market from adjusting. Keynes identified the main weakness of the economy at the aggregate level as being the lack of 'aggregate demand' for the output of the economy as a whole.

There are two main factors influencing the amount of employment that firms can offer: the wage rate (discussed in Chapters 18 and 21), and the demand for goods and services. If demand is high and the firm can readily sell its output, then it is more likely to take on new workers. Conversely, if aggregate demand for goods is low and the firm cannot sell its output, then it will not be able to carry on production and workers must lose their jobs. Keynes argued that aggregate demand was of overriding importance in determining the business environment in which firms made their hiring and firing decisions, and that neglecting it had led earlier economists into erroneous conclusions.

Keynes's emphasis on the importance of aggregate demand highlighted the cumulative rather than the self-correcting nature of market disturbances. Once firms begin to lay off workers, this is likely to have cumulative effects. The increase in unemployment will reduce aggregate demand and therefore make it more likely that other firms will start losing orders, and so have to make their workers redundant. In addition, business expectations about the future tend to a large degree to be reinforcing. Once a climate of pessimism sets in, firms are less likely to embark on new investment programmes, and this too depresses aggregate demand.

Keynes's analysis also posed a challenge to conventional notions of thrift and prudential behaviour. In a period of high unemployment, the prudent person would reduce expenditure in order to save more as a protection against future uncertainties. Similarly, firms taking a pessimistic view of the future would not embark on new investment. From the point of view of aggregate demand, these are the worst possible responses, as they put downward pressures on consumption expenditure and investment at a time when demand is already too low. It is far better for everyone to go out on a spending spree during a recession in order to boost aggregate demand and give employers an incentive to start hiring more workers.

2.3   The argument for government intervention

As individual workers and firms cannot decide to boost aggregate demand during recessions, is there any other economic agent that can? The Keynesian answer to this is that governments both can and should intervene to influence aggregate demand. In times of recession when demand is low, the government should try to increase aggregate demand, and during booms when the economy is in danger of overheating, it should try to damp it down. Thus the government should try to counteract the cumulative nature of movements in the aggregate economy by acting in a countercyclical manner to smooth out fluctuations and maintain a high and stable level of employment.

The Keynesian theory thus provides a clear theoretical rationale for government intervention. One way of understanding this is to see the aggregate economy in terms of a prisoners' dilemma game, such as the one presented in Chapter 5. There it was shown how individual decision making in situations of interdependence can lead to inferior results for the players, compared with the co-operative outcome. If the prisoners could agree on a co-operative approach, the pay-off for each of them would be higher than if each made the decision individually.

Question

The prisoners' dilemma game shows how the presence of interdependence between decisions can crucially affect outcomes. Try to consider how different firms' expenditures and employment decisions might be interdependent.

The interdependence here comes from the fact that one firm's expenditure is another firm's income. If one firm increases its expenditure on machinery and raw materials, then another firm experiences this as an increase in orders and in income. If one firm employs more workers, then other firms experience this as an increase in demand for the consumer products that they make.

It follows from this that if there is a recession within a single country, and ignoring international influences for the moment, the best course of action for the economy is for firms to embark on a massive expenditure programme, generating jobs and incomes for workers which are then spent on their own products. If all firms do this, everyone benefits. This is the best option for society as it generates the greatest number of jobs. The trouble is that it is only worth it for any individual firm to do this if it feels confident that other firms will do likewise. In other words, any one firm has to feel optimistic about the economy in general before it is prepared to expand. If it expects to be the only firm that expands, then its new expensive capacity will be redundant and profits will fall. But if all firms take this view, then no one expands, and the economy stays in a recession. On the other hand, if a firm could let other firms start the process of generating activity, it could initially benefit from the increased employment and incomes available to spend on its output without having to be the first to take the risk of embarking on expensive investment. In this case, its profits would be even greater because it would benefit from the general increase in activity without having to incur the costs of investment at that stage.

This prisoners' dilemma game is shown in the pay-off matrix in Figure 16.5. In order to represent an aggregate economy in a 2 × 2 matrix, we have to imagine just two firms, each deciding in the recession whether to start straightaway on an expensive investment project, or whether to wait and see if the economy improves first. Firm A is shown in the lower left-hand cells and Firm B is shown in the upper right-hand cells. The pay-offs in the matrix denote the level of profits for each firm. It is to be understood in this game that a high level of profits would allow the firms to offer more employment. Remember that it is the structure of pay-offs that is significant in game theory; the actual numbers in the pay-off matrix are arbitrary and have been chosen to illustrate the internal structure of the prisoners' dilemma game. In this matrix you will find that it is in both firms' interest not to invest immediately but to wait and see. If they both do this, however, the outcome is the worst possible for the society overall as neither firm invests and total profits are only £40. In this case, because both firms wait and do nothing until the recovery occurs, the outcome is that the recovery does not happen. If both firms were to go ahead, however, and invest immediately, each firm would earn £100 and the recovery would be underway.

Figure 16.5 **The decision to invest during a recession represented as a prisoners' dilemma game**

To understand this, consider first the situation for Firm A. Should Firm A invest now or should it wait and see? Consider what it should do if it expects Firm B to invest now. If it expects Firm B to invest straightaway, then its pay-off is £100 if it also goes ahead and invests now, or £110 if it waits. The pay-off is higher if it waits because it is not having to increase its own expenditure in order to benefit from the upturn in activity arising from Firm B's increased investment expenditure. If it expects Firm B to wait and see, Firm A's pay-off is £10 if it goes ahead and embarks on the new investment, and £20 if it also waits. Here again, the pay-off to Firm A is higher if it waits to see if there is going to be a general upturn before committing its own expenditure. If it invests now, its pay-off is only £10 because it has increased its expenditure, but as the other firm has not, its own investment was premature. Thus, whatever Firm A expects Firm B to do, it will be better off waiting to see whether there is an improvement before it commits itself to increased expenditure. The same line of reasoning applies to Firm B.

This example using the prisoners' dilemma may seem rather artificial as, to keep the matrix simple, I have had to present an entire economy as if it were composed of just two firms. The point it illustrates is nonetheless crucially important, as it shows the interdependence of expenditure decisions by economic agents. If all agents increase their expenditure, then aggregate demand is increased and the economy moves out of recession. If just a few economic agents increase expenditure, then the effect on aggregate demand is negligible and the economy remains stuck in a recession. This expenditure may take the form of consumption expenditure, investment expenditure, government expenditure or export expenditure. In the pay-off matrix, I concentrated on firms' investment expenditure, but the conclusion of the prisoners' dilemma game applies to all forms of expenditure: the best outcome for society as a whole occurs when firms (and other economic agents) increase their expenditure together in order to pull the economy out of recession; however, if expenditure decisions are taken individually, this best outcome is impossible and so the economy stays stuck in recession.

The solution to the dilemma posed by the prisoners' dilemma game is the co-operative outcome. One way of securing the co-operative outcome is to have a benevolent external agency which ensures the best solution. If an external agency can coax firms to increase their investment, for example by giving tax rebates or special investment grants, then this gets over the paradox of the prisoners' dilemma. According to the Keynesian argument, the government admirably performs this role of a benevolent external agency which co-ordinates the actions of other agents.

Consider what would happen in the prisoners' dilemma game if the government were to offer a £20 investment grant to firms as an inducement to get on with their investment. The grant means that the pay-off to investing straightaway is increased by £20. What difference would this make to the outcome of the game?

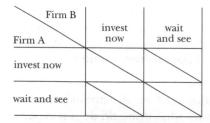

Figure 16.6 **Pay-off matrix for showing the decision to invest during a recession when the government offers an investment grant of £20**

Exercise 16.1

Enter the values of the pay-offs in the blank pay-off matrix in Figure 16.6 after the government offers firms a £20 investment grant.

What will be the outcome of this version of the game?

I hope you worked out that the pay-off to investing now is increased by £20 for both firms. This means that the pay-off to investing now when the other firm also invests is raised to £120, and the pay-off to investing now when the other firm waits is raised to £30. The result is that both firms choose to invest now irrespective of what the other firm does. The reason is that the relative pay-off to investing now as opposed to waiting has been raised. Both firms invest, and so the recession is a thing of the past!

Keynes did not present his argument in the form of a prisoners' dilemma game, but as a new economic model for understanding the relationship between aggregate demand and the level of output and employment. The revolutionary policy implication of Keynes's theory, however, was that it provided a persuasive argument for government intervention in the economy along the lines that I have just presented.

This is one of those instances in economic history where a new model of the economy resulted in an entirely new approach to economic policy making. The government was now thought to be able to introduce policy changes which would have enormously beneficial effects on the performance of the economy, and with this new-found power came a set of responsibilities for steering the course of the economy.

Instead of leaving well alone, the government now was to respond to the economic requirements of the moment by adjusting policy in a discretionary manner in order to 'fine tune' the economy. Keynesian economic theory thus provided an economic rationale for discretionary economic policy such that governments would assess current requirements and then make policy changes in accordance with these.

This required the government to have a set of economic objectives. An ultimate economic objective might be some acceptable level of economic well-being, but expressed like this such an objective is hard to pin down. A more specific economic objective would be expressed in terms of some desirable rate of growth, or an acceptable rate of unemployment or inflation. Sometimes a government has distributional objectives, such as greater equality in the distribution of incomes.

Different governments have different objectives, and these objectives may change in the course of time. During the 1950s and 1960s most western governments attached a high value to the objective of low unemployment, but during the 1980s and early 1990s the prime economic objective became the control of inflation.

Definitions

Discretionary economic policy

Discretionary economic policy requires the government to make policy changes on the basis of its judgement of current and future economic circumstances.

Economic objectives

A government's economic objectives are the specific objectives of its economic policy programmes, normally expressed in terms of the rate of unemployment, rate of inflation and/or rate of economic growth. Sometimes distributional objectives are included.

Definitions

Policy instrument

Policy instruments are economic variables which are directly controlled by the government. For example, tax rates might be an instrument of policy.

Policy target

Policy targets are economic variables which are only indirectly and approximately subject to control by the government. For example, tax revenues might be a policy target; these are influenced by tax rates but also by other factors.

The policy variables that are amenable to direct government control are sometimes called policy instruments. For example, the rate of income tax is a policy instrument as it is directly controlled by the government. A policy target is not under direct government control, but governments nonetheless try to influence it using the policy instruments at its disposal. For example, tax revenues may be a policy target which governments try to control using an instrument such as the tax rate, but they are influenced by other factors too.

The widespread acceptance of what came to be regarded as a Keynesian approach to discretionary policy making embodied these basic distinctions between economic objectives, policy instruments and policy targets. Sometimes objectives shifted, and sometimes aspects of policy making were moved from one category to another as priorities and constraints changed. Furthermore, the distinction between instruments and targets is not always watertight. For example, a long-standing issue within monetary theory is whether either the rate of interest or the money supply can be regarded as an instrument or a target of monetary policy (this was discussed in Chapter 11). But underlying this general approach to policy making was the belief that governments would and should respond to changing economic circumstances by making discretionary changes in its economic policy.

2.4   Income inequalities do matter

Once Keynesian economics had established an argument in favour of government intervention in the economy, boosting aggregate demand in times of recession and curbing it in times of boom, theorists also developed other functions for active state involvement. Keynes's emphasis on the need for increased aggregate demand during recessions highlighted the way in which inequalities in the distribution of income affect the level of aggregate demand. As Chapter 3 explained, the proportion of income that is spent rather than saved depends on the level of income. Those with a higher income spend a smaller proportion, whereas those on lower incomes tend to spend a higher proportion of their income. It follows from this that a redistribution of income via taxes from the rich to the poor will increase aggregate demand and so will help to make the aggregate economy function more efficiently.

Such redistributive programmes are especially important for helping to counteract the effects of the economic cycle. During a recession, the high levels of unemployment mean a sharp reduction in purchasing power for those without a job, and so this reduces aggregate demand. Welfare programmes of payments for those without work thus serve not only the humanitarian purpose of giving support to those in greatest need, but also help to boost aggregate demand and hasten the time when jobs become available again. During the boom, less is paid out in welfare programmes as the numbers of unemployed fall, and tax revenues rise with the higher level of economic activity.

Thus, Keynesian macroeconomics came to have a predisposition towards a more egalitarian approach to the distribution of income. This follows partly from its concern with maintaining a high and stable level of aggregate demand, and partly from its concern with unemployment, as it is the unemployed who have to bear the brunt of structural change and exogenous shocks impacting on the economy. But the links between

Keynesian economics and redistributive policies run deeper than this. Keynesian economics is also associated with a more general commitment to the aspirations and ethos of the welfare state. Whether and to what extent the welfare state has contributed towards redistributing incomes is an issue that has been much debated, and it is discussed in Chapter 23. The point here is that the proposals of William Beveridge for a social insurance model of welfare in the UK, encompassing all individuals in society, were based on the fundamental assumption that full employment could be maintained. It was this assumption of full employment that underwrote the insurance principle that everyone in society would be a paid-up member of the national insurance scheme, and so would be entitled by right to social insurance protection when in need. The importance of this link is illustrated by its partial erosion during the 1980s and 1990s: with growing unemployment, the original connection between the welfare state and the insurance principle was subject to attack as critics of the welfare state tried to redefine and curtail its sphere of operations.

For these reasons Keynesian economics is connected with a more general political stance of attempting to reform what it sees as the worst ills of capitalism. Keynesian economics was adopted by a broad swathe of social democratic thinking which attempts to save capitalism from its own worst evils. According to this position, relatively equal societies are not only more just; they are also more efficient in that everyone contributes productively, while everyone shares to some degree in the wealth so produced. It is therefore actively concerned to make capitalist economies work both more efficiently and more fairly, without fundamentally challenging the entrepreneurial ethos or the market allocation of resources. It values the political freedoms and the material advantages that are thought to accompany a relatively free system of markets in industrial capitalist societies, but it is also critical of what it sees as the shortcomings of an excessive reliance on market allocation. It therefore espouses a balance of the market mechanism and active state involvement to try to assure a less unequal distribution of the economic rewards and penalties associated with the inevitable process of structural change.

2.5   A new concept of the aggregate economy

Another implication of Keynes's theory was that it provided a new notion of the 'aggregate economy' as the macroeconomy. I have used this term a number of times so far in this chapter, but I now want to pause for a moment to consider what it means.

The aggregate economy refers to the national economy as a structured set of economic relations between all economic agents. This implies a notion of the total economy as an aggregation (or adding up) of all the individual transactions within the economy, which in turn implies a process of aggregating over all economic agents. As previous chapters have emphasized, there are many different kinds of agents. When we aggregate across the economy, however, we are abstracting from many of these differences and visualizing the economy as composed of a small number of different types of agents. There are *consumers,* who are the people who purchase the final output comprising goods and services. There are *workers* who sell their labour. There are *firms* which produce the final output. And there is the *government.*

Thinking of the aggregate economy in this way also implies a process of aggregating across markets. One such aggregated market is the market for all goods and services. This market includes all the traded goods and services, from motor vehicles, clothing and consumer goods to insurance services, meals out and shoe repairs. Another aggregated market is the labour market, where all labour is traded. The other aggregated market is the money market, as you learnt in Chapter 11. Looking at the economy in the aggregate, therefore, it is composed of three main markets: the goods market, the labour market and the money market. The core of macroeconomics is concerned with trying to understand the various ways in which these three aggregated markets interact, and how employment and output are determined in a world of economic transactions denominated in money terms.

This aggregate macroeconomy also reinforces the notion of the national economy. Here the extent of the macroeconomy is determined by national boundaries. The government which intervenes to reduce unemployment is the national government, which has a particular responsibility for the performance of the national economy. Thus, Keynesian macroeconomics also helped to identify the national economy as being composed of a distinct set of economic relationships that are amenable to systematic analysis, and which is the particular concern of the national government. For this reason, Keynesianism carried with it a distinct political agenda which emphasized national priorities and a nationally bounded view of government intervention.

This section has argued that Keynesianism was based on a technical innovation in economic analysis, in that it introduced the idea of the aggregate economy and the importance of aggregate demand in determining the level of output and employment. However, because of its challenge to *laissez-faire* ways of thinking, together with its arguments about the central importance of government policy in guiding the economy through the worst manifestations of capitalist instability, it was also embedded in a broader political and social agenda which set out to reform capitalism's own worst evils. It was associated with a concern to diffuse more widely the material benefits of industrialized economies, and to provide assistance to those who, through no fault of their own, were forced to bear the brunt of the massive dislocations to which the economy was periodically prone.

3   The resurgence of economic liberalism

3.1   Market adjustment

This view of the national economy and the role of government policy making persisted as a new orthodoxy throughout the 1950s and 1960s. In the post-1945 era of economic reconstruction, both its economic analysis and its wider political assumptions were broadly acceptable to governments and electors alike in the industrialized countries. Looking back on those decades, they appear successful in comparison with both earlier and later standards. As Figure 16.4 showed, unemployment in the main industrialized countries was low during this period. Growth rates were also high by historical standards, as Chapter 20 demonstrates. Income disparities between these richer countries on the one hand and non-industrialized countries on the other were very large, but there was a general expectation that in the course of time, these differentials would be reduced.

Looking back on this period, some economists have seen it as a kind of 'Golden Age', when macroeconomic performance achieved high and fairly stable levels of employment and growth by historical standards. It is a moot point as to whether this period of relative stability was achieved by the advance in economic thinking secured by the Keynesian revolution, or whether it was simply the result of the unique circumstances of post-war reconstruction. Either way, the relative success of those years led to a widespread expectation that, in future, the path of economic expansion need not be marked by the distress brought by the inexorable pattern of cyclical recessions, and by the harrowing experience of growing unemployment and the visible presence of poverty.

In retrospect, these years seem successful, but the pattern of cyclical activity was only muted, not defeated, and at the time there was considerable concern that the progress of economic growth was still subject to cyclical swings. If you look again at Figures 16.3 and 16.4, you will see that there was indeed a cyclical pattern in unemployment.

Question

How would you describe the pattern of unemployment in the period from the late 1940s to early 1970s that is shown in Figure 16.3?

In Figure 16.3 the UK unemployment rate shows a cyclical pattern during the period from the late 1940s to the early 1970s, with peaks in 1947 (2.3%), 1952 (1.7%), 1958/59 (1.7/1.8%) and 1963 (2.0%). Unemployment then rose in 1967 to 1.8% and carried on rising until the next peak in 1971/72 at 2.6%.

Furthermore, the years of low unemployment seemed to coincide with years of rising inflation. Figure 16.7 reproduces the UK unemployment graph of Figure 16.3 for the post-1950 period, but it also includes a red line showing the rate of inflation during these years.

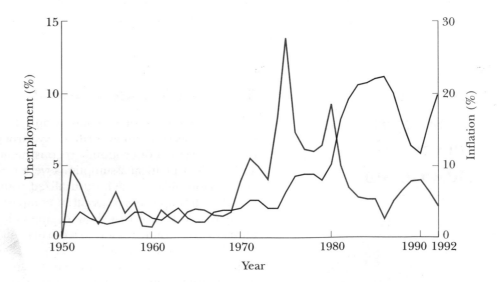

Figure 16.7   **UK unemployment and inflation, 1950–92**

Source: As for Figure 16.3

Question

In Figure 16.7, what is the relationship between inflation and unemployment for the UK during the 1950s and 1960s? Which are the years of low unemployment and of high inflation?

Figure 16.7 suggests that years of low unemployment are associated with high inflation. The years 1951, 1955/56, 1961 and 1965/66 were marked by relatively low unemployment and high inflation. This inverse relationship between unemployment and inflation gave rise to the view that there was a 'trade-off' between unemployment and inflation: that reductions in unemployment could be secured only on the basis of increases in the rate of inflation. At a theoretical level this led to a re-examination of the links between the price level and aggregate demand. This in turn led to a more sceptical approach to the feasibility of conducting permanently expansionary policies in order to keep unemployment low. It also provided a fertile ground for more substantial theoretical criticisms of the Keynesian approach to take root.

Another disturbing trend was also in evidence during this period. In Figure 16.3 you will see that, excluding the peak in 1947, each cyclical peak in unemployment is higher than the previous one. Looking at the four peaks in 1952 (1.7%), 1959 (1.8%), 1963 (2.0%) and 1971/72 (2.6%), each has a higher rate of unemployment than the one before it. In 1967, Milton Friedman delivered an influential lecture to the American Economic Association in which he argued that the trade-off was itself a delusion: that inflation had to rise by increasing amounts in order to get the same reductions in the level of unemployment, and that eventually there would be no trade-off at all: 'there is always a temporary trade-off between inflation and unemployment; there is no permanent trade-off. The temporary trade-off comes not from inflation *per se*, but from unanticipated inflation, which generally means, from a rising rate of inflation' (Friedman, 1968, p.11). There is more on this debate in Chapter 24.

During the 1970s the trade-off broke down in the UK as both inflation and unemployment were on a rising trend. In the OECD as a whole, inflation rose from 8.0% average during 1970–74 to 13.5% in 1980, and the unemployment rate rose from 3.5% in 1974 to 5.7% in 1980 (*OECD Economic Outlook*, June 1994). The old trade-off between unemployment and inflation seemed a thing of the past and Friedman's prediction seemed to be proved correct. Suddenly economists had to explain how rising unemployment and slow growth was compatible with rising inflation – stagflation as it was called.

On this issue there were two main answers. Some economists explained stagflation in terms of the two oil price shocks which fed inflationary pressures around the world via the higher price of oil. Other economists explained stagflation in terms of the inflationary effects of the Keynesian policies of the earlier period. Governments, they argued, had injected inflationary pressures into the system via government spending, so economic agents had come to expect inflation and anticipate its effects. But, by anticipating it, they were also nullifying its effectiveness in stimulating economic growth. Economists continued to argue over the causes, but governments responded to stagflation by trying to reduce government

Definition

Stagflation

The combination of *stag*nating growth and high in*flation* is known as stagflation.

expenditure. In this recriminatory atmosphere, anti-Keynesian views began to develop and received a more sympathetic hearing.

During the period of the 1980s and 1990s, *laissez-faire* views became influential again at the policy level. The resurgence of economic liberalism during this period is associated with the economic and political writings of economists such as F.A. Hayek, as well as Milton Friedman, both of whom had always been sharp critics of Keynesianism and the growth of the state. Hayek and Friedman resuscitated the pre-Keynesian view that markets work more efficiently in co-ordinating economic activities than any other means yet discovered, and they also linked this to a statement of the overriding political importance of individual freedom. According to this view, the growth of state involvement in the economy entailed a reduction of individual freedoms as well as a throttling of the market mechanisms which secure an equilibrium between demand and supply. This emphasis on the fundamental importance of market price signals – including wage rates – in allocating resources to where they are most highly valued, led them to stress the dangers of government intervention and persistent inflation in distorting these price signals.

Three main aspects of this distortion were emphasized. First, it was argued that the extensive system of government taxes and subsidies had distorted relative prices. Goods and services receiving a subsidy were priced lower than warranted, and those that were taxed carried a price higher than the true cost (see Chapter 10). The high marginal rates of income tax discouraged effort and initiative, and high welfare payments to those out of work deterred people from accepting realistic wages and returning to work.

Second, they argued that unemployment was the result of wages being out of line with the requirements of demand. The main culprit here was the monopoly practice of trade unions in bargaining for wages that were too high and which distorted the necessary relativities between different trades and occupations.

Third, it was argued that these distortions were compounded by Keynesian policies of increasing aggregate demand, which had simply stoked up inflation, which in turn further distorted price information. In a situation of rising prices it can be difficult for economic agents to know when any particular price rise is due to the shortage of the good in question or to general inflationary pressure. For this reason, Friedman and Hayek argued that the control of inflation – not the reduction in unemployment – should be the prime policy objective. They argued that government attempts to reduce unemployment by increasing aggregate demand had been unsuccessful, as this had simply raised the rate of inflation, which would, in the long run, cause such a misallocation of resources that unemployment would eventually be that much greater:

> Full employment has come to mean that maximum of employment that can be brought about in the short run by monetary pressure. This may not be the original meaning of the theoretical concept, but it was inevitable that it should have come to mean this in practice. Once it was admitted that the momentary state of employment should form the main guide to monetary policy, it was inevitable that any degree of unemployment which might be removed by monetary pressure

should be regarded as sufficient justification for applying such pressure. That in most situations employment can be temporarily increased by monetary expansion has long been known. If this possibility has not always been used, this was because it was thought that by such measures not only other dangers were created, but that long-term stability of employment itself might be endangered by them. What is new about present beliefs is that it is now widely held that so long as monetary expansion creates additional employment, it is innocuous or at least will cause more benefit than harm.

(Hayek, 1978, p.54)

Hayek argued that government expenditure had an inbuilt tendency to go on rising. Reflationary measures thus outweighed contractionary measures, with a long-term upward movement in prices and eventually in unemployment itself. Hence Hayek and Friedman argued that the prime objective of economic policy should be a stable – ideally a zero – level of inflation. This would provide a stable monetary environment in which the price mechanism would succeed in allocating all resources – including labour – to those uses where they were most highly valued.

Hayek and Friedman emphasized the monetary causes of inflation and argued that a proper rein on the money supply would bring down the rate of inflation. These views came to be known as monetarism, and were extremely influential at the policy level in countries such as the UK and Chile.

Given their opposition to interventionist government policy and the discretionary policy making of the Keynesian era, anti-Keynesian economists such as Hayek and Friedman were also opposed to discretionary policy. They argued that policy makers lacked the wisdom and the knowledge needed to exercise discretion in day-to-day policy making. In addition, they argued that vesting such enormous power in the hands of policy makers was inconsistent with a liberal defence of individual freedom. Accordingly, they recommended the use of policy rules rather than discretion, so that policy makers would have to adhere to agreed rules or guidelines in the conduct of policy.

Monetarism provides an ideal example of a rule-based policy in that it prescribed a constant rule in the form of a fixed annual increase in the money supply. The government's responsibility, it argued, was to follow the monetary rule and not allow the money supply to increase at a faster rate than that prescribed. An additional advantage of this rule, it was argued, was that it was transparent for all to see, thus providing a visible yardstick according to which the success of government policy could be measured. A widely publicized adoption of this monetarist prescription was the Medium Term Financial Strategy introduced by Margaret Thatcher's government in the early 1980s.

Along with this argument that the government's first priority is to control inflation, monetarism also stressed that the attempt to control unemployment is futile. It rejected the Keynesian argument that the level of unemployment is related to the level of aggregate demand, and reiterated the pre-Keynesian argument that unemployment is caused simply by incorrect wage rates. According to this view, the only way to reduce

Definitions

Monetarism

Monetarism is an economic theory which holds that inflation is a monetary phenomenon which has monetary causes. It argues that there is a close correlation between the money supply and the rate of inflation, and that the money supply can be used as an instrument of policy in order to control the rate of inflation, which is seen as the primary economic objective.

Policy rules

Economic policy is subject to rules when the government has no discretion in the implementation of policy but must adhere to fixed rules or strict policy guidelines.

unemployment is to reduce wage pressure by freeing labour markets, reducing union power, repealing legislation which protected workers' rights, and reducing welfare payments. This resurgence of *laissez-faire* thinking and the development of monetarism thus emphasized a 'market-clearing' view of exchange transactions, that markets are essentially self-adjusting in the sense in which Keynes had earlier challenged. At the level of macroeconomic theory, this also led to the development of a new school of anti-Keynesian economics known as 'New Classical' macroeconomics, so called because of its affinities with pre-Keynesian classical thinking (see Chapter 18). The New Classical approach stressed that, left to themselves, markets do adjust so that demand and supply are always in equilibrium. Hence unemployment must be the result of wages being too high, and so should properly be regarded as voluntary unemployment in that it results from the optimizing choices made by individual workers.

Thus, just as the growth of Keynesianism was attached to a broader political stance, so was the resurgence of economic liberalism. In spite of the attachment to *laissez-faire* principles, monetarism implied that government policy was not so much in abeyance as taking another form – that of deflating the economy. Making the control of inflation into the prime economic objective while curtailing workers' rights and emphasizing free market outcomes, imposed deflationary pressures on the economy which inevitably hit hardest those sections least able to defend their position. Whilst providing economic opportunities for some, the emphasis on individual freedom and individual responsibility bore most heavily on those whose livelihood was jeopardized by the economic dislocations of that period and by the financial stringency following the implementation of monetarist policies.

3.2   Government intervention at fault

We have seen that the free market position argued that governments had been addressing the wrong issue using the wrong economic theory. But we have also seen that it went even further in arguing that the theoretical foundation which had supported the idea of active discretionary policy making was unsustainable. It challenged the public interest view of the state that governments could operate as a benevolent external factor in ameliorating economic conditions. It challenged this notion by questioning the assumption that the government can function as an external agent which pursues the public interest. This criticism was noted in Chapter 10, where the private interest view of the state was contrasted with the public interest view. Here I shall draw out some of the implications of this debate for macroeconomic policy. In doing this I am also providing another example of the power of different models in economic theory and policy making. Previous chapters have shown how different models provide different ways of interpreting economic issues. Here at the macro level we find that the resurgence of economic liberalism provided a challenge to what had become the economic orthodoxy by providing a different set of interpretations which fundamentally changed current perceptions of the requirements of economic policy.

The first problem with the public interest view of the state, it was argued, relates to how the public interest is known in the first place. In democratic countries, electors vote for a broad programme of policies, and it is not possible for governments to know how they should rank individual policies. Indeed, it is not always possible to derive any consistent overall ranking of aggregate policies from the individual preferences of the electorate, even if all those preferences are fully known to the government (which they are not in practice). This problem is known as Arrow's impossibility theorem, after the work of the US economist Kenneth Arrow in the area of social choice theory. It has proved a difficult conundrum for social choice theorists, and has made many economists much more sceptical of the ways in which elected governments can claim a mandate for their policies based on the preferences of those who voted them into power. Chapter 22 explains this problem.

The second problem relates to the motivation of the government as an 'agent'. One rather cynical answer put forward by the free market position and 'public choice' school of economists, is that governments are composed of individuals who pursue their own self-interest. The civil servants or bureaucrats employed in government departments seek their own self-interest by trying to enlarge their own departments because this is where their power and prestige are based. Government departments therefore have an inbuilt tendency to grow in size because this is the means by which government employees or 'bureaucrats' enhance their own careers.

Furthermore, in electoral democracies, politicians look after their careers by ensuring that they are re-elected. This involves irresponsible expenditure programmes designed to buy electoral popularity, often in the run-up to an election, causing what is sometimes known as the 'electoral business cycle'. The outcome is a series of extremely short-term measures to manipulate a boom in time for an election, but with little attention to the long-term requirements of the economy. In addition, electoral popularity requires giving in to the organized special interest lobbies which spend considerable time and money trying to press their own case with the government. Far from being disinterested benevolent agents, politicians are 'captured' by the various powerful pressure groups which enrol government support for their own sectional interest. For these reasons, the free market position is extremely sceptical of political arguments which purport to be promoting the public interest, and emphasize instead that governments pursue their own, and not the public, interest.

These arguments provided another criticism of discretionary policy, and suggested yet again that policy rules would offer better control of government actions. Far from government being a benevolent solution to the prisoners' dilemma game, it came to be seen as one of the players in a strategic game, seeking to maximize its own pay-off. Recasting government as a player in a game yields very different results and undermines the original Keynesian view that governments should take discretionary action. As Chapter 5 explained, an important aspect of game theory is its recognition of the interdependence of decisions. This means that in making a decision, the players have to think ahead and consider the effects of their actions on the other players, and take their expected reactions into account. This strategic approach therefore recognizes the central importance of agents' expectations. Earlier economic theories had assumed that agents' expectations about the future would be based pretty much on what had happened in the past. The new interest in expectations in the context of strategic decision making showed that this was an unrealistic assumption to make (see Chapters 20 and 24).

The implications of taking agents' expectations into account within a strategic policy framework can be illustrated by thinking about a government's decision on whether to reflate the economy. According to the old way of thinking, a reflationary programme would reduce unemployment, although at the cost of some inflation. Taking into account strategic reactions, however, undermines this by showing that if private agents anticipate the government's plans, all that happens is the inflationary consequence without the improvement in employment.

Consider a game where the government has the choice of reflating or not reflating. The other player in this game is taken to be all other economic agents. Their choice is whether to act on the expectation that the government will reflate, or the expectation that the government will not reflate. A crucial aspect of this game is that it takes on board the argument mentioned above that the effects of injections of demand on the level of unemployment and inflation depend on whether or not they are anticipated by agents. Thus, the trade-off between inflation and unemployment deteriorates every time agents expect inflation to rise. (The details of this analysis are explained in Chapter 24.) This game is shown in Figure 16.8, where the pay-off (for both sets of players) is the rate of unemployment. Low levels of pay-off are therefore desirable.

Government \ Other economic agents	expect not reflate	expect reflate
not reflate	10	20
reflate	5	15

Figure 16.8   **Matrix showing unemployment as pay-off in different policy regimes**

Consider first the case where agents expect the government *not* to reflate. If the government does not reflate, then unemployment remains at 10%, but if it does reflate, then unemployment falls to 5%. The reduction in unemployment is the result of agents being taken by surprise as they do not expect a reflation to take place, and is an example of the trade-off between unemployment and unexpected inflation.

Now consider what would happen if agents expect that the government *will* reflate. The expectation of inflation now results in a worse trade-off between unemployment and inflation, and so even a non-reflation will result in a worse unemployment rate of 20%. However, if the government does reflate, this reduces unemployment to 15%.

Question

What would a rational government do in a situation represented by the matrix shown in Figure 16.8?

Whatever the public expects, it is always rational for the government to reflate. This means that reflation is the dominant strategy, as it is the preferred option for the government no matter what private economic agents expect. But in this case, what are economic agents most likely to expect the government to do, if they are also rational? The answer to this must be that agents will expect the government to reflate. This means that the final outcome will be in the bottom right-hand cell at 15% unemployment – which is not the best outcome.

The problem is that the government will achieve the best outcome if it can persuade everyone else that it is going to stick with a low inflation policy, come what may, while actually reneging on that commitment. But as everyone knows that it can do better by secretly defaulting on its own policy statements, no one will believe those policy statements in the first place. The

Definition

Definition

Policy credibility

A policy has credibility if other economic agents believe that the government is totally committed to carrying out that policy, come what may.

problem here is that policy credibility is lacking because other agents recognize that the government clearly has an incentive to renege on its own stated commitments.

In common with other strategic games, a solution to the impasse of policy credibility is provided by 'precommitting' the government to keeping to its declared policy statements, as this would then make its policy credible. It has been suggested that one form of precommitment would be to impose 'rules' on government policy rather than allowing a degree of choice or 'discretion'. In this way the policy rules function as a form of precommitment because the government is unable to renege on them. For example, rules about the money supply (if they were believed) would function as a precommitment that the government will not renege in the fight against inflation. Pegging the domestic currency to another currency, as in the European Exchange Rate Mechanism (ERM), provides another example of a policy rule. The operation of the Gold Standard provides yet another example where individual currencies were tied to gold at a fixed rate.

The efficacy of policy rules depends on whether the government really is bound by the rules come what may, and also on whether the rules are indeed appropriate for policy in all circumstances. The examples provided in the previous paragraph are a mixed bag in terms of both of these requirements.

Reflection

To what extent do you think these examples illustrate the efficacy of policy rules as opposed to policy discretion?

This consideration of the merits of rules versus discretion in the design of policy has had far-reaching effects in macroeconomic debates, as it suggests that in some circumstances government policy may be more effective if it had less freedom of manoeuvre to respond to the immediate circumstances of the moment. It also highlights the importance of the institutional structure of policy making in imposing political or other constraints on government freedom of action. Thus, it is sometimes argued that having an independent central bank in control of monetary policy reduces the area of discretion for the government, especially if the central bank is provided with mandatory instructions (see Chapter 28). Either way, the debate is far removed from earlier Keynesian arguments which simply assumed that governments were sufficiently well motivated and well informed to pursue the public interest in macro policy making.

3.3   Income inequalities are necessary

We have seen that the free market position is critical of the view that the state can act as a benevolent external agent that can plan for the public interest. In addition, we have seen that it places considerable reliance on market forces in allocating resources both at a micro and macro level. Consistently with these arguments, it also criticized the social democratic position that mature capitalist societies should, on political, social as well as economic grounds, try to avoid excessive inequalities in the distribution of income and wealth. Although not opposed to all aspects of the welfare state, the free market position argued that the welfare state – the 'nanny state' – had become too large and was causing an erosion in the market incentives that are a necessary feature of capitalist societies. It therefore argued for a reduction in the activities of the welfare state, and for a withdrawal of the state from as many areas of welfare provision as possible. It encouraged the idea of private insurance and private, rather than state, provision of services such as health and education.

In the area of income distribution, it argued that inequalities are a vital part of the operation of the price mechanism. According to this kind of analysis, people should be paid according to the labour market's monetary evaluation of their abilities. People with higher skills and experience should, properly, receive the full monetary equivalent of their greater value. Furthermore, to tax the highly paid groups at a higher rate than low-paid groups is to interfere with this market process and distort market signals. This would eventually result in a lower rate of output from society as a whole, since the higher-paid need to receive the full value of their higher earnings in order to be encouraged to work to full effect. Thus, allowing the distribution of income to derive from the operation of free markets would result in the greatest increase in income and output for the society as a whole. In the fullness of time, it was argued, the poor would benefit from this too, because when the effects of this increased wealth creation had 'trickled down', they would actually be better off than under a system of government redistribution to tax the rich and subsidize the poor. The Keynesian belief that redistributive policies can help to make the macroeconomy function more efficiently is argued to be a myth based on a fundamental misunderstanding of the role of market signals. These ideas influenced policy at many levels in a number of countries, including the UK, where tax reductions benefited top incomes the most.

Similarly, in the case of unemployment, it is inefficient to tamper with market evaluations. Unemployment, it is argued, is caused by wage rates being too high. The solution, therefore, is to let wages fall. To featherbed the unemployed by giving welfare payments for too long simply takes away the incentive to look for work, and makes the unemployed reluctant to accept the only jobs – the low-paid ones – that are available to them. The result of overgenerous welfare payments, together with wage rates that are too high relative to the skills offered, are the twin causes of persistent unemployment. Once again, it is argued, government schemes to help the unemployed turn out to have made the situation worse.

3.4   Approaches to the aggregate economy

In view of these criticisms, it is not surprising that the re-emergence of economic liberalism was also associated with theoretical attacks on the Keynesian macro model of the economy and its emphasis on the central role of the level of aggregate demand. There were basically two kinds of criticism.

The first argued that the notion of the aggregate economy was misconceived unless it could be derived rigorously from the behaviour of the individual economic agents who comprise it. This criticism is akin to Margaret Thatcher's well publicized argument that 'there is no such thing as society'. In each case, the fundamental element in the analysis is the individual person exercising choice and rationality in the various aspects of life, and so it makes no sense to try to look at society as a composite whole unless it can be understood as the summation of all the individual members. As a result of this criticism, there have been many attempts to ground the relations of the macro economy in the individual behaviour of the rational agents who comprise it. One area where this has taken place is in the field of expectations. As we have seen, once the expectations of private agents with respect to government policy are taken on board, this can overturn the results of previous economic theories.

The other criticism made of Keynes's formulation of the aggregate economy is that, in stressing the role of aggregate demand, it overlooked the significance of aggregate supply. It is debatable as to whether this criticism should properly apply to Keynes's own economics rather than to a bowdlerized version that became popular in the period of Keynesian orthodoxy. The point itself, however, is now accepted among economists in the sense that, at the aggregate as well as the micro level, supply-side factors have to be analysed in conjunction with demand-side factors. As later chapters explain, however, acknowledging the importance of aggregate supply still leaves scope for disagreement over the actual specification of the supply side of the economy, the proper role for supply-side policies, and the relationship between aggregate demand and aggregate supply.

These criticisms of Keynesian arguments at both the theoretical level and the policy level resulted in a more market-oriented approach to policy in many countries during the 1980s and early 1990s. Different governments enacted different kinds of changes which reflected this reversal to a more *laissez-faire* approach, but, in spite of this diversity, clear tendencies can be seen.

At the policy level, inflation came to be seen as a more pressing problem than unemployment. This resulted in a political toleration of high levels of unemployment that would have been regarded as unacceptable during the 1950s and 1960s. At the same time, government policy was not held to be accountable for these high levels of unemployment, which were viewed as the responsibility of individual workers who had held out for unrealistically high wages. This shift was accompanied by moves to reduce the power of trade unions at all levels in the UK, from national arenas for formulating policy right down to the factory floor.

Government involvement in the economy was reduced in many different ways. Aggregate demand was no longer seen as a key policy variable for controlling the level of output and employment. Instead, inflation was to be controlled using monetary policy – sometimes using the money supply as an instrument (as in the Medium Term Financial Strategy in the UK) and sometimes using the rate of interest as the main instrument. Government was to exercise greater financial rectitude, spending and borrowing less so that the government debt could be substantially reduced. In this way fiscal policy – that is, expenditure and tax policy – was used to control the level of government borrowing, a new target of policy, thus indirectly supporting the fight against inflation. Individual initiative and enterprise were to be fostered by reducing direct personal taxation, encouraging the take-up of private pension and insurance schemes, and reducing the provisions of the welfare state.

In the face of this radical movement for economic change, Keynesianism seemed to have little new to offer. It was associated with a tired regime of endless government interference that seemed to have done more harm than good. The new economic era was to be based on low taxes and individual gain, initiative and enterprise. The new view was confident that the fruits of this programme would be increased economic efficiency and improved prospects of material gain for those who could satisfy the market with the right product at the right price. The revival of economic liberalism was therefore also associated with a wider political programme that made its economic recommendations appeal to a broad populist base. It stressed the advantages of economic freedom and the liberty of the individual – freedom from state restrictions and liberty for individuals to play the market for the biggest stakes. Its political appeal lay in a new notion of 'popular capitalism', a broadly based property-owning democracy with share shops on the high street, and bright new shopping malls at every turn.

Figure 16.9 **Emerging from recession? A derelict factory site bought for housing, Bedfordshire, 1993**

Source: Network/Martin Mayer

4 Issues for the 1990s and beyond

4.1 Macroeconomic performance

By the early 1990s, over fifty years after Keynes published *The General Theory*, the fundamental issue of the role of the state in the management of the macroeconomy was still unresolved. The 1980s had seen some successes in terms of increased growth and the control of inflation, yet by the early 1990s the industrialized economies were once again in recession, with high rates of unemployment and non-employment, and with incomedistributions that were in some cases more unequal than at the beginning of the 1980s. Inflation in the OECD countries had fallen from the high of 13.5% in 1980 to 3.6% in 1993. Unemployment, however, which was at 5.7% in 1980, never again fell below 6%, and by 1994 had reached 8.5% (*OECD Economic Outlook*, June 1994). This experience helped to raise yet again some very basic questions about the relation between anti-inflation policy and unemployment. It also raised some fundamental questions about the functioning of labour markets, and the ways in which different policy frameworks and institutions of the labour market affect unemployment rates and non-employment rates in different countries.

Reflection

Looking again at Figure 16.7, do you think there is any evidence for the return of the inflation/unemployment trade-off in the UK during the 1980s and early 1990s? Chapter 24 addresses this issue.

These events showed that the economic cycle of recession and boom had not been defeated. The periodic nature of economic fluctuations is analysed in Chapter 25, and various theoretical approaches are reviewed there. Although the question of the recurring pattern of cyclical activity was an old one which derives from a period prior to Keynes's writing, other developments and theoretical issues for the macroeconomy in the 1990s were new or were reappearing with a renewed sense of urgency.

At the level of macro theory, this debate between a broadly *laissez-faire* approach and a broadly Keynesian approach has been continued by the development of two fundamentally different theoretical positions within macroeconomics (see Chapter 18). The New Classical approach to macroeconomic theory has incorporated the commitment to market clearing and the overriding importance of individual preferences. Its attachment to market clearing is in accord with its emphasis on perfectly competitive markets and the adjustment of price so that demand and supply are always equal. In this framework, involuntary unemployment of the sort that Keynes analysed is impossible.

By contrast, the New Keynesian approach attempts to refine what it sees as Keynes's original insights by taking account of modern theoretical developments. It emphasizes problems of co-ordination and market failure, and argues that, in the real world, markets do not behave like perfectly competitive markets. It therefore explores the implications of imperfectly competitive markets at the macro level, as well as the possibility of 'sticky prices' that do not adjust in the presence of market disequilibrium to secure market clearing. In addition, New Keynesian theories emphasize the significance of institutional differences in labour markets as a way of explaining how markets appear to function so differently in different contexts.

In some ways, the fundamental issue here is basically yet another version of the old one: whether *laissez-faire* or active government intervention is best able to secure low inflation with high and stable levels of output growth and employment within a social fabric of norms and expectations that have broad political support. But this stark opposition between *laissez-faire* and state involvement is also oversimplified in that all industrialized economies involve a significant state sector and would be unable to function without the institutional infrastructure provided by the state. As Chapter 10 showed, government final consumption and social security transfers are a sizeable proportion of GDP in all the industrialized economies (Table 10.2). At the macroeconomic level, even relatively non-interventionist states have found it difficult to stand by and let market forces alone determine economic outcomes. Withdrawal of the state by reducing government expenditure and taxes would have effects on the level and composition of aggregate demand

and on the financial position of specific interest groups. Even where such reductions are politically acceptable to electorates in principle, it may be extremely hard for governments to withdraw in practice, as President Reagan found when the US budget deficit was increasing in spite of his anti-government stance.

Rather than counterposing such a stark dichotomy between *laissez-faire* and interventionist policies, more recent debates have come to recognize that what is often at stake concerns the forms and mechanisms of policy measures, and not just the absolute size of the government sector. The debate over rules versus discretion, for example, concerns the appropriate mechanisms for securing particular targets or objectives. The debate over expectations and strategic games provides a model of the government as a player in a game, and these insights from game theory cannot be reduced to the simple dichotomy of intervention or abstention, as so much depends on the credibility of announced policy.

Running through many of these more recent debates is a keener awareness of the place of institutions in providing the context within which the big policy issues have to be debated. Thus, different institutional contexts in different countries contribute significantly to different standards of performance. For example, although unemployment rates for the OECD countries were worse on average during the 1980s and early 1990s than during the 1970s, there was considerable variation across countries; in 1993 Japan was at one extreme with the lowest rate of 2.5%, while Spain had the highest at 22.4% (OECD, 1994). This issue of institutional structure also links in with the question of the ways in which an economy can be seen as a form of 'organized' capitalism, as discussed in the previous chapter, and the extent to which institutions encourage economic agents (including the government) to contribute to outcomes which are congruent with the public interest.

Within this framework of continuing analytical debate, three major areas can be identified. First, economies are becoming increasingly open to international competition, and this has raised questions about the greater openness of national economies; second, issues of macroeconomic performance and distributional outcomes are again subject to considerable debate; and third, questions of the sustainability of continuous economic growth are being raised more urgently than ever before. A brief outline of these three areas concludes this final section of the chapter.

4.2   International competition and co-operation

I explained in Section 2.5 that Keynes's analysis of unemployment was set largely in the context of the national economy. From the nineteenth century until the 1930s, the international economic environment had been a very open one; freedom of trade had been the economic orthodoxy, and protectionist policies which favoured domestic over foreign goods were not widespread. This era was underpinned by the Gold Standard, under which currencies were freely convertible into gold. With the economic turbulence of the 1930s and then the onset of war, this changed and individual countries became less open to international trade and financial dealings. This more protectionist era was reflected in macroeconomic models in which the individual national economy was taken to be a relatively self-contained economic entity.

In the recent period, international competitive pressures and the abandonment of protectionist and regulatory policies have meant that the international economy is more open than ever before (see Chapter 12). This is having profound implications for our understanding of the functioning of national economies. It is no longer possible to envisage the national economy as a relatively closed economic system, even if this assumption is then later relaxed. For this reason, in the chapters that follow, the aggregate economy is taken to be an open economy that is subject to influences from the wider economic environment.

The first point to notice is that aggregate demand includes other countries' export demand for the output of the domestic economy. Thus, an increasingly important component of the demand for a country's output is determined by world trading conditions and lies beyond domestic control. In recent years this fact has been brought home to the countries of western Europe and North America by the phenomenal growth and export competitiveness of the countries of the Asian Pacific Rim – China, Hong Kong, Singapore, Indonesia, Japan, South Korea and Taiwan – which are leading to a decline in the manufacturing sectors of the older industrialized countries. As Chapter 1 explained, this has led some economists to speculate that the centre of gravity of the world economy is moving inexorably eastwards.

Changes in exchange rates produce an element of instability in trading markets, and can make a country's goods either more or less competitive internationally for reasons that are unrelated to conditions at home. For this reason, different exchange rate mechanisms have been set up at various times to try to eliminate unnecessary disturbances in exchange rates, and to enable governments to try to fix the external value of the currency. During the 1980s, for example, some countries in what is now the European Union set up the Exchange Rate Mechanism (ERM) in order to try to fix the exchange rates of their currencies within certain stipulated bands (see Chapter 19).

At a time of intense currency speculation, the activities of the international money markets are shown on television screens as an item of global newsworthiness. But this is to make particularly visible at crucial moments what is in fact going on all the time. Capital funds are now extremely mobile on a global basis, and fund managers will seek out any possibilities for profitable use. If exchange rates are expected to change by even a small amount, or if there are even small differences in the rate of interest available in different countries, then foreign exchange dealers and money managers will be moving funds around. With such large amounts of money, even very small differences in the rate of return per pound spent can result in large total profits for those who can react fast. This explains how little control governments may have over exchange rates and domestic interest rates.

In previous episodes of the economic cycle, changes in employment and output were closely related. During the recession, output and employment fell while unemployment rose. Similarly, during the upturn and boom, output and employment rose while unemployment fell. The 1980s and early 1990s have shown, however, that an economy can continue to grow over time in terms of output whilst offering only a small increase, or even a fall, in the number of jobs. This decoupling of employment opportunities and output growth means that unemployment and non-employment are not likely to be resolved by relying on steady output growth alone, as output growth by itself may not generate enough new jobs. One reason for this change is the increasingly international nature of competition, and the growth of output in the new industrializing countries. In order to compete, firms in the industrialized economies are having to upgrade their skills requirement and utilize more capital-intensive methods deploying newer technology. The result is the massive fall in the demand for unskilled labour that has taken place in the industrialized economies.

One consequence of this is that the industrialized economies cannot rely on increasing aggregate demand in order to create more jobs, as higher demand in the absence of improved productive capacity simply sucks in more imported goods. What has become crucially important are supply-side measures to increase the competitiveness of domestic output. Here again, though, as Chapters 18 and 21 explain, there is a sharp contrast between the *laissez-faire* approach of 'flexible' labour markets designed to depress wages, and more structural remedies to address issues such as skills and education, and the financing and development of more competitive technologies. Furthermore, shifts in aggregate demand will have implications for the longer-term supply-side potential of the economy. An economy that has had its productive capacity damaged by previous demand shocks may be less able to invest and innovate in the new products and processes of tomorrow. This then raises in acute form the relation between short-term demand management and long-term supply potential (see Chapters 18 and 20).

In this increasingly competitive international economic environment, countries have become more interdependent. It has always been the case that one country's balance of payments surplus is another country's balance of payments deficit, and that one country's currency appreciation is another country's depreciation. Furthermore, if one country increases its imports from another country, then, in turn, that supplying country is now better able to afford to purchase exports. But the increasing interdependence has raised new policy issues, including questions about strategic games and policy co-ordination at an international level (see Chapter 28). In addition, these international interdependencies also imply different distributional outcomes for the different countries.

4.3   Distributional issues

We have seen several times in this chapter that macroeconomic performance and distributional questions intersect. The opportunities open to economic agents and the constraints within which they have to work are inevitably affected by the larger economic environment around them. In part this environment relates to the state of the national economy and the economic policies of the national government. In addition, though, it also links in with wider international economic developments which may seem quite remote and beyond anyone's direct control. Thus distributional issues find their way into many chapters in this book, but in Chapters 21 to 23 distributional issues are given the prime focus.

To what extent would the chance of finding employment in Europe in the early 1990s be enhanced by reductions in wages? And what impact would this have on the distribution of income within the national economy? Evidence from the USA suggests that reductions in wages for unskilled workers during the 1980s had the effect of reducing unemployment there, but at the cost of an increase in the degree of inequality. This suggested to many economists that the main route to lower unemployment in Europe was via greater 'flexibility' of labour markets. Yet although the rate of unemployment was low in the USA, the rate of non-employment there seems broadly comparable with the high-unemployment countries. There are also counter examples to the case of the USA. For instance, low-paid workers also experienced a fall in wages in Canada, yet unemployment remained high in the early 1990s. Furthermore, in Sweden there was an increase in the wages of the low-paid during the 1980s, yet until 1993 unemployment was lower than in the USA (OECD, 1994).

An alternative avenue for increased employment prospects lies in reskilling and a more educated workforce, but here too distributional issues intervene. How is the extra training and education to be financed? What are the respective roles and responsibilities of government, firms and workers in the ongoing process of retraining during a period of high unemployment and structural change? And how do retraining requirements relate to the higher education system and the funding provisions for university students? Once again, the relation between the private and public sectors is much debated, as Chapter 21 examines.

Fundamental questions are also being asked about the role of the welfare state, and whether its prime justification is on moral/altruistic grounds, or whether it is based on economic efficiency or even political expediency. The resurgence of economic liberalism brought with it harsh criticisms of the welfare state, as we saw above, but they were countered by those who wished to re-establish general principles for the welfare state. J.K. Galbraith argued that the revival of economic liberalism is not neutral with respect to different groups in society, but directly favours the well-off. Those with secure jobs, good incomes and some savings are the ones who have most to lose from inflation and the least to lose from the presence of unemployment. They are the ones who pay the taxes which provide the welfare programmes for the poor, so they are the ones who will gain from reductions both in taxation and in the welfare state. This is how Galbraith, a long-time Keynesian, puts it in his analysis of the tax-reducing policies of President Reagan:

> From the foregoing comes the broad attitude toward taxes in our time and, in substantial measure, toward government in general. The fortunate pay, the less fortunate receive. The fortunate have political voice, the less fortunate do not. It would be an exercise in improbably charitable attitude were the fortunate to respond warmly to expenditures that are for the benefit of others. So government with all its costs is pictured as a functionless burden, which for the fortunate, to a considerable extent, it is. Accordingly, it and the sustaining taxes must be kept to a minimum; otherwise the liberty of the individual would be impaired.

> And politicians faithfully respond. To run for office promising better services for those most in need at even higher cost is seen by many, if not quite all, as an exercise in political self-destruction.

> *(Galbraith, 1992, pp.46–7)*

Here Galbraith argues that the discourse of economic liberalism conceals the fact that it is an ideology for the well-off and the comfortable, for what he calls the 'contented majority' who ignore the needs of a minority – the 'underclass'. On the other hand, the costs of this kind of social exclusion may prove too high. This concern about the political wisdom of allowing an underclass to develop has furnished arguments for the continuation rather than the attenuation of the welfare state.

The 1990s therefore saw a renewed debate on redistribution, social security and the future of the welfare state. A number of economists and other social scientists have worried aloud that too great an emphasis on material self-interest as the motivation of individual actions may be an inappropriate framework for the design of policy towards social security and public services. They suggest that economies do not function solely on the basis of individual self-interest, and that one role of social security provision may be to reinforce social cohesion and solidarity. This debate is explored in Chapters 22 and 23.

4.4   Sustainable economic growth

An assumption underlying analysis of the aggregate economy and distributional issues is that continuous economic growth is something worthwhile that policy makers should legitimately aim for. Economic growth usually brings rising average living standards, and it is generally assumed that it will also produce rising absolute standards for all, even for the poorest, although recent trends have cast some doubts on this. A problem facing economists and policy makers in the 1990s is, therefore, how to facilitate economic growth and rising economic prosperity without periodically reverting to recession. How can policy makers promote stable and lasting economic growth with an acceptable distribution of the economic gains and losses?

Just occasionally, this assumption about the desirability of economic growth is questioned, and these questions come from two quite different sources. One set of questions comes from those who are concerned that continuous growth, as recorded in terms of changes in measurable GDP, does not give an accurate picture of levels of well-being. It is argued that well-being comes from a variety of sources, and that measurable GDP is but one; to over-concentrate on GDP to the neglect of other elements of well-being may contribute towards a reduction of well-being overall.

One aspect of well-being may include living and working in an unpolluted environment. Thus, it is possible for well-being to decline even though measures of GNP are increasing. This environmental example provides a telling illustration of the problem that well-being may not be properly measured by GNP. It also reminds us that continuous economic growth is premised on the continuing availability of the earth's resources, and that environmentalists are constantly arguing that this premise is unfounded. This points to the second source of questioning: the worry about whether there can be sustainable economic growth such that the process of growth does not jeopardize its own future. This also involves issues of intergenerational equity, concerning the rights and obligations of the present generation vis-à-vis future generations. Given that our decisions now will affect the earth that we bequeath to future generations, to what extent should their possible needs be taken into account in current decision making?

In this environmental issue, distributional implications and economic analysis are again intertwined, as Chapter 27 explains. If the present generation feels that it should not deplete scarce resources but should leave them for future generations, this will have distributional implications both within and across countries. For example, curtailing present rates of growth now will favour most those individuals and countries which have already achieved a relatively high standard of living.

Just as economists are trying to understand the interconnections of the global economy and the implications of this for individual economies, so environmentalists are trying to understand the global interconnections of ecological issues. These two sets of concerns are interrelated in the concern for sustainable growth, as both economists and ecologists try to grapple with complex sets of interdependencies. Furthermore, for both economists and ecologists, the actual processes under examination are not reversible, as the path of development taken today will constrain the path of development that is possible tomorrow.

5   Conclusion

This chapter has introduced some of the themes covered in later chapters of this text by emphasizing the interconnections between aggregate economy analysis and distributional issues, and showing that these interconnections are important both within and between economies.

One implication arising from this survey is that economic analysis and values are sometimes closely related. Technical economic analysis, views about the proper role for government and individual economic agency, and the realm of ethical values, are all so closely interlinked that the boundaries between analysis and values may become fuzzy at times. Discussions as to whether a sharp reduction in wages will reduce unemployment soon merge into the question of whether it is right, reasonable or even politically judicious for large sections of the population to be subjected to rapidly deteriorating standards of living. Discussions as to whether highly mobile international capital makes governments powerless to administer monetary policy within their own frontiers, often slide into debate about whether governments ought to resist such attacks on their economic sovereignty.

Thus, economic controversies are based on unresolved value differences as well as unresolved issues of fact and analysis. Data analysis is crucially important for economics, and Chapter 26 introduces the topics of regression analysis and econometrics which establish statistical techniques for testing economic theories against time series data. In spite of the centrality of these statistical techniques, economics as an academic discipline is nonetheless characterized by a kind of pluralism – a plurality of theories, views and values – that does not always sit comfortably with its own self-image of objective scientific endeavour. But that image too is also under reassessment, as the social sciences more generally take on board the implications of new approaches right across the academic spectrum which stress the open-ended and unresolved nature of much intellectual enquiry. Within this more sceptical environment, claims to truth and knowledge also need to be understood in terms of their own intellectual and political context. So too with this text, which is conditioned by its time and place in reflecting current debates in economic policy.

PART 10

CHAPTER 17

MACROECONOMIC MODELLING

AGGREGATE DEMAND AND STABILIZATION POLICY

by Vivienne Brown

1 Aggregate demand and economic policy

If an economy goes into recession, should governments try to do anything about it? If unemployment rises, should governments try to stimulate more jobs in the economy? If economic activity is rising rapidly and the economy shows clear signs of overheating, should governments take any countermeasures? Questions such as these have attracted very different kinds of answers.

The change in economic thinking ushered in by the dominance of Keynesian approaches to economic management, resulted in largely affirmative answers to all these questions in the advanced industrialized economies during the 1950s and 1960s. Governments could effectively intervene in the economy, it was thought, by influencing the level of aggregate demand. As Chapter 16 explained, during the 1970s and 1980s a much more cautious view began to prevail about the effectiveness of Keynesian policies to 'fine tune' the economy using demand management policies. Doubts were raised about the inflationary consequences of such policies, and their harmful effects on the government's own financial position. During this period, a much greater stress came to be placed on problems of the supply side of the economy in generating the right conditions for sustained growth in a competitive world market. With the 1990s, however, came yet another fierce recession and rising unemployment, with the result that fundamental questions were again raised about the role of government policy in countering the worst effects of recession.

In order to examine these issues, we need to have a view of how the aggregate economy works, and how the government's activities impact on the rest of the economy. In this and the following chapter, a model of the aggregate economy will be presented which can be used as a framework for discussion of these issues, and this model will then be put to use in many of the later chapters. This chapter will develop a model of the demand side of the aggregate economy and will examine issues relating to government stabilization policies. Chapter 18 will add the supply side to develop the full aggregate demand/aggregate supply (*AD/AS*) model, and will then examine different supply-side policies. Chapter 19 will extend the *AD/AS* model by exploring more fully the ways in which international influences affect domestic policy options, and then Chapter 20 will set the whole analysis in a longer historical perspective by looking at longer-term trends and issues.

The overriding concern which drives all these chapters is the unstable nature of economic growth, with its attendant problems of boom and recession, inflation and unemployment. Since 1945, positive rates of growth have been the norm for the advanced industrialized economies, but the actual rate of growth has varied considerably, with some years of even negative or negligible growth. Figure 17.1(a) shows the rate of growth of gross domestic product (GDP) for the countries of the European Union, USA and Japan for the period 1961–92, and Figure 17.1(b) gives the same data for the UK, Germany, France and Italy. The figures show percentage real growth rates. The most striking feature of Figure 17.1 is the jagged nature of the lines, showing how rates of growth have fluctuated over this thirty-year period. The highest rate of growth recorded was 12.9 per cent in Japan in 1968, and the lowest was −2.7 per cent in Italy in 1975 following the first oil price rise, although the USA and the UK each experienced a fall of −2.5 per cent in 1982 and 1991 respectively. If growth is negative and GDP is falling, an economy is in severe recession.

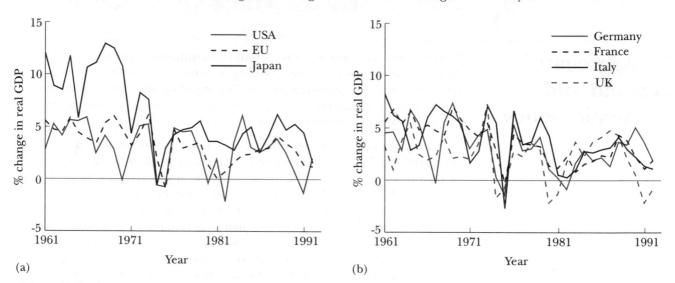

(a)

(b)

Figure 17.1   **Annual percentage change in real GDP, 1961–92**

Note: figures for Germany and the EU for 1992 include the former GDR.

Source: *European Economy* (1993) no. 54, Table 10, p. 191

Looking at these data as a whole, the fluctuations seem to come in a loosely regular pattern lasting approximately 4–6 years from peak to peak. The precise timing varies across countries, and the combined series for the 12 European countries has the effect of smoothing the pattern of fluctuations. Very roughly, however, the peak years when the rate of economic growth was at its height for most of the countries were the mid 1960s, the later 1960s, the early 1970s, the late 1970s and the late 1980s. Some countries also had a short-lived peak in the mid 1980s. Note too that growth rates were declining over this period overall: in Europe, growth fell from 4.8 per cent annual average for 1961–70, to 3.0 per cent for 1971–80, to 2.3 per cent for 1981–90. Similarly, in the USA over these decades, the growth rate fell from 3.8 per cent to 2.8 per cent down to 2.5 per cent, while for Japan it fell from 10.5 per cent to 4.5 per cent to 4.2 per cent.

These data tell a fundamental story about the changing fortunes of these countries. In this chapter I shall be focusing on the short-run fluctuations in growth – the recurrent ups and downs – and whether governments can smooth out these fluctuations by influencing the level of aggregate demand. The next section will examine how aggregate expenditure fluctuates during the course of the economic cycle. Section 3 will develop a model of aggregate demand and the factors that influence it – this is the theoretical heart of the chapter. Section 4 turns to the policy implications by examining how fiscal policy and monetary policy may be used to stabilize the economy. A criticism of such policies is that they lead to excessive government spending and rising government debt. Section 5 therefore looks at government finances and the growth of budget deficits and government debt in the late 1980s and early 1990s.

2   Aggregate expenditure and fluctuations in economic activity

At various points in this text we have stressed the importance of economic agents who take economic decisions. Chapter 2 introduced the circular flow of income diagram representing households, firms and government as the main economic agents in an economy. Later chapters have expanded on these agents, their institutional complexity and the kinds of constraints and possibilities that they face. In this section I am going to build on this analysis by looking at the ways in which the expenditure of these agents helps to account for the fluctuations in economic growth that are shown in Figure 17.1.

2.1   The components of aggregate expenditure

Chapter 2 explained the various components of aggregate expenditure. The largest component of expenditure is *consumption expenditure*. In the UK this amounts to about 59–63 per cent of GDP. Consumption expenditure includes the expenditure of households on all goods and services such as clothes, food, cars, domestic appliances, meals out, leisure activities, DIY, and so on. *Investment expenditure* by firms includes capital expenditure on items such as land, factories and machines, and also changes in stocks. In the UK, investment expenditure amounts to about 14–18 per cent of GDP. Stockbuilding is a small but very variable component of expenditure as it normally takes the brunt of unexpected changes in sales, falling rapidly in times of rising consumption expenditure and increasing rapidly with the onset of recession. *Government expenditure* refers to government exhaustive expenditure (defined in Chapter 10, Section 4.2) and includes items such as education, health, transport and defence. (Note that here government expenditure includes both current and capital expenditure, whereas in Chapter 2 it referred only to current expenditure because government capital expenditure was included in investment.) In the UK, government expenditure is around 23–26 per cent of GDP.

These three forms of expenditure – consumption expenditure, investment expenditure and government expenditure – are the three components of *domestic expenditure*. In addition, net foreign expenditure on domestic output is given by the value of exports less imports. In the UK, expenditure on imports and exports each amounts to about 22–28 per cent of GDP.

Total expenditure on domestic output thus equals the sum of consumption, investment and government expenditures, together with expenditure on exports less imports, i.e. aggregate expenditure on domestic output (AE) = consumption expenditure (C) + investment expenditure (I) + government expenditure (G) + exports (X) – imports (H), or

$$AE = C + I + G + X - H$$

Sometimes aggregate expenditure is expressed as the sum of domestic expenditure (DE) and net foreign expenditure (FE), i.e.

$$AE = DE + FE$$

We thus have two alternative but equivalent expressions for aggregate expenditure. In addition, both these expressions are equal to the total output produced in the domestic economy, or the gross domestic product, GDP. Remember from Chapter 2 that there are three equivalent approaches to measuring GDP – the expenditure, output and income approaches. Each one measures a country's GDP at a different moment in the circular flow.

As a result, we can also express the different expenditures as components of GDP, i.e.

$$\text{GDP} = DE + FE, \text{ and}$$

$$\text{GDP} = C + I + G + X - H$$

As GDP can be decomposed into expenditure components, this means that an analysis of the fluctuations in GDP can be carried out by examining the fluctuations in expenditure. This is the subject of the following section.

2.2   Fluctuations in aggregate expenditure

Section 1 showed how growth rates fluctuate. Since GDP can be expressed in terms of the components of expenditure, it is possible to analyse fluctuations in GDP by looking at the fluctuations in expenditure. Statistically, any change in GDP must equal the sum of the changes in the expenditure components; that is, if

$$\text{GDP} = DE + FE, \text{ then}$$

$$\Delta\text{GDP} = \Delta DE + \Delta FE$$

For example, if GDP changes by \$3 billion, then the sum of the changes in expenditure must also equal \$3 billion.

This relationship also holds for percentage changes. Any percentage change in GDP can be decomposed into the expenditure components. Consider the case where GDP increases by 5 per cent. In this example, the increase in domestic expenditure could be equivalent to 3 per cent of GDP, and the increase in net foreign expenditure equivalent to 2 per cent of GDP. Alternatively, the increase in domestic expenditure may be equivalent to 6 per cent of GDP, whereas the fall in foreign expenditure is equivalent to -1 per cent of GDP.

Contributions to GDP growth

In calculating the percentage contributions to GDP growth accounted for by the expenditure components, all the percentage changes are calculated in terms of GDP in the base year.

Thus, in calculating

$$\% \, \Delta\text{GDP} = \% \, \Delta DE + \% \, \Delta FE$$

each percentage is calculated in terms of the base level of GDP.

If the subscript t1 represents the current year and the subscript t0 represents the base year, then

$$\left(\frac{\text{GDP}_{t1} - \text{GDP}_{t0}}{\text{GDP}_{t0}} \times 100 \right) = \left(\frac{DE_{t1} - DE_{t0}}{\text{GDP}_{t0}} \times 100 \right) + \left(\frac{FE_{t1} - FE_{t0}}{\text{GDP}_{t0}} \times 100 \right)$$

For example, suppose you have the following data:

	t0	t1
GDP	150	165
DE	140	146
FE	10	19

To find contributions to growth:

$$\left(\frac{165 - 150}{150} \times 100\right) = \left(\frac{146 - 140}{150} \times 100\right) + \left(\frac{19 - 10}{150} \times 100\right)$$

$$10\% = 4\% + 6\%.$$

In this case, GDP growth is 10 per cent; domestic expenditure has contributed 4 per cent, and net foreign expenditure has contributed 6 per cent.

Exercise 17.1

Calculate the contributions to GDP growth for the following hypothetical example:

	1994	1995
GDP	400	420
DE	380	408
FE	20	12

Table 17.1 shows data for the USA, Japan and the countries of the European Union. This table gives forecast data on the contributions to changes in real GDP growth provided by domestic expenditure and net foreign expenditure for the period 1992 to 1995. These calculations were published in 1993 during a time when Europe and Japan were in recession.

Table 17.1 shows the expenditure contributions to growth by decomposing the overall growth rate into domestic expenditure and net foreign expenditure. The USA was undergoing a period of growth in the early 1990s – its growth rate in 1992 was 2.6 per cent. In this year domestic expenditure was contributing 2.9 per cent GDP growth, and net exports were making a negative contribution of −0.3 per cent. Growth was fuelled by rising domestic expenditure, which was growing faster than GDP in each of the years shown. As a result of a rapid growth in imports compared with exports, net foreign expenditure was making a negative contribution to GDP growth.

The Japanese economy, however, was in recession during these years, with GDP forecast to fall in 1993 by −0.5 per cent. Japanese recovery was impeded by the rising value of the yen, which made exports uncompetitive on world markets. Europe was in recession in this period, but here both domestic expenditure and net foreign expenditure were expected to make a contribution to growth over the period 1993–95. Buoyant growth in the USA and the Asian countries (outside Japan) was providing export

Table 17.1 **Contribution to real GDP growth, 1992–95 (per cent of real GDP in the previous year)**

	1992 (actual)	1993 (forecast)	1994 (forecast)	1995 (forecast)
USA				
DE	2.9	3.6	3.6	2.9
FE	−0.3	−0.8	−0.5	−0.2
Total = GDP	2.6	2.8	3.1	2.7
Japan				
DE	0.8	−0.4	0.9	2.5
FE	−0.2	−0.0	−0.4	−0.2
Total = GDP	0.7	−0.5	0.5	2.3
Europe				
DE	1.2	−1.4	1.0	2.3
FE	−0.0	1.2	0.5	0.3
Total = GDP	1.1	−0.2	1.5	2.6

Note: Components may not add up precisely to GDP due to rounding.

Source: *OECD Economic Outlook* (1993) no. 54

opportunities for the countries of Europe, and so it was expected that exports would grow at a slightly faster rate than imports.

As another example, consider the case of the UK boom and recession in the 1980s and early 1990s. The UK boom peaked in 1988, with an annual growth rate of 5.0 per cent per year, and then the economy went into deep recession earlier than other European countries, with negative rates of growth in 1991 and 1992. Table 17.2 shows contributions to changes in real GDP growth for the UK in the period 1986–92.

Table 17.2 **Contribution to real GDP growth, UK, 1986–92 (per cent of real GDP in the previous year)**

	1986	1987	1988	1989	1990	1991	1992
DE	4.8	5.3	7.9	3.0	−0.7	−3.4	0.4
FE	−0.5	−0.5	−2.9	−0.8	1.1	1.2	−0.9
Total = GDP	4.3	4.8	5.0	2.2	0.4	−2.2	−0.5

Source: *Economic Trends Annual Supplement* (1994)

Question

Table 17.2 shows the contributions to UK GDP growth from domestic expenditure and from net foreign expenditure. How would you describe the changes shown in this table?

Table 17.2 shows that the boom during 1986–88 was fuelled by a sharp rise in domestic expenditure, which grew by 7.9 per cent of GDP in 1988. By 1989 the contribution to growth from domestic expenditure had fallen to

3.0 per cent. In the following two recession years, domestic expenditure made a negative contribution to growth (−0.7 per cent and −3.4 per cent respectively). By 1992 it had picked up and was contributing 0.4 per cent.

Note also what is happening to net foreign expenditure as domestic expenditure fluctuates over the cycle. As domestic expenditure contributes positively towards growth during 1986–88, net foreign expenditure makes a negative contribution of −0.5 per cent to −2.9 per cent because, as incomes rise and domestic expenditure increases, the net trade balance deteriorates and imports rise relative to exports. Although not shown in this table, in 1988 imports rose by 12.6 per cent of the previous year's level, whereas exports rose by only 0.5 per cent. The opposite pattern is discernible during the recession: as the domestic expenditure contribution falls from 7.9 per cent in 1988 to −3.4 per cent in 1991, the net foreign expenditure contribution increases from −2.9 per cent to 1.2 per cent of GDP. In 1992, with an improvement in the rate of growth, the net foreign expenditure contribution once again deteriorates to −0.9 per cent. This relationship shows that, in the UK economy, improvements in the growth rate tend to be associated with a worsening trade balance as imports rise relative to exports.

In order to probe a little more into the increased expenditure which fuelled the UK boom, we need to examine the changes in the components of domestic expenditure. This is shown in Table 17.3, which shows the contributions to growth provided by the components of domestic expenditure in the UK during the period 1986 to 1992.

Table 17.3   **Contribution to growth from domestic expenditure, UK, 1986–92 (per cent of real GDP in the previous year)**

	1986	1987	1988	1989	1990	1991	1992
C	4.0	3.2	4.6	2.0	0.4	−1.4	−0.0
I	0.4	2.2	3.5	0.2	−1.9	−2.4	0.1
G	0.4	−0.1	−0.2	0.8	0.8	0.3	0.3
Total = *DE*	4.8	5.3	7.9	3.0	−0.7	−3.4	0.4

Note: Components may not add up precisely to *DE* due to rounding.

Source: *Economic Trends Annual Supplement* (1994)

Which elements fluctuate most over this period? The boom in 1988 was associated with increases in both consumption and investment expenditure. Consumption expenditure contributed 4.6 per cent of the growth in GDP in that year, whilst investment expenditure contributed 3.5 per cent. After 1988, both these items fell, but note how much more investment expenditure fluctuates. In 1986 investment contributed 0.4 per cent to GDP growth, whereas in 1988 it contributed 3.5 per cent. By 1991 this contribution had fallen to a negative −2.4 per cent. Such large swings in firms' investment expenditure help to account for the cyclical nature of economic activity. (Economic cycles are examined further in Chapters 20 and 25.) In this particular instance of the UK economy, even though investment expenditure is about one-quarter the size of consumption expenditure, the swing in its contribution to growth was greater. This difference is highlighted by the fact that consumption expenditure in 1991 was 1.6 per cent higher than it was in 1988, whereas investment expenditure was 23 per cent less in 1991 than in 1988.

The reasons, first for the increase, and then for the decline in private sector expenditure, involved a number of factors. These include the deregulation of the financial sector in the UK, which made credit more readily available, together with a series of tax reductions which increased real incomes for the better off. Both of these changes contributed towards a rapid rise in consumption expenditure. Accompanying this was an investment boom and a sharp rise in the private housing market which raised the capital values of existing houses and, in the deregulated financial climate, further encouraged an increase in indebtedness as people borrowed against the increased value of their house. An important factor that contributed towards the onset of recession was the increase in the rate of interest, which had the effect of substantially raising the costs of servicing the new private sector debt, including firms' investment and home ownership. With the boom over, asset prices such as house prices fell considerably. Private sector indebtedness then resulted in a record rate of bankruptcies and company liquidations, and, as Chapter 3 explained, many UK households found themselves in a position of 'negative equity', where the value of debt exceeded the value of their assets.

This section has shown how expansions and recessions are associated with sharp changes in the various elements of aggregate expenditure. The statistical evidence for the UK from 1986 to 1991 reveals an expansion of private sector expenditure followed by a sharp fall. Other expansions and recessions at other times and in other countries may show different patterns of volatility in the components of aggregate expenditure.

3   Aggregate demand

3.1   The components of aggregate demand

The previous section showed how the components of aggregate expenditure are subject to short-run fluctuations. These data were based on statistical estimates of GDP which measure the actual amounts that economic agents purchase; they are after-the-event, or *ex post*, measures of expenditure. To understand the fluctuations in GDP in terms of the fluctuations in the component items of aggregate expenditure makes good sense, because GDP can be interpreted in terms of the expenditure measure of national income.

The data do not say anything, however, about the direction of causation between these economic variables. We don't know, for example, whether a fall in investment causes GDP to fall, or whether it is the result of the fall in GDP. In order to be able to say anything about the direction of causation, we need to have a model of the relation between GDP and expenditure based on the *plans* of households, firms and governments – that is, before the expenditure actually takes place. This section will develop an analysis of such expenditure plans. In order to differentiate between planned and *ex post* expenditures, I shall continue to use the term expenditure for *ex post* expenditure, but I shall refer to planned expenditure – *ex ante* expenditure – as aggregate demand.

The previous section showed that there are four main components of aggregate expenditure: consumption expenditure, investment expenditure, government expenditure and net foreign expenditure. Aggregate demand also comprises these same categories, but this time they refer not to actual *ex post* expenditures that have taken place, but to planned *ex ante* demands.

Definition

Aggregate demand

Aggregate demand refers to the sum total of economic agents' planned demand for goods and services produced within the domestic economy (or a specified economic area).

Hence, the components of aggregate demand are consumption demand, investment demand, government demand, export demand and import demand, i.e.

$$AD = C + I + G + X - H, \text{ where}$$

C is consumption demand

I is investment demand

G is government demand

X is export demand

H is import demand

In this expression, the = sign is no longer an identity but represents a functional relationship.

Each of these components of aggregate demand relates to the plans of a different set of economic agents. Thus, the factors influencing aggregate demand are many and varied. In simple macro models we need to limit ourselves to highlighting the main ones. These influences are grouped below as components of (a) domestic demand and (b) net foreign demand.

Domestic demand

Consumption demand

Consumption was introduced in Chapter 3. Consumption demand depends on the level of current real domestic income and the real value of assets such as homes, works of art and equities. As households see their income or wealth rising, their consumption demand will also tend to increase. We should stipulate that current income refers to disposable income, i.e. post-tax income. In addition, a longer time horizon would be more relevant for many households' budgeting plans. This would mean, for example, that a low-income household which expected higher income in the future is more likely to plan to spend a higher proportion of current income now than a household which did not expect future income to improve. The amount by which consumption demand increases for any given increase in real income depends on the marginal propensity to consume, also explained in Chapter 3. The marginal propensity to consume is the proportion of any additional income that is spent on consumption; that is,

$$\text{MPC} = \frac{\Delta C}{\Delta Y}$$

Consumption demand also depends on the rate of interest. Normally, it is expected that an increase in the rate of interest would reduce consumption demand, as it increases the cost of borrowing.

Investment demand

As we saw above, firms' investment includes two elements, namely capital investment in new buildings and machinery, and stocks and work in progress. When firms plan their investment demand, they take into account the rate of interest, as this represents the cost of paying back loans. In addition, firms are influenced by general business expectations. The investment function was introduced in Chapter 2. It shows a negative relation between the rate of interest and the level of planned investment.

This means that if the rate of interest rises, then investment will decrease as firms find it more expensive to finance their investment plans.

Government demand

Government demand for goods and services includes the real goods and services that are necessary for the functioning of services such as the education system, the health service, the civil service, and so on. In simple models of the aggregate economy, it is conventional to assume that government plans are given; in other words, it is assumed that government plans are dependent on factors lying outside the economic model.

Net foreign demand

Export demand

Many factors lie behind the demand for a country's exports. In simple macro models, however, the main factors determining planned export demand are taken to be real income in the rest of the world, the domestic price level relative to world prices, and the exchange rate. A rise in world income implies an increase in plans to export domestic goods. A rise in domestic prices makes exports less competitive. If the exchange rate appreciates, this means that the value of the domestic currency increases relative to other currencies. When this happens exported goods become more expensive in terms of foreign currencies and so the demand for them falls. Exactly the converse sequence occurs if the exchange rate depreciates, leading to a rise in export demand.

Import demand

Similarly, in modelling import demand, the demand for imported goods is taken to depend on the level of domestic income, the real value of assets, and the rate of interest. As income and real wealth increase, so too does the demand for imported goods. Different countries have very different propensities to import goods when real incomes are rising. The *marginal propensity to import* is measured by the proportion of any increase in real income which is spent on imports, i.e.

$$\text{MPI} = \frac{\Delta H}{\Delta Y}$$

In addition, imports are affected by the ratio of world prices to domestic prices, and the exchange rate. Anything which makes world prices lower relative to domestic prices results in increased imports. An appreciation of the domestic currency makes imports cheaper, and so it causes the demand for them to rise. In the expression for aggregate demand, imports are presented as a negative item, whereas exports are a positive item.

This summary of the components of aggregate demand shows that it refers to the total demand of all economic agents, and includes foreign and domestic demand for a country's domestic output. As you can see, this involves disparate plans and expectations from a very wide range of different agents all over the world, from the weekly spending plans of a wage earner or pensioner, to the multi-billion investment decisions of large multinational corporations. It also includes government spending plans, from the pens and pencils of children at school to big building projects on roads and hospitals. The object of macroeconomic analysis is to see how all these varied and independent decisions mesh together to form an aggregate demand which, although beyond the forecasting powers of anyone to predict precisely, nonetheless conforms to certain underlying economic principles.

3.2   The aggregate demand function

The value of an elementary economic model is that it simplifies the complexity of the real economy by focusing attention on the central economic relations involved. The previous section has shown that there are very many influences operating on the level of aggregate demand. From the point of view of understanding the mechanisms at work behind short-run economic fluctuations, however, one particular influence on the level of aggregate demand is highlighted and placed at the centre of analysis, and this is the level of prices in the domestic economy.

As a first step towards building an aggregate model of the economy, attention is directed simply to the relationship between the level of aggregate demand and the price level. Will aggregate demand increase or decrease when the domestic price level changes? In asking this fundamental question, and in focusing exclusively on the relationship between just two economic variables, I am simplifying the situation by assuming that all other variables remain unchanged. I am making the standard assumption of *ceteris paribus* here, which allows me to concentrate on the single relationship between aggregate demand and the price level. Later in the chapter I will relax this assumption and examine what happens once we recognize that, in any real world situation, events do not just happen one by one, but very often all at once.

Definition

Aggregate demand function

The aggregate demand function describes the relation between aggregate demand and the domestic price level, on the assumption that all other economic variables are held constant. The *AD* function shows the total amounts that all economic agents – households, firms and governments – plan to purchase at different levels of domestic prices, when everything other than the price level is held constant.

The aggregate demand function is the name given to this simplified economic relation between aggregate demand and the domestic price level for any country. The previous section examined all the individual components of aggregate demand. Now we need to see how these individual components of demand are affected by the level of domestic prices.

Consider the case where the domestic price level rises: the GDP deflator shows that on average, say, prices in the domestic economy have risen by 5 per cent over the past year. What is likely to happen to the various components of aggregate demand in this case? The first thing to remember is that price is really a relative concept. This means that price changes always imply some sort of standard of reference; if prices go up, they are rising in relation to something else. Focusing on the national economy as though it were detached from the rest of the world may obscure this, hiding from view the significance of changes in the domestic price level compared with price changes taking place in the rest of the world. As the emphasis here is on the open economy trading in a highly competitive world, changes in the domestic price level have to be understood relative to price levels operating in other countries.

If one country's price level rises, and prices in the rest of the world stay the same, this means that the country's goods are now relatively more expensive on the world market. If a country's goods become more expensive, then its net foreign demand will decline. Exports become more expensive and so demand for them will fall. Imports become cheaper in the domestic market and so the demand for imports will rise. If imports rise and exports fall, then net foreign demand falls. As net foreign demand is a component of a country's aggregate demand, this means that aggregate demand also falls.

This shows that aggregate demand falls as the domestic price level rises. Households, firms and governments plan to purchase less of that country's output in response to the increase in its own price level. Note that this relation is an inverse one: aggregate demand and the domestic price level are moving in opposite directions. This inverse relation implies that if the price level falls, then aggregate demand will increase.

Question

Why would aggregate demand increase if the domestic price level fell?

If the domestic price·level falls while world prices remain unchanged, then domestic goods become cheaper than goods produced elsewhere. Exports become cheaper on world markets, and imports become more expensive in the domestic market. In this case, the demand for exports will increase and the demand for imports will fall. This implies that net foreign demand will increase and so too will aggregate demand.

To summarize: for an economy that is open to international trade, there is an inverse relation between its domestic price level and aggregate demand for its output. But remember the assumption of *ceteris paribus*: it is assumed that everything else remains the same, including the level of world prices. If other factors were to change at the same time, they would have to be taken into account and so would complicate the analysis. Thus the inverse relationship derived here is a first step on the road to building a realistic model of the aggregate economy. It does not capture much of the complexity of the real world, but it does provide us with a straightforward and important relationship between the domestic price level and the level of aggregate demand.

As with many other functional relationships in economics, it is useful to be able to represent the aggregate demand function on a diagram, as in Figure 17.2. The vertical axis represents the domestic price level, and the horizontal axis represents real output (GDP). As the relationship between aggregate demand and the level of domestic prices is an inverse one, the aggregate demand curve is drawn downward sloping from left to right.

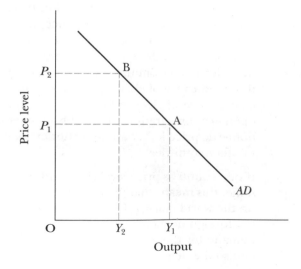

Figure 17.2 **The aggregate demand curve**

Consider a point such as A on the aggregate demand curve. At this point, aggregate demand is Y_1 and the domestic price level is P_1. Now consider what happens if the price level rises from P_1 to P_2. In this case, the country's goods become less competitive on the world market and its net trade balance deteriorates. Aggregate demand falls to Y_2 and there is a movement along the *AD* curve from A to B.

Figure 17.2 therefore shows an aggregate demand curve for an economy that is open to international trade, and where the inverse relation between aggregate demand and the domestic price level is the result of the international relative price effect. There is, however, an additional explanation for the inverse shape of the aggregate demand curve, and this links up with the money market which was explained in Chapter 11. If the domestic price level changes, then this may well have repercussions in the money market. This issue is controversial, as it depends on the extent to which the domestic monetary authorities are able to control the money supply. As Chapter 11, Section 5 explained, this is still subject to dispute.

Chapter 11 explained how an increase in the price level causes the demand for nominal money balances to increase. The reason for this is that people need more money to carry out their accustomed number of transactions. If the monetary authorities can fix the nominal stock of money, this implies that there is now an excess demand for nominal money balances at the original rate of interest. As Figure 11.6 (reproduced here as Figure 17.3) showed, this results in a rise in the rate of interest as bonds are sold in the attempt to increase nominal money balances. The demand for money curve has shifted to the right from L_1 to L_2, but there is also a movement back along the new demand curve as the rise in the interest rate chokes off the increased demand. The final outcome is a higher rate of interest with the original nominal stock of money.

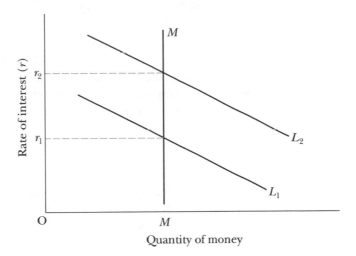

Figure 17.3 **Money market equilibrium with exogenous money supply**

Thus, an increase in the price level is associated with a higher rate of interest if the nominal money supply is exogenous. But the higher rate of interest in turn affects aggregate demand. Investment expenditure will be cut back because the cost of borrowing for firms increases. Similarly, households are likely to cut back on purchases if the rate of interest rises, because this will increase their borrowing costs. Many home owners will face higher mortgage repayments, and this will force them to cut back on their consumption demand. The higher rate may also precipitate a more pessimistic mood about future prospects for the economy, and this too will have a depressing effect on aggregate demand.

A fall in the price level will have the opposite effect. If the stock of nominal money remains constant in the presence of a fall in the domestic price level, then the demand for nominal money balances will fall, and this will result in downward pressure on interest rates. Lower interest rates will tend to increase aggregate demand by reducing the cost of borrowing and by promoting a more optimistic mood in the economy.

The effects of a changing domestic price level on interest rates thus works to reinforce the international price effect. In both cases, there is an inverse relation between the components of aggregate demand and the domestic price level. This is summarized in Figure 17.4.

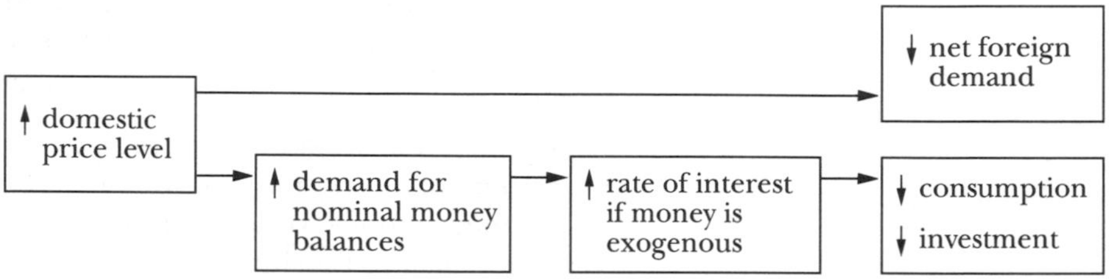

Figure 17.4   The inverse relation between the price level and aggregate demand

This interest-rate effect illustrates the difficulty of trying to work strictly within a *ceteris paribus* assumption, in that it shows that it is not always possible to hold everything else constant because of the close interdependencies that exist between economic variables. The effect of a changing price level on interest rates shows that, on certain assumptions about control of the nominal money stock, interest rates are determined by factors which are themselves influenced by the price level, and so it is not possible to hold interest rates constant as we consider the effects of changes in the price level.

Again, it must be stressed that this version of the aggregate model is a first approximation to the complexity and interdependence of a real economy, and the model itself has to be used flexibly. In particular, as Chapter 19 explains, the rate of interest is subject to international pressures. Furthermore, it is well to remember the discussion of Chapter 11, which cautioned that agreement is still lacking over the extent to which the monetary authorities are able to control the nominal stock of money, even in the absence of changes in the price level. An alternative view of the money market stresses that an increase in the price level may not automatically lead to an increase in interest rates. If the money supply is endogenous and cannot be controlled directly by the authorities, then an increase in prices does not necessarily lead to an excess demand for money because the money supply adjusts to the increased demand. This case was shown in Figure 11.8, where the rate of interest is unaffected by the increase in demand for nominal money balances.

Exercise 17.2

To check that you have understood the discussion so far, explain why you would expect aggregate demand to increase when the domestic price level falls. Illustrate your answer with an aggregate demand diagram.

3.3   Shifts in aggregate demand

The previous section showed how the aggregate demand function is based on the simplifying assumption that everything other than the domestic price level is held constant. This section will consider the impact on aggregate demand of changes in the other variables – the exogenous variables – which are held constant along the length of the *AD* curve.

These exogenous variables are those that are not influenced by the domestic price level. As the various components of aggregate demand are quite disparate, so are the different influences upon it. All these factors have already been referred to in Section 3.1 in the course of explaining the component parts of aggregate demand. Any change in these variables will be represented diagrammatically by a *shift* of the entire aggregate demand curve.

The UK boom in the late 1980s

Consider the case of the consumer boom in the UK during the late 1980s. Rapidly appreciating asset values led to an increase in the real wealth of households which, in the new climate of financial deregulation, facilitated an increase in consumer indebtedness that financed a consumer boom. This event corresponds to an increase in aggregate demand at every level of domestic prices. This is represented diagrammatically by a rightward shift in the *AD* curve, showing that aggregate demand increases at every level of domestic prices. This is shown in Figure 17.5.

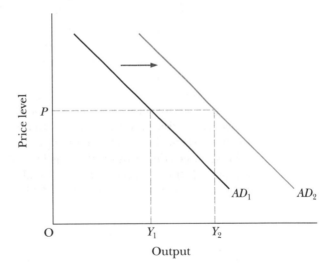

Figure 17.5 **A shift in the *AD* curve resulting from a consumer boom**

The original *AD* curve is shown as AD_1. At the original price level *P,* the level of aggregate demand is shown as Y_1. With an increase in house prices and increased availability of consumer credit, aggregate demand at the existing price level increases to Y_2. This is represented diagrammatically by a rightward shift in the *AD* curve from AD_1 to AD_2.

After a time, the boom came to an end and asset prices fell. Consumers now found that they were the victims of a debt overhang or negative equity, such that the value of their assets fell below the value of their enlarged debt. A period of retrenchment followed in which aggregate demand fell sharply, shifting the *AD* curve back leftwards towards AD_1 in Figure 17.5.

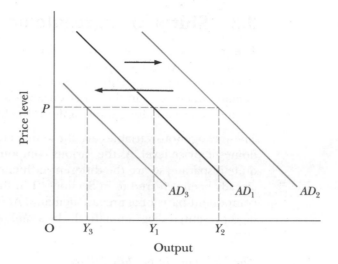

Figure 17.6   *AD* falls as the consumer boom comes to an end

An even deeper recession might have taken aggregate demand below its original level. In Figure 17.6 the addition of AD_3 to Figure 17.5 shows this situation. At the original price level, aggregate demand has fallen to a level Y_3, which is below the original level Y_1.

This analysis of the UK consumer boom shows how the *AD* curve shifts in response to a change in real asset values, one of the exogenous variables which was held constant when the curve was drawn.

The appreciation of the yen in the early 1990s

Another exogenous variable is the country's exchange rate. If this changes, the *AD* curve will shift. Consider the case of Japan in the early 1990s, when it was faced with an appreciation of the yen at a time when it was struggling to come out of recession. An appreciation of the yen implies that imports become cheaper, as each yen now exchanges for more units of foreign currency. As the yen is now more expensive for foreigners wishing to import Japanese products, this also means that exports become more expensive on world markets. The response of exports and imports to these changes in relative prices depends on the elasticity of export demand and import demand. If these demands are reasonably elastic, then the value of net exports (exports minus imports) will rise in response to the price changes.

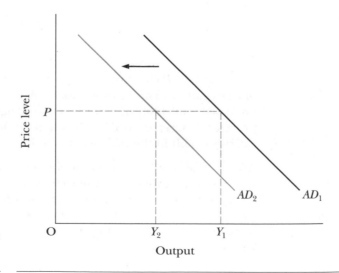

Figure 17.7   A fall in *AD* in Japan following the appreciation of the yen in the early 1990s

(The precise requirements in terms of the elasticities are explained in Chapter 19.) The outcome for aggregate demand in Japan was that it fell overall. This is illustrated in Figure 17.7.

The original aggregate demand curve is shown as AD_1. The appreciation of the yen causes net foreign demand for Japanese goods to deteriorate. The outcome is a fall in aggregate demand, shown as a leftward shift in the AD curve from AD_1 to AD_2. At the existing price level, the level of aggregate demand falls from Y_1 to Y_2.

The opposite case of a depreciation of the currency is illustrated by the events of 1992–93 for a number of countries including the UK, Italy, Spain, Portugal, Sweden, Finland, Australia and Canada. In these cases, a lower value of the currency facilitated an increase in exports and a reduction in imports, thus helping to boost aggregate demand.

High interest rates in Europe in the early 1990s

Following the overheating of the German economy after reunification, the rate of interest in Germany was raised to control inflation. Countries whose currencies were pegged to the deutschmark also had high interest rates in order to maintain their existing exchange rates. These high interest rates led to a fall in consumption expenditure and investment expenditure as households and firms found that the cost of borrowing had risen. Figure 17.8 shows the effects of a high interest rate policy on the level of aggregate demand.

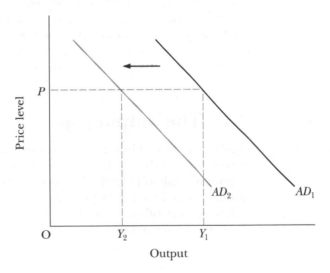

Figure 17.8   A fall in *AD* following high interest rates in Europe in the early 1990s

In Figure 17.8 the original aggregate demand is AD_1. As a result of German reunification, interest rates rise and this has the effect of reducing aggregate demand. The fall in aggregate demand is shown as a leftward shift in the AD curve from AD_1 to AD_2.

Exercise 17.3

1   What is the effect on aggregate demand if there is a crash in a country's stock market?

2   What is the effect on a country's aggregate demand if there is a rise in prices in the rest of the world?

In order to simplify the analysis of complex events, I have been taking a single event at a time, exploring the implications of each change taken on its own. The last two examples, however, illustrate how such events are often combined. A country's exchange rate and interest rate are often closely connected, as you will learn further in Chapter 19. For example, in 1992 the UK left the Exchange Rate Mechanism (ERM) of the European Monetary System (EMS) and allowed its currency to depreciate. At the same time the UK government was able to reduce interest rates because it was no longer committed to supporting the parity of the pound against the deutschmark by maintaining a high interest rate. (A high interest rate attracts financial capital into the country, which increases the demand for pounds and so strengthens the exchange rate.) Thus, two sets of events took place together: the pound depreciated and the rate of interest fell. Each of these effects contributed towards increasing aggregate demand, thus helping to pull the UK economy out of its deep recession. Diagrammatically, this would be represented by a larger shift in the *AD* curve to the right than would have been the case if either of these events had happened without the other.

In this case, both events were working in the same direction. This is not always the case, however. Consider the example of the European recession in the early 1990s. I have already noted the depressing effects of high interest rates in Europe which reduced aggregate demand. At the same time, there was something of an upturn in world trade. Strong growth in some Asian countries held out the prospect of increased exports for other countries. Thus, for the European countries, there were simultaneous pressures tending both to reduce aggregate demand and to increase it. In this case, the final outcome for each country would depend on the precise combination of these two opposing forces.

4   Stabilization policies

4.1   The output gap

Figure 17.1 showed how recurrent booms and cycles characterize the performance of the industrialized economies. These short-run fluctuations in growth result in periods when economic resources are being underutilized, followed by periods when they are being overutilized. Instead of having a smooth growth path where resources are being fully utilized all the time, the actual rate of growth fluctuates around the potential rate of growth, lying above it during booms and below it during recessions. Figure 17.9 shows an estimate of actual and potential rates of growth in the European Union from 1970 to 1993.

The actual rate of growth shown in Figure 17.9 is based on observed and forecast growth rates in member countries of the European Union. The graph shows the familiar picture of short-run fluctuations. Recessions occurred in the mid 1970s, early 1980s, and early 1990s. The potential growth rate represents an estimate of the growth rate implied by the full utilization of capital resources. This is not an observable variable but has been estimated on the basis of a number of assumptions about the growth of capital, and about what can reasonably be regarded as a full utilization of resources. This line showing potential growth is much smoother than the line showing actual growth, but it shows a declining trend from the 1970s to the 1990s.

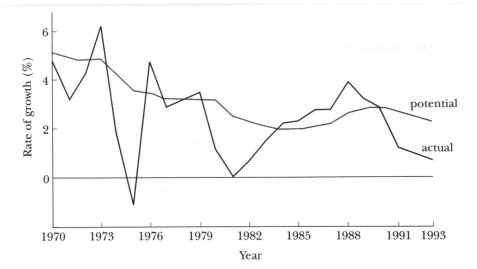

Figure 17.9 **Actual and potential rates of growth in the EU, 1970–93**

Source: *European Economy* (1993) no. 54, p.21

The potential growth that is lost/gained as a result of short-run fluctuations is shown on the figure by the vertical difference between potential growth and actual growth. Inspecting the figure carefully shows that the growth forgone during recessions is greater than the extra growth gained during booms. Thus, the cyclical fluctuations result in greater negative deviations from potential output than positive ones. In other words, short-term fluctuations in growth result not only in the inconvenience of an unstable growth path, but of a lower level of GDP than would be the case if growth could be maintained steadily without deviating from the potential full capacity rate. The *output gap* is the loss in output resulting from short-run fluctuations, given the longer-term productive potential of the economy.

The output gap may be even larger than this estimate of the output gap suggests. If the extent of each recession affects longer-term decisions to invest in new capital equipment, then productive potential is not independent of the pattern of cyclical fluctuations. In this case, it is possible that in the absence of such sharp short-term movements, the long-term productive potential might be greater than it actually is. This impact of short-run events on the longer run is discussed further in Chapters 18, 20 and 24.

4.2   Stabilization policies

Evidence on the output gap has suggested to many economists that governments should attempt to find ways of trying to smooth out short-term economic fluctuations by stabilizing the economy around its long-term growth path. Policy designed to smooth out short-term fluctuations is known as stabilization policy.

Keynesian economists have argued that governments should use stabilization policies to smooth the economic cycle and to reduce unemployment. They have argued that the best way to do this is to control the level of aggregate demand, boosting it in times of recession and reducing it during booms.

Stabilization policies cover many different aspects of policy, but three broad approaches have been identified.

Definition

Stabilization policy

This refers to the policy of attempting to smooth out the short-run economic cycle by controlling the level of aggregate demand.

Definition

Automatic stabilizers

These are the changes in government revenues and expenditure that are induced by fluctuations in economic activity. The automatic stabilizers operate contracyclically in smoothing economic fluctuations.

Automatic stabilizers

Tax revenues are the main automatic stabilizers. (Remember from Chapter 2 that net tax revenues include transfer payments.) Some components of government revenue respond automatically to the state of the economy without any further government intervention. Even though tax rates and unemployment benefit rates may be fixed, a recession or boom will induce changes in the total amounts paid in taxes and unemployment benefits. Tax revenues fall during a recession and rise during a boom, and unemployment payments increase during a recession and fall during a boom. These induced changes operate automatically in responding to the effects of the economic cycle. They are stabilizers because their effect works in the opposite direction to the movement of aggregate demand. If the economy moves into recession, incomes and aggregate demand fall, but the fall in tax revenues and the rise in unemployment benefits help to counteract the reduction in aggregate demand.

The OECD has estimated that, on average, government revenues in the OECD countries fluctuate with a slightly larger amplitude than that of national output. Table 17.4 provides data on the relation between unemployment benefits and government expenditure for the OECD countries in 1991.

Table 17.4   **Unemployment benefits and government expenditure, OECD countries, 1991**

	Unemployment benefit expenditure		**Increase in unemployment benefits following a 1 percentage point increase in the unemployment rate**		**Average unemployment benefit**
	as % of:		**as % of:**		**as % of:**
	government expenditure	GDP	government expenditure	GDP	average earnings plus employers' social security
United States	1.5	0.5	0.2	0.1	13.3
Japan	0.7	0.2	0.4	0.1	18.4
Germany	3.0	1.4	0.6	0.2	34.3
France	3.2	1.6	0.3	0.2	30.1
Italy	1.0	0.5	0.1	0.1	7.7
United Kingdom	1.7	0.6	0.3	0.1	15.4
Canada	8.1	4.1	0.8	0.4	61.4
Australia	4.0	1.5	0.4	0.2	24.2
Austria	1.8	0.9	0.6	0.3	46.8
Belgium	5.8	2.4	0.3	0.2	22.9
Denmark	5.5	3.2	0.6	0.3	47.5
Finland	3.6	1.7	0.4	0.2	40.1
Ireland	6.3	2.8	0.5	0.2	29.5
Netherlands	4.5	2.5	0.5	0.3	42.5
Norway	2.2	1.2	0.4	0.2	34.2
Spain	7.0	2.9	0.4	0.2	30.4
Sweden	0.8	0.5	0.6	0.3	47.8
Switzerland	0.4	0.1	0.8	0.3	46.3
Total of above countries	3.4	1.6	0.4	0.2	32.8

Source: *OECD Economic Outlook* (1993) no. 53, p.39

The first two columns show unemployment benefits as a percentage of government expenditure and GDP. The next two columns show the effect of a 1 percentage point increase in the unemployment rate on the total amount of unemployment benefit (as a percentage of government expenditure and GDP). The final column shows average unemployment benefit as a percentage of average earnings plus employers' social security payments. The country with the highest payments, according to these measures, is Canada, which pays out 4.1 per cent of GDP in total, and where the average benefit equals 61.4 per cent of the average earnings measure. Switzerland pays out the smallest amount in unemployment benefits as a percentage of GDP; since the average benefit is as high as 46.3 per cent, this must be the result of low unemployment. Unemployment benefits in the UK are well down the list at 0.6 per cent of GDP, and the UK has the third lowest average unemployment benefit at only 15.4 per cent of the average earnings measure.

As Table 17.4 shows, the automatic stabilizers vary considerably in size across different countries. The larger the size of the public sector, then the greater the role that the automatic stabilizers can play, but the overall effectiveness of the stabilizers depends also on the structural characteristics of the economy and the extent to which it is open to foreign trade. The OECD has calculated the effect of the automatic stabilizers on the smoothing of fiscal policy. Simulations suggest that the automatic stabilizers have the effect of reducing the amplitude of fluctuations by about one-quarter of what they would have been in the larger European economies. The consequent reduction in the cumulative output loss during a recession is estimated at about one-half. In the smaller European economies, the automatic stabilizers are less effective in smoothing the cycle because the economies are more exposed to foreign trade. Conversely, in the USA the automatic stabilizers have a proportionately greater effect because it is a larger and therefore more closed economy with trade forming a smaller proportion of GNP, though the stabilizers themselves are small (*OECD Economic Outlook*, 1993, no. 53, p.42).

Discretionary policies to 'fine tune' the economy

A major aspect of stabilization policy concerns the use of specific policy changes in response to the economic situation. These changes are sometimes known as 'discretionary' policy measures because their implementation requires a government decision. The two main types of discretionary policy are fiscal policy and monetary policy. Both are designed to work by changing the level of aggregate demand, increasing it during recessions and reducing it during booms.

Fiscal policy

An expansionary fiscal policy increases the level of aggregate demand. This could take the form of an increase in government expenditure, a reduction in taxes, or some combination of the two. Examples of increased government expenditure include infrastructure projects on roads, railways and the environment, or specific building projects relating to education and health programmes. These are classic Keynesian 'pump-priming' expenditures designed to influence aggregate demand and have a direct effect on employment.

Definition

Fiscal policy

This refers to a government's policy with regard to the balance between expenditure and taxation.

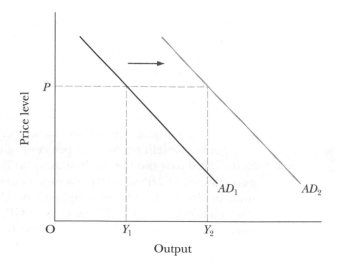

Figure 17.10 **An expansionary fiscal policy increases the level of aggregate demand**

Figure 17.10 illustrates an example of expansionary fiscal policy involving an increase in government expenditure. Aggregate demand increases from AD_1 to AD_2, and the level of income increases from Y_1 to Y_2 at the original level of prices.

Part of the Keynesian argument concerning the effectiveness of these policies relates to the 'multiplier' effect of such expenditures. The argument is that the government's own expenditure provides only the first round of increased expenditure. The recipients of increased government contracts or government salaries in their turn increase their consumption demand, and the recipients of this increased purchasing power are in turn able to increase their demand for goods and services, and so on.

The final increase in aggregate demand is therefore larger than the initial increase in government expenditure that caused it. As a pebble dropped into a pool produces a series of ripples, so too, it is argued, does an increase in aggregate demand. The initial increase in demand provides incomes and jobs to people who go out and spend more. Their increased demand in turn provides incomes and jobs for others, who in their turn increase demand. Adding up all these ripples of increased demand across the economy produces an overall increase in aggregate demand that is greater than the original increase which set off the process in the first place. This cumulative effect is measured by the demand multiplier.

Demand multiplier

The demand multiplier is the ratio of the final change in aggregate demand to the initial change in demand which brought it about. It shows by how much the initial change in demand has been multiplied to create a new level of aggregate demand, i.e.

$$\text{demand multiplier} = \frac{\text{final } \Delta \text{ in aggregate demand}}{\text{initial } \Delta \text{ in aggregate demand}}$$

For example, if government demand increases by £5 billion and the final increase in aggregate demand is £10 billion, then the multiplier = 10/5 = 2. In this case the multiplier is 2 because the final change in aggregate demand is twice the size of the original increase in demand which brought it about.

The demand multiplier also applies to changes in other components of aggregate demand. For example, if investment increases by £3 billion and the final increase in aggregate demand is £4.5 billion, then the multiplier is 1.5.

The demand multiplier shows how changes in government demand may have a magnified effect on final outcomes. (This theme is developed further in Chapters 25 and 26.) The size of these multipliers is a matter of considerable empirical and theoretical debate.

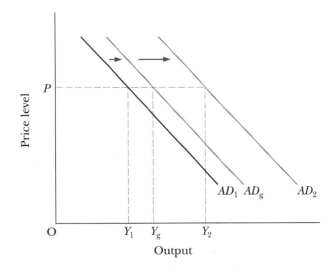

Figure 17.11 **The multiplier effect of an increase in government demand**

Demand multipliers can also be illustrated using the *AD* diagram. In Figure 17.11 the original aggregate demand is shown by AD_1. Government demand is then increased in order to boost economic activity, and the initial change in aggregate demand is shown by the new *AD* curve, AD_g. The level of income rises from Y_1 to Y_g at the original level of prices. This is shown by the horizontal distance $Y_g - Y_1$. In time the first-round effects of the increase in government expenditure give rise to second- and third-round effects and so on, until gradually all the induced changes in aggregate demand have worked their way through the economy. The final level of aggregate demand is at AD_2, and the level of income is at Y_2. The overall increase in income at the original level of prices is given by the distance $Y_2 - Y_1$. Using the multiplier formula,

$$\text{demand multiplier} = \frac{\text{final } \Delta \text{ in } AD}{\text{initial } \Delta \text{ in } AD}$$

From Figure 17.11, this is equivalent to:

$$\text{demand multiplier} = \frac{Y_2 - Y_1}{Y_g - Y_1}$$

Thus, the ratio of the distances between the aggregate demand curves gives the value of the demand multiplier. The greater the distance between the final *AD* curve and the initial *AD* curve, relative to the distance between the first-round *AD* curve and the initial *AD* curve, the greater is the demand multiplier.

Exercise 17.4

The government increases expenditure on new hospitals by £20 billion. Using the *AD* diagram, show the final effect on total output at the existing price level if the multiplier is 3.

Reducing taxes can have a similar effect to an increase in government expenditure in terms of boosting aggregate demand, but the composition of the goods and services purchased will be different. Probably some of the increased disposable income will be saved or spent on imports rather than being spent on domestic output, and this will reduce the final effect on aggregate demand. The impact on the distribution of income may be different too. The recipients of the tax reduction may well not be the same as the beneficiaries of the increased expenditure; the reason for this is that higher income groups tend to be strong beneficiaries of tax cuts, whereas lower- and middle-income groups tend to benefit particularly from expenditure programmes. The size of the public sector will be affected, however, because a policy of tax reductions rather than expenditure increases will result in a smaller overall size of the public sector. But in terms simply of the effect on aggregate demand, reducing taxes and increasing government expenditure shift the *AD* curve in the same direction.

Monetary policy

Discretionary policy may also include monetary policy, which attempts to influence monetary conditions such as the rate of interest, the money supply and the availability of credit. In addition, governments may also target a particular exchange rate. The conduct of monetary policy may be the formal responsibility of the government (as in the UK at the time of writing) or an independent central bank (such as the Bundesbank in Germany), but, as Chapter 19 explains, the conduct of monetary policy is now closely tied up with exchange rate policy. The mobility of international financial capital means that it is not possible to determine domestic monetary policy independently of exchange rate policy.

Monetary policy is important for stabilization policy because it affects the availability and price of credit, and this influences aggregate demand. If the rate of interest goes up, then credit becomes more expensive and this puts a brake on consumption demand and investment demand. The traditional Keynesian view of monetary policy was that it should be used in conjunction with fiscal policy to control aggregate demand. Interest rates should be lowered in a recession in order to boost demand, and raised in the boom to damp it down. Monetary policy was, however, generally regarded as inferior to fiscal policy as a means of controlling aggregate demand, in that it worked indirectly via the effects of interest rate and money supply changes and so its effects were thought to be less certain.

Definition

Monetary policy

Monetary policy involves influencing monetary conditions such as the rate of interest, the money supply or, sometimes, the exchange rate. It may be directed at changing real variables such as output or employment, or it may be aimed at controlling inflation.

Exercise 17.5

The government introduces an expansionary monetary policy by reducing interest rates. What effect will this have on aggregate demand?

The demise of fine tuning

Traditional demand management policies in the 1950s and 1960s involved a combination of fiscal and monetary policy. Expansionary fiscal policy used alone with an unchanged nominal money supply implies an increase in the rate of interest. This means that expansionary fiscal policy with an unchanged money supply is less effective than if accompanied by an accommodating monetary policy. Monetary policy can be accommodating in two different ways. First, in the case of an exogenous money supply (see Chapter 11, section 5.2), the government might directly introduce an expansionary monetary policy by increasing the supply of money. Second, in the case of an endogenous money supply (see Chapter 11, section 5.3), the government might accommodate monetary growth by not increasing interest rates to restrict the endogenous monetary expansion.

Demand management had to confront the problem of inflation in the 1970s. Monetarist economists such as Milton Friedman argued that expansionary demand management policies had contributed towards inflationary pressures. Expansionary monetary and fiscal policies had led to increases in the money supply, it was argued, and this had made inflation worse. Consequently, during the 1980s and early 1990s there was a shift in policy priorities in many countries away from using demand management to stabilize the economy. Instead, fiscal and monetary policies were to be used to control inflation, using high rates of interest and a reduced commitment to government expenditure.

Thus governments turned away from using Keynesian-style policies to boost aggregate demand, although their anti-inflation policies may still be analysed using the aggregate demand model. These anti-inflation policies correspond to the case considered above in Figure 17.8, where a tight monetary policy results in a fall in aggregate demand represented by a leftward shift of the *AD* curve.

The stabilization and inflation objectives of monetary policy sometimes imply contradictory movements in the rate of interest. Stabilization may well require a loosening of monetary policy with a reduction in interest rates, whereas the control of inflation requires a tightening of monetary conditions and high rates of interest. Faced with this choice, the European countries in the early 1990s chose the latter option.

Discretionary policies to 'coarse tune' the economy

In spite of disenchantment with fine-tuning policies, the presence of growing unemployment and widespread recession in the early 1990s predisposed a number of economists to investigate the possibilities for 'coarse tuning' the economy in the medium term. With restrictive monetary policies in operation to control inflation, and the implications of this for low rates of growth in the medium term without any significant improvement in unemployment, proposals to coarse tune the economy were put forward in the mid 1990s (Drèze and Malinvaud, 1994).

The macroeconomic policy proposals to coarse tune the European economy included lower rates of interest and an acceptance of the automatic stabilizers. In addition, the authors suggested some medium-term structural changes. These included making the welfare state more efficient, tax subsidies on the low paid by means of reductions in employers' social insurance contributions, public investment programmes such as housing, urban renewal, public transportation systems and trans-European transport and telecommunications networks, and a reconsideration of distributional fairness as between labour and capital, including both wage restraint on the part of workers and more rigorous European-wide policies to redress tax evasion on internationally mobile capital.

This approach to coarse tune the economy represents a more recent development of Keynesian instincts to redress high unemployment by increasing aggregate demand, but it was tempered with the recognition that expansionary fiscal policies were not practical in the current climate in Europe, where monetary stringency to reduce inflation was well entrenched. In addition, it recognized that the existing budgetary position of European governments was such that increased budget deficits along traditional Keynesian lines were not a feasible option. This issue of budget deficits is examined in Section 5.

4.3 Implementing stabilization policies

In the earliest and simplest Keynesian models it was often assumed that governments could stabilize the economy by adjusting policy and then watching the economy respond to these discretionary measures. The reality is far removed from this optimistic picture.

One problem is that of time lags in the policy-making process. Governments have first to identify the problem, then assemble the appropriate information, then announce the new policy measures, then wait for this to have an effect and, finally, wait for the results to materialize in the published statistics. Even this is an excessively optimistic view. One possibility is that unexpected events may occur which throw the whole policy off course. Another possibility is that economic relationships change anyway – many economic relations are not stable over long periods of time, and it is well-nigh impossible to know when changes are going to take place. For example, who would have forecast the reunification of Germany that took place in 1990, or the disintegration of the former Soviet Union? This is how the UK Treasury explained it in one of their public briefing papers:

> Useful as textbook models are in providing an understanding of how an economy works, they often suggest that a government has much more control over its economy than it can ever have in practice. In such models the government has to decide on a fiscal policy, particularly the difference between its spending and taxation, and a monetary policy as to the level and rate of growth of the money supply. In some models the government's role is simply one of solving a set of mathematical equations which represent the working of the economy. The solution will then tell it the combination of policy instruments to use to obtain the desired objectives of full employment, stable prices and a high and sustainable level of economic growth.

> The reality of economic management is complex: the economic behaviour of consumers, producers and other agents tends not to conform to simple predictable relationships which remain stable over time; the time it takes to gather information means that neither the government nor anyone else can really know what is

happening to the economy contemporaneously; and there are lags, sometimes quite long, between policy actions and their effects. An attempt at fine tuning the economy in the way described by the simplest economic models would be like trying to drive a car with unreliable steering and only partially effective brakes by looking in the rear-view mirror.

(Economic Briefing, 1993, no.5, p.1)

Governments, you might say, are bound to be defensive. But the points made in this extract are serious ones. Furthermore, although not noted in this UK Treasury *Briefing*, this model of policy making does not take into account the complications arising from the expectations of other economic agents and the problems of policy credibility discussed in the previous chapter. The government might announce that they are taking steps to speed up the process of recovery, but if agents don't believe that recovery is going to take place, or still feel nervous about the timing of a recovery, then they will not increase their expenditure. At worst, private agents might reduce their expenditure in the face of what they see as an unwarranted government spending increase, hence nullifying the expansionary effect. This extreme response – called 'crowding out' – is discussed further in Chapter 19.

Policy credibility is thus crucially important for policy to be successful. It requires that agents believe that the government will stick with the stated policy, but this depends on the expectations that agents have about the future and about the government's consistency in pursuing its objectives. A government might reduce interest rates to stimulate activity, but if firms believe that the government will shortly raise them again because of fears about renewed inflation, they will not respond to the interest rate reduction by increasing their investment. As in strategic games, governments have to take into account the effect of their policies on economic agents, and anticipate the effects of these reactions when formulating policy.

Finally, fears about the financial implications of stabilizing the economy by increasing aggregate demand have also made policy makers more cautious. Milton Friedman's criticisms that stabilization policies would lead to increasing government debt which would undermine the control of inflation, helped to introduce a more critical approach to Keynesian demand management policies. His arguments that an enlarged government debt would tend to put upward pressure on interest rates showed the internal limits to stabilization policies: government policies to increase demand would come up against their own limits if they increased interest rates, as this would in turn tend to reduce private sector sources of aggregate demand.

The outcome of these criticisms is that most economists are more sceptical now of the ability of governments to manage the economy and smooth out fluctuations. In spite of this, discretionary policies are still used in a range of different circumstances, not all of them corresponding to notions of Keynesian demand management.

5   Fiscal stance and budget deficits

5.1   Fiscal stance

Definition

Government financial balance

The government financial balance (or budget balance) shows the difference between government receipts and expenditure. A financial surplus (or budget surplus) implies that receipts exceed expenditure, whereas a financial deficit (or budget deficit) implies that expenditure exceeds receipts.

Fiscal policy refers to the balance between government expenditure and taxation. The overall effect of fiscal policy on the level of aggregate demand is known as the 'fiscal stance': if policy increases aggregate demand then fiscal stance is expansionary, and if it reduces aggregate demand it is contractionary. Fiscal stance is normally measured with reference to the government financial balance, or the difference between revenues and expenditure, which is generally expressed as a percentage of GDP.

An expansionary fiscal stance is one which shows a fall in the government financial balance – that is, an increase in the budget deficit or a reduction in the budget surplus. A contractionary fiscal stance represents an increase in the budget surplus or a reduction in the budget deficit.

Question

If stabilization policy is successful in smoothing the economic cycle, what would you expect to happen to the government financial balance (or budget balance) over the course of the cycle?

If discretionary fiscal policy is contracyclical, then the budget balance will deteriorate during the recession and improve during the period of renewed growth. The government increases spending/reduces taxes during the recession and reduces spending/increases taxes during the boom. If the smoothing were exact, and if stabilization were the only objective of discretionary fiscal policy, then the budget surpluses in expansionary years would exactly offset the budget deficits in times of recession, with the result that the net budget balance would be zero over the full course of the cycle. In fact, stabilization policy is only one of the objectives of government budgetary policy; other objectives will include welfare provision, the maintenance of social infrastructure, and some degree (however limited) of distributional fairness. Furthermore, during times when the economy is growing well, the government may for political reasons prefer to reduce taxes rather than improve the budget balance.

In addition, as we saw above, it is not the case that the good years necessarily balance out the bad ones, as this depends crucially on what is regarded as the norm or full capacity rate of growth. The estimate of the output gap in Figure 17.9, for example, based on an estimate of the potential rate of growth, shows that the output lost during the recession years is greater than that gained during the boom years. Finally, as argued above, stabilization policy is never administered perfectly. There are always errors of judgement and problems of timing, not to mention political shortsightedness and pragmatic responses to the immediate problems of the moment. Some economists have identified what they call the 'political business cycle', where governments stimulate an expansion in aggregate demand during the run-up to an election, and then impose the inevitable programme of retrenchment when they feel secure from electoral pressure. The result of all these factors is that although the budget balance tends to improve in years of expansion and deteriorate in years of recession, the budget does not balance in the long term, and problems of growing budget deficits reappear from time to time.

Budget deficits are financed either by government borrowing or by printing money. Borrowing involves selling government securities (bills and bonds) to the central bank, which then sells them to private sector agents (open market operations – see Chapter 11, Section 5). The cash raised by these sales provides the government with the cash required to meet its commitments, but as it is matched by a reduction in cash held by the private sector there is no overall effect on the money supply. Printing money also involves the sale of securities to the central bank in exchange for cash, but this time the securities are not resold by the bank. In this case the increased cash holdings are not met by reductions elsewhere, and so there is a corresponding increase in the monetary base and, hence, in the money supply.

5.2   Budget deficits and indebtedness

During the early 1990s, the government budget balance in many countries was deteriorating, and this renewed earlier fears about the effects of increasing government indebtedness. In 1993 the general government deficit was estimated at about 4.5 per cent of GDP in the countries of the OECD, and somewhat higher in Europe at about 6.8 per cent of GDP. These years were a time of negative or sluggish output growth, so tax revenues were falling while unemployment compensation was rising. There was therefore a significant cyclical element to the deterioration in the budget position of many countries, reflecting the effects of the recession on government finances. In addition, however, it was estimated that the underlying structural or cyclically adjusted deficits were worsening significantly, showing that the deterioration in government finances was not entirely the result of the recession. According to OECD calculations, the cyclical element of the deficit amounted to about 1 per cent of GDP for the OECD countries, leaving about 3.5 per cent due to changes in the underlying or structural budget position. For the European countries, the cyclical element was about 1.8 per cent of GDP, leaving about 5 per cent of GDP due to structural causes.

Adjusting the government budget balance

The recorded government budget balance shows the difference between government revenues and expenditure. This raw budget balance is generally regarded as a poor measure of fiscal stance because it does not take into account the effects of cyclical fluctuations.

The structural – or cyclically adjusted – budget balance

The structural budget balance gives an estimate of the budget balance that would be operative if the economy were at its trend level of output. It thus provides a measure of the balance which adjusts for the effects of the cycle. It is calculated by subtracting the cyclical component of the budget from the actual budget, i.e.:

> Structural or cyclically adjusted balance = actual balance – cyclical component

Inevitably in a calculation of this sort, there is wide scope for disagreement as to how the cyclical component should be calculated. Part of the problem is that it is impossible to know exactly what the full capacity rate of growth is at any point in time, as this is a hypothetical construct. Without a knowledge of the full capacity or trend rate of growth, it is not possible to estimate the degree of cyclical variation from it. Figure 17.9 showed an estimate of the European output gap using a measure of the potential rate of growth based on the growth of the capital stock, but other measures such as full employment of labour can also be used. Further, it is not always clear when cyclical movements are absorbed into changes in the trend. Changes that appear to be cyclical at first may become part of the longer trend if they persist for a period of time. For example, it is not always clear when some types of unemployment should be regarded as cyclical or as trend unemployment. (Issues of trend and cycle are discussed again in Chapters 20 and 26.)

In addition, economies are frequently being blown off course by exogenous shocks. Events such as the two oil price rises during the 1970s, financial deregulation during the 1980s, the liberalization of the economies of Russia and Eastern Europe, and the reunification of Germany, imply far-reaching economic changes that shift the trend rates of growth for other countries. With such large structural changes taking place within national economies, the notion of the government structural budget deficit becomes harder to operationalize.

The cyclical and structural components of the budget deficits for the OECD countries are estimated regularly on the basis of announced changes in fiscal policy, with some adjustment to reflect past records of implementation. Estimates for the period 1992 to 1994 (published in 1993) are shown in Figure 17.12 on a four-quadrant diagram to show the estimated mix of cyclical and structural deterioration that was expected over this period.

For any individual country, each of the structural and cyclical balances could either improve or worsen. This means that there are four possibilities for each country: an improvement on both the structural and cyclical components, a deterioration on both the structural and cyclical components, or an improvement on one component and a worsening of the other one. These four possibilities can be displayed in the four quadrants of Figure 17.12, in which the vertical axis measures changes in the structural component and the horizontal axis shows changes in the cyclical component.

The countries with an improved structural balance and cyclical balance (in the top right-hand quadrant) were the USA and Canada, whose economies were growing relatively rapidly at that time. All other countries, apart from Norway, experienced a worsening in the cyclical component, reflecting the continuation of recession or only sluggish recovery for these economies in the early 1990s. Most countries lie in the top left-hand quadrant, indicating that they were forecast to improve their structural budget positions at a time when the cyclical component was deteriorating. This means that discretionary fiscal policy was forecast to be contractionary for these countries, even though they were in recession. The countries in the bottom left-hand quadrant all had a small deterioration in the structural element at a time when the cyclical element was also deteriorating. Sweden has the greatest cyclical deterioration. The area to the left of the dotted line in Figure 17.12 includes all those countries for which the net effect of the change in the structural and cyclical balances was to worsen the overall budget balance.

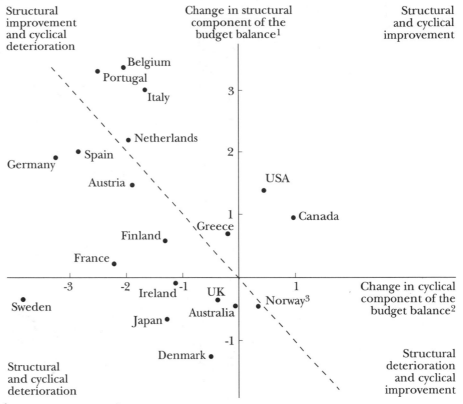

Figure 17.12 **The fiscal stance for OECD countries, 1992–94**

Source: *OECD Economic Outlook* (1993) no. 53, p.6

[1] Refers to the change in the cyclically adjusted general government budget balance.

[2] Refers to the difference between the change in the overall budget balance and the cyclically adjusted budget balance.

[3] Refers to Norway's mainland economy.

Countries to the right of the dotted line experienced an overall improvement in their budget balance.

Thus, during the early 1990s those countries in recession were showing reluctance to adopt expansionary discretionary fiscal policies. This was in part due to the general demise of Keynesian thinking, and a sceptical attitude towards the potential for fine tuning the economy. It was also the result of problems of financing the deficits amid anxieties about the general deterioration in budget deficits and the concomitant growth in public indebtedness that was taking place during this period. The Maastricht Treaty had included agreed 'reference values' for all European countries as part of the preparation for European monetary union. These values required that general government borrowing should not exceed 3 per cent of GDP and that the public debt should not exceed 60 per cent of GDP. During the period 1989 to 1993, the deterioration in budget deficits was such that not one European country could be found within both these reference values at the end of 1993. This is shown in Figure 17.13, which shows government borrowing and public debt as a percentage of GDP for (a) the countries of the European Union, and (b) the other OECD countries.

Figure 17.13(a) includes a dotted line which represents the Maastricht 'reference values' of 3 per cent government borrowing and 60 per cent public debt. Whereas five countries – the United Kingdom, Germany, France, Spain and Denmark – had been within these values in 1989, by 1993

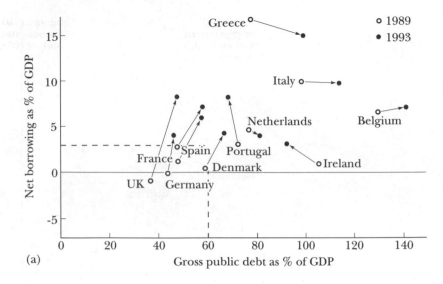

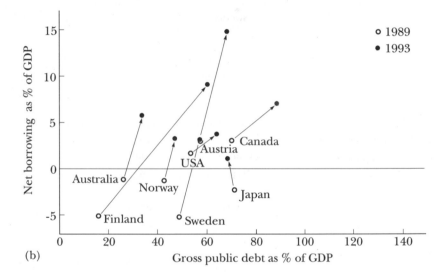

Figure 17.13 **Government borrowing and debt as % of GDP, 1989 and 1993: (a) European Union, (b) other OECD countries**

Source: *OECD Economic Outlook* (1993) no. 54, p.16

this was no longer the case and not one country fulfilled both reference values. Whether or not these reference values might be thought appropriate for countries in recession, the political impetus behind the Treaty meant that European governments were anxious to try to improve their budget positions in the direction of the Maastricht agreement, and so were reluctant to engage in discretionary expansionary policies, especially as the high real rates of interest at the time were making the servicing of the debt more expensive.

During this period most countries were experiencing a longer-term deterioration in their public finances, such that fears were being raised about the future burden involved in servicing the existing debt, let alone stabilizing it or even reducing it. If the government debt rises too fast, then the interest payments start to take up an increasing proportion of GDP, and eventually the government's financial position may become unsustainable. The debt ratio (the ratio of debt to GDP) increased for most OECD countries from the late 1970s to the early 1990s. The figures are shown in Table 17.5 for selected years from 1978 to 1995.

Table 17.5   **Debt ratios for EU and OECD countries, 1978 to 1995, % of nominal GDP**

	1978	1985	1990	1995 (forecast)
USA	39.2	48.1	55.4	64.1
Japan	41.9	68.7	69.8	72.4
UK	58.7	52.7	34.7	56.4
Belgium	68.8	122.3	130.7	144.8
Italy	62.4	84.3	100.5	118.0
EU	42.3	57.4	58.1	76.1
OECD	41.0	55.4	58.7	70.7

Source: *OECD Economic Outlook* (1993) no. 54, p.154

For both the EU and OECD as a whole, debt ratios grew during the 1980s, stabilized during the late 1980s, but then grew again during the 1990s. For the European countries, debt ratios increased by about 80 per cent as a proportion of GDP over this period. The USA debt ratio was consistently below the EU and OECD averages, but it still grew by over 60 per cent as a proportion of GDP. Japan's debt history was more varied: it grew more rapidly than the EU and OECD during the 1980s, but then it more or less stabilized so that its expected level by the mid 1990s corresponded more closely to the EU and OECD levels. The UK's debt ratio fell from 1978 to 1990, but thereafter rose by about 60 per cent. Even so, its projected 1995 level was just below its 1978 level and was still the lowest of any OECD country except Australia and Norway, which had projected debt levels of 41.3 per cent and 54.2 per cent respectively. Belgium was the country with the highest debt ratio in the OECD. Its debt ratio was the highest in 1987 and after that period it more than doubled. Italy had the second highest debt ratio.

Comparing this table with Figure 17.12 shows that it was some of the high-debt countries in the early 1990s that were making the strongest efforts to secure improvements in the structural balance. Belgium and Italy both improved the structural balance by 3 per cent or more. Portugal, with a projected debt ratio of 71.4 per cent in 1995, also improved the structural deficit by over 3 per cent, and the Netherlands, with a debt ratio of 82.8 per cent, improved its structural deficit by over 2 per cent. At the other end of the scale, three of the countries with a slight increase in the structural deficit were those with the lowest debt ratios (UK, Australia and Norway).

5.3   Policy implications

By the early 1990s there was considerable pressure – both economic and political – for governments to constrain budget deficits in a significant way and put into reverse the increase in debt ratios. It should be remembered that this was happening at a time when these economies were in recession and the only input to expansion was coming from the automatic stabilizers.

Exercise 17.6

Bearing in mind the analysis of aggregate demand in earlier sections of this chapter, what are the likely outcomes of policies to reduce the structural and cyclical components of the budget deficit at a time when the economy is in recession? Illustrate your answer using the *AD* diagram.

If the economy is in recession, this means that aggregate demand is low or falling. In these circumstances, stabilization policy requires that fiscal policy should be directed to reversing this decline by boosting aggregate demand. This could be achieved by increasing government expenditure or reducing taxes. Thus, cutting the deficit at a time of recession means working against the automatic stabilizers, and reducing aggregate demand further. If, for reasons of controlling inflation or maintaining financial discipline, it is necessary to reduce the government deficit, then this will tend to reduce aggregate demand.

At such a time, however, it is extremely difficult to cut government expenditure, as it raises wider issues about equity and the welfare role of government expenditure, as the early 1990s debates show. To reduce the cyclical component requires cutting unemployment benefits at a time when public sympathy is likely to be resistant to increasing the hardships of the unemployed. Reducing the structural component appears to require redefining and reducing the sphere of public responsibility in the traditional welfare areas of health, education and pension payments, although gains in efficiency are also sought. Such cuts may also result in reduced government support in areas of education, training and infrastructure that are important for macroeconomic efficiency and the reduction of structural unemployment in the future. In combination with demographic trends that result in additional claims on welfare services, the result is a knotty issue of competing economic and political demands upon the state. One possible solution to maintaining government expenditure and reducing the budget deficit would be to raise taxation, especially as one reason for the increase in government deficits in the early 1990s derived from an earlier period of tax cutting. This, however, was unacceptable both to those who wished to reduce the role of the state and those who wished to see an expansionary fiscal stance.

If the scope for fiscal policy in boosting aggregate demand is weak, this raises the question of the role of monetary policy. If inflation is low, there is a place for an easing of monetary conditions and reducing the rate of interest. In terms of financing the government's debt, a lower rate of interest reduces the cost of interest payments on the debt. Here the government is to some degree dependent on the international financial markets and the view that is taken of the government's credibility. If the strategy for reducing the deficit is regarded as credible in financial markets, then it is easier for interest rates to fall, and a fall in real interest rates will help to promote recovery. But if such credibility is absent, and the government is not believed to have a coherent policy for reducing the deficit and stimulating non-inflationary growth, then it is harder for interest rates to fall, and this impedes recovery.

Such credibility is especially significant in view of the potential inflationary implications of rising government indebtedness. The problem is that the government deficit may be financed by printing money, which itself contributes to inflationary pressure. The mechanism in this case is that the government sells securities to the central bank in return for cash; this extra cash then enlarges the monetary base, which in turn leads to an increase in the money supply. In normal circumstances there is generally thought to be little correlation between budget deficits and inflation, but the experience of hyperinflations has shown how massive government deficits have been monetized and how this has fed the inflationary spiral.

There is a great temptation for an indebted government deliberately to tolerate a degree of inflation in order to erode the real value of its own debt. Given this temptation, any anti-inflation policy in these circumstances has to be doubly convincing in order to establish credibility for the government's policy. Thus we see again the importance of the credibility of policy, and the close interconnections between fiscal and monetary policy.

6   Conclusion

This chapter has examined the demand side of the macroeconomy. It has looked at the different components of aggregate expenditure and has shown how they can fluctuate over the course of an economic cycle. The chapter has derived the aggregate demand function and has shown how this can be represented diagrammatically. The chapter has also looked at the difficulties involved in stabilization policy, the interlinking of fiscal and monetary policy, and growing budget deficits and debt ratios.

The diagrammatic analysis of the *AD* curve has proceeded by examining what would happen to aggregate demand at a given level of domestic prices. In spite of this diagrammatic restriction, the analysis repeatedly had to refer to the enduring problem of the relationship between stabilization policies and inflation. Thus the next step in building a model of the macroeconomy is to incorporate changes in the price level, and to examine the effects of different policies on the level of domestic prices. In order to do this it is necessary to combine our analysis of aggregate demand with aggregate supply. This is the subject of the following chapter.

CHAPTER 18

AGGREGATE SUPPLY AND SUPPLY-SIDE INTERVENTION

by Mary Gregory

1 Introduction

1.1 Introducing aggregate supply

In the previous chapter you studied aggregate demand in the economy, looking in turn at each of the main groups whose spending decisions determine the level of aggregate expenditure. The analysis of aggregate demand is one of the key elements in our picture of the overall functioning of the macroeconomy, and an essential building block in the model of the whole economy which we are assembling. Aggregate demand, however, is only one part of the story. You will remember from Chapter 1 that the most widely used national macroeconomic indicator is GDP, or national output, with GDP per head of population as the most common measure of national standards of living. Our task in this chapter is to build forward from the analysis of aggregate expenditure to the determination of GDP.

You have already been introduced in Chapter 2 to the concept of macroeconomic interactions through the circular flow of income. The discussion there showed how the production of national output generates incomes, in the form of the wages and salaries, profits and rents paid out by firms. When these incomes are spent, the resulting purchases take up the output from firms. In this way, production creates incomes that in turn give rise to expenditure which purchases the output from the production activities. The circular flow gives an initial perspective on the way in which expenditure decisions and output decisions interact to shape macroeconomic outcomes. Once we have completed our analysis of aggregate supply in this chapter, we will be able to combine aggregate supply with aggregate demand. This will give us a much more powerful tool-kit for analysing the determination of national output and the sources of macroeconomic fluctuations.

How national output is determined matters not only for its intellectual interest but also for the role of macroeconomic policy. Chapter 16 has already outlined the major shifts in the approach to macroeconomic management from the Keynesian era in the 1950s and 1960s, when macroeconomic policy was largely identified with demand management, to the last twenty years, when first monetarism and then conservative macroeconomics have been to the fore. In this chapter I will show how the differing views on the functioning of the macroeconomy and on the role of macroeconomic policy are based on differing analyses of the behaviour of aggregate supply.

Our first task is the development of the second of our main building blocks, the aggregate supply curve. However, the analysis of aggregate supply is neither straightforward nor uncontroversial, and this will be reflected throughout the chapter. Two distinctions will be of fundamental importance to us. The first concerns the representation of market structure. As Parts 3 and 4 demonstrated, the price and output decisions of firms vary considerably, depending on the type of market situation in which they are involved. We shall see that the view we take on these price and output decisions has major implications for the analysis of aggregate supply and for the macroeconomic outcomes that we derive. The macroeconomics of imperfect competition are very different from the macroeconomics of competitive markets.

The second major distinction will be between short- and long-run aggregate supply. You have already met the concepts of the short and long run in Chapter 4, when you studied the organization of the firm. There, the short run was the period in which a firm's buildings and equipment were taken as fixed, along with the available technology; in the long run capacity too could change, and the entry or exit of firms could take place. The distinction between the short and the long run is, however, a perfectly general one. The short run is the period during which at least one variable is held fixed, so that while adjustments to some variables occur, at least one remains unchanged. The variable held constant differs across models, as we shall see. In the long run, full adjustment of all variables has taken place. Each of the approaches that we will be examining uses the distinction between short- and long-run aggregate supply, but they differ in important ways on the characterization of the short run and the nature of the transition to the long run.

1.2   Structure and aims of the chapter

The aggregate supply schedule links the rate of production in the economy to the overall price level, showing the level of output that would be produced at different price levels. Equivalently, it shows the price level that would be required for producers to supply each level of output.

The economy's aggregate output depends on the quantity of factor inputs which firms find it profitable to use, and the accompanying output decisions that they make. The main elements in our analysis will therefore be wage and employment determination, and the production and pricing decisions of firms.

You will remember from Book 1 that there is no single 'correct' model of price determination for the firm. Game theory, monopoly, imperfect competition and perfect competition each have their place as the market situation of the firm varies. The firm may be a price-setter or a price-taker, and the level of output it chooses will vary with this. Similarly, the labour market can be regarded as approximately competitive, with firms paying the going wage rate, as set by the market. Or wages may be the outcome of a bargaining process, and at least partially insulated from market forces.

To keep the discussion reasonably uncluttered, I will group the various possibilities into two broad categories. The first approach is based on imperfect competition – the view that the modern firm, although subject to competitive pressures, has at least some degree of choice over the price it charges for its product and the wages it pays to its employees. The basis for this view is the observation that many firms sell differentiated products, which gives them a degree of market, or monopoly, power, and some

Definition

Aggregate supply schedule

The aggregate supply schedule (*AS*) shows the levels of aggregate output which producers will supply at different price levels.

discretion in price setting. Similarly, wage setting is often formalized through collective bargaining. Alternatively, management itself may choose the wage and salary rates on offer. The firm is thus viewed as a price- and wage-setter. These features, of imperfect competition in product markets and wage bargaining or wage setting by firms, broadly characterize the 'New Keynesian' approach to macroeconomics.

The second approach to aggregate supply will be the 'competitive' or New Classical approach. This has its microeconomic basis in the model of perfect competition, where prices and wages are regarded as set by impersonal forces of the market, which balance demand and supply. Individual firms and workers are then price- and wage-takers with no market power or bargaining power. This approach puts market forces firmly at centre stage, with prices adjusting continuously and effectively to maintain a balance between supply and demand. I shall refer to this frequently as 'competitive market clearing'.

The remainder of the chapter will be in four main sections. Sections 2 and 3 will develop the New Keynesian and 'competitive' approaches in turn. These sections will be at a fairly abstract theoretical level, as we strip each model down to its essentials. This is to allow us to pinpoint the key assumptions in each approach and the ways in which these influence the analysis. In Section 4 aggregate supply and aggregate demand will be combined to give a brief overview of the ways in which they provide an effective framework for the study of macroeconomic fluctuations and stabilization policy. This is taken up further in Chapter 20. Section 5 will give an overall perspective on the debates about aggregate supply, reviewing the microeconomic foundations of the differing approaches and contrasting their implications for macroeconomic policy.

2   A New Keynesian approach: wage bargaining and price setting

Definition

Sticky wages and prices

Wages and prices are said to be sticky when they do not adjust instantaneously to equate demand and supply.

The starting point for the New Keynesian approach to aggregate supply is the observation that in a modern economy firms are typically wage-setters and price-setters. That is, they exercise at least a degree of choice or discretion over the wages they pay and the prices they charge for their products, rather than implementing a going wage or price set by the impersonal forces of the market. In addition to wages and prices being set on a partially discretionary basis, they may not be adjusted smoothly and continuously as demand and supply conditions alter. Wages and prices are characterized by stickiness.

I will concentrate first on the role of wage setting, examining the process by which wage rates are determined. This will emphasize two essential features. First, under wage setting the wage outcome, and therefore the level of employment, will not be at the level which a competitive market would establish. Second, the process of wage adjustment can be expected to be sluggish. After wage setting we will look at firms' decisions on price, again establishing the same two features. These features of wage and price setting and stickiness in adjustment will be the main elements in our version of a New Keynesian aggregate supply story. Section 2.1 will develop the approach to wage setting and wage stickiness. Section 2.2 will review the price-setting process. Section 2.3 then derives the aggregate supply schedule on the New Keynesian view, and Section 2.4 summarizes briefly.

2.1   Wage setting through collective bargaining

In Europe (outside the former centrally planned economies) collective bargaining is the dominant mode of wage determination. Table 18.1 shows that in most western European countries in 1990, over 70 per cent of the workforce were covered by collective agreements, although in the UK and in some other countries of the OECD the proportion is lower. We will therefore centre our analysis on wage setting under collective bargaining and its influence on wage outcomes.

Table 18.1   **Trade union density and collective bargaining coverage rates, 1990**

Country	Trade union density (%)	Collective bargaining coverage (%)
Austria	46	98
Belgium	51	90
Finland	72	95
France[1]	10	92
Germany[2]	32	90
Netherlands	26	71
Norway	56	75
Portugal[3]	32	79
Spain	11	68
Sweden	83	83
Switzerland	27	53
UK	39	47
New Zealand	45	67
Australia	40	80
Canada	36	38
USA	16	18
Japan[4]	25	23

Note: figures refer to percentages of wage and salary earners.
[1] 1985. [2] 1992. [3] 1991. [4] 1989.

Source: *OECD Employment Outlook* (1994) Chart 5.1

It is worth noting, however, that the bargaining approach to pay setting does not apply only to situations of formal collective bargaining. Even where a personalized salary is set for the individual employee, with no formal representational procedures – as is often the case at management level – negotiation or bargaining may still occur, explicitly or even implicitly. Employees are costly to replace. If they quit, work experience, training and knowledge of the job and the firm go out of the door with them. In addition to the obvious expenses of recruitment, the firm faces the costs of training replacements and the loss of the expected profits from the expertise of experienced employees. These costs of labour turnover give the incumbent employee a degree of bargaining power. This may be reflected in the wage outcome purely on the employer's calculation and without any face-to-face negotiation or confrontation. Further development of these ideas can be found in Akerlof and Yellen (1986) and in the 'insider-outsider' model of Lindbeck and Snower (1988).

Reflection

How is pay determined for groups with which you are familiar? Does it involve bargaining, either directly or indirectly?

The wage bargain

Unions exist to represent groups of employees in negotiations with the employer, their collective role redressing the bargaining weakness of the isolated individual. Above all, union members look to their union to secure wage increases on their behalf. Our main proposition is that wage bargaining raises wages above the level which would otherwise be established. The bargaining power which the union can derive from collective representation, backed by the power of collective action, in general secures a higher wage. This situation is illustrated in Figure 18.1, where the L_S schedule represents the minimum wage acceptable to employees individually (their labour supply curve) and BW the wage which the union is able to obtain through collective bargaining. The vertical distance between the two curves represents the wage increase which the union achieves. For example, at employment level L, the increase is $W_1 - W_2$.

Since the impact of unions on wages is an important and challenging issue, many studies have sought to estimate the size of any wage mark-up attributable to collective bargaining. The existence of a wage premium, or positive wage mark-up, is almost universally confirmed, and estimates of its size vary from under 10 per cent to 20 per cent or more. The classic work on this was Lewis (1963) for the USA; the evidence is extensively reviewed in Lewis (1986), and in Layard, Nickell and Jackman (1991, Chapter 4). Chapter 21, Section 3.2 discusses this issue further.

However, establishing a role for union bargaining power must not be taken to imply that market forces are irrelevant. The ability of unions to raise

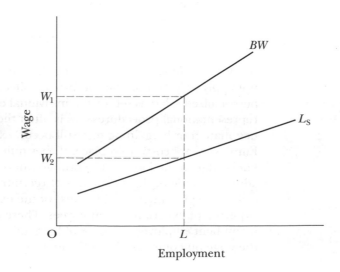

Figure 18.1   **Individual labour supply and collective bargaining over wages**

wages is strongly influenced by the level and also the trend in unemployment. High unemployment weakens union bargaining power. More subtly, when unemployment first starts to rise, most of the unemployed are still experiencing only a short spell without work. From their own and the employer's point of view, they are fully available for work. However, when unemployment has been high for some time, the numbers of long-term unemployed rise disproportionately, and their impact on wage setting has been demonstrated to be lower than for the short-term unemployed. In this way, both the level and the trend, or composition, of unemployment influence wage setting. With collective bargaining, therefore, labour market conditions still influence wage setting, but their impact is filtered in quite complex ways through union bargaining power. (This issue is explored in Layard, Nickell and Jackman, 1991, and, at a simpler level, in Layard, Nickell and Jackman, 1994.)

The higher wages established through collective bargaining must, other things being equal, reduce the level of employment which the firm can profitably sustain. We will return to this point later.

The process of collective bargaining in itself uses up resources, notably the time and energy of the negotiators on both sides. Because of these costs of negotiation, agreements normally apply for a specified period. In Britain, over 90 per cent of wage settlements are reported to be of twelve months' duration, with settlements for shorter or longer periods usually associated with a one-off switch of the settlement date (Gregory, Lobban and Thomson, 1985). A similar pattern of annual settlements applies in much of Europe. In the USA, where wage negotiations are often marked by prolonged and costly disputes, and where inflation has been generally lower over the post-war period, unionized wage contracts frequently run for three years, with only limited interim adjustment.

Reflection

Do you regard an annual wage review as the norm? Can you think of situations in which it might be more frequent?

The second major implication of wage setting through collective wage bargaining is therefore that it introduces greater fixity into wages, a fixity which increases with the length of the contract period.

Renewing the wage bargain

The wage bargain typically specifies the nominal or money wage. While the participants will have expectations about trends in prices, these cannot be perfectly foreseen. Any unforeseen change in the price level while the agreement is in force therefore results in a change in the real wage. This is extremely important, since it is the real wage that is the basis for economic decisions on labour supply and labour demand.

For example, if the price level rises over the contract period, the real value of the wage is eroded. This is a favourable development from the employer's viewpoint, since revenue rises while wage costs are fixed. But conversely it is unfavourable for the employee, whose standard of living is reduced. Contract renewal gives the union the opportunity to seek an adjustment to wages to offset the intervening change in prices. Since the firm's

Definitions

Nominal/money wage and real wage

The money or nominal wage is the wage expressed in terms of current money value. The real wage is the money wage adjusted for any change in the price level. If W is the money wage and P the price level, then the real wage is expressed as $\frac{W}{P}$.

profitability has risen, the employer will be able to concede the wage rise. In terms of Figure 18.1, both the L_S and BW curves will shift upwards when contracts are renewed at a higher wage after the price level has risen. Note that, in order to isolate the effect of a price rise, we are treating other cost and demand conditions as constant.

In viewing wages as set predominantly through collective bargaining, we therefore have to conduct the analysis in two stages: the short run, during which wages are taken as pre-set, fixed in nominal terms in the contract, and consequently varying in real terms as prices change; and the long run, when all contracts have been revised in the light of the price changes.

2.2   Price setting

It is frequently said that the pricing decision is one of the most important which firms have to make, and it is certainly obvious that many firms are price-setters, choosing the price which they charge for their product. As with wages, many prices are adjusted only at intervals, rather than on a continuous basis. Moreover, prices often seem not to be adjusted upwards when demand is high, or downwards when it is slack, as the operation of market forces would suggest.

Reflection

When was the last price change of:

1   your newspaper;

2   a first-class stamp;

3   a visit to the cinema?

In a much-quoted study, Cecchetti (1986) has documented the long intervals between changes in the cover price of magazines in the USA. Cecchetti shows that the price of the typical magazine on American news-stands is allowed to erode by 25 per cent in real terms (relative to prices in general) before adjustment. In other words, when inflation is at an annual rate of 4 per cent, the typical magazine changes its cover price every six years.

The concept of 'mark-up pricing' is often used to describe the pricing behaviour of firms with market power. Prices are set to cover costs and give the firm a satisfactory profit margin. While an adequate rate of profit must be achieved in the long run, the mark-up can be varied in the short run to reflect market conditions, the firm's market strategy, or the costs of price adjustment. In the short run, therefore, prices may be sticky; in the long run they will adjust fully to establish the required profit margin.

Reasons similar to the costs of negotiation for wage stickiness have been suggested as the source of price stickiness. In changing prices firms incur costs, which have come to be referred to collectively as 'menu costs'. These are the costs of revising and reprinting price lists (such as menus!), re-labelling, issuing new catalogues, adjusting slot machines, entering new prices into computerized systems, and similar operations. The decision on price adjustment involves weighing the costs of changing against the costs, in terms of forgone profits, of retaining a price which is no longer optimal.

Even for a rigorously profit-maximizing firm, price stickiness may be the appropriate outcome (Mankiw, 1985). Since the magazine cover is reprinted for each issue, menu costs cannot explain the fixity of price noted by Cecchetti. More generally, it seems clear that the costs of changing price must be much smaller than the costs of varying output in response to changing demand. Investigating the reasons why many prices are sticky, and why firms often seem to reduce output rather than cut prices, remains an area of active research for macroeconomists.

2.3   Short- and long-run aggregate supply

In this section we examine how employment and output are determined according to the New Keynesian view. I shall focus first on a world of collectively bargained wages, leaving aside for the moment possible price rigidities. Wage rigidity due to collective bargaining turns out to have powerful implications for the determination of output and employment.

Short-run aggregate supply

For the employer the crucial measure determining whether it is profitable to maintain or expand employment is the real wage. Once the level of the money wage has been determined in the wage settlement, any rise in the price of the firm's output reduces the real wage. This makes it profitable to expand output and employment. The firm's employment and output rise when the real wage falls.

This is shown as the upward-sloping short-run aggregate supply schedule (*SAS*) in Figure 18.2. The *SAS* curve shows the level of output that firms are willing to produce when the price level rises, *but money wages are held fixed* at the level agreed in the contract. It is the fixity of the money wage, implying the erosion of the real wage as price rises, that makes additional employment and increased output profitable and the *SAS* curve upward-sloping. The *SAS* schedule is short-run only, as it assumes that the money wage, set in the previous round of collective bargaining, remains unchanged.

Question

What will happen to the *SAS* when the money wage changes?

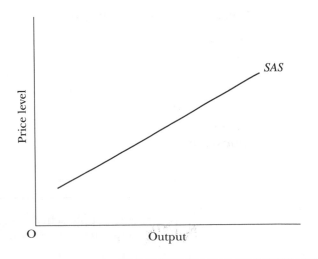

Figure 18.2   **The New Keynesian short-run aggregate supply curve**

The *SAS* is based on a given money wage, so it must be redrawn whenever the money wage is adjusted as contracts are renewed. In Figure 18.3, SAS_1 represents aggregate supply when the wage remains at its initial level W_1. This repeats the curve from Figure 18.2. When a higher wage, W_2, is negotiated, the *SAS* curve shifts upwards to SAS_2. Reading vertically up Figure 18.3 from the output axis, firms are now willing to supply their previous rates of output only at a higher price, to cover the higher wage costs. Or, equivalently, reading horizontally from the price axis, with the higher wage firms will be willing to supply less output at any price.

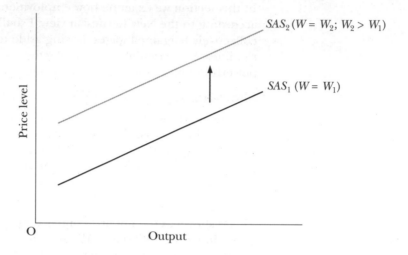

Figure 18.3 **A shift in the New Keynesian short-run aggregate supply curve**

So far I have established that with fixed money wages but a rising price level, the *SAS* curve is upward-sloping. An alternative, and more extreme, New Keynesian view adds the menu-cost story of price rigidity. If, because of menu costs, firms hold prices fixed while wage contracts keep money wages fixed, then the *SAS* curve is perfectly horizontal. Output will expand, or contract, in the short run with no change in prices – that is, output on these assumptions is infinitely elastic. Clearly this is a very strong, and over-restrictive, assumption to apply to all prices and therefore to the price level in general. However, to the extent that prices are sticky, the *SAS* curve will be flatter.

Long-run aggregate supply

Moving now to the long run, we are considering the time period in which wage and price rigidities cease to apply. The long-run aggregate supply schedule traces out the level of output which firms will choose to produce, at alternative prices, once all contract wages have been reviewed and adjusted to the new prices.

Question

Once wages have adjusted, what shape would you expect the long-run aggregate supply schedule to take?

The long-run aggregate supply schedule (*LAS*) is vertical, and independent of the price level, as shown in Figure 18.4. This may initially seem a surprising result, but its rationale should soon be clear. Workers want a high real wage – that is, they want the wage to be high relative to prices. Firms, on the other hand, want prices to be high relative to wages – that is, a low real wage. These objectives conflict, but agreement can be reached, its exact terms depending on the bargaining power of the two sides. Let that be at point A on the *LAS* in Figure 18.4, when the price level is P_A, and let us call the money wage at that point W_A.

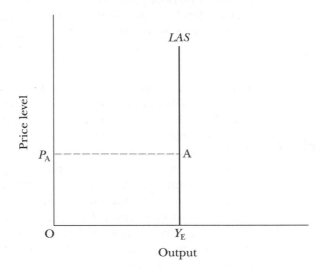

Figure 18.4 **The New Keynesian long-run aggregate supply curve**

Now suppose the union forces a wage increase. Since this represents an increase in costs, the employer must at some stage respond by raising prices, to restore profit margins. This price rise erodes the gain in the real wage intended, and initially achieved, by the wage rise. If the union responds by pushing up the wage again, a further round of price increases follows. This process can be stopped only when wages and prices are again mutually consistent – that is, when the real wage is restored to the initial equilibrium level. At that point employment and output are also restored to their original levels.

The crucial point is that money wages and prices can be mutually consistent at *any* level, provided they remain in line with each other. If prices rose to $100P_A$, a money wage of $100W_A$ would restore the original real wage. In the long run, the optimal rate of output is independent of the price level. The *LAS* schedule is vertical.

2.4   Review

The main features of the New Keynesian approach to aggregate supply can now be summarized. Its starting point is the view of the typical firm as engaging in wage bargaining and price setting. Because wages are set through collective bargaining, they tend to be fixed for the duration of the wage contract. This gives rise to a short-run *SAS* curve which is upward-sloping. When prices rise while wages are fixed, employment and output rise. When prices fall with wages fixed, employment and output fall. In the long run, however, wages must adjust to higher prices, and prices must adjust to wages, so the *LAS* is vertical.

Issues which we have not yet addressed directly are: what level of employment is implied by the *LAS* on the New Keynesian view, and how does this relate to full employment as understood in traditional Keynesianism? And what measures does it suggest for governments wishing to promote employment? These are questions that will be addressed in the final section of the chapter. Before turning to them, we will consider a rather different approach to the analysis of macroeconomic aggregate supply, namely the approach on which UK government policy has been largely based since the early 1980s. The next section develops this alternative view of aggregate supply based on competitive market clearing.

3   The competitive approach: market clearing in competitive markets

The key to the competitive or New Classical approach is its view of markets. Market prices are seen as adjusting smoothly to balance supply and demand, and markets clear continuously. The emphasis is on the power and efficiency of competitive markets. The competitive model in this view is not only the best description of the way real-world markets work, it also provides the ideal. Rigidities, monopoly power, bargaining and strategic behaviour are either unimportant, merely frictions which transitorily interrupt the smooth functioning of markets, or, if important, they are to be eliminated. This view of the intrinsic effectiveness and desirability of competitive markets has found support from many governments over the past decade. (See the discussion of perfect competition in Chapter 7.)

Since the key elements of the competitive approach may be less intuitively obvious than in the case of the New Keynesian approach, I will give a relatively extended discussion of its analytical underpinnings. As with the New Keynesian approach, I will start with the labour market, wages and employment. Section 3.1 will discuss the functioning of the competitive labour market, to establish how wages and employment are determined in that context. (Note that Chapter 21 will provide a more extended discussion of labour market models.) In Section 3.2 I turn to the determination of aggregate supply, drawing on what has just been established about wages in a competitive labour market to analyse the firm's output decision. I then examine how employment and output respond to a change in the price level, to derive the New Classical aggregate supply schedules under the competitive approach.

3.1   The competitive labour market

In this section we will look in turn at the three essential elements in the functioning of the competitive labour market: labour supply, labour demand, and the outcomes for wages and employment. The market is an aggregate one, but the supply and demand schedules are the outcome of decisions by individual workers and firms. It is these micro-level decisions which we will analyse. The analysis of labour supply will consider the individual's decision on how much employment to seek and accept, given the wage on offer. In looking at labour demand we will examine how many workers the firm will wish to employ at alternative wages. In the third sub-section we bring these together to establish the wage and employment outcomes in the competitive market.

Figure 18.5 gives a simple representation of the aggregate labour market in the competitive view. The horizontal axis measures the number of units of labour, L, and the vertical axis measures the real wage, written explicitly as $\frac{W}{P}$ – that is, the money wage, W, adjusted to real terms by deflation by the price level P. The following sections examine this model in more detail.

Labour supply

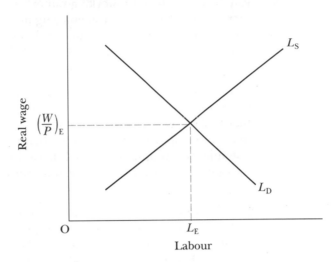

Figure 18.5   **The competitive aggregate labour market**

In Figure 18.5 the labour supply curve, L_S, is shown as upward-sloping; a higher level of the real wage increases the supply of labour in the economy, inducing more people to offer themselves for employment and accept work.

Question
Would you wish to work longer hours if the wage rate available was higher? Try to think carefully about the reasons for your decision.

You may not find it immediately obvious that labour supply should respond in this way to a higher wage. One of the main effects of a higher wage is to make individuals and households better off, and you may feel that this gives you the opportunity to work less, say four shifts instead of five, or to cut out weekend work or some overtime; or perhaps second earners will choose to pursue leisure or voluntary activities rather than add to household income. These arguments suggest that labour supply might be reduced when a higher wage is on offer. On the other hand, a higher wage means a more attractive return for the effort involved in each hour's work; leisure becomes more 'expensive' in terms of the income forgone. From this angle, taking advantage of the higher wage by working more hours seems a plausible response.

These reactions are, in fact, both correct. Each pinpoints one aspect of the way in which the wage influences labour supply, and they pull in opposite directions. The first effect is the *income* effect, which tends to reduce labour supply, since we are better off, and the second is the *substitution* effect, which increases labour supply as leisure becomes more expensive. Let us look in more detail at the reasons for these conflicting effects.

We have a fixed number of hours in the day available to us, and have to make the choice of how much of our time to allocate to work, which gives us our income and therefore our material standard of living, and how much to keep as leisure time, in which to enjoy both the standard of living our income buys for us, and the other aspects of life that we value. When a higher wage is on offer, we can derive a higher income from the same number of hours of work. Alternatively, we can maintain our income at the current level while working fewer hours and enjoying more leisure. Or we can divide the benefit, working rather less but still sufficient to earn an increased income while also enjoying more leisure. In general, since both income and leisure are desirable in themselves, the reaction to greater opportunities is to take more of both. This is the income effect. It leads us to take an increase in leisure, so reducing our labour supply.

On the other hand, a higher wage means that each period spent working becomes more worthwhile, in terms of the extra consumption purchases that it allows us to make. Equivalently, the 'cost' of leisure increases – that is, its opportunity cost rises – because we lose more, in terms of potential consumption, for each period in which we choose not to work. This gives the incentive to substitute work for leisure, increasing labour supply.

The impact of a higher wage on labour supply is therefore inherently ambiguous, depending as it does on the balance between these two offsetting effects. In drawing the L_S schedule upward-sloping, we are *assuming* that the substitution effect is more powerful than the income effect. If we regard the income effect as more powerful, the schedule becomes backward-bending, as in Figure 18.6, where labour supply falls as the wage rises.

So far I have talked, rather evasively, about the quantity of labour supplied at different wage levels. In the aggregate labour market, labour supply comprises two parts: the supply of hours, by people in work; and the supply of workers, through entry or return to work by those out of the labour force. In terms of the supply of hours, a backward-bending labour supply curve is eventually to be expected; as the wage rate rises ever higher, sooner or later we will take more leisure time and reduce our labour supply. This is the evidence of the long run of history. As wages have risen since the Industrial Revolution, average weekly hours have fallen by up to one-half. On the other hand, higher wages induce more *participation*, particularly by retirees and home-makers.

I have discussed the labour supply decision in some detail. You will see later in the chapter that it plays a crucial role in the concept of unemployment and the types of macroeconomic policies advocated by the competitive approach.

Labour demand

Turning now to the other side of the labour market, we will consider the firm's demand for labour. We will concentrate on the short run, when capital stock and technology are taken as fixed, and the firm can vary its rate of output only by varying its labour input. This focus on the short run is purely to keep matters simple. The implications for the relationship between labour demand and the wage has the same essential features, after a more elaborate analysis, if we allow capacity to vary. (Note that here we

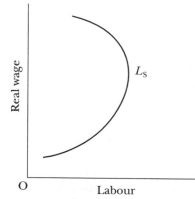

Figure 18.6   **Backward-bending labour supply**

have reverted to the definition of the short run in terms of non-adjustment of capital, which is standard in production theory, rather than the definition in terms of non-adjustment of nominal wages which we were using in the previous sub-section.)

The labour demand curve in Figure 18.5, labelled L_D, shows the number of workers the firm would wish to employ at different levels of the real wage. (The analysis could also be conducted – as in Chapter 21 – in terms of the number of labour hours supplied and demanded.) The curve is downward-sloping, as the firm will employ more workers when the wage is lower. The reason for this is that the firm is assumed to face diminishing returns to labour, as the variable factor. As explained in Chapter 4, Section 4, and in Chapter 14, Section 4, diminishing returns implies that the marginal product of labour declines as each additional unit of labour is added to a given capital stock. Note that marginal product here refers to the marginal physical product of labour (MPP_L).

The implication of diminishing returns to labour is that if the wage is lowered, the firm will demand more workers, since it can profitably employ them; or, equivalently, that the firm will be willing to take on more workers only if the wage is lowered.

Market equilibrium

Market clearing is central to the competitive approach. In Figure 18.5 the labour market clears at employment level L_E and real wage $\left(\dfrac{W}{P}\right)_E$, where labour demand just equals labour supply. This is an equilibrium outcome in that firms obtain all the workers they wish to employ at wage $\left(\dfrac{W}{P}\right)_E$ and all workers wishing to be employed at that wage find a job.

The crucial feature of the competitive labour market model is that neither excess demand for workers by firms, nor excess supply of labour from unemployed workers, can persist. Excess demand for labour by employers, as when the real wage is below its equilibrium level at $\left(\dfrac{W}{P}\right)_L$ in Figure 18.7,

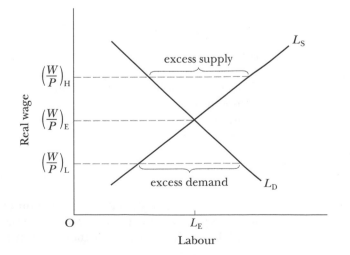

***Figure 18.7* Equilibrium in the competitive aggregate labour market**

will lead to the bidding up of money wages as employers compete against each other for workers. This raises the real wage, simultaneously reducing labour demand and increasing labour supply. This process continues until the excess demand has been eliminated.

Similarly, excess supply, in the form of more workers seeking jobs than there are jobs on offer at a wage such as $\left(\dfrac{W}{P}\right)_H$ in Figure 18.7, will lead to lower wages being offered and accepted. This downward pressure on money wages will persist until the real wage has been pushed back to its market-clearing level. This balancing of labour demand and labour supply through wage flexibility is the essence of the competitive market-clearing approach.

The competitive market-clearing approach has powerful implications both in the aggregate and at the level of the firm. In the aggregate, we can see that there is one, and only one, level of employment that is consistent with equilibrium in the labour market. This level is L_E. Only this level allows employers to obtain all the workers they wish at the going wage while simultaneously giving a job to all those seeking work at that wage. 'Full employment' has a natural, and quite specific, interpretation in this context: it is the level of employment at which labour demand and labour supply are equalized at the market-clearing real wage.

When it operates in a competitive environment, the firm becomes a wage-taker. It must pay the market-clearing wage $\left(\dfrac{W}{P}\right)_E$. Any firm offering less will lose its workforce, since employment is available for all seeking it at $\left(\dfrac{W}{P}\right)_E$.

Equally, not only is there no incentive to pay more, as the firm can obtain all the workers it wishes at this wage, but paying more would put it at a competitive disadvantage.

You will have noticed that in drawing these strong implications we are simply following through in a labour market context the predictions of the model of perfect competition developed for the product market in Chapter 7.

3.2 Aggregate supply in the competitive approach

The labour market is the first of our building blocks in the analysis of the competitive approach to aggregate supply. The next step is to build forward from the labour market outcome which we have just derived to the output decision of the firm.

From employment to output: the production function

We have just established that, in the competitive approach, each firm is a wage-taker, as market forces require it to pay the market-clearing wage. The firm's level of employment is then determined by its labour demand curve

L_D. This is shown in Figure 18.8, where L_E is the level of employment chosen by the firm. (Remember that here we are considering firm-level employment, not aggregate employment.)

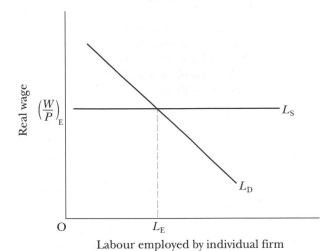

Figure 18.8   **Employment in the competitive firm**

With its level of employment determined, the firm's rate of output follows directly from its production function. This is shown in Figure 18.9, where the horizontal axis again measures the firm's level of employment, L, and the vertical axis measures its output (Y) determined by a standard production function of the type you have seen before with diminishing returns to labour, $Y = f(L)$. With employment at L_E, the firm's output is Y_E.

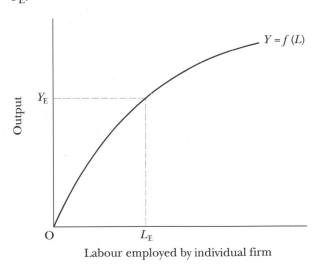

Figure 18.9   **Output by the competitive firm**

Confronting the price level

The final step in the analysis is to return to the macroeconomic level and examine how these equilibrium levels of employment and output are affected by the price level. In the competitive approach the answer is: 'not at all'; the aggregate supply schedule is vertical. As I spell out the reasoning leading up to this short and simple answer, you will recognize it as similar in a number of respects to the argument I used above to establish that the *LAS* in the New Keynesian case is also vertical.

Suppose the price level were to increase. With the money wage unchanged, the real wage would be eroded. This would result in a situation such as $\left(\dfrac{W}{P}\right)_{\mathrm{L}}$ in Figure 18.7. Again, the resulting increase in labour demand (along the aggregate L_D curve) and fall in labour supply (along the aggregate L_S curve) creates an excess demand for labour. This puts upward pressure on the money wage as employers bid against each other for scarce labour. This process continues until the excess demand has been eliminated, which happens only when the real wage has been restored to its equilibrium value, $\left(\dfrac{W}{P}\right)_{\mathrm{E}}$.

Question

How big is the rise in the nominal wage as compared to the original price rise?

The money wage will then have risen in exactly the same proportion as the price level. For example, if the price level were initially to double to $2P$, the money wage would also have to double to $2W$, to restore the real wage $\dfrac{W}{P}$ to its equilibrium level $\left(\dfrac{W}{P}\right)_{\mathrm{E}}$, at which supply and demand are equal. Since the market-clearing wage is unchanged, the firm's employment remains unchanged, and with it the level of output. In the competitive market-clearing model, employment and output are invariant to the price level. The *AS* curve is vertical, as shown in Figure 18.10.

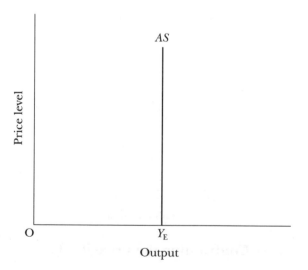

Figure 18.10   **A vertical aggregate supply curve**

Short-run aggregate supply

After the emphasis on the distinction between short- and long-run aggregate supply in the discussion of the New Keynesian approach in Section 2, you will be wondering whether the *AS* schedule we have just derived in the competitive approach is short- or long-run. A first answer is that in one respect it is both, and that there is no meaningful distinction in this model between the two. Remember that I defined the short run as the period during which some relevant variable is held fixed, so that only a partial adjustment can be made. The long run involves full adjustment. In the competitive approach, as I have just described it, markets function flexibly. There are no rigidities systematically preventing the market from establishing the equilibrium price. A distinction between the short run and the long run is unnecessary.

While this is the essential spirit of the competitive approach, the concept of a vertical aggregate supply schedule, where total output does not vary with the price level, poses a major problem for adherents of the competitive approach. That problem is the persistence of macroeconomic fluctuations or the business cycle. As Chapter 16 showed, there is consistent evidence, across countries and time periods, that output and prices move together over much of the cycle, rising together on the upswing and pausing or reversing together during recessions. (When prices are rising on a long-term basis, as has been the case throughout the post-war period, the cyclical movement in prices is more accurately described in terms of rising or falling inflation rather than rising and falling prices. The difference is not important in the present context.)

This problem has been readily acknowledged by the main group who adopt the competitive approach, the New Classical school. In response to it they have devised a model of an upward-sloping short-run aggregate supply curve which still retains the essential feature of competitive markets, namely that prices adjust flexibly to balance demand and supply. The central idea, attributable to Robert Lucas, has come to be known as the 'imperfect information' or 'price surprises' model. The individual producer, who sells in a competitive market, keeps a close and continuous watch on the price at which the product is being bought and sold on the market, without of course having any power to influence it. Producers are also consumers, and purchase a wide range of other goods. However, it is impossible to monitor all these prices continuously, as they move with shifting demand and supply conditions as well as any general inflation.

Producers have imperfect information about the overall level of prices. In particular, when they observe a rise in the price of their own product, they do not know whether this is a relative price change, affecting their product specifically, or whether it is part of a general inflationary trend. But a relative price change calls for an expansion of output, while general inflation does not. Producers face the problem of extracting the 'signal' of a relative price shift from the 'noise' of general inflation. They must make their output decisions on the basis of the price they observe for their own product relative to their best expectation about prices in general. Therefore, when prices overall rise unexpectedly, producers individually interpret this as a rise in their own relative price. Each firm increases its output and total output rises. Aggregate supply increases when the price level rises unexpectedly.

This confusion about prices can only be a short-run situation. If the price surprise turns out to be purely temporary, output reverts immediately to its equilibrium level. If the change in the price level is permanent, then as soon as producers become aware of this they revise their price expectations upwards. The *SAS* schedule 'jumps' upwards.

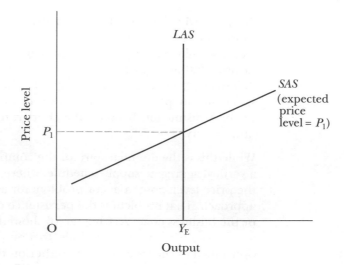

Figure 18.11   **Short- and long-run New Classical aggregate supply**

With the new situation fully incorporated into producers' expectations about the price level, output reverts to its 'full information' long-run level.

This is illustrated in Figure 18.11, where *SAS* is the short-run aggregate supply schedule. It is drawn for an expected price level of P_1, equal to the initial actual price level, and is upward-sloping, as producers vary output in response to 'price surprises'. Whenever expectations are revised, the *SAS* curve shifts upwards or downwards by the same amount. The aggregate supply schedule derived above is now labelled as the long-run supply schedule, *LAS*, where in the long run there are no price surprises and we have a full-information equilibrium.

You will see that Lucas's approach introduces yet another type of short run. The fixed element now is information or knowledge about the general price level. In the short run, producers form their best expectation about the general level of prices, and base their output decisions on the observed price of their own product relative to this. When price surprises occur, they respond by varying output. In the long run there is full information, and no price surprises.

This, and other ideas which Lucas has contributed to New Classical macroeconomics, can be followed up in Lucas (1981). A useful critique is Hoover (1988).

4   Combining aggregate supply with aggregate demand

In the preceding sections two very different views of the nature and functioning of the macroeconomy, the New Keynesian and the competitive or New Classical view, have generated essentially similar views of aggregate supply. The *AS* schedule is vertical and independent of the price level in the long run, but upward-sloping and varying in the same direction as the price level in the short run. In this section we will take advantage of these similarities to gain some initial insights into the functioning of the economy as a whole, combining the *AS* schedules with the *AD* schedule developed in Chapter 17. A number of general conclusions emerge from this, which are widely accepted. In the remaining section we will return to the differences between the two approaches, in terms of their interpretation of the functioning of the economy, and their policy approaches.

The three basic schedules are combined in Figure 18.12. *AD* is the downward-sloping aggregate demand curve familiar from Chapter 17. *LAS* is the long-run aggregate supply curve, which is vertical at Y_E, the economy's equilibrium level of output, once all adjustments have been completed. The intersection of the *AD* and *LAS* curves, at point A, gives the initial equilibrium price level, P_E, at which total demand just equals the economy's aggregate level of output. The mechanism through which the price level balances aggregate demand with total output is already familiar to you from Chapter 17. Variation in the price level, along the *AD* schedule, alters international competitiveness, and therefore the levels of exports and imports. In addition, changes in the price level may influence domestic interest rates, which in turn will affect aggregate demand. Adjustment in the price level can continue, altering expenditures, competitiveness and trade flows, until demand just equals output.

SAS is the short-run aggregate supply curve. The concept of the short run has to be defined for each approach. In the New Keynesian model, *SAS* traces out the level of output that would be supplied at different price levels, with the contract money wage held fixed. In the New Classical model, *SAS* shows the response of output to prices, given the expected price level. In both approaches, however, it is upward-sloping, and takes its initial position from the equilibrium price level, P_E.

Several further variables do not appear explicitly, but can be determined. Since the diagram relates to the product market, wages and employment are hidden. However, employment has to generate output level Y_E, and therefore its equilibrium level, L_E, for the economy as a whole is implied through the production function. This employment level, L_E, has to be associated with a particular value of the real wage. Given the price level P_E, the required level of the money wage is determined as W_E in Figure 18.5. Similarly, the expected price level does not appear explicitly, but must be equal to the actual level, P_E.

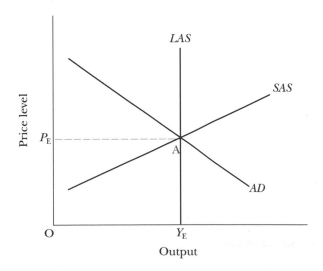

***Figure 18.12*   A composite view of the aggregate economy**

4.1   Analysing a demand expansion

We will now trace the effects of a change in the level of aggregate demand. Figure 18.13(a) repeats Figure 18.12, but with *AD*, *SAS* and P_E re-labelled with a subscript '1'. Aggregate demand is now increased, due for example to a monetary or fiscal expansion, or a world boom raising demand for exports. This shifts AD_1 outwards to AD_2, leading to upward pressure on prices at the initial level of output. The economy moves along the short-run aggregate supply schedule SAS_1 to point B, where both prices and output are above their initial levels, at P_2 and Y_2 respectively. The expansion of demand leads to an increase in output with rising prices. This is the typical upswing phase of a demand-led boom.

However, these can be short-run effects only. As the price level rises, the short-run supply curve cannot remain at SAS_1. Money wage contracts are renewed, or price expectations revised, shifting the *SAS* curve to SAS_2 by the vertical distance $P_2 - P_1$, corresponding to the rise in the actual price level. This is shown in Figure 18.13(b), with the new equilibrium at point C.

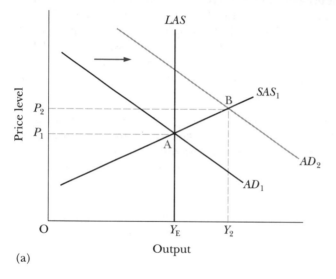

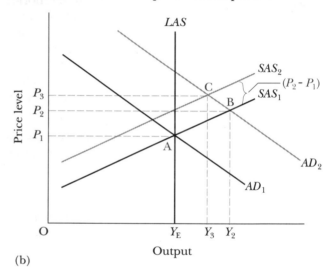

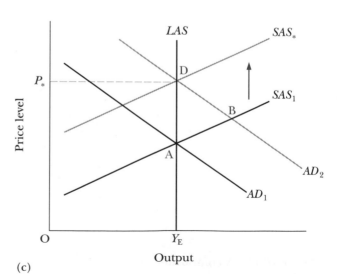

Figure 18.13   **Analysing a demand expansion**   (c)

This new position at C has two striking features. First, the price level is again higher, at P_3, than at the previous point B. The adjustment process, shifting the *SAS* curve, reinforces the initial price rise. However, the upward pressure on prices no longer comes from the demand side (*AD* is unchanged at AD_2) but from the supply side, through the shift of *SAS*. Price push replaces demand pull as the motor-force for the continuing rise in prices. Moreover, output is now lower, at Y_3, than previously. The expansion of output is being reversed. In this second phase, therefore, the price level continues to move upwards while output falls. The expansion phase of the boom is over, but the price rises continue.

However, the adjustment process set in motion by the demand expansion has not yet reached a conclusion. At C price push has increased the price level further, to P_3. This implies a further erosion of the real wage, or price surprise, and hence a further upward adjustment of *SAS*, bringing yet another upward push to the price level. Does this price spiral, i.e. the situation where rising prices lead to further rises, continue indefinitely, or what is required for it to come to an end? And how far does output fall? You will see from the figure that as the adjustments continue, they become progressively smaller: P_2 to P_3 and higher price levels, and Y_2 to Y_3 and lower output levels.

In Figure 18.13(c) the process ends at point D, when output has contracted back to its long-run equilibrium level of Y_E and the price level has risen to P_*. This is the price level at which demand is back into balance with long-run aggregate supply, Y_E. In terms of the diagram, the upward shift of *SAS* along the AD_2 curve continues until SAS_* reaches the intersection of AD_2 with *LAS*.

In terms of the economic processes underlying Figure 18.13(c), the progressive rise in the price level, through price push, reduces aggregate demand: competitiveness falls, interest rates may rise, and aggregate demand continues to fall until it is back into balance with the sustainable rate of output, Y_E. The excess demand generated by the initial expansion has been eliminated by higher prices. The increased demand induced an expansion of output, but on a purely temporary basis. The only permanent effect is a higher price level.

We have two stories of the adjustment process. In New Keynesian terms, wages are finally restored to their equilibrium real level when the rise in money wages, and therefore in the *SAS* curve, exactly matches the rise in prices. When the real wage is restored to its equilibrium level, employment and therefore output revert to Y_E. In New Classical terms, price surprises are eliminated when the excess demand has been eliminated and price expectations catch up with the actual price level. This occurs when demand equals output at its long-run level Y_E.

The response of the economy to an expansion of aggregate demand therefore comes in two phases. Initially there is an upswing in which both output and prices rise. However, this is only a temporary phase. The rising prices bring further price push, and output begins to contract. After the adjustments are completed, the increase in aggregate demand has no permanent effect on output. The only long-run consequence of the increase in demand is that the price level is permanently higher.

Exercise 18.1

Explain what would happen during the converse process of deflation following a demand contraction that has been initiated, for example, by a tight monetary policy. Illustrate your explanation with a diagram.

Before you conclude that demand management can achieve nothing except changes to the price level, a cautionary point should be noted. While the mechanism just described is perfectly general, the demand expansion was launched when output and employment were already at their long-run equilibrium rates. While this is the natural starting point for a theoretical analysis, it is not necessarily the starting point for practical policy! The central message remains, however: demand expansion raises prices, and expansion ahead of the sustainable rate of output will eventually be dissipated in higher prices.

Exercise 18.2

Using a diagram, examine the implications of an increase in aggregate demand for an economy with output below the long-run equilibrium level.

4.2   Analysing a supply shock

The concept of a supply shock, and its impact on output and prices, has been familiar since the dramatic increases in the world price of oil made by OPEC (the Organization of Petroleum-Exporting Countries) in the 1970s. These initiated an upsurge of inflation world-wide, accompanied, in many oil-importing countries, by the first significant recession of the post-war period. From the point of view of oil users (but not the oil producers!) the OPEC price increases were a negative supply shock. A much earlier, gruesome example was the Black Death, the plague which spread across much of western Europe in the middle of the fourteenth century, causing the deaths of one-third of the population, and resulting in a severe shortage of labourers to work the land. A less extreme example is the loss of productive capacity due to the destruction of physical plant, or the exhaustion of agricultural land or natural resources. More subtly, plant and equipment may suffer premature obsolescence because of the pattern of technical change.

Supply shocks can, however, also be positive, for example due to the discovery of a new natural resource, or a technological breakthrough which increases the economy's overall productivity. Fortunately, the long run of history indicates that, while adverse shocks can be extremely abrupt and unpleasant, positive supply shocks are on balance more common and more durable.

Exercise 18.3

Would you classify tighter standards of environmental regulation as an adverse supply shock, if they require firms to reduce their emission of pollutants?

A useful first distinction is between supply shocks which impact primarily on *LAS* and those affecting *SAS*. We will take them in that order.

Shifting long-run aggregate supply

You will remember that we derived the economy's long-run rate of output, Y_E, through the production function. This was shown for the firm in Figure 18.9, and is redrawn for aggregate output in Figure 18.14. Unlike Figure 14.4 in Chapter 14, the aggregate production function here is drawn for a given level of capital input, K, so that output Y is a function of labour input, L. So I will write this relationship as: $Y = g(L)$. A positive supply shock brings an upward shift in the production function; more output is produced at each level of employment. Output increases from Y_1 to Y_2 at an aggregate employment of L. A positive supply shock can occur either through an increased use of capital, or through improvements in technology, increasing the output obtainable from existing resources.

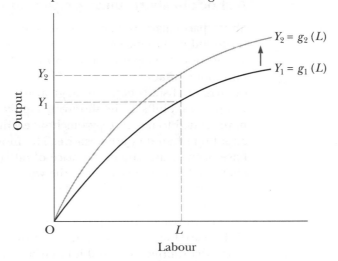

Figure 18.14   A shift in the aggregate production function

Let us now look at the effects of this in the *AD/AS* framework. Figure 18.15(a) shows the *AD* and *LAS* schedules as before, with the sustainable rate of output now labelled Y_E^1, and the long-run aggregate supply schedule LAS_1. For clarity, the *SAS* curve is omitted. Equilibrium is at A, where aggregate demand is equal to the initial equilibrium rate of output, Y_E^1, at

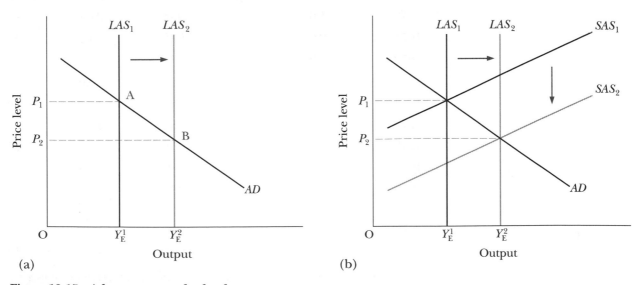

(a)   (b)

Figure 18.15   A long-run supply shock

price level P_1. A positive supply shock shifts the long-run aggregate supply schedule outwards, to LAS_2. The price level, at B, the new intersection with AD, is now lower, at P_2. This is a key result: an increase in long-run aggregate supply brings increased output and a lower price level. Conversely, an adverse supply shock reduces the economy's long-run rate of output and puts upward pressure on the price level. With supply shocks, output and price move in opposite directions.

SAS plays a less central role in this process. The increase in supply puts downward pressure on the price level, to which wage setting and price expectations adjust, shifting the SAS schedule downwards, as shown in Figure 18.15(b).

A shock to short-run aggregate supply

Shifts, particularly outwards, in the long-run aggregate supply curve are of profound importance for macroeconomic well-being, and are often treated as part of the analysis of growth rather than fluctuations. Indeed, you may have noted that the analysis in the last sub-section was closely related to the discussion of shifts between no-growth equilibria in Sections 4 and 5 of Chapter 14. Shifts in the short-run supply schedule, on the other hand, have tended to be more pyrotechnic events, and to attract particular attention when they are negative. The most spectacular recent instances have been in the case of the price of oil. Table 18.2 shows the huge changes that have occurred in the world oil price, both upwards and downwards, over the past two decades. Supply shocks affecting SAS tend to be known as 'price shocks' when, as with the oil price, their impact is primarily through the supply price of a commodity. The objective of the OPEC cartel was to force up the oil price; control of output, and the power to restrict supplies, enabled it to enforce the higher price successfully for more than a decade.

Table 18.2 **The price of oil (OPEC average) 1970–93**

	$ per barrel	Annual % change		$ per barrel	Annual % change
1970	1.6	—	1982	34.4	−4
1971	2.0	25	1983	29.9	−13
1972	2.2	10	1984	28.6	−4
1973	2.6	18	1985	28.0	−2
1974	9.9	281	1986	15.6	−44
1975	10.9	10	1987	17.1	10
1976	11.9	9	1988	13.5	−21
1977	12.8	8	1989	16.9	25
1978	13.1	2	1990	21.0	24
1979	19.0	45	1991	17.9	−15
1980	31.9	68	1992	17.5	−2
1981	35.9	13	1993	15.2	−13

Source: *National Institute Economic Review, Statistical Appendix*, various issues

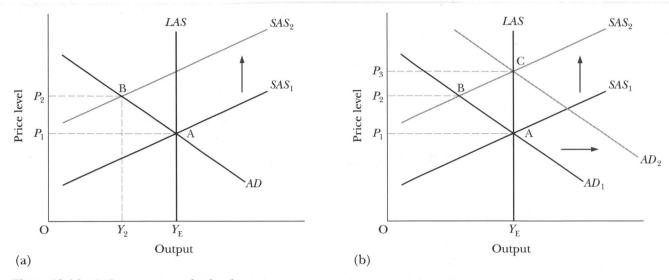

Figure 18.16   **A short-run supply shock**

I will illustrate the case of an oil price increase for an oil-using economy. When the price of oil rises, both mark-up and competitive pricing require a corresponding rise in the supply price of final output. In Figure 18.16(a) this is shown by the upward shift of the short-run aggregate supply schedule, from SAS_1 to SAS_2. This now intersects AD at point B. The immediate effect of the shift of SAS is twofold. The price level rises to P_2, and output falls to Y_2. The oil price increase is both inflationary, in its effect on prices, and deflationary, in its effect on output. This unhappy combination of outcomes has come to be known as *stagflation*.

The economy now faces a harsh dilemma. At point B, output Y_2 is below productive potential Y_E. (I am regarding Y_E as unchanged by the oil price rise, ignoring effects such as the premature scrapping of high-cost capacity.) The issue is the route by which output can be restored to Y_E. If no action is taken, as in Figure 18.16(a), this adjustment process has to be deflation, with the low level of output and employment putting downward pressure on prices and money wages, pushing SAS back towards its original level SAS_1. The price level stabilizes only when output is back at Y_E. At that point the price level is restored to P_1. Notice, however, that the oil price remains at its new level. In order for the overall price level to revert to P_1, other cost elements, such as money wages, have to be reduced. The same point can be seen if we think about the effects of the oil price rise on wages and employment. The rise in the oil price means that producers can offer only a lower level of employment at the old real wage. If employment is to expand again, the real wage must be reduced. This requires a fall in money wages.

Since this deflationary adjustment is likely to be protracted and painful, a demand expansion is a tempting possibility. Figure 18.16(b) shows AD shifted outwards to AD_2, restoring output to its long-run level Y_E, but now at point C where the price level is still higher, at P_3. This achieves the same required reduction in the real wage, but by a demand-induced further rise in the price level. The downward adjustment of money wages is avoided, but at the cost of a permanently higher price level.

Exercise 18.4

For oil-consuming countries the plummeting of the oil price in the mid 1980s was a major macroeconomic windfall. You should now be able to trace its effects on inflation and output. What policy responses would you expect this to encourage?

4.3   The open economy

So far I have not directly addressed the issue of the open economy. While the major issues involved in the open economy lie more on the demand side, with exports and imports, aggregate supply is affected in two important respects.

In Chapter 17, imports were purchased as part of consumption or investment expenditure – that is, as final goods. But most economies also import substantial quantities of raw materials and other intermediate goods for further processing. As inputs into domestic production they are an element of costs, and their prices affect the position of the *SAS* schedule. When they rise, the *SAS* curve shifts upwards. This is exactly the analysis which we have just developed for the price of oil. In open economies, import prices fluctuate for two reasons. World prices change with global demand and supply conditions. Moreover, the price of imports to the domestic economy is affected by the exchange rate, which can change abruptly and by substantial margins. This will be discussed more fully in Chapter 19. Imports tend to be one of the major sources of 'price shocks'.

Import prices also influence aggregate supply through a second, less direct, channel. Consumers too are purchasers of foreign-produced goods and are affected by their prices. For consumers, the price level that determines the real wage is the weighted average of the prices of domestic and imported consumer goods, where the two categories are weighted by their shares in expenditure. In most countries in western Europe the share of imports is one-quarter or more. To emphasize this role of import prices, the real wage as seen by the employee is often termed the real consumption wage.

Definition

Real consumption wage

The real consumption wage $\left(\dfrac{W}{P_c}\right)$ is the nominal wage deflated by the price of consumer goods, including imports.

A rise in the cost of imported consumer goods reduces the real consumption wage. Whether wages are bargained or not, compensating money wage increases are required to protect real purchasing power. If these money wage adjustments go through, the *SAS* curve shifts upwards. If they do not, labour supply will be adversely affected, reducing employment and long-run output. When employees gain wage rises to restore the real consumption wage, the economy is described as being characterized by *real wage resistance*, or *real wage rigidity*. The implications of this for competitiveness and therefore for the effectiveness of an exchange rate devaluation are explored more fully in Chapter 19. For present purposes, we note that in the open economy external influences, working through import prices, affect aggregate supply as well as aggregate demand.

5 Macroeconomic analysis and policies: a comparison of approaches

This final section will compare and contrast the two approaches developed above – the New Keynesian and the competitive. I will first compare the 'world view' underlying each, drawing out their points of divergence over the functioning of the macroeconomy and the outcomes it generates. Their implications for unemployment are particularly crucial, and will be discussed in Section 5.2. This leads, in Section 5.3, to a review of the policy problem as each side sees it, and their policy approaches. The final part, Section 5.4, offers a critique, and some more speculative thoughts about future lines of development.

5.1   The microfoundations

I have already emphasized that the competitive and New Keynesian approaches derive from very different world views. The essence of the competitive approach is the central role for market forces as the powerful and efficient mechanism by which prices balance supply and demand in all markets. This ensures that markets tend to clear continuously. Any persistent imbalance, involving excess supply or demand – such as unemployment – must derive from a malfunction of the market. The sources of malfunction are distortions to competition, caused, for example, by monopoly power of firms or unions, or government intervention. Distortions to competition thwart efficient market outcomes and should be eliminated. According to the competitive approach, the competitive market mechanism is both the most appropriate descriptive model and the ideal market form.

In the New Keynesian view, on the other hand, the model of perfect competition, where firms and workers are price- and wage-takers, is not appropriate to much of the modern economy. When market power is widely present, in many forms, in both labour and product markets, imperfect competition is the appropriate model. Market conditions impinge on wage- and price-setting processes, but are not decisive in determining the outcomes. While idealized forms of competitive markets can be supported on grounds of efficiency, they are not the most suitable representation of the real world.

The previous sections have shown, however, that in both views the *LAS* is vertical; there is a unique level of output and employment to which the macroeconomy tends, once all adjustments have worked through. The fundamental question is: do the two approaches lead to the *same* long-run outcomes? Or are the conceptual differences between them reflected in substantive differences? For reasons I will now discuss, the answer is that the two approaches envisage different outcomes, even in the long run.

5.2   Unemployment: the NRU and the NAIRU

We saw in Section 3 that the key element determining the long-run rate of output in the competitive approach is the equilibrium level of employment. This is the outcome of the process of market clearing in the labour market, where the real wage adjusts to equate the labour demand of firms with the labour supply from employees. The production function then translates this equilibrium level of employment into long-run aggregate supply. In the terminology originally introduced by Milton Friedman, these equilibrium or long-run levels have come to be known as the 'natural rates' of employment and output. The implications of the assumption of market clearing in competitive labour markets are best seen through their implications for unemployment. Since the process of market clearing implies demand equal to supply, any worker seeking a job at the market-clearing wage (on the labour supply curve) is matched by an employer willing to employ at that wage (on the labour demand curve). Therefore unemployment must also be an equilibrium. Any worker who is without a job at the natural rate of unemployment (NRU) is *voluntarily unemployed.*

Let us examine precisely what this means. Unemployment is voluntary when people who are available for, and seeking, work, choose not to accept employment at the going market wage. This 'natural rate' of unemployment involves two main groups. The first are those seeking work who have decided to reject what is currently on offer, and to continue to search for a better job. Both jobs and workers are heterogeneous, making 'job matching' important, and requiring a search to locate a suitable match. This 'frictional' unemployment associated with job search is both voluntary – reflecting decisions by workers seeking to do the best for themselves – and socially efficient, in that it helps achieve a proper match of job-holders with jobs. The second group are those, probably with low potential earnings, for whom employment may bring an insufficient improvement, or even a deterioration, in their financial position. While they may feel frustrated by this, unemployment is still voluntarily chosen as the least unsatisfactory of the disagreeable alternatives.

Voluntary unemployment is thus a valid and important concept. However, in the competitive approach it is the *only* type of unemployment consistent with a properly functioning labour market. Any unemployment in excess of this must be due to market distortions, such as the monopoly power of unions, frustrating the efficient working of the labour market.

In the New Keynesian view, on the other hand, with price setting and wage bargaining, equilibrium requires *mutual consistency* between wages and prices for both firms and workers. For firms, the prices they are setting for their products give an adequate mark-up over the wages they pay. For workers, the wages agreed are satisfactory, given the prices they face. This mutual consistency is necessary to prevent upward or downward pressure on prices and wages, and the emergence of a wage-price spiral. Because of this property, the long-run levels of employment and output in the New Keynesian view are based in the clumsily named non-accelerating-inflation rate of unemployment (NAIRU).

The element that is crucially *not* involved in the NAIRU is market clearing in the competitive sense. Equilibrium for firms and workers in setting wages and prices involves mutual accommodation of others' requirements. While this equilibrium is achieved through the changing level of unemployment, which alters the balance of bargaining power, compatibility between firms and workers does not require compatibility with the needs or aspirations of the unemployed. Labour market conditions, as reflected in unemployment, have only an indirect impact on the wage bargain.

Moreover, the level of unemployment implied by the NAIRU will be systematically *higher* than natural rate unemployment. You will remember

Definition

Natural rate of unemployment

The natural rate of unemployment (NRU) is the rate of unemployment when the labour market clears (at the natural rate of employment). At the NRU all unemployment is voluntary.

Definition

Non-accelerating-inflation rate of unemployment

The non-accelerating-inflation rate of unemployment (NAIRU) is the level of unemployment at which wage and price setting are mutually consistent, and the inflation rate is constant.

that with collective bargaining the wage is higher than the individual's supply price of labour. (In Figure 18.1 the bargained wage schedule lies above the labour supply curve.) With collective bargaining the wage is higher and therefore employment is lower than in the competitive situation. The success of collective bargaining in raising wages reduces the level of employment. Unemployment at the NAIRU is higher than at the NRU.

Is this additional unemployment voluntary or involuntary? In an immediate sense it must be involuntary. These are workers who are willing to work for the negotiated wage (indeed, for less than it) and who see apparently comparable people in employment at these wages. Firms are seen to be 'rationing' jobs at the negotiated wage. In a competitive situation the excess supply would put downward pressure on the wage, inducing an expansion of employment. Because of the bargaining equilibrium, firms do not reduce the wage, and would not expand employment even if the unemployed were to offer to work for a lower wage. The unemployment is involuntary, in that the unemployed would accept work at the going wage.

But in another sense the extra unemployment is also voluntary. The unemployed do not break away from the system, taking or even creating employment outside the sphere of collective bargaining in a competitive or unregulated sector. The higher wage established through collective bargaining creates the incentive to wait for a vacancy there. For this reason the unemployment is sometimes referred to as 'queuing' or 'wait' unemployment. The logic of queuing becomes even more compelling when we remember the continual turnover in the labour market. Every week some employees retire or leave the labour force, others leave their jobs, new jobs are created, while current ones are destroyed. Vacancies, replacements and recruitment mean that, for the individual, waiting can be the sensible strategy. But in the aggregate, jobs are not available for everyone. The distinction between voluntary and involuntary unemployment turns out not to be particularly helpful.

The NRU and NAIRU therefore represent different concepts of unemployment, arising from the different world views underlying them. How these differences are reflected in the respective policy agendas is the topic of the next section.

5.3   Supply-side policies

Although the NRU and NAIRU are the equilibrium rates of unemployment for the macroeconomy, this need not imply that they are set by the inexorable workings of the economic system, and therefore immutable. If we feel that the levels of unemployment at the NRU or NAIRU are too high, are there policies that will reduce them? This is an aspect of a wider question. When the *AS* and *AD* schedules were combined in Section 4, it was clear that the level of output is ultimately determined by the rate which the economy can sustain at the NRU or the NAIRU. A demand expansion brings only a temporary increase in output, with a sustained rise in prices, while an outward shift of the *AS* curve raises output and reduces the price level. If a sustained outward shift in supply can be achieved, then, at least in principle, demand can

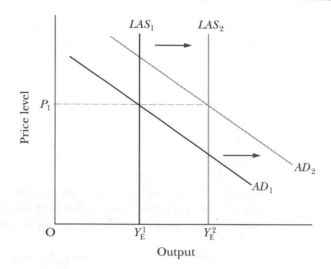

Figure 18.17 **Simultaneous demand and supply expansion**

expand continuously without upward pressure on prices. Figure 18.17 illustrates this.

An increase in demand from AD_1 to AD_2 can be accommodated at constant price level P_1 by the shift in aggregate supply from LAS_1 to LAS_2. The question to be addressed in this section, therefore, is: are there measures which government can take to help bring this about, through reducing the NRU or NAIRU, or otherwise? This brings us to the analysis of supply-side policies. We will approach this in two stages: labour market policies aimed at the NRU and NAIRU respectively, and then supply-side policies more widely.

Since the major practical measures in these directions have been taken in the UK over the past decade, this section will tend to focus on these. However, trends in the EU in the early 1990s, including issues highlighted in the Delors Report on unemployment, suggest that this pattern may be increasingly followed. A useful review of developments affecting the UK labour market in a comparative context is Barrell (1994).

Labour market policies and the NRU

For the competitive approach, the first role for policy intervention is to ensure that the labour market functions efficiently, with minimal distortions, to allow unemployment to approach the natural rate. Promoting labour market flexibility has been a continuing policy theme in Britain since 1979, and has prompted a wide range of measures. The most high-profile of these, and the one to which the government has attached the highest priority, has been the reduction of the power of trade unions. Measures aimed at this have included the progressive restriction of union actions in support of industrial disputes, the removal of their immunity from claims for civil damages arising out of strikes, and the abolition of the closed shop. Union power, on any measure, has fallen dramatically in Britain over this period. However, since unions have also been in retreat in other countries, notably the USA, it remains a matter of debate how far their decline in Britain is attributable to the more stringent legal framework, and how far to the rise in unemployment, or wider economic and social changes.

A second source of wage inflexibility is minimum wage regulation, seen as preventing wages adjusting to their market-clearing levels, or 'pricing workers out of jobs'. Wages Councils, which from the early years of the century had prescribed minimum rates of pay in a number of traditionally low-paying industries, had their powers reduced, and in 1993 were finally abolished (except for agriculture). With their demise, the only approximation to minimum wage regulation in Britain was eliminated. Trends in the EU in this area are unclear. In 1991 the European Commission delivered an Opinion that each member state should have in place some form of minimum wage protection. While Opinions are not binding, they are often a prelude to a legally binding Directive. On the other hand, in most countries of the EU, with the conspicuous exception of France, the levels of minimum wages have tended to be eroded over the 1980s (Gregory and Sandoval, 1994).

As a further thrust against the wage inflexibilities introduced by collective bargaining, the rescinding of the 'fair wages' resolution, which required private companies working on government contracts to adhere to pay rates set in the relevant collective agreement, was of considerable symbolic, if not practical, importance.

The natural rate itself will be reduced if job acceptances can be increased. Shorter periods of job search mean fewer workers searching at any time, and lower unemployment. I mentioned above that job search unemployment, to secure a good match of the worker with the job, is socially efficient. If increased efficiency in the search process can reduce search durations and therefore unemployment, there is a clear social gain. The establishment of Job Centres has been aimed at this; the functions of publicizing vacancies and helping to achieve job matches are separated from the payment of unemployment benefit. However, when job acceptances are accelerated because income support is curtailed, the social gain from the reduction in unemployment is less clear.

Efforts to reduce unemployment by raising job acceptances have focused on reform of the benefit system. Over the 1980s and early 1990s the rules on benefit entitlement have been made progressively more stringent, and the level of benefits has not kept pace with the growth of earnings. This is reflected in a fall in the 'replacement ratio', the level of income entitlements when out of work relative to average earnings (Dilnot and Walker, 1989). The influence of the level of benefits on unemployment has been a source of dispute. While large effects have been claimed (Minford, 1983), the weight of evidence seems to be that the level of benefits has little impact, although the structure of the benefit system has an important role in the differing patterns of unemployment between countries (Atkinson and Micklewright, 1991).

Greater labour market flexibility, through the labour demand side, has also been encouraged in Britain through reduced employment protection and lower benefits for temporary employment. However, potentially the most significant development, in response to the persistently high levels of unemployment in much of western Europe over the past decade, is the focus on the high social contributions levied on employers. These raise the level of labour costs, and may permanently lower employment, in addition to making European industry potentially uncompetitive on world markets. These issues feature prominently in the Delors Report on unemployment in the EU and are an area of active concern in the European Commission and, increasingly, member countries.

Policy implications of the NAIRU

Unlike the competitive view, the NAIRU approach has not received recent political endorsement. The discussion of policies therefore has to be more abstract, without the same basis in current measures.

The main feature which distinguishes the NAIRU from the competitive approach is the emphasis on the role of bargaining. While reducing trade union power might seem to fit the NAIRU approach, the main argument of New Keynesian theorists is that reducing the NAIRU implies structuring collective bargaining in the most economically efficient way, minimizing wage-push. It has been argued that the degree of centralization or co-ordination in wage bargaining has a U-shaped effect on employment, and conversely on the NAIRU. That is, when bargaining is carried out by a small number of 'encompassing' organizations, the inflationary consequences are reduced; it becomes easier to recognize that 'one person's pay rise is another person's price rise'. Highly decentralized bargaining, on the other hand, is similarly favourable in its limited inflationary consequences because small, localized bargaining groups are weak. The NAIRU, it is therefore conjectured, will be highest where bargaining is dominated by a moderate number of medium-sized unions (Calmfors and Driffill, 1988; Rowthorn, 1992). These ideas are relatively new and do not yet provide a sufficient basis for urging a reform of the structure of collective bargaining, although this could be a longer-term implication. Similarly, the NAIRU approach can be made the basis of a case for a revival of incomes policy, albeit in new forms (Layard, 1986).

More generally, since unemployment in the NAIRU view is seen as at least partially 'involuntary', there tends to be a greater emphasis on the urgency of the problem and on interventionism as part of a solution. In particular, a strong case can be made within the NAIRU framework for the integration of the benefits system with an active labour market policy, including placements, training and skills (Layard, Nickell and Jackman, 1991, Chapter 10; and 1994, Chapter 12).

Developing the supply side

The second link in the aggregate supply chain, the production function, opens up the issue of improving the productive efficiency of the economy as a whole, and promoting economic growth. There are numerous facets to this, often as much microeconomic as macroeconomic in character. You have met some of these already, such as deregulation and competition policy, privatization and regulation, industrial policy, and research and development. The important issue of education, skills and training is taken up in Chapter 21.

Exercise 18.5

President Norma's newly elected government in a major industrial democracy takes the competitive approach and decides to use demand-side policies to cut inflation, and supply-side policies to reduce unemployment.

1   Give some examples of policy measures, on both the demand and the supply sides, that would be appropriate to these objectives.

2   Draw an *AD/AS* diagram and use it to explain the effects of this combination of demand-side and supply-side policy measures on output and the price level.

Exercise 18.6

The government of President Norma loses the election to President Hilary, whose government takes the New Keynesian approach and decides to use demand-side policies to boost output and supply-side policies designed to maximize the degree of centralization or co-ordination in wage bargaining. However, the opposition parties force the government to compromise on the supply-side legislation so that the outcome is a labour market dominated by a moderate number of medium-sized unions.

Draw an *AD/AS* diagram showing the effects of this combination of demand-side and supply-side policy measures on output and the price level.

5.4   A concluding perspective

The analysis of aggregate supply gives considerable insight into the functioning of the macroeconomy. Combined with aggregate demand, as in Section 4, it gives an effective framework for analysing macroeconomic fluctuations, a framework which will be used extensively in later chapters. To conclude our discussion, this section will probe for weaknesses in the representations of aggregate supply as we have developed them. Then, in the light of some emerging doubts, I will offer some more speculative comments about possible future lines of development.

SAS and macroeconomic fluctuations

The central problem for macroeconomics remains the explanation of fluctuations in output, employment and prices or inflation, represented by the business cycle. Within the framework we have developed, cyclical movements are explained through the short-run aggregate supply schedule, given either demand or supply shocks. The two approaches I have discussed both derive an upward-sloping *SAS* schedule, although through different routes.

In the New Classical or competitive approach, output responds to a rising price level in the short run, as the producer/consumer cannot accurately observe the movement of overall prices. Since the competitive view is based on the establishment of correct prices by the efficient functioning of markets, 'wrong' decisions, to expand output erroneously, cannot be based on 'wrong' prices. They must be based on wrong perceptions of what are perfectly correct prices. Hence misperceptions play a crucial role. But while certain types of information can be costly to acquire, leading to the use of rules of thumb or other sources of error, it is not clear that this applies to the general price level, or rate of inflation. Retail prices are one of the most promptly and highly publicized macroeconomic indicators. Moreover, the typical cyclical upswing is of many months', even several years', duration and credulity is stretched to accept that misinformation could be so systematic and so persistent. While the tendency for output and prices to rise and fall together is incontrovertible, the adequacy of the misperceptions theory as an explanation of cyclical fluctuations seems in doubt.

The New Keynesian approach avoids the straitjacket of perfectly functioning markets. For the explanation of short-run supply responses its central element is money wage rigidity, due to the costs of negotiation, which leads to the erosion of the real wage as prices rise, and therefore to the expansion of employment and output. However, two criticisms can be levelled at this, one theoretical and the other practical. In terms of analytical acceptability, since the erosion of the real wage systematically disadvantages employees, an unanswered question is why they voluntarily enter into, and renew, contracts with this undesirable feature. Many forms of indexation are easily devised to adjust wages as prices change. Even if they could be criticized on detailed implementation, it is hard to accept that they would not still be an improvement over no adjustment at all. Yet such schemes are rare, with even Italy's *scala mobile* being withdrawn by 1992. The reason for the infrequent use of wage indexation may well lie in the second objection to the wage rigidity approach: that it does not fit the facts. In order for the expansion of employment and output to take place, the real wage must fall. The real wage should move *counter-cyclically*, falling as output rises. But the evidence is that real wages rise on a relatively constant trend, and to the extent that a cyclical pattern is present, it is *pro-cyclical* – that is, real wages and output move in the same direction. To explain this along New Keynesian lines would seem to require that nominal wages should be flexible and prices sticky, rather than the reverse.

A fascinating discussion of these difficulties and leading economists' worries about them can be found in Klamer (1984).

Equilibrium unemployment and hysteresis

A key concept for both approaches is the equilibrium rate of unemployment, the NRU or NAIRU. In each case this determines the economy's long-run rate of output, independently of the level of demand. A change in demand causes a temporary change in output and the price level, along the *SAS* schedule. Output, however, eventually returns to its long-run level, and the only permanent effect of the demand change is on the price level.

This separation of equilibrium unemployment, and the economy's potential output, from any influence of demand is increasingly coming into question. Much of western Europe has undergone a period of sustained deflation since the early 1980s, deriving from the determination to control inflation, both as desirable in itself and as a prerequisite for economic and monetary integration. This deflation has been accompanied by persistently high unemployment, much higher than in previous decades and, equally tellingly, higher than in the USA, where comparable deflation has not occurred. This suggests that the reduction in output and employment caused by the demand deflation may have extremely long-lasting, if not permanent, effects. This influence of past actual unemployment rates on current equilibrium unemployment is known as hysteresis (Blanchard and Summers, 1986).

Definition

Hysteresis

Hysteresis refers to the situation where an economy's long-run equilibrium depends on the short-run path of adjustment.

The effect of hysteresis is illustrated in Figure 18.18. Initial equilibrium is at point A, with output at its long-run level Y_E^1. A contractionary demand policy shifts AD_1 to AD_2, reducing output along *SAS* to point B. In the adjustment process discussed above, the deflation would reduce wages and prices still further, shifting *SAS* downwards, and back to equilibrium at point C, where

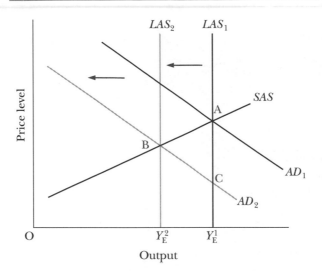

Figure 18.18   **The effect of hysteresis on long-run output**

output is restored to its original level Y^1_E. The hysteresis approach, on the other hand, suggests that the loss of output becomes permanent, with LAS_1 shifting inwards to LAS_2 and equilibrium output reduced to Y^2_E.

Two mechanisms have been suggested through which hysteresis may operate. The first involves capital stock and the rate of innovation. During a sustained recession, plant is scrapped and capacity is reduced and may even be closed down altogether. Any subsequent expansion of demand finds firms capacity-constrained, and supply responses inhibited. Moreover, during periods of capacity reduction, when no new equipment is being installed, innovations are not being made and long-term competitiveness is damaged. The second suggested channel is similar, but centres on the labour force. Persistently high unemployment brings long-term unemployment, and attrition of the skills and morale of the unemployed. This again permanently reduces sustainable output.

The tantalizing, and admittedly speculative, policy implication is that, if sustained demand deflation has brought higher actual and therefore equilibrium unemployment, might a sustained recovery of demand reverse the process?

The methodological implication is that analysing aggregate demand and aggregate supply separately may lead us to overlook some powerful interactions. Aggregate demand and aggregate supply schedules give us powerful tools for analysing the functioning of the macroeconomy, but we may eventually move beyond this framework.

PART 11

CHAPTER 19

MACROECONOMIC POLICY AND PERFORMANCE

ECONOMIC POLICY IN AN OPEN ECONOMY

by Andrew Stevenson

1 Introduction

1.1 Domestic policy and the exchange rate in open economies

In 1991, the UK's first – and last – full year of Exchange Rate Mechanism (ERM) membership, the economy contracted by 2 per cent, unemployment rose by more than half a million people and business leaders felt gloomy about the chances of recovery. Yet interest rates remained stuck at 10.5 per cent, offering consumers no incentive to increase their spending by saving less and borrowing more, and businesses no prospect of a lower sterling exchange rate to improve their competitiveness in world markets. Membership of the ERM committed the UK government to keeping interest rates high enough to maintain the sterling exchange rate within its prescribed range and so precluded the use of monetary policy – lower interest rates – to reflate the domestic economy.

On 16 September 1992, however, the UK government suspended sterling's membership of the ERM. UK interest rates quickly dropped to 6 per cent and sterling depreciated 15 per cent against the deutschmark. Almost immediately output began to grow again.

This historical episode illustrates perhaps more clearly than any other the principal theme of this chapter. With today's highly integrated world capital markets the monetary authorities can pursue an exchange rate target and implement whatever monetary policy this requires, or they can follow the monetary policy that is appropriate to domestic economic conditions and permit the exchange rate to find whatever level market forces dictate. They can target the money stock or the exchange rate, but not both.

A key condition for the emergence of this dilemma is that capital markets are much more international than they were in the 1950s and 1960s. For example, it is now a straightforward matter for UK residents to buy shares in a Japanese company or borrow from a French bank. This is an aspect of the increasing 'openness' of the world economy which is covered in greater detail in Section 1.2. Section 2 develops a model of foreign exchange markets and the determination of exchange rates by focusing on the role of trade flows and changes in imports and exports. The influence of trade flows makes itself felt mainly in the long run, so in Section 3 I introduce capital movements into the analysis in order to explain what drives exchange rate fluctuations in the short run.

The ground is now prepared for an analysis in Section 4 of the implications of alternative exchange rate regimes for the operation of monetary and fiscal policies. This is the analytical core of the whole chapter. Under fixed exchange rates, monetary policy on certain assumptions is powerless, while the effectiveness of fiscal policy at least in the short run is enhanced. The position is reversed under flexible exchange rates as the impact of monetary policy is reinforced while fiscal policy is ineffective. Hence the central result of the analysis: once international capital movements are brought into the picture, the authorities can control either the money stock or the exchange rate, but not both.

This outcome raises the question, 'Which should the authorities seek to control – the money stock or the exchange rate?' The arguments for and against adopting an exchange rate target as the centrepiece of macroeconomic policy are assessed in Section 5. The chapter concludes with a discussion in Section 6 of the ERM and the prospects for macroeconomic policy in the wake of its virtual collapse in 1993. (For an excellent review of many of the issues discussed in this chapter, see Pilbeam, 1992.)

1.2   The increasing 'openness' of the world economy

The definition of an open economy is one which carries out economic transactions with the rest of the world. The most obvious example of such transactions would be the sale of exports to and the purchase of imports from the rest of the world. Thus, the simplest measure of 'openness' of an economy is the share of foreign trade in a country's GDP. Table 19.1 sets out this indicator for a number of major economies.

Table 19.1   Share of trade in GDP in selected countries (%)

	1950	1960	1970	1980	1990
UK	26.00	20.10	21.88	26.00	26.02
USA	4.12	4.66	5.53	10.44	10.54
Italy	9.50	13.86	15.24	22.03	19.45
France	15.01	12.61	15.54	22.17	23.01
Germany	12.12	18.73	21.60	28.80	33.00

Source: *International Financial Statistics Year Book*, various years

These economies have generally become increasingly open over the post-war period, especially during the 1960s and 1970s. To a large extent, this trend reflects the post-war dismantling of the trade barriers which had been set up during the protectionist 1930s, described in Chapter 14. The GATT agreements, together with the setting up of regional free trading blocs such as the European Union, have reinforced this process of trade liberalization. Clearly, some economies are much more open than others. The USA is one of the least open of the Western economies. This is primarily because of both the size and the diversity of that country's economy, which makes it much more self-sufficient, reducing the potential gains from trade. The European economies are much more open, and this reflects both the growing degree of economic integration due to the European Union and the fact that these economies are not particularly rich in raw materials, and therefore much less self-sufficient than the US economy. Note also the rapid growth of trade in the case of the German economy, which reflects its importance as an example of export-led growth.

However, this is only half the story, since Table 19.1 focuses only on the importance of foreign trade transactions. Even more spectacular has been the increasing volume of international capital transactions over the post-war period. By capital transactions, I mean the international purchase and sale of financial assets. This can be in the form of residents of one country buying stocks and shares of a company or a government of another country, or alternatively, it can simply involve the switching of a bank account. Capital has become increasingly 'mobile', in a number of senses (see Chapter 11, Section 6.2). There are fewer foreign exchange controls imposed by individual countries. The UK finally abolished all capital controls in 1979, and European capital markets were further liberalized with the introduction of the Single Market in 1992. In addition, domestic financial markets have seen a considerable degree of deregulation and liberalization.

At the same time, with the development of global communications and the associated improvements in market information, capital transactions can now be effected much more quickly and more cheaply than, say, 20 years ago. These factors have combined to render exchange rates much more sensitive both to international interest rate differentials and to expectations about the future course of exchange rates. As we shall see, this is of central importance to the operation of domestic monetary policies. It is clear from Table 19.2 that the major economies are now much more open to international capital transactions than was the case in the mid 1970s. Note in particular the importance of capital movements in the case of the UK economy, where international transactions in bonds and equities amounted to almost seven times the size of UK GDP in 1990. An alternative measure of the importance of capital movements is the fact that in 1991, total world foreign exchange transactions averaged $880 billion a day, 60 times the volume of world trade. (See Bank of England, 1993.)

Table 19.2 **Cross-border transactions in bonds and equities[1] as a percentage of GDP**

	1970	**1975**	**1980**	**1985**	**1990**
USA	2.8	4.2	9.3	36.4	92.5
Japan	—	1.5	7.0	60.5	118.6
Germany	3.3	5.1	7.5	33.9	57.5
France	—	—	8.4[2]	21.4	53.3
Italy	—	0.9	1.1	4.0	26.7
UK	—	—	—	367.5	690.1
Canada	5.7	3.3	9.6	26.7	63.8

— not available.

[1] Gross purchases and sales of securities between residents and non-residents.
[2] 1982.

Source: Bank of International Settlements (1992) p.193

As a first step in providing a framework for analysing the current debates about exchange rate policy, it will be helpful to review and build upon the model of exchange rate determination which was outlined in Chapter 11.

2   The foreign exchange market, exchange rates and trade flows

2.1   Exchange rates: definitions and measurement

The *exchange rate* is the rate at which one currency is exchanged for another. It can therefore be regarded as the price of a unit of one currency in terms of another currency. In the UK it is customary to express the exchange rate as the number of units of foreign currency required to buy one unit of domestic currency, for example £1 = $1.50. A fall in the exchange rate is a depreciation and a rise in the exchange rate is an appreciation.

A *bilateral exchange rate* is the exchange rate between two currencies, and this is the kind of exchange rate which is most frequently cited in the media. Figure 19.1 shows the sterling/dollar rate and the sterling/ deutschmark rate for the period from 1976 to 1993. Note the appreciation of sterling against both the dollar and the deutschmark in the late 1970s/early 1980s, as the counterpart of Mrs Thatcher's domestic monetary policy. When Mrs Thatcher came to power, she afforded a high priority to reducing inflation by controlling monetary growth through high interest rates. In accordance with this anti-inflationary strategy, sterling was allowed to appreciate substantially. During the rest of the 1980s, sterling's steady depreciation against the deutschmark was interrupted only briefly by the strategy, adopted by Chancellor of the Exchequer Lawson, of pegging the exchange rate to the deutschmark. The substantial depreciation against the dollar in the early 1980s reflects the remarkable strength of the dollar in this period, which I discuss in greater detail later in this chapter.

The international pattern of bilateral exchange rates should always be consistent across financial centres and across currencies. Thus, if the £ is trading at $1.55 in New York it should also be trading at $1.55 in Tokyo. If exchange rates are not consistent with each other in this way, then

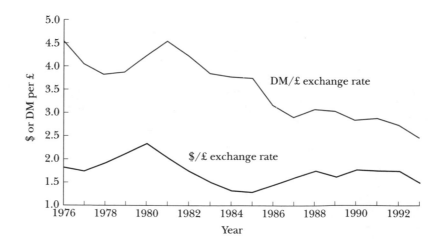

Figure 19.1   **UK bilateral exchange rates, 1976–93**

Source: *Financial Statistics*, various years

there is scope for profitable *arbitrage*, which means buying and selling currencies until the exchange rates are brought into line with each other.

Bilateral exchange rates show only the relative price of one currency in terms of another. If we are interested in the overall strength or weakness of a given currency, then we would need to have a measure of a country's exchange rate against the average of all other currencies. In this case we would require a measure of the *effective exchange rate*. The effective exchange rate is a weighted average of a country's exchange rate against all its trading partners where each bilateral exchange rate is weighted according to its share of the domestic country's trade. The effective exchange rate is expressed as an index.

Both bilateral and effective exchange rates as defined above are *nominal exchange rates.* This is to be contrasted with a country's *real exchange rate* which takes into account relative price levels. The bilateral real exchange rate is the ratio of two countries' price levels, translated into a common currency via the nominal exchange rate. Thus, we have

$$e' = e \cdot \frac{P}{P_F}$$

[handwritten annotation: bilateral real xchange rate = nominal x r · domestic price / foreign price]

Definitions

Bilateral real exchange rate

The bilateral real exchange rate is the nominal bilateral exchange rate multiplied by an index of domestic prices and divided by an average foreign price index.

where e' is the bilateral real exchange rate between the two countries, e is the nominal exchange rate, P_F is the price level in the foreign country, and P is the domestic price level. The real exchange rate can be taken as a measure of price competitiveness between the two countries. Price competitiveness is determined by the real exchange rate, not the nominal exchange rate. Thus, it is quite possible for a change in the nominal exchange rate to be offset by a change in domestic prices, leaving the real exchange rate (and therefore competitiveness) unchanged. For example, a 5 per cent depreciation of the nominal exchange rate will not affect the real exchange rate, if it is accompanied by a 5 per cent increase in domestic prices (relative to world prices).

Effective real exchange rate

The effective real exchange rate is the nominal effective exchange rate multiplied by an index of domestic prices and divided by an average foreign price index.

It is also possible to construct an effective real exchange rate, which would provide a measure of the domestic country's price competitiveness *vis-à-vis* the rest of the world. This would be a trade-weighted average of the relevant bilateral real exchange rates. The construction of such an index is complex since it needs to take into account price level changes in all of the domestic country's trading partners.

Finally, if the nominal exchange rate were exactly such as to equalize the purchasing power of a unit of domestic currency in both countries, that is, such that £1 could buy the same basket of goods in both countries, then the real exchange rate would be unity, and the nominal exchange rate would be generating what is known as *absolute purchasing power parity.*

Reflection

If you have travelled abroad, does your experience suggest that purchasing power parity holds?

Casual empirical evidence suggests that absolute purchasing power parity does not customarily hold, since travelling abroad shows that some countries are 'cheap' while others are 'expensive'. This is simply a way of saying that the domestic currency's real exchange rate is relatively high in the former case and low in the latter case.

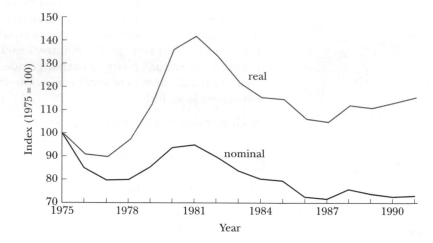

Figure 19.2 **UK effective exchange rates, 1975–91 (1975 = 100)**

Source: *International Financial Statistics Year Book* (1993) pp.718–19

Figure 19.2 sets out the nominal and real effective exchange rate indices for the UK. Note that both the real and nominal exchange rates fluctuate considerably, and note in particular the experience of the late 1970s/early 1980s, where both the real and nominal exchange rates for sterling appreciated significantly.

Exercise 19.1

You will note from Figure 19.2 that the real exchange rate appreciated by more than the nominal exchange rate in the period from 1978 to 1981.

1   What does this imply about UK inflation as compared to the rest of the world?

2   What would be happening if the nominal exchange rate appreciated and the real exchange rate depreciated at the same time?

2.2   A simple model of exchange rate determination

Exchange rates are determined in the foreign exchange market, which exists because of the currency needs of individuals and institutions involved in international trade or international capital transactions. In this section, I present a simple model of the exchange rate, similar to that outlined in Chapter 11. It is based on the limiting assumption that there are no capital transactions (that is, capital is completely immobile). This simplifies the discussion in the first instance, but I relax the assumption in Section 3.

Question

What did Chapter 11 suggest were the main factors influencing the demand for and supply of foreign exchange?

The demand and supply of foreign exchange in this simple model is directly related to the financing needs of importers and exporters. For example, a UK importer buying goods from the USA will have to buy dollars in order to pay the US exporter. Generally, individuals would not buy foreign exchange directly on the foreign exchange market, but rather would work through a bank, which would, in turn, work through a foreign exchange broker.

The key point to note about these transactions is that they must involve the exchange of one currency for another; when selling one currency, an institution must necessarily be buying another currency. Thus, factors affecting the demand for domestic currency in the foreign exchange market are equally factors affecting the supply of foreign currency, and vice versa.

Let me now set out a simple model of the foreign exchange market with the aid of Figure 19.3.

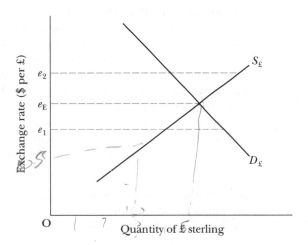

Figure 19.3   A simple model of exchange rate determination

In Figure 19.3, we measure units of the domestic currency along the horizontal axis, and the exchange rate (denominated as the number of units of foreign currency per unit of domestic currency – in this case, dollars per unit of pounds sterling) along the vertical axis. $D_£$ shows the demand for domestic currency in the foreign exchange market to be a downward-sloping function of the exchange rate, while $S_£$ shows the supply of domestic currency on the foreign exchange market to be an upward-sloping function of the exchange rate.

Looking first at the demand for domestic currency, the simplest explanation for the downward-sloping $D_£$ schedule relates to competitiveness and the demand for domestic exports. Looking back at the equation for e' above, you can see that for given P and P_F, a fall in e implies both a nominal and a real depreciation. This increases competitiveness and therefore increases the foreign demand for domestic exports. For example, suppose a UK manufacturer was producing a car which sold for £10 000 in the UK when the exchange rate was £1 = $1.50. This car would then sell for $15 000 in the USA. Suppose now that the exchange rate depreciates to £1 = $1.25. With the sterling price of the car unchanged, the dollar price would fall to $12 500, increasing the attractiveness of the car in the US market. We would therefore expect US imports of British cars to increase. US importers would therefore require more sterling to finance these purchases. Thus, a fall in the exchange rate has increased the demand for sterling in the foreign exchange market. You may be aware that I am making an assumption here about the price elasticity of demand for UK exports, and I return to this point later.

Similarly, the supply of sterling on the foreign exchange market reflects domestic demand for dollars, since in order to buy dollars, sterling holders have to sell sterling. A rise in the exchange rate is an appreciation, which, for given dollar prices, must reduce the sterling price of goods imported from the USA. This will increase UK demand for US exports, increasing the demand for dollars and therefore increasing the supply of sterling on the foreign exchange market. Again, the price elasticity of demand for the goods concerned has implications for this analysis.

We now have the ingredients of a simple model of exchange rate determination. At an exchange rate such as e_1 in Figure 19.3, the demand for sterling is greater than the supply. This can be taken to mean that exports exceed imports. In the foreign exchange market, the price of sterling is bid up – that is, the exchange rate begins to appreciate. As this happens, export demand (and therefore the demand for sterling) falls, while import demand (and therefore the demand for dollars and the supply of sterling) rises. This continues until the exchange rate reaches its equilibrium value of e_E. An analogous story applies to an exchange rate such as e_2, where import demand exceeds exports, and the exchange rate depreciates.

Note that in the above example, the authorities do not intervene at all in the market, and thus the exchange rate is said to be *freely floating*. Also, as the exchange rate rises to its equilibrium, the demand for sterling is falling and the supply of sterling is rising. This reflects falling exports and rising imports as competitiveness is reduced by the appreciating exchange rate. Thus, at the equilibrium exchange rate e_E, exports are equal to imports, which, in the absence of capital transactions, implies balance of payments equilibrium.

Of course, there are other factors besides the exchange rate which affect exports and imports. The exchange rate is important because it affects competitiveness, but we have already seen in Section 2.1 that it is the *real* exchange rate rather than the nominal exchange rate which is the appropriate measure of price competitiveness. Thus, it is possible for competitiveness to increase at a given nominal exchange rate, if domestic prices fall relative to world prices (each expressed in their own respective currencies).

Definitions

Exchange rate appreciation

Under flexible exchange rates, a rise in the exchange rate is market-led, reflecting an excess of demand over supply, and is described as an appreciation.

Exchange rate depreciation

A market-led fall in the exchange rate, reflecting an excess of supply over demand, is described as a depreciation.

Question

If foreign prices were to rise and domestic prices remain constant, what will happen to the demand for sterling?

In these circumstances exports will rise shifting the demand curve to the right, and imports will fall, shifting the supply curve to the left. Try drawing this for yourself. Under floating exchange rates, the result is an appreciation of the domestic currency. This is an interesting example, because it highlights one property which is frequently claimed for flexible exchange rates – namely that it insulates the domestic economy from the effects of world inflation. Since the appreciation described above will tend to reduce import costs, world inflation is prevented from being 'imported' into the domestic economy.

Competitiveness, however, as you know from Chapter 12, is not simply a matter of relative prices. Certain non-price aspects of competitiveness (for example, styling, marketing, after-sales service, reliability) are also likely to be important. For example, much of Italy's success in promoting export industries in the 1950s and the 1960s has been ascribed as much to fashion and style as to price competitiveness. Similarly, perceived reliability may be one of the factors behind the international success of the Japanese car industry.

Domestic and foreign income levels are also likely to be important in determining trade flows. Increasing incomes abroad will tend to increase demand for the domestic country's exports, simply because of market growth. Similarly, increasing domestic income will tend to increase the demand for imports.

Note that changes in any of these factors (other than changes in the nominal exchange rate itself) will affect exports and imports and therefore *shift* the demand and supply curves in Figure 19.3, with consequences for the nominal exchange rate.

Exercise 19.2

1   In the light of the above, what do you think are the likely consequences for a country's exchange rate, if its income growth is consistently above that of its trading partners.

2   How do you reconcile your answer with the experience of rapidly growing countries with customarily strong currencies, such as Germany?

Intervention in the foreign exchange market

Until now, I have assumed that the authorities do not intervene in the foreign exchange market, and that they let market forces determine the exchange rate. Turning to Figure 19.4, suppose that the authorities wish to stabilize the exchange rate at its current level, e_E. So long as the demand and supply curves remain at $D_{£1}$ and $S_£$, there is no need for the authorities to do anything.

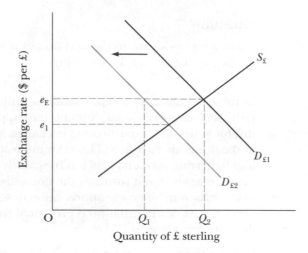

Figure 19.4 **Intervention in the foreign exchange market**

Question

What will happen if world income falls?

This means that, other things remaining equal, domestic exports will fall, shifting the demand curve to the left, say to $D_{£2}$. There is now excess supply of sterling (equal to $Q_2 - Q_1$) at the old exchange rate, and under floating rates this would lead to a depreciation to e_1. If the authorities wish to prevent this, they can intervene in the foreign exchange market, buying sterling (equal to the excess supply $Q_2 - Q_1$). However, if the authorities are buying sterling, they are necessarily selling foreign exchange. The authorities' stock of foreign exchange is called the *foreign exchange reserves*, and intervention to prevent a depreciation depletes their stock of reserves.

Another way of describing what is happening here is to say that the domestic country is running a balance of payments deficit equal to $Q_2 - Q_1$, and that this is being financed by the authorities running down their stock of foreign exchange reserves. In the long run, if the deficit persists, the authorities will need to carry out domestic policies to remove the deficit (for example, reducing domestic demand) or opt for a currency devaluation, that is, lower the exchange rate they are willing to defend (which would in turn remove the deficit by making exports more competitive).

Exercise 19.3

Starting from balance of payments equilibrium, what form of intervention would be required to peg the exchange rate if:

1   there was a sudden switch in tastes away from domestic exports, and

2   world inflation surged ahead of domestic inflation?

Finally, it is worth noting that these intervention policies have implications for the domestic money stock. When the authorities buy sterling (that is, when the balance of payments is in deficit), this reduces the amount of

Definition

Revaluation and devaluation

Under a system of fixed exchange rates, a decision by the authorities to stabilize the exchange rate at a higher level (to raise the exchange rate they are willing to defend) is a revaluation, while a decision to stabilize the exchange rate at a lower level (to reduce the exchange rate they are willing to defend) is a devaluation.

sterling in circulation and therefore reduces the domestic money supply. Alternatively, when the balance of payments is in surplus and the authorities sell sterling to peg the exchange rate, then the domestic money supply is increased.

Are the monetary consequences of exchange rate intervention avoidable? To some extent they are, if the domestic authorities undertake offsetting action. Such policies are referred to as *sterilization* policies. One possibility is that a surplus country might sell bonds domestically, to 'mop up' the domestic monetary consequences of exchange rate intervention using open market operations as described in Chapter 11, Section 5.2. A problem, however, is that domestic residents need to be persuaded to buy these bonds, and this will normally require some increase in domestic interest rates. Furthermore, as we shall see, once we introduce capital movements into the picture, such sterilization policies become distinctly problematical.

A major limitation of this simple model of exchange rates is that it assumes that there are no capital movements. But before rectifying that weakness in Section 3, I want to explore two developments of the simple model. The first concerns the speed of adjustment of exports and imports to changes in the nominal exchange rate, while the second takes up the distinction between nominal and real exchange rates in the context of the *AD/AS* model.

2.3   Exports, imports and exchange rates: further considerations

Exchange rates and trade elasticities

The model outlined in the previous section explained the slopes of the demand and supply curves of domestic currency in the foreign exchange market with reference to the effects of competitiveness on exports and imports. A rising exchange rate reduces competitiveness and thereby reduces exports (and the demand for domestic currency in the foreign exchange market).

However, it is important to note that these demands and supplies reflect the *values* (in terms of domestic currency) rather than simply the *volumes* of exports and imports.

Question

Would you expect an exchange rate depreciation to improve the external trade balance?

Let me focus first on exports. The first point is that the domestic currency value of exports is determined by their price multiplied by their quantity. Suppose that there is a fall in value of the domestic currency. On the assumption that exporting firms maintain the same price in domestic currency, then the foreign currency price of exports must have fallen. Demand for exports will increase, to a degree dependent on the price elasticity of demand facing the exporting firms in foreign markets. It is assumed here that firms face downward-sloping demand curves in their export markets. In terms of domestic currency, the value of exports must increase, and it will increase by more, the more elastic is the demand for exports.

However, turning to imports, the picture is slightly different. In this case, the foreign exporter will be likely to keep prices constant in foreign currency terms. This implies that import prices in domestic currency terms will rise, causing demand for imports to fall. Whether the value of imports rises or falls will depend on the price elasticity of demand for imports. If demand is elastic, the fall in demand will be proportionately greater than the increase in price, reducing the value of imports. However, if demand is inelastic, then demand will fall by proportionately less than price increases, thus *increasing* the value of imports.

The general conclusion from the above argument is that an exchange rate depreciation will be the more likely to increase the value of net exports (i.e. exports minus imports), the greater is the price elasticity of demand for exports and imports. If elasticities are very low, then it is possible for a depreciation actually to decrease the value of net exports. This conclusion is embodied more formally in what have come to be known as the Marshall–Lerner conditions, which state that for a fall in the exchange rate to increase the value of net exports (and for a rise to reduce it), the price elasticities of demand for imports and for exports must sum to greater than one (for a clear account of the elasticities approach, see Williamson and Milner, 1991).

Even this result is dependent on a number of important assumptions. The most important is that it requires the supply of both imports and exports to be infinitely price elastic, i.e. the supply curves to be horizontal. This is likely to be the case for imports, so long as we are dealing with a 'small country'. For example, an increase in UK demand for bananas is unlikely to push up the world price of bananas. However, it is much less likely to be the case for exports. Domestic exporters are likely to be operating on an upward-sloping aggregate supply curve in the short run and thus, as exporters increase output, export prices will rise, offsetting the competitive edge afforded in the first place by the depreciation. This effect is going to become all the more significant the nearer an economy is to full capacity. For such an economy, on the vertical long-run aggregate supply curve, a fall in the exchange rate will not increase net exports because the economy does not have the spare resources to meet the increased export demand. Under these circumstances, for the exchange rate reduction to 'work', it will need to be accompanied by some deflationary demand-management policies to 'make room' for the increased exports by reducing home demand.

Returning to the demand elasticities, is it reasonable to assume that the Marshall–Lerner conditions hold? Empirical evidence suggests that, in general, the sum of the import and export demand elasticities for developed countries lies somewhere between 1.5 and 2.5, thus satisfying the Marshall–Lerner conditions. However, these elasticity measurements are over a 2–3 year period, when demand patterns have time to adjust. Over a shorter period, it is probable that the demand elasticities are much lower. One reason for this may simply be that it takes time for consumers to switch allegiance away from the brand of one country's producer to that of another country. An additional reason may lie in the existence of contracts, and the lag before they are renegotiated.

These factors imply that the Marshall–Lerner elasticities will be lower in the short run than they are in the long run. Indeed, it has been estimated that long-run elasticities of demand in international trade are roughly double what they are in the short run. This can have implications for the value of net exports following a devaluation, namely that 'things can get worse before they get better'. This phenomenon is known as the 'J-curve' as illustrated in Figure 19.5.

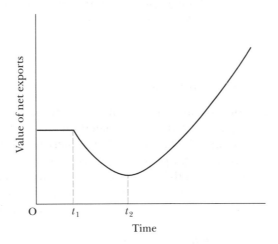

***Figure 19.5*   The 'J-curve'**

Measuring time along the horizontal axis and the value of net exports on the vertical axis, we assume the fall in the exchange rate takes place at time period t_1. The value of net exports initially falls. In domestic currency terms this could reflect, say, domestic importers continuing to purchase from abroad in the short run even in the face of increased import prices. In foreign currency terms, it could reflect lower export prices, but relatively inelastic export demand in the short run. However, once demand patterns begin to adjust to the new exchange rate at t_2, the value of net exports begins to rise. The time period $t_2 - t_1$ may be around nine months, and the time profile of the whole adjustment process traces out the letter 'J'.

There are other reasons why export and import volumes may respond sluggishly to an exchange rate change. For example, assuming that markets are not perfectly competitive and that there exists a degree of oligopoly, exporting firms might not reduce foreign currency prices in line with the exchange rate fall (preferring instead to increase their profits in terms of domestic currency), while foreign import-competing firms might cut their prices to match whatever price reductions the exporting firms did put into effect. Such pricing policies would leave export volumes largely unchanged.

Finally, we should note the importance of initial entry costs in international trade. An exporter seeking to enter another market abroad may need to engage in fairly heavy marketing in order to get a foothold in the foreign market. Besides market research and advertising, there are also the costs involved in setting up a marketing organization. These once-for-all costs involved in establishing a 'beach-head' in the foreign market have potentially important implications for the response of trade flows to exchange rate changes. Once an exporter has incurred these costs, they cannot be retrieved. Hence the firm is unlikely to retreat from a market because of an unfavourable change in the exchange rate in the short run, since re-entering the market will incur the same entry costs all over again. What this implies is that trade flows are unlikely to respond much to small changes in the exchange rate, especially if they are expected to be temporary. For example, in the first half of the 1980s, Japanese firms successfully penetrated a number of US markets, taking advantage of the soaring dollar to enable them to cover their entry costs. However, when the dollar depreciated in the second half of the 1980s, this penetration was not reversed. Japanese exporters had successfully established their beach-head in the USA and this was not to be lightly discarded, even in the face of an appreciating yen (for a clear account of the beach-head effect, see Krugman and Obstfeld, 1994).

Nominal versus real exchange rates

For a decline in the nominal exchange rate to be effective in increasing net exports, it must be translated into a real fall – that is, it must not be accompanied by an offsetting increase in domestic prices. However, there is a real danger of precisely this happening, since a nominal reduction tends to increase the domestic currency price of imports. If imported inputs are an important component of domestic costs, then an exchange rate reduction carries with it a clear inflationary threat. This threat is all the more serious if domestic wages respond to the increase in import prices, pushing domestic prices up even further.

I want to investigate this possibility further by reference to Figure 19.6, which depicts the *AD/AS* model built up in Chapters 17 and 18.

Question

How are the aggregate demand and aggregate supply curves influenced by changes in the nominal exchange rate?

Chapter 17 showed that the aggregate demand curve is a downward-sloping function of the domestic price level. In an open economy, an important reason for this is that net exports increase as domestic prices fall and competitiveness increases. Each aggregate demand curve is drawn for a given nominal exchange rate, and the discussion you have just worked through implies that a nominal reduction will cause the aggregate demand curve to shift to the right. The short-run aggregate supply curve is upward sloping and is drawn for a given level of wages and other input costs. If some inputs are imported, the aggregate supply curve is drawn for a given nominal exchange rate, and will shift upwards in response to a fall in the nominal exchange rate. Let me work through these relationships slowly.

Suppose we now begin from point A in Figure 19.6, with domestic income and output at Y_1 and the domestic price level at P_1. Now assume a fall in the nominal exchange rate. At a given domestic price level, this increases competitiveness and net exports, and the aggregate demand curve shifts to the right to AD_2. Note that even if no inputs are imported, this will raise prices to a degree dependent on the slope of the aggregate supply curve

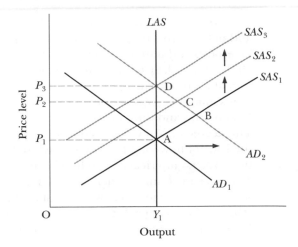

Figure 19.6   The response of aggregate supply to a fall in the nominal exchange rate

and the economy would move to point B. However, if some inputs are imported, then the aggregate supply curve will shift upwards, say to SAS_2, in response to the exchange rate fall. This takes the economy to a point such as C, where prices are higher at P_2, and therefore net exports are lower, than at point B. The effect of the nominal reduction on the real exchange rate has been diluted by the increase in the domestic price level.

However, there is an additional factor which can further weaken the effectiveness of the reduction in the nominal exchange rate, and this concerns the response of wages to the increase in import prices.

The key point here lies in workers' attitudes to real wages. In Chapter 18, Section 4.3, Mary Gregory defined the real consumption wage. In order to analyse the impact of exchange rate changes we need a second concept, the real product wage.

Definition

Real product wage

The real product wage is the nominal wage deflated by the price of domestic output.

It is the real product wage which affects profitability of firms and their demand for labour (and therefore the level of employment). On the other hand, it is the real consumption wage, the nominal wage deflated by the price of goods consumed domestically, which affects the standard of living of workers. In a closed economy, the real consumption wage might diverge from the real product wage because of taxation. In an open economy, changes in import prices can similarly drive a wedge between consumption and product wages.

Following a reduction in the nominal exchange rate, import prices (in domestic currency terms) rise. This increases the consumption price index by an amount dependent on the share of imports in domestic consumption, and therefore reduces the real consumption wage. If there is real wage resistance such that workers act to defend their real consumption wage, they will seek increases in their nominal wage. If they are successful, this will have the effect of putting upward pressure on the real product wage, which in turn will reduce the demand for labour, reducing output and employment at a given price level. In summary, the aggregate supply shifts from SAS_2 to SAS_3. In terms of Figure 19.6, the economy moves to point D where real income has fallen back to its original level. All that the nominal exchange rate fall has achieved is an increase in the domestic price level to P_3.

What this analysis shows is that the short-run increase in competitiveness and net exports brought about by a fall in the nominal exchange rate can be eroded and ultimately removed by its inflationary consequences. This is all the more likely to happen in economies where workers show a great deal of real wage resistance, or where there is a significant degree of wage indexation. Under these circumstances, net exports increase only temporarily, and the long-run effect is solely to increase domestic prices. The degree of real wage resistance is, of course, an empirical matter, as is the issue of how long it takes to reach the long-run equilibrium. As regards the former, empirical research indicates a high degree of real wage resistance in countries such as the UK and Australia, in contrast to countries such as Japan, where real wage resistance has been found to be low (Layard *et al.*, 1991). As regards the latter issue, the National Institute model of the UK economy indicates that it takes around four years for a nominal exchange rate reduction to be offset by the resultant domestic inflation (see Artis and Lewis, 1991).

The corollary of the above argument is that, if nominal exchange rate reductions ultimately serve only to increase the domestic price level, then nominal increases become a potentially effective anti-inflation weapon. Thus, a higher exchange rate reduces import prices, reducing both input costs and some consumer prices. So long as workers do not seek to increase their real consumption wage in the face of this, then the real product wage should fall, reducing inflationary pressures in the economy.

3   Exchange rates and the capital account

The simple model of exchange rates developed in the last section may provide a relevant explanation of exchange rates in the medium term, but it does not provide a convincing account of how the foreign exchange market works in the short run. It is now time to introduce capital movements into our model, since capital transactions now play a dominating role in the foreign exchange market.

Capital transactions are concerned with international lending and borrowing, which generally takes the form of the international sale and purchase of financial assets. We can divide such transactions into short- and long-term capital movements. Long-term capital movements include direct investment (most importantly the financing of investment projects by multi-national companies) and portfolio investment (principally the purchase and sale of long-term bonds and equity). However, it is short-term capital movements which are a much more volatile element in capital movements. Short-term capital movements refer to transactions in short-term assets, frequently bank accounts. It is generally this kind of activity which is involved when we refer to highly mobile international capital.

In analysing capital movements, it is useful to think of a world where there is a large number of portfolio holders (such as international fund managers) seeking to maximize the rate of return on their portfolios by allocating their funds between assets denominated in different currencies, taking into account the expected rates of return of these assets and their perceived riskiness.

There are two principal factors which taken together measure the relative rate of return of assets denominated in different currencies – relative interest rates and expected exchange rate changes. Interest rates will have a more significant effect on capital flows the closer substitutes are domestic and foreign assets. For example, if UK and German assets were very close substitutes and assuming that the exchange rate was not expected to change, then an increase in German interest rates would bid funds away from the UK into Germany. This would bid up UK rates and bid down German rates. The closer substitutes are the two sets of assets then the nearer will their interest rates be bid to equality.

In the limiting case where assets are perfect substitutes, domestic and foreign interest rates would have to be equal. This is sometimes referred to as *perfect capital mobility*. It is certainly the case that the development of international capital markets, associated with financial deregulation and advances in information technology, has increased the degree of capital mobility quite remarkably. However, so long as some assets are regarded as riskier than others and other factors such as taxation treatment differ between countries, then financial assets will not be perfect substitutes between countries. Under these circumstances, the riskier assets, for example, will have to yield higher interest to compensate portfolio holders, and this is called the *risk premium*.

Interest rates are not the only factor motivating short-term capital movements. Portfolio holders will also take into account *expected* future changes in exchange rates in assessing the relative rates of return of alternative assets. As an example, consider a UK investor deciding between holding a UK (sterling denominated) asset bearing 6 per cent, and a US (dollar denominated) asset bearing 8 per cent. In the absence of exchange rate expectations, the US asset is bearing a risk premium of 2 per cent.

Question

Suppose now that the market forms the expectation that the dollar is going to depreciate with respect to sterling in the coming year by 5 per cent. How will this affect our investor's calculations?

First, the actual interest payment (assuming it is paid at the end of the year) will be worth 5 per cent less in sterling terms. This is, however, a minor adjustment, on its own reducing the effective rate of interest from 8 per cent to 7.6 per cent (i.e. 95 per cent of 8 per cent). Much more significant is the fact that the capital invested will be worth 5 per cent less in sterling terms, if the expected dollar depreciation comes about. It is this expected capital loss which dramatically reduces the rate of return on the dollar asset as compared with the sterling asset, more than offsetting the nominal interest differential between the two countries. In this example, £100 invested in the UK at 6 per cent is worth £106 (£100 × 1.06) at the end of the year. By contrast, the same £100 invested in the US asset, and then converted back into sterling at the end of the year is worth only £102.60 (£100 × 1.08 × 0.95). In other words, the expected effective rate of return on the dollar asset is reduced by the expected depreciation of the dollar over the year, and since this rate of return is now below that of sterling assets, investors would be likely to switch their funds out of dollars and into sterling.

Uncovered interest parity condition

The relationship between exchange rate expectations and interest rates under perfect capital mobility is highlighted in the concept of the uncovered interest parity condition. It is important to note that this condition assumes that domestic and foreign assets are perfect substitutes. In that limiting case, in the absence of any expected change in exchange rates, we would expect domestic and foreign interest rates to be equal. That is,

$$r = r_F$$

where r is the domestic (or, in the above example, the UK) interest rate, and r_F is the 'world' (or the US) interest rate.

Now suppose that markets form the view that the sterling exchange rate is going to change in the coming year, where that expected change is denoted by $(\Delta e)_*$. If $(\Delta e)_*$ is positive, then markets are expecting a sterling appreciation. This would generate a capital inflow, increasing the demand for sterling in the foreign exchange market. This would serve to bring about the uncovered parity condition that

$$r = r_F - (\Delta e)_*$$

or alternatively, that

$$r - r_F = -(\Delta e)_*$$

What this condition states is that if the domestic currency is expected to appreciate, then the domestic interest rate should be below the world interest rate by an amount equal to the expected appreciation.

This condition can be amended to take into account less than perfect capital mobility, by adding a term to denote the risk premium. Thus, where domestic and foreign assets are imperfect substitutes, we have

$$r - r_F = -(\Delta e)_* + x$$

where x is the risk premium. If x is positive, then domestic assets are deemed to be riskier than foreign assets.

Figure 19.7 shows the short-term (Treasury bill) interest rate differential between the UK and Germany from 1976 to 1992. As this differential is positive, UK interest rates have been consistently higher than German rates over the period.

The above analysis suggests that there are two possible reasons for the UK–German interest rate differential. One reason is that the assets of the two countries might not be perfect substitutes, and that UK assets bear a risk premium over German assets (i.e. the risk premium, x, is positive). The second reason is that markets might consistently have been expecting sterling to depreciate with respect to the deutschmark over the period, perhaps because of the UK's higher inflation rate, i.e. the expected change in the exchange rate, $(\Delta e)_*$, is negative. Under such expectations, international investors would require higher UK interest rates as a reward for holding a depreciating currency.

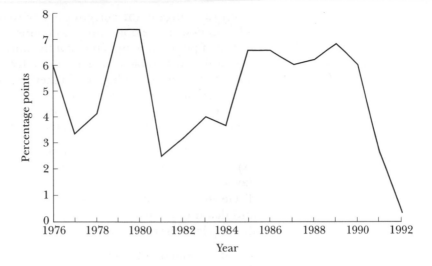

Figure 19.7 **UK–German interest differential, 1976–92**

Source: *International Financial Statistics Year Book* (1993) p.97

The course of the UK–German interest differential before and after the UK's entry into the ERM affords an interesting example of how exchange rate expectations might affect interest rates. Before sterling joined the ERM in 1990, markets felt that sterling was likely to depreciate, and UK interest rates reflected this sentiment. However, once sterling entered the ERM, market sentiment changed. Membership of the ERM offered the prospect of greater exchange stability for sterling, with the intervention rules greatly reducing the chances of a member currency depreciating. As the expectations of a sterling depreciation receded, so the UK authorities were able to allow domestic interest rates to fall towards German levels in the months following sterling entry into the ERM in October 1990.

Clearly, short-term capital movements can be crucially important in explaining day-to-day changes in exchange rates. Consider once more the behaviour of international asset-holders and let us assume that the assets in their portfolios are imperfect substitutes. The demand for any given asset will be a positive function of its expected rate of return, and a negative function of the rate of return on alternative assets.

Question

What will happen to the sterling exchange rate if the interest rate on UK assets rises?

There is now excess demand for sterling in the foreign exchange market. This will bid up sterling's exchange rate, which increases the relative price of UK assets in international portfolios and therefore removes the excess demand. The net result of the increase in UK interest rates is a sterling appreciation.

Similarly, an expected change in the exchange rate must affect the current exchange rate. If portfolio holders expect a currency to depreciate in the future, this will reduce demand for that currency, reducing the exchange rate today. Indeed, the current price of any asset may embody all the information currently available which could affect the future price of that asset. Any new information (which we might call 'news') must therefore lead to a change in the current price of that asset. An obvious source of relevant news is credible announcements by the authorities about the future course of policy. It is arguable that the appreciation of sterling in 1979–81 was partly attributable to a 'Thatcher effect' whereby markets anticipated restrictive monetary policy and higher interest rates, and this caused the exchange rate to rise in advance of such measures being adopted. (This is not the only explanation of this episode. North Sea oil similarly engendered expectations of a sterling appreciation at that time.)

Thus, increased capital mobility has meant that interest rates, exchange rate expectations, and new information have become important determinants of day-to-day fluctuations in the exchange rate. However, all of the above discussion has assumed that the authorities are conducting a 'clean' float, and that they are not intervening in the foreign exchange market. What are the implications of increased capital mobility for intervention policies?

The development of international capital markets has made it very difficult for one country's authorities to 'peg' effectively the exchange rate by means of intervention policies alone. The potential scale of capital movements is now so large relative to the foreign exchange reserves of most individual countries that they do not have the financial 'muscle' to out-buy or out-sell the market. For example, suppose the authorities attempt to set the exchange rate at a level which the market believes to be too high (or alternatively sets interest rates at a level which is too low for that exchange rate). There will be a large-scale capital outflow. To maintain the exchange rate by means of intervention, the authorities would have to purchase all the sterling being sold as the counterpart of the capital outflow, and it is unlikely that they would have sufficient reserves to do this. This is not to say that the authorities cannot determine their exchange rate, but in order to do so, they must implement domestic monetary policies consistent with their exchange rate target, so that the market accepts the exchange rate as credible. It is to a discussion of the interrelationships between exchange rates and domestic macroeconomic policies that I turn in the next section.

4   Monetary policy and fiscal policy in an open economy

In this section I analyse how monetary and fiscal policies operate in a small open economy with capital mobility. The aim is to compare the effectiveness of monetary and fiscal policies under fixed and freely floating exchange rate regimes. A high degree of capital mobility is the crucial assumption. (Note, however, that we are not making the extreme assumption of perfect capital mobility, which would imply the domestic interest rate must be tied to the world interest rate in the long run.) We have just seen that the authorities cannot hope to 'peg' the exchange rate by means of intervention in the foreign exchange market unless they are following a domestic monetary policy which is believed by agents in that market to be consistent with their exchange rate target. The implication is that the authorities can control monetary policy (setting the money supply or interest rates) or the exchange rate but not both. This is indeed the key result of the analysis of this section. In an open economy with international capital mobility, the authorities face a dilemma: they can control domestic monetary policy provided they permit the exchange rate to respond freely to market forces or they can fix the exchange rate provided they implement whatever monetary policy can win credibility on the foreign exchange market. Let us see how it is that the authorities find themselves in this situation.

4.1   Interest rates, aggregate demand and the balance of payments

It should be clear from the earlier discussion that the current account and the capital account of the balance of payments are affected by largely different sets of factors. (The balance of payments is explained in Chapter 12, Section 2.1.)

The current account is principally determined by domestic aggregate demand relative to world demand, domestic prices relative to world prices, and the exchange rate. Thus, under fixed exchange rates, increasing domestic aggregate expenditure and increasing domestic prices (for given world income and prices) will tend to push the current account into deficit. If the authorities do not intervene in the foreign exchange market to support the currency, this will tend to lead to a depreciation. After a considerable lag, this depreciation would tend to push the current account back towards balance, though not in the short run.

The capital account, on the other hand, is likely to be affected in the short run by interest rate differentials and exchange rate expectations. Thus, an increase in domestic interest rates will tend to attract a capital inflow as international investors take advantage of the improved opportunities in domestic financial markets. At the same time, however, if, at a given level of interest rates, investors expect that the domestic currency is likely to depreciate in the near future, then they will wish to withdraw their funds into a stronger currency, generating a short-term capital outflow. Indeed, as I suggested in Section 3 above, it is frequently expected changes in economic policies rather than the actual implementation of economic policies which is important in affecting the exchange rate.

4.2   The balance of payments and the money supply

It is also the case that balance of payments flows feed back on domestic policy, and in particular on the money supply, as I explained in Section 2.2. Under a balance of payment surplus, the authorities are buying foreign exchange and selling domestic currency on the foreign exchange market. In the case of the UK, this would mean that the Bank of England was selling sterling and accumulating foreign exchange. This, therefore, increases the supply of sterling in circulation, unless the authorities take some offsetting action by introducing sterilization policies. For example, the Bank of England could attempt to 'mop up' this increased money supply by open market operations, i.e. by selling bonds to holders of sterling. If this was successfully achieved, then the financial counterpart of the balance of payments surplus would be increased bond holdings rather than an increase in the money supply.

There are two points to be noted about this. The first is that it gives a clue about how inflation can spread internationally under fixed exchange rates. A high inflation country is likely to be running a balance of payments deficit with respect to a low inflation trading partner for reasons of competitiveness discussed in Section 2. Under fixed exchange rates, not only will the price of imports into the low inflation country be rising, but also its money stock will be increasing as a counterpart of its surplus. In the absence of effective sterilization policies, this will be inflationary. In fact, this has been a recurring problem for the German authorities, since low German inflation can be undermined by excessive monetary growth arising out of its surplus. It was precisely this dilemma which contributed to the breakdown of the ERM in September 1992 (see Section 6).

The second point is that effective sterilization measures are virtually impossible if international capital is highly mobile. If a surplus country attempts to sterilize by selling bonds, then domestic residents need to be induced to buy the extra bonds. This will entail some fall in bond prices, i.e. an increase in interest rates (see Chapter 11, Section 3.3). This will, in turn, induce a capital inflow, regenerating the initial balance of payments surplus. Thus, under conditions of international capital mobility, surpluses and deficits are likely to be reflected in changes in the domestic money supply. In fact, as we shall see below, it is a short step from this analysis, to demonstrate the key result of this chapter, signalled in Sections 1 and 4.1, that under these circumstances, the authorities cannot control both the money stock and the exchange rate. They can target either, but not both.

4.3   Monetary and fiscal policies under fixed exchange rates

The ground has now been prepared to analyse how the effectiveness of monetary and fiscal policies is affected by open economy considerations. In so doing, the focus will largely be on the short-run impact of policy when the impact of capital movements is crucially important, although in the longer term the adjustment of the current account becomes an important consideration. Fixed exchange rates are considered first. This means that the authorities have decided to target the exchange rate.

Question

Bearing in mind the dilemma facing the authorities which I outlined at the start of this section, what does targeting the exchange rate imply for domestic monetary policy?

The logic of the authorities' position is that they will be unable to control domestic monetary policy. Figure 19.8 shows the standard AD/AS model derived in Chapters 17 and 18. Starting from point A, associated with AD_1 and SAS_1, I assume that the balance of payments is in initial equilibrium. Suppose aggregate demand is now increased by either fiscal policy or monetary policy such that AD_1 shifts to AD_2, moving the economy to point B. At this point, the domestic economy exhibits both a higher income level and a higher price level, and for both these reasons, it is likely that net exports have fallen, pushing the current account into deficit (or reducing its surplus). However, the outcome for the balance of payments as a whole depends critically on what has happened to domestic interest rates and capital movements, and this in turn depends on whether aggregate demand has been increased by fiscal policy or by monetary policy.

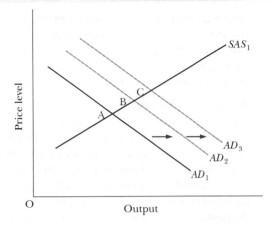

Figure 19.8 **Monetary and fiscal expansion under fixed exchange rates**

Suppose first that aggregate demand has been increased by means of expansionary monetary policy with fiscal policy kept neutral. Two preliminary points need to be clarified. First, fiscal policy is neutral when the government adopts a fiscal stance which is neither expansionary nor contractionary (see Chapter 17, Section 5.1). Second, there are two main techniques of monetary policy depending on whether the money supply is exogenous or endogenous. If the money supply is *exogenous*, it is set by the authorities (in the absence of the open economy consideration I am about to explain). An expansionary monetary policy would then involve the authorities' injecting cash into the banking system where it would be used to support a multiple expansion of credit, as a consequence of which the interest rate would fall (see Chapter 11, Section 5.2). If the money supply is *endogenous*, it is the outcome of lending decisions by the commercial banks taken in the light of the interest rate which is directly set by the authorities. An expansionary monetary policy would then involve a reduction in the interest rate, and an expansion of the money supply as the commercial banks advance more loans (see Chapter 11, Section 5.3).

In either case, the domestic money stock would have increased and the domestic interest rate would have fallen. In the absence of capital mobility, the authorities would only have to worry about the current account deficit. So long as this was not too large, the exchange rate could be pegged by intervention (i.e. buying sterling and selling foreign exchange). The domestic monetary effects of this intervention could be sterilized, and the aggregate demand curve would remain at AD_2, at least in the short run. (Note, however, that in the long run the authorities would face a foreign exchange reserves constraint if the current account deficit persisted.)

However, under capital mobility, lower interest rates (and therefore the position of aggregate demand and AD_2) becomes much less sustainable. Lower domestic interest rates lead to a substantial capital outflow. In the face of this, the authorities cannot peg the exchange rate by sterilized intervention. If the exchange rate is to be defended, the interest rate must be raised back towards its original level, shifting the aggregate demand back towards AD_1. Another way of telling the same story is that the expansionary monetary policy has provoked a massive capital outflow, which has reduced the money supply. The greater is the degree of capital mobility, the greater will be the capital outflow, and the greater will be the offsetting fall in the domestic money stock. Under perfect capital mobility, the money supply, the interest rate and the aggregate demand curve all assume their original positions, and monetary policy is completely ineffective. Thus, under fixed exchange rates, the authorities lose control of the money supply and interest rates to an extent dependent upon the degree of capital mobility.

By contrast, the effectiveness of fiscal policy accompanied by a neutral monetary policy may be enhanced under fixed exchange rates, at least in the short run, in those cases where the money supply is exogenous. Under an exogenous money supply, a neutral monetary policy, one that is neither expansionary nor contractionary, means that the authorities are leaving the money supply unchanged. Returning to Figure 19.8, if the initial fiscal expansion was unaccompanied by any increase in the money stock, then domestic interest rates must have increased (as excess demand is generated in the money market). Under capital mobility, this will generate a capital inflow with results which are the opposite of the monetary policy case. The capital inflow increases the domestic money stock and reduces interest rates back towards world levels. This effectively means that the effects of the expansionary fiscal policy are being reinforced by the monetary and interest rate consequences of the capital inflow. Thus, in Figure 19.8 the aggregate demand curve will be shifted further to the right, say to AD_3, making fiscal policy even more effective.

Question

Does that conclusion seem at all odd, given the earlier discussion of the balance of payments?

The notion of fiscal expansion generating a balance of payments surplus, even in the short run, may seem counter-intuitive. Certainly, the expansion will cause the current account of the balance of payments to move towards deficit, as increased domestic spending sucks in imports. The point is that this is more than offset by a short-run capital account surplus reflecting the higher domestic interest rates associated with the fiscal expansion. However, unless there is perfect capital mobility (that is a perfectly elastic supply of world capital funds available to be borrowed by the domestic country), then it is unlikely that the domestic economy will be able to borrow indefinitely to finance its current account deficit at a given interest. In the long run, it will come under pressure to take measures to correct the current account deficit.

In an economy where the money supply is endogenous and the government uses interest rates as the instrument of monetary policy, the outcome may be different. Insofar as a neutral monetary policy implies pegging domestic interest rates, this actually accommodates an increased money supply in response to an increased transactions demand for money. Fiscal policy would still be expansionary, as shown in Figure 19.8, but the balance of payments would now be in deficit. This is because the authorities have prevented the interest rate from increasing, and therefore there has been no capital inflow. This implies more acute financing difficulties for the authorities.

4.4   Monetary and fiscal policies under flexible exchange rates

How are these results altered by operating under flexible exchange rates? Figure 19.8 is again relevant. The authorities still face the problem of being able to control domestic monetary policy or the exchange rate but not both. The difference is that this time they have decided to target the money supply (if it is exogenous) or the interest rate (if the money supply is endogenous) and allow market forces to determine the exchange rate. As we shall now see, flexible exchange rates do more than merely permit the authorities to pursue the monetary policy of their choice; they actually increase the effectiveness of monetary policy.

Start from point A and then allow an increase in aggregate demand from AD_1 to AD_2. On the demand side of the model, the results under flexible exchange rates are neatly reversed from the fixed exchange rate case. If the increase in aggregate demand stems from expansionary monetary policy, then again this will tend to cause a balance of payments deficit. The difference is that under flexible exchange rates the result will be a fall in the exchange rate. This will ultimately lead to an increase in net exports, which constitutes a further increase in aggregate demand, shifting AD_2 to AD_3 and moving the economy from B to C. Thus, the impact of monetary policy is strengthened by its exchange rate consequences. (Note that in this case, the current account will be moved into surplus due to the depreciated exchange rate, and because of this, in the long run the exchange rate may rise back towards its original level.)

Exercise 19.4

In the light of this analysis, would you expect excessively expansionary monetary policy to be more inflationary under fixed or flexible exchange rules?

Now suppose that the movement from AD_1 to AD_2 reflects expansionary fiscal policy with a neutral monetary policy. In that case it is once more possible that, in the exogenous money supply model, this could result in a rise in the domestic interest rate sufficient to generate a balance of payment surplus. Under flexible exchange rates, this surplus would cause the exchange rate to appreciate. This would then render exports less competitive, and net exports would eventually fall, moving aggregate demand back from AD_2 towards AD_1. Indeed, under perfect capital mobility it will move all the way back. Here is a mechanism for 'crowding-out' of the type introduced in Chapter 17, Section 4.3, where a rise in government spending merely causes an equivalent fall in private spending. Attempted fiscal expansion is thwarted by a rising exchange rate, so that increases in government expenditure are matched by falling net exports leaving aggregate demand overall unaffected. (Again, in the longer run, the deterioration of the current account could be expected to lead to an offsetting depreciation of the currency.)

Once more, it might seem a little counter-intuitive that fiscal expansion can actually appreciate the currency even in the short run, when it is almost certainly going to push the current account towards deficit. Again, the key lies in the behaviour of interest rates and the capital account. Fiscal expansion places upward pressure on interest rates, causing the capital inflow which appreciates the currency.

The position is reversed, however, in the <u>endogenous</u> money supply model. In this case, when an expansionary fiscal policy is accompanied by a neutral monetary policy, this means that the authorities peg the interest rate. The consequence is that the money supply increases in line with the increase in aggregate demand caused by the fiscal expansion. The results are similar to those of a monetary expansion: the balance of payments goes into deficit and there is a fall in the exchange rate.

Finally, before we leave this analysis, it is important to examine the possible response of aggregate supply in the face of these exchange rate adjustments. Earlier in the chapter, it became clear that the aggregate supply curve, as well as the aggregate demand curve, is shifted by an exchange rate change, and that the extent of this shift will be determined by the importance of imports both as inputs and as final consumption goods, and by the degree of real wage resistance on the part of workers (Section 2.3).

Let me confine the analysis to the case of restrictive monetary policy, with the aid of Figure 19.9. If the money supply is reduced and the rate of interest rises (say, as part of an anti-inflation strategy), then this will shift the aggregate demand curve to the left, from AD_1 to AD_2. This will cause an appreciation of the currency, which will reduce net exports and reinforce the leftward shift of the aggregate demand curve, say to AD_3. As things stand, this takes the economy to point B, reducing both income and employment, and the price level. However, the appreciation also reduces the domestic currency price of imported inputs and consumer goods, which will tend to shift the aggregate supply curve downwards, by an amount largely determined by the importance of imported inputs and the degree of wage indexation. Thus, the economy may end up at a point such as C. The fall in output and employment is much reduced, and prices have fallen even further. If import costs are an important component of inflation, restrictive monetary policy can be doubly effective as an anti-inflation strategy, if the exchange rate is allowed to appreciate as part of this strategy.

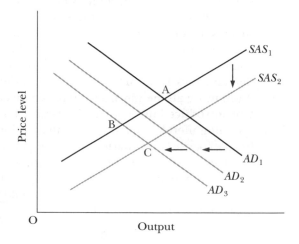

Figure 19.9 **Restrictive monetary policy under flexible exchange rates**

4.5   Two examples

The 1980s have seen two significant examples of the role of the exchange rate in macroeconomic policy. The first concerns the role of sterling as part of the anti-inflationary strategy of the early 1980s. The second concerns the experience of the dollar in the face of US macroeconomic policy under President Reagan.

Sterling in the early 1980s

When Mrs Thatcher came to power in 1979, she made a strong commitment to implement anti-inflationary policies. The anticipation of these policies as well as their implementation, caused sterling to appreciate significantly in nominal terms, and even more spectacularly in real terms (see Figures 19.1 and 19.2). This episode is significant for two reasons.

First, the extent of sterling's appreciation, and its subsequent reversal after 1981, is evidence of exchange rate 'overshooting'. It is a feature of many asset markets, including the foreign exchange market, that an initial shock can cause asset prices (or exchange rates) to overshoot their long-run equilibrium, before adjusting back in the longer run. This has been attributed to the fact that goods and factor markets adjust much more slowly than do asset markets. Thus, following some disturbance, asset markets apparently over-adjust, until real markets (and the general price level) have time to adjust.

Second, the episode might be regarded as a good example of the two sets of disinflationary effects that an exchange rate appreciation can impart. First, it reduces relative import costs, which reduces inflationary pressures, perhaps through wages as well as input costs. Second, it reduces demand pressures by reducing export demand. Certainly, inflation fell very substantially in the UK in the early 1980s – from 18.5 per cent in 1980 to 5.6 per cent in 1983. However, it can also be argued that some of the output costs of reducing inflation through exchange rate appreciation can be substantial and long-lasting. Since the fall in demand hits the export sector, this is likely to affect manufacturing disproportionately. In 1979–81, manufacturing output fell by almost 15 per cent and did not recover its 1979 level until 1988. As output growth falls, there may be hysteresis effects on productivity and therefore on competitiveness and future export growth (see Chapters 18 and 24 for accounts of hysteresis). Similarly, loss of capacity in the downswing may be less easily replaced in the upswing. In short, the economic costs of disinflation through exchange rate appreciation may be long-lasting.

The dollar under President Reagan

In the period from 1979 to 1985, the dollar appreciated in nominal terms by 45 per cent, and in real terms by 48 per cent. The experience of the soaring dollar is interesting for two reasons.

First, it affords an example of how expansionary fiscal policy and tight monetary policy can combine to produce an appreciating exchange rate. The US budget deficit rose from $16 billion in 1979 to $204 billion in 1986, while monetary policy remained tight, with interest rates averaging more than 10 per cent over the period, as compared with an average of 6 per cent in Germany. Capital flowed into the USA and the exchange rate appreciated. At the same time, one would expect fiscal expansion and a real appreciation to show in a deteriorating current account, which is exactly what happened. The US current account went from a small surplus of $200 billion in 1979 to a massive deficit of over $160 000 billion in 1987.

Second, international concern over the ever-rising dollar was sufficient to induce the governments of the major world economies to attempt some co-ordinated action to effect a 'soft landing' for the dollar, given the widespread view that the dollar had clearly 'over-shot' its equilibrium value. The first meeting of finance ministers resulted in the Plaza Accord, which was partly an attempt to reach co-ordinated exchange market interventions, and partly an attempt to 'talk the dollar down' by changing market expectations. The dollar then depreciated rather sharply, and a subsequent meeting in Paris issued the Louvre Accord which was an attempt to stem the decline of the dollar. The recognition by the major economies that there were potential gains to be derived from policy co-ordination is an important legacy of the dollar episode (Chapter 28 discusses international policy co-ordination).

5   Fixed exchange rates versus flexible exchange rates

The analysis of the previous section showed how the relative effectiveness of monetary and fiscal policies is affected by the choice of exchange rate regime. The discussion now moves on to assess the relative merits of fixed and flexible exchange rates. This will also serve as an introduction to the final section of this chapter, which considers the operation of the ERM and the experience of sterling within it.

The principal argument in favour of a regime of fixed exchange rates is that it removes an important element of risk from international trade. Import and export deals are frequently struck well in advance of delivery and payment. Thus, given that prices have to be agreed in one currency, a change in the exchange rate between the date of the contract and the date of payment will change the agreed price in the other currency.

Three points are worth noting about this argument. First, the burden of exchange risk is borne by the party in whose currency the price is not fixed. Since importers are generally invoiced in the exporter's currency, this means that importers must bear the exchange risk. Second, importers may win, as well as lose, through exchange rate changes. It is the existence of risk which is the disincentive, and this will only be important to the extent that traders are risk-averse. Finally, at least for short-term contracts, the existence of the forward exchange market enables traders to hedge against exchange risk (at a cost). In these markets importers can buy foreign exchange for delivery in the future at an exchange rate agreed today. However, forward exchange markets generally focus on three- and six-month contracts, and more medium-term exchange risks remain.

A second argument for fixed exchange rates concerns the role of speculators in the foreign exchange market. It is held that flexible rates means unstable rates. Against this, proponents of floating rates argue that flexibility does not mean volatility, on the grounds that the actions of speculators should ensure that exchange rates are always at, or at least adjusting towards, their equilibrium value. Speculators, on this view, buy when the price is 'too low' and sell when the price is 'too high'. Speculators who consistently make mistakes will go out of business.

This reply can be questioned. Frequently asset markets are driven by the 'herd' instinct, where speculative surges in the market can feed upon themselves and market expectations become self-fulfilling. A closely-related notion is that of a 'speculative bubble' where even rational speculators know that the exchange rate is, for example, rising progressively away from equilibrium, but the belief that the bubble is not quite ready to burst means that speculators perceive the prospect of a further capital gain which is just enough to compensate them for the risk of the bubble bursting prematurely. In any case, speculators may also be rational, but act on false information. The so-called 'finance minister' problem arises when a government leads the market to believe that a particular policy change is about to happen, affecting exchange rate expectations and therefore the current exchange rate, but then proceeds to renege on this policy announcement. The exchange rate then adjusts back. In all these cases, the exchange rate is driven, at least in the short run, away from its long-run equilibrium value, distorting both the trading position and the domestic price level of the economy.

What about the case for flexible exchange rates? An important argument is that flexible exchange rates automatically correct balance of payments surpluses and deficits, leaving the authorities free to pursue domestic objectives of growth, employment and price stability. This is sometimes described, particularly by opponents of the European Monetary System (EMS), as the retention of economic sovereignty. Indeed, it was argued in Section 4 that monetary policy becomes a powerful anti-inflationary weapon under flexible exchange rates.

However, the above argument can be turned on its head. It may be that the balance of payments acts as a *disciplining* device on governments. In particular, governments face the temptation to run fiscal deficits and to finance these by printing money in the sense explained in Chapter 17, Section 5.1. Under fixed exchange rates, this would result in balance of payments difficulties which would require the government to implement deflationary policies. Under flexible exchange rates, this discipline would be removed. Indeed, it can be argued that the adoption of a fixed exchange rate target adds credibility to a government's anti-inflation strategy. This was one of the central arguments behind UK membership of the ERM. Given the dominating position of the German economy in the ERM, joining the ERM was seen as lending credibility to UK anti-inflation policies, since this was seen as linking UK anti-inflation policy to that of Germany. If UK inflation rose significantly above that of the European economy, this would require a domestic policy response, perhaps through increased UK interest rates. Under flexible exchange rates, sterling would simply be allowed to depreciate. From the point of view of workers and employers in the UK, a fixed exchange rate would mean that increasing inflation would not be underwritten by a falling exchange rate. Rather, they would face falling competitiveness abroad and possibly higher interest rates and unemployment at home. This, it was argued, makes domestic anti-inflation policy much more credible, and therefore much more effective.

The above argument loses some of its appeal if the government of the domestic country can enforce a resolute and credible anti-inflationary monetary policy, since under flexible rates, monetary contraction may generate an over appreciation of the currency in the short run, with strong deflationary consequences. The UK in the early 1980s provides an example (Section 4.5).

A second argument for a regime of flexible exchange rates is that it serves to insulate the domestic economy from foreign shocks. For example, if there is recession abroad, this can spread to the domestic economy through falling demand for domestic exports. However, under flexible exchange rates, the exchange rate of the domestic economy would tend to depreciate, increasing the competitiveness of domestic exports and offsetting the effects of falling foreign income levels. The domestic economy would therefore, at least to some extent, be insulated from the foreign recession. A similar argument can be put forward regarding world inflation. If domestic inflation is lower than world inflation, then the domestic currency will tend to appreciate, reducing import prices, and therefore insulating the domestic economy from foreign inflation.

Once again, this argument can be turned on its head. It may be that there are certain foreign influences from which the economy should *not* be insulated. Once more, the ERM affords a possible example. It may be preferable for a high inflation country (e.g. the UK) to fix its exchange rate with respect to a low inflation country (e.g. Germany), so long as low inflation is afforded a high policy priority and if the high inflation country is perceived to have something of a credibility problem with respect to anti-inflation strategies.

It should be clear from this discussion that there are substantial arguments for and against adopting a fixed exchange rate as the centrepiece of macroeconomic policy. In a sense, this mirrors the fluctuating role of the exchange rate in UK economic policy in recent years. The UK's experience in the ERM has kept the exchange rate at the centre of the stage, and it is to this that I now turn in the final section.

Exercise 19.5

I have outlined two arguments in favour of fixed exchange rates and two arguments in favour of flexible exchange rates.

1   State briefly, in one sentence for each argument, the two arguments in favour of fixed exchange rates. Do not worry about any qualifications or criticisms of the arguments at this stage.

2   State briefly, in one sentence for each argument, the two arguments in favour of flexible exchange rates. As before, do not worry about any qualifications or criticisms of the arguments.

3   Now for some of the objections to the arguments. Give one reason for questioning each of the two arguments in favour of fixed exchange rates.

4   Give one reason for questioning each of the two arguments in favour of flexible exchange rates.

6   The ERM

6.1   The historical context: Bretton Woods and after

For about half of the period since the Second World War, the world economy operated under a system of broadly fixed exchange rates, which was known as the Bretton Woods system. This was the centrepiece of a new framework for international monetary relations which was established following an international monetary conference held in Bretton Woods, New Hampshire in 1944. Each country's exchange rate was to be fixed (within 1 per cent either way of a central parity) to the US dollar, with the dollar being pegged to the price of gold, at $35 per ounce. The system was not one of completely fixed exchange rates, since individual countries could negotiate an exchange rate change if its balance of payments entered 'fundamental' disequilibrium, devaluing the currency if the rate was too high, and revaluing it if it was too low. For example, following a succession of substantial UK balance of payments deficits, sterling was devalued by 14 per cent in 1967 (from $2.80 to $2.40). The Bretton Woods system was, therefore, an 'adjustable peg' system, where one-off exchange rate adjustments were within the rules.

The relatively successful operation of the Bretton Woods system over most of its life was partly attributable to the imperfect mobility of international capital over most of this period. The continuing existence of foreign exchange controls substantially restricted international capital movements which made it easier for the authorities of a given country to peg their exchange rate by means of official intervention in the foreign exchange market. Such intervention was more likely to be successful under foreign exchange controls, since these controls restricted the amount of speculative pressure which could be generated against a currency.

Thus, a key difference between the Bretton Woods era and the present day is that, over much of the earlier period, the exchange rate was regarded as a separate policy instrument which could be adjusted without severely constraining the use of other policy instruments (monetary and fiscal policy). The conclusion of Section 4 was that nowadays with more internationally mobile capital, the authorities find it very difficult to peg the exchange rate effectively by means of intervention alone. An exchange rate target needs to be accompanied by appropriate domestic monetary policies.

The breakdown of the Bretton Woods system in 1971 was followed by a general move to floating exchange rates. Individual countries were no longer committed to keeping their exchange rates fixed by means of official intervention in foreign exchange markets or by interest rate policy. That is not to say that since 1971 all exchange rates have been freely floating. In the first place, even though a given exchange rate may appear to be floating freely, it may not be a 'clean' float. This means that, although an exchange rate changes day to day, the authorities are nevertheless intervening in the market in order to smooth out these changes. While some countries opted for such a 'managed float', others have chosen to fix their exchange rates either with respect to one key currency, usually the dollar, or to a trade-weighted 'basket' of currencies. Since 1971, the EU has attempted to move towards a more stable exchange rate environment, in the first instance by means of what was effectively a joint float against the dollar in the 1970s (an arrangement which became known as the 'snake in the tunnel'). This was the forerunner of the European Monetary System and the Exchange Rate Mechanism. The key point to note is that, following the breakdown of the Bretton Woods system, there has not emerged a widely accepted exchange rate regime for the world economy as a whole.

6.2   The ERM in outline

The establishment of the European Monetary System in 1979, following a conference held at the Hague in 1978, was motivated by a number of factors. Fundamentally, it must be seen in the context of the ultimate objective of Economic and Monetary Union, where all members of the EU share a common currency and exchange rates become immutably fixed. More immediately, however, it provided a mechanism for increased exchange rate stability within the EU.

So far as exchange rates and monetary policy are concerned, the most important aspect of the EMS is the Exchange Rate Mechanism (for a comprehensive discussion of the breakdown of the ERM, see Artis and Lewis, 1993). The ERM is the mechanism whereby exchange rates of the EU currencies are stabilized with respect to each other. The main element is that all bilateral exchange rates must be stabilized within bands of the agreed central bilateral rates (these bands were fixed at 2.25 per cent until 1993). Once bilateral rates reach these bands, the two central banks concerned must intervene in the market to push the exchange rate back towards its central rate.

The central parities of the bilateral rates were agreed at the outset, but these were able to be changed by negotiated agreement. Such 'realignments' were quite common in the first half of the 1980s, but became much less frequent as the system 'bedded down'. Thus, between 1979 and 1983 there were seven realignments, while between February 1987 and September 1992 there were none. Realignments are a key element in the system, since they render the ERM an adjustable peg system, rather than a system of irrevocably fixed exchange rates.

The UK did not join the ERM until October 1990, and then only stayed within the ERM until September 1992. In the course of the summer of 1992, some of the weaker currencies within the ERM, particularly sterling and the lira, came under increasing speculative pressure. Then on 12 September, the lira was devalued by 7 per cent. This was followed by the dramatic events of 16 September, when, in an attempt to defend sterling's position, interest rates were increased first from 8 per cent to 10 per cent, and then a further increase to 15 per cent was pre-announced. This was not sufficient to bolster market confidence in sterling and the UK suspended its membership of the ERM that evening. Sterling depreciated immediately by 16 per cent, and the lira followed sterling in leaving the ERM. At the same time, the peseta was devalued by 5 per cent. In November, the peseta and the escudo were devalued by 6 per cent, and in January 1993 the punt was devalued by 10 per cent. This was followed by further devaluations of the peseta and the escudo in May. Finally, a wave of speculative pressure against the franc in the summer of 1993 led to a widening of all parity bands within the ERM to 15 per cent. Given that member currencies could now fluctuate against each other by as much as 30 per cent, the ERM could no longer be regarded as a form of fixed exchange rate system.

6.3 ERM – an assessment

The ERM can be seen as something of a hybrid system, between fully flexible and fully fixed exchange rates, trying to secure the best of both worlds in the short run, while preparing a path to monetary union and a single European currency in the long run.

The perceived fixed exchange rate benefits were mainly twofold. First, a more stable exchange rate environment provides an encouragement to trade. Research by Artis and Taylor (1989) confirms that nominal exchange rates have been more stable under the ERM and also that real exchange rates have been more stable, perhaps indicating some convergence of inflation rates. This is indeed the second perceived advantage of the ERM – that high inflation countries can improve their inflation performance. The argument here is that Germany is the low inflation 'leader' in the system, and that by fixing their exchange rates to the deutschmark, the high inflation countries gain some increased credibility for their anti-inflation policies. It is certainly the case that inflation rates have fallen in member countries under the ERM, with France and Italy bringing their rates down quite markedly. However, as Pilbeam (1992) points out, over the same period, inflation rates have also fallen elsewhere.

It was hoped to achieve these benefits without jettisoning the possibility of one-off exchange rate adjustment (realignments) if real exchange rates were getting uncomfortably out of line. For example, a high inflation country could quite quickly become seriously uncompetitive with fixed nominal exchange rates. These tensions explained the regular round of realignments in the system up to 1987, whereafter there were no further realignments until the events of 1992.

To some extent, the hybrid nature of the system contributed to its virtual collapse in 1993. First, the absence of realignments after 1987 while inflation differentials remained pushed real rates seriously out of line. Yet one of the reasons why countries did not seek a realignment in the face of this was that they did not want to sacrifice the anti-inflation credibility for which they had striven so hard in the earlier 1980s.

Second, the system was subjected to an *asymmetric shock* in the form of German reunification. This was essentially an inflationary shock which impinged on Germany but not directly on the rest of Europe. (A symmetric shock would be, for example, a substantial oil price increase, which would hit all the ERM countries in largely the same way.) Germany's preferred response to this shock would have been a deutschmark revaluation, but other members (particularly France) resisted this, again partly on the grounds of the credibility argument. In the absence of such a realignment, Germany increased domestic interest rates, placing other ERM countries under pressure to follow, in order to keep their exchange rates within the ERM parity bands. This meant, particularly in the case of the UK, that domestic monetary policy was constrained from pursuing domestic objectives. German rates were rising just at the time when the UK authorities were attempting to reduce rates in order to encourage a recovery from domestic recession.

These tensions damaged the credibility of the whole system, and specific currencies now came under speculative attack. It is interesting to note that the currencies of those economies most closely integrated with the German economy (for example, the Dutch guilder) did not come under attack.

At this point, two particular features of the system become important. First, in a system of narrow bands, when a currency comes under speculative pressure, speculators are essentially taking a one-way bet. When a currency reaches the floor of its bands, the only question is whether the floor is going to be adjusted downwards. There is no risk of the ceiling being adjusted upwards. If the realignment occurs, speculators win, if it does not, they are not significantly worse off. Moreover, it is difficult for countries to use interest rates in order to defend a currency when there are expectations of a realignment. This is because the expectation of, say, a 5 per cent capital gain in the next month translates into a very high annual rate of return. Thus, it requires quite unrealistically high interest rates to compensate portfolio holders for this expected one-off devaluation.

The second feature of the system worth noting is the pattern of intervention by the central banks of the member countries when currencies come under pressure. The central bank of the weak currency is constrained by its finite stock of foreign exchange reserves, but this does not apply to the strong currency. Thus, intervention by the Bundesbank usually implied purchases of the weak currency, and sales of deutschmarks. If this intervention was not sterilized, then this results in an increasing German money supply, with the threat which that carries for domestic inflation.

This is a central issue in the operation of the ERM. I have already mentioned the anti-inflation benefits of fixed exchange rates for other members of the ERM. The counterpart of this for the German economy is less comfortable. If the Bundesbank supports other currencies (and therefore keeps non-German inflation rates lower), this is at the risk of that intervention increasing the German money supply and generating domestic inflation. When the German economy was strong, and when interventions could be sterilized, this was not necessarily a problem. However, a larger scale of intervention at a time when German inflation was increasing due to reunification, as was the case in 1992, put the system under much greater strain.

It should be clear from the above that at least some of the reasons for the effective collapse of the ERM in 1993 can be traced back to the fact that the ERM was essentially a half-way house between fully flexible and fully fixed exchange rates. (For an interesting discussion of the lessons of the ERM breakdown for alternative exchange regimes, see the Bank of England, 1993.) In that sense there are a number of similarities between the ERM and the Bretton Woods system. Moreover, in the same way that increasing capital mobility was weakening the operation of the Bretton Woods system in its later years, so it has become apparent that in today's world of highly mobile capital, such a half-way house is difficult to sustain. Flexibility within narrow bands with the escape clause of possible realignments presents speculators with a one-way bet, while wider bands seriously weakens the credibility and therefore the anti-inflationary benefits of the system. This suggests the conclusion that the EU should opt for fully flexible rates or go directly towards a single currency. The latter may be a more attractive proposition for those countries with fully established low inflation credentials, and whose economies may already be closely integrated. For other economies, such as the UK, the single currency option could involve an extremely painful adjustment. Perhaps a more palatable alternative is that of exchange rate flexibility, at least in the immediate future. In that case the authorities must establish and maintain the credibility of their anti-inflation strategy, without the aid of a fixed nominal exchange rate. It is in this context that the arguments for establishing an independent central bank become all the more relevant (see Chapter 28).

7 Conclusion

This chapter has analysed the implications of the openness of economies for the effectiveness of monetary and fiscal policies. The nature of the exchange rate regime has emerged as a decisive factor. Under fixed exchange rates the authorities cannot control the money supply. They must therefore choose between a monetary target and an exchange rate target. This result depends crucially on the assumption that capital is internationally mobile. A subsidiary theme of the chapter is that the world has in fact moved in this direction. The consequence is not only that monetary and exchange rate targets are incompatible but also that fixed exchange rate systems, however appealing their perceived benefits, are hard to sustain. The choice facing European policy makers is therefore between a single currency and floating exchange rates, while no world-wide exchange rate system has emerged to replace Bretton Woods.

CHAPTER 20

MACROECONOMIC POLICIES IN HISTORICAL PERSPECTIVE

by Nick Crafts

1 Introduction: macroeconomic performance and problems

The objectives of this chapter are the following:

- To develop an historical perspective on macroeconomic performance that will permit a deeper understanding of success and failure.

- To illustrate the fundamental problems facing policy makers in seeking to manage the economy.

- To explore further the determinants of the rate of economic growth discussed in Chapter 14.

This work will take us beyond the confines of the short run both in the types of economic model to be considered and also in the data to be reviewed. The approach will have two features that are relatively uncommon in macroeconomic textbooks, namely (1) the chance to explore famous crises from the past using basic theoretical ideas, and (2) a focus on the impact of short-run shocks and policy choices on long-term economic performance.

The first question to answer is, of course, 'what happened?'. As we shall see, history shows a wide range of outcomes including episodes of growth without inflation, slump with price deflation, hyperinflation, full employment and mass unemployment. Awareness of the range of past performance is one key ingredient in addressing a second question, 'how good is a country's present performance?', although this knowledge clearly needs to be supplemented by an assessment of the conditions under which it would be feasible to emulate the best results from the past.

Probably the most common reason for (generally spurious) comparisons of economic performance is to score party political points about the effectiveness of economic policy, as in the rough and tumble of Prime Minister's Question Time in the British House of Commons. This prompts two further closely related questions worth exploring in some detail and with some care, namely, 'how far is economic policy responsible for short- or long-term outcomes such as recessions or differences in growth rates?' and 'what explains failures in the design of economic policy for stabilization?'.

1.1 Macroeconomic performance: an historical overview

Research by economic historians has produced a wealth of data from which this section draws some edited highlights. Inevitably, we must consider a good deal of quantitative information. In doing so, the objective will be to extract key points rather than to drown in a sea of minute detail.

Table 20.1   **Growth rates of real GDP (% per year)**

	1870–1913	**1913–50**	**1950–73**	**1973–89**
Australia	3.5 (0.9)	2.2 (0.7)	4.7 (2.4)	3.1 (1.7)
Austria	2.4 (1.5)	0.2 (0.2)	5.3 (4.9)	2.4 (2.4)
Belgium	2.0 (1.0)	1.0 (0.7)	4.1 (3.5)	2.1 (2.0)
Canada	4.1 (2.3)	3.1 (1.5)	5.1 (2.9)	3.6 (2.5)
Denmark	2.7 (1.6)	2.5 (1.5)	3.8 (3.1)	1.7 (1.6)
Finland	2.7 (1.4)	2.7 (1.9)	4.9 (4.3)	3.1 (2.7)
France	1.5 (1.3)	1.1 (1.1)	5.0 (4.0)	2.3 (1.8)
Germany	2.8 (1.6)	1.3 (0.7)	5.9 (4.9)	2.1 (2.1)
Italy	1.9 (1.3)	1.5 (0.8)	5.6 (5.0)	2.9 (2.6)
Japan	2.3 (1.4)	2.2 (0.9)	9.3 (8.0)	3.9 (3.1)
Netherlands	2.3 (1.0)	2.4 (1.1)	4.7 (3.4)	2.0 (1.4)
Norway	2.1 (1.3)	2.9 (2.1)	4.1 (3.2)	4.0 (3.6)
Sweden	2.2 (1.5)	2.7 (2.1)	4.0 (3.3)	2.0 (1.8)
Switzerland	2.1 (1.2)	2.6 (2.1)	4.5 (3.1)	1.3 (1.0)
UK	1.9 (1.0)	1.3 (0.8)	3.0 (2.5)	2.0 (1.8)
USA	3.9 (1.8)	2.8 (1.6)	3.6 (2.2)	2.7 (1.6)
Arithmetic average	2.5 (1.4)	2.0 (1.2)	4.9 (3.8)	2.6 (2.1)

Note: figures in parentheses indicate per capita growth rates.

Source: Maddison (1991) pp.49–50

Question

Consider Table 20.1, which contains a fundamental description of economic growth in advanced countries since 1870. What surprises you most in the table? How would you describe the relative performance of the UK?

Assessment of relative growth performance is a topic which is developed in Section 4. For the moment it seems appropriate simply to note that the UK's growth rate of output per head is persistently below average. As to the biggest surprise of Table 20.1, there could well be a wide range of responses but I suspect the most popular might be to pick out the exceptionally rapid growth of the 'Golden Age' (1950–73). Explanations for this unusual experience will be reviewed in Section 4.

Other important points to note from Table 20.1 are the following:

- Growth in output per head is the norm for these countries (even in the war and depression-hit period 1913–50): the average rate over 1870–1989 is about 1.9 per cent per year.

- Japanese growth during the 'Golden Age' was phenomenal but has not been sustained at the same rate in the last twenty years.

- While in general the range of growth rates in each period appears fairly small, the accumulative effect over these lengthy intervals adds up to a serious impact on relative income levels (see Section 4).

Although growth is the normal expectation, Figure 20.1, based on data for the same sixteen countries, reminds us that the aggregate growth rate of the advanced economies fluctuates considerably, as Chapter 17 noted for the period 1961–92. Even in the Golden Age, we find a wide range from 1.1 per cent in 1958 to 8.5 per cent in 1951. In 15 years out of the 119 graphed, aggregate GDP for the Group of 16 fell and so the growth rate was negative: on a conventional definition the advanced economies were in recession. Three more points stand out:

- the absence of recessions in the Golden Age;
- the severity of the 1930s Great Depression;
- the huge decline in output at the end of the Second World War.

The contraction in output in 1945–46 associated with military rundown has different implications for living standards from that of 1930–32 and may in some ways be more comparable with the declines in output in Eastern Europe in the early 1990s (see Section 2.4).

Question

Compare Figures 20.1 and 20.2. What are the main differences between the experience of the UK and that of the Group of 16?

The comparison shows two interesting features. First, the UK has many more recession years than do the sixteen countries in aggregate. This may seem to suggest that the UK experiences greater instability than the average. In fact, this kind of comparison is misleading and this is not the case – similar results obtain for other countries viewed in isolation. The greater stability of the aggregate group comes from the tendency of downturns in individual countries to be imperfectly correlated. Second, the relatively mild

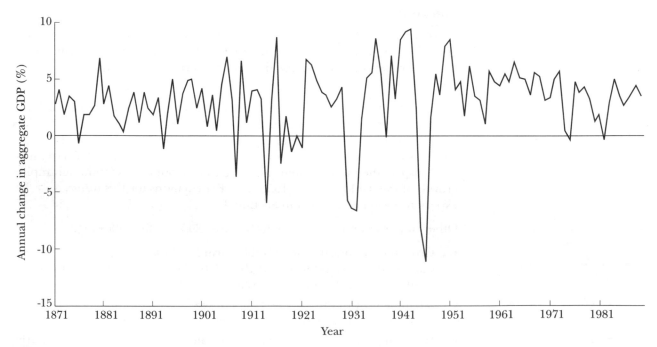

Figure 20.1   **Fluctuations in the momentum of growth, sixteen countries, 1871–1989**

Source: Maddison (1991)

contraction in the UK in the early 1930s stands out. The fact that the UK suffered much less than countries like the USA in the Great Depression is intriguing and will call for some explanation in Section 3.

Table 20.2   **Output fluctuations (%) (standard deviations)**

				Relative to post-1945	
	Pre-1914	**Inter-war**	**Post-1945**	**Pre-1914**	**Inter-war**
	(1)	**(2)**	**(3)**	**(1)/(3)**	**(2)/(3)**
Australia	6.30	4.85	1.93	3.3	2.5
Canada	4.47	9.80	2.22	2.0	4.4
Denmark	3.02	3.41	1.88	1.6	1.8
Germany	3.35	10.19	2.30	1.5	4.4
Italy	2.52	3.59	2.05	1.2	1.8
Japan	2.42	3.13	3.11	0.8	1.0
Norway	1.85	3.49	1.76	1.1	2.0
Sweden	2.43	3.74	1.45	1.7	2.6
UK	2.12	3.47	1.62	1.3	2.1
USA	4.28	9.33	2.26	1.9	4.1

Note that the American data for pre-1914 are of poor quality and may substantially exaggerate the volatility of output; revisions have been proposed but are the subject of unresolved controversy.

Source: Backus and Kehoe (1992) p.871

Table 20.2 provides some more formal evidence of the relative severity of cyclical fluctuations in economic growth in different countries and epochs by showing standard deviations for different periods. (The standard deviation

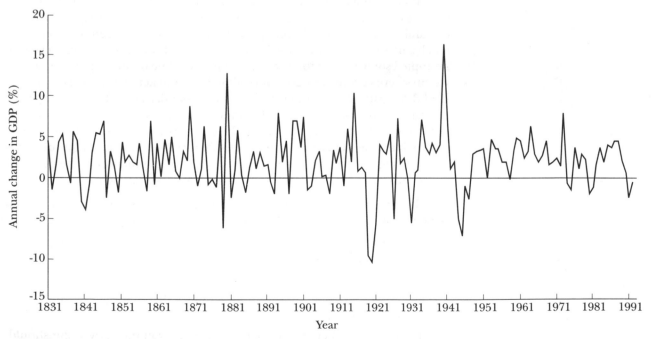

Figure 20.2   **Annual change (%) in UK GDP, 1831–1992**
Sources: Mitchell (1988); *Economic Trends*, various years

was explained in Chapter 9.) This will be useful when we consider the role of economic policy in promoting stability. Not surprisingly, the inter-war period emerges as having by far the worst experience for every country, except Australia. Perhaps less expected is that fluctuations were greater in the pre-1914 than in the post-1945 period, even though this included the OPEC shocks of the 1970s. A further glance at Table 20.2 will reinforce this perspective for the UK. Again, despite common perceptions to the contrary, the data in Table 20.2 confirm that the UK does not exhibit unusual volatility.

Table 20.3   **Inflation rates (%)**

	Mean			**Standard deviation**		
	Pre-1914	**Inter-war**	**Post-1945**	**Pre-1914**	**Inter-war**	**Post-1945**
Australia	−0.40	0.35	6.72	3.89	6.28	4.80
Canada	0.56	−1.05	5.05	3.46	4.63	2.53
Denmark	−0.05	−0.38	6.34	2.38	5.99	1.95
Germany	0.87	−1.28	3.74	3.91	5.33	2.08
Italy	0.69	1.80	7.96	3.82	10.89	4.15
Japan	3.56	0.27	4.57	5.39	7.62	4.26
Norway	0.74	−3.27	5.65	3.99	7.78	4.54
Sweden	0.40	−2.74	6.35	4.02	8.60	3.09
UK	0.09	−1.07	6.92	2.43	4.94	4.96
USA	−0.34	−1.29	4.22	3.04	6.25	1.47

Source: Backus and Kehoe (1992) pp.878–9

Table 20.3 adds inflation to the picture, looking both at average or mean rates and their variability as measured by standard deviations. The most recent period stands out in every country as much more inflationary than the other two: the data for Germany exclude the hyperinflation of the early 1920s which is examined in Section 3. Indeed, sustained inflation in peacetime is very much a new feature in the post-1945 period. This unwelcome arrival certainly prompted some to long for a return to the discipline of the Gold Standard, a system where currencies were convertible into gold at fixed rates. The pre-1914 data, which come from the classic Gold Standard era (1870–1913), do indicate that this was a period of low average inflation but they also show instability in inflation comparable to the recent past. In so far as the welfare costs of inflation stem from its unpredictability rather than its magnitude, this evidence suggests that for many countries the higher inflation of the post-war period may not have been as serious a problem as is often believed.

The changing experience of inflation is underlined by looking at the long-run evidence for the UK in Figure 20.3. Several points are worth remembering:

- Years of falling prices were actually quite common in the nineteenth century and on into the 1930s.
- The inflationary decade of the 1970s stands out as an aberration.
- The rate of inflation has varied much more than has the rate of economic growth.

Finally, the contrast between Britain and Germany in the early 1920s should be noted. At the very moment when Germany experienced hyperinflation, the British price level was falling dramatically!

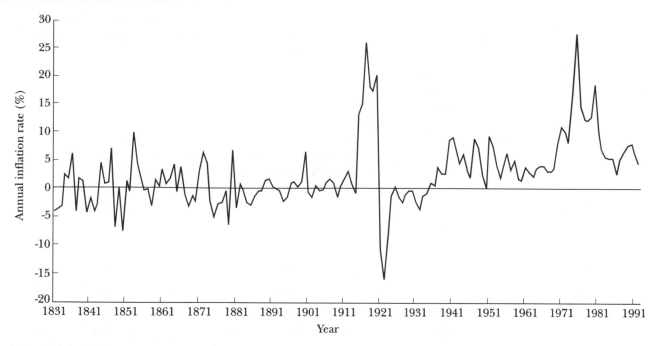

Figure 20.3 **UK inflation (GDP deflator), 1831–1992**

Source: Mitchell (1988); *Economic Trends*, various years

Figure 20.4 displays the UK unemployment rate since 1921, adjusted to allow for differences in the available statistics. These adjustments are large particularly where comparisons between the inter-war period and the recent past are concerned. Taken together with Figures 20.2 and 20.3 these data suggest the following:

- The unemployment rate tends to rise in recessions and fall in years of relatively rapid growth.
- In any particular period, relatively low unemployment and a boom tend to be associated with rising inflation.

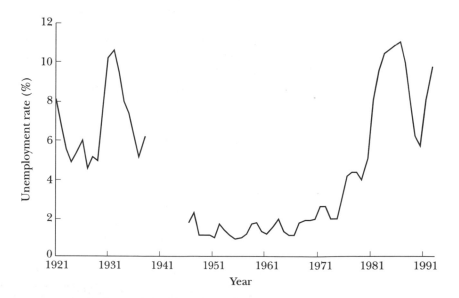

Figure 20.4 **UK unemployment rate: adjusted to a consistent basis, 1921–92**

Source: Crafts and Woodward (1991), updated using *Economic Trends*

- The level of unemployment which seems to be consistent with fairly stable inflation has changed markedly over time, being very low in the early post-war years but much higher recently.
- The British unemployment experience of the 1980s appears to be worse even than that of the 1930s.

Although levels of unemployment vary, there are often strong common features in changes in unemployment across the advanced countries, particularly at times of large macroeconomic shocks. Table 20.4 demonstrates this by showing data for the Great Depression and the years following the second OPEC oil shock when in each case there was a recession followed by recovery.

Table 20.4 **Standardized unemployment rates (%)**

	1929	1933	1937	1979	1983	1989
Australia	8.2	17.4	8.1	6.2	9.9	6.1
Austria	5.5	16.3	13.7	2.1	4.1	3.6
Belgium	0.8	10.6	7.2	8.2	12.1	8.1
Canada	2.9	19.3	9.4	7.4	11.8	7.5
Denmark	8.0	14.5	11.0	6.0	11.4	7.2
Finland	2.8	6.2	2.6	5.9	5.4	3.4
France	—	—	—	5.9	8.3	9.4
Germany	5.9	14.8	2.7	3.2	8.0	5.6
Italy	1.7	5.9	5.0	7.6	8.8	10.9
Japan	—	—	—	2.1	2.6	2.3
Netherlands	1.7	9.7	10.5	6.6	12.0	8.3
Norway	5.4	9.7	6.0	2.0	3.4	4.9
Sweden	2.4	7.3	5.1	2.1	3.5	1.4
Switzerland	0.4	3.5	3.6	0.3	0.9	0.5
UK	7.2	13.9	7.7	5.0	12.4	8.3
USA	3.1	24.7	14.2	5.8	9.5	5.2

Note that these data are standardized as far as possible to a common international definition whereas those of Figure 20.4 are standardized over time to current UK conventions.

Source: Maddison (1991) pp.260–5

1.2   Macroeconomic management: some perennial problems

The traditional view of economic fluctuations saw great scope for governments to stabilize the level of economic activity through demand management. If the aggregate supply curve is upward sloping in the short term, then stabilizing demand helps to stabilize output and employment. Success in this depends on a great deal of accurate information and the ability to act quickly in the face of shocks. Ill-timed or excessive interventions may make things worse, not better, and some shocks allow only unattractive policy options.

Question

For advanced countries the 1970s were characterized by big increases in the price of raw materials including, most obviously, oil. By contrast, the early 1930s saw the opposite coupled with a massive decline in world trade. How would the impact of these different shocks on the UK be represented on an *AD/AS* diagram?

The answer to this is quite straightforward but its implications are nevertheless important and we will return to them in Section 2. The 1970s shock is captured by the shift from SAS_1 to SAS_2 in Figure 20.5, raising prices from P_3 to P_4 and reducing output from Y_E to Y_2. This movement from A to B results in stagflation with falling output accompanied by rising prices. The 1930s shock can be seen as a shift from SAS_1 to SAS_3 as a result of lower raw material costs, plus the bigger shift from world trade decline of AD_1 to AD_2, together leading to a fall in prices to P_1 and in output to Y_1. This movement from A to C results in deflation with falls in both prices and output.

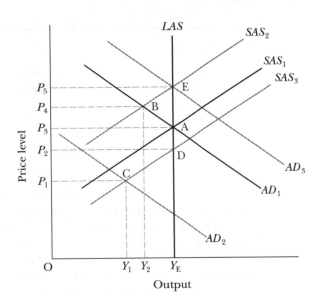

Figure 20.5   **Aggregate supply and aggregate demand**

Note that in the second, 1930s style, case the 'Keynesian solution' of stimulating demand back towards AD_1 appears very attractive; the outcome at D combats the fall in output without pushing prices up beyond their earlier level. In the first case, however, raising demand to AD_3 restores output to Y_E by moving to E, but only by accepting still higher prices at P_5. In this 1970s type stagflationary environment, traditional Keynesian responses seem much less appealing.

A serious problem arises in that encouraging policy makers to use discretionary intervention creates the opportunity for misuse of policy for short-term political ends. In particular, this may create inflation and overall welfare losses. This is the conclusion of the influential Barro-Gordon (1983) model which is represented in the pay-off matrix in Figure 20.6.

This model is similar to the one in Chapter 16, Section 3.2. Here the public is assumed to be worse off if inflation deviates from its expected rate (−1 in the top right and the bottom left quadrants). The government gains from

Public Government	zero expected inflation	high expected inflation
zero actual inflation	0 / 0	−1 / −2
high actual inflation	−1 / 1	0 / −1

Figure 20.6   The Barro-Gordon model

surprise inflation which temporarily lowers unemployment (1 in bottom left quadrant); this situation corresponds to a rightward shift in the *AD* curve causing both inflation and an increase in output. The government, however, loses from higher anticipated inflation which annoys voters with no compensating output gain (−2 and −1 in right quadrants); this situation corresponds to a rightward shift in the *AD* curve plus a corresponding upward shift in the *SAS* curve, causing prices to rise but with no change in output.

Exercise 20.1

1   Given the pay-offs in the Barro-Gordon model, explain why it is better for the government to have inflation.

2   Would you believe a promise by the government not to create inflation?

3   Which quadrant of the matrix shows the outcome?

4   Show the outcome using an *AD/AS* diagram.

The implication of the exercise is that, unless the government can make binding commitments, they will break promises not to create inflation. We should expect that their optimal strategy will be anticipated by the public and will thus lead to inflation but without raising output. A rule that cannot be broken would avoid the problem because there would be no possibility of imagining that surprise inflation could benefit the government: hence rules are better than discretionary policy according to this line of argument.

What is the downside risk of committing yourself to a policy rule? The most obvious is that it is no longer possible to respond to adverse demand shocks. In other words, there is a trade-off between the welfare losses from inflation if discretion exists and from possible unemployment if there are rules for maintaining low inflation. Even more worrying is that, if the 'wrong sort of shock' occurs, the policy rule may exacerbate its effects. The discussion in Unit 19 of ERM membership in the face of German unification illustrated this point: other European governments were stuck with the commitment to maintain existing exchange rates with the Deutschmark, at a time when the resulting high interest rates worsened their recession. A more graphic example discussed in Section 2.2 concerns adherence to the Gold Standard during the Great Depression of the 1930s.

In sum, macroeconomic policy is formulated by economists whose understanding is limited by an inability to perform controlled laboratory experiments and by governments who wish to get re-elected. All this makes policy errors only too likely.

More specifically, the key problem areas which lead to departures from a world of full employment and price stability are the following:

- exercise of discretion by short-termist politicians;

- unwelcome shocks from abroad;

- relying on a policy rule which has unfortunate consequences;

- incomplete information and forecasting errors.

1.3   Trend and cycle

Given a time series of observations for GDP, it is often useful to separate out a trend component from cyclical fluctuations. The trend can be thought of as the underlying rate of growth to which the economy will return once the temporary impact of shocks, policy errors and other short-term disturbances has evaporated. If the trend is thought of statistically, in terms of a constant proportionate rate of growth, then it can be estimated by regression methods. Regression is explained in Chapter 26.

Traditionally, economists have tended to think of the trend rate of growth as reflecting the improvement of productive potential, i.e. the growth of aggregate supply over time, with short-run fluctuations arising from changes in the pressure of demand, and they have often worked with models in which the trend rate of growth is a constant. If a reliable estimate of the trend rate of growth can be obtained, this is a key piece of the data with which to make policy. In particular, by comparing actual and trend output, an estimate of the 'output gap' can suggest the appropriate stance for policy to manage aggregate demand. In practice, things are not quite so simple, and recent developments in macroeconomics have tended to be critical of this approach, as the remainder of this section suggests. (A relatively accessible introduction can be found in Balke (1991).)

First, it should be stressed that trend rates of growth may vary over time. This poses quite serious measurement difficulties in practice and tends to imply that forecasting productive potential over long periods is subject to wide margins of error.

A second reason to be cautious about the traditional dichotomy between trend and cycle develops the point that transient shocks may have long-term implications. One way in which this may happen is through the changes in economic institutions and policy frameworks to which they give rise. The most obvious example is the aftermath of war, but the severe depression of the 1930s and the OPEC shocks of the 1970s may also have had quite profound impacts, as later sections explain.

Third, it may also be that some shocks affect the supply side and the subsequent trend rate of growth. Maddison (1991) argues that the 1970s saw just such shift to a lower trend growth rate in the OECD. We shall return to this point in Section 3.

Exercise 20.2

Review the data in Table 20.1 and Figure 20.1. Does Maddison's claim seem plausible? Can you think of any reasons why trend growth rates fell after 1973? Illustrate your answer using an *AD/AS* diagram.

It has been argued by the Real Business Cycle (RBC) theorists that some fluctuations which originate on the supply side may not require intervention to remedy welfare losses from market failure. An accessible introduction to this approach by a leading proponent and a leading sceptic can be found in Plosser (1989) and Mankiw (1989). This school of thought would claim that fluctuations in the level of economic activity generally do not reflect market failures but rational responses of households and firms faced with changing conditions, notably through 'technology shocks', which may be positive or negative.

The essence of RBC theory is that individuals make choices in a framework which includes the opportunity to switch activities between time periods in response to price signals. If, at a time of low activity, we observe households working less, consuming less but having more time for non-market work and leisure, this could simply all be a result of the substitution effect of a lower real-wage rate. In such a situation, unemployment represents household preferences, and so policy intervention would not be required. An example might be a case where the price of a primary producing economy's chief export crop falls as a result of its replacement in world markets by the invention of a synthetic substitute. This would be an example of a negative technology shock.

How seriously should we take this suggestion? It does not seem a good explanation of major crises. It is incredible even to economists sympathetic to RBC views that the Great Depression of the 1930s reflected technology shocks, and that welfare could not have been raised by economic policy intervention (Lucas, 1987, p.71). In normal times, however, RBC views may have some value, as Table 20.5 suggests.

Table 20.5 **Contributions of demand and supply shocks to fluctuations in growth and inflation, 1960–88 (%)**

	Growth		Inflation	
	Demand	**Supply**	**Demand**	**Supply**
OECD	43.3	56.7	45.2	54.8
G7	48.3	51.7	44.4	55.6
France	54.5	45.5	27.8	72.2
Germany	31.0	69.0	68.2	31.8
Japan	25.7	74.3	60.9	39.1
UK	76.0	24.0	48.3	51.7
USA	56.7	43.3	25.9	74.1

Source: adapted from Sterne and Bayoumi (1993)

Question

Check the plausibility of Real Business Cycle ideas by examining the data in Table 20.5. Do they seem to support the suggestion that the government should not seek to smooth out most fluctuations?

Table 20.5, which is based on a careful econometric study, finds that supply shocks are of slightly greater importance than demand shocks in explaining variations in OECD growth and inflation. Given that at least some of the demand shocks reflect policy errors, this suggests that, in the absence of policy intervention, the majority of shocks would originate on the supply side and that government neither can nor should try to stabilize output completely.

2 Case studies of stabilization failure

This section reviews some episodes of macroeconomic crisis. The historical notes provided are intended to be no more than thumbnail sketches and are written so as to highlight ideas encountered in Chapters 17–19 and in Section 1 above. References are given to fuller and more balanced accounts.

2.1 German hyperinflation, 1918–23

The inflation in early 1920s Germany is deservedly famous. By the end of November 1923, a one-kilo loaf of rye bread cost 428 billion marks. At the end of the war in 1918, currency in circulation was 33 billion marks; this had grown to 608 million trillion marks by December 1923. The best modern academic study can be found in Webb (1989). Table 20.6 displays some details of the inflationary experience.

Table 20.6 **Hyperinflation in Weimar Germany**

	Wholesale prices (1913 = 1)	Real M0 (1913 = 1)	Real govt debt (bn mks 1913)	Real budget deficit (bn mks 1913)
1919 I	2.74	2.63	54.1	1.50
1919 II	3.08	2.49	50.0	3.39
1919 III	4.93	1.59	32.1	1.98
1919 IV	8.03	1.18	17.3	0.78
1920 I	17.09	0.65	10.9	0.35
1920 II	13.82	0.93	14.2	1.19
1920 III	14.98	0.91	14.8	1.65
1920 IV	14.40	1.03	16.0	0.74
1921 I	13.38	1.07	17.5	0.20
1921 II	13.66	1.12	18.4	1.82
1921 III	20.67	0.82	12.4	1.23
1921 IV	34.87	0.65	8.7	0.92
1922 I	54.33	0.47	5.62	0.50
1922 II	70.20	0.45	4.15	0.30
1922 III	287.0	0.22	1.20	0.58
1922 IV	1475.0	0.17	0.95	0.83
1923 I	4888.0	0.23	1.30	1.05
1923 II	19385.0	0.22	0.68	1.09
1923 III	23900000.0	0.26	0.47	2.64
1923 IV	1261600000000.0	0.09	0.21	1.93

Source: Holtfrerich (1983); Webb (1986, 1989)

Several features of Table 20.6 should be noted:

- The inflation slowed, restarted and then accelerated spectacularly.
- During the inflation, the government ran large budget deficits yet the real value of its outstanding debt was almost completely wiped out.
- Although the nominal money supply soared, prices rose much more, so that the real money supply fell dramatically.

In a proximate sense, the inflation resulted from the massive rise in the money supply and the excess demand for goods this provoked. As inflationary expectations took hold, people tried to avoid holding money. This added further to the inflationary pressure and is reflected in the falling real value of M0 as the price level rose even faster than the money supply.

Webb (1989, p.v) rightly points to more deep-seated causes: 'The inflation did not happen because the Reichsbank's printing press had a faulty tachometer. It happened because the German government faced irreconcilable demands from labour, industry, and the Allies. The German government chose the policies that led to inflation because they appeared to offer lesser evils in the short run.'

As might be expected, the policy regime in place during the hyperinflation did not contain rules to discipline politicians. There was a floating exchange rate and, unlike the modern Bundesbank, the Reichsbank was not independent. It freely purchased government debt, thereby translating the growing government deficit into the monetary base of the economy. The public recognized that this created inflation and so expectations of inflation increased when additional public expenditure unmatched by new taxes was announced.

Early Weimar governments were coalitions of centrist parties threatened by extremists on both the left and the right. Raising additional taxation was very difficult politically. Nevertheless, by 1920 sufficient had been done to persuade the financial markets that the public finances and thus monetary growth were basically under control. In May 1921 the Allies announced reparations demands amounting to an initial flow of about 10 per cent of national income. When it became clear that taxes were not to be further increased, monetary growth and inflationary expectations were revived. Failure fully to meet reparations demands then provoked in 1923 the French invasion of the Ruhr and the final acceleration of inflation, with excess demand exacerbated now by falling aggregate supply.

Question

Stabilization was achieved and the hyperinflation ceased at the end of 1923. Reviewing the above and the analysis of Figure 20.6, what would have been required to bring this about?

The basic ingredient had to be a credible commitment by government to curtail its borrowing and the monetization of its debt. This was achieved by a return to the fixed exchange rate Gold Standard system, by the introduction of strict limits on purchases of government debt by the Reichsbank and, conditional on this, by the 1924 Dawes Plan which reduced reparations and provided a large international loan.

2.2   The Great Depression of the early 1930s

The Wall Street Crash of October 1929 and the slump which followed it are legendary. Figure 20.1 demonstrated the severity of the downturn; no such catastrophe followed the similar Wall Street Crash of October 1987. Naturally such momentous events raise a huge range of issues in the historical literature. Here the focus is narrowed to three related questions which illuminate the abstract arguments of Section 1. These are:

1   Why did output decline so dramatically in the USA?

2   What were the implications of the US slump for other countries?

3   Why did Britain escape so lightly by comparison?

Among major countries, the slump in the United States was the most severe of the 1930s and that in the UK the least. Table 20.7 shows that American prices and output both fell abruptly during 1929–33. The contraction in the money supply and investment were both pronounced and, most famous of all, so was the collapse in stock market prices. A good recent overview of the US experience is in Romer (1993).

Table 20.7   **The UK and USA in the Great Depression**

	Y	X	C	I	P	M0	M3	Equity prices
UK		£m 1938 prices			1929 = 100	£m		1938 = 100
1929	4216	986	3765	461	100	558	2542	113
1930	4210	849	3822	463	99.6	565	2549	91
1931	3980	684	3863	454	97.2	555	2523	71
1932	4008	669	3839	396	93.7	560	2571	68
1933	4046	678	3937	409	92.5	613	2782	84
1934	4334	704	4051	498	91.7	627	2721	102
1935	4496	794	4163	518	92.6	626	2874	113
1936	4633	771	4285	565	93.1	658	3080	131
1937	4834	810	4357	584	96.6	699	3205	122
USA		$bn 1929 prices			1929 =100	$bn		1941–43 = 100
1929	104.4	5.2	79.0	16.2	100	7.1	46.2	260.2
1930	95.1	4.0	74.7	10.5	96	6.9	45.2	210.3
1931	89.5	2.9	72.2	6.8	85	7.3	41.7	136.6
1932	76.4	2.1	66.0	0.8	77	7.8	34.8	69.3
1933	74.2	2.2	64.6	0.3	75	8.2	30.8	89.6
1934	80.8	2.7	68.0	1.8	80	9.1	33.3	98.4
1935	91.4	2.8	72.3	8.8	79	10.7	38.4	106.0
1936	100.9	3.0	79.7	9.3	82	12.2	42.9	154.7
1937	109.1	4.0	82.6	14.6	83	13.4	45.0	154.1

Source: Mitchell (1988); US Bureau of the Census (1960)

It is widely accepted that the American Great Depression resulted from demand shocks and that errors in monetary policy played a substantial part in precipitating the crisis. Precise attribution of the relative importance of the various components of the demand shock is still highly controversial. Factors which undoubtedly mattered included uncertainty coming from the volatile behaviour of stock market prices which, together with rising real debts, hit consumer spending. In addition, investment was held back by problems in the financial sector (Calomiris, 1993), and housebuilding investment was drastically reduced as earlier overbuilding was corrected (Hickman, 1974).

An important aspect of the American depression was the powerful impact of badly designed economic policy responses in the face of unexpected shocks, exacerbated by a fragile banking system. Initially, very restrictive monetary policy sought to restrain the stock market boom of the late 1920s. Failure to change policy rapidly when recession set in led to waves of bank failures, a further contraction of the money supply and a 'scramble for liquidity' as the public sought to convert bank deposits into currency (compare M0 and M3 in Table 20.7). Then, from Autumn 1931 until Spring 1933 expansionary policy was effectively precluded by the Gold Standard. After 1933 monetary expansion aided recovery.

What stood in the way of better policy making? To an extent, problems resulted from lack of appropriate data and experience. More fundamentally, the decentralized decision-making structure of the Federal Reserve System (Central Bank) made decisive and rapid counter-cyclical monetary policy very difficult, and the policy rule (Gold Standard) severely limited freedom of action (Eichengreen, 1992).

How did all this affect other countries? Most obviously it cut back demand for other countries' exports and curtailed American foreign lending, thus undermining balance of payments positions abroad. More subtly, but more importantly, impacts came through the Gold Standard system of fixed exchange rates based on convertibility of currencies into gold, as the excellent introductory survey by Newell and Symons (1988) reveals.

Deflation in the large US economy led to the prices of internationally traded goods falling generally by about 25 per cent between 1929 and 1932. Restrictive American monetary policy induced similar policy elsewhere to protect convertibility and the fixed exchange rate, and exposed other fragile banking systems to bank failures. Unilateral expansionary initiatives, whether monetary or fiscal, threatened the exchange rate via their implications for the balance of payments and were thus precluded by the Gold Standard. Restoration of internal balance and international competitiveness needed large falls in both prices and wages. Thus economies were pushed down the short-run *AS* curve as output fell in response to the deflationary policies, and as aggregate demand declined.

In these circumstances, in the absence of co-ordinated international reflation, leaving the Gold Standard and allowing the currency to depreciate made a lot of sense. This restored policy makers' discretion to use stabilization policy, permitted unilateral monetary expansion and interest rate cuts, and removed the need for further falls in prices and wages. Figure 20.7 shows the relationship between industrial production and exchange rates. Those countries whose exchange rate depreciated the most, were also the ones whose output increased. This figure clearly illustrates the different outcome for countries who left gold (like Sweden) and recovered, and those that did not (like France) who remained mired in depression.

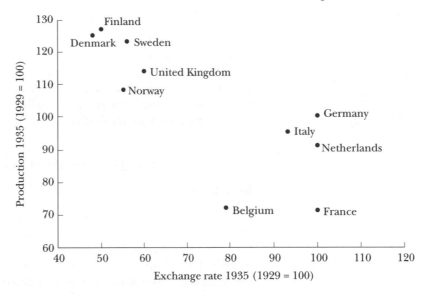

Figure 20.7 **Changes in exchange rates and industrial production, 1929–35**

Source: Eichengreen and Sachs (1985)

In 1925, returning to the Gold Standard had looked highly desirable as a rule which would prevent inflation; thinking of the German experience, the Governor of the Bank of England called the system 'knaveproof'. By 1931, adherence to this policy rule in the face of the shock of the world depression inflicted deep wounds, and discretion in economic policy seemed much more desirable.

The UK experienced a relatively early recovery. This was despite the apparent downward inflexibility of wages much remarked by contemporaries. Moreover, Keynesian demand stimulus through fiscal policy was deliberately eschewed. Compared with the USA, the favourable circumstances were rather to be found in being forced out of the Gold Standard in September 1931 when the £ sterling depreciated in value, also in the absence of bank failures, and much more buoyant investment opportunities in housebuilding. Accordingly Table 20.7 shows that M3 fell only very slightly in 1930–31 and rose appreciably in 1932–33, while prices fell much less and investment was much more resilient than in the USA.

Changes in economic policy, which included imposition of a general tariff on manufactures and heavy rearmament expenditure, also promoted recovery in the short run by increasing aggregate demand. There were, however, adverse consequences of the new policy framework for long-term growth, particularly through the lowering of competitive pressures on British firms to pursue productivity improvements (Broadberry and Crafts, 1992). This may be quite a good example of a cyclical shock with implications for future trend growth.

Question

Can you think of reasons why the aftermath of the 1987 stock market crash was less severe than that in 1929?

The Wall Street Crash is often talked of as the reason for the Great Depression. Clearly, this is too simplistic given the different experience 60 years later. This section suggests some reasons why the late 1980s did not see a repeat of the early 1930s. Most obviously, the policy response was very different. Mindful of the lessons of the earlier experience, monetary authorities around the world co-ordinated an immediate easing of monetary policy which helped to stimulate aggregate demand. Equally important, the world was not locked into the Gold Standard. Finally, it is doubtful that, in the absence of restrictive monetary policy, the 1929 crash would have had devastating consequences for the American economy.

2.3 Third world debt and macroeconomic shocks

Macroeconomic disturbances in the OECD countries have a fallout in the developing world and tend to have a particularly strong impact on countries who have relied heavily on foreign borrowing. The 1980s debt crisis is familiar (see Chapter 1) but it should not be forgotten that the 1930s also saw similar problems. In each case Latin America was heavily involved and a brief comparison of the two episodes is quite instructive. A still useful introduction to these issues can be found in Allsopp and Joshi (1986).

Three aspects of both these OECD recessions were crucially important for debtor developing countries in that

- demand for exports by OECD countries was cut back;
- primary product prices fell relative to manufactures;
- real interest rates rose steeply.

These developments weakened the balance of payments, and reduced real incomes and output in the debtor developing countries. In addition, in the 1980s the situation was complicated by the OPEC oil price shock of the late 1970s which added to the problems of oil importers till the mid 1980s and which, when reversed in 1986, then undermined the balance of payments of oil exporters.

From the point of view of debtor countries, the important relation is that between the rate of growth of export revenues and the interest rate on the debt. The higher is export growth relative to interest rates, the more can be borrowed while servicing existing debt, maintaining the debt/export ratio and sustaining creditworthiness.

A sudden move to a world of high interest rates and falling export revenues implies the need to cut back imports and create an export surplus just to service existing debt while maintaining the debt/export ratio. Once it is no longer possible just to roll over debts, then, to pay back, the government needs to create both an export surplus and a fiscal surplus. A shock of this kind is in fact much the same as the announcement of large reparations, and the stabilization problems are very similar to those which confronted Germany in the early 1920s.

As Figure 20.8 suggests, the macroeconomic shock to Latin American debtor countries, reliant as they were on the USA market, was much larger in the early 1930s than in the 1980s. Yet Figure 20.8 also shows that the subsequent economic recovery after 1932 was much stronger than that after

1983. Most of the difference can be attributed to the strikingly different policy response by governments in both lender and debtor countries.

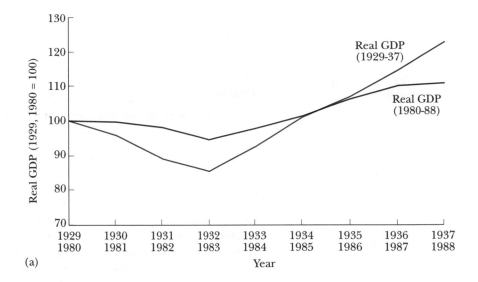

(a)

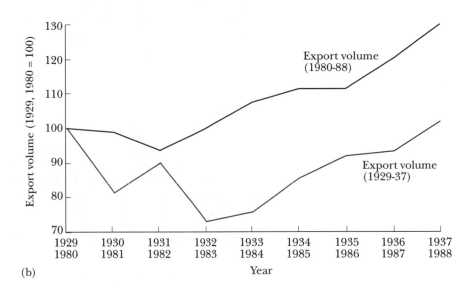

(b)

Figure 20.8   **(a) Latin American growth and (b) Latin American export volume in the 1930s and the 1980s**

Source: Maddison (1985); Inter-American Development Bank (1992)

In the 1930s there was a very high incidence of default on the debt which was mostly owed to private bondholders. Thus, by the end of 1935, $1163.7m out of $1523.8m owed to the USA was delinquent. The typical strategy adopted by Latin American governments also included leaving the Gold Standard and seeking to sponsor domestic industrialization through a variety of protectionist and state-centred measures. This amounted to an escape from the deflation of aggregate demand which the world shock and the service of their debts would otherwise have imposed.

In the 1980s, although there was much rescheduling of debt payments, there was little unilateral default. Most of the debt was owed to western banks and, fearful of the consequences of repudiation for the stability of their monetary systems, the lender countries exerted enormous pressure on debtor governments not to default. Instead they were pressed to introduce deflationary measures of approved stabilization and reform programmes geared to eventual repayment. In the least favourable cases (e.g. Argentina), the debt crisis degenerated into German style hyperinflation; in the more favourable outcomes, a stabilization was achieved and repayment maintained but with unfortunately low domestic investment (e.g. Mexico).

Question

To which aspects of the discussion of Section 1 does this experience relate?

These episodes are vivid examples of the economic management difficulties created by unanticipated external shocks. Here the shock comprises the fall in export demand plus the rise in interest rates. They also represent cases where the shocks had long-term consequences for trend growth rates in the debtor countries, particularly through their impact on the quantity and quality of investment. Here the long-term consequences were rather different from those in the short term. The protectionist economic development strategies which stemmed from the 1930s experience, proved seriously damaging to long-term growth prospects because they involved an inefficient use of resources, in the way discussed in Chapter 13. The supply-side reforms (including privatization and reduced protectionism) emanating from negotiations for rescheduling/relieving debt burdens in the 1980s may turn out to enhance long-run growth potential.

2.4   The transition from communism to capitalism in the early 1990s

The ending of the communist regimes in Eastern Europe was greeted at the time with euphoria and the widespread expectation that this heralded a much improved economic performance in these backward economies. In fact, the immediate macroeconomic performance was bitterly disappointing, as Table 20.8 reports. The inflation rates far exceed anything seen in the West in the past 40 years while, taken at face value, the collapse of output was of the same order of magnitude as in the Great Depression in the United States. A good introductory interpretation of this experience can be found in UNECE (1992, pp.39–56).

Question

Why might the official data of Table 20.8 overstate the true falls in output?

There is no doubt that a very serious contraction in output occurred but there are reasons to think these figures exaggerate. In particular, new private sector activity is under-recorded, the services sector is imperfectly monitored and, as a result, the declines in output of the state-owned manufacturing enterprises are given too much weight in the statistics. It should also be remembered that the welfare implications are not the same as they would be if similar declines were seen in the OECD. Rather, as at the end of a war, much of the output no longer produced may have been of very little or no value to consumers.

Table 20.8   **Changes in output and inflation in Eastern Europe**

	1989	1990	1991	1992
Real GDP (% change)				
Bulgaria	–1.9	–9.1	–11.7	–7.7
Czech and Slovak Republic	1.4	–0.4	–15.9	–7.1
Hungary	–0.2	–4.0	–12.0	–4.6
Poland	0.2	–11.6	–7.0	1.0
Romania	–6.9	–7.4	–13.7	–15.4
Russia	1.9	–3.6	–11.0	–20.0
Ukraine	4.1	–3.4	–10.0	–14.0
Consumer price inflation (% per year)				
Bulgaria	6.4	26.3	334.0	128.0
Czech and Slovak Republic	2.3	10.8	58.7	10.9
Hungary	17.0	28.9	35.0	23.0
Poland	251.1	585.8	70.3	43.0
Romania	0.9	7.4	161.0	210.0
Russia	2.4	5.2	90.4	1750.0
Ukraine	2.2	4.2	84.2	1600.0

Source: European Bank for Reconstruction and Development (1993)

Although the large falls in output were a very unwelcome surprise, economists had generally predicted that there would be a period of initial inflation and suspected that in some cases this would prove hard to control. Introduction of a market economy required price liberalization and implied an end to the rationing and forced saving of the communist period. This constituted a 'monetary overhang', i.e. the accumulated money balances were far higher than would willingly be held in a market economy at the initial price level. A large, one-off increase in the price level could be expected when prices were freed and was necessary to restore equilibrium.

Stabilizing the inflation after this initial phase posed problems similar to those in Weimar Germany and required similar disciplines on policy makers in the fledgling democracies. Starting out with an inadequate tax base in most cases and subservient/inexperienced central banks in some instances, large budget deficits which were monetized and which led to a high velocity of circulation of money were always a danger and hyperinflation very possible.

Question

Using the aggregate supply/aggregate demand framework, can you suggest reasons for the substantial output falls in Table 20.8?

It seems clear that both supply and demand factors were involved in the slump. Attempts at quantification are still in their infancy but the key problems have been identified. Leftward shifts in both short- and long-run *AS* came from three sources: temporary effects of redeploying resources, consequences of rising energy prices, and shortages of credit for working capital. Leftward shifts in *AD* came from declining export demand in the former COMECON trading area and also from deflationary policy when stabilization programmes were implemented. Demand management was horrendously difficult given the rapidly evolving structure of these economies, the effects of the power struggle in Russia and the lack of information about likely behaviour in the new circumstances.

A final aspect of the experience of transition should be borne in mind, namely the difference between the short- and long-run implications of policy choices. In order to have any chance of long-run growth and development as market economies, short-term economic pain was unavoidable. Transitory inflation in the elimination of excess money balances and unemployment from restructuring the economy were necessary components of change. In judging the transition, future generations will focus more on the quality of the policy reforms in relation to long-run growth and stability than the size of the initial output decline.

2.5 Macroeconomic management in the UK, 1983–93

In the mid 1980s, the UK had strong output growth, high unemployment and moderate inflation. During the late 1980s and early 1990s this phase was followed by a 'boom and bust cycle' in which first of all unemployment fell sharply and inflation began to accelerate. Then growth faltered, the economy slid into a lengthy recession while unemployment returned to mid-1980s levels and inflation fell to a thirty-year low. Look again at Figures 20.2, 20.3 and 20.4 to remind yourself of the details.

The background to this experience is the extensive policy change and experimentation carried out by the Thatcher governments. This is well described in Johnson (1991). Two key elements of this programme should be noted:

- the search for a policy rule to prevent inflation;
- supply-side reforms aimed at increasing trend growth and lowering the equilibrium level of unemployment.

The 1970s saw a very high level of inflation in the UK. Unfavourable commodity price shocks played a part as did over-ambitious unemployment targets, but many observers and the incoming Thatcher government took the view that the underlying problem was misuse of discretionary fiscal and monetary policy. The initial response of the new government was the Medium Term Financial Strategy which publicly set 'binding' money supply growth and budget deficit targets. Inflation fell steeply in the context of recession and commodity price falls but in practice the monetary targets were not achieved, were regularly adjusted and lacked credibility. When inflation increased again, the alternative rule on offer was to join the ERM and tie monetary policy to that of the independent Bundesbank. This was eventually done in October 1990.

Supply-side policy was aimed at improving efficiency and incentives through lowering direct taxation, and through privatization, de-regulation, and trade union reforms reducing unemployment benefits relative to earnings. The outcome was a major shakeout of labour in the early 1980s and a big rise in manufacturing labour productivity. As recovery took hold, there was a large expansion of personal credit lent by the newly de-regulated financial sector to increasingly optimistic households. Also unemployment began to fall in 1986 but was still above the (now lower?) equilibrium level.

Question

Table 20.9 reports a very typical economic forecast from 1987, together with the actual out-turn. The forecast turned out to be seriously wrong. What problems do you think may have confounded the forecasters?

Table 20.9   **London Business School UK economic forecast, October 1987, and actual out-turn (in parentheses)**

	GDP growth (% per year)	Inflation (% per year)	Unemployment (000s)
1987	3.0 (4.8)	2.9 (4.2)	2902 (2807)
1988	3.2 (5.0)	4.3 (4.9)	2738 (2275)
1989	3.1 (2.2)	4.6 (7.8)	2725 (1784)
1990	2.9 (0.4)	4.7 (9.4)	2674 (1623)
1991	3.2 (-2.2)	4.4 (5.9)	2587 (2287)

Source: *Economic Outlook* (1987); *Economic Trends Annual Supplement* (1994)

The basic reasons for forecasting errors are inaccurate data, a mis-specified economic model, unanticipated shocks and unforeseen changes in economic policy. All these played a part. Later data revealed that demand was growing much more quickly than was realized in October 1987. Central to this was consumer spending whose growth was very strong indeed and was fuelled by readily available credit. The old equations to predict consumer spending were no longer relevant but there was insufficient experience of the new liberalized financial system to replace them adequately and in the new conditions the personal savings ratio turned out to be extremely volatile. The forecasters' difficulty is reflected in Figure 20.9.

The demand growth was excessive and the economy soon was perceived to be overheating whereupon interest rates were raised dramatically, also shown in Figure 20.9. As growth in demand slowed in response to this, adverse shocks appeared in the form of the Gulf War and German unification. The latter's effect on the UK was made deflationary by the decision to join the ERM, itself an unknown at the time of the forecast in Table 20.9.

Now put yourself in the Chancellor of the Exchequer's shoes in the late 1980s. Designing an appropriate stabilization policy was not easy. Recall the discussion of trend and cycle in Section 1.3. At this point, estimates of potential output growth were very sensitive to methods of trend estimation.

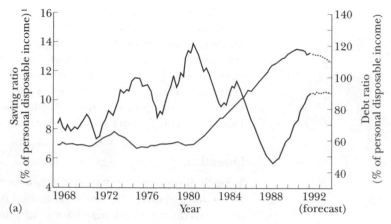

(a)

¹ four quarter moving average

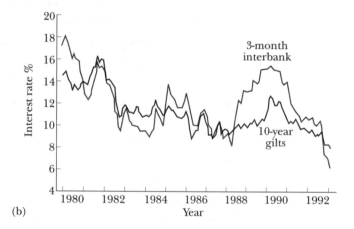

(b)

Figure 20.9 **(a) UK personal sector debt and saving ratios and (b) UK interest rates**

Source: HM Treasury (1993b)

Moreover, the policy reforms of the early 1980s may have raised productivity growth, but how much of this involved transitory elements? Reform of the labour market may have changed the equilibrium level of unemployment, but again it was not known by how much. Forecasting consumer demand growth had been made extremely difficult by the deregulation of credit which in turn made monetary targets unworkable. In 1987 it was still not obvious if and when overheating would occur or, in other words, how large was the remaining output gap.

After the failure of monetary targets, the pressure grew to adopt the alternative rule, membership of the ERM, which after all seemed to be working well for other countries. Here too the Chancellor's luck was out. In the context of German unification and the associated upwards move in ERM country interest rates, the UK can be seen to have adopted this rule just as the wrong sort of shock materialized. The ERM became a force for deflation much as had the Gold Standard of the early 1930s.

2.6   A perspective on the case studies

The five examples above comprise a sorry story of economic failures ranging from the unpleasant to the disastrous. Taken together they amply illustrate the perennial problems outlined in Section 1.2. Nevertheless, it must be remembered that these are exceptional episodes and do not represent anything like the average experience.

In fact, the data in Tables 20.1, 20.2 and 20.3 are consistent with an optimistic view of macroeconomic history in which on balance conditions have improved. Recent fluctuations have been less severe than formerly, inflation has been more predictable and income levels have been much higher than those of our ancestors. Even the standard of economic policy making seems better than that of the inter-war period. Indeed, a marked contrast with the problems of these case studies is to be found in the happy experience of the 'Golden Age' (1950–73) which is reviewed in detail in Section 3.

In sum, four themes stand out in the examples considered here:

- Good policy requires accurate information about key economic variables and relationships; this is sometimes unavailable.

- Economic policy makers have to cope with unforeseen shocks which imply that the optimal design of policy rules changes over time.

- Accordingly, there is a crucial recurrent question of how much discretion to allow policy makers.

- The short-run recovery and long-run growth consequences of stabilization policy decisions may be very different.

3   Comparisons of growth and productivity performance

Recall that Table 20.1 displayed a wide range of growth rates across the OECD countries: in the post-war period sustained growth in real GDP per person has been as high as 8.0 per cent in Japan during 1950–73 and as low as 1 per cent in Switzerland between 1973 and 1989. This raises several questions which this section addresses, namely:

- What are the proximate sources of growth?

- How should we evaluate growth performance?

- Why did OECD growth accelerate during and slow down after the Golden Age?

3.1   International comparisons of income and productivity

Since the mid 1970s there has been a major research effort directed at obtaining better measures of relative output and productivity levels across countries. The problem which investigators have to confront is how to convert output measured in the currency of one country into that of another. Chapter 19 showed that using prevailing exchange rates (which are influenced by interest rates, currency speculation etc.) for this purpose can lead to highly inaccurate results. What is required is a 'purchasing power parity (PPP) exchange rate' which reflects how high internal prices in one country are relative to the other. Estimating these PPP exchange rates is, of course, tricky and runs into problems of choice of the weights for different items, and the issue of the comparability of the goods and services in terms of quality.

Table 20.10   **Levels of GDP per person ($ at 1985 US prices)**

	1950	1973	1989
Australia	5931	10331	13584
Austria	2852	8644	12585
Belgium	4228	9416	12876
Canada	6113	11866	17576
Denmark	5224	10527	13514
Finland	3480	9072	13934
France	4149	10323	13837
Germany	3339	10110	13989
Italy	2819	8568	12955
Japan	1563	9237	15101
Netherlands	4706	10267	12737
Norway	4541	9346	16500
Sweden	5331	11262	14912
Switzerland	6556	13167	15406
UK	5651	10063	13468
USA	8611	14103	18317

Source: Maddison (1991), pp.6–7

Caution is therefore required in using Table 20.10 but the broad picture it shows is probably reasonably reliable and these data are the best currently available using PPP exchange rates. Several features of this table are well worth noting.

- There are some big changes in the rank order of countries over time. Japan was 16th in this list in 1950 and 4th by 1989; by contrast the UK was 5th in 1950 but only 12th in 1989.

- All countries experienced a large increase in per capita income during these 40 years; even in the UK the 1989 level was 2.4 times the 1950 level whereas in Japan it was 9.7 times the 1950 level.

- Despite common perceptions to the contrary, the difference in real GDP per person between the UK and continental European countries was quite small. In 1989 West Germany and France were only 3.9 per cent and 2.7 per cent respectively above the UK level.

- In general, the gap between the United States and other countries has narrowed appreciably since 1950. France, for example was 48 per cent of the US level in 1950 but 76 per cent by 1989, while Japan progressed from 18 per cent of the US level in 1950 to 82 per cent in 1989.

Table 20.11   **Estimates of comparative levels of value added/hour worked in manufacturing**

(a)   Comparisons with the United States (USA=100)

	Brazil	France	Germany	India	Japan	Korea	UK
1950	19.1	38.3	32.4	4.0	11.8	4.7[1]	38.2
1960	35.6	48.0	58.6	5.3	19.5	7.8	44.0
1973	39.8	73.3	79.6	5.0	49.2	11.4	52.4
1979	35.9	88.7	95.8	5.0	62.6	14.7	53.5
1989	28.4[2]	91.0	83.8	5.7[2]	73.9	18.7	61.9

[1]Estimate for 1953. [2]Estimate for 1987.

(b)   Comparisons with the United Kingdom (UK=100)

	France	Germany
1950	76.7	88.8
1960	90.3	115.7
1973	113.3	126.8
1979	134.1	151.0
1989	120.4	117.4

Source: van Ark (1993), with subsequent
revisions advised by the author

Table 20.11 offers another comparison based on PPP exchange rates. This is the best available study of relative labour productivity.

Question

Looking back to the discussion of purchasing power comparisons in Chapters 1 and 2, can you think of problems in making comparisons between countries in Table 20.11, part (a)?

The comparisons between countries at similar stages of development are the most reliable for two reasons. First, the range and quality of goods produced is more similar. Second, the differences in price structures are much smaller which makes the weighting problem less severe. In part (a) of the table, strictly speaking only bilateral comparisons between the individual countries and the USA are valid. The goods compared to estimate the PPP exchange rate will vary as will the choice of weights. The direct Germany/UK comparison of part (b) is the more accurate one, although the indirect one which was published much earlier is often quoted. Table 20.11 cannot be used for precise comparisons of, say, Korea, Brazil and France but the relativities it shows can be taken as crude approximations.

Taking Table 20.11 at face value, what does it tell us? As in Table 20.10, a striking aspect of these data is the dramatic 'catching-up' of the USA since 1950, when the American manufacturing productivity lead was at an all-time high. The UK is seen to have a relatively disappointing performance, being overtaken by France and Germany during the Golden Age, but it regained some ground during the 1980s. Korea, a much-discussed Newly

Industrializing Country (NIC), has clearly embarked on a catch-up of the West but at the end of the 1980s still had a productivity level relative to the USA similar to that of Japan in the 1950s.

Japan's catching-up of the USA is very impressive, although perhaps the figures do not quite match common perceptions of Japanese prowess. There are two reasons for this. One is that the figures are per hour; the Japanese worked about 25 per cent more hours per year than Americans in 1989 so that on a per worker basis productivity was similar. The second is that Japanese productivity by sector is quite variable; in electronics and motor vehicles the Japanese are well ahead but these sectors are not by any means typical of the whole.

3.2   The proximate sources of economic growth

Growth in real income and output per person requires increases in labour productivity. In turn, these result from the use of additional capital per person and from greater efficiency in the use of factors of production (obtained via better technology, improved organization of production, etc.). Increases in the amount of capital available come from net investment which should be thought of in a broad sense to include not only plant, equipment, etc., but also the skills and expertise of the labour force, i.e. human capital. These proximate sources of growth explain how growth comes about but not why. More fundamental reasons for why growth rates differ relate to the determinants of international differences in capital accumulation strategies and in efficiency of factor usage. These are to be found in incentive structures, institutions and political decision making, which are discussed in Section 4.

The best known empirical studies of the proximate sources of growth are based on the idea of growth accounting pioneered in the 1950s by Abramovitz, Denison and Kendrick and most prominently continued of late by Maddison. Growth accounting seeks to assess the contributions of capital and labour to output growth, and then it attributes the remaining growth to total factor productivity (TFP) growth. TFP growth comes from greater efficiency of factor use. Some of Maddison's most recent estimates are shown in Table 20.12.

Table 20.12   **Why growth rates differed: a growth accounting view (% per year)**

	Capital input	Labour	(Education)	TFP	GDP
	(1)	(2)		(3)	(1)+(2)+(3)
1950–73					
France	1.84	0.18	(0.39)	3.02	5.04
Germany	2.27	0.15	(0.19)	3.50	5.92
Japan	2.93	2.51	(0.52)	3.83	9.27
UK	1.75	0.01	(0.20)	1.27	3.03
USA	1.37	1.17	(0.48)	1.11	3.65

Table 20.12 (continued)   **Why growth rates differed: a growth accounting view (% per year)**

	Capital input	Labour	(Education)	TFP	GDP
	(1)	(2)		(3)	(1)+(2)+(3)
1973–87					
France	1.48	−0.24	(0.56)	0.92	2.16
Germany	1.28	−0.49	(0.05)	1.01	1.80
Japan	2.29	0.66	(0.45)	0.78	3.73
UK	1.12	−0.19	(0.41)	0.82	1.75
USA	1.24	1.31	(0.44)	−0.04	2.51

Source: derived from Maddison (1991)

Growth accounting

You have already come across this technique in Chapters 1 and 14. Here is the theory behind it. The increase in output due to capital (or labour) equals the change in the amount of capital (or labour) employed, multiplied by its marginal product. That is

$$\Delta Y = \frac{\Delta Y}{\Delta K} \cdot \Delta K + \frac{\Delta Y}{\Delta L} \cdot \Delta L$$

This can be rearranged as follows:

$$\frac{\Delta Y}{Y} = \left(\frac{\Delta Y}{\Delta K} \cdot \frac{K}{Y}\right) \cdot \frac{\Delta K}{K} + \left(\frac{\Delta Y}{\Delta L} \cdot \frac{L}{Y}\right) \cdot \frac{\Delta L}{L}$$

The original expression has been divided through by Y. The first expression on the right-hand side has been multiplied top and bottom by K, and the second term top and bottom by L.

If factors are paid their marginal products, as in perfectly competitive markets, then the expressions

$$\left(\frac{\Delta Y}{\Delta K} \cdot \frac{K}{Y}\right) \text{ and } \left(\frac{\Delta Y}{\Delta L} \cdot \frac{L}{Y}\right)$$

can be approximated by the shares in national income of profits (30 per cent) and wages (70 per cent). These approximations were used by Maddison. TFP growth is then calculated as the excess of actual growth over that predicted using the second equation above. The contributions of capital and labour are estimated using the factor shares to weight their growth rates.

Chapter 14 discussed a number of problems with the growth accounting approach, notably the lack of attention paid to investment in human capital which should really be treated as an additional factor of production with an important impact on output. In Table 20.12, human capital was measured by 'education', which is merely an adjustment to the labour input based largely on years of schooling. This is highly unsatisfactory as a measure of the growth of human capital. Future work will have to improve on this to allow for vocational training and the important externalities of both education and training (O'Mahony, 1992). The data in Table 20.12 undoubtedly attribute too little to *broad capital formation* (i.e. comprising both physical and human components) and too much to TFP.

What are the robust findings of Table 20.12? First, the most important is that the biggest differences in growth rates over time or across countries in the OECD are not due to physical capital accumulation. Despite that, Japan does stand out as investing more than the others and reaping rewards from this. Second, measured TFP growth varies widely but falls markedly in all cases in the second period accounting for most of the slowdown in growth after the Golden Age. Third, the negative growth in labour inputs in Europe but not elsewhere since 1973 is an interesting difference reflecting declining hours worked both from more holidays and higher unemployment.

What accounts for the variations in TFP growth? Maddison (1991) argues that, in all cases but the USA, a good deal of the post-1973 slowdown is due to the exhaustion of the gains coming from freer trade, redeployment of resources out of agriculture, and diffusion of American technology and organizational methods which had been very important in the 1950s and 1960s. The TFP growth decline after 1973 is not yet fully understood and for the USA remains something of a mystery.

The differences between countries in TFP growth in the Golden Age are quite remarkable. Obviously, scope for productivity gains from catch-up and reconstruction varied a great deal between, say, Germany or Japan and the UK. Also, differences in measured TFP growth partly reflect investments in training, R & D etc., which are not well measured by growth accounting; for example, these probably account for a significant part of the difference between Germany and the UK (Bean and Crafts, 1995). Finally, the UK seems to have been less efficient in the use of its factors of production than were other countries and, in a famous pioneering growth accounting exercise, Denison (1968) concluded that weak TFP in the UK reflected poor management and unfortunate industrial relations.

3.3   Normalizing for catch-up

Question

Would a league table of growth rates compiled from Table 20.1 tell you who had done well and who had not?

The answer is: not necessarily. There are two main reasons for this. First, growth potential may have varied between countries for reasons beyond their control. Second, there may be trade-offs between fast growth and other objectives of economic policy such as having an extensive welfare state about which voters in different countries would not make the same decisions. This sub-section follows up the first of these two points.

In Section 3.1 it was noted that 'catch-up' of the United States was a key feature of post-war growth. Tables 20.13 and 20.14 provide some quantification of this hypothesis. Underlying these numbers is an analysis of growth across countries in different periods which took into account growth of factors of production and then estimated the relationship between the initial productivity gap with the United States and subsequent growth of TFP. Table 20.13 reports the statistical prediction of what the normal impact of these effects would be on growth given the productivity gap for selected countries at the start of each period.

Table 20.13   **Growth in real GDP/hour worked: bonus potential from catch-up and reconstruction (% per year)**

	1950–60	1960–73	1979–88
Australia	1.2	0.5	0.4
Canada	0.2	0.3	0.3
France	2.1	1.0	0.3
Germany	2.9	1.0	0.3
Italy	2.4	1.2	0.4
Japan	4.0	2.2	0.9
Sweden	1.3	0.8	0.3
UK	1.6	0.8	0.5
USA	0.0	0.0	0.0

Source: Crafts (1992)

The results in Table 20.13 emphasize the importance of allowing for differential catch-up potential in comparing growth rates over time or across countries. Particularly in the early post-war years, one reason for slower British economic growth was the lesser potential growth from catch-up and reconstruction. The table also confirms, through the much lower figures in 1979–88, that exhaustion of catch-up potential appears to be a significant factor in the OECD growth slowdown of the past 20 years.

The unusually fast catching-up of the USA by other OECD countries in the 1950s and 1960s was aided by a more rapid and complete technology transfer than had been possible previously, as Nelson and Wright (1992) stressed in an influential survey article. Some of the key changes were noted in Chapter 12; they include lower trade barriers and a growing integration of the world economy, the growth of R & D spending and college education in the OECD generally, the increased role of multinational companies and a reduction in the American advantages derived from the natural resources and large domestic market.

Nevertheless catch-up is not the whole tale nor is catch-up automatically achieved, as economic historians have always stressed. As Abramovitz (1986, p.389) put it, 'Social capability [for catch-up] depends on more than the content of education and the organization of firms … it is a question of the obstacles to change raised by vested interests, established positions and customary relations among firms and between employers and employees'.

This point is reinforced by a look at Table 20.14, which is derived from an econometric prediction in Barro and Sala-i-Martin (1991) of the normal rate of closing the gap with the leader in the OECD countries. The table includes Latin American countries, which in 1950 had a smaller productivity gap with the USA than Japan.

Table 20.14   **Growth in real GDP/hour worked: actual and forecast convergence with the USA in GDP/hour, 1950–87 (USA = 100)**

	Actual	Forecast
Argentina	28	50
Australia	78	81
Brazil	25	29
Canada	92	86
Chile	33	53
Colombia	28	38
France	94	58
Germany	80	47
Italy	79	48
Japan	61	27
Mexico	27	35
Peru	20	34
Sweden	82	67
UK	80	73

Source: Crafts (1992)

The two key results in Table 20.14 are:

• Some OECD countries do much better at catching up than others.
• The Latin American countries, especially Argentina and Chile which had productivity levels comparable with many European countries, under-perform given their 1950 starting points.

These points are considered further in Section 4.2.

3.4   Economic policy in the Golden Age

Trend economic growth in OECD countries in the years 1950–73 was exceptionally strong and certainly far outstripped the achievements both of the inter-war period and the last 20 years. This prompts the linked questions: what roles did the post-war settlement and the economic policy arrangements which emerged thereafter play in this outcome?

Table 20.15   **Gross non-residential investment in the 1930s and the 1950s (% GDP)**

	1929–38	1950–59
France	12.1	13.8
Germany	9.8	16.2
Japan	13.6	20.1
Netherlands	14.0	18.2
UK	6.0	11.3

Source: van de Klundert and van Schaik (1993)

Question

Table 20.15 shows a marked rise in investment in the 1950s. What do you think might explain this?

The rise in investment shown in Table 20.15 could simply reflect the favourable technological situation but many writers have been inclined to ascribe to policy and institutional developments a significant part in the story (Glyn *et al.*, 1990). High levels of economic activity and investment did not, however, reflect massive demand stimulus by governments as Keynesians might have thought necessary. Nevertheless, although good performance should not be attributed to active demand management, the avoidance of policy errors by the Americans on the scale of 1928–31 was a crucial element in maintaining the favourable state of affairs. Also, elastic supplies of raw materials and energy were available to obviate the threat of adverse commodity price shocks, making macroeconomic management easier than in the 1970s.

Two features may have supported the incentive to invest despite the much higher direct taxes which characterized the post-war world and might otherwise have depressed investment. First, macroeconomic management in the Bretton Woods period may have been conducive to high levels of confidence (Boltho, 1982). Second, in many countries reconstruction was based on successful deals concluded between capital and labour. These helped to ensure wage moderation in return for high investment and provided effective monitoring and commitment devices for both sides to sustain high investment in the absence of serious shocks (Eichengreen, 1994).

The conditions which favoured high investment could be expected to have a different impact on growth in the short and long run if there are diminishing returns to capital, as was argued in Chapter 14. This is probably one of the reasons why growth slowed down in the 1970s but was so strong in the 1950s. It should be remembered, however, that diminishing returns to investment in broad capital (i.e. including human as well as physical capital) will tend to appear only quite slowly. Thus, the effect of higher incentives to invest at the outset of the Golden Age would last for decades rather than years.

In sum, in the 1950s and 1960s a number of factors combined to promote a higher trend rate of growth based on rapid catch-up with strong investment and productivity growth. Favourable policy developments played a part and were brought about by the war and Pax Americana. At the same time, the absence of adverse shocks made the policy makers' task easier than before or since.

4   Further exploration of comparative growth and productivity

While Section 3.2 looked at the proximate sources of growth, this section probes a little deeper to consider some underlying reasons for falling behind or forging ahead. Supposing that we had correctly attributed the sources of growth to capital, TFP etc., this would still leave unresolved the issue of why investment or productivity growth differed.

A common response would be to highlight some aspect of Abramovitz's 'social capability' but even this would still beg the question. Perhaps the single most popular explanation for British relative economic decline in the post-war period is inadequate management (Alford, 1988). Similarly, Porter (1990) in his famous business school study referred to in Chapter 12 highlights this, together with a list of further aspects of 'social capability' in his discussion of why countries lack competitiveness. For an economist, however, such a response raises the further issue of how this could persist – why were poor managers not removed by the entry of new firms or through the capital market by takeover, or failing this, why did government not make an appropriate policy intervention?

In other words, economists tend to presume that people are rational and that profitable opportunities for change are not neglected for long. Nevertheless, there are a number of well-recognized ways in which market failures occur, and more recently economic analysis has highlighted possibilities of government policy failure and persistent differences in growth and productivity performance.

Ideally, it would be nice to explain why *equilibrium* growth rates and/or productivity levels would differ. Research on this topic is still in its infancy, however, and the following sections can do no more than suggest some possibilities centring on two questions:

- Why are there substantial differences between market economies in growth rates of income per person?
- Are the sources of strong productivity performance also responsible for international competitiveness?

Reflection

Pratten (1976) found that multinationals operating in both countries had labour productivity levels 27 per cent higher on average in Germany than in the UK. Can you suggest explanations for this? No explicit answer will be provided here but both the following sections explore related issues.

4.1   Institutional influences on broad capital formation

Investment, whether in skill formation, research and development or physical plant and equipment, depends on expected returns. These will be influenced by the cost of capital, the tax regime and the extent to which the investor can appropriate the returns for her/himself. Each can differ between countries. There certainly may be market failures to worry about, since there are likely to be positive externalities to investment in broad capital, and some investments are in public goods. Typically, a significant part of investment in education and research is paid for by government.

A recent assessment of European technological activity concluded that Germany was a strong performer with a dynamic system compared with the relatively myopic system in the UK (Patel and Pavitt, 1988). This judgement was based on managerial capabilities, educational standards, established in-house expertise and commitment to new technologies. The data in Table 20.16 seem consistent with this view and also indicate that there are large variations in innovation activities.

Table 20.16   **Research and development (R & D) and patenting**

(a) R & D expenditure as a percentage of GDP

	1964	**1970**	**1980**	**1989**
France	1.8	1.9	1.8	2.3
Germany	1.6	2.1	2.4	2.9
Japan	1.5	1.8	2.2	3.0
UK	2.3	2.2	2.2	2.2
USA	2.9	2.6	2.4	2.8

(b) Share of non-American patents granted in USA (%)

	1938	**1950**	**1958**	**1979**	**1988**
France	9.2	15.5	10.4	7.9	6.8
Germany	38.2	0.6	25.6	22.7	17.4
Japan	1.5	0.03	1.9	27.8	41.3
UK	22.7	36.0	23.4	10.8	8.1

Source: OECD (1991), (1991a), Englander and Mittelstadt (1988), Nelson and Wright (1992) and Pavitt and Soete (1982)

Private sector R & D expenditure was where the big shortfall lay in Britain in the 1980s – in 1988 this was 1.5 per cent of industrial GDP compared with 2.2 per cent in Germany and 2.1 per cent in Japan (Stoneman, 1991). Important reasons for this were to be found in the capital market. British firms are uniquely exposed to the danger of hostile take-over which entails the exit of existing top management (Jenkinson and Mayer, 1992). This might be expected to dampen their enthusiasm for long-term investments. Mayer (1992) found this to be the case. After a careful review of the evidence, he concluded that large firms, which are important in high-technology industries, felt compelled to maintain dividends and forgo investment opportunities in R & D and training, unlike other European firms.

In the 1960s the UK invested a higher fraction of GDP in R & D than anyone except the USA, but assessments of this investment have tended to be highly critical. Much of the funding was government money and a very high fraction of that was related to defence and particularly to aerospace. Here the problems seem to have been little spin-off to other sectors, the political difficulties of killing white elephants quickly, lack of cost control, and the political attractions of glamorous projects which crowded out more mundane expenditures to enhance information flows and technology transfer in the private sector.

Comparisons of productivity in plant surveys and examinations of relative productivity by industrial sector have tended to find that a considerable part of the post-war British productivity gap has been due to inadequate training of the workforce. For example, O'Mahony (1992a) found about 60 per cent of the gap between British and German manufacturing labour productivity at the end of the 1980s was explained in this way. Table 20.17 shows the decline in apprenticeship in Britain and, implicitly, the lack of adequate alternative training modes leading to the much lower proportion of qualified workers in the British than in the German labour force in 1987.

Table 20.17   **Some aspects of British and German training**

(a) Apprentices in engineering relative to total employment (%)

	UK	Germany
1938	12.1	10.6
1950	4.4	8.0
1980	3.4	7.1
1989	1.6	7.5

Source: Broadberry and Wagner (1994)

(b) Qualification proportions and relative wage rates of the manufacturing labour force (1987)

	Qualifications (%)		Wage rate relative to unskilled	
	UK	Germany	UK	Germany
Higher level	6.7	6.0	1.748	2.218
Upper intermediate	4.4	8.2	1.345	1.710
Lower intermediate	26.3	56.4	1.165	1.176
None	62.6	29.4	1.0	1.0

Source: O'Mahony (1992)

Reflection

Think about the differences in British and German vocational training shown in Table 20.17. Does the table offer any clue as to the reason for the relative shortfall in qualifications in the British labour force? Does your own experience shed any light on this issue?

The academic literature stresses three immediate reasons for the relatively low level of training of the British workforce. First, as Table 20.17 reveals, British wage structures shaped by trends in post-war collective bargaining have tended to compress skill differentials, which has reduced the incentive for workers to train (Prais and Wagner, 1988). Second, UK firms seem to be more exposed to high job turnover and to worry much more about other employers poaching their newly trained staff in the absence of employers' organizations able to police the situation. Third, there has been a lack of effective government action to combat these market failures (Soskice, 1989).

Question

So why wasn't government intervention the route to solving these problems of making adequate long-term investments in broad capital?

A full answer to this question would require a very big book. Nevertheless, one important point should be made which permits some useful insights. Politicians are interested in votes and there may be few votes to be gained and many to be lost by attempting appropriate correction of market failures. The forgone benefits would typically be widely diffused and quite small to any individual relative to the costs of organizing to lobby for them or to monitor their effective delivery. Vested interests who might be hurt by intervention are typically in the opposite position. Yet no single firm or household can, on its own, reform or buck the system whose presence may owe a good deal to historical accident.

4.2   Eurosclerosis, rent-seeking and rent-sharing

The discussion at the end of the last section has been elaborated at some length by Olson (1982) in a book referred to in Chapter 15. He hypothesises that long-established democratic societies will develop 'sclerotic tendencies' in the form of continuing growth in the number of interest groups which will tend to inhibit their growth performance, for example, by slowing down necessary redeployment of resources from old-technology 'sunset' industries to high-tech 'sunrise' industries. A period of totalitarian government and/or foreign occupation will purge society of these growth-retarding organizations and lead to a subsequent period of faster growth. Olson thus provides a rationale for the old bar-room joke that it would have been better for Britain to lose the war.

Despite its intuitive appeal, this hypothesis has been subject to much criticism and, in its crude form, is probably unacceptable. Three points should be remembered. First, encompassing (or, as Chapter 15 calls them, 'peak') organizations such as the Confederation of British Industries or Trades Union Congress, unlike lobbies representing small groups (trade association, craft union), will tend to give more weight to societal rather than narrow sectional interests, and thus their relative strength matters. Second, by making commitments and giving up discretion, government may be able to limit the power of the interest groups; for example, by signing up to international agreements like GATT or the Treaty of Rome. Third, associations which are interest groups may also perform functions which are socially beneficial, perhaps effective self-regulation or the internalizing of externalities. There is, however, some value in following up Olson's thesis, even though it is inadequate as a general explanation of 'falling behind and forging ahead'. Two examples will illustrate this.

First, consider the contrast between British and German industrial relations in the post-war period. The German system comprising 16 industrial unions established in 1949 was a direct consequence of Nazism, war and occupation. The UK entered the post-war world with its traditional system of craft unions and shop stewards still intact and with politicians of both parties firmly of the view that industrial relations reform was a no-go area (Flanagan *et al.*, 1983). This epitomizes the Olson hypothesis. Did it matter for growth and productivity?

Yes, probably it did play a part in Britain's relatively slow catch-up growth and in the lower productivity of multinationals in the UK. Theory suggests that a single union will have more concern about the overall profitability and productivity of a firm than one representing a small subset of the workforce. Case studies give ample evidence of the inhibiting effects of British industrial relations on productivity gains from technological progress and eliminating restrictive practices (Prais, 1981). Econometric investigations attribute a large part of the relative improvement in British manufacturing productivity in the belated catch-up of the 1980s to changed working practices and staffing levels brought about by reductions in trade union bargaining power and reforms of industrial relations (Bean and Symons, 1989; Haskel, 1991).

Yet these studies make another point very strongly. Namely, that increasing competition in product markets particularly from potential imports provided a crucial impetus to the 1980s productivity improvement. In essence, this reduced the rents which were available to be shared between capital and labour and had partly been taken in the form of jobs for more union members, i.e. overstaffing. Further afield, protectionist economic policies and inadequate competition, stemming from disillusionment with the world economy, are probably a central component of Latin America's 'catch-up failure', reflected in Table 20.14.

This leads us to the second example, the thinking behind the Single Market (1992) programme of the European Union. In the early 1980s, Olson's analysis seemed to many to be particularly insightful for European countries and gave rise to the suggestion that 'Eurosclerosis' was responsible for poor growth in the EC (now the EU). One response was the 1992 initiative to remove non-tariff barriers to trade, such as preferential treatment for home suppliers tendering for government contracts, and sheltering home producers through 'consumer safety' legislation. The 1992 programme could be expected to reduce sclerotic tendencies in the following two ways:

* increasing competition;
* reducing national governments' discretion to give in to lobbying.

Table 20.18 **Estimates of potential economic gains from the European single market (% GDP)**

1	Direct gains from removing frontier controls	0.3
2	Direct gains from eliminating other restrictions (e.g. on public procurement, safety rules)	2.4
3	Productivity increases from subsequent rationalization of production	2.1
4	Productivity increases from additional competitive pressure to reduce costs	1.6
	Total	6.4

Source: adapted from Emerson (1988)

Question

Check that Table 20.18 does show that the European Commission expected the Single Market Programme to attack Eurosclerosis. Are there reasons to think that Olson himself would be sceptical of these estimates?

The first two components in the table are conventional specialization (welfare triangle) gains from lowering trade barriers (see Chapter 14). The third and fourth components of the welfare gains forecast in Table 20.18, which comprise more than half the total, come from the anticipated productivity improvements due to more competition, i.e. from reduced Eurosclerosis. Clearly, the firm closures and job shakeouts implicitly envisaged by these estimates would hurt vested interests. Yet the European Commission itself has a lot of discretion in implementing the proposals and has shown itself influenced by lobbying in the past. Moreover, member governments and their lobbyists are likely to believe they can cheat without effective monitoring or sanctions. Peck (1989) develops these points in detail.

4.3   International competitiveness

Much politicians' rhetoric, and a good deal of the hype surrounding 1992, refers to the international competitiveness of industry. The term is usually ill-defined but reference is generally made to the country's world market share and/or balance of external payments position. Intuition, or a reading of Porter (1990), might suggest that this will necessarily bear a strong relation to good performance in growth and productivity improvement, and thus to the same factors that we reviewed in the preceding sections. In fact, the links are less close than you might imagine and world market share in manufacturing is not something to become unduly concerned about.

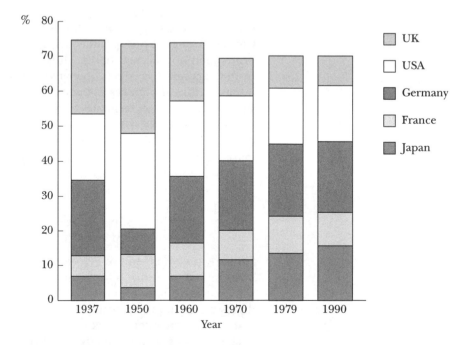

Figure 20.10 **Shares of world trade in manufacturing (%)**

Source: Brown and Sheriff (1979); *Monthly Review of External Trade Statistics* (1991); Maizels (1963)

Figure 20.10 shows dramatic changes in the pattern of world trade in the post-war period. Here common perceptions are largely correct. The notable developments are the rise of the Japanese share, the continued strength of Germany, the steep decline in the UK's share and the erosion of the US position. These changes are broadly in line with the relative growth and productivity performance described in Sections 3.1 and 3.2. Perhaps less widely recognized is that the big decline in the British share took place well before the 1980s, and that Japan has not yet caught up Germany in world market share.

Question

Compare Figure 20.10 with Tables 20.10 and 20.11. What does this tell you about the connection between world market share in manufacturing and output per person?

Evidently any relationship is somewhat loose. Two points should strike you. First, Germany and France had roughly the same income level at the end of the 1980s but France had less than half Germany's manufactured exports. Second, Germany's labour productivity in manufacturing was less than 85 per cent of the US level yet its exports were 25 per cent higher.

A little reflection provides some reasons for these apparently conflicting facts. The absolute size and openness to international trade of these economies varies somewhat. The overall trading relations that they have with the rest of the world depend also on their positions with regard to raw materials and invisible earnings, where the UK, for example, has traditionally been stronger than Germany. Finally, and most importantly, high labour productivity does not, as Chapter 12 noted, translate directly into competitiveness.

Changes in competitiveness can be expected to influence the volume of exports relative to imports and thus the balance of external payments. Competitiveness, appropriately defined, relates to relative costs of production not market shares. Thus changes in competitiveness will emerge from the combined effects of changes in relative productivity, relative inflation rates and moves in the exchange rate. Figure 12.7 in Chapter 12 showed the Treasury estimates of relative UK unit labour costs. Look back at this – remembering that a rise in the index implies improvement – and compare it with Table 20.11. Relative British labour productivity was markedly better at the end of the 1970s and particularly strong improvement was in fact registered in the early 1980s. Did this lead to improved competitiveness? – clearly not. The reasons for this are to be found particularly in exchange rate movements which were strongly influenced by changes in oil prices, monetary policy and eventually the decision to join the ERM at DM 2.95.

Similarly, a comparison of Figure 20.11 with Table 20.11 is also revealing. The general tendency is for economies with relatively low labour productivity to have lower wage costs which will substantially offset their disadvantage in productivity. The correlation is by no means perfect, of course. To a considerable extent this reflects short-term influences on exchange rates, with Germany in its post-unification phase noticeably out of line by having high labour costs.

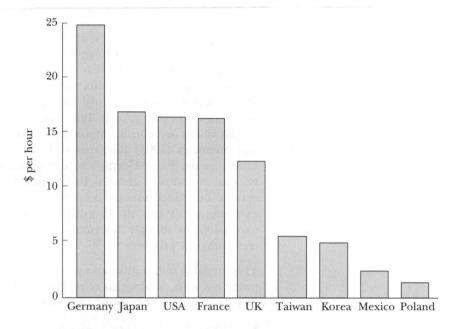

Source: data from Morgan Grenfell, Economics Department, 1994

Figure 20.11   Labour costs in manufacturing, 1993

Should nothing else change, then relatively weak productivity growth, compared with that in other countries, can be expected to lead to losses of competitiveness and adverse trends in the balance of payments. However, this can readily be compensated by a depreciation of the real exchange rate and this would be the normal medium-term result.

The real implication then is that weak productivity performance will tend to raise the price of imports relative to exports, and that this will tend to reduce real income growth, partly offsetting any increases in real GDP. For example, I estimated (Crafts, 1993, p.58) that, during the Golden Age, Germany and Japan enjoyed real income gains from terms of trade effects equivalent to 0.5 per cent and 0.4 per cent per year respectively more than did the UK. So weak UK productivity performance had costs in terms of real income growth. This should not be confused with problems of international competitiveness which result from mistakes in monetary and exchange rate policies.

5   Stabilization and growth in historical perspective

In the last part of this chapter I shall attempt to do two things:

- Bring together the work of Sections 1 and 2 with that of Sections 3 and 4, i.e. juxtapose stabilization and growth thus emphasizing the links between the short and the long run.

- Remind you of the value of a historical perspective when considering current economic performance and policy options.

5.1   Stabilization policies and the long-run growth rate

Question

Construct an argument to support the view that it is only supply-side rather than stabilization (demand-management) policy which affects long-run growth.

This result is suggested by analysis of a conventional *AD/AS* macroeconomic model of a small open economy. Key features of the model include a vertical long-run *AS* curve and an inability to influence the real interest rate which is determined in world markets. In this case, changes in the stance or mix of fiscal and monetary policy, or the choice of a different policy rule, will have no effect on the equilibrium volume of either output or capital. It is quite common to find in the literature results which are consistent with this prediction. For example, Alesina and Summers (1993) find that countries with independent central banks have – as the Barro-Gordon model would expect – lower inflation but at no cost in terms of growth. In the very long run the *AS* curve is still vertical but shifts outward as productive potential increases based on exogenous TFP growth. Investment is a passive component of this expansion, its volume determined by the real interest rate and technological progress.

This model is rather misleading when considered from an historical vantage point and with the insights of recent contributions to the theory of economic growth. Two points are worth remembering:

• Models which include both human and physical capital suggest that circumstances which independently promote higher investment have a quite long-lived effect on growth because diminishing returns only set in slowly.

• In a more realistic model, expected returns to investment could well depend on the macroeconomic policy stance of the government, which at the very least will affect the perceived risks of capital accumulation.

Reflection

Think about the second of these points. Can you think of historical cases to support this claim? Are there some suitable examples earlier in this chapter?

In fact, if we consider possible conflicts and spillovers between managing aggregate demand and promoting long-run growth, we have already encountered three interfaces which will flesh out the argument.

First, everyone accepts that hyperinflation is incompatible with sustained economic growth. As in Weimar Germany, hyperinflation tends to distort investment decisions and to provoke capital flight. Accordingly, the World Bank takes it as axiomatic that macro-stabilization to prevent hyperinflation is a necessary condition for a successful transition to growth in Eastern Europe in the 1990s (Fischer, 1992). On the other hand, as we saw in Section 2.4, an overriding concern with short-term price stability and full employment at all costs would effectively have ruled out economic reform in the former communist world.

Second, we have already noted the suggestion in Boltho (1982) that the macroeconomic policy framework of the Golden Age encouraged investment by reassuring people that there would be no repeat of the demand shocks of the 1930s. As with the first point, this should be seen as an argument that stability promotes investment and growth rather than that the route to faster growth is aggressive demand management.

Third, the experience of the UK during the 1980s revealed several important tensions between improving the supply side and short-term macroeconomic policy including the following:

1   Deregulating financial institutions and liberalizing foreign exchange transactions could be expected to have raised the quantity and quality of investment but made short-term macroeconomic forecasting much harder.

2   Allowing the free float of the pound in the early Thatcher years was consistent with a monetarist counter-inflation strategy but risked the hysteresis effects discussed in Chapter 18, involving a permanent contraction in the manufacturing base and, in consequence, lower future productivity growth (Krugman, 1987).

3   Adopting the ERM policy rule implied that short-term demand management would have to switch to relying on fiscal rather than monetary policy. This potentially conflicted with the government's stated aim of promoting investment and enterprise by promising business a stable low tax regime, because active fiscal policy would tend to involve changing tax rates.

5.2   Concluding comments

In this final section I wish simply to underline a few of the lessons from history that strike me from this survey. Please regard these as points whose validity you may wish to debate rather than as definitive conclusions.

First, it is important to have a yardstick for judging macroeconomic policy and performance. In this respect, the Golden Age (1950–73) is not an appropriate benchmark. Rather, it was the result of a unique (and thus unrepeatable) set of circumstances. Taking a longer historical view, the OECD experience of the last 20 years is quite respectable. Contrary to popular opinion, lessons are learnt from previous policy errors, and both post-1945 reconstruction of the world economy and the response to the stock market crash of 1987 are good examples of this.

Second, while the attractions of demand management were vastly oversold in the 1950s and 1960s, it would be wrong to suppose that policy is completely neutral in its economic effects and is always powerless to affect output in the long run. Moreover, big shocks do happen (1931, 1973, 1990, etc.) and, when they do, flexible policy responses are required.

Third, policy choices and institutional arrangements have substantial impacts on long-run growth performance which varies greatly across countries. The reasons for poor growth performance are often, at bottom, political and turn on the obstacles to creating better incentives for investment in broad capital.

Finally, history clearly tells us that policy and institutions have mattered both for growth and for stabilization. We know something of what to try and what to avoid. Unfortunately, we know much less about how deliberately to create an appropriate framework conducive to improved performance. Historical accident seems generally to have played a large part and, at any point, the past constrains the present through its legacy of vested interests and conventional wisdom.

PART 12
CHAPTER 21

by Francis Green

LABOUR IN THE ECONOMY
THE LABOUR MARKET

1 Introduction

A financially-starved student goes down town one day, knocks on a factory door and asks if there is any work going: perhaps there is a half-day's labouring to be done, perhaps not. Across the globe a 40-year-old man goes to work in an office in one of the large Japanese corporations: he has been working there already for 20 years and confidently expects to do so for 20 more. These two people are doing the same thing in one general respect: they are both participating in a labour market.

They seem poles apart. On the one hand, the student works just a few hours in return for equivalent wages and may never again return to have any relationship with the company. Here the labour market is similar to the market for, say, apples in a street market: a consumer exchanges money for apples and after the exchange is done, provided there is no fault with the apples, that is that. The only difference is that apples are exchanged rather than, in the case of the student, a few hours work. On the other hand, the Japanese worker benefits from the 'nenko system' which guarantees lifetime employment in the firm for a proportion (largely male) of the Japanese work-force. The relationship between the worker and the firm is still an exchange of work for wages, but its long-term character is likely to have very different implications from that of the 'casual' labour market of the student.

Most workers participate in labour markets that lie between the poles of the casual labour market and the nenko system. Some jobs are more stable and secure, and are regarded as long-lasting or even as 'permanent', in contrast to others which are subject to a greater likelihood of closure and are typically more short term. But of course many 'permanent' jobs cease to exist in the event of dismissals for misconduct or more commonly, redundancy. Even the seemingly 'safe' IBM, which for a century or so never made any workers redundant anywhere in the world, had in the changed circumstances of the early 1990s to declare massive redundancies.

So while it is correct, if somewhat trite to define a labour market as the place where wages are exchanged for labour, it is already clear that one striking feature of labour markets is that they vary so much according to their length and degree of permanence. What else is special about labour markets that merits our exclusive attention in this chapter? Probably you can think of a number of answers to this question, but I wish to emphasize three significant points.

First, in a labour market, the money that is being exchanged is wages (or salaries) and these form a very large part of most people's income. On average about 60 per cent of income in the UK derives from the reward to labour (excluding self-employment, *Key Data*, 1993, Table 9.6). Hence the factors which determine wages have a great effect on income distribution. Moreover, our welfare is directly linked to our employment prospects. When unemployment looms as a result of labour market failure, it is a matter of great concern.

A second reason why the analysis of labour markets needs to be special is that the wages paid to an employee do not automatically guarantee that a satisfactory job is done from the firm's point of view. When we buy apples from a street seller it is relatively easy to see if any are rotten and insist on replacements if necessary. By contrast, to motivate workers to work in return for their wages requires that they be managed somehow. The economic analysis of labour markets cannot properly be considered completely separately from the issue of worker motivation. Later on in the chapter we shall be considering a model which highlights the consequences of this link between wages and worker motivation.

The third reason why labour markets are different from many others in the modern day is that their scope is geographically far less wide than other important markets. We have become accustomed to thinking in global terms in relation to the money market or to many product markets: UK-based banks, for example, by no means confine their operations to UK lending. Yet firms based in a particular country or area largely recruit their work-forces from that area. For many types of work, those below the highest grades, that area is usually taken to be the town and its surroundings: for the purposes of local-economy statistical analysis, the UK Department of Employment delineates 'Travel-To-Work Areas' on the map. For other types of work the market may be national in scope (this would largely be true of the market for senior managers). For some the market may indeed be international, but international recruitment is still relatively rare. The exception to this must, however, immediately be stated: where there is large-scale migration of labour, it is more appropriate to think of the market as international, if not global. Yet despite occasional mass migration, the fact that labour markets remain distinctly national is evident, if only from the different wages paid to the same type of labour in different countries. In developing countries, wages are typically a small fraction even of unskilled manual workers' wages in the industrialized world. And even between countries of the advanced industrialized world there remain distinct differences in wages and conditions of work, because of the relatively high economic, social and political barriers to migration. In this chapter I shall primarily, though not exclusively, draw my examples from the British labour market.

In the light of these special characteristics of labour markets, the aim of this chapter is to address three broad questions about how they operate:

1   What are the determinants of wages and employment? Why do some workers get paid more than others?

2   Why do labour markets often 'fail'? By 'failure' I mean here that in some way supply is not equated to demand. One major instance of such failure is large-scale unemployment, which is the difference between the aggregate supply of workers and the total amount of employment. I shall be examining several possible explanations for this.

3   Finally, how do institutional interventions in the free operation of labour markets affect their performance? I mean by 'institutions' here anything other than individual workers or firms. This includes trade unions, employer organizations and the various arms of government.

I shall begin the analysis of these questions by elaborating on the perfect competition or 'competitive' model of the labour market introduced in Chapter 18, Section 3. The chief reason for beginning with this is that many current official policy analyses and positions emerge broadly from this approach. For example, it is normally assumed, if not proved, that minimum wage legislation tends to raise wages at the expense of employment. This is part of a wider view that much unemployment is linked to workers pricing themselves out of jobs. A related policy has been to reduce the power of unions, which are thought also to contribute to inefficiency and to high wages at the expense of the jobs of the unemployed. Another related policy is that as far as possible, access to training in firms should be determined by employers' and employees' choices; this has led to support for a 'training market'. All these conclusions can be drawn from the perfect competition model. They amount to four distinct but related themes which I shall return to examine in detail later in this chapter: wages legislation, trade unions, unemployment and training.

As the chapter proceeds, you will see that, although there are useful insights to be gained from the perfect competition model, most of the assumptions needed to underpin this model are unrealistic. Nevertheless, the model can serve us as a benchmark against which to contrast the assumptions of alternative models based on imperfect competition, which I regard as the normal or most widespread structure of the labour market. You may judge these assumptions for yourself.

2   The perfectly competitive labour market

The perfect competition model is primarily an analysis of a 'spot market' in which an amount of labour (measured, say, in hours) in the present is sold for wages. Both the price of labour – the wage rate per hour – and the level of employment are determined by the intersection of demand and supply, just as in many commodity markets. A number of assumptions form the starting point of this model:

- A1: Buyers and sellers of labour are price takers: they cannot individually alter wages.

- A2: All participants are perfectly informed: workers know the available job and wage opportunities, while firms know the potential workers in the labour market.

- A3: Workers can move freely between jobs or in and out of work.

- A4: Labour hours, once purchased from the workers, are used without problem as effective labour to produce output.

- A5: Firms aim to maximize profits.

2.1   The demand for labour

The demand for labour is the demand for a factor of production. It is commonly referred to as a 'derived demand' since the labour is wanted not for itself but for the profits which it brings to the company. Let us consider how the demand for labour is determined in principle by a firm using just this one variable factor, labour, to produce an output, aiming to maximize profits. Recall that the marginal physical product of labour (MPP_L) is the extra output produced by utilizing an extra unit of labour, and that it declines as labour input increases (Chapter 18, Section 3.1). In the analysis here we are particularly concerned with the marginal revenue product (MRP) which is related to the MPP_L.

If P is the price of the product we can write:

$$MRP = P \times MPP_L$$

Because we assume that in perfect competition the firm is a price taker, the decline in MPP_L means that the MRP curve is also declining. The MRP curve is illustrated in Figure 21.1.

Definition

Marginal revenue product

The marginal revenue product (*MRP*) is the extra revenue obtained by the firm from employing an extra unit of labour.

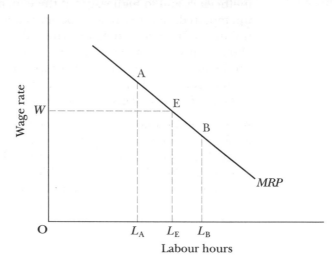

Figure 21.1 **The firm's demand for labour, under perfect competition**

Suppose that the market wage rate is given by *W.* The theory of the firm's demand for labour may now be simply stated: the firm that maximizes profits will demand labour up to the point where the wage equals the marginal revenue product, or:

$$W = MRP$$

This is illustrated by point E in Figure 21.1, where employment is L_E. How do we know this is the optimal amount to employ? We can reason by considering alternative points. At A with only L_A employed, the MRP is above *W.* This means the firm could get extra profits by employing one more unit of labour, since the extra revenue, *MRP,* is greater than the cost, *W.* Conversely, at B, with *MRP* below *W,* the firm could get more profits by cutting a unit of labour, since the cost saving, *W,* is more than the lost revenue, *MRP.* Thus, neither A nor B are points at which profits are maximized; but at E, no change in employment could raise profits further.

Definition

Demand for labour

The demand curve for labour in the perfectly competitive model is given by the marginal revenue product curve.

If now the wage rate were raised or lowered, the profit maximizing firm would simply alter its employment according to its *MRP* curve. The curve thus traces out the demand for labour.

Not all firms are the same, of course, and so their labour demand curves may have different slopes and shapes, but they are expected to be downward sloping. Hence, when we aggregate all firms to obtain the market demand for labour, we would also have a downward-sloping demand curve. This is a key conclusion emerging from the analysis and it will be used again, below. But before leaving this topic I want to draw your attention to some loose terminology I have been using so far: in talking about labour I have not discussed different types of labour such as carpenters, labourers, managers, etc. Implicitly I have been assuming all labour is the same. Nevertheless, the same arguments can apply to any specific type of labour, leading to the conclusion that there are downward-sloping demand curves for each type.

Exercise 21.1

The proposition that the demand for labour rises when the wage rate falls is widely believed. Can you trace the steps in the argument leading to that conclusion?

2.2   Labour supply

We turn next to look at the underlying determinants of labour supply. These can be divided into: (a) the factors determining overall labour supply, and (b) the factors determining the supply of a particular type of labour, relative to alternative types of labour. Let us look at each in turn.

Overall labour supply

Within any country the ultimate boundary affecting labour supply is population. In Table 21.1 I have compiled some summary data for the UK. You will see that although there are over 57 million people, only some 28 million are in the work-force (meaning that they are either employed or officially unemployed). A number of factors play a part in determining this overall figure. There are social factors, to do with attitudes towards women and to young or old people working, which have changed gradually over the years. There are technical factors such as the availability of washing machines which have made work in the home more productive than in earlier times, thereby in principle freeing up time for paid work. There are political factors such as the availability of state-financed child care facilities, or the provision of full-time education or higher education. And there are private economic factors such as the availability of private sources of income that may alter the incentive to work. Someone with a large private income will be able to afford the cost (in terms of lost wages) of not going to work.

Table 21.1   **UK population and labour statistics, 1990**

	Thousands
Population	57 411
Work-force	28 478
Work-force in employment	26 923

Source: *Key Data* (1993)

Labour supply to a particular line of work

We now turn to consider the supply of potential workers to particular kinds of work. It is this theory of supply, together with the demand for particular types of labour, that provides an explanation of relative wages – that is, wages in one job relative to those in another. This is crucial both for reasons of distribution and for reasons of economic incentives.

Suppose we consider two jobs, A and B, with the same skill requirements but with differing conditions of work: job A has worse conditions than B. This might mean more risky, or less pleasant work surroundings in some way. Job B might, for example, be window cleaning, while job A is window cleaning on high-rise buildings. The supply of high-rise window cleaners is going to depend on the wages and riskiness of the high-rise jobs *relative to* those for the ordinary window cleaners. A typical supply curve might be as in Figure 21.2.

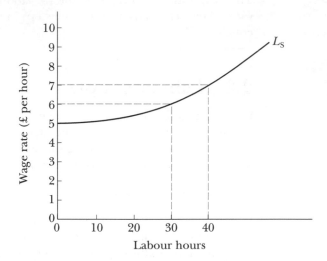

Figure 21.2   **Labour supply for high-rise window cleaning**

Suppose that workers could get £5 per hour for ordinary window cleaning. Assuming no one prefers the extra risks of high-rise work, labour supply L_S will be zero for any wage at or below £5. At £6, however, a certain number (30) are prepared to accept the risk of an hour's high-rise work. At a wage of £7 more workers (40) are induced to forego the safer job for the extra reward. The variation in workers' attitudes towards the risk is causing the relative supply curve to be upward sloping.

2.3   The supply and demand for labour and 'compensating wage differences'

Let us now put our supply and demand curves together. Pursuing the same example, the market demand for high-rise window cleaners will be downward sloping, as for any labour. The determination of wages and employment is shown in Figure 21.3.

It is assumed in this figure that a process of free-market bidding will sooner or later lead to a market equilibrium with supply equal to demand at a level of 35, with a wage rate of £6.50 per hour. There is thus a wage premium of £1.50 or 30 per cent compared to ordinary window cleaning, which is the 'compensating wage difference', representing the market valuation of what it takes to induce workers to assume the extra risk of high-rise work.

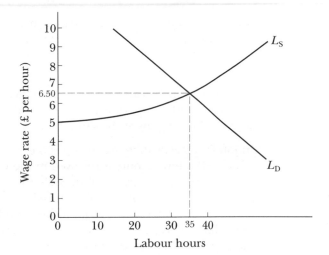

Figure 21.3 **The determination of wages and employment in high-rise window cleaning, under perfect competition**

Exercise 21.2

Show, using the demand and supply diagram, what would happen to high-rise window cleaners' wages and employment on completion of a new high-rise office block in town.

2.4   Human capital

One over-simplification with the model of labour markets so far is that we have ignored differences in skill. Yet skill differences account for a good proportion of wage differences, for the simple reason that the supply of workers to jobs with specialized skills is restricted. Arguably, a few jobs require rare abilities that can be developed but not acquired if not already present – not everyone can acquire the skill to participate in professional tennis, for example. Nevertheless, most jobs use skills that require greater or lesser amounts of education and training. The theory of human capital says that people will have an incentive to acquire skills (or 'human capital') if it gives them access to high-paying jobs. Suppose that we consider two further jobs, C and D. Job C pays more than D but it requires an extra year's

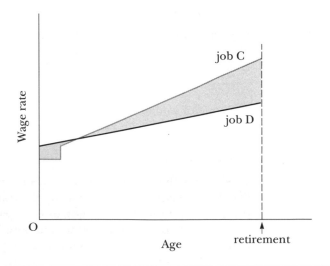

Figure 21.4 **Age–wage profiles, and the investment in human capital**

training. The pay differential thus 'compensates' for the disadvantage of having to take an extra year's training, in an analogous way to our window cleaner example with the high-rise worker compensated for the extra risk.

But what precisely is the disadvantage of this training? We can picture this by looking at how wages might hypothetically alter over a lifetime of work, as in Figure 21.4 (not drawn to scale on the lower axis). Suppose two people start on the two jobs at the same age.

In job D, a steady increase in wages is expected through to retirement. In job C only a low income is received in the year whilst training (perhaps from a government grant). But, while the starting wage is the same as for job D only a year behind, it is pictured as increasing more rapidly over the lifetime. The differentials of job C over job D increase over time. The total red coloured area is the benefit of the extra training. The cost, however, is the grey coloured area. This cost represents the opportunity cost of the lost wages during the early period. To be added to this are the fees incurred for the training, and any other 'out-of-pocket' costs, and the total costs represent the 'disadvantage' of the training.

Put in this way, this is really a theory of investment, very similar to any investment in physical capital. A firm buys a machine and thereby incurs costs in the present. It expects that the machine will produce extra revenues and profits in the future, these being the pay-off to the investment. Similarly, the pay-off to the individual of undergoing education or training is the extra wage to be gained later on. There will also, in the case of training, be a pay-off to the firm that provides the training for its work-force, in the form of greater productivity from that work-force. The only difference, then, between investment in physical capital and investment in human capital is that, whereas physical capital could be sold off to another user, it is difficult or impossible to sell human capital once acquired, except in a slave society.

Monetary advantage is not the only reason for education and training. The theory of human capital stresses the monetary rationale but this need not exclude other 'non-pecuniary' factors. These must include the satisfaction of studying (I hope you agree) and the potential future rewards of being more educated or trained, perhaps with a more satisfying job.

Exercise 21.3

What are the costs and benefits, as you see them, and roughly when are they likely to occur, of studying a degree level course, such as an Open University course. Which of these might in principle be quantifiable?

Thinking of human capital acquisition as an investment, the particular case of training presents an important problem. Much training, to be effective, needs to be done in and by firms rather than schools. The basic question this poses is: who pays for the training?

One way for the individual to pay for firm-based training is to work for the firm but receive lower wages during the training period. At the extreme, trainees might receive no wages, or even pay the firm for the training received. The underlying assumption here is that the trainees (or their families) own sufficient funds for living expenses during the training period, or else that they gain access to funds through the capital market. You might want to judge for yourself how realistic that assumption is, and we shall return to it later (see Section 5).

An alternative is for the firm to pay for the training fees, and to pay the trainee a full wage while training – in this case the opportunity cost of the training is the lost current output. The firm has an incentive to pay for training if it has good reason to believe the trainee will continue to work for the firm. When the training is in skills specific to the firm – for example, acquainting sales staff with the company's products – that seems reasonable. Where, however, the training is in 'transferable skills' which could be used in other firms, and where job mobility is relatively easy, rational firms will be reluctant to fund training since other firms can bid away trained workers for slightly higher wages. So transferable skills must be paid for by the trainees themselves through reduced wages, in return for the prospect of higher wages in the future.

2.5   Summary and implications of the perfect competition model

The analysis began with five economic assumptions, A1 to A5, to which I have now added another:

- A6: Potential trainees have access to perfect capital markets.

Question

What answers are given by the perfect competition model to the three broad questions I asked in the introduction?

Taking the first question, wage differentials are explained as the outcome of the individual choices underlying the supply of and demand for labour. In sum, the wages of one job may be more than another's because:

1   there is a 'compensating difference' in the conditions of work, e.g. due to riskiness or unpleasantness, or

2   the job requires particular skills which are costly to acquire. Workers must incur these costs through undergoing education or training. Only those that choose to do so receive the compensating rewards of better paid jobs.

Second, markets 'fail' to match supply with demand only when some outside (non-market) force prevents the free adjustment of prices and wages to achieve equilibrium. Unemployment, therefore, is ultimately due to workers insisting on wages being too high.

Finally, the only aim of government intervention should in this view be to support free market processes. For example, within such a framework it is easy to rationalize attempts to limit the power of trade unions to affect wages. And governments should support a training market in which individuals and firms judge for themselves the value of training, rather than directing training from above.

I want now to end this section with an illustration of these general arguments against all other forms of intervention, by examining the case that is made against the state attempting to raise the wages of the low-paid. In many countries (the UK is an exception) there is a national minimum wage applying to all jobs. Economists basing their argument on the demand and supply framework have usually argued that this must reduce employment in those jobs where the minimum wage comes above the market wage.

The argument is illustrated in Figure 21.5 which gives the supply and demand for labour hours in the low-pay sectors of the economy. If the government imposes a wage W_M, where the market would otherwise settle on a wage W_E, employment (measured in hours of work) in these jobs is restricted to L_M. The benefit to workers who keep their jobs is the increased wage rate, but there are $L_E - L_M$ hours of work no longer available. The extent of this shortfall is determined by the size of the wage rise and by the elasticity of labour demand.

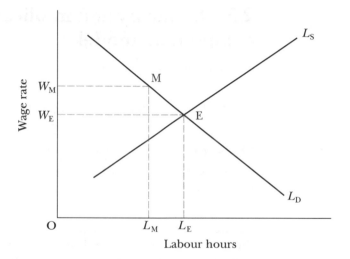

Figure 21.5   The effect of minimum wage legislation on employment, under perfect competition

On the basis of this analysis it is commonly argued that minimum wage legislation would be detrimental to economic efficiency even if it reduces inequality. It might also be argued that the legislation would exacerbate inequality: if large numbers of people were made unemployed and if they received low state benefits, this could more than outweigh any benefits to equality from raising the pay of those in work.

The development of UK government policy over the last decade has been consistent with these general conclusions. In Britain, minimum wage legislation only ever applied to a minority of the work-force – those in industries thought to be unprotected by unions and covered instead by Wages Boards and Councils. The chief areas covered were clothing, agriculture, retail trades and catering. After 1986 protection was limited to over 21-year-olds, and even for adults holiday pay was excluded from regulation. This was a precursor to the eventual abolition of all the councils in 1993 except that for agricultural workers.

3   Imperfectly competitive labour markets

3.1   Minimum wage legislation again

For the rest of this chapter I am going to be dismantling the perfect competition model, by considering what happens in a number of cases when the assumptions are dropped and new ones inserted. This will bring us to a more detailed examination of the policy issues I have highlighted. With the issue of minimum wage legislation fresh in mind from the previous section, it is appropriate to begin with assumptions A1 and A2, two assumptions that were crucial to deriving the policy conclusion that argued against market intervention. In particular I want to question the proposition that firms cannot individually alter wages. This proposition is illustrated by the horizontal curve L_{S1} in Figure 21.6, which shows an infinitely elastic supply of labour hours to a firm at the going wage rate. For two related reasons this assumption may be false. Let us assume that a firm offers to employ workers at a wage less than W. Would anybody work for the firm? The answer is yes. First, there may be many workers who lack information about what jobs and wage offers are available elsewhere – so they accept the job or, simply, continue working for the firm if they already worked there. Second, even if they have information about better-paying jobs they may face transport and other costs that render it not worthwhile to switch jobs. Some workers may leave the company, or fewer workers would apply, so on balance the firm that offers lower wages will get some labour but less than before. In other words, competition is not perfect and the supply curve of labour to a particular firm is likely to be upward sloping. This is illustrated by the curve L_{S2} in Figure 21.6.

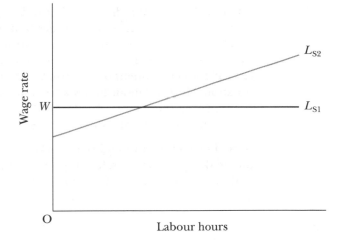

Figure 21.6 **Labour supply curves of a single firm.** L_{S1}: **labour supply to a firm under perfect competition;** L_{S2}: **labour supply to a firm under imperfect competition**

The fact that the labour supply curve, L_{S2}, slopes upwards means that we must now reconstruct the analysis of the firm's employment decision. This is done in Figure 21.7.

I start with a labour supply curve, L_S, which is upward sloping like curve L_{S2} in Figure 21.6. The firm which aims to maximize profits would be failing to do so if it set employment, measured in labour hours at point C on Figure 21.7 where the *MRP* equals W_C. If it lowers employment by one hour the amount of labour cost saved equals the wage rate, W_C, plus the reduction in the wage bill for remaining hours worked. Hence the amount saved is greater than the revenue lost (the *MRP*) and its profits would rise. Instead, the firm calculates the marginal factor cost (*MFC*) of labour.

Definition

Marginal factor cost

The marginal factor cost (*MFC*) of labour is the extra cost of employing an extra unit of labour.

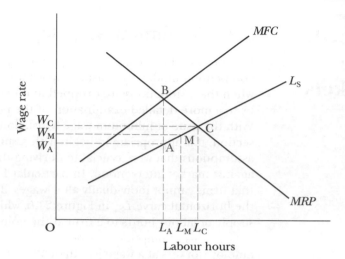

Figure 21.7 Minimum wages under imperfect competition

Because the supply curve of labour is upward sloping, the *MFC* is equal to the wage rate (the cost attributed to the one extra person/hour) *plus* the small change in the wage bill for all the other hours worked. That is, the *MFC* must be above the wage rate. A numerical example will serve to illustrate this point. Suppose a firm employs 100 hours of labour for £5 per hour. Its total wage bill is therefore £500. If it were to increase the hours worked to 101, it might need to raise its wage rate to, say, £5.05 in order to attract the extra unit of labour. The new wage bill is then $101 \times £5.05 = £510.05$. Hence the cost of the extra hour is £10.05, greater than the wage rate for one hour's work.

A typical *MFC* curve is drawn in Figure 21.7, above the labour supply curve at every point. The analysis continues that only when the *MFC* equals the *MRP* will profits be maximized – as illustrated by point B in the figure. Why? An analogous argument can be used to that which was used above in the case of perfect competition (Figure 21.1) to prove that $W = MRP$ in that situation. Here, if labour hours were lower than at B, profits could be raised by increasing them, since $MRP > MFC$. Conversely, if labour hours were higher than at B, profits could be raised by lowering them since $MFC > MRP$.

Note, however, that when hours worked are determined in this way the wage rate is W_A, given by the relevant point on the supply curve – that is, A. It is evident that both wages, W_A, and employment, L_A are *lower* than at C where $W = MRP$, the perfect competition position.

Consider, now, the impact of minimum wage legislation where the minimum wage is set at W_M, above the level W_A that the firm would otherwise choose. In this case we can say that the firm would employ labour hours L_M, greater than L_A. Why? Because there is no advantage for the firm in employing less. At M the *MRP* is greater than the minimum wage rate W_M, so any cutbacks in hours would lead to a fall in profits. The point is that the minimum wage prevents the employer from reducing the wage bill for remaining workers, which would otherwise have been the reason for lowering hours worked. On the other hand, the firm would not raise hours worked because that would mean raising wages above W_M and, the *MFC* being above *MRP* at that point, this would also lower profits. Hence M must be the profit-maximizing point under the minimum wage legislation.

Question

How does this conclusion differ from that obtained in the perfect competition model?

The conclusion is in striking contrast to that obtained in the perfect competition model. Up to the value W_C, any increase in the minimum wage brings unequivocal benefits to workers, in the form of both higher wages and greater employment levels, while removing some of the profits of companies. Once W_C has been reached, however, any further rises in the minimum wage would lead to falls in employment, in line with the perfect competition model.

As a result of this analysis, we can only conclude that the effect of minimum wage legislation on employment is uncertain from the point of view of economic theory. If the perfect competition model is correct, or if the minimum wage is pushed too high (above W_C), we would expect a reduction in employment. But, if the imperfect competition model with an upward-sloping labour supply curve facing the firm is correct, and the minimum wage is not pushed excessively above the free-market level W_A, we should expect an increase in employment. Only careful empirical investigation will be able to show us which effect is valid, and the conclusion could be different for different countries. Most empirical studies have been done for the US labour market, where there is currently no consensus as to the impact on employment. A number of recent studies show little or no effect in either direction. The impact of the abolition of the Wages Councils in Britain has yet to be assessed at the time of writing.

3.2   Trade unions and the labour market

Perhaps the most unrealistic aspect of the model of perfect competition in the labour market is the view that labour market actors – firms and workers – all act independently and are unable to influence prices or wages (assumption A1). This may be a fair approximation in a few minor sections of the economy, but for the most part in many countries wages and conditions are the subject either of collective negotiations between trade unions and employers, or sometimes between groups of unions and employers. If not the subject of collective bargaining, they are often regulated by explicit legal or implicit customary codes. In addition, many millions of people in Europe are employed by governments whose behaviour cannot simply be likened to a profit-maximizing firm. In all these cases, the simple notion of labour supply and labour demand outlined in Section 2 is inapplicable.

Here we shall look at some of the ways in which the presence of trade unions changes the picture. Table 21.2 gives an approximate idea of unions' potential influence in some different countries in the mid 1980s. It gives the union density, defined as the number of union members as a percentage of potential union members. (Note that these data were compiled on somewhat different definitions from those given in Chapter 18, Table 18.1.) While it might be reasonable as a first approximation to disregard unions in the USA (it had a union density of only 16 per cent), in most of Europe, especially in Scandinavia, this would be seriously unrealistic. (As Table 18.1

showed, although density is low, collective bargaining coverage is high in France.) Nevertheless, UK unions have been substantially cut down in size in the last decade and a half. The union density of 43 per cent shown for 1985 in Table 21.2 is actually a point on a slippery slope in which density has fallen from over half in 1980 to about 35 per cent by 1991. This fall is in the context of adverse economic conditions (high unemployment) and a series of anti-union pieces of legislation, starting with the 1980 Employment Act, which successfully limited the ability of unions to recruit new members and reduced their power in relation to management.

Table 21.2   **Union density in 1985**

	%
Australia	51
Canada	30
France	18
West Germany	37
Ireland	46
Italy	40
Japan	29
Netherlands	29
Sweden	88
UK	43
USA	16

Source: Sapsford and Tzannatos (1993) p.249

The perfect competition theory essentially regards unions' impact on the market as detrimental; hence the evident policy conclusion is to reduce their influence. There are two main bases for the argument. First, it is assumed that unions raise wages, thus moving the firm up its labour demand curve, as in Figure 21.5, to point M, thereby displacing employment from the unionized to the non-unionized sector of the economy. What is not clear is how far up the curve the unions would want to force wages. It is hardly reasonable to think of unions aiming to push wages up indefinitely. Assuming they had the power to raise wages, but assuming also that they are aware of the downward-sloping labour demand curve, they would want to limit the use of that power so as not to sacrifice too much employment. But how much is 'too much'? This is not an easy question, because it depends on what sorts of workers have power in unions – is it the older workers with relatively secure jobs, who would want to raise wages substantially, or is it the more marginal younger workers whose jobs are less safe?

Empirical estimates of unions' impact on wages are hard to obtain, but what economists can find is an estimate of a union/non-union wage differential for otherwise similar workers. In Britain, the best estimates of this lie in the range 10 per cent to 15 per cent for manual workers, though these are subject to quite wide margins of error. For non-manual workers the estimated impact on wages is much lower, and arguably zero. Taken together, these estimates would not indicate a vast amount of employment displacement. If the elasticity of demand for manual workers were especially high – for example, as high as one – this would mean that unions' impact on pay caused a 10 per cent to 15 per cent displacement of manual employment.

A second reason why policy makers might want to reduce unions' influence is if they slow down innovations and lower productivity by enforcing restrictive practices within companies. Here the argument is that in order to protect their jobs, unions prevent the introduction of labour-saving innovations, and hinder the substitution of one kind of labour for another.

Set against these negative connotations as to the economic effects of unions, there are also reasons to expect that unions might have a positive impact on productivity. American writers Freeman and Medoff argue that unions provide a collective 'voice' to speak to management and that this can improve productivity (Freeman and Medoff, 1984). Without a union an aggrieved worker may have little choice but to remain unhappy or quit the firm. A union helps sort out the grievance and hence lowers labour turnover. Lower labour turnover reduces the costs of hiring replacements and provides more incentives for firms to train their employees. Moreover, unions acting in co-operation with management can find ways to improve efficiency that are eventually beneficial. In so far as unions do raise wages, this can also keep up worker morale and hence worker effort (I come back to this point later). Finally, it is often recognized that upward pressure on wages may stimulate efficiency gains from improved management. In the short run higher wages from a newly organized union can 'shock' a sleepy management into better performance. But perhaps more important is the long-run effect attributed to unions that have been successful in keeping wages high in Germany. This is to force management to adopt strategies for high skills and high productivity. Arguing that managers given the choice will often opt for a low-wage route to competitiveness, high wages that unions impose could act as a barrier to this route. Instead management will opt for high value-added products that require high levels of research and development, sustained investment and continued training for the work-force.

For all these reasons it is theoretically possible that the presence of unions can raise the marginal physical product of labour (MPP_L) and hence the marginal revenue product which is the basis of the demand for labour curve. A conceivable scenario is then illustrated by Figure 21.8. The initial

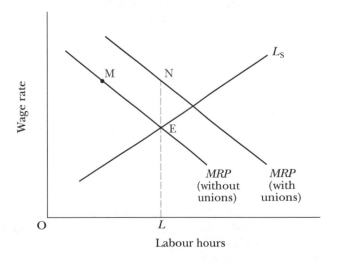

Figure 21.8 **Unions' impact on wages and employment**

point is E, the intersection of the labour supply curve L_S and the marginal revenue product curve in the absence of unions. Now examine the impact of unions. On the one hand they may raise the wage rate, which in the absence of any changes in efficiency would lower employment accordingly, at point M. However, where unions also raise the *MRP*, this would in itself raise employment. Putting the two effects together results in an ambiguous effect. As drawn at point N the net result is no impact on employment, but depending on the extent of unions' impact on the MPP_L, the employment effect could be positive or negative.

In view of the conflicting theories about unions' impact on productivity, economists have sought to estimate the empirical effects. The results are not clear-cut, but the balance of evidence suggests that in a significant number of cases the impact on productivity is positive. That does not mean to say that it always is or will be: this is one of those many areas in economics when the answer cannot be predicted by theory and may differ empirically from circumstance to circumstance.

Thus far we have considered the impact of unions on wages and on productivity in companies. In addition, unions can have an effect on other aspects of the labour market. For example, studies have found quite consistently that unions tend to compress wage differentials. This should not be too surprising, because much of the union movement has been historically rooted in an ideological commitment to equality. But also we should remember too that unions have had, and still have in a number of countries, a considerable indirect influence over labour markets and the economy generally via their impact on policy and on law making. This means that a complete assessment of unions should not be too narrowly focused. It should not rest simply on the theoretical and empirical issues looked at here, even though they are important for our analysis of labour markets.

3.3   Segmentation and segregation in the labour market

Segmentation and wage differentials

While the perfect competition model suggests that wage differentials in the economy reflect skill differences or 'compensating' differences in work conditions, such a conclusion has often seemed at odds with the reality observed by empirical labour economists. Starting in the USA in the late 1960s, observers began to notice an intransigent 'segmentation' of jobs – initially a dual system of two segments. In one segment, the primary labour market, were 'good jobs' – ones with reasonably high wages, some prospects for improvement including access to training, relative job security, high fringe benefits and long job tenure. In the secondary labour market were 'bad jobs' with the converse, i.e. low pay, high turnover and relative insecurity, with few other benefits. Such segmentation has also been observed in other countries. One way of seeing this in Britain is to note the considerable differences in average wages in different industries. If we restrict ourselves to any of the four groups for which evidence is shown in Table 21.3, it is apparent that jobs in, say, the energy and water supply industries pay well, while the distribution, hotels and catering industry is an area of low pay.

Table 21.3   **Average hourly pay (excluding overtime) of full-time employees, Great Britain, 1992 (£)**

	Males		Females	
	manual	non-manual	manual	non-manual
Agriculture, forestry and fishing	4.12	6.79	3.63	—
Energy and water supply	8.00	12.32	—	7.26
Metal extraction and manufacture, and chemical industries	6.50	10.68	4.62	6.65
Engineering, vehicles and metal goods industries	6.25	9.92	4.42	6.11
Other manufacturing industries	5.90	9.80	4.10	6.20
Construction	5.95	9.61	—	5.44
Distribution, hotels and catering	4.96	7.68	3.66	5.02
Transport and communications	5.86	9.94	5.39	6.51
Banking, finance, insurance, etc.	5.50	12.47	4.98	7.09
Other services (including government)	5.26	10.24	4.18	7.65

Source: *New Earnings Survey* (1992) Part C

There are many empirical studies by economists which attempt to explain differences in wages. It is common for such studies to focus on differences in skill levels and on compensating factors, these being the factors suggested by the perfectly competitive model of the labour market. But although such factors do play a role, the studies almost invariably leave unexplained some of the variation in wages between industries. The remaining variation may be thought of as reflecting elements of segmentation, wherein there are notable barriers to entry preventing workers in less good jobs transferring to the better ones. This implies a rejection of the assumption A3 of perfect labour mobility. Here are three factors preventing such mobility that economists have looked at.

1   There may be barriers to obtaining the necessary skills for a primary-sector job.

2   Groups of workers may seek to protect their privileged status by exerting artificial barriers to their occupation. Professional workers may use artificially high qualifications standards; trade unions may use industrial muscle to protect their craft status.

3   Sometimes associated with such barriers, discrimination on grounds of sex, race or disability is used to keep certain groups out of an occupation by rejection or, more usually, by discouragement.

Exercise 21.4

Make a list of some other factors which in your experience prevent labour mobility.

Occupational segregation and male/female differentials

An enduring and striking feature of labour markets in all countries is the lower pay received by female workers. This is evident in every industry in Britain, as you can see from taking another look at Table 21.3. Table 21.4 shows that the ratio of female to male earnings is less than 100 per cent in all countries listed. However, there is a considerable variation in the extent to which women are disadvantaged: of the countries shown, female workers fare best in Sweden and worst in Japan. This variation suggests that women's disadvantages in the labour market are linked to the social and economic environment, which varies from country to country.

Table 21.4 **Ratio of female to male hourly earnings, manual workers in manufacturing, mining and construction industries**

	%
Austria	70
France	73
Germany	73
Japan	49
Sweden	87
UK	73
USA	68

Source: Rowthorn (1992)

One of the major explanations that writers have given for the low pay of women is their concentration into relatively few occupations. As women's labour is over-supplied to these occupations there is no market pressure for a rise in pay. This unbalanced supply of female labour comes from the exclusion of women from many high-paying occupations. This process I should like to refer to as *horizontal segregation*. Horizontal segregation is an instance of labour market segmentation, where the host of social and economic forces limiting the access of women to the high-paying occupations constitutes the source of labour immobility. Note, however, that segmentation can occur independently of such segregation and is conceivably quite separate.

The horizontal segregation of women is supplemented by *vertical segregation*, whereby males are disproportionately found in higher grades and females in lower grades, within any particular occupation or industry. This is a most obvious source of pay inequality. The reasons for the disparity range from overt discrimination to more subtle limitations placed upon women via their role in domestic labour. Some idea of how extensive horizontal and vertical segregation is in Britain can be gleaned from looking at Table 21.5. Note the predominance of female workers amongst the lower-ranking occupations (in terms of expected pay levels), such as personal service workers and unskilled manual workers. Nearly three-quarters of women workers are to be found either in these occupations or among junior and intermediate non-manual workers. Moreover, these figures conceal further concentrations of women among the detailed occupations subsumed within each group of the table.

Table 21.5   Proportion of female workers, Great Britain, 1992

	%
All workers	47
Managers and professionals	30
Intermediate non-manual workers	62
Junior non-manual workers	76
Personal service workers	82
Foremen and supervisors	17
Skilled manual workers	10
Semi-skilled manual workers	41
Unskilled manual workers	64

Source: *Quarterly Labour Force Survey* (1992) Spring

Both segmentation and segregation are contributory causes of inequality in the labour market. Moreover, artificial barriers to labour mobility and the under use of women in many areas of the labour market are evident aspects of inefficiency. The case for active government intervention, contrary to the perfect competition model, is strong. Some policies directed at these features of the labour market are:

1   To subsidize the acquisition of skills through education and training. (I shall discuss later the reasons why this cannot be left to the market.)

2   To prevent artificial barriers to entry into the professions by ensuring that qualifications where used as entry criteria are justified, i.e. to regulate the profession from outside.

3   To use education and training to counteract forms of socialization that support the gender-identification of jobs.

4   To proscribe acts of direct discrimination in selecting on grounds of sex or other characteristics. Into this category in Britain, for example, come the 1970 Equal Pay Act and the 1975 Discrimination Act.

3.4   Efficiency wages: three models

So far in this chapter I have looked at the complications that arise when assumptions A1, A2 and A3 are replaced by various alternatives. Now I want to turn to assumption A4, in order to show why it too plays a crucial role in the perfect competition model. I have already alluded briefly, in discussing the role of unions, to the possible effect of higher wages in eliciting greater effort through improved 'morale' and hence motivation of workers. This effect is one example of a range of models for labour market analysis entitled, a bit misleadingly, efficiency wage models

The common conclusion of efficiency wage models is that higher wages can raise productivity. So we will in effect be dropping assumption A4. We will address the fact that, once the labour contract has been agreed, it is

Definition

Efficiency wage models

Efficiency wage models recognize that there is a causal link between the wages paid and the efficiency with which labour is managed and motivated. Thus, higher wages raise productivity.

impossible for employers to monitor the effort that is put in during every minute of the day. Some way of *managing and motivating labour* has to be found. In this section I want to look at three such models.

The morale effect

In the first model, it is argued that better wages may lead to improved relations between employers and workers. The 'morale' effect arises from observations made by a number of sociologists of the workplace, but it is probably a phenomenon well-known to many managers. The idea recognizes that the employees in a workplace are not just a set of individuals – they are a collective body, and individual behaviour is affected by the work norms of the group. These work norms help to delineate what is expected of workers and what is considered a fair rate of effort. In these circumstances, an exchange of 'gifts' can occur in which the employer pays wages above the minimum that would be necessary to keep employees from quitting the firm, and workers respond by exceeding the production targets that management sets for them. Thus, up to a point it pays the employer to pay a 'good' wage, above the basic minimum: the extra morale results in greater productivity that more than covers the extra expense.

The nourishment effect

A second argument as to why higher wages might improve productivity applies primarily in circumstances found in impoverished Third World countries. In fact it was here, in the context of Third World agriculture, that the relationship between wages and productivity was first noticed by modern economists. The argument is straightforward. It simply states that higher wages enable a better standard of living for the work-force. This permits improved diets and leads to stronger and healthier workers. Where, therefore, a firm's work-force is relatively stable and also largely manual it is able to get greater productivity from the work-force by keeping it healthy. For such firms it pays – in terms of profits – to treat the workers well.

There are obvious limits to this argument. It could not apply where there is a high turnover of workers – it is no good from the firm's point of view to create a healthy work-force for other firms. It would not apply where there is a reasonable level of welfare benefits or other sources of income that allow good nourishment independent of wages from work. For this reason it is not an argument we would expect to be relevant in the industrial world except perhaps in pockets of extreme poverty.

The worker discipline effect

A third, and more general argument builds from the proposition that work itself is disliked by workers, and that the only reason people go to work is for the wages. This proposition underlies the approach of most economists. We can immediately object that many workers gain satisfaction from their jobs. Nevertheless, there is a large class of work which is essentially alienating or unpleasant. Moreover, it remains a reasonable starting point to suggest that if workers could have the same wages but without having to put in the effort, they would frequently choose to do so.

In 1915, Henry Ford instituted a further dramatic change in his automobile factory near Detroit. I say 'further' because he had only recently introduced his revolutionary assembly line techniques to car production. Now he suddenly raised the wages of shop floor workers from $3 to $5 a day. Furthermore, he maintained this would increase his profits. From the point of view of much conventional economics based on the simple perfect competition model this makes little sense. But it is possible to see Ford's reasoning in the context of the theory of efficiency wages. Probably part of the story was to do with the morale effect outlined above. It may also be due to the 'worker discipline effect'.

The idea behind the worker discipline effect is that workers cannot be monitored closely every minute. They must be induced to continue supplying effort when not observed by a manager or supervisor. But if work is unpleasant and disliked, why work? In such circumstances, the 'rational' worker would choose to minimize on effort, except for one matter: the risk of being caught shirking and consequently dismissed. From the firm's point of view this discipline must be sufficiently strong to motivate effort from the work-force. This necessitates:

1   That there is some chance of workers who are not working properly being caught. In other words, there must be some supervisors to direct and monitor workers in their daily tasks. These supervisors add to the costs of production.

2   The threat to dismiss shirking workers (or otherwise penalize them) must be serious.

It is in the latter point that the importance of wages comes in. Suppose that wages are low – at or not much above the income that workers would get easily from elsewhere, either from state benefits or from other easily available employment. Then there is not much to lose from being dismissed. The 'cost of job loss' – the difference between wages and the income that could be obtained if dismissed – must be sufficient to make dismissal a real danger. Otherwise, why would workers work? The problem Henry Ford found amongst his work-force prior to his raising wages, was that there was a great deal of disenchantment with the work itself, and consequently a low level of effort and high turnover (either from dismissal or from workers simply leaving due to being fed up). By upping the stakes, Ford made the cost of job loss considerable for his work-force. His confidence in the profit-increasing reason for his move lay in his expectation that at $5 a day he would have a more loyal, harder-working work-force whose overall productivity would increase by more than the extra wage cost.

Reflection

If you have had personal experience of the workplace, either as a manager or as a shop-floor employee, you might care to consider the relevance of these models. How closely was the effort you put in monitored by your supervisor? Did your employer pay at or above the bare minimum necessary to keep people from quitting? Did the rate at which people were paid affect their commitment and effort? If so, why?

Having looked at these three reasons why high wages can lead to higher productivity, I now ask: what implications does this have for our analysis of labour markets? I shall look at two answers to this question: the first leads to a modification of our analysis, while the second introduces the subject of unemployment.

3.5   Implications of efficiency wage models

First implication: the elasticity of demand for labour

Recall that the marginal revenue product of labour (*MRP*) curve is the basis of the derived demand for labour, because the profit-maximizing condition for the perfectly competitive firm is to employ workers up to the point where the *MRP* equals the wage rate. This proposition remains true. But we must now recognize that firms could change the *MRP*, for any value of *L*, by changing the wage rate. The higher the wage rate the greater is the effort and productivity of the marginal worker (and, also, of the average worker). Therefore, the marginal physical product of labour (MPP_L) could change when the wage is changed.

In Figure 21.9 the wage rate is initially W_0. The curve labelled *MRP* ($W = W_0$) is the appropriate marginal revenue product curve for that wage rate. Profits are therefore maximized at labour hours L_0. The firm could choose to raise wages to W_1, but if so it would be incorrect to say that employment would fall to point B. Rather, since at each level of labour hours the MPP_L is higher due to the efficiency wage effect, the whole *MRP* curve shifts upwards. In the diagram, maximum profits would instead be obtained at point C and labour hours L_1.

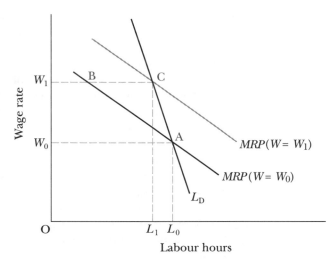

Figure 21.9   **Demand for labour, with efficiency wages**

Figure 21.9 thus illustrates that the demand for labour curve in this case (joining points A and C and labelled L_D) is less elastic than the *MRP* curve as a result of the efficiency wage effect. Indeed, if you reflect a little, you could see how the *MRP* curve could conceivably have shifted up sufficiently to ensure *no* cut in hours worked or even a rise coincident with the wage rise. Whether that would happen depends on the strength of the efficiency wage effect, which would differ according to circumstances.

Question

At this point it is worth checking your understanding of the above analysis against a possible confusion that sometimes occurs. Consider the following two statements:

1   The basic model tells us that the marginal revenue product of labour is equal to the wage.

2   The efficiency wage model tells us that the marginal revenue product of labour (as well as the marginal physical product of labour) is affected by the wage.

These two statements are both valid, but are making different propositions. Can you see how they are different?

The answer is that the first proposition is a condition that ensures the firm is maximizing its profits. It would be true, under perfectly competitive conditions, whether or not efficiency wage forces were important. The second is a causal statement about what determines marginal productivity: the fact that wages are thought to have an impact is the hallmark of efficiency wage models. The statement would be true even if the firm were not at its profit-maximizing position.

Second implication: a rationale for unemployment

For our second implication, I want to introduce the topic of unemployment for the first time in this chapter, in order to examine an interesting conclusion that follows from efficiency wage models in contrast to the perfect competition model. Recall that, in the latter, it was assumed that labour markets cleared by means of wage adjustments which equate supply and demand. Figure 21.3 depicted a cleared labour market. The same arguments apply to the labour market as a whole. In the perfect competition model, then, there is no explanation of why unemployment occurs, other than to imply that if unemployment exists, wages must have failed to adjust to the market-clearing rate. In brief: unemployment could always be eliminated by lowering wages sufficiently.

Consider now the impact of the worker discipline effect. This tells us that, in a world where work is disliked and supervision less than perfect, it would be impossible to motivate workers to work if there was no unemployment. Workers would see that there is little or no cost to being dismissed because at full employment they could immediately get a job elsewhere at the same wage. Only if there is a risk of spending some time on the dole, with consequent low income, would workers be induced to work rather than shirk.

This basic insight can be used to show that there must be a certain amount of unemployment to keep the economy at work – perhaps a rather surprising conclusion.

Figure 21.10 is an adaptation of the demand/supply framework applied to the aggregate labour market, but amended to account for the worker discipline effect.

I assume for simplicity a fixed work-force, which is depicted by the vertical line L_S. The *MRP* is the marginal revenue product of labour curve which is drawn in the usual way assuming that workers once employed put in the required effort. In terms of the perfect competition model, equilibrium would occur at point F with everyone employed.

However, our above argument has shown that the trouble is that *no worker would choose to work at the wages paid at point* F. Instead, we can plot a relationship between the level of wages and the level of employment as follows.

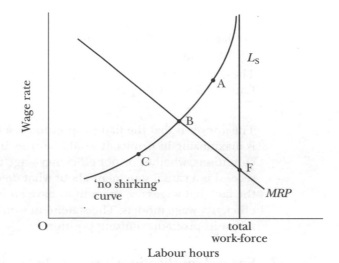

Figure 21.10 **Unemployment from the worker discipline effect**

For a relatively high level of employment (e.g. point A) a dismissed worker would experience a relatively short unemployment spell. Hence a high wage level is needed to motivate workers – a low wage and workers would choose to shirk.

By contrast, at a low level of employment (e.g. point C) the consequence of dismissal could be a long period out of work. Therefore a much lower wage level is needed to get people to work. Joining up points such as A and C, we have the 'no shirking curve', meaning that this gives for each level of employment and unemployment the wage that employers must pay to elicit proper effort from their workers. Point B, the intersection of the 'no shirking' curve with the *MRP* curve, is the point where employers will be maximizing their profits. Hence B is the equilibrium for the economy. Firms will have no incentive to employ more (or less) workers since the wage equals the *MRP*.

Exercise 21.5

At point B, the equilibrium, there are unemployed workers. Why can they not offer to work for lower wages than existing workers and so get jobs?

This equilibrium with unemployment has been arrived at without assuming that trade unions or governments or any other outside agent manipulates wages. The only departure from the perfect competition model is to drop assumption A4, and replace it with a simple model of worker motivation.

Intervention: could government eliminate unemployment?

The perfect competition model counselled no active market intervention, owing to its conclusion that full employment was the normal outcome from unfettered market processes. Later we shall examine some rationales for intervention to reduce unemployment. However, the rather striking conclusion of the model we have just looked at is that it may be counter-productive for government to attempt to reduce unemployment. Assume, for the moment, that government policies can alter the level of employment in Figure 21.10. Ask what would be the consequence of raising employment beyond point B. Answer: a considerable disruption of effort. In a prescient paper written not long after the 1930s depression years, the Polish economist Kalecki questioned whether big business or governments under their influence would ever want to eliminate unemployment entirely, even if they would try to reduce it below the levels of the 1930s depression years (Kalecki, 1943). In the mid 1960s, when the British economy seemed to operate successfully enough with only a few hundred thousand unemployed, Kalecki's fear appeared misplaced. It was widely assumed then that Keynesianism could ensure full employment. Now no one is so sure, after two decades of rising unemployment. It seems likely that the risk of months, even years, on the dole has been a motivating factor for many workers in Britain and elsewhere.

However, we should not necessarily conclude that it is government's job in support of business enterprise to maintain a suitable level of unemployment, even if the model helps to explain the relaxation of the objective of full employment which no government could fail to emphasize in the 1950s and 1960s. First, there is no suggestion that the currently very high levels of unemployment across Europe are necessary for worker motivation, and nothing in the current argument speaks against aiming for reduction in these levels. Second, it must be remembered that the model is built on an assumed world of alienating disliked work, where motivation to work comes primarily through the fear of lost wages. But there are many lines of work where this is not the case, and there are other more positive forms of motivation, including the provision of more challenging and satisfying work. Encouraging and enabling these other routes to worker motivation would therefore also be a valid form of government intervention. If successful, it would open the door to macroeconomic policies aimed not just at reducing unemployment but at genuine full employment.

4   Instability and unemployment

Underlying the very high levels of unemployment to which I have just referred is a persistent feature of the modern era: economic fluctuations and instability. Fluctuations in product markets inevitably lead to fluctuations in the labour market. If the supply curve of labour is steady, it is relatively simple to see from our supply and demand curves that in the perfect competition model, such fluctuations are met by wage and employment changes. If, for example, demand for labour falls, the

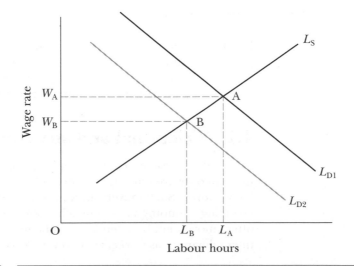

Figure 21.11   **Fluctuating labour demand in a fully flexible perfectly competitive labour market**

predicted consequence is a fall in wages and employment. This is illustrated by the move from A to B in Figure 21.11, where the wage rate falls from W_A to W_B and hours worked from L_A to L_B.

Yet two stylized facts speak strongly against this simple model. First, and most obviously, for more than the last two decades the UK and most other western countries have had growing unemployment – evidence that the labour market is failing to clear. Figure 21.12 shows the rise of unemployment in a number of countries. (The data have been averaged for several time periods to bring out trends: hence they fluctuate less than on Figure 1.5.) Second, there is scant evidence of a major response of real wages to unemployment. Some studies have shown a slowing down of real wages in times of high unemployment, but the degree of sensitivity of real wages to unemployment is not great. Average real wages in the UK continued to rise over the 1980s and early 1990s despite the large rise in unemployment.

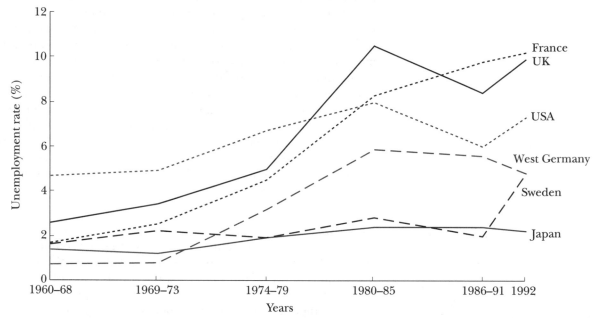

Figure 21.12 **Unemployment rates for France, West Germany, Japan, Sweden, UK and the USA, 1960–92**

Source: *OECD Economic Outlook*, various years

Let us look more closely into the factors underlying unemployment. The persistent presence of unemployment is a manifestation of the imperfect nature of labour markets. I will begin by making a distinction between three types of unemployment: 'frictional', 'structural' and 'demand-deficient'.

4.1 Frictional and structural unemployment

Frictional unemployment is a consequence of labour mobility. All the time many people are wanting to switch jobs, or are moving in and out of the labour force. Such movement would be inevitable and desirable in any changing economy so as to match resources to where they are needed. Very often, movement between jobs will be interrupted by a short-term spell of unemployment as workers search for alternative employment. At the same time, firms will generally have short-term vacancies they fill after looking for suitable applicants. The worker's search process and the firm's recruitment process take a while, and as a result zero unemployment is not feasible. Frictional unemployment is the name we give to the unemployment associated with this search for jobs. In Britain, we now look back on the years of the middle and late 1960s as an era of effectively full employment, but even then there were at all times a few hundred thousand people officially unemployed.

Where, however, the unemployed worker's search for jobs is proving difficult while at the same time firms are having trouble filling their vacancies, even after a period of intensive search, we refer to the resultant unemployment as *structural unemployment*. The idea here is that there are some social or physical barriers in the way of matching the unemployed to the available jobs.

One example is the geographical barrier. Suppose job vacancies are to be found in East Anglia, while in the north there are large areas of unemployment. Especially if the vacancies are for relatively low-paying jobs, it may not be worthwhile for an unemployed person to move to East Anglia from the north in search of employment, given the high moving costs.

Perhaps a more intractable barrier is the skills barrier. Where one industry declines and another expands, the unemployed ex-employees of the declining industry will generally not have the skills appropriate for the expanding industry. To match the worker to the job would necessitate a period of retraining. With no intervention in the market, we have already seen how it can become impossible for individuals to obtain the necessary retraining, even if (a strong condition) there are jobs to be had at the end of the training period. Often the result of industrial decline is prolonged spells of unemployment.

Structural unemployment is likely to be serious at times of economic crises, when there is massive industrial decline and relocation (see Chapter 25). Its extent is linked not only to failures within the labour market, such as the skills problem just mentioned. It is exacerbated by rigidities in the housing market. In the UK, the boom and bust cycle in house prices, has not helped those wishing to move to gain employment. In many countries of the newly-capitalist Eastern Europe, a good deal of housing (and other welfare services) have been linked to jobs in the old communist enterprises, rendering job mobility that would necessitate often moving house quite impossible.

4.2   Demand-deficient unemployment, wage rigidity and flexibility

Even though frictional and structural unemployment are important, I do not suggest that all the unemployment we see in the present day can be categorized in this way. Demand-deficient unemployment arises whenever there is a fall in the aggregate demand for products and for labour, while at the same time wages are slow to adjust.

The various possible origins of a cut in aggregate demand, such as a fall in investment or consumer spending, or contractionary fiscal or monetary policies are discussed in Chapters 17 and 24. Here, the question I am going to address is: what factors might affect the extent of wage rigidity and its opposite, wage flexibility?

Here are some arguments that have been put forward:

1   Some employers enter into explicit or more often implicit long-term contracts with their workers. The deal is that in 'good times' while order books are full and demand for labour is high, workers do not exploit their advantage by demanding large wage rises. Instead they forgo such rises as a sort of insurance premium to be set against the risk of 'bad times'. The firm, in its turn, is happy to accept this insurance: in return for limited promises not to make workers bear the full cost of future crises – that is, by bearing extra losses in recession – it gains higher profits at other times.

I should think you will agree with me that this will hardly stand as a comprehensive account of wage rigidity in national labour markets, especially as employers have in recent decades shown little reluctance to shed workers in large numbers. Nevertheless, there are cases of explicit long-term contracts involving two years, and even the more standard one-year deal is still a long time in relation to the rapid fluctuations that occur in some labour markets. Moreover, we can see how firms wishing to maintain a reputation as a 'good employer', in order more easily to recruit the best workers in good times, will be reluctant to make savage cuts in wages or employment during recessions. This was how the reputation of IBM was built until it was forced recently to renege on its implicit promise never to declare workers redundant.

2   A second, and more generally applicable argument is that unions and workers are often as much concerned with *relative* wages as with their *absolute* real wage. (The relative wage is their wage relative to other groups of workers, while the absolute real wage represents a measure of the volume of commodities that the wage could buy.) Employees are concerned about their relative wage with good reason: they judge their market worth in terms of the market values of other comparable groups.

Reflection

In your own job, if you have one, do you assess your wage more in absolute terms or relatively to other employees?

What then, will workers do in response to cuts in labour demand? The answer depends on whether they act independently or in a collective manner. Moreover, as we shall see, if they bargain collectively in a union it depends crucially whether and how far the different unions in an economy are co-ordinated.

Individual wage constraints

Where unions are absent or very weak, and also where employers are largely independent agents (not regulated by employer organizations or government), we should expect to see wages fluctuating with the changing demand for labour. Employers constrained by losses or low profits propose pay cuts in order to reduce costs. Employees feel obliged to accept them in order to save their jobs. Such is the conception most closely embodied by the US labour market of the last decade which has experienced comparatively less unemployment than European countries but declining wages for millions of workers.

Encompassing unions

At the opposite end of the individual/collective spectrum is the situation where all workers are members of unions, and the unions co-ordinate their bargaining with employers who are also nationally co-ordinated. In such a situation, a national wage deal can be struck. Since the co-ordinating bodies 'encompass' unions representing all members of the work-force there is likely to be pressure for the deal to involve employment for all. We would therefore expect to find such an economy with wages that are relatively flexible in response to macroeconomic fluctuations and with little unemployment.

This situation is most closely realized by the centralized bargaining arrangements of the Scandinavian 'corporatist' countries. In Sweden, for example, the main labour organization, the LO, deals directly with employers' federations. In Sweden wages are found to be relatively flexible, and unemployment remained very low until the early 1990s while elsewhere it soared (see Figure 21.12).

Independent union bargaining

Wage flexibility has been found to be most problematic in the intermediate part of the spectrum. Remember that unions are concerned to defend their members' interests, which include their relative wages. Consider a strong union that bargains independently with an employer. The union will attempt to maintain or increase wages and as far as possible their members' employment. The employer responds by maintaining or increasing the price of the product, which it can do in an imperfectly competitive market. This single price increase only affects the union's members marginally, but when many firms are doing the same there is a general upward pressure on prices.

The net effect for other workers is either or both of two outcomes. If all employers raise prices, which they could if the level of product demand is maintained at a high level, there is a built-in inflation. Indeed, inflation will accelerate if the situation persists. Though there may be full employment, inflation is unstable and also the weaker unions can lose out by not having such large wage increases as the strong unions. If, on the other hand, all employers cannot raise prices, due for example to competitive pressures and to monetary constraints on demand, many firms will instead introduce job cuts. The choice, therefore, is a traditional one: inflation or unemployment. But the terms of that choice are made worse by presence of strong bargaining units such as large unions and large employers, without the necessary national co-ordination between the bargaining units.

Let me sum up what I have said in this and the previous section about the causes of unemployment.

1   There is unemployment due to 'efficiency wages': in a world where work is alienating, intrinsically unrewarding and imperfectly monitored, a certain level of unemployment is always going to be necessary to maintain work discipline.

2   There is frictional unemployment associated with the normal processes of job search and recruitment.

3   There is structural unemployment, often occurring in periods of major industrial upheaval, when there are jobs available in the aggregate but the unemployed are not matched to the available vacancies.

4   Unemployment can rise if there emerges a deficiency of aggregate demand. The extent of any rise in unemployment depends in part on how flexible or rigid is the labour market, and this in turn depends on the degree of co-ordination of bargaining units (unions and employers). On the other hand, this is not all there is to say about unemployment: a full explanation requires also an understanding of the macroeconomic factors that can lead to aggregate demand deficiencies (see Chapters 17 and 24).

Notwithstanding 1, reasons 2–4 suggest several ways in which governments can intervene to keep unemployment down. These are considered in the next section.

4.3   Labour market flexibility and government intervention

Whatever the cause of unemployment, there is generally a choice of ways for governments to intervene, with varying distributional consequences. In every case, we could say that the government is trying to make the labour market 'more flexible', in the sense of restoring labour market equilibrium in response to macroeconomic fluctuations. To an extent, labour market flexibility is a widely-held objective, but economists and politicians differ over the appropriate form of flexibility. Let us look at this choice in respect of policies addressed at remedying each source of unemployment.

As regards frictional unemployment, government can make the market more efficient by providing counselling and information services to employees, and recruitment services to employers. Particularly if these services are non-discriminatory they can have a beneficial effect on equality, as well as on efficiency.

However, governments can also affect frictional unemployment by changing the amount of benefit payable while unemployed. A lower benefit will make it more costly to remain unemployed searching for jobs, leading people to take jobs they otherwise would have turned down. Conversely a high benefit might induce workers to hang on indefinitely waiting for the ideal job to come along. There is little evidence that, in practice, benefit levels in the UK account for more than a small fraction of total unemployment. In addition, the level of unemployment benefits (relative to earnings) has tended to fall in the past 15 years or so whilst unemployment has tended to rise. Whether reducing benefits improves the working of the labour market cannot be answered definitely. Even if frictional unemployment is reduced, the job match may be less adequate; that is, workers may be induced to accept jobs less well suited to them than if they had waited longer.

As regards structural unemployment, we can also delineate two broad ways to intervene. One way is actively to support the reallocation of labour from declining to growing industries. The chief instrument here is state support for intensive retraining. Such a policy has long been a feature of successive governments in Sweden which have been committed to the goal of full employment. The geographical dislocations can also be reduced by regional policies aimed at moving the firms to the workers rather than the other way round. Regional policies work by giving firms subsidies or tax breaks as incentives to locate in deprived areas.

The alternative government policy is to attempt to reconstruct free market forces by removing the impediments to their action. Thus, if workers are to move from one occupation or industry to another, this can be done by allowing wages to fall in the first and/or rise in the second, enabling individuals to respond appropriately to the incentives for relocation and retraining. The philosophy here, then, would be to free up the housing market and the 'training market'. Moving house would, in this view, be easier if there were an active and substantial private rental sector. Moving jobs might be facilitated if individuals had access to loans to fund their training – hence, for example, the UK government's provision of Career Development Loans (I describe these below). This approach to restructuring the labour market is likely to be less beneficial to individual workers, because they have to bear the full cost of the adjustment process rather than share it with firms or government. How far it improves the labour market by reducing structural unemployment remains an open empirical question.

Finally, governments also have a crucial role to play in <u>tackling demand-deficient</u> unemployment. On the one hand they may try to regulate fluctuations in aggregate demand using appropriate macroeconomic policies. On the other hand, governments can affect the level of wage flexibility. The analysis I described above suggests again two alternative routes for success in this respect. Governments could ensure that unions and employers work together in a co-ordinated fashion, engendering a corporatist framework for both wage bargaining and policy making. This approach is linked to a general philosophy of seeking a degree of consensus among the various interest groups in society (unions, employers' chambers of commerce and so on), and of laying down a legal and institutional framework which constrains these groups to take account of wider needs than just those of their own members (see Chapter 24). Alternatively, governments could move to recreate the conditions for a free individualistic labour market, assisting employers in attempts to reduce wages where there is excess labour supply. Either policy could achieve the objective of making overall wages more responsive to macroeconomic fluctuations. The first alternative, however, is likely to be the more egalitarian response, for two reasons. First, unions are for the most part committed to lower wage dispersion, so there is liable to be less income inequality among those in work. Second, in the free labour market approach, governments need to ensure that the incomes of those out of work are kept low, since otherwise there is little fear of unemployment.

5   Training interventions and institutions

We have by now seen, in the previous two sections, a clutch of features of imperfect labour markets, and in each case there was an argument for some kind of intervention to improve efficiency and/or equity. In this final section I want to look at one more salient aspect of the imperfect labour market: the problem of the acquisition of skills through training. We have just seen that training is an important ingredient in policy approaches to reducing structural unemployment. But training has a wider significance in addition to unemployment policy. Achieving an adequate level of training is often taken as the key to improving the productivity of the work-force. In terms of the *AD/AS* model, training the work-force shifts the long-run aggregate supply curve to the right, resulting in increased output at a lower level of prices. Further, ensuring the widest opportunities for skill acquisition is vital for the achievement of greater social and economic equality. I shall first look at the central obstacles surrounding training in an imperfect labour market, and then consider how various institutions surmount these obstacles and how in principle the government might intervene.

One linchpin of the perfect competition model of Section 2 is the view that there is a viable market through which individuals can acquire transferable skills. As long as the prospective wages of jobs with the newly acquired skills are high enough to make an adequate return on the 'investment' in the necessary training, individuals will choose to do so. Hence, it is concluded that the wage premium accruing to the more skilled jobs is the appropriate market reward for incurring the costs of training. Central to this thesis was assumption A6 (Section 2.5), that individuals could borrow sufficient funds on the capital market.

This assumption is unrealistic because the uncertainty involved in economic life severely constrains the borrowing, except perhaps in a small number of instances where the chances of failure or drop out are slim and job prospects are guaranteed. Banks are either unwilling to lend, when they have no physical collateral, or else may charge especially high rates. For many, if not most, types of training, borrowing is not possible. The only way it can happen is if the firm pays for the training. In fact most training within enterprises in Britain is paid for by firms, not employees. In the vast majority of cases it is the firm that pays the fees for employees' training courses, and relatively few employees take a pay reduction while receiving training.

Here then is the problem. As noted above (in Section 2.4), profit-maximizing firms will not invest in training their workers in transferable skills if they fear losing their investment through labour turnover. Mobility of labour means that training creates an 'external benefit', a new skill that is valuable for industry as a whole but not necessarily for the firm that pays for it. It is hard to see how the cost of training can be linked to the benefits if all firms act independently. The problem is another example of the prisoners' dilemma (see Chapter 5). Suppose that there are two non-co-operating firms in an industry, and substantial labour mobility between the firms. Suppose, too, that a skilled work-force brings greater profits. It would be good for both firms if both engaged in training, but without co-operation each could gain by not training (thus saving on training costs) and 'poaching' trained workers from the other firm. As a result both firms decide not to train, which is the worst outcome for both.

What, then, is the way out of the dilemma? Evidently, there is a case for some form of intervention to ensure provision of training is 'adequate'. I shall here look at some possible government policies or institutional mechanisms for avoiding the problem.

5.1   A 'training market'

One approach is for the government to try to resolve the problem of the individual's inability to borrow. This would be favoured if it is felt advantageous not to intervene in the labour market itself, which has broadly been the approach of the UK government in the last decade. Career Development Loans (CDLs) are an example of this approach. These are loans from private banks, subsidized by the government in that it pays the interest until three months after the end of any training course. By improving the functioning of the capital market, the aim is to enable individuals to fund their own training. In terms of our model of training decisions outlined above (Section 2.4), this could work in principle if individuals were well-informed and had access to jobs in a situation of reasonably full employment. In this case, there is in effect a 'training market' operating within the labour market for jobs. People can pay for training that is supplied either by firms or by educational institutions. With respect to CDLs, however, uncertainty about unemployment, together with far from perfect information about the benefits of training, accounts for a relatively slow take-up of this facility: only some 27,000 loans were granted altogether in the first four years after 1988.

5.2   Direct state intervention

A straightforward way to avoid an externality is for government to intervene directly in the funding of training by implementing its own schemes. The Youth Training Scheme (YTS) has been the most widely used vehicle in Britain. Since its inception in 1983 over a million young people have gone through YTS or its successor, 'Youth Training'. Nevertheless, critics have frequently questioned the quality of training provided, seeing YTS more as a response to mass youth unemployment or as a means of lowering youth wages. While the schemes improved during the 1980s, the same accusation has been made of the training quality provided by Employment Training (ET) schemes for the long-term unemployed.

Nevertheless governments can make a substantial contribution to work-based skills acquisition. In Britain the Training Opportunities Scheme (TOPS) was often successful in creating high-level skills (Payne, 1991). In Singapore, as in other countries of the Pacific Rim, central state intervention to subsidize and motivate training has been decisive in the 'upskilling' of the work-force.

State interventions such as these necessarily involve considerable costs, and the need to apportion these costs fairly and to minimize the drain on central taxation, has led some governments to set up a 'pay or play' system of intervention, designed to make the industry that benefits from the training bear the costs. An example of this is the Industrial Training Board (ITB) system, which was set up in Britain in 1964. The ITBs were given the power to raise a levy from firms in the industry under their control, in order to fund training within the industry. Those firms that provided training were then reimbursed from the ITB. Those which did not train but benefited from the higher skills had to pay the levy. In principle this was an efficient way to avoid the externality. The system has even been exported successfully, for example to Hong Kong, but in Britain it worked less well in practice. On the one hand the ITBs were widely charged with excessive bureaucracy. On the other hand, it has been argued that many firms, especially small ones, did not see the need for much training. Consequently, many ITBs began to lose the political support of businesses. The conflict between the wishes of policy makers, the needs of employees and the strategic needs of employers can be the rock on which many schemes of government intervention founder. Most ITBs were abolished in the later 1980s.

5.3   The nenko system

In Japan, as observed in the introduction to this chapter, it is common for a proportion of the male labour force to stay with one employer throughout a whole career. Zero mobility is less common in other western nations, but zero or low mobility is certainly found for certain groups of work. Those employed by governments may typically work for long periods, or even a complete career, for one sector of government.

Where labour turnover is low, it is expected that firms (or the government agency as employer) can make a judgement as to the amount of training that will maximize profits (or value to the government service) and provide the necessary funding since they will receive the benefits. At the same time, workers are rewarded within firms for acquiring higher skills, and are motivated to train. These factors help to account for the high level of training that occurs within Japanese firms, especially when compared with firms in the USA where workers tend to stay with their companies for much shorter periods.

5.4   'Corporatist' intervention

Finally, let us note the resolution to the externality problem obtained in Germany. In Germany there is a 'dual' system, whereby most young people not entering higher education gain apprenticeships. They attend school for part of the week, and get work-based training and work the rest of the week. The system is widely regarded as effective, and one of the reasons is that pressure is brought on firms to participate. The pressure to participate, and the regulation of the training itself, comes as much from industry level and regional organizations such as chambers of commerce and trade union groupings, as from central government. Training is also monitored by statutory works councils in firms. Unlike in an individualistic system where all firms and workers act independently, the opportunity for firms to 'free-ride' by 'poaching' skilled labour while not contributing to training effort is limited.

The striking aspect of the institutional mechanisms found in Germany is that the intervention is tri-partite, involving representation of workers, employers and government, rather than hierarchical or 'top-down'. This tri-partite regulation of the labour market is the hallmark of 'corporatism', the political and institutional system discussed in Chapter 15 involving organizations on both sides of industry as well as government in many areas of policy formation and economic regulation. The system is found in different shapes and guises in a number of advanced industrial countries in Europe, such as Germany, Austria and the Scandinavian countries.

6   Conclusion

If nothing else, I hope this chapter will have shown how complex labour markets are in reality, far from the simple perfect competition model of supply and demand. As a general rule, though with exceptions, each time I introduced an element of complexity questioning the assumptions of the perfect competition model, I developed an alternative model designed to capture some known feature of actual labour markets. Moreover, with each new model I arrived at a rationale for government intervention in one form or another on grounds of economic efficiency. To take some examples, governments have a case for intervening to remove the externalities involved in job-related training, to regulate unemployment (but not to reduce it to zero), to remove or minimize barriers to labour mobility between sectors of the labour market, to tackle structural rigidities such as those resulting from chronic decline of industries, or to impose a wage minimum on the labour market.

Each form of intervention should improve the economic efficiency of certain aspects of the labour market. But within this objective we have also seen that alternative forms of intervention are likely to have varying implications for economic inequality. Take, for example, the issue of labour market flexibility. Allowing or forcing wages to fall may help to clear the labour market in an area of declining industries, especially if benefits are also lowered. The alternative way to avoid unemployment is to assist workers directly with retraining for expanding industries and assist firms to locate in declining areas. These are two policies with the same objective of full employment – but they have manifestly different implications for income distribution. The next chapter turns the focus from labour markets to a broader discussion of income distribution.

PART 13

CHAPTER 22

by David Bailey and Shaun Hargreaves Heap

DISTRIBUTION AND INTERVENTION

VALUES AND DISTRIBUTION

1 Introduction

Did you know that begging is a criminal offence in Britain? In Henry VIII's time they cut off the beggar's ears. The normal punishment today is a £50 fine or three days in prison. We only know this because beggary is in the news. It has become visible on British streets over the last decade in ways that few, if any, people can remember. Twenty years ago beggars were rare in Britain. Now any traveller on the London Underground can testify to their numbers: often young, many clearly in acute need.

The (re)appearance of beggars on the streets is a symptom, albeit a particularly dramatic one, of something which affects increasing numbers in Britain: poverty. The growth of poverty is related to a recent move towards greater income inequality in the UK, and the extraordinary thing about

Figure 22.1 **Begging on the London Underground**

both is that they reverse the earlier trends of the post-war period (and most earlier periods this century) towards less poverty and greater equality. How has this come about? Should anything be done about it? These are the questions addressed by this chapter.

The definition and measurement of poverty is controversial and we begin Section 2 by considering a variety of measures for the UK and other countries. The discussion then moves on to the causes of poverty, looking first at those cases where people are poor because they are not in work. The poor who are in work are discussed in Section 3 where we consider recent changes in the distribution of earnings, in particular the increase in the number of relatively low-paid jobs.

Should anything be done about poverty and inequality in the distribution of income? Section 4 addresses this question. Plainly, this can be a highly charged and complex issue. Economics has tended to approach it in a particular way. Interventions to redistribute income from the rich to the poor appear to imply a judgement that making the poor better-off more than compensates for making the rich worse-off, that is, they involve interpersonal comparisons of welfare or well-being. The question which economists ask then becomes: How does a society come to have an ethical standard which will enable it to make these judgements?

Perhaps members of a society will agree on such a standard. More likely, perhaps they will agree to resolve their disputes via the ballot box. Or perhaps, in the absence of any agreement, they will decide to do nothing at all (as the New Right recommends). We consider these possibilities and are inclined to doubt any general or simple answer. Even when a society agrees to a standard, there is the troubling matter of how far it stretches. Global inequalities in income are more extreme than those within any single country. To illustrate the enormity of this gap, the investment bank of Goldman Sachs generated profits of £2.6 billion in 1993 which were distributed among 161 partners mainly in New York and London. In 1993 the GDP of the Republic of Tanzania, one of the poorest countries in the world, was £2.2 billion and this was distributed among 25 million people. If ethics demand that something be done about begging in London, do they also demand that something be done about this disparity?

Section 5 returns to questions of measurement, this time with respect to inequality, and links them, following the discussion in Section 4, to the different ethical reasons for being concerned with income distribution. In particular, this section shows how measures of inequality embody different views on how to compare the welfare of different people.

Section 6 considers whether all our ethical concerns in this area do turn on such interpersonal comparisons of welfare. It is not clear that they are the only issue. There is also the concern to see people's rights respected. Consider, for example, the inequalities of income associated with race and gender. Concern with gender or racial inequality rather than inequality *per se*, seems rooted in the thought that everyone has rights, for example to equal treatment before the law or in the labour market, and these groups' rights are being violated. If this is the case, then alternative measures of inequality and policy interventions may become appropriate, highlighting the importance of being clear over *why* inequality is a matter of ethical concern.

In short, this chapter is concerned with unravelling one of the extraordinary developments in recent years, the growth of poverty and inequality, and with revealing what is at issue when a society decides what if anything should be done about such a change.

2 The incidence and causes of poverty

Definitions

Absolute poverty

A person (or household) is in absolute poverty if their income or expenditure is below a specified real level.

Relative poverty

A person (or household) is in relative poverty if their income or expenditure is below a specified proportion of average (mean or median) income or expenditure.

Before we can survey changes in poverty we need to measure it. And, as Chapter 9 argued, we cannot measure without making some value judgements. This section therefore begins with some problems of measurement.

2.1 The measurement of poverty

The definition and measurement of poverty is controversial and it is helpful at the outset to introduce a broad distinction between 'absolute' and 'relative' poverty. Suppose the judgement as to whether a person is in poverty depends on his or her income level. Someone is in absolute poverty when their income falls below some defined and fixed level, whereas they are in relative poverty when their income is low relative to that of other individuals in society. To illustrate how these two ways of looking at poverty might differ, consider what will happen to each when all incomes in society are growing. The numbers in absolute poverty will decline because everyone's income is rising relative to the absolute standard by which poverty is judged. In comparison, income growth may or may not lower relative poverty: it all depends on whether those at the lower end of the income scale find their incomes growing faster or slower than other incomes. If all incomes grow at the same rate then nobody's relative income changes and relative poverty remains the same.

Question

Why should we worry about relative poverty?

At first glance, the concept of relative poverty may seem less worrying than absolute poverty. If we mean by poverty some state where it is difficult for individuals to function as human beings, then it seems natural to think of some absolute physical requirements which have to be satisfied. In this context whether other individuals on average have more or less of these requirements is of no consequence; and yet this is taken into account by measures of relative poverty. However, a functioning human is also a social being and this entails being able to engage in enterprises which are similar to those of other people. So poverty can also arise when incomes fall significantly relative to those of others.

Consider the use of a television. Plainly one can live without a television since it is not a physical necessity. Yet functioning as a social being is made more difficult in many societies without one. How could you discuss with neighbours and friends the latest episode of a favourite soap opera, or share the horror of what is going on in Bosnia or indeed argue about the influence of TV violence? Naturally some people function socially without a television, but you will see the point. Human beings do not live by bread alone and they are deprived when their opportunities for social interaction are diminished by relative poverty.

Definitions

Headcount index

The headcount index is the percentage of the population whose income per head is below a specified level, or poverty line.

Poverty gap

The poverty gap is the percentage by which the income of the average poor person falls short of the poverty line.

Whether a poverty level is established 'absolutely' or 'relatively', there must be a method for measuring the incidence of poverty with respect to that level. Unfortunately this is not as simple as it might seem. One method of measurement is to count the number of people whose income or expenditure falls below the chosen poverty level. This gives us the headcount index. Alternatively it may be interesting to know *how far* the typical poor person falls below this line. This is measured by calculating the average difference between the poverty line and the expenditure or income of the poor, and then expressing this figure as a proportion of the poverty line to yield what is known as the poverty gap. These measures are widely used, but both have their problems.

Comparing poverty measures

In order to illustrate these problems, imagine a hypothetical community in which there are five people out of a total population of 50 living below the official poverty line of $50 per week, half the average income. Their weekly incomes are as follows:

A	$40
B	$30
C	$20
D	$30
E	$40

Exercise 22.1

Calculate the headcount index and the poverty gap.

Now suppose that the income of an individual living below the poverty line is increased but not by enough to take this individual out of poverty. For example, suppose that C's weekly income is increased from $20 to $30. One might argue that in some fundamental sense poverty has been reduced, and we would wish to see this reflected in the chosen index of poverty. Yet the headcount index will not change. Only if the increase in C's income had been enough to lift C above the poverty line would this measure have registered a fall in poverty.

The poverty gap indicator performs better, registering a fall.

$$\frac{\$10 + \$20 + \$20 + \$20 + \$10}{5} = \$16$$

$$\frac{\$16}{\$50} \times 100 = 32 \text{ per cent}$$

However, this measure of poverty can fail to move in the right direction if the individual is taken out of poverty by the increase in income. That depends on whether the individual's income was above or below the average income of the poor. The poverty gap indicator falls only if the individual whose income is increased started out with an income below average for the poor. For example, if C's income is increased from $20 to $52, the poverty gap falls from 36 per cent to 30 per cent. However if A's income increases from $40 to $52 the poverty gap actually increases to 40 per cent though the headcount index has fallen. Check both of these calculations for yourself. So neither the headcount index nor the poverty gap can be relied upon always to move in the right direction.

Exercise 22.2

Suppose C, the poorest, loses (a) $5, (b) $15 to A. Poverty would seem to have worsened. What happens to the poverty gap and the headcount index in each case?

Such problems suggest that the results using both measures should be treated cautiously. In practice the use of either measure also requires further difficult decisions. For instance, should one calculate the incidence of poverty using data on expenditure or income? Expenditure may seem to provide the better guide to an individual's welfare, but if an individual gains a sense of well-being through saving as well as spending then income may be the more appropriate measure.

So far in our discussion we have talked about individuals. However, most individuals live in multi-person households. What difference does this make for our analysis of poverty? Some economies of scale are present in households, since often the size of the house (and hence rent or mortgage repayments) does not increase in proportion to the number of people living in the house. If expenditure must only increase by 40 per cent to enable a two-person adult household to be just as well off individually as a single person, then one could argue that it is as if the larger household contains 1.4 adults. Actual numbers of persons can in this way be converted into equivalent numbers. Similarly, the costs of maintaining a particular standard of living do not increase as rapidly when the number of children in the household increases as when the number of adults goes up. Naturally, the age of the children must be taken into account in this exercise, and it may also be sensible to give a lower weight to retired individuals than to prime-age adults. Therefore, when looking at household poverty, it is more appropriate to use income or expenditure per 'equivalent adult' rather than simply using a per capita figure.

This is perhaps enough by way of a caution on some of the difficulties related to measuring poverty, so let us turn to some actual measures and what they reveal about poverty in the UK and elsewhere.

2.2   Poverty in the United Kingdom

What has happened to poverty in the United Kingdom since 1979? We consider household absolute poverty first. A common absolute standard for judging household poverty is the real income level available to households of different types on the standard benefit (income support, previously supplementary benefit); and we take the real level of this benefit in a particular year, 1979, as our 'absolute' standard for all years.

The proportion of all households with income (net of housing costs) below this value was 7.6 per cent in 1979 and 7.0 per cent in 1989. This suggests a slight decline in absolute poverty. However, the use of income figures for pensioners may be misleading (in so far as some are dissaving and hence spending above their income), so it is interesting to look at non-pensioner households. Here the proportion of households below the 1979 benefit level was 4.5 per cent in 1979 and 6.6 per cent in 1989. Non-pensioner household absolute poverty has been rising, and the increase in begging may be explained as an understandable if illegal response to such absolutely low income levels. In fact for some sub-groups within this category the proportion in absolute poverty is startlingly high: for instance 9.7 per cent of single person households were in absolute poverty in 1989 (compared with 7.2 per cent in 1979) (Social Security Committee, 1992/93).

Table 22.1 shows individual (as opposed to household) poverty. As before we can set an absolute level for income and calculate the number of people with income that falls short of this value. If the standard for absolute poverty is taken as the income level which was 40 per cent of the average income level in 1979, then the number of people in absolute poverty rose from 1.3 million to 1.6 million over the decade of the 1980s. Or if income levels are calculated net of housing costs, then the numbers in absolute poverty rose from 1.7 million to 2.6 million. In other words, the numbers with very low absolute income grew by about 1 million people over the decade.

Table 22.1   **Number of individuals below various proportions of average income, UK (millions)**

Proportion of average income (%)	Before housing costs (BHC)			After housing costs (AHC)		
	1979[1]	1988/89[1]	1988/89[2]	1979[1]	1988/89[1]	1988/89[2]
	(1)	(2)	(3)	(4)	(5)	(6)
40	1.3	1.6	4.5	1.7	2.6	6.1
50	4.4	3.8	10.4	5.0	5.3	12.0
60	9.8	8.3	16.0	10.4	9.9	16.8
80	21.4	17.0	25.6	21.6	17.6	25.7
100	32.0	24.6	34.7	31.8	24.5	34.3
Total no. of individuals	54.0	56.0	56.0	54.0	56.0	56.0

[1] Calculated with respect to 1979 real average income.

[2] Calculated with respect to 1988/89 average income.

Source: Department of Social Security (1992)

Question

What conclusions may we draw about *relative* poverty from Table 22.1 (columns 1, 3, 4 and 6)?

Comparing columns 1 and 3, and 4 and 6 in Table 22.1 shows the change in the number of individuals in relative poverty reinforcing the picture of the 1980s as a decade of growing deprivation for those at the bottom of the income distribution. The number of people living on less than half the national average income rose from 4.4 million to 10.4 million between 1979 and 1989. Thus if half the average income level is taken as a rough and ready measure of what is required for an individual to participate in a meaningful way in society, then the number 'outside' society grew by a devastating 6 million people over this period.

The extraordinary thing about this growth in poverty is that it took place during a period when most people in employment enjoyed very significant increases in real incomes. So why did the numbers in poverty increase?

The interaction between rising unemployment between January 1979 (4.1 per cent) and January 1989 (7 per cent), and the changes in the benefits offered by the welfare state, accounts for some of this growth. For instance when individuals lose their jobs now, the extent to which their income is replaced by social security benefits is less than was previously the case. Unemployment benefit now rises in line with the retail price index rather than as previously being indexed to average earnings. Over time the real earnings of those in work have risen, with the result that the relative position of those reliant on benefit has deteriorated. For those who have been unemployed for more than a year, and they numbered over 1 million in the late 1980s and early 1990s, unemployment benefit has not been payable (in 1994 the period was reduced to six months). Such individuals are eligible at most for income support (IS), which is a means tested benefit. As such, there is some stigma attached to it, and not all those who are eligible take up their entitlement, further worsening the situation.

Throughout the 1980s unemployment was high by historical standards and this contributed to the incidence of poverty in a variety of less direct ways. For example, the wives of unemployed men are much more likely to be unemployed than wives of employed men. This may partly reflect a disincentive effect of the way the benefit system operates: if the potential earnings of the wife are low, the household may feel that it is hardly worth her working given the loss of benefit that would ensue. More significance, however, attaches to the state of the local labour market; the lack of employment opportunities affects both spouses. Likewise, economic recession is associated with increased staying-on rates at school, while those who leave school and fail to find employment are less likely to leave home than those with jobs. Both effects contribute to the greater incidence of poverty as unemployment rises. Furthermore, the lack of employment for young people can have serious long-term consequences, creating a dynamic of poverty driven by an inability to accumulate human capital and valuable work experience and to develop those characteristics desired by employers such as reliability, initiative and commitment.

2.3   Poverty in the European Community

Let us now put the British experience in the 1980s in an international perspective. Table 22.2 gives information on poverty rates in certain EC countries in the early 1980s. The poverty line is constant and is equal to 50 per cent of mean equivalent expenditure in the given base year, and expenditure is measured in 1980 prices. Thus it provides a comparable measure of the incidence of absolute poverty in different countries.

Table 22.2   **Poverty in the European Community**

	Poverty rates (%)	
	base year	end year
Germany, 1978–83	10.3	9.7
Spain, 1980–85	20.3	19.1
France, 1979–85	18.0	13.1
Ireland, 1980–87	18.5	18.7
Italy, 1980–85	12.1	12.4
Netherlands, 1979–85	6.9	9.5
UK, 1981–85	14.0	16.2

Source: Eurostat (1990)

Question

What do you think is the most striking difference between the countries in Table 22.2 in the incidence of absolute poverty?

Perhaps the most striking difference is that the UK and the Netherlands were the only economies to register substantial increases in poverty. Note too that this rise in absolute poverty for all households in the UK conflicts with the 1979–89 data in Section 2.2. This is because unemployment in the UK was higher in 1985 (10.8 per cent) than in 1989.

2.4   Poverty in the USA

What has happened to poverty in the USA over the last 30 years? Using an absolute measure based on income, the poverty rate fell in the economic expansion of the mid 1960s and early 1970s from 20% in 1963 to 11.6% in 1972/73. Since then, however, only elderly households, for whom the absolute poverty rate fell from 32.6% in 1963 to only 10.2% in 1988, have continued to experience a decline in the incidence of poverty. In the somewhat depressed macroeconomic conditions from the mid 1970s to the mid 1980s, the poverty rate increased among non-elderly households from 10.7% to 11.6%. The poverty rate tends to vary contra-cyclically, since a decline in employment increases income inequality. The US expansion of the late 1980s, which saw the unemployment rate fall from 7.4% in 1984 to 5.45% in 1988, however, was associated with a smaller than expected fall in the poverty rate of non-elderly households from 13% in 1984 to 12.2% in 1988, and for young families the poverty rate remained stuck at 15.6% (Cutler and Katz, 1991). This suggests that other factors were at work. Indeed, there were important changes in the distribution of earnings for reasons which are similar to those which we discuss in Section 3 for the UK.

2.5   Poverty in developing countries

To compare the extent of absolute poverty in different developing countries, the 1990 *World Development Report* of the World Bank used two poverty levels: at per capita incomes of $275 and $370. Since using official exchange rates to convert each country's per capita income into a common dollar measure can be misleading, the study used 1985 dollar purchasing power parity exchange rates (see Chapter 20). The report published results using the headcount index and the poverty gap measure for both poverty lines.

The total number of very poor in these low-income countries in 1985 was 633 million (18 per cent of the population of the developing world) and of the poor 1116 million (one third of the population of these countries). Sub-Saharan Africa and South Asia had 30 per cent of their people in the very poor category and about 50 per cent in the poor category. Even the most successful of the developing regions (East Asia and Latin America) had a tenth of their people in the very poor category, and a fifth in the poor category. Poverty gaps were typically about 30 per cent (*World Development Report*, 1990, Tables 2.1, 3.2 and 3.3).

What characteristics were associated with the probability of being poor in these countries? Typically, it was found that the incidence of poverty was higher in rural areas, particularly where the land is arid, infertile and mountainous. Poverty is more likely amongst large families, though one needs here to allow for two-way causation, with poverty leading to larger families, both voluntarily as insurance against old age and other adversities of life, and involuntarily as a result of a lack of knowledge of, and access to, effective methods of birth control. The poor lack capital, both human and physical; landlessness is a prime factor in accounting for poverty, and low endowments of human capital resulting from poor nutrition and inadequate schooling mean that such individuals are confined at best to low-paid earning opportunities such as unskilled labourers, self-employment in the informal sector, or as scavengers, hustlers, criminals and prostitutes. They also have less access to publicly provided goods and services, e.g. agricultural extension services, and lower ability to make use of such opportunities when they are provided. Women and children are especially disadvantaged.

Though the picture painted above is a gloomy one, there are some bright spots. Over the medium term in some countries there have been significant reductions in the proportion of their populations below the poverty line, and at the same time marked improvements in important socio-economic indicators such as under-5 mortality rates. For example in Indonesia over the period 1970–87, the headcount index of poverty fell by 2.34 percentage points each year from an initial level of 58 per cent and the under-5 mortality rate by 3.3 per cent per year; and in Costa Rica over the period 1971–86 the headcount index fell by 1.41 percentage points per year from an initial level of 45 per cent and child mortality by a massive 9.7 per cent per year (*World Development Report*, 1990, Table 3.5). The evidence suggests that addressing the problem of poverty in the long run requires increasing the human capital of the poor; improving and maintaining the economy's total capital including its physical infrastructure; and generally encouraging economic growth.

3   The distribution of earnings in the UK

The growth of poverty in the UK has been accompanied by an increasing inequality in the distribution of earnings over the last 20 years. This section considers the evidence and then some explanations.

3.1   Changes in the distribution of earnings in the UK since 1970

The story that we shall relate is one of increased inequality in the structure of earnings in Britain from the late 1970s onwards. This is the case for the distribution of earnings of both men and women, and within different age groups. The one bright spot is that there has been a narrowing of the gap between male and female earnings, and we shall have more to say about this in Section 6. British experience is not unique; in the USA for instance, real wage gains have been virtually non-existent over the last two decades for many workers with poor educational qualifications and little human capital, and the share of the highest earners has increased markedly.

First we outline two measures of inequality. Look at Figure 22.2a, which shows a hypothetical frequency distribution (see Chapter 9, Section 3.1), with the numbers receiving a particular level of income measured along the vertical axis, and the income level along the horizontal axis. Figure 22.2b displays the same information in a different format, measuring on the vertical axis the total number of individuals whose income is no greater than a particular level of income. (Note that the vertical scale is smaller on Figure 22.2b than on 22.2a.)

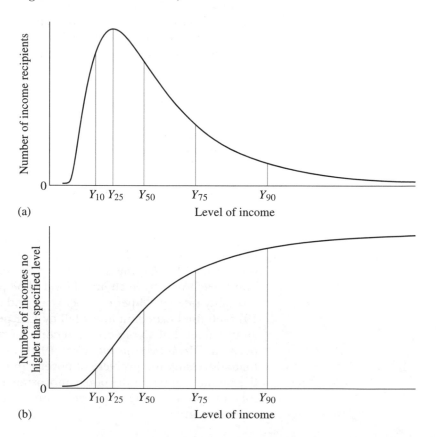

Figure 22.2 **Two measures of income inequality**

One approach to inequality would be to compare two points on this distribution. Let Y_p be the income accruing to the income recipient who is at the p percentile point of the income distribution, that is, p per cent of the recipients have an income no greater than Y_p and $(100 - p)$ per cent receive incomes no smaller than Y_p. It is convenient to divide the income distribution into blocks of equal size. We might use ten equal blocks, or *deciles*, so that the people receiving the lowest 10 per cent of incomes fall within the lowest decile group and so on. Similarly, a *quartile* is one of four blocks of incomes, the lowest quartile group consisting of people receiving the lowest 25 per cent of incomes and so on. For example Y_{90} is the income of the person located at the highest decile of the income distribution, 10 per cent of the sample having earnings greater than this, and Y_{10} is the income of the person located at the lowest decile, 10 per cent of the sample having earnings smaller than this. A measure of the inequality of the distribution would be the ratio of Y_{90} to Y_{10}. I will call this the *decile ratio*. Assume for example that this ratio is 4; then basically what this figure is telling us is that the income of a representative high earner is four times higher than that of a typical low earner.

Alternatively, instead of a single income, we could take a range of income. We then normalize this, that is, relate it to the distribution as a whole by expressing it as a percentage of median income. An example of such a measure of the dispersion of the distribution would be the *relative interquartile range* which is given by:

$$\frac{(Y_{75} - Y_{25})}{Y_{50}} \times 100$$

The larger is the value of this measure, the more spread out are incomes in the middle of the distribution.

These measures help to throw some light on the changes that have occurred in the distribution of incomes in the UK over the last 25 years. Evidence from the annual *New Earnings Survey* suggests that after narrowing somewhat in the 1970s the distribution of earnings has become increasingly dispersed. The behaviour of the decile ratio and the relative interquartile range for men and women are depicted in Figures 22.3 and 22.4. The gross hourly

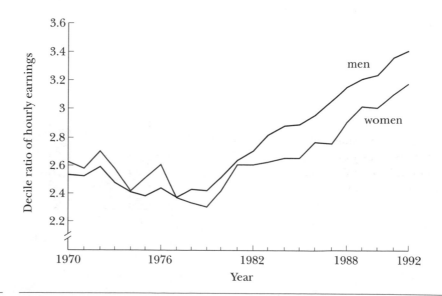

Figure 22.3   **Ratio of hourly earnings at the highest decile to those at the lowest decile, men and women, UK, 1970–92**

Source: *New Earnings Survey*, various years

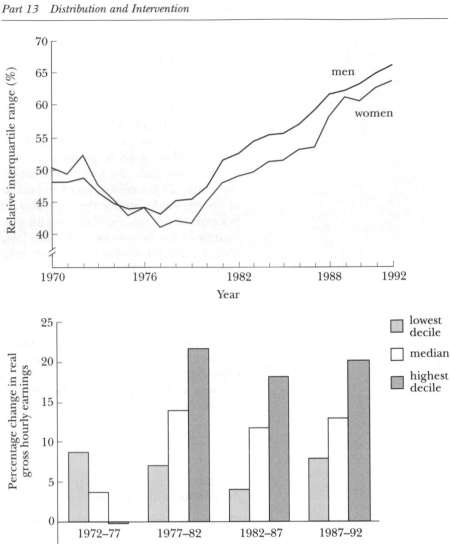

Figure 22.4 Relative interquartile range of hourly earnings, men and women, UK, 1970–92

Source: *New Earnings Survey,* various years

Figure 22.5 Percentage changes in real gross hourly earnings at different points on the male earnings distribution, Great Britain

Source: *New Earnings Survey,* various years

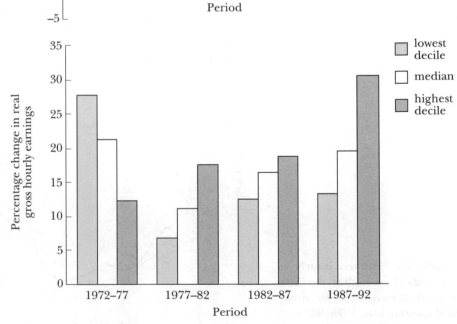

Figure 22.6 Percentage changes in real gross hourly earnings at different points on the female earnings distribution, Great Britain

Source: *New Earnings Survey,* various years

earnings of the male at the highest decile were 3.41 times larger than those of the male at the lowest decile in 1992, compared to a multiple of only 2.53 in 1970 (Figure 22.3), whilst the interquartile range has widened in percentage terms from 48.2 per cent in 1970 to 66.3 per cent in 1992 (Figure 22.4). A similar picture also emerges for the distribution of female earnings.

There have also been quite startling changes in the growth of real hourly earnings at different points of the earnings distribution. Figures 22.5 and 22.6 show that real earnings for both men and women at the lowest decile grew more rapidly than real earnings at both the median and at the highest decile between 1972 and 1977. However, since then the relative position of the lowest-paid has deteriorated to a remarkable degree. Take another look at Figures 22.5 and 22.6. Notice that for each sub-period 1977–82, 1982–87 and 1987–92 real earnings growth for both men and women was lowest for the lowest decile and highest for the highest decile. Between 1987 and 1992, for both men and women real earnings growth at the lowest decile was about 40 per cent of the increase at the highest decile.

Earnings also became more dispersed within age groups in the 1980s as can be seen in Figures 22.7 and 22.8, which show the ratio Y_{90}/Y_{10} for men and

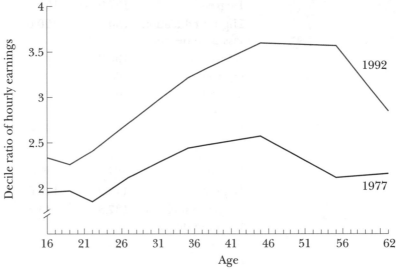

Figure 22.7 Decile ratio of hourly earnings for men by age, Great Britain, 1977 and 1992

Source: *New Earnings Survey,* various years

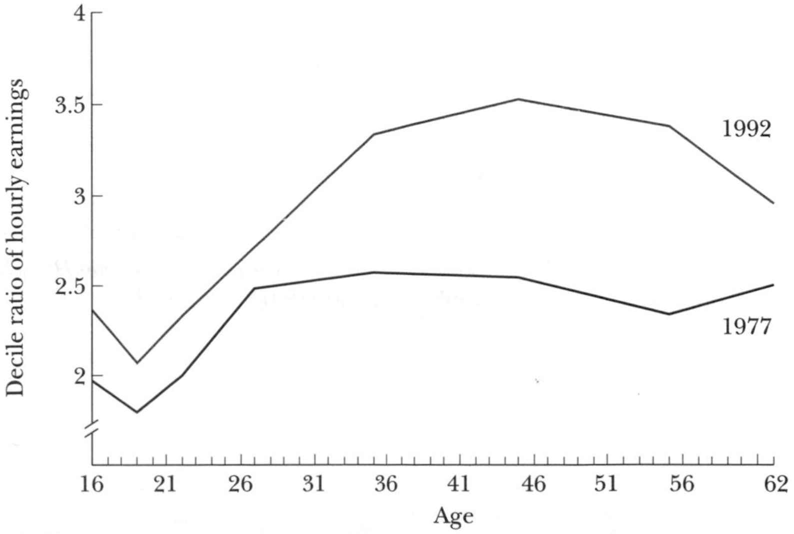

Figure 22.8 Decile ratio of hourly earnings for women by age, Great Britain, 1977 and 1992

Source: *New Earnings Survey,* various years

women, by age, for 1977 and 1992. A proportionately greater increase in Y_{90}/Y_{10} is observed for prime-age men and women than for other age groups. Earnings also became more dispersed across educational groups. The relative pay of the more highly educated declined in the 1970s, and rose again in the 1980s. In Table 22.3 the average earnings of workers with different educational qualifications are depicted as a percentage of the average earnings of workers with O level or equivalent qualifications (the examinations taken at about age 16). For instance the earnings of a male graduate were 78% higher than the earnings of a man with O level or equivalent qualifications in 1971, only 41% higher in 1980, but 75% higher in 1991. The corresponding figures for women were: 78% higher in 1971, 61% higher in 1980 and 82% higher in 1991. Furthermore, despite rising participation, children from professional households are still six or seven times more likely than their manual counterparts to enter higher education.

Table 22.3   **Relative earnings by educational qualification, Great Britain, selected years 1971–91**

Men	1971	1976	1980	1986	1991
Degree	177.9	154.2	140.8	152.5	174.6
Higher education less than degree	130.1	120.6	116.5	117.8	131.0
A level or equivalent	106.2	98.1	100.0	104.0	113.1
O level or equivalent	100.0	100.0	100.0	100.0	100.0
CSE, craft, etc.	89.4	91.6	92.2	86.1	84.1
No qualification	78.8	85.0	86.4	85.1	87.3
Women	**1971**	**1976**	**1980**	**1986**	**1991**
Degree	178.2	179.0	161.2	168.8	182.4
Higher education less than degree	137.8	146.7	136.9	144.8	162.6
A level or equivalent	104.2	106.7	100.0	110.4	109.3
O level or equivalent	100.0	100.0	100.0	100.0	100.0
CSE, craft, etc.	95.0	95.2	92.2	95.8	90.7
No qualification	74.4	86.7	86.4	90.6	80.2

Notes: earnings are median earnings in each category relative to median earnings of those with O level or equivalent. A level examinations are typically taken at age 18. The data for 1971 and 1976 are based upon gross annual earnings, and for the other years on usual gross weekly earnings of persons aged 20–69 in full-time employment.

Source: calculated from data in *General Household Survey* (1980) Table 6.6; (1986) Table 9.19; and (1991) Table 10.12

3.2   Accounting for changes in the structure of earnings

To account for the changes in the UK distribution of earnings that have occurred over the last two decades, and similar changes that have taken place in other advanced economies such as France, Japan and the USA (see Katz *et al.*, 1993; Levy and Murmane, 1992), we need to consider the role of demand-side factors, supply-side factors and institutions. Despite the limitations of the perfectly competitive demand and supply model in explaining developments in labour markets (Chapter 21), it is helpful to begin by considering the extent to which individual choices in response to changes in the conditions of demand and supply suggest explanations for some but by no means all of the changes that have occurred in the distribution of earnings.

Changes in relative wages can originate from either the supply or demand side (see Chapter 21, Sections 2.1 and 2.2). Increased governmental support for further and higher education such as lower tuition fees, more scholarships or increased maintenance grants will reduce private costs and shift the supply curve of educated labour to the right from S to S_1 on Figure 22.9. The result, *ceteris paribus*, is an increase in the proportion of the labour force with more education and a corresponding fall in their relative pay.

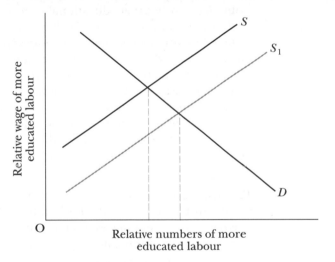

Figure 22.9 **An increase in the relative numbers of more educated labour**

On the demand side, the relative pay of the educated would be increased by such factors as: changes in the composition of demand that led to the expansion of sectors which were more intensive in the use of more educated labour, such as professional services; or technological change within a given sector of the economy which raised the relative demand for more highly educated labour at given factor prices, for example increased mechanization or computerization. Both types of change would be associated with a rightwards shift in the demand schedule from D to D_1 in Figure 22.10. In the short run the supply curve S_S will be relatively inelastic, given the time lag involved in expanding the supply of skilled labour through education and training. Initially, therefore, the main impact would be felt on relative wages rather than on relative quantities with the new short-run equilibrium position at point B. However, in the long run supply S_L would be more elastic, as more individuals are induced to acquire additional years of schooling as a result of the increase in the returns to

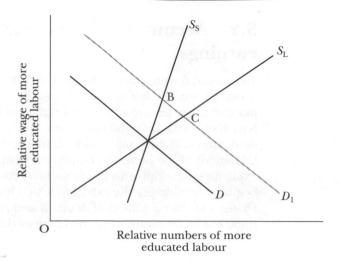

Figure 22.10 **The effects of an increase in the demand for more highly educated labour**

education. The relative pay of the more educated falls somewhat and the new long-run equilibrium position occurs at point C in Figure 22.10.

Throughout the period under consideration the stock of more educated labour in the UK increased relative to the stock of the less educated, although the relative growth in supply of the more educated was less rapid in the 1980s than in the 1970s. By itself this slowdown in relative growth would have meant that educational differentials narrowed less rapidly in the 1980s than they would otherwise have done. The fact that they actually widened might be explained by changes in labour demand favouring the more skilled and/or technological change biased in their favour. Support for these explanations can be found in the decline of the manufacturing sector, increased competition from newly industrializing countries in industries such as textiles, clothing and footwear, and in the increasing significance of computerization and information technology generally in the production process. It seems, then, that the forces of supply and demand can go some way towards explaining changes in the structure of UK earnings.

The institutional environment in which the wage setting process takes place is also influential. In the 1970s when the UK earnings distribution narrowed, incomes policies of an egalitarian form were in operation for a substantial part of the time. Legislation favourable to the operation of trade unions was also introduced during the Wilson and Callaghan administrations, and union membership and density (that is, union members as a proportion of the labour force) rose to a peak of 13.3 million and 52.8 per cent respectively in 1979.

The period since 1979 has been much less favourable to organized labour. The recession of the early 1980s with its massive destruction of manufacturing capacity and jobs, the anti-union stance of much of the industrial relations legislation of the 1980s and an increased willingness amongst employers to de-recognize unions have led to substantial declines in both the number of trade unionists and in union density. Unions lost about 3 million members in the 1980s and union density had fallen to 37.6 per cent in 1990. Unionization tends to be higher amongst manual workers, who are less well-paid on average than non-manual workers, and a wide range of empirical evidence suggests that unions raise the relative pay of their members above the level it would otherwise have been. Consequently, these changes, along with the abandonment of incomes policies, help to account for the widening of the earnings distribution in the 1980s.

Two developments are likely to reinforce these inegalitarian changes in the distribution of earnings. The first is the abolition, outside agriculture, of the Wages Councils, which had set minimum rates of pay in a range of low-paying industries, in some cases since before the First World War. Second, the Conservative government's opt-out of the Social Chapter of the Maastricht Treaty may marginally increase the flexibility of the labour market but at the cost of greater inequality in the distribution of incomes.

4   Who cares about inequality?

Should anything be done about the growth in inequality discussed in the last two sections? Our analysis certainly suggests that there are policies which would reverse those changes. For instance, the government could further promote the acquisition of human capital skills, or it could introduce more generous unemployment benefits. The question is whether there is any inclination towards taking policy action in favour of greater equality.

We are personally in no doubt that something ought to be done, but this is not simply a matter for two economists to decide. These are public policy decisions, and society must decide whether it wants to undertake these policies. This immediately raises a question, which we focus on in this section, about how such social (as opposed to individual) choices are made. How, given a possible range of individual opinions, does a society form a judgement in such matters?

4.1   The problem of interpersonal comparisons of welfare

A concern with inequality reflects a normative judgement (see Chapter 7, Section 6), that a less unequal distribution of income is to be preferred to a more unequal one. As we suggested in Section 1, this seems to entail ethical judgements about how to make interpersonal comparisons of well-being. The point is that when income is redistributed the poor gain and the rich probably lose. So how does society weigh the rich's loss against the poor's gain? Where does society get such an ethical standard from?

To understand how economists think about this problem, we first need to consider in rather more depth the concepts of welfare and utility introduced in Chapter 7. Economists, as you know, tend to associate people's well-being (or welfare) with the degree to which their preferences are satisfied. Levels of satisfaction, for an individual, are called 'utility', as Chapter 7 explained. Economists therefore often represent a person's preferences by a so-called utility function; so that a person's well-being becomes synonymous with their utility level, and the issue we are addressing becomes how to make interpersonal comparisons of utility.

For this purpose, it is important to remember that utility is an ordinal variable (see Chapter 9). A utility function therefore assigns utility numbers to the various possible bundles of goods and services that you might consume. The function is constructed in such a way that it gives a higher utility number to one bundle whenever you prefer it to another. In other words, economists like to say that when you prefer bundle a to bundle b, it is 'as if' each bundle gave you utility and you chose bundle a because it gave more utility than bundle b (and their reason for doing this is that it enables individual choice to be modelled using simple mathematics).

These utility functions vary across the population because people have different preferences between goods now (for instance some of us prefer apples to bananas while others prefer bananas to apples), and also intertemporally (for instance some of us prefer to spend income now rather than save while others look more to the future). They are also personally arbitrary in the sense that if you prefer a to b then any utility number can be assigned to a so long as it exceeds the number assigned to b.

This is at once both a strange and an innocent way of analysing well-being and it is important to be clear about where the strangeness starts and the innocence stops. It is innocent in the sense that there is *no* implied connection with the social philosophy of <u>utilitarianism</u>. This was a philosophy that also believed that individual well-being could be captured by an index of that person's pleasure, and it argued that society should be organized in such a way as to maximize the aggregate sum of these individual pleasures in society. As such, it presumes that one person's pleasure (or utility) experience can be compared with another – otherwise there is no way of calculating the sum of the individual pleasures in any society. However, although the economists share (at least in a metaphorical sense) this representation of people as utility or pleasure machines, glowing, as it were, more or less brightly as their consumption enables preferences to be more or less satisfied, this does not thereby commit them to the view that these utility or pleasure units of inner glow are interpersonally comparable. Since utility numbers attached by economists to any consumption bundle are personally arbitrary there is no way that my personally arbitrary (except for the ranking) utility number for any commodity can be compared with another person's equally arbitrary utility number. In fact, the social philosophy of utilitarianism simply begged precisely the question that we want to answer here: namely how do societies actually make these interpersonal comparisons.

Note that this way of looking at the world does not mean that economists automatically assume people are selfish. A person's well-being is associated with the satisfaction of his or her preferences but these preferences can, for instance, be other-regarding or altruistic, with the result that a person's utility rises not just as that person consumes more but also as the consumption of other people increases.

Nevertheless, the model is strange, largely because it (apparently) ignores other influences on a person's well-being. For example, people often think that well-being depends not only on satisfying their preferences, but also on being satisfied with their preferences in the first place. Indeed there is a long tradition in Western philosophy that associates well-being with a sense of autonomy, which comes from feeling that one holds one's preferences to be one's own. In turn, this serves to highlight a general and troubling insouciance in the model with respect to where preferences come from. Are people born with them? This hardly seems plausible if the preferences refer to commodities like Levis 501s or Ford Escorts. Yet, if they are the product of socialization or they change with experience, then there must be some doubt over whether satisfying a momentary set of preferences is really the same as well-being in the large.

Likewise, it is not clear that the language of preference satisfaction always captures why or how people act. People often care not just about whether a preference is satisfied but *how* it is satisfied, and it is not always clear that this is another type of preference. For instance, when someone values 'honour' do they just have a rather particular kind of preference? Similarly there are certain types of action that generate well-being which simply cannot be accounted for in terms of preference satisfaction. Consider spontaneity. This is plausibly a source of well-being for some people, yet these people could not hold that they had a preference for spontaneity which they acted upon because this would be self-defeating. After all, could you intend to act spontaneously, without by definition not being spontaneous?

We should note, finally, that within this utility framework, we can find situations where redistributions do not require these tricky interpersonal comparisons. There are some cases where the rich are actually made better-off through giving income to the poor and so the conflict between the utility of rich and poor does not arise. The rich may be altruistic, for instance, and so positively value, for themselves, the improvements in the welfare of the poor. More important perhaps, and quite independent of altruistic motives, there may be externalities between the welfare of the rich and the poor because they live in close proximity. There are public health connections, which our Victorian forebears were conscious of and which we are just rediscovering as diseases like tuberculosis resurface in London and New York. Poor environments are breeding grounds for diseases like TB and they do not respect the boundaries of poor neighbourhoods. This provides a powerful incentive for the rich to care about the welfare of the poor: enlightened self-interest.

4.2   Making interpersonal comparisons in a pluralist democracy

Leaving aside 'easy' cases where no conflict of interest arises, let us return to our main question. Accepting for the sake of argument the economists' utility framework, how can a society get the ethical standard which will allow it to decide whether making the rich worse-off is justified by the gain in the welfare of the poor?

There may be societies in which the answer to this question seems unproblematic, because people share an ideology or religion which provides, at least implicitly, an ethical standard of comparison. In plural societies, however, there is a variety of ethical views. Consider, for instance, some contrasting views on social justice that circulate in Anglo-American and other plural societies.

Concepts of social justice

One strongly argued position in the Anglo-American debate on social justice holds that, whatever outcomes emerge from voluntary exchanges in markets, they are just. This is because market outcomes are seen as respecting individual freedom (see for instance Nozick, 1974). So on this account there is no general need to make interpersonal comparisons of welfare because whatever distribution of income emerges from voluntary exchange, it is fine.

However, others believe that social justice requires rather more. At the least, it demands that individuals be treated impartially and a simple way of discovering what impartiality might demand is to conduct a thought experiment which puts you behind a 'veil of ignorance'. The device operates in the following way. You are asked to compare different possible social arrangements (i.e. sets of individual outcomes) without knowing what position you will occupy under each possible arrangement. So, for instance, you must rank a case where there are no redistributive policies with a case where there is some redistribution, with a case where there is more redistribution, and so on across all possible arrangements; and you know only that you stand an equal chance of being someone 'rich' as someone 'poor' in each of these possible arrangements of incomes. Thus you are forced to be impartial. In these circumstances, a particularly risk-averse person is likely to have a keen eye for the position of the poorest person in each possible arrangement and so opt for the one which treats the poorest person best (see Rawls, 1972). Alternatively, an indifference to risk will lead a person to opt for the arrangement with the highest average income and so on.

Indeed the possibilities seem endless here, because even if one accepts that the veil of ignorance is a useful device, there is still further room for dispute. We assumed above that the poorest person could be identified by their income level. In fact, Rawls believes that everyone needs certain primary social goods and that people will choose the arrangement which gave the most of these goods to the person who was poorest in terms of these goods. On his account, income is only a highly visible proxy for these goods. But is income a good proxy? Sen (1985), for instance, prefers to use the notion of 'capabilities' as the basis for individual comparisons. This would take account of other aspects of a person's situation (including their rights) since in his view it would, for example, be wrong to count an income of £10 000 for one person as the same as £10 000 for another person when the two people have very different physical attributes. The £10 000 does not give the person with a disability as many 'capabilities' as the other person and so should not be judged morally equivalent. But will people agree on how to assess a person's capabilities? What is the appropriate monetary trade-off for physical or mental disabilities? Should a distinction be made between people who are born with disabilities and those who suffer them as a result of their own actions, say, while drinking and driving? It is clear, then, that people can hold very different views on standards of social justice. So how should we choose between conflicting standards?

Voting on ethical standards

We may appear to be over-dramatizing this problem because pluralism and differences of view are often accommodated through a democratic procedure. There are, after all, political parties which embody different ethical positions and which compete with each other for our votes on this and other bases; and the party (or parties) which are most persuasive form the government and enact their policies. It is as simple as that!

However matters are not quite so simple. People must agree to resolve their differences in this way by the ballot box and it is not always clear that they will or, if they do, that it will generate a coherent solution to the problem. With majority voting, there is a problem if there are permanently dissatisfied minorities. In addition, there is a potential problem of democratic 'incoherence'. Democratic incoherence arises when there is no single stable outcome from majority voting. To see the problem, consider an example where there are three possible social arrangements, x, y and z, and there are three individuals, A, B and C. Each outcome (or arrangement) will specify a particular income level for each of the three individuals, and we assume each individual has a different view regarding the relative justice of these possible social outcomes.

The views of A, B and C are captured by the following orderings (or rankings), with the most preferred outcome appearing first and the least preferred appearing last. One possible key to these orderings is that outcome x favours A, while y favours B and z favours C. In addition A cares more about B's welfare than C, while B cares more about C than A and C cares more about A than B. Alternatively A, B and C might simply have different ethical standards which lead them to rank the alternatives in these different ways. Here are the orderings.

A: [x, y, z]

B: [y, z, x]

C: [z, x, y]

Question

Now suppose there is a system of majority rule, so the outcome which emerges is the one which secures the votes of a majority (i.e. two people in this instance). Which outcome is the winner?

Consider the possible coalitions of two voters which might emerge around particular outcomes. For example, a coalition of A and B could form to deliver outcome y in preference to outcome z because both A and B prefer y to z. However, it is not a stable coalition because C has the incentive and can persuade A to join him or her in a coalition which secures x rather than y because both prefer x to y. But this coalition in turn is unstable because B would prefer z to x and can persuade C to join him or her in a coalition to secure z rather than x. But the moment this coalition forms, we know it will not last because A can entice B away into a coalition which delivers y rather than z because A and B both prefer y to z; and so on. Work through these alternatives for yourself. You will see that no stable coalition of two voters will emerge, with the result that we will observe either a form of political paralysis where no decision is made, or political instability as one coalition gives way to another and the society cycles through each of the three options.

This difficulty has been variously interpreted by social scientists. The problem can in fact be stated in a very general form and is the subject of a famous theorem in economics called the Arrow Impossibility Theorem (Arrow, 1963a). For our purposes, we draw the inference that democracy will only provide a procedural solution for resolving disputes of this sort where the disagreements are less sharp than those captured above.

At first sight, this conclusion may seem less than helpful. Indeed it may appear to suggest, in effect, that democracy is really only useful for resolving disputes when there are no significant disputes in the first place! But first impressions are misleading.

First, this model of what happens in a democratic polity is heavily dependent on the economist's view of individuals as preference satisfiers. Voting, as a device for aggregating preferences, is all that democracy consists of on this view, whereas other traditions often see voting as a relatively minor part of the proceedings. For example, democratic politics might plausibly be as much about debate, dialogue and persuasion as they are about voting procedures. People engage in debate where ideas are explored and minds are changed. Indeed if people want to be satisfied *with* their preferences (as well as seeing them satisfied), the political arena is one place where they have the opportunity to review, discuss and assess one aspect of those preferences.

Second, even when the voting model of democracy is accepted, it is only certain types of disagreements which create problems for democracies. For example, the problem of 'cycling' between different outcomes does not arise when everyone's differences of opinion can be fitted along one dimension, say the commonly used left–right political spectrum, and where distance from one's preferred spot on this spectrum determines how one rates alternatives, as Exercise 22.3 illustrates.

Exercise 22.3

1   Suppose x refers to a left-wing outcome, y refers to a centre outcome and z refers to a right-wing outcome. Do A's, B's and C's preferences above make sense for people who rank alternatives exclusively along a left–right spectrum?

2   Suppose a three person democracy (A, B and D) contains people with the following preferences:

A: [x, y, z]

B: [y, z, x]

D: [z, y, x]

What outcome will emerge under a system of majority rule?

Despite these more optimistic arguments, it would be foolish not to recognize that many disagreements in plural societies run 'deeper' than a one-dimensional dispute, and they do not always dissolve with debate and dialogue. So what should be done when democracy cannot guarantee either the rights of minorities or coherent decisions?

4.3   Agreeing to disagree with *laissez-faire*?

An influential answer to this question, associated with the New Right, is that the democratic state should not concern itself with issues where there are such 'deep' and recalcitrant disagreements. After all, there is no compulsion for the state to intervene and if the people in whose name the state acts cannot agree on what should be done, what could be more natural than not acting? On this view the state might, as a result, withdraw from redistributive activities because this is exactly the area where disagreements are likely to be too sharp for democratic resolution. Indeed in plural societies, it is tempting to think that most people would only agree that the state should promote economic efficiency and so, following this logic and picking up another theme from the arguments of the New Right, the state might be expected to promote competitive markets since they further economic efficiency. In short, the state would adopt a *laissez-faire* stance in support of a competitive market system and steer clear of redistribution.

Suppose that people do indeed agree that governments should promote economic efficiency. Is this objective best served by a *laissez-faire* attitude by governments? We address this question, partly because an affirmative answer forms part of the influential New Right thinking sketched above, and partly because it is also important for societies where there is ethical agreement over redistribution. If efficiency is best served through *laissez-faire*, then there will be a trade-off between the two objectives of efficiency and equity, since any intervention in support of the distributional objective will work against *laissez-faire* and hence the objective of efficiency. Thus, the society will need to decide to what extent it wishes to favour the pursuit of one objective over the other. However, if efficiency is not promoted by *laissez-faire*, then, conversely there need be no trade-off between the objectives and intervention may be able to promote both equity and efficiency.

The connection between *laissez-faire* and efficiency may appear to be established by the proposition that competitive markets with clear property rights (which usually means private property relations) generate a Pareto optimal allocation of resources (see Chapter 7). It is tempting to conclude from this proposition that there is no need for governments to interfere in markets on grounds of efficiency. They should just leave things to the free play of market forces as these will deliver Pareto efficient outcomes. However, this conclusion does not automatically follow.

First, the connection between *laissez-faire* and perfect competition with well-defined property rights is weak because there is no guarantee in the absence of government intervention either that a perfectly competitive economy, once established, will remain a competitive economy; or that clear property rights can be maintained without significant government support via a law enforcement system. There may, for instance, be natural tendencies towards oligopolization and monopolization in some markets (see Chapter 6); so the maintenance of competitive conditions may well require significant intervention (see Chapter 8). Likewise, the government is likely to have to provide certain public goods (for instance a legal system to uphold clear property rights) or to make further interventions to compensate for other sources of market failure such as externalities (see Chapter 10). In other words, a so-called 'night-watchman state', charged with upholding competition and property rights, might have to be significantly involved in the economy.

Second, it is not clear that the sense of efficiency which most concerns people can be equated with the notion of Pareto efficiency. A part of this difficulty arises because Pareto provides a static criterion of efficiency. We know only that when it is satisfied there is no way to reallocate resources so as to make one person better-off without at the same time making another person worse-off. It is possible for a society to be concerned with a more dynamic sense of efficiency, for instance, whether competitive markets deliver appropriate rates of growth (see Chapter 12 and in particular the debate with the Austrian school on the nature of competition). Here we wish to draw attention to a slightly different problem of interpretation associated with this sense of efficiency.

What seems to make the Pareto criterion attractive for those concerned with efficiency in a static sense is the thought that if you do *not* have it, then in principle, you could make at least one person better-off through a reallocation of resources without making anyone worse-off. Since it seems somewhat crazy to forego such an opportunity for making people better-off without harming anyone, and it is only when you have Pareto efficiency that these possibilities have been exhausted, Pareto optimality appears very attractive.

However, what needs emphasizing is that the move to a Pareto-efficient allocation from a non-Pareto one *only in principle* creates the possibility of making at least one person better-off without making another person worse-off. *In practice* the move from a non-Pareto-efficient allocation to a Pareto efficient one can make some people worse-off. This possibility arises because, as Chapter 7 showed, there are generally several Pareto-efficient allocations of given resources. Thus, as Exercise 22.4 demonstrates, it is only with a movement to some but not all the possible Pareto-efficient allocations that everyone is made better-off.

Exercise 22.4

Consider Figure 22.11 which is very similar to Figure 7.21. The frontier AB traces the Pareto-efficient allocations of food between two social groups. C is a non-Pareto-efficient allocation – food is wasted. Mark on Figure 22.11 the range of points along AB which can be reached from C without making one group worse off.

A concrete illustration of this problem comes from the Uruguay Round of the GATT treaty. These negotiations aim to remove the trade barriers that distort markets away from the competitive ideal type, precisely so as to capture the gains which come from moving towards a Pareto-efficient allocation of resources. (However, remember the qualification about 'second best' policies, explained in Chapter 7, Section 6.3: making one market highly competitive only reliably moves an economy towards Pareto efficiency if all the other markets are already perfectly competitive.) Table 22.4 provides estimates of how income levels will increase in different parts of the world as a result of the Uruguay Round reductions.

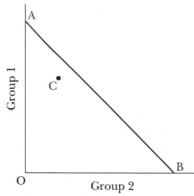

Figure 22.11 **Allocation of food between two competing groups**

Table 22.4   **Winners and losers from the GATT round (predicted % change in real income by 2002)**

	Effect of GATT	Full free trade
Low income Asia	0.6	1.3
China	2.5	4.5
India	0.5	1.8
Upper income Asia	2.6	8.2
Indonesia	0.7	2.6
South Africa	0.6	0.1
Other Africa	−0.2	−0.9
Maghreb	−0.5	−2.3
Mediterranean	−0.4	−2.4
Gulf region	−0.5	−1.0
Brazil	0.3	0.4
Mexico	0.0	−0.4
Other Latin America	0.6	0.4
USA	0.2	0.3
Canada	0.2	0.0
Australia	0.1	1.0
Japan	0.9	2.7
EU	1.4	2.8
EFTA	1.4	3.0
Eastern Europe	0.1	−0.1
Former USSR	0.1	0.9

Source: OECD and World Bank, reproduced in the *Independent on Sunday*, 3 October 1993

Question

Look carefully at the winners and losers in Table 22.4. Do you think the gains of the winners outweigh the losses of the losers?

The table reveals clear gains overall, as one would expect from the theory explained in Chapter 13, but interestingly not all regions will enjoy those gains. In particular, some of the poorest countries in the world stand to lose income. Why? One of the features of the Uruguay Round is the reduction in the protection for agriculture world-wide and this will have the effect of reducing some of the famous food mountains produced by the EU. In the past, much of the agricultural surpluses of the EU (which were encouraged by the protection of European agriculture) have been sold on world markets and this has tended to lower the world price of food. Once the protection is removed under the Uruguay Round and European agriculture contracts, the sale of European surpluses on world markets will fall and the price of food will rise. This, in turn, will adversely affect many of the low income countries that are not self sufficient in food and which have traditionally bought much of their food on world markets.

The lesson to be drawn is that, if what makes Pareto efficiency an attractive characteristic of competitive markets is the realization of the *potential* gains available to all which come from moving from a non-Pareto allocation, then governments will often have to intervene to redistribute the gains in order to ensure that those potential gains are actually realized *by all.* Otherwise, it is quite likely that some people will be harmed by the move towards Pareto optimality. Hence a concern with efficiency may require the government to take a view on distribution. Therefore, it may actually be logically impossible, without some further agreement over equity, to be motivated only by static efficiency considerations.

Unfortunately, this leaves the discussion of how pluralist society decides on its response to inequality in an inconclusive state. It appears from Arrow that the ballot box is not always a solution and neither, it seems now, is the retreat of the state. However, there are other ways of responding to the problem of instability identified by Arrow by restricting the scope of government decision making in ways which stop short of the New Right's 'night-watchman state'. For instance, instability could be avoided by drawing the boundaries of the state so as to include groups of people who do not disagree 'deeply' with one another, that is by having an appropriate plurality of democratic states (or devolved decision-making units), each formed among people who do not disagree with each other in this 'deep' way.

Thus Arrow's result might usefully inform the discussion over what has become known in the European Union as the issue of 'subsidiarity' (that is, the discussion over the assignment of decision-making powers to the different levels of the state, from the supranational through national to the local government level). Different types of decision making should be targeted at the level at which there is sufficient agreement to avoid the problem of instability.

Equally, it might help answer the question posed at the beginning of this chapter concerning how far such ethical considerations stretch. In so far as groups must share a common ethical view for them to be able to intervene to redistribute income among themselves then the possibilities for redistribution are largely determined by the scope of those ethical agreements. At the moment, to judge from the preponderance of national decision-making units, these agreements typically only stretch as far as the boundaries of the nation state. Indeed perhaps, as traditional sources of allegiance and solidarity between people have waned in the post-industrial societies of Europe and North America, the agreement does not even stretch this far; and this might explain in part why many nation states seem recently less inclined to make redistributive interventions.

Thus it seems there may be no general answer to the question of how pluralist societies respond to inequality. Nevertheless, what does seem clear is that groups which share a sufficient ethical agreement to motivate intervention will want to know to what extent their views on distribution are respected by the actual outcomes in society. We therefore turn in Section 5 to ways of measuring inequality.

5   Measuring inequality

5.1   The Lorenz curve and the Gini coefficient

The measures we used earlier in connection with poverty and the distribution of earnings are easily calculated and are readily available, but they have a weakness. They concentrate on a limited number of points of the distribution, and so they ignore a substantial amount of information. In this section we consider several alternative measures which take account of all points of the distribution:

1   the standard deviation (*SD*),

2   the coefficient of variation (*CV*), and

3   the Gini coefficient (*G*).

There also exist other measures of inequality, and a more comprehensive discussion can be found in Atkinson (1983) and Sen (1973).

The standard deviation is a measure of the degree of dispersion of a distribution and was discussed in Chapter 9, Section 3.2. It is given by:

$$SD = \sqrt{\frac{\sum (Y_i - \overline{Y})^2}{n}}$$

where Y_i is the income of individual i, $\overline{Y}$ mean income, and n the number of individuals. Incomes that lie further away from either side of the mean contribute disproportionately to the measure and *SD* will be smaller when incomes are bunched around the mean than when they are more dispersed around the same mean. The standard deviation is dependent upon the mean of the distribution. If you compare two distributions of income which only differ in that each person's income is twice as large in the second distribution as it is in the first, then the standard deviation of income of the second distribution will be twice as large as the standard deviation of the first distribution. To overcome this problem, we normalize (that is, get rid of the size effect just described) by dividing the standard deviation by the mean of the distribution, thereby obtaining a measure known as the *coefficient of variation* (*CV*):

$$CV = \frac{SD}{\text{mean}}$$

The standard deviation and coefficient of variation have the property of being sensitive to transfers from richer to poorer income recipients which do not reverse their position in the income distribution: transferring £1 of income from a richer to a poorer individual will lead to a reduction in inequality as measured by the *SD* and *CV*. It is desirable for measures of inequality to possess such a property; and it is called the Pigou–Dalton criterion, named after two British economists, one of whom (Dalton) was Chancellor of the Exchequer in the UK Labour government of 1945–50.

A useful diagrammatic device for depicting the nature of the distribution of income is the Lorenz curve. To construct a Lorenz curve we measure along the vertical axis the cumulative proportion of total income, and along the horizontal axis the cumulative proportion of income recipients, having ranked the income recipients in order starting from those with the lowest incomes. The Lorenz curve then depicts the relationship between these two variables.

Let us use the following information about the distribution of family income in the USA in 1980 to construct a Lorenz curve. The families in the lowest quintile group of the income distribution (i.e. the bottom 20%) received 5.2% of aggregate money income; those in the second quintile group received 11.5%, those in the third quintile group 17.5%; those in the fourth quintile group received 24.3%; and those in the highest quintile group 41.5%, whilst the richest 5% of households received 15.3% of aggregate income (US Bureau of the Census, 1993, Table 702).

Summing these figures, we find that the poorest 40% of families received 16.7% of aggregate income; the poorest 60% of families received 34.2% of aggregate income; the poorest 80% of families received 58.5% of aggregate income; and 84.7% of income accrued to 95% of families. Plotting these points on a diagram, we have a Lorenz curve depicting the distribution of family income for the USA in 1980. This is shown in Figure 22.12. If income was equally distributed, the Lorenz curve would coincide with the diagonal on Figure 22.12.

Reflection

Before you read on, work out for yourself why this is so. Hint: look carefully at the axes.

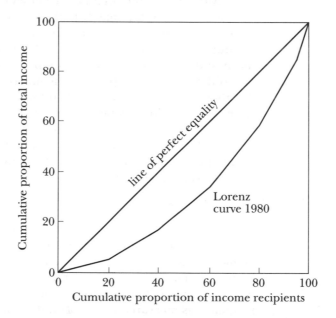

Figure 22.12 **Lorenz curve for the USA, 1980**

Source: US Bureau of the Census (1993) Table 702

Since the diagonal line represents equally distributed income, the further away the Lorenz curve is from the diagonal, the more unequal is the income distribution. Now try Exercise 22.5.

Exercise 22.5

The distribution of family income in the USA in 1991 was as follows: the lowest quintile group received 4.5% of aggregate income; the second quintile group received 10.7%; the third quintile group received 16.4%, the fourth quintile group received 24.3%, and the highest quintile group 44.1%

with the top 5% receiving 17.1%. Construct a 1991 Lorenz curve, using Figure 22.12 as a model.

Having constructed the Lorenz curve for 1991, compare it to the 1980 curve. What conclusions would you draw from this comparison about changes in the distribution of income in the USA in the 1980s?

Associated with the Lorenz curve is a measure of inequality known as the Gini coefficient. This can be explained by looking at the Lorenz curve diagram again. The Gini coefficient is the ratio of the area between the diagonal and the Lorenz curve (the area marked A in Figure 22.13) to the area of the triangle beneath the diagonal (the area A + B). It varies between 0 in the case of perfect equality and 1 when all the income accrues to a single individual. The more the Lorenz curve is bowed down from the diagonal, the more unequal is the distribution of income, and hence the larger will be the value of the Gini coefficient.

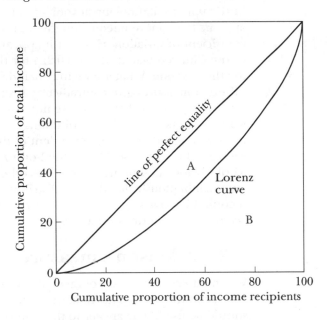

Figure 22.13 **The Lorenz curve and the Gini coefficient**

The Gini coefficient has a neat economic interpretation. A value of 0.3 can be interpreted as meaning that if two incomes are drawn at random from the income distribution, then we would expect that on average the difference between them to be 60 per cent of mean income in the economy (twice the value of the Gini coefficient times 100). In this way the Gini coefficient is a particularly helpful measure when our ethical interests relate to the typical relative income differences in a society. In addition a transfer from a richer to a poorer person which leaves unchanged the rank position of all individuals will lead to a fall in the value of the Gini coefficient.

Before reading further, you should work through the following exercise to consolidate what you have learned so far.

Exercise 22.6

On a remote Pacific island there are 10 households, whose incomes, measured in thousands of units of the local currency, are as follows: 4, 6, 8, 8, 8, 9, 10, 14, 16, 17. Total income is 100; hence mean income is 10.

1   Plot a Lorenz curve for the distribution of household income for this Pacific island.

2   Calculate the values of the standard deviation and coefficient of variation for the above data (look back at Chapter 9, Section 3.2 for how to do this).

3   Now assume that following some economic shock, incomes are affected, and we now have the following ranked set: 5, 5, 7, 8, 8, 9, 12, 14, 15, 17. Plot the Lorenz curve for the new distribution, and compare it with the initial Lorenz curve.

4   Calculate the values of the standard deviation and coefficient of variation for the above data.

Were you somewhat surprised when you compared your two Lorenz curves for the above exercise by the ambiguous results you obtained? The two Lorenz curves intersect at the lower end, again in the middle and coincide in the upper tail. Looking at your summary statistics, the first distribution appears to be more unequal on the basis of the standard deviation and coefficient of variation. However it appears in fact less unequal on the basis of the Gini coefficient which is 0.224 for the initial distribution and 0.226 for the new one. What are we to conclude about inequality, since the different measures give contradictory results? The results we have derived for our hypothetical example are not just a theoretical curiosity. Typically when we rank alternative distributions as more or less unequal, we find that the rankings will not be independent of the particular measure of inequality we have chosen to use. Only if the Lorenz curve for one distribution lies wholly below the Lorenz curve of the other distribution will we be able to say unambiguously that the first distribution is more unequal than the second. Like our simple measures of poverty, these measures of inequality are not as straightforward as they might seem at first sight.

5.2   Atkinson's measure of inequality

When different measures of inequality point to different directions of change in the income distribution, as they did in the example above, which should be used? The answer to this question must depend on why one is interested in inequality in the first place. In turn this takes us back to Section 4 and the specific ethical consensus in a society which is responsible for that concern. In particular what we would like to be able to do is match a society's ethical standpoint with an appropriate measure.

In some cases this is easy. For example it follows from the discussion in Section 5.1 that the Gini coefficient would be appropriate for a society which uniquely placed value on reducing relative income differences. But it is not so easy to see what precise sort of ethics are being represented in other measures. However, some progress is possible. Let us recall from Section 4 that judging the ethical appropriateness of an income distribution seems likely to involve interpersonal comparisons of welfare. Now consider the following thought experiment: £1 is transferred from someone who is rich to someone, say, who has half his or her income. However, in the course of the redistribution some part of the £1 is lost (you can think of it as the administrative cost of the transfer) with the result that only a fraction (β, pronounced beta) of the amount taken from the richer person goes to the poorer person.

Now let us focus precisely on the type of interpersonal comparison of welfare which is being made, by asking at what value for β you would be just indifferent as to whether the transfer of income took place or not. For that value of β, we will then define ε (pronounced epsilon) such that $\beta = 0.5^\varepsilon$. (Note that ε does not mean elasticity here, but is a number which indicates ethical views.) Hence if $\varepsilon = 1$, you would be indifferent between taking £1 from an individual and giving 50p to an individual whose pre-transfer income was half that of the first individual; on the other hand, if $\varepsilon = 2$, then $\beta = 0.25$ and the leakage could be as high as 75p before you became indifferent to the transfer. In other words, ε is an index of your ethical attitude towards inequality: the higher the value of ε, the greater is your aversion to inequality and the greater the leakage you would be prepared to accept in order to transfer income from a richer to a poorer person.

Atkinson (1983) has developed a measure of inequality which specifically incorporates value judgements of the above type. This measure is complex, but here is a flavour of the idea. For a given distribution of income the Atkinson measure of its inequality will be higher the larger the value of ε. Furthermore, if you compare two distributions of income using Atkinson's measure, it is not unusual to find that one distribution appears to be more unequal at low values of ε, and the other one at higher values. This will indeed be the case whenever the Lorenz curves for the two distributions intersect. Atkinson noted that the Lorenz curves for the distribution of income in West Germany and the United Kingdom in the 1960s intersected once, with the shares of both the lowest and highest income groups being higher in Germany than in the UK. The implication of this is that his measure gave a lower value for the UK at low values of ε but once ε rose above 3, the British distribution was measured as more unequal than the German.

Let us assume that as an individual's income increases, the utility of income and hence the welfare of this individual also increases but at a diminishing rate. If we also assume, like the utilitarians, that adding up the utilities of different people is possible, and that the welfare of society is given by the sum of the welfare (utilities) of the individuals making up the society, then Atkinson's measure turns out to have an interesting interpretation. Since the marginal utility of income is assumed to fall as income increases, transferring income from a richer to a poorer person reduces the utility of the richer person by less than it increases the utility of the poorer person, and social welfare increases. Hence comparing two economies with the same mean income, social welfare will be higher in a society in which income is equally distributed than in one where there is some dispersion of income.

To be specific, we can define the concept of the equally distributed equivalent income (Y_{EDE}). This is the level of per capita income which, if received by all individuals in the society, we would regard as yielding the same amount of total social welfare as obtained with the actual distribution. Atkinson's measure of inequality is then given by:

$$A = 1 - \frac{Y_{EDE}}{Y}$$

which can be interpreted as one minus the proportion of current income which if distributed equally would give the same level of social welfare as the current distribution.

If we are prepared to make the ethical judgements required to set ε, Atkinson's measure calculates A; and when, say, A turns out to be 0.2, this means we would only need a per capita income, provided that it was equally distributed, equal to 80 per cent of the mean income in the economy to achieve the same level of social welfare as in the actual economy.

Table 22.5   **Alternative measures of changes in earnings inequality for men: heads of households age 25 to 54 years, working year-round, full-time for selected countries**

		Gini	Atkinson		
			$\varepsilon = 0.5$	$\varepsilon = 0.8$	$\varepsilon = 1.5$
USA	1979	0.258	0.057	0.094	0.254
	1986	0.298	0.074	0.120	0.341
Canada	1981	0.222	0.043	0.071	0.148
	1987	0.253	0.057	0.091	0.185
Sweden	1981	0.180	0.029	0.045	0.079
	1987	0.190	0.032	0.049	0.082
Australia	1981	0.208	0.040	0.065	0.155
	1985	0.212	0.042	0.067	0.146
W. Germany	1981	0.195	0.033	0.054	0.114
	1984	0.204	0.034	0.053	0.097

Source: Green *et al.* (1992) Table 5

Table 22.5 shows that changes in distributions do register different changes according to the chosen measure of inequality. It shows Gini coefficients beside three calculations of Atkinson's measure which assume increasing levels of ethical concern as we move from a low ε to a higher one. While all the measures point to the same direction of change in a number of economies, they notably yield conflicting indications in Australia and West Germany. For Australia, the first three measures register an increase in inequality from 1981 to 1985, but the last measure suggests a reduction; for West Germany the Gini coefficient and the Atkinson measure with $\varepsilon = 0.5$ show an increase, whereas the Atkinson measure based on the higher values of ε suggests a reduction in inequality. Nevertheless in cross country comparisons for the later year, the Lorenz curves do not intersect and as a result there is a clear ranking by all measures: from the most to the least unequal, it reads USA, Canada, Australia, West Germany and Sweden.

6   Are individual income levels all that count?

The last sub-section sought to build a measure of inequality that falls (rises) when there is a redistribution of income which society judges increases the welfare of the recipient by more (less) than the donor's welfare declines. This requires that the society decide when the welfare gain of the poor person outweighs the welfare loss of the richer person. The virtue of Atkinson's measure is that it allows for different societies to form different judgements regarding these interpersonal comparisons and so build different measures of inequality to inform their public debates.

The worry to which we return in this section is that there may be more to a society's ethical consensus than these interpersonal comparisons of welfare allow. First, the approach implicitly associates an individual's welfare with his or her income and it is possible to have a view of individual 'welfare' which depends on more than income (and what it can buy). We mentioned earlier the complication of physical disabilities. Here is another. Suppose your income is £100 a week and you decide to spend every night at home watching the TV, is your 'welfare' unchanged when the government declares a curfew making it illegal to venture out at night? Your income has not changed and you were going to stay in the house anyway, nevertheless you might plausibly feel 'worse-off' because the government has taken away certain rights which you previously enjoyed even though you did not exercise them.

Second, the approach seems to assume that ethical concerns attach only to outcomes. The outcomes are captured by our various income levels, and ethical interest is focused on the distribution of those incomes across the population. However, it is perfectly plausible that ethical interest stretches beyond outcomes. A society may be concerned with the fairness or rightness, for instance, of the procedures or processes which have been responsible for these outcomes. It is not always the particular level of income for an individual which we find ethically offensive but how it was derived. Consider why people typically believe that raising a tax on the rich to help the poor is very different, even when it has the same effect upon income levels, from a situation where the poor steal from the rich.

What links both worries is the idea that ethical concerns may include a respect for the rights of individuals, and simple measures of the distribution of income in our society will be inadequate for this task. The development of further measures to cover these wider concerns will depend on what rights interest us. In the UK many people believe that individuals have rights to equal treatment and so they are particularly concerned that differences in outcomes should not arise *simply* because of differences in the sex or race of the individuals. Let us take the case of gender discrimination.

The wage an individual receives is determined by many factors: personal characteristics such as physical strength, intellectual ability, health status, years of education and experience, gender and ethnic origin; the nature of the occupation, including the training required, its non-pecuniary aspects such as danger, stress, boredom, and whether it offers scope for independent action and the exercise of initiative; the characteristics of the firm in which the worker is employed such as its size, market power and profitability, geographical location and the state of the local labour market, and whether it bargains with a trade union over pay and conditions.

On average women earn less than men. Prior to equal pay and opportunities legislation in the 1970s, the average hourly earnings of women in full-time work in the UK were just over 60 per cent of those of men; since the mid 1970s the corresponding figure has hovered around 75 per cent as Figure 22.14 shows. Earnings on Figure 22.14 are average hourly earnings, excluding overtime, of full-time employees aged 18 or over, whose pay was not affected by absence, except for 1971–73 where age is 21 or over.

The earnings differential shown in Figure 22.14 reflects in part the fact that the average man possesses more earning-enhancing characteristics than the average woman. Since many women have discontinuous periods of

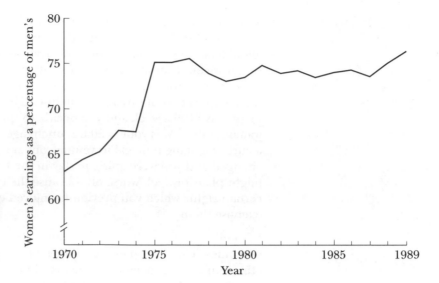

Figure 22.14 **Women's earnings relative to men's, Great Britain, April of each year (%)**

Source: *New Earnings Survey,* various years

participation in the labour force as a result of child rearing and other family responsibilities, there is less incentive for them to invest in skill acquisition and training, particularly since human capital depreciates rapidly when it is not being utilized. However, as a result of the existence of wage discrimination, a given set of characteristics is associated with a lower level of earnings for a woman than for a man.

In order to measure the extent of such discrimination, we may ask the following hypothetical question: given her characteristics, what would the average woman have been paid had she been male? By comparing these hypothetical earnings with both male and female actual earnings, we may then decompose the differential into a part due to differences in endowments and a part due to discrimination. British estimates of the extent to which female earnings would be higher in the absence of such discrimination vary from as little as 5 per cent to in excess of 20 per cent (Greenhalgh, 1980; Wright and Ermisch, 1991).

However wage discrimination is not the only handicap which women face in the labour market. Women are over-represented in low status, low paying occupations (Chapter 21). It has been estimated that more than 40 per cent of women would have to change occupation for the two distributions to be similar. These occupational differences are again the result of both differences in traits and of discrimination by employers. One British study has suggested, that in the absence of discrimination in access to occupations 16.5 per cent of women would be in managerial and professional jobs and 23 per cent in semi-skilled and unskilled manual jobs compared to the actual figures of 5.1 per cent and 39.9 per cent respectively (Miller, 1987).

The willingness of women to invest in human capital to increase their potential market wage is, therefore, not only affected by role specialization and the division of labour within the household, but also by the expectation that the return to such investments will be adversely affected by subsequent discrimination in both access to good jobs and wages. British evidence suggests though that making the occupational distributions by gender more similar would only have a small impact (approximately 5 per cent) in reducing the gender wage gap: intra-occupational factors predominate in accounting for the gap. Given that a major role is played by the depreciation of skill that occurs during periods of non-participation in explaining both female occupational attainment and earnings, there seems little likelihood of there being a major improvement in the economic status of women without there being a significant reallocation of household duties within the family.

Thus it is possible to gauge the extent of inequality even when ethical concerns come from a different tradition. This brief discussion also suggests what is perhaps a general point about policies directed at inequality. It seems likely that policies for tackling inequalities which offend against a shared ethics based on rights are going to be more difficult to construct and implement than the kind of redistributions of income which will satisfy an ethics founded on interpersonal comparisons of welfare.

7 Conclusion

The measurement of inequality is no simple matter. We have argued that how inequality is measured ought to depend on why people are interested in inequality in the first place. For this reason we have used a variety of measures to plot the changes in the distribution of income over the last 10–15 years in several countries. Some of those changes are quite extraordinary. In particular, in the UK, there is now significant poverty. The causes are complex and are bound up with changes in the provisions of the welfare state, the growth of unemployment, and technological change which has outpaced the upgrading of human capital. Nevertheless, something could be done about it. The question is 'should it or will it be done?' We have not tried to answer this question in a definitive way. Rather we have focused on the conditions that have to be satisfied for any group of individuals to take collective action (make social choices) and we have considered some arguments, particularly those of the New Right, which might lie behind a failure to act. The next chapter turns to the mechanisms of redistribution.

CHAPTER 23   REDISTRIBUTION

by Maureen Mackintosh

1   Introduction

> In past times, the economically and socially fortunate were, as we know, a small minority – characteristically a dominant and ruling handful. They are now a majority not of all citizens but of those who actually vote. ... They will be called the Contented Majority.
>
> ...
>
> For a considerable, though by no means the entire range of public services, the supporting taxes fall on the contented; the benefits accrue to others. ... There follows a highly understandable resistance to all taxation.
>
> *(Galbraith, 1992, pp.15, 44)*

> The new jobs for Britain's middle classes – and even more worryingly for their children – are part-time, self-employed or fixed contract. ... The freedom promised by markets has created new swathes of anxiety that did not exist before. ... Two men living in the same street and saving the same amount can have vastly different pension funds on retirement. The commuter in his or her suburban or green-belt villa is dependent upon a cheap mass transport system, decades of neglect imply an upward spiral of fares. The middle classes ... in successive elections over the 1980s have gradually been withdrawing support from the party that is the source of their ills.
>
> *(Will Hutton, The Guardian, 2 August 1994)*

J.K. Galbraith, the eminent US economist, and Will Hutton, a London-based economic journalist, share the view that support for public services from middle-income citizens depends upon the benefits they gain from them. But they draw different conclusions from that view. Galbraith argues in *The Culture of Contentment* that the voting majority in the USA gains little from public welfare spending, and feels secure without it. Hence the support for tax cuts. Will Hutton suggests that in Britain people on middle incomes feel increasingly economically *in*secure as public services and benefits decline in an era of economic recession and job 'flexibility' – and that this in turn may affect voting patterns.

This chapter explores these closely interrelated issues of risk and redistribution. The risk of destitution, whether it be through loss of income or assets, ill health or old age, is addressed in different societies in various ways, including private insurance, mutual societies and tax-financed social insurance. Such schemes shift income from all those insured, to those in immediate need: in that sense they are redistributive. But there is a more common sense of redistribution. Redistribution is generally taken to mean a transfer of resources – by the state or private charity – from the better off to the less well off, in pursuit of greater equality or the relief of poverty. This distinction between insurance and redistribution seems clear in principle, but in practice the ideas become closely intertwined in the debate on social security and public services.

This chapter addresses three aspects of this debate. The most difficult question is, why do societies redistribute income or wealth? What is the mixture of motives, for tax payers, donors and governments? Can we identify patterns of ethical concern, individual self interest and the pursuit of economic efficiency which seem to explain observed patterns of redistribution?

To address this, we need to answer two related questions. First, between whom do societies really redistribute? Are contributors redistributing to *themselves*, from good times to bad, from young to old? Or from those who are securely better off to those who are persistently poor? I will use some of the techniques you learned in Chapter 22 to explore these issues. And second, what are the economic effects of redistribution? Does a trade-off between efficiency and equity, of the sort discussed in Chapter 22, mean that redistribution reduces economic efficiency? Or can it, on the contrary, improve economic growth by promoting social cohesion?

As Chapter 22 noted, these issues are deeply contested since they imply winners and losers, and since the very measures and models we use to investigate them turn on differences in values. Furthermore, patterns of redistribution within particular societies become embedded in economic institutions – such as state benefit systems, health services and the insurance industry – which themselves influence our views of what is right and possible. So answers, however tentative, to the questions about motives for redistribution need to include an understanding of these institutions and the pressures to which they respond.

I begin by considering this interrelation between redistributionary motives and changing redistributive institutions over time, including some economic efficiency arguments for state involvement in welfare. Sections 3–5 then consider the redistributive and economic effects of tax/benefit systems and – as a case study of public services – of health services in industrialized countries, using UK and comparative evidence. Finally, Section 6 turns to the most contested issue of all: the redistribution of wealth.

2   Redistribution: public and private means

2.1   Motives and institutions

We can learn something of *why* we redistribute income by looking at *how* we do it. All economies, however developed their market systems, also redistribute resources by non-market means, both within households and across them. Through a variety of complex mechanisms, children, the infirm, the elderly and those unable to find work may be supported by their fellow citizens.

Reflection

Before you read on, think about that last statement. What redistributive mechanisms and institutions outside the household can you identify in societies you know?

Here are some possible answers, ordered roughly from smaller to larger institutions. But assumptions about scale can be misleading. I personally know some global extended family networks!

Mutual help between friends

Extended family networks

Mutual aid and group savings organizations

Trade union assistance schemes

Private insurance and pension schemes

Charities, national and international

State social security and public service provision

Development aid from richer to poorer countries

Redistributions forced by foreign powers

This is a curiously mixed list. Some institutions on it are very personal, indeed private, such as helping friends. Others are 'public' in the sense of being undertaken by the state (social security, for example, and foreign invasions). And some are non-profit organizations such as charities and trade unions. One odd item out seems to be the private insurance companies. These are hardly 'non-market' institutions. Yet private insurance is certainly a major form of cash redistribution in industrial economies. (The other odd item, foreign intervention, is discussed in Section 6.)

These forms of redistribution suggest two sorts of motives. The first is ethical or altruistic. Donating to charity falls mainly in this category. And *one* motive for voters' supporting state-financed social security and public services may be a genuine desire to prevent destitution or lack of access to basic services by the poor.

The second sort of motive may be self interest, and here things get more complicated. For recipients of redistribution, the self interest motive speaks for itself – and not all those recipients may be poor. Subsidies for rail commuting and home ownership are common examples of 'middle class welfare'. So one model for understanding redistribution may be drawn from the private interest view of the state (see Chapter 10, Section 4.1). If we understand the state as an arena for competition between private interests, then we would expect redistribution by the state to follow the tracks of political power: either voting majorities or influential lobbies. This was the assumption behind Galbraith's argument above.

The self interest of the better off may also directly motivate redistribution. As Chapter 22 noted, it may be in the interests of the comfortable to ensure widespread immunization, clean drinking water and sanitation. They may also recognize that an efficient economy requires the education of all citizens, not just those who can pay. These examples both turn on the existence of externalities (Chapter 10, Section 2.3): public health and education benefit the wider society, not just their individual recipients. The well off may also support redistribution through fear of criminality and violent revolt.

Furthermore, even the apparently fortunate may fear unemployment or homelessness, and just about everyone fears ill health. So the better off may support a safety net against the day when they may need it. Since there are limits to the extent to which private insurance can provide such a safety net, self interest may sustain tax-financed provision.

Exercise 23.1

Can you see a similarity between this argument and the views of John Rawls on social justice, discussed in Chapter 22?

Redistribution, therefore, may be motivated by personal need or acquisitiveness, ethical open-handedness or a sense of shared risks. It seems likely that redistributive institutions which persist – especially those which persist in deeply divided societies – may be those which succeed in appealing to a mixture of these motives. How have these institutions evolved?

2.2   From voluntary action to social security (and back again?)

> That charity was a central preoccupation for medieval men and women is indisputable. In England alone some 220 hospitals were founded in the twelfth century and some 310 in the thirteenth. The donors who endowed and maintained them were granting gifts, allocating property, bestowing food, money, clothes and spiritual care upon strangers. …
>
> *(Rubin, 1987, p.1)*
>
> The researchers believe the medieval concept of charity has no place in the modern world.
>
> *(Commentary on Voluntary Action report, The Guardian, 6 October 1993)*

While national comprehensive state-based social security systems date only from the late nineteenth century, and are limited to a small number of industrialized countries, charity and mutual aid appear to be as old and as widespread as human history. 'Charity' carries, as the first quotation notes, an implication of caring for strangers – though it might also imply patronage for known dependants. 'Mutual aid' suggests rather a sharing of risks among those known and trusted – an implication of assistance among equals. But the categories overlap, as anyone knows who has travelled within less developed countries and been 'adopted' and cared for within the mutual aid networks of strangers.

Charity can be understood as gift-giving, but gifts are two-edged. They can be an expression of moral or religious belief, an altruistic commitment to the welfare of others. But they also, as anthropologists have stressed, tend to create obligations in their wake. The idea of giving to strangers as an expression of moral values has been used to interpret activity which seems inexplicable in terms of pure self interest: an example is a study of voluntary blood doning by the sociologist Richard Titmuss (1970). On the other hand, recipients of charity may feel demeaned by dependency on the goodwill of the giver – on gifts they are unable to repay. Hence the modern deprecation of charity – expressed in the second quotation above – as compared to social security to which people have rights.

Mutual aid schemes, like charity, focus on life's necessities: food, shelter, coping with illness, paying for essential ceremonies such as weddings and funerals. Collective local savings schemes, for example, are common throughout sub-Saharan Africa. So important to economically vulnerable people are these patterns of risk spreading that, in periods of social upheaval, new forms tend to be invented.

Historians record just such a pattern during the industrial revolution in Europe. As industrial cities grew, and people were torn out of old social relationships, they created new patterns of mutual assistance. The early trade unions, often in association with churches, created Friendly Societies. Small in size, these societies fulfilled a social role, as well as encouraging saving: initially for decent burial, later for unemployment, sick pay and medical care. Some even managed payments in disablement and old age. By the mid nineteenth century, it has been estimated that half the population of England and Wales belonged to such societies, and similar societies in France claimed 2 million members by the turn of the century (de Swaan, 1988, pp.143–4).

Throughout Europe, economic development brought a shift in the pattern of insurance from these small-scale schemes to larger private and state ventures. Some large private ventures retained the 'mutual' form – such as the British Building Societies – while others became profit-making ventures. Meanwhile governments took a more active role. Within about 50 years, from the 1880s to the 1930s, most European governments set up national compulsory social insurance schemes to address the hazards of destitution due to old age, ill health and disability, and unemployment (de Swaan, 1988, p.152). Along with direct public service provision these schemes were greatly extended after the Second World War. Risk spreading, by the later part of the twentieth century, had become nationalized in Europe in two senses: through national-scale private insurance schemes, and through state provision.

Note the emphasis on risk and insurance. While the effect of social security may be redistributive from rich to poor – a matter considered carefully below – much of the explicit justification for its establishment was cast in the language of insurance. The widespread cross-national acceptability of the new schemes seems to have been rooted in a broadening sense of shared risk (Goodin and Dryzek, 1987). As the growth of industrial cities made the risks to different social classes more interdependent, so growing wage employment spread the vulnerability to unemployment across classes. Furthermore, two major wars spread insecurity to the better off throughout Europe, increasing the acceptability of risk-spreading among regions and social classes. Economic destitution lost some of its association with personal failure. Finally, the experience of wartime planning also encouraged acceptance of a wider role for the state.

Limits to the nationalization of risk?

And there many people thought it would rest. The 'nationalization' of risk was associated with the rise of national states, and with a level of confidence in their probity and administrative capacity. The legitimacy of the state as an agent of risk-sharing became intertwined, especially in the aftermath of the Second World War, with a more explicitly social-democratic emphasis on the state as an agent of greater economic equality.

This set of ideas – equality, risk-sharing and the legitimacy of the state as social agent – which sustained the welfare state came under world-wide attack in the 1980s. Three challenges emerged to the post-war consensus. First, rising government budget deficits brought fears of a fiscal squeeze: the financing of social security via taxation seemed to be pressing against a political and economic limit (OECD, 1988, 1994a). Second, there was evidence of a generally declining social and political commitment to sharing risk and reducing inequality, in favour of acceptance of greater inequality and the privileging of freedom of action (see Chapter 22).

And third, there was a rising mistrust of the state as a social and economic agent. The state was increasingly characterized as inefficient and unresponsive, and resistance developed to the use of public services for purposes of social control. Indeed, the inflexibility of state social provision is widely identified as a source of social exclusion. State services can be captured by existing beneficiaries, including the middle classes, and exclude new groups in need. For example, most social security schemes are patterned along gender lines, limiting women's access to benefits. And, although systematic research on social security and 'race' is really only available for the USA, there is evidence that European state social security systems contain strong elements of institutional racism, e.g. the partial exclusion of 'guest workers' from benefits, and racist application of rules (Ginsberg, 1992).

All this has added up to a considerable coalition against state domination of welfare. The economic literature increasingly focuses on the extent to which the state does *not* monopolize provision. There is in fact a varying balance across Europe between state, charitable and private provision for pensions, disability insurance and health care, although the state generally dominates unemployment provision and means tested poverty relief. Whether the current debate signals a real retreat by states from redistributive and social security activities in the industrialized West is much disputed. But the shift in ethical discourse has been unmistakable. There is a new emphasis on self-reliance and charitable or 'third sector' organizations as sources of social provision. The idea of the 'mixed economy of welfare' – variously interpreted – expresses this shift.

2.3   Analysing risk and insurance

So what can economic analysis contribute to this contestation of the proper boundaries between public and private action in redistribution? One useful contribution is to analyse the strengths and limitations of private insurance. This analysis asks, in a way I hope is by now familiar, what are the most common market failures in private insurance, and how could the state intervene to overcome them? The analysis therefore falls within the 'public interest' view of the state, begging for the moment the question of the effectiveness of state intervention in practice.

Probability and private insurance

Insurance works on probabilities. Private insurance companies spend large sums of money trying to work out the probabilities of various calamities occurring to identifiable groups of people. Over large groups of people, probabilities of particular occurrences can become rather stable and predictable. I do not know if I will fall ill and be unable to work next year, but it is possible to work out with reasonable precision what percentage of a large group of people rather like me in age and general health status will become ill.

So insurance works by identifying groups with predictable probabilities of incurring a problem, and charging them all a sum which allows the unlucky ones to receive compensation. Let us take the example of sickness benefit insurance payments made if you fall ill while working. Suppose that a private insurance company knows that there is a 0.5 per cent chance of someone like you being off work in any month, and pays £800 if you are. Then the premium will be 0.5% × £800 plus a share of the insurance company's administrative costs including normal profit.

Exercise 23.2

Suppose that a group of people including you have a 1 in a 100 chance of being ill in any year, and that the average cost to the insurance company is £2500 per illness episode, plus £5 per person for administration. What is your annual premium?

Formally, if the probability of requiring a given compensation, Z, is p, and the administrative costs are A, then the premium is:

$$pZ + A$$

If you can afford it, and are sufficiently foresighted to worry (over 30 years of age?) then you will pay. That is the principle of private insurance. To make it work, several conditions are essential.

First, enough people have to be insured to make the calculated probabilities reliable. This condition is called the law of large numbers. Among small groups of people, the proportion who will be ill at any time will vary greatly from year to year. But with very large groups, the average sickness rate becomes much more predictable. As a result, risks can be pooled efficiently. A problem faced by Friendly Societies and their kind is that they may be too small to generate a predictable level of shared risk, so a chance combination of problems can overwhelm them.

Second, the probability that one individual needs compensation has to be independent of the probability of the same problem for others. My becoming ill must not influence your state of health, for example, otherwise the average will not be stable for the group. So infectious diseases are a problem. This is a second problem for small mutual aid societies. In nineteenth-century Europe, for example, a local trade union mutual aid society would be most needed when the largest local employer collapsed, but then the fund would be rapidly bankrupted, since all would lose their income together. Similarly, a local disaster – flood or fire or infectious disease – rapidly overwhelms the resources of local mutual aid societies just when most needed.

Third, the probability of the insured disaster must be less than one. If $p = 1$, then the problem is certain to happen. If you are already sick or disabled, health insurance to cover the condition would cost at least as much as the treatment. This means the most vulnerable people in society can find certain forms of insurance inaccessible.

Fourth, people must not be able to influence the probability of the insured event occurring. Hence pregnancy is hard to insure against, and so is unemployment. This source of market failure is called 'moral hazard'. The market fails to work efficiently in this case because the insurance company lacks good information on the intentions of the insured person.

Fifth, the insurer also needs good information about the risks attached to each individual. Otherwise, some high risk people may represent themselves as low risk, and so pay insufficient premiums. This in turn pushes up costs for others. If the result is that the truly low risk individuals find average premiums rising to a point where insuring is not worthwhile, then low risks will drop out, further raising the cost to others. This market failure is called 'adverse selection'.

Barr (1993) provides a more detailed discussion of the conditions for efficient private insurance.

Question

What does this analysis suggest about the likely boundaries of private insurance?

These conditions for efficient private insurance are stringent. Taken together, they suggest that private insurers are likely to fight shy of unemployment insurance (because of moral hazard). They are also likely to avoid, or charge very big premiums to, high risk individuals (such as medical insurance for those over 70, or young inexperienced male drivers), or for insurance against new and unpredictable risks (such as AIDS).

The conditions also imply distributional problems with private insurance. The highest premiums may be demanded of those on low incomes, as the example of pensioners' medical insurance suggests. Combined with the fact that private insurance is a marketed service, hence the demand reflects incomes, this implies that some people cannot acquire private insurance, however much they want or need it. So if others in society want them insured, other forms of redistribution are necessary.

Social insurance

Private insurance is therefore problematic in some areas of major social concern: unemployment, old-age pensions for the low paid and unpaid, chronic disability and health insurance. For these categories, private insurance is unlikely to be sufficient if society – however defined – wishes all its members to be insured. Some people will be excluded by lack of income, others by the nature of the risks themselves – given the market failures in private insurance – or by their particular probabilities of succumbing to them.

These problems can be used to explain the spread of social insurance. Have a careful look at the definitions now. On these definitions, the state can in principle provide 'private' insurance. But social insurance would not be viable for a private insurer, because it covers (privately) uninsurable risks.

Definitions

Social insurance

Social insurance refers to compulsory and universalistic insurance systems, to which all in certain categories compulsorily contribute, and from which contributors suffering from defined contingencies, such as unemployment, receive benefit.

Private insurance

Private insurance by contrast is non-universalistic: access to it is based on actuarial calculation of risk and acceptance of individual application, and it can be provided by independent profit-seeking or non profit companies.

So how can the state insure the uninsurable? The state has two major advantages over private insurers: its capacities for investigation and compulsion. By compelling universal coverage, the state can prevent low risk people from refusing to enter a pooled system, and thereby reduce the costs of universal coverage. Investigative powers are used in areas where moral hazard is seen as serious, for example, to enforce a test of 'genuinely seeking work' as the price of unemployment benefit.

One explanation from economic theory, therefore, for the rise and persistence of social insurance is a response to insurance market failures. The boundaries between social and private insurance are contested in theory and shifting in practice as the insurance industry develops. You should note, however, that social insurance schemes in practice combine risk pooling – true insurance – and redistribution from rich to poor. Risk pooling requires only that people make a common flat-rate payment, based on average costs of the scheme. Social insurance payments, however, are often income-related, which implies that there is redistribution between the better off and poorer in costs of access to the scheme, as well as redistribution towards those who fall ill or unemployed.

The persistence of social insurance may perhaps be explained by its capacity to combine efficient insurance with rich-to-poor redistribution. It can be 'sold' politically as both an efficient safety net and an ethical system, and has the additional advantage that as contributors people have rights to the benefits: there is no stigma of charity.

2.4   Social assistance and public services

Social insurance does however have gaps. By definition, insurance systems – private and social – only cover contributors for the risks for which they are designed. There will, therefore, be people who are not eligible for benefits because they could not or did not contribute, or suffered from uninsured (possibly new or unforeseen) risks. Hence, most industrialized countries have other benefits which try to fill in these gaps.

There are two types of non-insurance cash benefits. One is *universal benefits*, paid by right to certain categories of people whether they have contributed or not. The most common are family benefits of various types, paid to adults supporting children. The other type is social assistance. Social assistance implies an ethical commitment to redistribute income from the better off to the poor, though the better off may still be motivated by a fear that they may one day need the system.

The balance between social insurance, social assistance and universal benefits within public social provision varies across industrialized countries. Table 23.1 suggests, however, that social insurance is the dominant category. On these definitions benefit trends have generally reinforced social insurance, but the UK has seen a sharp shift towards means testing.

Definition

Social assistance

Social assistance is the general term for benefits which are means tested, that is, access to the benefits requires an income below a given threshold.

Table 23.1   **Types of publicly funded benefit, 1960 and 1986, selected countries (% of total benefits)**

Country	Year	Social insurance (including medical)	Social assistance	Family allowance
West Germany	1960	66.7	6.6	2.0
	1986	78.1	5.2	3.1
Sweden	1960	71.3	12.2	10.7
	1986	84.1	0.5	4.6
Japan	1959–60	50.8	12.7	0
	1986	72.9	8.2	0.4
UK	1959–60	71.0	10.8	5.4
	1986	59.1	24.4	6.7
USA	1959–60	61.5	15.4	0
	1986	62.6	19.3	0

Note: percentages do not add to 100 because of omission of an 'other' category, including benefits for public employees and war victims.

Source: Barr (1992) pp.761–2; ILO (1992)

The definition of social insurance used in constructing Table 23.1 is, however, broader than the formal definition in Section 2.3, in order to make the data reasonably comparable across countries. The problem arises because some industrialized countries (such as Germany) have social insurance funds for health care, while others (such as Sweden) support universal health care access out of general taxation. Once social insurance fund contributions are graduated by income and those unable to pay are subsidized, the distinction between social insurance and tax-financed universal benefits loses much of its force. The most important distinction for the economic analysis of redistribution, brought out in Table 23.1, is that between universalistic (social insurance or tax financed) systems and means tested assistance.

In a number of industrialized countries, health care is not only financed, but also provided, by the state: the benefits are provided *in kind*, that is, free or subsidized at the point of use. Education is frequently supplied in the same way. For example 93 per cent of UK children go to state schools (*Social Trends*, 1994). These big public services also have much in common with social insurance in terms of motivation: they are universalistic and compulsory, so consumer sovereignty is overridden. You cannot choose in Britain not to educate children – though you may teach them at home – nor can you opt out of your right of access to the National Health Service and its tax cost to you.

How can the overriding of consumer sovereignty, whether through social insurance or public provision, be explained? Section 5 returns to this question. A partial explanation might be found in externalities, as Section 2.1 noted. Another possible reason could be the problem of public goods (Chapter 10, Section 2.3).

Question

Is education a public good?

Education does not fit the economists' technical definition of a public good. It can be easily divided up for purchase – as in private schools – and a classroom place occupied by one child is not available for another. Very similar arguments apply to much of health care. Hospital care, like education, is *rival* (more for me, less for you), and it is *excludable* (I can consume some without letting you in). So, both can be – and are – sold on markets. Market failures of the public good type do not provide a satisfactory explanation of these compulsory public services.

It seems rather that society must, in some sense, deem health care (whether health insurance or direct provision) and education sufficiently important that people should be forced to consume them – and provide them for their children – whether they wish to or not. Richard Musgrave, the US public finance economist, calls such goods and services merit goods (Musgrave and Musgrave, 1984, p.78).

The choice between provision in kind by the state on the one hand, and enforcement and finance of universal access on the other, is not the focus of this chapter. The concern is rather with the motivations and redistributive effects of the whole varied package of universal and means tested, cash and in-kind provision.

Definition

Merit goods

Goods are called merit goods if society seeks to encourage their consumption, overriding the preferences of the individual consumer.

3   The tax/benefit system

Given the emphasis on social insurance (in a broad sense) identified above, how redistributive are tax/benefit systems? This section addresses that question for *cash* benefits, only using UK and comparative data. Section 5 returns to benefits in kind.

3.1   A baseline for redistribution

To measure redistribution we need a baseline against which to measure it. One way to find one is to use the three economic circuits – state, market and domestic – distinguished by Jane Wheelock in Chapter 3, Figure 3.11, to classify the institutions through which redistribution occurs (Table 23.2).

On Table 23.2, column 1, plus the factor incomes in columns 2 and 3, plus non-profit insurance payments (that is, the elements above the red line), constitute the primary income distribution. This is the income distribution among households generated by the labour market and by ownership of capital, financial assets (including insurance) and land. The other activities in columns 2 and 3 then constitute redistribution through some form of public (state or charitable) action, and result in a secondary income distribution which can be compared to the primary one. Column 4 activities are largely missing from statistics (apart from inheritance), but are relevant to measuring redistribution, since we are really interested in the standard of living of people, not of 'households'. These are useful working definitions, but as Section 4 shows, the distinction between primary and secondary distributions is not wholly straightforward.

Definitions

Primary income distribution

The primary (or market) income distribution is the distribution of incomes produced by factor markets and asset ownership before taxes and transfers.

Secondary income distribution

The secondary income distribution is the income distribution after taxes and transfers.

Table 23.2   Access to resources in mixed economies

Type of resources	Sector			
	market/private		state/public	households and kin
	profit seeking	non profit		
	(1)	**(2)**	**(3)**	**(4)**
Cash	Factor incomes	Factor incomes	Factor incomes	
	Insurance payments	Insurance payments	Cash transfers and tax allowances	Cash transfers
		Subsidies and grants	Subsidies and grants	
Kind	Payments in kind	Benefits in kind	Benefits in kind	Shared consumption
		Subsidized goods and services	Subsidized goods and services	Gifts
				Inheritance

Source: reworked from Rein and Rainwater (1986) p.15

3.2   Redistribution in cash: taxes

The difference between the primary and secondary income distributions is largely determined by taxes and benefits. I will start from the tax side, using UK data. The context for the discussion is the growing inequality of earnings and rising poverty levels in the UK analysed in Chapter 22.

Most public services and benefits are paid for by taxes, divided in Table 10.1 in Chapter 10 into taxes on income (including social security contributions and the community charge) and taxes on expenditure (including VAT and customs and excise duties).

Question

How does the level of taxes you pay relate to your level of income?

Definitions

Progressive taxes

Taxes are progressive if the proportion of income paid in tax rises with income.

Proportional taxes

Proportional taxes have average tax rates which do not change with income levels.

Regressive taxes

Taxes are regressive if the proportion of income paid in tax falls as income rises.

If the proportion of your income paid in taxes rises with your income, then the tax system is said to be progressive. Income tax systems are usually structured to be progressive. So for example, UK tax bands in 1994 were: a tax free allowance which varied according to marital status and a number of other factors, then successive tax bands of 20 per cent, 25 per cent and 40 per cent on higher incomes. The 40 per cent top rate was much lower than the 98 per cent top rate (on unearned income) in 1978. The progressivity of the UK income tax system was reduced by social security (National Insurance) contributions which were subject in 1994 to an income ceiling above which nothing further was payable.

Not all taxes are progressive: some are proportional, or even regressive, falling hardest on the poor. The Community Charge, or 'poll tax', instituted first in Scotland in 1989, and abolished in 1993, was a rather notorious example of a regressive tax on income. In a local area, everyone paid the same sum of money except the small number qualifying for income-related exemptions, generally from 80 per cent of the tax. Hence in most cases the lower your income, the higher the proportion of your income paid in poll tax, and this was widely resented.

Figure 23.1   **Poll taxes have twice caused riots in Britain: (top) Richard II appeases the poll tax rebels on the death of Wat Tyler, Smithfield, June 1381 and (bottom) poll tax demonstration, London, March 1990**

Furthermore, the formal income tax banding is only part of the story. There are many ways legally to avoid tax (never mind illegal evasion). Tax breaks on certain types of financial investment, and tax expenditures (such as tax relief on some mortgage interest) favour the better off, and this reduces the progressiveness of income tax in practice.

So how about taxes on expenditure? If all goods and services were taxed at the same rate, and everyone spent all their income, taxes on spending would be proportional to income. However, many systems of indirect taxation exempt goods which are seen as important necessities. For example, in Britain in 1994, VAT was not charged on food, children's clothing and books and newspapers – and the proposal to impose it at full rate on domestic fuel met Parliamentary defeat. These exemptions are for distributional reasons: they lessen the impact of the taxation on those on low incomes. On the other hand, as Chapter 3 showed, lower income households tend to spend a higher proportion of their income than others, which raises their taxes on expenditure relative to income.

If we divide UK tax paying households into deciles, then Figure 23.2 shows for 1991 the proportion of tax paid on average by households in each decile group. The households are ranked by 'equivalent' disposable income (see Chapter 22, Section 2.1).

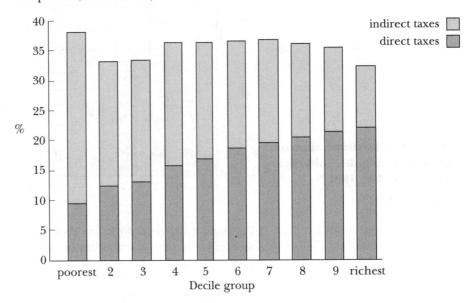

Figure 23.2 **Taxes as percentage of gross income by decile group, UK, 1991**

Source: *Economic Trends*, May 1993, adjusted following Hills (1993) p.85

Question

What does Figure 23.2 tell us about the progressivity of the British tax system?

At the extremes, the British tax system is regressive: the poorest decile group paid on average the highest proportion of their income in taxes, and the richest decile group the lowest. In the middle, the system is roughly proportional, with progressive income tax largely outweighed by regressive indirect taxes. The regressive impact of indirect taxes is magnified because, while the long-term poor live largely within their means, those in the lowest decile group whose incomes have temporarily or recently dropped, and the retired, spend from savings thus raising their expenditure and taxes relative to income.

3.3 The UK tax/benefit system

Figure 23.2 showed tax payments from gross income, including cash benefits. Despite a somewhat regressive tax system, the UK tax/benefit system as a whole may still be redistributive between rich and poor if those on low primary incomes gain more from benefits than they pay in taxes. As Figure 23.3 shows, in 1991, the lowest half of the income distribution received substantially more absolute cash benefits than those on higher incomes, both from social insurance (contributory) and from means tested benefits. Again, however, the lowest decile group did worse than the somewhat less poor.

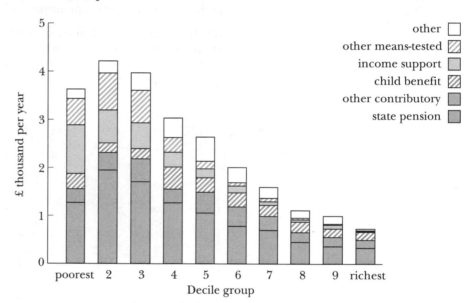

Figure 23.3 **The distribution of cash benefits to households by decile group, UK, 1991**

Source: Hills (1993) p.15

Putting the two sides together then, we would expect that in any year, the secondary income distribution in the UK would be more equal than the primary distribution. Figure 23.4 tests this proposition: the bar chart compares average 'original' income (before taxes and benefits) with 'post tax' income after cash benefits and direct and indirect taxes for 1991.

Question

What does Figure 23.4 show concerning the redistributive impact of the UK tax/benefit system?

The system does redistribute 'vertically' between rich and poor. It has a substantial proportional effect at the bottom (the households in the lowest decile group gain on average £1779 or 153 per cent over their primary income, and the second decile group gain 108 per cent), and a substantial absolute effect at the top (the top decile group loses only 31 per cent of primary income but this is worth £14 544).

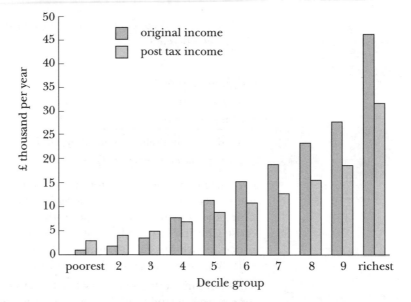

***Figure 23.4*   Original and post tax average incomes of households by decile group, UK, 1991 (£)**

Source: *Economic Trends*, May 1993, adjusted following Hills (1993)

As you know from Chapter 22, the measures you choose matter. So check the above result and also put to work the techniques in Chapter 22, with the following exercise.

Exercise 23.3

Table 23.3 shows the percentage shares of households in total incomes by quintile groups (two deciles), in 1992, before and after taxes and cash benefits. Table 23.4 shows the Gini coefficients for a range of years for original and post-tax income, and for disposable income (after cash benefits and direct taxes, before indirect taxes).

1   Calculate the cumulative shares and draw the Lorenz curves for the two columns in Table 23.3 and interpret the results.

2   Explain what we learn about pre- and post-tax inequality and redistribution from Table 23.4

***Table 23.3*   Shares of total original and post-tax incomes of households by quintile group, UK, 1992**

Quintile groups	Original income	Post-tax income
Bottom	2	6
2nd	6	11
3rd	16	16
4th	26	23
Top	50	44

Note: households ranked by 'equivalent' disposable income see Section 3.2.

Source: *Economic Trends* (1994)

Table 23.4   **Gini coefficients for original, disposable and post-tax income, UK, selected years**

	1979	1984	1989	1992
Original income	44	49	50	52
Disposable income	27	28	34	34
Post-tax income	29	30	37	38

Note: data for households ranked by 'equivalent' disposable income.

Source: *Economic Trends* (1994)

Even if the tax/benefit system reduces inequality in one year, it still might not be redistributive over the longer term. It might be redistributing over time chiefly within social classes rather than between the 'lifetime rich' – those with the highest lifetime incomes – and the 'lifetime poor'. The two processes are not easy to distinguish, since a higher proportion of the elderly than of the general population tend to be poor.

These lifetime effects are very hard to analyse empirically, but Figure 23.5 is drawn from a study which uses computer modelling to trace the lifetime implications of the current system: i.e. it models what would happen over time if the current UK tax and benefit system was maintained unchanged. The study shows that the current system is redistributive over time. Figure 23.5 includes the distribution of health and education benefits in kind, discussed in Section 5. It shows that the 'lifetime rich' receive most of their benefits on a self-financed basis, though even in this group, some individuals receive net benefits paid for by others. In the poorest decile group, more than half of average benefits represent redistribution from other tax payers. The same study shows that overall those in decile groups 6–10 pay more in tax than they receive in benefits, but this is not true of all individuals in these groups. Figure 23.5 also shows that total lifetime benefits received are more or less the same for each lifetime income decile group. In other words, the groups get much the same benefits in total over their lifetimes, but pay very differently for them. Taxation is more progressive on a lifetime basis than in a single year, but benefits are less focused on the poor.

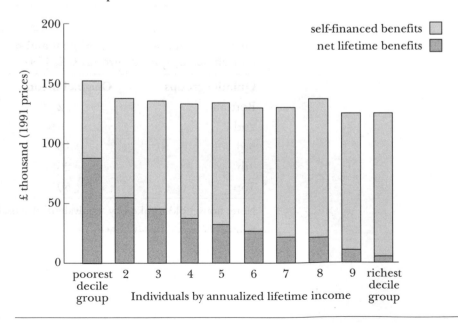

Figure 23.5   **Lifetime benefits and taxes, 1991 UK tax and social security system**

Source: Hills (1993) p.20, derived from LIFEMOD simulation model

3.4   Comparing tax/benefit systems

How does the redistributive effect of the UK tax/benefit system compare with other industrialized countries? I use here some comparable data from the Luxembourg Income Study (LIS) to compare the UK with three other countries. West Germany and Sweden are wealthier European countries than the UK; and both are, in the terms explained in Chapter 15, examples of 'organized' capitalism. Both have extensive welfare systems, but Sweden, a socially rather homogenous country, has a reputation for a particularly generous and redistributive approach. The USA on the other hand, although also a wealthy country, has an 'unorganized' economic system – in that sense more like the UK – with a much less universalistic welfare system than the other three.

Table 23.5 provides some data on the structure of incomes in the four countries. The categories are slightly different from our previous ones. The table shows 'market incomes' (primary income) including occupational pensions, as a percentage of gross incomes including cash benefits. It also gives net cash income (disposable income) after direct taxes; the effect of indirect taxes is not available.

Table 23.5   **The relative importance of income sources and direct taxes, selected countries, early 1980s (average value as % of average gross income)**

	West Germany	Sweden	UK	USA
Wages and salaries	63.1	64.5	72.0	75.8
Self employment income	16.7	3.7	4.5	6.7
Property income	1.1	2.7	2.7	5.8
Factor incomes	*80.9*	*70.8*	*79.3*	*88.3*
Occupational pensions	2.3	0.0[1]	2.5	2.6
Market incomes	*83.3*	*70.8*	*81.7*	*90.8*
Child benefits	1.4	1.3	2.2	0.0
Means tested benefits	0.6	4.4	2.1	1.3
Other cash benefits	14.5	23.6	12.9	6.8
Total cash benefits	*16.5*	*29.2*	*17.2*	*8.0*
Other cash income	0.2	0.0	1.1	1.2
Gross income	*100.0*	*100.0*	*100.0*	*100.0*
Income tax	14.8	28.5	13.6	16.5
Payroll tax (employees)	7.7	1.2	3.3	4.5
Net cash income	*77.5*	*70.2*	*83.1*	*79.0*

[1] Occupational pensions do exist in Sweden, but are included in cash benefits in the data.

Note: figures may not add exactly to totals because of rounding.

Source: O'Higgins *et al.* (1990) p.31

Question

What differences between countries stand out in Table 23.5?

Striking differences include Sweden's high direct taxes, and high levels of non-means tested cash benefits; the USA's low benefit levels relative to income; the importance of self employment income (which tends to be highly unequal) in West Germany, and the importance of property income (also typically unequal) in the USA. As a result, the potential scope the government has for redistributing income in an equalizing direction (the government's 'impact potential') seems greatest in Sweden. You can test its effects with reference to Table 23.6.

Question

Compare the factor income and post-tax income shares in Table 23.6. Subtract the factor income share from the net cash income share at the bottom, and vice versa at the top. Does Sweden in fact have the most redistributive tax/benefit system of the four countries?

Table 23.6   **Income shares of quintile groups of people, selected countries, early 1980s (%)**

	West Germany	Sweden	UK	USA
Factor incomes				
Lowest quintile group	2.3	6.5	4.0	4.2
Top quintile group	44.7	33.2	36.3	38.8
Net cash income				
Lowest quintile group	13.1	16.4	12.4	9.0
Top quintile group	36.2	24.2	30.6	32.0

Note: individuals are ranked by family gross income to form quintiles.

Source: O'Higgins *et al.* (1990) p.41

Your results should show that on these data the West German tax/benefit system is the most redistributive at the bottom, in the sense of generating the largest percentage point change in income share. This is in part because Sweden starts with a much less unequal distribution of factor incomes than West Germany, so its considerable redistributive activity has a somewhat smaller percentage effect. The USA, as might be expected, is least redistributive at the lower end. At the upper end the impact of the Swedish system stands out more.

Chapter 22 made a sharp distinction between inequality and poverty. So far, we have been measuring the effect of the tax/benefit system on income inequality. What about poverty relief? How successful are these countries in reducing relative poverty via their benefit systems?

Table 23.7 compares pre- and post-transfer poverty rates for the four countries in the early 1980s: that is, the percentage of individuals in households with net income below 50 per cent of median income. The table shows up the relative lack of success of the US benefit system in dealing with poverty, and the variability of success in other countries by family type. Furthermore, it demonstrates the concentration of pre-benefit poverty in elderly households, and the very great success of the Swedish benefit system in dealing with this. No system completely removes single parent poverty, which has a particularly serious effect on women.

Table 23.7 **Percentage of people who are poor by types of household, selected countries, early 1980s**

		Percentage of persons who are poor in				
		total	elderly families	single parent families	two parent families	other families
West Germany	Pre-transfer	28.3	80.3	34.8	12.9	20.1
	Post-transfer	6.0	9.3	18.1	3.9	5.4
	% reduction	78.8	88.4	48.0	69.8	73.1
Sweden	Pre-transfer	41.0	98.4	55.0	21.3	30.5
	Post-transfer	5.0	0.1	9.2	5.0	7.0
	% reduction	87.8	99.9	83.3	76.5	77.0
UK	Pre-transfer	27.9	78.6	56.3	17.6	12.8
	Post-transfer	8.8	18.1	29.1	6.5	4.1
	% reduction	68.5	77.0	48.3	63.1	68.0
USA	Pre-transfer	27.3	72.0	58.5	16.0	15.4
	Post-transfer	16.9	20.5	51.7	12.9	9.8
	% reduction	38.1	71.5	11.6	19.4	36.4

Source: Smeeding *et al.* (1990) Table 3.5, p.67

4 The economics of cash redistribution

4.1   Explaining cash redistribution

So what does this analysis of the data on redistribution suggest about explanations? Look back for a moment to Hutton and Galbraith in Section 1, and their emphasis on voting. Under majority voting, we would expect the middle income voters to exercise power. If voting tends to be polarized between the better off and the poorer, then the 'swing' voters in the middle choose the government, a proposition familiar to Labour and Conservative politicians in Britain.

We might therefore expect redistribution to favour the centre of the income spectrum, taking resources from both rich and poor. In the data just set out there is some evidence of this phenomenon – known as 'Director's law' after the economist Aaron Director, who first stated it – in the relative disadvantage of the poorest income decile in the UK in both taxes and benefits; in the fairly substantial level of redistribution from higher incomes; and in the gaps in the safety nets in all four countries. In the UK and the USA in particular, there is evidence of persistent and worsening disadvantage among the poorest.

However, the extent and persistence of social insurance programmes suggest they have widespread support. The best explanations of this draw on a mixture of ethics, the acceptability of a system providing equal right to all contributors, and a sense of shared risk. The public campaigns of the 1930s and 1940s which influenced the post-war British social insurance legislation focused on security, equal access and equal minimum standards, rather than on overtly redistributive objectives (Glennerster, 1990), and the middle classes were brought into the social insurance net for the first time. In the USA, social security pensions form the element of welfare that, Galbraith notes, is least under threat from voters.

Social insurance systems seem to be particularly solid in countries of the 'organized capitalism' type such as Germany and Sweden. 'Organized' systems tend to generate more egalitarian primary income distributions than 'unorganized' systems, and also tend to sustain more inclusive welfare systems. Conversely, the UK, with a more 'unorganized' economic system, shifted sharply away from social insurance towards means tested benefits as unemployment and primary inequality rose in the 1980s (Henley and Tsakalotos, 1993; Green *et al.*, 1994). Between 1978/79 and 1988/89, means tested benefits as percentage of total benefits rose from 8.4 per cent to 18.1 per cent, and the government shifted from avoiding further means testing in the 1970s to treating 'targeting' as an objective in the 1980s (Barr and Coulter, 1990).

There seems to be a paradox here. Means tested benefits are the most immediately redistributive form of benefits, since they are paid only to those in need. One might therefore expect them to predominate in countries with the greatest ethical concern with equality. But the opposite appears to be the case. It is the countries where inequality rose most rapidly in the 1980s – the USA and the UK – which are moving towards a more limited and stratified benefit system, which sets up as far as possible an institutional division between privatized provision for the better off and means tested welfare for the poor. As Section 3 showed, these systems are in fact less redistributive than more inclusive systems.

One reason why this may be so is suggested by Galbraith's arguments in *The Culture of Contentment*. In countries where benefits become stratified in this way, the middle income voters may cease to feel a commitment to welfare provision and withdraw support for adequate provision. Another is that in socially highly stratified countries such as the UK, means tested benefits have long carried a social stigma which, along with complexity of conditions, reduces take-up substantially. Take-up rates appear to be over 80 per cent for the main safety net benefit (currently Income Support) but only around 50–60 per cent for benefits available to low income families in work (Fry and Stark, 1991; Dorsett and Heady, 1991). Furthermore, means testing is administratively expensive: in the UK in 1991 11.8 per cent of the funds for Income Support, and 42.2 per cent of the Social Fund (both means tested) went on administration but only 1.3 per cent of pension spending.

In explaining redistribution via complex tax/benefit systems, therefore, it seems useful to look to the extent of social integration and perceived social solidarity. As the memory of wartime has receded in Western Europe, the sense of shared risks has waned. Social institutions such as benefit systems may focus social solidarity or conversely reinforce stratification in the face of economic stress.

4.2 Economic effects of means testing

Question

Look back at Section 3. What assumption was I making in that section about the effects of taxes and benefits on the primary, original or 'market' income distribution?

I have been implicitly assuming that taxes and benefits do not affect the primary distribution. But you should certainly know enough economics by this stage to be wary of that assumption. So much economic analysis is about analysing responses of people and firms to economic incentives that it is quite natural to ask, how do they respond to taxes and benefits? Surely the original income distribution would be different had social security not existed? These questions lie behind proposals for the privatization of parts of social security. This section considers some of the economic effects of benefits at the lower end of the income distribution.

The poverty trap

Do taxes and benefits help people out of poverty or trap them in it? To answer that question, we first need to distinguish between average rates of tax – as in Figure 23.2 – and marginal tax rates.

Definition

Marginal tax rates

Your marginal tax rate is the tax rate you pay on additional income as your income rises.

Question

At what point in the income distribution do you think that people pay the highest *marginal* rates of tax?

To think about this question, forget about indirect taxes for a moment, and consider the interaction of direct taxes and benefits. In Britain, when your income is below a certain threshold – which depends upon your household circumstances – you are usually eligible for means tested benefits. When your income rises – for example, if you work longer hours – you start to lose these benefits. You can think of this benefit withdrawal as a tax: for each rise in income, you lose a certain amount of benefit. In Britain in the 1980s, the tax rate could in a significant number of cases be over 100 per cent: you actually lost more in benefit than you gained in income over a particular income range. Reform instituted in 1988 reduced the numbers subject to marginal tax rates of greater than 100 per cent, but continuing high rates of benefit withdrawal constitute what has become known as the poverty trap.

Figure 23.6 illustrates the problem. The figure has post-tax income on the vertical axis, and original income on the horizontal axis. The red dashed diagonal line shows the points where the two are equal, i.e. there is no taxation or benefits. A (simplified) income tax schedule would give an individual a net income along the line OAB. Up to original income level Y_{O1} your income is free of tax; after that, you pay a fixed proportion of your income in tax. Now suppose that the benefit system gives you a minimum net income of Y_{N1} at zero original income. However, above original income Y_{O2}, those benefits start to be withdrawn rapidly as income rises. If the effect is that net income follows the path FGHB, then between G and H, that is between original incomes of Y_{O2} and Y_{O3}, the marginal tax rate is

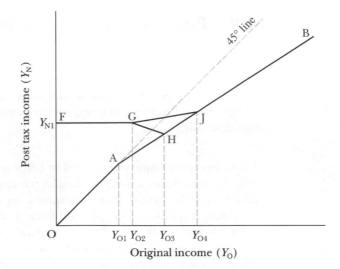

Figure 23.6   The poverty trap

Source: based on Brown and Jackson (1990) p.465

over 100 per cent. Above Y_{O2} there is no point in working to raise your income unless you can get well above Y_{O3} in one fell swoop.

That is the worst kind of poverty trap. A less drastic one is shown by the net income path FGJB. Here, the marginal tax rate is never over 100 per cent. But between G and J, or original income Y_{O2} and Y_{O4}, it is very close to 100 per cent: you keep very little of any additional earnings. And these high tax rates spread out over a larger original income range than in the first case.

The implication is that with means tested benefits, many people at the low end of the income distribution face the highest marginal tax rates in the country. That is the cost of the relative redistributive effectiveness of means tested benefits. Social insurance and universal benefits which are not means tested do not create a poverty trap because they are not withdrawn as income rises.

The unemployment trap

We can think of the impact of these high marginal tax rates on incentives to take paid work at all as a second 'trap', the unemployment trap. People are caught in an unemployment trap when their income in work is little higher – or even actually lower – than their income on benefits. On this basis it has been suggested that benefits are a major cause of unemployment, and benefit cuts proposed as a method of reducing unemployment (Minford *et al.*, 1985).

One measure of this unemployment trap is the replacement ratio: the ratio of income when out of work to (post-tax and transfer) income in work. This is an area of economic analysis where the questioning in Chapters 3 and 9, about the household as against the individual as unit of analysis, is relevant. Much research has focused on the incentives to work of the first earner in a household, usually a man. The broad conclusion has been that higher replacement ratios lengthen the duration of unemployment somewhat, but the magnitude of the effect on unemployment rates is not great (Barr, 1993, p.203). Disaggregating people within households and by household type does however pick out two groups whose work incentives seem to be affected by the current benefit structure in the UK.

Married women appear to be the group whose labour supply is most responsive to tax and income changes, in part because they are very conscious of the opportunity cost of their paid work in terms of domestic caring, in part because of women's relatively low wages, and in part because benefits depend on the couple's joint income. Women partners of unemployed men are therefore deeply affected by the unemployment trap. If the couple loses benefits when the woman takes a paid job, there may be very little incentive for her to work, and this may be one (but only one) factor in the tendency for couples in Britain to polarize between two-earner and no-earner couples (Hills, 1993).

The second group facing serious employment disincentives within the British system are lone parents, overwhelmingly women. Figure 23.7 demonstrates the problem. This is a simulation which shows net income per week at different hours of work at a lower paid job for a single parent with two small children, on different assumptions about child care costs and receiving maintenance from the other parent. A 'poverty plateau', illustrating the poverty trap, and the effect of child care on employment incentives stand out here. Britain has a low rate of employment of lone parents, as compared to married women, and as compared to the EU average (Hills, 1993), at least in part because of the relative lack of publicly funded child care.

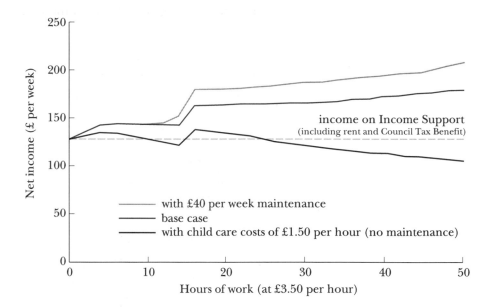

Figure 23.7   Net income by hours of work for a lone parent

Source: Hills (1993) p.27

Means tested benefits therefore have a considerable economic cost because of the disincentive to earn, and the trapping of people into low incomes. Shifts towards increased means testing are likely to worsen this and other disincentives. For example, the elderly in the UK became increasingly dependent on means tested benefits as the value of the old age pension fell relative to earnings (Chapter 22). If most savings must be spent before elderly people are eligible for benefits, then in the medium term the incentive to save is also reduced. Recently the view that state pensions must discourage savings has been used to argue for their abolition, although research on disincentive effects is inconclusive. We now turn to a parallel debate over the public/private boundary and redistribution in health insurance and health care.

5   Health care and redistribution

In addition to cash benefits, governments spend large sums on benefits in kind, especially health and education. This section considers health care as a case study of the redistributive effects of public services, including social insurance for health care, using some cross-country comparative data. I will ask two distinct questions about health care and redistribution. First, are health care systems redistributive in the sense tested for the tax/benefit system: do lower income people receive more health care than they pay for, and higher income people less? And second, do health care systems redistribute effectively from the healthy to the ill?

At the same time, I want to use the case of health care to explore further the importance of institutions and the willingness to redistribute. This section argues that the apparent willingness to redistribute through public health care spending is deeply influenced by the perceived importance of health care to the quality of people's lives, and also by the serious market failures displayed by private health care markets.

5.1   Efficiency and access in health care systems

Industrialized countries finance health care through a mix of public and private financing. The details of the systems are complex, each having evolved historically from a patchwork of earlier schemes, and this makes cross-country comparison difficult. Figure 23.8 shows recent OECD data on the mix of public and 'non-public' (including charitable) funding, and Figure 23.9 shows health expenditure per head for the same countries, compared on the basis of PPP exchange rates (Chapter 19, Section 2.1).

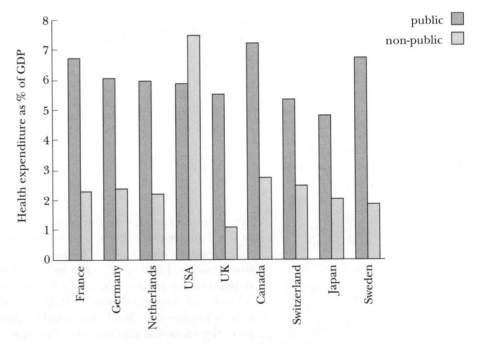

Figure 23.8   **Health expenditure by sector as % of GDP, selected OECD countries, 1991**

Source: OECD (1994a)

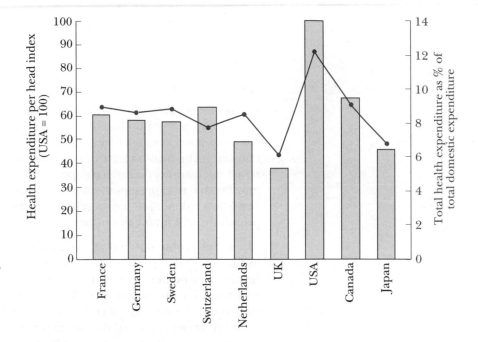

***Figure 23.9* Total health expenditure per head, and as % of total domestic expenditure, selected OECD countries, 1990**

Source: OECD (1994a)

Question

Compare Figures 23.8 and 23.9, and summarize the differences in health care financing between the countries shown.

The USA, the UK and Japan stand out as unusual. The USA spends far more than any other country, absolutely and relatively, and is far more heavily weighted towards private provision than any other country, while still making very substantial public health expenditures. The UK and Japan have low relative spending, and the UK strikingly low absolute spending. The predominance of public finance is greatest in the UK and Sweden. Similarities include a substantial public spending role in most countries, a clustering of most continental European countries in terms of share of health spending in total domestic spending, and a public/private financing mix in all the countries shown.

So how might we explain the high level of government health spending? A possible explanation already introduced is market failure in health care.

Market failures in health care

Question

What do you think are likely to be the main market failures in health care? Look back at Sections 2.2 and 2.4 for some hints.

Health care markets are problematic in a number of ways. There are problems of consumer sovereignty – do we know what we are 'buying'? – and of risk – do we know when we will need to buy it? Unfortunately the answer to both questions is often, no. Medical knowledge is heavily, though not exclusively, concentrated in the medical professions. And however much we could and should be better informed about our health, it is hard to see how that semi-monopoly on information could be broken. The implication is that the health care market cannot be fully efficient: you will remember from Chapter 7 the importance of consumer knowledge to the efficient operation of competitive markets.

Furthermore, since we cannot be sure when we will need medical care, health care is best purchased through some form of insurance to spread risk. You have already encountered in Section 2 two of the main market failures in the health care insurance market. One is 'adverse selection'. Since the insurers do not have 'perfect information', high risk individuals may be able to represent themselves as lower risks than they are. If as a result low risk people are overcharged, they may drop out. Result, rising premiums and inefficient insurance.

The other problem is 'moral hazard': there are health conditions I can influence. I cited pregnancy above. Another illustration is a recent debate in Britain on whether persistent heavy smokers should receive publicly funded treatment for smoking-related illness. However, a further complication is that moral hazard can afflict doctors too. Where medical care is paid for on a fee-for-service basis and doctors determine the quantity and type of treatment, then doctors (and hospitals or clinics generally) have incentives to over-treat. Research shows that this is a factor in the rapid escalation of the unit costs of medical treatment, including higher medical incomes, which is evident in private insurance systems and particularly acute in the USA (Ham *et al.*, 1990). This is an important reason for the high US health care spending shown in Figure 23.9.

Given this level of market failure, there is an efficiency case for intervention, though previous chapters have contained warnings about assuming that governments can always do better than even flawed markets. Governments are unable to remove the information problems in health care: patients will continue to be poorly informed. What they can potentially do is to find regulatory or other methods to reduce incentives for cost escalation and over-provision. How they choose to try to do this in different countries depends in part on their approach to the other main motive for intervention: universalizing access.

Access to health care

Across the industrialized countries, governments have sought to widen access to medical care as incomes have risen. Newly industrialized countries such as South Korea are now pursuing the same goal. There are basically two ways in which this can be done: publicly financed universal health care access, funded either through taxation or social insurance schemes; or partial (income tested) funding for those on low incomes. These distinctions provide a rather different set of divisions among countries: the USA and the Netherlands both take the latter approach (though within very different regulatory frameworks) and had respectively 43 per cent and 73 per cent of their population covered by public schemes in 1987. The other countries in Figure 23.9 had over 90 per cent of their populations under public coverage of in-patient health care costs (OECD, 1990). When access to health care through private finance is put together with the public health finance, only the USA among these countries fails to achieve near-universal coverage.

5.2   Health care and redistribution: finance

To explore the redistributive effects of health care we need, as for the cash benefit system, to look at both who pays for and who benefits from care. This discussion draws on a study of a sample of OECD countries' data from the mid 1980s (Doorslaer *et al.*, 1993). On the finance side, the study asks the question: is the total system of health finance progressive or regressive? The study uses an index based on the Lorenz curve to answer the question. The principle is illustrated in Figure 23.10.

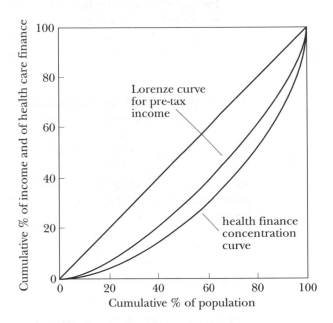

Figure 23.10   **Analysing the progressiveness of health care finance**

Source: based on Doorslaer and Wagstaff (1993) Figures 3.5 and 3.6

Figure 23.10 is the Lorenz curve diagram, with one addition. One of the curves – drawn here closer to the diagonal – is the familiar Lorenz curve for pre-tax income. The other curve is a health finance concentration curve. This plots the cumulative proportion of total health care finance (both public *and* private) paid by the population ranked by pre-tax income. Where the latter lies outside the former, then health care finance is progressive: lower income groups pay a lower proportion of their income for health care than higher income groups. Where the health finance concentration curve lies inside the Lorenz curve for pre-tax income, then finance is regressive: the burden falls relatively more heavily on the poor. If the two curves coincide, health finance is proportional.

The study concluded that only three countries in the study sample had even marginally progressive health care financing systems (the UK, Ireland and Portugal). Sweden was not studied, but Denmark's finance was mildly regressive. The most regressive health finance was in those countries with private funding-dominated systems (such as the USA), but France, where the dominant system is social insurance, also has quite regressive funding, as does the Netherlands. The largely tax-based UK financing, it is interesting to note, emerges as mildly progressive – despite the somewhat regressive tax system analysed in Section 3 – in part because of its small private insurance element. Additional private cover is concentrated among the better off. If those with higher incomes were allowed to opt out of the NHS into private insurance, the finance would be regressive.

5.3   Equity and redistribution in health spending

> ... the better off appear to receive more health care under the NHS relative to need than the less well off ... The NHS therefore, along with other systems of public health care, appears to favour the better off.
>
> *(Le Grand, 1982, pp.30–1)*
>
> Put together with the fact that so much health care expenditure is redistributive, from rich to poor and from healthy to sick, the spectre of rising costs presents a huge challenge to the current social equilibrium.
>
> *(Besley and Gouveia, 1994, p.248)*

If health finance tends to be regressive, is the effect countered by progressive health benefits? It is easy to become confused in trying to answer this question, because the literature contains two distinct standards – or baselines – against which we might measure health care benefits. The first quotation above, from a book on the social class distribution of public service benefits which generated much subsequent research, captures the most common frame of debate: it compares actual benefits to a standard of complete equality: equal treatment for equal need. The second quotation acknowledges an alternative, less researched question: how are benefits distributed relative to those which the poor could have purchased from their own income? It is the *second* of these questions which provides a parallel for the discussion of cash benefits in Section 3.

I will examine first some empirical answers to both questions. I will then go on to reflect upon why the terms of the research and debate have developed so differently for cash benefits and health benefits – and why that may be changing.

It is by now well established that *health* varies systematically with social class. Those on higher incomes enjoy on average better health and longer life expectancy. Furthermore, a narrower distribution of incomes, whether over time in one country, or cross-culturally, appears to be associated with narrower class differences in mortality (Wilkinson, 1994). The need for health care is therefore biased towards those on lower incomes, and we require a measure of equity in expenditure which recognizes this bias.

The comparative study cited above uses indices of morbidity (ill health) constructed from interview data in the sample countries. (Alternative indices were based on chronic health problems, limiting chronic illnesses, and on individuals' self assessment of their health.) These indices confirmed that the poor have worse health in all the sample countries, with the UK and the USA standing out as having particularly large health inequalities (Wagstaff and Doorslaer, 1993).

Why should lower income people gain less from universal access health care systems than the better off? One reason is that the opportunity costs of using the system – travel, time off work and resultant loss of income – all weigh most heavily on the poor. Other reasons include discrimination, and lack of information and confidence on the part of lower income users; these last are likely to be worse in more class-divided societies. Where insurance systems involve co-payments by individuals, these can prove a barrier for the poor. We might therefore expect a bias away from equal care for equal need.

Le Grand's study quoted above showed a bias towards the better off, who appeared to receive more care in relation to need. Some subsequent studies have failed to identify this bias, and the issue for the UK remains in dispute. The method used by the comparative study quoted above is to construct 'standardized expenditure figures' for each income group in each country. These figures show what the expenditure on each income group would have been if the group had had the morbidity and the age distribution of the population as a whole. If health care were equitable, each decile of the population would then get one tenth of the standardized expenditure, since the effects of differing need have been removed. If it is not equitable, we can draw one more cumulative curve, this time for standardized expenditure against population (Figure 23.11). The gap between the curve and the diagonal, as a proportion of the total area under the diagonal, measures the extent of pro-rich inequality of health care (Wagstaff and Doorslaer, 1993).

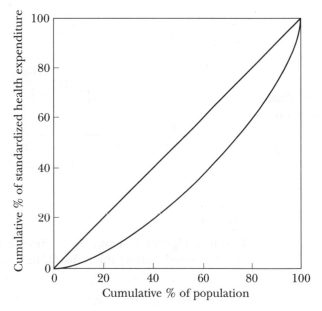

Figure 23.11 **A standardized expenditure concentration curve to measure health care inequality**

Source: based on Wagstaff and Doorslaer (1993) p.75

The results for the sample of countries turn out to be sensitive to the precise indicator of ill health used, and seem likely to understate bias against the poor, since the poor are more likely to have several conditions at once, and to receive poorer treatment once in the system. However – partly because of this problem – the conclusion that in the USA and the UK there is a bias towards the better off seems a robust one. In the other countries, the results are inconclusive.

Question

I have concluded above that the evidence shows, first, that UK health financing is marginally progressive, and second, that health spending has an anti-poor bias. What does this tell us about the over all redistributiveness of UK health care?

So far, we know that health care redistributes from healthy to ill, but not with complete equity in relation to need. But it still may be the case that the poor do considerably better than they would if they purchased health care from their cash incomes. There is much less research on this, but if we assume that health care is something people value – which seems reasonable, since they seek it – and if we are prepared to measure its value to them by its cost of provision – a much more debatable proposition – then we can examine the effects of in-kind benefits in exactly the same way as cash benefits. Figure 23.12 adds benefits in kind – largely health and education – received by each decile group of the population to the data displayed in Figure 23.4.

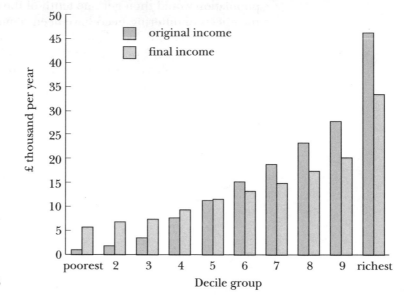

Figure 23.12   **Original and final average incomes of households by decile group, UK, 1991**

Source: *Economic Trends*, May 1993, adjusted following Hills (1993) p.85

Question

Compare Figures 23.4 and 23.12. How do benefits in kind – included in 'final income' – affect the redistributiveness of the UK tax/benefit system?

They increase it. The benefits in kind are an important addition to the standard of living of households in the lowest three deciles as compared to original income. Public expenditure on health, like education, is enormously redistributive in the rich-to-poor sense: as indeed one would expect if it is distributed anywhere close to equally in a deeply divided society.

5.4   Merit goods and redistribution

The conclusion that health care expenditure tends to be strongly redistributive can be generalized to most industrialized countries. Why have these societies and governments been willing to use health care in this way? The answer must partly lie, it seems, in the nature of health care itself. We seem generally to attach a strong value to universal health care access, presumably because health is key to people's capacity to be active citizens and consumers. The concept of merit goods (Section 2.4) captures some of this moral weight attached to health care. Le Grand, in a later discussion (1991a), points out that one reason why we are generally more concerned with equality of access to health than to, say, television is because illness is seen as largely beyond our control: a matter of need, not demand.

But then food is basic too, and we do not supply it in this way, preferring cash benefits for food expenditure. Le Grand is inclined to think we would be better to redistribute more in cash and less in kind, hence circumventing the middle class 'capture' of public services.

> ... what is being argued here, essentially, is that redistribution policy should concern itself less with subsidising services and more with 'subsidising' the poor – or rather acknowledging the poor's legitimate claim on a greater share of the nation's income or wealth.
>
> *(Le Grand, 1987, p.106)*

One argument for this reform might be that reducing poverty would reduce ill health, since the general standard of living has a very large impact on health outcomes. But would it work? One problem is that a shift away from socialized health care – social insurance or public provision – to private insurance would leave some people uninsured, because of the problems of insurance coverage explained above. Since there are strong efficiency reasons for socializing health insurance, as just explained, there are efficiency costs to privatizing access.

Exercise 23.4

One efficiency issue has yet to be discussed for health. Does socialized health insurance or public health care provision contribute to the poverty trap? How would privatizing access to health care affect it?

Furthermore, the shift would require both a very large rise in cash benefits relative to their current levels, and social acceptance of a situation where health care depended upon income, since people would be purchasing it. It is this latter effect which seems to contravene long established social values. Besley and Gouveia (1994, p.249) suggest that, 'The US social equilibrium has traditionally taken it for granted that the poor deserve less health care than the middle classes.' European governments and voters appear – judging by the outcome – to take the alternative view that health care should be close to egalitarian.

But equal provision is a very high standard to set in unequal societies. In countries characterized by strong inequalities of income and wealth, power and status – that is, most countries – we would expect markets *and* other economic institutions to reflect that inequality to some extent. If one looks, for example, at the setting up of the NHS in Britain, one can see its institutions as a form of social settlement among different interest groups, with its tax-financed structure no doubt being influenced by the absence at the time of a lobby of strong private medical insurers and its universal scope being achieved in part by a favourable financial settlement for the powerful medical consultants' lobby. Furthermore, if we apply 'Director's law' (Section 4.1) to health care finance, then we would expect the settlement to suit those on middle incomes.

In this context it is impressive how redistributive health care has become. The combination of the efficiency and risk-reducing benefits of social insurance, the cost advantages of government regulation or provision, and the social commitment to universal access has made it one of the most redistributive activities in industrialized countries. Furthermore, the social insurance approach (including inclusive tax-financed systems) is – as for cash redistribution – markedly more redistributive in cross-national comparisons than health care systems such as the US which target public benefits on the poor alone (Besley and Gouveia, 1994).

Challenges to the social insurance approach to health care are emerging, as an earlier quotation suggested, precisely because of its redistributiveness in a period of perceived fiscal pressure. It seems highly unlikely that willingness to undertake cash redistribution is as great. Because of this patterning in attitudes, inclusive health care may be one of the most durable forms of redistribution.

6   Assets and institutions: problems of wealth redistribution

The chapter so far has largely been about redistribution starting from the primary income distribution. It has shown that redistribution of income – in cash and kind – is extensive, and in industrialized countries largely occurs through the benefit system and the big public services. Not all of this redistribution by any means is between well-off and poor, in the sense of persisting social classes, much being redistribution across people's own lifetimes. And much 'welfare' spending goes to the middle classes. The extent to which all this activity reduces poverty varies greatly, and furthermore, there are limits to cash redistribution imposed by the impact on economic incentives.

6.1   Primary income and the distribution of wealth

An alternative to this type of redistribution is to try to change the primary income distribution itself.

Question

How can a country's primary income distribution be changed? To help you to think about this, look back at Section 3.1.

The primary income distribution is generated by factor markets and asset-ownership. 'Assets' in this statement refer to the stock of land, productive capital, invested financial assets and human capital. Chapter 22 noted that inequalities generated in the wage labour market can be traced back in part to inequalities in human capital, and Chapter 12 suggested that differences in economic success between countries can be traced partly to the same roots.

Shifts in asset ownership therefore greatly influence primary incomes. *Which* assets matter depends on the level of economic development. At low levels of industrialization, land ownership is key. In England and Wales in the later seventeenth century, land accounted for nearly half of household wealth; by the 1970s the proportion was below 5 per cent (Smith, 1993). As industrialization proceeds, the pattern of equity ownership, the pattern of self employment, and the extent and spread of education and training become increasingly important determinants both of average incomes and of their distribution.

The distribution of assets is hard to measure because data are often not required for tax purposes, and because information about the *wealthy* is always hard to come by. In industrialized countries, data on asset ownership distinguish marketable wealth – including portfolios of financial assets and housing – and a broader definition of assets including the value of occupational pensions. Financial assets are strongly concentrated in the higher income deciles: in the UK in 1991/92 over half of households had non-pension financial assets of £455 or less, and financial asset holdings only rose sharply for households with incomes over £25 000 per year. Pension and housing wealth however is spread more widely. The Inland Revenue calculates that the wealthiest 5 per cent own 37 per cent of the marketable wealth, and 30 per cent of wealth including occupational pensions (Banks *et al.*, 1994). By 1991, 73 per cent of employees in the UK had some non-state pension rights, and the spread of occupational and private pension schemes – which held 32 per cent of total stock market equities – had made the financial markets a matter of concern for a majority of households (Dilnot *et al.*, 1994).

Over the twentieth century, the distribution of these categories of assets has tended to become more equal in industrialized countries. Estimates suggest that for England and Wales the concentration of household wealth peaked early in the century, with 87 per cent held by the wealthiest 5 per cent, and that concentration then fell steadily until the 1980s, though it seems possible that the long-term trend has now been reversed.

Definition

Wealth

An individual's wealth is the present value of their expected real lifetime income.

While the discussion so far has used 'assets' and 'wealth' interchangeably, economic theory considers wealth not so much in terms of identifiable assets, but rather in terms of the capacity to generate income, as the definition shows. The concept of the present value of future income is explained in Chapter 27, along with the associated concept of discounting. The fundamental idea is that income in the future is generally worth less to people than income now. Hence, income expected in the future needs to be discounted – reduced in value – to allow for this positive time preference (Chapter 11). The resultant value in the present of an individual's income is then their wealth – what they are 'worth'.

Defining wealth in this way points up the importance of human capital (see Chapter 21, Section 2.4), which is omitted from wealth statistics since it is so hard to measure. Since people are not – or should not be – bought and sold, there is no direct measure of their 'worth', and future incomes are subject to uncertainty, though they can be estimated. Expected future incomes depend on several kinds of variables: original endowments of assets (at birth); subsequent accumulation through savings and investment in human or physical capital (partly a matter of choice and temperament); and luck. Luck is quite clearly a factor: two largely identical individuals making similar choices can have very different fates. As two public sector economists put it (Atkinson and Stiglitz, 1987, p.267): 'Some people work for a firm that goes bankrupt; other people invest early in Rank Xerox'. Rank Xerox is a classic example of a firm whose share prices took off as a result of an innovation, in this case the plain paper copier; early investors did well.

So measured asset distribution at any moment in time is only an imperfect indicator of wealth distribution. It omits human capital, and how people use their assets. Despite the data problems, however, it is not hard to establish that countries which have highly inegalitarian asset distributions generally also have highly inegalitarian income distributions.

One explanation links inequality to industrialization. Industrialization is expected to be associated at first, as in Britain, with rising inequality in both senses. The industrialization process is expected to be patchy and economically disruptive, generating wide divisions between new entrepreneurial incomes and new low wage employment. Later, broadening participation in industrial labour markets and rising mass consumption – underpinned by social security programmes and public investment – will exert an equalizing force.

A comparison between industrializing countries suggests, however, that that story is too simple. Consider Latin American industrializers, such as Brazil or Mexico, on the one hand, and East Asian industrializers such as Taiwan or South Korea on the other. Table 1.2 in Chapter 1 compared the income distributions of Brazil and South Korea, on the basis of the share of the richest and the poorest groups. And Section 4.1 of Chapter 1 used the example of the Amazon basin deforestation to illustrate how highly unequal societies, with a high concentration of wealth and power, tend to reproduce those inequalities as they develop.

Reflection

Have a look back at that case study of Brazil before you read on.

Now contrast the story told there with a number of aspects of South Korean development. South Korea has, like Brazil, had a repressive government over long periods of its industrialization, which suppressed much dissent, repressed labour organization and provided until recently very little 'welfare' such as health care and social security. However, assets have been much more evenly distributed in South Korea than in Brazil. In particular, human capital has been spread widely through South Korean society by extensive education and training. And a land reform after the Second World War broke up large land holdings, and established widespread smaller scale land ownership.

On this foundation, South Korea built a labour intensive industrialization path which has expanded access to wage incomes. As industrialization proceeded, high levels of training and education allowed productivity and wages to rise. The outcome is, not egalitarian, but far less unequal than Brazil. A similar story can be told about Taiwan, another rapid industrializer in East Asia. Again, the underpinning of *relatively* egalitarian growth was a highly redistributive land reform undertaken in the aftermath of the Second World War and the Chinese revolution (which brought the Nationalists, and the Americans, to Taiwan), and widespread education and training (Wade, 1990).

Two lessons can be drawn from this comparison. One is about a possible 'trade-off' between efficiency and equity. The discussion of responses to economic incentives suggested that income redistribution can have economic costs – though there may also be benefits, such as better health. The East Asian story suggested that *asset* redistribution may have a number of dynamic efficiency *benefits*: that over time, there may not be a trade-off at all.

The other lesson is about the extreme conditions which may be necessary to achieve rapid asset redistribution of an egalitarian sort.

6.2 Asset redistribution

The land reforms in both the cases cited above were undertaken in the aftermath of war, and under pressure from a foreign power – the USA. In both cases, they were politically motivated, aiming to break up old power blocks. The effect was to drive the elite into a search for new power bases, in industry and government, and to create a basis for later industrialization. But these land reforms are special. Only a few major land reforms have been achieved in recent history, and these have generally been associated with intense political upheaval: collectivization in China for example. It generally takes an unusual mixture of crisis and political ruthlessness to push through a major asset redistribution such as a land reform.

The earlier discussion of motives for redistribution might suggest that this is a puzzle. In highly inegalitarian countries, the asset-less are in the large majority. So why is drastic asset redistribution so unusual? There are a number of possible answers, and they are all about power and the resistance of institutions to change. Asset ownership is generally associated with power and influence, and radical reforming governments are often 'tamed' in office by accommodations with powerful interests. Furthermore, the level of inequality in a society influences people's ideas about what is acceptable: ideas and experience are not independent. In effect, the primary distribution of income emerges from the basic structures of society: its ownership patterns and employment structures. And these basic structures are hard to manipulate as circumstances change.

Partly as a result, wealth taxation has been relatively unusual in industrialized countries, though inheritance tax in the UK contributed to the break up of large landed estates. The main wealth taxes in OECD countries have been property taxes, individual and corporate taxes on net wealth, and estate, inheritance and gift taxes. Their share of total tax revenue for OECD countries varied in the late 1980s between 10–11 per cent in the UK and the USA (because of the importance of local property taxes) to 1–2 per cent in West Germany and Sweden (Smith, 1993, p.101). The long-term trend to greater equality of wealth in the UK post-1945 has been more the result of pensions schemes and spreading education and skills than of wealth taxation.

A tentative conclusion seems to be that – except in periods of acute upheaval – institutional reforms which spread new assets in an inclusive fashion are more likely to 'stick' than attempts at direct asset redistribution. Examples might be pensions schemes in the private sector and, more controversially, 'social capital' accumulated by people in public sector pension rights. In the 1970s, the UK Royal Commission on Income and Wealth considered state pension rights as an asset. de Swaan, quoted earlier in this chapter, also sees state pensions as part of people's 'social capital'.

Adding the value of state pension rights to other assets makes asset distribution appear more equal. The reversal of commitments to state pension provision in the face of fiscal pressures has, however, reduced the estimated value and reliability of such social capital as an element of assets.

7   Conclusion

The central message of this chapter is the close link between values, institutions and the distributions of incomes and wealth. The distribution of wealth is deeply embedded in the institutions of a society, and – though it changes massively over long periods – is hard to change suddenly by policy intervention. The primary income distribution, generated by a society's assets and economic activity, is redistributed through institutions – public services and tax and benefit systems – which also have histories. Furthermore, in unequal societies, redistributive institutions are probably easier to destroy than to build and sharp wealth redistributions (and hence income redistributions) generally emerge from violent upheaval. These may be egalitarian shifts: 'under such conditions anyone's future might be your own' (Goodin and Dryzek, 1987, p.66). However, such upheavals can also create redistribution in a highly inegalitarian direction – as may be happening in parts of Eastern Europe – and the implication of this chapter is that those new distributions too, once 'set', will be slow to change.

PART 14

CHAPTER 24

by Graham Dawson

MACROECONOMICS AND ECONOMIC CHANGE
UNEMPLOYMENT AND INFLATION

1   Introduction

In the late 1970s and early 1980s, policy makers throughout the large OECD economies abandoned the goal of full employment which had guided macroeconomic policy throughout the 1950s and 1960s and made their first priority the elimination of inflation. They did so because they believed that inflation does more damage to the economy than unemployment.

The UK economy since 1979 has been a test case for this change of policy because it has undergone what are probably the two most severe disinflations among the large OECD economies. Among the G7 economies only Italy had a worse inflation record in the 1970s. Yet by 1993 the UK inflation rate was below Germany's, a more dramatic turnaround than any other European nation, or the USA or Japan, has experienced.

But the fall in inflation has been accompanied throughout OECD economies by recession and a rise in unemployment. This raises the central questions of this chapter. Do policy makers face a trade-off between unemployment and inflation? To put it another way, is higher unemployment the price that has to be paid to get inflation down? And, if it is, is it a price worth paying? The former UK Chancellor of the Exchequer Norman Lamont was in no doubt about the answers.

> Rising unemployment and the recession have been the price we have had to pay in order to get inflation down – but that is a price well worth paying.
>
> *(House of Commons, 16 May 1991)*

Apart from acknowledging that disinflation is far from painless, Lamont was implicitly retreating from the much more audacious claim put forward by one of his Thatcherite predecessors, Geoffrey Howe, almost exactly ten years earlier.

> Some people think we can choose between inflation and unemployment. Let inflation rise a bit they say to get unemployment down. But it doesn't work like that. The two go together. Higher inflation means higher unemployment. It's like an addictive drug, the more you get the more you need and the more damage it does to you.
>
> *(Budget broadcast, 10 March 1981)*

What Howe seemed to be saying was that inflation causes unemployment. It is not, on this view, a question of tolerating higher unemployment for the sake of lower inflation. Unemployment does not rise when inflation falls: 'the two go together'. What is more, unemployment rises as a consequence of earlier inflation. So here is the strongest possible case for trying to eliminate inflation – that it is also the way to achieve reduced unemployment.

The principal aim of this chapter is to try to clarify the relationships between unemployment and inflation which constrain macroeconomic policy. I start by asking which is the more serious problem – inflation or unemployment? What exactly *is* the price that is paid when unemployment is high – and who pays it? Why does getting inflation down matter? So Section 2 assesses the costs of unemployment and inflation in an attempt to decide which is the more serious problem.

Next, I turn to the difference of view between Howe and Lamont: is there a trade-off between unemployment and inflation or does inflation cause unemployment? Until the early 1970s there was general, if not quite universal agreement among most macroeconomists and policy makers that there was an inverse relationship between unemployment and inflation. This view, developed originally by the economist A.W. Phillips in the 1950s, is explained in Section 3. However, a handful of dissidents such as Friedman (1968) argued that the observed trade-off was no more than a statistical association between low unemployment and high inflation which would collapse if policy-makers attempted to exploit it. As the 1970s wore on and inflation rose without any reduction in unemployment, many economists came to believe that Friedman had been vindicated. Friedman's theory, which introduces the concept of inflationary expectations, and its development into the 'rational expectations' hypothesis form the subject matter of Section 4.

The current position is that the '1960s orthodoxy' has developed into New Keynesianism, according to which there does exist a trade-off between inflation and unemployment, albeit only in the short run, while Friedman's critique has been developed into the competitive or New Classical approach. In an extreme form, the competitive approach argues that there may be no trade-off even in the short run. The differences between these schools of thought were explained by Mary Gregory in Chapter 18, where she traced their implications for unemployment by examining the New Classical natural rate of unemployment and the New Keynesian NAIRU. Here I develop, in Sections 5 and 6, an alternative perspective on both the natural rate approach and the NAIRU which interprets unemployment and inflation as manifestations of social conflict over the distribution of income.

2   The costs of unemployment versus the costs of inflation

2.1   The costs of unemployment

Let me give the first words on the costs of unemployment to some unemployed people interviewed as part of a research project (Dawson, 1992). 'I received ten minutes' notice on being made redundant.' Initially unemployment can feel like liberation: 'I felt better – money in the bank – less tired – plenty of fresh air – an opportunity to do things with my life without the frustrations and claustrophobia of factory life.' But a couple of years on it can be a different story: 'depressed and insecure, no success in finding even part-time work to supplement savings.' 'Yes, whenever I get a sufficient amount or come into money I spend it fast, mostly on drink. I seem to panic when I have money to spend.' 'To survive this unwanted gap in one's life one has to be drunk or half-crazy most of the time it seems.' 'I feel like an autistic child in relation to other working folk.'

For many people, those words may be enough to imply that full employment is the only objective of macroeconomic policy worth pursuing. Would policy makers not do better to listen to some of the victims of their policies than to peruse another table of economic statistics? Perhaps it is an unjust response when confronted with observed injustice to a minority – the people who are unemployed – to look for evidence that unemployment also adversely affects the well-being of the rest of society. But, since there *are* economic statistics which highlight the damage unemployment does to the economy as a whole, it is important to look at them as part of a complete picture of the problem.

The principal cost which unemployment imposes on society as a whole is the loss of output which would have been produced if resources had been fully employed. The simplest approach to measuring this output loss is to assume that everyone who is out of work would, if found a job, produce as much as the average person already in employment. But unemployed people tend to be less skilled than the labour force as a whole, so that, other things being equal, the average product method may exaggerate the scale of output loss.

On the other hand, there are reasons why the average product method might underestimate the output loss. When recorded unemployment rises, other symptoms of spare capacity emerge. Part-time work falls (without adding to the officially recorded unemployment figures) and so too does overtime working. There is usually a decline in the participation rate, the percentage of the population of working age who declare themselves to be part of the labour force by seeking work, because the poor prospects of finding a job discourage people from trying. An increase in hidden unemployment occurs, when firms 'hoard' labour even though there is nothing for the workers concerned to do.

A more promising approach, introduced in Chapter 17, is therefore to extrapolate the trend rate of output growth under full employment through the years of unemployment, and to measure the 'output gap', the amount by which actual output during the years of high unemployment falls short of full employment output. Using an output gap method, Okun concluded that 'a reduction in unemployment ... has a much larger than proportionate effect on output' (Okun, 1970, p.140). Okun's method takes into account the hidden spare capacity associated with recorded unemployment. The estimates of the output loss using this method depend upon the level of unemployment chosen as an approximation to feasible full employment. The results of Okun's approach to measuring the 'output gap' used in an EC research study are shown in Table 24.1. The low and high estimates are made by comparing output in the early 1980s with output during two earlier periods of relatively low unemployment which act as feasible approximations to full employment. The low average unemployment of the years 1968–73, before the first oil price shock, yields a high estimate of output loss, while the higher average unemployment of 1974–79 yields a low estimate.

Table 24.1 **Output loss estimates (% of GDP)**

	Germany		France		Italy		UK	
	low	**high**	**low**	**high**	**low**	**high**	**low**	**high**
1980	—	6.7	6.1	13.3	3.4	6.8	3.0	6.5
1981	3.0	10.3	9.6	16.7	7.1	10.4	9.5	13.1
1982	8.0	16.0	12.0	19.1	9.5	12.8	12.3	15.8
1983	13.4	20.6	14.1	21.2	13.5	16.8	13.7	17.2

Source: Junankar (1985) Tables 4.10–4.13, pp.40–1

Clearly, the cumulative output costs of unemployment are substantial. For example, by 1983 the output of the German economy was (on the high estimate) a fifth lower than it would have been if the economy had been running at full capacity. For all four economies, by 1983 the output gap had reached more than 10 per cent, or, in other words, each economy produced 10 per cent less output than it was capable of producing at full employment. Nevertheless, you might feel that the loss of goods that might have been produced but were not and never will be is a somewhat intangible, hypothetical deprivation. But this loss of potential output has serious effects on people's well-being. In the circular flow model of the economy, output equals income (Chapter 2). So in principle every member of the labour force (and their dependants) may bear some of the output costs of unemployment in the form of a reduction in income. People's incomes are lower on average than they would be if there were full employment. The *incidence* of output loss, or the impact of unemployment on the distribution of income, depends in part upon the extent to which social security benefits compensate unemployed people for the loss of earned income.

The fiscal cost of unemployment represents that part of the incidence of output loss which is in principle placed on taxpayers. For most OECD economies, each one per cent increase in unemployment raises the amount paid out in unemployment benefit by 0.2 or 0.3 per cent of GDP (see Chapter 17, Table 17.4). Then there is the loss of income tax revenue when people lose their jobs. However, the government could decide to offset some of the distributional impact of the output loss by allowing the automatic stabilizers to operate unhindered (see Chapter 17). The rise in unemployment in the early 1990s did in fact lead to a deterioration in the public finances of many OECD countries.

This leaves most of the output loss to fall on unemployed people. It is not easy to generalize about the degree of financial hardship imposed on unemployed people and their families, because national benefit systems vary, in terms of both the 'replacement ratio' – unemployment benefits as a percentage of previous earnings – and conditions of eligibility. In the USA during the 1980s, for example, married couples where the previously employed partner was paid close to average US earnings, were likely to face a replacement ratio somewhere between 45 per cent and 66 per cent. For the UK most unemployed people – single or married couples with no children – were looking at replacement ratios of less than 60 per cent unless earnings when last in work had been very low. The only group likely to be 'better off on the dole' comprised married couples with four or more children previously on less than half average male manual earnings (about four per cent of unemployed people came into this category). A replacement ratio as high as 80 per cent still means the loss of a fifth of income from work, typically from an already low income. So unemployment has a severely regressive effect on the distribution of income.

The further effects of unemployment are less susceptible of investigation and quantification by the standard methods of economics. Still, it is clear that many unemployed people and their families experience a deterioration in their psychological well-being, ranging from anxiety and boredom to severe depression and despair. Even if the majority of unemployed people are still able to get a lot out of life, this may mean, not that unemployment is only a trivial setback, but that considerable moral strength has been invested in coming to terms with a major crisis. There is a greater incidence of physical ill-health among unemployed people, although the degree to which this reflects a previous record of poor health continues to be a matter of academic dispute.

The question of a link between unemployment and crime is a controversial one. What *can* be said is that joblessness is a significant factor in explaining criminal behaviour among young single men with a prior disposition to criminal activity. The collapse in the demand for unskilled male labour throughout industrial countries over the last twenty years or so has led some young men in urban areas to leave the regular labour market altogether and make a living from illegal activities such as dealing in drugs.

There is no doubt that unemployment seriously damages the health of the economy and the well-being of unemployed people. But governments in many industrial nations seem to believe that inflation carries an even more alarming health warning. What are the economic arguments for this position?

2.2   The costs of inflation

> We are committed to achieving price stability because it is a necessary precondition for the sustainable growth of output and employment. ... Sound money – price stability – is about jobs and investment; it is about living and welfare standards.
>
> *(Eddie George, Bank of England, August 1993)*

This statement of the benefits of price stability, the gains from eliminating inflation, implies that the costs of inflation are slow output growth and hence unemployment and low living standards. Eddie George, Governor of the Bank of England, is typical of many policy-makers throughout the industrial world who see price stability as the key to long term economic growth and prosperity. In this section, I am going to set out the arguments underlying this view and then present some evidence on the link, if there is one, between inflation and output growth.

The most influential argument for the belief that inflation inhibits economic growth is called the inflationary noise argument and it states that without price stability markets cannot allocate resources efficiently. According to *The Economist*, 'the best inflation rate … means zero because anything higher interferes with the fundamental function of prices – their ability to provide information about relative scarcities' (February 22, 1992). Inflation distorts the transmission of price signals, so it is said to resemble the 'noise' or background interference which distorts the transmission of radio signals. If you think back to Chapter 7 on perfect competition, you will recall that changes in the conditions of supply and demand – changes in the relative scarcity of resources and in the relative popularity of products – cause price changes which act as signals to consumers and producers.

This is where the inflationary 'noise' comes in. Friedman (1977) argued that as inflation rises so does its volatility, with the consequence that 'an additional element of uncertainty is, as it were, added to every market transaction' (p.466). Economic agents might confuse a price rise that is merely part of the general inflationary background with a price rise that signals a real change in relative scarcity. For example, suppose that a firm buying copper as input to a production process observes a price rise in a highly inflationary environment. If the price rise genuinely signals a change in relative scarcity but the firm dismisses it as 'noisy', it will waste this newly scarce material. If, on the other hand, the price rise is purely inflationary or noisy but the firm misinterprets it as a scarcity signal, it will incur extra costs in needlessly economizing on copper, perhaps by searching for a substitute or a possible alternative supply.

The implication is that high inflation, by undermining static allocative efficiency, should also slow down economic growth. Hence we can evaluate the inflationary noise argument by asking a fairly straightforward factual question: Is high inflation positively associated with low economic growth? Stanners (1993) undertook a particularly careful survey of the evidence, some of which is reproduced in Table 24.2.

Table 24.2   **Inflation and GNP growth in 44 countries, 1980–88**

	Ordered by:				
	Increasing inflation			**Decreasing growth**	
country	inflation (% pa)	growth (% pa)	country	inflation (% pa)	growth (% pa)
Japan	1.3	4.0	Thailand	3.0	6.8
Netherlands	2.3	1.3	Pakistan	6.9	6.3
Germany	2.8	1.7	Turkey	40.5	5.4
Thailand	3.0	6.8	Indonesia	9.4	5.2
Austria	4.0	1.8	Morocco	7.5	4.7
USA	4.2	3.2	Kenya	9.7	4.2

Table 24.2   **Inflation and GNP growth in 44 countries, 1980–88 (continued)**

	Ordered by:				
	Increasing inflation			**Decreasing growth**	
country	inflation (% pa)	growth (% pa)	country	inflation (% pa)	growth (% pa)
Belgium	4.6	1.4	Japan	1.3	4.0
Canada	5.1	3.4	Tunisia	8.2	3.4
UK	6.1	2.7	Canada	5.1	3.4
Norway	6.2	3.2	Colombia	24.4	3.3
Denmark	6.6	1.9	Finland	7.4	3.2
Average	*4.2*	*2.9*	*Average*	*11.2*	*4.5*
Pakistan	6.9	6.3	Norway	6.2	3.2
France	7.1	1.9	USA	4.2	3.2
Finland	7.4	3.2	Australia	8.1	3.2
Sweden	7.5	2.1	Israel	116.0	3.1
Morocco	7.5	4.7	UK	6.1	2.7
Australia	8.1	3.2	Spain	9.9	2.6
Ireland	8.2	2.5	Paraguay	22.2	2.6
Tunisia	8.2	3.4	Ireland	8.2	2.5
Indonesia	9.4	5.2	Ecuador	31.0	2.5
Kenya	9.7	4.2	Portugal	18.9	2.2
Spain	9.9	2.6	Italy	11.3	2.1
Average	*8.2*	*3.6*	*Average*	*22.0*	*2.7*
Italy	11.3	2.1	Sweden	7.5	2.1
New Zealand	11.5	1.9	Brazil	198.8	2.1
Nigeria	12.1	1.2	Denmark	6.6	1.9
Guatemala	12.5	0.1	France	7.1	1.9
Philippines	13.9	1.2	Costa Rica	28.4	1.9
South Africa	14.1	1.5	Peru	82.1	1.9
El Salvador	15.7	−0.7	New Zealand	11.5	1.9
Syria	15.8	1.2	Austria	4.0	1.8
Venezuela	16.1	1.2	Germany	2.8	1.7
Greece	18.5	1.4	South Africa	14.1	1.5
Portugal	18.9	2.2	Belgium	4.6	1.4
Average	*14.6*	*1.2*	*Average*	*33.4*	*1.8*
Paraguay	22.2	2.6	Greece	18.5	1.4
Columbia	24.4	3.3	Netherlands	2.3	1.3
Zambia	27.1	1.0	Nigeria	12.1	1.2

Table 24.2   **Inflation and GNP growth in 44 countries, 1980–88 (continued)**

	Increasing inflation			Decreasing growth	
country	**inflation (% pa)**	**growth (% pa)**	**country**	**inflation (% pa)**	**growth (% pa)**
Costa Rica	28.4	1.9	Venezuela	16.1	1.2
Ecuador	31.0	2.5	Philippines	13.9	1.2
Turkey	40.5	5.4	Syria	15.8	1.2
Uruguay	53.9	−0.2	Zambia	27.1	1.0
Mexico	73.5	1.0	Mexico	73.5	1.0
Peru	82.1	1.9	Guatemala	12.5	0.1
Israel	116.0	3.1	Uruguay	53.9	−0.2
Brazil	198.8	2.1	El Salvador	15.7	−0.7
Average	*63.4*	*2.2*	*Average*	*23.8*	*0.8*

Source: Stanners (1993) Table 1, p.82

I have set out these data in detail so that you can look at the variability of inflation and growth experience internationally. Table 24.2 shows average inflation and growth in 44 countries for 1980–88. Figure 24.1 plots average inflation against average growth rates for a longer period for nine OECD countries.

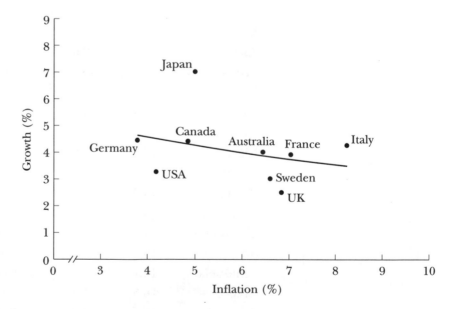

Figure 24.1   **Inflation and GNP growth, nine countries, 1950–87**

Source: Stanners (1993) Figure 4, p.85

Question

Does the evidence assembled in Table 24.2 suggest that low inflation is a necessary precondition for high economic growth?

The answer seems to be no. The countries in the very low inflation group headed by Japan have an average inflation rate of 4.2 per cent, and exhibit an average growth rate of 2.9 per cent, which is actually lower than the 3.6 per cent achieved by the next group with an average inflation rate of 8.2 per cent. True, growth falls to 1.2 per cent for the next group as inflation rises to 14.6 per cent. The position is reversed however for the next group which combines the highest average inflation rate of 63.4 per cent with growth rates which average 2.2 per cent. Conversely, while the highest growth group do have the lowest average inflation, the dispersion within that and the other groups is considerable. Finally, the dispersion of the points in Figure 24.1 is such as to make the 'best fit' line unreliable. Stanners concludes from a statistical exploration of his data that the evidence does not support the argument that low inflation, let alone price stability, is a necessary precondition for high economic growth.

Perhaps the explanation of the inflationary noise argument's failure to survive this confrontation with the evidence lies in its unwarranted assumption that price changes are the only source of information about relative scarcities available to economic agents. The rational firm is hardly likely to interpret a price rise as a signal of increased demand unless it is confirmed by other aspects of its specialist knowledge of its own market, such as an unusually rapid depletion of its stocks of finished products.

Economists have identified several other possible costs of inflation. The declining competitiveness of UK manufacturing industry has sometimes been explained as the consequence of relative inflation, that is, a higher inflation rate in the UK than in other industrial countries. It is worth noticing at once that, unlike inflationary noise, this is not even in principle an argument for achieving price stability throughout the industrial world. At most, the international competitiveness argument establishes that it is desirable for a high inflation economy with a deteriorating trade performance to disinflate in order to undercut the average inflation rate of its industrial competitors. The UK appeared to be in this position as its share of world exports of manufactured goods fell from 20 per cent in 1954 to 9 per cent twenty years later while its inflation rate was higher than those of its main industrial competitors. However, more recent developments have left the international competitiveness argument looking rather unpersuasive.

Question

Look back at Paul Auerbach's discussion of international competitiveness in Chapter 12, in particular his comments on Figures 12.7 and 12.8. Does that discussion support the argument that a loss of international competitiveness is one of the costs, or adverse effects, of inflation?

I think two points made in Chapter 12 are worth recalling. First, the UK's improved export cost competitiveness in the 1980s and early 1990s was not reflected in a better balance of trade record, while Japan and Germany combined trade surpluses with a deterioration in measured competitiveness. Second, the explanation is probably that non-price factors such as design quality, delivery dates, after-sales service and product reliability are at least as important as price in determining international competitiveness.

You have already encountered the concept at the heart of the next argument for eliminating inflation: menu costs. Mary Gregory discussed them in connection with New Keynesianism in Chapter 18, Section 2.2. The menu costs of inflation are the resources used in revising not only menus, of course, but catalogues, price tags, vending machines and so on. Efforts to quantify the menu costs of inflation have produced low figures. One estimate puts the menu costs of an annual UK inflation rate of 20 per cent at no more than 0.1 per cent of GDP (Minford and Hilliard, 1978). The menu costs of inflation at the rates experienced in the major industrial economies over the years since the second world war seem to be much too low to make any contribution to justifying a policy goal of price stability.

Let us turn from the possible output costs of inflation to its redistributive effects. Unemployment has an unequivocally regressive effect on the distribution of income. Is the same true of inflation? The picture is quite complicated because there are several different routes along which the inflationary process might affect income distribution, making some individuals or groups better off while making others worse off. As you will see in Section 5.2 below, redistributive effects play a role in partisan theories of macroeconomic policy making. In class terms, inflation tends to redistribute income away from the capitalist class towards the working class. If rising wage awards are driving inflation, then inflation increases the share of wages in national income at the expense of profits. Inflation also erodes the value of non-indexed financial assets which are disproportionately held by the upper middle class. So inflation can have a progressive impact on income distribution.

J. M. Keynes on inflation and unemployment

Cartoon by BIF from Peter Pugh and Chris Garratt, *Keynes for Beginners*, Icon Books Limited, 1993

On the other hand, many more people are now affected by financial asset values because of the spread of pensions schemes. And inflation can undermine the living standards of low income groups relying on state benefits. In many economies, social security benefits such as unemployment benefit and old age pensions are indexed to rise with inflation. However, if such benefits are tied to the consumer price index when average wages are rising more rapidly, pensioners and other recipients will experience a decline in their standard of living relative to that of the employed population. It is important to notice that the problem here is not inflation but the choice of method of indexation.

There do not seem to be any thoroughly convincing grounds for believing that moderate inflation causes serious damage to the economy or disturbs the distribution of income in unequivocally undesirable ways. The case against 'learning to live with moderate inflation' ultimately rests upon the fear that it might accelerate into hyperinflation, which undeniably plunges the economy into chaos. Perhaps policy makers are risk averse, trading off recession now against the chance, however remote, of total economic collapse some time in the future. The problem is that, for people who lose their jobs or cannot find work in the first place, recession now is hard to distinguish from economic collapse.

Learning to live with hyperinflation? In the German hyperinflation of 1923, the mark lost so much value that it was cheaper to paper walls with it than to buy wallpaper

3   Inflation, unemployment and expectations

3.1   The Phillips curve

Definition

The Phillips curve

The Phillips curve is a graph showing a trade-off between unemployment and inflation: the lower the rate of unemployment, the higher the rate of inflation.

The fundamental dilemma confronting economic policy makers is whether government intervention in the economy will improve its performance or make things worse. Whatever the area of economic policy under consideration, there is no escape from the disturbing thought that any policy intervention itself might do more harm than good. The idea of a trade-off between unemployment and inflation is directly relevant to this dilemma in the macroeconomic field. This trade-off, expressed in the Phillips curve analysis outlined below, was developed in the 1960s into a guide for policy makers whose main objective was full employment: 'one could achieve and maintain a permanently low level of unemployment merely by tolerating a permanently high level of inflation' (Mankiw, 1990, p.1647). Since the late 1970s, however, economic policy in industrial countries has been dominated by the belief that policy intervention based on the assumption of a trade-off between unemployment and inflation will only make things worse – adding to inflation without bringing unemployment down.

The main aim of this section is therefore to examine the question whether there is a trade-off between unemployment and inflation which can be exploited by policy-makers. There is however another, more theoretical, aim informing this section. In Chapters 17–19 you were introduced to a theoretical framework for analysing macroeconomic issues and policies which uses the concepts of aggregate demand and aggregate supply. On reading this section you may wonder how the Phillips curve relates to *AD/AS* analysis. After introducing the Phillips curve, I will therefore 'translate' it as it were, into the language of *AD/AS* analysis.

The logical first step in answering the question whether there is a trade-off between unemployment and inflation is to inspect the annual rates of inflation and unemployment over a reasonably long period of time and see if unemployment comes down when inflation goes up and vice versa. This is almost exactly what Phillips (1958) did for the British economy, initially for the period from 1861 to 1913. I said *almost* exactly because, while we think of inflation as a rise in the general level of *prices*, Philips plotted the rate of

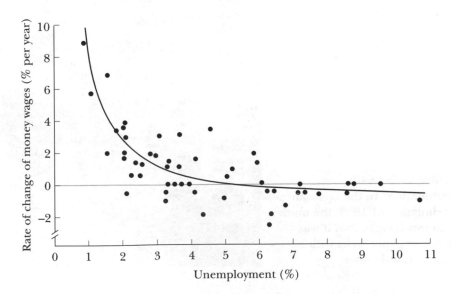

Figure 24.2 **The original Phillips curve for the British economy, 1861–1913**

Source: Phillips (1958)

wage inflation against the unemployment rate. The result was quite a good fit for an initially steep curve becoming gradually flatter (Figure 24.2). The same curve fitted the data for the years 1948–57 almost as well, suggesting that there was indeed a trade-off between unemployment and inflation over the last hundred years.

The next question is, what does this empirical relationship mean? How is it to be explained? The interpretation offered by Phillips is an application of supply and demand analysis to the labour market. Suppose initially that wages are stable (the rate of wage inflation is zero) and the labour market is in equilibrium. If the demand for labour falls, unemployment above equilibrium in the form of an excess supply of labour drives down its 'market price' or, in other words, leads to fall in the general level of wages. If instead the demand for labour rises, excess labour demand brings unemployment below its equilibrium level and initiates wage rises.

Phillips' (1958) paper stimulated further research into the relation between unemployment and inflation. Price inflation as distinct from wage inflation was also found to be negatively correlated with unemployment and it became customary to think of the Phillips trade-off in these terms. This was more useful for policy-makers because unemployment and (price) inflation were in the 1960s, as in the 1990s, two of the central macroeconomic problems they faced. The Phillips curve now presented policy-makers with a range of options from which to choose the optimal, or least undesirable, combination of inflation and unemployment. For example, the inflation rate that would have to be tolerated to achieve full employment could simply be read off a Phillips curve diagram such as the one shown in Figure 24.2. The popularity the Phillips curve quickly won with policy-makers is shrewdly commented on by Humphrey (1986, p.15).

> … the Phillips curve appealed to policy-makers because it provided a convincing rationale for their failure to achieve full employment with price stability – twin goals that were thought to be mutually compatible before Phillips' analysis. When criticised for failing to achieve both goals simultaneously, the authorities could point to the Phillips curve as showing that such an outcome was impossible and that the best one could hope for was either arbitrarily low unemployment or price stability but not both.

3.2 Two theories of inflation

This is an appropriate point to relate the Phillips curve to the *AD/AS* framework which you studied in Chapters 17–19. Putting these two economic models side by side, so to speak, will also enable me to introduce two theories of inflation: demand pull and cost push. Let us start by considering the case of a government which wants to reduce unemployment and is prepared to live with an increase in inflation to do so. A set of expansionary monetary and/or fiscal policy measures is therefore introduced and the economy duly moves along its Phillips curve upwards and to the left from A to B in Figure 24.3. Inflation has indeed risen and unemployment fallen. When inflation is caused in this way, by an expansion of aggregate demand, it is known as *demand-pull* inflation.

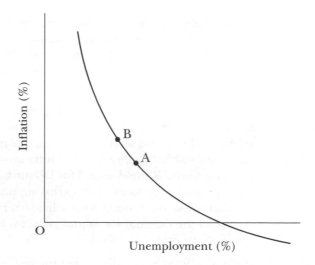

Figure 24.3 **An expansionary movement along the Phillips curve**

Question

How can we represent on an *AD/AS* diagram the effect of a monetary and/or fiscal expansion on the price level and the level of output?

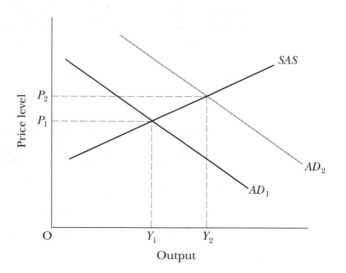

Figure 24.4 **Demand-pull inflation**

In Figure 24.4 the monetary/fiscal expansion, represented by the shift in the *AD* curve from AD_1 to AD_2, causes the price level to rise from P_1 to P_2 while output also rises from Y_1 to Y_2. The explanation lies in the shape of *SAS* curve, which slopes upwards. So the effects of an expansion in aggregate demand when the *SAS* curve is upward sloping correspond to a leftward movement along the Phillips curve. This upward sloping short-run aggregate supply curve is characteristic of both the New Keynesian and the New Classical schools of thought discussed in Chapter 18.

In the New Keyensian strategy, the aggregate demand expansion is reflected in a rise in prices which, while money wages are fixed by contractual agreements, leads to a fall in real wages. Firms therefore hire more labour and use it to increase output. So an expansion of aggregate demand raises the price level and output and reduces unemployment. The *AD/AS* framework captures the changes in the price level and in output, while the Phillips curve relates inflation (the rate at which the price level is changing) and unemployment. The *AD/AS* framework and the Phillips curve are two ways of seeing the same sequence of events. While the Phillips curve represents the effects of changes in aggregate demand, the *AD/AS* analysis explains how those effects have come about, in terms of changes in the short run equilibrium level of output or national income.

It was not much more than a decade after Phillips had reported his discovery of a trade-off between unemployment and inflation going back almost a century that it appeared to break down. Plotting the time path of inflation against unemployment for the UK economy reveals a relationship in the 1970s that cannot be depicted by the downward sloping Phillips curve and cannot readily be explained in terms of demand pull (Figure 24.5).

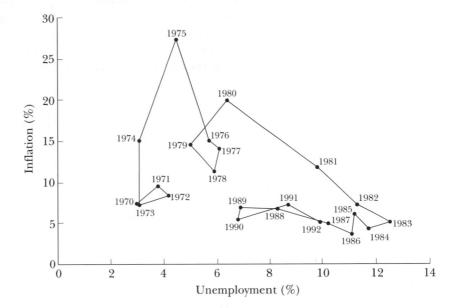

Figure 24.5 **Inflation and unemployment in the UK, 1970–92**

Source: *OECD Economic Outlook,* various years

Question

Are any of the inflationary episodes of the 1970s surveyed in Chapter 20 evident in Figure 24.5? Did the Phillips curve cease to exist or do traces of it continue to be observable? Does Figure 24.5 reveal any sign of the anti-inflationary priorities of policy-makers in the 1980s?

I think the first and second oil price shocks of the 1970s are quite clearly visible, in the steeply rising movements of the curve in Figure 24.5 for 1973–75 and 1979–80. And you can see that the increase in inflation of the years 1973–75 and 1978–80 was not associated with a fall in unemployment. In the early 1980s a trade-off between inflation and unemployment seems, however, to reappear on Figure 24.5.

Question

Thinking back to Chapter 18 again, how would you draw a short run *AD/AS* diagram showing an increase in inflation accompanied by a fall in output as occurred in the 1970s? This time the diagram should depict an increase in the costs of production, resulting from the oil price rises.

An increase in the price level accompanied by a fall in output can be shown by shifting the short run *AS* curve upwards or to the left, from SAS_1 to SAS_2 in Figure 24.6. Two factors might explain an economy-wide increase in the costs of production. Higher input costs, usually in the costs of imported raw materials or fuel, and higher wage rates would both reduce profits if the price level is unchanged, with the consequence that producers would be willing to supply less output at each and every price level. But producers will in fact attempt to pass on some of the cost increases to consumers in the form of higher prices and the economy will settle at a new equilibrium, with a higher price level, P_2, and lower output, Y_2. When inflation occurs in this way, it is classified as *cost-push* inflation.

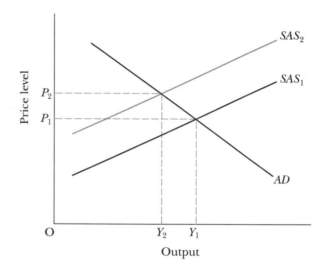

Figure 24.6   **Cost-push inflation**

How can cost-push inflation be represented in terms of the Phillips curve? The empirical relationship between unemployment and inflation had become more complex than that observed by Phillips for the British economy from 1861 to 1913. The Phillips curve analysis could easily be modified to reflect the more complex unemployment-inflation relationship now observed throughout the industrial world. Basic supply and demand analysis has shown you that curves shift if there is some change in the conditions we hold constant in drawing the original curve. Perhaps all that had happened was that the Phillips curve had shifted outwards or to the right? For example, the oil price rise of 1979 could be seen as shifting the UK Phillips curve in this direction. Higher oil prices fed through into higher prices in general, so that any given unemployment rate was associated with a higher inflation rate than before as noted in the discussion of Figure 24.5.

However, there are in fact two segments of the time path plotted in Figure 24.5 that slope downwards like a Phillips curve, one only briefly in 1975–77, the other over the years 1980–83. These Phillips curve remnants, if you like, are interesting because they may reflect the response of policy-makers to the cost-push inflationary episodes which shifted the Phillips curve outwards.

Question

What policy measures might have initiated these movements downward and to the right on Figure 24.5? How can an *AD/AS* diagram show the effects of the relevant policy measures?

It seems that policy makers wished to reverse the inflationary consequences of the increases in imported raw material prices. Certainly, the movements downwards and to the right are consistent with their using contractionary monetary and/or fiscal policies to trade higher unemployment for lower inflation.

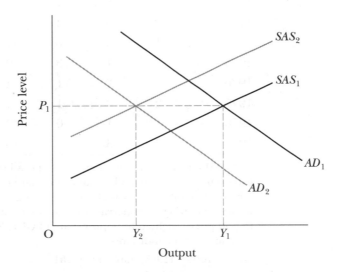

Figure 24.7 **A contractionary demand response to higher import prices**

In terms of *AD/AS*, once higher import prices had shifted the *SAS* curve, as in Figure 24.7, governments introduced contractionary monetary and/or fiscal policies to shift the *AD* curve leftwards to AD_2 so that the new equilibrium pegged the price level at P_1, accepting the trade-off of Keynesian or demand deficient unemployment generated by the fall in output equal to $Y_1 - Y_2$. Finally, the following exercise asks you to consider what will happen if policy makers are more concerned with unemployment than inflation.

Exercise 24.1

Suppose that governments had instead responded to the import price rise by trying to prevent a rise in unemployment. How can this be illustrated on an *AD/AS* diagram? What happens to prices?

3.3   Explaining inflation

I want to conclude this section with a brief look at the causes of inflation in large OECD economies in the 1970s. This will offer a wider international perspective on the response of policy makers to 1970s inflation which will provide a cue for an examination in Section 4 of some theoretical developments concerning the Phillips curve. Brown (1985, pp.98–9) identifies four potential causes of inflation – expenditure pull, monetary growth, import-price cost push and wage push – and adds their disinflationary counterparts. Table 24.3 shows the number of inflationary and disinflationary impulses of each type per year for eleven large OECD economies.

Table 24.3   **Inflationary and disinflationary impulses in 11 OECD economies, 1970–79 (number of impulses)**

Year	+M	+E	+W	+I	−M	−E	−W	−I
1970	2	1	3	3	5	3	0	1
1971	8	3	3	1	2	4	2	3
1972	9	3	1	0	0	1	2	2
1973	2	4	4	9	4	0	1	0
1974	1	3	6	11	6	5	0	0
1975	5	1	3	0	3	3	2	11
1976	1	6	1	4	4	2	7	2
1977	2	0	1	4	3	6	1	3
1978	4	1	0	0	5	1	4	8
1979	3	3	1	10	4	2	0	0

Note: +M = increase in rate of growth of broad money; +E = increase in rate of growth of money GDP and rise in profit share of value added in manufacturing; +W = increase in rate of growth of hourly earnings and fall in profit share of value added in manufacturing; +I = increase of more than one per cent in rate of change of import price weighted by import share of GDP. Negative headings imply the opposite movement of the indicators.

Source: Brown (1985) Table 4.2, p.101

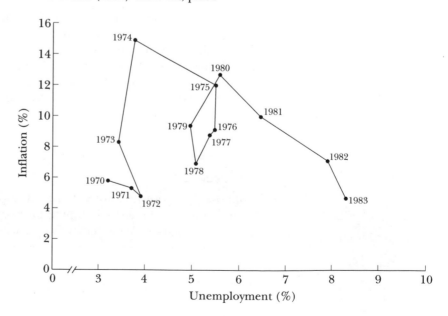

Figure 24.8   **Inflation and unemployment in the large OECD economies, 1970–83**

Source: Dawson (1992)

Question

Examine Table 24.3 in conjunction with Figure 24.8. Are any traces of a downward sloping Phillips curve discernible in Figure 24.8? If so, is it possible to link up any of the inflationary/disinflationary impulses with significant movements along, or shifts of, the Phillips curve for large OECD economies?

What really stand out in the early 1970s are the 17 inflationary impulses coming from monetary expansion in 1971 and 1972. The next set of inflationary impulses of any note are the 20 import-price observations for 1973 and 1974. So it seems that import-price cost push tells the truth, but not the whole truth, about the outward shift of the Phillips curve from 1972 to 1974. Monetary expansion in most of the major industrial economies in 1971–72 increased the demand for and hence the prices of primary products on world markets. The acceleration in world inflation led to a defensive reaction by OPEC countries, concerned at the erosion of the real value of their financial assets, adding a further cost-push twist to the demand-pull inflation already set in motion by monetary expansion. This can be interpreted as a shift outwards of the Phillips curve in the early 1970s. The only other concentration of inflationary impulses occurs at the time of the second oil price shock in 1979. This time however there was no preceding monetary expansion to speak of. Again the early 1980s suggest a reassertion of the inflation/unemployment trade-off along a shifted curve.

In fact, after 1973, there are more *dis*inflationary monetary impulses than inflationary ones – more in each year of the 1970s except 1975. So it is reasonable to conclude that the oil-importing economies reacted to the oil price shocks by monetary contraction designed to contain their inflationary impact. This implies a trading-off of lower inflation against higher demand deficiency or Keynesian unemployment. The question is: why did governments react to the oil price shocks of the 1970s in this way?

There are, I think, three reasons. First, as we saw in Section 2, policy-makers judged inflation to be a more serious problem than unemployment. Second, some economists argued that the inflation of the 1970s was ultimately the consequence of misguided expansionary policies in the 1960s (and early 1970s). They claimed that the Phillips curve broke down because policy makers tried to exploit the trade-off to secure permanently lower unemployment. After I have discussed this view in Section 4, we will be in a position to consider the third reason in Section 5 . This is the argument, particularly influential in the early 1980s, that inflation could be reduced and perhaps even eliminated altogether without any increase in unemployment at all.

4   Inflation and expectations

4.1   The expectations-augmented Phillips curve

In Section 3, we saw that the unemployment/inflation trade-off appeared to break down in the early 1970s. This was not in itself fatally wounding to the Phillips curve analysis because it was possible to interpret the combination of rising inflation and unchanged or even rising unemployment as a series of short-run Phillips curves shifting outwards. However, some economists had always been sceptical of the Phillips trade-off on theoretical grounds and they seized upon its empirical difficulties as confirmation of their misgivings.

The theoretical deficiency of the Phillips curve analysis, according to Friedman (1968) and Phelps (1967), concerned its microeconomic foundations, in particular the assumptions it incorporated about the behaviour of economic agents in the labour market. Friedman argued from two main premises. First, he assumed that the demand and supply of labour were functions, not of the nominal wage rate but of the real wage rate, that is, nominal wages divided by prices, W/P. Second, he proposed that in bargaining over wage rates, workers use their experience of past inflation to predict future price rises and aim to anticipate these in wage settlements. Friedman's conclusion was that, while there is a trade-off between unemployment and inflation in the short run, a permanently lower level of unemployment cannot be secured by accepting a higher rate of inflation.

Friedman's analysis of the labour market exemplifies what Mary Gregory in Chapter 18 referred to as the competitive approach (see Chapter 18, Section 3). Accordingly, he assumed that workers and unemployed people are rational economic agents no less than the profit-maximizing firms they deal with. In other words, the analysis abstracts from considerations of social norms and the psychological pressures of unemployment and from wage bargaining institutions. It presents decisions to accept or reject job offers, to remain in or give up a job, as matters of individually weighing up the disutility of working against its financial rewards. Friedman believed that government intervention to try to trade-off higher inflation for permanently lower unemployment would change agents' expectations and their behaviour in a way that would only make matters worse.

Let us remind ourselves of how a demand expansion works in the absence of expectations. Policy makers might suppose that a moderate increase in inflation would reduce unemployment through a relatively simple causal mechanism. A monetary expansion increases the demand for goods, causing a general rise in prices. Nominal wage rates are slow to respond, so real wage rates fall, persuading employers to move down their labour demand curves and recruit the extra workers they need to increase output. Unemployed people do not incorporate past inflation into their expectations, assuming prices will be stable in the next year. They are willing to work at the unchanged nominal wage rates on offer and unemployment falls. This combination of rising inflation and falling unemployment is shown by a movement upwards and to the left from A to B along the short-run Phillips curve PC_1 in Figure 24.9.

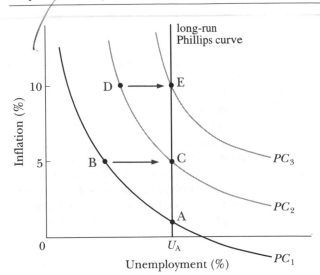

Figure 24.9 The expectations-augmented Phillips curve

Once we stop and think about this, it immediately seems implausible and indeed Chapter 18 has already suggested that this kind of short-run outcome cannot be a long-term equilibrium. If people are calculating their prospective rewards from employment – and in the competitive labour market model people are rational agents who do exactly that – it is no more than common sense to adjust the money wages on offer for inflation. A rational agent would fail to do so only if there had been so little inflation that the adjustment was not worth the effort. Once we have decided to model people's decisions in the labour market as those of rational agents, we are more or less committed to incorporating expectations of inflation into their behaviour.

That is just what Friedman did. He argued that the process of trading off higher inflation for lower unemployment worked only on the assumption that people did not bother to form expectations about future inflation or that their expectations were mistaken. Once the newly recruited workers incorporate last year's inflation into their expectations of inflation in the next year, they either decide it is not worth working and leave their jobs or negotiate higher nominal wage rates. Either way, unemployment returns to its original level but at the new rate of inflation. This is how the short-run Phillips curve PC_1 shifts outwards to PC_2 as the economy moves from B to C on Figure 24.9.

Policy makers, the story continues, interpret their failure to secure a permanent drop in the unemployment rate as a sign that their choice of expansionary monetary medicine was correct but the dosage was too low. The course of treatment is therefore repeated and the economy moves along PC_2 from C to D while workers are surprised by the new, higher rate of inflation. But, once again, as soon as this inflation rate is used as the basis of expectations, the prospect of low real wages reverses the fall in unemployment and the short-run Phillips curve shifts to PC_3 as the economy moves from D to E. The outcome is the original unemployment rate combined with a higher inflation rate, showing that in the long run there is no trade-off between unemployment and inflation. The long-run Phillips curve is vertical at U_A, joining the points the economy returns to after each expansionary phase – A, C and E.

This argument should, I hope, remind you of the concept of the natural rate of unemployment and the associated vertical long run *AS* curve, introduced in Chapter 18, Sections 3.2 and 5.2. The natural rate of unemployment was defined there by Mary Gregory as the rate at which the labour market clears. Friedman, who originated the concept, noted that it reflected some institutional characteristics of the labour market, such as 'the cost of gathering information about job vacancies and labour-availabilities, the costs of mobility and so on ...' (Friedman, 1968, p.8). Of the other institutional factors mentioned by Friedman, attention has tended to focus on social security benefits. The level of unemployment benefits influences people's individual labour supply curves. If the level of benefit is increased, the urgency of finding work might be diminished, increasing the number of people out of work when the labour market is in equilibrium – that is, the natural rate of unemployment.

In the short run, expansionary monetary or fiscal policies can reduce the actual rate of unemployment below this long-run equilibrium, or natural, rate even in a competitive model. It follows that the natural rate will prevail only in the absence of expansionary policies. *The natural rate hypothesis*, as this first result of Friedman's analysis is called, states that there is no permanent trade-off between unemployment and inflation because in the long run unemployment returns to its natural rate. The vertical long-run Phillips curve is the diagrammatic representation of the natural rate hypothesis. If expected inflation is the same as last year's inflation, then, in the absence of expansionary policies pushing the economy along a short-run Phillips curve, actual inflation this year will be the same as last year and hence the same as expected inflation and the economy is in equilibrium at the natural rate of unemployment. Table 24.4 shows how Figure 24.9 could be interpreted in the light of this model.

Table 24.4 **Actual and expected inflation and changes in unemployment**

Year	Expected inflation (last year's actual inflation) (%)	Actual inflation (%)	Change in unemployment
1	1	5	falls A → B on PC_1
2	5	5	rises B → C, PC_1 to PC_2
3	5	10	falls C → D on PC_2
4	10	10	rises D → E, PC_2 to PC_3

Question

On this model, how could policy makers maintain unemployment below its natural rate in the long run ?

This can be done only by continually expanding aggregate demand, so that the rate of inflation is always accelerating. Workers are therefore constantly surprised by inflation: always, if you like, a year behind in their expectations. This leads to *the accelerationist hypothesis* which is the second of Friedman's results. It states that unemployment can be maintained below its natural rate only by constantly accelerating inflation (see Figure 24.10). As people's expectations chase after actual inflation, inflation must accelerate to keep ahead of those expectations. Attempts to peg unemployment below its natural rate will eventually provoke hyperinflation.

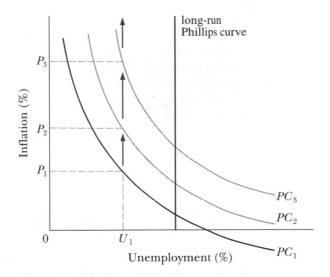

Figure 24.10   The accelerationist hypothesis

The natural rate and accelerationist hypotheses both depend on Friedman's assumption that expected inflation is precisely equal to last year's inflation. However, while it came to be widely believed in the early 1970s that inflationary expectations were the main cause of the outward shift of the observed Phillips curve, the analysis of those expectations underwent a major revolution.

The main problem with Friedman's approach, known as *adaptive expectations*, was that it committed economic agents to making easily avoidable errors in forecasting inflation. Under adaptive expectations, in forming expectations about the future course of an economic variable, agents rely solely on past values of that variable. True, they can calculate a weighted average of inflation over the past few years, the greatest weight being attached to last year's inflation and so on. They can also learn by their mistakes, incorporating an error-learning mechanism to adjust forecasts by some fraction of the discrepancy between last year's expected inflation and last year's actual inflation – hence the term adaptive expectations. For example, if expected inflation is 6 per cent and the outcome is actually 10 per cent, then the expected inflation rate for next year will be revised upwards.

This procedure works reasonably well if the rate of inflation is stable or changes only slowly but during variable inflation it is far too mechanical a procedure and locks agents into systematic errors, such as constantly being surprised by ever-accelerating inflation. In any case, it is just intuitively implausible to suppose that people would focus solely on past inflation to the exclusion of obviously relevant 'background' information, such as the election of a government committed to fighting years of high inflation or the move from national currencies to a single European currency. Surely, it came to be thought, the rational agents who inhabit economic models can do better than adaptive expectations.

4.2   Rational expectations

The rational expectations hypothesis was advanced by Muth (1961), although its significance for macroeconomic theory and modelling was not fully exploited until the 1970s. Muth's basic premise was that 'information is scarce, and the economic system generally does not waste it' (1961, p.316). This probably does not seem particularly remarkable but Muth went on to argue that the information relevant to the formation of inflationary expectations included knowledge of the structure of the model of the economy being used by policy makers. Carter and Maddock (1984) explain the significance of this step:

> The innovation introduced by Muth was to consider the expected price as endogenous to the model, and generated by the model itself....The agents in the market are assumed to know the structure of the model ... and to use this information in order to form their expectations. ... This information includes of course the precise structure of the model.
>
> *(Carter and Maddock, 1984, p.30)*

So now it seems that 'agents in the market' such as people in work negotiating wage claims and unemployed people deciding on job offers are being assumed to know the precise structure, expressible in a series of equations for forecasting the future course of output, inflation and so on, of the economic model used by policy makers. Since economists are notoriously prone to error in making such forecasts, it seems implausible to assume that people with no professional interest in them routinely do better.

However, proponents of rational expectations insist that there is no suggestion that all or most individual people in the real world actually form their expectations of inflation in any systematic way. According to Minford and Peel (1983), all that is being claimed is that the *typical individual* 'utilizes efficiently the information available to him in forming expectations about future outcomes'. Since this a belief about the 'typical individual', it 'cannot be falsified by examples of behaviour by any actual individual'. As long as enough real people who 'contribute a dominant proportion of the variability in aggregate behaviour' make efficient use of all the available information, 'this would be sufficient to generate aggregate behaviour that exhibited rationality' (Minford and Peel, 1983, pp.4–6). What this amounts to is the claim that irrational ways of forming expectations, being randomly distributed across a large sample of the population, cancel out, so that the aggregate outcome is *as if* all agents were rational.

Question

If agents form their price expectations rationally, it seems that they cannot be surprised by a change of macroeconomic policy. Looking back to Figures 24.9 and 24.10, how would this affect the outcome of the strategy of repeated expansions of aggregate demand to peg unemployment below its natural rate?

Under adaptive expectations, the policy reduced unemployment below its natural rate only temporarily, until agents adjusted to the new inflation rate. But, if they form their price expectations rationally, they can never be surprised by any systematic policy. So their expectations of inflation will always be accurate and unemployment will not fall below its natural rate even temporarily. The policy will be entirely ineffective. For example, in connection with expansionary monetary policy, Minford and Peel (1983, p.19) argue that if the government changes the money supply rule which they are following, output (and hence unemployment) will not be affected because the new monetary stance is 'incorporated into people's expectations … and cannot cause any surprises'.

The effect of introducing adaptive expectations into the analysis of the relationship between unemployment and inflation was to curtail the trade-off to the short-run. It seems that the impact of introducing rational expectations into the analysis is more dramatic: there is no trade-off at all because systematic policy has no effect on output and unemployment. This is the extreme competitive model of the economy once again with a vertical short-run as well as long-run *AS* curve (see Chapter 18, Section 3.2). Does macroeconomic theory really show that macroeconomic policy has no effect on the economy?

5   Inflation, disinflation and conflict

5.1   Painless disinflation

In this section I want to return to the question I raised at the end of Section 3: why did governments react to the oil price rises of the 1970s by trying to move their economies downwards and to the right along their respective Phillips curves? I offered three reasons in answer to that question. The first, that inflation was adjudged from the mid 1970s to be a more serious problem than unemployment, we have already considered in Section 2. We have just finished looking at the second reason, the belief that the upsurge in inflation in the 1970s was the consequence of policy makers' attempts to exploit the unemployment/inflation trade-off in the 1960s. This has prepared the ground for the examination of the third reason, that there was after all no trade-off, that inflation could be reduced without causing an increase in unemployment.

By the late 1970s, unemployment and inflation in most OECD economies were both uncomfortably high. So the dilemma facing policy makers was how to decide which of these problems to tackle first. The trade-off approach would have held out the unappealing prospect that, whichever problem was given priority, the cost of alleviating it would have been making the other one even worse. But policy makers, particularly in the UK and the USA, were encouraged to take a more optimistic view of the situation confronting them. For the development of expectations theory offered the chance, it seemed, to solve one of the problems without exacerbating the other at all: to eliminate inflation at no cost in higher unemployment. If agents formed their expectations rationally and, the argument went, one other condition to be discussed below was met, disinflation could be painless.

Rational expectations theory asserts that agents can never be surprised by systematic macroeconomic policy. They incorporate policy rules not only into their forecasts of future inflation but also into their behaviour. So, for example, they react to a contractionary monetary policy by anticipating its downward effect on the rate of inflation, thereby bringing about that effect as they negotiate contracts of various kinds on the assumption of lower inflation. Agents' reactions to policy make the disinflationary policy work without affecting output. Price inflation falls but no wage gap opens up and so there is no change in the level of unemployment. If policy makers are convinced that they can rely on agents' reacting to policy in this way, they will be much more inclined to tackle inflation without worrying about their policies' effects on unemployment.

Exercise 24.2

To check that you have understood the discussion so far, try filling in Figure 24.11. This is a pay-off matrix, but here, as with Figure 16.6 in Chapter 16, the pay-offs are the same to both parties. The quadrants of the matrix identify the outcomes of the government's inflationary and disinflationary policies, given the reaction of the other economic agents in the economy. The left-hand quadrants show what happens to unemployment and inflation if agents allow themselves to be surprised. The right-hand quadrants show the outcomes if agents rationally anticipate policy effects. I have completed the top left-hand quadrant. You should fill in the others.

Figure 24.11 **Matrix for predicting the effects of inflationary and disinflationary policies on unemployment and inflation**

Government policy \ Agents' reactions	no reaction	full anticipation
reflate	unemployment falls inflation rises	
disinflate		

The implication of the exercise, which you should complete before reading on, is that an expansionary monetary policy to reflate the economy and reduce unemployment is successful if agents fail to react by anticipating upward price level effects, but that under rational expectations (and one further condition explained below) agents anticipate an acceleration in the rate of inflation, thereby bringing it about and leaving the level of unemployment unchanged. A contractionary monetary policy to eliminate inflation works painlessly, without adding to unemployment, provided agents anticipate the downward pressure on prices, but in the absence of this reaction unemployment will rise, at least in the short run.

As I noted above, painless disinflation requires more than the rational expectations hypothesis. The further condition is the assumption that all markets, including the labour market, clear continuously and immediately in response to shocks, or unexpected changes in the conditions of supply and demand. The rational expectations hypothesis plus the market-clearing assumption make up the competitive approach in macroeconomic thought

(Chapter 18, Section 3). The policy implication of this approach is that disinflation can be painless.

What do New Classical economists have to say about events in the labour market following the announcement of a disinflationary policy stance? In practice it seems that involuntary unemployment might occur, because wage contracts in imperfect labour markets do not permit real wage rates to fall instantaneously to market-clearing levels. However, Patrick Minford (1985), a prominent New Classical economist in the UK, suggests that there is a residual non-union labour market where wage rates are free to adjust without delay, thereby clearing the labour market as a whole of excess supply. In other words, when workers lose their jobs in the unionized labour market they can always take a wage cut and find a job in the non-unionized labour market. So any increase in unemployment as a consequence of disinflationary policies is voluntary and the disinflation therefore painless. This is the extreme New Classical, or competitive approach.

In the event, however, the disinflation of the early 1980s was far from painless. Unemployment in OECD economies rose sharply, remained high for the rest of the decade and was associated with an increase in long-term unemployment. In terms of the unemployment–inflation trade-off, it is interesting to measure the *sacrifice ratio* for each economy. This is the ratio of the cumulative increase in unemployment to the overall fall in inflation. The cumulative rise in unemployment is found by adding the percentage point rise in unemployment for each year of disinflation. The overall fall in inflation is measured from peak inflation (sometime in 1980–82) to the lowest rate achieved by 1986, both measured in percentage points. These cumulative sacrifice ratios for selected OECD economies during the disinflation of the early 1980s calculated according to the formula

$$\text{sacrifice ratio} = \frac{\text{cumulative rise in unemployment}}{\text{fall in inflation}}$$

are shown in Table 24.5. For example, in Austria a five percentage point rise in unemployment accompanied each fall in inflation of one percentage point, while in the USA each one percentage fall in inflation was achieved at a cost of a four percentage point rise in unemployment.

The question is, was the rise in unemployment voluntary, as New Classical economists claim? There are two reasons for saying no. The first concerns the market-clearing assumption, while the second relates to the rational expectations hypothesis.

The market-clearing assumption has been challenged in a number of ways, of which I want to recall just two from earlier chapters, one relating to the goods market, the other to the labour market. The essential point is that there are good reasons for prices and wages in the real world to be 'sticky', that is, to fail to respond quickly to changes in the conditions of demand or supply in order to clear the market. Economists who stress this aspect of markets belong to the New Keynesian school of macroeconomic thought (see Chapter 18, Section 2). Take the goods market first. Imperfectly competitive firms may fail to restore equilibrium because they balance the benefits of changing prices against the costs. These costs are called menu costs, not altogether happily, because they comprise more than the cost of the chalk used up by your local bistro (Chapter 18, Section 2.2). As Mankiw (1990, p.1657) puts it, 'these menu costs include the time taken to inform

Table 24.5   **Sacrifice ratios in selected OECD economies in the disinflation of the 1980s**

Country	Sacrifice ratio: cumulative percentage point rise in unemployment per one percentage point fall in inflation
Belgium	17.91
Germany	15.20
Netherlands	9.92
Denmark	7.66
Japan	7.00
France	6.67
Austria	5.15
Italy	5.07
UK	4.35
USA	4.34
Finland	3.78
Sweden	3.44
Norway	1.63
Switzerland	0.81

Source: Dawson (1992) Table 15.2, p.183

customers, the customer annoyance caused by price changes and the effort required even to think about a price change.' While total menu costs of inflation seem small (Section 2.2 of this chapter) they may be great enough for individual firms in imperfectly competitive markets to be reluctant to lower their prices when the demand for their goods declines as a consequence of disinflationary policies. So here is a New Keynesian reason for believing that many firms in the economy may react to disinflationary policies too slowly to make those policies work painlessly.

Turning to the labour market, Chapter 21 explained the concept of efficiency wages. So I just want to comment briefly on their significance in the context of disinflation. Employers pay efficiency wages to raise productivity, for example, through the worker discipline effect. The argument goes that you are less likely to shirk and risk dismissal if the opportunity cost of losing your job – that is, the income you earn from it – is high. So this gives firms a motive for not cutting wages in a recession, even in the face of the persistent unemployment that emerged during the 1980s.

The significance of menu costs and efficiency wages is twofold. First, they offer an explanation for the failure of agents other than trade unions or workers to anticipate policy effects by making price adjustments. So the unemployment associated with disinflation is not a voluntary choice by workers or their representatives. Second, there is no reason to believe that menu costs and efficiency wages are confined to the unionized sector of the labour market. These New Keynesian arguments, based on a model of imperfectly competitive markets, raise doubts about the New Classical argument that wage cuts are always possible in the non-unionized sector.

The second challenge to the New Classical argument concerning painless disinflation concerns the rational expectations hypothesis itself. It is not so much an objection to the New Classical approach as such, as a matter of drawing attention to a difference of view among rational expectations theorists themselves. According to the standard interpretation of the rational expectations hypothesis, a necessary and sufficient condition for painless disinflation is that the government should follow a systematic policy which agents can discover. Ideally, the government should announce its policy clearly and unambiguously. However, there is another, more stringent, specification of the condition put forward by Sargent (1983) according to which the government's unequivocal commitment to a systematic policy is necessary but not sufficient. The further condition is that 'the change in the rule for the pertinent variable must be widely understood and uncontroversial' (Sargent, 1983, p.114). It is the words 'and uncontroversial' that matter here. They imply that agents must accept the validity of the economic model that guides policy makers, not just understand it. Disinflation will be painless, or at least 'low cost', to the extent that there is a consensus in favour of the government's model of the economy and hence its disinflationary strategy.

Why does Sargent add the extra condition? The original version of rational expectations theory states that macroeconomic policy changes the price level (while leaving the real economy unaffected) to the extent that agents adapt their behaviour to the policy rule they discover. But, Sargent insists, the mere discovery of the rule is not enough. We are all familiar with rules – school rules, speed limits and so on – which we understand perfectly well but either deliberately break or simply ignore. It is one thing to understand that the government would like us to reduce our prices or our wage demands but quite another actually to do it. So Sargent seems to be right. The implication is that painless disinflation requires (a) that markets clear and (b) that expectations are rational in the sense that agents share the government's policy objective and its model of the economy. How likely is it that these conditions will be met in real world economies?

In order to answer that question, I want to introduce two more theoretical perspectives: conflict models of the inflationary process and partisan theories of macroeconomic policy making.

5.2   Inflation, markets and conflict

Conflict theorists tend to see inflation, not so much as the problem, but rather as the outcome of attempts to solve the prior problem of a distribution of income which economic agents believe to be inequitable. A microeconomic illustration might clarify the basic idea. Suppose that a monopoly raises the price of its product. This redistributes income from consumers to the monopolist (see Chapters 6 and 8). But many of the consumers themselves work on the production side in other markets exhibiting varying degrees of monopoly power, so they will try to reverse the redistribution of income by raising the price of their goods or services, some of which will be purchased by the beneficiaries of the original monopoly price rise. The inflationary process is under way.

At the macroeconomic level, it is useful, particularly in two-party representative democracies, to see this conflict over the distribution of income as a struggle between workers and capitalists (for example, Rowthorn, 1977). Workers aim to shift income distribution in their favour by demanding higher wages, the owners of capital raise prices in order to defend the initial income distribution and a wage-price spiral evolves. Or capitalists raise prices to increase profits, only to encounter higher wage demands as workers seek to hold on to the initial income distribution and a price-wage spiral takes off.

Where does the government come into this process? Partisan theories of macroeconomic policy maintain that governments pursue policies which redistribute income in favour of their supporting constituencies. According to Hibbs (1987) an increase in US unemployment is associated with a fall in the income shares of the two poorest quintiles and a rise in the shares of the two richest quintiles. Minford (1985) argues that inflation redistributes income in the opposite direction by eroding the value of financial assets (other than those that are indexed against inflation) which are most likely to be held by the upper middle class. Moreover, in the UK inflation throughout the 1970s appears to have increased the share of wages in national income at the expense of profits (Brown, 1985). So the first priority of left-of-centre governments has traditionally been to cut unemployment, while right-of-centre governments are mainly concerned to reduce inflation.

True, a disinflationary policy may be common to parties from both sides of the political divide, perhaps because fears of a currency crisis prompt left-of-centre parties into wanting to be seen to be tough on inflation. In those circumstances, a left-of-centre government would be expected to favour a relatively slow fall in inflation to a low but still positive target rate with the intention of minimizing the increase in unemployment, while a right-of-centre government would be more likely to seek a relatively rapid elimination of inflation even at the cost of a sharp rise in unemployment.

A disinflationary policy rule announced by a right-of-centre government might therefore be interpreted by workers as an attempt to sustain, or to bring about, a distribution of income they regard as unjust or exploitative. Such a policy might be perceived as seeking to deflect the costs of economic adjustment away from the right-of-centre government's constituency, which will be the principal beneficiary of the swift elimination of inflation and will be relatively unscathed by an increase in unemployment.

The high unemployment cost of disinflation is therefore now explicable as the consequence of economic agents' attempts to resist policy. If, given competitive markets, all that is required for painless disinflation is that a policy rule is discovered by economic agents who form their expectations rationally, then the explanation of rising unemployment is that the government is either failing to follow a coherent policy or has given ambiguous signals about it. Yet throughout the 1980s the governments of the major OECD nations made their anti-inflationary objectives very clear.

On Sargent's interpretation of rational expectations, however, mere understanding is not enough. The policy rule must be uncontroversial, in the sense that agents must share the government's objective of eliminating inflation and its belief in the validity of its model of how the economy works. In economies where some agents perceive disinflation as a partisan move in the struggle over income distribution, the policy objective will be anything but uncontroversial. And the availability of a competing model of the economy reinforces the likelihood of resistance to partisan policies.

Agents might in the aggregate act as if they believe in an economic model in which firms delay price adjustments out of a desire to avoid menu costs, rather than one which postulates continuous market clearing throughout the economy.

If we were to interpret Sargent's conditions for the rationality of expectations with extreme stringency, they could be met only in an economy entirely without conflict over the distribution of income or disagreement over the way in which the economy works. It is, I think, more realistic to regard the fulfilment of Sargent's conditions as a matter of degree. It follows that the combination of inflation and unemployment – and the macroeconomic performance of the economy in general – will be improved to the extent that there exists a consensus over the distribution of income, the way in which the economy works and hence the direction of macroeconomic policy. I want you to conclude this section by completing an exercise which will test this hypothesis. But first I must give you some background information.

In fact, you already have most of it, from Chapters 15 and 21. In Chapter 15 Grahame Thompson distinguished two forms of capitalism, one of which is the 'organized capitalism' exemplified by the German economy. In labour markets terms, this is reflected in a corporatist approach involving centralized bargaining arrangements where 'the peak organizations of labour and employers are brought together at a national level, usually under government auspices, to decide systematically on wage levels, and often other aspects of economic activity' (Section 3.1). It is noted in the same section that centralized bargaining tends to produce lower levels of unemployment. Similarly, in Chapter 21, Section 4.2 Francis Green suggests that in a corporatist economy, where national wage deals can be struck by nationally co-ordinated unions and employers, we 'would expect to find such an economy with wages relatively flexible in response to macroeconomic fluctuations and with little unemployment'.

There is some disagreement about the precise specification of a corporatist economy and hence about which economies are correctly classified as such. However Soskice (1990) reviewed labour market institutions in a number of economies and estimated their 'degree of centralization' in terms of the effectiveness of co-ordination in practice rather than the formal location of wage bargaining. On this basis, the most highly centralized economies are Japan, Austria and Switzerland, followed by Sweden and Norway and then Germany and the Netherlands. In the following exercise, inflation and unemployment data are provided for three of these economies, namely Japan, Sweden and Germany, and for three decentralized or non-corporatist economies, these being France, the UK and the USA. Note that these data are based on OECD standardized definitions of unemployment and inflation. The UK data therefore differ somewhat from the unemployment and inflation data for the UK presented in Chapters 16, 17 and 20.

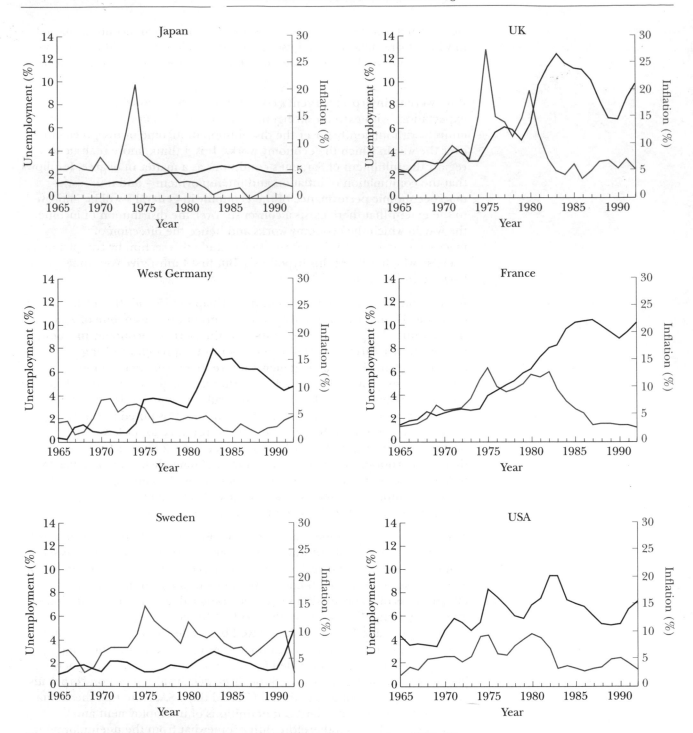

Figure 24.12 **Inflation and unemployment in selected economies, 1970–92**

Source: *OECD Economic Outlook,* various years

Exercise 24.3

Consider the data on inflation and unemployment shown in Figure 24.12.

1   Sum up each economy's record on inflation and unemployment (briefly), let's say in one sentence for each economy.

2   Are there any outstanding features common to all, or most, of the economies?

3   Is the performance of the three corporatist economies (Japan, Germany and Sweden) on (a) inflation and (b) unemployment systematically better than that of the three non-corporatist ones (France, the UK and the USA)?

4   Summarize in your own words the argument, derived from Sargent's conditions for rational expectations, for expecting corporatist economies to out-perform non-corporatist ones.

6   Unemployment

6.1   Demand deficient unemployment, the natural rate and the NAIRU

In this section I want to pull together some strands of thought about unemployment. Several explanations of unemployment have been discussed in previous chapters. In Chapter 16 Vivienne Brown explained how our understanding of unemployment was revolutionized by John Maynard Keynes in the 1930s. Keynes argued that the mass unemployment of the 1930s was caused by a deficiency of aggregate demand and was therefore involuntary on the part of unemployed people. Only government intervention to reflate the economy could reduce unemployment. A different explanation was discussed by Mary Gregory in Chapter 18. On a competitive view of the labour market, unemployment is voluntary.

In Chapter 21 Francis Green identified four categories of unemployment summarized in Section 4. Where work is alienating and imperfectly monitored, unemployment may occur due to the worker discipline effect. There is frictional unemployment associated with the time lags normally involved in job search and recruitment. Structural unemployment emerges if there is a mismatch between the available vacancies and the skills of unemployed people. And finally there is demand deficient unemployment.

What I want to do now is to consider these explanations of unemployment in the light of concepts debated in this chapter, specifically the natural rate of unemployment, and unemployment as the cost of disinflation. I have suggested that the disinflation brought about by the UK recession of the early 1980s – and I think the same is true of the recession of 1990–92 – entailed a cost in terms of higher unemployment. In this context the trade-off between inflation and unemployment appears to be as robust as ever; governments can move their economies downwards and to the right along a short-run Phillips curve. The increases in UK unemployment in these two recessions were, I would argue, increases in demand deficient unemployment; high interest rates caused a fall in aggregate demand for goods and for labour while wages (and prices) were slow to adjust. But there was more to the course of UK unemployment in the 1980s than this.

Table 24.6 **GDP growth, inflation and unemployment UK 1980–92**

	GDP growth (%)	Inflation (%)	Unemployment (%)
1980	−2.0	18.5	5.1
1981	−1.2	10.1	8.1
1982	1.7	7.0	9.6
1983	3.8	5.6	10.5
1984	1.8	5.4	10.7
1985	3.8	5.4	10.9
1986	3.6	2.6	11.1
1987	4.4	5.1	10.0
1988	4.7	6.5	8.1
1989	2.1	7.8	6.3
1990	0.5	8.0	5.8
1991	−2.2	6.2	8.1
1992	−0.9	4.4	9.8

Note: the data in Table 24.6 are based on UK definitions, and therefore differ from the data in Figure 24.12, based on standardized OECD definitions.

Source: *Economic Trends Annual Supplement*, various years; Layard, Nickell and Jackman (1991); Crafts and Woodward (1991)

Question

Is there anything about the data in Table 24.6 to suggest that demand deficiency does not tell the whole story about UK unemployment in the 1980s?

If all unemployment could be explained as the consequence of demand deficiency, it would be the case that when output falls, unemployment rises and when output increases, unemployment falls. What happens in the labour market would depend closely on what happens in the goods market. This is consistent with the data for the recession of the early 1980s. However, from 1982 output resumed its growth yet unemployment remained high, only falling to 10 per cent in 1987. This raised doubts about the adequacy of demand deficiency as an explanation of unemployment. The trading off of rising unemployment against falling inflation along a conventional short-run Phillips curve in the early 1980s gave way to a period of persistently high unemployment accompanied by a somewhat uneven inflation performance. One reaction to this situation was to look to either the natural rate hypothesis assuming competitive markets, or the NAIRU assuming imperfectly competitive markets, for an alternative explanation of unemployment.

The reason why either the natural rate of unemployment or the NAIRU may offer an explanation is that they are both liable to change in response to changes in labour market institutions and the other structural factors on which each depend. Which structural factors matter depends on your model of the labour market, as Chapter 18 Section 5 explained. Both the natural rate and the NAIRU are long-run equilibrium rates of unemployment, but that does not mean that they are fixed forever. They are rather different types of equilibrium – only the natural rate assumes that the labour market clears and that all unemployment is voluntary – but both are equilibrium rates in the sense that they reflect the structure and institutions of the labour market when the inflation rate is stable, in the absence of expansionary or contractionary pressures.

When these structures change, so do the equilibrium rates of unemployment. So it is important to be able to estimate the total impact on the natural rate of unemployment or the NAIRU of, for example, changes in the cost of gathering information about job vacancies, in the value and availability of social security benefits, and (in the case of the NAIRU) on wage bargaining institutions. In other words, it is important to be able to measure the equilibrium unemployment rate and how it changes over time.

There is general agreement that the long term equilibrium rate of unemployment whether calculated as the natural rate or the NAIRU 'has risen significantly in Britain since the mid 1960s. In fact all the evidence confirms this whatever the method of calculation' (Knight, 1987, p.268). Any empirical estimate of the rate is specific to the model of the economy being used. Layard and Nickell (1985, p.77) estimated the NAIRU from within a model of imperfectly competitive markets where firms are price makers. Their figure for the NAIRU during the years 1980–83 is 10.47 per cent. Layard (1986, p.164) detected a slight upward trend to 1986, when the NAIRU was put at 11.7 per cent. Matthews and Minford (1987), on the other hand, assume that the labour market clears and that all unemployment is voluntary. On this basis, unemployment at the natural rate rose sharply from 2.1 million in 1979 to 3.7 million in 1981, before falling to 1.6 million by 1986. So on one estimate the NAIRU rose slightly during the early 1980s, while on another the natural rate fell significantly.

Look back now at the data in Table 24.6. Suppose, after all, that demand deficient unemployment had fallen during the mid 1980s, as it should have done in view of the growth of GDP. It follows that the failure of total unemployment to fall in line with the putative decline in demand deficient unemployment could be explained as the outcome of a rise in the NAIRU. A higher NAIRU would have offset lower demand deficient unemployment. So far, perhaps, so good. However, for this story to be truly convincing, we must find changes in structural and institutional factors to account for the supposed rise in the NAIRU. If, for example, the level of social security benefits increased or their accessibility improved, or if trade union power increased, the apparent rise in the NAIRU would be explained. In fact the very opposite is true. Unemployment benefits fell relative to wages, particularly after the abolition in 1982 of the earnings-related supplement. Legislation curbed the power of the trade unions and their membership fell, implying a weakening of their capacity to raise their members' wages. Taxes on labour were reduced by the abolition of the national insurance surcharge.

It seems reasonable to conclude that neither the natural rate hypothesis nor the concept of the NAIRU help greatly in explaining the persistence of high unemployment throughout the mid 1980s. But I turned to these concepts of equilibrium unemployment only because demand deficiency could not account for that phenomenon. Where do we go from here?

6.2   Hysteresis

The answer is that events in the mid 1980s led economists to a concept which mirrors the perplexing records of UK and European unemployment at that time. It seemed as though unemployment, having risen to about 10–11 per cent of the labour force in the early 1980s, had simply got stuck at that level. Perhaps unemployment was high throughout the mid 1980s just because it had reached such a high level in the early 1980s? Was there some mechanism or process that might cause actual unemployment to become locked into the high level to which demand deficiency had driven it by 1981? Might this apply to the natural rate or the NAIRU, too, not just to actual or total unemployment?

That the natural rate or NAIRU at any particular time might depend on what had happened to actual unemployment at previous times had in fact been predicted as long ago as 1972:

> The transition from one equilibrium to the other tends to have long-lingering effects on the labour force, and those effects may be discernible in the equilibrium rate for a long time ... the natural unemployment rate at any future date will depend on the course of history in the interim ... such a property is sometimes called 'hysteresis'
>
> *(Phelps, 1972, p. xxiii)*

The concept of hysteresis was introduced and defined in Chapter 18, Section 5.4. Economists set about the task of testing for the existence of this effect by asking two main questions. Is it supported by the facts: that is to say, is there a systematic statistical association between actual unemployment at a particular time and the natural rate or NAIRU at a later time? If so, what are the mechanisms or processes that might transform this association into an explanatory theory? The answer to the first question is that the current equilibrium unemployment rate does seem to be a function of past values of actual unemployment (Jenkinson, 1988; Blanchard and Summers, 1988). But this is only the beginning of the story, because correlation does not entail causation. In other words, the fact that the natural rate or NAIRU tracks the course of actual unemployment does not mean that a rise in actual unemployment causes the subsequent rise in the equilibrium unemployment rate. There could, for example, be a third factor which exerts a causal influence on both.

However, three mechanisms have been suggested which might explain hysteresis effects: which might, that is, explain why a period of high unemployment might set in motion processes which raise the long-term equilibrium rate. Two concern the labour market, while the third applies to the goods market. First, the insider–outsider hypothesis divides people involved in the labour market into insiders who experience uninterrupted employment and outsiders who suffer repeated spells of unemployment (Lindbeck and Snower, 1988a; Blanchard and Summers, 1988). Outsiders have little influence on wage bargaining. Since they are perceived as less employable than insiders, they will probably be unable to 'price themselves back into jobs' by offering to work for lower wages when output turns up after a recession. Instead, insiders will be able to turn the increase in the demand for labour to their own advantage by pushing for higher wage settlements. It is therefore arguable that high unemployment in the early 1980s, by creating more outsiders, in effect reduced the labour supply in subsequent years and thereby raised the equilibrium rate of unemployment.

The second hysteresis effect in the labour market concerns long-term unemployment. As unemployment rose in the early 1980s, the number of people without a job for a year or more increased as a percentage of the total number of unemployed people. The long-term unemployment hypothesis holds that the skills of people who suffer long-term unemployment atrophy and their attitude to work deteriorates (Price, 1988). The experience of failure in job applications eventually discourages them from searching for work. Once again the effect is to reduce the labour supply and raise the natural rate or the NAIRU.

The third mechanism applies to the goods market. The physical capital hypothesis is based on the fact that high unemployment tends to be associated with a fall in the productive capacity of the economy. Investment in new capacity is discouraged by the low levels of business confidence instilled by disinflationary policies, and the existing capital stock is diminished as firms go out of business or close some of their branch factories. The consequence is that economic recovery will very quickly set off inflationary pressures. For example, firms will soon be operating at full capacity and will then be obliged to respond to any further increase in demand for their goods by raising prices because capacity has not been increased by investment. Also, workers in such firms will be in a strong bargaining position to push for higher wages. So the natural amount of unemployment 'needed' to keep the inflation rate stable will rise.

These are reasonable grounds for believing that high unemployment in the early 1980s cast a long shadow over the rest of the decade, keeping the equilibrium unemployment rate and actual unemployment higher than they otherwise would have been. This hysteresis effect has an important implication for policy. Hysteresis in fact undermines the whole concept of the natural rate of unemployment and of the NAIRU since both, if you recall, are supposed to be dependent on structural and institutional factors in the labour market rather than the level of aggregate demand. But the logic of the hysteresis argument is that both the natural rate and the NAIRU are in part dependent on past levels of actual unemployment, including demand deficient unemployment caused by disinflationary policy measures. This means that policy makers cannot assume that a brief period of unemployment above the equilibrium rate will eliminate inflation and enable unemployment to return quickly to the natural rate. We have already seen that disinflation is far from painless, and the existence of hysteresis effects means that the costs of getting inflation down may last much longer than policy makers have tended to assume.

Can we now draw together this discussion of unemployment, relating Francis Green's categorization of types of unemployment in Chapter 21, the analysis of aggregate demand deficiency in Chapters 17 and 18, and the concepts of the natural rate the NAIRU and hysteresis explored further in this chapter? We might tell a story about the 1980s and early 1990s along the following lines. There is a base line of unemployment due to the worker discipline effect, frictions in the labour market and mismatch between the skills of unemployed people and those required by vacancies. It seems clear that the increases in unemployment in the early 1980s and early 1990s were caused by deficiencies of aggregate demand engineered by policy makers whose objective was to reduce inflation. The persistence of high unemployment for much of the 1980s when output growth was strong seems to me to be most convincingly explained by the hysteresis or long-lasting effects of the high level of demand deficiency at the start of the decade.

7   Conclusion

Unemployment and inflation are the headline issues of macroeconomic policy making, reported by the media month by month and year on year. This chapter has focused on these issues of short run macroeconomic policy. Perhaps the most fundamental question is 'Which is the more serious problem – unemployment or inflation?', for until we answer that question we cannot decide what the first priority of policy should be. Should we aim for full employment or price stability? In Section 2, I reviewed the evidence on the costs of unemployment and the costs of inflation. Unemployment is both inefficient, representing a loss of potential output, and inequitable, damaging the well-being of unemployed people. There does not seem to be any conclusive evidence for believing that moderate inflation has serious adverse effects on the economy and the case for eliminating it rests on a reluctance to take the risk, however small, of its acceleration into hyperinflation. So it seems to me that unemployment is the more serious problem and full employment a more worthwhile goal than price stability.

But do we really have to choose between cutting unemployment and fighting inflation? Price stability is seen by some policy makers on the political right as a means, rather than an alternative, to economic growth and full employment. The relationship between unemployment and inflation was discussed in Sections 3 and 4. It is clear that the trade-off between unemployment and inflation, expressed by the Phillips curve, applies only to the short run. Once the inflationary expectations of economic agents are recognized to adjust in the long run, as they were first by Friedman and then by rational expectations theorists such as Sargent, the trade-off collapses.

The New Keynesians and New Classicals agree on this point, differing essentially on the manner in which – and hence on the speed with which – the labour market reflects the adjustment of inflationary expectations. This difference of approach to the labour market leads to conflicting views of the costs of disinflation, discussed in Sections 5 and 6. The slow adjustment of imperfectly competitive markets persuades the New Keynesians that disinflation is likely to be costly in terms of a prolonged rise in demand deficient unemployment. The New Classicals see markets as adjusting more rapidly. While some New Classical theorists admit the possibility of a short-run trade-off, there is an extreme New Classical – or competitive – approach which argues that the rapid adjustment of competitive markets makes disinflation painless, at least in principle.

I have tried to advocate an alternative approach, based on the suggestion that the incorporation of inflationary expectations into the analysis of macroeconomic policy does not go far enough in recognizing the *agency* of economic agents. Perhaps economic agents, on both sides of the labour market, have their own objectives and priorities, which grow out of a recurring conflict over the distribution of the national income. If so, disinflation will incur a substantial unemployment cost unless there is a consensus on the importance of eliminating inflation.

CHAPTER 25

ECONOMIC FLUCTUATIONS AND TECHNOLOGICAL CHANGE

by Andrew B. Trigg

1 Introduction

In the East End districts of Poplar, Millwall, Greenwich, Deptford, Limehouse and Canning Town, at least 15,000 workmen and their families were in a state of utter destitution, and 3,000 skilled mechanics were breaking stones in the workhouse yard (after distress of over half a year's duration) ... I had great difficulty in reaching the workhouse door, for a hungry crowd besieged it ... They were waiting for their tickets, but the time had not yet arrived for the distribution. The yard was a great square place with an open shed running all round it, and several large heaps of snow covered the paving-stones in the middle. In the middle, also, were little wicker-fenced spaces, like sheep pens, where in finer weather men worked; but on the day of my visit the pens were so snowed up that nobody could sit in them. Men were busy, however, in the open shed breaking paving-stones into macadam. Each man had a big paving-stone for a seat, and he chipped away at the rime-covered granite with a big hammer until he had broken it up, and got his day's pay – three pence and an allowance of food. In another part of the yard was a rickety little wooden house, and when we opened the door of it, we found it filled with men who were huddled together shoulder to shoulder for the warmth of one another's bodies and breath. They were picking oakum and disputing the while as to which could work the longest on a given quantity of food – for endurance was the point of honour. Seven thousand ... in this one workhouse ... were recipients of relief ... many hundreds of them ... it appeared, were, six or eight months ago, earning the highest wages paid to artisans.

(The Morning Star, 1867, quoted in Marx, 1867, p.625)

This report, quoted by Karl Marx in Volume 1 of *Capital*, gives some insight into the effects of the economic recession which hit the UK economy in 1866. The workers, who had 'six or eight months ago' worked as well-paid artisans, were put out of work because one of the main casualties of this recession was the iron shipbuilding industry, the main employer at the time in London's East End. These workers, like many others in different countries and at different times, suffered from the vagaries of what economists call the business cycle.

Throughout the history of capitalism there have always been cycles – booms and recessions, peaks and troughs – in economic activity. These have been shown in Chapter 20 to be endemic to market economies. An important question to be asked, therefore, is 'What determines these booms and recessions?'. There is no simple answer, but a number of much-disputed theories.

In this chapter I shall examine a selection of these theories by making use of the techniques developed in previous chapters – in particular the aggregate demand/aggregate supply diagram. Each of these theories is associated with the name of a great economic thinker – John Maynard Keynes, Karl Marx, Milton Friedman and Joseph Schumpeter. The theoretical frameworks outlined in this chapter will not necessarily have the same structure, however, as those originally developed by the writers associated with them. There is a difference between Keynes and Keynesian, and between Marx and Marxian. The term Keynesian is often used as a very loose term for theories which include aggregate demand as a main determinant of economic activity. The Keynesian theory of the business cycle, which this chapter will concentrate on, is much more mechanical than the theory envisaged by Keynes himself and a little less complicated. The term Marxian usually refers to theories which are influenced by Marx's original work without being entirely faithful to it. In this chapter a Marxian theory of the business cycle will be developed. The term Schumpeterian, however, does closely refer to the theory of the business cycle developed by Schumpeter himself, and the term monetarist closely refers to Milton Friedman's monetary theory of the business cycle.

There are some significant differences between the four approaches covered in this chapter. First, in the Keynesian, Marxian and Schumpeterian theories the business cycle is endogenous to capitalism. As capitalism develops, its internal workings automatically generate fluctuations in economic activity. For the monetarist theory, however, business cycles only occur because of exogenous shocks to the market system. These exogenous shocks are caused by government interference in the economy.

A second difference concerns the extent to which the theories seek to provide a complete explanation of the cycle. The Keynesian, Marxian and monetarist theories can all be used to provide complete explanations for the whole of the cycle. In contrast, the Schumpeterian theory explains only part of the cycle.

The relative merits of these different approaches is not merely a matter of academic interest. Economists and politicians alike would desperately like to know the causes of economic cycles. Once the causes are identified, the relevant policy prescription can be developed. If, for example, we hold with the Keynesians that fluctuations in investment provide the reason for cycles, then some form of government intervention to influence investment might be desirable. If, however, we hold with Friedman that fluctuations in the money supply drive the cycle, then some form of government control of the money supply is desirable. An additional question to be addressed in this chapter, therefore, is 'How can and should policy makers respond to booms and recessions?'.

The relevance of the aggregate demand/aggregate supply diagram to economic cycles is explained in Section 2. Some simple facts that are common to many business cycles will be considered in order to show how this diagram can be applied. In the rest of the chapter the competing theories of the business cycle will be introduced and compared. In developing this discussion I shall look at empirical evidence on economic

Definition

Capitalism

Capitalism is an economic system based on free markets in which private owners of the means of production (that is, capital) employ labour to provide goods and services for profit.

cycles from a number of countries, with particular emphasis on the UK during the 1980s. My intention, however, will not be to test these theories, but merely to illustrate how they might be applied.

2 Cycles and aggregate demand

The main indicator that economists use to measure economic cycles is the level of output. During the recession phase of a cycle output will decline, and during a boom phase it will increase. Other indicators, such as the level of employment, can also follow a cyclical path, but the most commonly used indicator is output.

Question

What examples are there in recent years of periods in which output has contracted?

The most recent example is the recession in the world economy in the early 1990s. In 1991, for example, output in the UK contracted by 2.2 per cent (*International Financial Statistics Year Book*, 1994). In Figure 25.1 the three most recent recessions are shown for West Germany, the UK, and the USA.

The vertical axes show the rate of growth of output, and the horizontal axes the relevant time periods. The use of data on rates of growth to analyse periods of recession has already been introduced in Chapter 17. The horizontal line drawn on each diagram represents a zero growth rate of output. If the curve which tracks the growth of output falls below this line, then there is negative output growth. In West Germany, for example, the rate of output growth fell to −1.3 per cent in 1975. This means that there was a recession in which the West German economy contracted by 1.3 per cent in 1975. Figure 25.1 shows that all three countries experienced recessions in the mid 1970s, the early 1980s and the early 1990s.

Between the recessions shown in Figure 25.1 there are periods of growth which can be referred to as boom phases of the business cycle. Before the recession of the early 1990s, for example, West Germany experienced a boom rate of output growth of 4.9 per cent in 1990, the UK an output growth of 5 per cent in 1988, and the USA an output growth of 3.9 per cent in 1988. All three economies have clearly followed a cyclical path in which periods of growth have been followed by periods of contraction.

The different phases of the cycle are shown in Figure 25.2. For simplicity this diagram looks at differences in the level of output, but, as we have seen above, the rate of growth of output is often used as the indicator of economic activity. Output initially increases from point A to point B. This is a boom period, or what Schumpeter (1939) referred to as the prosperity phase of the cycle. Point B is a turning point, as output stops rising and begins to fall. The recession phase of the cycle (from B to C) covers the period when output has begun to fall. From C to D output falls further and the depression phase is entered. Finally, there is another turning point at point D, where output enters the recovery phase (from D to E). Output returns to its original level at point E. An economic cycle is therefore usually characterized by a systematic pattern of fluctuations in the level of output over time.

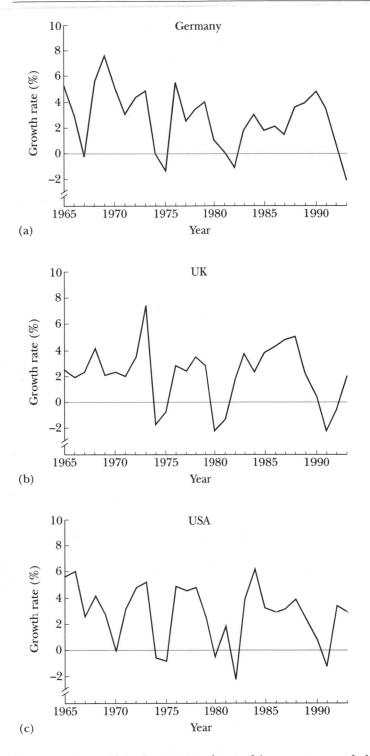

Figure 25.1   The rate of growth of output in West Germany, the UK and USA, 1960–92 (GDP at constant prices, percentage change from previous year)

Source: *International Financial Statistics Year Book* (1994)

How can the model of aggregate demand/aggregate supply be used to explain this cycle? Is it fluctuations in aggregate demand or aggregate supply that drive the cycle in output? In his classic study, *The Trade Cycle* (1959), R.C.O. Matthews argued that fluctuations in aggregate demand are the most important factor. There is a simple reason for this. Matthews observed that in most business cycles both output and prices tend to increase during a boom and fall during a depression. In the Great Depression of the 1930s, for example, Sherman (1991) has shown that there

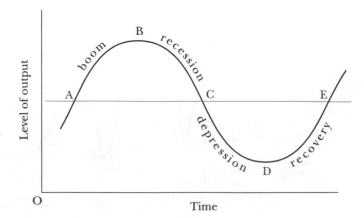

Figure 25.2   **A typical business cycle**

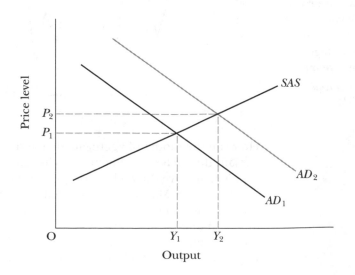

Figure 25.3   **Prices during a typical business cycle**

was a contraction of both output and prices. Figure 25.3 shows the path that prices will take if the economy moves in the direction suggested by Matthews.

Between points A and B (the boom phase) the price level increases, but not by as much as output, as Figures 25.2 and 25.3 are drawn to suggest. This cyclical pattern followed by prices can be explained by looking at fluctuations in aggregate demand. Consider the aggregate demand/ aggregate supply diagram in Figure 25.4.

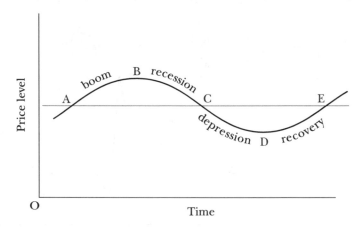

Figure 25.4   **An increase in aggregate demand**

First, let us assume that the boom phase of the cycle is driven by an increase in aggregate demand, without for the moment considering its precise components. This increase in aggregate demand, which is represented on the diagram by a rightward shift of the aggregate demand (*AD*) curve, has a twofold effect. It increases output (Y_1 to Y_2), since firms supply more output to meet the extra demand; and it increases prices (P_1 to P_2), because there is initially excess demand which induces suppliers of goods to increase prices to clear the market.

To complete the picture Figure 25.5 shows the movements of aggregate demand which would generate the other phases of the business cycle, shown in Figures 25.2 and 25.3 above.

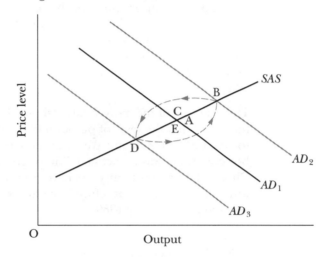

Figure 25.5 **Movements in aggregate demand during a typical business cycle**

The initial increase in aggregate demand is shown between points A and B. This is the boom phase of the cycle, in which both output and prices increase. A turning point exists, however, at point B; for some reason, to be investigated later, aggregate demand moves back towards its original level. This is the recession phase of the cycle, between points B and C. The reduction in aggregate demand now reduces output and prices back to their original level. Points A and C are the same point on Figure 25.5, because on Figures 25.2 and 25.3 output and prices are each the same at points A and C.

During the depression phase of the cycle, aggregate demand falls further, moving the economy to point D on Figure 25.5. Output and prices fall together to the bottom of the cycle, where a new turning point exists. The green shoots of recovery are expressed in an increase in aggregate demand which moves the economy from D to E – back to the original level of output and prices.

Fluctuations in aggregate demand can therefore be used to provide an explanation of fluctuations in both output and prices during the business cycle.

Question

Using the *AD/AS* diagram, show why fluctuations in aggregate supply are not consistent with Matthews' observations about the movements of prices and output during the business cycle.

Movements in aggregate supply cannot explain the movements of output and prices over the business cycle if prices and output move in the same direction. If you draw the *AD/AS* diagram and shift the short-run aggregate supply curve to the right (or downwards), this will increase the level of output, but the level of prices will fall. This is not consistent with Matthews' observation that prices rise during the boom phase of the cycle, suggesting that the main factor which causes economic cycles is the level of aggregate demand.

Prices and output do not always move in the same direction, however. An important example is the oil price shock in the mid 1970s. You should recall from Chapter 20 that an increase in the price of oil shifts the short-run aggregate supply curve to the left (or upwards), thereby increasing prices and reducing the quantity of output. This explains the occurrence of stagflation – high unemployment and high inflation – in the mid 1970s. In the more recent recessions of the early 1980s and early 1990s, however, inflation tended to fall only after a reduction in output had taken place.

The example of the early 1980s is shown in Table 25.1. In this period we have seen that the level of output fell – there were negative rates of growth – for the USA, the UK and West Germany (Figure 25.1). Unlike the 1930s, however, there was no actual fall in prices. As has been pointed out in Chapter 24, the post-war years have been characterized by permanent inflation. Table 25.1 therefore looks at the rate of price inflation during the recession in the early 1980s.

Table 25.1 **Changes in prices and output in the early 1980s (%)**

	USA		**UK**		**West Germany**	
Year	**Output growth**	**Inflation**	**Output growth**	**Inflation**	**Output growth**	**Inflation**
1980	−0.5	9.6	−2.2	19.8	1.0	4.3
1981	1.8	8.9	−1.3	11.7	0.1	4.2
1982	−2.2	6.9	1.7	7.1	−1.1	4.7
1983	3.9	3.3	3.7	4.9	1.9	3.3

Source: *International Financial Statistics Year Book* (1994); Layard, Nickell and Jackman (1991) pp.526–32

In the USA the contraction of output in 1980 was followed by a reduction in the rate of inflation from 9.6 per cent in 1980 to 8.9 per cent in 1981, and down to 6.9 per cent in 1982. Instead of there being a cut in actual prices, as in the 1930s, there was a cut in the rate of increase in prices. In the UK the fall in the rate of inflation was more dramatic over this period. From a rate of 19.8 per cent in 1980 inflation fell to 7.1 per cent in 1982. In West Germany the reduction in output by 1.1 per cent took place in 1982, with a reduction in inflation from 4.7 per cent in 1982 to 3.3 per cent in 1983. It should be noted, however, that there is a time lag between a change in output and its effect on prices. The relationship between output and prices during the course of the business cycle is not as straightforward as Figures 25.2 and 25.3 suggest.

3 Investment and aggregate demand

One of the most important components of aggregate demand is private investment – investment conducted by firms. This is not because the absolute amount of money spent on investment is large. In the 1991 UK national accounts, for example, investment only represents 16.6 per cent of GDP while consumer expenditure represents 64 per cent of GDP (see Chapter 2, Table 2.7). Investment is important because it fluctuates substantially during the course of cycles. This is illustrated in Figure 25.6, which shows the rate of growth of output and private investment in the UK during the 1980s.

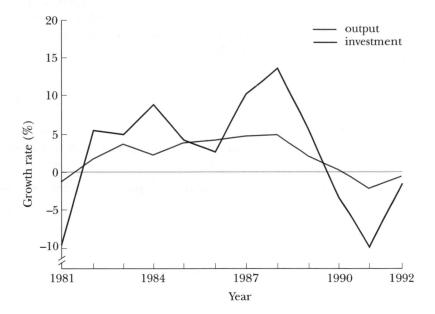

Figure 25.6 **The rate of growth of output and investment in the UK, 1981–92**

Source: *International Financial Statistics Year Book* (1994); *OECD Quarterly National Accounts* (1994)

During the peak of the boom the UK economy enjoyed growth rates in output of around 5 per cent in 1987 and 1988. During the subsequent recession the UK economy contracted by 2.2 per cent in 1991 and by 0.6 per cent in 1992. The fluctuations in investment over this period were much more violent. In 1988 the growth rate of investment peaked at 13.5 per cent, but contracted by nearly 10 per cent in 1991.

In view of these violent fluctuations, a number of economists have concentrated on investment as the driving force of the business cycle. Their approach is to argue that fluctuations in investment generate fluctuations in aggregate demand, which consequently result in fluctuations in output and prices.

In this part of the chapter two leading variants of this approach will be considered. In each approach an additional factor which determines fluctuations in investment is introduced. First, according to the Keynesian approach, the main factor is the rate of change of output. Secondly, a Marxian approach identifies the rate of profit as the main factor.

3.1   The Keynesian approach

The Keynesian approach to investment in the business cycle has two main building blocks: the multiplier and the accelerator. The multiplier has already been introduced in Section 4.2 of Chapter 17. Keynes's solution to the Great Depression of the 1930s was for governments to increase government spending and hence aggregate demand in order to stimulate economic recovery. The multiplier expresses the idea that the final increase in aggregate demand is larger than the initial increase in government expenditure that caused it. The same is true of an initial increase in any of the components of aggregate demand, including investment. Let us suppose that the expectations of entrepreneurs become more optimistic and they increase their investment in new plant and equipment.

The initial effect of an increase in investment is that additional workers would be employed to make the new plant and machinery. These workers would spend their additional income on goods and services. Additional workers would then be employed to produce these new goods and services. This further batch of additional workers would also spend their extra income on goods and services. The effect of the initial increase in aggregate demand – the demand for new plant and machinery – would *multiply* throughout the economy. It would have knock-on effects on the income and consumption of workers throughout the economy. The effect of an initial increase in aggregate demand on the total national income of an economy is measured by the demand *multiplier*, which can be expressed as a simple equation:

change in output = multiplier × change in investment

Assume that the multiplier takes on a value of 2. This means that if investment increases by 1 unit, then output will eventually increase by 2 units.

Exercise 25.1

A new hospital is built at a cost of £200 million. If the multiplier is 2.5, what will be the effect on output?

Definition

Keynesian accelerator

The Keynesian accelerator measures the amount of net investment (additional capital stock) required to produce a unit increase in output.

The second building block of the Keynesian approach to the business cycle is the accelerator. This concept captures the notion that the main factor that influences the level of investment in the economy is the *rate of change* in output. An important distinction was made in Chapter 2 between a stock and a flow. A stock represents something constant at a particular point in time, such as a machine or a factory – referred to as capital stock. Investment is a flow which represents additions to, or changes in, the capital stock. It involves the movement through time of new machinery from the machine manufacturer to the factory which uses the machinery. *Gross investment*, which I will refer to simply as *investment*, denotes the purchase of new machines. We can think of it as the outcome of two sets of decisions. First, investment decisions taken to replace worn-out plant and machinery in order to maintain the capital stock at a constant level are referred to as *replacement investment*. Second, investment decisions taken to increase the capital stock are referred to as *net investment*.

Why would the firm increase its capital stock? A plausible answer is that the firm increases its capital stock because there has been an increase in the demand for its product. There is, therefore, a relationship between increases in demand and increases in capital stock (net investment). Moreover, as we saw in Figure 25.6, fluctuations in investment are of a much greater magnitude than changes in output. This raises the question of why changes in demand and hence output lead to much greater changes in investment.

Suppose that a firm has 50 machines, each of which produces 2 units of output per period. Each year 10 machines wear out and have to be replaced. (This implies that the entire capital stock has to be replaced every five years.) Now suppose that demand increases from 100 to 110. An additional 5 machines are needed to produce the extra 10 units of output, and so net investment is 5. Gross investment therefore increases from 10 to 15 (10 for replacement and 5 for net investment). So a 10 per cent increase in demand has led to a 50 per cent increase in investment.

Let me develop this example to illustrate another point about the accelerator. What if the demand remains at 110 units next year? Net investment falls to zero and gross investment falls back to the replacement investment. This shows that the higher level of investment can be maintained only if output continues to expand; once output stabilizes, even at the higher level of 110 units, net investment is zero and the only investment comes from replacing worn out equipment.

The Keynesian accelerator models this relationship between net investment and the rate of change of output demanded using a simple equation:

$$\text{net investment} = \text{accelerator} \times \text{change in output}$$

The amount by which net investment changes when output increases in response to a change in demand depends on the size of the accelerator, which in turn depends on the technical nature of the production process and the capital:output ratio. Suppose that the value of the accelerator is $\frac{1}{2}$. This means that for every increase in output by 2 units, the amount of capital needs to increase by 1 unit; in this case the capital:output ratio is $\frac{1}{2}$. This accelerator relationship can be expanded from the behaviour of an individual firm to the economy as a whole. Aggregate net investment responds to changes in aggregate demand according to an aggregate accelerator.

Exercise 25.2

Assume that the accelerator has a value of 3. If output increases by 300 units, what will be the consequent level of net investment?

How can these two building blocks, the multiplier and the accelerator, be used to formulate the Keynesian theory of the business cycle? The key components of this theory are shown in Figure 25.7. Let us assume, as a starting point for this flow diagram, that there is an increase in output which generates, via the Keynesian accelerator mechanism, an increase in investment as firms require more capital stock to achieve the increase in output. This increase in investment then generates, via the multiplier, an increase in output. In the boom phase of the business cycle these two mechanisms, the accelerator and multiplier, feed off each other to generate increases in output and investment. Conversely, in the downturn phase of a business cycle, reductions in output and investment feed off each other in the opposite direction. Each reduction in output generates a reduction in investment (via the accelerator) which generates a reduction in output (via the multiplier).

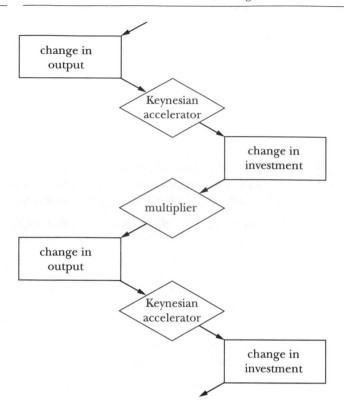

Figure 25.7   The Keynesian multiplier-accelerator model

Question

Why did the boom come to an end? Is there something about the nature of the accelerator that explains why this happened?

There is a clue in the numerical example given above: investment declines as soon as output stabilizes at a constant level. But why should output stabilize? Suppose that output grows by the same amount this year as it did last year, i.e. by 2 units. The accelerator equation above tells us that, in this case, net investment will be the same this year as it was last year. Without an increase in net investment, there is no multiplier effect. Output therefore stabilizes next year and, with no additions to the capital stock needed, investment declines to a level sufficient to cover replacement. A downward spiral of falling output and investment then ensues, until once again a turning point is reached. Unless output grows at an ever increasing rate, investment will fluctuate and the economy will undergo a cycle of boom and recession.

A numerical example of the multiplier-accelerator model

The Keynesian theory of the business cycle can be demonstrated in detail using a numerical example. Here we combine the accelerator model with the multiplier model to show how increases in output can lead to fluctuations in investment (via the accelerator), and fluctuations in investment lead to further fluctuations in output (via the multiplier) and so on. Table 25.2 shows a hypothetical case designed to illustrate the interaction of the accelerator and the multiplier.

In each period, once the new level of output is known, the change in output (i.e. ΔY) can be calculated. This then gives the required net investment (net I) according to the accelerator model where, in this case, we assume that the accelerator is $\frac{1}{2}$, i.e.

$$\text{net investment} = \tfrac{1}{2}\,\Delta Y$$

Note that this implies a level of capital, K, which ensures a constant capital:output ratio of $\frac{1}{2}$. Replacement investment (replacement I) is required because the capital stock needs replacing every five years. Gross investment (gross I) is the sum of net investment and replacement investment. The final column in Table 25.2 shows the change in gross investment between the two periods (ΔI). According to the multiplier formula, the increase in output in any period is given by the previous period's increase in investment multiplied by the value of the multiplier, here taken to be 2.

In Table 25.2 the economy starts in period 1 with a constant output level of 200 units and zero net investment. The desired capital stock is 100, and with replacement investment of 20 each year the entire capital stock is replaced every five years. Thus, in the absence of exogenous shocks, the economy could reproduce itself indefinitely as shown for period 1.

Table 25.2   The multiplier-accelerator model

Period	Y	ΔY	K	Replacement I	Net I	Gross I	ΔI
1	200	0	100	20	0	20	—
2	230	30	115	20	15	35	15
3	260	30	130	20	15	35	0
4	260	0	130	20	0	20	−15
5	230	−30	115	20	−15	5	−15
6	200	−30	100	20	−15	5	0
7	200	0	100	35	0	35	30
8	260	60	130	35	30	65	30
9	320	60	160	20	30	50	−15

Now let's consider what happens in period 2 if there is an exogenous increase of 30 units of output. According to the accelerator model this requires net investment of 15 (i.e. $\frac{1}{2} \times 30$) and gross investment of 35 (i.e. $20 + 15$). Note that this implies an increase in investment of 15 (i.e. $\Delta I = 15$) and an increase in the capital stock to 115. From this period on we shall let the model run and see what happens.

Period 3: The effect of the increase in investment in period 2 is to increase output in period 3. As the multiplier is 2, the increase in output is 30 (2×15), so in period 3 output is increased from 230 to 260. This again requires net investment of 15 and gross investment of 35, so in this period gross investment remains unchanged. Note that although output has increased, investment has remained constant. This illustrates an important aspect of the accelerator model, namely that increases in investment occur only if output increases at an increasing rate.

Period 4: With gross investment in the previous period remaining constant, output in this period remains constant at 260, and net investment is therefore zero. This implies gross investment of 20 and a fall in investment of 15 compared with period 3. The implication for the following period is that output falls by 30 to 230.

Period 5: Since output has fallen to 230, net investment is –15 which, with replacement investment of 20, implies a gross investment of only 5. Investment thus falls by 15 for a second time, and output in period 6 falls from 230 to 200.

Period 6: With output having fallen to 200, net investment is again –15 and gross investment again is only 5. This time, however, the change in investment is zero, so output for the following period is unchanged.

Period 7: Output is unchanged at 200, so net investment is zero. But what happens to gross investment? Remember that capital equipment lasts for five years and then has to be replaced. Until now the economy has been in the situation where exactly one-fifth of the capital stock needed replacing each year, thus requiring a steady stream of replacement investment of 20 each year. But in period 2 an extra 15 units were invested and their life ended in year 6. This means that in year 7, in order to maintain the existing capital stock, replacement investment is 35 not 20. This also illustrates an important aspect of investment, that current investment is influenced by the past pattern of investment as well as by changes in current output.

Period 8: As the previous period's investment increased by 30, current output increases by 60 to 260 and this implies net investment of 30. In this period replacement investment is again 35, reflecting the increased investment in period 3. Gross investment is 65, again implying an increase of 30. This means that next period's output will increase by 60 to 320.

Period 9: With output at 320, net investment is 30. Replacement investment is 20, so gross investment is 50.

An examination of Table 25.2 reveals that the level of output has followed a cyclical path. Figure 25.8 shows this path over the nine periods.

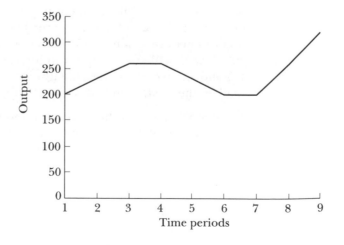

Figure 25.8   **The cyclical path of output in Table 25.2**

Exercise 25.3

Will output continue to rise in the hypothetical case shown in Table 25.2? Calculate the level of output for periods 10–14.

This numerical example shows how the interaction of the accelerator and the multiplier can cause fluctuations in the level of output without any assistance from outside forces. The specific path of output depends on the actual values chosen for this example, and particularly on the values of the accelerator and the multiplier which were held constant throughout the course of the cycle in this illustration, itself a restrictive simplifying assumption. (You might like to experiment to see how output fluctuations change with alternative values of the accelerator and multiplier.) The result here is a rather stylized and exaggerated picture of the process of fluctuations, but nonetheless the general point holds that the combination of an accelerator mechanism and the multiplier process can result in cycles of greater amplitude than would be the case if either one operated in the absence of the other.

3.2   Investment and consumption in the 1980s

The multiplier-accelerator model can be used to give some insight into the business cycle fluctuations of the UK economy in the 1980s. Figure 25.6 shows that the boom in investment that occurred in 1987 and 1988 was followed by a severe contraction in the early 1990s. Why did this contraction of investment take place?

The accelerator model suggests that movements in aggregate demand might explain why the investment cycle took place. One component of aggregate demand that might be important is household consumption, since this makes up about two-thirds of GDP. Figure 25.9 shows the growth rates of household consumption and investment during the 1980s.

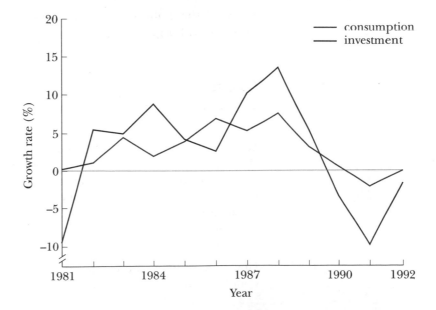

Figure 25.9   **The rate of growth of household consumption and investment in the UK, 1981–92**

Source: *OECD Quarterly National Accounts* (1994)

These figures do not either prove or disprove the multiplier-accelerator model of the business cycle. In performing a test of any model of the business cycle, there are many more variables than those considered here which must be taken into account. Nevertheless, it appears that investment and household consumption tended to move together during the course of the 1980s business cycle. During the boom phase of the cycle the growth rates of both investment and household consumption increased. The household consumption growth rate increased from 2.0 per cent per annum in 1984 to 7.5 per cent per annum in 1988. Investment increased from a growth rate of 2.6 per cent in 1986 to 13.5 per cent in 1988. In 1991, however, during the recession phase of the cycle, household consumption fell by 2.2 per cent and investment by 9.8 per cent.

This approximate movement together of investment and household demand is consistent with the multiplier-accelerator model. Via the accelerator each increase in the rate of growth of demand could be adjudged to generate an increase in investment. By the multiplier these increases in investment could fuel further increases in demand, which fuel further increases in investment, and so on. It should also be noted that the fluctuations in UK investment during the 1980s are much more pronounced than the fluctuations in demand, as the multiplier-accelerator predicts. The multiplier-accelerator provides a possible explanation of the boom in the UK economy during the 1980s.

3.3   Government intervention

The account I have given so far of the structure of the Keynesian model and the seemingly inevitable business cycle fluctuations of the 1980s must seem rather pessimistic. Can nothing be done to iron out the vagaries of the business cycle? The former contemporary of Keynes, James Meade, has recently lamented that economic depression is 'being treated once again as in pre-Keynesian days as a cyclical Act of God. It is impossible to convey what hell this has caused for an old Keynesian' (Meade, 1994, p.8).

However, the multiplier-accelerator model can in principle provide an opportunity for government intervention to prevent recessions from taking place.

Question

What form might this government intervention take?

We have seen that the root cause of cycles is to be found in this model in the uneven pattern of investment, which amplifies the effects of an exogenous disturbance. Net investment fluctuates because of changes in output, and replacement investment fluctuates because of previous fluctuations in gross investment. These changes in investment in their turn exercise a disproportionate effect on output via the working of the multiplier.

Government intervention may attempt to stabilize output by ensuring counteracting changes in other forms of expenditure in order to nullify the effects of the changes in investment. Stabilization policy was introduced in Chapter 17 as a way of controlling aggregate demand so that the economy is protected from swings in economic activity. This requires that the government introduces changes in non-investment forms of expenditure, leaving total demand relatively constant.

For example, if investment increases by 50, then other forms of expenditure – consumption expenditure, government expenditure and net foreign expenditure – have to fall by 50 in order to leave total expenditure unchanged. If investment is booming, then the government could introduce deflationary measures to reduce other forms of expenditure: the government could raise interest rates, increase taxes and reduce its own expenditures. On the other hand, if investment is falling, then that is the time to inject some extra demand into the economy, say by lowering interest rates, reducing taxes, and increasing government expenditure.

Chapter 17 examined some of the difficulties standing in the way of this kind of stabilization policy, and explained how many western governments and economists have become more sceptical of the prospects for 'fine tuning' the economy in this way. In addition, there are three fundamental problems with the multiplier-accelerator model. First, it is very difficult to measure both the accelerator and the multiplier. Both involve complex statistical methods which look at the relationship between output and investment. All statistical estimates involve errors, and this will always make it very difficult to develop precise policy prescriptions.

Secondly, the difficulty of estimating the multiplier and accelerator coefficients is compounded by the problem that they may not be stable over time. Investment depends on the expectations of entrepreneurs, which can be very unstable. In the late 1980s, for example, the frenzied optimism of the UK boom in 1986/87 was quickly followed by a period of pronounced pessimism in the early 1990s. The volatile psychology of markets is something that Keynes himself emphasized. Since expectations are based on such 'shifting and unreliable evidence, they are subject to sudden and violent changes' (Keynes, 1936, p.315).

The accelerator model, in which investment mechanically depends on fluctuations in demand, was developed by Samuelson (1939) and is categorized as Keynesian, in the sense that it represents one interpretation of Keynes. This means that it is part of the tradition which follows from Keynes but is not part of his own work. Some economists, such as G.L.S. Shackle, prefer to emphasize other aspects of Keynes's work, in particular the role of expectations and the 'animal spirits' of both producers and consumers (Ford, 1990). The precarious nature of expectations and investment provides an important qualification to the accelerator model.

Thirdly, the accelerator does not take into account the reserves of capacity that can exist at the start of an upturn in economic activity. If a large proportion of factory space and machinery has been lying idle due to lack of demand, the firm may simply bring this excess capacity into operation if the economy picks up. The accelerator may therefore be very small at the start of an economic upturn.

For some writers such as Michal Kalecki, a Polish contemporary of Keynes, the accelerator does not work for most of the business cycle. For Kalecki (1954) 'it is well known that large reserve capacities exist, at least throughout a considerable part of the cycle, and that output may therefore increase without an actual increase in existing capacities' (p.285). Firms often tend to keep large reserves of capacity because this gives them the flexibility to respond to sudden changes in demand or to new competition from other firms.

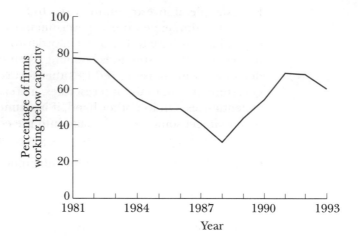

Figure 25.10 **Percentage of firms working below capacity in the UK, 1981–94**

Source: CB1 (1994)

Question

Look at Figure 25.10. Does this graph provide any evidence of excess capacity in the UK during the period 1981–94? If so, at what stage in the economic cycle is it most apparent?

Figure 25.10 shows the proportion of firms in the CBI's 1994 *Industrial Trends Survey* which have reported that they are not using the full capacity of their capital stock, and it provides some evidence of the existence of excess capacity in the UK over the period 1981–94. At the start of the period, in 1981, 77 per cent of the firms surveyed were working below full capacity. During the course of the 1980s this proportion dropped, so that in 1988, at the peak of the boom, 31 per cent of firms were not producing at full capacity. It seems that the accelerator is mainly of relevance in periods such as 1988 when the majority of firms are operating at full capacity.

In view of the problems associated with examining the effect of demand on investment, it is worth considering an alternative approach in which profits are a determinant of investment.

Reflection

Summarize in one paragraph the main thrust of the Keynesian theory of the business cycle. Key words here are investment, output, multiplier and accelerator.

3.4   The Marxian approach

There are many variants of the Marxian approach to the analysis of fluctuations in economic activity. The most orthodox approach is Marx's 'Law of the falling rate of profit', which has been subject to much controversy since the publication of the third volume of *Capital* (1894). The fundamental idea of this law is that fluctuations in investment are determined primarily by movements in the rate of profit.

The fact that a firm makes £200 million profit in a particular year is a poor indicator of how well the firm is doing. It is more helpful to compare this volume of profit to the volume of capital which the firm has invested. For example, if the firm has a capital stock of £200 million, then the rate of profit is 100 per cent. For each pound invested another pound of profit is received. The firm is doing well, since it would not get a rate of return of 100 per cent by investing its money in a bank or building society. If, on the other hand, the firm had invested in a capital stock of £2000 million, the profit rate would be only 10 per cent. It might have been easier for the firm to put its money in an interest-paying bank account rather than going to the trouble of building a factory and employing workers.

Exercise 25.4

A firm produces agricultural machinery using a capital stock valued at £400 million. Its annual profits are £200 million. What is the rate of profit?

The rate of profit is important not only as a motivation for investment, but also as a source of funds. As Marglin and Bhaduri (1990, p.183) point out, 'Today's profits are, on the one hand, a primary source of saving for the accumulation of business capital. Tomorrow's profits, on the other hand, are the lure which attracts the investor'. A fall in the rate of profit discourages firms from investing, since it both cuts off the funds for investment and reduces expectations of the future profitability of investment. A study by Klein and Moore (1985) confirms that firms use movements in the profit rate as a benchmark for judging the future profitability of their outlays.

How can the profit rate be used to construct a theory of the business cycle? For Marx the seeds of such a theory are provided by his observation that capitalists always strive to accumulate capital. 'Accumulate, accumulate! That is Moses and the prophets!', wrote Marx in Volume 1 of *Capital* (p.558). This ceaseless striving to accumulate capital, according to Marx, will in the long run undermine the profit rate. In the above example, a firm which made £200 million profit and had a capital stock of £200 million enjoyed a profit rate of 100 per cent. When the capital stock increased to £2000 million the profit rate fell to 10 per cent. Since the profit rate is the ratio between total profits and the capital stock, a long-run increase in the capital stock leads to a tendency for the profit rate to fall.

The long-run tendency for the rate of profit to fall has been adapted by Michal Kalecki to construct a theory of the business cycle. This theory is often said to embody the same original insights as Keynes's *General Theory*. Supporters of Kalecki have claimed that he discovered the central principles of the *General Theory* prior to and independently of Keynes. Unlike Keynes, however, Kalecki was not part of mainstream economics. Whereas Keynes went to Eton and Cambridge, Kalecki went to Gdansk Polytechnic. Whilst Keynes was tutored by the great Cambridge economist, Alfred Marshall, Kalecki was schooled in the 'underworld' (as Keynes referred to it) of Rosa Luxemburg and Karl Marx. Kalecki's model is distinctly Marxian in flavour but contains some important similarities with the Keynesian model.

Kalecki's model is built around an investment equation in which investment is a function of the rate of profit. There are a number of other factors which influence investment, but I shall concentrate here solely on the components which make up the profit rate (more detail is provided in Trigg, 1994).

The core of Kalecki's investment equation has the form:

net investment = accelerator × change in rate of profit

This accelerator reflects the effect of a change in the rate of profit on investment. If the rate of profit increases then there is positive net investment; if it falls, there is negative net investment.

A comparison of Kalecki's equation with the earlier equation for the accelerator reveals that Kalecki's accelerator is similar to the Keynesian output accelerator. However, whereas the Keynesian accelerator looks at the effect of *changes in output* on investment, the Marxian accelerator in Kalecki's equation looks at the effects of *changes in the rate of profit* on investment.

The Marxian accelerator is consistent with Klein and Moore's (1985) observation that changes in profitability affect investment decisions. If the profit rate starts to fall, then firms will start to downgrade their expectations of future profitability and scale back their investment plans. The relationship between investment and the rate of profit is shown in Figure 25.11.

Definition

Marxian accelerator

The Marxian accelerator measures the amount of net investment expenditure by firms in response to a unit change in the rate of profit.

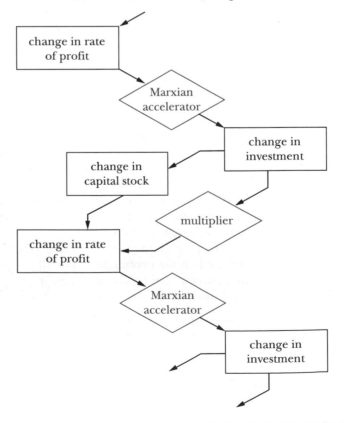

Figure 25.11   **The Marxian investment-accelerator model**

The flow diagram takes as its starting point a change in the rate of profit. Assume that this change is positive: the rate of profit increases, which means that via the accelerator net investment will be positive. There are two consequences of this change in investment: (a) an increase in total profits via the multiplier; and (b) an increase in capital stock.

The resultant change in the rate of profit depends on which of these two factors is dominant. Either the increase in total profits is dominant, in which case the rate of profit falls, or the rate of profit is dragged downwards by a burgeoning capital stock. The consequent change in the rate of profit will then generate a new level of net investment via the Marxian accelerator.

Using these interactions between investment and the rate of profit, Kalecki generates a similar pattern of cyclical fluctuations to the Keynesian multiplier-accelerator model, but for different reasons. Figure 25.12 provides an illustration of a business cycle in which there are fluctuations in investment and the capital stock. Investment here refers to net and replacement investment.

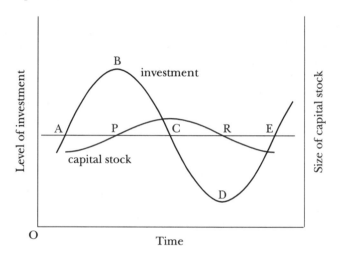

Figure 25.12 **Kalecki's theory of the business cycle**

There are four main stages to the business cycle, and these are shown in Figure 25.12:

Between points A and B: there is a boom phase in which investment increases. By a multiplier process very similar to that used by the Keynesians, increases in investment generate increases in aggregate demand which generate increases in profits. The relationship between aggregate demand and profits is a very important component of Kalecki's theory.

Between points B and C: at point B the cumulative boom in investment and profits comes to an end, because the capital stock has increased as a result of the investment boom. At point P the capital stock is increasing more rapidly than total profits and the profit rate therefore starts to fall, inducing a turning point in the direction of investment. A downward spiral of reductions in investment generates reductions in aggregate demand (via the multiplier), which further reduce profits so that there are additional downward impacts on investment.

Between points C and D: the downward spiral of falling investment and profits continues. With investment below the level for replacement, the capital stock starts to fall.

Between points D and E: at point R, the capital stock is falling at a sufficient rate to improve the profit rate and hence investment. An upturn takes place.

Kalecki's theory of the business cycle can be illustrated by looking at the movement of the rate of profit in the UK at the end of the 1980s. In Figure 25.13 the 'rate of return on capital in the business sector' is used as a very rough indicator of the rate of profit. The annual percentage change in this profit rate is compared with the rate of growth of investment.

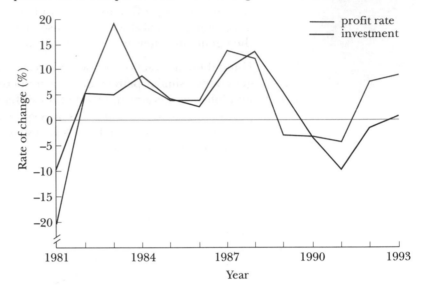

Figure 25.13   The rate of growth of investment and the annual percentage change in profit rate in the UK, 1981–93

Source: *OECD Quarterly National Accounts* (1994); *OECD Economic Outlook* (various years)

Question

What can be inferred from Figure 25.13 about the relation between movements in the profit rate and in investment in the UK over the period 1981–93?

It can be seen that the movements in the rate of profit and in investment moved quite closely together during the course of the 1980s. The peak in the growth rate of investment of 13.5 per cent in 1988 was preceded by a peak growth rate for the rate of profit of 13.8 per cent in 1987. Once the two variables peaked, both followed the same downward path during the late 1980s. In 1991 the rate of profit contracted by 4.2 per cent and investment by 9.8 per cent.

These observations are broadly consistent with the Marxian approach. As investment increased, this could have stimulated the rate of profit (via the multiplier); and as the rate of profit increased, this could have further stimulated investment (via the accelerator). Similarly, the recession phase of the cycle could have been triggered by a slowdown in the profit rate. Once the profit rate had peaked in 1987, due to an accumulation of the capital stock, the slow-down in its rate of increase could have started to temper business investment plans. The slow-down in the rate of increase of investment in 1988 could have heralded a new downward path for both investment and the rate of profit. However, this provides only an illustration of how the Marxian approach could be used to interpret the fluctuations in the late 1980s. The fact that investment and the rate of profit moved together over this period does not prove any causation between the variables. They may have moved together without having had any influence on each other. Perhaps other unobserved variables were driving investment. We saw earlier, when discussing the Keynesian approach, that the rate of growth of demand can also explain the fluctuations in investment.

In any case, if we wished to test the Kalecki model it must be stressed that the model developed here is only a very simplified version of Kalecki's system. The model does, however, highlight some key components of his theory of the business cycle. Like Marx, Kalecki saw the rate of profit as a key determinant of the business cycle. To quote Malcolm Sawyer (1985), 'both saw that during a trade cycle, it would be a decline in the rate of profit which would be an important trigger in the downswing' (p.164).

Unlike Marx, who was not particularly interested in policy proposals, Kalecki suggested several, the first of which was also recommended by the Keynesians. If the government stimulates aggregate demand through increasing its own spending, this will boost the profits of capitalists and stimulate their investment. For Kalecki (1945), however, there also 'comes into the picture another contradiction of the capitalist system formulated by Marx in his law of the falling rate of profit' (p.385). Even though the government has stimulated aggregate demand, it may still not prevent a downturn in economic activity because the profit rate, and hence investment, may fall. The logical conclusion is that the government should intervene to increase investment. Kalecki advocated that 'state-owned factories should be built to fill the deficiency in private investment' (p.385). For Kalecki, a socialist solution is necessary to solve the problem of the business cycle.

In the next section a different type of theory is developed which explicitly incorporates the behaviour of individual agents in the economy.

Reflection

Summarize in one paragraph the main thrust of the Marxian theory of the business cycle. Key words here are accumulation, capital stock, profits and expectations.

4   Money and aggregate demand

The Keynesian and Marxian approaches to the business cycle do not explicitly take price movements into account. That is not to say that Marx, Keynes or Kalecki ignored prices in their writings. The point is simply that the core models of the business cycle which I have derived from their work do not include the price mechanism as a key component. The main focus of such models is on the explanation of movements in the real volume of investment and output over the business cycle. However, since we know from Figure 25.3 that prices fluctuate over the business cycle, it follows that some consideration should be given to theories in which prices play a central role.

A major twentieth-century economist who has incorporated prices into his theory of the business cycle is Milton Friedman. In emphasizing the importance of prices, Friedman gives equal importance to an additional variable, namely money. He develops a linkage between money and prices over the business cycle by making use of the *quantity theory of money*, developed by Irving Fisher (1911). A very simplified version of Friedman's model is presented in this section.

The quantity theory of money is formulated around a simple identity:

$$MV = PY$$

where

M = the stock of money

V = velocity of circulation (the average number of times each unit of money is used for making transactions)

P = the average price level, and

Y = the flow of real goods and services (real national income)

The left-hand side of the identity (MV) represents the amount of money needed for transactions in the economy over a given period. Since the stock of money (M) changes hands a number of times in a period (depending on the size of V), the amount of money needed for transactions is MV. Suppose that, in a simple economy in which monetary transactions take place between firms and households, the velocity of circulation has a value of 4. If the amount of money needed for transactions during a particular period is 100, this means that people will hold a money stock of 25. Since the 25 circulates four times around the economy during the period, this is sufficient to provide the means of exchange for the 100 worth of transactions.

On the right-hand side of the quantity equation, real national income (Y) multiplied by the average price level (P) gives nominal national income: the money value of goods and services sold.

The basis of Friedman's interpretation of the quantity equation is his assumption that there will be a stable demand for money. Perhaps you can recall the transactions demand for money from Chapter 11, Section 4.1. The transactions demand has none of the volatility associated with the speculative demand for money emphasized by Keynes (Chapter 11, Section 4.2). Individuals will tend to demand or hold the same amount of money each week for transaction purposes. This means that the velocity of circulation, the speed at which money circulates around the economy, will also tend to be stable. If people reduced their transaction demand for money each week, this would mean that the velocity of circulation would increase – the transactions balances would have to circulate more quickly for the economy to function.

If the demand for money and hence the velocity of circulation are stable, what happens when the supply of money increases? If the stock of money M increases and V is unchanged, MV must increase and, by the quantity equation, so too must PY. Friedman's point is essentially a very simple one: if the supply of money increases while velocity and the demand for money remain unchanged, some people are going to find themselves with greater money balances than they are willing to hold and will get rid of them, by spending more. With V a stable component of the quantity equation, economic fluctuations originate in M, the stock of money. Assume that the government increases the money stock in some way, for example by paying its own public sector workers more wages. It could print more money to make this possible (see Chapter 11, Section 5.2 and Chapter 17, Section 5.3). The resultant increase in money balances leads to a general increase in production. Consumers throughout the economy spend more money on goods and services and assets.

In the short run this increase in aggregate demand generates an increase in output. There is, however, an additional consequence of the increased demand. Shopkeepers are able to charge higher prices for the goods which consumers demand. Eventually these increases in price choke off the new demand, and it returns to its original level. This scenario has been considered in Chapter 18, where a vertical long-run aggregate supply curve means that in the long run shifts in aggregate demand have no impact on the level of output.

In the quantity equation the increase in the money stock (M) first causes an increase in national income (Y) which then leads to an increase in prices (P). This increase in prices reduces the level of national income back to its previous level. A business cycle in output and prices has been generated by the increase in the money supply. For Friedman, governments generate cycles by changing the money supply. The usual pattern is for an upturn in economic activity to be generated by an increase in the money supply. The inflation which this generates then causes the government to force down the rate of increase in the money supply, and the economy overshoots in the opposite direction with a downturn in economic activity. The reduction in inflation associated with this downturn generates a recovery phase, and the cycle retreads its familiar steps.

The monetary theory of the business cycle can be illustrated by looking again at the UK economy during the 1980s. Figure 25.14 shows movements in the rate of growth of output, the rate of growth of the money supply (M4), and the inflation rate.

The rate of growth of the money supply fluctuates substantially over this period, increasing from a rate of 12.4 per cent in 1982 to rates of between 17 and 19 per cent in 1987, 1988 and 1989. These large increases are then followed by smaller increases in the money supply of 5.6 per cent in 1991 and 3.1 per cent in 1992. What is clear from these figures is that the money supply follows a cyclical path during the 1980s.

There is also some evidence that these changes in the money supply can be related to changes in output and inflation. The period in which the money supply grew quickly (between 1987 and 1989) was also characterized by a

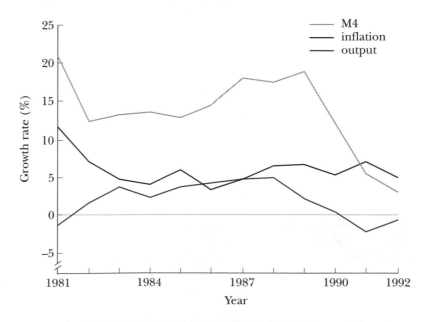

***Figure 25.14*   Growth rates of output, money supply and inflation, 1981–1990**

Sources: *International Financial Statistics Year Book* (1994); Layard, Nickell and Jackman (1991); *Annual Abstract of Statistics* (various years)

boom in output growth, which increased from a low of 2.3 per cent in 1984 to 5 per cent in 1988. During this period inflation virtually doubled, from 3.5 per cent in 1986 to 6.8 per cent in 1989. Increases in the money supply could plausibly have generated higher growth rates of output which could then have fuelled increases in inflation. Eventually, however, the boom in output came to an end. The increase in inflation could have generated a reduction in the real money supply so that each pound held by consumers had less purchasing power. The consequent reduction in aggregate demand could have caused a fall in output. Once again it should be noted that these observations do not prove or disprove Friedman's theory: they are merely consistent with the monetary theory of the business cycle.

The policy conclusions that can be drawn from this monetary theory of the business cycle are very different from those that can be derived from the Keynesian and Marxian traditions. A pronounced business cycle such as that which occurred in the UK in the 1980s is not attributable to forces which are endogenous to capitalism, but can be attributed to the relaxation in control of the money supply by central government. In this view, the responsibility lay not with capitalism but with the profligate finance minister, Nigel Lawson. For Friedman, markets only undergo cyclical fluctuations because of government interference with the money supply. If the stock of money was allowed to grow at a steady rate, the economy could grow at a stable and healthy rate.

One problem with the monetarist approach is that there are many different measures of the money supply (see Chapter 11). The first, M0, provides the simplest measure, since it comprises notes and coins circulating in the economy. As the indicators increase from M0 to M4, the number of items included in the measures also tends to increase. M4, the measure used in Figure 25.14, also includes deposits held in bank deposit and current accounts, together with deposits in building society accounts. There has been some dispute among economists as to which of these measures is the most reliable indicator to use in policy making. To check whether it matters for the monetarist theory of the business cycle that there are so many different measures of the money supply, Figure 25.15 shows the movements of the two extreme measures (M0 and M4) during the 1980s.

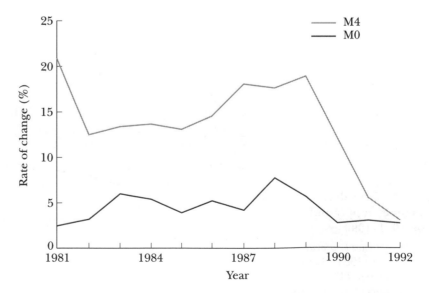

Figure 25.15   **Growth rates of different measures of the money supply, 1981–89**

Source: *Economic Trends Annual Supplement* (1995)

Question

Does Figure 25.15 suggest any ways in which the existence of different measures of the money supply might cause problems for the monetarist theory of the business cycle?

Two observations can be made. First, the two lines show that different measures of the money supply grow at different rates. The cyclical growth path of M4 is much more pronounced than that of M0. The second observation is that despite these differences, both measures of the money supply followed the same pronounced downward growth path in the late 1980s. The start of the recession in the late 1980s was characterized by pronounced falls in both measures of the money cycle. Regardless of which measure is used, the 1980s recession involved a cyclical growth path for both measures of the money supply. This does not mean that the recession was caused by the fall in money supply growth rates, but only that the data can be interpreted to be consistent with Friedman's theory.

There is a further problem with Friedman's theory. Even though government intervention is seen as the cause of business cycles, governments still have to intervene to stabilize the economy, if only to keep the growth of the money stock steady. A key area of controversy for the monetary theory is over the interpretation of the 1930s depression. Friedman argues that the reason for the depth of the 1930s depression was the poor response of the US Federal Reserve. According to him, if the Federal Reserve – the US central bank – had increased the supply of money after the 1929 stock market crash, the Great Depression would not have occurred.

This type of monetary injection was also recommended by various commentators after the stock market crash of 1987, only on this occasion it was in fact carried out by the governments of many industrial economies. We have seen above that for the UK M4 was growing at a rate of 14.5 per cent in 1986. The stock market crash of 1987, however, brought with it the threat of a sharp downturn in economic activity. To prevent this downturn, interest rates were held at a low rate, thereby allowing money to be acquired cheaply in the UK economy. We have also seen that in the three years following 1986 the money supply grew at a markedly high rate.

With hindsight, these increases in money supply, in the hope of preventing a downturn, were somewhat foolhardy. The relaxed monetary policy generated an increase in the money stock which helped to fuel a boom in economic activity, an increase in inflation, and an eventual recession in the early 1990s when interest rates were raised to bring inflation down. In 1991 the UK experienced the deepest recession since the 1930s. The money stock should perhaps have been stimulated after the 1929 stock market crash, but not after the 1987 crash. Policy makers find it very difficult to know when such policy measures are necessary.

Reflection

Summarize in one paragraph the main thrust of Friedman's monetary theory of the business cycle. Key words here are government, money, prices and output.

5   Innovations and technology

A theory of the business cycle which does not fall within the Keynesian–monetarist nexus is that usually associated with Joseph Schumpeter. In this section I shall introduce Schumpeter's theory, present some empirical evidence relating to part of the theory, and consider some of its problems.

5.1   The Schumpeterian approach

Schumpeter developed a theory of the business cycle in which innovations are the most important factor. You may recall from Chapter 6 that an innovation can represent the introduction of a new product or method of production.

Innovations disturb the economy because they represent major discontinuities rather than small incremental changes in economic activity. A new railway line, for example, is either built or not built. The disturbance created by such an innovation, if it goes ahead, is so profound that it can revolutionize methods of production or transportation and can create an economic cycle. To quote Schumpeter (1951), 'If there can be a purely economic cycle at all, it can only come from the way in which new things are, in the institutional conditions of capitalist society, inserted into the economic process and absorbed by it' (p.131). Innovations form part of Schumpeter's process of creative destruction, which was introduced in the context of monopoly power in Chapter 6. A railway will destroy the economic basis of the canal system, for example, but this change will be creative because of the widespread economic opportunities associated with the railway.

The reason for the extent of the disturbance created by an innovation is that there is often a great deal of social resistance to it. In the case of a new railway there may be resistance from those who have to live near to it. For example, Crewe junction – one of the largest railway junctions in the UK – was originally planned to be in Newcastle-under-Lyme, on the western side of Stoke-on-Trent. The factory owners who lived in the area, however, were not prepared to tolerate the disturbance which the railway junction would have caused.

This type of social resistance often results in innovations being temporarily halted. How easy, for example, would it be for a motor car which does not run on petrol to become the market leader? There would be resistance from existing car manufacturers, oil companies, and the makers of components for both industries. (This point may remind you of the discussion of path dependency in Chapter 15.) The consequence of this social resistance is that innovations tend to cluster. The delay in the introduction of an innovation means that all the possibilities which it would generate are held up. Its introduction can open the floodgates such that a wave of new innovations takes place.

For Schumpeter this clustering of innovations generates movement away from economic equilibrium. By equilibrium he does not mean a situation in which demand is precisely equal to supply. There is instead a neighbourhood of equilibrium, which means there is equilibrium in a very broad and approximate sense. The movement between neighbourhoods of equilibrium in response to a clustering of innovations is referred to by Schumpeter as a primary cycle.

Definition

Primary cycle

The primary cycle is a cycle of economic activity driven by innovations.

The primary cycle is characterized by two stages: boom and recession. In the boom stage there is a clustering of innovations, such as those associated with a railway boom. The building of the new railway increases both the demand for raw materials by producers, and the demand for goods and services by workers employed in its construction. There will be multiplier effects as a result of the new innovation, after a time lag between the initial increase in demand and the ability of firms to expand output. As part of this process there is also an expansion in credit, because producers wishing to take part in new activity have to borrow money to fund their participation.

Eventually, however, the railway is built and the boom comes to an end. The output satisfies the demand which the innovation generated. The revenues from the additional output are used to pay off the credit that was taken out during the boom. A recession takes place as the economy struggles back to a new equilibrium. A good example of this process of boom and recession is provided by the great railway bridges that were built as part of the railway boom in the UK. Whole towns were temporarily erected to build these projects. In one such project on the England–Scotland border, the town is reported to have had a hotel, public houses and even a barber's shop. Today there is no evidence that such a town ever existed, apart from the record books. All that stands is the railway bridge to which it was devoted. The finishing of the railway ended the boom in economic activity for which the town was erected. Once the project was finished, a process of readjustment and recession took place. The barber had to move elsewhere to ply his trade.

The movement between the two equilibria is characterized by a boom caused by the introduction of innovations and a recession which occurs once the effects of the innovations have been absorbed by the economy.

In addition to this primary cycle, Schumpeter also identifies a secondary cycle. There is a mass psychology which governs the way in which business people perceive the size of the boom and extends the amplitude of the cycle, as is shown in Figure 25.16, further than is justified by the primary cycle. Not only does the boom expand beyond the realms of the primary cycle, but once a turning point takes place business people also over-react to the extent of the downturn. The economy embarks on a depression. For Schumpeter the recession turns into depression because of the over-reaction of business people to the primary cycle.

Definition

Secondary cycle

A secondary cycle is based on the over-reactions of business people to the primary cycle.

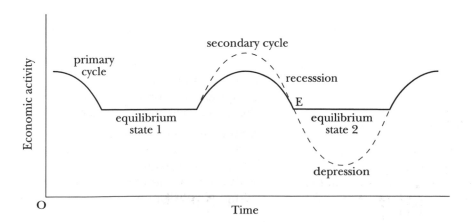

***Figure 25.16* Primary and secondary cycles**

Source: Oakley (1990) p.173

However, Schumpeter struggled to come up with a reason why the economic system should recover from the depression phase. He called this the 'problem of the recovery point' (Schumpeter, 1939, p.151). A depression, according to Schumpeter, feeds upon itself and can in principle run on indefinitely. The best prospect for recovery lies once again in the mass psychology of markets – in expectations. At the bottom of the cycle there is what Schumpeter calls 'depression business'. Some people do well out of depressions. An increase in unemployment can cause the failure of a grocer whose customers are unemployed workmen. However, his market is not completely annihilated, and if he disappears there is room for other grocers to expand. Another example might be the tyre industry. During the recession of the early 1990s the demand for cars fell. A spin-off from this was that people kept their cars for longer periods of time and needed to replace worn-out tyres. Some tyre companies did quite well, despite the economic climate. The point to be made here is not that there is any additional market for tyres or groceries, but that if some firms do well in a depression this may help expectations to recover. This is important because it is business expectations which amplify the primary cycle into the secondary cycle.

The problem with this recovery mechanism is that the increase in expectations for the odd tyre manufacturer might not be enough to restore expectations in the economy as a whole. The tyre industry may constitute such a small proportion of total industry that if the economy is in the doldrums across all sectors, it may not recover without something more drastic. Schumpeter offers a mechanism by which the economy might recover, but no automatic stabilizers to correct a business cycle downturn. It could be argued, however, that Schumpeter's theory has succeeded in identifying a problem with the way in which markets function. If Schumpeter's theory of the secondary cycle is correct, then a more complete theory, such as that developed by Kalecki or Friedman, may be imposing a regularity on the business cycle which does not exist.

5.2   Applications of the Schumpeterian approach

In addition to formulating a theoretical explanation of the business cycle, Schumpeter contributed to our empirical knowledge of cycles. Some intensive empirical work on the history of business cycle fluctuations led him to observe cycles of different amplitude and duration. The best known of these cycles is associated with the name of the Russian economist Nikolai Kondratieff, who was head of the Moscow Business Conditions Institute in the 1920s. Like most Russian economists of his time, Kondratieff was purged by Stalin – the last record of him is that he appeared as a key witness in one of Stalin's show trials in March 1931. The official Soviet Russian Encyclopaedia dismissed his theory of cycles in a single sentence: 'This theory is wrong and reactionary' (Solomou, 1987).

Schumpeter did not think so. He argued that there is considerable evidence for the existence of Kondratieff cycles. Schumpeter argued that the industrial revolution generated a Kondratieff cycle over the period 1783–1842; the age of steam and steel (railways) generated one for the period 1842–1897; and the period after 1897 also heralded a new

Definition

Kondratieff cycle

A Kondratieff cycle is a cycle that lasts between 50 and 60 years.

Kondratieff based on electricity and heavy engineering. Other writers in the Schumpeterian tradition have identified Kondratieff cycles during similar time periods to Schumpeter, and have suggested in addition the existence of a fourth Kondratieff starting in 1948. These cycles, based on the introduction of major innovations, are often referred to as *long waves*. Like waves hitting the shore, one Kondratieff cycle will inevitably be followed by another.

A major problem with long-wave analysis is that there are only four long waves to work with. Since long waves of fifty or so years are thought to be endemic to a capitalist market system which has only existed for about 200 years, there could only have been four long waves. Any statistician will confirm that a sample of four is not a very good data set on which to test a theory.

Nevertheless, proponents of the long-wave theory have endeavoured to use empirical evidence to show that such long waves have taken place since the inception of capitalism. For example, van Duijn (1983) concentrated on the growth rates of industrial production for a number of countries. Table 25.3 presents his findings for the second, third and fourth long waves.

Table 25.3   **Growth rates of industrial production in van Duijn's long-wave upswings and downswings (%)**

	United Kingdom		USA		Germany[1]	
2nd Kondratieff						
upswing	1845–1873	3.0	1864–1873	6.2	1850–1872	4.3
downswing	1873–1890	1.7	1873–1895	4.7	1872–1890	2.9
3rd Kondratieff						
upswing	1890–1913	2.0	1895–1913	5.3	1890–1913	4.1
	1920–1929	2.8	1920–1929	4.8	1920–1929	
downswing	1929–1948	2.1	1929–1948	3.1	1929–1948	
4th Kondratieff						
upswing	1948–1973	3.2	1948–1973	4.7	1948–1973	9.1
	France		Italy		Sweden	
2nd Kondratieff						
upswing	1847–1872	1.7				
downswing	1872–1890	1.3	1873–1890	0.9	1870–1894	3.1
3rd Kondratieff						
upswing	1890-1913	2.5	1890–1913	3.0	1894–1913	3.5
	1920–1929	8.1	1920–1929	4.8	1920–1929	4.6
downswing	1929–1948	–0.9	1929–1948	0.5	1929–1948	4.4
4th Kondratieff						
upswing	1948–1973	6.1	1948–1973	7.9	1948–1973	4.7

[1] 1948–1973: West Germany.

Source: van Duijn (1983) Table 9.7

Each Kondratieff is made up of an upswing and downswing. For example, during the third Kondratieff the USA displays growth rates of between 5.3 and 4.8 per cent during the upswing, and a growth rate of only 3.1 per cent during the downswing. For the fourth Kondratieff, supposedly driven by mass production and the motor car, van Duijn only presents growth rates for the upswing, which are as high as 9.1 per cent for Germany. According to long-wave theory, the period after 1973, not yet fully documented, has been a period of downswing in the world economy. We have seen earlier that this has indeed been a period of downturn relative to the post-war boom, so it does appear to be consistent with the existence of a fourth long wave.

Question

Are there any periods that have been left out in Table 25.3?

A weakness in van Duijn's data in Table 25.3 is that the period around the First World War, 1913–1920, is not included. As Tylecote (1992) has reported, this period is regarded by van Duijn to be merely an 'interruption' to the upswing associated with the third Kondratieff. However, the war period had a detrimental effect on the growth rate of output during a supposed upswing in the long wave. For Solomou (1987a), once growth rates for this period are included, the existence of the third Kondratieff is brought into question.

This example provides an important warning to any economist for whom the long wave provides an attractive explanation of fluctuations in economic activity: it is possible to present the data to fit in with a preconceived view of what has happened. Tylecote (1992) has also pointed out that van Duijn is less keen to take out the period of the American Civil War in 1865. The rapid growth of the USA economy during the period 1866–72 could have taken place merely due to post-war reconstruction, but for van Duijn this growth is due to the long-wave upswing.

These examples show that history and its interpretation can be a very uncertain business. As economists we need to provide summaries and generalizations across periods of time; but we also need to take into account the importance of historical events which do not fit into our theories. The problem with sweeping theories such as the long-wave theory is that there is a danger of engaging in research which ignores the importance of historical events.

Having voiced this warning, some consideration can be given to more recent research into long waves. We have seen that the period after 1973 should, according to the long-wave theory, have seen a downturn in industrial activity. Since some evidence for this post-1973 downswing exists, this raises the question whether it will be followed by an upswing in economic activity.

It has been argued by Reati (1992) that a new upswing phase in the long wave should take place from 1995 onwards. The main seeds for this recovery are provided by the technological revolution associated with computers, electronic goods and telecommunications. For the upswing to take place in the mid 1990s, this technological revolution must start to take place during the downswing phase of the long wave. By way of comparison, the introduction of techniques of mass production – which fuelled the (post-

1948) fourth Kondratieff – took place during the 1920s, part of the downswing phase of the third Kondratieff. Similarly, the computer-based revolution of the 1970s and 1980s could have sown the seeds for the fifth Kondratieff. Table 25.4 provides evidence for an increase in the activity of three sectors which Reati considers important.

Table 25.4 **Indications of the spreading of the technological revolution, 1975–89 (data in constant 1985 prices)**

	Variable	Office and data processing machines; instruments		Electrical goods		Communication services	
		% share		% share		% share	
		1975	1989	1975	1989	1975	1989
Germany	VA	2.7	3.0	10.4	14.4	3.6	5.1^3
	Inv	3.9	4.1	9.4	11.9	5.2	7.2^3
France	VA	3.3	4.6	7.5	10.3	3.0	6.0
	Inv	2.7	4.1	6.7	7.5	5.3	4.3
Italy	VA	1.8^2	2.7	6.5^2	8.0	2.3^2	3.3
	Inv^1	2.5	2.5	6.7	9.7	5.7^2	7.1^3
UK	VA	1.1	3.6	8.6	10.0	4.9	3.9
	Inv	1.5	3.3	5.7	8.0	7.0	7.0^3
USA^6	VA^4	5.7	7.9	6.3	9.0	4.3	5.5^4
	Inv^4	4.3	7.4	4.5	10.6	9.1	7.8^4
Japan	VA^3	2.7	3.8	3.4	17.7	3.1	2.3^3
	Inv^4	3.4	4.9	5.8	16.7	4.7	2.8^4

[1] Base year 1980

[2] Ycar 1980.

[3] Final year 1988.

[4] Final year 1987.

Source: Reati (1992) p.261

Comparisons are made between 1975 and 1989 for six different countries; the variables considered are value added (VA) and investment (Inv). For example, in the UK the share of total manufacturing investment by the electrical goods sector increased from 5.7 per cent in 1975 to 8.0 per cent in 1989. The share of value added increased from 8.6 per cent to 10 per cent. This pattern of increase for electrical goods is found in all of the countries considered over this period. For office and data processing machines and optical instruments there is also a clear pattern of increase. Only communication services provide any exceptions, with Japan for example showing a reduction from 3.1 to 2.3 per cent for value added and 4.7 to 2.8 per cent for investment. The general pattern is still, however, in favour of an increase in the share of communication services.

A problem with this interpretation is that the boom in the late 1980s ended with a recession throughout the world economy. The question to be asked (at the time of writing in 1994) is whether this recession merely provided a

Source: Tam Dougan

short blip in this long-run recovery, or whether it will become so deep that the long-run recovery becomes nothing more than a pipe dream.

From a policy point of view there would be a number of problems, even if an upswing in the long wave were to take place. New technologies can result in a loss of jobs. If a secretary can type more letters with a word processor than with a typewriter, then the introduction of the former will mean that there are fewer jobs for secretaries. The problem, therefore, is that the fifth Kondratieff could be characterized by mass unemployment in certain countries even in its upswing phase. In response, Reati recommends the imposition of cuts in hours of work for workers in employment. In the UK, for example, there were 2.8 million unemployed in 1993. If each of the 20 million or so employed workers took a cut of five hours per week, this would amount to 2.8 million jobs (assuming a 35-hour week after the reduction in hours).

At the touch of a button I have eliminated all unemployment in the UK. Or have I? The workers already in employment may resist a cut in their weekly income, and the employers may object to having to pay fixed costs, such as national insurance, for more workers. There would need to be some sort of social contract between capital and labour.

This left-of-centre interventionist approach is not the only policy response to long-wave analysis. For some economists on the right of the political spectrum, an interventionist approach could make things much worse than if the economic system is left to its own devices. Schumpeter himself can be placed firmly on the right of the political spectrum. He was a virulent anti-socialist who, for example, was implacably opposed to the Roosevelt New Deal, a US public spending programme introduced in response to the Great Depression in the 1930s (see Catephores, 1994). For Schumpeter the process of creative destruction which generates economic cycles should not and cannot be interfered with by governments. His prediction in the 1930s that an upswing would eventually arrive provided part of the basis for his opposition to the Roosevelt New Deal. If one believes, as he did, that an upturn will automatically arrive, then the logical conclusion is that there is no need for government intervention.

It follows that both the left and right of the political spectrum can make use of the long-wave approach, depending to some extent on the point of the cycle in which we find ourselves. During a recession economists on the right of the political spectrum, such as Schumpeter, are attracted by long-wave theory because it suggests that capitalism could recover from its downturn. Even during a boom period writers on the left find the long-wave approach pertinent because it might predict the imminent crisis of capitalism.

6   Conclusion

This chapter has presented a menu of four different theories of the business cycle, each associated with the name of a great economic thinker. From John Maynard Keynes we inherit the notion that fluctuations in aggregate demand provide the driving force behind economic cycles. In this approach investment is the main determinant of fluctuations in economic activity; and in turn investment is dependent on the strength of demand in the economy. For Karl Marx investment is also the main determinant of cycles, but for him it depends on fluctuations in the rate of profit. According to Milton Friedman, government intervention generates fluctuations in the money supply which result in fluctuations in economic activity. For Joseph Schumpeter, on the other hand, economic cycles are driven by fluctuations in technological change. New innovations such as the railway or the microchip provide the basis for fluctuations in economic activity. Each theory selects a different variable – demand, profit rates, money or innovations – as the main determinant of the business cycle.

By way of illustration it has been shown that with respect to the UK economy in the 1980s there is some evidence that each of these theories is consistent with observable movements in the data. Indeed it could be argued that the reason for such a multiplicity of theories of the business cycle is the richness of empirical evidence available. It should also be noted that the method of comparison has been very simple, making use of purely descriptive statistics. To test the explanatory power of a theory would require the use of much more sophisticated statistical techniques, some of which are introduced in the next chapter.

In addition to considering some empirical evidence on the business cycle, this chapter has also considered the implications of each theory for policy formulation. Both the Keynesian and Marxian approaches suggest that government stimulation of aggregate demand is needed to iron out the vagaries of the business cycle. The Marxian approach also suggests the need for socialist intervention in the form of state-run factories. The monetarist approach suggests the opposite: that governments should refrain from intervention in the economy. It has also been shown that the Schumpeterian approach is so general that it enables economists on both the left and right of the political spectrum to draw their own conclusions. In this approach, the business cycle can either be viewed as an essential and unavoidable part of long-run capitalist expansion, or as an avoidable phenomenon which governments can and should prevent.

Each of the theories considered has been shown to have its own shortcomings. In both the Keynesian and Marxian approaches the multiplier and accelerator are perhaps too unstable to be a useful guide to policy. For the monetarist approach, the problems associated with defining the money supply raise doubts about its reliability as a guide to policy.

Finally, the Schumpeterian approach, with its layers of different cycles, is arguably too complex for meaningful empirical investigation. Deciding which of these theories should be used to construct policy proposals is a matter for reasoned discussion and empirical investigation. This chapter has, I hope, provided a useful introduction to the debate.

PART 15

CHAPTER 26

by Andrew B. Trigg

DATA AND ECONOMIC FORECASTING

DATA ANALYSIS AND FORECASTING

1 Introduction

Throughout this text a number of theories have been developed which are based on the relationships between economic variables. The consumption function (Chapter 3), for example, models the relationship between income and consumption, whilst the quantity theory of money (Chapter 25) models the relationship between money and prices. In this chapter I shall introduce some statistical techniques which economists use to estimate these relationships using real world data. These techniques provide the basis for the science of econometrics – the application of statistical techniques to economics.

The aim of the chapter is to show how two statistical techniques, the methods of *correlation* and *regression*, can be used to develop and improve the quality of economic analysis. Having first explained these techniques, the chapter will then illustrate their importance in economics by looking at the problem of forecasting. Estimating a relationship between two variables provides a basis for making some forecasts of their future path. The methods introduced in this chapter provide the core methodology for many of the forecasting models used by City analysts and governments.

The chapter will also look at an application of these statistical techniques to the simulation of the impact of economic policy. A consumption function for the Japanese economy will be estimated and used to provide an estimate of the Keynesian income multiplier. By modelling the relationship between income and expenditure, a simulation will be conducted to look at the impact of the Japanese government's public expenditure programme in the early 1990s.

A particular type of real world data will be used for this introduction to statistical methods. As Chapter 9 explained, there are two main types of data which economists use: cross-section and time series data. The former, which was the main focus of Chapter 9, is information which relates to one particular point in time. By taking a cross-section the researcher can compare, for example, the unemployment rate in different regions for a particular year. This enables a comparison of different regions. Conversely, time series data looks at observations over an extended period of time. The unemployment rate for a particular region could be observed for 20 or so years in order to gain an insight into its long-run path. Instead of asking the question, 'Is Northern Ireland more depressed than Greater London?', the question 'Has Northern Ireland improved its prosperity since the 1960s?' might be asked.

For the rest of this chapter I shall concentrate on time series data, because this is the form of data most widely used in macroeconomics, which forms the main focus for Book 2. For example, economists look at time series data for unemployment and inflation to test the Phillips Curve (Chapter 24); and for money and inflation to test Milton Friedman's monetary theory of the business cycle (Chapter 25). By looking at variables over time, some insight can be gained into the explanatory power of economic theories.

Analysing relationships between economic variables involves looking at data for two or more variables. In Chapter 9, Section 4.1, you saw how to represent data for two variables on a scatterplot. We shall be using scatterplots in many places in this chapter. So, if you need to remind yourself about them, now is the time to look back at Chapter 9.

Wherever possible I have tried to limit the amount of mathematics used in this chapter. Some of the calculations which you may find interesting and useful to work through have been put in the Appendix so as not to detract from the main purpose of the chapter, which is to help you gain an intuitive understanding of how data analysis is performed by economists.

2   Regression and correlation

The historical basis for modern econometrics can be traced back to a railway platform in Ramsgate, England, towards the end of the nineteenth century. A statistician called Francis Galton (1822–1911) was pondering a scatterplot of the results of his survey of the heights of parents and their children. The brainwave which suddenly struck him was that these observations looked as though they were distributed around a straight line (Kennedy, 1983).

To explain what is meant by this I have conducted a survey of the heights of seven daughters and their mothers. (These daughters were those who happened to be working on the corridor where I work at the time of writing this chapter.) The results are shown in Table 26.1. Figure 26.1 shows these observations displayed on a scatterplot, with the heights of daughters shown on the horizontal axis, and the heights of mothers shown on the vertical axis.

Table 26.1   **Results from a survey of seven women**

	Height of daughter	**Height of mother**
Observation 1	5' 4"	5' 2"
Observation 2	5' 7"	5' 1"
Observation 3	5' 6"	5' 3"
Observation 4	5' 5"	5' 2"
Observation 5	5' 5"	5' 1"
Observation 6	5' 4"	5' 0"
Observation 7	5' 1"	5' 0"

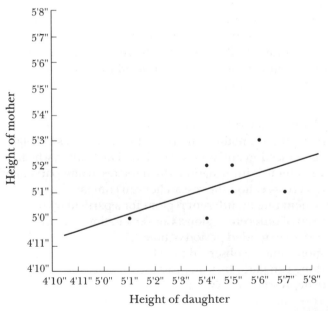

Figure 26.1   **The heights of seven mothers and daughters**

Each observation is shown by a dot on the scatterplot, and a straight line has been drawn through them, as suggested by Francis Galton. It is drawn so as to go as near as possible to the dots, but so as to leave dots evenly distributed on each side of it. This line can then be used to talk about the relationship between the heights of daughters and their mothers. The slope of this line indicates how the height of a mother tends to vary with that of her daughter. The line slopes up from left to right to show that tall daughters tend to have tall mothers. But, the rule only holds in general, because not all observations lie exactly on the line; there are some tall daughters who have short mothers, as observation 2 shows.

What, it might be asked, does this have to do with economics? Well, in the same way that the relationship between heights of mothers and daughters can be compared, this can also be done for economic observations, such as income and expenditure. In Figure 26.2 an example is given using observations on household disposable income and expenditure over the period from 1950 to 1992 for the UK. This information was used by Jane Wheelock in Chapter 3 to estimate a consumption function. It is repeated here to show how a line can be useful when fitted to economic data.

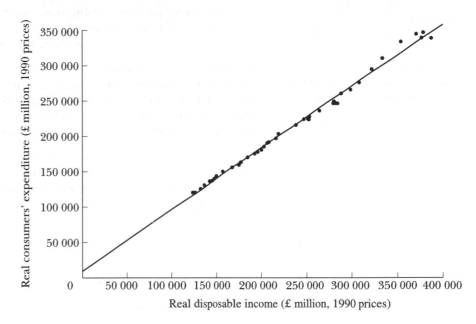

Figure 26.2   **The consumption–income relationship, UK, 1950–92**

Source: Central Statistical Office

This line provides a summary of the relationship between income and consumption expenditure. If real disposable income in the UK, for example, were about £150 billion at 1990 prices, then by using the summary line real consumption could be predicted to be about £140 billion. If disposable income were, on the other hand, about £300 billion, then real consumption could be predicted to be about £270 billion. This line slopes up from left to right, showing that consumption increases with income, but has a slope less steep than it would have if consumption took up the whole of income. As you will see in the last section of this chapter, the estimation of this type of summary line can be very useful for simulating the impacts of economic policies.

This type of summary line is known as a 'regression line'. (In Chapter 9 it was called a line of best fit.) Whenever we draw such a line, we are interested in its direction, its slope and how well it fits the data. In this part of the chapter I will show how such a regression line can be precisely estimated without a ruler and guesswork. This is important because where to place the line when using a ruler depends on subjective judgement. To quote Harper (1991, p.157): 'It would be much better if a mathematical method of drawing the line could be devised instead of leaving it to the artistic whim of the individual'.

A mathematical method for drawing the line will be developed by first looking at the relationship between variables in a simple diagram. The notion of *correlation* between variables will be introduced, before turning to the precise details of how the regression line is estimated.

2.1   Correlation

In Figure 26.2 observations on income and consumption in the UK are not widely dispersed over the whole scatterplot. They are narrowly spread around the regression line such that it can be adjudged to provide a good representation of the relationship between income and consumption. As income increases over time, the regression line can be used to summarize the consequent path of consumption. Since consumption and income, in this example, are closely related to each other around a straight line, there can be said to be correlation between the two variables.

Figure 26.3 shows three types of correlation. For ease of exposition the variables are referred to as x and y. A convention is to use x to refer to the horizontal axis, and y to refer to the vertical axis. We use lower case x and y, not capitals, here, in order not to get confused with variables such as incomes for which we use capital Y elsewhere in the text.

In Figure 26.3(a) there is *zero correlation* – no discernible relationship between x and y. In part (b) there is *positive correlation*. As x increases y also tends to increase. In part (c) there is *negative correlation*. As x increases y tends to decrease.

Definition

Correlation

Correlation is the extent to which two variables are related to one another around a straight line.

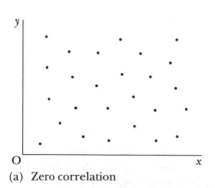

(a) Zero correlation

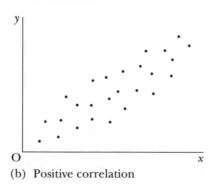

(b) Positive correlation

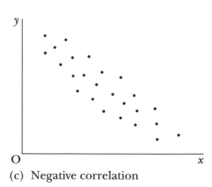

(c) Negative correlation

Figure 26.3   **Different types of correlation**

Questions

What examples are there in economics of pairs of variables which display:

1   Positive correlation?

2   Zero correlation?

3   Negative correlation?

The consumption function provides an example of positive correlation. As household income increases over time, household consumption also tends to increase (Figure 26.2).

An example of negative correlation is shown in Figure 26.4. These observations show the relationship between government investment and consumption in the UK over the period 1970–87. The vertical axis shows government consumption as a percentage of GDP, whilst the horizontal axis shows government investment as a percentage of GDP. As government investment increases government consumption tends to fall – there is negative correlation.

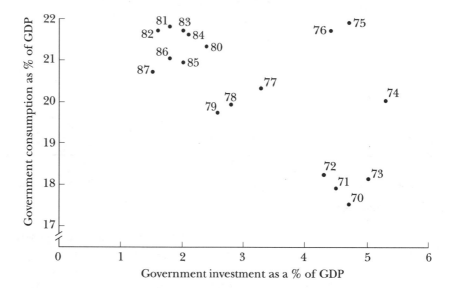

Figure 26.4   Government investment and consumption in the UK, 1970–87

Source: *Economic Trends Annual Supplement* (1989)

An example of near zero correlation is displayed by the relationship between inflation and growth rates of output across a number of economies over the period 1980–88. These are shown in Figure 26.5. There is no discernible correlation between inflation and growth per head of population over this period. It would be very difficult to fit either an upward sloping or downward sloping line to this scatterplot. Graham Dawson discussed this issue in Chapter 24.

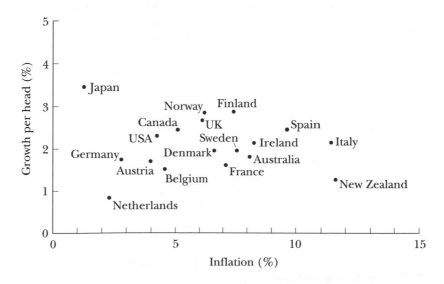

Figure 26.5   Inflation and growth per head in 18 countries, 1980–88

Source: Stanners (1993)

In addition to providing an indication of the *sign* (positive or negative) of the straight line relationship between variables, correlation shows the strength of the relationship. In Figure 26.6 examples are given of *weak* positive correlation and *strong* positive correlation. The nearer the observations lie to a straight line, the stronger the correlation. In Figure 26.6(a) the observations are fairly widely dispersed in a broad band (weak correlation) compared to Figure 26.6(b) where the observations are more narrowly concentrated along a narrower band (strong correlation).

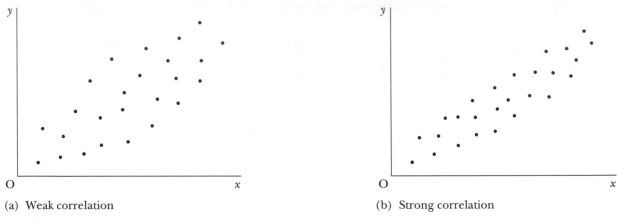

(a) Weak correlation   (b) Strong correlation

Figure 26.6   **Weak and strong correlations**

The scatterplot diagram can thus be used to show the nature of correlation between variables. Correlation can be zero, positive or negative, and weak or strong. There is, however, a fundamental problem with this approach. Although the scatterplot diagram provides an important picture of the variables, its interpretation can be imprecise. You have to use your visual judgement as part of the interpretation to decide what sort of correlation there is. Where the correlation is not very strong, people may disagree about its visual interpretation.

A more precise method is needed which does not rely on individual judgement. Figure 26.7 provides a basis for explaining how we can move from a visual judgement of correlation to a precise measure of first the sign and then the strength. For simplicity, I shall once again label the axes of the scatterplot x and y. This scatterplot is then divided in Figure 26.7 into four quadrants. To do this two straight lines are needed, one for x and the other for y. These lines are drawn by calculating the means of x and y. The mean, defined in Chapter 9, is calculated by dividing the sum of the observed

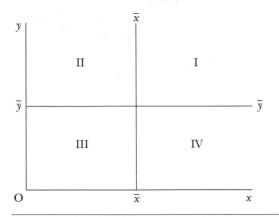

Figure 26.7   **The four quadrants**

values of the variable by the number of observations. It is what we often talk about as their average. The mean of 4 and 8, for example, is 6. This is calculated by adding together 4 and 8 to get 12 and dividing by 2, the number of observations. The mean of x is written $\bar{x}$ and the mean of y, $\bar{y}$.

The means $\bar{x}$ and $\bar{y}$ are represented on Figure 26.7 by the two red lines. The vertical line represents $\bar{x}$, the mean of x, and the horizontal line represents $\bar{y}$, the mean of y. Once these lines are constructed, there are four quadrants on the scatterplot diagram.

I will now show that the nature of the correlation between x and y depends on the quadrants in which most of the observations fall. Take a look at the examples of positive and negative correlation in Figure 26.8.

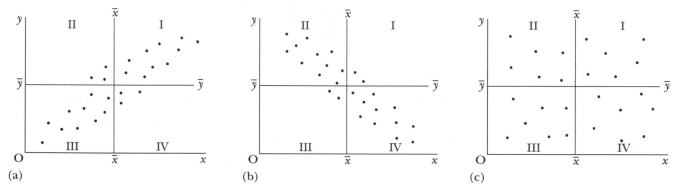

Figure 26.8 **Correlation and the four quadrants**

In part (a) the observations tend to be concentrated in quadrants I and III. This means that there is positive correlation – as x increases y tends also to increase. If, on the other hand, observations are concentrated in quadrants II and IV there is negative correlation – as x increases y tends to decrease (see part b). With zero correlation observations are distributed equally between the four quadrants (part c). The allocation of an observation to a particular quadrant depends on the answer to the following two questions:

1 Is x more than or less than the mean value, $\bar{x}$?

2 Is y more than or less than the mean value, $\bar{y}$?

There are four possible answers (if for simplicity we ignore values of x and y equal to their means):

> Quadrant I: x is **more** than $\bar{x}$ and y is **more** than $\bar{y}$
>
> Quadrant II: x is **less** than $\bar{x}$ and y is **more** than $\bar{y}$
>
> Quadrant III: x is **less** than $\bar{x}$ and y is **less** than $\bar{y}$
>
> Quadrant IV: x is **more** than $\bar{x}$ and y is **less** than $\bar{y}$

Asking the question whether x is more or less than $\bar{x}$ is the same as asking whether x is to the right or left of the vertical line on the scatterplot. Similarly, asking the question whether y is more or less than $\bar{y}$ is the same as asking whether y is above or below the horizontal line.

The covariance

I can now use these quadrants to develop a statistical indicator – called the covariance – which will tell us the sign of a correlation, that is, whether it is positive or negative. This will also be a stepping stone to measuring the strength of correlation. I will start by developing a procedure for allocating observations to quadrants. This can be done by calculating the difference between each observation and its mean. These differences are also known as deviations from the mean. You may recall that this calculation was introduced in Chapter 9. The difference between x and its mean is $(x - \bar{x})$ whilst the difference between y and its mean is $(y - \bar{y})$.

If a value of x is above $\bar{x}$, then the difference $(x - \bar{x})$ is positive. If, on the other hand, a value of x is less than $\bar{x}$, then the difference $(x - \bar{x})$ is negative. Similarly, if a value of y is above $\bar{y}$, then the difference $(y - \bar{y})$ is positive. And if a value of y is less than $\bar{y}$, then the difference $(y - \bar{y})$ is negative.

By finding out whether these deviations are positive or negative each observation can be allocated to one of the four quadrants, as shown in the first two columns of Table 26.2.

Table 26.2

Quadrant	$(x - \bar{x})$	$(y - \bar{y})$	$(x - \bar{x})(y - \bar{y})$
I	+	+	+
II	−	+	−
III	−	−	+
IV	+	−	−

Comparing Table 26.2 and Figure 26.8 shows that in quadrants I and IV the deviation $(x - \bar{x})$ is positive (x is to the right of the vertical line). In quadrants I and II the deviation $(y - \bar{y})$ is positive (y is above the horizontal line).

The third column in Table 26.2 multiplies the two deviations together in order to get $(x - \bar{x})(y - \bar{y})$. Note that for quadrants I and III the entries for $(x - \bar{x})(y - \bar{y})$ are positive. This is because in quadrant I both deviations are positive and in quadrant III both deviations are negative (a negative multiplied by a negative yields a positive). In quadrants II and IV, however, the values of $(x - \bar{x})(y - \bar{y})$ are negative (a positive multiplied by a negative yields a negative).

We are now ready to calculate the covariance. For any set of observations, the positive and negative values in the final column of Table 26.2 can be averaged to find out whether the overall correlation between x and y is positive or negative. The average of this column is defined in statistics as the covariance between x and y. If the covariance is negative, then the correlation between x and y is negative – so a major proportion of the observations appear in quadrants II and IV of the scatterplot diagram. If, on the other hand, the covariance is positive, then quadrants I and III dominate, and the correlation is positive.

Having explained the concept of covariance in this way, I can now sum it up in a formula, which only uses algebra which you have already seen.

$$\operatorname{cov}(x, y) = \frac{\Sigma(x - \bar{x})(y - \bar{y})}{n}$$

Here, Σ means the summing up of all values of $(x - \bar{x})(y - \bar{y})$, and n is the number of observations.

Definition

Covariance

The covariance between two variables, x and y, is written cov (x, y). It provides an indicator of the type of correlation which exists between x and y. Where the covariance is positive, there is a positive correlation between x and y. Where the covariance is negative, so is the correlation.

I can now explain covariance once again using the elements of this formula. The sign of the covariance depends on which values of the term $(x - \bar{x})(y - \bar{y})$ dominate: negative or positive. As I have shown, this is the same as asking in which quadrants observations tend to be found. If most observations are in quadrants I and III on Figure 26.8, then most of the values of $(x - \bar{x})(y - \bar{y})$ will be positive. Averaging over these values, the covariance will be positive.

On the other hand, if there is negative correlation, then observations tend to be found in quadrants II and IV. This will yield lots of negative values for $(x - \bar{x})(y - \bar{y})$ so that their average, the covariance, will be negative. A negative covariance therefore means that there is negative correlation between x and y.

In the Appendix, Section A1, I give an illustrative example of how the covariance can be calculated. You could either turn to the Appendix and work through it now, to help your understanding of this section, or keep reading and work further on the covariance later.

2.2   Measuring correlations

While the covariance tells us the sign of a correlation between two variables, it does not tell us how strong that correlation is. This is because the size of the covariance is influenced by other factors besides the strength of the relationship between the correlation.

Let me illustrate the problem by an example. Compare scatterplots (a) and (b) in Figure 26.9. They both chart the relationship between income and purchases of milk for a sample of eight households. In (a) milk purchases are measured in pints, in (b) they are measured in litres, so (b) shows exactly the same purchases as (a) but with the y variable measured in different units. Whether we measure purchases of milk in pints or litres, does not make any difference to the relationship between income and milk consumption, so any meaningful measure of the strength of a correlation must give the same answer in both cases. The unit of measurement of milk, however, changes the way the scatterplots look and therefore, as you can see, also changes the slope of the regression line we draw through them.

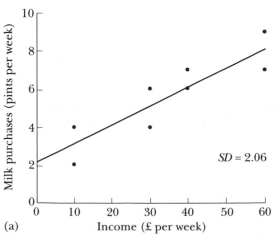
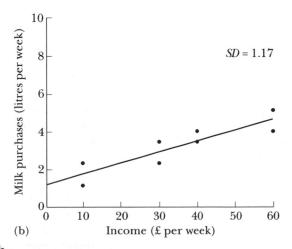

(a)

(b)

Figure 26.9   **Scatterplots of income and purchases of milk**

So we need a measure of the strength of a correlation, which gives the same answer for both scatterplots. All the y values plotted on (b) are just $\frac{9}{16}$ of the corresponding values plotted on (a) because one pint is $\frac{9}{16}$ of a litre. So when we calculate the covariance in (b), it will turn out to be $\frac{9}{16}$ of that we would get from (a). To get a measure of the strength of a correlation, we need to scale the covariance appropriately so as to take account of the different units in which y is measured on the two scatterplots. We can do this by using the standard deviation introduced in Chapter 9. If we simplify the notation in Chapter 9 a little, and use lower case x, we can define the standard deviation as

$$\text{standard deviation } (SD) = \sqrt{\frac{\Sigma(x - \bar{x})^2}{n}}$$

It shows the spread of the set of n values of x from the mean $(\bar{x})$.

When we change the units in which a variable is measured, the standard deviation also changes proportionately. I have indicated the standard deviations of y on scatterplots (a) and (b) in Figure 26.9, so you can see how they differ. This means that we can use the standard deviation of the variable y as a scaling factor. If we divide the covariance by the standard deviation of y (milk purchases), we will get a measure that will take the same value whatever scale we use for y.

There is a similar scaling issue for the x variable (income). If we change the units in which it is measured, from pounds to pence for example, this must not change our measure of the strength of the correlation between x and y. We can ensure that it does not by using the standard deviation of x as another scaling factor, and dividing the covariance of x and y by that too.

We call this 'normalizing' – the process of getting rid of a scaling problem by dividing by an appropriate scaling factor. You have met it already in Chapter 22, Section 5.1. There the standard deviations of income distributions were normalized by dividing by their means. Here, we are normalizing the covariance of two variables, by dividing by each of their standard deviations.

Definition

Correlation coefficient

The correlation coefficient, R, measures the strength and sign of correlation between two variables x and y.

The result of these calculations is the correlation coefficient, which measures both the strength and the sign of a correlation. It is worked out by dividing the covariance by the standard deviation of each of the variables.

$$\text{correlation coefficient } R = \frac{\text{cov }(x, y)}{SD(x)\ SD(y)}$$

The correlation coefficient varies between −1 and 1, taking the value −1 when there is a perfect negative correlation, 1 when there is a perfect positive correlation and 0 when there is no correlation between the two variables. Correlation coefficients between these extremes register some correlation, with observations spread about but not exactly on a regression line.

Scatterplots (a)–(f) in Figure 26.10 illustrate different values of the correlation coefficient. In (a), all the points lie exactly on a straight line sloping upwards so there is a correlation coefficient of 1. In (b), the points again lie on a straight line but sloping downwards so there is a correlation coefficient of −1. In (c), the points have no linear relationship, so the correlation coefficient is 0. In (d), where the points lie around but not

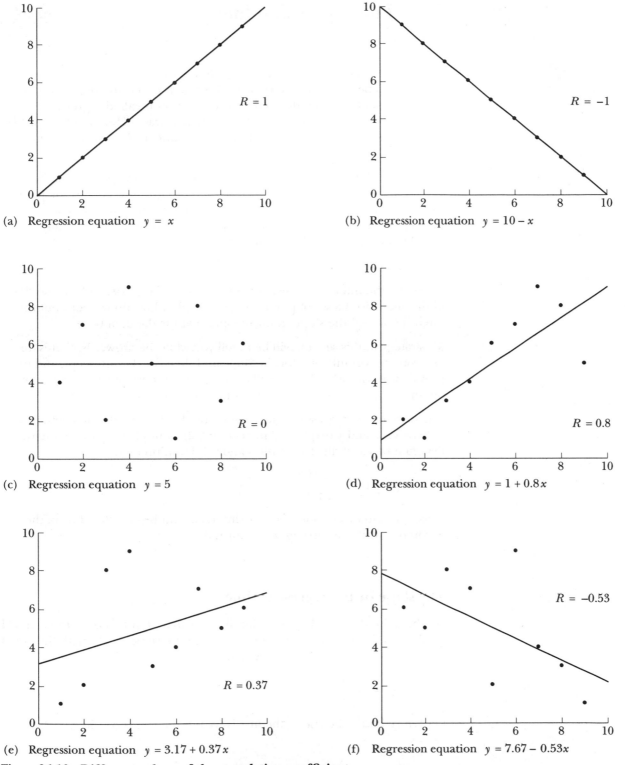

Figure 26.10   Different values of the correlation coefficient

exactly on a straight line, the correlation coefficient is 0.8; while in (e) there is only a rather weak linear relationship to be seen and the correlation coefficient is 0.37. In (f) there is a stronger linear relationship but in the opposite direction, and the correlation coefficient is –0.53.

2.3   The regression line

Now that I have shown how to plot the observations for x and y on a scatterplot diagram, and introduced the concept of correlation, the objective is to specify a summary line, a line which summarizes the relationship between these variables. This line is called the regression line, and the area of research devoted to its estimation is called regression analysis. To quote the eminent econometrician, David Hendry (1993, p.14): 'economists have found their Philosopher's Stone; it is called regression analysis ... '.

We want to plot the line that fits the data best. Unless we have a perfect correlation, that is all the data does lie on a straight line, then some points will deviate from any line we fit. We are aiming to find the line that minimizes these deviations. As you already know from Chapter 9, any straight line can be written in the form:

$$y = a + bx$$

where a is the intercept where the line starts on the y-axis, and b is the slope of the line. Given a set of points on a scatterplot, how do we work out the intercept, a, and the slope, b, for the line that fits the data best?

My strategy in this section will be to tell you what the answer is, that is, to give you the formula first for the slope and then for the intercept, and then provide you with what I hope will be an intuitive sense of why we work them out that way, following on from the discussion of correlations.

The slope of the regression line is measured by the correlation coefficient, R, between x and y (explained in Section 2.2) multiplied by the standard deviation of y and divided by the standard deviation of x.

$$\text{slope} = b = \frac{R \cdot SD(y)}{SD(x)}$$

Once you know the slope, then the intercept can be calculated from the means of x and y, according to the formula

$$a = \bar{y} - b\bar{x}$$

The slope of the regression line

So why is the slope of the regression line calculated in this way? To get a feel for this, think back to the way you calculated the slope of a straight line on a graph (Chapter 9, Section 4.2). You used the formula

$$\text{slope} = b = \frac{\text{rise}}{\text{run}}$$

On Figure 26.11, the rise of the line is Δy and the run is Δx. So

$$b = \frac{\Delta y}{\Delta x}$$

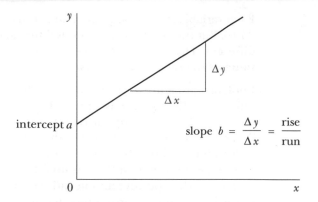

$$\text{slope } b = \frac{\Delta y}{\Delta x} = \frac{\text{rise}}{\text{run}}$$

Figure 26.11   **The rise and the run**

The run of the line Δx, is captured by the standard deviation of x. Why this should be so is suggested by Figure 26.12 which shows two different sets of observations for x and y.

In scatterplot (b) of Figure 26.12 the standard deviation of x is greater than in scatterplot (a). This is because the standard deviation measures the spread of x around its mean, and the deviations from the mean are larger in (b) than in (a). The more spread out the observations of x, the greater the standard deviation and hence the greater the 'run' associated with the regression line.

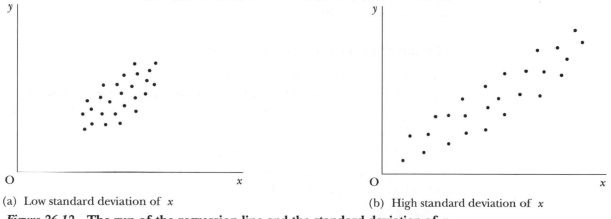

(a) Low standard deviation of x

(b) High standard deviation of x

Figure 26.12   **The run of the regression line and the standard deviation of x**

So the run of the regression line is captured by the standard deviation of x. What then should we use for the rise of the regression line? Can we use the standard deviation of y? In fact the rise of the regression line is a bit more complicated. It reflects two influences: the spread of the y variable, and the extent to which x and y are related. To see this, consider the following questions.

Questions

Look back at the different scatterplots in Figure 26.10. All the scatterplots show the same set of x values and y values, but in different combinations to produce different sets of points.

1   What does having used the same set of values say about the standard deviations of x and y in the different diagrams?

2   What determines the slope of the regression lines?

Each variable has the same standard deviation on each scatterplot in Figure 26.10. But the regression lines fitted through each set of points are clearly different. They have different slopes, even though the spread of x and y values is the same in all the diagrams.

Look first at Figure 26.10 (d) and (e). In (d) the correlation coefficient is quite large, though not as large as 1 since the fit is not perfect. In (d) the regression line slopes upwards quite steeply, while in (e), where the correlation coefficient is smaller, the slope is less steep. In (c), there is no correlation, and the line is just horizontal, with no rise at all; that is, it has zero slope showing that there is no relation between x and y. In (a) and (b), we have perfect positive and negative correlations respectively, and the rise of the line is equal in magnitude to the whole spread of y; (f) is an example of a negative correlation, where the correlation is not perfect, and the regression line slopes less steeply downwards than in (b).

These scatterplots show that the rise depends on the correlation coefficient between the two variables. With a low correlation coefficient only some of the standard deviation of y is picked up in the rise of the regression line. The correlation coefficient, R, is a number between 1 and -1. Its magnitude tells you the proportion of the standard deviation of y that goes into the rise of the regression line, and its sign tells you whether the rise is positive or negative. The rise is captured by multiplying the standard deviation of y by the correlation coefficient.

The intercept of the regression line

Finally, to understand the intercept of the regression line, look back at Figure 26.8. The regression line will always travel through the point where the vertical ($\bar{x}$) and horizontal ($\bar{y}$) red lines meet. At this point the equation for the line is:

$$\bar{y} = a + b\bar{x}$$

Since we know $\bar{y}$, $\bar{x}$ and b, the intercept a can be derived by taking $b\bar{x}$ from both sides of the equation to give:

$$\bar{y} - b\bar{x} = a$$

and therefore

$$a = \bar{y} - b\bar{x}$$

This section has provided a hopefully intuitive account of how the regression line can be estimated. It should also be mentioned that the procedure outlined in this section has a particular name. It is called the *method of least squares*. This is because it draws the line which minimizes the sum of the squares of the deviations of the line from the observations it summarizes. If you wish to find out more about this method you may want to look at the more mathematical descriptions of regression methods found in introductory statistics textbooks (e.g. Quadling, 1987). For the purposes of this text, however, an understanding of the approach taken in this chapter will suffice.

The Appendix to this chapter (Section A2) explains how the expression for the slope of the regression line can be put in a form which allows you to calculate the line from a data set, and provides an example of such a calculation.

Exercise 26.1

Assume that you have collected some observations on income and consumption, for the last 20 years, for a country which you consider to be of interest. Explain in words the steps involved in fitting a regression line to show the relationship between income and consumption.

2.4   The fit of the regression line

Once a regression line has been calculated the econometrician needs to know how well it fits the data. Regression lines do not, in general, fit their data perfectly. Some points will deviate from the line as in Figure 26.13. The aim in fitting a regression line is to minimize these deviations. More exactly, it is to find the line for which the sum of the squares of those deviations is the lowest possible for any straight line – that is why it is called 'least squares' regression. But for some sets of data such a line will fit the data better than for others. For all data sets, the regression line will be the line of best fit, but is it a line of good fit? A measure which indicates how well a line fits the data is R^2, the square of the correlation coefficient, often called the coefficient of determination.

Definition

R^2

The R^2 measures the goodness of fit of a regression line.

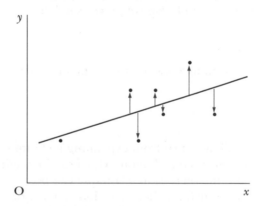

Figure 26.13   **Deviations from a regression line**

The R^2, like R, captures the strength of the relationship between x and y. Unlike R, it is always a positive number between 0 and 1, telling you how closely the points cluster around the regression line. The stronger the correlation between x and y, the higher the value of R^2. If there is no correlation between x and y, then R^2 is 0; if the fit is perfect then R^2 is 1.

Within any set of data, the y values will vary. Some of that variability will correspond in a linear fashion to variations in x and be picked up by the regression line. But there will also be variations that correspond to deviations from the regression line, as in Figure 26.13. The R^2 measures how much of that variability is picked up by the regression line. When the R^2 is 1, all the variability in y is picked up by the regression line and there are no deviations from the line. When the R^2 is 0, none of the variability in y corresponds to the regression line and any variation in y is due to deviations from the regression line. For values of R^2 between 0 and 1, the R^2 tells us what proportion of the variability in y is picked up by the regression line. The higher the R^2, the better the fit.

Exercise 26.2

Suppose that two variables take identical values for all observations – each value of x is exactly equal to the corresponding value of y. What would be the value of R^2? What are the slope and the intercept of the regression line?

The extremes of 0 and 1 are limits between which the R^2 can vary. For an econometrician who has fitted a regression line the question 'What is the R^2?' is asked in order to find out how well the regression line fits the data. The nearer to 1 the better the fit; the nearer to 0 the worse the fit. If, for example, the R^2 is equal to 0.96 this means that 96 per cent of the variability of y is summarized by the regression line relating y to x. Only 4 per cent of the variability of y is not represented by the regression line. A lower value of R^2, say if it was equal to 0.04, would mean that only 4 per cent of the variability of y is summarized by the regression line.

In practice some judgement is needed in interpreting the R^2. If, for example, it took a value of 0.52 does this mean that the regression line is a line of good or bad fit? Whilst the line summarizes over half the variability of y, there is also about a half of the variability not represented by the regression line. An example of how the value of R^2 is calculated is given in the Appendix to this chapter (Section A3). Working through that, now or later, should help you to consolidate this section.

Reflection

Explain in a few sentences the importance of R^2.

3   Time series data

I will now turn from explaining techniques to considering their use. One of the main contributions which can be made by this chapter is to demonstrate how the regression technique can be used to model time series data. This is data which is collected by looking at a particular variable at different points in time: for example, 1960, 1961, 1962, etc. Time series data can be contrasted with cross-section data, which provided the main subject matter for Chapter 9. This latter type of data is drawn from a number of different observations at a particular point in time.

Exercise 26.3

Consider the following types of data:

1   US rate of profit, 1960–93.

2   UK monthly household expenditure, January 1992–December 1992.

3   Unemployment rates for the 52 US states, 1993.

4   South African interest rates, 1980–93.

5   UK household expenditure, 7000 households from the *Family Expenditure Survey*, 1992.

Which of these data sets are time series and which are cross-section?

One of the main problems with using time series is the lack of consistency of data collection across years. Assume, for example, that we wished to construct a time series for unemployment rates over the last 20 years in the UK. The problem is that the statisticians who collect and process this data continually revise and modify their methods. They attend statistics conferences where they learn and develop new techniques and procedures. The construction of a consistent time series is not their most important objective. They want to construct the best estimate of the unemployment rate for a particular year.

Moreover, revisions to the published unemployment rate may not be the sole preserve of statisticians. During the 1980s, the method for calculating the UK unemployment rate changed on about 30 occasions. There has been much dispute over whether these changes were due to the influence of politicians, wanting to lower the official unemployment rate by changing its method of calculation.

The further one tries to go back in constructing a time series of data, the more problems may be faced. Not only can the methods of calculation change, but old series of data may be replaced by new series. A good example of this is the change in the method of classifying industries in the UK *Census of Production* in 1979. If I want to look at the output of individual industries, I have to construct two sets of time series data. One series runs from 1968 to 1979; the other from 1980 to the present. The system of classifying the data has changed so radically that it is not possible to construct a continual time series of data from 1968 to the present.

Even if a consistent time series of data is available, there are also some specific modelling problems which arise. I shall mention two of these problems. The first problem concerns the linear nature of the regression line. A linear regression line could be specified for the relationship, say, between investment for a particular country (I) and time (t).

$$I = a + bt$$

The variable t takes on values 1, 2, 3, etc. as time progresses. Given observations of investment over a number of time periods, assume that a regression line has been fitted to the data. The coefficient b, the slope of the regression line, shows the effect of a change in time on investment. Indeed, between any time period and the next, the change or increment in investment (ΔI) is equal to the constant amount b. This is because $\Delta t = 1$ between one period and the next, so the slope is:

$$b = \frac{\Delta I}{\Delta t} = \Delta I$$

This amounts to a linear growth model of investment. In each period investment grows by the same amount b. A container being filled with water at a constant speed can provide a useful analogy to the linear model of investment (Figure 26.14).

When the tap is turned on, the same amount of water runs into the container regardless of the level of water in the container. The analogy is that the water falling out of the tap can be thought of as investment, with the amount of water in the container representing the capital stock. Regardless of the level of capital stock, the same amount of investment is injected into the economy according to the linear model of investment.

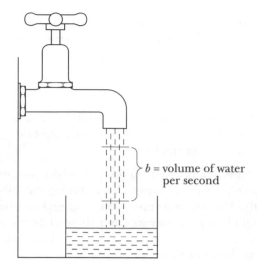

Figure 26.14   **Tap water falling into a container – an analogy to the linear growth model**

Source: Wuyts (1994)

However, as investment increases in each period, the capital stock which is being added to will accumulate. There will be more and more factory space and machinery to produce products for the market place. The economy's capacity will continually increase. The problem with this linear model is that this increase in capacity is not taken into account – investment always increases by a constant amount equal to b. The Keynesian economic theory discussed in the previous chapter tells us that, as the capital stock accumulates, the economy may produce too much capacity and hence the level of investment may falter. In other words, the level of investment in one period is not independent of the level of investment in the previous period. The linear regression line does not allow for such relationships. Investment is unlikely to grow by a constant amount in each period as the linear model assumes.

This relationship between the level of investment in different time periods can apply to many types of time series data. For example, the level of government spending in one period may well be related to the level of government spending in the next period. The level of money supply in one period is plausibly related to money supply levels in previous periods. This happens frequently in time series data because they refer to historically connected processes. The path of investment over several periods represents a process in time with its own history. It would be surprising if the observations of investment in different time periods were not connected, since they are part of the same process. Unfortunately, because of their linear nature, regression lines do not take into account such connections.

A second problem with time series modelling is how to interpret correlation between variables. Just because two variables are correlated, this does not necessarily mean that movements in one are *caused* by variations in the other. If x is correlated with y this does not mean that x determines y. Correlation between variables does not necessarily imply causation. There may be *spurious correlation* between variables. A classic example is the discovery by a well known UK econometrician that there is correlation between cumulative rainfall in the UK and the rate of inflation (Hendry, 1993). The R^2 between these two variables is high, taking a value of 0.98, indicating that a large proportion of the variation in these variables is captured by the regression line fitted between them. There is obviously no causation between these variables. Inflation is not caused by wet weather, nor is wet weather caused by rising prices. The correlation between these variables is spurious.

Even if correlation is not spurious and some economic relationship between variables is plausible, the direction of causation is not always obvious. It may be the case, for example, that there is correlation between observations on profits and investment. A case could be made for causation in either direction. An increase in profits could encourage firms to invest more, and an increase in investment could generate a climate in which more profits can be made. There is no substitute for economic theory when interpreting the correlation between economic variables.

Reflection

List the problems noted above associated with using regression analysis on time series data.

4   Forecasting

One of the most important applications of the regression line is in the field of forecasting. For economists who work on the compilation of forecasts of economic activity, the regression line is an essential tool. In this section, some time series data is used to show how a regression line might be used for forecasting purposes.

The example which is chosen is that of gross domestic product for the Japanese economy in the 1980s and early 1990s. There is no particular reason for choosing Japan as an example, except that there have been some interesting developments in policy in recent years which lend themselves to empirical analysis. Figure 26.15 shows a scatterplot of Japan's GDP over a sample period, 1980–91.

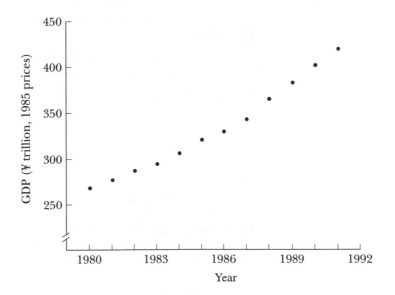

Figure 26.15   Japanese GDP, 1980–91

Source: OECD (1993)

Imagine that you are an economist wishing to forecast the movement of Japan's GDP during the period after 1991. In order to achieve this you would need to identify any regularity in the variations of GDP over the period. If the data displays a regular path, then it could be inferred that this path will also be followed in later years outside the sample period.

In Chapter 20 Nick Crafts introduced the notion of the trend line. An economy's output may undergo business cycle fluctuations, but it should also display a trend over time. This trend line is used to capture any regularities in the movement of an economy's output over time. In previous chapters the methods used to estimate this trend line were not explicitly discussed; but in the analysis that follows a trend line is estimated using regression techniques.

In the previous section the notion of a trend was introduced in the context of time series movements of investment. A trend variable t is usually given values 1, 2, 3, etc., representing each period of analysis. Over the period 1980–91, for example, the trend variable could take the value 1 in 1980, the value 2 in 1981, and so on. To estimate the trend line, the variable being considered (in this case Japan's GDP) is regressed on the trend variable. The procedure followed and the results of this regression are set out in the Appendix to this chapter (Section A4).

It can thus be reported that the estimated trend line for Japan's GDP over the period 1980–91 has the structure:

$$\text{GDP} = 242 + 13.8t$$

This line shows the trend which GDP in Japan followed over the period in question. The slope of this line tells us that the trend increase in GDP is ¥13.8 trillion each year. For each increase in time by one year, there is estimated to be a ¥13.8 trillion increase in GDP.

Before showing how this trend line can be used for forecasting, the R^2 can be reported. It takes a value of 0.98. This means that the trend line summarizes 98 per cent of the variation of Japan's GDP during the 1980s. The line provides a very good fit, which means that we should have a great deal of confidence in using it for forecasting purposes.

Question

How might you use this trend line for forecasting purposes?

The way in which the line can be used for forecasting is very straightforward. If you were an economist in Japan in 1992 and you wanted to forecast the GDP over that year and the ensuing years, then all that is required is to plug the trend values for these years into the equation for the trend line. In 1992 the variable t would be equal to 13, such that the forecast GDP would be

$$\hat{y}_{92} = 242 + (13.8 \times 13) = 421 \text{ trillion yen}$$

The term $\hat{y}_{92}$ represents the forecast value of GDP for 1992. The prediction of ¥421 trillion for GDP in 1992 compares with values of 418 in 1991 and 401 in 1990. The trend which GDP has been following in previous periods is *extrapolated* onto the subsequent forecast period. A similar extrapolation could be made for 1993 by plugging in the value of 14 for t in the trend line equation.

Exercise 26.4

Using the above trend line, what would be your forecast of Japan's GDP in 1994?

The forecasting procedure can be shown in a different light by drawing the regression line onto the scatterplot diagram (see Figure 26.16).

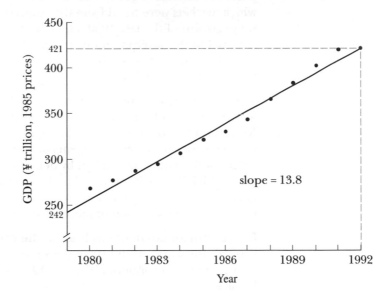

Figure 26.16   **Using a trend line to forecast Japanese GDP**

Source: OECD (1993)

The intercept (242) and the slope of the line (13.8) are displayed together with the observations for which the line provides a fit. Also shown is the forecast GDP of ¥421 trillion for 1992.

What stands out from this picture is that actual GDP deviates from the trend line in a quite systematic manner. In the early 1980s, GDP is above the trend but falls below it during the middle part of the decade. At the end of the decade, GDP moves above the trend line. The Japanese economy is displaying business cycle fluctuations around the trend line. Like most advanced economies the Japanese economy experienced a recession in economic activity in the early 1980s, and a pronounced boom in economic activity in the late 1980s. (Note that the term recession is used here to refer to a slowdown in GDP growth relative to the trend line, and not a cut in output as in Chapter 25.)

It should be noted that the occurrence of business cycle fluctuations is the same problem referred to in the previous section as the historical connectedness of data. The use of a regression/trend line for prediction assumes that the change in GDP is the same each year (¥13.8 trillion) or rather, since the regression line is not a perfect fit, that changes in GDP above or below the trend cancel each other out and do not show a regular pattern. In fact the deviations in Figure 26.16 show a cyclical pattern. When the Japanese economy was going through a recession in the early 1980s, there were successive years with GDP lying below the trend line. In the later boom, GDP was above the trend line for a number of successive years. There are, therefore, potential problems with fitting a trend line for the whole of the 1980s since there are two distinctly different historical processes – recession and boom. There are turning points in these historical processes which cannot be captured by a single linear equation.

Two alternative trend lines could be fitted to the data. First, it could be argued that the end of the 1980s represented a structural break from previous periods of growth. The Thatcher/Reagan revolution in the 1980s, which had some impact in Japan, could be argued to have heralded a new period of unbridled growth for market economies – a new golden age in which markets were freed from the restrictions of state interference. The rapid growth of the late 1980s could set the pace for future economic activity. On this interpretation, a trend line that is relevant to the 1990s should be fitted through the late 1980s only, since there was a structural break in the mid 1980s.

A second interpretation is that the strength of the boom in the late 1980s was due to the relaxation of credit restrictions – also part of the Thatcher/Reagan revolution – which took place in Japan during this period. It became easier for economic agents to borrow money, which meant that the extent of the boom was fuelled by debt. On this interpretation the boom was 'artificial' since it was based on borrowed money. In the end such activity cannot be sustained. A more realistic long-term trend would be based only on the period of more moderate growth in the early 1980s.

Either of these two positions leads to the conclusion that a trend line through the whole of the 1980s does not capture the long-term growth path of the Japanese economy. If the late 1980s provide a sustainable structural break with the past, then a new trend line is needed starting in this period. A break in a trend of this kind is called a segmented trend. If, on the other hand, the late 1980s provide an 'artificial' aberration, then a trend line for the early 1980s provides the most reliable guide to future trends.

The procedure used to calculate the segmented trend lines is shown in the Appendix, Section A5. I shall concentrate on the resultant regression lines, which are shown in Figure 26.17. Each line has been fitted to the scatterplot diagram.

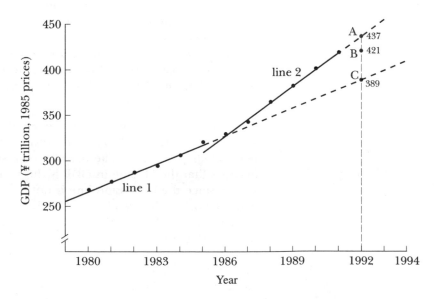

Figure 26.17 **Segmented trend lines, Japan's GDP, 1980–91**

Source: OECD (1993)

Line 1, the trend line for the early 1980s, is flatter than line 2, the trend line for the late 1980s. The equations for these lines are:

Line 1: $y = 255 + 10.3t$

Line 2: $y = 309 + 18.3t$

Notice that the coefficient for the slope of the first line (10.3) is less than the coefficient for the slope of the second line (18.3).

These lines can be used to provide different forecasts of GDP in 1992 and beyond. The following forecasts can be made:

Line 1: $\hat{y}_{92} = 255 + (10.3 \times 13) = 389$

Line 2: $\hat{y}_{92} = 309 + (18.3 \times 7) = 437$

For Line 1 the year to which the forecast applies (1992) is represented by period 13. For Line 2 this year is represented by period 7. These forecasts are shown on Figure 26.17. The forecast using Line 1 is represented by point C, the forecast using Line 2 by point A, and the original forecast using the trend line across the whole time series by point B.

Which of these forecasts you choose is a matter for theoretical discussion. If you believe there has been a structural break in the mid 1980s then one of the segmented trend lines should be used (forecast A or C). An econometrician who chooses forecast A may be said to have a more optimistic view of the sustainability of the late 1980s boom. An econometrician who chooses forecast C may have a more pessimistic view of this boom, arguing that it must come to an end, such that the economy will return to a low growth path. The original trend line, for the whole period, provides something of a middle ground between these two approaches. Instead of fitting segmented trend lines you could simply take a look at Figure 26.16 and make a subjective assessment. Since output for 1990 and 1991 seems to be moving above and away from the trend line, you might be tempted to think that it will shortly move back again.

You may regard what I am about to do now as something of a cheat, but it will reveal the importance of choosing the right trend line. I will now consider, with the benefit of hindsight, the *actual* performance of the Japanese economy during 1992 and 1993. The actual observations are shown as black dots in Figure 26.18, together with the forecasts made using the three trend lines.

For both 1992 and 1993 the best forecasts are made by the full trend line, based on the whole of the sample period. Forecast B (B_{92} and B_{93}) is considerably nearer the actual observations than forecast A (A_{92} and A_{93}) or forecast C (C_{92} and C_{93}).

This is not to say, however, that plotting the segmented lines is not potentially useful. The Japanese economy moved very sharply into recession during 1992. The rate of growth for 1991 was 4.2 per cent, whereas for 1992 it was 1.9 per cent. In 1993 the rate of growth was 0.1 per cent. Line 1, based on the low growth rates of the early 1980s may provide an indication of where the economy in this example could be moving in the longer term. If GDP grows at a low rate for any length of time, say more than 5 years, then the economy will move back towards Line 1. In this scenario, in which the late 1980s expansion turns out to be an aberration, the trend line based on it proves increasingly unrealistic.

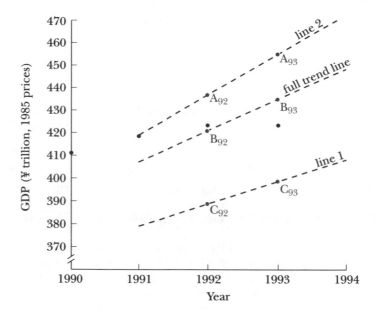

Figure 26.18 Forecasts with three different trend lines

Source: OECD (1993)

You may also have felt that Line 1 was not given a fair chance in this contest. When we talk about returning to the lower growth rates of the 1980s, this could still be from a higher base level of GDP as a result of the high growth rates on the late 1980s. In other words, as Nick Crafts pointed out in Chapter 20, Section 1.3, short-term changes or shocks can have long-term effects. In this case we would draw a trend line with the same slope as that of line 1 for the early 1980s, but starting from one of the data points we have for the end of the 1980s, whenever we judge the aberration of the late 1980s to be over. You could try drawing in such a line by hand and judging whether you think that would predict GDP for the 1990s better than any of the other lines I have drawn. The point to emphasize here is that forecasting is not just a mechanical exercise. The use of mechanical models such as the regression line is important, but an equally important factor is the judgement of the forecaster. One of the most experienced forecasters in the UK, Paul Ormerod, points out that

> macro-economic models are unable to produce forecasts on their own. The proprietors of the models interfere with their output before it is allowed to see the light of day. These 'judgmental adjustments' can be, and often are, extensive. Every model builder and model operator knows about the process of altering the output of a model, but this remains something of a twilight world, and is not well documented in the literature.
>
> *(Ormerod, 1994, p.103)*

This part of the chapter has shown how the techniques of regression can be used for forecasting purposes. By fitting trend lines to time series data, forecasts can be made of the likely path of economic activity. In the next section an additional application of regression techniques is explored, namely the simulation of policy.

"We'll soon give you our estimates of the strength of the economy. But remember, sir: it's not an exact science."

Source: Cartoon by Ed Fisher. Copyright, 1995, Harvard Business Review. Reprinted by permission of Ed Fisher

5   Simulation

A distinction can be made between simulation and forecasting. A simulation is much less ambitious than a forecast. It focuses on one policy measure and provides an estimate of the impacts it is likely to generate. This assumes that all other aspects of policy are unchanged. It incorporates the assumption of *ceteris paribus* – other things being equal. A forecast, on the other hand, tries to provide the best possible estimate of future events given all available information.

As before, assume that you are an economist trying to anticipate events in Japan for the period beyond 1991. You know from the last section that Japan's economy moved into recession in 1992 and 1993. In response to the recession, Japan's government introduced a number of fiscal packages throughout 1992 and 1993. In the analysis that follows I shall concentrate on the largest of these, a fiscal package worth ¥8.5 trillion or £49 billion of government spending. This amount of money is reported to have been equal to 1.8 per cent of the GDP of Japan (*Financial Times*, 14 April 1993).

In this section an attempt is made to simulate the impacts of this Japanese fiscal push. My aim is merely to illustrate how regression techniques might be used in carrying out such a simulation. The results should be treated with caution because a number of simplifying assumptions will be made.

In order to simulate the impacts of the fiscal package, the figures given by the *Financial Times* will have to be made consistent with the data used in this chapter. The data I have been using for Japan have been calculated in 1985 constant prices and in terms of trillion yen. Japan's GDP in 1992 was ¥426 trillion at 1985 constant prices. If the fiscal package in April 1993 represented 1.8 per cent of Japanese GDP, then its magnitude in 1985 constant prices is ¥7.7 trillion: 1.8 per cent of ¥426 trillion. Because it is calculated in 1985 rather than 1992 prices, this figure is less than the figure of ¥8.5 trillion quoted by the *Financial Times*.

How then can the impacts of a ¥7.7 trillion increase in government spending be simulated? In the previous chapter a Keynesian theory of the business cycle was presented in which the multiplier and accelerator work together to generate cycles in economic activity. For simplicity, I shall now use just the multiplier to simulate the impacts of the Japanese package. You will recall from Chapter 17 that the multiplier is based on the relationship between household income and expenditure. If government spending increases, then more people are employed and they consume extra goods and services with their new incomes. People employed making these additional goods and services also consume more out of their additional income. The proportion of extra income which people spend is crucial to the size of the multiplier.

The first part of the simulation requires a little algebra. Recall from Chapter 17 that

$$Y = C + I + G$$

where

Y = income,

C = consumption,

I = investment, and

G = government spending.

This is the Keynesian identity which says that national income is made up of consumption, investment and government spending. An additional term could also be added for exports and imports, but for simplicity I will assume for the moment that there is a closed economy with no outside trade.

An important building block for the estimation of the multiplier is the consumption function. As explained in Chapter 3, the consumption function models the relationship between income and consumption. I will use the following equation for the consumption function.

$$C = a + cY$$

Household consumption (C) is a linear function of income (Y), in which the slope, c, is the marginal propensity to consume (MPC). The intercept, a, is the amount of consumption which is not dependent on income.

Substituting the second equation into the first yields the expression

$$Y = a + cY + I + G$$

Subtracting cY from both sides of the equation gives

$$Y - cY = a + I + G$$

This can be rewritten as:

$$(1 - c)\ Y = a + I + G$$

and now dividing both sides by $(1 - c)$ yields

$$Y = \frac{1}{1 - c}\ (a + I + G)$$

The multiplier is the expression $\frac{1}{1-c}$. The higher the value of c, the lower is the size of the multiplier's denominator, $1 - c$, and hence the higher the size of the multiplier itself. A change in government spending (G) will affect income (Y) according to the size of the multiplier $\frac{1}{1-c}$. If Japan increases its government spending by ¥7.7 trillion, then the multiplier can be used to estimate the effect on income.

Exercise 26.5

Calculate the multipliers associated with the following imaginary countries.

(a) Country A has a consumption function, $C = 12 + 0.4Y$.

(b) In country B the MPC is 0.6.

(c) In country C the MPC is 0.9.

Did you have any worries about the definition of the MPC which you have just used in Exercise 26.5? If you looked back at Chapter 3, you may have been reminded that the consumption function developed there related consumption not to national income, but to households' *disposable* income after tax Y_d. As Jane Wheelock noted in Chapter 3, it is disposable income which seems likely to be the income total most closely related to consumption decisions. So the consumption function in Chapter 3 is written:

$$C = a + bY_d$$

and this seems the best equation to use for estimation purposes. So can we adapt our model of the multiplier to include the concept of disposable income?

One way to do this is to suppose that a proportion t of income comes back to the government in taxes. Then we can specify the relation between national income and disposable income as:

$$Y_d = Y - tY = (1 - t)\ Y$$

This additional equation tells us that the relationship between c, the marginal propensity to consume out of national income, and b, the MPC from disposable income, is as follows:

$$C = a + bY_d = a + b(1 - t)Y$$

The expression $b(1 - t)$ is therefore the same as c in my earlier consumption function. The effect of the taxes is to scale down the MPC from disposable income to give the MPC from gross income. I can therefore rewrite the multiplier

$$\frac{1}{1 - c} \text{ as } \frac{1}{1 - b(1 - t)}$$

We now have a model we can use for estimation. Note that this simulation has two distinct parts. First we have developed a mathematical model in which $\frac{1}{1 - b(1 - t)}$ is specified to be a quantitative expression for the multiplier. Next comes a statistical procedure by which the multiplier can be estimated for the Japanese economy.

An empirical estimation of the multiplier for Japan's economy can be attempted by looking at a time series of observations on household disposable income and consumption expenditure during the 1980s (see Table 26.3). A line can be fitted between these observations, its slope being the marginal propensity to consume (MPC).

Table 26.3   **Real income and consumption data for Japan, 1980–91 (¥ trillion, 1985 constant prices)**

Year	x disposable income	y consumption
1980	189	160
1981	195	162
1982	202	170
1983	208	175
1984	214	180
1985	221	186
1986	229	193
1987	235	201
1988	246	211
1989	257	220
1990	264	230
1991	273	236

Source: OECD (1993)

Since the method of regression has already been covered at length in the appendix of this chapter, I shall not include the table and calculations for estimating this consumption function. Suffice it to say, in practice, economists do not usually follow such a long-winded approach. The calculations are completed much more quickly on a computer, or even using a fairly basic calculator.

I can therefore report that using a computer, a regression line has been estimated for the data in Table 26.3, which has a slope of 0.93. I can also report that the R^2 is equal to 0.99, which means that the regression line provides a very close fit. Since the MPC is the slope of the consumption function it follows that:

MPC = b = 0.93

This means that for every additional yen of income obtained by households after taxes, 0.93 yen will be consumed. In other words 93 per cent of additional net income is directed to the consumption of goods and services. For the purposes of calculating the multiplier, however, we need to scale down the MPC out of disposable income using the tax rate. I will assume that t, the tax rate on additional income is 15 per cent. Then the marginal propensity to consume out of national income c is

$$c = b(1 - t) = 0.93(1 - 0.15) = 0.79$$

One additional adjustment is also needed. It is necessary to calculate the proportion of additional income spent on Japanese goods and services. If consumers buy goods from abroad, this will not have any multiplier effect on the Japanese economy. Assume that about 20 per cent of Japanese consumption is of products which are imported. This means that the MPC for domestic consumption should be scaled down by a further 20 per cent. For every ¥100 spent on consumption, ¥20 will be directed to imported goods and services. Since 20 per cent of 0.79 is 0.16, the domestic value of the MPC is 0.63 (calculated by taking 0.16 from 0.79). The multiplier can then be calculated by the formula:

$$\text{multiplier} = \frac{1}{1 - 0.63} = \frac{1}{0.37} = 2.7$$

This means that for every additional yen of government spending, ¥2.7 of additional income is created for the Japanese economy. Indeed, for the fiscal package of ¥7.7 trillion, the impact on income would be 2.7 multiplied by 7.7, a simulated increase of ¥20.8 trillion. This increase represents a 4.9 per cent simulated increase in Japan's GDP. According to this simulation, if such an impact were to take place, Japan's economy could as a direct result be approaching a return to the heady days of the late 1980s when growth rates were above 5 per cent.

This simulation should, of course, as I have intimated, be interpreted with a great deal of caution. It is only meant as an illustration of how regression analysis can be used to simulate the impacts of government policy. The first point to note is that consumption functions estimated on time series data always over-estimate the marginal propensity to consume. Just because consumption and income increase each year, it does not mean that all the increase in consumption is due to this year's additional income. The two variables may be correlated but consumption may increase for other reasons. According to Milton Friedman, households plan their consumption according to their expected lifetime income (their wealth). A temporary increase in income, such as that induced by Japan's fiscal package, will not have much affect on the wealth of consumers. Their consumption may not, therefore, increase to the extent suggested by the above consumption function.

An additional limitation of the above consumption function is that it models the effect of only one variable on consumption, namely income. There are many other factors which may affect household consumption, such as the number of children in a household, the type of accommodation and so on. If these factors are correlated with income, and evidence suggests that they are, then the above regression line does not provide the best possible estimate of the MPC. A technique which can model the correlation between consumption and many variables (more than two) could usefully serve this purpose. This type of analysis is called *multiple regression*, and provides the focus for much of modern econometrics.

Even if a more sophisticated method for estimating the size of the MPC were used, there is still uncertainty over its accuracy as a guide to the future. The fitting of a regression line is always based on past values of variables. There is never any guarantee that variables will follow the same pattern in the future as was displayed in the past. Whilst evidence suggests that the sun will always rise each morning, this by itself does not provide any guarantee that it will. Just because the MPC was 0.79 in the 1980s, we cannot be certain that it will take this value in the 1990s. Indeed, evidence suggests that the recession of the early 1990s induced a faltering in consumer confidence. The risk of job loss and high interest rates provided a climate in which consumers were unwilling to part with the same share of their income as in the past. This means that the value of the MPC estimated over past data can prove to be very inaccurate. Inevitably, econometricians have to let their data and models do the talking, but there is also a need for subjective judgement of the reliability of such models.

6   Conclusion

This chapter has provided a basic introduction to the method of regression analysis. By introducing the notion of correlation between variables, an intuitive account has been given to the mathematical formulae used to estimate a regression line. In addition the coefficient of determination, or R^2, has been shown to be a useful indicator for the goodness of fit which regression lines provide.

The importance of regression techniques to economic analysis has been demonstrated using time series data for Japan in the 1980s. In addition to estimating trend lines for forecasting purposes, I also conducted a simulation of a Keynesian fiscal package in the early 1990s. I also discussed the extent to which this type of analysis can be said to be useful, with specific reference to the problems associated with time series data.

There are of course many more problems with regression analysis, and a myriad of methods used to overcome them, than have been covered in this chapter. In particular there is a vast literature associated with statistical testing and regression analysis. By giving an introduction to regression analysis, this chapter has merely provided an initial taste of one of the key statistical techniques which economists use.

Appendix

This appendix provides some exercises and examples to demonstrate how you can, in practice, work out some statistical concepts discussed in the text. Working through them should help you to grasp the ideas in Section 2 more clearly, and to understand the calculations behind the applications of regression analysis in Section 4. I start with the promised example of calculating a covariance. I then explain how the formula for the slope of the regression line, discussed intuitively in the text, can be used to calculate the regression line for a small data set. A demonstration is also provided of how the R^2 can be estimated. Finally, I work through the estimation of the trend line and the segmented trends for Japan in Section 4.

Section A1   Calculating the covariance

An example can be used to illustrate how the covariance is calculated. Assume for simplicity that there are five observations of the variables x and y. Figure 26.19 shows a scatterplot of these observations.

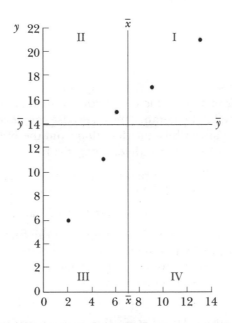

Figure 26.19   **An example of positive correlation**

This scatterplot shows that x and y look to be positively correlated. Four of the observations are in quadrants I and III. This positive correlation can be confirmed by calculating the covariance between x and y. To do this the values of x and y are displayed in Table 26.A1.

Table 26.A1   **Data for calculating the covariance**

x	y	$x - \bar{x}$	$y - \bar{y}$	$(x - \bar{x})(y - \bar{y})$
2	6	−5	−8	40
5	11	−2	−3	6
6	15	−1	1	−1
9	17	2	3	6
13	21	6	7	42
$\Sigma x = 35$	$\Sigma y = 70$			$\Sigma(x - \bar{x})(y - \bar{y}) = 93$
$\bar{x} = \dfrac{35}{5} = 7$	$\bar{y} = \dfrac{70}{5} = 14$			$\text{cov}(x,y) = \dfrac{93}{5} = 18.6$

The first step is to calculate the means of *x* and *y*. The first column is added up such that the sum (Σx) is equal to 35. The mean is calculated by dividing 35 by 5, the number of observations. It follows that $\bar{x}$, the mean of *x*, is equal to 7. Using the same method of calculation the mean of *y* is calculated to be 14.

The next step is to calculate the deviations from the mean for both *x* and *y*. The third column shows numbers calculated by subtracting $\bar{x}$ from *x* for each observation. On the first line, for example, the mean, which is equal to 7, is taken from the value for *x*, which is 2, to yield a value for $(x - \bar{x})$ of −5. The fourth column is constructed by following the same procedure for *y*.

Once the deviations from the mean are calculated, the final column for $(x - \bar{x})(y - \bar{y})$ can be constructed. To do this the elements in the third and fourth columns are multiplied together. It can be seen that four of the entries in this column are positive. Moreover, these are the observations which lie in quadrants I and III in Figure 26.19. The observation which lies in quadrant II is represented by a value of −1 in the final column. This is because the deviation from the mean of *x* is negative whilst the deviation from the mean of *y* is positive (a positive times a negative yields a negative).

That *x* and *y* display positive correlation in this example is confirmed by averaging the values in the final column of Table 26.A1. This average, $\frac{\Sigma(x - \bar{x})(y - \bar{y})}{n}$, is the covariance of *x* and *y* and it takes a value of $\frac{93}{5}$ = 18.6. Four of the observations in the final column are positive, so it is not surprising that their average, the covariance, is positive. This positive value shows us, without looking at the scatterplot, that there is positive correlation between *x* and *y*.

Section A2   *Estimating the regression line*

Section 2 sought to provide an intuitive account of how the regression line can be understood and estimated. The formula used in that section for the slope of the line can in fact be simplified algebraically to provide an equation which you can use directly to estimate the regression line for a set of data. I described the slope of the regression line in Section 2 as

$$\text{slope} = b = \frac{R \cdot SD\,(y)}{SD\,(x)}$$

In Section 2.2, I wrote out the correlation coefficient *R* as

$$R = \frac{\text{cov}\,(x, y)}{SD\,(x)\ SD\,(y)}$$

If you substitute that expression for *R* into the equation for the slope and cancel out *SD(y)* you get:

$$b = \frac{\text{cov}\,(x, y)}{SD\,(x)\ SD\,(x)} = \frac{\text{cov}\,(x, y)}{\text{var}\,(x)}$$

since the standard deviation was defined as the square root of the variance (see Chapter 9).

Finally, if you put back into that last formula the definitions for the covariance and variance in terms of deviations from the mean, you will find that

$$b = \frac{\dfrac{\Sigma(x - \bar{x})(y - \bar{y})}{n}}{\dfrac{\Sigma(x - \bar{x})^2}{n}} = \frac{\Sigma(x - \bar{x})(y - \bar{y})}{\Sigma(x - \bar{x})^2}$$

The last formula, the result of cancelling out n, is composed of familiar elements which you have seen before in calculating the covariance. I am now going to show how it can be used to estimate some regression lines.

The regression line and its R^2 can be calculated by adding two further columns to Table 26.A1. In Table 26.A2 the squares of the deviations from the mean of both x and y are calculated.

Table 26.A2   **Data for an example regression line**

x	y	$x - \bar{x}$	$y - \bar{y}$	$(x - \bar{x})(y - \bar{y})$	$(x - \bar{x})^2$	$(y - \bar{y})^2$
2	6	−5	-8	40	25	64
5	11	−2	-3	6	4	9
6	15	−1	1	−1	1	1
9	17	2	3	6	4	9
13	21	6	7	42	36	49
$\Sigma x = 35$ $\Sigma y = 70$				$\Sigma(x - \bar{x})(y - \bar{y})$ $= 93$	$\Sigma(x - \bar{x})^2$ $= 70$	$\Sigma(y - \bar{y})^2$ $= 132$
$\bar{x} = 7$ $\bar{y} = 14$				cov (x,y) $= 18.6$	var (x) $= 14$	var (y) $= 26.4$

On the first line, for example, the deviation −5 is squared to give a value for $(x - \bar{x})^2$ of 25. Once the values of $(x - \bar{x})^2$ are summed up, the *variance* of x is calculated by dividing the sum by 5. The slope of the regression line, b, is calculated by dividing the covariance of x and y by the variance of x, or directly from the equation above as:

$$b = \frac{\Sigma(x - \bar{x})(y - \bar{y})}{\Sigma(x - \bar{x})^2} = \frac{93}{70} = 1.33$$

The intercept can then be calculated as:

$$a = \bar{y} - b\bar{x} = 14 - (1.33 \times 7) = 4.69$$

These slope and intercept estimates can be used to draw the regression line on Figure 26.20.

The line starts at 4.69 and rises according to the slope, 1.33. For every increase in x of 1, there is an increase in y of 1.33.

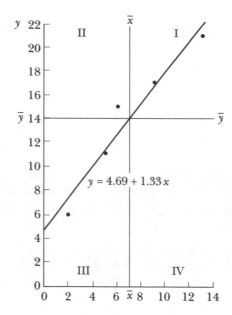

Figure 26.20   An example regression line

Section A3   Estimating the R^2

Continuing with the example in Section A2, to find out how well the regression line fits the data, the R^2 can be calculated by making use of the final column of Table 26.A2. The R^2 is the square of the correlation coefficient. Since

$$R = \frac{\text{cov } (x, y)}{SD (x) \; SD (y)}$$

we can calculate R^2 as

$$R^2 = \frac{(\text{cov } (x, y))^2}{\text{var } (x) \; \text{var } (y)}$$

Since var (x) is the $SD(x)$ squared and var (y) is the $SD(y)$ squared, we can rewrite that as

$$R^2 = \frac{(\Sigma(x - \bar{x})(y - \bar{y}))^2}{\Sigma(x - \bar{x})^2 \, \Sigma(y - \bar{y})^2}$$

when we cancel out the n by which top and bottom are both divided.

Using the formula for the R^2 we have the result that:

$$R^2 = \frac{(\Sigma \, (x - \bar{x})(y - \bar{y}))^2}{\Sigma(x - \bar{x})^2 \, \Sigma(y - \bar{y})^2} = \frac{93^2}{70 \times 132} = 0.94$$

An R^2 of 0.94 means that 94 per cent of the variability of y is summarized by the regression line. The remaining 6 per cent is not summarized by the line. This shows that the regression line fits the observations very well.

Section A4   Estimating a trend line for Japan's GDP, 1980–91

Next, I turn to the calculations underlying Section 4. A trend line for
Japan's GDP can be estimated by specifying the relationship between
variables x and y. Let y be the observations of real GDP for Japan over the
period 1980–91. The variable x can be a variable which captures the
movement of time. Let period 1 be 1980, period 2 is 1981, and so on. In
Table 26.A3 the first column contains the time periods 1 to 12 (variable
x), whilst the second column contains GDP (variable y).

Table 26.A3   Data for estimating Japan's GDP trend line, 1980–91

Year	x	y	$x - \bar{x}$	$y - \bar{y}$	$(x - \bar{x})(y - \bar{y})$	$(x - \bar{x})^2$	$(y - \bar{y})^2$
1980	1	267	−5.5	−64.75	356.13	30.25	4192.56
1981	2	276	−4.5	−55.75	250.88	20.25	3108.06
1982	3	285	−3.5	−46.75	163.63	12.25	2185.56
1983	4	293	−2.5	−38.75	96.88	6.25	1501.56
1984	5	305	−1.5	−26.75	40.13	2.25	715.56
1985	6	320	−0.5	−11.75	5.88	0.25	138.06
1986	7	329	0.5	−2.75	−1.38	0.25	7.56
1987	8	342	1.5	10.25	15.38	2.25	105.06
1988	9	364	2.5	32.25	80.63	6.25	1040.06
1989	10	381	3.5	49.25	172.38	12.25	2425.56
1990	11	401	4.5	69.25	311.63	20.25	4795.56
1991	12	418	5.5	86.25	474.38	30.25	7439.06
	$\sum x = 78$	$\sum y = 3981$			$\sum(x - \bar{x})(y - \bar{y})$ $= 1966.55$	$\sum(x - \bar{x})^2$ $= 143$	$\sum(y - \bar{y})^2$ $= 27654.22$

$$\bar{x} = \frac{78}{12} \qquad \bar{y} = \frac{3981}{12}$$
$$= 6.5 \qquad = 331.75$$

Source: OECD (1993)

The task is to fit a regression line between the time and GDP variables.
Recall from Table 26.A2 that the line is fitted by calculating some
additional columns. These can be most easily calculated by using a
calculator, or if available a computer program. By finding the sum of all
the columns the slope of the regression line is calculated such that:

$$b = \frac{\Sigma(x - \bar{x})(y - \bar{y})}{\Sigma(x - \bar{x})^2} = \frac{1966.55}{143} = 13.8$$

Similarly, the intercept is:

$$a = \bar{y} - b\bar{x} = 331.75 - (13.8 \times 6.5) = 242$$

and the R^2 is:

$$R^2 = \frac{(\Sigma(x - \bar{x})(y - \bar{y}))^2}{\Sigma(x - \bar{x})^2 \; \Sigma(y - \bar{y})^2} = \frac{1966.55^2}{143 \times 27\,654.22} = 0.98$$

1980–85

A segmented trend line can be calculated by taking the first six observations of Japan's GDP and letting the trend variable take values between 1 and 6 (Table 26.A4).

Table 26.A4   **Data for estimating Japan's trend line, 1980–85**

Year	x	y	$x - \bar{x}$	$y - \bar{y}$	$(x - \bar{x})(y - \bar{y})$	$(x - \bar{x})^2$	$(y - \bar{y})^2$
1980	1	267	−2.5	−24	60.0	6.25	576
1981	2	276	−1.5	−15	22.5	2.25	225
1982	3	285	−0.5	−6	3.0	0.25	36
1983	4	293	0.5	2	1.0	0.25	4
1984	5	305	1.5	14	21.0	2.25	196
1985	6	320	2.5	29	72.5	6.25	841

$$\Sigma x = 21 \qquad \Sigma y = 1746 \qquad\qquad \begin{array}{ccc} \Sigma(x-\bar{x})(y-\bar{y}) & \Sigma(x-\bar{x})^2 & \Sigma(y-\bar{y})^2 \\ = 180 & = 17.5 & = 1878 \end{array}$$

$$\bar{x} = \frac{21}{6} = 3.5 \qquad \bar{y} = \frac{1746}{6} = 291$$

The following can then be calculated:

$$b = \frac{\Sigma(x-\bar{x})(y-\bar{y})}{\Sigma(x-\bar{x})^2} = \frac{180}{17.5} = 10.3$$

$$a = \bar{y} - b\bar{x} = 291 - (10.3 \times 3.5) = 255$$

$$R^2 = \frac{(\Sigma(x-\bar{x})(y-\bar{y}))^2}{\Sigma(x-\bar{x})^2 \; \Sigma(y-\bar{y})^2} = \frac{180^2}{17.5 \; \times \; 1878} = 0.99$$

1986–91

A segmented trend line for the second period can be calculated by again letting the trend variable take on values from 1 to 6 for these years (Table 26.A5). Try the calculations for yourself this time.

Table 26.A5   **Data for estimating Japan's trend line, 1986–91**

Year	x	y	$x - \bar{x}$	$y - \bar{y}$	$(x - \bar{x})(y - \bar{y})$	$(x - \bar{x})^2$	$(y - \bar{y})^2$
1986	1	329	−2.5				
1987	2	342	−1.5				
1988	3	364	−0.5				
1989	4	381					
1990	5	401					
1991	6	418					

$$\Sigma x = \qquad \Sigma y = \qquad\qquad \begin{array}{ccc} \Sigma(x-\bar{x})(y-\bar{y}) & \Sigma(x-\bar{x})^2 & \Sigma(y-\bar{y})^2 \\ = & = & = \end{array}$$

$$\bar{x} = \qquad \bar{y} =$$

Exercise 26.6

Estimate the slope and intercept of this segmented trend line, together with its R^2, by filling in the missing columns of Table 26.A5.

PART 16

ECONOMIC POLICY AND THE LONGER TERM

CHAPTER 27

SUSTAINABLE DEVELOPMENT

by Giles Atkinson

1 Introduction

In June 1992, the world's politicians descended on Rio de Janeiro, Brazil to attend the United Nations Conference on Environment and Development, known as the Earth Summit. They were joined by thousands of other delegates eager to exert an influence on the proceedings. The Earth Summit had been over-dramatically hailed by some as 'the last chance to save the Earth'. But even allowing for the hype, the environmental problems debated in Rio do have global ramifications for the way in which human populations intend to use the environment to meet their economic development goals in the future. The wide range of concerns can be summarized in a phrase you first met in Chapter 1: the need for *sustainable development* – development that generates current human well-being without imposing significant costs on future generations.

The objectives of this chapter are threefold. The first is to convey the scale of environmental change, or more accurately global environmental degradation, and to introduce the concept of sustainable development as a response to it (Section 2). I will illustrate the problem by focusing on deforestation and its consequences – such as global warming and biodiversity loss.

The second objective is to show that economics is at the heart of discussions regarding sustainable development (Section 3). The environment is seen by economists as a form of capital: environmental capital. Our decision to degrade the environment erodes our ability to satisfy the well-being of future generations, so that it has been proposed that sustainable development requires the maintaining of environmental capital. Economics also helps us to look for the most efficient way to meet this constraint whilst ensuring that the current generation can still meet its own needs as far as possible.

The final objective is to examine the prospects for policy to promote sustainable development (Section 4). Global problems require global solutions, and the role of international co-operation is crucial. Unfortunately, it would be naive to think that such co-operation is the inevitable result of an appeal for the global good. Countries with large amounts of environmental capital tend to be those that are not in a position to conserve. Conversely, those countries that are in a better position to shoulder the burdens of sustainable development are those with less environmental capital. Solutions must be politically feasible, reconciling conflicting economic interests.

2   Sustainable development

2.1   Deforestation

Deforestation, the *permanent* clearing of forest lands by human populations, is not a new phenomenon. It is reckoned that when the Romans landed in Britain nearly 2000 years ago most of the land was covered by broad-leaved forests (Gradwohl and Greenberg, 1988). By 1992, total forest cover was about 10 per cent of land area in what is now the UK, which represents an increase in forest cover from those levels which prevailed at the beginning of this century. This experience is common to many industrialized countries. In the European Union, forest cover was on average 25 per cent of land area in 1992. As Table 27.1 shows this masks country variations, from Portugal where 40 per cent of total area was under forest cover to Ireland where forest cover was only 5 per cent.

Table 27.1   **Relative forest cover in EU countries, 1992**

	Total land area (million hectares)	**Forest cover (%)**
Portugal	9.2	40
Spain	49.9	31
Germany	34.9	30
France	55.0	27
Italy	29.4	23
Belgium/Luxembourg	3.3	21
Greece	13.1	20
Denmark	4.2	12
UK	24.1	10
Netherlands	3.4	9
Ireland	6.9	5
European Union	233.4	25

Source: Moran (1994)

However, current concerns about deforestation have shifted to other types of forests – in particular to tropical broad-leaved (hardwood) forest of which 80 per cent is tropical rain forest. By and large these tend to be located in so-called developing countries or regions, particularly Amazonia, central Africa and south-east Asia. Tropical rain forests are defined by ecologist Norman Myers as 'evergreen/partly evergreen forests in areas receiving over 100 mm rain in any six months for two out of three years, with a mean annual temperature of over 24°C' (Myers, 1990). Other important characteristics of forests are determined by the degree to which the forest has been disturbed by human activity. *Primary forest* is forest which has not been disturbed by humans. In such forest, growth has reached a climax where tree death will equal tree growth. *Secondary forest*, on the other hand, is forest which has been disturbed by human activity, but has the ability to exhibit net growth.

Where rates of cutting are persistently greater than the ability of the forest to grow back, an ever-decreasing forest area will result. Table 27.2 shows some measurements of deforestation, surveying 87 countries in the tropics.

Column 3 gives an 'opening balance' for land area under forest in units of 1000 hectares in 1980. Column 4 gives the 'closing balance' in 1990. The final column translates these data into an average annual rate of deforestation. As the column shows, although deforestation is occurring throughout the tropics, the pressures tend to be concentrated in particular regions or continents.

Table 27.2   **Estimates of tropical forest area and rate of deforestation for 87 countries**

Region or sub region	Countries in region	Forest area (thousand hectares)		Deforestation (% per year)
		1980	**1990**	
Latin America	32	923 000	839 900	0.9
Central America and Mexico	7	77 000	63 500	1.8
Caribbean sub region	18	48 800	47 100	0.4
Tropical South America	7	797 100	729 300	0.8
Asia	15	310 800	274 900	1.2
South Asia	6	70 600	66 200	0.6
Continental south-east Asia	5	83 200	69 700	1.6
Insular south-east Asia	4	157 000	138 900	1.2
Africa	40	650 300	600 100	0.8
West Sahelian Africa	8	41 900	38 000	0.9
East Sahelian Africa	6	92 300	85 300	0.8
West Africa	8	55 200	43 400	2.1
Central Africa	7	230 100	215 400	0.6
Tropical Southern Africa	10	217 700	206 300	0.5
Insular Africa	1	13 200	11 700	1.2
Total	87	1 884 100	1 714 800	0.9

Source: World Resources Institute (1992); adapted from Pearce and Warford (1993) Table 5.7

Questions

On Table 27.2:

1   Which regions have the highest rates of deforestation?

2   Which region has the largest absolute deforestation in terms of hectares lost?

Scanning the final column it is clear that if we are interested in relative rates of deforestation then the most marked losses are in Central America and Mexico, insular and west Africa and Asia. However, Latin America has the largest absolute deforestation rate in terms of hectares lost. If these rates of deforestation are continued into this decade and the next, forests in these regions are set to dwindle almost to exhaustion.

Why then does deforestation matter? Tropical forests provide a rich array of functions, which will be lost when forest land is permanently cleared of trees. Such losses have implications for areas within tropical countries but also affect the well-being of the world as a whole. I will focus on the two global issues: the role of forests as a habitat for flora and fauna; and forests as stores of carbon dioxide and as fixers (or sequestrators) of carbon.

Why deforestation matters: biodiversity

Forests provide an important habitat for plants and animals collectively known as biological diversity or biodiversity. Tropical deforestation is a proximate cause of the mass extinction of species. I use the term 'proximate cause' because there are forces driving the deforestation itself, including unequal land tenure and poverty (see Chapter 1).

Biological diversity can be defined in several ways. The best known is *species diversity*, the number and variety of species. There are other definitions such as *genetic diversity*, which refers to the genetic information contained not only

Figure 27.1   **Amazonian deforestation for cattle ranching**

in each different species but also within individual members of each particular species. In addition, there is *ecosystem diversity*, which refers to the variety of habitats, communities and ecological processes. Tropical forests represent one type of ecosystem within which resides a myriad of different species, each containing its own unique genetic information. In fact, as Swanson (1990) reports, about half the world's species live in the world's tropical forests. Countries which contain a relatively large proportion of the world's species diversity are sometimes referred to as 'megadiversity countries' and include Brazil, Zaire, Mexico, Indonesia, Colombia and Madagascar. Table 27.3 indicates the extent of deforestation in these countries during the 1980s. Tables 27.4 and 27.5 provide an indication of threatened animal and plant species relative to known species in these countries.

Table 27.3   **Deforestation in 'megadiversity countries' as a percentage of forest land**

Country	Forest area (thousand hectares)		Deforestation (% per year,
	1980	**1990**	**1981–90)**
Brazil	514 480	489 330	0.5
Colombia	51 700	43 550	1.7
Indonesia	116 900	111 180	0.5
Madagascar	13 200	11 700	1.2
Mexico	43 350	38 000	1.3
Zaire	177 590	174 070	0.2

Source: World Resources Institute (1992)

Table 27.4   **Known and threatened[1] animal species, number, 1990**

Country	Mammals		Birds		Reptiles		Amphibians		Freshwater fish	
	known species	threatened species	known species	threatened species	known species	threatened species	known species	threatened species	known species	threatened species
Brazil	394	24	1567	123	467	11	487	0	—	9
Colombia	358	25	1665	69	383	10	375	0	—	0
Indonesia	479	50	1500	135	—	13	—	0	—	29
Madagascar	105	53	250	28	259	10	144	0	—	0
Mexico	439	26	961	35	717	16	284	4	—	98
Zaire	409	22	1086	27	—	2	—	0	700	1

[1] Threatened species are either endangered, vulnerable, rare or indeterminate.

— not available.

Source: World Resources Institute (1992)

Table 27.5 **Known and threatened plant taxa,**[1] **1991**

Country	No. of plant taxa	No. of rare and threatened plant taxa	Rare and threatened plant taxa per 1000 existing taxa
Brazil	55 000	240	4
Colombia	45 000	316	7
Indonesia	—	—	—
Madagascar	10 000 to 12 000	193	16–19
Mexico	20 000	1111	56
Zaire	11 000	3	0

[1] Threatened species are either endangered, vulnerable, rare or indeterminate. Taxa: native plant species found in the country.

— not available.

Source: World Resources Institute (1992)

Exercise 27.1

1   From Table 27.3, which country suffered the greatest absolute deforestation in terms of hectares lost?

2   From Table 27.4, which country has the greatest number of threatened species (mammals, birds, etc.)?

3   From Table 27.5, which country's plant taxa face the highest risk?

Deforestation matters because biodiversity is lost as a result. It seems reasonable to ask why the loss of biodiversity matters. The answer is not easy but many would agree that biodiversity provides important economic, social and ecological services. For example, plant diversity is an important source of genes for the development of new crop species that are integral to productive agricultural systems. Another benefit of biodiversity is that cures for fatal diseases such as AIDS might lie in the genetic information of plants indigenous to tropical forests. To take one example, World Resources Institute (1992) reports that in the USA, an effective anti-cancer drug was developed from the bark of the yew trees found in the ancient forests of the Pacific Northwest. In Madagascar, a plant called the rosy periwinkle has also been proven to have anti-cancer medicinal properties. Indeed, in 1985 plant-derived drugs had an estimated retail value of $43 billion. Loss of plant species could translate into significant economic costs.

Possibly as important, but less clearly established, is the suggestion that biodiversity may help to maintain the stability and resilience of ecosystems after shocks and stresses. Yet it would be inaccurate to portray the state of knowledge concerning the functions of biodiversity as anything but incomplete. Nevertheless, the uncertainty surrounding the consequences of biodiversity loss is seen by many as a source of global concern in itself. While there is no consensus estimate of species loss, many biologists believe that a process of mass extinction is being experienced. Some estimates suggest that at least 27 000 species per annum are being lost in tropical forests alone

(Myers, 1992). This does not include species lost in other ecosystems such as coral reefs, wetlands and islands (which may push the annual species loss beyond 30 000). If these trends continue, as much as 20 per cent of all species could be lost within the next 30 years.

A counter-argument is that the developed countries of the north have depleted much of their diversity without any catastrophic or serious effects. Perhaps the developing nations in the south could follow the same model of development. However, this would be a strategy with highly uncertain pay-offs because the globalized costs of successive conversions of land and loss of diversity are probably increasing. While early conversions and extinctions left plenty of diversity and thus had little impact, this is not true of later conversions which are eating into an ever-decreasing stock of diversity. What is clear is that species extinction is an irreversible process – lost species cannot be recreated. Even if it were possible to restore biodiversity eventually, the time frame for this reversal would be millions of years (Wilson, 1992).

Why deforestation matters: climate change

Forests serve important climatic functions. By assimilating carbon dioxide through the process of photosynthesis, trees (and vegetative matter) help to stabilize the climate. Forests therefore provide a sink for the emissions of carbon dioxide (the most significant greenhouse gas in the atmosphere in terms of volume), and hence play their part in slowing global warming. Moreover, when forests are cleared, the trees are often burnt, releasing additional carbon dioxide into the atmosphere. Yet the economic activities that usually replace forestry, such as permanent agriculture or pasture, do not replace these carbon-fixing functions.

Global warming refers to an increase in mean global temperature as a result of the 'greenhouse effect'. The greenhouse effect is a natural process by which energy from the sun passes through the atmosphere. Heat is radiated back from the earth but is partially blocked by atmospheric gases, usually called 'greenhouse gases' (GHGs) because they cause the atmosphere to warm. Global warming is not caused solely by deforestation. Indeed, deforestation probably contributes only 15–20 per cent of GHGs (carbon dioxide, ozone, water vapour, chlorofluorocarbons (CFCs), methane and nitrous oxide) in the atmosphere. Carbon dioxide is more usually emitted from the burning of fossil fuels such as oil and coal to meet our energy needs. At the moment these emissions occur predominantly in the industrialized north.

The atmosphere can assimilate (absorb and process) some but not all of these GHGs. Competing human activities 'use up' the earth's capacity to absorb carbon dioxide and other GHGs. This intensifies the 'greenhouse effect' and global temperature may rise. It has been estimated that, if nothing is done to stop the trend of emissions, global mean temperature will rise by between 0.2 per cent and 0.5 per cent a decade. However, there are many scientific uncertainties in this field. While there is evidence that the climate has changed since the industrial revolution, this slight warming is consistent with natural variations rather than being induced by humans. The uncertainty surrounding the predicted rate of warming leaves plenty of scope for fierce debate concerning the gravity of effects that may (or may not) take place. In fact, some scientists have reasoned that global warming is a myth or at least is so uncertain that we are not under any obligation to take remedial action.

Pearce and Warford (1993) outline some of the possible effects of climate change.

- Increases in regional temperature may have an effect on crops through reductions of soil moisture and the risk of summer drought. Changes in regional rainfall might occur; for example, arid zones might become even more arid.

- Increases in temperature could cause the oceans to expand and ice sheets to melt. This may cause sea levels to rise by 3 to 10 centimetres a decade if no action is taken to prevent climate change. Low lying land by the sea is put at risk. In the UK, one of the areas at risk is around the Wash in East Anglia.

Exercise 27.2

State in a few sentences what you understand by the terms biodiversity loss and global warming. How are these problems related to tropical deforestation?

While some ecologists claim that global environmental change is potentially life-threatening to humans, such apocalyptic visions are not required in order to argue that significant costs are entailed by allowing this change to proceed unhindered. The implication can be drawn that further economic development should be undertaken only if it is sustainable.

2.2   Sustainable development and time preference

The term 'sustainable development' has become something of a buzz phrase, but what does it actually mean? In this section I discuss the definition of sustainable development and some of the philosophical issues it raises.

A definition of 'sustainable' is not hard to agree on; it means long lasting or enduring. Development is slightly harder to define for it means different things to different people. It might generally be agreed that development refers to an increase in human well-being. However, human well-being cannot be directly measured, and in practice, development is often narrowly defined as increasing real gross national product per head of the population. This definition is sometimes broadened to consider improvements in other aspects of the 'quality of life' such as those embodied in social indicators which reflect, for example, the education and health of people within a country.

The most commonly cited public definition of sustainable development emanated from the World Commission on Environment and Development (WCED, or the 'Brundtland Commission') in 1987. Sustainable development is development that, ' ... meets the needs of the present without compromising the ability of future generations to meet their own needs' (WCED, 1987, p.8). So sustainable development is development that generates current human well-being without imposing significant costs on the future. For the Brundtland Commission, significant costs are translated into the inability to meet future development needs. For Pearce and Warford (1993) sustainable development is development that secures an increase in the well-being of the current generation provided that future well-being does not decrease. This effectively takes the same form as the Brundtland definition but substitutes 'welfare' for 'needs'. What it implies is that we should not trade-off well-being now for a loss of well-being in the future.

If accepted as a worthwhile social goal, sustainable development implies that development should be evenly distributed across generations. This does not mean that economic progress is sacrificed so that each generation is guaranteed equal levels of well-being. What it means is that progress must not be reversed at a future date. The way in which the current generation is using the environment may represent one way in which potentially large costs are being passed on to the future. In this sense, we may be buying our development at the expense of our descendants. The suggestion that this is not an acceptable trade-off raises philosophical issues concerning fairness or justice which are not easy to resolve.

Sustainable development is therefore based on the concept of *intergenerational justice* which refers to distribution across generations. This is distinct from distribution within a generation, or intragenerational justice, discussed in Chapter 22. It is worth noting that environmental problems also impose significant costs on the present generation, which does raise questions of intragenerational justice. For example, pollutants emitted from power stations such as sulphur dioxide generate significant current costs in terms of adverse effects on human health and in some cases death from respiratory problems. Some current environmental problems and possible solutions were discussed in Chapter 10. Possible connections between current inequalities and the problems of achieving sustainability are discussed towards the end of this chapter.

The concept of intergenerational justice has been debated at length by philosophers, political scientists, economists and environmentalists. The basic problem, as the economist and philosopher John Broome (1992) points out, is how to weigh up against each other goods and bads that occur at different times. In assessing environmental projects, one common approach discussed further in Section 3 is to add up the costs and the benefits of the project over time and to compare the two. But this is not a satisfactory decision rule if the benefits largely accrue to the current generation and the costs fall on the future. How can we value benefits and costs which have yet to occur?

We are all familiar with the sort of decisions individuals make in this regard. An individual may, for example, compare the costs of doing a degree with the future benefits. *Discounting* is a technique for comparing the worth of goods and bads which occur at different times by expressing future benefits and costs in terms of an estimate of their *present value*. One of the basic principles on which discounting is based is positive time preference (Chapter 11, Section 2.2). For example, it was suggested there that, other things being equal, you would probably prefer £100 cash now to £100 cash in a year's time. In other words, £100 in a year's time is worth less to you than £100 now. So positive time preference means that current

Definition

Sustainable development

Sustainable development can be defined as an increase in human well-being that is not later reversed: development that is lasting.

benefits are preferred to future benefits which are, at the time they occur, of the same magnitude. This is not the sole reason for discounting but it is the rationale that often receives the most attention in analyses of sustainable development. This is because it deals with impatience on the part of individuals or society: a preference for the present over the future.

Discounting

Discounting provides a technique for measuring the degree to which future benefits are worth less than current benefits. In Chapter 11, Section 2.2 it was explained that positive time preference underlies the payment of interest on loans. Suppose that you are willing to postpone spending £100 if someone pays you 10 per cent interest in return for borrowing the money for a year. The rate of interest you are willing to accept represents the rate at which you are discounting the benefits of spending £100 because they are postponed for one year.

We can measure the effects of discounting using a formula derived from the concept of compounding explained in Chapter 1. Discounting can be thought of as compounding in reverse: the longer the postponement the less you value the future benefits.

The present value, *PV*, of a future benefit, *FB*, is given by the formula

$$PV = \frac{FB}{(1 + r)^t}$$

where *r* is the discount rate (in this example the interest rate) and *t* stands for the number of years which elapse before the benefit becomes available (in this example the duration of the loan). The discount rate is expressed as a decimal rather than a percentage – in this example, 0.1 for 10 per cent. So the present value of £100 in a year's time is:

$$PV = \frac{£100}{1.1} = £90.91$$

Exercise 27.3

To see how this discounting formula relates to compound interest, calculate the value of £90.91 invested for a year at a 10 per cent interest rate.

Let us apply the discounting formula to a hypothetical case involving environmental costs and benefits. A golf club wishes to extend its course and one option is to buy a small copse and fell the trees. The landowner is offered £12000 and is told that refusal would lead the club to adopt an alternative plan leaving no prospect of a future sale of the copse. An ornithological trust which wishes to preserve the habitat of a rare bird offers the landowner a grant of £3000 a year for 5 years. The landowner is on the point of accepting the grant, for £15000 easily outbids the golf club's £12000. However, his daughter is an economist and, home for the weekend, explains discounting.

The present value of £3000 a year for 5 years, assuming once again a discount rate of 10 per cent, is calculated as follows. The formula is:

$$PV = \frac{FB}{(1 + r)^t}$$

We can calculate the present value of each separate £3000 payment. So after one year ($t = 1$):

$$PV = \frac{£3000}{(1 + 0.1)} = £2727$$

The second payment, after two years ($t = 2$) has a present value:

$$PV = \frac{£3000}{(1 + 0.1)^2} = £2479$$

Over the five years, the total present value of the grant to the landowner is:

$$PV = \frac{£3000}{1.1} + \frac{£3000}{(1.1)^2} + \frac{£3000}{(1.1)^3} + \frac{£3000}{(1.1)^4} + \frac{£3000}{(1.1)^5}$$

$$= £2727 + £2479 + £2254 + £2049 + £1863 = £11\,372$$

Assuming the landowner wants to maximize his income and has positive time preference and a 10 per cent discount rate, he sells the copse to the golf club.

The limitations of discounting are discussed below but one problem is worth mentioning here. A discount rate of 10 per cent is fine for the purposes of a hypothetical example. But how should we choose a discount rate when discounting a real environmental project? This is a crucial question. For example, if the landowner applied a discount rate of 5 per cent, the present value of £3000 a year for 5 years is £12 990 and he would therefore accept the grant from the ornithological trust.

The rate of interest you are willing to accept in return for postponing spending indicates the rate at which you are discounting future spending compared with current spending. In deciding on a rate at which to discount the future benefits of a conservation project, for example, it is therefore reasonable to take an interest rate as a starting point. But should we think of the benefits of the project as postponed consumption and choose an interest rate households might expect to receive from a bank or building society? Or should we regard the benefits as the return on an investment (in the resources of production used in the project) and take an interest rate firms might face in borrowing to finance the investment? And how should a society's discount rate differ from our individual time preference rates? There are no easy answers. The choice of discount rate remains controversial, and is discussed further in the next section.

Exercise 27.4

Consider two environmental projects, such as cleaning up a polluted lake and setting up a recycling plant, which have the benefits shown in Table 27.6. Which has the greater present value of the benefit stream, if a discount rate of 10 per cent is assumed?

Table 27.6

	Cleaning up lake	Recycling plant
Year 1	£1500	£3500
Year 2	£2000	£3000
Year 3	£2500	£2500
Year 4	£3000	£2000
Year 5	£3500	£1500

The use of discounting has received significant criticism from environmentalists because it biases decision making towards policies and projects that yield immediate benefits. In contrast, as Exercise 27.4 showed, policies or projects that yield benefits which only occur relatively far into the future rather than providing quick returns will be judged in an unfavourable light. For example, the extent of deforestation and the losses entailed might suggest that a project to reforest areas that have been cleared might be desirable. However, trees take a long time to grow. Under a regime of discounting a programme of afforestation would not fare very well relative to an alternative project that yielded its benefits sooner. The opportunity costs of afforestation – the loss of immediate benefits from the alternative project – would appear too high.

The implication of this line of thought is that there is a tension between the concept of intergenerational justice, and hence sustainable development, and the use of discounting in evaluating future benefits. Discounting favours the present over the future. But we may feel that, morally, the well-being of future generations should be given equal consideration to that of the current generation. We might derive such a principle from a concept of fairness: either fairness in outcomes, or fairness in what is intrinsically right. Chapter 22, Section 4.2 discussed John Rawls' concept of social justice as impartiality between individuals. We could extend this impartiality across time, in arguing that the well-being of each generation should be equally valued. This implies, as Broome (1992, Chapter 3) notes, that the rate of discount applied by society to future well-being – the social rate of discount – should be zero.

Concepts of intergenerational justice underpin the argument for sustainable development. Against these arguments for an equal consideration of future welfare some commentators have raised the problem of uncertainty. We, the current generation, do not know what future generations will want, so perhaps discounting future benefits is a reasonable response to this uncertainty.

Uncertainty is discussed further in Section 3, but two points may be made here. First, it is reasonable to assume that basic needs will probably remain the same. For example, if the environment does provide unique life-support functions then it is reasonable to make the assumption that future generations will value these functions and therefore value their preservation. Second, we can conceptualize concern for future generations, even though we do not know what they will want, by thinking in terms of the choices left available to them. Development that is not sustainable indicates that the current generation is 'closing off' choices that future generations would otherwise be free to make, thus narrowing their opportunities.

We can now turn to the question of how the current generation can secure sustainable development. We have already seen that one way to achieve this might be to use a zero social discount rate in making decisions that affect the future. There are, however, other ways by which we can assess the obligations of this generation towards the future. Can it, for example, compensate the future for imposing costs? The current generation holds a stock of environmental capital which can be used to derive well-being now and into the future. However, using up this capital by degrading environments erodes the opportunities of future generations. Is it feasible to compensate them for this loss?

3 An economic framework for environmental policy

3.1 The environment as 'capital'

This section explores some of the implications of the concept of sustainable development within a framework of economic analysis. Much of economics is concerned with a search for scientific objectivity (an issue discussed further in Chapter 28). Yet, as our earlier discussion revealed, development is a value term concerning the well-being of individuals and society. Sustainable development also embodies a value judgement regarding how we should treat future generations. Such value judgements are inevitable, and rather than being avoided, they should instead be explicitly recognized. Let us begin from a familiar value judgement in economics, the concept of Pareto efficiency or the Pareto principle (Chapter 7, Section 6.2). In this framework each individual starts off with an initial endowment of inputs of productive resources which determines his or her well-being. Any change in economic activity is judged in relation to this initial well-being. The Pareto principle states that society is better off if a change in the allocation of inputs or outputs of economic activity leaves at least one person better off *without* making someone else worse off. This gain is known as a Pareto improvement and when all such gains have been exhausted, then Pareto efficiency is achieved.

When the Pareto principle is used to analyse the efficiency with which resources are allocated between current and future generations, it can generate implications which are somewhat similar to those of sustainable development. In order to think about intergenerational concerns, the definition of endowments needs to be expanded so that it includes environmental resources. In particular, it is the time path of environmental resources that is of interest. Where these resources are being used up, then this particular endowment will be decreasing. Consequently, there is less to be passed on to future generations, which decreases the economic opportunities open to them to meet their development goals. This violates the requirement for sustainability as laid out in the Brundtland Commission's report. It also contradicts the Pareto principle extended to consider future generations. No gain in current well-being can be achieved at the expense of future well-being.

What this amounts to is a requirement that an increase in well-being today does not lead to a reduction in well-being tomorrow. The endowments we have tomorrow must generate at least as much well-being as our current endowments. A large part of these endowments consists of various forms of productive capital.

Definition

Capital

Capital is an endowment that yields a stream of benefits over time.

The most common example of capital is manufactured capital such as machines. However, when capital is defined in this way, knowledge is also capital – human capital, as explained in Chapters 14 and 21. Environmental resources are capital, too. When available, these resources provide flows of ecological services that contribute to human well-being over time. Environmental capital takes many forms, including tropical forests, which provide a habitat for an abundance of living things. Thus biodiversity preservation can be viewed as a service flow from the forest which is in turn seen as a capital asset.

An economic approach to sustainable development therefore couches the main requirement for sustainability in terms of non-declining endowments, or capital, over time. An important issue is whether or not the composition of the total stock of capital can be permitted to change. If so, then sustainability might be promoted in other ways than by preserving environmental capital. However, even if this is possible, future generations must still be compensated for loss of environmental capital with some other form of capital, i.e. gains must compensate losses. As the following sections show, it is far from clear that we are in a position to determine the appropriate level of compensation for the loss of environmental resources.

3.2 Compensating the future

Capital provides a stream of benefits over time. Thus, capital provides a return and it is from this return that current and future generations are believed to derive well-being. In Chapter 4, Neil Costello described the production function which specified the way in which inputs such as raw materials and manufactured capital are transformed into outputs through production processes:

$$Q = f(F_1, F_2, \dots , F_N)$$

The same principle could apply here. However, this time Q is human well-being and the Fs are forms of environmental and manufactured capital. The basic idea is that if we have less of one particular capital component then, other things being equal, we would expect to generate less well-being. A simple rule for sustainability suggested in Section 3.1 is that capital should be left intact, that is, productive capacity should not be eroded. This might be achieved via capital bequests: the current generation must pass on a capital stock that in terms of its productive capacity is at least as large as it inherited.

But does this mean that the composition of the capital stock must remain unchanged? Must we have as much of each F, or can the Fs be substituted for each other? The example in Chapter 4 suggested that in general each of the inputs can be combined in many different ways with each of the other inputs. For example, more skilled chefs make it possible to use fewer raw materials because of the reduction in waste. Let us turn this example around and suppose that there is a long-term shortage of the raw materials. It would be possible, in principle, to maintain the output of meals by recruiting more skilled chefs to make the reduced quantity of raw materials 'go further'. What has happened here is that the restaurant has substituted one input, the skill and knowledge of chefs, for another, raw materials. Economists tend to assume that inputs or productive resources – the Fs – are easily substitutable one for another. It is not unusual for a firm to substitute new technology for labour. However, it may in practice be very hard to replace the loss of environmental capital (raw materials) with human capital (skill and knowledge). The extent to which human and manufactured capital can be substituted for environmental capital is a highly contentious issue.

Tropical deforestation represents the loss of environmental capital. The current generation is passing on a physically smaller stock of tropical forests than it inherited. However, this does not necessarily imply unsustainable development. Whether it does so will ultimately depend on whether or not future generations can be compensated for this loss of capacity. This in turn depends on whether the 'productive capacity' of tropical forests can be substituted by alternative forms of capital (such as machines and knowledge). The legitimacy of development based on replacing environmental capital with 'produced' capital is a major source of disagreement between (some) economists and environmentalists. The former argue that the loss of one particular capital asset does not matter insofar as its services can be provided by a substitute asset. Environmentalists, on the other hand, stress the uniqueness of environmental capital.

This debate has its roots in an interchange that occurred in the early 1970s, between the 'Club of Rome' (an international non-governmental organization) and economists studying the use of natural resources. The argument presented by the 'Club of Rome' in *The Limits to Growth* (Meadows *et al.*, 1972) was that development could not be sustained indefinitely because the world's supply of non-renewable resources such as oil, gas and metals is finite. The ultimate exhaustion of these resources implied a physical limit to economic growth. This pessimistic vision of the future led to a flurry of research intended to reassess the human plight, which was given further stimulus in 1973 by the four-fold increase in the international price of oil.

Oil is a non-renewable resource which means that the extraction of one unit today means there is one less unit of oil to extract tomorrow. The question was how to use this valuable energy source without depriving future generations of a means of generating well-being. The answer according to economist John Hartwick was that 'oil economies' should invest a certain portion of oil revenues in alternative forms of capital. 'Hartwick's rule', as this principle has become known, works on the assumption that future generations can produce as much well-being without oil provided that the current generation passes on the means to achieve this (Hartwick and Olewiler, 1986). An increasing quantity of manufactured capital can replace the decreasing amounts of environmental capital represented by oil. Extended to our tropical forests example, then, deforestation could be condoned if the proceeds are reinvested in other forms of capital. The largest proximate cause of deforestation is the clearing of land for use in agriculture. Agricultural production might form the basis of the compensation that is required for sustainable development. Another example is associated with the cutting of forests for sale as timber. If part of the proceeds of timber sales are reinvested, then development might be sustainable without tropical forests.

Does this sound plausible? If so, then most environmentalists and many scientists would appear to be unduly pessimistic concerning the ability to compensate the future for deforestation. Instead, a radically changing environment might be viewed as an inevitable outcome of the development process. Yet the view that it is possible to compensate future generations for the loss of environmental capital by bequeathing greater quantities of other forms of capital is a debatable assumption, not an established fact. I will proceed here, however, by accepting that assumption for the sake of argument.

The next step is to try to assess the level of compensation that is required when environmental capital such as tropical forest is depleted. Cost–benefit analysis is a technique which can be used to evaluate the economic implications of cutting down tropical forests. This in turn requires a method of measuring economic values which is explained in Section 3.3. However, this method is not without its critics and so, in Section 3.4, I will consider an alternative view which holds that there is too much uncertainty surrounding exactly what it is we lose when tropical rain forests are destroyed for cost–benefit analysis to be an appropriate technique.

3.3   Measuring economic values

In the previous section I discussed the issue of compensating future generations for the loss of environmental capital. It seems that justice requires that we make such compensation and, if we assume that there is some substitutability between forms of capital, it is possible, at least in principle, to do so. However, it might turn out in practice that the scale of compensation entails a sacrifice of living standards which the current generation would be unwilling to make. The problem is then to decide whether it is worth investing in the manufactured capital designed to replace the environmental capital which has been degraded. Will the rate of return – the stream of future benefits from the new capital – be sufficient to offset the losses in future well-being incurred through the degradation of environments? It is the social rate of return that is relevant here, that is, the stream of benefits (net of costs) to society as a whole.

In order to assess the social rate of return from preserving environments such as tropical forests, some measure of their economic value is needed. How, you might ask, can the value of a forest be measured? There are no markets for forests; no auction rooms in which the forces of demand and supply work out the market price. In the absence of such mechanisms environmental economists have developed their own methods of measuring environmental values.

Definitions

Direct use values

Direct use values are the direct benefits people derive from their use of the environment.

Indirect use values

Indirect use values are the indirect benefits people derive from the environment.

There are three main classifications of environmental values. The first concerns the direct use values associated with the environment. In the case of tropical forests these *direct use values* include the harvest of forest produce, fuelwood and timber. Use values are also related to tourism ('ecotourism') where sites of outstanding natural beauty can be visited by tourists. Also many people derive pleasure from watching wildlife films. Although they may never actually visit the area filmed, this pleasure can also be regarded as a use-value.

The second type of environmental value is that of indirect use values. Examples would be the storing of carbon in forests, and providing a habitat for biodiversity. The evaluation of these functions is sometimes conceptualized in terms of the damage done by losing the service. In the case of carbon storage, the damage would be the contribution to global warming that may occur as a consequence of the increase in carbon emissions into the atmosphere.

The third class of values are non-use values. These are based on the ethical views which people may hold in connection with the environment. The main non-use value is existence value: the valuing of something in and of itself rather than for its uses. People clearly value the existence of species such as elephants, mountain gorillas or humpback whales, or they value whole ecosystems such as rain forests. Donations to environmental groups represent one mechanism by which existence values are revealed in people's behaviour. It is hard to separate existence value in practice from use value, since it is human preferences which are being expressed in both cases. However, the very remoteness of some environments for which pledges are made might justify the idea of 'existence value' as a separate category.

These different measures of environmental values provide the basis for cost–benefit analysis, a widely used economic framework which may be applied to evaluate environmental issues. In simple terms cost–benefit analysis involves the comparison of the costs and benefits of an environmentally sensitive activity. The concept of opportunity cost, explained in Chapter 11, is relevant here. The opportunity cost of an economic activity is the benefit which would have been gained from the activity forgone. In the case of deforestation, for example, the opportunity costs of conserving the forest are the benefits of an alternative use of the land such as agriculture. If those benefits are greater than the assessed value of the forest, there is a net gain associated with cutting down trees and developing the land for agriculture. Losers can be compensated for the loss of forests and there is still a net gain to human well-being. However, the discussion of environmental values, above, implies that the calculation must include the non-market values just outlined: it must be a full *social* cost–benefit analysis.

An example of how social cost–benefit analysis can be applied is provided by the case of the Amazonian tropical forest. Amazonia is a vast area of tropical forests in South America extending into six countries: Brazil, Colombia, Peru, Venezuela, Ecuador and Bolivia. Brazil accounts for two-thirds of the Amazonian forest (which also corresponds to a significant proportion of global tropical forests). In assessing the economic value of this forest there are two dimensions to be considered. First there are the domestic benefits associated with the forest. Within Brazil policy makers will try to maximize the net domestic benefits of policy towards forests. These domestic benefits are those which a sovereign country can 'capture' for its own development. There will be domestic benefits associated with both conservation and development. However, if we assume that these two benefit streams will be mutually exclusive, each land-use policy will involve forgone domestic benefits. So Brazil will seek to choose the option yielding the greater net benefits.

What are the domestic benefits of conservation? These will vary depending on the conception of conservation that is adopted. 'Strict' conservation or preservation leaves environments as wilderness. This rules out many direct uses of these areas, such as ecotourism, or sustainable harvest of timber. However, these benefits are exactly the kind of value that the country can appropriate. Indirect uses might also include domestic benefits, such as flood protection functions. The scientific evidence is disputed but one argument is that forests, by preventing soils from washing away after severe

Definition

Non-use values

Non-use values are benefits from the environment which are unrelated to its use.

rainfall, thereby prevent the sedimentation of rivers and flooding. The domestic benefits of development are perhaps easier to assess. These refer to the benefits derived from a change in land use to some other activity. Typically, this may involve clear cutting forest (as opposed to sustainable harvesting), and either selling this once and for all timber harvest, or burning it and then using the land for agricultural production.

The consideration of indirect use values is a required step in the full evaluation of the benefits of conservation. Matters are even further complicated when we turn to the second dimension: global costs and benefits. The environmental effects of conservation or deforestation do not respect national boundaries. The whole world benefits from, for example, carbon storage. Global benefits may also be derived from the pure existence of a unique ecosystem such as a forest.

In order to weigh up the costs and benefits of the conservation of tropical forests a common unit of analysis must be found. One way to achieve this is to put monetary values on costs and benefits. Pearce (1992) undertook just such an exercise in Amazonia. First, he estimated the monetary value of this tropical forest as a carbon sink – a receptacle for storing carbon. The annual global benefit is described in terms of the damage that would have been caused by carbon dioxide emissions if the forest did not exist. This he calculated to be $3.9 billion per annum. The second part of his calculation looked at Amazonia as a unique natural asset. Amazonia is a true focal point for global environmental concerns. There may be non-use value associated with the knowledge that this forest is conserved. Estimates of non-use value are not easy to obtain but, working from a number of studies that are available, Pearce derives a 'very conservative' estimate of $8 per adult per annum. The next step is to estimate how many individuals hold this value, which Pearce assumes to be 400 million (corresponding to the adult population of the richest nations of the world). This yields a non-use value of $3.2 billion per annum.

These values should be compared with the revenues (net of costs of production) that farmers in the Amazon now obtain from forestry. On the basis that these revenues are about 20 per cent of gross output in the forestry sector in Amazonia, an annual figure of $3.2 billion is obtained. This provides an estimate of the net benefit from preservation of the Amazonian forests in the region of some $3.9 billion per year. This estimate is based only on carbon sink value and non-use value. If the value of biodiversity were also considered then this would consolidate Pearce's findings. Note, however, that there is nothing 'concrete' in the numbers discussed here. What they illustrate is the possible magnitude of monetary values of tropical forests relative to those values we customarily think of as relevant to economics: e.g. those that pass through markets (such as timber and agricultural production).

This example can be restated in more general terms. Global benefits, associated with conservation can be written B_g. The 'host' country will consider the domestic costs of conservation C_h. These are the forgone development benefits associated with forestry or agriculture (in other words the opportunity cost of forest conservation). C_h will be weighed up against the domestic benefits of conservation, B_h. Deforestation occurs because within the host country:

$$C_h > B_h$$

so that the host country would have incurred net costs, $C_h - B_h > 0$, had it decided to conserve and forgo the benefits of changing land uses. In Pearce's example the net costs of conservation C_h were \$3.2 billion (the value of forestry activity in Amazonia). Pearce assumed that $B_h = 0$. There are no domestic benefits from conservation in his model.

Where the environmental resource is unique, as in the case of Amazonia, we would expect the global benefits B_g to be large. What Pearce found was that global benefits actually might exceed the net domestic costs of conservation:

$$B_g > C_h - B_h$$

where B_g = \$3.9 billion + \$3.2 billion.

We know that:

$$C_h - B_h = \$3.2 \text{ billion}$$

since B_h is assumed to be zero.

So there is a global net benefit of conservation:

$$B_g - (C_h - B_h) > 0$$

How can it be ensured that this global net benefit is achieved? This problem is complicated by the inherent conflict between the developing country (the 'host' to the forest) and the population of richer countries benefiting from conservation, implied by the model just set out.

In contrast to the example of the global commons defined in Chapter 10, which includes the atmosphere and the world's oceans, the forest as we have seen is slightly different. Forests provide global benefits but are within the sovereignty of particular countries (although within countries ownership will probably be poorly defined). While the world benefits from the conservation of tropical forests, it is unlikely that a country facing a choice regarding its land-use policy will attach much weight to these values. Conserving the environment is more likely to be regarded as a luxury that simply cannot be afforded. So, individuals and countries in the relatively low-income developing world may not value the services of environmental resources. Rather, at low levels of income, people may be willing to trade-off environmental quality for increased income. However, at some higher level of income people are less willing to accept the trade-off, and wish to use their increased incomes to improve environmental quality. Hence, the demand for environmental benefits is biased towards the rich.

In the face of this conflict of interest, one way of achieving the net global benefits identified by the model is for richer countries to compensate the host country interests for the loss of domestic revenues that occur due to conservation. The compensation principle is based on *incremental cost*. The aim of the principle of incremental cost is to compensate host countries for the benefits that they cannot appropriate and hence to ensure a shift in host country decision making to reflect global well-being. In the formula set out above these benefits are designated C_h because, as the forgone benefits of developing the forest, they are the opportunity cost to the host country of its conservation. The amount of compensation is determined by $C_h - B_h$, that is, the cost to the host country of forest conservation net of any benefits that conservation might bring it. In Pearce's model the figure of \$3.2 billion is further described as gross incremental cost because B_h is set at zero. Net incremental cost subtracts from the compensation a positive estimate of the domestic benefits of conservation. These might consist of tourism revenue from visitors to the forest.

Another adjustment to net incremental cost might be made for the distortions introduced by host country governments. These distortions help to stack the odds in favour of projects that involve forest clearing. In this way unsustainable practices are actively subsidized by government policy. For example, during the 1970s and part of the 1980s, the Brazilian government granted subsidized credit to projects that involved forest clearance, in particular claiming land for the ranching of livestock. The credit subsidy lowered the (private) rate of return that a project needed to earn in order for it to be profitable. Many of these subsidy schemes are now being dismantled, but significant losses have already been incurred.

The need for compensation reflects a disparity between the domestic value of forested land and the global value of forested land. The argument is essentially the same as one which was introduced in Chapter 10. There, the example of petrol use illustrated the argument that the marginal private benefit (or cost) of a polluting activity such as car use diverged from the marginal social benefit (or cost). The result was an overuse of cars relative to the social optimum. In the example discussed in this section, for private benefit read domestic or host country benefits and for social benefit read global benefits. The result is an over-exploitation of tropical forests.

The difference lies in the policy prescription that emerges. In the car example, a 'green' tax was suggested to equate the social benefit of pollution with the private benefit of pollution. This is the *polluter pays principle* and it states that it is the polluter who must compensate the victim for the costs that he or she imposes. If the polluter pays principle were applied in the Amazonian example, a country wishing to cut down its forest would have to compensate the world for the loss of the global benefits. The country would have to accept that indigenous forests are a sink for carbon dioxide emissions mainly emanating from elsewhere in the world. The polluter pays principle is a powerful rationale behind market-based environmental policies such as pollution taxes. But given that the host country effectively owns the forest the polluter pays principle would not be enforceable.

The concept of incremental cost is therefore based on the *victim pays principle*. It is the victim who makes the payment – the rest of the world which compensates the host country – in order to avoid the costs caused by deforestation. Both the polluter pays principle and victim pays principle are illustrations of Coase's Theorem (Coase, 1960). Coase argued that where property rights were clearly defined, government intervention should not be necessary to enforce the appropriate payments. However, in the forest example it is unlikely that the incremental cost will be paid without government intervention. More to the point, it is unlikely that the transfer will be made in the absence of co-operation between many governments. No single country has an incentive to make this payment, unless the motivation of that donor country was one of altruism towards other nations. Nevertheless, it is in the global interest that this transfer is made, because inaction can do irreversible damage to attempts to secure sustainable development. The longer we wait to deal with the problem, the greater are the costs which are passed on to the future. The prospects for international policy co-operation will be discussed in Section 4.

Definition

Coase's Theorem

Coase's Theorem states that an efficient solution to pollution externalities is bargaining between the polluter and victim. Either the polluter or victim could compensate the other depending on the ownership of the property affected. As long as property rights are defined, no government intervention should be required.

Question

How would you summarize the main implications of Pearce's cost–benefit analysis for the conservation of tropical forests?

The Pearce example and the subsequent discussion of incremental cost provided a powerful rationale for conservation of tropical forests. However, it was one which recognized that a trade-off between conservation and deforestation might be possible and desirable. In cases where the costs of conservation outweigh the benefits, this analysis would suggest that society is better off pursuing a more general objective of sustainability. Deforestation could be permitted but the proceeds would be reinvested elsewhere. While some environmentalists would find this suggestion of a potential trade-off unacceptable on, say, moral grounds, another line of reasoning highlights the degree of error associated with the estimates of benefits. This position, which is often based on the lack of unequivocal scientific evidence surrounding the precise losses associated with the destruction of ecosystems, will be discussed in the next sub-section. A possible way of reconciling the two approaches, based on the idea of safe minimum standards, will then be considered.

3.4   Uncertainty and safe minimum standards

In undertaking a cost–benefit analysis of a conservation project, economists attempt to weigh up the costs and benefits of two scenarios, destroying or degrading some piece of environmental capital and conserving it, on the assumption of other things being equal. In other words, we try to predict two possible future courses of the world by assuming that the only difference between them is that in one the environmental capital is destroyed and in the other it is conserved. In reality, other things will change but, since we are concerned with the future, we cannot possibly know for certain what those changes will be. In this section I want to examine four main sources of this uncertainty: the life-support functions of ecosystems, the irreversibility of some environmental processes, technological progress and population growth. I will then discuss a possible policy response to uncertainty: safe minimum standards.

Life-support functions of ecosystems

In the previous section, it was suggested that the economist's concept of indirect use benefits encapsulates the so-called life-support functions of ecosystems. In principle, the importance of ecosystems in regulating life could be evaluated alongside more traditional economic variables such as those market-traded services provided by ecosystems. In reality, however, knowledge of the natural world is seriously incomplete. So, while it is believed that biodiversity plays a critical role in preserving ecosystems from shocks and stresses, little is known about the role of particular species or groups of species over time in the provision of these services (Barbier *et al.*, 1994). In fact, out of a possible 30–50 million species in the world, only about 1.4 million have actually been identified.

A suspicion also remains that there is more to the total value of an ecosystem than the sum of the values of individual functions. The economist's taxonomy of values, set out in Section 3.3, is regarded by ecologists as a set of secondary values. Ecologists describe the forest ecosystem as the primary value, where the 'component parts of an ecosystem are contingent on the existence and functioning of the whole' (Turner, 1993). This might not seem too far removed from an analysis of a tropical rain forest as a capital asset that supplies numerous service flows. The difference is that ecologists stress that the total value is more than just the sum of the parts. The 'extra' bit represents the 'glue' value of an ecosystem: in other words, the ecosystem is holding the functions together, and that is a function in itself. There is therefore some disagreement between economists and ecologists over the scope of cost–benefit analysis in measuring the value of ecosystems: economists need to consider whether they accept the concept of a primary value and can recognize it within their calculations.

Irreversibility

Tropical deforestation is an irreversible process, in that this valuable asset cannot simply be built up again later. For example, outside the realms of science fiction species extinction cannot be reversed. In effect, biological diversity is non-renewable and its loss is therefore technically irreversible. Not all environmental resources are characterized by irreversibility. Air quality can be improved through the control of emissions of pollutants from, for example, power stations. Water quality can also be improved. However, there may come a threshold point where damage becomes irreversible. Such threshold effects imply that continued environmental degradation beyond the threshold level renders damage costs infinite.

Irreversibility can also refer to the feasibility of imposing a technically reversible solution. Global warming is very likely to be feasibly irreversible, because of the pressures of growing population and economic growth. An expansion of human numbers caused by population growth increases the pressure on natural resources, while economic growth may increase resource requirements per head of population. Both result in increased energy use and, as more fossil fuels are burnt, emissions of GHGs are increased. Even if countries commit themselves to reducing emissions of GHGs, concentrations of these gases in the atmosphere would still increase for some time to come (although this will vary with the degree of commitment). Some warming of global temperatures may already be inevitable even if action were to be taken now. Global warming might also be feasibly irreversible simply because current generations may find the adjustments required unpalatable in terms of current sacrifice. Because of the uncertainty of outcome associated with environmental change, they may prefer to carry on 'business as usual'.

However, uncertainty may be a reason for action rather than inertia, a view which is the basis of a decision-making rule known as the *precautionary principle*. This principle argues on the grounds of uncertainty for the conservation of environmental resources such as biodiversity and tropical forest habitats even if cost–benefit analysis suggests that development would be beneficial. This is especially urgent where the degradation of resources is irreversible.

Technological progress

Sustainable development, as we saw in Section 2.2, is connected to the notion that the current generation should aim to bequeath to the future at least as much capital as it inherited. Two schools of thought were identified: one believes that it does not matter what form this bequest takes, while the other believes that particular components of environmental capital must form part of this bequest. The assumption behind the second view is that these resources are unique and their contribution to development cannot be replaced by substitutes. I now want to explore this debate further by examining the possibility of technological progress. Technological optimists (or 'cornucopians') claim that improved technology will always look after the interests of future generations. They regard the concept of sustainable development as irrelevant, because technological progress ensures the current generation is always poorer than those that follow.

Technological progress expands the opportunities open to the future, enhancing the production and consumption possibilities of an economy by raising the productivity of capital. One way to think of this is that greater output can be obtained for the same level of inputs; this implies the same Qs for fewer Fs in Section 3.2. This reduces the onus on the current generation to pass on to the future as much capital as it inherited and hence constitutes an argument in favour of discounting. It also raises another possibility. Environmental capital which is currently thought to be the unique provider of certain benefits may not be seen in this light in the future, because of the development of substitute goods or substitute processes made possible through technological breakthroughs. The technological optimists would argue that history is full of such instances.

Fuel use in the developing world provides an example. The burning of biomass such as fuelwood is an essential source of energy in many developing countries, mostly in rural and poorer urban communities. It is estimated that fuelwood provides 62 per cent of energy requirements in Africa and 34 per cent in Asia. In some sub-Saharan African countries it accounts for up to 90 per cent of total energy consumption. Natural forests and woodlands provide the bulk of fuelwood needs and although fuelwood and charcoal production accounts for only 10 per cent of total forest depletion, it is a powerful erosive force at the forest edge. The size of this threat in terms of energy use will depend upon the availability of substitute fuels (e.g. kerosene) but also on technological measures, such as fuel efficient stoves that increase the productivity of the scarce resources. When more efficient stoves are introduced into the household, more energy is produced from a given amount of fuelwood. Forest depletion falls, and labour is released for other economic activity.

While technological optimists are convinced of the pervasiveness of improved technologies in overcoming constraints on development, surprisingly little is known about how such changes actually come about. According to the theory of induced innovation, the development of new technologies is a response to pressing problems. For example, population pressures, it is argued, have a 'forcing effect' on agricultural productivity increases. So farming systems changed from 'shifting cultivation' to 'long fallow periods', to 'short fallow farming and cropping rotations with organic manuring', to 'modern intensive monocultures' based on high-yield crops and the application of irrigation, fertilizers, insecticides and pesticides (Pearce, 1990). This latter structural change is characteristic of what has become known as the 'Green Revolution'. Increasing demand increases the price of agricultural products and so farmers respond to this change in incentives by adapting their farming techniques.

Can technological change mitigate the potentially serious effects from the loss of tropical rain forests and other ecosystems by replacing, for example, critical life-support functions? Some technological optimists argue that it can, although it is largely a question of faith. In fact, environmental resources have in the past provided the key for technological change. Section 2.1 indicated the role of plant diversity in providing the genetic information needed to develop new types of grains.

Technical solutions to the global warming process have been put forward. One suggestion is the emission of particles such as dust into the atmosphere, which would have a cooling effect on climate by reflecting back the sun's radioactive rays. However, most scientists regard any attempt to deliberately control the global climate with suspicion. Similarly, sulphur dioxide from the burning of fossil fuels may help to mitigate the global warming process by reflecting radiation from the sun. Sulphur dioxide is transformed in the atmosphere by chemical reactions to form sulphate aerosols, which reflect radiation in the same way as dust particles but are probably more powerful coolants. However, sulphur dioxide is a pollutant, both in its own right and as a precursor to acid rain, which is a significant source of damage to human health, buildings, materials and ecosystems. In addition, sulphate aerosols contribute to visibility loss (such as at the US Grand Canyon).

The benefits of technological change are themselves uncertain. Chlorofluorocarbons (CFCs) were hailed as a technological breakthrough when discovered in the 1930s and were found to have multiple uses in foam packaging, refrigerators and aerosol sprays. What could not have been anticipated at the time of discovery was that CFCs would play the major role in the depletion of the ozone layer, which blocks the sun's radiation. Depletion of the ozone layer increases the risk of skin cancers and cataracts due to increased exposure to the sun's ultraviolet rays. CFCs are also a powerful greenhouse gas.

Population growth

Technological progress can play an important role in relieving human pressure on environmental resources. Population growth has the opposite effect. Other things being equal, population growth increases the human pressure on environmental resources. An expanding human population requires habitat and resources. In the case of agriculture, only if the effects of technological progress offset the effects of population will pressure on land be relieved.

Question

Refer to Table 27.7. What has happened to world population levels over the period 1950–90? How is world population expected to change from 1990 to 2025?

Table 27.7 **World population size and growth: actual and future**

Region	Population size (millions)				Average annual population change (%)		
	1950	1990	1995	2025	1975–80	1985–90	1995–2000
World	2516	5292	5770	8504	1.73	1.74	1.63
Africa	222	642	747	1597	2.88	2.99	2.98
North and Central America	220	427	453	596	1.47	1.29	1.09
South America	112	297	326	494	2.28	2.01	1.71
Asia	1377	3113	3413	4912	1.86	1.87	1.68
Europe	392	498	504	515	0.45	0.25	0.23
USSR (former)	180	289	299	352	0.85	0.78	0.64
Oceania	13	26	28	38	1.49	1.48	1.24

Source: World Resources Institute (1992)

Table 27.7 shows that world population levels doubled from 1950 to 1990. Between 1990 and 2025 world population is estimated to increase by just over 60 per cent. Stabilization in world population at around the 10–12 billion mark may only occur by the middle of the twenty-first century.

In contrast to the technological optimists, the 'neo-Malthusians' are pessimistic regarding our prospects. In the early nineteenth century, Thomas Malthus argued that the population of England was limited by the availability of food. Populations expanded so long as food supplies allowed. It follows that any progress that could be made by improving agricultural practices would induce further population growth. Human populations were doomed to live at the biological minimum, the standard of living consistent with human survival and adequate functioning but no more. With the benefit of hindsight it is clear that Malthus underestimated the capacity for improvements in technology to outstrip the increased demand for food that population growth brought.

The neo-Malthusians are so called because they have reintroduced the idea of absolute limits on population and economic growth in terms of increased environmental pressures. An increase in economic activity, it is argued, increases the amount of resources that are dragged through the economic system, so that, for example, a greater absolute amount of energy is required although energy per unit of GNP might stay constant. The idea of upper limits to population levels and levels of economic activity is still central to the claims of some ecologists and neo-Malthusians. Humans compete for resources on a finite planet. The pressure is determined both by the scale of economic activity and the number of humans. If economic activity or population are to expand they may do so at the expense of ecosystems such as tropical forests. Ecologists argue that there is an upper limit to this process whereby the 'integrity' or quality of ecosystem functions are seriously compromised.

It has been calculated that the global human population directly or indirectly appropriates about 25–40 per cent of the global ecosystem (Vitousek *et al.*, 1986). As indicated in Table 27.7, the natural world will have to accommodate multiples of present population pressure within several decades. The proposed upper limit to this process is sometimes linked to the ecological notion of 'saturation points'. A saturation point is the maximum population that a given area can sustain. At low levels of population, food and space are relatively abundant allowing rapid increases in population. At higher levels of population, the rate of growth begins to taper off and population approaches the saturation point. This ecological concept is commonly applied to animal and plant species where the only constraint is that the population survives indefinitely. Biologist Paul Ehrlich has claimed that a sustainable global population at the current average living standard in the developed world would be as low as 2 billion, a fraction of the actual world population. Any estimate of sustainable population is highly sensitive to the degree of optimism that is adopted with respect to technological progress. Ehrlich's claims err on the side of extreme caution.

The idea of an upper bound to economic activity and population size is anathema to technological optimists. They would argue such reasoning falls into the same traps as Malthus's original hypothesis and is based on a static unchanging view of the world. Of course both views are caricatures of the world in which we live. So while history informs us of many instances where human pressures on the environment have been eased by technological progress, population growth is nonetheless implicated in the deforestation process. However, the past is not necessarily a good guide to the future. Some would argue that maintaining environmental capital, as embodied in tropical forests, in fact represents a cautious view of the ability of improved technology to absolve us of our responsibilities towards the future. On the other hand it is usually argued that forest loss and biodiversity loss are not susceptible to technological fixes.

I will go on to investigate appropriate policy responses to the conservation of environmental capital. While I have stated that population pressures have been suggested as one reason for deforestation it is less clear what this implies for public policy. It can be wrongly interpreted as a rationale for control over household fertility decisions, although more usually policy prescriptions have focused on increasing the flow of information concerning birth control, and the role of female rights and access to education. However, in Section 4 I will effectively by-pass these particular controversies and take population growth as given in order to look at alternative policies that have been suggested for the maintenance of environmental capital. The purpose of this sub-section has been to highlight the central role attributed to population pressures by some environmentalists and ecologists.

Exercise 27.5

1   Summarize the main dangers in allowing cost–benefit analysis to be a guide to decision making regarding the environment and sustainable development.

2   Summarize the main difference between the views expressed by technological optimists and neo-Malthusians.

Safe minimum standards

So what is an appropriate policy response to the levels of uncertainty just outlined? One approach is the development of safe minimum standards (SMS), a concept proposed by Ciriacy-Wantrup (1952) as a guiding rule for nature conservation. In this framework, sustainable development, defined in terms of the conservation of environmental capital, is placed beyond the reach of routine trade-offs with other social goals such as higher living standards. The basic idea is that we should avoid irreversible damage to the environment unless the social costs – the loss of the benefits of development – are intolerably large.

A policy rule from safe minimum standards

Pearce (1992) provided an example where the benefits of clearing land for an alternative activity are known, along with the benefits of conservation. Normally, it might be expected that while the benefits of development may be known with some reasonable degree of certainty, conservation benefits will be uncertain. Fortunately, it is not required that the magnitude of these conservation benefits is known in order to draw conclusions for policy. The only information that we do require is that yes (Y) benefits do exist or no (N) benefits do not exist for both conservation and development. Let us label conservation benefits P and development benefits D. So development benefits, which are known, are written B_D. B_D can be interpreted as the costs of conservation. B_P is now the benefits of conservation which are not known. Pearce *et al.* (1990) have analysed the decision-making rule which can be drawn out of this available information in terms of the following matrix:

	Y	N	Maximum loss
Develop (D)	B_P	0	B_P
Conserve (P)	$B_D - B_P$	B_D	B_D

The matrix describes a combination of four possible choices. Each is characterized by its own loss, that is, its opportunity cost. These are:

* (D, Y) develop the land when there are benefits of conservation. This entails losses of B_P.

* (D, N) develop the land when there are no benefits of conservation. This entails no losses, hence the entry of 0.

* (P, Y) conserve when there are benefits of conservation. The loss here is equivalent to the forgone development benefits minus the benefits of conservation.

* (P, N) conserve when there are no benefits of conservation. Losses are the forgone development benefits.

In the face of uncertainty and irreversibility the decision rule to follow is to minimize the maximum loss, a procedure known as the minimax solution. This means that developing the land can only be justified where B_D is extremely large outweighing high estimates of the unknown conservation benefits.

Bishop (1993) conceives of SMS along similar lines to Pearce's analysis set out above. Bishop's example is that 90 pence worth of biodiversity cannot be given up for a pound's (£) worth of coffee. If we were rigidly sticking to the rules of cost–benefit analysis then we would not reach the same conclusion, because there would be a net gain of 10 pence from growing coffee. Hence, the SMS decision rule demands caution when assessing the benefits of conservation relative to the benefits of development.

The effect of SMS is to reverse the bias in environmental decision making. Instead of assuming that environmental resources are there to be developed unless there is some strong reason for believing the development to be unsustainable, the approach is to make conservation the preferred option unless the forgone development benefits are intolerably large. However, what is meant by 'intolerable' is left unclear, though Bishop would intend it to reflect substantial costs. The SMS rule still requires conservation and hence sustainable development to compete for funding with other worthwhile social objectives. The magnitude of 'intolerable' costs is still determined by the current generation. Hence in the extreme, if the present generation does not care about the future, any current sacrifice for conservation may seem intolerable. The SMS approach still implies some system of weighting so perhaps we are back where we started. There is no escaping value judgements about the well-being of different generations.

4   The need for international co-operation

If preserving environmental capital is required for sustainable development, then this requires that countries which have run down their natural capital compensate countries which still retain natural capital. The former can be thought of as countries in the 'developed north' with relatively high levels of other forms of capital, while the latter are countries in the 'developing south' with relatively little other capital. The richest 20 per cent of the world's population, most of whom live in the north, have 82.7 per cent of global income (United Nations Development Programme, UNDP, 1992). In contrast, the poorest 20 per cent have only 1.4 per cent. In 1960–70 these respective shares were 70.2 per cent and 2.3 per cent indicating that economic disparities have increased.

4.1   Aid and the environment

Existing aid flows

What are the implications of existing north–south aid flows for sustainable development? About 70 per cent of overseas development assistance (ODA) is bilateral, that is, given directly from one country to another. These transfers are not intended to secure sustainable development. They derive from a mixture of humanitarian motivations, historical ties with developing countries, and sometimes the objective of securing benefits (Thirlwall, 1994). Much of total aid flows to the richest 40 per cent of developing countries, who are relatively high military spenders and have relatively low provision for priority programmes that aim to supply basic needs (UNDP, 1992). It would seem that ODA is often poorly targeted, if our objective for assistance is to foster development amongst the poorest citizens of the world. The United Nations sets a uniform target for ODA of 0.7 per cent of GNP.

Question

Consider Table 27.8. To what extent have developed countries met this aid target?

Table 27.8 **Total ODA as a percentage of GNP: selected countries and regions**

Country or region	As % of GNP		
	1970 actual	1990 actual	adjusted target[1]
Canada	0.41	0.44	0.69
Japan	0.23	0.31	0.87
USA	0.31	0.19	0.76
European Union	0.36	0.41	—
France	0.46	0.52	0.65
Germany	0.33	0.42	0.74
Netherlands	0.60	0.93	0.58
UK	0.42	0.27	0.53
Nordic countries	0.34	0.90	0.80
OECD countries	0.33	0.33	0.70

[1] Adjusted target is 0.7 multiplied by one plus the percentage difference between the donor's 1989 GNP per capita and the average GNP per capita of all donors.

Source: UNDP (1992)

Table 27.8 indicates that few developed countries donate anything approaching this target. However, a more equitable basis for determining the magnitude of transfers would be to allocate the burden of the 0.7 per cent ODA requirement on the basis of GNP weightings (UNDP, 1992). This would mean that economies with relatively large GNP per capita would contribute a correspondingly greater proportion of total GNP as aid. The adjusted target column of Table 27.8 shows how this would alter the structure of allocations.

A critique of ODA can also be made on environmental grounds. Not only do funds often end up financing a project with dubious development and economic benefits but they also appear to work against sustainable development. One of the most conspicuous examples of this are some large-scale hydroelectric dam projects which have contributed to deforestation, changes in downstream water quality, the flooding of forested land and the displacing of rural populations.

Turner (1990) suggests that poverty is the enemy of sustainable development. By encouraging short-term decision making in order to ensure immediate survivability, poverty forces people away from actions that would ensure sustainable livelihoods. For example, poverty tends to encourage subsistence farming on marginal lands with poor soil productivity. The soil quickly erodes and is exhausted of nutrients so that farming activity soon has to switch to other land, creating a vicious spiral of poverty and environmental degradation. In so far as aid packages raise incomes and alleviate poverty, environments may benefit.

There are now pressures to ensure that the environmental sensitivity of aid projects is taken into account. An alternative to traditional projects is to give developing countries technological know-how as aid. The technological gap that exists between the developed and developing world is seen as a major cause of wealth and income disparities between the two regions. The encouragement of soil conservation methods and improved farming technologies is one way in which this gap could be closed. However, some have voiced concern that developing countries do not have the technical or the institutional capacity to absorb the potentially large resource transfers that are proposed as part of 'sustainability packages'.

The environment-indebtedness link

In 1990, the total external debt of developing countries stood at $1350 billion in contrast to a mere $100 billion in 1970 (UNDP, 1992). The major impact of this debt is in Latin America and sub-Saharan Africa where debt is respectively 50 per cent and 100 per cent of GNP. Servicing debt has become a severe problem in these regions. Environmentalists have argued that the crisis of international debt is deepening environmental problems, which in turn worsens the debt problem. For example, in order to earn foreign exchange with which to repay external debt, indebted countries will seek to increase exports of natural resources such as timber. Yet, although the timber industry is implicated in deforestation, the international trade of timber is probably only responsible for 10 per cent of deforestation. There is in fact little evidence for a positive relationship between debt and environmental degradation. Deforestation is caused by more fundamental driving forces, such as land tenure arrangements, population pressures and the mismatch between domestic and global benefits. Other mechanisms whereby debt can *indirectly* contribute to environmental degradation have been proposed. For example, where the obligation to service debts lowers the standard of living and competes with other uses of a country's GNP, environmental objectives may be downgraded (Pearce *et al.*, 1995).

'*Debt-for-nature*' swaps might be seen as one mechanism for tackling the compensation issue. A debt-for-nature swap reduces the debt obligations of a developing country to a developed country in return for the conservation of certain environmental resources. A creditor purchases the protection of a rain forest (or some other environmental asset) in return for retiring part of the country's debt. The emphasis in countries such as Costa Rica, Ecuador, Zambia and Madagascar where debt-for-nature swaps have been initiated has been on achieving a particular conservation goal. The policy is not intended to resolve the problem of indebtedness itself.

4.2   Problems of international co-operation

It is clear that any international agreement for sustainable development must be mutually beneficial in order for a sufficient number of countries to sign up. Yet such international co-operation is intensely problematic in a very unequal world. First, the compensation might not be forthcoming, or at least donors might not be willing to give sufficient quantities of compensation. Second, the potential recipients may not be willing in principle to give up what they see as a right to use their environments how they see fit.

An international strategy to conserve environmental capital therefore requires the creation of new and additional transfers specifically designed as environmental aid or environmental compensation. An example of an international agency designed to facilitate environmental 'aid' flows is the Global Environmental Facility (GEF), which was set up in 1990, by the World Bank, the United Nations Environment Programme (UNEP) and the

United Nations Development Programme (UNDP). The aim of the GEF is to shift the emphasis of decision making on to the consideration of global benefits in addition to local benefits. Specifically the GEF was established in order to:

- protect the ozone layer;
- protect international water resources;
- protect biodiversity; and
- ensure a decrease in GHG emissions.

International attention has also shifted to the negotiation of global agreements to promote the conservation of environmental capital. Four major agreements emerged from the Earth Summit. One was a huge document called *Agenda 21* described as a global 'masterplan for sustainable development' (Grubb *et al.*, 1993). Individual governments carry the responsibility to implement the requirements set out in this document. Overseeing the progress of each is a new international body set up during the Earth Summit: the Commission for Sustainable Development (CSD). However, although each sovereign government must report to the CSD, this body has no international legal status and therefore cannot actually *force* countries to comply with *Agenda 21*.

The other agreements reached at the Earth Summit covered climate change (the Framework Convention on Climate Change, FCCC), biodiversity conservation (the Convention on Biodiversity, CBD) and deforestation (the Forest Principles). It is important not only for developing countries to sign up to these conventions (which for the most part they have done) but also for the developed world to share the burden of implementation. Any agreement will be worthless if the developing countries do not find it in their interests to comply. Rapid population growth and economic growth will conspire against any attempts by the developed world to bring into effect a unilateral agreement. For example, increasing emissions of GHGs would negate the actions of countries attempting to decrease their own emissions. I want now to look more closely at the Convention on Biodiversity in order to illustrate some of the conflicts that might arise in attempting to implement international agreements to secure sustainable development.

The convention on biodiversity

The CBD committed countries to the conservation and sustainable use of biological resources. However, biodiversity conservation was designated as an issue of national sovereignty to be determined within national boundaries, which raises doubts as to the actual commitment to conservation that will result. National governments may decide that maximizing domestic or host country benefits requires reneging on the sustainability constraint. Ensuring compliance may necessitate changing the economic incentives that key decision makers face. In particular, it will require the creation of new and additional funds to finance compensation in accordance with the principle of incremental cost.

However, there is no mention of global benefits in the convention. The CBD states that compensation is the difference between how much a country spends on biodiversity preservation *without the* CBD and what it would have to spend *with the* CBD. The sustainability constraint operates without any reference to the magnitude of global benefits. In a sense, this fits in with an approach based on positive but uncertain benefits, perhaps based on a notion of SMS. The absence of specific reference to global benefits was, however, largely a concession to political conflicts between the developed countries and the developing countries.

The developing nations of the south regard an emphasis on global benefits to be against their interests, implying an obligation to provide stores of biodiversity in forests and other ecosystems for the global good rather than to develop these resources for their own domestic benefit. An illustration of this is the furore that surrounded the convention on the protection of the world's forests. This was due, in the main, to the protestations of India and Malaysia who were implacably opposed to the idea that their forests should be preserved as a sink for the GHG emissions of the developed world (Grubb *et al.*, 1993). The developed countries had already threatened the capacity of the globe to absorb GHGs by increasing their own emissions in the past and had largely depleted their forests. Agarwal and Narain (1992) argue that the thinking behind various suggested international environmental conventions which would include the FCCC and the CBD is a form of 'environmental colonialism'. They argue that the problem of sustainable development as the conservation of environmental capital originated in the 'excessive' consumption of the developed world and in particular the USA. Developing countries have their own environmental priorities based on preventing desertification, land and water degradation and declining prices of the natural resources that they trade on international markets. Although some of these concerns are not unrelated to concerns surrounding deforestation, the critique indicates that international agreements are not necessarily easily achieved even if new and additional funds are made available.

The political will of the developed world to provide adequate compensation and therefore to share the burden of implementation of international conventions can also be questioned. No actual magnitudes for compensation were agreed at the Earth Summit. The signing of the CBD was almost scuttled by the reluctance of three key signatories – the USA, UK and Japanese governments – to commit themselves to an agreement that left open-ended the monetary sums that might be required to save the world's biodiversity. Japan and the UK wavered but eventually signed the CBD during the summit. It took just over a year and a change of President for the USA to sign. The Earth Summit coincided with the US presidential elections and a serious downturn in global and US economic activity. Short-term economic concerns are often in conflict with policies that require sacrifice on the part of current generations, and this is a major obstacle to the achievement of sustainable development.

Although many figures have been bandied about, the true magnitude of the sums ultimately required is simply not known. Credible estimates have looked at the costs of improving the monitoring and conservation of remaining wildernesses (of which closed tropical forests form part), the costs of decreasing emissions of GHGs particularly carbon dioxide (by switching to less polluting fuels or reducing energy use) and additional ODA for conventional development needs. Pearce *et al.* (1993) suggest a figure of about $50 billion per annum. At the time of the Earth Summit a figure of $100 billion per annum was considered as a reference level. The Global Environmental Facility has an annual budget of $2 billion.

Given the ambiguous legal status of these new international agreements, countries may either renege altogether on compensation by not ratifying the conventions in their own parliaments or use ambiguities in the conventions to their own advantage. The fact that countries often prefer to allocate blame for global environmental change to other countries does not augur well for the success of international co-operation. The classic example is the emphasis of the developed world on future projected rates of economic growth and population growth in the developing world. Conversely, the developing world focuses on 'over-consumption' in the developed world. The real danger is that these conflicts will lead countries to let environmental events simply unfold in front of them. If the global costs of environmental degradation are increasing, then solutions will become more expensive. These increasing costs will be passed on to future generations, contrary to the notion of sustainable development.

Exercise 27.6

The Convention on Biodiversity (CBD) seeks to maintain global biological resources. What problems lie in the way of the successful implementation of this convention?

---

5   Conclusion

Sustainable development has been defined as human well-being generated now that is not reversed in the future. I have devoted most attention to the view that the way to achieve this social goal is to maintain environmental capital, using as an example tropical deforestation and its implications for biodiversity loss and global warming. One approach to conserving such environmental capital focuses on the role of discount rates in decisions that affect future generations. I have concentrated on analysing the most efficient ways to maintain capital, illustrating this with the global and national costs and benefits of tropical forest conservation. This led me to a compensation rule based on incremental cost, which in turn is based on the principle that the victim pays. A key factor in the implementation of such strategies is the political will required to fund these solutions and the role of international institutions to broker such trades.

Perhaps the most persistent theme of this chapter has been uncertainty. At the scientific level, the effects of biodiversity loss and the likelihood of global warming are hard to predict. At the philosophical level considerable uncertainty surrounds the concept of intergenerational justice: the problem of how to strike the right balance between the needs of the current generation and those of future generations. At the political level, the self-interest of nations threatens to disrupt efforts at international policy co-operation to secure sustainable development. I have tried to show how economics can help to guide policy in the context of uncertainty by making the concept of sustainable development as precise as possible, by devising ways of evaluating the costs and benefits of alternative courses of action, by identifying key aspects of uncertainty and by drawing out policy rules such as safe minimum standards from alternative assumptions.

CHAPTER 28

ECONOMIC INTERDEPENDENCE AND POLICY CO-ORDINATION

by Graham Dawson

1 Introduction

In his evidence to the Macmillan Committee on Finance and Industry on 5 December 1930, Keynes looked forward to the day when monetary policy 'will be utterly removed from popular controversy and will be regarded as a kind of beneficent technique of scientific control, such as electricity' (Keynes, 1930, p.263).

Those words, at once forceful and elegant, are a typically Keynesian expression of confidence in the power of scientific knowledge and the benevolence of public policy. Guided by the expert advice of economists, policy makers would bring jobs to a jobless world as swiftly and reliably as electricity was bringing light and warmth to almost every home in the country. In this chapter I am going to examine two macroeconomic policy issues which challenge this optimistic picture of economic policy.

Sixty years on, monetary policy seems further than ever from being perceived as a 'beneficent technique'. People who lost their jobs as a consequence of the 'monetarist experiment', conducted with particular determination in the UK and the USA, carried placards which read, 'If this is the cure stop treating us'. Keynes himself seems to have combined a deep distrust of politicians (whom he saw as subject to the vagaries of 'popular controversy') with, as his biographer Robert Skidelsky (1992, p.288) puts it, 'a belief in scientific expertise and personal disinterestedness which now seems alarmingly naive'. This combination of a private interest view of politicians with a public interest view of expert officials (to use the terms developed in Chapter 10, Section 4.1) led Keynes to advocate the autonomy of the Bank of England from the whims of politicians. Public distrust has since tended to spread from politicians to public officials, but the debate on the desirability of an independent central bank lives on.

GUY FAWKES
**The only person
to enter Parliament
with honest intentions**

Is an independent central bank – that is, a central bank with a constitutional guarantee of freedom from political control in its conduct of monetary policy – a vital precondition of vigorous macroeconomic performance? I discuss this issue in Section 2. The perceived failure of the UK authorities – the government and a politically subservient central bank – to control monetary growth and inflation is contrasted by some commentators with the apparent success of the Bundesbank, the independent central bank of Germany, in keeping inflation low. As a result the Bundesbank has emerged as a model for the European Central Bank envisaged under European Monetary Union.

Section 3 turns to another long-lasting issue dear to Keynes's heart: the reform of the international monetary system. Can experts formulate a workable set of arrangements for co-ordinating the macroeconomic policies of individual nations and of supra-national blocs such as the EU? A brief historical survey reveals that only limited progress has been made. The current system of flexible exchange rates faces the intractable problem of a conflict of interest between currency speculators who benefit from exchange rate volatility and manufacturing firms whose long-term planning requires exchange rate stability.

Three proposals for an international monetary system for the twenty-first century are then outlined, and it becomes clear that an evaluation of their relative merits is problematic. The proposals cannot be evaluated in isolation from the theoretical perspectives or research programmes from which they draw their characteristic assumptions and methodological principles. Worse, they are based on different interpretations of what the problem is and ultimately on different value judgements about the world distribution of income and wealth.

This reflection leads us to question both aspects of Keynes's policy optimism: the scientific content and the benevolence. Section 4 draws on both these issues of monetary policy to argue that theory choice and policy recommendation are not the straightforward processes they are represented to be in the mainstream tradition of positive economics. Positive economics is rooted in the view that economics shares certain essential features with the physical sciences and can be summed up in three main principles: that economic theories can be tested against observations of the real world; that the history of economic thought exhibits scientific progress; and that value judgements introduce a subjective or personal element into economic policy prescriptions. I end the chapter by examining some of the doubts that have been expressed about these principles.

2   Central bank independence

2.1   Economic interdependence and central bank independence

The interdependence of national economies is sharply exhibited in the foreign exchange market. For example, in a system of fixed exchange rates the monetary authorities of an economy with a higher rate of inflation than those of other members of the system will find its currency under speculative pressure. A short-term response is to push up domestic interest rates, but the authorities may take a longer view and seek to reduce the inflation rate to the average of other economies in the fixed exchange rate system. But what if there is an election on the horizon? Will the government be able to resist the temptation to take risks with inflation in order to keep interest rates low and voters happy? One way out of this dilemma might be to hand over monetary policy, and hence the responsibility for controlling inflation, to a central bank which is guaranteed a sufficient degree of independence from the elected government to discharge its anti-inflationary duties unhindered by political calculations.

This response to economic interdependence raises two main questions. First, do independent central banks have a better track record on inflation than politically subservient ones? After a quick survey of the institutional context of the UK, US and German central banks, I want to examine UK monetary policy to see if it is possible to ascribe its repeated failures to control inflation to the fact that the UK central bank is subservient to elected politicians. The German record on inflation is much better, and the German central bank is independent, but we must be careful not to jump to the obvious conclusion. There are many other differences between the UK and Germany which might affect their contrasting records on inflation. We must also be careful not to assume that keeping inflation down is the only goal of macroeconomic policy.

This leads to the second main question about central bank independence. Is it desirable in a representative democracy to allocate inflation policy to an institution whose directors, however technically competent they may be, are not elected? While a full investigation of the political issue of the democratic control of monetary policy is outside the scope of this chapter, I will examine two relevant issues. First, is there an economic price to be paid for whatever success against inflation independent central banks may achieve? And second, how independent of political and value judgements is the expert knowledge which economists, such as those advising the directors of an independent central bank, might claim to possess? This second question, which bears on a principal theme of this chapter – the methodology of economics as a policy science – is considered in Section 4 in the context of a discussion of the scientific status of economic knowledge and the role of values and moral principles in economics.

Comparative central banks

The central bank is sometimes referred to as the 'government's bank'. In the UK the Bank of England is directly accountable to the government of the day and hence ultimately to the voting population. However, the US and German central banks, the Federal Reserve and the Bundesbank, are constitutionally independent of the elected governments. European Monetary Union (EMU) involves the creation of a politically independent European Central Bank (ECB) at the heart of a European System of Central Banks (ESCB), in which all the participating national central banks will also be independent of their respective governments.

The establishment of the Bank of England was a matter of historical expediency, and from the start it was the government's bank. In 1694 a syndicate of wealthy individuals raised £1 200 000 to lend to the government of William and Mary, which was heavily in debt because of war with France. The syndicate planned to issue notes, but fear of opposition from parliament led to the omission of any reference to this in the Act authorizing the establishment of the Bank. The Bank appears to have made the most of its strong bargaining position a few years later, when the government's need for further loans enabled it to become the only corporate body to be granted the right to issue bank notes – and hence effectively the sole note-issuer – in England and Wales. Other banks were permitted to issue notes only if they had fewer than six partners (and would therefore be severely limited in the amount of cash they could raise to back the note issue). The nationalization of the Bank in 1946 formalized its duty to implement the government's monetary policy. In 1994 the Bank was allowed greater openness in explaining interest rate policy decisions, and it now publishes a quarterly inflation report which on at least one occasion has questioned government policy on interest rates. These measures were taken to re-establish the credibility of UK monetary policy, and perhaps to prepare for the Bank's eventual independence as part of the ESCB.

Figure 28.1 **The Bank of England, the United Kingdom's central bank**

In marked contrast to the Bank of England's origins, the US Federal Reserve System was set up in 1913 as a policy response to a series of failures in the private banking system. There are twelve regional Federal Reserve Banks, each responsible for supervising the banking system in its region and each represented on the Federal Reserve Board, which formulates and implements the monetary policy which it believes is most appropriate to the needs of the US economy. The Federal Reserve Bank, or 'Fed', has constitutional independence and its policies have frequently brought it into conflict with the US president. On occasions, however, the Fed has yielded to political pressure. For example, in 1980, a presidential election year, interest rates were reduced after pressure from the White House. The economy recovered from a brief recession, even though inflation remained at the rate that had prompted the original increase in interest rates.

Similarly, the Bundesbank is in principle entirely independent of political control. It implements monetary policy in pursuit of its objective of maintaining the value of the Deutschmark through price stability (which is defined in practice as an annual inflation rate of 0–2 per cent). Once again, political pressure can cause the central bank to abandon its preferred policy. For example, at the time of German reunification the Bundesbank gave in to the government of Chancellor Kohl by accepting a rate of conversion of the Ostmark to the Deutschmark of one to one.

The subservience of the Bank of England exemplifies the centralization of power in the executive arm of the UK government. The independence of the Fed reflects a constitutional bias against such centralization and towards a system of checks and balances. The Bundesbank's position is the consequence of a fear of a return to the hyperinflation which led to the virtual collapse of the German economy in 1922–23. It is worth noting that the Bundesbank is in one sense less independent of political control than the Fed. The Bundesbank is not free to depart from the objective of price stability, which was imposed upon it by the government when it was established. It therefore lacks the discretion enjoyed by the Fed to select the monetary policy that it considers to be most appropriate to economic conditions. It is precisely this lack of discretion over the objective of monetary policy – its commitment to a fixed policy rule – that is thought by some commentators to underlie the Bundesbank's perceived success. So the question of central bank independence is an aspect of the larger issue of rules versus discretion discussed by Nick Crafts in Chapter 20.

2.2   UK monetary policy: targets and techniques

UK monetary policy is a record of almost unmitigated failure, which provides a sharp contrast to the perceived success of the Bundesbank in controlling inflation. To what extent should its anti-inflationary reputation be attributed to the independence of the Bundesbank from political control?

The primary objective of monetary policy throughout the industrial economies is to control inflation. The policy shift in the early 1980s in favour of low or even zero inflation was based on the monetarist assumption that controlling the rate of growth of the money supply was a necessary and sufficient condition for reducing or eliminating inflation. The money supply was therefore seen as an intermediate target on the way to the objective of price stability (for the distinction between targets and objectives, see Chapter 16, Section 2.3).

It is not just the selection of a monetary target that matters; its public announcement is itself an important part of the policy. By committing itself before the tribunal of the financial markets to a formal target, the government seeks to enhance the credibility of its anti-inflationary stance. No government wants the humiliation of failing to achieve its stated aims, so a public monetary target is likely to persuade people that policy makers are serious in their anti-inflationary resolve. On the assumption that expectations are important – that is, policy is more likely to work if people act on the belief that it is working – it follows that the proclamation of monetary targets increases the chances of success of a disinflationary policy stance (see Chapter 24 on expectations). The next question is, which measure of the money supply should be targeted?

Chapter 11 drew a distinction between narrow money (M0) and broad money (M4). These became the only official monetary aggregates (Bank of England, 1994), although figures on M0 were not published until 1984. In 1979 the UK government chose to target sterling M3 (£M3) which comprised: (a) cash; (b) sight and time deposits with the banks provided they were in sterling; and (c) certificates of deposit (see Chapter 11).

So £M3 was a measure of broad money but not as broad as M4. It was chosen because it seemed to be correlated with inflation in a way that some economists interpreted as an indication of a causal link.

There are other possible monetary targets too. Thinking back to Chapter 19, another candidate for targeting is the exchange rate. Suppose, first, that the money supply is exogenous, or within the government's direct control, and the government is operating a fixed exchange rate policy – that is, it has a target range for the external value of sterling, such as 6 per cent either side of £1 = DM2.95. If the government permitted the money supply to grow too quickly, the rate of interest would fall, making sterling less attractive on the foreign exchange markets. In order to prevent sterling falling below its target range against the Deutschmark, the UK government would have to reduce the rate of growth of the money supply. So an exchange target might work as effectively as a money supply target in restraining monetary growth before inflation accelerates.

Next, suppose that the money supply is endogenous, or beyond the direct control of the government. The government can instead set interest rates to influence the demand for money. If sterling is uncomfortably close to its 'floor' against the Deutschmark, this might indicate a lack of confidence on the foreign exchange markets about the prospects for UK inflation. An interest rate rise to boost sterling will also exert downward pressure on inflation. Once again, an exchange rate target is in principle as effective an anti-inflationary discipline as a money supply target.

There remains a further set of possible monetary targets. In Chapter 11 I suggested that, rather than thinking in terms of a sharp dichotomy between money and non-money, we should make use of the concept of a 'spectrum of liquidity' along which are placed assets of varying degrees of 'moneyness'. Some of the less liquid assets may be more reliable indicators of future inflation than the money supply itself. These assets include equities and, for the UK with its high level of owner occupation and deregulated financial markets, houses.

As Pepper (1990) shows, it is reasonable to monitor changes in the price of assets such as houses as a potential cause of inflation, not merely an early symptom:

> The rise in asset prices was an important cause of the consumer boom in 1987 and 1988. People became more wealthy. Some spent a portion of their capital gains … there was also direct borrowing to finance consumption. People's confidence had risen and this made them more willing to borrow rather than wait until expenditure could be financed out of income in the future.
>
> *(Pepper, 1990, pp.49–50)*

The UK government therefore has a range of possible monetary targets: two official measures of the money supply, the sterling exchange rate, and asset prices. What instruments or techniques are available to the monetary authorities in their attempts to hit the particular monetary target, or set of targets, they have selected?

Chapter 11 noted that there are in principle two main avenues open to the government in trying to control the money supply. It can operate on the demand side of the money market by setting the rate of interest, or it can work directly on the supply side. It may help to distinguish these if I draw an analogy between the supply or 'production' of money by the financial services industry – banks, building societies and so on – and the production of a good by manufacturing industry.

Question

Suppose that the government wanted to control the number of new cars purchased next year. Can you suggest three methods of government intervention in the car market that might achieve this aim?

On the demand side, the government could raise car prices through higher taxation, or use subsidies to reduce the cost of alternative means of transport. Working through the price mechanism in this way roughly corresponds to the use of interest rates in the money market. A second demand-side method is rationing: limiting the quantity per time period a household may purchase, as with food rationing in the UK during and after the Second World War. However, rationing as a technique of monetary policy – direct control of the quantity of money – has been used in the UK on the supply side, for example by instructing banks to keep their lending beneath a stipulated ceiling. The other supply-side technique I am going to discuss is monetary base control.

Reflection

Look back at Section 5.2 of Chapter 11 and remind yourself of the money multiplier model of credit creation by banks.

The banks' ability to create new deposits by making loans depends on their having sufficient reserves of liquid assets to cover expected cash withdrawals by customers. These cash reserves are known as the monetary base, and the monetary authorities could in principle control the amount of money, or credit, created by the banks by regulating the availability of notes and coins to the banks and their customers. In a sense the monetary base is the raw material of the money supply industry, as noted by Friedman in evidence to the UK Treasury and Civil Service Committee in 1980. After dismissing monetary control through interest rates as inefficient, he went on: 'Far easier to control the output of motor cars by controlling the availability of a basic raw material, say steel, to the manufacturers – a precise analogy to controlling the money supply by controlling the availability of base money to banks and others' (Friedman, 1980, p.58).

Suppose, for example, that UK banks are operating a 10 per cent liquidity ratio, giving a money (or credit) multiplier of 10. If the monetary authorities were now to confiscate some of the cash held by the banks, there would eventually be a reduction in deposits – i.e. in the money supply – equal to ten times the size of the 'lost' cash.

However, in practice monetary base control has never been more than a twinkle in the eyes of commentators such as Friedman. The fundamental problem is that monetary base control is easily evaded, as US experience with reserve base requirements in the 1960s illustrates: transactions were recorded in overseas branches of US banks. Exchange controls – limits on the amount of foreign currency a US or UK resident can buy – could in principle prevent evasion of this kind, but they were abolished in the UK in 1979 and their re-imposition is a long way from the political agenda. Gowland (1990) therefore concludes that 'without exchange control, reserve base control could not operate in the UK' (p.64).

How effective have the techniques actually used by the UK monetary authorities been in achieving their chosen targets?

2.3   Of booms and bubbles and busts: a brief history of UK monetary policy since 1951

While the techniques of monetary policy adopted by successive UK governments reflect ideological bias to some degree, learning from experience explains most of the major changes. Broadly speaking, quantity controls or rationing appealed to the interventionist instincts of left-of-centre governments, while right-wing governments which favoured free market principles felt more comfortable using the price mechanism, or interest rates. The review of UK monetary policy which follows draws on Gowland (1978, 1990), Pepper (1990), and the Bank of England (1994).

The 1950s was a period of political consensus, reflected in the fact that Conservative governments sought to control the growth of credit by rationing. Bank lending was subject to ceilings, and hire purchase controls stipulated the minimum deposit and the maximum repayment period. However, there were no formal monetary targets, and the ceilings on bank lending were not legally enforceable, the assumption being that 'moral' argument would persuade the banks to comply. Perhaps the collectivist spirit of the Second World War still influenced the minds of politicians, who believed that banks would put the national interest (in the form of the need sometimes to curb inflationary pressures) above the profit motive. Greater use was made of credit ceilings in the 1960s, especially by Labour governments after 1964.

In 1971 a new policy known as Competition and Credit Control was announced by the recently elected Conservative government. This signalled a switch to interest rates as the main technique of monetary control. In this change of regime, free market ideology was probably less influential than experience, for it was widely believed that ceilings had become ineffective. The problem, as with all forms of rationing, was evasion. For example, parallel markets had developed among newly established financial institutions to which the credit ceilings did not apply. Secondary banks, finance companies and hire purchase companies were set up with the aim of extending credit to customers who had been refused loans by the major banks because they had reached their credit ceilings. Such forms of evasion undermined the reliability of the money supply figures provided by the major banks as indicators of inflationary pressures.

In 1971 credit ceilings were replaced by 'a system under which *the allocation of credit is primarily determined by its cost*' (Bank of England, 1971, original emphasis). The target was M3, and the technique was to use interest rates. However, by 1972 M3 was growing at an annual rate of 22 per cent, rising to 27 per cent in 1973 (compared to its average rate of growth in the 1960s of 6–8 per cent). The cause of this loss of control over the money supply was the authorities' reluctance, at a time of accelerating inflationary expectations, to raise nominal interest rates sufficiently high to deter borrowers.

The response of the monetary authorities to the loss of control over the money supply was to return to ceilings, to rationing, but this time of deposits rather than lending. From 1973 there was a penalty: if a bank breached its ceiling, it had to place 'supplementary special deposits' – extra cash – with the Bank of England. In 1976 the Labour government introduced an explicit monetary target for the growth of sterling M3, with the aim of enhancing its anti-inflationary credibility in the financial markets. Had the authorities at last discovered a meaningful target and an effective technique for achieving it?

The answer is no. Once again the problem with ceilings was evasion, and in 1980 the Conservatives introduced the Medium Term Financial Strategy (MTFS). This involved:

(a) a return to interest rate policy as the main technique of controlling bank lending to households and firms; and

(b) a medium-term approach to monetary targeting: a series of targets was set for sterling M3, stretching initially over a four-year period (see Table 28.1).

Table 28.1   **The Medium Term Financial Strategy**

	Target growth rate £M3 (%)	Actual growth rate £M3 (%)
1980–81	7–11	17.9
1981–82	6–10	13.6
1982–83	5–9	11.7
1983–84	4–8	8.2
1984–85	6–10	11.6
1985–86	5–9	16.5
1986–87	11–15	20.5

Source: *Bank of England Quarterly Bulletin*, various issues

The original MTFS targets are shown in the first four rows of Table 28.1. As you can see, the rate of growth of £M3 exceeded the target in all four years, although its rate of growth did fall. Moreover, a significant part of the high £M3 growth in 1981–82 reflected the ending of the distortion to the official money supply figures caused by the evasion of ceilings on bank liabilities. The real problems for the MTFS began when it was extended into the mid 1980s, and even though the target range was revised upwards for 1986–87, the outcome was still well above the upper limit.

This led to the discrediting of broad money supply targets. It was argued in some quarters that because £M3 included bank deposits held as savings, it was misleading to assume that broad money growth above target was inflationary. It would be better, so the argument went, to focus on narrow money which is unambiguously held for transactions purposes. In 1984 the government announced a narrow money target, M0, consisting basically of cash.

Figures for £M3 ceased to be published after 1987, and attention shifted to the exchange rate as 'one of the indicators the authorities took account of in deciding monetary policy, and for a period an informal attempt was made to constrain sterling within a narrow trading range just below DM3 = £1' (Bank of England, 1994). This approach was formalized on the UK's entry into the Exchange Rate Mechanism (ERM) in 1990. However, the high interest rates needed to sustain sterling within its trading range came to be widely regarded as inappropriate for the domestic economy, and the government suspended sterling's membership of the ERM in 1992 (see Chapter 19).

By 1994 there were two official measures of the money supply, M0 and M4, which are 'monitored' rather than formally targeted, as indicators of inflationary (or disinflationary) pressures.

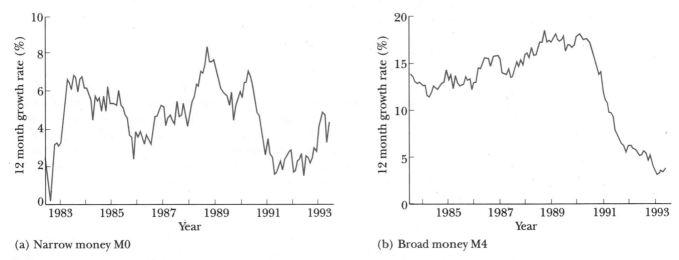

(a) Narrow money M0

(b) Broad money M4

Figure 28.2   **Growth rates of narrow and broad money, UK, 1982–93**

Source: *Economic Briefing* (1993) no.5, August

Question

Look at Figure 28.2, reproduced from Chapter 11. What would be your forecast for inflation in 1994 on the basis of (a) M0 and (b) M4?

The strong, if erratic, growth of M0 from early 1991 suggests that inflation was due to accelerate, while M4 during the same period shows only a weak upturn after a fairly sharp fall. So would the inflation rate take off, or would it at most just edge up a little? There is no alternative but to exercise judgement. However, this undermines the purpose of monetary targets, namely to enhance the credibility of anti-inflation policy by minimizing opportunities for discretion (see Section 2.1 above). In making a decision, the authorities consider the exchange rate and asset prices as well as money supply data and also the level of wage settlements. The clear and simple target suggested by monetary theory has been superseded by a pragmatic acceptance of the complexity of the economy.

So what is our judgement on the techniques of monetary control? Interest rate policy continues to be the technique on which the authorities rely for major policy adjustments (Bank of England, 1994).

Exercise 28.1

Revise your knowledge of the effects of interest rates by answering the following questions.

1   How does a change in interest rates affect consumption and investment through savings and borrowing?

2   How does a change in interest rates affect prices via the exchange rate?

Four historical episodes provide evidence for a tentative judgement on the efficacy of interest rate changes in controlling the rate of growth of the money supply. The first two are booms or 'bubbles'. The switch to interest rates in 1971 contributed to the 'Barber boom' (so called after the UK Chancellor of the Exchequer in office at the time), with the money supply out of control and inflation accelerating. This might have been averted if the authorities had been willing to raise nominal interest rates to unprecedentedly high levels. During the 'Lawson boom' of the mid 1980s (discussed in Chapter 20) the problem was that in the early stages of the boom, interest rates were set too low for the domestic economy, in order to curtail the rise of sterling against the Deutschmark. These two episodes are sometimes cited by advocates of an independent central bank for the UK. A central bank charged with achieving price stability but otherwise free from political interference would not be reluctant to set interest rates to whatever level was appropriate for domestic monetary conditions.

However, the other two episodes cast doubt on politicians' alleged unwillingness to use interest rates for corrective tough action on the economy. In the recession of 1980–81, policy makers raised interest rates with the intention of eliminating the relatively high inflation rates persisting since the boom of 1971–72. Inflation fell, but only after a drop in output and a rise in unemployment, and oddly the causal chain seemed to miss out the money supply, which grew outside its target range. In the recession of 1990–92 the growth rates of M0 and M4 were severely cut back by high interest rates. Once again, however, output and jobs were lost and money supply growth was not brought under control until a year or so after interest rates had been raised. It seems, therefore, that high interest rates work only if they are high for long enough to shock economic agents into adjusting their behaviour in ways that have adverse effects on output and jobs.

Was it considerations of political reputation or was it technical incompetence that first of all permitted excessive monetary growth and then sought to eliminate its inflationary consequences even at the cost of recession? Some commentators have argued that central banks free from political control are able to pursue a more consistent monetary policy which avoids lurching from boom to bust while maintaining a low rate of inflation.

2.4   Independent central banks and macroeconomic performance

In this section I examine three pieces of research relevant to the relation between the independence of the central bank and macroeconomic performance. The first (Barro and Gordon, 1983a) makes explicit the context of the rules versus discretion debate, and implies that independent central banks are likely to achieve lower rates of inflation. The second (Alesina and Summers, 1993) offers a relatively straightforward empirical test of this hypothesis, while the third (Epstein, 1992) presents a richer model of the relations between the politico-economic structure and the central bank.

Barro and Gordon's (1983a) model is based on a full private interest view of the state. The basic model was set out in Chapter 20, Section 1.2. In this model politicians are motivated by self-interest and respond to voters. The implication is that, if given the chance, policy makers create more inflation than people expect, because that has the effect of increasing the rate of economic growth and hence the popularity of politicians. Policy makers can do this under a discretionary monetary regime where they are not bound by a fixed rule such as 'set interest rates to whatever level is required in order to maintain price stability'. The problem is that under a discretionary regime voters come to expect the authorities to act in this way, so the rate of inflation needed to surprise people rises. The psychology here is the same as that which is implicit in Friedman's expectations-augmented Phillips curve (Chapter 24). Barro and Gordon infer from their model that discretionary monetary regimes will tend to be associated with higher average inflation rates. Accordingly, their policy recommendation is that 'the equilibrium rates of inflation and monetary growth can be lowered by shifts from monetary institutions that allow discretion to ones that enforce rules' (pp.101–2).

An added twist to the plot is that the biggest inflation surprise occurs when the authorities, having established a reputation for being tough on inflation, 'cheat' by expanding the money supply and thereby engineering an increase in the rate of economic growth. Firms and workers are slow to revise their assumption that the authorities are bound by an anti-inflationary rule and therefore fail to adjust their behaviour to take account of the inflation that will eventually ensue. So the monetary growth has a major impact on the real economy, on output and jobs. Of course, this cheating destroys the policy maker's reputation, which can only be restored by another lengthy period of anti-inflationary rectitude, the 'punishment interval'. Repeated interactions of this sort between the policy maker and private agents may reinforce the anti-inflationary rule:

> … it is possible that reputational forces can support the rule. That is, the potential loss of reputation – or credibility – motivates the policymaker to abide by the rule. Then, the policymaker forgoes the short-term benefit from inflation shocks in order to secure the gain from low average inflation over the long term.
>
> *(Barro and Gordon, 1983a, p.102)*

Three possible regimes are distinguished on the basis of this analysis. The preferred strategy is to follow a rule, without cheating, because this yields the lowest average inflation over the long run. It is plausible to see the Bundesbank as a policy maker in this category. The second best strategy is to follow the rule most of the time but to lapse, or cheat, occasionally, which brings the short-term benefits of inflation shocks but at the cost of a higher long-run average inflation rate. In recent years the Fed has approximated this middle position, maintaining the freedom to depart from a tough anti-inflationary rule when the economy is felt to require an expansionary policy stance, but in practice guided by a belief in the importance of containing inflation. The worst scenario is to rely on the policy maker's discretion, because expansionary episodes require higher and higher inflation to surprise private agents. The subservience of the Bank of England and the inconstancy of the authorities seems to place the UK in this situation.

Barro and Gordon present a clear hypothesis which is amenable to empirical testing: a fixed policy rule reduces the average inflation rate over the long term. Policy will be guided by such a rule only if there exists an appropriate institutional framework, and an independent central bank is one obvious constitutional device for guaranteeing firmness of purpose in monetary policy. So it is plausible to interpret Barro and Gordon (1983a) as presenting the hypothesis that an independent central bank will secure the lowest average inflation rate over the long term.

This hypothesis is put to a direct empirical test by Alesina and Summers (1993). The point of ensuring the independence of the central bank is that 'delegating monetary policy to an agent whose preferences are more inflation averse than are society's preferences serves as a commitment device that permits sustaining a lower rate of inflation than would otherwise be possible' (p.151). In so far as high inflation has adverse effects on output, this will improve the growth rate. Furthermore, an independent central bank, by behaving more predictably – that is, in accordance with a fixed rule – might insulate the economy from the political business cycle and reduce partisan shocks to policy following elections (see Chapter 24). Greater stability might reasonably be expected to enhance the rate of economic growth.

The fundamental problem in testing the hypothesis that independent central banks reduce inflation and increase growth is measuring the independence of central banks. Alesina and Summers (1993) use the average of two indices of political independence and economic independence. Political independence is defined as the central bank's ability to set its policy objectives without interference from the government and is measured in terms of:

> factors such as whether or not its governor and the board are appointed by the government, whether government representatives sit on the board of the bank, whether government approval for monetary policy decisions is required and whether the 'price stability' objective is explicitly and prominently part of the central bank statute.
>
> *(Alesina and Summers, 1993, p.153)*

Economic independence is defined as 'the ability to use instruments of monetary policy without restriction' (p.153). The average index of central bank independence is shown in the second column of Table 28.2. Of the large economies, Germany has the most independent central bank.

Table 28.2   **Central bank independence and economic performance**

Country	Average index of central bank independence	Average inflation (%), 1955–88	Average real GNP growth (%), 1955–87
Spain	1.5	8.5	4.2
New Zealand	1.0	7.6	3.0
Australia	2.0	6.4	4.0
Italy	1.75	7.3	4.0
United Kingdom	2.0	6.7	2.4
France	2.0	6.1	3.9
Denmark	2.5	6.5	3.3
Belgium	2.0	4.1	3.1
Norway	2.0	6.1	4.0
Sweden	2.0	6.1	2.9
Canada	2.5	4.5	4.1
Netherlands	2.5	4.2	3.4
Japan	2.5	4.9	6.7
United States	3.5	4.1	3.0
Germany	4.0	3.0	3.4
Switzerland	4.0	3.2	2.7

Source: Alesina and Summers (1993)

A number of measures of economic performance were plotted against the measure of central bank independence. The principal result is that the greater the independence of the central bank, the lower is the average inflation rate for the period 1955–88 (see the third column of Table 28.2, and Figure 28.3).

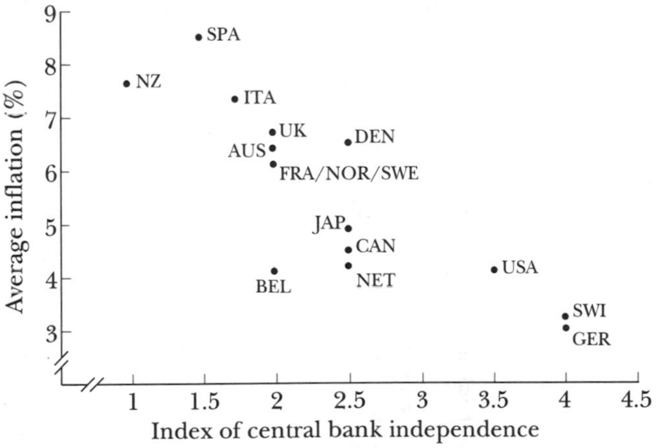

Figure 28.3   **Central bank independence and average inflation, 1955–88**

Source: Alesina and Summers (1993) p.155

The outcome is very different for growth. There is no relation between the degree of independence enjoyed by the central bank and the rate of economic growth (fourth column of Table 28.2). Confirm this by drawing the scatter plot for yourself.

Accordingly, Alesina and Summers (1993) conclude that there is 'some presumption that the inflation benefits of central bank independence are likely to outweigh any output costs' (p.15). Note that this view goes beyond the factual claims about the relations between central bank independence and inflation and growth. Alesina and Summers are making a judgement about the desirability of central bank independence.

This conclusion is rejected, in respect of both the facts about and the desirability of central bank independence, by Epstein (1992). Epstein develops a model of central banking which draws on the ideas of Marx, Keynes and Kalecki which Andrew Trigg introduced in Chapter 25. This 'contested terrain' approach is based on two principles:

1   The state – and hence the central bank – is seen as a terrain of class, and intra-class, conflict.

2   Structural factors such as the structure of the labour market act as a constraint on policy.

In this model, monetary policy is determined by four main factors: capital–labour relations; industry–finance relations; the position of the domestic economy in the world economy; and the degree of central bank independence. Epstein questions both the political and the economic desirability of central bank independence and, in connection with the economic issue, presents evidence which casts doubt on the significance of Alesina and Summers' (1993) finding that central bank independence has no effect on average rates of GNP growth. On the question of political desirability, Epstein (1992, p.2) argues that 'the expanded role of non-democratic central banks seems certain to damage the liberal democratic structure of European and US capitalism'. On the issue of economic desirability, Epstein asks whether independent central banks will impart a 'deflationary bias' to the world economy, trading off growth for lower inflation.

This seems to be a straightforward question of fact. Are independent central banks associated with slower growth, or are they not? Epstein's answer to this question is illustrated in Figure 28.4, which shows that 'more independent central banks tend to be associated with higher GNP gaps' (1992, p.19).

Figure 28.4   **Central bank independence and GNP gaps, 1970–84**

Source: Epstein (1992)

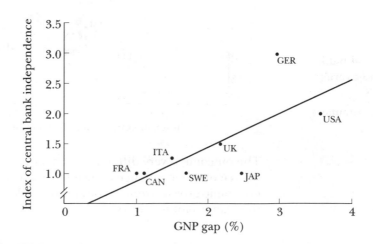

So we do not, after all, have quite the direct conflict of evidence that seemed likely, for two different measures of economic growth performance are being used. While Alesina and Summers (1993) opt for a simple average growth rate over the period 1955–88, Epstein (1992) calculates the output gap for the much shorter period 1970–84. The output gap (see Chapters 17 and 24) measures the shortfall of actual output against potential output and is calculated according to the formula:

$$\text{GNP gap} = \left(\frac{\text{potential GNP}}{\text{actual GNP}} - 1 \right) \times 100$$

It is not possible to say that one interpretation of the phrase 'economic growth performance' is right and the other wrong. However, I think it is reasonable to point out that Alesina and Summers' long period includes much of what Nick Crafts in Chapter 20 refers to as 'the Golden Age'. During this period there were no macroeconomic problems comparable to the oil price shock for central banks, independent or otherwise, to deal with. We might therefore find out more about the difference in approach by focusing more narrowly on difficult times which presented policy makers with a harsher choice. The problem after the oil price rises of 1974 and 1979 was deciding whether to accommodate the inflation that followed in order to keep the economy as close to full employment as possible, or to stifle the inflation with tight monetary policy, whatever the cost in terms of higher unemployment. It is plausible that the previously latent or hidden differences in approach between independent and subservient central banks manifested themselves in systematically different policies. If so, they might be captured by Epstein's (1992) narrower focus, while remaining submerged in Alesina and Summer's (1993) broader historical perspective.

Should central banks be independent? The answer depends upon several factors. It seems to be agreed that independent central banks are associated with lower inflation. So perhaps it is reasonable to conclude that central banks ought to be independent if either there is no output cost of the lower inflation they will achieve, or the benefits of lower inflation outweigh the costs of achieving it. But this latter judgement raises the accountability issue. As Epstein makes clear, an independent central bank is a non-democratic institution. Are we willing to allow a non-elected group of central bank officials to decide on behalf of society as a whole whether reducing inflation is a more urgent priority than encouraging the growth of output and employment?

3   The search for an international monetary system

3.1   Policy co-ordination and exchange rate regimes

How do policy measures taken in one country affect the economy of another? Let me remind you of some of the main ways in which policies can be transmitted across frontiers, which were explained in Chapter 19. I will make two assumptions. First, there is a considerable degree of capital mobility, so that monetary expansion or contraction in one country can affect interest rates in another. Second, prices and wages are 'sticky', or substantially less than perfectly flexible, so that macroeconomic policy can affect real output and not just the price level in the short run.

In a world of capital mobility and sticky prices, domestic policy can have external effects through interest rates and either the balance of payments or exchange rates, depending on the exchange rate system in operation. Take interest rates. A monetary expansion in, say, Japan, reduces domestic interest rates. In so far as capital is internationally mobile, the Japanese money supply constitutes part of the world money supply, so it does the same thing for other national economies too. The further effects of domestic policies depend on the exchange rate system.

For example, under flexible exchange rates, a monetary or fiscal expansion in Japan will, other things being equal, lead to a depreciation of the yen, or, from the point of view of its trading partners, an appreciation of their currencies against the yen. This decline in price competitiveness might cancel out the increase in Japan's demand for imports caused by the monetary expansion. If exchange rates are fixed, the monetary expansion increases Japan's demand for imports and hence real output in other national economies.

To what extent have national policy makers co-ordinated their macroeconomic decision making in response to the effects of the international transmission of policies?

Bretton Woods 1947–73

The Bretton Woods system of international payments was in operation during the 'Golden Age', 'an era of unprecedented sustained economic growth in both developed and developing countries' (Adelman, 1991). During this period the increase in living standards, i.e. in real gross domestic product per head of the population, in OECD economies was 4.9 per cent and averaged 3.3 per cent in developing economies.

Bretton Woods was a system of fixed exchange rates based on the US dollar. Central banks were committed to intervention in the foreign exchange markets to maintain their national currencies within 1 per cent above or below their par value, or central parity, against the US dollar. Par values could be changed only in the event of a 'fundamental disequilibrium' on the balance of payments, a condition that was interpreted sufficiently stringently to make realignments infrequent. Sterling, for example, was devalued only three times, in 1949 and twice in 1967. The Bretton Woods system eventually collapsed in 1973 when member countries pursued incompatible monetary and fiscal policies. This made it impossible to maintain the fixed parities.

Why was Bretton Woods so successful while it lasted? An interesting interpretation is offered by Davidson (1992–3). Keynes argued that traditional exchange rate systems failed because they placed the burden of adjustment on the debtor nations, i.e. those with balance of payments deficits. This led to a deflationary bias, since the solution to a balance of payments deficit under fixed exchange rates is to reduce aggregate demand. In order to avoid releasing persistent deflationary forces on to the global economy, it was necessary to transfer the burden of adjustment from debtor to creditor nations:

> It is characteristic of a freely convertible international standard that it throws the main burden of adjustment on the country which is in the *debtor* position on the international balance of

payments – that is, on the country which is (in this context) by hypothesis the *weaker* and above all the *smaller* in comparison with the other side of the scales which (for this purpose) is the rest of the world.

(Keynes, 1941, p.27)

Under the Bretton Woods system the USA was the major creditor and would have amassed a surplus of international reserves if the burden of adjustment had in fact, and not merely in principle, been placed on debtor nations. The European economies needed to import capital equipment to replace that destroyed during the Second World War. The resulting trade deficits would have led to debts on a scale that could only have been repaid at the cost of a sacrifice of living standards that would have threatened social unrest. However, the USA chose to disburse the surplus through Marshall Aid and other foreign grants and aid to debtor countries.

There is no need to be starry-eyed about US motivation to find some merit in this aid programme. Chomsky (1992), quoting Hogan (1987), argues that the foundation of policy was US planners' vision of a 'Grand Area', a region believed to be 'strategically necessary for world control'. From this perspective the primary motivation for the Marshall plan was the need 'to avert "economic, social and political" chaos in Europe, contain Communism (meaning not Soviet intervention but the success of the indigenous Communist parties), prevent the collapse of America's export trade, and achieve the goal of multilateralism' (Hogan, 1987, pp.42–3, quoted in Chomsky, 1992, p.47).

The point is not to indict US neo-imperialism but to suggest that the success of Bretton Woods is to be explained at least in part as the consequence of a powerful nation's foreign policy ambitions in a particular set of historical circumstances rather than the design features of the prevailing international monetary system. It would be dangerous to assume, as we will see that Davidson (1992–3) seems at times to do, that creating institutions which impose the burden of adjustment on the creditor nation will guarantee an international monetary system conducive to economic growth. Perhaps institutional design cannot compensate for an unwillingness on the part of creditor nations to accept the responsibility for adjustment.

Flexible exchange rates from 1972

The switch to flexible exchange rates meant, by definition, less intervention in the foreign exchange markets, but nevertheless it is best understood as a move from one form of policy co ordination to another: from policy co-ordination through state intervention towards policy co-ordination through the spontaneous order of the market. Policy makers believed that national governments would be able to pursue monetary and fiscal policies designed in response to conditions in their domestic economies, leaving market forces to respond to and in effect co-ordinate the outcomes of these policies through the standard medium of price movements – in this case, changes in exchange rates.

However, relying on exchange rate movements to co-ordinate national economic policies is likely to be hazardous when world capital markets are closely integrated, as they were by the early 1980s. You have already seen that capital flows can generate an uncomfortable degree of volatility in exchange rate movements (Chapter 11, Section 6.2 and Chapter 19, Section 3). As Andrew Stevenson explained in Chapter 19, Section 4.5, in the early 1980s the combination of an expansionary fiscal policy and a tight monetary policy in the USA led to a capital inflow which caused the US dollar to appreciate.

The US dollar's real effective exchange rate (see Chapter 11, Section 6.1 and Chapter 19, Section 2.1) appreciated from 84.7 in 1980 (1982 = 100) to 112.8 in 1985 in response to the tight money/loose fiscal policy mix. In 1985 US fiscal policy was tightened up and the outstanding dollar debt became a source of unease on the foreign exchange markets. By 1989 the dollar had depreciated to a real effective exchange rate of 76.1. This degree of exchange rate volatility is the consequence of capital account or speculative transactions determining market trends. The problem is that exchange rate movements have very different implications for exporting firms and currency speculators. Exporters would prefer exchange rate stability (to eliminate exchange rate risk – see Chapter 19, Section 5), while it is exchange rate volatility that provides opportunities for profitable speculation.

The further effect of flexible exchange rates in the context of integrated world capital markets is to accentuate the global business cycle. When current accounts drive exchange rate movements, countries running deficits have to deflate their economies. These deficits must be reflected in surpluses for other countries, leaving them free to expand their economies. With deficit economies deflating and the others expanding, the global business cycle will be muted. However, when capital accounts drive exchange rate movements, the global business cycle is likely to be accentuated. High interest rates in one country lead to interest rate rises elsewhere in an effort to remain competitive in the struggle for internationally mobile capital.

The consequence is that, far from liberating national monetary and fiscal policies, flexible exchange rates driven by speculative transactions have forced governments into explicitly co-ordinating policies. At the Plaza Accord of 1985 the G5 finance ministers (from the USA, Japan, Germany, France and the UK), agreeing that the US dollar, although already falling, was over-valued, sought to drive it down both by intervention on the foreign exchange market and by changes to macroeconomic policy. It was understood that the USA would adopt a more restrictive fiscal policy while Germany and Japan would follow a more expansionary course. The dollar continued to fall at much the same rate. In 1987 G7 finance ministers (G5 plus Canada and Italy) signed the Louvre Accord, expressing the view that the dollar had fallen far enough and that exchange rates should stay as they were. But the dollar's fall continued into 1988.

International policy co-ordination through the spontaneous order of the market has led in practice to an intolerable degree of exchange rate volatility and hence to explicit efforts at policy co-ordination by national governments, albeit ad hoc and ineffectual.

European monetary union

During the 1980s the currencies of the then EC member states, except the UK, were linked in a fixed exchange rate system, the ERM. The ERM was established to secure monetary stability throughout the EC. This involved, first, keeping exchange rates stable to reduce exchange rate risk, i.e. the chances of a large and sudden exchange rate fluctuation altering the competitiveness of a country's internationally traded output. It was also hoped that ERM membership would oblige member states to reduce their inflation rates through the pursuit of tight monetary and fiscal policies, instead of allowing currency depreciation to offset relative inflation.

In the early 1980s currency realignments were frequent, largely because of inflation rate differentials. But the implementation of tough disinflationary measures by France in 1983 introduced some stability into the ERM. Realignments became less frequent and anti-inflationary domestic policies were widely adopted. The Bundesbank's anti-inflation credibility helped the Deutschmark to emerge as the anchor of the ERM in this period. By the late 1980s the removal of capital controls and the prospect of EMU (see Chapters 14 and 19) had combined to secure a period of tranquillity inside the ERM.

However, turmoil returned to the foreign exchange markets in the early 1990s. German reunification led to a fiscal expansion accompanied by higher interest rates, with the consequence that interest rates had to be raised elsewhere to protect weaker currencies from speculative pressures. A misguided decision on the central parity compounded the difficulties for sterling, which had joined the ERM in 1990, and its membership was suspended in 1992. In the second half of 1993 the ERM itself was virtually in abeyance, the bands having been widened from 2.25 per cent to 15 per cent either side of the central parity.

Policy co-ordination and exchange rate regimes

What conclusions can be drawn about policy co-ordination and exchange rate regimes? The fate of fixed and flexible exchange rate systems alike seems to depend on the role played by the most powerful participant economy.

The success of Bretton Woods had less to do with intrinsic design features than with the historical circumstances of the cold war. The major creditor nation recycled surpluses for political reasons.

The switch to flexible rates encountered difficulties in the context of international capital mobility and the consequent preponderance of speculative transactions over the current account of the balance of payments. Exchange rate volatility reached unacceptable levels as the largest economy in the system in effect exported its domestic policy imbalance.

The ERM calmed the exchange rates of EC members for a while because, after the French franc crisis of 1983, macroeconomic policies were co-ordinated. But once German fiscal policy was forced out of step with the rest by the exigencies of reunification (and, to some degree, policy misjudgements), the system virtually collapsed.

So it seems that no fixed exchange rate regime has been strong enough to impose macroeconomic policy co-ordination on participant economies, and flexible rates have failed to act as a substitute for formal policy co-ordination. Policy co-ordination has to come first, and while it lasts exchange rate fluctuations can be confined within tolerable limits. The irony is that the circumstances that would make it possible for a fixed exchange rate system to work also suggest that it would not be needed, for the same set of circumstances would make it unlikely that flexible exchange rates would exhibit disquieting fluctuations.

On the other hand, it is arguable that the desire to preserve a fixed exchange rate system gives greater urgency to the co-ordination of macroeconomic policies before speculative pressures build up an irresistible momentum. Can this motive be reinforced by formal, institutionalized arrangements, perhaps even incorporating sanctions? Is there a role in such a formal system for the reintroduction of capital controls or other curbs on speculation? And how can the responsibility for adjustment be placed on creditor nations as much as on deficit countries? These are some of the questions to be investigated in Section 3.2.

3.2   An international monetary system for the twenty-first century?

The aim of this section is to compare three proposals for reforming the world's monetary system: a fixed exchange rate system for the three major economies; a system of target zones rather than the narrow bands of conventional fixed exchange rate regimes; and a system which attempts to recreate in formal institutional arrangements the successful formula 'stumbled upon' by Bretton Woods, by placing the burden of adjustment on creditor nations.

McKinnon's fixed nominal exchange rate system

McKinnon (1988) proposed a system of fixed nominal exchange rates based on purchasing power parities for the major world economies, i.e. the USA, Japan and Germany. If the EU member states proceed with Maastricht all the way to European monetary union, McKinnon's system would apply to the USA, Japan and the EU. The proposal calls for fixed nominal exchange rates within a narrow band, with the domestic macroeconomic policies of the three participants subordinated to defending those 'sustainable purchasing power parities'. The PPP exchange rate, introduced by Andrew Stevenson in Chapter 19, is the exchange rate that would equalize the purchasing power of a unit of one currency in two countries by offsetting differences between their domestic price levels. The result is that, under McKinnon's fixed exchange rate regime, £1 would buy the same basket of goods in any country in the system – that is, there would be purchasing power parity between currencies. A country's PPP exchange rate could change only if its domestic price level changed relative to those of other members of the exchange rate system. So PPP exchange rates would be determined, at least in the long run, by inflation rates (rather than, for example, speculative pressures). McKinnon's proposal implies that member countries would be committing themselves not only to defending fixed nominal exchange rates but also to maintaining a common inflation rate. The US, Japanese and EU central banks would be instructed to 'adjust their domestic money supplies to maintain these nominal exchange rate parities and, concomitantly, maintain the same rates of domestic price inflation in internationally tradable goods' (McKinnon, 1988, p.87). The outcome, McKinnon believes, would be an end to the exchange rate turbulence that disrupted international trade in the 1980s.

McKinnon's proposal is based on the monetarist model of the economy. In this model, changes in the money supply affect output and employment in the short run, causing business cycles, as Andrew Trigg explained in Chapter 25. In the long run, however, changes in the money supply and hence aggregate demand have no effect on output and employment; the long-run aggregate supply curve is vertical (see Chapters 18 and 24).

How can the authorities respond to an external shock when monetary policy is subordinated to defending a fixed exchange rate? McKinnon's solution is based on the competitive model of the macroeconomy, outlined by Mary Gregory in Chapter 18. Suppose that the economy suffers a loss of export markets. The real exchange rate depreciation that is needed to sustain output and employment is unobtainable.

Question

Is there any other way in which the economy, according to the competitive model, might adjust to the adverse supply shock?

The fall in demand for exports leads to a fall in demand for labour. In a competitive labour market, this causes real wages to fall to maintain unemployment at its natural rate. If McKinnon's system has led member economies to converge on price stability, money wage cuts will be necessary.

Once the purchasing power parity rates have been fixed, they will never need to be changed, provided each central bank adheres to its monetary rule, because even real or supply-side shocks cannot have any impact on the full employment level of real output.

So we cannot evaluate McKinnon's proposal in isolation from the monetarist research programme as a whole, including the assumption of competitive markets.

Williamson's target zones for fixed real exchange rates

Williamson and Miller (1987) proposed a system of target zones for the real effective exchange rates of a limited number of major currencies. The zones would permit currencies to move 10 per cent either side of their central parities, the width of these bands reflecting an acknowledgement of the impossibility of calculating central parities with any degree of precision. These parities would be fundamental equilibrium exchange rates (FEERs), where each currency's FEER is defined as the exchange rate which allows the economy to be in both internal and external balance. The initial parities would be open to occasional adjustments in response to supply shocks or inflation differentials.

National governments would be committed to well-defined rules regarding both monetary and fiscal policies, aimed at restricting the growth of nominal domestic demand to the rate consistent with internal and external balance. Williamson's definition of external balance as 'a current account balance that is sustainable and appropriate in the light of thrift and productivity' (Williamson, 1992–3, p.202) is problematic because there are doubts about what exactly is being introduced by the use of the value-laden term 'thrift'. His definition of internal balance as 'the lowest unemployment rate consistent with control of inflation' (p.202) is more openly controversial, since here Williamson is relying on the concept of the NAIRU (see Chapter 18, Section 5.2) and therefore effectively giving priority to the control of inflation over the pursuit of full employment.

Williamson's strategy is essentially to update the Bretton Woods system to repair what he sees as its main faults. The first was the absence of the 'limited exchange rate flexibility' that would have allowed the system to endure in the face of supply shocks and speculative crises. The second was its bias towards accelerating inflation due to the failure to recognize the concept of the NAIRU.

The theoretical framework supporting Williamson's proposal is an 'eclectic view of macroeconomic theory that combines short-run Keynesian truths with the long-run reality of the neutrality of money' (p.182). Later, he explains that the 'intellectual origins of these proposals clearly lie in the interwar work of Keynes ... modified to take into account the vertical long-run Phillips curve' (p.186).

So, as with McKinnon's monetarism, an evaluation of Williamson's proposed international monetary system involves a consideration of the theory or model of the world economy on which it is based. But notice the new twist to the argument. Williamson clearly regards competing Keynesian and monetarist theoretical frameworks as sufficiently fluid to permit combining elements from each into a novel eclectic model which is neither purely Keynesian nor purely monetarist. Moreover, there seems to be an underlying assumption that there is such a thing as scientific progress in economics: 'I count myself among those economists comfortable in recommending policies based on the best theories and evidence currently available, rather than a purist who insists in principle on total certainty and logical consistency' (Williamson, 1992–3, p.191). What I think this means for Williamson is that there is a coherent body of macroeconomic theory in which progress is made by using monetarist insights to refine the original Keynesian foundation.

Davidson's plan for an international money clearing unit

Davidson's proposal is to establish an international money-clearing unit (IMCU) to fulfil two functions of money in international trade: those of a unit of account and a medium of exchange. IMCUs would be used in a clearing institution 'to keep the payments score among the various trading nations plus some mutually agreed upon rules to create and reflux liquidity while preserving the international purchasing power of the international currency' (p.158).

IMCUs would be held only by central banks and would be convertible into domestic currencies, initially at a rate chosen by each nation and therefore – to avoid disruption to trade – based on the existing exchange rate structure. The exchange rate between each domestic currency and the IMCU would be fixed, changing only to reflect permanent increases in real unit labour costs. In this way the long-term purchasing power of the IMCU would be stabilized.

An innovative feature of the IMCU system is its incorporation of a trigger mechanism to encourage creditor nations to spend credit balances accumulated from running current account surpluses once they have reached levels agreed in advance to be excessive. Creditor nations could spend these surpluses in three ways:

- by buying goods produced by other members of the system;
- by undertaking direct foreign investment projects; and
- by making transfers (foreign aid) to deficit members.

In these ways the burden of adjustment would be placed on creditor nations, with the aim of avoiding the deflationary bias which Davidson, following Keynes, believes to be the major design fault of traditional fixed exchange rate systems.

There are two features which differentiate Davidson's proposal from those of McKinnon and Williamson. The first is the theoretical framework which informs the IMCU system. McKinnon and Williamson believe that the free market economy will achieve equilibrium at full employment or at least the natural rate of unemployment – admittedly, for Williamson only in the long run. Davidson, however, does not believe that free market economies show any tendency either in the short run or the long run towards full employment equilibrium.

The second distinctive feature is that only Davidson addresses the problems of less developed countries (LDCs), seeking to change '*the arbitrary and inequitable international distribution of income and wealth*' (p.177, original emphasis). A principal objective of the IMCU system is to guarantee a level of world aggregate demand consistent with full employment in LDCs. Placing the responsibility for adjustment on creditor nations is also intended to stimulate foreign direct investment in and unilateral transfers to LDCs.

This difference between McKinnon and Williamson on the one hand and Davidson on the other introduces another new twist to the argument. It had seemed that their proposals could simply be understood as competing solutions to the same problem, but it is now clear that they do not agree on what the problem is. Only Davidson defines the problem to include the issue of the global distribution of income and wealth, and only the IMCU system has any place for LDCs. So different economists see 'the problem' in different ways, which presumably reflect their different moral and political values.

This calls into question the idea of scientific progress in economics, for it suggests that we cannot necessarily assume that different theories which apparently address the same problem actually interpret it in the same way. The situation is more complicated than a choice, based on agreed criteria, among several rival routes to an agreed destination. The diversity of theories might be grounded in something deeper than the choice of the best means to a common end. Perhaps the idea of a plurality of theoretical frameworks eventually converging on a single right way of doing economics must be abandoned? Perhaps another metaphor is more apt, that of a conversation reflecting intrinsically different and equally sustainable viewpoints.

So a question that arises from this comparison of three proposals for reforming the international monetary system concerns the nature of economic reasoning itself. How should we interpret the activities of economists?

4
Macroeconomics, methodology and postmodernism

The question at the end of the last section concerns the methodology of economics: that part of the discipline devoted to the study of how economists seek to understand and explain economic events, processes, behaviour and institutions. Methodological debate draws on a branch of philosophy known as epistemology or the theory of knowledge. An assumption made by many epistemologists is that there exist foundations of knowledge: certain distinguishing features shared by the products of successful scientific investigations. If so, we can ask whether the theories put forward by economists satisfy these criteria and hence can be accepted as scientific knowledge. The question of whether economics is a science can therefore be interpreted as the question of whether the testing of theories in economics has access to the same foundations of knowledge as the testing of theories in, say, physics.

Lying behind this debate is an anxiety that economics, as a social science, might be distorted by political or ideological bias in a way that prevents it from attaining the objectivity of the disciplines everyone agrees to be scientific. Economists might be unable to resist the temptation to drop the disinterested pursuit of truth in favour of the rhetorical devices of political debate. The standard defence against this is the idea that it is possible to define an economic method which has enough in common with the natural sciences for economics properly to be regarded as a science. This idea is summed up in the phrase 'positive economics'. In this section I want to discuss three principles which I think define the concept of positive economics, and to consider the degree to which the products and procedures of economic reasoning exemplify these principles. It is beyond the scope of this section to argue for a definite answer to this question, but I hope it will be possible to give you an idea of the main issues it raises, and of some of the positions which economists and philosophers have defended.

4.1   Can economic theories be tested against observations of the real world?

The first principle of positive economics is that:

> The claim that economics is scientific stands or falls ... on the claim that economists can improve their ability to understand and predict events in the real world by stating theories, subjecting the theories to the test of real-world observations and by improving the theories in the light of what is learned thereby.
>
> *(Lipsey, 1989, p.15)*

This statement about the scientific status of positive economics contains two assumptions which might be questioned. Lipsey claims that it is possible to confront a theory directly with a set of observations of the 'real world'. This assumes, first, that theories can be subjected to empirical testing of a potentially decisive nature. A particular theory is tested against a set of observations and, if necessary, improved. But the discussion of McKinnon's proposal for a fixed nominal exchange rate system suggested some problems. McKinnon's argument does not constitute a *particular* theory that can be evaluated in isolation from the larger theoretical perspective or research programme from which it draws its methodological principles and fundamental assumptions. And the idea that the larger perspective can be decisively tested against real-world observations faces the problem that it takes more than one set of observations to undermine confidence in a theoretical framework.

The second assumption is that the real world exists as something apart from the theory of it that economists are trying to assess. This assumption is challenged by the argument that what we take to be reality depends on the way we select from and organize the mass of appearances presented to us by our senses. This is the nominalist conception of economic modelling introduced by Grahame Thompson in Chapter 2, where it is contrasted with realism. The metaphor that realism draws upon is that of stamping or imprinting: the real world actively imprints its contours on our passive senses. The nominalist approach regards our senses and our minds as active, bringing organizing principles and theories to bear on the chaos of appearances. We construct reality. A clear example from economic reasoning is provided by Wendy Olsen in Chapter 9.

Question

Do you see a connection between the nominalist interpretation of economic modelling and Wendy Olsen's critical comments in Chapter 9, Section 2 on the positivist assumptions that underlie much official data collection?

The difficulty is that the observations of the real world are themselves informed by the theoretical perspective we are seeking to test. Does the real world include economies which display a tendency, perhaps evident only in the long run, towards equilibrium? Is money neutral in that world? The observations monetarists would accept as relevant to the assessment of McKinnon's proposal are not 'raw' data or 'brute' facts. They are, and have to be, selected and organized according to the central principles of the monetarist research programme. Showing that fixed nominal exchange rates would have undesirable effects in a 'real' world where money is not neutral would cut no ice with monetarists.

This does not mean that we should jump to the conclusion that economic theories cannot be evaluated at all. We must continue to test theoretical arguments against empirical data, while bearing in mind that empirical tests of broad frameworks frequently prove inconclusive.

Exercise 28.2

Now turn to Chapter 25, Section 6 (don't worry – it's only a page!).

1   Why does Andrew Trigg believe that his empirical testing of four theories of the business cycle has proved inconclusive?

2   Why does he think that further testing might tell us more about the explanatory power of each theory?

3   What other criterion for judging these theories does he suggest?

4.2   Does the history of economic thought display scientific progress?

The second principle of positive economics, already hinted at in the quotation that illustrated the first principle, is that scientific progress is possible in economics. The basic idea is that testing theories against observations makes it possible to improve them. Perhaps there is nothing exceptionable in that, but it tends to be elaborated into a more ambitious, and more controversial, claim. This further argument is that economics makes progress by extending and enriching a standard model to cover new and initially puzzling phenomena. In connection with the stagflation of the 1970s, Lipsey (1989, p.774) comments as follows: 'Such was the pace of theoretical and empirical research ... that within a very few years, the phenomenon of stagflation was explained by, and incorporated into, conventional macro models'.

The assumption here is that macroeconomics is a coherent body of knowledge – a set of conventional macro models – which can be endlessly refined in the light of new observations. True, the existence of competing theoretical perspectives is not overlooked. But they, too, are seen as contributing to the advancement of economic knowledge. They provide opportunities and resources for scientific progress, through the use of insights originating in one perspective to improve the ability of another to withstand empirical testing. Williamson's eclecticism is an example. Those who believe in scientific progress tend to think that ultimately economics will converge on a single research programme. Or perhaps the view is that there already is one, with any alternative to the conventional or mainstream theoretical perspective being dismissed as 'more of a state of mind than a serious research programme' (Rogers, 1993, p.1318).

The idea of progress to ultimate convergence on a single paradigm presupposes a foundations theory of knowledge. Particular modes of thinking, such as the discipline of economics, are applications to a specific area of human experience of very general principles of thought which constitute the foundations of all knowledge. The task of a relatively new discipline like economics is to grope its way towards a set of methodological guidelines which can be verified by tracing their origins in the foundations of knowledge. As economists realize that some theoretical perspectives cannot be warranted in this way, they will discard them one by one until only the truly rational or scientific method is left.

This idea of narrowing the focus of inquiry through a single method or perspective is typical of modernism, a cultural movement particularly characteristic of the early twentieth century out of which positive economics emerged. The alternative image of an array of competing 'ways of seeing' is typical of postmodernist thought. In economics the leading proponent of the latter perspective is Donald McCloskey, whose ideas on rhetoric, analogy and metaphor were introduced by Grahame Thompson in Chapter 2. Postmodernism is a trend of thought or intellectual fashion or even a 'spirit of the age', not a tightly knit group of thinkers with an agreed manifesto. But there are certainly some common threads running through most postmodernist writing which imply that there is no single right way of doing economics, a doctrine known as methodological pluralism.

Postmodernism, as the name implies, is best understood as a reaction to modernism, which is summed up (perhaps too succinctly) by McCloskey as follows:

> Round about 1920 in the West certain philosophers came to believe that their subject could be narrowed down to an artificial language; certain architects came to believe their whole subject could be narrowed to a cube; certain painters came to believe that their whole subject could be narrowed to a surface. Out of this narrowness was supposed to come insight and certitude.
>
> *(McCloskey, 1990, p.5)*

The philosophers referred to by McCloskey were known as 'the Vienna circle', from the place where they discussed philosophy, or as 'logical positivists', from the nature of their doctrines. That is why, when those ideas reached economics around 1950, they were formalized as positive economics. McCloskey's argument is that modernism – and hence positive economics – is not exactly wrong, but rather too narrow a conception of rational thought whether in scientific inquiry or artistic endeavour.

The discussion in Section 2.4 of some recent research into the comparative macroeconomic performance of economies under independent central banks is an illustration of methodological pluralism. The 'official' line, which clearly exemplifies a positivist style of thought, assumes that price stability is the supreme goal of macroeconomic policy and that central bankers are impartial experts on the technical question of how to achieve it. However, one model of central banking in an international context takes a radically different line on the desirability of central bank independence, from a point of view which gives a much higher priority to issues concerning the distribution of income and wealth. This alternative view draws on the 'contested terrain' model of central banking, which disaggregates the capitalist class into finance and industry, and presents the central bank as the terrain of intra-class as well as inter-class conflict. Accordingly, the policy of the central bank in such models depends upon the relative power of finance, industry and labour (Epstein, 1992). Perhaps there will continue to be a diversity of incompatible schools of thought in economics as long as within society there are different social groups with conflicting interests.

This alternative image of incompatible viewpoints calls into question the idea of objective expert knowledge. Competing theoretical frameworks seem particularly likely to persist, furthermore, where they are associated with different values which people hold. It is time to consider the third principle of positive economics.

Exercise 28.3

Look back to Chapter 18, Section 5.1. Does anything Mary Gregory says about the New Keynesian and New Classical approaches strike you as an obstacle to their eventual convergence into a single perspective on macroeconomics?

4.3   Do economic policy recommendations necessarily reflect subjective value judgements?

The third principle of positive economics is moral scepticism, expressed in the pair of statements below:

> *Positive economics* deals with objective or scientific explanations of the working of the economy.
> *Normative economics* offers prescriptions or recommendations based on personal value judgements.
>
> *(Begg, Fischer and Dornbusch, 1991, p.10)*

Underpinning this distinction is the idea that personal value judgements are merely subjective tastes which cannot be changed by rational argument or scientific inquiry and so cannot belong to the body of human knowledge. Their inferior epistemological status is captured by their description by some positivist economists and philosophers as 'wishful thinking'. The implication is that value judgements can only distort scientific investigation.

Can this sharp distinction between positive and normative economics be maintained? Positive economics, its proponents argue, is a collection of factual statements about the way in which the economy works, which can reasonably claim the status of scientific knowledge. Their objectivity is protected by their being demarcated very sharply from normative economics, in which personal value judgements give rise to proposals about how we would like the economy to work. While this distinction may seem attractive, it has some unfortunate implications. In particular, I want to suggest that it tends to reduce choices among policy recommendations to matters of tastes.

I think you will see what I mean if I sketch in a bit of background in moral philosophy. The distinction between positive statements and normative judgements is characteristic of a certain interpretation of reason and of the scope for rational thought. This is the instrumental conception of reason, according to which subjective or personal feelings provide us with wants, needs or desires, while reason gives us the means to achieve them. The eighteenth-century Scottish philosopher David Hume, a friend of Adam Smith's, put it rather memorably: 'Reason is, and ought only to be, the slave of the passions, and can never pretend to any other office than to serve and obey them' (Hume, 1906, Book II, Chapter iii, pp.414–15).

The passions dictate to us what we want and reason tells us how to get it. For example, your 'passions', inflamed no doubt by advertising, might tell you that you must have the new fragrance from Karl Lagerfeld or some item of men's grooming from Aramis – reason does not come into wanting such things. Rational thinking shows you how to get what you want in the world as it is. So, when it comes to understanding the world – for instance the way in which the economy works – reason, in the shape of scientific investigation, can in principle come up with a picture of how things really or objectively are, whether we like them that way or not. Provided economists remain within the bounds of the positive, their advice deserves to be treated as expert knowledge and the conduct of monetary policy will be no less scientific an endeavour than the generation and control of electricity.

However, this instrumental interpretation of positive economics is increasingly being seen as problematic. Positive economics attained its pre-eminence in the discipline at a time when there was probably a greater degree of consensus than exists today over the ultimate ends of economic activity. In the 'Golden Age' of 1950–73, not only was trend GNP growth in the OECD countries higher than it is today, but there also seems to have been less questioning of GNP growth as the supreme goal of economic policy. Concerns about environmental pollution and non-renewable resource depletion were less prominent in public debate. In such circumstances interpreting value judgements as expressions of subjective feelings was unlikely to 'destabilize' the objectivity of knowledge, since there were broad areas of agreement on values.

By contrast, the discussion in Section 3 of Davidson's proposed IMCU revealed that values entered into the definition of the policy problem. The differences between Davidson's IMCU proposal and the international monetary systems advocated by McKinnon and Williamson include a difference in value judgements about the issue of the world distribution of income and wealth. From the perspective of positive economics, the proposals to reform the world monetary system cannot therefore be regarded as competing scientific solutions to the same problem. From within that perspective, the choice among them cannot be determined by scientific principles, but is ultimately a matter of value judgements. If these judgements in turn are wholly personal or subjective, as the moral scepticism inherent in positive economics insists that all value judgements are, then economic debate is constructed upon highly subjective foundations which are not themselves amenable to rational debate.

We might be willing to accept this conclusion. The radical wing of postmodernism, exemplified by the French philosopher Derrida, among others, argues that each one of us creates his or her own reality and that there is no criterion for judging one reality to be better or more authentic than any other. A central theme of this tradition of postmodernist thought is 'the celebration of fragmentation, particularity and difference' (Squires, 1993, p.2). Postmodernism is an expression of a culture in which something approaching a consensus over values has been replaced by a number of competing views about the desirability of different kinds of economic activity, perhaps reflecting ethnic, gender, age, regional and class differences among people. If at the extreme there are as many 'realities' as there are individuals, what counts as economic knowledge in my world might not do so in yours.

Curiously, therefore, too sharp a distinction between positive and normative, reason and passion, threatens to open the door to a radical subjectivism. This in turn seems to confront us with an unappealing dilemma. Either we defend positive economics as a discipline relevant to policy at the expense of installing a single set of values as the 'right' one, or we acknowledge the heterogeneity of values at the expense of rational policy debate. My instinct is that something must have gone wrong if we find ourselves facing such unattractive choices. The problem seems to me to lie in the instrumental conception of reason, and the assumption behind it that normative judgements are personal or subjective in a sense that places them beyond the reach of rational reflection.

This interpretation of reason simply does not, I suggest, do justice to situations of moral conflict, reflection and uncertainty with which I think most people are familiar. It fails to distinguish between subjective tastes, such as a liking for toffee fudge ice cream, and moral principles, such as loyalty, responsibility, sympathy or a sense of duty. Every motive or desire, every spring of action, is regarded as a 'passion', a subjective feeling. This seems to me to restrict excessively the scope of reasoned argument and critical reflection in human affairs. For we *do* revise our normative judgements, and even our feelings about moral matters, in the light of experience. Consider, for example, the discussion of begging which opens Chapter 22.

Reflection

What was your immediate emotional reaction if you recently met someone begging? Can you imagine finding out some new information that would lead you to feel differently about the person, and perhaps to revise any moral judgements or 'policy prescriptions' you might have formed?

I think it is quite easy to do so. You might imagine being jolted out of your first unsympathetic reaction by a story of catastrophic misfortune or injustice or, on the other hand, having second thoughts about your first generous impulse after learning of laziness or other sources of income.

Chapter 22 also contained a discussion of *laissez-faire* (in Section 4.3) which I want to use to illustrate how our feelings about moral issues are typically based on assumptions concerning matters of fact. Let us suppose that I take the view that government intervention in the economy should be kept to a minimum. It is possible to hold this principle dogmatically, in a 'whatever the consequences' frame of mind. But it is equally possible to be circumspect in one's commitment to this normative principle and to revise it in the light of new information. I might take it for granted that a free market economy will lead to the highest possible level of GNP per head without increasing the degree of inequality. If a policy of *laissez-faire* opens a much bigger gap between rich and poor than anyone had expected, I might *feel* differently about it. I might qualify my commitment to the principle of minimum government intervention. Our feelings about moral questions can be modified by reasoned argument on the basis of new information.

This gives normative judgements something in common with economic theories: both are susceptible to revision after we confront them with data or evidence or experience. I am not saying that we put our economic theories to the test of experience in the same way as we revise our moral principles in the light of experience. I am suggesting that the relation between economic theories and normative judgements is too subtle and complicated to be captured by a simple dichotomy between objective knowledge and subjective feelings, between reason and the passions. Our normative judgements and even our feelings about moral issues are subject to critical reflection as a kind of 'testing' in a way that our subjective tastes are not.

Amartya Sen has argued for the importance of a 'careful assessment of aims, objectives, allegiances, etc., and of the conception of the good' (Sen, 1987, p.42). In order to illustrate the 'careful assessment' characteristic of moral reasoning, I want to consider a hypothetical example based on Sen (1976). Suppose that you are promoted by your transnational employer to manage a salmon farm in a country run by a regime which tortures its political opponents. Soon after you get there, you become deeply uneasy at the disappearance, presumably to face torture and death, of people you know. You consider the options which seem to be open to you: return home; continue to manage the farm; join a non-violent campaign for the release of political prisoners; or work for the violent overthrow of the regime. You might try to calculate what it is in your own interest to do and rank the options as in column 1 of Table 28.3. But should self-interest be your guiding principle? You try another ranking, based on your conception of what would be the 'most moral' thing to do (column 2). Can you live up to such a rigorous moral code? A careful assessment of your past behaviour, the likely consequences of the different courses of action, and your capacity for moral and physical courage leaves you in little doubt that your actual decision will reflect the ranking shown in column 3.

Table 28.3   **Ranking moral choices**

(1)	(2)	(3)
Self-interest	**Most moral**	**Actual**
Manage farm	Non-violence	Return home
Return home	Armed struggle	Manage farm
Non-violence	Return home	Non-violence
Armed struggle	Manage farm	Armed struggle

Nevertheless, you are aware that a person of greater moral courage would join a non-violent campaign for the release of the political prisoners. This suggests that moral choices prompt us into more than a process of critical reasoning and self-examination leading to alternative rankings of the four options. We may also rank the rankings themselves, perhaps in the order 2, 3, 1.

The idea that the scope of reason is confined to the discovery of reliable means to ends determined solely by subjective feelings therefore seems to me to be too narrow. Reason is also concerned with bringing our beliefs, experiences, feelings and values into some sort of harmony or coherence. In that case we can begin to work out a role for values or normative judgements in economics without compromising its claim to be a systematic and rational form of inquiry.

Exercise 28.4

Chapter 22, Section 4.2 contains a brief discussion of the views on equality of Nozick, Rawls and Sen.

1   Can you find in that discussion any evidence for the view that a commitment to equality might be a subjective taste?

2   Do any of the points considered there suggest to you that a commitment to equality might be a matter of principle and as such amenable to reasoned argument and critical reflection?

5   Conclusion

I have tried to keep two storylines running through this chapter, one about the interdependence of national economies and the scope for policy co-ordination, and the other about the methodology of economics or the nature of economic theorizing. Two areas of policy co-ordination have been discussed. First, the independence of central banks might make national monetary policies more uniformly anti-inflationary, but at the cost of sacrificing other macroeconomic objectives such as growth or full employment. There is also a loss of democratic accountability, which may appear rapidly if electorates are less averse to inflation or more averse to unemployment than policy makers. Secondly, three alternative reforms of the world financial system reflect differences in policy objectives as well as in theoretical frameworks. Should the world's monetary system be designed to achieve financial stability alone or to go further and aim to secure full employment in LDCs?

These two discussions of macroeconomic policy co-ordination raised doubts about the reasonableness of interpreting economics as a source of 'beneficent techniques of scientific control', to use the phrase quoted from Keynes in the Introduction to this chapter. It suggested that value judgements and choice of theoretical frameworks are closely interlinked. I went on to argue, however, that value judgements should not be seen as beyond the scope of critical reflection. Economic theory is deeply influenced by the demands of economic policy, and the future development of economics will contain much debate on the proper links between theory, politics and moral values.

ANSWERS TO EXERCISES

Chapter 1

Exercise 1.1

The increase from 1970 to 1973 is 22.15% in total, or 6.90% on average per year (each to the nearest two decimal places).

Exercise 1.2

$$1\% \quad = \frac{1}{100} = \text{one-hundredth} = 0.01$$

$$7\% \quad = \frac{7}{100} = \text{seven-hundredths} = 0.07$$

$$50\% \quad = \frac{50}{100} = \text{one-half} = 0.5$$

$$55\% \quad = \frac{55}{100} = \text{eleven-twentieths} = 0.55$$

$$120\% \quad = \frac{120}{100} = \text{one and one-fifth} = 1.2$$

$$250\% \quad = \frac{250}{100} = \text{two and a half} = 2.5$$

12% of 4000 = 480

70% of 4000 = 2800

135% of 4000 = 5400.

Exercise 1.3

In five years, that is in Y_6, the income per head will be:

$$Y_1(1 + r)^5 = 12\,000\,(1 + 0.03)^5 = 12\,000(1.03)^5 = 12\,000 \times 1.159274 = 13\,911.29$$

or approximately $13\,900.

Chapter 2

Exercise 2.1

$$\frac{\text{US}\$163\,500\text{m}}{7.8\text{m}} = \text{US}\$20\,962$$

Exercise 2.2

$$\frac{\pounds430\text{m}}{107.5} \times 100 = \pounds400\text{m}$$

Thus there would have been no change in real GDP. The apparent (nominal) increase would have been purely the result of inflation.

Exercise 2.3

$$\frac{£574\,146m}{140.5} \times 100 = £408\,645m \text{ (rounded)}$$

This is not quite the same figure as in Table 2.2: it is about £80m out because of rounding errors.

Exercise 2.4

Income is a flow, while population is a stock. This makes it difficult to be too definitive about measures of per capita income.

Exercise 2.5

£574 146m − £83 023m + £5878m = £497 001m

Exercise 2.6

1   £497 329m + £77 340m − £77 668m = £497 001m

2   It indicates that UK nationals earned more income abroad than foreign nationals earned in the UK.

Exercise 2.7

1   $C = 90.76$; $I' = 41.54$; $I'' = 1.91$; $G = 29.77$; $X = 67.63$; $H = 66.15$; net exports = +1.48; GDP = 165.46 (all figures US$ billion).

Exercise 2.8

Your completed table should read as follows:

Table 2.8 (completed)

Expenditure		Income	
Consumers' expenditure	367.9	Income from employment	329.8
General government final consumption	121.9	Income from self-employment	57.5
Gross domestic fixed capital formation	95.4	Gross trading profits of companies	60.7
Value of physical increases in stocks	−5.3	Gross trading surplus of public corporations	3.1
Total domestic expenditures	579.9	Gross trading surplus of government enterprises	0.1
Exports of goods and services	135.1	Rent	44.1
less Imports of goods and services	−140.4	Imputed change for consumption of non-trading capital	4.5
Statistical discrepancy	−0.4	Total domestic income	499.8
GDP at market prices	574.1	*less* Stock appreciation	−2.8
Adjustment to factor cost	77.1	Statistical discrepancy	—
GDP at factor cost	497.0	GDP at factor cost	497.0

Chapter 3

Exercise 3.1

Consumers' expenditure will be £20 001 million, £30 001 million and £40 001 million respectively.

Exercise 3.2

Examples of 'inferior goods' might include the following:

Developed world	Third World
Black and white televisions	Basic foodstuffs such as rice and millet
Public transport	Bicycles
Public housing	Traditional forms of housing
Matches	

Exercise 3.3

The independent variables mentioned are the price of meat, the prices of substitutes like fish, income level, and the desire for a healthy diet.

Exercise 3.4

Your completed table should read as follows:

Table 3.5 (completed) **Shifts in the demand curve for strawberries**

Change in variable	Effect on demand curve
Decrease in national income.	Decrease in demand for strawberries at all prices. Demand curve shifts to left.
Increase in national income.	Increase in demand for strawberries at all prices. Demand curve shifts to right.
Rise in price of substitute goods (e.g. raspberries, or cherries).	Demand curve shifts to right.
Fall in price of substitute goods.	Demand curve shifts to left.
Rise in price of complementary goods (e.g. cream).	Demand curve shifts to left
Fall in price of complementary goods.	Demand curve shifts to right
Change in socio-economic preferences in favour of strawberries (e.g. advertising campaign).	Demand curve shifts to right.
Change in socio-economic preferences away from strawberries (e.g. due to pollution of crops).	Demand curve shifts to left.

Exercise 3.5

Factors leading to an increase in demand for owner-occupied housing during the 1980s: relatively high inflation, availability of credit (due to financial deregulation), cuts in subsidies to public sector housing, tax concessions for owner-occupiers, subsidies for council house buyers.

Factors leading to a decline in demand at the start of the 1990s: falling incomes, rising unemployment rates throughout the country, high interest rates leading to high mortgage repayments, young households unable to afford to purchase, forced sales.

Chapter 4

Exercise 4.1

1   The production function summarizes the relationship between inputs and outputs. For a given state of technology it shows the maximum output that can be produced from different combinations of inputs.

2   In the context of firms' production activities, division of labour means the dividing up of any work process into specialized activities undertaken by different people in order to increase the quantity of output available from given inputs.

3   The short run is the period in which not all factors of production are variable. The long run, in contrast, is the period in which all factors of production can be varied.

Exercise 4.2

1   The long-run average cost curve (see Figure 4.9) shows the lowest unit costs that can be obtained at all the relevant levels of output. This can be thought of as representing the optimum combination of factors of production.

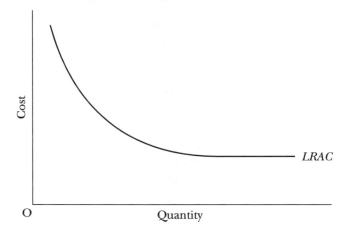

Figure 4.9   **The long-run average cost curve**

2   Short-run average costs differ from long-run average costs because in the short run some factors of production are fixed in quantity.

3   See Figure 4.10. $SRAC_n$ indicates that there are many short-run average cost curves bounded by the *LRAC*.

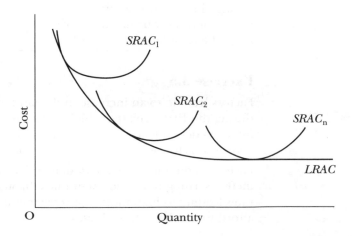

Figure 4.10   **The relation between short-run and long-run average costs**

4 In these circumstances long-run average costs rise, but because cheaper factors can replace the more expensive factors, long-run average costs do not rise by the full amount of the increase in the factor price.

5 The figures in Table 4.5 should be as shown below.

Table 4.5 (completed)

Level of output (no. of units per day)	Total cost (£)	Average cost (£)	Marginal cost (£)
1	50	50	50
2	90	45	40
3	150	50	60
4	220	55	70

Chapter 5

Exercise 5.1

See Figure 5.12.

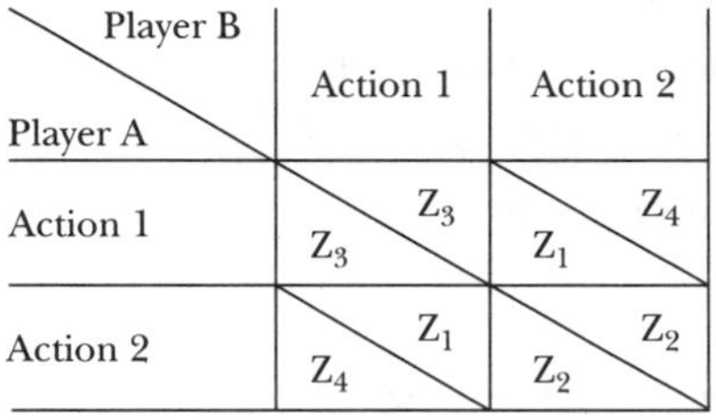

Figure 5.12 **Pay-off matrix showing the general form of the prisoners' dilemma game**

The structure of pay-offs (Z_1, Z_2, Z_3, Z_4) takes the form of $Z_1 < Z_2 < Z_3 < Z_4$

Exercise 5.2

Table 5.1a (completed) **Deriving an oligopolist's marginal revenue: case (a)**

Price	Expected quantity demanded	TR	MR
£5.00	100	£500.00	—
£4.98	101	£502.98	£2.98
£4.96	102	£505.92	£2.94
£4.94	103	£508.82	£2.90
£4.92	104	£511.68	£2.86
£4.90	105	£514.50	£2.82

Exercise 5.3

Table 5.1b (completed)   **Deriving an oligopolist's marginal revenue: case (b)**

Price	Expected quantity demanded	TR	MR
£5.00	100	£500.00	—
£5.01	99	£495.99	£4.01
£5.02	98	£491.96	£4.03
£5.03	97	£487.91	£4.05
£5.04	96	£483.84	£4.07
£5.05	95	£479.75	£4.09

Chapter 6

Exercise 6.1

40 + 20 + 10 + 5 + 5 = 80 per cent.

Exercise 6.2

We know that:

average cost (AC) = 1

quantity (Q) = 5

price (P) = 10

Hence:

total cost $(TC) = Q . AC = 5$

total revenue $(TR) = Q . P = 50$

total profit $= TR - TC = 50 - 5 = 45$

Note that the . here means 'multiplied by'.

See Figure 6.19.

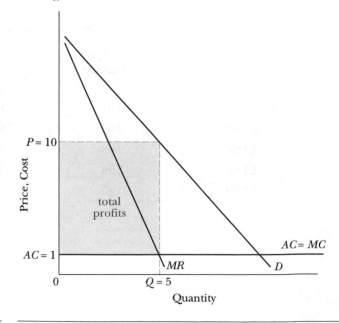

Figure 6.19 **Calculating supernormal profits**

Chapter 7

Exercise 7.1

(a)   See Table 7.1 (completed) for the additional columns.

Table 7.1 (completed)

Quantity	Marginal cost (£)	Average variable costs (£)	Average total costs (£)
0	—	—	—
1	5	5	17
2	3	4	10
3	1	3	7
4	3	3	6
5	5	3.4	5.8
6	7	4	6
7	9	4.7	6.4
8	11	5.5	7

(b) 6 shirts per day.

Exercise 7.2

See Figure 7.22.

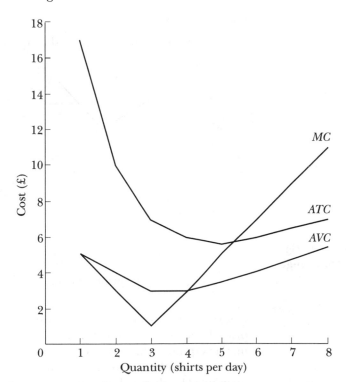

Figure 7.22 **Short-run marginal cost, average variable cost and average total cost curves.**

Note that the *MC* curve cuts the *ATC* curve only approximately at its lowest point, since curves drawn from discrete points only approximate the relationships between smooth curves such as those on Figures 7.8 and 7.9.

Exercise 7.3

Table 7.3 (completed)   **Short-run industry supply: shirts per day**

Price (£)	By manufacturer 1	By manufacturer 2	Total
5	5	6	11
7	6	7	13
9	7	8	15

See Figure 7.23 for the graphed data.

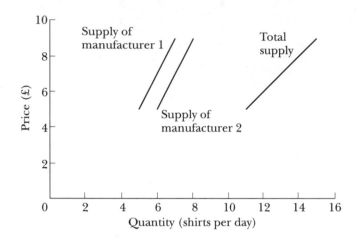

Figure 7.23 **Deriving a short-run supply curve**

Exercise 7.4

Figure 7.24 shows the change in the equilibrium market price.

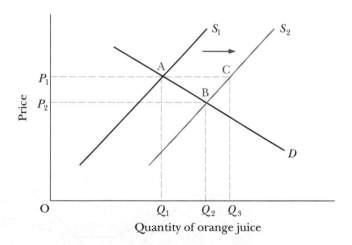

Figure 7.24 **A shift to the right in the supply curve for orange juice**

Unexpectedly warm weather increases the supply of orange juice at any price, hence the supply curve moves to the right from S_1 to S_2. The new market equilibrium at B will be at a lower price with a higher quantity sold. Consumers will move along their demand curve to the new price (P_2) and quantity (Q_2). It may help to envisage unsold orange juice piling up at the old price (P_1) where supply now exceeds demand. That is, there is excess supply measured by the distance AC at P_1. If some suppliers reduce price to clear their warehouses, others will have to follow, and demand will increase as price falls until the new equilibrium is reached. But the model only really tells us how the two equilibria, A and B, differ. It is a comparative static model.

Chapter 8

Exercise 8.1

AB is 90 per cent of competitive output. AK is 5 per cent of the competitive price. Hence ABEK is 5 per cent of 90 per cent = 4.5 per cent of the value of sales (price times output) at the competitive equilibrium C.

Exercise 8.2

By definition, the price elasticity of demand ε_D is:

$$\varepsilon_D = \frac{\text{proportionate change in quantity}}{\text{proportionate change in price}} = \frac{\dfrac{\Delta Q}{Q}}{\dfrac{\Delta P}{P}}$$

By rearranging this equation, you should be able to extract:

$$\Delta Q = \varepsilon_D \cdot \frac{\Delta P}{P} \cdot Q$$

If ΔP is given, then ΔQ is related directly to ε_D. So the triangle loss $0.5 \times \Delta P \Delta Q$ is directly proportional to the demand elasticity. If the elasticity is doubled, the loss is doubled. Generally, the larger is ε_D, the larger is ΔQ. Therefore the output of the newly monopolized industry falls as ε_D rises, reducing the distributive effect of a given price change.

Exercise 8.3

If merger raises prices, this will *benefit* rival firms – they will face a relaxation of price competition in the market – unless the higher price is achieved by first driving rivals partly or entirely from the market.

Exercise 8.4

(a) The cost saving amounts to 5p per unit on sales of one billion units, which is equal to £50 million. This is all additional profit.

(b) The profit margin is unchanged at 10p per unit and there is therefore no profit increase on the initial sales of one billion units. Since a 5 per cent reduction will lead to a 2.5 per cent increase in volume, the number of units sold increases by 25 million. With a profit of 10p per unit, the increase in profits is therefore £2.5 million. The benefit is proportional to the increase in sales. It is therefore also proportional to the price elasticity of demand. Thus, if the elasticity is doubled, the profit gain will double.

The profit reward is therefore twenty times greater in case (a) than case (b), illustrating the potentially much stronger incentives for cost reduction associated with price-cap regulation.

Chapter 9

Exercise 9.1

Here are the percentages filled in on Table 9.1.

Table 9.1 (completed)   **Frequencies and percentages of different tenure types**

Value label	Value	Frequency	Percentage
Owned outright	1	2301	22
Owned with mortgage	2	4918	48
Local authority rented	3	1843	18
Housing association rented	4	306	3
Rented from employer	5	111	1
Rented private unfurnished	6	392	4
Rented private furnished	7	355	3
Other rented	8	21	<1
Data are missing	9	17	<1

Did you calculate 70% 'owners' (22% + 48%) and 30% 'tenants'? This would give the bar chart in Figure 9.25.

This is one reasonable answer to the exercise but it is rather uncritical. Those with mortgages are not fully owners, and only 22 per cent of people live in houses owned outright. A more critical approach could point out, furthermore, that the question implicitly assumes that all residents of an owner-occupied house equally 'own' it. Similarly, it assumes that all individuals living in rented accommodation are actually paying the rent. But diversity in people's household roles might mean that one person paid the mortgage or rent, while others lived there without owning or renting it. These data exclude children under 16.

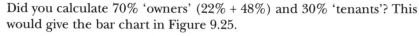

Figure 9.25   Bar chart of tenure types collapsed into two categories

Exercise 9.2

3.54 could be a value: for example it could be a wage rate (£3.54 per hour) among several rates paid to a sample of workers. But it could not be a frequency: frequencies are counts, and therefore are integers (whole numbers) ranging from zero upwards.

Exercise 9.3

Figure 9.26 shows the histogram drawn from the data provided.

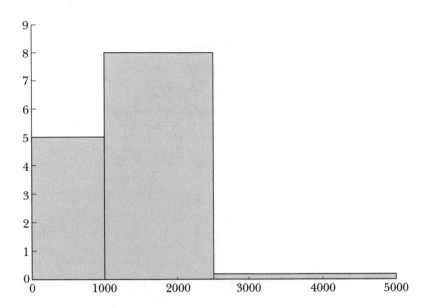

Figure 9.26 **Drawing a histogram**

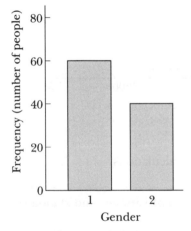

Figure 9.27 **Bar chart of frequencies: gender**

Exercise 9.4

'Gender', as a variable, is at the categorical level of measurement. Its frequencies could be described in a table such as the one below:

Table 9.12 **Variable: gender**

Category	Value	Frequency
Male	1	60
Female	2	40
Total		100

The mode here is *male* or '1'. There is no median, since the male and female categories are not ranked. And there is no mean, because it makes no sense to add up the values 1 and 2 for men and women, since these are just nominal (arbitrary) labels. We could use a bar chart of frequencies (Figure 9.27). As in all such bar charts, the frequency (or count) goes on the vertical axis and the variable name goes on the horizontal axis.

Exercise 9.5

The histogram is shown in Figure 9.28. The graph has been given a maximum value so it can be read, and the break in the axis shows where the axis has been truncated. Many skewed variables are not given a specific maximum value, and in the case of trade unions a few unions exceed 1 million members, so only a truncated axis can provide a readable graph.

To calculate the height of the bars, create a table as before, and calculate the height by dividing the count in each interval by the width of the interval.

Size of trade union	Number of unions	Width of interval	Height
<1000	140	1000	0.140
1000 – 2499	49	1500	0.033
2500 – 4999	27	2500	0.011
5000 – 9999	18	5000	0.004
10 000 – 1.5 million	71	10 000[1]	0.007

[1] Arbitrarily chosen truncated interval. If the interval had been wider the height would have been lower since it is the area which measures the frequency.

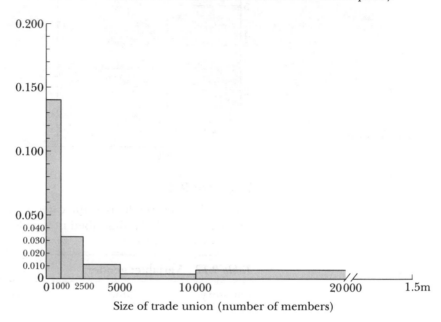

Figure 9.28 **Histogram showing size of trade union, UK, 1989**

Exercise 9.6

Table 9.5 (completed) shows the results of the calculations.

Table 9.5 (completed) **Example of the calculation of variance and standard deviation**

Person	Income X_i	(Income – mean) $(X_i - \overline{X})$	Squared difference $(X_i - \overline{X})^2$
Jane	50	−25	625
Sunil	100	25	625
Jim	40	−35	1225
Arnold	110	35	1225
Sum	300	0	3700
Mean income	$\frac{300}{4} = 75$		
Variance			$\frac{3700}{4} = 925$
Standard deviation			$\sqrt{925} = 30.4$

Exercise 9.7

The scatterplot is shown in Figure 9.29. You could try to draw an approximate line of best fit through the points. Notice that at low levels of income households are spending their savings: there is negative saving.

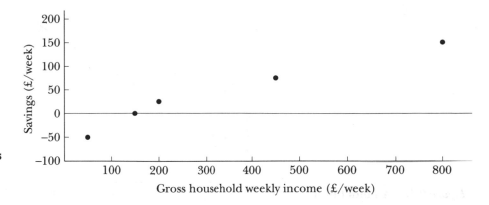

Figure 9.29 **Scatterplot of gross weekly household income against savings**

Exercise 9.8

Table 9.9 (completed) shows the calculations.

Table 9.9 (completed) **Estimates of expenditure from the equation for the consumption function in Figure 9.10**

Gross income per week	Calculation	Estimated expenditure
£100	$67.81 + (0.49 \times 100)$	£116.81
£200	$67.81 + (0.49 \times 200)$	£165.81
£300	$67.81 + (0.49 \times 300)$	£214.81

Exercise 9.9

I hope you saw that you need to plot at least two points on the line and then draw a line connecting them. There is no point going into the non-positive points of the graph either; stop the line where it hits an axis of your graph. The points I would plot are (0, 2000), where the first figure is the value for *P* and the second for *Q*, and perhaps (100, 500). The demand curve should then look as in Figure 9.30. It has a negative slope of −15.

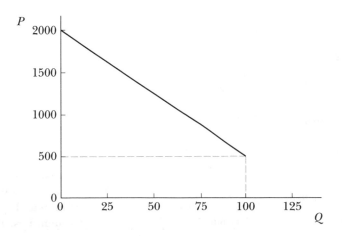

Figure 9.30 **The demand curve graphed**

Exercise 9.10

The graph of the wage model should look like Figure 9.31. The independent variable here is *hours worked*, and the dependent variable is the *weekly wage*.

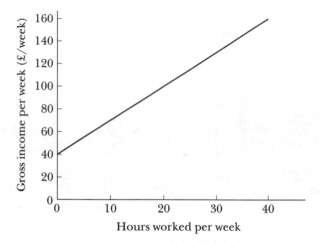

Figure 9.31 **A model of a weekly wage**

Exercise 9.11

The *y*-intercept is 7.56. The line has a slope of 0.04. Your calculations should work from the estimated *y*-intercept of about 7 or 10. The height of the line when *x* is 1000 is about 40. (Use a straight edge or ruler to read this from the *y*-axis.) Suppose you guessed 7 for the intercept. The rise then is about 40 − 7 = 33. The run is exactly 1000. The slope is

$$\frac{33}{1000} = 0.033$$

If you guessed 10 for the intercept you should have 0.03 for the slope. If you guessed 5 for the intercept you should have 0.035 for the slope. If you guessed the height of the line at *x* = 1000 to be 50, then your slope estimates will be higher. The line's equation is in fact:

$$EXP = 7.56 + 0.04 \times INC$$

Exercise 9.12

The bar charts should look like Figures 9.32 and 9.33.

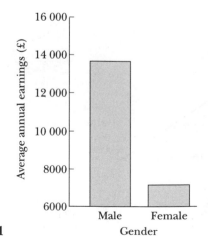

Figure 9.32 **Bar chart of means: average annual earnings of men and women, UK, 1991**

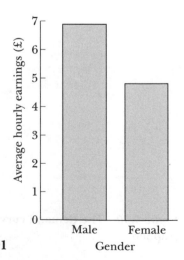

Figure 9.33 **Bar chart of means: average hourly earnings of men and women, UK, 1991**

Exercise 9.13

1   See Figure 9.34. A distribution which has the same mean but a smaller standard deviation is narrower than the distribution in Figure 9.24. It will therefore be taller, if the distributions are the same size: more cases will be clustered close to the mean.

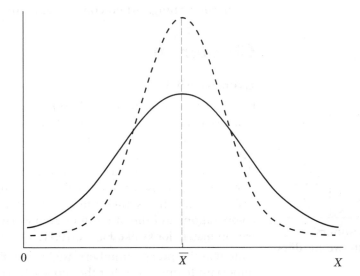

Figure 9.34 **Two non-skewed distributions with the same mean and different standard deviations**

2   Figure 9.35 shows sketches of the two distributions. The men's distribution has a higher mean and is more dispersed.

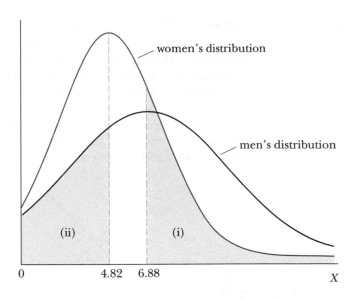

Figure 9.35 **Overlapping distributions of men's and women's hourly earnings**

3   The overlap between the distributions implies that some women have pay rates which exceed those of some men. The larger the overlap, the larger is this group. In Figure 9.35, some women have pay rates which exceed men's average earnings: the shaded area labelled (i). Furthermore, some men earn below women's average pay rates: the shaded area labelled (ii) in Figure 9.35. Thus the statement that 'women's pay rates are lower than men's pay rates' is a generalization to which there are exceptions.

4   If earnings were skewed, with more people on low wages, then the graphs might have even more overlap at higher income levels. The mode and the median would lie below the mean income in both the men's and the women's distributions. Comparison of the two means would not reflect the skewness, and indeed *median* earnings is widely used as a measure of the central tendency of earnings data, rather than mean earnings, when comparing earnings distributions for this reason.

Chapter 10

Exercise 10.1

Herder A \ Herder B	co-operate	defect
co-operate	100 / 100	120 / 10
defect	10 / 120	20 / 20

***Figure 10.11*   A prisoners' dilemma game with two herders**

Consider two herders: A and B. Suppose that they consider that they have equal rights to use the land, and they know that if they 'co-operate', i.e. use the land equally up to its carrying capacity without deterioration, then the pay-offs are 100 each. That is, they make 100 a year each from their herds. If they both continue to push up cattle numbers (they 'defect'), then in the year in question their returns fall to 20 each. If one behaves co-operatively, and the other cheats, then the one who cheats does slightly better than with co-operation, and the other does even worse than if both defect. Then the pay-off matrix looks like Figure 10.11.

Note that the precise numbers used in the figure do not matter. The important features are that the top left hand corner should sum to more than the numbers in each other quadrant, so that 'co-operate' is the best joint outcome, and that the best strategy for each herder should nevertheless be to 'defect' whatever the other does.

Exercise 10.2

Figure 10.12 shows that the scrubbing equipment shifts the *MPC* curve upwards to MPC_1 because it raises power station costs. The effect is to raise the market price of power to the user, and to reduce output (P_{a1} and Q_{a1} as compared to P_a and Q_a). At the same time the gap between the *MSC* and the *MPC* curve is reduced. This is because the drop in rain acidity, as a result of the scrubbing, decreases the external costs of power generation, so the *MSC* curve moves closer to the *MPC* curve. I have assumed some gap remains: residual acidity and/or the environmental effects of the scrubbing medium.

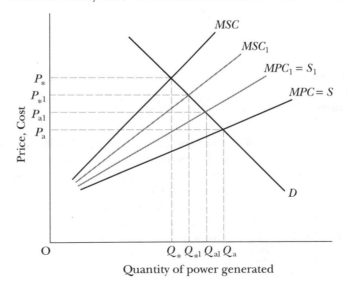

***Figure 10.12*   The effects of scrubbing equipment on the private and social costs of power generation**

Chapter 11

Exercise 11.1

Money provides a means of payment, a store of wealth, and a unit of account.

Exercise 11.2

1 (a) The rise in UK real incomes leads to an increase in the demand for imports from the USA at the existing exchange rate, £1 = a (Figure 11.13). This causes sterling to be sold (the quantity supplied to increase) in order to acquire dollars to buy the additional imported goods. So the supply curve shifts outwards from $S_{£1}$ to $S_{£2}$. This lowers the equilibrium exchange rate to £1 = b.

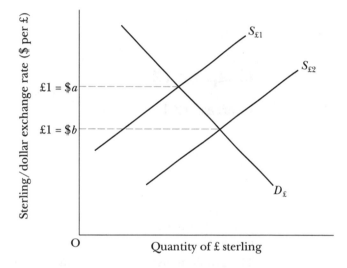

Figure 11.13 **The effect of a rise in UK real incomes on the foreign exchange market for sterling**

(b) The rise in UK prices relative to US prices leads to a fall in the demand for UK exports to the USA. This reduces the demand for sterling by holders of US dollars at the existing exchange rate of £1 = a (Figure 11.14). The demand curve therefore moves to the left, from $D_{£1}$ to $D_{£2}$. The equilibrium exchange rate falls to £1 = c.

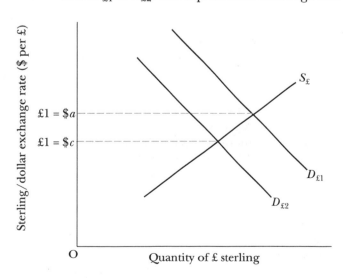

Figure 11.14 **The effect of relatively high UK inflation on the foreign exchange market for sterling**

2   (a) The price in US $ = 1.5 × £20 = $30.

(b) The price in US $ = 1.2 × £20 = $24.

(c) There will be a 35% increase in the demand for the £ sterling. The fall in the exchange rate and hence the $ price is 20%. The formula for the price elasticity of demand is:

$$\varepsilon_D = \frac{\text{proportionate change in quantity demanded}}{\text{proportionate change in price}}$$

Let us call the proportionate change in demand x. Then

$$\varepsilon_D = \frac{x}{20\%} = \frac{x}{-0.2} = -1.75$$

so, $x = -1.75 \times -0.2 = 0.35 = 35\%$.

Chapter 12

Exercise 12.1

(a) $\dfrac{25 - 20}{25} = 0.2$

(b) $\dfrac{45 - 30}{45} = 0.33$

Situation (b) represents, on this measure, a greater degree of monopoly power, that is a greater proportionate difference between price and marginal cost.

The problems associated with this measure include the practical difficulties in gathering the relevant information about firms' marginal costs. But the gap between price and marginal cost is also hard to interpret. Is it the result of static monopoly power, or a temporary reward for innovation? Furthermore, if monopoly generates X-inefficiency (Chapter 10) costs will rise, and the gap between price and marginal cost will be reduced. So the measure will fail to indicate monopoly power in those circumstances.

Exercise 12.2

Between 1975 and 1980 the RULC in domestic currencies increased, indicating faster unit cost increases in the UK than abroad. Since 1980 it improved (that is, fell) three times, once during the recession of the early 1980s, again after the mid-1980s boom, and finally during the early 1990s. As far as the exchange rate-corrected indicator is concerned, this was on a more or less continuous downward (improving) trend between 1980 and 1986, indicating the relative depreciation of sterling over that period. Since then, it rose at the beginning of the 1990s and then fell dramatically during 1992 and 1993.

Chapter 13

Exercise 13.1

If P_w were above P_a, then domestic production at world prices (indicated by the supply curve) will be greater than domestic demand ($Q_t > C_t$ on Figure 13.12). As a result, the good would be exported by the home economy. The gain in going from autarky to free trade is C. Consumers lose A + B, and firms gain A + B + C.

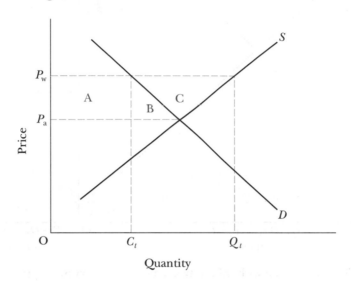

Figure 13.12 **The effects of a world market price above the domestic market price**

Exercise 13.2

1   A tariff raises the price of a good in the home economy above the world price. This reduces home demand below the quantity demanded at the world price. So the demand for imports (the gap between home demand and home supply at the world price) falls. Hence the supply of imports exceeds demand at the old world price. The world price must fall to reduce the quantity of imports supplied.

2   Point b in Figure 13.5 is the demand for imports once the tariff is in place, at the price including the tariff ($P_w^t + t$). Point a is the supply of imports. Suppliers of imports get the local price less the tariff, P_w^t. Consumers pay the local price including the tariff ($P_w^t + t$). Supply and demand will balance at the import level where supply at the world price (P_w^t) is equal to demand at the tariff-inclusive price ($P_w^t + t$), i.e. where the vertical distance between S_w and D_h is equal to t.

Exercise 13.3

Figure 13.13 illustrates this case. Since S_w is horizontal at the world price P_w, the tariff and resultant drop in demand for imports from $C_f - Q_f$ to $C_t - Q_t$ has no effect on world price. The free trade world price P_w^f is equal to the world price with a tariff P_w^t. Area H has vanished, since it resulted from the difference between P_w^t and P_w^f.

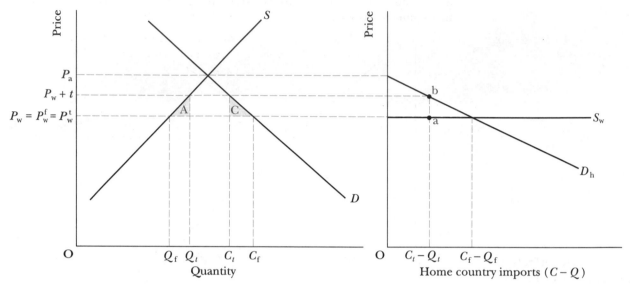

Figure 13.13   **Tariffs and welfare with infinitely elastic foreign export supply**

Exercise 13.4

In the situation in pay-off matrix 2, foreign will not choose P whatever home does, since it makes a loss either way (-2 or -1) as opposed to zero (0 or 0). Given that foreign chooses N, home will always choose P, gaining 5 rather than 0. So $\{P, N\}$ is the only equilibrium.

Exercise 13.5

In pay-off matrix 3, home will always choose P, since this is better than N whatever foreign does. Given that, foreign will prefer N to P, since it gets zero rather than a loss (-2). So $\{P, N\}$ is a unique equilibrium.

Exercise 13.6

Home will choose P since this is always better than N. Similarly, foreign can always choose P for exactly the same reason. Their situation is symmetrical, and $\{P, P\}$ is the unique equilibrium.

Chapter 14

Exercise 14.1

$$\text{intra-WE trade propensity} = \frac{\left(\dfrac{\text{intra-WE trade}}{\text{WE GDP}}\right)}{\left(\dfrac{\text{total WE trade}}{\text{total world trade}}\right)}$$

The intra-WE trade propensity is the share of Western Europe's GDP devoted to intra-WE trade divided by the relative importance of Western European countries' trade in world trade.

Exercise 14.2

The first thing to do is to determine the shares S_D, S_P and S_N in the base case, and the new shares after each change. These are shown in Table 14.6 in each case. To calculate the shares simply divide each subtotal by the overall total (thus for the base case, S_D is $1000/2000 = 0.5$).

Table 14.6

	Base case totals	share	(a) totals	share	(b) totals	share	(c) totals	share	(d) totals	share
S_D	1000	(0.5)	900	(0.45)	1000	(0.500)	850	(0.425)	1000	(0.476)
S_P	400	(0.2)	500	(0.25)	550	(0.275)	500	(0.250)	500	(0.238)
S_N	600	(0.3)	600	(0.30)	450	(0.225)	650	(0.325)	600	(0.286)
Total	2000	(1.0)	2000	(1.00)	2000	(1.000)	2000	(1.000)	2100	(1.000)

(a) is a case of unambiguous trade creation: S_P rises, S_D falls.

(b) is a case of unambiguous trade diversion: S_P riscs, S_N falls.

(c) is a more complex case: S_P rises and S_D falls, but S_N also rises slightly. So this might be a mixture of trade creation (£100) and external trade creation (£50). But it could also reflect creation (£50) plus diversion (£50) outweighed by external trade creation of £100. We can in fact never separate these three effects unambiguously.

(d) is a case of trade creation: S_P rises and S_D falls. Looking at shares alone might also suggest some diversion because S_N falls. No trade is really diverted, however, because the total non-partner imports do not change. This is why I said above that shares allow the approximate identification of effects. The moral is that we should, strictly speaking, not consider just shares, but also absolute amounts of trade.

Exercise 14.3

(a) $9\% \times \dfrac{2}{3} = 6\%$

(b) $15\% \times \dfrac{1}{3} = 5\%$

Firm B / Firm A	invest now	wait and see
invest now	120 / 120	110 / 30
wait and see	30 / 110	20 / 20

Figure 16.10 **Pay-off matrix showing the decision to invest during a recession when the government offers an investment grant of £20**

Chapter 16

Exercise 16.1

A completed version of the blank matrix in Figure 16.6 is shown in Figure 16.10. The dominant strategy equilibrium in Figure 16.10 is for both firms to invest now.

If Firm A expects Firm B to invest, the pay-off to Firm A for investing now is £120 compared with £110 for waiting. If Firm A expects Firm B to wait, the pay-off to investing now is £30 as opposed to £20 for waiting. Thus, whatever Firm A expects Firm B to do, its best option is to invest now. The same reasoning applies to Firm B, and so both firms invest now.

Chapter 17

Exercise 17.1

GDP increased by 5 per cent. *DE* increased by 7 per cent of GDP and *FE* by −2 per cent of GDP.

Exercise 17.2

There are basically two reasons why aggregate demand increases when the domestic price level falls. The first is related to the competitiveness of domestically produced goods relative to other goods on the world market. If domestic prices fall, then export demand will increase and import demand will fall. This implies that net foreign demand increases. As net foreign demand is a component of aggregate demand, this means that aggregate demand will rise. This is shown in Figure 17.14 as a movement along the *AD* curve from A to B. At the original level of prices P_1, the level of aggregate demand is given by Y_1. At the lower level of prices P_2, aggregate demand has increased to the level shown as Y_2.

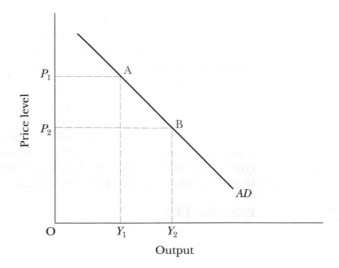

Figure 17.14 **A fall in the domestic price level**

Second, there may also be an effect on the rate of interest resulting from the fall in the domestic price level. If the money supply is exogenous, a fall in domestic prices will reduce the demand for nominal money balances. This creates excess supply in the money market, which in turn exerts a downward pressure on the rate of interest. If the rate of interest does fall, this will tend to stimulate both consumption demand and investment demand as the cost of borrowing is now lower. The increase in aggregate demand is represented diagrammatically by a downward movement along the *AD* curve, thus reinforcing the effect shown in Figure 17.14.

Exercise 17.3

1   If a country's stock market crashes, then the securities quoted on the stock exchange fall dramatically in value. Holders of these securities now have reduced wealth holdings, and so there is a fall in real wealth right across the economy and in other countries too. This reduction in real wealth will reduce both consumption demand and investment demand. The result is a fall in aggregate demand which is represented diagrammatically by a leftward shift of the *AD* curve.

2   If there is a rise in world prices, then the domestic output of a country becomes more competitive on world markets. Export demand increases as foreign demand rises, and import demand falls as domestic households and firms switch their expenditure from foreign goods to domestically produced goods. The result is that there is an increase in aggregate demand for the economy's output. This is represented diagrammatically by a rightward shift of the *AD* curve.

Exercise 17.4

The increase in government demand is shown by a rightward shift of the *AD* curve from AD_1 to AD_2 in Figure 17.15, where the horizontal distance $Y_2 - Y_1$ equals £20 billion. If the multiplier is 3, the final increase in output at the existing price level must be £60 billion, as shown by the final *AD* curve AD_3. Note that the distance $Y_3 - Y_2$ is £40 billion, i.e. twice $Y_2 - Y_1$.

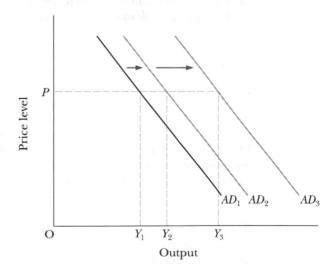

Figure 17.15 **Aggregate demand and the multiplier**

Exercise 17.5

If the government reduces interest rates, this will ease the cost of borrowing. This in turn results in an increase in consumption demand and investment demand. The resultant increase in aggregate demand is represented diagrammatically by a rightward shift of the *AD* curve.

Exercise 17.6

Reduction of the cyclical and structural components of the budget deficit implies a contractionary fiscal stance which results in a reduction in aggregate demand. If the economy is already in recession, then aggregate demand is already falling. Reducing the budget deficit at a time of recession therefore results in a greater decline in aggregate demand than would otherwise have been the case. This case is illustrated in Figure 17.16.

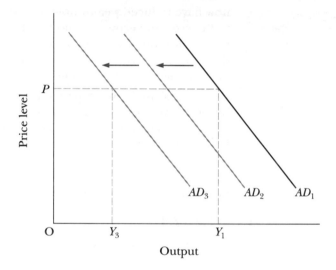

Figure 17.16 **A contractionary fiscal policy during a recession**

The recession is illustrated by a leftward shift in the *AD* curve from AD_1 to AD_2. The contractionary fiscal policy results in reducing aggregate demand even more; this is shown by the leftward shift in the *AD* curve from AD_2 to AD_3. The overall outcome is that the *AD* curve shifts from AD_1 to AD_3, and the level of aggregate demand at the existing level of prices falls from Y_1 to Y_3.

Chapter 18

Exercise 18.1

A demand contraction implies a reduction in output below the long-run equilibrium level (assuming a long-run equilibrium as the initial position). In Figure 18.19 *AD* falls from AD_1 to AD_2. This movement from A to B involves a fall in both prices and output; the fall in prices implies a rise in real wages. In the long run, there will be a return to the equilibrium output Y_E and a lower price level at C. In the New Keynesian version of the movement from B to C, the reduction in output and employment at B puts downward pressure on bargained money wages. This causes real wages to fall until the economy arrives at point C, the long-run equilibrium, as *SAS* shifts from SAS_1 to SAS_2. In New Classical terms, the *SAS* curve shifts from SAS_1 to SAS_2 as producers revise their price expectations downwards in the light of the fall in prices.

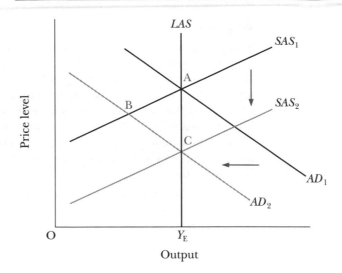

Figure 18.19 **Demand deflation in a fully employed economy**

Exercise 18.2

An economy with output below the long-run equilibrium is shown in Figure 18.20, with AD_1 intersecting SAS at price level P_1, and output Y_1 below the long-run level Y_E. A demand expansion – perhaps following a reduction in interest rates, a fiscal expansion or a rise in world incomes – could increase AD from AD_1 to AD_2. Prices and output would then increase to P_2 and Y_E respectively.

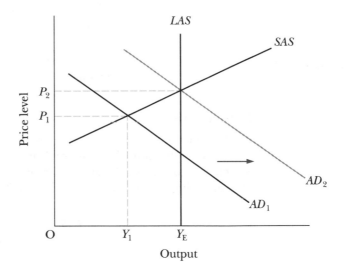

Figure 18.20 **Demand expansion in an under-employed economy**

Exercise 18.3

Tighter standards of environmental regulation constitute an adverse supply shock because the reduction of pollutants would increase the costs of production. In the longer period, however, the effects are less certain. Firms would have an incentive to find cheaper ways of reducing pollutants, and so in time the extent of the AS shift would be reduced. Furthermore, to the extent that natural resources are being conserved for future use, *very* long-run production prospects might even be enhanced.

Exercise 18.4

The fall in the price of oil results in a fall in the supply price of aggregate output, in both the mark-up and competitive models. This implies a fall in the *SAS* curve from SAS_1 to SAS_2 in Figure 18.21, showing the fall in prices and a rise in output as the economy moves from A to B. There is now overfull employment which starts to push up costs and nominal wages. Higher costs result in higher prices, and so the *SAS* curve starts to move back to the original SAS_1, returning the economy back to A. Nominal wages and prices both rise during this process, but real wages are higher at A than before the oil price fall.

If policy makers wish to avert this return to the original price level, then *AD* has to be reduced to AD_2, which implies a lower price level than the original one; here the economy is at C.

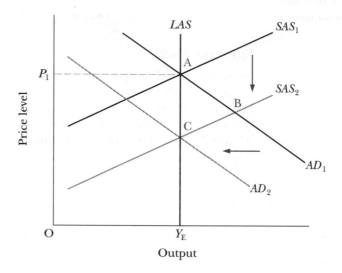

Figure 18.21 A fall in oil prices shifts the *SAS*

Exercise 18.5

1 Contractionary monetary policy would involve raising interest rates, while contractionary fiscal policy might take the form of tax increases or cuts in government spending. Supply-side policies might include retraining, anti-union legislation, and competition policy.

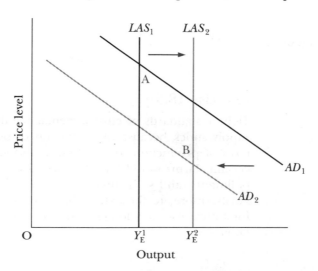

Figure 18.22 Demand- and supply-side policies in the long run: an expansion of output

2 The full effect of this package of policy measures will become apparent only in the long run because the supply-side reforms are intended to reduce the NRU. The demand contraction shifts the *AD* curve inwards from AD_1 to AD_2 and sets off an adjustment process which shifts the *SAS* curve downwards from SAS_1 to SAS_2, as shown in Figure 18.19 and explained fully in the answer to Exercise 18.1. The difference this time is that the *LAS* curve shifts outwards from LAS_1 to LAS_2 in Figure 18.22 in response to the supply-side measures. The new long-run equilibrium is therefore at point B in Figure 18.22, with the price level lower and output and employment greater than at the original equilibrium point A.

Exercise 18.6

Once again the full effect of this package of policy measures will become apparent only in the long run because this time the effect of the supply-side reforms is to raise the NAIRU.

The demand expansion shifts the *AD* curve outwards from AD_1 to AD_2, while the *LAS* curve shifts inwards from LAS_1 to LAS_2 in response to the compromise supply-side measures (Figure 18.23). The new long-run equilibrium is therefore at point B, with the price level higher and output lower than at the original equilibrium point A.

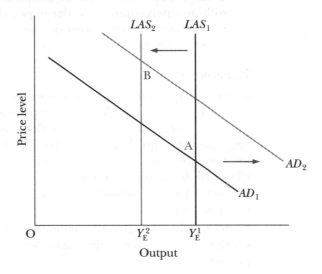

Figure 18.23 **Demand- and supply-side policies in the long run: a contraction of output**

Chapter 19

Exercise 19.1

1 The fact that sterling's real exchange rate appreciated more than its nominal exchange rate implies that UK inflation was higher than inflation in the rest of the world.

2 An appreciation of sterling's nominal exchange rate at the same time as a depreciation of its real exchange rate would imply that UK inflation was lower than inflation in the rest of the world.

Exercise 19.2

1 If a country's income growth is consistently above that of its trading partners, its demand for imports will outstrip its trading partners' demands for exports, and its exchange rate will therefore depreciate.

2 The experience of rapidly growing countries with customarily strong currencies such as Germany might be explained in terms of the competitiveness of its internationally traded manufactured goods, particularly, in view of the strong currency, the non-price aspects of competitiveness.

Exercise 19.3

1 A sudden switch in tastes away from domestic exports would shift the demand curve for the domestic currency to the left, causing the exchange rate to depreciate in the absence of intervention. In order to peg the exchange rate, the authorities would have to buy the domestic currency in sufficient quantities to equal the excess supply.

2 If world inflation surged ahead of domestic inflation, the price competitiveness of internationally traded domestic output would increase and, other things being equal,

(a) foreign demand for exports would increase, shifting the demand curve for the domestic currency to the right, and

(b) domestic demand for imports would fall, shifting the supply curve of the domestic currency to the left.

Both of these changes would cause the exchange rate to appreciate without intervention. In order to peg the exchange rate, the authorities would have to sell the domestic currency in sufficient quantities to offset the excess demand for domestic currency.

Exercise 19.4

Expansionary monetary policy is more likely to be inflationary under flexible exchange rates. Monetary expansion leads to a depreciation of the exchange rate, which increases the demand for exports and hence aggregate demand. A further source of inflationary pressure is the increase in import costs associated with the depreciating currency, the effects of which will be amplified in the presence of real wage resistance. This will shift the *SAS* curve upwards. Neither of these effects are present under fixed exchange rates.

Under fixed exchange rates monetary expansion causes a capital outflow which reduces the domestic money stock and hence diminishes inflationary pressures.

Exercise 19.5

Here are my one-sentence summaries.

1 • Since exchange rate movements change import and export prices, fixed exchange rates reduce the risks associated with international trade.
 • Fixed exchange rates reduce instability caused by speculation on the foreign exchange market.

2 • Since flexible exchange rates automatically correct deficits and surpluses on the balance of payments, the authorities are free to pursue domestic macroeconomic goals such as growth and jobs.
 • Flexible exchange rates protect the economy from external shocks.

3 • One objection is that importers may win as well as lose through exchange rate movements.

- The principal objection is that speculation tends to move currencies towards their equilibrium values, thereby reducing instability.

4 - The balance of payments, under fixed exchange rates, acts as a constraint on governments, curbing irresponsible fiscal policies.

- Some external influences may benefit the economy and so it should not be insulated from them.

Chapter 20

Exercise 20.1

1   Whatever the public expects, it is always better for the government to have inflation. If the public expects zero inflation, then (reading down the left side) the pay-off for the government is 0 if actual inflation is zero and 1 if actual inflation is high. Inflation is therefore preferred.

If the public expects high inflation, then (reading down the right side) the pay-off for the government is −2 if actual inflation is zero and −1 if actual inflation is high. Again, inflation is preferred.

2   If the government's preferred option is to have inflation, then would you believe a promise by the government not to create inflation? Presumably not.

3   Economists expect economic agents to behave rationally. In the Barro-Gordon model, it is rational for the public to expect the government to create inflation because they know that inflation is the government's dominant strategy. In this case, the outcome is the bottom right-hand cell (−1,0) with high expected inflation and high actual inflation.

4   In terms of the *AD/AS* diagram Figure 20.12, the government keeps on with expansionary policies to increase *AD*, but the public anticipates this and so the *SAS* curve shifts upwards. The outcome is an inflationary spiral with no increase in output. This is shown in Figure 20.12 as the movement from A to B; the price level increases from P_A to P_B but output remains constant at Y_E.

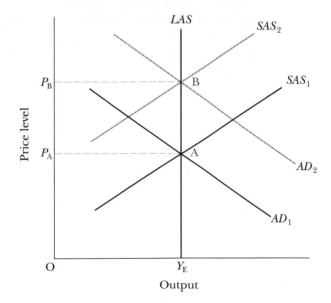

Figure 20.12 **The Barro-Gordon model illustrated using the *AD/ AS* diagram**

Exercise 20.2

The trend rate of growth appears to be lower for the period 1973–89 than for the immediately preceding period 1950–73. The oil shock of 1973 may have contributed to this. In Figure 20.13, the *SAS* curve shifts up to SAS_2 as a result of the oil price rise, taking the economy in the short run to point B. Whether this event affects the trend growth rate depends on whether the *LAS* also shifts to the left, reducing output in the long term to Y_E^2 at point C, or whether domestic adjustments involving reductions in real wages are sufficient to restore output in the long term back to the original equilibrium level Y_E^1 at point A.

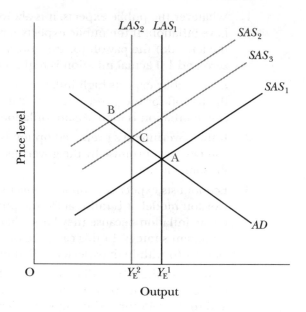

Figure 20.13 **The effect of the oil price shock, 1973**

Although the growth rate for the period 1973–89 is below that for 1950–73, it is, however, still high by historical standards and is greater than for the periods 1870–1913 and 1913–50. Thus, the period 1973–89 may represent a return to an even longer historical trend rate of growth. In this case, it is the period 1950–73 which is exceptional. This period might be explained by fundamental supply-side changes shifting the *LAS* to the right, sustained by a stable growth in *AD* underpinned by the post-war consensus about policy objectives.

Chapter 21

Exercise 21.1

The demand for labour is a derived demand which means that it is valued for what it can be used to produce, rather than for its own sake. The marginal revenue product (*MRP*) is the extra revenue obtained by the firm from employing an extra unit of labour.

$$MRP = P \times MPP_L$$

where MPP_L is the marginal physical product of labour. Diminishing marginal returns causes the MPP_L to decline and because it is assumed that a perfectly competitive firm is a price taker, the *MRP* is also declining.

Profit maximization ensures that firms will employ labour up to the point where

$$W = MRP$$

Hence (with labour as the only variable factor of production) the demand curve for labour is the same as the *MRP* curve, and therefore declining as labour increases. Accordingly, a fall in wages leads a profit-maximizing firm to employ more labour.

Exercise 21.2

After the completion of the new office block, the demand curve for high-rise window cleaners shifts outwards from L_{D1} to L_{D2}, as shown in Figure 21.13, resulting in an increase in both wages and employment.

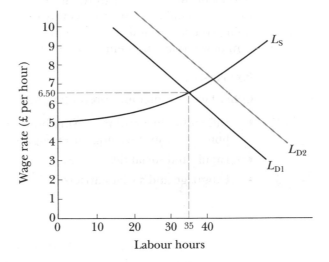

Figure 21.13 **An increase in the demand for high-rise window cleaning**

Exercise 21.3

My brief list of costs would include the following:

- Time spent studying means less potential work time and accordingly perhaps less current income. Also there will be a sacrifice of domestic labour time, with, for example, less time spent on household responsibilities, or at leisure.

- There will be direct costs such as fees, stationery items and perhaps books. In addition there may be other costs associated with the need to have somewhere quiet to study.

Perhaps we should add the mental anguish involved in having to tackle difficult material or in completing assessments – and also the possible strain on family life!

My list of benefits would include:

- Improved future job prospects, in terms of a reduced chance of future unemployment.

- A future potential to earn higher wages.

- A future potential to do a more intrinsically satisfying job.

- In the present I would gain the intellectual satisfaction from studying.

One could, in principle, estimate the future wage benefits and employment prospects obtained as a result of doing the course. Perhaps you will be pleased to learn that economic research generally indicates a considerable economic return, for example, to getting degrees, with evidence of some increase through the 1980s compared to the 1970s. You could also estimate reasonably well the costs to you in terms of the time taken in studying. On the other hand it is hard to quantify the consumption benefits and costs of doing courses, even if your judgement as to whether to start the course cannot avoid taking them into account.

Exercise 21.4

Other factors sometimes preventing mobility would include:

- Difficulties involved in moving house (including buying and selling houses), or in travelling far enough to where the jobs are.

- Family and social ties.

- Language and social barriers.

Exercise 21.5

If some workers offered to work for wages below the equilibrium point B on Figure 21.10, the employer would deduce that once employed it would not be worthwhile for workers to work properly. The employers would expect the workers to shirk and take the chance of being caught, since the cost of being caught is not so great with such low wages. Even if the workers would prefer to work at these wages, rather than remain unemployed indefinitely, they would find it impossible to convince the prospective employers of their intentions as, with imperfect monitoring of the workplace, the promise of 'good' behaviour could not be guaranteed. Any such promise would have to be disregarded if the employer is rational and if it is recognized also that workers are rational. All this, of course, applies strictly to a world of alienating and unsatisfying work, where unemployment is the prime disciplinary measure against shirking.

Chapter 22

Exercise 22.1

The headcount index is

$$\frac{5}{50} = 10 \text{ per cent}$$

The average difference between the poverty line ($50) and the income of the poor is

$$\frac{\$10 + \$20 + \$30 + \$20 + \$10}{5} = \$18$$

The poverty gap measure expresses this as a proportion of the poverty line

$$\frac{\$18}{\$50} \times 100 = 36 \text{ per cent}$$

Exercise 22.2

(a) Neither measure changes. The headcount index remains at 10 per cent. The poverty gap does not change since the redistribution does not affect the average income of the poor.

$$\frac{\$5 + \$20 + \$35 + \$20 + \$10}{5} = \$18$$

$$\frac{\$18}{\$50} \times 100 = 36 \text{ per cent}$$

(b) The measures move in opposite directions. The headcount index falls:

$$\frac{4}{50} = 8 \text{ per cent}$$

This is because A has shifted over the poverty line. For the same reason the poverty gap increases.

$$\frac{\$20 + \$45 + \$20 + \$10}{4} = \$23.75$$

$$\frac{\$23.75}{\$50} \times 100 = 47.5 \text{ per cent}$$

Exercise 22.3

1 A's preferences on this account make perfect sense: they capture a committed left winger. He or she prefers the left-wing outcome to a centre one, which in turn is preferred to the one furthest away on the political spectrum, the right-wing outcome. Likewise B's preferences are intelligible: they represent someone whose preferred position is just right of centre and so right-wing policies are closer to this person's preferred position than are the left-wing ones, hence [y, z, x]. However, C's preferences (of [z, x, y]) do not fit into this scheme because they correspond to a right winger who likes right-wing outcomes best of all but who prefers left-wing outcomes to centre ones. There is, of course, nothing wrong as such with someone holding such preferences. They simply do not fit into this constrained left–right pattern for

disagreements because a right winger on this account should prefer centre outcomes to left-wing ones since the centre is closer to his or her preferred right-wing position than is the left-wing one.

2   In these circumstances, y beats all comers as a majority prefer it to both x and z.

Exercise 22.4

Between points F and G, on Figure 22.15 each group can have more than at C; at F and at G, Group 1 and Group 2 respectively benefit without damaging the other. Between A and F Group 2 loses relative to C, and between G and B Group 1 loses. All points from A to B are Pareto efficient.

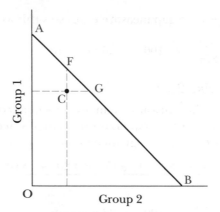

Figure 22.15 **Moves to a Pareto efficient position which leave neither group worse off**

Exercise 22.5

When you plotted the US Lorenz curve for 1991, you should have found that it lay wholly below the corresponding curve for 1980, providing us with strong evidence of increasing inequality during the Reagan and Bush presidencies. Figure 22.16 plots both curves on the same figure.

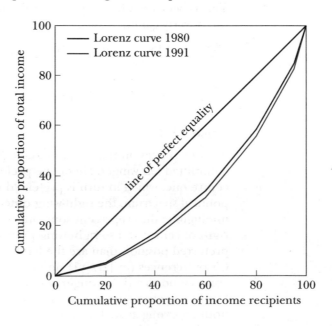

Figure 22.16 **Lorenz curves for the USA, 1980 and 1991**

Exercise 22.6

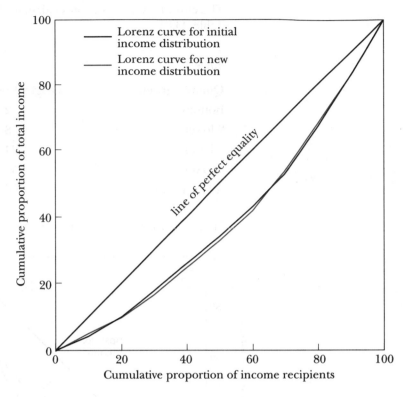

Figure 22.17 **Lorenz curves for the Pacific island**

1   Figure 22.17 shows the Lorenz curve for the initial income distribution.

2   Standard deviation = 4.074, and coefficient of variation = 0.4074.

3   Figure 22.17 also shows the Lorenz curve for the new distribution of incomes.

4   Standard deviation = 4.025, and coefficient of variation = 0.4025.

Chapter 23

Exercise 23.1

Both arguments turn on uncertainty about our own fate, which may lead us to support social arrangements which offer considerable security to the least well-off.

Exercise 23.2

Your premium is 1 per cent of £2500 = £25, plus £5 = £30 per year.

Exercise 23.3

1 The cumulative percentages calculated from Table 23.3 are given in Table 23.8.

Table 23.8

Quintile group	Original income	Post-tax income
Bottom	2	6
2 lower	8	17
3 lower	24	33
4 lower	50	56
All households	100	100

Figure 23.13 shows the Lorenz curves for original and post-tax income.

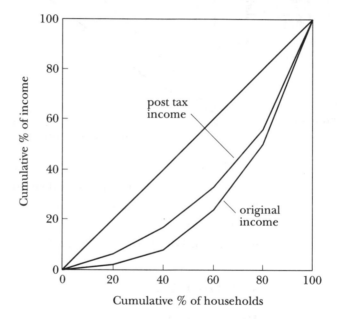

Figure 23.13 **Lorenz curves for original and post-tax income of households by quintile group, UK, 1992**

The curve for post-tax income lies wholly within the curve for original income, showing that post-tax incomes are more equal than original incomes, hence the tax/benefit system is redistributive.

2 The Gini coefficients on Table 23.4 show that original income by decile group in the UK became steadily more unequal between 1979 and 1992, as did inequality of both disposable income and post-tax income. In each year, disposable income (after benefits and direct taxes) was considerably more equal than original income, but post-tax income (allowing for indirect taxes) was more unequal than disposable income.

Exercise 23.4

Socialized health care does not create a poverty trap since the benefits are not means tested. A shift to privatized access to health care associated with increased use of means tested cash benefits would worsen the poverty trap.

Chapter 24

Exercise 24.1

If governments wished to prevent a rise in unemployment after a rise in import prices had shifted the short-run *AS* curve upwards, then they could have introduced expansionary monetary and/or fiscal policies. These would shift the *AD* curve to AD_2 on Figure 24.13, so that the new equilibrium takes the price level up to P_2 but with unchanged output and unemployment Y_1.

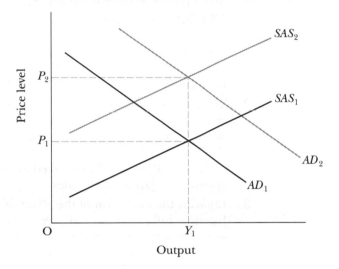

Figure 24.13 **An expansionary demand response to higher import prices**

Exercise 24.2

Figure 24.14 shows the completed version of Figure 24.11. There is a discussion of the results of this exercise below Figure 24.11.

Figure 24.14 **The effects of reflationary and disinflationary policies on unemployment and inflation**

Government policy \ Agents' reactions	no reaction	full anticipation
reflate	unemployment falls / inflation rises	unemployment unchanged / inflation rises
disinflate	unemployment rises / inflation falls	unemployment unchanged / inflation falls

Exercise 24.3

1   Japan: Inflation remained fairly steady until 1973 and quickly subsided from the high peak in 1974 to approximate to price stability in the 1980s; unemployment remained below 3% for the entire period.

West Germany: The inflation rate has been relatively steady, peaking at only 8% in 1971 and not exceeding 5% after 1975; a long period of full employment ended in the early 1970s, unemployment rose to a peak of 8% in 1983 and then fell back below 5%.

Sweden: The inflation rate accelerated from 1968 to peak in 1975 and remained relatively high until a sharp fall in 1992; unemployment remained below 3% until 1991.

UK: The volatility of the inflation rate is striking, almost quadrupling in 1973–75 and doubling in 1978–80, with a sharp fall in between and an even sharper one to 1984; unemployment did not exceed 5% until 1976 but never fell below 5% after that, being stuck at or just above 10% for much of the 1980s, with a dip in the late 1980s.

France: There have been two spells of double-digit inflation (1974–75 and 1979–82), the latter being followed by a strong downward trend; the long-run upward trend in unemployment has displayed surprisingly little cylical variation and remained around 10% from the early 1980s.

USA: Inflation, never rising above 10%, exhibited a gradual upward trend from 1965 to 1975, peaked again in 1980 and has since receded below 5%; unemployment dipped below 5% in the late 1960s, was on an upward trend to the early 1980s, with peaks in 1971, 1975 and 1982/83 falling back to approximately 5% in the late 1980s, then rising again.

2   The effects of the two oil price shocks of 1973–74 and 1979 are clearly visible in the inflation rates of most countries, although the second one does not seem to have made any impact on inflation in Japan and Germany. An upward trend in unemployment rates from the early 1970s to the mid 1980s can be observed everywhere, although it is only barely apparent in Japan and Sweden.

3   (a) With the exception of the effect of the first oil price shock on the Japanese inflation rate, two corporatist economies – Japan and Germany – are the star performers on inflation. The Swedish record, however, is no better than those of the non-corporatist economies.

(b) The star performers on unemployment are the two corporatist economies, Japan and Sweden, although unemployment in Sweden rose sharply in the early 1990s. However, Germany shares with the non-corporatist economies a broadly similar pattern of increasing unemployment rates until the mid 1980s followed by declines of varying rapidity.

4   Sargent's interpretation of rational expectations theory implies that painless disinflation requires that the policy rule is not only understood by economic agents but is also uncontroversial. The centralized wage bargaining institutions characteristic of corporatist economies are probably more conducive to the formation of a consensus on policy objectives.

Chapter 25

Exercise 25.1

Output will increase by £200 million × 2.5 = £500 million.

Exercise 25.2

300 × 3 = 900 units of new net investment.

Exercise 25.3

No, output won't continue to rise. In period 9 investment has fallen from 65 to 50. This fall in investment of 15 has the effect in period 10 of reducing output by 30 to 290 which in turn results in net investment of −15 (see Table 25.2 (completed)). Replacement investment is only 5, because gross investment was only 5 in period 5; only 5 machines were purchased then, so there are only 5 needing to be replaced now. (Note that these machines purchased in period 5 are the oldest of the 160 machines in use – that is, the capital stock in period 9. You can check this by adding up gross investment for periods 5 to 9 inclusive.) Since replacement investment is only 5, there is gross investment of –10 and surplus capital stock is scrapped. The fall in investment compared with the previous period is 60, which induces output to fall even further by 120 to 170 in period 11. Again there is gross disinvestment (–55) and investment is 45 less than in period 10. By the multiplier process, output in period 12 falls again to 80.

Table 25.2 (completed)

Period	Y	ΔY	K	Replace- ment *I*	Net *I*	Gross *I*	ΔI
10	290	−30	145	5	−15	−10	−60
11	170	−120	85	5	−60	−55	−45
12	80	−90	40	35	−45	−10	40
13	160	80	80	65	40	105	115
14	390	230	195	50	115	165	60

In period 12, the process of decline begins to go into reverse by (a) a smaller decline in net disinvestment, and (b) the need for increased replacement investment stemming from the earlier surge in gross investment in period 7. So in period 12, although gross investment is still negative (–10), it represents a substantial increase over period 11, and so the multiplier effect for period 13 is positive with an increase in output of 80.

In period 13 the tide really turns: (a) the increase in output implies net investment of 40, and (b) replacement investment rises to 65 as a result of the depreciation of the large gross investment made in period 8. As a result, gross investment in period 13 is 105, the highest yet, and the resulting 115 increase in investment over the previous period implies a staggering 230 increase in output in period 14. Again we see how the interaction of the accelerator and the multiplier can cause fluctuations in the level of output.

Exercise 25.4

$$\text{Rate of profit} = \frac{200}{400} \times 100 = 50\%.$$

Chapter 26

Exercise 26.1

The first step in this exercise would be to check the correlation between income and consumption, for the country of interest, using a scatterplot diagram. This will give some indication as to whether there is sufficient correlation to warrant the estimation of a regression line. If the two variables appear to be correlated, then the correlation coefficient can be calculated, along with the standard deviations of the two variables. Using these, the slope of the regression line can be calculated. Once you have the slope, there is sufficient information available to then calculate the intercept.

Exercise 26.2

If x and y are identically distributed, then R^2 takes the value of 1. There is perfect correlation. The regression line fits perfectly through the points, starting at the origin, so the intercept is zero. The points lie on a diagonal line from the origin, so $b = 1$.

This can also be stated in algebra. If the line is

$$y = a + bx$$

then $y = x$ implies that a must be zero and b must equal 1.

This extreme case was shown in Figure 26.10(a).

Exercise 26.3

1, 2 and 4 are time series, 3 and 5 are cross-section.

Exercise 26.4

To make a forecast for 1994 the variable t is equal to 15. It follows that

$$\hat{y}_{94} = 242 + (13.8 \times 15) = 449 \text{ trillion yen}$$

Exercise 26.5

The formula for the multiplier is $\frac{1}{1-c}$ where c is the marginal propensity to consume (MPC). Using this formula the multipliers for each country are:

(a) $\dfrac{1}{1-c} = \dfrac{1}{1 - 0.4} = \dfrac{1}{0.6} = 1.67$

(b) $\dfrac{1}{1-c} = \dfrac{1}{1 - 0.6} = \dfrac{1}{0.4} = 2.5$

(c) $\dfrac{1}{1-c} = \dfrac{1}{1 - 0.9} = \dfrac{1}{0.1} = 10$

Exercise 26.6

Table 26.A5 (completed) shows the results of the calculations of the last five columns, and their totals.

Table 26.A5 (completed) **Data for estimating Japan's trend line, 1986–91**

Year	x	y	$x - \bar{x}$	$y - \bar{y}$	$(x-\bar{x})(y-\bar{y})$	$(x-\bar{x})^2$	$(y-\bar{y})^2$
1986	1	329	−2.5	−43.5	108.75	6.25	1892.25
1987	2	342	−1.5	−30.5	45.75	2.25	930.25
1988	3	364	−0.5	−8.5	4.25	0.25	72.25
1989	4	381	0.5	8.5	4.25	0.25	72.25
1990	5	401	1.5	28.5	42.75	2.25	812.25
1991	6	418	2.5	45.5	113.75	6.25	2070.25
	$\Sigma x = 21$	$\Sigma y = 2235$			$\Sigma (x-\bar{x})(y-\bar{y})$ $= 319.5$	$\Sigma (x-\bar{x})^2$ $= 17.5$	$\Sigma (y-\bar{y})^2$ $= 5849.5$

$\bar{x} = \dfrac{21}{6}$ $\quad \bar{y} = \dfrac{2235}{6}$

$\quad = 3.5$ $\qquad = 372.5$

From these you can calculate:

$$b = \frac{\Sigma(x - \bar{x})(y - \bar{y})}{\Sigma(x - \bar{x})^2} = \frac{319.5}{17.5} = 18.3$$

$$a = \bar{y} - b\bar{x} = 372.5 - (18.3 \times 3.5) = 309$$

$$R^2 = \frac{(\Sigma(x - \bar{x})(y - \bar{y}))^2}{\Sigma(x - \bar{x})^2 \, \Sigma(y - \bar{y})^2} = \frac{319.5^2}{17.5 \times 5849.5} = 0.997$$

Chapter 27

Exercise 27.1

1   Brazil: 25 150 000 hectares.

2   Indonesia: 227 species.

3   Mexico: 5.6 per cent of existing taxas are rare or threatened.

Exercise 27.2

Biodiversity loss may mean a loss of species diversity, genetic diversity or ecosystem diversity. Global warming is the increase in mean global temperature believed to be caused by an increase in 'greenhouse gases' which trap energy from the sun in the earth's atmosphere. Tropical deforestation causes the extinction of species through the loss of habitats and contributes to the increase of carbon dioxide in the atmosphere, the most prevalent greenhouse gas.

Exercise 27.3

Based on the discussion in the Appendix to Chapter 1, £90.91 invested at 10 per cent per year will be worth in one year's time

£90.91 (1 + 0.1) = £100

So the present value in the example in the text is the sum you would need to invest now to achieve £100 in a year's time at your required rate of interest. This is what was meant by saying that discounting is compounding in reverse.

Exercise 27.4

The present value of the benefits from cleaning the lake is calculated as follows:

$$PV = \frac{FB}{(1 + r)^t}$$

So over the five years, the present value of the stream of benefits is:

$$PV = \frac{£1500}{1.1} + \frac{£2000}{(1.1)^2} + \frac{£2500}{(1.1)^3} + \frac{£3000}{(1.1)^4} + \frac{£3500}{(1.1)^5}$$

$$= £1364 + £1653 + £1878 + £2049 + £2173$$

$$= £9117$$

Similarly, the present value of the benefits from a recycling plant is calculated as follows:

$$PV = \frac{£3500}{1.1} + \frac{£3000}{(1.1)^2} + \frac{£2500}{(1.1)^3} + \frac{£2000}{(1.1)^4} + \frac{£1500}{(1.1)^5}$$

$$= £3182 + £2479 + £1878 + £1366 + £931$$

$$= £9836$$

The recycling plant has the greater present value because the main benefits of cleaning the lake, not being available until well into the future, are heavily discounted.

Exercise 27.5

1 We do not know enough about the natural world to be sure that the concept of indirect use value captures the life-support function of ecosystems. Furthermore, environmental processes may be either technically or feasibly irreversible. Technological progress leads some to argue that worries about the degradation of environmental capital are misplaced, but the effects of technological change are uncertain. Population growth may stimulate technological innovation or it may set upper limits to sustainable economic growth. All of these considerations introduce acute uncertainty into the cost–benefit calculation.

2 Technological optimists believe that future generations will enjoy higher living standards (GNP per head) than the current generation, because technological progress will raise GNP at a faster rate than population growth. The neo-Malthusians believe that saturation points impose upper limits on population and economic growth.

Exercise 27.6

The donor countries of the north might not be willing to contribute adequate compensation for forgoing the benefits of development. The countries of the south might be unwilling to surrender the right to exploit their own environmental resources.

Chapter 28

Exercise 28.1

1 A rise in interest rates reduces consumption and investment by making saving more attractive and increasing the cost of borrowing.

2 A rise in domestic interest rates relative to those overseas leads to a net inflow of capital and consequently to an appreciation of the exchange rate, which reduces import prices and hence, other things being equal, domestic prices.

Exercise 28.2

1 The empirical tests of Chapter 25 have proved inconclusive because each of the theories is to some extent 'consistent with observable movements in the data'.

2 More sophisticated statistical techniques might tell us more about the explanatory power of each theory.

3   The usefulness of each theory as a guide for policy is suggested as a further criterion of comparison. From this point of view, all four theories have shortcomings.

Exercise 28.3

The fact that the New Keynesian and New Classical approaches derive from different micro-foundations – assumptions about the way in which the labour market works – which in turn reflect 'very different world views', suggests that convergence might be problematic.

Exercise 28.4

1   Perhaps the position ascribed to Nozick, that 'whatever outcomes emerge from voluntary exchanges in markets, they are just', sounds like the expression of a subjective taste, since it does not seem to allow any scope for revision in the light of new information.

2   While it is clear that people do have strong feelings about abstract ideals such as equality or justice, it is hard to imagine having a subjective taste or any kind of emotional attachment for semi-technical ideas such as income as a proxy for primary social goods or capabilities. The debate about the object of individual comparison – whether it ought to be income as a proxy for primary social goods or capabilities – suggests that there is scope here for critical thought.

REFERENCES

Serials

Anuário Estatístico do Brasil, Sao Paolo, Government of Brazil (annual).

Annual Abstract of Statistics, London, HMSO for Central Statistical Office (annual).

Bank of England Quarterly Bulletin, London, Bank of England (quarterly).

Bulletin of Labour Statistics, Geneva, International Labour Office (annual).

Economic Briefing, London, HM Treasury (twice yearly).

Economic Outlook, London Business School (monthly).

Economic Survey of Europe, Geneva, United Nations Economic Commission for Europe (annual).

Economic Trends, London, HMSO for Central Statistical Office (monthly).

Economic Trends Annual Supplement, London, HMSO for Central Statistical Office (annual).

Europa World Year Book, London, Europa Publications (annual).

European Economy, Brussels, Commission of the European Communities (irregular).

Family Expenditure Survey, London, HMSO for Central Statistical Office (annual), also CSO *Family Expenditure Survey*, 1961– (computer file).

Financial Statistics, London, HMSO for Central Statistical Office (monthly).

General Household Survey, London, HMSO (annual).

Great Britain Annual Abstract of Statistics, London, Central Statistical Office (annual).

Industrial Policy in OECD Countries, Annual Review, Paris, OECD (annual).

International Financial Statistics Year Book, Washington DC, International Monetary Fund (annual).

International Trade, Geneva, GATT (annual).

Key Data, London, HMSO for Central Statistical Office (annual).

Monthly Digest of Statistics, London, HMSO for Central Statistical Office (monthly).

Monthly Review of External Trade Statistics, London, HMSO (monthly).

National Westminster Bank Quarterly Review, London, National Westminster Bank (quarterly).

New Earnings Survey, London, HMSO (annual).

OECD Economic Outlook, Paris, OECD (twice yearly).

OECD Employment Outlook, Paris, OECD (annual).

OECD Main Economic Indicators, Paris, OECD (monthly).

OECD Quarterly National Accounts, Paris, OECD (quarterly).

Quarterly Labour Force Survey, London, HMSO (quarterly).

Social Trends, London, HMSO for Central Statistical Office (annual).

United Kingdom National Accounts, London, HMSO for Central Statistical Office (annual).

World Development Report, Oxford and New York, Oxford University Press for World Bank (annual).

World Economic Outlook, Washington, International Monetary Fund (twice yearly).

World Economic Survey, New York, United Nations, Department of International Economic and Social Affairs (annual).

Other references

Abramovitz, M. (1986) 'Catching up, forging ahead, and falling behind', *Journal of Economic History*, vol.46, no.2, pp.385–406.

Adelman, I. (1991) 'Long term economic development', *Working Paper no.598*, California Agriculture Experiment Station, Berkeley, March.

Agarwal, A. and Narain, S. (1992) *Global Warming in an Unequal World: a Case of Environmental Colonialism*, New Delhi, Centre for Science and Environment.

Airlines (1993) Key Note Report, 9th edn, Hampton, Middlesex, Key Note.

Akerlof, G. and Yellen, J. (eds) (1986) *Efficiency Wage Models of the Labor Market*, Cambridge, Cambridge University Press.

Alesina, A. and Summers, L.H. (1993) 'Central bank independence and macroeconomic performance: some comparative evidence', *Journal of Money, Credit and Banking*, vol.25, no.2, pp.151–62.

Alford, B.W.E. (1988) *British Economic Performance, 1945–1975*, London, Macmillan.

Allen, M. (ed.) (1990) *The Times 1000: 1990–91*, London, Times Books Ltd.

Allsopp, C.J. and Joshi, V. (1986) 'The international debt crisis', *Oxford Review of Economic Policy*, vol.2, no.1, pp.i–xxxiii.

Amsden, A. (1989) *Asia's Next Giant, South Korea and Late Industrialization*, Oxford, Oxford University Press.

Ark, B. van (1993) *International Comparisons of Output and Productivity*, Groningen, University of Groningen.

Armstrong, P., Glyn, A. and Harrison, J. (1984) *Capitalism since World War II: the Making and Breakup of the Great Boom*, London, Fontana.

Arrow, K. (1963) 'Uncertainty and the welfare economics of medical care', *American Economic Review*, vol.52, no.6.

Arrow, K. (1963a) *Social Choice and Individual Values*, 2nd edn, New Haven, Cowles Foundation.

Artis, M.J. and Lewis, M.K. (1991) *Money in Britain: Monetary Policy, Innovation and Europe*, Hemel Hempstead, Philip Allan.

Artis, M.J. and Lewis, M.K. (1993) 'Après le déluge: monetary and exchange-rate policy in Britain and Europe', *Oxford Review of Economic Policy*, vol.9, no.3, pp.36–61.

Artis, M.J. and Taylor, M.P. (1989) 'Exchange rates, interest rates, capital controls and the European Monetary System: assessing the track record', in Giavazzi, F., Micossi, S. and Miller, M. (eds) *The European Monetary System*, Cambridge, Cambridge University Press.

Atkinson, A.B. (1983) *The Economics of Inequality*, 2nd edn, Oxford, Clarendon Press.

Atkinson, A.B. and Stiglitz, J. (1987) *Lectures on Public Economics*, Maidenhead, McGraw-Hill.

Atkinson, A. and Micklewright, J. (1991) 'Unemployment compensation and labor market transitions: a critical review', *Journal of Economic Literature*, no. 4, December.

Backus, D.K. and Kehoe, P.J. (1992) 'International evidence on the historical properties of business cycles', *American Economic Review*, vol.82, no.4, pp.864–88.

Bairoch, P. (1982) 'International industrialisation levels from 1750 to 1980', *Journal of European Economic History*, vol.11, no.2, pp.269–334.

Baker, S., Smith, G. and Weiner, E. (1993) 'The Mexican worker', *Business Week*, 19 April, pp.38–44.

Balassa, B. (1975) 'Trade creation and diversion in the European Common Market', in Balassa, B. (1975a).

Balassa, B. (ed.) (1975a) *European Economic Integration*, Amsterdam, North-Holland.

Baldwin, R. (1989) 'The growth effects of 1992', *Economic Policy*, no.9, October, pp.247–82.

Baldwin, R. (1993) 'On the measurement of dynamic effects of integration', *Empirica*, vol.20, pp.129–48.

Balke, N.S. (1991) 'Modelling trends in macroeconomic time series', *Federal Reserve Bank of Dallas Economic Review*, May, pp.19–33.

Bank of England (1971) *Competition and Credit Control*, London, Bank of England.

Bank of England (1993) *Bank of England Quarterly Bulletin*, vol. 33, no.4, November.

Bank of England (1993a) *Bank Briefing*, August, London, Bank of England.

Bank of England (1994) *Monetary Policy in the UK*, May, London, Bank of England.

Bank of International Settlements (1992) *Annual Report*, Basle, BIS.

Banks, J., Dilnot, A. and Low, H. (1994) 'The distribution of wealth in the UK', *IFS Commentary*, no.45, London, Institute of Fiscal Studies.

Barbier, E.B., Burgess, J.C. and Folke, C. (1994) *Paradise Lost: the Ecological Economics of Biodiversity*, London, Earthscan.

Barr, N. (1988) 'The Phillips Machine', *LSE Quarterly*, vol.2, no.4, pp.305–37.

Barr, N. (1992) 'Economic theory and the welfare state', *Journal of Economic Literature*, vol.XXX, June.

Barr, N. (1993) *The Economics of the Welfare State*, 2nd edn, London, Wiedenfeld and Nicholson.

Barr, N. and Coulter, F. (1990) 'Social security: solution or problem?', in Barr *et al.* (1990).

Barr, N. *et al.* (1990) *The State of Welfare: the Welfare State in Britain Since 1945*, Oxford, Clarendon Press.

Barrell, R. (ed.) (1994) *The UK Labour Market: Comparative Aspects and Institutional Developments*, Cambridge, Cambridge University Press.

Barro, R.J. (1991) 'Economic growth in a cross section of countries', *Quarterly Journal of Economics*, vol.106, no.2, pp.407–44.

Barro, R.J. and Gordon, D. (1983) 'A positive theory of monetary policy in a natural-rate model', *Journal of Political Economy*, vol.91, no.4, pp.589–610.

Barro, R.J. and Gordon, D.B. (1983a) 'Rules, discretion and reputation in a model of monetary policy', *Journal of Monetary Economics*, vol.12, July, pp.101–22.

Barro, R.J. and Sala-i-Martin, X. (1991) 'Convergence across states and regions', *Brookings Papers on Economic Activity*, vol.1, pp.107–58.

Bean, C. and Crafts, N.F.R. (1995) 'British economic growth since 1945: relative economic decline ... and renaissance?', *CEPR Discussion Paper*, no.1092, London, Centre for Economic Policy Research.

Bean, C. and Symons, J. (1989) 'Ten years of Mrs T', *CEPR Discussion Paper*, no.316, London, Centre for Economic Policy Research.

Beason, R. and Weinstein, D. (1994) 'Growth, economies of scale, and targeting in Japan, 1955–90', Harvard Institute of Economic Research, Discussion Paper 1644.

Begg, D., Fischer, S. and Dornbusch, R. (1991) *Economics*, London, McGraw-Hill.

Bernal, J.D. (1965) *Science in History, vol. 2: The Scientific and Industrial Revolutions*, Cambridge, Mass., MIT Press.

Besley, T. and Gouveia, M. (1994) 'Health care', *Economic Policy*, no.19.

Best, M.H. (1990) *The New Competition: Institutions of Industrial Restructuring*, Cambridge, Polity Press.

Binks, M. and Coyne, J. (1983) *The Birth of Enterprise: an Analytical and Empirical Study of the Growth of Small Firms'*, Hobart Paper 98, London, Institute of Economic Affairs.

Bird, D., Stevens, M. and Yates, A. (1991) 'Membership of trade unions in 1989', *Employment Gazette*, vol.99, no.6, pp.337–43.

Bishop, R. (1993) 'Economics, efficiency, sustainability and biodiversity', *Ambio*, vol.22, no.2–3, pp.69–73.

Blanchard, O. and Summers, L. (1986) 'Hysteresis and the European unemployment problem', *NBER Macroeconomics Annual*, vol. 1, Boston, Mass., National Bureau of Economic Research.

Blanchard, O.J. and Summers, L.H. (1988) 'Hysteresis and the European Unemployment Problem', in Cross (1988).

Boltho, A. (1982) 'Growth', in Boltho, A. (ed.) *The European Economy: Growth and Crisis*, Oxford, Oxford University Press.

Bowen, H., Leamer, E. and Sveikauskas, L. (1987) 'Multi-country, multi-factor tests of the factor abundance theory', *American Economic Review*, 77, pp.791–809.

Bradshaw, D. (1993) 'Two heads are better than one', *Financial Times*, 29 May.

Braudel, F. (1982) *The Wheels of Commerce*, London, Collins.

Braverman, H. (1974) *Labour and Monopoly Capital: the Degradation of Work in the Twentieth Century*, New York, Monthly Review Press.

British Household Panel Survey (computer file), ESRC Research Centre on Micro-social Change, Colchester, ESRC Data Archive, 1993.

Broadberry, S.N. and Crafts, N.F.R. (1992) 'Britain's productivity gap in the 1930s: some neglected factors', *Journal of Economic History*, vol.52, no.3, pp.531–58.

Broadberry, S.N. and Wagner, K. (1994) 'Human capital and productivity in manufacturing during the twentieth century', *CEPR Discussion Paper*, no. 1036, London, Centre for Economic Policy Research.

Broome, J. (1992) *Counting the Costs of Global Warming*, Cambridge, White Horse Press.

Brown, A.J. (1985) *World Inflation Since 1950*, Cambridge, Cambridge University Press.

Brown, D. (1972) *Bury my Heart at Wounded Knee: an Indian History of the American West*, London, Pan Books.

Brown, V. (1992) 'The emergence of the economy', in Hall, S. and Gieben, B. (eds) *Formations of Modernity*, Cambridge, Polity Press.

Brown, C. and Jackson, P. (1990) *Public Sector Economics*, 4th edn, Oxford, Blackwell.

Brown, C.J. and Sheriff, T.D. (1979) 'De-industrialization: a background paper', in Blackaby, F.T. (ed.) *De-industrialization*, London, Heinemann.

Buigues, P., Ilzkovitz, F. and Lebrun, J.-F. (1990) 'The impact of the internal market by industrial sector: the challenge of the member states', *European Economy*, special edition 1990, *Social Europe*, Commission of the European Communities: Directorate-General for Employment, Industrial Relations and Social Affairs and Directorate-General for Economics and Financial Affairs.

Burda, M. and Wypolosz, C. (1993) *Macroeconomics: a European Text*, Oxford, Oxford University Press.

Burke, T., Genn-Bash, A. and Haines, B. (1988) *Competition in Theory and Practice*, London, Croom Helm.

Caballero, R.J. and Lyons, R.K. (1989) 'The role of external economies in US manufacturing', National Bureau for Economic Research, *Working Paper* 3033, July.

Caballero, R.J. and Lyons, R.K. (1990) 'Internal versus external economies in European manufacturing', *European Economic Review*, vol.34, June, pp.805–30.

Calmfors, L. and Driffill, J. (1988) 'Centralisation of wage bargaining and macroeconomic performance', *Economic Policy*, no. 6, pp.13–61.

Calomiris, C.W. (1993) 'Financial factors in the Great Depression', *Journal of Economic Perspectives*, vol.7, no.2, pp.61–85.

Cannan, E. (1932) 'The demand for labour', *Economic Journal*, vol.XLII, pp.357–70.

Carson, C.S. (1975) 'The history of the United States national income and product accounts: the development of an analytical tool', *Review of Income and Wealth*, series 21, no.2, pp.153–81.

Carter, M. and Maddock, R. (1984) *Rational Expectations: Macroeconomics for the 1980s?*, London, Macmillan.

Catephores, G. (1994) 'The imperious Austrian: Schumpeter as a bourgeois Marxist', *New Left Review*, no. 205, pp.3–30.

CBI (1994) *Industrial Trends Survey*, London, CBI.

Cecchetti, S. (1986) 'The frequency of price adjustment: a study of the news-stand prices of magazines', *Journal of Econometrics*, vol.31, pp.255–74.

Cecchini, P. (1988) *The Costs of Non-Europe*, London, Wildwood House.

Central Statistical Office (1992) *Business Monitor PA 1002: Report on the Census of Production 1990*, summary volume, London, HMSO.

Central Statistical Office *Family Expenditure Survey*, 1961– (computer file), Colchester, ESRC Data Archive, 1992.

Child, J. and Smith, C. (1987) 'The context and process of organizational transformation – Cadbury Limited in its sector', *Journal of Management Studies*, vol.24, no.6, pp.565–93.

Chomsky, N. (1992) *Deterring Democracy*, London, Vintage.

Ciriacy-Wantrup, S.V. (1952) *Resource Conservation: Economics and Policy*, Berkeley, University of California Press.

Coase, R.H. (1960) 'The problem of social cost', *Journal of Law and Economics*, vol.3, October, pp.1–44.

Commission of the European Communities (1988) 'The economics of 1992', *The European Economy*, no.35; also in Emerson, M. (1988) *The Economics of 1992*, Oxford, Oxford University Press.

Commission of the European Communities (1993) 'Recent economic trends', *European Economy, Supplement A*, no.5.

Corbett, J. and Mayer, C. (1991) 'Financial reform in Eastern Europe: progress with the wrong model', *Oxford Review of Economic Policy*, vol.7, no.4, pp.57–75.

Cowling, K. (1982) *Monopoly Capitalism*, London, Macmillan.

Crafts, N.F.R. (1992) 'Productivity growth reconsidered', *Economic Policy*, vol.15, pp.387–426.

Crafts, N.F.R. (1993) *Can De-industrialization Seriously Damage Your Wealth?*, London, Institute of Economic Affairs.

Crafts, N.F.R. and Woodward, N.W.C. (1991) 'The British economy since 1945: introduction and overview', in Crafts, N.F.R. and Woodward, N.W.C. (eds), *The British Economy Since 1945*, Oxford, Clarendon Press.

Cross, R. (ed.) (1988) *Unemployment, Hysteresis and the Natural Rate Hypothesis*, Oxford, Basil Blackwell.

Crow, B. and Thomas, A. *et al.* (1983) *Third World Atlas*, Milton Keynes, Open University Press.

Cutler, D.M. and Katz, L.F. (1991) 'Macroeconomic performance and the disadvantaged', *Brookings Papers on Economic Activity*, no.2, pp.1–74.

Daly, M. and McCann, A. (1992) 'How many small firms?', *Employment Gazette*, February, pp.47–51, HMSO.

David, P.A. (1985) 'Clio and the economics of QWERTY', *American Economic Review Papers and Proceedings*, vol.77, no.2, pp.332–7.

Davidson, P. (1992–93) 'Reforming the world's money', *Journal of Post Keynesian Economics*, vol.15, no.2, pp.153–79.

Dawkins, R. (1986) *The Blind Watchmaker*, Harlow, Longman.

Dawson, G. (1992) *Inflation and Unemployment: Causes, Consequences and Cures*, Aldershot, Edward Elgar.

De Melo, J. and Panagariya, A. (1993) *New Dimensions in Regional Integration*, Cambridge, Cambridge University Press.

de Swaan, A. (1988) *In Care of the State*, Cambridge, Polity Press.

Denis, H. (1904) *Histoire des Systèmes Économiques et Socialistes*, Paris, V. Giard and E. Brière.

Denison, E.F. (1967) *Why Growth Rates Differ*, Washington, Brookings Institution.

Denison, E.F. (1968) 'Economic growth', in Caves, R.E. (ed.) *Britain's Economic Prospects*, London, Allen and Unwin.

Department of Social Security (1992) *Households Below Average Income: a Statistical Analysis, 1979–1988/89*, London, HMSO.

Dibben, M. (1993) 'Fair deals from the counter revolution', *The Observer*, 7 November.

Dicken, P. (1992) *Global Shift*, 2nd edn, London, Peter Chapman.

Dickson, M. (1991) 'How Nucor is stealing a march on the big mills', *Financial Times*, 29 May.

Dilnot, A., Disney, R., Johnson, P. and Whitehouse, E. (1994) *Pensions Policy in the UK: an Economic Analysis*, London, Institute of Fiscal Studies.

Dilnot, A. and Walker, I. (eds) (1989) *The Economics of Social Security*, Oxford, Oxford University Press.

Dixit, A.K. and Nalebuff, B.J. (1991) *Thinking Strategically: the Competitive Edge in Business, Politics, and Everyday Life*, New York, Norton.

Doorslaer, E. van, and Wagstaff, A. (1993) Equity in the finance of health care: methods and findings', in Doorslaer *et al.* (1993).

Doorslaer, E. van, Wagstaff, A. and Rutten, F. (eds) (1993) *Equity and Finance in the Delivery of Health Care: an International Perspective*, Oxford, Oxford University Press.

Dore, R. (1992) 'Japanese capitalism, Anglo-Saxon capitalism: how will the Darwinian contest turn out?', *Occasional Paper* no.4, Centre for Economic Performance, London School of Economics.

Dornbusch, R. and Edwards, S. (eds) (1991) *The Macroeconomics of Populism in Latin America*, Chicago, University of Chicago Press.

Dorsett, R. and Heady, C. (1991) 'The take-up of means tested benefits by working families with children', *Fiscal Studies*, vol.12, no.4.

Drèze, J.H. and Malinvaud, E. (1994) 'Growth and employment: the scope for a European initiative', *European Economy – Reports and Studies*, no.1, pp.75–106.

Drèze, J. and Sen, A. (1989) *Hunger and Public Action*, Oxford, Clarendon Press.

Drysdale, P. (1986) 'The Pacific basin and its economic vitality', in Morley, J. (ed.) *The Pacific Basin: New Challenges for the United States*, New York, Academy of Political Science, Columbia University.

Duijn, J.J. van (1983) *The Long Wave in Economic Life*, London, Allen and Unwin.

Edwards, J.S.S. and Fischer, K. (1991) 'Banks, finance and investment in West Germany since 1970', *Discussion Paper*, no.497, London, Centre for Economic Policy Research.

Eichengreen, B. (1992) *Golden Fetters*, Oxford, Oxford University Press.

Eichengreen, B. (1994) 'Institutions and economic growth: Europe after World War II', *CEPR Discussion Paper*, no. 973, London, Centre for Economic Policy Research.

Eichengreen, B. and Sachs, J. (1985) 'Exchange rates and economic recovery in the 1930s', *Journal of Economic History*, vol.45, pp.925–46.

Elbaum, B. and Lazonick, W. (1986) *The Decline of the British Economy*, Oxford, Clarendon Press.

Emerson, M. (1988) *The Economics of 1992*, Oxford, Oxford University Press.

Englander, A.S. and Mittelstadt, A. (1988) 'Total factor productivity: macroeconomic and structural aspects of the slowdown', *OECD Economic Studies*, vol.10, pp.7–56.

Epstein, G.A. (1992) 'Political economy and comparative central banking', *Review of Radical Political Economics*, vol.24, no.1, pp.1–30.

Ericson, R.E. (1991) 'The classical Soviet-type economy: nature of the system and implications for reform', *The Journal of Economic Perspectives*, vol.5, no.4, pp.11–28.

European Bank for Reconstruction and Development (1993) *Economics of Transition*, vol.1, no.3.

Eurostat (1990) *Poverty in Figures: Europe in the Early 1980s*, Institute of Social Studies Advisory Service (ISSAS), Luxembourg, Office for Official Publications of the European Communities.

Fagerberg, J. (1988) 'International competitiveness', *Economic Journal*, no.98, June, pp.355–74.

Feinstein, C.H. (1972) *National Income, Expenditure and Output of the United Kingdom, 1855–1965*, Cambridge, Cambridge University Press.

Fischer, S. (1991) 'Economic reform in the USS and the role of aid', *Brookings Papers on Economic Activity*, no.2, pp.289–301.

Fischer, S. (1992) 'Stabilization and economic reform in Russia', *Brookings Papers on Economic Activity*, vol.1, pp.77–111.

Fischer, S. and Gelb, A. (1991) 'The process of socialist economic transformation', *The Journal of Economic Perspectives*, vol.5, no.4, pp.91–106.

Fisher, I. (1911) *The Purchasing Power of Money*, London, Augustus M. Kelly.

Flanagan, R.J., Moene, K.O. and Wallerstein, M. (1993) *Trade Union Behaviour, Pay Bargaining, and Economic Performance*, Oxford, Clarendon Press.

Flanagan, R.J., Soskice, D.W. and Ulman, L. (1983) *Unionism, Economic Stabilization and Incomes Policies: The European Experience*, Washington, Brookings Institution.

Flynn, J., Dwyer, P. and Toy, S. (1994) 'Finally, the pay-off from Thatcher's revolution', *Business Week*, 21 February, pp.14–16.

Ford, J.L. (ed.) (1990) *Time, Expectations and Uncertainty in Economics: Selected Essays of G.L.S. Shackle*, Cheltenham, Edward Elgar.

Freeman, C. (1982) *The Economics of Industrial Innovation*, London, Francis Pinter.

Freeman, R.B. and Medoff, J.L. (1984) *What Do Unions Do?*, New York, Basic Books.

Friedman, M. (1962) *Capitalism and Freedom*, Chicago, University of Chicago Press.

Friedman, M. (1968) 'The role of monetary policy', *American Economic Review*, vol.58, pp.1–17.

Friedman, M. (1977) *Inflation and Unemployment: the New Dimension of Politics*, IEA Occasional Paper no.51, London, Institute of Economic Affairs.

Friedman, M. (1980) Evidence submitted to Treasury and Civil Service Committee, *Memoranda on Monetary Policy*, Session 1979–80, vol.1, HC 720, July, London, HMSO.

Fry, V. and Stark, G. (1991) 'New rich and old poor: poverty, take-up and the indexation of the state pension', *Fiscal Studies*, vol.12, no.1.

Galbraith, J.K. (1975) *Economics and the Public Purpose*, London, André Deutsch.

Galbraith, J.K. (1992) *The Culture of Contentment*, Harmondsworth, Penguin.

Ganguly, P. and Bannock, G. (1985) *UK Small Business Statistics and International Comparisons*, London, Harper and Row.

Geroski, P. and Jacquemin, A. (1986) 'Industrial change, barriers to mobility, and European industrial policy', *Economic Policy*, no.1, pp.169–205.

Gershuny, J. (1978) *After Industrial Society*, London, Macmillan.

Ginsberg, N. (1992) *Divisions of Welfare*, London, Sage.

Glennerster, H. (1990) 'Social policy since the Second World War', in Barr *et al.* (1990).

Glyn, A., Hughes, A., Lipietz, A. and Singh, A. (1990) 'The rise and fall of the Golden Age', in Marglin, S.A. and Schor, J.B. (eds) *The Golden Age of Capitalism*, Oxford, Clarendon Press.

Goldschmidt-Clermont, L. (1987) *Economic Evaluations of Unpaid Household Work*, Geneva, International Labour Organisation.

Goodin, R. and Dryzek, J. (1987) 'Risk sharing and social justice: the motivational foundations of the post war welfare state', in Goodin, Le Grand *et al.* (1987).

Goodin, R., Le Grand, J. *et al.* (1987) *Not Only the Poor: the Middle Class and the Welfare State*, London, Allen and Unwin.

Gowland, D. (1978) *Monetary Policy and Credit Control: the UK Experience*, London, Croom Helm.

Gowland, D. (1990) *Understanding Macroeconomics*, Aldershot, Edward Elgar.

Gowland, D.H. (1985) *Money, Inflation and Unemployment: the Role of Money in the Economy*, Brighton, Wheatsheaf.

Gradwohl, J. and Greenberg, R. (1988) *Saving the Tropical Forests*, London, Earthscan.

Green, F., Henley, A. and Tsakalotos, E. (1994) 'Income inequality in corporatist and liberal economies: a comparison of trends within OECD countries', *International Review of Applied Economics*, vol.8, no.3, pp.303–31.

Green, F. and Sutcliffe, B. (1987) *The Profit System*, Harmondsworth, Penguin.

Green, G., Coder, J. and Ryscavage, P. (1992) 'International comparisons of earnings inequality for men in the 1980s', *Review of Income and Wealth*, series 38(1), pp.1–25.

Greenhalgh, C.A. (1980) 'Male–female wage differentials in Great Britain: is marriage an equal opportunity?', *Economic Journal*, vol.90, pp.751–75.

Gregory, M., Lobban, P. and Thomson, A. (1985) 'Wage settlements in manufacturing 1979–84: evidence from the CBI Pay Databank', *British Journal of Industrial Relations*, vol.23, no.3.

Gregory, M. and Sandoval, V. (1994) 'Low pay and minimum wage protection in Britain and the EC', in Barrell, R. (ed.) (1994).

Grubb, M. *et al.* (1993) *The Earth Summit Agreements*, London, Earthscan.

Haaland, J.I. and Norman, V.D. (1992) 'Global production effects of European integration', in Winters, L.A. (ed.) *Trade Flows and Trade Policy After '1992'*, Cambridge, Cambridge University Press.

Ham, C., Robinson, R. and Benzeval, M. (1990) *Health Check: Health Care Reforms in an International Context*, London, Kings Fund Institute.

Hamilton, C.B. and Winters, L.A. (1992) 'Trade with Eastern Europe', *Economic Policy*, April, no.14, pp.78–116.

Hannah, L. and Kay, J.A. (1977) *Concentration in Modern Industry: Theory, Measurement and the UK Experience*, London, Macmillan.

Hardin, G. (1968) 'The tragedy of the commons', *Science*, vol.162,13 December.

Harper, W.M. (1991) *Statistics*, 6th edn, London, Pitman.

Harrison, P. (1987) 'A tale of two stoves', *New Scientist*, May, pp.40–3.

Hartwick, J.M. and Olewiler, N.D. (1986) *The Economics of Natural Resource Use*, New York, Harper and Row.

Haskel, J. (1991) 'Imperfect competition, work practices and productivity growth', *Oxford Bulletin of Economics and Statistics*, vol.53, pp.265–79.

Hay, D.A. and Morris, D.J. (1991) *Industrial Economics and Organization: Theory and Evidence*, Oxford, Oxford University Press.

Hayek, F. (1937) 'Economics and knowledge', *Economica*, no.4, pp.33–54.

Hayek, F. (1948) 'The meaning of competition', reprinted in Hayek, F. (1976).

Hayek, F. (1948a) 'The use of knowledge in society', reprinted in Hayek, F. (1976).

Hayek, F. (1949) *Individualism and Economic Order*, London, Routledge.

Hayek, F. (1976) *Individualism and Economic Order*, Chicago, University of Chicago Press.

Hayek, F.A. (1978) 'Full employment, planning and inflation', in *A Tiger by the Tail*, Institute of Economic Affairs, London, pp.53–60; originally published in *Studies in Philosophy, Politics and Economics*, London, Routledge, 1967.

Hendry, D.F. (1993) *Econometrics: Alchemy or Science?*, Oxford, Blackwell.

Henley, A. and Tsakalotos, E. (1991) 'Corporatism, profit squeeze and investment', *Cambridge Journal of Economics*, vol.15, pp.425–50.

Henley, A. and Tsakalotos, E. (1993) *Corporatism and Economic Performance*, Aldershot, Edward Elgar.

Hewitt, T. (1992) 'Brazilian industrialisation', in Hewitt, T., Johnson, H. and Wield, D. (eds) *Industrialisation and Development*, Oxford, Oxford University Press.

Hibbs, D.A. (1987) *The Political Economy of Industrial Democracies*, Cambridge, Mass., Harvard University Press.

Hickman, B.G. (1974) 'What became of the building cycle?', in David, P. and Reder, M. (eds) *Nations and Households in Economic Growth*, London, Academic Press.

Hills, J. (1993) *The Future of Welfare: a Guide to the Debate*, York, Joseph Rowntree Foundation, November.

HMSO (1985) *United Kingdom National Accounts: Sources and Methods*, 3rd edn, London, HMSO for Central Statistical Office.

HM Treasury (1993) *The Government's Expenditure Plans 1993–94*, London, HMSO.

HM Treasury (1993a) *Treasury Bulletin*, vol.4, no.2, London, HMSO.

HM Treasury (1993b) *Financial Statement and Budget Report*, London, HMSO.

Hobbes, T. (1651) *Leviathan, or the Matter, Forme and Power of a Commonwealth Ecclesiastical and Civil* (quotation from the Fontana edn, 1962).

Hogan, M. (1987) *The Marshall Plan*, Cambridge, Cambridge University Press.

Hogan, W.W. (1991) 'Economic reforms in the Soviet states of the former Soviet Union', *Brookings Papers on Economic Activity*, no.2, pp.303–19.

Holtfrerich, C.L. (1983) *The German Inflation, 1914–1923*, Berlin, de Gruyter.

Hoover, K. (1988) *The New Classical Macroeconomics: a Sceptical Inquiry*, Oxford, Blackwell.

Huff, D. (1991) *How to Lie with Statistics*, London, Penguin.

Hume, D. (1906) *A Treatise of Human Nature* (quotations from the 1978 edn, ed. Selby-Bigge, A.H., Oxford, Oxford University Press).

Humphrey, T. (1986) *From Trade-offs to Policy Ineffectiveness: a History of the Phillips Curve*, Richmond, Va., Federal Reserve Bank of Richmond.

ILO (International Labour Office) (1992) *The Cost of Social Security*, Thirteenth International Enquiry 1984–1986, Geneva.

Inter-American Development Bank (1992) *Economic and Social Progress in Latin America*, Washington DC, Johns Hopkins Press.

Ito, T. (1992) *The Japanese Economy*, Cambridge, Mass., MIT Press.

Jacquemin, A., Buigues, P. and Ilzkovitz, F. (1989) 'Horizontal mergers and competition policy in the European Community', *European Economy*, no.40.

Japan Statistical Association (1987) *Historical Statistics of Japan*, vol.3, Tokyo.

Jenkinson, T. (1988) 'The Nairu: statistical fact or theoretical straight jacket?', in Cross (1988).

Jenkinson, T. and Mayer, C. (1992) *Boardroom Battles*, Oxford, Oxford Economic Research Associates.

Johnson, C. (1991) *The Economy Under Mrs Thatcher, 1979–1990*, Harmondsworth, Penguin.

Junankar, P.N. (1985) *Costs of Unemployment*, Brussels, Commission of European Communities.

Kalecki, M. (1943) 'Political aspects of full employment', in Kalecki, M. (ed.) *Selected Essays on the Dynamics of the Capitalist Economy 1933–1970*, Cambridge, Cambridge University Press, pp.138–45.

Kalecki, M. (1945) 'Full employment by stimulating private investment?', reprinted in Osiatynski, J. (ed.) (1990) *Collected Works of Michal Kalecki, vol. 1, Capitalism: Business Cycles and Full Employment*, Oxford, Clarendon Press.

Kalecki, M. (1954) 'The theory of economic dynamics', reprinted in Osiatynski, J. (ed.) (1991) *Collected Works of Michal Kalecki, vol. 2, Capitalism: Economic Dynamics*, Oxford, Clarendon Press, pp.207–338.

Katz, L.F., Loveman, G.W. and Blanchflower, D.G. (1993) *A Comparison of Changes in the Structure of Wages in Four OECD Countries'*, Cambridge, Mass., National Bureau of Economic Research, working paper no.4297.

Kay, J.A. (1993) *Foundations of Corporate Success*, Oxford, Oxford University Press.

Kendrick, J.W. (1970) 'The historical development of national income accounts', *History of Political Economy*, vol.2, no.2, pp.284–315.

Kennedy, G. (1983) *Invitation to Statistics*, Oxford, Basil Blackwell.

Kennedy, P. (1988) *The Rise and Fall of the Great Powers: Economic Change and Military Conflict from 1500 to 2000*, London, Fontana.

Keynes, J.M. (1930) Evidence to the Macmillan Committee, reprinted in *The Collected Writings of John Maynard Keynes, Vol.XX Activities 1929–31: Rethinking Employment and Unemployment Policies*, London, Macmillan (1981).

Keynes, J.M. (1934) 'Poverty in plenty: is the economic system self-adjusting?', reproduced in *The Collected Writings*, vol.13, *The General Theory and After, Part I Preparation*, London, Macmillan, 1973.

Keynes, J.M. (1936) *The General Theory of Employment, Interest and Money* (quotations from the London, Macmillan edn, 1967).

Keynes, J.M. (1941) 'Activities 1940–4. Shaping the post-war world: the Clearing Union', reprinted in Moggridge, D. (ed.) (1980) *The Collected Writings of John Maynard Keynes*, vol. XXV, London, Macmillan.

Kiguel, M. and Liviatan, N. (1992) 'Stopping three big inflations', *Policy Research Working Papers*, WPS 999, Washington, World Bank.

Klamer, A. (1984) *The New Classical Macroeconomics: Conversations with New Classical Economists and their Opponents*, Brighton, Harvester Wheatsheaf.

Klein, P. and Moore, G. (1985) *Monitoring Growth Cycles in Market Oriented Countries*, Cambridge, Mass., Ballinger.

Klundert, T. van de and Schaik, A. van (1993) 'On the historical continuity of the process of economic growth', *CEPR Discussion Paper*, no.850, London, Centre for Economic Policy Research.

Knight, K.G. (1987) *Unemployment: An Economic Analysis*, London, Croom Helm.

Kolko, G. (1968) *The Politics of War*, New York, Vintage Books.

Komiya, R. (1990) *The Japanese Economy: Trade, Industry and Government*, Tokyo, University of Tokyo Press.

Kosai, Y. (1986) *The Era of High Speed Growth*, Tokyo, University of Tokyo Press.

Kregel, J., Matzner, E. and Grabher, G. (eds) (1992) *The Market Shock*, Vienna, Austrian Academy of Sciences/Research Unit for Socio-Economics.

Krugman, P. (1987) 'The narrow moving band, the Dutch disease and the competitive consequences of Mrs Thatcher', *Journal of Development Economics*, vol.27, no.1, pp.41–55.

Krugman, P. (1991) 'History and industry location: the case of the manufacturing belt', *American Economic Review Papers and Proceedings*, vol.81, no.2, pp.80–3.

Krugman, P.R. and Obstfeld, M. (1994) *International Economics, Theory and Policy*, 3rd edn, London, HarperCollins.

Layard, R. (1986) *How to Beat Unemployment*, Oxford, Oxford University Press.

Layard, R. and Nickell, S. (1985) 'The causes of British unemployment', *National Institute Economic Review*, February, pp.62–85.

Layard, R., Nickell, S. and Jackman, R. (1991) *Unemployment: Macroeconomic Performance and the Labour Market*, Oxford, Oxford University Press.

Layard, R., Nickell, S. and Jackman, R. (1994) *The Unemployment Crisis*, Oxford, Oxford University Press.

Le Grand, J. (1982) *The Strategy of Equality: Redistribution and the Social Services*, London, Allen and Unwin.

Le Grand, J. (1987) 'The middle class use of the British social services', in Goodin, Le Grand *et al.* (1987).

Le Grand, J. (1991) 'Quasi-markets and social policy', *Economic Journal*, no.101.

Le Grand, J. (1991a) *Equity and Choice*, London, HarperCollins.

Leontief, W.W. (1953) 'Domestic production and foreign trade; the American capital position re- examined', *Proceedings of the American Philosophical Society*, 97, pp. 332–49.

Levy, F. and Murmane, R.J. (1992) 'US earnings levels and earnings inequality: a review of recent trends and proposed explanations', *Journal of Economic Literature*, vol.30, pp.1333–81.

Lewis, H.G. (1963) *Unionism and Relative Wages in the United States*, Chicago, University of Chicago Press.

Lewis, H.G. (1986) 'Union relative wage effects', in Ashenfelter, O. and Layard, R. (eds) *Handbook of Labor Economics*, Amsterdam, North- Holland.

Liebenstein, H. (1966) 'Allocative efficiency and X-efficiency', *American Economic Review*, vol.56, pp.392–415.

Likierman, A. (1988) *Public Expenditure*, London, Penguin.

Lindbeck, A. and Snower, D. (1988) *The Insider-Outsider Theory of Employment and Unemployment*, Cambridge, Mass., MIT Press.

Lindbeck, A. and Snower, D. (1988a) 'Union activity, unemployment persistence and wage-employment ratchets', in Cross (1988).

Linder, S.B. (1986) *The Pacific Century*, Stanford University Press.

Lipsey, R.G. (1989) *An Introduction to Positive Economics*, London, Weidenfeld and Nicolson.

Lipsey, R. and Lancaster, K. (1956) 'The general theory of the second best', *Review of Economic Studies*, vol. 24, pp.11–32.

Lorenz, C. (1994) 'Nationality should still count', *Financial Times*, 11 February, p.13.

Lucas, R. (1981) *Studies in Business Cycle Theory*, Oxford, Blackwell.

Lucas, R.E. (1987) *Models of Business Cycles*, Oxford, Blackwell.

Maddison, A. (1985) *Two Crises: Latin America and Asia 1929–38 and 1973–83*, Paris, OECD.

Maddison, A. (1991) *Dynamic Forces in Capitalist Development*, Oxford, Oxford University Press.

Mahar, D. (1989) *Government Policies and Deforestation in Brazil's Amazon Region*, Washington, World Bank.

Maizels, A. (1963) *Industrial Growth and World Trade*, Cambridge, Cambridge University Press.

Mankiw, G. (1985) 'Small menu costs and large business cycles: a macroeconomic model of monopoly', *Quarterly Journal of Economics*, no.400, pp.529–39.

Mankiw, G. (1990) 'A quick refresher course in Macroeconomics', *Journal of Economic Literature*, XXVIII (4), December, pp.1645–60.

Mankiw, N.G. (1989) 'Real business cycles: a new Keynesian perspective', *Journal of Economic Perspectives*, vol.3, no.3, pp.79–90.

Marglin, S.A. and Bhaduri, A. (1990) 'Profit squeeze and Keynesian theory', in Marglin, S.A. and Schor, J.B. (eds) *The Golden Age of Capitalism*, Oxford, Clarendon Press.

Marshall, R. and Tucker, M. (1992) *Education and the Wealth of Nations*, New York, Basic Books.

Marx, K. (1867) *Capital*, vol.1 (Chapter 6 quotations from the 1912 edn, Chicago, Kerr; Chapter 25 quotations from the 1954 edn, London, Lawrence & Wishart).

Marx, K. (1894) *Capital*, vol.3, reprinted 1981, Harmondsworth, Penguin.

Maskin, E. and Tirole, J. (1988) 'A theory of dynamic oligopoly, II: price competition, kinked demand curves, and Edgeworth cycles', *Econometrica*, vol.56, pp.571–99.

Matthews, K.P.G. and Minford, A.P.L. (1987) 'Mrs Thatcher's economic policies, 1979–87', *Economic Policy*, 5 October, pp.57–101.

Matthews, R.C.O. (1959) *The Trade Cycle*, Cambridge, Cambridge University Press.

Mayer, C. (1992) 'The financing of innovation', in Bowen, A. and Ricketts, M. (eds) *Stimulating Innovation in Industry*, London, Kogan Page.

Mayer, C. and Alexander, I. (1990) 'Banks and securities markets: corporate financing in Germany and the UK', *Discussion Paper*, no.433, London, Centre for Economic Policy Research.

McCloskey, D.N. (1986) *The Rhetoric of Economics*, Brighton, Harvester Press.

McCloskey, D.N. (1990) *If You're So Smart: The Narrative of Economic Expertise*, Chicago, University of Chicago Press.

McKinnon, R.I. (1988) 'Monetary and exchange rate policies for international financial stability: a proposal', *Journal of Economic Perspectives*, vol.2, pp.83–103.

McRobie, G. (1981) *Small is Possible*, London, Jonathan Cape.

Meade, J.E. (1994) *Full Employment Without Inflation*, London, Social Market Foundation.

Meadows, D.H., Meadows, D.L., Randers, J. and Behrens, W. (1972) The 'Club of Rome', *The Limits to Growth*, London, Earth Island.

Miller, P.W. (1987) 'The wage effect of occupational segregation of women in Britain', *Economic Journal*, vol.97, pp.885–96.

Minford, A.P.L. (1985) *Unemployment: Cause and Cure*, Oxford, Basil Blackwell.

Minford, A.P.L. and Peel, D. (1983) *Rational Expectations and the New Macroeconomics*, Oxford, Martin Robertson.

Minford, P. (1983) *Unemployment: Cause and Cure*, Oxford, Martin Robertson.

Minford, P. *et al.* (1985) *Unemployment: Cause and Cure*, 2nd edn, Oxford, Blackwell.

Mintzberg, H. (1989) *Mintzberg on Management: Inside our Strange World of Organizations*, New York, Free Press.

Mirowski, P. (1989) *More Heat than Light*, Cambridge, Cambridge University Press.

Mitchell, B.R. (1988) *British Historical Statistics*, Cambridge, Cambridge University Press.

Mitchell, S. (1981) 'Introduction', in Mitchell, S. (ed.) *The Logic of Poverty*, London, Routledge and Kegan Paul.

Moore, J. (1983) quoted in Kay, J.A., Mayer, C. and Thompson, D. (eds) (1986) *Privatisation and Regulation: the UK Experience*, Oxford, Clarendon Press.

Moran, D. (1994) 'Forestry', in Pearce, D.W. *et al.*, *Blueprint 3: Measuring Sustainable Development*, London, Earthscan.

Musgrave, R. and Musgrave, P. (1984) *Public Finance in Theory and Practice*, 4th edn, New York, McGraw-Hill.

Muth, J.F. (1961) 'Rational expectations and the theory of price movements', *Econometrica*, vol.29, pp.315–35.

Myers, N. (1990) 'Tropical forests', in Leggett, J., *Global Warming: the Greenpeace Report*, Oxford, Oxford University Press.

Myers, N. (1992) 'Biodiversity preservation and the precautionary principle', *Ambio*, vol.22, no.2–3, pp.74–9.

Nelson, R.R. and Wright, G. (1992) 'The rise and fall of American technological leadership: the postwar era in historical perspective', *Journal of Economic Literature*, vol.30, no.4, pp.1931–64.

Nemetz, P. (1990) *The Pacific Rim: Investment, Development and Trade*, 2nd edn, Vancouver, University of British Columbia Press.

Netting, R. (1981) *Balancing on an Alp*, Cambridge, Cambridge University Press.

Newell, A. and Symons, J. (1988) 'The macroeconomics of the interwar years: international comparisons', in Eichengreen, B. and Hatton, T. (eds) *Interwar Unemployment in International Perspective*, Dordrecht, Kluwer Academic Publishers.

Newlyn, W.T. (1950) 'The Phillips/Newlyn hydraulic model', *Yorkshire Bulletin of Economics*, September.

Nolan, P. (1993) 'China's post-Mao political economy: a puzzle', *Contributions to Political Economy*, vol.12, pp.71–97.

Norheim, H., Finger, K.M. and Anderson, K. (1993) 'Trends in the regionalisation of world trade, 1928–1990', in Anderson, K. and Blackhurst, R. (eds) *Regional Integration and the Global Trading System*, Hemel Hempstead, Harvester Wheatsheaf.

North, D. (1993) *Institutions, Institutional Change and Economic Performance*, Cambridge, Cambridge University Press.

Northedge, A. (1990) *The Good Study Guide*, Milton Keynes, The Open University.

Nozick, R. (1974) *Anarchy, State and Utopia*, Oxford, Blackwell.

O'Higgins, M., Schmaus, G. and Stephenson, G. (1990) 'Income distribution and redistribution: a microdata analysis for seven countries', in Smeeding *et al.* (1990).

O'Mahony, M. (1992) 'Productivity and human capital formation in UK and German manufacturing', *National Institute of Economic and Social Research Discussion Paper*, no.28.

Oakley, A. (1990) *Schumpeter's Theory of Capitalist Motion*, Cheltenham, Edward Elgar.

OECD (1982) *Historical Statistics, 1960- 1980*, Paris, OECD.

OECD (1988) *The Future of Social Protection*, Paris, OECD.

OECD (1990) *Health Care Systems in Transition*, Paris, OECD.

OECD (1991) *Main Science and Technology Indicators*, Paris, OECD.

OECD (1991a) *Basic Science and Technology Statistics*, Paris, OECD.

OECD (1992) *Historical Statistics, 1960–1990*, Paris, OECD.

OECD (1992a) *International Direct Investment: Policies and Trends in the 1990s*, Paris, OECD.

OECD (1993) *OECD Economic Surveys: Japan*, Paris, OECD.

OECD (1994) *The OECD Jobs Study: Facts, Analysis, Strategies*, Paris, OECD.

OECD (1994a) 'New orientations for social policy', *Social Policy Studies*, no.12, Paris, OECD.

Okun, A. (1970) 'Potential GNP: its measurement and significance', Appendix, *Political Economy of Prosperity*, Washington, DC, Brookings Institution.

Olson, M. (1982) *The Rise and Decline of Nations*, Newhaven, Conn., Yale University Press.

Olson, M. (1988) 'The productivity slow-down, the oil shocks, and the real cycle', *The Journal of Economic Perspectives*, vol.2, no.4, pp.43–69.

Ormerod, P. (1994) *The Death of Economics*, London, Faber and Faber.

Ostrom, E. (1990) *Governing the Commons*, Cambridge, Cambridge University Press.

Parkin, V. (1991) *Chronic Inflation in an Industrialising Economy: the Brazilian Experience*, Cambridge, Cambridge University Press.

Patel, P. and Pavitt, K. (1988) 'The international distribution and determinants of technological activities', *Oxford Review of Economic Policy*, vol.4, no.4, pp.35–55.

Pavitt, K. and Soete, L. (1982) 'International differences in economic growth and the international location of innovation', in Giersch, H. (ed.) *Emerging Technologies*, Tübingen, Mohr.

Payne, J. (1991) *Women, Training and the Skill Shortage: the Case for Public Investment*, London, Policy Studies Institute.

Peacock, A. and Wiseman, S. (1961) *The Growth of Public Expenditure in the United Kingdom*, Princeton, Princeton University Press.

Pearce, D.W. (1990) 'Population growth', *Blueprint 2: Greening the World Economy*, London, Earthscan.

Pearce, D.W. (1992) 'Deforesting the Amazon: toward an economic solution', *Ecodecision*, vol.1, pp.40–50.

Pearce, D.W., Barbier, E. and Markandya, A. (1990) *Sustainable Development*, London, Earthscan.

Pearce, D.W., Fankhauser, S., Adger, W.N. and Swanson, T. (1993) 'World economy, world environment', *World Economy*, vol.15, no.3, pp.295–314.

Pearce, D.W., Moran, D., Maddison, D. and Adger, W.N. (1995) 'Debt and environment', *Scientific American*, vol.272, no.6, pp.28–32.

Pearce, D. and Turner, K. (1990) *The Economics of Natural Resources and the Environment*, Hemel Hempstead, Harvester Wheatsheaf.

Pearce, D.W. and Warford, J.J. (1993) *World Without End: Economics, Environment and Sustainable Development*, New York, Oxford University Press.

Pearce, J. (1981) *Under the Eagle: US Intervention in Central America and the Caribbean*, London, Latin American Bureau.

Pearson, J., Barnathan, J., Hinchberger, B. and Wehrfritz, G. (1993) 'Many Third World players are going world class', *Business Week*, 12 July, pp.40–3.

Peck, M.J. (1989) 'Industrial organization and the gains from Europe 1992', *Brookings Papers on Economic Activity*, vol.2, pp.277–99.

Pepper, G.T. (1990) *Money, Credit and Inflation*, research monograph no.44, London, Institute of Economic Affairs.

Perkins, D.H. (1986) *China: Asia's Next Economic Giant?*, Seattle, University of Washington Press.

Phelps, E.S. (1967) 'Phillips curves, expectations of inflation and optimal unemployment over time', *Economica*, vol.34, August, pp.254–81.

Phelps, E.S. (1972) *Inflation Policy and Unemployment Theory*, London, Macmillan.

Phillips, A.W. (1950) 'Mechanical models of economic dynamics', *Economica* (new series), vol. xvii, pp.283–305.

Phillips, A.W. (1958) 'The relationship between unemployment and the rate of change of money wage rates in the United Kingdom 1861–1957', *Economica*, vol.24, pp.283–99.

Pigou, A.C. (1920) *The Economics of Welfare* (quotations from the 4th edn, London, Macmillan, 1960).

Pilbeam, K. (1992) *International Finance*, London, Macmillan.

Pleck, J.H. (1979) 'Men's family work: three perspectives and some new data', *The Family Co-ordinator*, October.

Pliatsky, L. (1982) *Getting and Spending*, Oxford, Blackwell.

Plosser, C.I. (1989) 'Understanding real business cycles', *Journal of Economic Perspectives*, vol.3, no.3, pp.51–77.

Polanyi, K. (1944) *The Great Transformation: the Political and Economic Origins of Our Time* (quotations from the Beacon Press edn, Boston, 1957).

Policy Studies Institute (1992) *Credit and Debt: the PSI Report*, London, PSI.

Porter, M.E. (1990) *The Competitive Advantage of Nations*, London, Macmillan.

Posnett, J. (1992) 'Income and expenditure of charities in England and Wales', *Charity Trends*, HMSO.

Prais, S.J. (1981) *Productivity and Industrial Structure*, Cambridge, Cambridge University Press.

Prais, S.J. and Wagner, K. (1988) 'Productivity and management: the training of foremen in Britain and Germany', *National Institute Economic Review*, vol.123, pp.34–47.

Pratten, C.F. (1976) *Labour Productivity Differentials within International Companies*, Cambridge, Cambridge University Press.

Price, S. (1988) 'Unemployment and worker quality', in Cross (1988).

Quadling, D. (1987) *Statistics and Probability*, Cambridge, Cambridge University Press.

Rawls, J. (1972) *A Theory of Justice*, Oxford, Oxford University Press.

Reati, A. (1992) 'Are we at the beginning of a new long term expansion induced by technological change?', *International Review of Applied Economics*, vol.6, no.3, pp.249–85.

Reid, G.C. (1981) *The Kinked Demand Curve Analysis of Oligopoly*, Edinburgh, Edinburgh University Press.

Rein, M. and Rainwater, L. (eds) (1986) *Public/Private Interplay in Social Protection: a Comparative Study*, Armonk, New York, M.E. Sharp.

Robinson, J. (1978) *Economic Philosophy*, Harmondsworth, Penguin.

Robinson, J.P. *et al.* (1972) 'Everyday life in twelve countries', in Szalai, A. (ed.) *The Use of Time*, The Hague, Mouton.

Rogers, C. (1993) 'Mr. Keynes and the Post Keynesians: principles of macroeconomics for a monetary production economy', *Economic Journal*, vol.103, no.420, September, pp.1317–18.

Romer, C.D. (1993) 'The nation in depression', *Journal of Economic Perspectives*, vol.7, no.2, pp.19–39.

Rowthorn, B. (1992) 'Corporatism and labour market performance', in Pekkarinen, J., Pohjola, M. and Rowthorn, B. (eds) *Social Corporatism: a Superior Economic System?*, Oxford, Oxford University Press.

Rowthorn, R. (1977) 'Conflict, inflation and money', *Cambridge Journal of Economics*, vol.1, pp.215–39.

Rowthorn, R. (1992) 'Centralisation, employment and wage dispersion', *Economic Journal*, vol.102, no.412, May.

Rowthorn, R. *et al.* (1993) *Social Corporatism*, Oxford, Clarendon Press.

Rubin, M. (1987) *Charity and Community in Medieval Cambridge*, Cambridge, Cambridge University Press.

Sachs, J. and Larrain, F. (1993) *Macroeconomics in the Global Economy*, Brighton, Harvester Wheatsheaf.

Sadowski, Z. (1991) 'Privatization in Eastern Europe: goals, problems, implications', *Oxford Review of Economic Policy*, vol.7, no.4, pp.46–56.

Samuelson, P. (1939) 'Interaction between the multiplier analysis and the principle of acceleration', *Review of Economic Statistics*, no.21, May, pp.75–8.

Samuelson, P.A. (1969) 'The way of an economist', *International Economic Relations, Proceedings of the Third Congress of the International Economics Association*, London, Macmillan.

Sapir, A. (1992) 'Regional integration in Europe', *Economic Journal*, vol.102, no.415, pp.1491–506.

Sapsford, D. and Tzannatos, Z. (1993) *The Economics of the Labour Market*, Basingstoke, Macmillan.

Sargent, T.J. (1986) *Rational Expectations and Inflation*, New York, Harper and Row.

Sawyer, M.C. (1985) *The Economics of Michal Kalecki*, London, Macmillan.

Scherer, F.M. (1975) *The Economics of Multiplant Operation*, Cambridge, Mass., Harvard University Press.

Scherer, F.M. and Ross, D. (1990) *Industrial Market Structure and Economic Performance*, Boston, Houghton Mifflin.

Schmalensee, R. and Willig, R.D. (1989) *Handbook of Industrial Organisation*, Amsterdam, North-Holland.

Schumpeter, J. (1934) *The Theory of Economic Development*, Boston, Harvard (quotations from the Oxford University Press edn, New York, 1961).

Schumpeter, J. (1939) *Business Cycles*, 2 vols, New York, McGraw- Hill.

Schumpeter, J. (1942) *Capitalism, Socialism and Democracy*, New York, Harper.

Schumpeter, J. (1951) *Essays* (quotations from the 1989 edn, New Brunswick, Transaction Books).

Segal, N. (1987) 'The Cambridge phenomenon', in Ferguson, D. *et al.*, *Cambridge*, Cambridge, Covent Garden Press.

Sen, A. (1987) *Hunger and Entitlements: Research for Action*, Helsinki, World Institute for Development Economics Research of the United Nations University.

Sen, A.K. (1973) *On Economic Inequality*, Oxford, Clarendon Press.

Sen, A.K. (1976) 'Rational fools: a critique of the behavioural foundations of economic theory', *Philosophy and Public Affairs*, vol.6, Summer, pp.317–44.

Sen, A.K. (1985) *Commodities and Capabilities*, Amsterdam, North Holland.

Sen, A.K. (1987) *On Ethics and Economics*, Oxford, Blackwell.

Sen, A.K. (1987a) *On Ethics and Economics*, Oxford, Basil Blackwell.

Shapiro, C. (1989) 'Theories of oligopoly behaviour', in Schmalensee, R. and Willig, R.D. (eds), vol.1, pp.329–414.

Sherman, H.J. (1991) *The Business Cycle*, Princeton, Princeton University Press.

Sik, E. (1992) 'Networking in capitalist, communist and post-communist societies', extended version of paper presented at 4th International Karl Polanyi Conference, Concordia University, Montreal, November.

Skidelsky, R. (1992) *John Maynard Keynes, the Economist as Saviour 1920–1937*, London, Macmillan.

Smeeding, T.M., O'Higgins, M. and Rainwater, L. (1990) *Poverty, Inequality and Income Distribution in Comparative Perspective, The Luxembourg Income Study*, London, Harvester Wheatsheaf.

Smith, A. (1776) *An Inquiry into the Nature and Causes of the Wealth of Nations*, London (quotations from the Everyman edn, London, David Campbell Publishers, 1991; Chapter 8 quotation from the 1976 edn, eds Campbell, R.H. and Skinner, A.S., Oxford, Clarendon Press).

Smith, A. (1790) *The Theory of Moral Sentiments* (quotations from the 6th edn, eds Raphael, D. and MacFie, A., Oxford, Clarendon Press, 1976).

Smith, R. (1993) *Personal Wealth Taxation: Canadian Tax Policy in a Historical and International Setting*, Canadian Tax Foundation, Toronto.

Smithin, J.N. (1990) *Macroeconomics After Thatcher and Reagan*, Aldershot, Edward Elgar.

Social Security Committee (1992/93) *Low Income Families 1979–1989*, Second Report Session, H.C. paper 359, London, HMSO.

Soete, L.L. (1979) 'Firm size and inventive activity: the evidence reconsidered', *European Economic Review*, vol.12, pp.319–40.

Solomou, S.N. (1987) 'Kondratieff, Nikolai Dmitrievich', in Eatwell, J. (ed.) *The New Palgrave*, London, Macmillan.

Solomou, S.N. (1987a) *Phases of Economic Growth, 1850–1973: Kondratieff Waves and Kuznets Swings*, Cambridge, Cambridge University Press.

Solow, A. (1989) 'Is there a global warming problem?', in Dornbusch, R. and Poterba, J. (eds) *Global Warming: Economic Policy Responses*, Cambridge, Mass., MIT Press.

Soskice, D. (1989) 'Wage determination: the changing role of institutions in advanced countries', *Oxford Review of Economic Policy*, vol.6, no.4, pp.36–61.

Soskice, D. (1990) 'Wage determination: the changing role of institutions in advanced industrialized countries', *Oxford Review of Economic Policy*, vol.6, no.4, pp.36–61.

Soskice, D. (1991) 'Wage determination: the changing role of institutions in advanced industrial countries', *Oxford Review of Economic Policy*, vol.6, no.4, pp.36–61.

Squires, J. (1993) 'Introduction', *Principled Positions: Postmodernism and the Rediscovery of Value*, London, Lawrence & Wishart.

Stanners, W. (1993) 'Is low inflation an important condition for high growth?', *Cambridge Journal of Economics*, vol.17, no.1, pp.79–107.

Sterne, G. and Bayoumi, T. (1993) 'Temporary cycles or volatile trends? Economic fluctuations in 21 OECD countries', *Bank of England Working Paper*, no.13, London, Bank of England.

Stone, R. (1951) 'The use and development of national income and expenditure estimates', in Chester, D.N. (ed.) *Lessons of the British War Economy*, Cambridge, Cambridge University Press.

Stoneman, P. (1991) 'The promotion of technical progress in UK industry: a consideration of alternative policy instruments', *Warwick Business School Research Papers*, no.11, Warwick, Warwick Business School.

Studenski, P. (1958) *The Income of Nations: Theory, Measurement and Analysis: Past and Present*, New York, New York University Press.

Sugden, R. (1986) *The Economics of Rights, Co-operation and Welfare*, Oxford, Blackwell.

Sugden, R. (1992) 'Anarchic order', in Hargreaves-Heap, S. *et al.*, *The Theory of Choice: A Critical Guide*, Oxford, Blackwell.

Svejnar, J. (1991) 'Microeconomic issues in the transition to a market economy', *The Journal of Economic Perspectives*, vol.5, no.4, pp.123–38.

Swann, D. (1992) *The Economics of the Common Market*, 7th edn, Harmondsworth, Penguin.

Swanson, T. (1990) 'Biodiversity', in Pearce, D.W. (1990).

Symes, D. (1992) 'Agrarian reform and the restructuring of rural society in Hungary', paper presented at Rural Economy and Society Study Group, University of Hull, December.

Thirlwall, A.P. (1994) *Growth and Development*, 5th edn, London, Macmillan.

Thomas, A. *et al.* (1994) *Third World Atlas*, 2nd edn, Buckingham, Open University Press in association with The Open University.

Thurow, L. (1992) *Head to Head: the Coming Economic Battle among Japan, Europe and America*, London, Nicholas Brealey Publishing.

Titmuss, R. (1970) *The Gift Relationship*, London, Allen and Unwin.

Townsend, H. (1968) *Scale, Innovation, Merger and Monopoly: an Introduction to Industrial Economics*, Oxford, Pergamon Press.

Tribe, K. (1994) 'Market economics and the economics of the market', in Thompson, G.F. (ed.) *The United States in the Twentieth Century: Markets*, London, Hodder and Stoughton in association with The Open University.

Trigg, A.B. (1994) 'On the relationship between Kalecki and the Kaleckians', *Journal of Post Keynesian Economics*, vol.17, no.1, pp.91–109.

Truman, E.M. (1975) 'The effects of European economic integration on the production and trade of manufactured product', in Balassa, B. (1975a), pp.3–39.

Turner, R.K. (1990) 'Environmentally sensitive aid', in Pearce, D.W. (1990).

Turner, R.K. (1993) 'Speculations on weak and strong sustainability', in Turner, R.K. (ed.) *Sustainable Environmental Economics and Management: Principles and Practice*, 2nd edn, London, Belhaven.

Tylecote, A. (1992) *The Long Wave in the World Economy*, London, Routledge.

UK Motor Industry (1993) Key Note Market Review, 3rd edn, Hampton, Middlesex, Key Note.

UN (1992) *World Investment Report: Transnational Corporations as Engines of Growth*, New York, UN Department of Economic and Social Development, Transnational Corporations and Management Division.

UN (1993) *World Investment Report*, New York, UN.

UNECE (United Nations Economic Commission for Europe) (1992) *Economic Survey of Europe, 1991–2*, New York, United Nations.

UNIDO (United Nations Industrial and Development Organization) (1993) *Industry and Development Global Report 1993/4*, Vienna, UNIDO.

United Nations Development Programme (1992) *Human Development Report 1992*, New York, UNDP.

US Bureau of the Census (1960) *Historical Statistics of the US*, Washington DC.

US Bureau of the Census (1993) *Statistical Abstract of the United States*, Washington DC, Government Printing Office.

US Department of Commerce (1975) *Historical Statistics of the United States: Colonial Times to 1970*, Washington DC.

van Ark, *see* Ark, van

van de Klundert, *see* Klundert, van de

Veblen, T. (1912) *The Theory of the Leisure Class*, London, Macmillan.

Vickers, J. and Yarrow, G. (1991) 'The British electricity experiment', *Economic Policy*, vol.6, no.1, pp.187–232.

Vitousek, P.M., Erlich, P.R., Erlich, A.H. and Matson, P.A. (1986) 'Human appropriation of the products of photosynthesis', *Bioscience*, vol.36, no.6, pp.368–73.

Wade, R. (1987) 'The management of common property resources: collective action as an alternative to privatisation or state regulation', *Cambridge Journal of Economics*, vol.11, no.2.

Wade, R. (1990) *Governing the Market*, Princeton, Princeton University Press.

Waelbroeck, M. (1992) 'Is the Common Market a free market?', in *Essays in Regulation*, Oxford, Regulatory Policy Institute.

Wagner, A. (1883) *Finanzwissenschaft* (quotations from Wagner, A. 'Three extracts on public finance', in Musgrave, R. and Peacock, A. (eds) *Classics in the Theory of Public Finance*, London, Macmillan, 1958).

Wagstaff, A. and Doorslaer, E. van (1993) 'Equity in the delivery of health care: methods and findings', in Doorslaer *et al.* (1993).

Waring, M. (1989) *If Women Counted: a New Feminist Economics*, London, Macmillan.

Webb, S.B .(1986) 'Fiscal news and inflationary expectations in Germany after World War I', *Journal of Economic History*, vol.46, no.3, pp.769–94.

Webb, S.B. (1989) *Hyperinflation and Stabilization in Weimar Germany*, Oxford, Oxford University Press.

Weick, K.E. (1979) *The Social Psychology of Organizing*, 2nd edn, Reading, Mass., Addison Wesley.

Wheelock, J. (1990) *Husbands at Home: the Domestic Economy in a Post-Industrial Society*, London, Routledge.

Whish, R. (1993) *Competition Law*, 3rd edn, London, Butterworth.

Wilkinson, R. (1994) 'Health, redistribution and growth', in Glynn, A. and Milliband, D., *Paying for Inequality*, London, IPPR and Rivers Oram Press.

Williamson, J. (1992–93) 'On designing an international monetary system', *Journal of Post Keynesian Economics*, vol.15, no.2, pp.181–92.

Williamson, J. and Miller, M. (1987) *Targets and Indicators: a Blueprint for the International Co-ordination of Economic Policy*, Washington DC, Institute for International Economics.

Williamson, J. and Milner, C. (1991) *The World Economy, a Textbook in International Economics*, Hemel Hempstead, Harvester Wheatsheaf.

Wilson, E.O. (1992) *The Diversity of Life*, London, Penguin.

Winters, L.A. (1987) 'Britain in Europe: a survey of quantitative trade studies', *Journal of Common Market Studies*, vol.25, pp.315–35.

Winters, L.A. and Venables, A.J. (1991) *European Integration: Trade and Industry*, Cambridge, Cambridge University Press.

World Bank (1992) *World Development Indicators*, Washington, World Bank [via the Socio-Economic Time Series Access and Retrieval System (STARS)].

World Bank (1993) *The East Asian Economic Miracle*, Washington, World Bank.

World Commission on Environment and Development (Bruntland Commission) (1987) *Our Common Future*, Oxford, Oxford University Press.

World Resources Institute (1992) *World Resources 1992–93*, Washington, DC, World Resources Institute.

Wright, R.E. and Ermisch, J.F. (1991) 'Gender discrimination in the British labour market: a reassessment', *Economic Journal*, vol.101, pp.508–22.

Wuyts, M. (1994) *Analysing Trends in Time Series Data*, Population and Development Teaching Texts, The Hague, Institute of Social Studies.

ACKNOWLEDGEMENTS

Grateful acknowledgement is made to the following sources for permission to reproduce material in this book:

Chapter 1

Figures

Figure 1.3: This table is reprinted with permission of the publisher from *The Pacific Rim: Investment, Development and Trade*, edited by Peter Nemetz (Vancouver: UBC Press, 1990). All rights reserved by the Publisher; Figure 1.8 (*top*): Susan Cunningham; Figure 1.8 (*bottom*): Mark Edwards/Still Pictures; Figure 1.9: *World Development Report 1992: Development of the Environment*, Oxford University Press, Inc., © 1992 The International Bank for Reconstruction and Development/The World Bank.

Tables

Table 1.1: Bairoch, P. (1982) 'International industrialisation levels from 1750 to 1980', in De Rosa, L. (ed.) *Journal of European Economic History*, vol. 11, no. 2, Banca Di Roma, Italy.

Cartoons

p.37: Banx.

Chapter 2

Figures

Figure 2.3: London School of Economics/Suntory-Toyota International Centre for Economics and Related Disciplines; Figure 2.4: Barr, N. (1988) 'The Phillips machine', in *LSE Quarterly*, Winter 1988, Basil Blackwell Ltd; Figure 2.5: *Punch*, 15 April 1953.

Tables

Tables 2.4, 2.5 and 2.6: adapted from CSO (1992) *Key Data*, 1992/3 edition, © Crown Copyright, reproduced with the permission of the Controller of Her Majesty's Stationery Office.

Chapter 3

Tables

Table 3.2: CSO (1992) *Social Trends 22*, © Crown Copyright, reproduced with the permission of the Controller of Her Majesty's Stationery Office.

Chapter 4

Figures

Figure 4.8: Birmingham City Council, Library Services, Archives Division.

Tables

Table 4.1: CSO (1992) *Great Britain Annual Abstract of Statistics*, © Crown Copyright, reproduced with the permission of the Controller of Her Majesty's Stationery Office.

Chapter 5

Text

'Dirty Dogfighting', *Financial Times*, 12 January 1993.

Chapter 6

Text

Reeves, P. (1993) 'Hardball in the software league', *The Independent on Sunday*, 26 September 1993.

Figures

Figure 6.2: Cowling, K. (1982) *Monopoly Capitalism*, Macmillan Press Ltd.

Tables

Table 6.6: Freeman, C. (1982) *The Economics of Industrial Innovation*, Pinter Publishers Ltd, © Christopher Freeman.

Chapter 7

Text

'Family values', *The Economist*, 25 Dec 1993 - 7 Jan 1994; Wainwright, M. (1994) 'Beer supping reform comes to successful head', *The Guardian*, 20 January 1994; 'The softening of software', *The Economist*, 8-14 January 1994; 'Seagate's watershed', *The Economist*, 13 November 1993; 'Chill in eastern US heats hogs, gas futures', *Toronto Globe and Mail*, 28 December 1993, Reuters, London; 'The basic issue', *The Economist*, 20 November 1993.

Figures

Figure 7.1: Daly, M. and McCann, A. (1992) 'How many small firms?', *Employment Gazette*, February 1992, © Crown Copyright, reproduced with the permission of the Controller of Her Majesty's Stationery Office.

Chapter 9

Figures

Figure 9.8: Crow, B., Thomas, A., Jenkins, R. and Kimble, J. (1983) *Third World Atlas*, Open University Press; Figure 9.10: *Family Expenditure Survey 1992*. Central Statistical Office. © Crown Copyright. Reproduced with the permission of the Controller of Her Majesty's Stationery Office; Figure 9.23: CSO (1992) *Key Data*, 1992/93 edition, © Crown Copyright, reproduced with the permission of the Controller of Her Majesty's Stationery Office.

Tables

Tables 9.1, 9.6, 9.7 and 9.11: *British Household Panel Survey, 1991*. The data used in this BHPS were made available through the ESRC Data Archive. The data were originally collected by the ESRC Research Centre on Micro-social Change at the University of Essex. Neither the original collectors of the data nor the Archive bear any responsibility for the analyses of interpretations presented here; Table 9.10: *Family Expenditure Survey 1992*. Central Statistical Office. © Crown Copyright. Reproduced with the permission of the Controller of Her Majesty's Stationery Office.

Chapter 10

Figures

Figure 10.6: Brown, C.V. and Jackson, P.M. (1990) *Public Sector Economics*, 4th edn, Basil Blackwell Ltd.

Chapter 11

Text

Kellaway, L. (1993) 'Twelve acorns for a haircut', *Financial Times*, 30 November 1993.

Figures

Figures 11.5 and 11.10: HM Treasury (1993) *Economic Briefing*, no.5, August. © Crown Copyright, reproduced with the permission of Her Majesty's Stationery Office.

Cartoons

p.79: Nick Baker.

Chapter 12

Text

United Nations, *World Investment Report: Transnational Corporations as Engines of Growth*, 1992, United Nations Publications.

Figures

Figure 12.3: Thomsen, S. (1992) 'Integration through globalisation', in Lomax, D.F. (ed.) *National Westminster Bank: Quarterly Review*, February 1992, National Westminster Bank plc; Figure 12.7: HM Treasury (1993) *Treasury Bulletin*, Summer 1993, vol.4, no.2, © Crown Copyright. Reproduced with the permission of the Controller of Her Majesty's Stationery Office; Figure 12.8: adapted from OECD (1993) *OECD Main Economic Indicators*, January 1993, © Organisation for Economic Co-Operation and Development.

Tables

Table 12.1: CSO (1992/93) *Key Data*, © Crown Copyright. Reproduced with the permission of the Controller of Her Majesty's Stationery Office; Table 12.2: adapted from Dicken, P. (1992) *Global Shift – The Internationalization of Economic Activity*, 2nd edn. Reprinted with permission from Paul Chapman Publishing Ltd, London. © Copyright 1992 Peter Dicken.

Chapter 13

Figures

Figure 13.3: Venables, A. (1992) 'Economic integration', in Ball, J. (ed.) *The Economics of Wealth Creation*, Edward Elgar Publishing Ltd.

Chapter 14

Figures

Figure 14.9: Reprinted from Barro, R.J. (1991) 'Economic growth in a cross section of countries', *The Quarterly Journal of Economics*, vol.CVI, no.425, Issue

2, by permission of The MIT Press, Cambridge, Massachusetts. © 1991 by the President and Fellows of Harvard College and the Massachusetts Institute of Technology.

Tables

Tables 14.1 and 14.2: Sapir, A. (1992) 'Regional integration in Europe', *The Economic Journal*, vol.102, no.415, November 1992, Basil Blackwell Ltd. © Copyright 1992 by The Royal Economic Society; Table 14.3: Haaland, J.I. and Norman, V.D. (1992) 'Global production effects of European integration', in Winters, L.A. (ed.) *Trade Flows and Trade Policy After 1992*, Cambridge University Press. © Cambridge University Press 1992; Table 14.4: Burda, M. and Wyplosz, C. (1993) *Macroeconomics: a European Text*, Oxford University Press. Reprinted by permission of Oxford University Press. © M.C. Burda and C. Wyplosz 1993; Table 14.5: Baldwin, R. (1989) 'The growth effects of 1992', in De Menil, G. and Portes, R. (eds) *Economic Policy: a European Forum*, vol.9, October 1989, Cambridge University Press. © Centre for Economic Policy Research and Maison des Sciences de l'Homme 1989.

Chapter 15

Text

Barham, J. 'University to offer course in corruption', *Financial Times*, 27 April 1993.

Figures

Figure 15.2: *Industry and Development: Global Report 1993/94*, United Nations Industrial Development Organization, Vienna.

Tables

Table 15.1: Corbett, J. and Mayer, C. (1991) 'Financial reform in eastern Europe: progress with the wrong model', *Oxford Review of Economic Policy*, vol.7, no.4, Winter 1991, Oxford University Press. Reprinted by permission of Oxford University Press. © Oxford University Press and The Oxford Review of Economic Policy Limited.

Chapter 16

Figures

Figure 16.1: Hulton Deutsch Collection; Figure 16.2: Network/Neil Libbert; Figure 16.4: OECD (1994) *The OECD Jobs Study: Unemployment in the OECD Area, 1950–1995*, © OECD 1994, The Organisation for Economic Co-operation and Development; Figure 16.9: Network/Martin Mayer.

Chapter 17

Figures

Figure 17.9: *European Economy*, 54, 1993, © ECSC-EEC-EAEC, Brussels/Luxembourg, 1993, Commission of the European Communities; Figure 17.12: OECD (1993) *OECD Economic Outlook*, 53, June 1993, © OECD 1993, The Organisation for Economic Co-operation and Development; Figure 17.13: OECD (1993) *OECD Economic Outlook*, 54, December 1993, © OECD 1993, The Organisation for Economic Co-operation and Development.

Tables

Table 17.1: OECD (1993) *OECD Economic Outlook*, 54, December 1993, ©
OECD 1993, The Organisation for Economic Co-operation and
Development; Table 17.4: OECD (1993) *OECD Economic Outlook*, 53, June
1993, © OECD 1993, The Organisation for Economic Co-operation and
Development.

Chapter 18

Tables

Table 18.1: OECD (1994) *Employment Outlook*, July 1994, © OECD.
Reproduced by permission of the OECD.

Chapter 19

Tables

Table 19.2*: Bank of England Quarterly Bulletin*, vol.33, no.4, November 1993,
© Bank of England 1993.

Chapter 20

Figures

Figure 20.9: HM Treasury (1993) *Financial Statement and Budget Report
1994-95*, © Crown Copyright, reproduced with the permission of the
Controller of Her Majesty's Stationery Office.

Tables

Tables 20.1, 20.4 and 20.10: Maddison, A. (1991) *Dynamic Forces in Capitalist
Development: A Long-Run Comparative View*, Oxford University Press, © Angus
Maddison 1991. Reprinted by permission of Oxford University Press; Tables
20.2 and 20.3: Backus, D. K. and Kehoe, P. J. (1992) 'International evidence
on the historical properties of business cycles', *American Economic Review*,
September 1992, vol.82, no.4, The American Economic Association.
Copyright © American Economic Association 1992; Table 20.11: adapted
from van Ark, B. (1993) *International Comparisons of Output and Productivity:
Manufacturing Productivity Performance of Ten Countries from 1950 to 1990*,
Groningen Growth and Development Centre, Monograph Series, no.1;
Tables 20.13 and 20.14: Crafts, N. (1992) 'Productivity growth reconsidered',
Economic Policy, 15, October 1992, Cambridge University Press; Table 20.17a:
Broadberry, S. and Wagner, K. (1995) 'Human capital and productivity in
manufacturing during the twentieth century: Britain, Germany and the
United States', in Crafts, N. and Toniolo, G. (eds) *Quantitative Aspects of Post-
war European Economic Growth*, Centre for Economic Policy Research/
Cambridge University Press; Table 20.17b: O'Mahony, M. (1992)
'Productivity levels in English and German Manufacturing', *The Institute
Economic Review*, no.139, February 1992, National Institute of Economic and
Social Research.

Chapter 21

Tables

Table 21.2: Sapsford, D. and Tzannatos, Z. (1993) *The Economics of the Labour
Market*, Routledge, © David Sapsford and Zafiris Tzannatos.

Chapter 22

Figres

Figure 22.1: Paul Baldesare/Photofusion.

Tables

Table 22.4: Huhne, C. (1993) 'Not everyone stands to get fat on Gatt', *Independent on Sunday*, 3 October 1993; Table 22.5: Green, G., Coder, J. and Ryscavage, P. (1992) 'International comparisons of earnings inequality for men in the 1980s', in *The Review of Income and Wealth*, vol.38, no.1, Copyright 1992 by the International Association for Research in Income and Wealth.

Chapter 23

Figures

Figure 23.1 (*top*): Mansell Collection; Figure 23.1 (*bottom*): Paul Lowe/Network; Figures 23.3, 23.5 and 23.7: Hills, J. with the LSE Welfare State Programme (1993) *The Future of Welfare: a Guide to the Debate*, © Joseph Rowntree Foundation; Figure 23.6: Brown, C.V. and Jackson, P.M. (1990) *Public Sector Economics*, 4th edn, Basil Blackwell Ltd, Copyright © C.V. Brown and P.M. Jackson 1978, 1982, 1986, 1990; Figure 23.10: Van Doorslaer, E., and Wagstaff, A. (1993) 'Equity in the finance of health care: methods and dealings', in Van Doorslaer, E., Wagstaff, A. and Rutten, F. (eds) *Equity in the Finance and Delivery of Health Care: An International Perspective*, by permission of Oxford University Press; Figure 23.11: Wagstaff, A. and Van Doorslaer, E. (1993) 'Equity in the delivery of health care: methods and findings', in Van Doorslaer, E., Wagstaff, A. and Rutten, F. (eds) *Equity in the Finance and Delivery of Health Care: An International Perspective*, by permission of Oxford University Press.

Tables

Table 23.3: *Economic Trends*, no.483, 1994, © Crown Copyright. Reproduced with the permission of the Controller of Her Majesty's Stationery Office; Tables 23.5, 23.6 and 23.7: Smeeding, T.M., O'Higgins, M. and Rainwater, L. (eds) (1990) *Poverty, Inequality and Income Distribution in Comparative Perspective: the Luxembourg Income Study* (LIS), Harvester Wheatsheaf, © 1990 M. O'Higgins, T.M. Smeeding and L. Rainwater.

Chapter 24

Figures

p.119: Hulton-Deutsch Collection; Figure 24.1: Stanners, W. (1993) 'Is low inflation an important condition for high growth?', in *Cambridge Journal of Economics*, vol.17, no.1, March 1993, © 1993 Academic Press Limited.

Tables

Table 24.2: Stanners, W. (1993) 'Is low inflation an important condition for high growth?', in *Cambridge Journal of Economics*, vol.17, no.1, March 1993, © 1993 Academic Press Limited; Table 24.3: Brown, A.J. assisted by Jane Darby (1985) *World Inflation Since 1950: An International Comparative Study*, Cambridge University Press, © The National Institute of Economic and Social Research 1985.

Chapter 25

Tables

Chapter 26

Figures

Chapter 27

Figures

Tables

Chapter 28

Figures

Cartoons

INDEX

Note: page numbers highlighted in bold indicate the page on which an entry is defined.